Encyclopedia of
SOCIAL WELFARE HISTORY
in North America

Editors

John M. Herrick and Paul H. Stuart

Associate Editors

John Graham
Enrique C. Ochoa
Ruth Britton

Editorial Assistants

Russell Bennett
Benson Chisanga

Encyclopedia of
SOCIAL WELFARE HISTORY
in North America

Editors

John M. Herrick
Michigan State University

Paul H. Stuart
University of Alabama

A SAGE Reference Publication

SAGE Publications
Thousand Oaks ▪ London ▪ New Delhi

To Kathleen and Joni

For information:

Sage Publications, Inc.
2455 Teller Road
Thousand Oaks, California 91320
E-mail: order@sagepub.com

Sage Publications Ltd.
1 Oliver's Yard
55 City Road
London, EC1Y 1SP
United Kingdom

Sage Publications India Pvt. Ltd.
B-42, Panchsheel Enclave
Post Box 4109
New Delhi 110 017 India

Printed in the United States of America on acid-free paper.

Library of Congress Cataloging-in-Publication Data

Encyclopedia of social welfare history in North America / edited by John M. Herrick and Paul H. Stuart.
    p. cm.
Includes bibliographical references and index.
ISBN 0-7619-2584-8 (cloth)
  1. Public welfare—United States—Encyclopedias. 2. Public welfare—Canada—Encyclopedias.
3. Public welfare—Mexico—Encyclopedias. 4. Social reformers—United States—Encyclopedias.
5. Social reformers—Canada—Encyclopedias. 6. Social reformersrs—Mexico—Encyclopedias. I. Herrick, John Middlemist.
II. Stuart, Paul H.
HV12.E497 2005
361.97′03—dc22

2004022284

04 05 06 07 08 09 10 9 8 7 6 5 4 3 2 1

Acquiring Editor:	Rolf Janke
Editorial Assistant:	Sara Tauber
Developmental Editor:	Yvette Pollastrini
Production Editor:	Kristen Gibson
Copy Editor:	Taryn Bigelow
Typesetter:	C&M Digitals (P) Ltd.
Indexer:	Sheila Bodell
Cover Designer:	Ravi Balasuriya

List of Contents

List of Entries

Reader's Guide

We provide this list to assist readers in locating entries on related topics. It classifies entries by country and category, although some entries may appear in more than one category.

Families and the Life Cycle

Aged

Employment and Labor

Children

List of Contributors

Abramovitz, Mimi
Hunter College-City University of New York

Achenbaum, W. Andrew
University of Houston

Agostoni, Claudia
Universidad Nacional Autónoma de México

Alvarez, Rodney R.
University of Central Florida

Anderson, Linnea M.
University of Minnesota–Twin Cities Campus

Andrews, Janice
University of St. Thomas

Arrom, Silvia Marina
Brandeis University

Baines, Donna
McMaster University

Beechem, Michael
University of West Florida

Beito, David T.
University of Alabama

Bella, Leslie
Memorial University

Bellamy, Donald F.
University of Toronto

Bennett, Russell L.
University of Alabama

Bergquist, Kathleen Ja Sook
University of Nevada–Las Vegas

Birn, Anne-Emanuelle
University of Toronto

Black, Allida
George Washington University

Blau, Joel
Stony Brook University, State University of New York

Bliss, Katherine
University of Massachusetts–Amherst

Blum, Ann
University of Massachusetts, Boston

Brachet-Márquez, Viviane
El Colegio de México, A.C.

Bradshaw, Cathryn
University of Calgary

Brilliant, Eleanor L.
Rutgers, the State University of New Jersey

Brownlee, Keith
Lakehead University

Buck, Sarah A.
Dona Ana Branch Community College/New Mexico State University

Burson, Ike
Mississippi State University

Burwell, N. Yolanda
East Carolina University

Carlton-LaNey, Iris B.
University of North Carolina-Chapel Hill

Carniol, Ben
Ryerson Polytechnic University

Carp, E. Wayne
Pacific Lutheran University

Carrillo, Hector
University of California–San Francisco

Casas Torres, Graciela
Universidad Nacional Autónoma de México

Cates, Jerry R.
University of Illinois at Chicago

Chandler, Susan Kerr
University of Nevada–Reno

Chisanga, Benson
University of Alabama

Christie, Nancy
Trent University

Church, Wesley T., II
University of Alabama

Collins, Cyleste Cassandra
University of Alabama

Contreras, Carlos Alberto
Grossmont College

Csiernik, Rick
University of Western Ontario

Cypher, James M.
California State University–Fresno

Dawson, Alexander
Simon Fraser University

De Vos, Paula
San Diego State University

D'Elia, Donald J.
*State University of
New York, New Paltz*

Delaney, Roger
Lakehead University

DeWitt, Larry W.
Social Security Administration

Di Matteo, Livio
Lakehead University

DiNitto, Diana M.
University of Texas-Austin

Donahue, Peter
University of Calgary

Duffy, Ann
Brock University

Durst, Douglas
University of Regina

Eisinger, Peter
Wayne State University

Esser-Stuart, Joan E.
*University of Miami Medical School/
Jackson Memorial Hospital*

Este, David
University of Calgary

Fixico, Donald
University of Kansas

Flores-Briseño, Guillermo A.
*Universidad Nacional Autónoma de
México*

Fox, Daniel M.
Milbank Memorial Fund

Frank, David
University of New Brunswick

Gates, Leslie
*Binghamton University-State
University of New York*

Gauss, Susan M.
University of Delaware

Genco-Morrison, Bianca
Albuquerque Public Schools

Ginsburg, Leon
University of South Carolina

Gledhill, John
University of Manchester

Gomes, Cristina
*Facultad Latinoamericana de
Ciencias Sociales-México*

González de la Rocha, Mercedes
*Centro de Investigaciones y
Estudios Superiores en
Antropologia–Occidente*

Goodwin, Joanne L.
University of Nevada-Las Vegas

Graham, John R.
University of Calgary

Gray, Erin
University of Calgary

Gripton, James
University of Calgary

Grob, Gerald N.
*Rutgers, the State
University of New Jersey*

Hagen, Jan L.
*University at Albany,
State University of New York*

Hall, Peter Dobkin
Harvard University

Harvey, Janice
Dawson College

Heilman, Elizabeth
Michigan State University

Herrick, John M.
Michigan State University

Hopkins, June
George Washington University

Horstman, Allen
Albion College

Jansson, Bruce S.
University of Southern California

Jennissen, Therese
Carleton University

Jones, Gareth A.
*London School of Economics
and Political Science*

Kallen, Evelyn
Queen's University

Karabanow, Jeff
Dalhousie University

Klaassen, David J.
University of Minnesota–Twin Cities

Klein, Jennifer
Yale University

Lai, Daniel
University of Calgary

Lee, Bill
McMaster University

Leighninger, Leslie
Arizona State University

Leighninger, Robert
Arizona State University

Lewis, Stephen E.
California State University–Chico

Lindenmeyer, Kriste
*University of Maryland–Baltimore
County*

Lindhorst, Taryn
University of Washington

Lundy, Colleen
Carleton University

MacDonald, Alison B.
Alberta College of Social Workers

Machtinger, Barbara
Bloomfield College

MacLaurin, Bruce
University of Calgary

Martínez, Elí Evangelista
*Universidad Nacional Autónoma de
México*

Maurutto, Paula
*University of Toronto at
Mississauga*

McCallum, Margaret
University of New Brumswick

McGilly, Frank
McGill University

McNeece, C. Aaron
Florida State University

Medina-Mora, María Elena
*Instituto Nacional de Psiquatría,
México*

Mesbur, Ellen Sue
University of Waterloo

Midgley, James
University of California, Berkeley

Miller, Jim
University of Saskatchewan

Montes de Oca Zavala, Verónica
Universidad Nacional Autónoma de México

Morrissey, Megan
University of Minnesota–Twin Cities

Nelson, Kristine
Portland State University

Neufeld, Alfred H.
University of Calgary

Nystrom, Nancy M.
Michigan State University

Ochoa, Enrique C.
California State University–Los Angeles

Oliver, Ellen
Memorial University

Padilla, Tanalís
Dartmouth College

Peebles–Wilkins,Wilma
Boston University

Pescador, Octavio Augusto
University of California–Los Angeles

Polzin, Michael J.
Michigan State University

Popple, Philip R.
University of North Carolina at Charlotte

Powell, Milton
Michigan State University

Quinn, Peggy
University of Texas–Arlington

Ramirez Solórzano, Martha Alida
Instituto Jalisciense de las Mujeres

Rayside, David
University of Toronto

Reisch, Michael
University of Michigan

Rice, James J.
McMaster University

Riches, Graham
University of British Columbia

Rivera-Garza, Cristina
Instituto Technológico de Estudios Superiores de Monterrey-Toluca

Samuels,Warren J.
Michigan State University

Sanchez, Miguel
University of Regina

Sanders, Nichole
Lynchburg College

Saunders, Marlene
Delaware State University

Schriver, Joe M.
University of Arkansas

Selmi, Patrick
University of South Carolina

Shaw, Greg M.
Illinois Wesleyan University

Shillington, Richard
Canadian Council on Social Development

Shragge, Eric
Concordia University

Simon, Barbara Levy
Columbia University

Splane, Richard B.
University of British Columbia

Stamp, Robert M.
University of Calgary

Stoner, Madeleine
University of Southern California

Stotzer, Rebecca L.
University of Michigan

Stuart, Paul H.
University of Alabama

Sullivan, Nancy
Memorial University of Newfoundland

Sussman, Sam
University of Western Ontario

Swift, Karen
York University

Taylor, Marcus
University of Alberta–Edmonton

Thorpe,Wendy L.
Nova Scotia Archives & Records Management

Tropman, John M.
University of Michigan

Turner, Francis J.
Wilfrid Laurier University

Ursel, E. Jane
University of Manitoba

Valentich, Mary
University of Calgary

Velcamp, Theresa Alfaro
Sonoma State University

Venturini, Vincent J.
Mississippi Valley State University

Waugh, Joan
University of California–Los Angeles

Welch, David
University of Ottawa

Wild, Timothy
City of Calgary

Williams, Heather
Pomona College

Wilson, Tamar Diana
University of Missouri, St. Louis

Winterdyk, John
Mount Royal College

Worthington, Catherine A.
University of Calgary

Wright, Glenn
National Archives of Canada, Ottawa

Yee, June Ying
Ryerson Polytechnic University

Zamora Díaz de León, Teresa
Universidad Nacional Autónoma de México

Ziliak, Stephen T.
Roosevelt University

Preface

Rationale

In the *Encyclopedia of Social Welfare History in North America*, we endeavored to bring together basic information on the history of social welfare in the three major countries that constitute North America—Canada, Mexico, and the United States of America. Our intention was to provide readers with information about how these three nations have dealt with social welfare issues, some similar across borders, others unique, as well as to describe important events, developments, and the lives and work of some key contributors to social welfare developments. If we have succeeded, the encyclopedia will be useful to beginning students of social welfare history as well as established scholars who are seeking to extend their investigations into new areas of inquiry.

This encyclopedia, the first of its kind, takes a *continental, tri-national* approach to its subject matter. Experts on the history of social welfare in Canada, Mexico, and the United States contributed entries to the volume. We have defined social welfare broadly, to include education, informal mutual assistance, the development of the social work profession, and voluntary charitable activities as well as state-supported public welfare activities. (The encyclopedia does *not*, however, attempt to cover the history of social work practice or the development of specialized education for social work or the other human services.) The coverage is broad and interdisciplinary; contributors include scholars from the fields of anthropology, economics, education, health sciences, history, labor and industrial relations, political science, social work, and sociology.

Much published research on social welfare policy and social welfare history takes a national approach, with perhaps a nod to developments in other countries. In choosing a continental focus for this encyclopedia, the editors hoped to encourage, in a small way, cross-national and comparative research. We hope that readers will find the encyclopedia a convenient guide and starting point for investigations of the development of social welfare history in any one of the three countries as well as for comparative studies.

Organization and Themes

The entries in the encyclopedia are, for the most part, chronological. In some cases, the entries are *sui generis*, unique to a particular country. In other cases, where appropriate, similar entries on two or on all three countries have been grouped together to facilitate cross-national comparisons. In addition, a Reader's Guide is provided, which groups entries by country and by topic.

Research Guides to studying social welfare history in Canada, Mexico, and the United States are provided in an appendix. Written by archivists, these guides introduce the reader to resources for further research, including archival depositories and printed primary sources in social welfare history in each of the three countries. Chronologies of important events in social welfare that are described in the entries are also provided. A chronology is presented for each of the three countries covered in this volume so that the reader can trace events in one country or compare developments in two or three countries at various points in time.

Editorial Process

Social work librarian Ruth Britton suggested a need for this encyclopedia. Surveying standard reference works showed a void in this area; hence, the project began. In planning this project, it was decided early on that its scope should be North American, including Canada, Mexico, and the United States. Our intention was to provide readers with information about how these three nations have dealt with social welfare issues, some similar across borders, others unique, as well as to describe important events, developments and the lives and work of some key contributors to social welfare. Associate editors for Canada and Mexico, both of them experts in the history of social welfare in those countries, were invited to join the project and contributors, both established and emerging scholars, were recruited.

Our intention was to bring together in one source basic information about themes, issues, events, and personalities that shaped North American social welfare, broadly conceived. In deciding what to include, we were selective, admitting early on that we could not cover every issue, policy, or personality that might be relevant. In particular, it was not possible to provide as much detail on the development of the helping professions, in particular social work, as some readers may wish. We hope the final product will provide readers with valuable information about national as well as cross-national social welfare history. And we hope that our work will encourage further study in this rich and complex field. The history of North American social welfare shows how three nations, each with a complex history, have chosen to deal with the provision of social welfare programs and services to their populations. Social welfare decisions in the past have affected the well-being of millions of people and individual and collective social welfare in the future remain a fundamental concern for all nations.

Acknowledgments

The editors are grateful for the opportunity to work together on this project. The editors' names are presented in alphabetical order and each of us appreciates the contribution of the other. We also wish to acknowledge the work of our Associate Editors for Canada and Mexico, John Graham and Enrique Ochoa, respectively, for their critical work in identifying experts to prepare entries and in providing editorial guidance to the contributors. We are grateful, too, to Associate Editor Ruth Britton, librarian emeritus of the University of Southern California School of Social Work, who first suggested the need for this project, and for her keen suggestions and editorial skills. And, of course, this project could not have been completed without the generous commitment of time and expertise by the authors of our many entries. The hard work of keeping track of authors' entries and generally keeping the project on track was done by our able editorial assistants, both of them students in the PhD Program in Social Work at the University of Alabama, Benson Chisanga and Russell Bennett. It is appropriate to admit that without their good work this project might not have been completed. Staff members of Sage Publications, in particular Sara Tauber, Rolf Janke, and Kristen Gibson, worked tirelessly and patiently with us to bring this work to completion. We are indebted to them. Our employing institutions, Michigan State University and the University of Alabama, generously provided time for editorial work and resources for scholarship. We particularly want to thank the administrators who provided release time for research and tangible resources. John Herrick would like to thank his colleagues in the College of Social Science and the School of Social Work for their unflagging support and encouragement and for the patient concern and support of his wife, Kathleen. Paul Stuart would like to thank his wife, Joan E. Esser-Stuart, for her assistance and support, as well as University of Alabama colleagues, including Provost Judy Bonner, Dean James P. Adams, Jr., and Jordan Kosberg, former chair of the PhD program, for the provision of time and resources in support of this project.

Note to Readers

This encyclopedia contains 180 original entries written by experts on social welfare in North America that discuss persons, topics, and organizations that were important in the development of social welfare policies, services, and institutions in the three major nations of North America—Canada, Mexico, and the United States. Topics such as child welfare policy or poverty have essays discussing the topic from each of the three nations included in the book, providing readers with cross-national comparisons. Other essays, such as those on Jane Addams, John Joseph Kelso, and the Mexico City Poor House, describe persons or institutions that were important for the development of social welfare in one of the three nations.

Editing an encyclopedia with a tri-national focus presented several challenges. Contributors of entries on Mexico and to some extent Canada used words in Spanish and French, respectively, to describe developments in those countries. We have italicized foreign words and provided English translations in parentheses except in cases where the meaning of the words seemed obvious from the context. Another question was the spelling of English words, since Canadian usage differs from United States usage. We have generally used contemporary United States English spellings for uniformity and consistency, except, of course, in the case of the names of organizations and the titles of books, articles, and journals. Canadian usage is unique; in some cases, Canadians spell English words in the same way that British people do, while in other cases, Canadian spelling is similar to spelling in

the United States. For example, in Canada the word "labor" is spelled "labour," while in the United States the word is spelled "labor." Both countries use the same spelling for "organization," however.

One of the purposes of this encyclopedia is to help people launch their own investigations in social welfare history. Thus, we see this encyclopedia as a place to begin investigations, rather than as a place to end them. Each entry ends with suggestions for Further Reading, for the most part recent writings on the topic of the entry that the reader can consult for more depth on the subject. Most of the longer entries include lists of collections of original unpublished documents or Primary Sources that are relevant to the subject of the entry. Many entries also include lists of printed documents produced during the times described in the entry. These are labeled Current Comment and provide the reader access to the thoughts and observations of persons who had a hand in the events described in the entry or who observed the events directly.

A Reader's Guide provides lists of the entries in this encyclopedia organized under several topical headings. We hope the Reader's Guide will enable users of the encyclopedia to identify entries that are relevant for their particular interests quickly. For the serious student, we have also provided an appendix with Research Guides to resources for historical research in each of the three countries—the archives and other depositories of unpublished primary sources, the major printed primary sources, and other materials needed to do original research on a topic. For the serious student of the history of social welfare in Mexico, a reading knowledge of Spanish is necessary. Similarly, a reading knowledge of French will be needed to seriously investigate many topics in Canadian social welfare history.

We hope readers will find this reference work to be easy to use and that it will become an important resource for anyone interested in learning about the history of social welfare in North America.

About the Editors

John M. Herrick has been a Professor in the School of Social Work and administrator at Michigan State University since 1973. Prior to that, he taught at King's College, the University of Western Ontario (Canada), the University of Illinois at Urbana-Champaign, and Macalester College, St. Paul, Minnesota. His research interests and research publications have been in the areas of social welfare/social work history, social welfare policy and services, and health care policy and services for the elderly. He teaches undergraduate and graduate students. For several years he was President of the Social Welfare History Group, a group of scholars who conduct social welfare historical research and promote interest in social welfare history among historians and social workers.

Paul H. Stuart is a Professor in the School of Social Work at the University of Alabama, where he has taught since 1987. Prior to that, he taught at the University of Wisconsin-Eau Claire, Washington University in St. Louis, and Augustana and Sioux Falls Colleges in South Dakota. He holds a MSW degree from the University of California, Berkeley, and an MA in History and a PhD in History and Social Welfare from the University of Wisconsin. His research interests include the history of Indian relations with the United States and the history of social welfare and social work in the United States. A former President of the Social Welfare History Group, he is the author of several articles, book chapters, and books, including *Nations within a Nation: Historical Statistics of American Indians* (Greenwood Press, 1987).

A

ABBOTT, EDITH (1876–1957)

Edith Abbott was born in the town of Grand Island, Nebraska, in 1876 and died in 1957. She and her younger sister Grace were major figures in the development of social work and social welfare in the twentieth century. Whereas Grace was an activist who helped create social programs, Edith was a scholar and policy analyst who devoted her career to the professionalization of social work and the modernization of public welfare in the United States.

Grace and Edith's father was an early settler of Grand Island, a small prairie town near the westward-reaching Overland Trail. A lawyer who became Nebraska's first lieutenant governor, he often discussed politics with his sons and his daughters. He and his wife, a former high school principal, stressed the importance of higher education and communicated to their children a respect for human rights (and women's rights) and an interest in social reform.

Edith Abbott received a BA from the University of Nebraska in 1901. When bad economic times ruled out full-time graduate school, she began teaching high school and attending summer sessions at the University of Chicago. There, the economist Thorstein Veblen recognized her potential, and she was offered a small scholarship to enroll full-time. Abbott received a PhD in economics in 1905. During her studies, she took courses on the legal and economic position of

women from Sophonisba Breckinridge, who had a law degree and a PhD in political science and taught in the university's Department of Household Administration. A strong bond developed between the two women, each seeing in the other similar interests and challenges— love of learning, a concern for justice and equality, and the frustration of seeking a satisfactory outlet for those commitments in a world that limited women's involvement outside the home.

Breckinridge influenced Abbott's choice of dissertation topic—women in industry—and encouraged Abbott's interest in combining scholarship with social reform by finding her a position with the Women's Trade Union League in Boston. She also encouraged Abbott's interest in research on such social reform topics as women's work and child labor. Abbott spent 1906–1907 studying at the London School of Economics. There she met Beatrice and Sydney Webb and increased her skills in social investigation and her exposure to reform. During part of her stay, she lived and worked in a London settlement house, learning about the lives of the urban poor. Her reaction to the activities of the English suffrage movement, however, showed her chosen role of analyst rather than activist; she wrote an article describing the important social actions that British women were taking, but acknowledged her lack of courage to serve in the campaign.

On returning from London, Abbott began teaching at Wellesley College. Within a year, Breckinridge and

Julia Lathrop, a Hull House resident, urged her to return to Chicago as assistant director of the social investigation department of the University of Chicago School of Civics and Philanthropy. The move to this school, which would eventually become the School of Social Service Administration at the University of Chicago, marked the beginning of Abbott's lifelong involvement in social work education and profession-building, grounded in her belief in the importance of social service research.

Directed by Breckinridge, the Department of Social Investigation sought to apply social science methods to the study of social problems, with the hope of ameliorating those problems. Abbott and Breckinridge conducted research and supervised the work of advanced graduate students. Together, the two produced studies of housing conditions, discrimination against immigrants and African Americans, and juvenile delinquency. As Abbott embraced the growing field of social work, she wanted social work students to have access to advanced social science courses and research facilities. She began to envision a profession grounded in a scientific approach to practice and social reform.

Abbott and her sister Grace took up residence in Hull House. They became part of a growing network of female reformers, including Lathrop, Jane Addams, Florence Kelley, and Lillian Wald. Soon, Abbott would become even more involved in training the professionals who would carry out the reforms.

Due in part to financial difficulties, as well as to Abbott and Breckinridge's belief that schools of social work could never become truly professional schools until they were housed in universities, the School of Civics and Philanthropy became part of the University of Chicago in 1920. Abbott became dean of the new University of Chicago School of Social Service Administration 4 years later. With Breckinridge at her side, she developed a curriculum that included political science, economics, law, and the study of immigration and labor problems. Abbott saw social work as a scientific discipline in its own right. Students were expected to go into the community and apply rigorous methods of social investigation, both to help individuals and to document needed policy change. To further bolster the school's academic status, Abbott

and Breckinridge launched the *Social Service Review,* a scholarly social work journal.

Abbott was convinced that professional schools had a major role to play in shaping and defining the social work profession. A master's degree was crucial to that definition. Her emphasis on scholarship and graduate education as the way to strengthen social work was seen as narrow by some and put her in conflict with members of the social work union movement of the 1930s and with the proponents of undergraduate social work education. But Abbott maintained her conviction that social work "will never become a profession except through the professional schools" (1942, p. 40).

Abbott was particularly interested in expanding the social work profession's role in the administration and staffing of public welfare agencies. This became a major focus of the Chicago school, distinguishing it from most other schools of social work. Abbott pioneered the development of public welfare as a field of professional expertise. She decried the inadequacies and politics of existing state poor laws. In the 1930s, she advocated for a modern state/federal public welfare system, staffed by professional social workers, to provide permanent general relief and categorical programs such as Aid to Dependent Children (ADC). When ADC and other assistance programs were established under the 1935 Social Security Act, the Chicago school played a major role in educating social workers for the new programs.

As one of Abbott's major legacies, Chicago school graduates became both caseworkers and administrators in public welfare programs, as well as heads of other schools of social work across the country. In tribute to her accomplishments, a former student noted: "Edith Abbott gave status to social work; students saw her . . . as a master of their profession" (Lillian Ripple, quoted in Costin, 1983, p. 230).

—*Leslie Leighninger*

See also Abbott, Grace; Hull House (United States); Immigration and Social Welfare Policy (United States); Lurie, Harry Lawrence; Mothers' Pensions (United States); Social Security (United States); Social Work Profession (United States)

Primary Sources

National Association of Social Work Records and Council on Social Work Education Records, Social Welfare History Archives, University of Minnesota, Minneapolis; Edith and Grace Abbott Papers, Regenstein Library, University of Chicago, Chicago, IL.

Current Comment

Abbott, E. (1942). *Social welfare and professional education* (Rev. ed.). Chicago: University of Chicago Press.

Further Reading

Costin, L. B. (1983). *Two sisters for social justice: A biography of Grace and Edith Abbott.* Urbana: University of Illinois Press.

Leighninger, L. (1987). *Social work: Search for identity.* Westport, CT: Greenwood.

Wright, H. (1954). Three against time: Edith and Grace Abbott and Sophonisba Breckinridge. *Social Service Review, 28,* 41–53.

ABBOTT, GRACE (1878–1939)

Grace Abbott, American social worker and second chief of the U.S. Children's Bureau, was born in Grand Island, Nebraska, the third of Othman Ali Abbott and Elizabeth Griffin Abbott's four children. Othman Abbot was a Civil War veteran, lawyer, and Nebraska's first lieutenant governor. Elizabeth Griffin Abbott had a Quaker background, was a graduate of the Rockford, Illinois, Female Seminary, and an active abolitionist and suffragist. Both parents valued education, although they were hampered by limited resources. Grace Abbott attended classes at the local high school and earned a degree from Grand Island College in 1898. She went to Broken Bow, Nebraska, to teach, but soon contracted typhoid and returned home. In fall 1899, she took a teaching position at Grand Island High School. Abbott continued her education by enrolling at the University of Nebraska during 1902–1903. Her older sister, Edith Abbott, encouraged Grace to take summer courses at the University of Chicago in 1906. Grace Abbott recognized the greater employment opportunities available for a woman in Chicago and consequently moved to the city in 1907. She began living at Hull House in 1908 and took a job with the Juvenile Protection Association. Her sister Edith also moved to the settlement house and the two became a formidable duo in the social welfare network led by Jane Addams, Sophonisba Breckinridge, Florence Kelley, Julia Lathrop, and Graham Taylor.

In 1909, Grace Abbott completed her master's degree in political science at the University of Chicago and became the first director of the Immigrants' Protective League, which had been founded in 1908 by Judge Julian Mack and University of Chicago professors Breckinridge and Ernest Freund. Among other activities on behalf of immigrants, Abbott testified before Congress in 1912 against a proposed literacy test. She also wrote *The Immigrant in Massachusetts,* a report sanctioned by the Massachusetts state legislature. Grace Abbott was a member of the Women's Trade Union League and chaired an Illinois committee in 1915 examining conditions for female prisoners.

The U.S. Children's Bureau's first chief, Julia Lathrop, offered Abbott several jobs with the agency, but she refused. Passage of the 1916 Keating-Owen Act restricting child labor changed her mind. Abbott moved to Washington, D.C., in 1917 to head the Children's Bureau's new division of child labor. On August 31, 1917, a North Carolina judge ruled the new law unconstitutional. The U.S. Supreme Court agreed in its *Hammer v. Dagenhart* decision delivered on June 3, 1918. Abbott stayed in Washington to work on preparations for the second White House Conference on Children to be held in June 1919. She accompanied Lathrop to Belgium, France, Great Britain, and Italy to observe the effects of World War I on children and to invite potential participants to the Washington conference. Abbott returned to Chicago after the Washington meeting ended. She worked as head of the Illinois commission on immigration, reestablished the Immigrants' Protective League, and taught at the University of Chicago's School of Civics and Philanthropy.

In 1921, Julia Lathrop asked Grace Abbott to return to Washington as the Children's Bureau's new chief. Always the astute politician, Lathrop did not announce her plans to step down until Abbott agreed to take the position. Endorsements from prominent Republicans such as philanthropist Julius Rosenwald, Wisconsin Senator Robert M. LaFollette, and Illinois Governor Frank Lowden made Lathrop's choice of Abbott very popular.

One of Abbott's first responsibilities was administration of the 1921 Sheppard-Towner Maternity and Infancy Act. The largest federal social welfare program developed to that date, Sheppard-Towner was designed to reduce the nation's high infant and maternal mortality rates. Despite the program's popularity, by the mid 1920s the American Medical Association (AMA) launched a campaign against the program. With the AMA denouncing Sheppard-Towner as "socialized medicine," Congress allowed the act to expire in 1929. But Sheppard-Towner taught Abbott and her supporters some important lessons about the effectiveness of preventive medicine and education for mothers and children. It also exposed the political resistance the Children's Bureau faced as it tried to expand under Abbott's leadership.

Despite such problems, Abbott was able to expand the Children's Bureau's influence in the United States and abroad. She served in an advisory role to the League of Nations, was president of the National Conference of Social Work from 1923 to 1924, and helped to organize the International Conference on Social Work in 1928. At President Herbert Hoover's 1930 White House Conference on Children, Abbott successfully resisted an attempt by the American Medical Association and the Public Health Service to remove all child health responsibilities from the Children's Bureau. Abbott publicly criticized Hoover for not doing enough to help the nation's children and their families during the Great Depression. She was happy to see Franklin Delano Roosevelt elected president in 1932 and agreed to stay on as Children's Bureau chief while her friend, Frances Perkins, settled in as secretary of labor. Abbott finally resigned from the bureau in early 1934 and took a position as professor at the University of Chicago's School of Social Service Administration. But her duties in Washington were not over. The Children's Bureau's new chief, Katharine F. Lenroot, asked Abbott to help develop the children's sections for the Committee on Economic Security. From 1934 to 1935, Abbott, along with Lenroot and bureau physician, Martha May Eliot, wrote the child welfare sections of what became the 1935 Social Security Act—Titles IV (Aid to Dependent Children), V (Maternal and Child Welfare), and VII (Social Security Board).

After leaving Washington for good, Abbott edited the *Social Service Review* and published *The Child and the State* (1938) outlining her views on the role of government in child welfare. Weakened by tuberculosis, Abbott died in Chicago at the age of 60 on June 19, 1939. She never married or had children, but acted for 16 years as guardian for her niece Charlotte and for most of her life as an advocate for other people's children. During her lifetime, Grace Abbott was an influential member of the social welfare reform movement rooted in Chicago's Progressive Era politics. Her leadership underscored the idea that children are a shared private and public responsibility.

—*Kriste Lindenmeyer*

See also Abbott, Edith; Aid to Dependent Children/Aid to Families With Dependent Children (United States); Child Welfare Policy (United States); Hull House (United States); Lurie, Harry Lawrence; Mothers' Pensions (United States)

Primary Sources

Edith and Grace Abbott Papers, Regenstein Library, University of Chicago, Chicago, IL; Records of the U.S. Children's Bureau (Record Group 102), National Archives & Records Administration, College Park, MD.

Current Comment

Abbott, E. (1939, September). Grace Abbott: A sister's memories. *Social Service Review, 13,* 351–407.
Abbott, Grace [Obituary]. (1939, June 20). *New York Times*, p. 21.

Further Reading

Conway, J. K. (1971–1972, Winter). Women reformers and American culture, 1870–1930. *Journal of Social History 5,* 164–177.
Costin, L. B. (1983). *Two sisters for social justice: A biography of Grace and Edith Abbott.* Urbana: University of Illinois Press.
Lindenmeyer, K. (1997). *"A right to childhood": The U.S. Children's Bureau and child welfare, 1912–1946.* Urbana: University of Illinois Press.
Muncy, R. (1991). *Creating a female dominion in American reform, 1890–1935.* New York: New York University Press.

ABORIGINAL PEOPLE AND POLICY (CANADA)

After the creation of the Canadian state in 1867, aboriginal policy sought to discharge the federal government's obligations to aboriginal peoples at the lowest possible cost. In terms of the Inuit (formerly Eskimo) and Métis, the mixed-blood peoples of the West, this approach meant denying any federal responsibility for them. So far as Indian peoples, who are now usually referred to in Canada as First Nations, are concerned, the government's parsimonious approach meant securing land treaties as inexpensively as possible, implementing treaties on the cheap, using Christian missionaries to deliver social policy, attempting to refashion First Nations through cultural assimilation to make them economically self-sufficient and reduce government obligations, and trying to control Indians politically to avoid resistance to policy initiatives. The results have been to undermine First Nations and, eventually, provoke vociferous political resistance to government.

Post-1867 policy was based on earlier colonial experiments in treaty making, assimilation, and removing Indian status. Treaty making had been most consistent and advanced in Ontario, where a series of land-related treaties was negotiated between the 1770s and the early 1860s. These pacts usually exchanged exclusive aboriginal title to territory for compensation, which in the post-1818 period took the form of annuities or annual payments. An explicitly assimilative social policy was adopted in the same region in the 1830s by the British Indian Department, which, no longer finding Indians militarily useful in a post–War of 1812 world and wanting to reduce government's outlay for Indian affairs as much as possible, worked with Christian missionaries to encourage Indians to move into permanent villages and adopt agriculture and Christianity. In the 1840s, this "civilization" policy, as it was termed, was expanded to include government-sponsored and church-run residential schools. The final policy innovation of the colonial period was the adoption of a program to promote enfranchisement. Enfranchisement meant simply the abandoning of Indian status and life ways in favor of British Canadian citizenship and political rights. Enfranchisement was embodied in the Gradual Civilization Act of 1857, which encouraged voluntary enfranchisement. This trio of policies—land treaties, assimilation, and enfranchisement—constituted the foundation of the new nation's Indian policy after 1867, as the fledgling Dominion of Canada tackled a development agenda that included acquisition and integration of Hudson's Bay Company land in the West as rapidly as possible.

To pursue its policy of western development, the new Canadian government emphasized negotiation of treaties covering access to aboriginal land. Between 1871 and 1921, it concluded a series of agreements, known as the Numbered Treaties 1–11, which covered the West (except for most of British Columbia) and some parts of the North. Unfortunately, in implementing the treaties the government was generally dilatory and parsimonious in its approach. After 1921, it ceased making treaties until an upsurge in aboriginal resistance to exploitation of their territories forced a return to negotiations. Large portions of Canada—most of British Columbia and the North, northern Quebec, and the four Atlantic provinces—remained uncovered by land treaties in the twenty-first century.

Missionaries of the Roman Catholic, Anglican (Church of England), Methodist, and Presbyterian churches served as the delivery agents of most social policy for Indians until well into the twentieth century. They had their greatest impact in education, especially residential schooling, which was an important part of federal policy from 1883 until 1969. Unlike the United States, where the churches fell out of favor as school directors at the end of the nineteenth century, Canada relied on the missionaries until the middle of the twentieth century, when declining numbers in missionary ranks made the policy nonviable. The primary reason for the state-church collaboration in social policy was a combination of ideology and economics. Planners believed that education that had a strong Christian component would be more effective in the long run than secular instruction, and religious zeal meant that missionaries performed their duties for less than lay people. Moreover, since state policy relied heavily on an assimilative approach, missionaries were deemed to be effective agents of government policy.

Indian schools were ineffective pedagogical instruments, and residential schools especially did a great deal of damage. Reliance on the churches allowed government to shirk its oversight responsibilities as well as some expense, and missionaries sometimes relied more on zeal than training in the schools. The residential schools, in particular, failed both as educators and caregivers. With insufficient government funding and oversight, they provided inadequate care and instruction, permitted physical and sexual abuse of children, and produced students who were demoralized and ill equipped for life as workers or as marriage partners and parents. In the late twentieth century, revelations of abuse stimulated a public outcry and litigation involving 12,000 former residential school students by the end of 2002. Related social policies that owed much to the influence of Christian missionaries were campaigns to suppress traditional aboriginal ceremonies. In 1885, the Indian Act, the comprehensive federal legislation that attempted to regulate all aspects of First Nations peoples' lives, prohibited the Potlatch of West Coast First Nations, and in 1895 the attack was broadened to the summer ceremonials of Plains nations. The campaign of cultural suppression ended only in 1951.

Although educational and cultural policies have garnered most of the headlines, defective economic and political policies were equally misguided. Federal economic development policies for First Nations were always blighted by paternalism and parsimony, and in the prairie West in the late nineteenth century they were actually hindrances to economic progress on reserves. Between 1889 and 1897, a so-called "peasant farming" policy that required reserve farmers to do all their farmwork with hand tools stifled initiative just as Plains peoples were trying to make an adjustment from buffalo hunting to crop growing and ranching. The most glaring example of paternalism was the section of the Indian Act that required reserve farmers to secure a permit from the Indian agent before taking crops to town for sale. The 1888 severalty policy, a copy of the Dawes Act (1887) in the United States, attacked communal landholding and use by encouraging the conversion of reserves to freehold properties. The combination of Indian Act paternalism and underinvestment discouraged the development of economic initiative and turned Indian reserves into economic backwaters that by the late twentieth century resembled third-world communities.

Attempts at political control through the Indian Act revealed the same pattern. Beginning in 1869 and continuing until the 1960s, the Department of Indian Affairs attempted to regulate band councils through powers to depose chiefs and councillors as well as Indian agent oversight of band council meetings.

Government interference in First Nations' political behavior culminated in an amendment to the Indian Act, in force from 1927 until 1951, which made it illegal to raise or contribute money for pursuit of a claim. The prohibition effectively barred Indian leaders from using lawyers and made political organization and activity on a large scale extremely difficult.

Other aspects of First Nations social policy that proved disruptive concerned Indian status. Post-1867 legislation continued the colonial policy of enfranchisement, which meant abandoning Indian status and acquiring the rights and obligations of citizenship. Enfranchisement was simply political assimilation. In 1869, the enfranchisement legislation was broadened so that any woman with Indian status who married a male without it would lose her status, as would their children and descendants. Since status Indian males who married non-status women did not lose status, the provision was glaringly discriminatory. Although general enfranchisement legislation, which was voluntary, was not very effective, the gender discrimination provisions affecting women had the effect of stripping large numbers of people of their Indian status. The discrimination ended only in 1985 with an amendment to the Indian Act that ended the practice.

The various social policies followed from 1867 until the latter part of the twentieth century were consistent and destructive. They were in various ways motivated by the twin forces of ideology and parsimony: They sought to assimilate First Nations and save the federal government money. Unfortunately, they also retarded economic development, stifled political initiative, undermined Indians' confidence and sense of self-worth, and, eventually, provoked First Nations' political opposition.

Native campaigns against federal policy began to be effective by the 1970s. By then, provincial and national organizations, many of them headed, ironically, by residential school graduates, had emerged to give voice to First Nations' disenchantment and challenge government policy. Their campaigns in the courts and the political arena have frequently deterred governments from persisting with failed social policies. Their opposition, for example, was a major component in the government's 1969 decision to phase out church-managed residential schools. Similarly, political opposition eventually stopped the "sixties scoop," the policy of encouraging adoption of First Nations' children by non-Natives that both federal and provincial governments pursued for a time. In the 1980s and early 1990s, First Nations' political activity on the national stage was intense, as aboriginal organizations—First Nations, Inuit, and Métis—played major roles in a series of negotiations concerning renewal of Canada's Constitution.

In the early twenty-first century, aboriginal policy and aboriginal peoples in Canada were in a state of flux. The old paternalistic and assimilative policies, which never worked and created social pathology in First Nations communities and families, had been discredited and discontinued. No satisfactory substitute for them, however, had yet been found. In some social policy areas—especially education, child welfare, and some aspects of health care—the government encouraged the devolution of policy administration to First Nations. First Nations leaders, however, also wanted power over policy development, and the federal government and First Nations' political organizations continued to spar over control of these matters. They also were engaged in debate over the implementation of some form of aboriginal self-government and aboriginal land claims in many parts of the country where effective land treaties were never negotiated. In other words, Canada's policies for aboriginal peoples continue to be a work in progress.

—*Jim Miller*

See also Federalism and Social Welfare Policy (Canada); Rural/Northern Social Welfare (Canada); Social Welfare (Canada): Before the Marsh Report; Social Welfare (Canada): Since the Marsh Report

Primary Sources

Records of the Department of Indian Affairs (Record Group 10) of the Dominion of Canada, Library and Archives Canada, Ottawa, ON; *Indian Affairs Annual Reports, 1864–1990,* reprinted for many years in the *Sessional Papers* of the Parliament of Canada and available on the Library and Archives Canada website (www.collectionscanada.ca/).

Current Comment

Cairns, A. C. (2000). *Citizens plus: Aboriginal peoples and the Canadian state.* Vancouver: University of British Columbia Press.

Flanagan, T. (2000). *First Nations? Second thoughts.* Montreal, QC, and Kingston, ON: McGill-Queen's University Press.
Miller, J. R. (2004). *Lethal legacy: Current Native controversies in Canada.* Toronto, ON: McClelland & Stewart.

Further Reading

Dyck, N. (1991). *What is the "Indian problem"? Tutelage and resistance in Canadian Indian administration.* St. John's, NL:, Memorial University, Institute for Social and Economic Research.
Miller, J. R. (1996). *Shingwauk's vision: Canada's Native residential schools.* Toronto, ON: University of Toronto Press.
Miller, J. R. (1997). *Canada and the aboriginal peoples, 1867–1927.* Ottawa, ON: Canadian History Association.
Milloy, J. S. (1999). *A national crime: The Canadian government and the residential school system, 1879 to 1986.* Winnipeg: University of Manitoba Press.

ABORIGINAL PEOPLE AND POLICY (MEXICO)

The "Indian question," as it is often phrased, has been an important issue in Mexico since the arrival of Europeans in Mesoamerica during the 1520s. The Indian was the *sine qua non* of the colonial state's existence. Indian labor and tribute were the principal source of wealth that colonists found in Mexico, and the potential conversion of "heathen" souls was the overt mission that Castilians used to justify their conquest. *Conquistadores* (Spanish conquerors) and royal officials used the *encomienda* (a grant of Indian labor and tribute) and the *repartimiento* (a practice whereby adult indigenous males were required to contribute 45 days labor per year to the Crown) as a means of ensuring that the indigenous population was an easy source of wealth. At the same time, the Franciscan missionaries who installed themselves in Tlatelolco in the aftermath of the conquest (Bernardino de Sahagún being the most famous) worked tirelessly to learn Native languages, educate young members of the indigenous nobility, evangelize, and act as intermediaries between indigenous communities and royal officials.

Simultaneous desires to exploit and evangelize ultimately produced the most lasting indigenous institution of the colonial period, the *ejido* (communal land). After the 1520s, the indigenous population of Mexico dropped precipitously (perhaps by 95 percent), and in their efforts to resolve this crisis royal officials created a series of communal Indian villages, which resettled indigenous populations into towns where they would enjoy permanent access to the land, water, and forest resources. Other than royal and religious officials, nonindigenous peoples were generally banned from *ejidos*. In return for these grants, community members were required to do service for the Crown, and sometimes purchase goods through officially licensed vendors; but for the most part, the *ejido* provided indigenous peoples with some protection against the ravages of colonialism. *Ejidos* produced goods for local consumption, but they also produced much of the food consumed in urban areas, allowing residents to raise the capital they needed to pay tribute and other obligations. They also produced an important quality of indigenous life that persists today, as loyalties among indigenous Mexicans are still generally drawn according to village boundaries. The colonial state encouraged each village to develop vertical linkages with royal officials rather than horizontal linkages across regions, and encouraged rivalries among villages on questions of boundaries and forest and water rights. Many of these rivalries continue to this day.

Ejidos were often productive agricultural enterprises, but they were based on principles of corporate land tenure that came under attack during the late colonial and early republican periods. Eighteenth and nineteenth century liberals believed that all forms of landholding except private property were unproductive, and thus impediments to national development. They also saw the extent of *ejidal* holdings in Mexico as a serious impediment to the creation of a modern nation. In this, Mexican liberals, particularly after independence in 1821, often adhered to a series of ideas that would have an enormous impact on Mexico in the nineteenth century. During the colonial period, the Indian people had been categorized as a caste, inferior to Whites and Mestizos, but possessing legitimate rights to land due to their designation as Indians. During the nineteenth century, however, under the influence of thinkers such as Arthur de Gobineau and Herbert Spencer, Mexican liberals increasingly saw Indians as a race of inferior beings who should be eliminated in the interest of progress. Though some early nationalists called for the preservation of the traditional Indian rights, most liberals

during the nineteenth century supported the elimination of the *ejido* and the forced assimilation or destruction of indigenous cultures. At their worst, nineteenth century liberals supported genocidal practices, as happened during the dictatorship of Porfirio Díaz (1876–1911) with the forced relocation of the Yaquis from Sonora to the Yucatán, where they worked under slavelike conditions.

Some teachers and philosophers decried these practices. Francisco Pimentel and Justo Sierra both pressed the Mexican state to reject the view that the Indian was racially inferior and adopt policies oriented toward elevating and assimilating indigenous peoples into a modern nation. In 1909, Andrés Molina Enríques went so far as to declare the Indian superior to Whites. These voices remained isolated, however, until Mexico was convulsed by the 1910 Revolution, in which over a million Mexicans (10 percent of the population) lost their lives. Many believed that a key cause of the unrest had been indigenous Mexicans, who remained mired in poverty and represented probably about a third of Mexico's population. In an effort to undo this situation in 1917, President Venustiano Carranza created the Department of Anthropology under Manuel Gamio. This was the first of a series of agencies that would seek to solve the Indian problem through the careful application of social scientific knowledge about the Indian, signaling the birth of a movement known as revolutionary *indigenismo*, a political and literary movement that favored indigenous people. Unlike their antecedents, Gamio and those who followed him into the revolutionary state sought the complete incorporation of the Indian into the Mexican nation.

Revolutionary *indigenistas* rejected the reservation system as it was practiced in the United States as condemning Indians "to a slow, agonizing death." Instead, they argued that the Indian could and should be incorporated into the mainstream through education, the introduction of "modern" agriculture and living practices (such as "healthy motherhood," nutrition, and hygiene), and the distribution of land to indigenous communities so that they might become productive agriculturalists. At a time when in other countries the Indian was often represented as an immutable racial inferior, these activists rejected racism in favor of viewing Indians as potential citizens, whose backwardness resulted entirely from isolation and exploitation.

During the 1920s and 1930s, these efforts intensified, as the revolutionary state built thousands of schools, constructed roads, brought potable water and irrigation to Indian communities, and sent "cultural missionaries" throughout the country to teach the gospel of progress. These efforts peaked during the presidency of Lázaro Cárdenas (1934–1940), who distributed 18 million hectares of land to rural Mexicans. Cárdenas believed the Indian was simply a rural proletarian, and implemented programs that reflected this view. Although certain *indigenistas* during this era increasingly viewed indigenous peoples as oppressed nationalities with the right to cultural and political self-determination, they remained a small and often excoriated minority.

After 1940, *indigenismo* retreated from public view, mostly because the Mexican state adopted a conservative program of capitalist modernization and top-ranking officials lost interest in the Indian question. New educational and social programs during these years were rarely tailored to the specific needs of indigenous communities and typically failed. It was also at this time, however, that some innovative social and educational programs began to gather momentum. During the 1930s, officials working in the Department of Indian Affairs had undertaken Mexico's first efforts at bilingual education in a number of Indian boarding schools, and, in spite of official hostility at the federal level, these programs slowly expanded during the 1950s under the auspices of the National Indigenista Institute (*Instituto Nacional Indigenista*, or INI). Through coordinating centers in several states, INI officials gradually created a cohort of bilingual indigenous teachers, who went into indigenous communities as "cultural promoters," acting as teachers, scribes, and sometimes emerging as a new generation of political leaders in rural Mexico. These new elites rarely had the power to press for further land reform, as redistribution after 1940 was minimal, but they did oversee a series of agricultural, economic, and political programs in their communities, gradually building linkages between indigenous communities and the Mexican state.

These efforts accelerated after 1970, when President Luis Echeverría (1970–1976) committed new resources to indigenous communities during a period of political crisis. Unlike past projects though, his efforts took place at a time when indigenous movements were increasingly demanding not only land, but also cultural and linguistic self-determination. The leaders of these movements rejected efforts to assimilate the Indian in favor of the demand that indigenous peoples in Mexico be granted specific rights. Their demands were made public in a congress at Pátzcuaro, Michoacán, in 1975. At this meeting, indigenous leaders from throughout the country demanded cultural autonomy, official status for Indian languages, representation in government for ethnic groups, and an Indian university. Delegates also complained that the land, forest, and water resources they possessed were completely inadequate. In this, they mixed traditional rural complaints about poverty with a new series of demands for cultural rights. Some of these demands could be met fairly easily, and during the decade of the 1970s federal officials did grant land to some communities and expanded programs for bilingual and bicultural education. Others were more difficult, as federal officials repeatedly resisted efforts to enact laws that would truly grant indigenous groups the right to self-determination.

In 1990, President Carlos Salinas de Gortari (1988–1994) amended the Constitution to recognize Mexico as a multicultural nation, and gave indigenous peoples the right to protect and preserve their cultures. In practice, however, these reforms had little impact. Cultural self-determination remained an ill-defined political agenda, and federal officials were reluctant to cede their authority to indigenous groups. Recently, the leaders of Mexico's 56 major indigenous ethnicities met with federal officials to demand territorial division or autonomy for their groups, but they were rebuffed by officials who promised only programs to fight poverty. Local landowners, who often relied on poorly paid indigenous workers, were similarly reluctant to grant power to groups that might oppose them, and often used murder and intimidation to defend their interests. These practices were tied to the rise of movements like the Zapatista Army of National Liberation (*Ejército Zapatista de Liberación Nacional,* or EZLN), which rose in rebellion in Chiapas in 1994. The EZLN, like a number of recent movements in Mexico, mixed traditional peasant demands for more land and resources with an increasingly confrontational approach to cultural rights.

Critics of the EZLN pointed out that although its leaders claimed an indigenous following, it was hard to distinguish it from more traditional peasant movements. This confusion represented one of the serious challenges for Indian policy in Mexico, where the term "Indian" has always had a very vague meaning, and often simply was used to describe poor rural people. At present, the INI administers to the 5,282,347 Mexicans (6.8 percent of the population) who are described by the census as speaking Indian languages. Because this designation merely describes people who habitually speak indigenous languages, it leaves several million Mexicans who are bilingual and live in Indian communities (or sometimes outside of Indian communities) outside the category. This creates one of the problems that contemporary movements and policymakers struggle with. Unlike the United States, where Indian is a racial category, in Mexico no such clear-cut designation makes someone an Indian. As such, it is often difficult to determine exactly who should be able to claim the moniker "Indian," and what rights they should enjoy.

—*Alexander Dawson*

See also Land Reform (Mexico); Peasant Movements and Social Programs (Mexico); Poverty (Mexico); Rural Education (Mexico)

Further Reading

Aguirre Beltrán, G. (1992). *Teoría y práctica del la educación indígena.* Mexico City: Fondo de Cultura Económico. (Original work published 1973)

Díaz Polanco, H. (1997). *Indigenous peoples in Latin America: The quest for self-determination.* Boulder, CO: Westview.

Lomnitz, C. (2001). *Deep Mexico, silent Mexico: An anthropology of nationalism.* Minneapolis: University of Minnesota Press.

Tresierra, J. C. (1994). Mexico: Indigenous peoples and the nation-state. In D. L. Van Cott (Ed.), *Indigenous peoples and democracy in Latin America* (pp. 187–210). New York: St. Martin's.

ABORIGINAL PEOPLE AND POLICY (UNITED STATES)

The history of the aboriginal peoples in the Americas and the United States government has been a series of colonized treatments. In general, federal policy has resembled a pendulum that cycles in a positive direction toward American Indians and then swings in a negative direction. Initially, more than 500 Indian nations representing as many as 15 million people in North America encountered European colonization in the so-called New World. Major imperial powers—the Dutch, Russians, French, Spanish, and British—traveled to Native America during the 1500s and 1600s. By the late eighteenth century, British colonization had established itself permanently in what became known as New England. A colonial revolution resulted in the emergence of the United States. The new nation contended with British-Indian alliances that attempted to prevent American settlers from encroaching on Indian land.

As a new country, the United States attempted to earn recognition as a sovereign nation from the Indian nations, while the British sought Indians as allies. Relations between Indians and Americans were generally friendly as the new federal government adopted a diplomatic strategy of negotiating treaties of friendship, establishing boundaries, and getting the Indian nations to favor the United States instead of Britain. The first U.S. effort along these lines was the Treaty of 1778 with the Delaware. This treaty recognized the boundaries between the two nations, acknowledged mutual sovereignty, and rendered safe passage for Americans through Delaware land. President George Washington's administration sought Indian allies as friends against the threatening British influence that continued to linger after the American Revolution.

During Thomas Jefferson's presidency, the federal government tried to maintain a positive approach to Indian policy as U.S. citizens moved westward and more Indian nations in the interior of North America became involved with them. Jefferson had observed the successful farming among several Indian nations in the Virginia area. This led him to believe that Americans and the indigenous peoples could live side by side in building a new America based on agriculture. Indian nations whose economies depended more upon hunting would have to adjust culturally to a more agrarian lifestyle. The hunting tribes, however, disregarded Jefferson's notions and his administration began to focus on forming trade agreements with more Indian nations. Trade and gradual land acquisition became the objectives of Jeffersonian Indian policy.

Subsequently, however, the increasing pressure of U.S. settlement resulted in a new policy that proved harmful to aboriginal peoples. American expansion across the Appalachian Mountains and into Kentucky and Tennessee provoked war with the Indian nations. U.S. expansionists like Andrew Jackson, a frontier leader from Tennessee, believed that the Indian nations should surrender their land to U.S. settlers and move farther westward to prevent additional hostilities. Elected president in 1828, Andrew Jackson developed a policy of Indian removal that Congress endorsed in 1830. An estimated 94 treaties were signed between Indian nations and the United States during the removal era from the early 1820s to 1860, removing eastern Indian nations to west of the Mississippi River.

Near the Atlantic Seaboard, small Indian nations with diminishing populations were too weak to fight and they were removed easily via treaties. Most Indian nations, however, resisted removal, fighting for their land in the South, the Ohio area, and the Great Lakes region. Small skirmishes, battles, and wars like Tecumseh's campaign of 1812; the Black Hawk War of 1832; the Seminole Wars of 1817–1818 and 1835–1842; and the Little Crow War of 1862 completed the subordination of the eastern aboriginal peoples, who were forced to accept new land in the West called Indian Territory (now the states of Oklahoma, Kansas, and Nebraska).

The outbreak of the U.S. Civil War after 1860 resulted in federal disengagement from Indian affairs as the Union found itself busy dealing with the southern states. In fact, the Confederacy paid more attention to Indian nations as it tried to recruit them to join the South and several Confederate-Indian treaties were signed, including the Pike agreements (named after Albert Pike who negotiated Confederate treaties with the Seminole, Creek, Cherokee, Choctaw, and Chickasaw in Indian Territory). By this time, the United States found itself facing new conflicts with Indian nations in the West as U.S. settlers pushed into Kansas, Nebraska, Texas, and the Dakotas.

After the war, the United States developed a peace policy to negotiate more treaties with western Indian nations. Councils were held with aboriginal peoples and early agreements acknowledged hunting areas of the Plains Indian nations. A faction in President Ulysses S. Grant's administration opposed the peace policy and favored fighting Indians. It was pressure from settlers, ranchers, miners, and railroad companies that caused hostilities to erupt again. Throughout the 1860s and 1870s, Indian wars occurred on the Great Plains, in the Southwest, and in the Pacific Northwest. The Sioux War, especially the Battles of the Rosebud and Little Bighorn in 1876, marked the peak of hostilities between the United States and the Indian tribes even as the Apache and Navajo Wars in the Southwest and the Nez Perce War in the Northwest raged on. Finally, the Wounded Knee massacre of 1890 ended major hostilities between American Indians and the United States as the nineteenth century drew to a close.

New Indian policy emerged in the late 1800s. Passed in the form of the General Allotment Act of 1887, federal policy called for the individual allotment of nearly 200 reservations to members of the Indian nations. Most American Indians accepted or were forced to accept allotment of their land, although a minority escaped the process. Plains Indian hunters became farmers and ranchers, according to the allotment policy, but this did not work very well until the late twentieth century. The allotment policy enabled opportunists to exploit Indian people for their land and properties. Disarmed and disillusioned, American aboriginal peoples found themselves living within the American culture of individuality and Christianity. The White man's civilization was forced upon them.

Efforts to educate Indian youth at Indian boarding schools extend back to the early days of the 1600s and 1700s on the Atlantic Seaboard. Harvard University, William and Mary College, and Dartmouth College all educated Indian students. More than 100 Indian boarding schools were built during the nineteenth century with some—such as the Carlisle Indian School in Carlisle, Pennsylvania, and the Haskell Indian School in Lawrence, Kansas—becoming famous. Less well known is the fact that in the 1800s the Cherokee, Creek, Seminole, Choctaw, and Chickasaw tribes, known as the Five Civilized Tribes, built their own boarding schools in Indian Territory. The federal government boarding schools treated Indian students harshly, adopted military discipline, and punished Indian students for speaking their Native languages. The long history of boarding schools continues today, although many were closed during the 1970s as Indian nations began to construct their own schools.

The failure of Indian allotment as policy and the Great Depression resulted in a new policy, the Indian New Deal, beginning in 1934 with the Indian Reorganization Act (IRA). Tribal communities were allowed to form tribal governments patterned after the U.S. government and loans were made available to these communities. These efforts became the foundation of modern tribal governments that are more self-sufficient today. The IRA years continued until the outbreak of World War II. As many as 25,000 American Indian men entered the armed services during the war. Later, 10,000 to 12,000 served in the Korean conflict, and 43,000 served in Vietnam.

World War II convinced Congress that American Indians could live in urban areas, where jobs were available, at a time when reservation economies were suffering. An estimated 100,000 American Indians entered the relocation program, a federal effort to move aboriginal peoples from reservations and rural areas to cities. In the 1950s and 1960s, this urbanization policy seemed to fail. More important, termination policy, starting in 1954 with House Concurrent Resolution 108, called for the end of treaties and federal responsibilities for each Indian tribe, group, or community. Because of the complexity of the termination process, specific legislation was required to terminate a tribe. Without federal assistance, many Indian communities encountered serious problems, which resulted in strong dissent from new Indian leadership of young, college-educated Indians in urban areas. Many of these youth became members of the American Indian Movement (AIM), an activist organization started in 1968.

The 1970s saw increased Indian activism. President Richard Nixon advocated a changed federal policy of American Indian "self-determination." Enacted in 1975, self-determination still guides federal Indian policy. Substantial compensation for land claims and federal programs for housing, loans, educational assistance, and college scholarships enabled Indian nations and individuals to have more opportunities on nearly 300 reservations throughout the United States. By the late twentieth century, there were 562 federally recognized tribes and an Indian population of 2.3 million. American Indians were living better lives with more control over their own destinies. Having rebuilt their tribal governments, health care systems, and other programs to help their people, nearly 200 tribes have entered the gaming industry to supplement other tribal programs and to provide services for their people.

—*Donald Fixico*

See also Education Policy (United States); Homestead Act (United States)

Primary Sources

Records of the U.S. Bureau of Indian Affairs (Record Group 75), National Archives & Records Administration, Washington, DC, College Park, MD, and other regional records centers; Archives Research Room, Oklahoma Historical Society, Oklahoma City; Western History Collections, University of Oklahoma, Norman.

Current Comment

Kappler, C. J. (Ed.). (1904). *Indian affairs: Laws and treaties* (Vols. 1–2). Washington, DC: Government Printing Office.
U.S. Commissioner of Indian Affairs. (1824–1949). *Annual report(s)*. Washington, DC: Government Printing Office.
U.S. Department of Commerce. (1984). *Federal and state Indian reservations and trust areas*. Washington, DC: Government Printing Office.

Further Reading

Fixico, D. L. (2003). *The American Indian in a linear world: American Indian studies and traditional knowledge*. New York: Routledge.
Prucha, F. P. (1984). *The great father: The United States government and the American Indian*. Lincoln and London: University of Nebraska Press.
Washburn, W. E. (1971). *Red man's land, White man's law: A study of the past and present status of the American Indian*. New York: Charles Scribner's Sons.

ADDAMS, JANE (1860–1935)

Social reformer, peace activist, writer, organizer, and administrator, Jane Addams is best known for her founding of and long affiliation with the Hull House social settlement in Chicago and her peace activism in the early decades of the twentieth century. Born on September 16, 1860, in Cedarville, Illinois, Addams was the eighth of nine children born to John Huy Addams and Sarah Weber Addams, and one of four who survived to adulthood. Sarah Addams died when Jane Addams was just over 2 years of age.

Addams's father, a Quaker and a moderately well-to-do businessman, was active in Illinois politics, serving in the state senate from 1854 to 1870. He was a founder of the Illinois Republican party and was influenced significantly by Abraham Lincoln. Addams adored her father, who had been an ardent abolitionist, and credited him with her moral and intellectual development. In contrast, in her autobiography, Addams gave virtually no attention to her stepmother, Anna Haldeman, a widow with two young boys who married John Addams when Jane was 8 years old.

In 1877, following her father's wishes, Jane Addams enrolled in the Rockford Female Seminary, although she had long dreamed of attending Smith College. She finished at the top of her class in 1881, and was granted her degree a year later when the renamed Rockford College for Women became a degree-granting institution. Her years at Rockford were marked by intellectual rigor; and it was here that she met her lifelong friend and settlement cofounder, Ellen Gates Starr. Upon finishing her studies, Addams found only limited opportunities to apply her learning, a common dilemma among others of this first generation of college-educated American women.

About this same time, Addams faced a major personal crisis when in 1881 her father, at the age of 59, suddenly took ill and died. This event marked the beginning of an 8-year period in Addams's life in which she lacked direction and endured major health problems, including depression. Following surgery and a 6-month recuperation to correct a disabling spinal condition, her health improved significantly and she was able to tour England and Europe from 1883 to 1885. She returned to Europe in 1887 for a very different kind of tour, when she observed many social and religious movements occurring in England and on the continent and visited a number of philanthropic organizations. She ended her tour with a visit to Toynbee Hall in London, which had been founded by idealistic young social reformers who believed that by taking up residence in a poor section of London, they could learn about the poor and assist them by living in their midst. Although in her autobiography Addams identified the moment she decided "it would be a good thing to rent a house in a part of the city where many primitive and actual needs are found" (1910, p. 85) as occurring at a bullfight in Madrid in April of 1888, it is likely that she had begun to formulate her ideas about creating the settlement that was to become Hull House long before that actual date.

Upon returning to the United States, Addams and her friend and traveling companion, Ellen Gates Starr, began to search for a building and local support to launch their project. Their search ended with the establishment of Hull House, situated in an old mansion on the corner of Polk and Halstead streets in Chicago's Nineteenth Ward. The surrounding neighborhood was crowded with tenements, and was home to Greek, Italian, Irish, Polish, Russian, German, Sicilian, and other immigrants. Addams insisted they had no practical plans in mind after moving into their new home on September 18, 1889, but it is likely some ideas had already begun to form as both Addams and Starr had read widely on social movements. Addams envisioned a setting that served a dual purpose: to provide a means by which young educated persons could apply their learning, and to serve their neighbors trapped in urban poverty.

Strongly influenced by the ideas of John Dewey, an American educator, Addams believed residents of the settlement would learn by doing and by responding to the immediate needs of the surrounding neighbors. A kindergarten was started almost immediately, followed quickly by boys' clubs, women's clubs, and then a whole host of service clubs, primarily focusing on the needs of women and children. Addams also used the settlement as a venue to bring art and literature to the neighborhood, and Hull House became a place for the celebration of folk art from various ethnic groups.

Hull House also became a sociological laboratory, where residents carried out innumerable investigations on the surrounding tenements, sweat shop labor, child labor, and a host of other social problems.

An effective administrator, Addams attracted an impressive group to reside at Hull House, including Julia Lathrop, Florence Kelley, Grace and Edith Abbott, and Alice Hamilton. She herself was a skilled mediator who insisted that all sides on any issue be heard. Hull House frequently became the center of controversy as Addams and the residents took on a number of local causes, particularly related to labor organizing. Addams served a short time as the garbage inspector for the Nineteenth Ward, and led a campaign to unseat a corrupt city alderman. Inevitably, Addams's interests and influence expanded beyond the local neighborhood to encompass nearly every reform effort on the national scene from 1890 to 1925. She championed the cause of suffrage for women and was active in the Progressive party campaign of 1912. She became the first woman to head the National Conference of Charities and Correction in 1909, and in 1911 she became the first head of the National Federation of Settlements. She served on the founding executive committee for the National Association for the Advancement of Colored People (NAACP), and lent her support for the founding of the Urban League. Through these activities, Addams gained a national reputation and until about 1915 enjoyed high public esteem, being viewed as a model of female benevolence.

As early as 1907, Addams began to focus her attention on peace activism, which commanded nearly her whole attention after the start of World War I in 1914. She was elected chair of the Women's Peace party in 1915, and later that same year led the American delegation to the International Congress for Women, at The Hague, Netherlands. Throughout the war, Addams spoke in favor of mediated resolutions for international conflicts and against the use of arms. She continued her peace activism following the war, and in 1919 she was elected the first president of the Women's International League for Peace and Freedom, an organization that grew out of the 1915 Hague conference. Her peace activism was unpopular during the war and in the anticommunist hysteria that marked the early years of the 1920s. Popular opinion turned sharply against Addams during this time, when she was labeled unpatriotic and later branded as a socialist and communist. Many critics in the 1920s charged that Hull House had become a center for radicalism, and Jane Addams, once the most respected woman in America, had become "the most dangerous woman in America" (Davis, 1973, p. 251).

The Norwegian Nobel Committee recognized Addams's peace activism in 1931 by awarding her the Nobel Peace Prize, which she shared with Nicholas Murray Butler. This, along with new challenges posed by the deepening depression of the 1930s, helped to restore Addams's reputation at the end of her life. Despite failing health in her later years, she remained active until her death on May 21, 1935, at the age of 74.

—*Megan Morrissey*

See also Hamilton, Alice; Hull House (United States); Progressive Era (United States); Settlement Houses (Canada); Settlement Houses (United States)

Primary Sources

Jane Addams Papers, Swarthmore College Peace Collection, Swarthmore, PA; Ellen Gates Starr Papers, Sophia Smith Collection, Smith College, Northampton, MA.

Current Comment

Addams, J. (1902). *Democracy and social ethics.* New York: Macmillan.
Addams, J. (1909). *The spirit of youth and the city streets.* New York: Macmillan.
Addams, J. (1910). *Twenty years at Hull House.* New York: Macmillan.
Addams, J. (1930). *The second twenty years at Hull House.* New York: Macmillan.

Further Reading

Davis, A. F. (2000). *American heroine: The life and legend of Jane Addams* (Rev. ed.). Chicago: Ivan Dee. (Original work published 1973)
Elshtain, J. B. (2002). *Jane Addams and the dream of American democracy.* New York: Basic Books.
Linn, J. W. (1935). *Jane Addams: A biography.* New York: Appleton-Century.

AFRICAN AMERICANS AND SOCIAL WELFARE (UNITED STATES)

African American families and children have been both protected and endangered by social welfare legislation in the United States. Because of the heritage of slavery and segregation, African Americans have viewed government and voluntary social welfare programs ambivalently. Self-help programs have been significant for African Americans throughout their history. A discussion of specific social welfare programs will highlight the ways that African Americans were affected.

The first Africans to arrive on American soil did so as free, albeit indentured persons. They, like their White counterparts, were recognized as laborers. There existed no race-based differential; yet adherence to Christianity was required. But gradually, the recognition of race overshadowed the importance of religion and racial categorizing became ingrained as the primary identifying imperative for slavery. Massachusetts became the first English colony in North America to recognize slavery as a legal institution in 1641. Connecticut and Virginia followed in 1650 and 1661, respectively. The "peculiar institution" was to continue until the end of the Civil War, when the Confederate army surrendered in 1865.

Because of the understandable esteem that African American people held for the Emancipation Proclamation of January 1, 1863, it became one of the "most far-reaching pronouncements ever issued in the United States" (Quarles, 1969, p.116). The Emancipation marked the beginning of the end of the institution of slavery. Yet it was the passage of the Thirteenth Amendment in December, 1865 that abolished slavery. The Fourteenth Amendment, ratified in 1868, extended citizenship rights only to freedmen, leaving African American women subject to the same unequal status as White women.

Congress established the Bureau of Refugees, Freedmen, and Abandoned Lands in March 1865 in the War Department. Commonly known as the Freedmen's Bureau, this organization served emancipated African Americans and refugee Whites by alleviating suffering and acting as legal guardian. For example, the Bureau issued 21 million rations, approximately 5 million going to Whites and 15 million to Blacks. By 1867, there were 46 hospitals under the bureau staffed by physicians, surgeons, and nurses. The medical department spent over $2 million to improve the health of former slaves and treated more than 450,000 cases of illness (Franklin & Moss, 1994, p. 229).

Clearly a valuable service for many disparate and desperate people, the Freedmen's Bureau met with vehement opposition in the South and functioned in an atmosphere of hostility. The promotion of mutual confidence between African Americans and Whites was not to result from the Freedman's Bureau's efforts.

The bureau's school-founding work was especially troubling to Whites who thought this federal expenditure of funds excessive and wasteful because they believed that African Americans could not absorb book learning. Despite this agitation and hostility, the Freedmen's Bureau established over 4,000 schools for the freedmen and women.

The Freedmen's Bureau established a number of historically Black colleges and universities (HBCUs). Some of the most prominent included Hampton Institute, Howard University, St. Augustine College, Johnson C. Smith University, and Fisk University. Almost a quarter of a million former slaves received some education in over 4,000 schools through the efforts of the Freedmen's Bureau. Eventually, Congress refused to fund the Freedmen's Bureau and it ceased operations in 1872.

The Freedmen's Bureau failed former slaves in one very important regard—land acquisition. Second to freedom, former slaves needed land. They wisely understood that freedom without land in the rural South was hollow. Some land was redistributed to former slaves, but most was eventually restored to the former owners by presidential proclamations of amnesty.

In addition to land ownership, freedmen and women highly valued education. The Morrill Act of 1862 provided for the founding and maintenance of agricultural and mechanical colleges in the United States. Because there were no provisions for the racial distribution of these funds, only Virginia, Kentucky, Mississippi, and South Carolina directed any of these funds to African American students. There was some sporadic protest that gained little hearing. In 1890,

Congress passed a second Morrill Act that increased the original appropriations but withheld funds from any states that did not include African Americans in its benefits. The new Morrill Act of 1890 did not require that schools integrate, but allowed states to establish segregated colleges so long as the funds were equitably distributed between African American and White colleges. Within 6 years of this legislation, all of the former Confederate states except Tennessee had established separate land-grant colleges for African Americans. The equitable division of funds was, however, slow in coming and continues to elude those HBCUs that were funded under the Morrill Act of 1890. The segregation that was perpetuated by the Morrill Act of 1890 became a permanent fixture throughout the South, and the desire to segregate African Americans revealed itself in various forms of legislation and court decisions.

In 1896, the U.S. Supreme Court upheld the segregation that had been written into the new constitutions of the southern states. With its "separate but equal" decision, known as *Plessy v. Ferguson,* African Americans were increasingly disenfranchised. Segregation laws multiplied rapidly throughout the South covering a range of human and civil rights from separate drinking fountains and toilets to Jim Crow Bibles for African American witnesses in courts.

Keeping African Americans disenfranchised ensured a large, low-waged labor force and guaranteed southern plantations' productivity. The sharecropping system was essentially a recreation of a slave labor system for landless African Americans. This system dominated the southern landscape and influenced every aspect of the sharecropping family's life. Laws, policies, values, and attitudes continued to exacerbate the oppressive and impoverished state of African Americans. For most African Americans, the depression began long before the stock market crashed in 1929. In addition to the depression, many factors forced African Americans to live in fear and deprivation.

A lukewarm acknowledgment of the needs of the African American community came during the Franklin D. Roosevelt administration with a pool of advisers generally referred to as the "Black Cabinet." This fairly large group of African American advisers was constantly changing. These advisers were federal employees, but not high-level policymakers. Moreover, these individuals did not have easy access to the president and were often rebuffed or denied the opportunity to gain an audience with him, although the president's wife, Eleanor Roosevelt, encouraged their efforts. These Black Cabinet members were sometimes referred to as salesmen for the New Deal. Other times more favorably described as the Black brain trust, this group was composed of prominent professionals like well-known social workers E. Kinckle Jones, executive secretary of the National Urban League, who served as adviser on "Negro affairs" in the Department of Commerce and Lawrence Oxley who was the chief of the Division of Negro Labor in the Department of Labor.

The New Deal brought relief to many African Americans. The Social Security Act of 1935 was of extreme importance to the African American community. The exclusion of farmworkers and domestic servants from the Old-Age Insurance program, however, was devastating to African Americans because many were employed in these areas. Nonetheless, the Social Security Act provided tremendous assistance to a group of people who were disadvantaged in the work world.

The Aid to Dependent Children program of the 1935 Social Security Act (later named Aid to Families With Dependent Children, or AFDC) embraced the same discriminatory practices as its predecessor, the state mothers' pension programs. African Americans were subjected to a different set of eligibility standards in many states. Eventually, arbitrary policies such as the "home suitability clauses," "man-in-the-house rule," and "substitute father rules" were applied in ways that denied assistance to African American children.

Other social service programs of the New Deal shared some of the same discriminatory characteristics as the AFDC programs. The Civilian Conservation Corps (CCC), enacted in 1933, provided employment for the nation's youth through conservation projects in national and state parks. The CCC, one of the more popular aspects of the New Deal legislation, was strictly segregated, except for a few camps in New England. Slightly more than 15 percent of the Works Progress Administration (WPA) enrollees were African Americans. The various branches of the WPA included the Federal Arts Project, which enrolled African American writers and actors. Zora Neale Hurston and Langston Hughes were among the most prominent African American artists employed by the Federal Writers' Project.

Another New Deal program, the National Youth Administration (NYA), had a Negro Division headed by Mary McLeod Bethune, founder of Bethune-Cookman College and the only female member of President Roosevelt's Black Cabinet. The NYA afforded thousands of African American youth the opportunity to remain in school. Ten percent of all youth in the NYA were African American; and thousands who were not enrolled in school were given the opportunity to develop skilled trades via the NYA.

The Wagner Labor Relations Act of 1935 was one of the most significant New Deal measures to affect African Americans. This legislation guaranteed the right of collective bargaining and strengthened organized labor. Furthermore, this legislation gave the more militant labor organizers the strength needed to organize mass-production industries where large numbers of African Americans were employed, including steel, iron, automobiles, longshoring, shipping, and garment manufacturing.

Although some New Deal legislation positively affected the lives of African Americans, the Jim Crow system firmly remained intact throughout the South during the Great Depression and beyond. Scholars note that two contrasting developments occurred in the 1950s that severely threatened the Jim Crow system. These include the 1954 Supreme Court decision in the *Brown v. Board of Education* case that not only engendered hope but also the brutal murder of Emmett Till in 1955, which caused tremendous outrage. *Brown v. Board of Education* outlawed racial segregation in public schools and banned the doctrine of "separate but equal." Many states blatantly ignored the Supreme Court order whereas others sought ways to avoid adhering to it with few, if any, repercussions.

Between 1955 and 1965, several groups established themselves to repudiate American racism, setting the stage for the emergence of the modern civil rights movement. Groups arose in both the North and South to attack discrimination in housing, employment, and education. Student groups were prominent among

them. African Americans in the North were emboldened by the new political power that the vote, denied to most African Americans in the South before Congress enacted the Voting Rights Act of 1965, gave them. Furthermore, African Americans who provided the core support for the successful civil rights movement helped increase the probability of legislation that benefited the working poor of all races. The Civil Rights Act of 1964 and the Voting Rights Act of 1965 were the primary federal policy responses to the movement.

The Voting Rights Act of 1965 was designed to extend to all citizens equal voting rights and to provide federal examiners to monitor elections. Because it abolished literacy tests for voting, the law had a far-reaching impact on African Americans. Two years after passage of the Voting Rights Act, for example, African American registration in "Mississippi went from 6.7 to 59.8 percent, and in Alabama from 19.3 to 51.6 percent" (Quarles, 1969, p. 270).

Title VII of the Civil Rights Act of 1964 required the desegregation of public facilities and outlawed discrimination in employment on the basis of race, color, religion, gender, or national origin. It also established the Equal Employment Opportunity Commission (EEOC). As a result of this legislation, by the late 1960s African American women began to approach parity with White women in terms of employment in office work and compensation.

In addition to the 1964 Civil Rights Act and the 1965 Voting Rights Act, President Lyndon B. Johnson's Great Society initiative also invested in human capital through social programs aimed at providing opportunities for the poor. The War on Poverty programs included Upward Bound, Volunteers in Service to America (VISTA), Job Corps, and Head Start. Head Start, one of the most researched and evaluated childhood programs in America, often boasts significant gains in test scores among both African American and White children. The first major welfare reform in over 30 years took place with the 1996 Personal Responsibility and Work Opportunity Reconciliation Act (PRWORA). This legislation eliminated the welfare entitlement program Aid to Families With Dependent Children (AFDC) and replaced it with the Temporary Assistance for Needy Families (TANF) time-limited program. The time-limited component of TANF has potentially severe consequences for the 8 million children who are on welfare. This is especially true in a tight economy, where there are few jobs available to low-skilled workers.

Another policy that some project will have a major impact on African American children is the Multiethnic Placement Act (MEPA). Signed by President Bill Clinton in 1994, this law prohibits any foster care or adoption agency that receives federal funds from denying a placement solely on the basis of race. Further, this law increased opportunities for transracial adoptions. Transracial adoptions account for some 1,000 to 2,000 African American child placements annually. Contemporary scholars postulate that MEPA will "probably enable a small number of Caucasian foster parents to adopt minority foster children who have been in their homes since infancy" but will not significantly impact the number of children in foster placements. The pathos of this law, however, is that social workers are "being challenged to justify the placement of African American children with African American families and to justify the use of specialized minority programs, due to the restrictive laws limiting consideration of race" (McRoy, Oglesby, & Grape, 1997, p. 101).

Affirmative action, a term first used during the Johnson administration, has constantly been under attack. Much of the opposition is voiced through accusations of "reverse discrimination" and "unwarranted preferences." Defined as the set of public policies and initiatives designed to help eliminate past and present discrimination against ethnic minorities and women, affirmative action has come under attack most recently in the courts because opponents believe that it penalizes Whites. With two separate but parallel cases from the University of Michigan, the Supreme Court decided its first ruling on affirmative action in higher education admission in 25 years. The Court voted 5 to 4 to uphold the University of Michigan law school's affirmative action policy which favors achieving a diverse student body using a point system that takes race into account in overall admission scores. In the undergraduate case, however, the court ruled 6 to 3 that the point system violated equal protection provisions of the Constitution.

Economic retrenchment continues to be a significant problem for the United States as plants, mills, and factories close their doors and as large corporate agribusinesses overtake the small family farm. Access to opportunities for employment, education, adequate housing, food security, health care, and so on continues to be a challenge for ethnic and racial minorities. The historical record reveals social programs and policies that have worked. We are challenged to build on these programs and to advocate for a distribution of goods and services that does not continue to leave the same groups wanting, but that treats all U.S. citizens as resources worthy of the country's attention, preservation, and investment.

—Iris B. Carlton-LaNey

See also DuBois, W. E. B.; Frazier, E. Franklin; Progressive Era (United States); Roosevelt, Anna Eleanor; Rush, Benjamin; Wells-Barnett, Ida B.; Young, Whitney

Primary Sources

Records of the Women in Industry Service, Women's Bureau (Record Group 86) and Records of the Division of Negro Economics, General Records of the Department of Labor (Record Group 174), National Archives & Records Administration, College Park, MD; Julius Rosenwald Papers, Special Collections Research Center, University of Chicago Library, Chicago, IL.

Current Comment

Dubois, W. E. B. (1903). *Efforts for social betterment among Negro Americans.* Atlanta, GA: Atlanta University Press.
Lerner, G. (Ed.). (1972). *Black women in White America: A documentary history.* New York: Vintage.
McRoy, R., Oglesby, Z., & Grape, H. (1997). Achieving same-race adoptive placements for African American children: Culturally sensitive practice approaches. *Child Welfare, 76,* 85–104.
Ross, E. (Ed.). (1978). *Black heritage in social welfare, 1860–1930.* Metuchen, NJ: Scarecrow Press.

Further Reading

Carlton-LaNey, I. (Ed.). (2001). *African American leadership: An empowerment tradition in social welfare history.* Silver Spring, MD: NASW Press.
Franklin, J., & Moss, A. (1994). *From slavery to freedom.* New York: Alfred A. Knopf.

Martin, E., & Martin, J. (1985). *Helping tradition in the Black family and community*. Silver Spring, MD: NASW Press.

Quarles, B. (1969). *The Negro in the making of America*. New York: Collier.

AGING POLICY (CANADA)

Within the last 20 years, there has been a skyrocketing growth in the numbers of Canadians aged 65 and over. Census data from Statistics Canada show that in 1981, 2.4 million or about 10 percent of the Canadian population were age 65 years and over. In 2000, Statistics Canada reported a 62 percent increase to 3.8 million, resulting in 13 percent of the population being seniors. The elderly population in Canada is expected to grow in the next few decades. For example, it is projected that 17 percent of Canadians will be 65 years and over by 2016. By 2031, the percentage could be as high as 24 percent. The growth of the aging population has been particularly significant among the oldest of seniors. The number of Canadians aged 85 and over rose from 140,000 in 1971 to 400,000 in 2000. It is projected that by 2051, there will be almost 2 million Canadians aged 85 and over, a fivefold increase from the current figure. The aging trend of the Canadian population speaks to the importance of government policies that ensure the needs of older persons are being best met.

HISTORICAL DEVELOPMENT

Policies are often translated into specific social programs or social transfers for people in need. As early as 1906, the process of building policy to support the elderly in Canada began in the House of Commons, where members were agitated by concerns about the welfare of older workers. Parliamentary committees began to study the concept of old-age pensions, although there was not strong government support. In 1914, the Social Service Congress raised Canadians' awareness of the need for social security programs, including those that protected citizens from the poverty arising with old age. The end of the First World War and the return of the soldiers prompted the government to investigate an old-age pension system for Canada. After much debate about the type of old-age pension program to initiate, Parliament passed the Old Age Pension Act of 1927. This act, which involved a partnership with provinces, outlined eligibility, residence requirements, and the maximum amount recipients could receive. Although the dominion government passed this act in 1927, it took 9 years for all provinces to take part in the program.

This initial system of old-age pension had its flaws. The Marsh Report of 1942 pointed to administrative practices that limited the effectiveness of the program, including residence requirements and the condition that recipients had to be British subjects. The Old Age Pension Act stayed in place, however, until new legislation was introduced in 1951. This legislation, entitled the Old Age Security Act, created a universal program that was managed and financed by the federal government. This act allotted $40 a month to persons aged 70 and above who had lived in Canada for at least 20 years. The universal nature of this program began to take away the stigma of receiving social assistance in old age. During the same year, the Old Age Assistance Act was introduced. This program was for those aged 65 to 69 on a means-tested basis and was cost shared with provinces.

Even with these programs in place, more improvements were needed in the standard of living for the elderly. Although there was a private market in retirement pensions, a national system was needed to allow pensions to move with employees through job positions and across the country. As a response, the Canada Pension Plan (CPP) and Quebec Pension Plan (QPP) came into place in 1965. Both plans are similar in design, with the QPP being administered by the Quebec provincial government solely for workers in that province and the CPP being administered by the federal government for those in all provinces other than Quebec. These were contributory pension plans in which workers paid a percentage of their salary and received benefits after retirement. Both plans also offered survivor's pensions for the spouses of deceased pensioners, disability pensions, and children's and death benefits. Together, these pension plans covered 92 percent of Canada's workforce. For those ineligible for CPP or QPP, the Guaranteed Income Supplement Plan introduced in 1966 provided a guaranteed minimum income for retired persons on the basis of an income test. These programs provided a basis for present-day government programs to support Canada's elderly population.

CONTEMPORARY ROLES OF GOVERNMENTS

In view of the aging of its population, Canada has been quite well aware of the necessity to develop policies and programs to address the needs of the growing aging population. At the present time, policies and programs for this population are the responsibilities of both the federal and provincial or territorial governments, each of which has a minister responsible for seniors. In addition, both at federal and at most provincial government levels, there is an arm's-length advisory body providing input and advice on policies related to seniors. At the federal level, the National Advisory Council on Aging was established in 1980, with the objective of assisting and advising the Canadian government on policies and matters related to the aging of the Canadian population. The council consists of 18 members, representing different parts of Canada. The functions of the council include offering advice to the federal government, monitoring policy developments, and developing positions on various aging issues.

THE NATIONAL FRAMEWORK ON AGING

To better coordinate the development of policies and services for the aging population, the National Framework on Aging (NFA) was proposed in 1994 by the federal, provincial, and territorial ministers responsible for seniors. The framework is used as a tool to assist governments at all levels to respond to the needs of the aging population. According to the NFA's vision statement, Canada should promote the well-being of older people of all ages and in all aspects of life, and recognize the valuable contributions of seniors. Within the framework, five core principles are endorsed: dignity, independence, participation, fairness, and security. Associated with the NFA is a policy guide designed to help policymakers understand and respond to the needs and values of older persons. The policy guide

consists of policy questions to help the development of related policies in all sectors and across jurisdictions. These questions are framed to ensure that policies and related programs for older persons are consistent with the vision statement as well as the principles identified in the NFA.

In addition to the policy guide, another tool developed to facilitate the implementation of the NFA is the Seniors Policies and Programs Database (SPPD). Established in January 2000, this database provides a regularly updated system to assist governments and other organizations review and develop policies and programs related to seniors. This database can be used as a "coordination" tool for ensuring that governments at all levels are aware of the development of various policies and programs affecting seniors.

POLICIES AND PROGRAMS FOR OLDER PERSONS

Policies related to older persons can be categorized in three domains:

1. Employment and financial security: The focus of the policies and programs in this area is to ensure that older persons have the financial resources to meet their needs and to sustain their well-being. Examples of policies and related programs include Old Age Security (OAS), the Guaranteed Income Supplement (GIS), and Canada/Quebec Pension Plan (C/QPP). Eligible older adults living in some provinces and territories can also receive income supplements or age-related tax credits on top of the federal financial benefits.

2. Health care: The Canada Health Act (1984) forms the policy basis for providing universal health care coverage for all Canadians including the aging population. The Canada Health Act points to the five fundamental principles related to insured health care services and extended health care services that the provinces and territories must provide to receive the federal financial contributions under the Canada Health and Social Transfer (CHST). These principles are public administration, comprehensiveness, universality, portability, and accessibility. At the implementation

level, the actual delivery of health care services and determination of the extent of the health care coverage remain within the provincial/territorial jurisdiction. In view of this, provincial and territorial governments often develop their own policies, programs, and commission studies, particularly in the areas of primary care and long-term care needs of the aging population.

3. Community and social support: Each of the provincial and territorial jurisdictions has a variety of community support programs and services. Their purpose is to enhance the overall well-being of the aging population in the community and facilitate their independence for as long as possible. These programs and services cover an array of needs related to older persons such as housing assistance, service access, social support, services for persons with disabilities, guardianship, transportation, and continuous education and learning.

THE FUTURE OF AGING POLICIES

With the increasing aging of the Canadian population, the question is, are Canadians ready to face the challenges? Although there are policies and programs attempting to address the needs of the aging population for finance, health care, and community support, challenges and unanswered questions in each of these areas continue to surface, particularly in the context of shrinking financial resources. As the size of the workforce becomes smaller, the burden of providing financial support to older persons has created an ongoing debate on the future roles of the government. With major cutbacks in government spending, most of the financial security programs for older persons are no longer universal. This means that they only benefit those who are most in need financially, resulting in the general economic situation of older persons being left unattended. In 2001, the National Advisory Council on Aging (NACA) only gave a "B" grade rating to the "economics" of older Canadians, meaning that improvements are definitely needed to ensure that the elderly have adequate financial resources to sustain their well-being. The question of the affordability of Canada supporting a universal old-age security and

pension system, however, continues to surface in policy debates. Instead of expanding the current pension system, the federal government tends to put more of the onus on Canadians. This is mainly carried out through the policy of increasing tax exemptions for working Canadians when investing in the Registered Retired Saving Plans, which are set up for the purpose of saving for retirement incomes.

The Commission on the Future of Health Care, which was formed in 2001 to examine Canadian health care, pointed to the need for the system to be prepared for an increase in health needs associated with the growth of the aging population. Although some of the recommendations have identified national strategies for ensuring the health needs of the aging population and their care providers, it remains a controversial topic whether the federal government really has the resources needed to implement these recommendations. Also, there is an ongoing debate between provincial/territorial jurisdictions and the federal government on the sharing of power and responsibilities in providing health care. This continues to add another layer of complexity to the health care agenda in the context of the growing health needs brought forth by the aging population.

The provision of adequate community support programs and services is essential to facilitating the achievement of the ultimate goal of health and well-being as specified in the National Framework on Aging. Nevertheless, the shrinking of public funds continues to add pressure to community-based organizations in providing quality services. The financial responsibility for maintaining adequate and quality programs is gradually downloaded from the government level to the local level, creating further difficulties for local groups and communities. Despite the general recognition by both the government and community of the importance of the informal system in providing care and support to the aging population, systematic policies and programs to acknowledge and support the contributions of the family and informal caregivers are still lacking and require further development.

—Daniel Lai

See also Social Security (Canada); Women and Poverty (Canada)

Current Comment

Health Canada. (2004, January 26). *Canada Health Act: Overview* [On-line]. Available: www.hc-sc.gc.ca/medicare/chaover.htm

Health Canada. (2004, July 8). *Seniors policies and programs database* [On-line]. Available: www.sppd.gc.ca

Health Canada. (2004, September 19). *Principles of the national framework on aging: A policy guide* [On-line]. Available: www.hc-sc.gc.ca/seniors-aines/nfa-cnv/pdf/aging_e.pdf

Health Canada, Division of Aging and Seniors, National Advisory Council on Aging. (2003, September 30). *Interim report card: Seniors in Canada 2003* [On-line]. Available: www.hc-sc.gc.ca/seniors-aines/index_pages/naca_e.htm

Statistics Canada. (2004, April 4). *2001 Census of Canada* [On-line]. Available: www.statcan.ca/

Further Reading

Graham, J. R., Swift, K. J., & Delaney, R. (2003). *Canadian social policy: An introduction* (2nd ed.). Toronto, ON: Prentice Hall.

Guest, D. (1997). *The emergence of Social Security in Canada* (3rd ed.). Vancouver: University of British Columbia Press.

Health Canada. (2002). *Canada's aging population.* Ottawa, ON: Ministry of Public Works and Government Services Canada. Available: www.hc-sc.gc.ca/seniors-aines/pubs/fed_paper/pdfs/fedpager_e.pdf

Romanow, R. (2002). *Building on values: The future of health care in Canada.* Ottawa, ON: Commission on the Future of Health Care in Canada. Available: www.hc-sc.gc.ca/english/care/romanow/

AGING POLICY (MEXICO)

Today, the demographic aging process is a relevant topic for governmental institutions in Mexico. According to the data available at the beginning of the twenty-first century, there are 7.5 million older persons in Mexico and projections estimate that within five decades one-third of the total population will be at least 60 years of age. Additionally, government studies agree with international organizations that this phenomenon will have profound social and political consequences on Mexico. In response, the Mexican government created the National Committee for the Aging in 1999. Nevertheless, Mexico still does not have a consistent aging policy or a national gerontological plan.

The National Population Council (*Consejo Nacional de Población,* or CONAPO) is responsible for population policy in Mexico. CONAPO has focused on migration as well as a decrease in fertility and mortality and its effects on the general population. The agency's role in aging policy, however, has been limited to promoting study of the aging process in universities and other research centers. Aging policy in Mexico is currently coordinated by the Older Persons National Institute (*Instituto Nacional de Personas Adultas Mayores,* or INAPAM), previously *Instituto Nacional de la Senectud,* or INSEN), created as part of the Health Ministry in 1975. INAPAM was established as part of the Secretariat for Social Development (*Secretaría de Desarrollo Social,* or SEDESOL) and began its work in 2000. Once this change was made, the government adopted a new approach to aging—it was not regarded as an illness; on the contrary, older people were seen as integral and important participants in national social development. At the same time, the major political parties began to realize the future potential of the elderly population as voters and their needs were addressed in the political platforms of several parties.

SOCIAL SECURITY SYSTEM FOR OLDER PERSONS

Currently, aging policy in Mexico is linked to several agencies, both governmental and nongovernmental. The Social Security system has played an important role; for decades it has designed specific and differentiated programs for the retired population. Historically, however, the Social Security system has included only those workers employed under formal contracts by private firms and public agencies. An aging population of informal workers was and is excluded. The main agencies that provide services for the elderly are the Mexican Social Security Institute (*Instituto Mexicano del Seguro Social,* or IMSS) and the Social Security Institute for Government Workers (*Instituto de Seguridad y Servicios Sociales de los Trabajadores del Estado,* or ISSSTE). At the beginning of the twenty-first century, only 22 percent of the elderly received a pension from one of these agencies, and 94 percent of the IMSS pensions were equivalent to the minimum wage. In addition, about 49 percent of the elderly had health services coverage provided by one of the country's Social Security agencies; of these, 78 percent received coverage from IMSS and 19 percent from ISSSTE. These figures vary, however, according to the area of residence. Those affiliated with either IMSS or ISSSTE are concentrated in urban areas; there is a serious lack of services and coverage in rural areas. One of the greatest problems for studying aging in Mexico is the difficulty of understanding rural aging because existing research has an urban bias. Future research needs to address the issues of the rural elderly in order to present a more balanced view of all the elderly in Mexico.

In 1995, the IMSS privatized the pension system. Individuals now make contributions directly to private financial institutions that manage individual pensions. This changed the pension system from one based on intergenerational solidarity to a private and individual system that uses private financial institutions for its administration. In order to receive a pension, workers must make contributions for a period of 750 to 1,250 weeks. Whether or not the new pension system will be successful is unclear because it has not experienced heavy demand from retirees. Some problems are emerging because informal, rural, and low-income workers do not receive pension benefits. Also, the ISSSTE is currently experiencing a serious financial crisis as well as a change in ownership that could have an impact on the provision of health services, especially for the elderly.

Other agencies that offer services for elderly former workers are the Mexican Oil Company (*Petróleos Mexicanos,* or PEMEX), and some decentralized state agencies, whose retired workers have a privileged Social Security system. Not all these retirees have gerontological and geriatric programs, but the health services afforded these former workers are envied by many. In general, programs for the elderly are biased toward those who are physically and mentally healthy. There are few programs specifically aimed at the elderly who are ill and their caregivers. Mexico does not have good programs for strengthening the social networks of former workers, which could help them cope with health and social problems. Those services that do exist focus primarily on medical treatment and economic support.

OLDER PERSONS OUTSIDE THE SOCIAL SECURITY SYSTEM

Older persons without Social Security coverage may apply to other social services in case of need. Some of these are the Health Ministry (*Secretaría de Salud,* or SSA); INAPAM; the National System for the Integral Development of the Family (*Sistema Para el Desarrollo Integral Para la Familia,* or DIF); and special facilities located across the country. The Health Ministry can provide health services for all elders, but it does not have a geriatric services program. The most prestigious health agency is the National Nutrition Institute (*Instituto Nacional de la Nutrición Salvador Zubirán*), founded by Salvador Zubirán and named in his honor. The institute has the most widely acclaimed geriatrics clinic in Mexico, but it cannot meet the needs of all the elderly. INAPAM provides services for persons who can document their age as 60 years or older. It offers health services, psychological counseling, recreational programs, and discounts for purchase of prescription drugs and for the costs of cultural and entertainment events. INAPAM cannot hope to fulfill the needs of the elderly who suffer serious disabilities and of those who are very elderly—that is, over the age of 80. The National System for the Integral Development of the Family (DIF) provides social services to "vulnerable" populations, those who are extremely poor or severely marginalized, regardless of age. It operates nearly 40 nursing homes. Home-care services for the elderly are almost nonexistent in Mexico. Recent studies have found that long-term care services for the elderly are often understaffed and that they sometimes treat the elderly inappropriately, not as adults but as helpless children, thereby stigmatizing and demeaning them.

Services for the elderly are provided on the assumption that the elderly live with family members and enjoy good mental health. This assumes that family members will serve as intermediaries between the elderly and agencies that provide services to them. In the case of serious progressive illnesses resulting from chronic degenerative diseases, however, health agencies have no support personnel to provide home-based rehabilitation services. Personal care and the cost of therapy must usually be provided by the family or by the patient. In the case of mental illness or other neurological disorders, Social Security institutions rely on hospitals to provide care. Thus, it is clear that the current system is ill equipped to deal with the increasing number of aged persons expected in the near future. In 2000, there were 2 million disabled people in Mexico and 50,000 of them were 60 years old and over.

LOCAL SOCIAL POLICY FOR OLDER PERSONS

In several Mexican states, local governments have independent, uncoordinated health service systems for the elderly. Only a few states have social policies and services aimed at the elderly. In Mexico City, for example, there are special services and programs for the elderly: The current left-wing government offers all those over the age of 70 food pensions equivalent to $60 a month; the Health Ministry provides free drugs and vaccines to the elderly; and an advisory council is responsible for administering programs and services for the elderly.

Local programs for the elderly use family and community networks to improve the status of the elderly. Some programs aim to strengthen bonds between generations and social groups, as well as promote traditional culture and values and the rights of the elderly. This has made local governments national promoters of good social policies for the elderly. In Guadalajara, for example, the state university holds an annual event at which young and old come together to discuss problems and develop appreciation for one another. Other research centers and universities have promoted similar initiatives.

NONGOVERNMENTAL AND CIVIC PROGRAMS FOR OLDER PERSONS

Several nongovernmental programs provide social services for the elderly. The Private Assistance Board (*Junta de Asistencia Privada,* or JAP) includes over 430 private-sector institutions that provide medical and educational services for children, youth, and the elderly with mental or physical disabilities. The elderly are also eligible for daytime shelter, and some residential services are available for foreigners.

The elderly participate in a wide variety of services and programs. They also have become an important political constituency. As a group, the elderly are becoming more cognizant of their power and they are becoming more vocal in demanding that their needs be recognized by policymakers and others.

FINAL COMMENTS

Aging policy in Mexico is an elusive matter that tends to change according to governmental priorities. Since there is no agreed-upon government gerontological plan, policies and services for the elderly are not well coordinated. An effective national policy for the elderly should focus not only on the medical needs of the elderly but also on their social, cultural, and psychological needs. Aging policy must also be multidimensional if it is to reach the goal of improving the quality of life for the elderly.

—Veronica Montes de Oca Zavala

See also Social Security (Mexico)

Primary Sources

Archivo Histórico de la Secretaría de Salubridad y Asistencia, Mexico City; *Instituto Nacional de Estadística, Geografía e Informática* (www.inegi.gob. mx); *Consejo Nacional de Población* (www.conapo. gob.mx). Research is being conducted on the elderly and on the aging process at institutes in Mexico such as *Colegio de México, Universidad Nacional Autónoma de México* (UNAM), *Facultad Latinoamericana de Ciencias Sociales* (FLACSO), and *Centro de Investigaciones y Estudios Superiores en Antropología Social* (CIESAS).

Current Comment

Benítez-Zenteno, R. (1988). *Población y política en México.* Mexico City: Miguel Ángel Porrúa; Universidad Nacional Autónoma de México, Coordinación de Humanidades, Instituto de Investigaciones Sociales.

Gomez, C. (1997). Seguridad social y envejecimiento: La crisis vecina. In C. Rabell (Ed.), *Los retos de la población* (pp. 297–339). Mexico City: Facultad Latinoamericana de Ciencias Sociales; Juan Pablos.

Gutiérrez, L. M. (Ed.). (1996). *Salud del adulto mayor en México, estrategias y plan de acción.* Mexico City: Grupo Intersectorial de Salud del Adulto Mayor; OPS;

Secretaría de Salud, Dirección de Enfermedades Crónico Degenerativas.

Montes de Oca, V. (in press). *Redes comunitarias, género y envejecimiento. Participación, organización y significado de las redes de apoyo comunitario entre hombres y mujeres adultas mayores: La experiencia de la colonia Aragón en la ciudad de México.* Mexico City: Universidad Nacional Autónoma de México, Coordinación de Humanidades, Instituto de Investigaciones Sociales.

Further Reading

Gomez, C., & Montes de Oca, V. (in press). Aging in Mexico: Families, informal care and reciprocity. In P. Lloyd-Sherlock (Ed.), *Living longer: Aging, development and social protection.* London: Zed Publishers.

Ham Chande, R. (2003). *El envejecimiento en México: El siguiente reto de la transición demográfica.* Mexico City: Colegio de la Frontera Norte; Miguel Ángel Porrúa.

Laurell, A. C. (2000). Structural adjustment and the globalization of social policy in Latin America. *Journal of the International Sociology Association, 15*(2), 306–325.

Montes de Oca, V. (in press). *El envejecimiento en México: Un análisis sociodemográfico de los apoyos sociales y el bienestar de los adultos mayores.* Mexico City: Universidad Nacional Autónoma de México, Coordinación de Humanidades, Instituto de Investigaciones Sociales.

Montes de Oca, V., & Gomez, C. (Eds.). (in press). *Envejecimiento demográfico y políticas públicas para personas adultas mayores: México en Iberoamérica ante el nuevo siglo.* Mexico City: Universidad Nacional Autónoma de México, Coordinación de Humanidades, Instituto de Investigaciones Sociales.

AGING POLICY (UNITED STATES)

Under the "federal" system of government adopted in 1787, the public sector's responsibilities have been distributed across local, state, and national levels. In the early years of the republic, some localities and states took responsibility for the aged, but only when private charity and philanthropy or other sources of support were exhausted. After 1880, U.S. military pensions became the most important source of old-age relief. The federal government's role increased with the passage of the Social Security Act in 1935, and Medicare, Medicaid, and the Older Americans Act 30 years later. In recent decades, states have assumed more discretionary power in allocating resources, in part because conservatives have opposed nationwide senior citizen "entitlements."

GRASSROOTS INITIATIVES

Families and private agencies from the colonial era through the early decades of the republic bore most of the responsibility for caring for older people in need. Individuals were expected to make their own provisions for their later years. Consistent with the Elizabethan Poor Law of 1601, most colonial governments stipulated that families were to provide for their own vulnerable members. Black elders got support in slave quarters. Occasionally, citizens left bequests or built homes for their servants or indigent widows. In a few communities—Williamsburg, Virginia, in the 1680s, Philadelphia, Pennsylvania, in the 1700s—public funds were committed to erect almshouses, which offered shelter to the "worthy" elderly, as well as to orphans, criminals, and sick people. This was the extent of governmental attention to the elderly.

In the nineteenth century, grassroots efforts on behalf of the aged remained modest and tightly circumscribed. Seven states required older magistrates to step off the bench; these constituted the only public retirement policies before the Civil War. Eighteen of the 30 states by 1860 set penalties for family members who did not look after their aged kin. In the early twentieth century, Colorado, Ohio, and Kentucky made elder neglect a criminal offense. These laws were rarely enforced.

Local and state legislatures meanwhile raised funds for prisons, orphanages, and homes for the deaf and blind. As a result, almshouses increasingly became in effect old-age homes. By 1910, about 2 percent of the nation's elderly lived in almshouses; of the native-born inmates roughly 45 percent were at least 60 years old, as were 70 percent of all foreign-born almshouse residents. Going to the almshouse or poorhouse was a dreaded, dreadful prospect.

As railroad companies and large corporations began to institute pensions for employees, the public sector followed suit. Twenty states authorized disability and old-age pensions for schoolteachers; some municipalities covered police and firefighters. Only Arizona enacted an old-age assistance law prior to World War I, which was quickly ruled unconstitutional. Massachusetts legislators, suspecting that poverty among its elderly was growing, were relieved by experts who found that conditions for the aged poor living in the community were relatively good. Since reformers did not consider old-age dependency a problem, there was no need for state legislatures to act.

Paradoxically, the national government eschewed any responsibility for the aged while providing them the most support. Thomas Paine's proposal for governmental pensions was ignored in the 1790s, but President James Monroe addressed the plight of aging revolutionary war veterans. In 1818, the federal government granted pensions to soldiers who had served at least 9 months and required assistance. Support later was belatedly granted to veterans of the War of 1812 and the Mexican War and to their widows. Congress appropriated funds for a U.S. Naval Home in 1833 and a Soldiers' Home in 1851.

Civil War pensions became a major political issue. The number of pensioners rose sevenfold to 921,000 between 1886 and 1911. Congress authorized pensions in 1912 for any Union soldier who served 90 days and was at least 62. Age per se was deemed a disability. The provision claimed 18 percent of the federal budget. Southern states, teetering on bankruptcy, had to deal with Confederate veterans without federal assistance. Congress refused to draw an analogy between the plight of industrial veterans and military veterans—despite studies documenting the extent of old-age dependency by Lucille Eaves, Abraham Epstein, and others. It took an economic catastrophe, the Great Depression, to move the nation.

SOCIAL SECURITY BECOMES THE ENGINE FOR OLD-AGE POLICY MAKING

The economic consequences of the Great Depression and the political demands of senior activists in the Townsend Movement, a depression-era campaign for old-age pensions, led to the passage of the Social Security Act of 1935. Title I of the act promised old-age assistance up to $30 per month to qualified individuals over 65. Costs were to be covered with matching funds from states and the national government. Not only did Title I hasten the demise of the almshouse, but it established the first old-age entitlement in the United States: Older applicants could

appeal adverse decisions. Title II established an old-age insurance fund to which 40 percent of the workforce and their employers contributed. In 1939, coverage was expanded to include not only employees over 65 but also their dependents.

After World War II, old-age public policies increased benefits. A 1950 amendment to the Social Security Act increased Title II benefits by 77 percent. Disability provisions and early-retirement clauses were added to Social Security later in the decade. Medicare, which provided hospital insurance and coverage of some physician fees, became available in 1965 to Social Security beneficiaries. Another key piece of legislation was Medicaid, a medical program for the poor, which covered institutional care for the aged poor. In 1972, the Social Security Act was amended to add a cost of living index to Title II benefits. Congress added a new national program, Supplemental Security Income, to provide cash benefits to the poor elderly and disabled. Washington also monitored pension developments in the private sector. Corporate pensions became negotiable through collective bargaining, thanks to a Supreme Court ruling in 1949. The Keogh Act (1962) and Employee Retirement Security Income Act (1974), respectively, set guidelines for individual retirement plans and established fiduciary standards for larger pension systems.

The 1965 Older Americans Act made the Administration on Aging the nation's clearinghouse for new initiatives, such as underwriting centers to study aging at colleges and universities. To foster biomedical research, particularly in seeking a cure for Alzheimer's disease, Washington established the National Institute on Aging in 1974. A House Select Committee on Aging and a Senate Special Committee on Aging were created to consider new policy initiatives. More than 135 agencies in the federal government started special units on aging.

Washington did not act alone under the federal system. States, through the 1973 Comprehensive Services Act, gained more discretionary power in allocating funds through the creation of a network of Area Agencies on Aging. Some saw this act as a way to reduce Washington's penchant for spending by allowing officials and citizens at the local level to determine priorities. In retrospect, a shift in political thinking about public old-age policies occurred in the 1970s.

Neoconservatives urged individuals and private institutions to take more responsibility for dealing with the vicissitudes of age. By the late 1970s, even some liberal Democrats acknowledged that it was expensive to extend coverage and to liberalize entitlements. Jimmy Carter was the first president to tighten the disability rolls, but Congress chastised President Ronald Reagan's proposal for more harsh cutbacks. Nonetheless, the 1983 amendments to the Social Security Act managed to contain future costs while raising taxes, even as lawmakers endorsed the program's fundamental soundness. Hardliners wanted to go further. They continue to demand that Social Security be scrapped in favor of relying on private systems and individual savings.

The Bill Clinton administration attempted to revive national awareness of the needs of older people, but it did not get very far. After its Comprehensive Health Act was defeated, the administration lobbied with mixed success for more funds to cover prescription drugs. President Clinton elevated his first commissioner on aging, Fernando Torres-Gil, to the position of assistant secretary for health and human services. This was more than a symbolic gesture, for Torres-Gil had imaginative ideas on utilizing older people from diverse backgrounds as workers and volunteers. But the Administration on Aging has basically been checkmated for the past decade. Cutbacks in public programs once considered "sacred cows" are now feasible. Governments no longer issue bold agendas to utilize the diverse energies of the nation's elders.

—*W. Andrew Achenbaum*

See also Health Policy (United States); Social Security (United States); Supplemental Security Income (United States)

Primary Sources

Social Welfare History Archives, University of Minnesota, Minneapolis; Michigan Historical Collections, University of Michigan, Ann Arbor; Records of the Administration on Aging in the Records of the Social and Rehabilitation Service (Record Group 363) and Records of the Social Security Administration (Record Group 47), National Archives & Records Administration, College Park, MD.

Current Comment

Butler, R. N. (1975). *Why survive?* New York: Harper & Row.

Hall, G. S. (1922). *Senescence.* New York: D. Appelton.

Pifer, A., & Chisman, F. (Eds.). (1985). *The report of the Committee of Economic Security of 1935.* Washington, DC: National Conference on Social Welfare.

Further Reading

Achenbaum, W. A. (1978). *Old age in the new land: The American experience since 1790.* Baltimore: Johns Hopkins University Press.

Cole, T. R. (1992). *The journey of life.* New York: Cambridge University Press.

Haber, C., & Gratton, B. (1994). *Old age and the search for security.* Bloomington: Indiana University Press.

AID TO DEPENDENT CHILDREN/AID TO FAMILIES WITH DEPENDENT CHILDREN (UNITED STATES)

The Aid to Dependent Children (ADC) program, one of three public assistance titles of the 1935 Social Security Act, was a federal-state system of aid to children in need due to the absence of one or both parents. States were not required to participate, but, if they did, they had to meet federal standards to qualify for federal cost sharing. Federal standards, however, did not set a minimum payment level and states varied widely in the adequacy of benefits. Although benefits could be very low, federal ADC spending had no limit: All individuals who met a state's ADC eligibility criteria were entitled to federal subsidies. At first, ADC addressed only the needs of children, disregarding the needs of an impoverished parent or relative caretaker. By 1950, Congress had authorized federal sharing in additional payments to caregivers, and the program's name was changed to Aid to Families With Dependent Children (AFDC) to mark the shift. In 1962, Congress gave states the option to make AFDC payments to intact families in need because of unemployment (thus creating the AFDC-U program).

The original ADC program emerged from mothers' pensions, state programs for needy widows and other "respectable" women with children. The recipient mothers were expected to stay home to rear their children in accordance with moral standards. The proposed ADC program was framed in a similar manner: It was seen as a small and, with one exception, a comparatively uncontroversial program. One contentious aspect was the original Social Security bill's requirement that states provide benefits at a level to give recipients a decent standard of living. During debate over the bill, powerful, White, southern members of Congress forced the removal of the minimum standards provision both to contain welfare costs and to ensure that welfare payments were not high enough to disrupt White hegemony over the African American southern labor force.

By the 1960s, the small, relatively uncontroversial program of 1935 had developed into a huge and controversial one that dissatisfied both liberals and conservatives. Dramatic societal changes had altered the size and composition of the AFDC population as well as public perceptions of them in ways that bore little resemblance to the original mothers' pension picture. Mechanization of southern agriculture resulted in massive migration from the rural South to the urban North where many families then needed help. Changing social mores resulted in higher rates of marital dissolution and births out of marriage. Changing roles of women meant that staying out of the workforce to take care of children was not as sacrosanct a role as in the days of mothers' pensions, thus opening the door to demands that "mothers on welfare" go to work. In the 1960s, the size of the AFDC rolls increased at a pace critics considered explosive: from 3.1 million recipients in 1961 to 10.2 million recipients in 1971. Welfare rights advocacy efforts of the 1960s were but one of many factors playing a part in this expansion.

Advocacy for the rights of AFDC recipients was needed. By the 1950s, many states implemented highly oppressive practices meant to curtail the welfare rolls, for example, midnight raids and suitable home policies. In a carryover of mothers' pension thinking, state officials argued that public funds should not support immoral or unsuitable home settings for children. Thus, unannounced inspections and midnight raids

were made on female AFDC recipients' homes to see if a man was present, which could be evidence of an immoral relationship. Evidence of a man's visit or refusal to allow the inspection could result in immediate termination of benefits without right of appeal. Some states flagrantly discriminated against persons of color: paying lower benefit levels or refusing to accept applications from them. For example, for 15 years Arizona and New Mexico illegally refused to accept public assistance applications from Native Americans residing on reservations. Advocacy victories, including court decisions, by the end of the 1960s established a series of due process safeguards that greatly expanded applicants' ability to receive the AFDC benefits to which they were entitled.

Societal ambivalence toward AFDC is shown in post-1960s efforts to reform welfare. President Richard Nixon surprised the nation with a proposal to replace all welfare with a guaranteed income program called the Family Assistance Program (FAP). Although FAP failed, one portion was modified and enacted in 1972: the Supplemental Security Income (SSI) program. In enacting SSI, Congress federalized all the previously joint federal-state public assistance programs except for AFDC, which was left as before. Presidents Jimmy Carter and Ronald Reagan made efforts to fundamentally modify AFDC, but not until Bill Clinton's administration was AFDC radically changed. In 1996, Congress replaced AFDC with the Temporary Assistance for Needy Families (TANF) program. Federal block grants gave states increased discretion in designing their TANF programs to provide assistance to families with dependent children. For the first time, a ceiling was put on federal program spending, a limit was placed on how long a family could receive benefits, mothers were forced to quickly reenter the workforce after the birth of a child, and incentives and penalties were established for states to bring TANF rolls down. Highly controversial itself, TANF has fundamentally altered the manner in which support is provided to the nation's families with dependent children.

—*Jerry R. Cates*

See also Mothers' Pensions (United States); Poor Law (United States); Roosevelt, Franklin Delano; Social Security (United States), Social Welfare (United States): Since the Social Security Act; Supplemental Security Income (United States)

Primary Source

Records of the Social Security Administration (Record Group 47), National Archives & Records Administration, College Park, MD.

Current Comment

Abbott, G. (1938). *The child and the state.* Chicago: University of Chicago Press.

Piven, F. F., & Cloward, R. (1971). *Regulating the poor: The functions of public welfare.* New York: Pantheon.

Steiner, G. (1966). *Social insecurity: The politics of welfare.* Chicago: Rand McNally.

Further Reading

Bell, W. (1965). *Aid to Dependent Children.* New York: Columbia University Press.

Gordon, L. (1994). *Pitied but not entitled: Single mothers and the history of welfare, 1890–1935.* New York: Free Press.

Katz, M. B. (1996). *In the shadow of the poorhouse: A social history of welfare in the United States.* New York: Basic Books.

ALTMEYER, ARTHUR JOSEPH (1891–1972)

The career path of Arthur Altmeyer traced one of the main lines of influence through New Deal era social policy. As a former graduate assistant at the University of Wisconsin to the economist John R. Commons, Altmeyer became an important figure in the Wisconsin tradition of social reform. As secretary of the Wisconsin State Industrial Commission from 1922 to 1934, he administered Wisconsin's pioneering worker's compensation program and helped create its first-in-the-nation unemployment insurance system. An early adviser to Secretary of Labor Frances Perkins, Altmeyer served a 6-month stint as compliance director for the National Recovery Administration before being tapped in June 1934 by Perkins to be the second assistant secretary of labor. Altmeyer and Perkins jointly created the President's Committee on Economic Security, on which Altmeyer served as technical director, and during the second half of 1934 crafted the Franklin Roosevelt administration's Social Security proposals.

Taking a place on the three-person Social Security Board created in 1935 to administer the new Social Security Act, Altmeyer was the real force at the board. It was Altmeyer who had both the administrative background and theoretical grasp of social policy that was needed to make a successful start to this new federal undertaking. In January 1937, Altmeyer was elevated by President Franklin D. Roosevelt to be chairman of the board, and in 1946 he became commissioner for Social Security. During World War II, Altmeyer served as secretary to the War Manpower Commission and to the postwar International Refugee Organization. He also played a leading role in the expansion of social insurance to the nations of Latin America during the 1940s and 1950s.

Altmeyer was the key player in the legislative development of the 1939 amendments to the Social Security Act, which transformed the program from a narrow personal retirement system to a broad family-based social insurance program. The inclusion of additional workers under Social Security in 1950 and 1952 was the result of Altmeyer's careful policy research and planning. He fought against patronage in personnel selections in the Social Security Administration and for the principle that the agency had an affirmative duty to help applicants perfect their benefit claims. These ideas challenged traditional practices and put Altmeyer in conflict with powerful political forces, but he prevailed on both issues.

Working usually behind the scenes, Altmeyer shunned personal attention, once referring to his own personality as being "about as interesting as cold spinach." He had a theorist's intellectual grasp of social policy along with an administrator's skill at putting policy into practice, and an earnestness of purpose that made him seem stern and overly serious. From the inception of the Social Security program until his retirement in 1953, Arthur Altmeyer was the most influential figure in the development and evolution of the various programs under the Social Security Act. After his death in 1972, the main headquarters building of the Social Security Administration in Baltimore, Maryland, was renamed in his honor, a fitting tribute to the man who more than any other single individual shaped the Social Security program during its formative years.

—*Larry W. DeWitt*

See also Cohen, Wilbur Joseph; Social Security (United States)

Primary Sources

Arthur J. Altmeyer Papers, Wisconsin Historical Society, Madison; Records of the Committee on Economic Security, Social Security Board, and Social Security Administration (Record Group 47), National Archives & Records Administration, College Park, MD; an oral history interview with Arthur J. Altmeyer is available on the Social Security Administration website (www.ssa.gov/history/ajaoral.html).

Current Comment

Altmeyer, A. J. (1932). *The Industrial Commission of Wisconsin.* Madison: University of Wisconsin Press.

Altmeyer, A. J. (1966). *The formative years of Social Security.* Madison: University of Wisconsin Press.

Ferrero, R., & Altmeyer, A. J. (1957). *Estudio economico de la legislacion social Peruana y sugerencias para su mejoramiento.* Lima, Peru.

Many of Altmeyer's speeches and articles have been republished by the Social Security Administration on its Internet website (www.ssa.gov/history/collectalt.html).

Further Reading

Berkowitz, E. D. (1991). *America's welfare state.* Baltimore and London: Johns Hopkins University Press.

Derthick, M. (1979). *Policymaking for Social Security.* Washington, DC: Brookings Institution Press.

Witte, E. E. (1962). *Development of the Social Security Act.* Madison: University of Wisconsin Press.

AMERICAN PUBLIC WELFARE ASSOCIATION (UNITED STATES)

The advent of the Great Depression after 1929 with its resultant dramatic rise in poverty sparked a national advocacy movement to push for a federal response to the deepening crisis. In 1930, state welfare administrators and federal bureaucrats united to form the American Association of Public Welfare Officials (AAPWO). The mission of the new organization was to sponsor research and to advocate for social welfare policy legislation. Five years later, the group claimed its first legislative success with the passage of the federal Social Security Act in 1935. As a liaison between the federal government and state welfare administrators, the organization was deeply involved in the development and implementation of regulations for new Social Security programs such as Old-Age Insurance, Old-Age Assistance, Aid to the Blind, and Aid to Dependent Children.

Recognizing the need for a permanent organization that would advocate on behalf of public social welfare, the Rockefeller Foundation, a private philanthropy, granted AAPWO funding to establish a national office beginning in 1932. Frank Bane, then head of the Virginia Department of Public Welfare, became the first director of the renamed American Public Welfare Association (APWA). Bane would soon become the first director of the Social Security Administration. Bane established the APWA national office in Chicago, Illinois. Relocating from Washington, D.C., to Chicago allowed APWA to collaborate with some of the leading intellectuals in social welfare policy formulation, including Edith Abbott and Sophonisba Breckenridge at the University of Chicago School of Social Service Administration. In its early years, APWA counted in its membership many public welfare innovators, including Grace Abbott and Katharine Lenroot of the Children's Bureau; Frank Bane, Wilbur Cohen, and Robert Ball of the Social Security Administration; and Elizabeth Wickenden, who held a number of roles in federal social welfare agencies.

In just a decade, the organization doubled its membership to 70,000. In 1941, after the United States entered World War II, APWA was called on to expand its focus from emergency relief for the poor to the coordination of social welfare services to members of the armed forces and their families. As the organization evolved, it turned its attention to additional domains of public social welfare, most notably child welfare and services to the aging. Today, APWA has over 70 special interest areas that span a range of social welfare issues, including services to the disabled and Native American tribal issues in public welfare, adoption, and case management activities.

The APWA national headquarters remained in Chicago until 1974 when it relocated to Washington, D.C. In the 70 years since its inception, APWA has been a forum for research and discussion on public social services. Several APWA research projects have influenced federal social policy decisions, and from the earliest years of the association, it published research supportive of professional social casework or social work services. A 1956 study conducted by APWA provided the first documentation that families who received counseling from social service personnel had shorter stays on welfare. This finding was incorporated into the Social Security amendments of 1962, requiring state public welfare agencies to provide social services to needy clients.

In addition to numerous research projects that are detailed in monographs from the organization, APWA has also sponsored the dissemination of knowledge related to public welfare through regional and national conferences, and two national publications: the *American Public Welfare Association Newsletter* (now known as *The Washington Report*), and the journal *Public Welfare* (now known as *Policy and Practice*). Since the 1930s, APWA has also published a directory that provides information on state public welfare agencies and officials, and documents the evolution of social welfare programs and leadership.

In the midst of the latest round of welfare reform, and the increasingly negative societal view of "welfare," the organization adopted a new name in 1998. Now known as the American Public Human Services Association (APHSA), the organization continues to pursue its mission to promulgate and implement public policies that improve the lives of families.

—Taryn Lindhorst

See also The New Deal (United States); Social Security (United States); State Boards of Charities (United States)

Primary Sources

Records of the American Public Welfare Association, Social Welfare History Archives, University of Minnesota, Minneapolis (http://special.lib.umn.edu/ swha); Frank Bane Interview, Oral History Research Office, Columbia University, New York; Papers of Arthur Altmeyer, Robert Ball, Wilbur Cohen, and Elizabeth Wickenden, Wisconsin Historical Society, Madison.

Current Comment

American Public Welfare Association. (1941). *APWA: Our autobiography.* Chicago: Author.
Reports and documents produced over the 70-year history of the American Public Welfare Association are also available at the American Public Human Services Association office, Washington, DC, and on the World Wide Web (www.aphsa.org).

Further Reading

Viswanathan, N. (1961). *The role of the American Public Welfare Association in the formulation and development of public welfare policies in the United States: 1930–1960.* Unpublished doctoral dissertation, Columbia University, New York.

ASIAN AMERICANS AND SOCIAL WELFARE (UNITED STATES)

The social welfare of Asian Americans has been shaped by shifting labor needs, immigration policies, and a somewhat tenuous position as the "perpetual foreigner." Today, Asian Americans, those of Asian, Southeast Asian, and Indian subcontinent origin, constitute the fastest-growing minority group with 3.6 percent of the total United States population identifying themselves as "Asian" and another 0.6 percent as "Asian" and at least one other race. Comprising over 30 different ethnic groups, Asians have a history that spans more than 150 years in the United States.

Asians have come to the United States with much the same hopes and dreams as earlier European immigrants, pushed by economic need and drawn by opportunities that the West offered. There have been two significant waves of Asian immigration. The early wave was composed mostly of lone male contract laborers who came as sojourners from China and Japan, as well as from Korea, East India, and the Philippines. They left their families and homes to work the sugarcane fields of Hawai'i; the fruit orchards, vineyards, and mines of California; the fisheries in the Pacific Northwest; and the transcontinental railroad. The second wave, following the passage of the 1965 Immigration and Nationality Act, brought an educated middle class of professionals who arrived with their families and life savings. Unlike the earlier immigrants, they came to make a permanent home in the United States. Among the second wave were refugees from Southeast Asia, a more diverse group of varying national, economic, social, and educational backgrounds, all of whom at least initially believed their stay to be temporary. Although the experiences and circumstances of these two waves of Asian immigrants appear vastly different, they have shared a common history of being the "perpetual foreigner" in a country that has both welcomed them for their labor while resenting them for their presence and success.

FIRST WAVE

Early Chinese, Japanese, Korean, Filipino, and East Indians were denied citizenship, the right to establish families, and own land, and they often lived in segregated communities. The immigration of Asians to the United States began with Chinese in the mid 1800s, largely in response to the need for labor in the sugarcane fields of Hawai'i. The trans-Pacific immigration increased as laborers were recruited to the mainland as a "cheap" labor supply for agricultural work in California, fisheries in the Pacific Northwest, and to build the transcontinental railroad. The diversity of national origin within the labor force served as a control mechanism to minimize opportunity for workers to organize and to be held as leverage lest they demand higher wages or better conditions. Plantations recruited Japanese workers and paid them a lower wage as an example to disgruntled Chinese laborers, counting on language and cultural barriers as well as a history of national discord to dissuade organizing. Increasing anti-Chinese sentiment resulted in a complete halt to the immigration of Chinese laborers for a period of 10 years and the denial of naturalized citizenship with the passage of the Chinese Exclusion Act in 1882. Some 30,000 Japanese *kan'yaku imin,* or government-sponsored contract laborers, immigrated to the Hawai'ian islands between 1885 and 1894. Similarly, Filipino and Korean laborers were recruited as sources of "cheap" labor. Despite efforts to thwart solidarity based on ethnic and national isolation, Asian Americans have a history of organizing. Hawai'ian plantation workers were able to organize strikes, communicating in Pidgin English.

Living and working conditions for the Chinese and other Asian laborers were stark and dangerous.

They were often enlisted to do work that native-born laborers refused to do and at a lesser wage. Housing was substandard with many living in boarding houses and hotels that were overcrowded and unsanitary, and many were subjected to racial violence. For example, in October 1871, 19 Chinese were murdered by a mob of 500 in California. San Francisco was established as the gateway for the importation of Chinese labor on the mainland. San Francisco's Chinatown was overwhelmingly male and presumed to be rampant with prostitution, gambling, and illicit drug use. The few women who made the trip to Gold Mountain (the Chinese referred to California as *Sam Gaan* or Gold Mountain) were mostly wives of merchants and storekeepers. After the passage of the Chinese Exclusion Act of 1882, many of the laborers were stuck in California, destined to live out the remainder of their lives alone, isolated from family and home. The landowners realized that the men would be more content and productive if they had family with them and, therefore, encouraged the Japanese practice of importing "picture brides." Women were matched through arranged marriages with men they had never met and traveled across the Pacific to become a part of the labor economy.

The Gentlemen's Agreement of 1908, like the Chinese Exclusion Act of 1882, involved exclusion based on national origin. The Japanese were targets for much of the same xenophobia that the Chinese encountered because their agricultural successes were threatening to native Californians. The anti-Japanese sentiment resulted in the San Francisco school board's segregation of Japanese children and the passing of the Gentlemen's Agreement, which excluded immigration of any laborers who did not already have established farming interests. The number of Japanese who were able to enter dramatically declined although family members were allowed to join those already in the United States.

An immigration station, Angel Island, was being built to process trans-Pacific travelers when the great earthquake and fire of 1906 destroyed San Francisco's municipal records. "Paper sons" were born out of the flames, creating an opportunity for Chinese to sponsor "offspring" for immigration with false papers. Angel Island became a fortress where Chinese and other immigrants were interrogated and held for up to 2 years in order to prove their eligibility, the conditions so desperate that some committed suicide while waiting.

Korean, Filipino, and South Asian immigrants were among the first wave, but they were significantly fewer in number. Like the Japanese, the Koreans separated themselves into economic enclaves for survival. The Filipinos, or Pinoys, and East Indians were different from their East Asian counterparts in two significant ways: Many of them came with a certain degree of English proficiency and, as subjects of colonial rule, they were more Westernized. Religion was also a factor. Most Filipinos were Catholic because of the Spanish colonization and many of the Koreans were Christian and encouraged by missionaries to emigrate.

Despite the diversity of these early immigrants, they shared similar experiences of racial isolation, discrimination, and violation of their civil rights. They were refused service at restaurants, hotels, and stores and were segregated in movie theaters, public transportation, and housing. They were denied the right to vote, own property, intermarry, send their children to the same schools as White children, and legal recourse. They endured the anger, suspicion, and fear of a country that viewed them as perpetual foreigners. World War II was a watershed for anti-Asian sentiment and a time of reckoning for the United States to examine its own record regarding human rights. As a member of the Allied Forces, the United States was engaged in the preservation of freedom overseas, while its own laws and doctrine impinged on the rights of U.S. residents and citizens. Following Japan's attack on Pearl Harbor on December 7, 1941, President Franklin D. Roosevelt issued Executive Order 9066 forcing more than 120,000 Japanese in the United States into internment camps. Their civil liberties were circumvented in the name of national defense. Many of them were Nisei (U.S. born citizens). Eager to prove their loyalty, 9,507 Nisei men in Hawai'i volunteered for military service. They became members of the segregated fighting forces of the 442nd Regimental Combat Team and the 100th Battalion. Overall, some 33,000 Nisei fought in the United States armed forces. They were among the most decorated units, suffering high casualties fighting for freedom that the United States had denied them. President Harry Truman, addressing the returning Nisei soldiers of the 442nd, praised them: "You fought for the free nations of the world . . . you fought not only the enemy, you fought prejudice—and you won." This acknowledgment seemed empty when, upon returning from the internment camps, Japanese Americans found that much of what they previously had owned and worked so hard for was lost, and they were met with the same suspicion and distrust. They chose to quietly go about rebuilding their lives with many of the Issei (first-generation Japanese Americans) sliding into silence.

World War II impacted not only the Japanese, but also the Asian American community as a whole. The war was very personal for the Chinese and Filipinos who fought alongside White U.S. soldiers in Asia and Europe. They earned respect for their bravery and were proud to be recognized as more than houseboys, restaurant workers, and laborers. As members of the armed services, they were eligible to become citizens. The Chinese and Filipinos, as well as Koreans, found themselves having to defend themselves against generalized anti-Japanese discrimination, often resorting to signs and buttons for identification. The defense industry opened up opportunities for work in factories and Koreans, as former subjects of Japanese colonization, were invaluable as Japanese-language interpreters and teachers. Although the United States purportedly fought a war of moral principle against the Aryan supremacy doctrine of the Nazi regime, South Asians challenged the United States' exclusionary immigration and naturalization policies resulting in the establishment of a quota in 1946 and naturalization rights for East Indians. Similarly, pressure to repeal the Chinese exclusion laws mounted as China, allied with the United States and Japan, denounced the race-based imperialistic policies of the West. The repeal was enacted in 1943, establishing an immigration quota and naturalization rights for Chinese.

SECOND WAVE

The 1965 Immigration and Nationality Act paved the way for a major shift in immigration from Europe and Latin America to Asia. The act eliminated the national origins quota system and established a per-country limit based on hemisphere. The focus was on family reunification, meeting marketplace labor needs, and offering asylum. The new Chinese, Korean, Filipino, and East Indian immigrants arrived with an education or in pursuit of continuing their education. The "brain drain" of lawyers, doctors, nurses, engineers, computer programmers, pharmacists, academics, and entrepreneurs was a function of professionals seeking to improve their quality of life and not, as their predecessors, focused on merely meeting basic survival needs. Many, however, found themselves underemployed, forced out of their professional fields due to discriminatory credentialing and hiring practices and language barriers, and earning less than their native-born counterparts. They immigrated with their families, intending to establish new lives and homes, often hoping later to sponsor extended family. Instead, the Korean and East Indians have been forced to turn to entrepreneurial endeavors more out of necessity than inclination. They pooled their monies, invested in small businesses, and participated in ethnic economies as a strategy to circumvent segregated and racist systems. The Asian greengrocers, liquor store owners, and restaurateurs have replaced the Jewish, Greek, Polish, and Italian entrepreneurs who left the urban centers amidst the post–World War II White flight to the suburbs.

The suspicion and distrust of the earlier "yellow peril" has been replaced with the "model minority myth." According to the 2001 *Statistical Abstract of the United States,* Asian Americans as a whole perform well academically, with approximately 42 percent of all Asian American adults having completed at least a 4-year college degree. They also have a median family income of $52,826, which is higher than that of White families at $49,023. Their relative economic and educational successes have been held up as an example for other minorities, placing them in an untenable middleman position in comparison to African Americans, Latinos, and indigenous peoples.

Civil war in the Southeast Asian countries of Vietnam, Laos, and Cambodia and the United States' participation in these conflicts brought thousands of refugees to the United States. The year 1975 marked a mass exodus of refugees to Thailand and the Philippines, people seeking to escape genocide. The communist regimes sought to eliminate the educated middle class and those who had supported the U.S. military agenda. Many of the early refugees were professionals and high-ranking military officials who were airlifted out. Later refugees were from a less-educated working class, and if they survived the killing fields of Cambodia and the rape and plunder of Thai pirates, they arrived in America traumatized and often separated from family. The preliterate ethnic Mien and Hmong of Laos abandoned their mountain dwellings for urban centers in the United States where life was often incomprehensible. This cultural dissonance has contributed to their having the lowest level of education (61 percent with an elementary education or less in 1996) among Asian Americans as well as the highest dropout, unemployment, teen pregnancy, and poverty rates (in 2000 a reported 62 percent lived below the poverty line). The model minority myth has resulted in these communities being underserved and overlooked, although private and public social service agencies have attempted to respond to their needs.

The wars in Korea and Vietnam have also resulted in the international adoption of over 150,000 children to predominately White U.S. families. The welfare of these adopted children has been the subject of much conjecturing, research, and political debate.

Today, Asian Americans have become active participants in lobbying for equal rights and protection under the U.S. Constitution. Asian American college students supported the civil rights movement and calls for affirmative action. Sensei (third-generation Japanese Americans) fought for and won reparations and an official apology for the Issei and Nisei who were interned during World War II. The Asian Pacific American Labor Alliance (APALA), founded in 1992 and affiliated with the AFL-CIO, promotes social justice by fostering collaboration between the labor movement and the Asian American community. The welfare and needs of Asian American communities are as diverse as the people themselves. They are communities in transition. Japanese Americans marry outside the Japanese American community at a high rate and their families have been in the United States for multiple generations. The Chinese American community is somewhat polarized between the third and fourth generations—ABCs (American-born Chinese) and the newly arrived immigrants who sustain and keep viable the Chinatowns and ethnic enclaves in the larger cities. The Filipino and East Indian communities are more transparent, spread out into the suburbs. Economic and educational needs in the Southeast Asian communities are compounded by the loss of culture and identity, the first-generation parents fearing that their children are a "lost generation."

Regardless of ethnic origin, Asian Americans have inherited and maintained systems of support that are somewhat closed and resistant to outside intervention, affecting help-seeking behaviors and needs identification. Asian American communities have a history of establishing mutual aid associations—often defined by ethnicity, family name, or dialect. The Chinese began such self-help during periods of exclusion, and other immigrant and refugee communities have established similar organizations aimed to meet the bilingual/bicultural needs of their communities. Similarly, church-, temple-, and mosque-based outreach and support sustain Korean and East Indian communities. The myth of Asians as a model minority prevents an informed understanding of the issues and concerns that impact the welfare of this diverse group of people. Issues that affect their lives include racism and violence, affirmative action, immigration, English-language proficiency, discrimination, poverty and housing, health, gender violence, and mental health. Relevant social policy for Asian Americans must therefore take into account their diverse histories and complex ecological contexts.

—*Kathleen Ja Sook Bergquist*

See also Immigration and Social Welfare Policy (United States); Labor Movement and Social Welfare (United States)

Primary Sources

Asian American Studies Center, University of California, Los Angeles; Association for Asian American Studies, Cornell University, Ithaca, NY.

Current Comment

Fujiwara, L. H. (1998). The impact of welfare reform on Asian immigrant communities. *Social Justice, 25*(1), 82–104.

Hsiao, A. (1998). The hidden history of Asian-American activism in New York City. *Social Policy, 28*(4), 23–31.
Publications of the Asian Pacific American Labor Alliance (AFL-CIO), Washington, DC; the National Asian Pacific American Legal Consortium, Washington, DC; the Japanese American Citizens League (JACL), San Francisco, CA; and the Organization of Chinese Americans (OCA), Washington, DC.

Further Reading

Daniels, R. (1997). No lamps were lit for them: Angel Island and the historiography of Asian American immigration. *Journal of American Ethnic History, 17*(1), 3–18.
Kim, H.-c. (1994). *A legal history of Asian Americans, 1790–1990.* Westport, CT: Greenwood.
Takaki, R. (1989). *Strangers from a different shore: A history of Asian Americans.* New York: Penguin.
Wong, K. (2001). *Voices for justice: Asian Pacific organizers and the new labor movement.* Los Angeles: Center for Labor Research and Education.

ASSOCIATION FOR IMPROVING THE CONDITION OF THE POOR (UNITED STATES)

Founded in 1843 in New York City and modeled on British prototypes, the Association for Improving the Condition of the Poor (AICP) soon became an exemplar for urban reform and charity organizations throughout the United States. From its beginnings, the AICP embraced a complicated mission with three parts. Its founders, led by Robert M. Hartley, sought to establish an urban sanitation movement, provide immediate relief and access to jobs to poor neighbors, and contribute to their spiritual uplift. The AICP carried on its work for 97 years, until the Great Depression forced it and the Charity Organization Society of New York to merge in 1939, forming the still-extant Community Service Society of New York.

A RESPONSE TO CRISES

The men who created the AICP did so near the end of a prolonged economic depression that had begun with the panic of 1837. Urban dwellers in daily face-to-face contact with unemployed and hungry New Yorkers, the founders grasped the interconnection between poverty and contagion. Although dangerous diseases like cholera, typhus, and tuberculosis threatened all residents of the city, impoverished tenement dwellers suffered the worst toll. Disproportionate rates of mortality among newborns, children, and birthing mothers in poor neighborhoods spurred the creation of the AICP.

The founders of the AICP were merchants, doctors, and lawyers—White evangelical Protestants with Anglo-American backgrounds. They created the association to preserve civic cohesion in a city in which a rising proportion of residents were Catholic and Jewish immigrants from Ireland, Germany, and other countries with distinctly different political and cultural traditions from those of England and the United States.

The extreme and visible poverty of Black New Yorkers was another stimulus to creating the AICP. Hartley, the leader of the organization during its first three decades of advocacy, reform, and service, joined with other founders in establishing from the outset an inclusive approach to philanthropy, one that reached across racial, national, and religious lines.

SANITATION

Although the AICP was organized three decades before the germ theory was verified, its leaders and many volunteers documented the intimate interconnections between filth, morbidity, and mortality. Under Hartley's leadership, the AICP created free dispensaries (outpatient health clinics) and public baths in the early 1850s. After the Civil War, AICP continued these initiatives, forming the basis of New York City's public health care, clean water supply, and public baths.

Hartley and other founders also made direct appeals to real estate developers' consciences to build tenements with improved ventilation. When that campaign failed, the AICP built, in 1855, a model tenement of its own for Black working men and their families. The organization's leadership also undertook systematic investigation of tenements, realizing that public regulation would have to supplant moral suasion. In 1857, the association conducted a block-by-block study of defective dwellings, sewers, and streets throughout Manhattan. AICP lobbying, based on the 1857 survey data, led to a pioneering 1867 law establishing health and safety standards for tenements.

The investigations and advocacy of the AICP also highlighted the impurity of milk production and distribution. The first pure-milk legislation in the United States resulted in 1862 in New York City. Similarly, under the AICP's prodding, New York created a city department of health in 1866, complete with medical supervision and police powers. AICP surveys and lobbying also prompted regulation of the city's markets, slaughterhouses, and sewers.

When, in 1882, Robert Koch discovered the bacillus that caused tuberculosis, the leading cause of death in the nineteenth century, the AICP immediately devoted itself to curtailing the spread of the disease. The association offered public educational workshops, pamphlets, and exhibitions about tuberculosis treatment and prevention; low-cost medical examinations at AICP dispensaries; free nursing, dentistry, and nutritional education in public schools; and free medical and residential facilities for individuals and families directly infected.

IMMEDIATE RELIEF

Providing money, medicines, clothing, fuel, and vouchers for food to people deemed both indigent and worthwhile—that is, poor people found to be hardworking, ill, disabled, aged, or young—was central to the AICP's purpose. The organization continued to supply material relief to poor neighbors, even in the decades of the 1870s and 1880s, when social Darwinists and scientific philanthropy advocates condemned the indiscriminate giving of charity as inimical to the social good.

To assess the need and worthiness of New Yorkers for charity, the AICP copied innovative European and English charitable practices of the era, which Hartley studied firsthand before leading the AICP. Under Hartley's direction, New York City was divided, for friendly visiting purposes, into numbered sections that corresponded precisely with preexisting municipal ward and district divisions. Systematic monthly home visiting by hundreds of trained male volunteers, their filing of weekly and monthly reports, and regular supervision by the most senior of volunteers and Hartley characterized the AICP's method until the 1870s. Then, when bad health forced Hartley's retirement, two men took over, one the AICP's new executive director, and the other the first paid director of home visitation. The latter supervised a small, paid full-time staff of female home visitors and a trained volunteer corps, now made up of both genders. Their activities became an important model for casework in the emergent profession of social work.

In the new century, the AICP continued its provision of material relief and intensified its focus on helping people to find jobs. In 1909, the association collaborated with the Charity Organization Society of New York in founding the National Employment Exchange, a forerunner of public unemployment services. Later, in 1930, the AICP again joined with the Charity Organization Society of New York in lobbying for a bill that resulted in the New York State Old-Age Assistance Act. In the same year, the two groups cooperated with other agencies in financing the Unemployment Work Relief Bureau, a precursor of public emergency relief programs.

MORAL REFORM

What inspired successful businessmen and professionals of the 1840s to spend much of their free time and money on helping the urban poor? The founders of the AICP were motivated, in large part, by a profound and activist piety. They were evangelical Presbyterians, Methodists, Episcopalians, and Quakers who had been inspired in their youth by the spiritual revivals of the Second Great Awakening. The architects of the AICP had previous experience in Christian movements that had created urban church missions, bible tract societies, Sunday schools, and temperance campaigns in the first three decades of the nineteenth century. In building the AICP, they sought to extend their good works and prayer beyond the confines of the sectarian.

The AICP's friendly visitors coupled moral education with material relief during the first three decades of the organization's life. They employed prayer and moral suasion, together with money, food, fuel, medicines, and job referrals, in their fight against unemployment, indigence, alcoholism, family abandonment, and homelessness. When the founders were replaced by a newer generation of leaders in the 1870s, the AICP became a secular endeavor.

As proto-social workers and public health workers, AICP members refined a repertoire of practice and social reform methods that remain important today. Casework, intensive case management, home visiting, investigative social surveys, lobbying, case and issue advocacy, and public health education are part of the legacy of the AICP. In addition, Robert M. Hartley and his fellow founders demonstrated a dual devotion to science and faith that enabled their AICP successors to embrace vigorously and quickly the bacteriological revolution and the challenges of urban modernity.

—*Barbara Levy Simon*

See also Charity Organization Societies (United States); Hopkins, Harry Lloyd; Poverty (United States)

Primary Source

The Records of the Association for Improving the Condition of the Poor are in the Community Service Society of New York Papers, Rare Book & Manuscript Library, Butler Library, Columbia University, New York.

Current Comment

Hartley, I. S. (Ed.). (1882). *Memorial of Robert Milham Hartley*. Utica, NY: Press of Curtis & Childs [Printer].

Hartley, R. M. (1842). *An historical, scientific, and practical essay on milk as an article of human sustenance; with a consideration of the effects consequent upon the unnatural methods of producing it for the supply of large cities.* New York: J. Leavitt. Available: Rare Book & Manuscript Library, Butler Library, Columbia University, New York.

Riis, J. (1971). *How the other half lives: Studies among the tenements of New York.* New York: Dover. (Original work published 1890) Available: www.yale.edu/amstud/inforev/riis/title.html

Further Reading

Conkin, P. K. (1995). *The uneasy center: Reformed Christianity in antebellum America.* Chapel Hill: University of North Carolina Press.

Cunningham, H., & Innes, J. (Eds.). (1998). *Charity, philanthropy and reform: From the 1690s to 1850.* New York: St. Martin's.

Lubove, R. (1959). The New York Association for Improving the Condition of the Poor: The formative years. *New York Historical Society Quarterly, 43,* 307–327.

Rosenberg, C. S. (1971). *Religion and the rise of the American city: The New York City mission movement, 1812–1870.* Ithaca, NY: Cornell University Press.

B

BALL, ROBERT MYERS (B. 1914)

Robert Ball probably had a greater influence on the development of the Social Security system than anyone else in the second half of the twentieth century. A career civil servant who started with the Social Security Administration (SSA) in 1939 as a lower-level employee, he rose eventually to be appointed commissioner of the SSA by President John F. Kennedy in 1962. It was a position he held under three presidents until he retired in 1973.

Ball first came to notice when he took an assignment at the SSA as the lead instructor in the agency's training programs. His skills as an educator were immediately evident, but it was his grasp of the principles of social programs, and an unmatched ability to explain them in a clear way, that would become signal traits throughout his career. In 1948–1949, Ball was tapped to be the staff director of the Social Security Advisory Council. The work of this council resulted in the pivotal 1950 amendments to the Social Security Act, which Ball did more than anyone else to shape. These amendments increased the value of old-age insurance benefits and added the Aid to the Permanently and Totally Disabled public assistance program. This effort elevated Ball's status at the SSA and he was placed in effective charge of the agency's largest operational component. This opened the door to the other part of Ball's twin talents: his skills as an administrator. Ball

was also instrumental in smoothing the transition from the Harry S. Truman to the Dwight D. Eisenhower administrations, and in persuading skeptical Republicans within the administrations to support Social Security.

A strategic legislative thinker and a master at relations with Congress, Ball influenced every piece of Social Security legislation from 1950 through 1972. His patience and persistence, coupled with a thoroughgoing pragmatism, made him very effective on Capitol Hill. On the administrative side, Ball successfully guided the agency during the expansions of coverage in the early 1950s and the addition, in 1956, of disability benefits. In 1962, he engineered a reorganization of the SSA, which separated its welfare responsibilities, transferring these to a new Welfare Administration in the Department of Health, Education, and Welfare. Ball was in charge of the implementation of the Medicare program following its passage in 1965. This effort—which President Lyndon B. Johnson described as the most extensive peacetime undertaking in the nation's history—was a resounding success, further contributing to Ball's reputation as an able administrator.

Following President Richard M. Nixon's reelection in 1972, Ball retired from government. He went on to be one of the country's most active and prolific experts on Social Security, health care, and related topics. He was a senior scholar at the Institute of

Medicine of the National Academies from 1973 to 1980. In 1981–1982, Ball was the most important member of the National Commission on Social Security Reform (also known as the Greenspan Commission), whose report resulted in the 1983 amendments—the last major piece of Social Security legislation in the twentieth century.

Ball has been a frequent adviser to top Democratic political figures over the years. He worked in President Jimmy Carter's reelection campaign in 1980 and was an important adviser on Social Security to officials in the Bill Clinton administration. He continues today to write, educate, and advocate for Social Security. A cofounder of the National Academy of Social Insurance in 1986, Ball's eminence in the field of Social Security was unmatched by any other figure in the late twentieth century.

—Larry W. DeWitt

See also Social Security (United States)

Primary Sources

Robert M. Ball Papers, Wisconsin Historical Society, Madison; Records of the Social Security Administration (Record Group 47), National Archives & Records Administration, College Park, MD; an oral history interview with Robert M. Ball is available on the Social Security Administration website (www.ssa.gov/history/orals/balloralhistory.html).

Current Comment

Ball, R. M. (1952). *Pensions in the United States.* Washington, DC: Government Printing Office.
Ball, R. M. (1978). *Social Security today and tomorrow.* New York: Columbia University Press.
Ball, R. M., & Bethel, T. N. (1989). *Because we are all in this together: The case for a national long term care insurance policy.* Washington, DC: Families USA Foundation.
Many of Ball's speeches and articles have been republished by the Social Security Administration (SSA) on its Internet website (*www.ssa.gov/history/bobball.html*).

Further Reading

Ball, R. M. (2000). *Insuring the essentials: Bob Ball on Social Security.* New York: Century Foundation.
Ball, R. M., & Bethel, T. N. (1998). *Straight talk about Social Security.* New York: Century Foundation.

Berkowitz, E. D. (2003). *Robert Ball and the politics of Social Security.* Madison: University of Wisconsin Press.
Marmor, T. R. (1987). Entrepreneurship in public management: Wilbur Cohen and Robert Ball. In J. W. Doig & E. C. Hargrove (Eds.), *Leadership and innovation.* Baltimore and London: Johns Hopkins University Press.

BOWERS, FRANK SWITHUN BARRINGTON (1908–1992)

Born in London, England, on June 26, 1908, Bowers immigrated to Canada in his twenties, working as a ranch hand from 1932 to 1934. He then entered the Roman Catholic Oblate order, taking the name Swithun. After ordination, Father Bowers served as an assistant at St. Joseph's Church, in Ottawa, Ontario, from 1942 to 1946. At St. Patrick's College, University of Ottawa, he taught religion as a lecturer from 1945 to 1947, and was a professor of sociology from 1946 to 1947.

He was then chosen by the Oblates to establish a school of social welfare at St. Patrick's. He enrolled at the School of Social Work, Columbia University, New York, in June 1947 in an accelerated master's program. He completed it in December 1948. During the next 6 months, he prepared for the opening of St. Patrick's School of Social Welfare. The first class of 17 students began their programs in June 1949. In 1951, the school received its first accreditation from the American Association of Schools of Social Work (later the Council on Social Work Education). Within a few years, St. Patrick's had become the foremost social casework school in Canada. Father Bowers remained as director until 1971. In 1967, the school became affiliated with Carleton University in Ottawa and moved to the Carleton campus in 1972, where it continued as the Carleton University School of Social Work.

As a scholar, Father Bowers published over 30 articles. He is best known for his tripartite article, "The Nature and Definition of Social Casework," published in the U.S. journal *Social Casework* in 1949. For nearly two decades, his definition was the standard for both practitioners and social work educators. In 1949–1950, he completed advanced courses at the Institute of Psychology, University of Ottawa. He was awarded an honorary LLD from the University of Buffalo in 1961.

As founder and director of the St. Patrick's School of Social Welfare, Father Bowers had a major influence on the development of social work education within Canada. During the late 1950s and early 1960s, he and Charles Hendry, director of the School of Social Work at the University of Toronto, were the leading figures in the development and activities of the National Committee of Canadian Schools of Social Work, the forerunner of the Canadian Association of Schools of Social Work. Father Bowers was also elected to the board of directors of the American Association of Schools of Social Work and served on its Committee on Accreditation. He was active in the International Conference on Social Work, holding the office of treasurer. He gained an international reputation for his capacity to articulate his vision of social work practice and the social work profession.

His students knew him as a masterful teacher, a thought-provoking intellectual, and a gifted orator. He inspired in students and professionals the determination to offer compassionate human services in an accountable, rational fashion.

In 1968, having gradually withdrawn from the priesthood, he married Margaret Moores, a welfare worker from Newfoundland who had graduated from St. Patrick's in 1965. Following his retirement, they moved to Algarve, Portugal, where he wrote several articles on the history of Portugal under the name of Frank Bowers. On July 2, 1992, on a trip to Canada, he reunited with his friends in Three Hills, Alberta. Later that evening, he suffered a stroke. He had come full circle; there were no more words to be spoken. He died on July 13, 1992, in Calgary, Alberta.

—James Gripton and Mary Valentich

See also Cassidy, Harry; Hendry, Charles Eric; Small Systems Social Work (Canada); Social Work Profession (Canada); Urwick, Edward Johns

Further Reading

Bowers, S. (1949, October). The nature and definition of social casework: Part I. *Social Casework, 30,* 311–317.

Bowers, S. (1949, November). The nature and definition of social casework: Part II. *Social Casework, 30,* 369–375.

Bowers, S. (1949, December). The nature and definition of social casework: Part III. *Social Casework, 30,* 412–417.

Bowers, S. (1950). The nature and definition of social casework. In C. Kasius (Ed.), *Principles and techniques in social casework: Selected articles, 1940–1950* (pp. 97–127). New York: Family Service Association.

BRACE, CHARLES LORING
(1826–1890)

Charles Loring Brace is credited with originating family foster care in the United States. In 1853, he founded the New York Children's Aid Society (CAS) to rescue poor children from slums created by urbanization and immigration. An important figure in child welfare history, he was also a cultural leader in nineteenth century attitudes toward urbanization, poverty, and family life.

Brace was born in 1826 in Litchfield, Connecticut, the second child of John Brace and Lucy Porter. John had moved to Litchfield to assist his aunt, Sara Pierce, founder of one of the first schools in the United States to extend secondary education to women. His students included Harriet Beecher Stowe, who wrote *Uncle Tom's Cabin* (1852), and her sister Catharine Beecher, whose books defined women's new domestic roles.

The Braces moved to Hartford, Connecticut, when Charles was 7, and he grew up enjoying natural beauty and simple country pleasures. But he was also exposed to a vigorous intellectual climate that supported both the cult of domesticity and the evangelical movement that shaped family life and philanthropy in the nineteenth century. Brace's mother died when he was 14 and his older sister Mary took charge of the family.

As a teenager, Brace became a follower of Horace Bushnell, a Congregational minister whose ideas about the unconscious influence of family life on children's moral development profoundly influenced him. Bushnell advocated saving children from bad or irreligious families by placing them in good Christian families, inspiring Brace's later commitment to family foster care for poor children.

At Yale and the Yale Divinity School, Brace developed liberal religious and political views, questioning the idea of original sin, applauding the 1848 European revolutions, and opposing slavery. At 19, he decided to enter the ministry. Continuing his studies, Brace moved to New York to attend the Union Theological Seminary and began his work with the poor in the penitentiary, charity hospital, and almshouse on Blackwell's Island. As a young theological student, he wondered at the crowded streets of New York City. Nothing in his experience growing up in bucolic Hartford had prepared him for the noise, filth, and confusion of the immigrant-filled Five Points slum. He took every opportunity to escape to his friend and schoolmate Frederick Law Olmsted's farm on Staten Island. With Olmsted, who later designed New York's Central Park, Brace debated the ideas of Ralph Waldo Emerson about nature and country life. Emerson's views of the transforming power of nature, along with Bushnell's faith in the family, formed a core of idealism that supported Brace's almost mystical belief in the redeeming effects on vagrant children of Christian homes in the country.

In the spring of 1850, Brace and Olmsted went on a fateful walking tour of Great Britain. There, they visited the ragged schools of London and Edinburgh founded to provide religion and education to children too poor to attend regular schools. Continuing to Germany, Brace became enamored with the warmness of German home life, so unlike the formalism, coldness, and materialism he attributed to American households. In Hamburg, he found a model for his future work in the nearby *Rauhe Haus* (Rough House), a religiously inspired farm home for vagrant children operating on a family system. Near the end of his tour, Brace entered politically torn Hungary. Arrested and jailed for associating with Hungarian revolutionaries and possession of revolutionary literature, he regained his freedom with the assistance of a Catholic priest who smuggled his letters to the American consulate.

Once back in New York, Brace started to work with urban missionary Louis M. Pease, the founder in 1850 of the Five Points Mission. Brace's experiences with Lower Manhattan's adult alcoholics and prostitutes, however, soon convinced him of the need to intervene with children to institute lasting reform. Even those with parents, Brace felt, had no semblance of the family life he advocated for all Americans. In his column in the New York *Daily Times,* he campaigned for a school for vagrant children, such as those he had

seen in London and Edinburgh. Inspired by a similar effort in Boston, the full program of the New York Children's Aid Society (CAS) was outlined at its inauguration in March 1853.

Brace was especially drawn to the vigorous newsboys. He admired their independence and ingenuity while trying to polish their rough edges. He created the Newsboys Lodging House to shelter and reform them, and later encouraged them to join the "orphan trains," which took homeless youngsters west where they were often adopted by farm families and given opportunities and a fresh start. (Newsboys inspired publisher Horace Greeley's famous call to "Go west, young man" and many of Horatio Alger's books.) Admiring as he was of street boys, Brace had grave misgivings about the future potential of vagrant girls, as he believed that once besmirched, female virtue was impossible to regain.

Recognized as an important figure in New York society, Brace directly solicited the support of New York's first families, including the Roosevelts and Astors, and reached many other contributors through the CAS annual reports. He gathered many of his experiences and stories into his classic book, *The Dangerous Classes of New York and Twenty Years' Work Among Them* (1872), which recounted the founding and development of the CAS.

Brace's ideas varied little throughout his career. He was a national and international figure who corresponded with Henry Lloyd Garrison, John Stuart Mill, and Charles Darwin, developing his own theory of personality: He believed that each child was born with "gemmules" that could be nurtured toward good or bad. Brace's steadfast defense of the family as the "best asylum" and "God's reformatory" for poor and homeless children and his critique of the effects of institutionalization and orphanages led to the development of the cottage system in institutional care. In the 1880s, the National Conference on Charities and Correction recognized the superiority of family care over institutional care for dependent children. Although he was criticized for casual placement procedures, lack of supervision, and religious bias, Brace's ideas still shape modern family foster care.

—Kristine Nelson

See also Children's Aid Society (United States); Child Welfare Policy (United States); Religion and Social Welfare (United States)

Primary Sources

Brace, C. L. (1973). *The dangerous classes of New York and twenty years' work among them.* Silver Spring, MD: National Association of Social Workers. (Original work published 1872)

Brace, E. (Ed.). (1894). The life of Charles Loring Brace told chiefly in his own letters. New York: Charles Scribner's Sons.

Further Reading

O'Connor, S. (2001). *Orphan trains: The story of Charles Loring Brace and the children he saved and failed.* New York: Houghton Mifflin.

Wohl, R. R. (1969). The "country boy" myth and its place in American culture: The nineteenth century contribution. *Perspectives in American History, 3,* 77–156.

C

CANADIAN ASSOCIATION OF SOCIAL WORKERS

The Canadian Association of Social Workers (CASW) was created in 1926 as an organization of individual social workers. The CASW would promote professional standards, advocate for social work education, promote public support for the profession, publish a journal, and engage in research.

By 1938, the organization had over 500 members and branches in British Columbia, Ontario, and Manitoba. Most social work professionals, however, were women, and there was concern about their low status. CASW leaders thought that by drawing more men into the field, they would improve this status. Recruitment drives in the 1930s used pamphlets to argue that men were tougher and more rational and therefore would be better equipped for work in social administration and in corrections. This campaign created a gendered role differentiation within the Canadian social work profession that persisted to the end of the century.

Canada's welfare state expanded in the decades after the Second World War, and with this expansion the number of practicing Canadian social workers also increased, reaching over 2,000 by the 1950s. Under Canada's federal Constitution, most health and welfare services fall within provincial jurisdiction, so most social workers were working for provincial governments, local governments, and nonprofit agencies. As a result, provincial social work associations developed in all of the Canadian provinces. The need for a federated social work association, one that would parallel the federated structure of the Canadian Constitution, became evident. In 1985, CASW became a federated association of autonomous provincial social work associations. At first, a national board of directors was appointed by the provincial organizations, with larger provinces appointing a larger number of directors. As a result, the national association was dominated by the larger provinces and lacked a truly national perspective. A 3-year consultation culminated in a restructuring of the CASW into an organization with a governing board composed of one representative for each province. Member organizations originally participated through delegate assemblies until an annual joint meeting of the CASW board and the presidents of the member social work organizations replaced these in 1996.

CASW currently has a national membership of 18,928 social workers, consisting of the individual members of all the member organizations in the Canadian provinces and territories. The national office remains small, with an executive director, a social worker, and three support staff. Nonetheless, the association has undertaken a variety of initiatives, including international commitments, membership support, and social action. CASW is a member of the International Federation of Social Workers, and contributes to and supports that organization by paying membership dues, participating on the board, and assisting with the development of materials. CASW also tries to strengthen the social work profession in Canada by developing the professional code of ethics, creating standards and guidelines for various areas of practice, and distributing the *Canadian Social Worker* to all individual members. This journal is published in French and English. It features discussions of new areas of practice (e.g., HIV/AIDS, practice in interdisciplinary settings) and is the only bilingual social work journal in North America. CASW has also tried to influence federal government policies that affect the conditions faced by both social workers and their clients. For example, when a Conservative government was in power in the 1980s, CASW advocated equitable tax reform, defended federal cost sharing in provincial social programs, opposed free trade with the United States, and participated in peace initiatives. More recently, CASW has engaged in social action through participation in broader coalitions, such as Campaign 2000, the Canadian Coalition for Rights of Children, the National Coalition on Housing and Homelessness, and the Canadian Coalition of Organizations Responding to AIDS. Given CASW's limited financial and human resources, the national association finds this more effective than acting alone on specific issues, even if it attracts less publicity.

Canada's provincial social work associations, like their counterparts in medicine and nursing, have sought self-regulation and monopoly control over their field of practice. The various provincial associations have developed at varying rates toward this objective. Some provinces began with voluntary registration, but most have now moved toward requiring registration for use of the title of social worker and practice as a social worker. In three provinces—Prince Edward Island, Ontario, and British Columbia—registration is handled by one organization and membership support and social action are handled by another. In such situations, social workers may be required to join their regulatory organization, but they may choose not to join their professional association. In seven provinces, registration, membership support, and social action functions are combined. The Newfoundland and Labrador Association of Social Workers (NLASW), for example, handles all these functions. This situation, however, is fluid and varies with the definition of regulation in provincial legislation. Whether or not an independent regulatory body provides for it, self-regulation includes the establishment of minimum credentials for admission to the profession. In most instances in Canada, social workers must have at least a BSW degree to become registered social workers in their province. The exception is the province of Alberta, where social workers with 2-year college diplomas are admitted to the profession. Regulatory organizations are also responsible for investigating those accused of inadequate or unethical practice and disciplining them if necessary. The "registrars" (as the executive officers of social work's regulatory organizations are known) from jurisdictions across Canada also meet annually, but they lack the mandate to create their own national social work organization. In light of the potential for a national association of regulatory bodies in social work, the mandate of CASW may be extended to incorporate national considerations in support of provincial registration functions.

Variability in structure and required credentials across Canadian provinces presents a challenge for Canada's social work organizations, particularly in light of the free trade agendas of governments in Canada, Mexico, and the United States. International agreements require that workers be able to move freely between jurisdictions and that credentials be universally acceptable. Many fear that the diplomas accepted as the minimum requirement for admission to the social work profession in Alberta will become generally accepted everywhere. Free trade advocates also support the development of a competency-based definition of practice, so that social workers from any jurisdiction can be evaluated and admitted to the profession in their destination state or province without reference to their academic qualifications. Many social work educators are critical of this position, claiming that one cannot reduce the critical and reflective practice to a series of specific competencies. To do so, they suggest, would constitute de-skilling.

CASW's most significant recent initiative responded to these challenges. A national social work forum followed a major consultation in Quebec and a significant study of the human resource needs of the social work sector in Canada funded by Human Resources Development Canada. Representatives of social work education, social work regulation, and social work practice together addressed the "priority issues facing the profession" (Canadian Association of Social Workers, 2001, p. 3). The issues raised at the forum echoed those that were of concern to social workers when they first decided to create CASW almost 80 years earlier. Traditional concerns with professional identity, enhancing practice, and strengthening education were overlaid with contemporary concerns about the impact of budget cutbacks in social and health services, the declining quality of work environments for social workers, the relevance of traditional practice approaches in the context of an increasingly diverse society, expectations of effective practice in interdisciplinary settings, and the implications of globalization and free trade.

—Leslie Bella

See also Social Work Profession (Canada)

Further Reading

Bella, L. (1995). Gender and occupational closure in social work: Registration initiatives of Canada's anglophone social work associations. In P. Taylor & C. Daly (Eds.), *Gender dilemmas in social work: Issues affecting women in the profession* (pp. 107–124). Toronto, ON: Canadian Scholars' Press.

Bella, L. (1996). Profession as ideology: Doctors, nurses and social workers. In W. Kirwin (Ed.), *Ideology, development and social welfare: Canadian perspectives* (pp. 145–164). Toronto, ON: Canadian Scholars' Press.

Canadian Association of Social Workers. (2001, October). *Toward sector collaboration in social work*. A report on the Social Work Forum, Montreal, Quebec. Available: www.casw-acts.ca/SW-Forum/CdnSWForum-TowardSectorCollaboration.htm

Struthers, J. (1987). "Lord give us men": Women and social work in English Canada, 1918–1953. In A. Moscovitch & J. Albert (Eds.), *The benevolent state: The growth of welfare in Canada* (pp. 111–125). Toronto, ON: Garamond.

CANADIAN COUNCIL ON SOCIAL DEVELOPMENT

The social agency known since 1971 as the Canadian Council on Social Development (CCSD) has a record that reaches back to 1920 as the country's foremost agency for the promotion of the social well-being of Canadians. Its lineage is traceable through three predecessor councils: the Canadian Welfare Council (CWC, 1935–1968), the Canadian Council on Child and Family Welfare (CCCFW, 1930–1935), and the Canadian Council on Child Welfare (CCCW), which came into being in 1920. Although differences in the objectives, roles, and functions of the organization over the course of its history are thus manifest, unbroken threads of common purpose as a human service association make it appropriate to refer to the agency at any time in its history as the Council.

The Council's community service spans well over half of Canada's life as a nation. Social welfare needs of Canadians have emerged at every stage in the historical development of the nation and have elicited humanitarian responses from individual citizens, groups, and organizations under different auspices, with various concerns and diverse plans of action. The genius of the Council has been to provide a medium for concerted thinking, policy formulation, and advocacy on the social needs and aspirations of the Canadian people.

The leadership provided by the Council in the social development of the nation reflects the support of citizen membership in all regions of Canada, the community leaders who have served on its boards and committees, its highly competent professional and administrative staff, and the succession of gifted and committed professionals who, as executive directors (now presidents), have provided strong policy and organizational direction.

The Council advocated and firmly supported measures advanced by the national government during World War II to address the grave defects of the country's social and economic structures revealed during the depression of the 1930s. In the postwar years, the Council's research and advocacy were strongly influential in the succession of public measures that, by the early 1970s, had given Canada the status of a fully matured welfare state.

In subsequent decades, the Council pioneered efforts to address issues that included racism, Native rights, homelessness, family violence, and the many manifestations of social and economic inequity. It also promoted policy positions to counter neoconservative policies and procedures designed to weaken or eliminate the social welfare gains achieved in earlier times.

The Council moved strongly into the twenty-first century. Its leadership was evident in numerous social policy measures and programs: the creation of the Personal Security Index, the collaborative endeavor Preventing Crime through Social Development, work on the Progress of Canada's Children, and positive approaches in reducing dependency and increasing employability.

The Council continues as a major publisher in the social development field. It enjoys a wide and expanding measure of citizen, community, and governmental support in recognition of its sustained work for the advancement of social justice in Canada.

—*Richard B. Splane*

See also Davidson, George Forrester

Further Reading

Annual reports of the Canadian Council on Social Development, 1996–2003, are available on the Council's website (www.ccsd.ca/aboutus.html).

Splane, R. B. (1996). *75 years of community service to Canada: Canadian Council on Social Development, 1920–1995.* Ottawa, ON: Canadian Council on Social Development.

CASSIDY, HARRY (1900–1951)

Harry Cassidy was a well-known social welfare expert in both Canada and the United States during the 1930s and 1940s. Born in Vancouver, British Columbia, in 1900, he studied at the University of British Columbia where he received an undergraduate degree in economics and history before heading to the United States to receive a doctorate in economics from the Brookings Graduate School of Economics and Government in Washington, D.C., in 1926. After 3 years of teaching in the United States, in 1929 he returned to Canada where he worked as an assistant professor in the Department of Social Science (today, the Faculty of Social Work) at the University of Toronto.

Cassidy was a founding member of the League for Social Reconstruction that was established in 1932 to advocate for social reforms to alleviate the problems created as a result of the Great Depression. During the

1930s, Cassidy conducted or was involved in a number of seminal social studies in the areas of unemployment, housing, and labor conditions. At the time, he was one of only a few academics in Canada conducting research in the field of social welfare. In 1931, he was commissioned to carry out a study of relief administration in Ontario by the Unemployment Research Committee of Ontario, resulting in the report, *Unemployment and Relief in Ontario 1929–1932: A Survey and Report* (1932). He also collaborated in a study of labor conditions in the men's garment industry and a study to investigate housing conditions in Toronto. In 1934, Cassidy was lured to British Columbia where he became the director of social welfare for the province. During his tenure in this position, Cassidy was instrumental in preparing and planning for the implementation of provincial health insurance legislation. When these plans were shelved, Cassidy left to take up the position of director of the School of Social Welfare, University of California, Berkeley, which he held from 1939 to 1944.

Cassidy's work during the 1930s resulted in *Social Security and Reconstruction in Canada* (1943), which focused on the development of a comprehensive Social Security program for Canada. He followed up on this publication with *Public Health and Welfare Reorganization* (1945), an effort to encourage the development of provincial and local health and welfare services as part of a comprehensive system of national social welfare in Canada.

In 1945, Cassidy returned to Canada and took up the position of director of the School of Social Work at the University of Toronto where he remained until his untimely death in 1951. During his career, he was also involved in many other social reform activities. He served as director of training for the United Nations Relief and Rehabilitation Administration in 1944–1945 and as an adviser to the Canadian Department of National Health and Welfare in 1947.

—*Peter Donahue*

See also Bowers, Frank Swithun Barrington; Hendry, Charles Eric; Social Welfare (Canada): Before the Marsh Report; Social Welfare (Canada): Since the Marsh Report; Social Work Profession (Canada); Touzel, Bessie; Urwick, Edward Johns

Further Reading

Irving, A. (1981). Canadian Fabians: The work and thought of Harry Cassidy and Leonard Marsh, 1930–1945. *Canadian Journal of Social Work Education, 7*(1), 7–28.

Irving, A. (1983). *A Canadian Fabian: The life and work of Harry Cassidy.* Unpublished doctoral dissertation, University of Toronto, ON.

CHARITY ORGANIZATION SOCIETIES (UNITED STATES)

The London, England, Charity Organisation Society was the first to be established in 1869. The movement quickly made an impression in the United States, where, by the 1880s, the largest and most influential societies were located in Boston, New York, Philadelphia, Chicago, Indianapolis, and Baltimore. By the early twentieth century, charity organization societies were firmly entrenched in 104 American cities. Privately funded and administered, the societies were prominent in formulating welfare policy from the 1870s to 1929. Charity organization societies used "scientific" methods of organization, coordination, and investigation to solve the problems of poverty. Their legacy is twofold. First, the societies paved the way for the development of the modern welfare state through their innovative programs such as tenement house reform and championing preventive public health campaigns. Second, charity organization societies pushed the professionalization of social work through their development of the "case-method" approach to social welfare.

Charity organization societies were the institutional expressions of a major philanthropic reform movement, "scientific charity," that advocated placing all charitable relief on an efficient, scientific, and businesslike basis to cope with the destabilizing forces of industrialization in the late nineteenth century. The problems of urban poverty—a growing homeless population, masses of people thrown out of work by frequent economic depressions, and uncontrolled immigration—seemed to call for a recasting of welfare policy for a new and dangerous age. What were people entitled to? What was the state's responsibility? What was the role of private agencies? Charity organization societies were influential in defining the attitudes and the ideology that set the agenda for the discussion and formulation of welfare policy in the late nineteenth and early twentieth centuries.

Charity organization societies struggled to preserve the best of the old-style philanthropy with new methods. Everyone agreed that the immense wealth created by the new industrial economy was also creating great poverty, and with it, a widening gap between the rich and the poor. How to bridge the gap? The charity organization answer was to encourage the prosperous members of the community to acknowledge the mutuality of society, in a thoughtful and earnest manner. Thus, the early societies were made up of largely volunteer leaders and workers. The early programs tended to focus on punitive solutions to poverty, such as the elimination of the homeless from the city streets through enforced "beggary laws," and making sure that cash relief was given only under strict conditions.

Therefore, the charity organization movement proclaimed that charity should not be an unthinking act, that is, based on an automatic response to distress (such as giving a "pauper" a few dollars here and there), but rather should uplift, educate, and reform the recipient into a productive and independent member of society. The individual, with important exceptions, was held accountable for his or her actions. In a nutshell, charity organization combined elements of paternalism and individualism, social control and independent action, conflicting impulses that have characterized the policy and practice of social welfare from the nineteenth century to the present time.

Charity organization societies attracted numerous critics, including churches, religion-based charities, labor unions, and settlement house workers, who chastised the movement for being all head and no heart. One opponent described charity organization as being more of "an organization for the prevention of charity" than for the relief of genuine distress. An even more damning assessment came from the pen of the Boston poet John Boyle O'Reilly: "The organized charity scrimped and iced / In the name of a cautious, statistical Christ."

Undeterred by criticism, always controversial and contentious, the practitioners of "charity organization" strove to reform state and local, public and private charitable agencies, and their clients. The societies established and promoted stringent regulations for state, or public relief, thus discouraging abuse of taxpayer funds, especially by corrupt urban political machines. Simultaneously, the societies would invigorate and direct the private charitable sector. Indeed, charity organization was dedicated to the belief that most welfare was best handled by the private sector, with a limited but important role for the public realm, such as care for the mentally ill population.

Significantly, charity organization societies were allied with state and municipal reformers in the Gilded Age and Progressive Era, which often pitted a coalition of reformers against the urban boss-run machines in hard-fought elections. By the last decade of the nineteenth century, charity organizations' emphasis on solving poverty through individual reform was complemented by "preventive philanthropy." Charity organization societies became known for programs that not only encouraged self-help, but also promoted the establishment of community-based social services that would provide the environmental incentive for people to enjoy the benefits of independence. Often, the societies played a key role in the formulation of legislation related to health and welfare concerns.

The mechanics of charity organization require explanation. Each society was a separate entity, having its own constitution, governing central council, and central office. A city's neighborhoods were divided up into districts, with every district having an office, staffed by a district committee. The quality of the district committees' work was important to the societies' success or failure. The gathering and recording of information on people who applied for any sort of assistance was undertaken by "district agents" and then transmitted into personal histories of the clients and their families. This information was only as valuable as its availability. Successful charity organization societies shared vital statistics and information on the poor and the conditions of poverty with other like-minded charitable agencies, and worked together to create a registry or clearinghouse. Ideally, informed and humane decisions about proper aid to indigents would be rendered.

In the 1880s, societies emphasized the importance of "the friendly visitor," whose motto was "Not alms, but a friend." The visitor was a trained volunteer charity worker whose job it was to screen the applicants,

evaluate their situation, and recommend intelligent action to be taken by carefully selected agencies. By the 1890s, however, much of charity organization work was done by paid workers, the majority of whom were women. The first professional school for social work, founded under the auspices of the Charity Organization Society (COS) of New York City, was established in 1898. Later, the school was taken over by Columbia University.

The elite founders of the charity organization societies were among America's first "social scientists." They believed that the principles of science could be applied to solve social problems. COS leaders such as Robert Treat Paine and Annie Adams Fields of Boston; Josephine Shaw Lowell, Robert Weeks deForest, and Edward T. Devine of New York; and Mary Richmond of Baltimore, among others, argued that all decisions about charitable relief should be brought under the control of trained, objective caseworkers. Although Paine, Fields, Lowell, and deForest were upper-class philanthropists, their advocacy of the professional social worker would radically transform charitable and welfare practices by the early twentieth century. Largely because of their vigorous leadership, charity organization societies became influential in the university classroom, the business boardroom, and the legislative hall.

The charity organization movement had its own journals—*Charities, Charities and the Commons,* and *Survey.* Each society also published its own "annual reports." The societies were well represented in the welfare worker's professional group, the National Conference of Charity and Corrections. In 1911, they formed the National Association of Societies for Organizing Charity, later the Family Service Association of America. The majority of charity organization societies outlived their usefulness when many of their programs were taken over by the government after the devastating depression that commenced in 1929. Many changed their focus, however, and continued as family service agencies.

—Joan Waugh

See also Family Service Association of America (United States); Housing Policy (United States); Lowell, Josephine Shaw; Poor Law (United States); Poverty (United States); Religion and Social Welfare (United States); Scientific Philanthropy (United States); Social Work Profession (United States); Work Relief (United States)

Primary Sources

The Records of the National Association of Societies for Organizing Charity and its successor organizations may be found in the Records of the Family Service Association of America, Social Welfare History Archives, University of Minnesota, Minneapolis (http://special.lib.umn.edu/swha/). Additional materials may be found in the Mary Richmond Papers, Rare Book & Manuscript Library, Butler Library, Columbia University, New York (www.columbia.edu/cu/lweb/indiv/rare/) and in the Records of the Russell Sage Foundation, Rockefeller Archive Center, Rockefeller University, Sleepy Hollow, NY (www.rockefeller.edu/archive.ctr/).

Current Comment

Devine, E. T. (1922). *When social work was young*. New York: Macmillan.

Watson, F. D. (1922). *The charity organization movement in the United States: A study in American philanthropy*. New York: Macmillan.

Further Reading

Katz, M. B. (1986). *In the shadow of the poorhouse: A social history of welfare in America*. New York: Basic Books.

Waugh, J. (2001, Summer). "Give this man work!" Josephine Shaw Lowell, The Charity Organization Society of the city of New York, and the depression of 1893. *Social Science History, 25*(2), 217–246.

CHILDREN'S AID SOCIETY (UNITED STATES)

The emigration program of the Children's Aid Society of New York (CAS) was the forerunner of modern family foster care. It is credited with being the most extensive and important of the nineteenth century placing-out programs. Charles Loring Brace founded the CAS in 1853 to address the needs of an estimated 10,000 vagrant children crowding the streets of lower Manhattan. His work in New York City's impoverished Five Points slum convinced him that rescuing poor children from the influences of their parents and neighborhoods was the only hope of avoiding intergenerational poverty and the development of a hereditary lower class in the United States.

In 1852, Brace came up with the idea of a children's mission based on the free schools for poor children ("ragged schools") he had visited in Great Britain and a similar program in Boston. Brace wanted to help the children of Irish and German immigrants who, because of the death, disability, or absence of one or both parents, scratched out a living sweeping streets, selling newspapers, or begging and stealing.

Brace announced the new organization to the public in the New York *Daily Times* on March 2, 1853. At that time, he outlined the problem posed by street children, the inadequacy of existing efforts to aid them, and the proposed program of the society, successfully calling for public support. The eventual program of the CAS was fully outlined: religious meetings, industrial schools for girls, lodging houses for homeless newsboys, reading rooms, and placement in the country. Brace became increasingly convinced, however, that city life itself was harmful to children and observed an almost miraculous change in children sent to the country. After its third year, the emigration program, later dubbed the "orphan trains," became a dominant focus of the CAS. It was based on two principles: the superiority of the Christian family for the education and moral reformation of vagrant children and the need to follow the natural law of demand for labor in creating a large-scale program.

Recruitment, transportation, and placement of children in midwestern states remained constant throughout the century. Children were brought by their parents (usually single mothers), or handed over by children's institutions, and were taken in by CAS agents. Every 2 weeks, after bathing, receiving new clothes, and saying their goodbyes, groups of children boarded westward-bound trains. They marveled at the fruit trees, livestock, and abundance of food in their letters to the CAS, often wishing that they could bring their mothers and siblings to this land of plenty.

Upon arriving in a town that had expressed a desire to receive them, the children and local families assembled in a hall or church. A local committee screened applicants and farmers made their choices, sometimes checking teeth or feeling muscles to determine the suitability of a child. Often sibling groups were separated, the older children selected first, leaving the younger ones behind, crying. The children also looked over the farmers, noting the kindliness or hardness of their demeanor or the appearance of their horses. Once all selections had been made, the agents and remaining children reboarded the train to go on to the next town.

Although less than a quarter of the children sent west were young orphans, Brace's writings, largely directed at raising funds for the voluntary organization, emphasized their plight. Children brought in by families in crisis, and later older boys in search of work, made up the majority of child placements. Despite his vision of emigration as a permanent solution to urban poverty, about half eventually returned to New York. In addition, although not publicized, the CAS helped an almost equal number of families with children to relocate to the West. Throughout the nineteenth century, the CAS also continued serving large numbers of children through programs and placements within the city.

The financial crises of the 1850s put Brace at odds with the advocates of children's institutions, initiating a debate that endured for the rest of the century. The emigration program was vilified for snatching Catholic children to place them in Protestant homes and for exporting young criminals to the country. As the competition for funds among voluntary organizations increased, Brace's previously suppressed criticism of congregate institutions as cold and unnatural places that instilled children with questionable moral values and left them unable to perform simple domestic tasks, surfaced publicly.

After the Civil War, the methods and rhetoric of the CAS changed little. Increasingly challenged to defend his practices, Brace conducted fact-finding tours and solicited testimonials to assure his supporters that, despite the fact that many were unaccounted for, the children were treated kindly, doing well, and growing into upstanding citizens. Those who were mistreated, he argued, were free to seek better circumstances because they were not indentured. Nonetheless, criticism from the Catholic church, supporters of children's institutions, and western officials continued. The CAS responded by instituting more consistent and frequent supervision. But, as the demand for children's labor in the Midwest declined and as placements ranged

farther west and south, reports of abuse increased. By the early 1900s, the CAS emigration program had dwindled from a high of over 4,000 children placed in 1875 to 712 placed in 1902. Although the last train set out for Texas in 1929, the CAS continues to provide services to New York's children.

As a transitional program between the apprenticeship and indenture contracts of an agricultural economy and family foster care as we know it today, the emigration program profoundly affected ideas about children's needs and the appropriate setting for meeting them, spurring the development of similar programs in other United States cities and in Canada. Today, although the child welfare system places the vast majority of children in family foster homes, criticism of a lack of supervision, poor care, and abuse have spurred calls for the reestablishment of orphanages, reminders that the issues that ultimately caused the decline of the emigration program are far from resolved.

—Kristine Nelson

See also Brace, Charles Loring; Child Welfare Policy (United States); Religion and Social Welfare (United States)

Current Comment

Brace, C. L. (1973). *The dangerous classes of New York and twenty years' work among them.* Silver Spring, MD: National Association of Social Workers. (Original work published 1872)

Children's Aid Society of New York. (1971). *Annual reports, 1854–1963.* New York: Arno Press.

Further Reading

Holt, M. I. (1992). *The orphan trains: Placing out in America.* Lincoln: University of Nebraska Press.

O'Connor, S. (2001). *Orphan trains: The story of Charles Loring Brace and the children he saved and failed.* New York: Houghton Mifflin.

CHILD WELFARE POLICY (CANADA)

Child welfare in Canada developed as a response to the social and economic conditions of the nineteenth century. Once organized and legislated, its focus primarily centered on the care and relationships between parents, especially mothers, and their children. Two contradictory social traditions have been drawn upon as the basis for child welfare provisions: first, the doctrine of *parens patriae,* or the state as parent of the nation, and second the long-standing social tradition of viewing children as property of their parents. Efforts to find and maintain a balance between these two competing mandates characterizes child welfare policy historically and currently, although the potential of child welfare policy for influencing economic and social welfare policy has all but disappeared over the past century.

ORIGINS OF CANADIAN CHILD WELFARE

Dislocations caused by the Industrial Revolution and immigration to Canada, along with the emergence of an educated middle class and concern about both social and personal reform, created the conditions for the development of child welfare policy. Especially in urban centers, social reformers observed families uprooted, destitute, in transit, and mothers deserted or widowed. Toward the end of the nineteenth century, orphaned and destitute children sent for placement from Britain began to make their way to the streets of Canadian cities. These "street urchins" became a focus of concern for a new and growing group of middle class social reformers.

Various legislative efforts to address the problem of orphaned and abandoned children had already been made in the previous century. The Orphans Act (1799) provided for orphaned children to be indentured. The Ontario Industrial Schools Act (1874) attempted to define a neglected child, and the Children's Protection Act (1888) established the principle that representatives of the state could remove a child from the family if provisions for care were found unsuitable. During this period, legislation aimed at changing social conditions for a larger population of poor children was also developed. For instance, laws providing for compulsory public education and for regulating child labor were passed.

During the 1880s and 1890s, middle-class reformers focused attention on developing more personal services to identify and assist orphaned, delinquent, and neglected children. John J. Kelso, a Toronto journalist, is generally credited with spearheading the drive to create legislation and organizations to protect and provide services for this population of children. In 1891, the first Children's Aid Society was founded in Toronto, with Kelso as director. Soon after, in 1893, the

government of Ontario passed an Act for Prevention of Cruelty to Children. These developments expressed not only a concern for the safety of "street urchins" but also the reformers' interest in preserving social stability, a mix of interests captured in the motto of the first Children's Aid Society: "It is wiser and less expensive to save children than to punish criminals." Other Canadian provinces followed suit with similar legislation, although with somewhat different organizational arrangements. Quebec was the last province to develop legislation (1977), having vested the child protection function in the Catholic church until then.

Until early in the twentieth century, some social reformers continued to address child welfare issues by attempting to reduce the poverty of mothers. At the 1914 Social Service Congress, reformers succeeded in arguing for a "famous first principle" that no child should be removed from his or her home on grounds of poverty alone. Eventually, all provinces passed legislation providing for "mothers' pensions." Eligibility for pensions was tied to the "worthiness" of the applicant, however, and social workers tended to focus on working with and changing parents, and especially mothers, rather than changing the social and economic environment of families. In the first half of the twentieth century, investigations of child welfare "complaints" were a staple activity of mostly female child welfare workers. During this era, and particularly in the depression of the 1930s, workers, some of whom were volunteers, marshaled material support for poor families. Neglect rather than abuse was often the cause of their intervention. Workers also "placed" children in foster homes as well as in orphanages and other institutions. Gradually, these workers became more professionalized as social sciences emerged and as the developing profession of social work created schools and training programs. Few changes were made in this period to the original provincial laws.

ORGANIZATION OF SERVICES

In Canada, responsibility for health, education, and welfare services is provincial rather than federal. Child welfare, like other welfare programs, is legislated, organized, and delivered by each of the 10 provinces and 3 territories. In some jurisdictions, child welfare is a branch of provincial government. In others, private, nonprofit agencies are mandated by the provincial government to deliver services. One province, Nova Scotia, has a mix of both. Recently, some aboriginal organizations, or First Nations, have been mandated to deliver services through arrangements with provincial governments and federal authorities, involved because of their historical relationship with First Nations through the federal Indian Act.

Although there are now many jurisdictions with child welfare authority, the basic approach to the protection of children is fairly similar across the country. Generally speaking, child welfare services are residual, or "last chance" services. Poor people, immigrants, and single mothers have been overrepresented in the population of service users since the inception of formal services. Laws allow intervention by the state when this care is deemed not to be in the "best interests" of children. The issue of determining what circumstances justify intrusion of the state into the family, however, is an issue of ongoing social debate. As opinion shifts, policy also shifts, creating what has been termed a "pendulum" effect in child welfare policy.

From the inception of formal organization and legislation, child welfare has structured itself around four kinds of activities: investigation of allegations of child abuse and neglect; in-home support to families with children; alternate care for children whose families are deemed incapable, either temporarily or permanently, of providing "proper" care; and adoption services for children whose parents have died or have lost legal guardianship of their children. At times, one or more of these service areas has predominated over others, depending on the social, economic, and political context.

RECENT TRENDS

Beginning in the middle of the twentieth century, a series of changes in legislation and focus began. Attention to the "best interests of the child" as the first principle of child protection decision was among the first of these changes. In Canada, as elsewhere, the "discovery" of the battered child led to changes in the law, the most notable of which was the addition of mandatory report requirements in cases of suspected abuse and neglect. Beginning in the mid 1980s, a series of changes in child welfare legislation occurred across

the country. Attempts were made to specify the meaning of "best interests," to be accountable for removal of children from their own families, and to conduct more careful investigations into allegations of neglect and abuse. The release of the Badgley Report (1984), reporting a high rate of sexual abuse of Canadian children, produced new legislative and policy attention to this issue. Sixteen offenses were added to the sexual assault provisions of the Criminal Code of Canada (Federal Bill C-15), ranging from unwanted touching to assault with a weapon. These additions to the code did not relieve child welfare authorities of the responsibility to investigate complaints of sexual abuse of children but ensured that police would also be involved in such investigations and in laying criminal charges against alleged offenders. Patrick Johnston's book, *Native Children and the Child Welfare System* (1983), which demonstrated substantial overrepresentation of aboriginal children in care outside their homes, also raised questions about whether authorities were too intrusive and quick to remove children from the care of parents, especially in aboriginal communities. This report, among others, provided support for legislative changes mandating "least intrusive actions" of child welfare authorities consonant with protection of a child. For a period of time following this change, more resources for in-home support services were made available to child welfare organizations.

Over the past few years, public attention has been focused on child welfare processes and services by virtue of numerous well-publicized deaths of children known to protection authorities. The Gove Report (1995), for instance, recorded in great detail problems and errors leading to the death of Matthew Vaudreuill in British Columbia. Publicity and public opinion in reaction to media stories has helped to push the pendulum back in the direction of more frequent and intrusive intervention into families, with the result that the numbers of children in care are rapidly increasing in most provinces. Currently, investigation rather than in-home support is the prevalent activity in many agencies, and "risk assessment" tools and training have become common practice across the country. Child poverty, seen a century ago to be closely connected to child welfare issues, appears as a separate policy issue at the beginning of this new century, while both practice and legal mandates in child welfare focus on identifying potential risks to children posed by the behavior of their parents. The question for many who work in child welfare is whether safety and security of children can be assured apart from social welfare support for their families.

—*Karen Swift*

See also Kelso, John Joseph; Women and Poverty (Canada)

Primary Sources

"Complaint books" (showing how early social workers addressed child welfare issues), Metro Toronto Archives, Toronto, ON; John J. Kelso Papers, Library and Archives Canada, Ottawa, ON; also see provincial child welfare legislation and annual reports; current information on child welfare legislation can be found online (www.hrdc-drhc.gc.ca/soc pol./cfs/cfs.shtml/).

Current Comment

Committee on Sexual Offences Against Children and Youth. (1984). *Sexual Offences Against Children* [Badgley Report]. Ottawa, ON: Department of Supply and Services Canada.

Gove Commission. (1995). *Report of the Gove Enquiry into Child Protection in British Columbia* (Vols. 1–3). Vancouver, BC: Author.

Johnston, P. (1983). *Native children and the child welfare system* (Canadian Council on Social Development Series No. 147). Toronto, ON: Lorimer.

Social Service Council of Canada. (1914). *Proceedings of the Social Service Congress of 1914*. Ottawa, ON: Author.

Further Reading

Jones, A., & Rutman, L. (1981). *In the children's aid*. Toronto, ON: University of Toronto Press.

Sutherland, N. (1976). *Children in English Canadian society*. Toronto, ON: University of Toronto Press.

Swift, K. (1995). An outrage to common decency. *Child Welfare, 74*(1), 71–91.

CHILD WELFARE POLICY (MEXICO)

The concept of child welfare, as a distinct form of public assistance and as a standard of children's well-being, developed in Mexico in the late nineteenth century. Both meanings of child welfare were shaped by expanding state oversight of education and public health, influenced by international trends but also prompted by the project of modernizing Mexico's popular classes, most of whom were of mixed Spanish

and aboriginal descent. Additionally, professional and commercial elites linked to Mexico's export-led economic growth drew on legacies of religious charity while promulgating bourgeois notions of sentimental childhood through private beneficence. These factors established the foundations for persistent characteristics of Mexican child welfare policy and institutions to the present. Twentieth century programs in education and medicine developed within a highly centralized state sector, tying expansion and contraction of goals and services to shifting political priorities and national economic fluctuations. Mexico's cosmopolitan professional classes have worked largely through the state to adapt international standards of child health and welfare to a social context marked by extreme disparities between rich and poor, and between city and countryside. Despite the dominance of state institutions, myriad private initiatives, sometimes affiliated with public agencies or with religious organizations, have specialized and responded to changing needs in the interstices of the public child welfare system.

During Mexico's colonial period, late eighteenth century law and institutions marked a turning point in concepts of poverty, poor relief, and child welfare, formerly based on piety, patronage, and social hierarchies founded on race. The Mexico City Poor House, under secular administration, was established to intern and reform beggars through religious instruction and work, and the capital's foundling home admitted infants of all castes and classes. In 1806, an endowment founding a school within the poorhouse initiated the institution's gradual transformation into an orphanage. Long after Mexico's 1821 independence from Spain, family, ritual kin, and patronage networks remained the first recourse for the protection of children outside their families of origin. But in the capital, public orphanages, including a vocational school doubling as a correctional facility, sheltered, disciplined, and educated children of poor, often female-headed families.

After decades of divisive political conflict over the separation of church and state, Mexico's liberal legal reform of the late 1850s and early 1860s established the foundations for new concepts of child welfare by mandating secular public primary education and transferring to public administration charitable institutions, some serving a predominantly juvenile clientele. The short-lived Second Empire of the mid 1860s consolidated the liberal education agenda and founded a maternity hospital in the capital. Welfare administrators of the Restored Republic assigned the state a leading role in the formation of productive citizens through civic and vocational education, reorganized Mexico City orphanages and trade schools accordingly, and briefly operated the capital's first public day care centers. Civil codes fortified the state's paternal role by granting public institutions guardianship over orphaned inmates and expanding state authority in disciplining incorrigible minors. Nevertheless, elite participation in religious charities like the Society of Saint Vincent de Paul sustained links between piety and benevolence.

The government of Porfirio Díaz, 1876 to 1911, centralized and consolidated state oversight of child welfare while also encouraging private beneficence. While insisting on limited state responsibility for the poor, Díaz encouraged working-class mutual aid and private philanthropy, but also expanded public primary education and urban public health, federalized welfare administration, and built asylums and hospitals throughout Mexico. Under state patronage, the Mexico City medical college introduced specializations in obstetrics and pediatrics. Sentimental notions of childhood informed private initiatives for children and fostered elite women's leadership of charities for poor mothers and children, like the kindergarten founded by Mexico's first lady. Yet the concept of childhood as a protected life phase also prompted penal law reforms distinguishing stages of criminal responsibility for minors and legislation regulating child labor in Mexico's growing manufacturing sector. Despite the rupture of the Mexican Revolution, 1910–1920, Díaz's federal consolidation of education, medicine, assistance, and juvenile corrections laid the groundwork for the expansion of child welfare programs during subsequent decades of revolutionary reform.

In the aftermath of armed conflict, revolutionary principles of political inclusion and validation of Mexico's popular classes merged with international models of child saving and puerile culture to promote rapid development of public child welfare policies and programs between 1920 and 1940. The revolutionary Constitution of 1917 limited child labor and mandated universal public secular primary education. Optimistic

reformers saw children as the future citizens of a modern, competitive nation and looked to secular public education and medicine to build a healthy, skilled workforce. Loss of population during the revolutionary conflict prompted high-priority public health campaigns to reduce infant mortality. A growing network of clinics provided maternal-child health services. Public primary education under the Secretariat of Public Education became the delivery vehicle for teaching hygienics, modern domesticity, and child rearing, linking key factors influencing child development. Additionally, sociological analysis emphasizing economic causes of delinquency supported the 1926 foundation of Mexico City's juvenile court, based on U.S. models, to reeducate and reintegrate minors into the social and economic mainstream. The 1931 federal labor code incorporated educational and medical criteria for improving child development into restrictions on child labor. These measures promulgated and institutionalized definitions of childhood and adolescence as protected life stages, with public education and public health supporting optimum intellectual and physical development, and placed child welfare at the center of Mexico's developing welfare state apparatus.

During the presidency of Lázaro Cárdenas, 1934–1940, the revolutionary state articulated the concept of a right to social assistance and explicitly linked public child welfare to national economic development. After the Mexico City meetings of the seventh international Pan American Child Congress in 1935, state-sponsored extramural services such as kindergartens and factory crèches, mothers' clubs, and soup kitchens proliferated, initiating a transition from child-only to family-based services. The creation of the Secretariat of Public Assistance centralized oversight of child health and welfare programs. Initiation of federally administered training and certification for social workers, visiting nurses, and child care workers in public institutions professionalized services. Despite the consolidation and expansion of state programs, they remained concentrated in Mexico City.

During the 1940s, federal child welfare policy emphasized support of children within the family and encouraged legal regularization of families. The creation in 1943 of the Secretariat of Health and

Welfare fused public medical and assistance programs for children. After 1943, Social Security legislation extended federal benefits and medical services to formal sector workers and their families. Federal welfare administrators also encouraged a resurgence of public-private partnerships as well as private philanthropy to provide services to mothers and children.

The "Mexican Miracle," rapid economic growth of the 1950s and 1960s, underwrote significant gains in public education, increasing literacy rates and raising women's educational attainment, key indicators of child welfare. School breakfast programs, implemented by the National Institute for the Protection of Childhood, improved children's nutrition. Widespread immunization forestalled epidemic diseases. National rates of infant mortality also declined steadily. Mexican economic policy during this period, however, favored industry over agriculture, provoking high rates of migration to cities where underemployment and conditions in informal settlements exposed the weaknesses of national child welfare models linked to economic development.

Since the mid 1970s, Mexico's hosting of international forums on women, population, and children has reflected the influence of international standards of child welfare on national policy. Increasingly, Mexico's policy landmarks on behalf of children have responded to initiatives such as the 1979 International Year of the Child. Slow and uneven implementation, however, points to bureaucratic and financial obstacles afflicting the highly centralized state sector. Mexico's national debt crisis of the early 1980s, followed by deep cuts in federal spending, hyperinflation, and declines in real wages and living standards reversed long-term gains in child welfare. State retrenchment in social services, privatization of state enterprises, and shrinking public sector employment stranded a growing proportion of Mexican children outside safety nets of Social Security and public health. These structural effects increased the number of children living in poverty and focused attention on declining school attendance and rising child labor as family survival strategies, domestic abuse as a public health issue, and the problems of urban children working and living in the street.

In recent decades, Mexican child welfare policy has incorporated concepts of human rights and gender, with recognition of the special concerns of girls and female adolescents. Mexico ratified the United Nations Convention on the Rights of the Child in 1990 and reformed the Constitution to include child rights. In 1994, however, the United Nations Committee on the Rights of the Child gave Mexico a mixed evaluation. The concentration of public child welfare and health services in cities has left the countryside underserved, even as the termination of agricultural subsidies heightened migration to cities and to the United States. Despite a laudable percentage of children entering school, the number of children completing primary education varies by region, as do key child welfare indicators such as maternal, infant, and child mortality, with the highest rates in rural, indigenous communities. Under the North American Free Trade Agreement (NAFTA), unregulated industrial pollution and mushrooming shantytowns have created critical conditions for children along the U.S.-Mexican border. The urgent problems of street children and migrant minors and the resurgence of traffic in children have been met in part by church-based and nongovernmental organization (NGO) initiatives. Nevertheless, by international measures, Mexican child welfare in the areas of health and education has improved over the last quarter century. To address problems of recent focus such as domestic abuse, police violence against street children, drug use, HIV/AIDS, and the welfare of rural and indigenous children, newly articulated policy priorities establish ambitious goals that remain to be met.

—Ann Blum

See also Mother and Family Programs (Mexico); Social Reform and State-Building (Mexico); Women and Social Welfare (Mexico)

Primary Sources

Federal records of nineteenth and twentieth century institutions and agencies are in Mexico's national archives, the *Archivo General de la Nación*, and the historical archive of the federal administration of health and welfare, *Archivo Histórico de la Secretaría de Salubridad y Asistencia,* both located in Mexico City. Records of Mexico City's two principal orphanages, dating from the late colonial period to the early twentieth century, can be found in the Mexico City archives, the *Archivo Histórico del Ex-Ayuntamiento de la Ciudad de México.*

Current Comment

Secretaría de Desarrollo Social, Secretaría de Educación Pública, Secretaría de Salud. (2002). *Un México apropiado para la infancia y adolescencia: Programa de acción, 2002–2010.* Mexico City: Author.

Secretaría de Salud. (1993). *La atención materno infantil: Apuntes para su historia.* Mexico City: Author.

Further Reading

Arrom, S. M. (2000). *Containing the poor: The Mexico City Poor House, 1774–1871.* Durham, NC: Duke University Press.

Guy, D. J. (1998, July). The Pan American Child Congresses, 1916 to 1942: Pan Americanism, child reform, and the welfare state in Latin America. *Journal of Family History, 23*(3), 272–291.

Ward, P. (1986). *Welfare politics in Mexico: Papering over the cracks.* London: Allen and Unwin.

CHILD WELFARE POLICY (UNITED STATES)

Since the seventeenth century, child welfare policy in the United States has wavered between providing support for keeping families together and removing dependent children from their families and caring for them elsewhere. "Dependent children," in the language of the nineteenth century, and "children at risk," the phrase of the late twentieth century, refer to those whose families are unable to care for them and who have become the public's responsibility. Historically, five principal programs have provided for these children: outdoor relief, almshouses, orphanages, foster care and adoption, and public welfare.

OUTDOOR RELIEF

The colonists followed the European doctrine of *parens patriae,* which made the state the ultimate parent, responsible for all dependents, especially children. Consequently, local poor law officials provided needy families with direct aid or outdoor relief—the provision of goods such as food, clothing, and fuel. In addition, following English Poor Law (1601), they "placed out" or removed 5- to 6-year-old children from destitute and motherless homes and placed them with other families. They also indentured

or apprenticed children over the age of 7 by contract to work for other families in return for board, clothing, training, and education. The Elizabethan Poor Law established three fundamental tenets of American welfare policy: Families had prime responsibility for relief; public expense for relief was minimized; and a distinction between the deserving and undeserving poor was established that lasted until the federalization of welfare during the New Deal.

ALMSHOUSES

By the first quarter of the nineteenth century, industrialization and immigration created a vast amount of urban poverty. Responding to the inadequacy and expense of outdoor relief and the hostility to the poor, town officials built almshouses and committed families, paupers, the infirm, and the mentally ill, as well as lawbreakers and alcoholics. The majority of inmates were women, many with their children. In 1790, 1,000 children lived in almshouses; between 1880 and 1920, over 75,000 children resided in almshouses nationwide. The children came from the same background as in the prerevolutionary period: White, destitute, fatherless. Because they kept single mothers and their children within them, almshouses can be seen as a form of family preservation.

ORPHANAGES

Investigation of almshouses revealed children living in overcrowded, mismanaged, and squalid, conditions. During the 1850s and 1860s, child welfare reformers urged that "scientifically" administered orphanages replace almshouses. In 1861, Ohio passed the first law ordering the removal of children from the state's almshouses. The majority of states followed Ohio's example and, between 1865 and 1890, established state boards of charities to investigate charitable and correctional institutions. The preference in policies for dependent children shifted from almshouses to private, often sectarian, and public orphan asylums. Orphan asylums grew from 33 before 1833 to nearly 200 by 1860; 600 by 1890; 972 by 1910; and 1,321 by 1933. They were the product of epidemics, like cholera; the effect of the

Civil War in depriving so many families of fathers; the predatory practices of Protestant child-placers, such as the New York Children's Aid Society's Charles Loring Brace, which led Catholic and Jewish immigrant communities to create their own orphanages; and the poverty that arose as a result of the massive immigration, industrialization, and urbanization of the late nineteenth century. The vast majority of the children were not orphans; 90 percent had one parent living and most were White and poor.

In the last half of the nineteenth century, middle-class child reformers denounced orphanages for removing children from their families and placing them in large congregate institutions, which, they claimed, resulted in regimented routines that turned the youngsters into robots. This was an inaccurate accusation. The orphanages did a fairly good job of providing temporary material aid (long term if necessary) and then returning most children to their own parents after short stays. Still, in the face of criticism, many twentieth century orphan asylum managers "downsized" and turned to the "cottage system": small groups of children who lived together in family-like settings run by a matron. Orphanages continued to thrive through the 1930s, when more than 1,600 orphanages existed nationwide, housing approximately 144,000 children.

FOSTER CARE AND ADOPTION

Foster care and adoption, the out-of-home placement of children in family homes, became widespread in the twentieth century. The practice had its roots in the mid nineteenth century as an alternative to orphanages and took the form of indenture, in which the child worked for his or her keep; boarding out, which was a paid placement; or placement (adoption) in a "free" or unpaid home. The number of children in foster care and adoption did not surpass the number of orphanages until the late 1940s. These practices were exemplified by Charles Loring Brace's New York Children's Aid Society, which removed children from their family homes and put them on "orphan trains," destined for family farms in distant states, deliberately cut off from parents of origin.

PUBLIC WELFARE

The first half of the twentieth century witnessed a dramatic shift in policy from family dissolution to a return to the support of dependent children within their families. Prominent policies at the state level included the increasing regulation of private and state adoption agencies and the passage of mothers' pension laws, which gave widows money to support needy children in their own homes. At the federal level, the Great Depression destroyed the capacity of the states to provide adequate public welfare. In response, the federal government enacted the Social Security Act of 1935 (Public Law 74–271), a watershed in child welfare, which initiated a federal commitment to aiding dependent children and became the most successful measure to prevent children's out-of-home placement. Title IV of the act, Aid to Dependent Children (ADC), later amended and titled Aid to Families With Dependent Children (AFDC), grew out of mothers' pensions and set standards for the states to provide cash payments to support children.

Title V of the Social Security Act, later known as Title IV-B, also provided federal assistance in the provision of child welfare services, services that were later expanded in federal legislation as Public Law 93–247, the Child Abuse Prevention and Treatment Act of 1974, and Public Law 96–272, the Adoption Assistance and Child Welfare Act (AACWA) of 1980. Passage of Public Law 93–247 was fueled by the public outrage in the wake of the publication of C. Harry Kempe's *The Battered-Child Syndrome* (1962), which revealed widespread and unreported child abuse. The act provided states with funds to identify, prevent, and ameliorate the effects of abuse and neglect and established a National Center on Child Abuse and Neglect. AACWA, the first federal statute underwriting adoption, revolved around the concept of "permanency planning," the idea that state governments would be paid (75 percent) to make plans for children in long-term foster care—either to return them to their biological families or place them permanently with other families. The ineffectiveness of this statute led to the Adoption and Safe Families Act of 1997, an amendment of AACWA, again stressing the need for a speedy determination on permanency planning either by reunification with a family of origin or by adoption.

In the conservative political climate of the 1980s and 1990s and in the face of widespread dissatisfaction with AFDC, Congress passed the Family Support Act of 1988 (Public Law 100–485) and the Personal Responsibility and Work Opportunity Reconciliation Act (PRWORA) of 1996 (Public Law 104–193), the most radical reform of the nation's welfare program since ADC was created in 1935. PRWORA ended the federal entitlement program for poor families (AFDC), put time limits on receiving federal welfare assistance, required most recipients with young children to work, and turned over most decisions about child care to the states with a new block grant of federal funds, Temporary Assistance for Needy Families. In light of child welfare, data accumulated by 2001 strongly suggest that PRWORA has been successful, although some experts question the causes. Between 1993 and 1999, the poverty rate declined, from 15.1 percent to 11.8 percent. During the same period, the child poverty rate dropped from 20 percent to 15.5 percent.

—*E. Wayne Carp*

See also Aid to Dependent Children/Aid to Families With Dependent Children (United States); Brace, Charles Loring; Children's Aid Society (United States); Health Policy (United States); Juvenile Justice Policy (United States); Lathrop, Julia Clifford; Mothers' Pensions (United States); National Association of Social Workers (United States); Progressive Era (United States); Social Security (United States); Social Work Profession (United States)

Primary Sources

The Records of the U.S. Children's Bureau, Social Security Board Papers, and the Women's Bureau Papers are held by the National Archives & Records Administration, College Park, MD (www.archives.gov/index.html); the Records of the Child Welfare League of America, the National Committee for the Prevention of Cruelty to Children, and the Papers of Ernest E. Witte are held by the Social Welfare History Archives, University of Minnesota, Minneapolis (http://special.lib.umn.edu/swha/); in addition to its outstanding Oral History Collection, Columbia University in New York holds the papers of a number of prominent social work leaders, including Homer Folks, Mary Richmond, Helen Hall, and Gertrude Vaile (www.columbia.edu/cu/lweb/).

Current Comment

Abbott, G. (1938). *The child and the state: Legal status in the family, apprenticeship, and child labor.* Chicago: University of Chicago Press.

Bremner, R. H. (Ed.). (1970). *Children and youth in America: A documentary history* (Vols. 1–3). Cambridge, MA: Harvard University Press.

Proceedings of the National Conference on Social Welfare [and its predecessors]. (1874–1982). Available: www.hti.umich.edu/n/ncosw/

Further Reading

Blank, R., & Haskins, R. (Eds.). (2001). *The new world of welfare.* Washington, DC: Brookings Institution Press.

Carp, E. W. (Ed.). (2002). *Adoption in America: Historical perspectives.* Ann Arbor: University of Michigan Press.

Katz, M. B. (1996). *In the shadow of the poorhouse: A social history of welfare in America* (Rev. ed.). New York: Basic Books.

COHEN, WILBUR JOSEPH (1913–1987)

Wilbur Cohen, along with Arthur Altmeyer and Edwin Witte, was part of the group of Social Security pioneers who emerged out of the intellectual tradition of institutional economists at the University of Wisconsin. Cohen studied under Witte at Wisconsin and when Witte and Altmeyer formed the president's Committee on Economic Security (CES) in 1934 to draft the Franklin D. Roosevelt administration's Social Security proposals, Witte brought Cohen in as an eager young staffer. Immediately making himself indispensable at the CES, Cohen displayed the quick intelligence, gregarious personality, and restless energy that characterized him throughout his life. After the Social Security Act was passed, Cohen was hired as the first professional employee of the new Social Security Board created by Congress to administer the act.

At the board, Cohen became Chairman Arthur Altmeyer's personal legislative assistant. Despite his relative youth, Altmeyer relied heavily on Cohen as his emissary to Capitol Hill. Cohen's intellectual mastery of the subject matter of social insurance, his ability to explain technical matters in understandable language, and especially his agreeable personality, made him a very effective legislative liaison. Much of Social

Security policy in the first two decades of the program featured Altmeyer as the up-front policymaker and Cohen as the behind-the-scenes technician helping to get the board's proposals enacted into legislation.

With the coming of the Dwight D. Eisenhower administration in 1953, Cohen soon left government and went into academe, becoming a professor of public welfare administration at the University of Michigan. Although outside of government, Cohen was influential on Capitol Hill in lobbying for the passage of Social Security disability benefits in 1956. When the Democrats returned to power in 1961, President John F. Kennedy appointed Cohen as assistant secretary for legislation at the Department of Health, Education, and Welfare (HEW), reprising his earlier role of legislative liaison—this time at the cabinet level of government. In the Lyndon B. Johnson administration, Cohen would rise to become, first, undersecretary of the department, and then finally, secretary of HEW in 1968. The major education legislation of the mid 1960s was guided by his deft political hand, as were most of the early changes in the welfare area. In 1965, he was the essential man in the creation of the Medicare program, representing President Johnson on Capitol Hill and skillfully negotiating passage of the bill in Congress.

Leaving government a second time at the end of the Johnson administration, he returned to academe, becoming dean of the School of Education at Michigan; and in 1980 he moved to the LBJ School of Public Affairs at the University of Texas, where he remained until his death. During his academic career, Cohen was involved in many areas of social welfare policy, frequently testifying before Congress and cofounding the Social Security advocacy group SOS (Save Our Security) in 1979. Much of the key social welfare legislation of the 1950s, 1960s, and 1970s reflects his influence. In 1975 and 1976, Cohen was elected president of the American Public Welfare Association. Throughout his life, Wilbur Cohen was an active and effective advocate for the core causes that moved him: Social Security, health care, education, and welfare reform.

—Larry W. DeWitt

See also Altmeyer, Arthur Joseph; Social Security (United States)

Primary Sources

Wilbur J. Cohen Papers, Wisconsin Historical Society, Madison (www.wisconsinhistory.org/); Wilbur J. Cohen Papers, Lyndon Baines Johnson Presidential Library, Austin, TX (www.lbjlib.utexas.edu/); Wilbur J. Cohen Papers, Bentley Historical Library, University of Michigan, Ann Arbor (www.umich.edu/~bhl/).

Current Comment

Cohen, W. J. (1957). *Retirement policies under Social Security.* Berkeley: University of California Press.
Haber, W., & Cohen, W. J. (Eds.). (1948). *Readings in Social Security.* New York: Prentice Hall.
Haber, W., & Cohen, W. J. (Eds.). (1960). *Social Security: Programs, problems and policies.* Homewood, IL: Irwin.

Further Reading

Berkowitz, E. D. (1995). *Mr. Social Security.* Lawrence: University Press of Kansas.
Marmor, T. R. (1987). Entrepreneurship in public management: Wilbur Cohen and Robert Ball. In J. W. Doig & E. C. Hargrove (Eds.), *Leadership and innovation.* Baltimore and London: Johns Hopkins University Press.
Additional background information on Cohen can be found on the Social Security Administration website *(www.ssa.gov/history/wilburc.html).*

COMMUNITY DEVELOPMENT (CANADA)

The history of community development in Canada reflects the country's diversity and complexity. There are, however, significant themes that are important. These include the work of women, the development and sharing of knowledge, local activity embedded in and influenced by social movements, the importance of foreign influences and of institutions, particularly government and church, and finally the intersection and reciprocal influence of ideas and strategies. The six stories presented here reflect these themes.

THE WOMEN'S INSTITUTE

The Women's Institute, founded in the late 1890s in Ontario by Erland Lee and Adelaide Hunter Hoodless, was aimed at improving life, not only for women but also for all who lived in agricultural areas. The national organization focused on countrywide issues and chapters focused on local matters. From its inception, the Women's Institute was a source of education and skill development for rural women. Early education efforts focused on health, child, and family concerns. As the organization matured, members demanded a broader range of topics, including legal issues, especially family and property law; fundraising; effective meetings; parliamentary process; and later international women's issues, as well as skills to achieve more effective participation in community and national life. The Women's Institute played a key role in two world wars and the intervening depression, raising funds and assisting those in need locally, nationally, and internationally. In the 1940s, the organization sought and acquired group health insurance 20 years before Canada instituted universal health care. As the women's movement and urbanization developed, the Women's Institute decreased in importance. Nevertheless, it continues to work on traditional issues, particularly those of interest to rural people.

COOPERATIVE MOVEMENTS

With Canada's rapid settlement in the early 1900s came increased attempts by farmers to protect themselves against powerful corporate interests. In Saskatchewan, farmers battled the Canadian Pacific Railway and grain companies, eventually forming the Saskatchewan Grain Growers Company (SGGC) in 1908. In addition to its efforts to ensure justice for farmers, the SGGC, advocated for reforms, including a graduated income tax, nationalization of utilities and food processing plants, tariffs favorable to farmers, as well as striving for women's rights and universal health care. The SGGC was also instrumental in establishing farmer-owned elevator companies and (the still existent) Wheat Pool. Women like Violet McNaughton played key roles, convening kitchen table meetings that addressed local and national issues like the establishment of Canada's universal health care. Though similar to the adult education orientation of the more famous Antigonish movement, with its local study groups and reading circles, the cooperative farmers' movement was more heavily influenced by developments in the western United States and more closely

linked to political organizations like the Communist party and the Cooperative Commonwealth Federation. Early organizing efforts resulted in mergers with similar "farmer" organizations in other provinces and the creation of the National Farmers' Union (NFU) in 1969. The NFU continues to maintain a strong local focus while addressing issues of provincial, national, and, more recently, international concern.

Led by Fathers James Tompkins and Hugh MacPherson, and by Moses Coady of St. Francis Xavier University, the Antigonish movement emerged in the Antigonish region of Nova Scotia during the 1920s as an approach to social reform grounded in elements of adult education and cooperation, a social justice program with a basis in Catholic social teachings. Influenced by Canadian experiments in Saskatchewan and Quebec, as well as some in Great Britain and Scandinavia, it combined cooperative development and adult education to teach community members about their economic helplessness and methods to challenge it. Not the first to develop cooperatives, the Antigonish movement was the first to meld ideals of cooperation and adult education. Contemporary teachings and the support of the Catholic church were important to the movement as was support from the Nova Scotia government and the Carnegie Foundation. Its work continues at the Coady International Institute at St. Francis Xavier University.

THE COMPANY OF YOUNG CANADIANS

The Company of Young Canadians (CYC) emerged as a federal government initiative in 1965 aimed at putting the energy of youth to work in communities across Canada. It evolved into a nationwide, grassroots approach to community development with a wide variety of projects—civil rights and antipoverty activism; the development of food co-ops and youth drop-in centers; and outreach projects addressing problems associated with drug and alcohol use and violence. By 1974, it had over 400 workers. The CYC was shaped by both officials and citizens (clearly influenced by contemporary student and community activism, especially the U.S. Peace Corps and Volunteers in Service to America) and designed to be participatory, with strategies that were aggressively change oriented. The CYC worked with the alienated to improve communications between them and mainstream Canadian society. It took a social action approach that often focused on gaining power for disenfranchised communities. An initiative this broad and radical could not help but face organizational and political difficulties. In 1975—with criticism from politicians and business elites and internal squabbling—the CYC dissolved. Although its influence has never been formally evaluated, CYC projects contributed resources, stimulated community participation, and educated community members. A number of CYC workers went on to make contributions to their communities and country.

ANIMATION SOCIALE/ SOCIAL ANIMATION

Animation Sociale/Social Animation grew out of particular conditions in Quebec in the 1960s. A "quiet revolution" transformed the province from a conservative and cautious society to a dynamic and change-oriented culture. This was an era of "democratization" of political institutions and services, supported by federal funding and policies. A new, well-educated class was growing and demanding increased citizen participation. With financial support from the Roman Catholic church and the United Way, private agencies developed programs that supported the early *Animation Sociale* community development initiatives. Practitioners (*animateurs*) began working in rural and urban areas where communities faced harsh economic and social problems. Like other approaches, it drew on foreign influences such as the Christian socialist movement in France, Paulo Freire's consciousness-raising approach in Latin America, and the civil rights movement in the United States. *Animation Sociale* aimed "to bring order and purpose to community action. . . . The *animateur's* role [was] to inform, stimulate participation, and provide a rational planning approach" (Wharf & Clague, 1997, p. 31). Though criticized for failing to bring about fundamental social change, in the 1960s *Animation Sociale* triggered development of new forms of organizations and more political approaches to community practice, which resulted in the development of a grassroots leadership that persisted in local organizing. Many *animateurs*

went on to become involved in more radical social and political movements.

ABORIGINAL COMMUNITY DEVELOPMENT

It was only in 1951 that a revision of the federal Indian Act overturned many of the colonial strictures on aboriginal people and "allowed" them to organize effectively. While local issues such as housing and education were addressed, a broader focus quickly emerged, confronting the pervasive state control of Indians' economic, social, and cultural affairs. Leaders and spokespersons became increasingly vocal and able to relate the history of colonization as well as current realities. Leaders—men and women, educators and artists, politicians and social activists—created environments in which effective "aboriginal" community development could occur. Particularly important was George Manuel, who began as a local organizer of communities in British Columbia and went on to found the National Indian Brotherhood. The impetus of the activist orientation of the 1960s, underpinned by the civil rights movement in the United States and a "war on poverty" at home, stimulated general Canadian support for aboriginal organizing. During the late 1950s and early 1960s, many provinces initiated community development programs in rural and remote regions and aboriginal communities took advantage of the organizing opportunities. Though short-term funding meant that little in the way of immediate gains were made in material resources, the confidence and political awareness engendered by the local efforts resulted in the development and strengthening of provincial and national organizations.

CONCLUSION

As community development in Canada enters the twenty-first century, new issues are occupying increasing attention: the environment, and immigrant and refugee issues, for example. The men and women who are working in these areas will contribute their energy and ideas to the continuing story.

—*Bill Lee*

See also Community Economic Development (Canada)

Primary Sources

Company of Young Canadians Fonds, William Ready Division of Archives and Research Collections, McMaster University, Hamilton, ON; Marie Michael Library, Coady International Institute, St. Francis Xavier University, Antigonish, NS; Centre for the Study of Co-operatives, Resource Collections, University of Saskatchewan, Saskatoon.

Current Comment

Brown, L. (1972). *How we got where we are now: A short history of the farmers' movement in Saskatchewan.* Saskatoon, SK: National Farmers' Union.

Coady, M. (1939). *Masters of their own destiny.* New York: Harper & Brothers.

Elias, P. D. (1991). *Development of Aboriginal people's communities.* North York, ON: Captus.

National Farmers' Union. (1969). NFU Statement of Purpose. Available: www.nfu.ca/misc_files/NFU_Statement_of_Purpose.pdf

Further Reading

Ambrose, L. M. (2000). *Women's institutes of Canada: The first one hundred years 1897–1997.* Gloucester, ON: Tri-Co Printing.

Blondin, M. (1971). Animation sociale. In J. A Draper (Ed.), *Citizen participation: A book of readings* (pp. 159–170). Toronto, ON: New Press.

McFarlane, P. (1993). *Brotherhood to nationhood: George Manuel and the making of the modern Indian movement.* Toronto, ON: Between the Lines.

Wharf, B., & Clague, M. (Eds.). (1997). *Community organizing: Canadian experiences.* Don Mills, ON: Oxford University Press.

COMMUNITY ECONOMIC DEVELOPMENT (CANADA)

Community Economic Development (CED) practices and organizations have grown rapidly in Canada since the mid 1980s. CED is a strategy that has been developed primarily but not exclusively in response to the deterioration of local economies and lack of hope for revitalization from the outside—either from the private market through investment or the support of government programs. Through CED, community organizations have now become players in the process of economic development. These initiatives are often not-for-profit and are democratically managed. The outcomes are diverse, reflecting the different geographies, politics, cultures, and traditions of each region.

These have varied from the promotion of small-scale enterprises or training programs that were put in place to employ people who faced long-term unemployment, to loan funds to support CED initiatives, to planning initiatives that promote local economic development. The underlying goals are to find ways to revitalize local economies, ameliorate poverty through training and job creation, and to involve residents and other local actors in these processes. The partnerships created bring representatives from the private sector, unions, local institutions, and government together to build these initiatives.

Despite the huge variations in practice, the recent growth of CED has common roots. It is a response to the consequences of changes linked to shifts in the wider political economy. Two aspects are key. First, changes in the economy linked to what is popularly described as globalization have led to economic restructuring in many regions in Canada. Jobs have been lost, entire industries closed, natural resources like mining and fishing have disappeared. Low paying, less stable, and part-time work has replaced jobs that used to be available in the primary and manufacturing sectors. The consequence for those working and out of work has been an increase in poverty. Second, during the same period, both provincial and federal governments have cut back and redefined social programs. Consequently, individuals and communities were deprived of support for both income and services, and the community sector responded with innovative ways to organize support for the individuals affected by the new social and economic conditions. The contradiction here is that on the one hand local organizations have resigned themselves to the deterioration of social conditions and acted to fill the gaps and provide jobs. On the other hand, the new context has provided opportunities for the development of new local initiatives that have acted to increase citizen participation and, thus, enhance local democratic practices.

This reemergence of CED builds on older traditions and practices. Its antecedents vary depending on the region of the country. For example, in the 1920s in Nova Scotia, the Antigonish movement, led by Moses Coady and Jimmy Tompkins, used adult education as a means of establishing self-help groups and cooperatives. Similarly, in the 1930s, in Quebec and in the Prairie provinces, cooperative enterprises were a response to economic hardship faced by those living in both rural and urban communities. Some of these have grown into large cooperative businesses such as the *caisse populaire* (cooperative banks in Quebec), but their traditions of collective economic endeavors are part of the legacy that has been taken in hand by CED practitioners. The revival of community activism in the 1960s and related social movements provided another important root for the current CED revival. These movements created organizations of citizens that challenged both public and private power at the local level and created alternative, democratically managed local institutions. Thus, across the country, a tradition of local democratic participation and social innovation has deep roots that have contributed to organizational capacity to participate in CED practice.

The basic goal of CED is to use business development as a means of obtaining social ends. One of the most common practices is to create businesses that provide training and employment experience for unemployed people as a means to integrate them into jobs. Some of these types of programs create permanent jobs whereas others are transitional. Often these projects are connected to the social assistance programs of their respective provincial governments. The first CED project that used this strategy was the Human Resources Development Association (HRDA) in Halifax, Nova Scotia. Founded in 1977, the organization has created small businesses that are labor-intensive and do not require high skill levels. The purpose of these businesses was to provide an alternative to social assistance. In Quebec, *entreprises d'insertion,* or training businesses, provide training and time-limited work experience to those receiving *aide sociale* (social assistance). There are many types of businesses. Some, like Chic Resto-Pop, a community restaurant and hot meal service for schools, have a social vocation. It trains approximately 100 welfare recipients at a time.

Some CED organizations act to promote local economic development. They provide technical and financial assistance, including capital, to projects. One of the earliest of these was New Dawn Development Corporation in Sydney, Nova Scotia.

Incorporated in 1976, it responded to deteriorating economic conditions brought about by the downsizing and subsequent closure of the steel production and coal mining enterprises. It has developed real estate and housing and set up businesses. In the 1990s, it took over an old military base and developed homes for seniors. It has a large asset base and is an example of an organization that has developed many businesses for the purposes of meeting social and job creation needs.

Other CED organizations have become para-governmental. Montreal's CED organizations provide a good example. Beginning as local initiatives in working-class neighborhoods in the mid 1980s, coalitions of labor, community organizations, and businesses sought strategies to combat poverty and unemployment. Revitalization strategies were to be put in place through local organizations. These included efforts to save local businesses or create new ones to get people reemployed through the use of job training. In addition, the structures of these organizations involve the local population through representation of different sectors on their boards. The programs of the organization are designed to provide technical and financial support to both traditional and community businesses and to support programs designed to enhance local residents' entry into the labor market. Through a process of funding these organizations, the provincial government has gradually taken them over and they have become integrated into a provincial network of local development agencies with a specific mandate and stability. They are, however, still able to encourage and support local initiatives. Some CED initiatives are alternatives for community social development and have been created by groups that have been excluded from the mainstream economy such as aboriginal communities, women, immigrants, and those living with the consequences of being diagnosed with "mental illness." The following are examples of their CED practices. Aboriginal communities have struggled with competing paradigms of their traditional values and the pressures of participating in capitalist markets. Some communities have created successful joint ventures based on local resources such as forestry, whereas others have created cooperative enterprises in both rural and urban settings.

Women have established cooperatives and loan funds to create alternatives to the mainstream economy and enhance their autonomy. The values motivating these practices are in opposition to competition and build on relations of solidarity. For example, loan circles began in Montreal in the late 1980s to provide start-up capital, and technical and social support for women setting up small businesses. Immigrant women also have had success in establishing alternative enterprises. For example, Afghan Women's Catering was established in 1997 to alleviate the economic and social hardship experienced by Afghan women and their families, particularly as a result of the cutbacks in social assistance and services. Emphasis was placed on skills and capacity building through this catering collective. Another example is A-Way Express in Toronto. This business grew out of a movement of people who have contended with the mental health system and call themselves "psychiatric survivors." The business provides courier service, using public transportation. Despite its success as a business, it is far more than that. A-Way describes itself as an alternative business. It was established partially to counter the myth that people who have been institutionalized can never work, and to build a community of solidarity for these individuals. It provides a flexible work environment in which people can negotiate their hours based on their specific needs and capacities. In addition, it is democratically structured with the board of directors in the majority drawn from employees. The leadership and recent directors are among the so-called psychiatric survivors.

As CED grows as a social and economic strategy and receives greater recognition and financial support from government, practitioners are facing difficult issues. Will CED become a means of creating a different form of economic development that is locally controlled, ecological, and based on participatory democracy; or will it become a sector of the dominant economy that is different only because its jobs are unstable and keep people poor and on the periphery? These are the poles; the question is to which end CED will be pulled.

—Eric Shragge

See also Community Development (Canada)

Current Comment

Anderson, R., & Bone, R. M. (2000). First Nations economic development: The Meadow Lake Tribal Council. *Journal of Aboriginal Economic Development, 1*(1), 13–34.

Fontan, J.-M., & Shragge, E. (1996, October). Chic Resto-Pop: New community practice in Quebec. *Community Development Journal: An International Forum, 31*(4), 291–301.

Fontan, J.-M., & Shragge, E. (1998). Community Economic Development organizations in Montreal. *Journal of Community Practice, 5*(1, 2), 125–136.

Fraser, S. J. (2002). An exploration of joint ventures as a sustainable development tool for First Nations. *Journal of Aboriginal Economic Development, 3*(1), 40–44.

Further Reading

Lotz, J., & MacIntyre, G. (2002). *Sustainable people: A new approach to community development.* Sydney, NS: University College Cape Breton Press.

MacLeod, G. (1986). *New age business: Community corporations that work.* Ottawa, ON: Canadian Council on Social Development.

Shragge, E. (Ed.). (1997). *Community Economic Development: In search of empowerment* (2nd ed.). Montreal, QC: Black Rose.

Wharf, B., & Clague, M. (Eds.). (1997). *Community organizing: Canadian experiences.* Toronto, ON: Oxford University Press.

CONSERVATIVE VIEWS ON SOCIAL WELFARE

Although social welfare programs are typically identified with liberal approaches to public policy, there is also a conservative tradition and point of view about the development and maintenance of social welfare. That position is not necessarily one of blanket opposition to social welfare programs, but it is often one that is quite different from the liberal model of social welfare. The conservative approach has antecedents throughout the history of social welfare.

The conservative-liberal split, as it would be known in the United States, occurs in many different arenas of public life and in general concerns the role government should play in meeting the social, health, and economic needs of its citizens. The foundations of conservatism developed from the works of Edmund Burke, an eighteenth century English politician, who was opposed to the French Revolution. He was concerned about what he considered the excesses of that conflict, in particular what he perceived to be mob rule.

The conservative tradition also has its origins in the writings of Adam Smith, an economist, and author of the book, *The Wealth of Nations* (1776). Smith opposed government regulation of or involvement in the economy. A free market and the freedom of each individual to pursue his or her own economic interests were, in Smith's belief, the most important factors in developing a strong national economy. He believed that government efforts to influence the economy could interfere with the natural forces that make an economy efficient and promote economic growth.

In more recent times, conservative political leaders in the United States, such as Presidents Herbert Hoover, Dwight Eisenhower, and Ronald Reagan, have asserted that the role of government should be limited to basic functions such as international relations, defense, and governance of the money supply; that taxes should be low so that people have sufficient funds to pursue their own personal and economic objectives; and that government should be little involved in direct services to people. Such ideas were typical of the thinking in American government during the nineteenth and early twentieth centuries. These concepts are built into the U.S. Constitution and were altered only after the Great Depression of 1929. The depression led to executive and congressional action and Supreme Court decisions that gave the federal government a greater role in preserving the well-being of American citizens through programs such as Social Security and financial assistance to low-income families. These initiatives are the cornerstones of modern American social policy.

The conservative approach, however, remains viable and is often committed to the provision of human services. Many of the strongest supporters of human services programs as well as the largest contributors to voluntary social welfare programs in the United States would call themselves conservatives. They do not object to people being helped but they do object to extensive government involvement in providing that help. They believe that services ought to be provided by voluntary agencies supported by voluntary contributions. Churches and other religious institutions are ideal locations for the development and delivery of human services from the conservative perspective.

One of the earlier contemporary thinkers about conservatism was Russell Kirk, who wrote from the 1950s through the 1990s. Some of his principles have persisted, such as the belief in an enduring moral order; the value of adherence to custom, convention, and continuity; the principle of prudence; and the value of voluntary community as opposed to involuntary collectivism. Many conservative thinkers, such as Charles Murray, Milton Friedman, and Rose Friedman, also believe that minimal taxes themselves provide a social welfare benefit inasmuch as they leave money in the hands of the people. People should be able to design and purchase their own social welfare protections, something they are more likely to be able to do if they retain larger portions of their earnings. Murray and the Friedmans view government programs, which require significant amounts of taxation, as interfering with the best interest of citizens. Charles Murray identifies himself as a Libertarian. His positions on social welfare services are among the most radical in that he does not believe government should provide them at all.

Conservatives believe that people are better off on their own in pursuing their economic and social interests. According to many conservatives, citizens would be better served by saving their own money, buying their own retirement policies, and making their own decisions and plans for caring for themselves than they are by Social Security programs.

Although it is a political anathema to suggest that Social Security be abolished, as some conservative politicians have, many, including President George W. Bush, propose allowing U.S. citizens to invest some part of their Social Security contributions in securities as a way of promoting better growth for their retirement policies. It is their money, conservatives assert, and theirs to risk for their own possible gain. The contention is that a paternalistic government that protects its peoples' finances, whether or not they want them protected, runs counter to the values of a free society.

The ideas of Smith as well as the notions of more contemporary conservative thinkers suggest that programs such as Temporary Assistance for Needy Families, unemployment compensation, and even government-supported health insurance such as Medicaid and Medicare interfere with the unfettered use of their funds by citizens in the larger economy. Government ought to make sure the economy is strong, they would say, and when it is, people are able to buy their own protection, at the levels they want, with their own funds.

Some well-known contemporary conservatives include President George W. Bush and his political appointees, radio commentators such as Rush Limbaugh, and a whole group called neoconservatives by some, largely because they were earlier considered to be liberals. These neoconservatives, who do not use that term to describe themselves, include Irving Kristol, Norman Podhoretz, Nathan Glazer, Gertrude Himmelfarb, James Q. Wilson, and Thomas Sowell.

A special concern of many conservative social welfare thinkers is that the social welfare establishment, which they define as primarily liberal, does not provide accurate information on social problems. They attribute much of the blame to the media, which they believe have a liberal bias. They contend that the media distort many social problems such as homelessness and HIV/AIDS. They argue that instead of showing the homeless as the largely mentally ill, substance-abusing people that they are, the media focus on homelessness as a problem that can affect people who are hardworking, free of social pathology, and victims of a difficult economy or other circumstances beyond their control.

In the case of HIV/AIDS, some conservatives feel it is portrayed as a health problem that can affect anyone when, in fact, almost all AIDS patients are male homosexuals, intravenous drug users, or people who have sexual relationships with intravenous drug users or male homosexuals. They say treating HIV/AIDS as a disease that anyone can contract is liberal propaganda used to make services for special groups more acceptable. Conservatives also contend that the media have suppressed research showing that children who have a parent who stays at home rather than working grow up healthier and better functioning than children who participate in day care programs. It is not likely that all or even most conservative thinkers oppose services to the homeless, persons with AIDS, or day care for working parents. Many simply believe that these programs can foster dependency and interfere with effective family life. These critics also think that those receiving these social services ought to be more accurately described.

The basic difference between the conservative and liberal points of view about social welfare is often an argument about the role of government in providing aid. Liberal thinkers believe that government can and should help people directly. Conservative thinkers are skeptical about the ability of government to be helpful, in the long run, to those who need assistance. The conservatives often think that government programs to serve the disadvantaged may do more harm than good. Of course, conservative views on social welfare are varied and extensive. This summary provides some of the key ideas as well as some of the key thinkers in the conservative social welfare policy arena.

—*Leon Ginsburg*

Primary Sources

Ebenstein, W. (1960). *Great political thinkers: Plato to the present* (3rd ed.). New York: Rinehart; Hayek, F. (1976). *The road to serfdom.* Chicago: University of Chicago Press. (Original work published 1944); Kirk, R. (1955). *The conservative mind: From Burke to Eliot* (4th ed.). Washington, DC: Regnery; Smith, A. (1991). *The wealth of nations.* New York: Everyman's Library. (Original work, *An Inquiry Into the Nature and Causes of the Wealth of Nations*, published 1776)

Current Comment

Friedman, M., & Friedman, R. (1984). *Tyranny of the status quo.* New York: Harcourt, Brace, Jovanovich.
Murray, C. (1984). *Losing ground: American social policy, 1950–1980.* New York: Basic Books.
Sowell, T. S. (1995). *The vision of the anointed: Self-congratulation as a basis for social policy.* New York: Basic Books.

Further Reading

Gerson, M. (1996). *The essential neoconservative reader.* New York: Addison-Wesley.
Ginsberg, L. (1998). *Conservative social welfare policy.* Chicago: Nelson-Hall.
Jansson, B. S. (2000). *The reluctant welfare state: American social welfare policies—past, present, and future* (4th ed.). Belmont, CA: Wadsworth.
O'Gorman, F. (1973). *Edmund Burke: His political philosophy.* London: Allen and Unwin.

CONSTITUTION OF 1917 (MEXICO)

Mexico's Constitution of 1917 was one of the most progressive and socially reformist documents to be produced in the early twentieth century. Emerging from the Mexican Revolution of 1910–1920, the document addressed a broad range of concerns of workers, peasants, and middle-class reformers. Although the Constitution has been selectively implemented, it contributed to the legitimacy and stability of postrevolutionary Mexico and laid the basis for a nationalist welfare state.

President Venustiano Carranza called for the drafting of a new constitution in 1916. Delegates were elected and began meeting at the Constitutional Convention in Querétaro in December. The delegates, partisans of Carranza's government, represented a range of political interests yet were largely composed of urban-based, middle-class reformers with very little representation from Mexico's working classes and rural majority. President Carranza specifically barred representatives of popular revolutionary leaders Emiliano Zapata and Pancho Villa from the convention. Despite the fact that delegates were Carranza loyalists, the convention sought to greatly alter the previous Constitution of 1857 in contrast to Carranza's wishes.

The Constitution of 1917 that was submitted to President Carranza confirmed a separation of powers between the executive, legislative, and judicial bodies and basic freedoms of assembly, speech, petition, and press. It sought to strengthen local democracy and control. In addition to these basic principles, issues of national self-determination and social reform greatly influenced the delegates. This led to the inclusion of several provisions, such as Articles 3, 27, and 123, which laid the basis for a reformist and nationalist document.

The delegates saw land concentration and foreign control of natural resources as a significant obstacle to Mexico's national development. Article 27 laid the basis for the transformation of property rights by giving the nation the right to expropriate property and redistribute land when it was deemed of public utility. This article helped pave the way for significant land distribution programs, especially during the presidency of Lázaro Cárdenas (1934–1940), benefiting hundreds of thousands of Mexicans. Article 27 also gave the nation direct ownership of the country's natural resources and subsoil rights. This reversed the policies of the Porfirio Diáz administration (1876–1911) that allowed private and foreign companies direct access to the nation's national resources without government regulation or oversight. The United States government

and foreign oil companies pressured successive presidents to keep them from implementing this aspect of Article 27. When workers began to overtly criticize foreign oil companies, however, President Cárdenas used Article 27 to expropriate Mexico's vast petroleum reserves in 1938.

To address issues of poverty and inequality, the delegates drafted Article 123 to deal with labor and social welfare. Like Article 27, it went well beyond the modest proposals of President Carranza and even surpassed contemporary social provisions in industrialized countries. Article 123 called on Congress to pass legislation to allow workers the right to organize; to regulate the maximum workday to 8 hours and 6 days a week; to regulate child labor such that children between 12 and 16 years of age were not to work for more than 6 hours daily; to establish a one-month paid maternity leave following childbirth; to grant two special half-hour breaks to nursing mothers in the workplace; to establish a minimum wage that would meet the "normal needs of the life of the worker, his [sic] education, and his [sic] lawful pleasures"; and to establish equal pay for equal work to workers regardless of sex or nationality. Article 123 also encouraged states and the federal government to develop old-age pensions and accident and death insurance. In addition, the state was to have an important regulatory and intermediary role in labor-management relations.

The Constitution also mandated the establishment of state-run public education. Article 3 established that every individual had the right to receive an education. Primary and secondary education was to be free, secular, and compulsory. Education was described as important to "develop all of the faculties of being human and . . . instill in the student, at the same time, a love of country and awareness of international solidarity, in independence and justice." Higher education was deemed important for the development of the nation, and the federal government was empowered to help develop and fund universities.

The Congress had to pass enabling legislation before many of the Constitution's provisions were enacted. President Carranza and his successors were slow to implement some of the more progressive articles. In addition, business groups, landowners, the United States government, and other powerful interests lobbied to ensure that the more far-reaching articles remained unimplemented. The Constitution would be selectively implemented, yet it provided the legal basis for an activist and nationalist social welfare state.

The breadth and promise of the Constitution of 1917 led many to mobilize to pressure the government to develop social programs mandated by the document. The government has also utilized this breadth to address some demands of the popular sector without having to address systemic inequalities. The Constitution of 1917 helped to forge the legitimacy of the postrevolution governments, contributing to Mexico's social and political stability. But, as more socially oriented articles of the Constitution of 1917 have been amended or deemphasized, especially after the neoliberal reforms beginning in the 1980s, social movements have come to challenge the legitimacy of the government. The most prominent example of this is the Chiapas uprising that began in 1994, which came about, in part, in response to the implementation of NAFTA and to the reforms of Article 27 that ended land reform.

The Constitution of 1917 is a landmark document in Mexican history and provided the basis for far-reaching social reform. It led to stability and legitimated the dominant classes. As noted above, it has been selectively implemented. As a result, its promise remains unfulfilled.

—Enrique C. Ochoa

See also Education Policy (Mexico); Labor Movement and Social Welfare (Mexico); Land Reform (Mexico); Social Reform and State-Building (Mexico); Social Welfare (Mexico): Since 1867; Welfare Ministries in the Twentieth Century (Mexico)

Primary Source

An English version of the Mexican Constitution of 1917 can be found on-line (www.ilstu.edu/class/hist263/docs/1917const.html).

Further Reading

Brachet-Márquez, V. (1994). *Dynamics of domination: State, class, and social reform in Mexico, 1910–1990.* Pittsburgh, PA: University of Pittsburgh Press.

Knight, A. (1986). *The Mexican Revolution* (Vols. 1–2). Cambridge, UK: Cambridge University Press.

Mendiolea, G. F. (1957). Historia del Congreso Constituyenente de 1916–1917. Mexico City.

Niemeyer, E. V., Jr. (1974). *Revolution at Querétaro: The Mexican Constitutional Convention of 1916–1917.* Austin: University of Texas Press.

Ruíz, R. E. (1992). *Triumphs and tragedy: A history of the Mexican people.* New York: Norton.

CRIMINAL JUSTICE POLICY (CANADA)

The essential function of any criminal justice system is the maintenance of social control through the use of formal sanctions and rewards that the government has empowered the various elements a criminal justice system to exercise. The Canadian criminal justice system (CJS) is composed of three formal elements and a fourth informal element. The formal elements are the police (federal, provincial, and municipal), the criminal court system (federal and provincial/territorial), and the correction system (federal and provincial/territorial). How their respective mandates come into being is subject to much debate. The informal element, sometimes referred to as the "hidden element" of the CJS, is the public. The formal elements are virtually universal around the world. What varies between countries is the nature of how the various elements are organized and function.

The Canadian criminal justice system can trace its primary roots of influence to England and a modest influence from France. Although John Cabot (from Britain) arrived at Cape Breton Island in 1497, it was the French who first colonized what is now known as Quebec in 1604 with the arrival of Samuel de Champlain. The early settlers were mostly interested in exploiting the land for its rich furs. Because they settled and based most of their activities in Quebec, the French had a more significant impact on justice policy and administration in the province of Quebec. The French influence is still evident in the province's language and social, cultural, and legal ideologies and practices. Although the English, under the leadership of David Kirke, had captured Upper Canada (now known as Quebec) in 1629, they returned it to the French in 1632. The English tended to concentrate their fur-trading efforts further west and established themselves in Lower Canada (now known as Ontario).

The long history of rivalry between England and France also spilled over into the New World, and the eventual Battle on the Plains of Abraham in 1759 in Quebec, in which the French lost, resulted in the French influence being limited and largely concentrated in Quebec. During its formative years, some parts of western Canada resembled a wild frontier with no formal crime control infrastructure. With many of the new settlers coming from nefarious backgrounds, crime was not necessarily rampant; but for those who chose to commit crimes, there was no formal law enforcement structure. Thus, Canada's pioneer days were characterized by pockets of lawless land with little, if any, social justice or social welfare. As permanent settlements were established in what was formerly known as New France, however, many of the crimes familiar in the Old World quickly emerged in the new. The evolution of a formal criminal justice system finally came to fruition in 1867 with the signing of the British North America (BNA) Act.

With the signing of the BNA Act, Canada acquired sovereignty over its criminal justice system. It is not exactly clear whether the emergence of a formal crime control infrastructure was due to increasing crime rates or due to increased public perception of crime. Nevertheless, the act identified the division of responsibilities between federal and provincial governments. Under section 91 of the act, the federal parliament decided which behaviors constituted criminal offenses whereas Section 92 of the act gave provincial (or territorial) governments jurisdiction over law enforcement and the administration of the justice system. In 1982, the act was repatriated in the Constitution Act, which in Part 1 included the Canadian Charter of Rights and Freedoms.

Although life during the pioneer days of Canada was comparatively hard, a formal infrastructure to support all Canadians was lacking. The Constitution Act was designed to ensure that all Canadians irrespective of race, national or ethnic origin, color, religion, sex, age, or mental or physical disability would be treated equally and fairly under law. Since its inception, however, there has been an ongoing debate as to whether the various agencies and departments involved in the administration of justice policy actually function as a unified "system." This has perhaps been most clearly illustrated in Graham Packer's (1968) work in which he suggested that the values system underlying the administration of the criminal justice system reflects one of two approaches: the "crime control model" and the "due process model." The crime control model sees the primary purpose of the CJS as the protection of the public through the detection, apprehension, and incapacitation of offenders. People are seen as responsible for their actions and the system should be able to act swiftly, with surety and efficiency, when someone violates the laws of the land. The model places a high presumption of guilt and an emphasis on compensation for the victim of crime.

By contrast, the due process model emphasizes procedural fairness and the presumption of innocence. Under this model, the onus rests with the criminal court system to prove guilt. And, to protect the rights of all individuals, there are protocols and procedures in place to ensure that those accused of crimes receive a fair trial. These rights today are part of the Charter of Rights and Freedoms, Sections 7–15. For example, under Section 15, all Canadians are considered equal "before and under law and equal protection and benefit of law."

Although the Canadian CJS has evolved considerably since 1867, today it is generally characterized as representing a modified due process model. When examining Canadian crime statistics, however, it is apparent that the poor, underprivileged, aboriginals, and others who are economically, socially, and politically challenged are disproportionately represented in the CJS. These conditions exist in spite of the affirmative action programs under the equality rights section of the charter, which says that the law does not preclude any "program or activity that has as its object the amelioration of conditions of disadvantaged individuals or groups including those that are disadvantaged because of race, national or ethnic origin, colour, religion, sex, age or mental or physical disability."

The apparent intention of the framers of Confederation and its repatriation under the Constitution Act was to develop a CJS that was based on a "value consensus model" as opposed to a "conflict model." One of the key organizations for providing an independent and critical perspective of Canadian law was the Canadian Law Reform Commission, which became the Law Commission of Canada in 1997. The commission regularly reviews a wide range of legal issues as they pertain to social justice in Canada.

All elements of the Canadian CJS, whether at the municipal, provincial/territorial, or federal level have at some time or another been the subject of controversy. For example, over the years the Royal Canadian Mounted Police (RCMP) have experienced numerous internal operational problems, as have the penitentiary system and the judiciary. These incidents have prompted some to argue that the Canadian CJS reflects the conflict model. This perspective sees the CJS as a "state-initiated and state-supported effort to rationalize mechanisms of social control" (Taylor, Walton, & Young, 1975, p. 24).

The Canadian CJS, like that of virtually any developed country, is complex. To clearly define and describe the nature of the country's criminal justice policy and offer any comment on its relation to social welfare, it must be viewed within a theoretical context and within a context that is sensitive to the economic, political, and social climate.

Since the late 1980s, the Canadian CJS has encountered a number of challenges in fulfilling its mandate. These concerns have not only been expressed within the system but also through the voice of the public. This is perhaps most clearly evident in the call to replace the 1984 Young Offenders Act with the newly proposed Youth Criminal Justice Act as well as a stronger move toward greater victim compensation and involvement in the justice process with such initiatives as restorative justice, a return to greater community-based policing, and in some provinces (e.g., New Brunswick, Ontario, and British Columbia) a move toward the privatization of correctional institutions. Restorative justice emphasizes repairing the harm experienced by victims of crimes, often through restorative actions by the offender. Community-based policing implies a closer relationship between law enforcement officers and community residents. Privatization involves the transfer of governmental functions to private firms, often on a fee-for-service basis.

As long as social justice in Canada continues to be based on political laws as opposed to scientific laws, Canadian criminal justice policy will be bifurcated along social and economic lines. Even though the United Nations describes Canada as having one of the finer systems of social justice, those who are marginalized would argue otherwise. Yet, relative to countries that enjoy less economic and social stability, social justice and social welfare in Canada is still considerably more advanced.

—*John Winterdyk*

See also Race and Ethnic Relations (Canada)

Current Comment

Harris, M. (1986). *Justice denied.* Toronto, ON: Macmillan.

Further Reading

Packer, G. (1968). *Introduction to criminal law* (3rd ed.). Toronto, ON: Methuen.

Roberts, J. V. (2000). *Criminal justice in Canada: A reader.* Toronto, ON: Harcourt Brace.

Schmalleger, F., MacAlister, D., McKenna, P., & Winterdyk, J. (2000). *Canadian criminal justice today: An introductory text for the twenty-first century.* Toronto, ON: Pearson Education Canada.

Taylor, I., Walton, P., & Young, J. (1975). *The new criminology: For a social theory of deviance.* London: Routledge & Kegan Paul.

CRIMINAL JUSTICE POLICY (UNITED STATES)

Crimes are forbidden acts in which, at least in theory, society is the victim, along with the person who is robbed, cheated, assaulted, or otherwise harmed. Crime is also a legal concept that involves a political decision to prohibit certain behavior. Throughout recorded history, the usual punishments for criminals have been death, slavery, exile, maiming, or the payment of fines. Beginning with the Enlightenment, however, the philosophy of utilitarianism influenced criminal justice, calling for a hierarchy of penalties and punishment prescribed according to the gravity of the offense. Today, criminal justice has shifted to a neo-Kantian principle of "just deserts" or retribution. Most criminals today are sentenced to some form of probation supervision rather than imprisonment. The concept of imprisonment as rehabilitation took root in the latter part of the eighteenth century, gained popularity during the 1950s, waned in the 1970s, and made a gradual comeback in the 1990s.

Liberal ideologies about criminal justice are likely to be based on an assumption that most of the defects of human behavior have their origins in the social environment. Conservative ideologies assume that the primary cause of crime is inadequate control over a fundamentally flawed human nature. Radical ideologies, never very popular in America, are based on the view that crime is a result of the structure and dynamics of a capitalist economic system.

COLONIAL PERIOD

English settlers brought the "common law" with them to America, with the use of juries and grand juries, a strong emphasis on oral testimony in criminal trials, and a judge who played the role of a revered umpire. Colonial justice was also strongly influenced by religion; the Puritans and the Quakers had clear ideas about what a godly society should look like. The most common punishments, dispensed in public venues, were likely to be whipping, branding, hanging, and the pillory. Public rituals reinforced the legitimacy of criminal proceedings. Criminal penalties were exacted for "crimes" such as kissing one's wife in public, working on the Sabbath, and failing to regularly attend church. Blasphemy and fornication were treated severely, and buggery could result in hanging.

EARLY AMERICAN CRIMINAL JUSTICE

Between the American Revolution and the beginning of the twentieth century, criminal law and the criminal justice system were reformed to make them more congruent with republican ideals. Harsh, autocratic common law, an odd mixture of extreme legalism and extreme discretion, was gradually replaced with a more rational and just system. The Bill of Rights set the stage for the protection of essential human rights. Flogging and branding were abandoned for more humane punishments. The first American prison was opened in an old converted copper mine in Connecticut in 1773. The "penitentiary movement" began with the remodeling of the Walnut Street Jail in Philadelphia in 1790. Prisoners worked at hard labor and lived in solitary confinement, practices meant to both reform prisoners and deter future offenders. Silence was a rule

commonly enforced; inmates were to use their time for solitary reflection, contemplation, and Bible reading.

NINETEENTH CENTURY CRIMINAL JUSTICE

Important transformations occurred later in the nineteenth century. The criminal justice system, once run entirely by amateurs, gradually became professionalized. Whereas in colonial America no one worked full-time in criminal justice, by 1900 there were full-time judges, prosecutors, prison guards, and police officers. A number of riots swept the major cities in the 1830s and 1840s, giving rise to the establishment of professional police departments. Philadelphia and New York City established police departments in 1845; New Orleans and Cincinnati, in 1852; Boston, in 1854; and Baltimore, in 1857.

New reform efforts developed in the prisons. In 1844, the Correctional Association of New York was organized. The Prisoners' Aid Association of Maryland began in 1869. The John Howard Society, a voluntary advocacy and prisoners' rights organization, began in England in 1866, and a branch was established in Massachusetts in 1889. The National Conference of Charities and Correction, founded in 1874, provided a forum for leaders in corrections, as well as state charities.

The classic penitentiary had all but disappeared by 1850. It had never been popular in the South, where prisoners worked in chain gangs on state farms or were routinely contracted out to private employers who used them as cheap labor in mining and building railroads. "Good time" laws were a popular innovation in the mid nineteenth century, providing time off for good behavior. At the end of the Civil War, the great majority of inmates consisted of recently freed slaves.

THE MODERN ERA

By the beginning of the twentieth century, the indeterminate sentence was rapidly gaining support. It was consistent with a rehabilitative model of corrections, in which a person was typically sentenced to a minimum period of time, but would be released when rehabilitated. The idea of rehabilitation was attractive to the emerging profession of social work, but the principle of client self-determination effectively moved social workers out of adult corrections until after World War II.

In the postwar era, Americans' fear of crime grew, perhaps as a result of the tremendous social changes that had occurred. The result was a new "get tough" attitude about crime and criminals. The 1960s saw a dramatic increase in drug-related crime. Congress responded by creating a new federal agency, the Law Enforcement Assistance Administration, in 1968. It provided funding to state and local police jurisdictions to strengthen their crime-fighting capacity until it was abolished in 1982.

This eventually led to the "war on drugs" proclamation of President Richard Nixon in 1969, which resulted in increased funding for all aspects of law enforcement and corrections. The consequence of a national policy of "zero tolerance" has been a dramatic increase in the number of persons incarcerated, with little impact on the actual use of illicit drugs. Approximately 700,000 persons are arrested each year for marijuana offenses alone. Over 2 million people are incarcerated in the nation's jails and prisons, the highest rate of incarceration in the world. Eighty percent of those incarcerated in state prisons for drug offenses are ethnic minorities, primarily African Americans. African Americans are also represented disproportionately in other parts of the criminal justice system. The great majority of criminal offenders, however, are sentenced to probation, rather than prison.

In the mid 1970s, there was a shift away from rehabilitation in the criminal justice system, stemming in part from research indicating that prisons were not effective instruments of rehabilitation. The federal government temporarily abandoned its rehabilitative goals for federal prisoners, and many state governments followed suit. The few social workers that remained in the justice system worked in probation and parole, with private agencies assisting offenders and their (or victims') families, or in the juvenile justice system. A decade later, however, new rehabilitative initiatives were launched at both the federal and state levels, and social workers were slowly coming back into the field.

The federal government has been much more active in influencing criminal justice policy in recent years, especially through the provision of generous funding for special law enforcement projects at the community level. These projects include such things as equipment and technology assistance, "community policing," and concentrated drug law enforcement. The effect of these grants has been to focus local law enforcement efforts on federal priorities—such as reducing the supply of illicit drugs within the community. The events of September 11, 2001, have also led to increased emphasis at the local level on dealing with acts of terrorism.

The death penalty has been a continuing source of conflict in America. In the midst of controversial cases that led to declining public support, the NAACP (National Association for the Advancement of Colored People) Legal Defense Fund launched a moratorium campaign against the death penalty. In 1972, a U.S. Supreme Court opinion invalidated the Georgia death penalty law and affected similar statutes in other states. Capital punishment was effectively suspended for a time. Within 2 years, however, 35 states had passed new death penalty laws incorporating provisions that overcame the Court's objections. On January 1, 2003, there were 3,692 offenders on death row. Fifty-five percent were ethnic minorities, and 82 were juveniles.

Criminal justice policy in the United States has been shaped by changing economic and social conditions, including the extent and nature of crime, scientific discoveries, politics, and public opinion. The current war on drugs has had a profound impact on criminal justice policy. As our prisons filled with drug offenders, more treatment programs were routinely offered both in correctional settings and as alternatives to prison. Drug arrests have also fueled a phenomenal increase in the incarceration of women. At present, more than 3 percent of the adult population in the United States is under some form of correctional supervision, and we have surpassed both the former Soviet Union and the Republic of South Africa with the highest rate of incarceration in the industrialized world. It appears that drug arrests will guarantee the growth of our rapidly expanding correctional system well into the twenty-first century. Unfortunately, this growth will disproportionately affect racial and ethnic minorities.

—*C. Aaron McNeece*

See also Juvenile Justice Policy (United States); Rush, Benjamin; Substance Abuse Policy (United States)

Primary Source

Monkkonen, E. H. (1991). *Crime and justice in American history* (Vols. 1–2). Westport, CT: Meckler.

Current Comment

Currie, E. (1998). *Crime and punishment in America.* New York: Metropolitan Books.

Martinson, R. (1975). *The effectiveness of correctional treatment: A survey of treatment evaluation studies.* New York: Praeger.

Nixon, Richard M. (1969, July 14). Special message to the Congress on control of narcotics and dangerous drugs. In *Public papers of the presidents: Richard M. Nixon* (pp. 513–518). Washington, DC: Government Printing Office. Available: www.nixonfoundation.org/Research_Center/PublicPapers.cfm

Further Reading

Currie, E. (1993). *Reckoning: Drugs, the cities, and the American future.* New York: Hill and Wang.

Friedman, L. M. (1993). *Crime and punishment in American history.* New York: Basic Books.

Hindus, M. S. (1980). *Prison and plantation: Crime, justice, and authority in Massachusetts and South Carolina, 1767–1878.* Chapel Hill: University of North Carolina Press.

Miller, J. G. (1996). *Search and destroy: African-American males in the criminal justice system.* New York: Cambridge University Press.

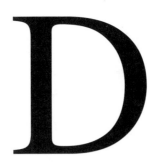

DAVIDSON, GEORGE FORRESTER (1909–1995)

George Forrester Davidson, a descendant of pioneer founders of Nova Scotia, Canada, received the education that prepared him for a brilliant career at the University of British Columbia (1924–1928) and Harvard University (1928–1932). Biographical studies of his life and work describe him as a model or exemplar in his lifetime and beyond in the fields of both social policy and public policy.

Davidson's creative linkages with social policy were evident in the positions he held in social planning and welfare fund-raising in Vancouver, British Columbia, in the 1930s and as executive director of Canada's leading social welfare agency, the Canadian Welfare Council, in the 1940s. During those years, he was also a lecturer at the School of Social Work, University of British Columbia, an active member of the Canadian Association of Social Workers, president of the Canadian Conference of Social Work, and president of the International Conference on Social Work. His linkages with social policy extended, as well, to the positions he held in public settings where, imbued with social welfare knowledge and social work values, he played a central role in the development of social programs that immeasurably enhanced Canadian society.

A high rating for George Davidson's leadership credentials in the area of public policy is equally sustainable. In association with his mentor and colleague, Harry Cassidy, and with a number of outstanding women in the social work field, he became a major contributor to a golden age of provincial social welfare programming in British Columbia in the 1930s and early 1940s.

From 1944 to 1972, Davidson held senior positions in the government of Canada. At the outset, he had a part in the development of the blueprint for the Canadian welfare state formulated at the Federal Provincial Conference on Reconstruction in 1945 and expressed in the conference's highly influential Green Book Proposals. As deputy minister in the federal departments of National Health and Welfare, and Citizenship and Immigration, his outstanding contributions in policy and administration led to his appointment to the very center of government: director of the Bureau of Government Organization in 1963 and secretary of the Treasury Board in 1964. He was thus in leadership positions in policy and program developments that by the early 1970s had given Canada the status of a fully matured welfare state.

Davidson's final position in the government of Canada was as president of the Canadian Broadcasting Corporation (1968–1972), to which he was appointed by the prime minister as a reflection of his broad understanding of human and social problems and his possession of the skills needed to administer a complex organization in a state of crisis. After four and a half years under his direction, the corporation had become a public broadcasting system that was serving Canada well.

Davidson was then able to accept senior appointments in the United Nations (1972–1986): first as an undersecretary general for administration and management and later as senior adviser to the Population Fund. His United Nations work crowned a lifetime of public service.

George Davidson's legacies endure in ongoing endeavors for humane social policy and rational public policy.

—*Richard B. Splane*

See also Canadian Council on Social Development

Further Reading

Splane, R. B. (2003). *George Davidson: Social policy and public policy exemplar.* Ottawa, ON: Canadian Council on Social Development.

DISABILITY POLICY (CANADA)

Disability policy typically refers to a number of clusters of policies for public programs directed at disabled people. The term "disabled people" is used rather than "people with disabilities" to reflect the definition of the term as adopted by Disabled Peoples' International. Such a pluralistic definition is particularly apt for Canada because it has a very decentralized form of governance as compared to most European countries and the United States. In Canada, prime constitutional responsibility for programs and policies of relevance to the well-being of disabled people (such as education, income support, employment preparation, supports for independent living, accessible environments, medical rehabilitation, and others) is vested in each of its 10 provincial and 3 territorial governments. The federal government's responsibility, in contrast, is quite limited.

Disability policy in Canada also can be of an "implicit" rather than "explicit" nature. This arises from Canada's parliamentary system of government and its practice of adopting "permissive" legislation. In contrast to "prescriptive" legislation that sets precise targets and time lines, the wording of permissive legislation provides governments considerable discretion in the kinds of new programs developed, along with when and how to introduce them.

Although permissive legislation and decentralized responsibility have the risk of contributing to major differences from one region to another, in fact the variance that exists (and there are real differences between the provinces) seems not much different from that found in other countries. This is largely because the different political cultures of the provinces also provide opportunities for innovation. Disability advocacy organizations, for example, have been able to persuade newly elected governments to adopt innovative approaches previously proved by the disability groups themselves. Such innovations, once adopted by one province, become examples for other provinces. The federal government, too, has played an important role by building on its responsibility to promote equality of opportunity for Canadians. It has provided grants to advocacy groups developing innovative initiatives and encouraged the spread of successful ideas through federal-provincial cost sharing and other means. The result has been an increasingly distinctive approach to disability widely recognized as among the most advanced in the world.

HISTORY

Early services for disabled people were developed in the absence of any particular policy. The very first was a special residence for women with mental disorders organized by the Catholic church in Quebec City in 1717. In 1747, the first hospital for "the sick, aged, incurable, insane and orphaned" was opened in Montreal, also by the church, and in 1835 the first public-funded "asylum" for people with psychiatric impairments was opened in St. John, New Brunswick. Early schools for deaf and blind children followed in the mid 1800s, and the first residential school for "idiots and feeble minded" in 1888 in Orillia, Ontario. All seem to have been modeled on programs previously developed in Europe and the United States.

Though provincial governments provided tax support for some, and operated others directly (such as residential institutions), there were no disability policies as such. Indeed, there were few health or welfare policies.

The first major disability policies were worker's compensation laws adopted by Quebec in 1909 and other provinces shortly after. These created a framework acknowledging the role of society in organizing and regulating rehabilitation services and financial support for workers injured in the workplace. The second important early policy development occurred during World War I, when, for the first time, the federal government became engaged with disability issues. The federal government, which had constitutional responsibility for the health of injured and sick war veterans, developed a network of rehabilitation hospitals and tuberculosis sanatoria for them. It also became involved in sharing the cost of public medical and rehabilitation services as the result of a tragic naval accident. A munitions ship from France, docked in the Halifax, Nova Scotia, harbor, caught fire and exploded, leveling much of the city and killing and injuring several thousand people. Broad public sympathy for the victims provided a context for the federal government to collect and channel funds for the cost of rehabilitation and other services for the victims with the support of provincial governments. Although this was an isolated instance, it served as a model for federal-provincial programs in later decades.

Few other disability policies were developed until after World War II. The most notable exception was adoption by several provinces of ill-conceived laws to sterilize "mentally defective" adults in the 1920s. The last of these was revoked in 1973.

An unprecedented expansion in kind and number of policies followed World War II. These were prompted by a series of social movements, each building on the advances of predecessors. All had as their aim, in one form or another, the inclusion of disabled people as valued members in normal community life. Disabled veterans were the first to press their case. Their central aim was to secure rehabilitation services as close to their home communities as possible (rather than in large veterans' hospitals), and in a way that would prepare them for community life. This led to development of early rehabilitation programs and services, integrating both medical and social approaches. The "polio movement" followed. Parents and professionals sought not only better disease prevention and medical rehabilitation services, but also access for affected children to regular school and camping opportunities. These forces led to the first federal-provincial conference on disability in 1952, in which agreement was reached on the cost sharing of vocational rehabilitation services by federal and provincial governments. The incentive of federal funds contributed to a rapid expansion in employment and training programs for disabled adults of working age across Canada.

The years following World War II also saw the development of new ideas for people with cognitive impairment. The province of Saskatchewan, in particular, became a world leader in community-based approaches to mental health services, demonstrating that it was possible to phase out reliance on large "mental hospitals." But the efforts of parents of children with intellectual impairments had the most sustained impact. Beginning in 1948, when the first local parent group was formed, this Canada-wide grassroots organization (now the Canadian Association for Community Living) pressed for the rights of their children to education, employment, and independent living. A second federal-provincial conference on disability in 1964, this one on "mental retardation," again contributed to a rapid expansion of community-based resources and opportunities. Special funding was provided for a series of demonstration projects, and financing of community services was made possible through a new federal-provincial cost-sharing mechanism called the Canada Assistance Plan. In the 1970s, the same association again prompted a nationwide series of demonstration projects, this time to place the emphasis on individualized services leading to community inclusion—the main ideas of which were adopted by provincial governments across Canada by the mid 1980s.

"Disability rights" became the watchword of the most recent major social movement, one led by a new generation of disability self-advocates composed mainly of people with motor and visual impairments. Beginning in the mid 1970s, they argued that disability was socially defined, and that the main issues confronting disabled people were barriers in the social and physical environment. This movement, along with other disability organizations, joined advocates representing women, aboriginal people, and those of racial minorities in seeking civil rights guarantees. The context could not have been better in that the federal and all provincial governments (except Quebec) had agreed to patriate Canada's Constitution, adding to it the Canadian Charter of Rights and Freedoms. The charter, adopted in 1982, guarantees equality before and under the law, and equal benefit of the law without discrimination on the basis of race, ethnicity, color, religion, sex, or disability. This made Canada the first country to have this kind of constitutional guarantee for its disabled citizens. As the highest law in the land, all other laws are subject to it. As a consequence, provincial as well as federal laws affecting disabled people have been amended and updated to ensure conformity with the charter.

CURRENT STATUS

Today's disability policies can be characterized as having a uniformly high level of commitment to fostering the equality of opportunity for community inclusion, yet there is considerable variability in the extent to which such ideals are implemented. For example, most provincial governments have programs that foster the inclusion of children with intellectual impairments in regular schools and classrooms. Yet, the extent to which such aspirations are implemented depends on both the philosophical commitment of a given government to such an ideal and the economic prosperity of the province. Similar discrepancies might also be noted in other important policy domains, whether in income support for disabled adults, the availability of technical aids, personal aides in support of independent living options, supported employment programs, and so on.

The federal government is involved in three ways. It has lead responsibility in areas of its jurisdiction including aboriginal peoples, the military, Crown corporations, and federally regulated private sector employers (e.g., banks, major transportation and communications industries), for which it enacts legislation such as the 1986 Employment Equity Act that provides for equal opportunity for disabled people.

Second, the federal government has a constitutional responsibility to seek equity of resources and opportunity for all Canadians. With the agreement of provinces and territories, it has established countrywide programs affecting disabled people, such as universal medical care, shared funding of various social initiatives, and the Canada Pension Plan (which has a disability benefit). Third, Canada, with the agreement of the provinces, adopted the Canadian Charter of Rights and Freedoms in 1982. This is the highest law of the land, with all other laws subject to it. The charter guarantees equality before and under the law, and equal benefit of the law without discrimination on the basis of race, ethnicity, color, religion, sex, or disability, making Canada the first country with this kind of constitutional guarantee. Both its provisions, and how the charter was formulated, speak to Canada's distinctive rights culture.

—*Alfred H. Neufeld*

See also Health Policy (Canada); Social Security (Canada)

Further Reading

Bickenbach, J. E. (1993). *Physical disability and social policy.* Toronto, ON: University of Toronto Press.

Crichton, A., & Jongbloed, L. (1998). *Disability and social policy in Canada.* Toronto, ON: Captus.

Enns, H., & Neufeldt, A. H. (2003). *In pursuit of equal opportunity: Canada and disability at home and abroad.* Toronto, ON: Captus.

Puttee, A. (Ed.). (2002). *Federalism, democracy and disability policy in Canada.* Montreal, QC, and Kingston, ON: McGill-Queen's University Press.

DISABILITY POLICY (MEXICO)

Many countries throughout history have considered disability to be a social problem. When understood in this manner, disability does not involve only an individual and his or her family, but an implied compact with every member of society and the government to provide adequate services. Historically, Mexico has conceptualized disability under the medical model paradigm grounded, at least in part, on Talcott Parsons's illness model in which medical interventions are intended to modify the person's condition without considering broader socioeconomic, attitudinal, and environmental factors. This approach assumes that any difficulties lie in the individual's deviation from what is considered as normal. The social welfare policies implemented by the federal government during the 1990s, however, modify this perception of persons with disabilities. The new approach, the social model of disability, considers disability a multifaceted condition located within the environment and society and not only in the person. At the end of 2000, of Mexico's 97 million inhabitants, 2,315,000 (2.31 percent) had some type of disabling condition (2.48 percent of men; 2.15 percent of women).

BACKGROUND

Disability has historically resulted from ignorance, social exclusion, extreme poverty, malnutrition, illiteracy, and demographic growth. In recent years, however, although there has been an increased frequency of chronic degenerative illnesses, paradoxically, the early detection and adequate management of various genetic diseases and congenital malformations has increased the life expectancy of the Mexican population.

At the end of 1980, the social welfare system did not provide adequate social attention to persons with disabilities. Public institutions did not include persons with disabilities in their programs and actions. Even though the Secretariat of Public Education (*Secretaría de Educación Pública*) generated important special education programs, such actions did not contemplate the inclusion of children with disabilities in the regular school system; nor did the labor market provide equal access to working opportunities.

Beginning in 1990, a new national policy was implemented that began to generate a culture of attention, respect, equity, and equality toward persons with disabilities. Between 1990 and 1994, the states of Aguascalientes, Campeche, Coahuila, and Nuevo León developed legal initiatives to favor persons with disability. Today, every state has its own laws regarding the treatment of this social group. In May 1995, for the first time in its history, the federal government of Mexico adopted the National Program for the Well-Being and the Incorporation of Individuals With Disability (*Programa Nacional Para el Bienestar y la Incorporación al Desarrollo de las Personas con Discapacidad*). This nationwide program seeks to eliminate discrimination against persons with disabilities, and to reduce urban barriers that impede or restrict their access to public or private facilities.

THE CURRENT SITUATION

Today, a new bio-psycho-social paradigm has replaced most of the ideas and societal attitudes derived from the historical concepts of "impairment," "disease," and "handicap." New proposals and programs for the development and social well-being of persons with disability are informed by this new paradigm.

In this spirit, Mexico's Constitution has been amended to prohibit "all discrimination motivated by . . . different capabilities"; similarly, the Constitution also establishes the right for every person to receive education, health protection, and housing. Article 123 states that "every person has the right to a dignified and profitable employment."

In 1999, the Mexican Senate committed itself to adhere to International Labor Organization Convention 159. Convention 159, concerning Vocational Rehabilitation and Employment of Disabled Persons, was adopted in 1983. Mexico ratified the convention in 2001. Since then, the Mexican Social Security Institute (*Instituto Mexicano del Seguro Social*) has supported diverse administrative actions, modifications, and legal actions to promote and increase the inclusion of persons with disability in the national labor force.

During the presidential administration of Vicente Fox (who assumed office in 2000), Mexico established the National Program for the Attention to Persons with Disability (*Programa Nacional de Atención a las Personas con Discapacidad*), 2001–2006, composed of six nationwide subprograms—Health, Labor Inclusion, Accessibility, Quality Services, Education, and Legislation and Human Rights. To implement and oversee these programs, two administrative entities were created: in December 2000, the Office for the Representation, Promotion and Social Inclusion of Persons with Disability (*La Oficina de Representación Para la Promoción e Integración Social Para Personas con Discapacidad,* or ORPISPCD); and, in February 2001, the National Consultative Council for the Social Inclusion of Persons with Disability (*Consejo Nacional Consultivo Para la Integración Social de las Personas con Discapacidad*). The latter office started operating with the aim of reorganizing and expanding Mexican social welfare policies related to disability issues, strengthening interinstitutional coordination, and enhancing the social position of individuals with disabilities through the participation of their nongovernmental organizations. The National Consultative Council for the Social Inclusion of Persons with Disability is composed of the Secretaries of Social Development, Communications, Public Education, Health, Labor, and Social Prevision, and representatives of the National System for the Integral Development of the Family (*Sistema Nacional Para el Desarrollo Integral de la Familia*, or DIF) and the ORPISPCD.

In November 2001, the Federal Law for Deaf Culture was passed to promote the creation of equal opportunities for the hearing impaired. In April 2003, as part of the National Program for Accessibility proposed by the federal government and coordinated by the Secretariat of Economy, a program was initiated to implement the Official Mexican Norm for the Accessibility of Persons with Disability to Public and Private Service Facilities. This project establishes regulations for the construction of public spaces to facilitate the activities and displacement of persons with disability without environmental restrictions and in a secure manner.

Subsequently, in April 2003, the 58th Legislature of Representatives approved the Federal Law for the Social Inclusion of Persons with Disability, setting a legal framework for strengthening the rights, responsibilities, and guarantees established by the Constitution, diverse international agreements, federal laws, regulations, and other normative documents. This initiative, at present under consideration by the Senate for ratification, would stimulate public policies promoting those programs that favor and guarantee the citizenship rights of persons with disability under a framework of equality and societal conscience toward human diversity. At the same time, it would require the federal government to designate financial resources to such programs. The legislation contains 144 articles included in 8 titles, all referring to the rights of persons

with disability in areas such as Prevention, Habilitation and Rehabilitation (Articles 8–25), Labor and Training (Articles 26–64), Education (Articles 65–82), Accessibility, Transportation and Housing (Articles 83–110), Accessible Housing (Articles 111–134), Culture, Recreation and Sporting (Articles 135–141), Entity of Control (Articles 142–143), and Sanctions and Defenses (Article 144).

Also during the 2000–2003 period, the 58th Legislature approved modifications to the Federal Penal Code, the Bank of Mexico Law, the United Mexican States Political Constitution, the General Civil Protection Law, and the General Law of Health. Recently, the House passed the presidential initiative for the Federal Law for Prevention and Elimination of Discrimination.

At the same time, during the last 2 years, different programs, agreements, and joint declarations involving education, labor, health, accessibility, and transportation, among others, have been established by the federal sector, institutions and organizations from the private sector, and various nongovernmental organizations (NGOs) to promote the equalization of opportunities and the quality of attention toward persons with disability within the national territory.

CONCLUDING CONSIDERATIONS

Advances in social policies affecting disabled people in Mexico are undeniable. Today, as a nation, Mexico has stronger social, political, and economic structures affecting persons with disabilities. Such structures will have a favorable impact on the recognition of the human rights of persons with disabilities and the creation of opportunities for them. Diverse social phenomena, however, such as the globalization of the economy, the democratization process, the economic crisis, the centralization of resources, and the concentration of services in only a few important cities, together with paternalistic and perhaps authoritarian attitudes, can hamper the positive impact of those social policies and programs created to benefit those with disabilities in Mexico.

—*Guillermo A. Flores-Briseño*

See also Social Security (Mexico)

Primary Sources

Asamblea Legislativa del Distrito Federal en Materia de Discapacidad; Legislación local y federal en materia de discapacidad; Compilación Realizada por la Comisión por los Derechos e Integración de las Personas con Discapacidad (2003); Comisión Nacional de los Derechos Humanos; Leyes de Integración Social Para las Personas con Discapacidad en las Entidades Federativas (1999), Secretary of Treasury and Public Credit, Mexico City; Programa Nacional Para el Bienestar y la Incorporación al Desarrollo de las Personas con Discapacidad (1995); Senado de la República, Foro Internacional Convenio 159: Readaptación Profesional y Empleo a las Personas con Discapacidad (1999).

Current Comment

Oficina de Representación Para la Promoción e Integración Social Para Personas con Discapacidad. (2003). Ley federal para personas con discapacidad. *Boletín de la Oficina de Representación Para la Promoción e Integración Social Para Personas con Discapacidad, 2,*(6). Available: www.discapacidad. presidencia.gob.mx

Programa Nacional de Atención a las Personas con Discapacidad. Available: www.discapacidad.presidencia.gob.mx

Further Reading

Flores-Briseño, G. A. (1999). El modelo médico y el modelo social de la discapacidad: Un análisis comparativo. In M. Ribeiro & R. E. López (Eds.), *Políticas sociales sectoriales: Tendencias actuales* (Vol. 2). Monterrey: Universidad Autónoma de Nuevo León.

Flores-Briseño, G. A. (2003). Societal attitudes toward persons with disabilities in the metropolitan area of Monterrey, Nuevo León. Unpublished doctoral dissertation, University of Texas at Arlington.

Parsons, T. (1951). The social system. Glencoe, IL: Free Press.

DISABILITY POLICY (UNITED STATES)

Policies related to disability reflect their historical and political context. They stipulate the programs, services, and benefits available to the disabled. These policies and the effects of their implementation interact with, and sometimes support or contradict, policies in other areas such as health care, housing, and education.

Disability can be defined as an impairment that prevents a person from participating in the activities expected for others of a similar age and situation. The lack of a clear, consistent definition of disability is a reflection of the fact that the United States has no integrated, comprehensive disability policy. Throughout the twentieth century, federal legislation regarding education, health, employment, and housing of the disabled was enacted with each law establishing its own criteria for participation. In some cases, the definitions and provisions for benefits in one program directly contradicted those mandated by other laws and policies.

BRIEF HISTORICAL OVERVIEW

Historically, the meaning of "disability" has depended on the context in which it was viewed. In biblical times, disability was sometimes seen as a punishment from God for the sins of people or their parents. Other cultures regarded people with disabilities as possessing certain supernatural traits; they were frequently regarded as shamans or those who had direct access to the gods.

During the eighteenth and early nineteenth centuries, people with disabilities who lived in small communities were simply absorbed into the community, often receiving care or protection from other residents. As an adult, the person could possibly find a role in greeting people, running errands, or serving as a friend for the elderly. No particular policy was required to manage disability when these circumstances prevailed.

Industrialization and Disability

As the United States became more industrialized in the late nineteenth and early twentieth centuries, those who had supported and cared for people with disabilities became more involved in the formal, paid work setting. Productivity was the key and people with disabilities generally did not fit the desired employee profile. Disabled people tended to lose their roles in the community as well as the protection the community had provided.

Institutions for people with disabilities became more prevalent. Those with visual or hearing disabilities were sent to schools for the blind or deaf to receive training in whatever work was deemed appropriate. For people with learning difficulties or mental disabilities, institutional living was intended to provide the care and training that might lead to a cure. In some cases, governmental funding was sought and secured to support such institutions.

One of the consequences of institutionalization was that people with disabilities were no longer highly visible and recognizable members of their communities. They were segregated from mainstream society. As familiarity decreased, acceptance by the community diminished as well. Families had few if any role models for raising children with disabilities, and they were increasingly pressured to institutionalize their children.

During the 1960s, people with disabilities and their families and supporters actively demanded better health care, appropriate housing and education, and the right to participate in their communities. The results of this activism can be seen in the variety of laws providing benefits and prohibiting discrimination.

Historically, disability has been seen as a curse, a medical issue, or a problem to be hidden away. Today, disability is regarded as a social construct. According to this perspective, if a building is universally accessible, the qualified person using a wheelchair or crutches will experience no barriers to participation in whatever activities are available. A disability that requires using a chair or other device is not viewed as impairment. It is simply a part of that person's unique self.

GENERAL LEGISLATION

During the Great Depression and after World War II, several laws were enacted that were designed to assist the elderly. Many of these also provided benefits for people with disabilities.

Social Security Act

In addition to providing funds for older persons, the Social Security Act of 1935 established the Aid to the Blind (AB) public assistance program to provide cash benefits to blind people. Eligibility requirements included a means test, meaning that receipt of benefits was restricted to blind people who were poor. Congress added Aid to the Permanently and Totally Disabled (APTD), a public assistance program that provided

cash benefits to disabled people in 1950. As was the case with AB, eligibility for APTD included a means test, limiting benefits to applicants who were poor. Congress added disability coverage to the Old-Age and Survivors Insurance program, creating Old-Age, Survivors and Disability Insurance (OASDI) in 1956. With the addition of Disability Insurance, workers who contributed to the Social Security trust fund, and who became blind or disabled prior to retirement age, would be eligible for Social Security Disability Insurance (SSDI) benefits if they were unable to engage in substantial gainful activity for at least 12 months. Financial need was not a criterion for receiving SSDI benefits.

Supplemental Security Income

In 1972, Congress combined three "adult" public assistance programs—Old-Age Assistance, AB, and APTD—to create Supplemental Security Income (SSI). SSI provided monthly payments for persons who had financial need and were blind, disabled, or elderly. A person need not have contributed to the Social Security system to qualify for SSI support but must have established financial need through a means test, meaning that benefits were restricted to persons who had a qualifying condition—old age, blindness, or disability—and were poor.

Medicare and Medicaid

The Social Security amendments of 1965 established the Medicare and Medicaid programs. The purpose of Medicare was to provide health insurance for qualified Social Security beneficiaries, including those who had disabilities. Income level was not a factor because this was not a means-tested or needs-based program. Medicaid is a public assistance medical care program for the poor, many of whom were also disabled. It was administered by the states with federal financial participation and under federal guidelines.

DISABILITY-RELATED LEGISLATION

Post World War II

During the Second World War, the use of medical technology saved the lives of many in the armed forces whose injuries would otherwise have resulted in death, many of whom had long-lasting disabilities. These disabled survivors returned home needing therapy, adaptive equipment, and suitable work and living arrangements. In some cases, what the veterans received was federally funded institutionalization in settings such as veterans' hospitals. Eventually, the rehabilitation profession developed to address the needs of those who could be expected to live for decades while coping with their disabilities.

The Disability Rights Movement

The civil rights activities of the 1960s attempted to secure equal rights to persons who had been damaged by racial discrimination. As people with disabilities observed and participated in this movement, they learned strategies and developed ideas about how their lives should and could be different. Disabled students at the University of California, Berkeley, successfully obtained the right to attend class, live near campus, and receive the assistance needed to participate fully in the university's activities. Over time, education, health care, housing, and employment issues were addressed by the disabled and their supporters with varying degrees of success.

Rehabilitation Act

One outcome of the disability rights movement was the Rehabilitation Act of 1973, which resulted in the creation of a nationwide network of independent living centers to provide advocacy and assistance for people with disabilities Another, and possibly better known, component of the Rehabilitation Act was Section 504. It prohibited any entity receiving federal funds from discriminating against people with disabilities, giving them the same legal safeguards as other groups.

Individuals with Disabilities Education Act

Parents of children with disabilities utilized prior legislation such as the Rehabilitation Act of 1973, as well as the strategies developed by the civil rights activists, to pressure legislators to pass the Education for All Handicapped Children Act of 1975. The name of this legislation was later changed to the Individuals with Disabilities Education Act (IDEA). The goal of IDEA was to provide a free, appropriate public education for children with disabilities.

Among other mandates, IDEA requires input from parents and a disabled student in establishing Individualized Education Plans (IEP). Early intervention programs were available to the families of children diagnosed with developmental problems. Students with disabilities were entitled to services until they graduated from high school or reached their 21st birthday.

Americans with Disabilities Act

The Americans with Disabilities Act (ADA) of 1990 was the most comprehensive legislation addressing the needs of people with disabilities. It prohibited discrimination against people with disabilities in nearly all aspects of their lives, including employment, education, transportation, and access to buildings.

Responsibility for implementation of the ADA was fragmented. The U.S. Department of Transportation investigated issues regarding air, rail, and bus travel and discrimination and promoted appropriate access and availability to all citizens, disabled or not. The U.S. Department of Labor tried to ensure that all qualified persons had the opportunity to obtain employment. Employers were required to provide necessary accommodations such as ramps, adaptive equipment, flexible work times, and other reasonable accommodations.

Olmstead Decision

In *Olmstead v. L.C.* (1999), the U.S. Supreme Court ruled that states must provide services for people with disabilities in the most integrated setting appropriate for their needs. The result of this decision is that people with disabilities can no longer be required to live in institutions to receive needed services. It is now possible for a person to live in her or his own home while still receiving services and participating in activities and programs formerly offered only to those in institutions.

—Peggy Quinn

See also Health Policy (United States); Social Security (United States); Supplemental Security Income (United States)

Primary Sources

Disability Rights and Independent Living Movement Archive, Bancroft Library, University of California, Berkeley (www.lib. berkeley.edu/LDO/bene55/disability.html); Society for Disability Studies, University of Illinois, Chicago (www.uic.edu/orgs/sds/ links.html); the U.S. Department of Justice, Americans with Disabilities Act home page (http://ada.gov/); National Council on Disability, Washington, DC (www.ncd.gov/).

Current Comment

Bowe, F. (1992). *Equal rights for Americans with disabilities.* New York: F. Watts.

Braddock, D. (Ed.). (2002). *Disability at the dawn of the 21st century and the state of the states.* Washington, DC: American Association on Mental Retardation.

Oriol, W. E. (2002, January/February). Olmstead decision brings major shift in disability care. *Aging Today 23*(1). Available: www.agingtoday.org/home/archives.cfm

Further Reading

Burkhauser, R. V., & Haveman, R. H. (1982). *Disability and work: The economics of American policy.* Baltimore: Johns Hopkins University Press.

Scotch, R. K. (1989). *From good will to civil rights.* Philadelphia: Temple University Press.

Trent, J. W., Jr. (1994). *Inventing the feeble mind: A history of mental retardation in the United States.* Berkeley: University of California Press.

DUBOIS, W. E. B. (1868–1963)

William Edward Burghardt DuBois, vigilant civil rights activist, educator, and prominent African American scholar was born in Great Barrington, Massachusetts, in 1868. He received undergraduate degrees from both Fisk and Harvard universities. After earning a master's degree from Harvard in 1891, he did post–master's studies at the University of Berlin in Germany before returning to Harvard to earn a doctorate in 1896. A believer in Marxist philosophy, he viewed socialism as the solution to the class and economic struggles in the Black community. He is noted for his pronouncements about the race problem in America, his postulations on the availability and preparation of leadership talent among African Americans ("the talented tenth"), his social research on living conditions in the Black community, and his emphasis on the acquisition of political power by African Americans through organized efforts. In 1905, he organized the Niagara Movement, the forerunner of the National Association for the Advancement of Colored People (NAACP). He encouraged the Black man to press for voting and political rights, to become entrepreneurial, to develop new employment opportunities, to make use of the media, to engage in health advocacy, and to attack crime. A student of history, philosophy, and economics, he used his knowledge to systematically study the African American community and to gather data that could be used to influence social change.

DuBois's writings have been very influential across race and class lines. A review of his book, *The Philadelphia Negro* (1899), published in the November 11, 1899, issue of *The Outlook,* provides insight into his effectiveness at using social research data to show the impact of racial discrimination on the quality of life in the Black community. Commenting on his chapter on employment opportunities, the review states: "It is this chapter that especially appeals to the conscience of the Nation" (p. 647).

DuBois was a brilliant and prolific writer of books, articles, and speeches on a range of subjects. He wrote critiques of the philosophies of African American leaders, such as Marcus Garvey and Booker T. Washington, and a tribute to Paul Robeson, the well-known singer and activist. Today, his often-cited message from his classic, *The Souls of Black Folk* (1903) is still reiterated: "The problem of the Twentieth century is the problem of the color line." The problem of the color line is a running theme in DuBois's writings and speeches. His polemical essay, "The Black Man Brings His Gifts," published in the *Survey Graphic* in 1925, uses fictionalized commentary to illustrate the difficulties of acceptance across class and racial lines.

DuBois emphasized the need for scientific approaches to understanding conditions in the Black community throughout his professorial career at Atlanta University in Georgia. DuBois left the United States and moved to Ghana in 1961. He died there 2 years later. His life and work are important for understanding the social welfare of African Americans in the United States.

—*Wilma Peebles-Wilkins*

See also African Americans and Social Welfare (United States); Progressive Era (United States)

Primary Source

W. E. B. DuBois Papers, Special Collections and Archives, W. E. B. DuBois Library, University of Massachusetts, Amherst.

Current Comment

Foner, P. S. (Ed.). (1970). *W. E. B. DuBois speaks* (Vols. 1–2). New York: Pathfinder.

Franklin, J. H. (1993). *The color line: Legacy for the twenty-first century.* Columbia: University of Missouri Press.

Further Reading

Lewis, D. L. (2000). *W. E. B. DuBois—The fight for equality and the American century, 1919–1963.* New York: Holt.

E

ECONOMIC CRISIS, FAMILY AND GENDER, 1980S TO THE PRESENT (MEXICO)

Mexico underwent a profound economic crisis from 1982 to 1986 characterized by high rates of inflation and a general contraction of the economy. Real wages declined dramatically. Formal employment began to lose ground, as jobs in the informal economy became one of the few alternatives for low-income persons. Informal economic enterprises, whose owners manage to escape state control and do not provide workers with social benefits that promote their families' well-being, served as a cushion for workers who could not find jobs in the formal economy. Between 1986 and 1988, profound economic restructuring took place. Wages continued to decline and inflation rose, reaching a peak of 159 percent in 1987. The privatization of state firms advanced rapidly and local markets were opened to the influx of foreign goods, which seriously impacted local manufacturing enterprises. As a result, many firms closed and numerous jobs were lost. Since reducing labor costs was an important way for local enterprises to become more competitive in the new open economy, wages continued their downward trend to the level of those in the *maquiladoras* (export-oriented factories) in the north of Mexico, which pushed wages about 60 percent lower than wages in the older industrial sector. The informal economy proliferated as employment in the formal sector declined.

The economic crisis produced significant private adjustments for families and household social organization, which had a significant gendered impact. The concept of "private adjustments" alludes to changes in the household economy and household division of labor that result from economic transformations and economic policies that are implemented during and after economic crises. Most private adjustments are damaging and not easily overcome even when the economic crisis formally ends and the health of the economy is supposed to be restored. On the contrary, most of the elements of adjustment taking place at the household level are part of a perverse process of cumulative disadvantage.

HOUSEHOLD RESPONSES TO THE CRISIS OF THE 1980s

One of the most relevant analytical tasks in the field of household and family research has been the study of household transformations in the context of economic change. Although household and family are distinct concepts, alluding to different types of relationships, the majority of households in Mexico are formed by kinship links. A large number of extended households, however, include non-kin among their members, and an increasing number of households absorbed non-kin producers of income during the worst years of the 1980s crisis. Economic crises and structural adjustment in Mexico have produced a process of social restructuring and profound private adjustments at the household level. Together with the hierarchical nature of households and the unequal distribution of resources and burdens, this requires a social and political economy approach to household and family research to highlight the linkages between change at the macro level of national economic policy and changes at the micro level of household organization.

Research conducted in Mexico has shown that urban households, as in many other Latin American countries, have gone through a process of restructuring and adjustment as the larger economy has experienced structural changes. Precrisis research showed that poor working families had difficulty surviving if they were dependent on a single wage earner because wages, even during boom economic periods, were too low to be considered a "family wage," one that could support a family. In such a context, household organization and a collective work strategy—with income coming from a number of different sources—were key elements for the survival of individuals and families. Before the crisis of the 1980s, poor people manipulated a wide range of resources. Wage labor coexisted with domestic work and resources came from participating in social exchanges. Households were conceptualized as contradictory social units in which gender and age hierarchies, solidarity, conflict, and confrontations between individual and collective interests coexisted.

Household responses to the crisis of the 1980s resulted in families resorting to "traditional" mechanisms for facing economic hardship. One of the most important household changes was the rise in the number of workers or income earners who had to participate in the labor market. This resulted in increased and unfair burdens on women. Because nearly all adult men were employed before the crisis began in 1982, their participation in the labor market did not increase as much as that of other household members. Adult married women with children increased their participation in the job market substantially and young, single women who were not employed outside the home had to do housework and provide child care. Many young males (14 years old and younger) had to drop out of school and enter

the job market. The use of the household labor force proved to be crucial for the overall household's survival. As the income of the male head of the household was reduced, household incomes decreased but not as much as individual wages. In addition to increasing the number of wage earners, urban households found new sources of income, such as informal jobs and self-employment in order to offset the fragility of their traditional wage sources. The wage-derived proportion of total household income diminished, while that of income from independent work increased. Together with the intensification of wage work, mainly through the participation of women and children, households increased their actual size (the number of members) as a result of the addition of adults as well as through the birth of new members. Consequently, the number of extended households increased, resulting in more housework for women. Consumption of goods such as clothing, services, house cleaning, and maintenance declined as families chose not to buy goods not deemed necessities. Income directed to health and education also decreased and did not recover when better times returned. Although one of the main goals of the new policies was to maintain adequate levels of food consumption, there were modifications in the patterns and levels of consumption, mainly through restrictive practices that resulted in reduced consumption of meat, fish, and dairy products and increased consumption of cheap animal protein such as eggs and tripe. Clothing, entertainment, education, and health care were restricted or eliminated to protect food consumption.

As the economy collapsed and went through major adjustments and restructuring, households became the scene of social restructuring and private adjustment. The economic crisis was "privatized." Women had to work harder, not only in the labor market but also in their homes, since household chores increased with the larger size of households. Lunch had to be made for members who left home to work, and clothes needed mending. Time and energy were needed to produce goods and services that were previously purchased in the marketplace. The impact of the crisis differed for various types of households. Larger, extended, and consolidated households had comparative advantages over small, often nuclear households in protecting income and consumption patterns.

SURVIVAL: AN ENDLESS HOUSEHOLD CAPACITY?

In spite of the relative success of household responses to the crisis, signs of the erosion of household survival capabilities were apparent. The more vulnerable households were those with the most children because their nutrition, health, and education levels were threatened. All household members had to work much harder and intensify the use of their remaining resources and assets, particularly the labor force of women and children. They had to work for lower wages and under worse conditions. The living conditions of the majority of urban households severely deteriorated. Saving for "emergencies" was impossible because all income was consumed. The chances of falling into destitution increased without the cushioning effects of savings to cope with illness, accidents, or death. Mutual help and assistance, relying on social exchanges, resulted in increasing demands on social networks. A future deterioration of the economy would encounter an already worn-out population. The 1990s provided the framework for increased difficulties and obstacles for the survival of poor families and households as employment opportunities diminished.

The 1995 economic crisis and its structural reforms disrupted household economies and made it difficult for families to survive. If their labor is the most important resource of urban poor people, their survival is threatened when they cannot find work. Although employment was precarious in the past, today's lack of jobs threatens many families.

This financial crisis signaled a watershed for Mexican labor markets because, for the first time since 1982, the population did not respond with a general intensification of work and informal employment. Although women's participation continued to rise, men's fell for the first time since the 1982 crisis. Unemployment among male youth reached unprecedented levels in 1995, reaching almost 30 percent in major metropolitan areas. The increasingly common situation of not finding a job, which primarily affects young males in urban Mexico, was having a strong impact on household capacity to supplement the low incomes of male and female heads through the participation of young family members in the labor market. In the past, they generated income when aging heads of households faced declining incomes. In the 1990s, the comparative advantages of consolidated households seemed to vanish as jobs became increasingly difficult to obtain. All types of household structures were struck by deprivation during the mid-decade crisis and were unable to recover to the levels of well-being they had achieved in the early years of the 1990s. The comparative advantages of larger, extended, and consolidated households practically disappeared. Instead, cumulative disadvantages, resulting from recurrent adjustments and restricted consumption, and the inability to convert the household labor force into a real asset, were part of the daily lives of the urban majorities. Labor exclusion diminishes the capacity of individuals to participate in self-provisioning, self-employment, and household production. The lack of regular incomes is a formidable obstacle for investing in materials and transportation, and there were more households that, because of a lack of resources to invest in social exchange, were being left out of social networks and, therefore, became increasingly isolated.

Labor exclusion is unfavorable to the operation of traditional household mechanisms of work intensification. After two profound economic crises, and two decades of restructuring and adjustment policies, poor households and families see their resources eroded and increasing challenges to their survival and reproduction. Private adjustments have taken place among the poor who are encountering many obstacles to fulfilling their needs. This has produced long-term and accumulated effects in every dimension of poor people's lives. The household, once understood as a cushion against economic shocks and crises, may have—in the context of labor exclusion—become an eroded portfolio of resources. From the 1980s to the first decade of the twenty-first century, Mexican families have experienced two decades of diminishing choices and added constraints, with differential gender effects and diminished options for the future.

—*Mercedes González de la Rocha*

See also Economic Policy (Mexico); Informal Economy (Mexico); International Social Welfare; Neoliberalism, Social Programs, and Social Movements (Mexico); Substance Abuse Policy (Mexico); Women and Social Welfare (Mexico)

Current Comment

González de la Rocha, M. (2000). *Private adjustments: Household responses to the erosion of work* (Conference Paper Series No. 6). New York: United Nations Development Programme.

Moser, C. (1996). *Confronting crisis: A comparative study of household responses to poverty and vulnerability in four poor urban communities* (Environmentally Sustainable Development Studies and Monographs Series No. 8). Washington, DC: World Bank.

Further Reading

Benería, L. (1992). The Mexican debt crisis: Restructuring the economy and the household. In L. Benería & S. Feldman (Eds.), *Unequal burden: Economic crises, persistent poverty, and women's work* (pp. 83–104). Boulder, CO: Westview.

González de la Rocha, M. (1988). Economic crisis, domestic reorganisation and women's work in Guadalajara, Mexico. *Bulletin of Latin American Research, 7*(2), 207–223.

González de la Rocha, M. (1994). *The resources of poverty: Women and survival in a Mexican city.* Oxford, UK: Blackwell.

González de la Rocha, M. (2001). From the resources of poverty to the poverty of resources: The erosion of a survival model. *Latin American Perspectives, 28*(4), 72–100.

ECONOMIC POLICY (CANADA)

Economic policy concerns decisions and actions of government regarding economic activity. The parameters for economic policy in Canada were created in 1867 with the birth of the federation under the British North America Act. The federal government was accorded "nation-building" powers like the regulation of trade and commerce, postal service, defense, navigation and shipping, and, most important, the raising of money by any mode of taxation. Provincial governments were accorded matters of "local concern," such as the management and sale of provincial public land, the running of hospitals and asylums, municipal institutions in the province, education, and direct taxation within the province in order to raise revenue for provincial purposes. Time has seen expenditure growth and the evolution of mainly provincial jurisdiction in natural resources, health care, and education. The pre-1900 government share of gross domestic product (GDP) was under 10 percent but by the late twentieth century it was nearly 50 percent—mainly as the result of the growth of health, welfare, and regulatory functions. Canadian economic policy since 1867 can be divided into distinct phases: nation-building (1867–1913), war and depression (1913–1945), the postwar welfare state (1946–1973), and the post-welfare era (1973 to the present).

NATION-BUILDING (1867–1913)

The nation-building phase (1867–1913) was marked by the National Policies, a triad of land, railway, and commercial policies aimed at making the Canadian West an investment frontier. Dominion land grants sought to settle the region with farmers, who behind the tariff barrier erected by the National Policy tariffs, would serve as a market for eastern Canadian manufactured goods. The crucial link was the transport corridor provided by a transcontinental railway—the Canadian Pacific Railway (CPR)—that erected a national economic space along an east-west axis. The CPR's completion in 1885 represented not only an impressive engineering achievement but also a significant joint public-private sector economic undertaking that fashioned an economic and social space parallel to the United States. Whereas nation-building was an interventionist phase for Canadian economic policy, domestic labor and social policies were more definitely of a laissez-faire nature. In terms of economic performance, slow economic growth during the 1870s and 1880s eventually gave way to the high growth of the wheat boom era after 1896.

WAR AND DEPRESSION (1913–1945)

The war and depression period (1913–1945) was a volatile time that paved the way for interventionist government economic policies in the postwar era. The need to finance World War I military spending paved the way for a shift in public finances as personal income taxes, business income taxes, and federal sales taxes were introduced. Despite the increased government presence in the economy due to wartime activity, the general policy environment was still one of minimal government intervention in economic activity aside from restrictions on collective bargaining and the imposition of conscription. Although the 1920s began with an economic downturn and labor unrest, the remainder of the 1920s saw an economic boom fueled by electrification and consumer durable spending.

The Great Depression of the 1930s highlighted the economic inequality resulting from industrialization, urbanization, and unemployment due to business cycle fluctuations. Fewer Canadians relied on farm or family when faced with job losses or illness. Relief was primarily a local undertaking and there was no comprehensive system of old-age security, unemployment insurance, or health care. The depression led to pressure for more government intervention and regulation of the domestic economy and also policies for freer international trade as the realization grew that trade barriers had worsened the depression.

Faced with the economic turmoil of the 1930s and deteriorating provincial public finances due to the burden of relief, the Rowell-Sirois Commission was appointed and its final report (1940) set the stage for postwar equalization transfers to the provinces and a modern unemployment insurance system. Moreover, the spread of Keynesian economic ideas regarding government management of the business cycle and the depression experience paved the way for interventionist government economic policy in the post–World War II era. Indeed, the first steps toward a comprehensive welfare state took place during this period with acts bringing about the first old-age pensions, unemployment insurance, and family allowances.

THE POSTWAR WELFARE STATE (1946–1973)

Canada entered the Second World War as an agricultural nation undergoing manufacturing and urban growth and emerged as an industrial nation largely as the result of explicit government management of resources during the wartime economy. The success of government economic management during World War II, the scars of the Great Depression, the fear of a return to depression in the aftermath of war, and Keynesian economic doctrine all led to the interventionist postwar welfare state (1946–1973). Canada's economic policies were part of an international trend toward more government intervention along with efforts to promote more international trade via lower tariff barriers. This period saw explicit domestic economic management policies in terms of fiscal and monetary policies to stimulate the economy during downturns.

There was also an expansion of public support for education, health, unemployment assistance, and social welfare. The postwar period saw provincial equalization payments, national pension plans, a system of Medicare, the growth of provincial transfers to municipalities, hospitals, and universities, and welfare programs by the provinces. The growth of an extensive array of social programs was supported by tax revenue from the postwar economic boom. Many of these programs also served the needs of the demographic bulge known as the "baby boom."

THE POST-WELFARE ERA (1973 TO THE PRESENT)

The oil price shocks of 1973 and 1979 brought the global "golden age" of prosperity to an end and the post-welfare era (1973 to the present) of Canadian economic policy began. With rising unemployment and inflation during the 1970s, governments ran deficits in an effort to maintain employment and programs. The federal government debt-to-GDP ratio rose from nearly 20 percent in the 1970s to about 70 percent by the 1990s before aggressive fiscal reduction policies took hold. The rising debt levels were aggravated during the 1980s by high central bank interest rates to fight inflation. The lethal combination of rising debt levels, slowing economic growth, and high interest rates crowded out government program spending and put pressure on social programs and transfers in health, education, and social welfare. For example, during the 1970s, federal transfers to the provinces for insured health services went from a cost-sharing arrangement to slow-growing block grants. The decline in federal transfers to the provinces eventually spilled over into declines at the municipal level, and the period of the 1990s, in particular, was one of austerity.

Policies to cope with the post–oil shock era included free trade, tax reform, deregulation, and expenditure reduction and have defined the current early twenty-first century policy environment in Canada. In general, the more interventionist policies of the post–World War II era were gradually assaulted by a more laissez-faire set of policies after 1973. Free trade with the United States in the late 1980s and the North American Free Trade Agreement (NAFTA) of the early 1990s were supposed to create larger markets for Canadian goods and services and allow Canadian firms to reap economies of scale and boost productivity. The reform of taxation at both federal and provincial levels saw a reduction in income tax rates during the 1990s in an effort to become more competitive with the United States. There was also consumption tax reform with the creation of the federal Goods and Services Tax in 1991. Deregulation in transportation and telecommunications sought to create more competition in these vital economic areas. Finally, there were expenditure reductions at both the federal and provincial levels in the 1990s that eventually saw a return to balanced budgets. The late 1990s finally saw an upturn in Canadian economic growth and performance.

The human cost of reduced spending on health, social welfare, and education, however, has created pressure in the early twenty-first century to address the consequences of cutbacks. This pressure has been accompanied by a new distrust of markets in the wake of the technology stock crash. Growing economic integration with the United States has also sparked economic concerns. The growth of tighter border security in the wake of 9/11 has the potential to harm trans-border commerce. Moreover, despite a decade of free trade, there are still disputes in the areas of softwood lumber, wheat marketing, and culture in which Canadians see themselves as increasingly participating in a lopsided arrangement given the economic dominance of the United States.

On the social policy side, the report of the Romanow Commission on health in 2002 has set the stage for new spending and reform of health care in an effort to begin repairing the tears in social fabric that occurred during the 1990s. There is growing concern about the shortage of public sector professionals in everything from health care to food and water inspection. The deteriorating physical infrastructure of cities is also a concern. The long-term success of these new policies will ultimately depend on continued economic productivity growth to generate the necessary tax revenues. Canadian economic performance during the first few years of the twenty-first century has been robust.

—Livio Di Matteo

See also Social Welfare (Canada): Before the Marsh Report; Social Welfare (Canada): Since the Marsh Report; Welfare Capitalism (Canada)

Further Reading

Gillespie, W. I. (1991). *Tax, borrow and spend: Financing federal spending in Canada, 1867–1990.* Ottawa, ON: Carleton University Press.

Norrie, K., Owram, D., & Emery, J. C. H. (2002). *A history of the Canadian economy* (3rd ed.). Scarborough, ON: Nelson Thomson Learning.

Perry, J. H. (1989). *A fiscal history of Canada: The postwar years* (Canadian Tax Paper No. 85). Toronto, ON: Canadian Tax Foundation.

Watkins, M. H. (1963, May). A staple theory of economic growth. *Canadian Journal of Economics and Political Science, 29,* 141–158.

ECONOMIC POLICY (MEXICO)

Since Mexico was integrated into the world economy in the sixteenth century, the Mexican economy has experienced several periods of rapid growth. A careful examination of the distribution of this growth, however, reveals a paradox of increasing wealth and inequality. Indeed, on more than one occasion Mexico experienced spectacular economic growth, as it did at the end of the eighteenth century and, again, at the end of the nineteenth century, but that growth was so unevenly distributed that those inequalities contributed to rebellions, upheavals, and in 1910, a full-fledged Revolution.

THE COLONIAL ECONOMY

The year 1519, the first year of the conquest of Mexico, signaled the beginning of a system in which Mexico would be incorporated into the world economy as a colony of Spain, mainly on the basis of mining, agriculture, and ranching. The conquest also introduced an economic system that relied for generations on the exploitation of Native peoples. Over the next 300 years, although Mexico emerged as a supplier of raw materials, most notably of silver, cochineal, sugar, tobacco, and other agricultural products, its economy was also characterized by an unequal economic system in which the Spanish colonizers and their descendants dominated the economic and political spheres and most non-Whites lived in poverty. The effects of this inequality would continue to be felt in Mexico for centuries.

Beginning in the 1760s, the Spanish Crown under the new Bourbon dynasty began implementing a series of policies geared to stimulating the economy and making it more efficient. Known collectively as the Bourbon reforms, one of the main goals was to boost the export of Mexico's raw materials. The reforms included the opening of new ports, abolishing trade monopolies, and stimulating production of Mexico's largest export, silver, and by 1810 Mexico was the most prosperous of Spain's colonies.

Although the Bourbon reforms stimulated economic growth and further integrated Mexico into the world economy, these policies were designed by the Spanish monarchs to extract more wealth for themselves. Thus, most people in the colony did not benefit from this economic growth. Whereas the in-country merchants, miners, and ranchers who benefited most from this economic growth were invariably of European origin, the workers in the rural sectors, mainly Natives and *Mestizos* (racially mixed populations), saw their real incomes drop. As Mexico's agricultural exports grew, increasing commercialization of agriculture led to an increasing concentration of landholding, thereby reinforcing Mexico's already unequal social system and leading to further insecurity in the countryside. Particularly vulnerable to these economic transformations were Natives and *Mestizos* in the *Bajío* region, where the land came under increasing assault as more areas of Mexico became integrated into the web of capitalist cultivation. By the late eighteenth century, the *Bajío,* encompassing a broad swath of territory to the north of Mexico City from Hidalgo to Queretaro, Guanajuato, and Jalisco, had become the "breadbasket" of Mexico. Paradoxically, this region also became a hotbed of violence. Natives and *Mestizos* rebelled when their way of life was threatened by the encroaching *haciendas* (the large, landed estates), the commercialization of agriculture, and the fluctuations of the international economy. Finally, a series of droughts, popular pressure, elite resentment of colonial restrictions, and a crisis in Europe came together in 1810 to spark Mexico's wars for independence. The breakdown of the colonial order unleashed the pent-up frustrations of tens of thousands of Mexicans, resulting in race and class warfare and elite infighting from which the country would take decades to recover.

THE NINETEENTH CENTURY: FROM ECONOMIC STAGNATION TO ECONOMIC GROWTH

By 1821, Mexico had achieved its independence, but the human and physical cost of the independence wars, combined with the inability of the various factions involved to forge consensus, contributed to such instability that no coherent and sustained public policy would be possible until well into the second half of the nineteenth century. The destruction of the wars, the collapse of the credit system, loss of investor confidence, perennial elite infighting, inefficient economic organization, and a lack of well-developed institutions led to almost half a century of economic stagnation. In an example of the difficulties Mexico had in re-establishing central authority, the presidency of Mexico changed hands 36 times from the 1820s to the middle of the 1850s, with the average tenure lasting only seven and a half months. With the silver industry—the engine of economic growth during the colonial period—in shambles, agricultural fields sacked, and textile mills shut down, investors withheld their capital and a vicious cycle of instability, lack of investment, and economic depression followed. In real terms, Mexico's gross domestic product shrank and would not recover its 1800 levels until 1860.

After stability was finally achieved in the second half of the nineteenth century, the attention of policymakers turned toward creating an institutional framework that would entice foreign investment, stimulate economic growth, and consolidate an export-led model of development. A new Constitution in 1857, with its emphasis on unleashing market forces and the sanctity of private property, outlined the new direction that Mexico would take for the next half century. This liberal economic model was at its apogee from 1876 to 1911, a period when President Porfirio Díaz and his advisers, known as the *Científicos,* for their belief in a scientific approach to public policy, ruled uninterruptedly. During this period, fueled by a new wave of agricultural and mineral exports, the Mexican economy grew at unprecedented rates. Among the major export products were sugar, cotton, henequen, copper, and petroleum. Railroads played a major role in binding Mexico's regions together, connecting mining sites and *haciendas* to their principal markets, and bringing new land into the realm of commercialized agriculture. The railroads also helped to bind the Mexican economy ever closer to the United States, Mexico's largest market and principal source of investment. Díaz's policies facilitated the expansion of large landholders, created a new class of industrialists and bankers, and attracted foreign investors to Mexico to such an extent that these foreign elites eventually owned a quarter of Mexico's arable land and dominated Mexico's petroleum and copper industries. Even more than during the Bourbon reforms of the late eighteenth century, the increased concentration of land ownership created such inequalities that class conflict sharpened as the twentieth century approached. By 1910, 75 percent of Mexico's cultivable land was dominated by the *haciendas,* several having expanded to more than 10 million acres. At the same time, 95 percent of Mexico's rural population no longer owned any land. In some regions, like the sugar-producing region of Morelos, the sugar *haciendas* became such an overwhelming economic force that they swallowed up the land of over 30 Native villages. As people lost their village land, they become temporary, low-wage laborers on the growing *haciendas*. The revolutionary Emiliano Zapata emerged from this region as a leader of Native peoples' efforts to recover their ancestral land that had been lost to the *haciendas*. Despite Mexico's impressive economic growth during this period, the distribution of this economic growth was so unequal that it led to the Mexican Revolution of 1910, a cataclysmic event that brought this model of economic development to a screeching halt.

THE AFTERMATH OF THE 1910 REVOLUTION AND THE RISE OF IMPORT SUBSTITUTION INDUSTRIALIZATION

After almost a decade of violence, dislocation, and economic contraction, policymakers of the postrevolutionary era ushered in a new inward-looking model of development that was in many ways a rejection of half a century of liberal economic policies. The Constitution of 1917 was the blueprint for this new economic model that would be characterized by the gradual implementation of nationalist economic policies designed to repossess natural resources, limit foreign investment, foster Mexican industry, and

engage in a far-reaching program of land reform. The implicit protection provided by the two world wars and the collapse of commodity prices during the Great Depression provided an impetus for Mexican policymakers to consolidate this model of development. From the late 1920s, an official party that would eventually become known as the Institutional Revolutionary party (*Partido Revolucionario Institucional,* or PRI) controlled the presidency and directed the nation's economic policy. Policymakers took back effective control over the nation's natural resources, expanded the building of infrastructure projects, became heavily involved in protecting and subsidizing agriculture and industry, and in general ushered in an era of unprecedented state involvement in the Mexican economy. Because the PRI centered on protecting national industry in order to industrialize the nation and diversify the economy, these policies are often referred to as Import Substitution Industrialization (ISI). Indeed, as Mexican economic policy centered on industrializing the nation after 1940, the state moved beyond involvement in energy and infrastructure and became a direct producer of industrial products. This trend accelerated as Mexico discovered new petroleum deposits in the 1970s. By 1982, the Mexican state was responsible for over 50 percent of economic activity. It owned steel mills, airlines, and truck manufacturers and had even nationalized the nation's banks. The model also led to a dual system of agriculture, with large, capital-intensive enterprises tied to international markets, and small agricultural plots often producing for subsistence.

While putting into place this state-led model of development, policymakers were also establishing a wide-reaching social safety net that included subsidized food, electricity, and health care. Despite a persistent gap between the nation's rich and poor, by 1982, when this economic model ran out of steam, Mexico's levels of poverty were on the decline, educational achievement rates were rising, illiteracy rates were declining, and social indicators in general were steadily moving in a positive direction. During this era, Mexico's Social Poverty Index, an index developed by James W. Wilkie, showed a steady decline in the percentage of the population that was ill-fed, ill-clothed, and ill-housed.

Though punctuated with periodic economic and political crises, this economic model provided the nation with relative stability for over six decades. Reliant on petroleum exports and international loans, this economic model provided the nation with economic growth until a confluence of factors led to its collapse. Because there were few checks and balances in the Mexican political system, this state-led economic model became laden with inefficiencies and corruption, and consequently many industries became a drain on the state. A precipitous decline in oil prices and a surge in world interest rates triggered the collapse in 1982.

THE COLLAPSE OF IMPORT SUBSTITUTION INDUSTRIALIZATION AND THE RISE OF NEOLIBERALISM

The model's collapse brought with it almost a decade of economic crisis and ushered in a new era of economic policymaking in Mexico. A new generation of U.S.-trained policymakers (mostly economists) consolidated their power, began dismantling the old economic order, and began developing policies of economic liberalization, deregulation, and massive privatization. In their efforts to "get prices right," the new policymakers reduced subsidies on energy, inputs, health care, and foodstuffs. In the countryside, subsidies that farmers had received for their corn and beans, for example, were slashed, while the prices they paid for fuel and fertilizers shot up. In urban areas, subsidies for tortillas and milk were cut, while the wages of workers declined by almost 50 percent. The loss of subsidies, combined with the severe economic contraction of the 1980s, pushed Mexico's social indicators in the opposite direction. Cuts in health care and educational expenditures led to a rise in infant mortality and a drop in educational attainment rates. Indeed, the structural adjustment policies that policymakers put into place had such severe social costs for the Mexican population that scholars dubbed the 1980s the "lost decade."

The signing of the North American Free Trade Agreement (NAFTA) in November of 1993 represented the culmination of this new market-oriented economic orthodoxy. Referred to also as neoliberal policies because they harken back to the liberal economic policies of the late nineteenth century, these policies are designed to entice foreign investment, stimulate economic growth, and consolidate an export-led model

of development. Investors flocked to Mexico and the Mexican economy once again began growing. But, in an ominous sign of the unequal growth that this new economy has generated, Maya Natives from Chiapas, calling themselves the *Zapatistas* after Emiliano Zapata's movement of 1910, rebelled against the Mexican government on January 1, 1994, unleashing a new round of political and economic crises. Just as foreign capitalists invested in Mexico when they perceived stability, they left just as fast during times of instability. By the end of 1995, so many investors had taken their money out of Mexico that the *peso* collapsed, bringing with it a new round of economic contraction with devastating social costs.

The election of Vicente Fox of the National Action party (*Partido de Acción Nacional*, or PAN) in 2000, the first non-PRI president since the Revolution of 1910, was a watershed political event, but it did not signal a shift in economic policy. The Fox administration has continued emphasizing market-oriented solutions to Mexico's problems. After the elections, Fox emerged as the lead promoter of the *Plan Puebla Panama* (PPP), an ambitious Inter-American Development Bank project intended to build the physical infrastructure needed to plug Mexico's poorest region, the south, and Central America into the NAFTA zone and attract foreign investment to that region.

In yet another sign of the unequal benefits these free-market policies have brought to Mexico, farmers on horseback forcibly occupied the Congress on December 10, 2002, and began mounting daily protests demanding a renegotiation of NAFTA provisions that were to end most agricultural tariffs in January of 2003. Though providing only 5 percent of Mexico's GNP, agriculture employs 22 percent of Mexico's workforce. The disappearance since the mid 1980s of the federal programs that provided financial assistance to rural producers, combined with the opening of markets to highly subsidized U.S. grain imports, have devastated Mexico's countryside. It is estimated that one million small farmers have left their land since NAFTA alone. It is yet to be seen whether this new era of market-opening policies will depart from Mexico's previous ones and finally ameliorate rather than exacerbate Mexico's inequalities.

—Carlos Alberto Contreras

See also Economic Crises, Family and Gender, 1980s to the Present (Mexico); Informal Economy (Mexico); International Social Welfare; Poverty (Mexico); Social Welfare (Mexico): Before 1867; Social Welfare (Mexico): Since 1867

Current Comment

Banco Nacional de México. *Review of the economic situation of Mexico* [On-line]. Available: www.banamex.com/eng/esem/index.html

United Electrical, Radio and Machine Workers International. *Mexican Labor News & Analysis* [On-line serial]. Available: www.ueinternational.org

Further Reading

Haber, S., & Bortz, J. L. (2002). *The Mexican economy, 1870 to 1930: Essays on the economic history of institutions, revolution, and growth.* Stanford, CA: Stanford University Press.

Semo, E. (1993). *The history of capitalism in Mexico: Its origins, 1521–1763.* Austin: University of Texas Press.

Wilkie, J. W. (Ed.). (1990). *Society and economy in Mexico.* Los Angeles: University of California, Los Angeles, Latin American Center Publications.

Wise, C. (Ed.). (1998). *The post-NAFTA political economy: Mexico and the Western Hemisphere.* University Park: Pennsylvania State University Press.

ECONOMIC POLICY (UNITED STATES)

THEORY

The central problem of social welfare history is whether one is dealing with people's beliefs or with what actually happened, each a matter of interpretation. Differences exist between arguable reality and our consciousness and modes of expression thereof. Disciples of a particular interpretation are uncomfortable with explanations or commitments not representing their fundamental tenets as sacred but interpreting them as serving some social control or psychic balm function or having some situational, utilitarian, pragmatic, or even political basis of meaning.

An interpretive base can represent either a particular system of belief or a particular endeavor to transcend all such systems and constitute an abstract, theoretical model for examining current developments. Instead of focusing on the language of debate, expressive of people's sentiments, one can identify what the language both expresses and contributes to the actual process of working out solutions to perceived problems.

The interpretive base adopted here commences with government used to establish the fundamental economic institutions. These institutions give effect to some notion of a good society, govern the structure of and operate through markets, and help govern whose interests will count. No transcendental, given system is presented to us; we continually engage in the social reconstruction of the economy and of government itself. The fundamental domain is the legal-economic nexus through which all this is worked out. One set of inputs comes from the aforementioned belief systems; another is the changing meaning of such terms as liberty, property, taking, and welfare.

The actual level of social welfare is a function of the sum of individual preferences somehow weighted by power. In expanded terms, then, the level of social welfare is a function of (1) the processes by which people develop preferences for private economic goods and for social policies and their respective outcomes, and (2) the processes by which some people's preferences count for more than others. Policy generating social welfare comprises many factors and forces; particular positions on issues are inputs to the policy-making process, though some weigh more than others. "Social welfare," thus, has had multiple and kaleidoscopic meanings.

Government must choose between Alpha and Beta when their claims are in the same field of action and conflict. The result is that one will have a right and the other not; welfare will be enhanced for the former and diminished for the latter. Some of these rights are called property. Other rights, or entitlements, are not called property but have the same effects on the distribution of welfare. This is true of regulation, deregulation, taxation, government spending, and, inter alia, social welfare programs.

The fundamental domain in which social welfare is worked out is the system of organization and control inclusive of the legal-economic nexus and the contest to control government and thus the purposes to which government is to be put.

HISTORY

From the Massachusetts Bay Colony to the present, economic policy has been a product of compromises between different conceptions of a good society. These compromises are typically driven by the vote-getting needs of politicians seeking elective office. In early Massachusetts, one key conflict was between those who sought a faith-based theocracy and those who favored a more freewheeling, and freer, commercial organization of society. The conflict between certain religious beliefs and the claims of rival economic claimants has persisted, along different and changing lines.

One further conflict was between those who believed in individual or family self-reliance and those who believed in using government to create opportunities for the disadvantaged through means different from but to the same effect as earlier government actions creating property rights and otherwise generating opportunities for the presently advantaged.

The early conflict between theocracy and a commercial society was succeeded by a conflict over the respective roles of agriculture and industry. This conflict, like the earlier one, was over the deepest meanings of welfare and thereby over the nature of the economic system then being constructed.

In the early nineteenth century, a controversial program of internal improvements was adopted at local, state, and federal levels of government. Canals, post roads, and harbors and ports and their attendant facilities were means of promoting the interests of certain groups. They succeeded in opening up vast new areas of the continent to exploration and occupation. They survived legal challenges that such programs did not represent a "public purpose." Somewhat earlier, the rationale of the institution of the corporation was not that of enabling entrepreneurial activity but of promoting certain public purposes. All of these programs and institutions were vehicles of promoting social welfare—though not all persons benefited; for example, the American Indians. Later, canals, railroads, and other transportation modes received government support.

Other actions centered on the Bank of the United States and eventually the Federal Reserve System and the system of land banks, that is, the provision of a convenient and reliable money supply and a set of financial institutions capable of relatively safely providing the supply of money. These institutions served the purposes of both the financial community—sometimes called "the money power"—and the social welfare of the whole community. Not only changes in banking were involved; money itself also was transformed from gold and silver to privately issued banknotes, to government-issued paper currency, to bursts of electronic energy transferring account balances.

Conflict over the nature of the monetary and banking system originated both from those who distrusted high finance and the people employed therein and from continuing conflicts over the nature of the system. These problems were further complicated by arguments over whether state debts from the postrevolutionary period should be repaid and, if so, by which level of government.

Comparable issues arose over protectionism—the tariff and other devices—and which level of government could impose particular taxes.

Some issues turned on property rights. Government was supposed to protect private property; it was also to determine whose interests would be protected as property. This was especially trying, first, when conflicting recognized property interests were at stake and, second, over slavery. Property was widely redefined and redistributed and thereby both helping to determine and to give effect to the evolving concept of welfare. Even antipolitical positions constituted political positions on the economic role of government.

The provision of social welfare was further extended by the development of various socioeconomic policies. One type of policy involved the treatment of labor. Protective labor policy—requiring, for example, that people be paid in lawful money and not company scrip redeemable only at company stores, that workers have safe working conditions, that wages and hours worked be reasonable, and that compensation be paid regularly—enhanced the welfare of the entire working population. Labor relations policy—legalizing and protecting the right to bargain collectively—enhanced the welfare of union members, not least in enabling their grievances to be aired in fair processes.

A second type of policy involved the promotion of social welfare benefits through the provision of financial security and other protections. Social Security, unemployment insurance, worker's compensation, and programs for the protection of the physically and mentally ill, the very old, the very young, the poor, the unemployable, and the disadvantaged were adopted. These programs remained controversial. Different philosophies of government, the good society, and social welfare were temporarily reconciled through changes in appropriations.

A third type of policy involved governmental supports for a wide spectrum of economic interests. These supports were given at all levels of government and included basic scientific research, applied research, and extension services, including demonstration projects and education in agriculture.

Whenever various groups felt endangered or perceived a serious problem, they took recourse to government as an instrument of conflict resolution and of problem solving. In the realm of ideas, absolutist notions of nonintervention ruled, though not unchallenged; in the domain of practice, pragmatism and politics reigned.

—*Warren J. Samuels*

See also Tax Expenditures (United States)

Current Comment

Barber, W. J., Rutherford, M., Medema, S. G., Johnson, M., & Samuels, W. J. (Eds.). (2000–2003). *Early American economic thought* (Vols. 1–15). London: Pickering & Chatto.

Chairman of the Council of Economic Advisors. (1950–). *Economic report of the president.* Washington, DC: Government Printing Office. [On-line 1995–]. Available: www.gpoaccess.gov/eop/

Further Reading

Dorfman, J. (1946–1959). *The economic mind in American civilization* (Vols. 1–5). New York: Viking.

Fine, S. (1956). *Laissez faire and the general-welfare state.* Ann Arbor: University of Michigan Press.

Friedman, M. (1962). *Capitalism and freedom.* Chicago: University of Chicago Press.

Galbraith, J. K. (1973). *Economics and the public purpose.* Boston: Houghton Mifflin.

EDUCATION POLICY (CANADA)

Canadian education policy has been characterized throughout its history by four underlying tensions. First, church-state relations affected education, with church control of schooling receding before secularization and state power over the past 200 years. Second, English-French linguistic tensions have been important. During the past century, diversity initiatives produced increased school rights for linguistic minorities, particularly French-speaking people. Third, federal-provincial jurisdictional disputes have characterized the development of education in Canada, with both the constitution and political realities favoring provincial dominance. Finally, both Britain and the United States have influenced Canadian education. Initially, British influences were stronger, but these have been increasingly subjugated by educational ideas from the United States.

COLONIAL BEGINNINGS OF CANADIAN EDUCATION

Church initiatives led to the earliest schools and colleges in the North American colonies that later became part of the Dominion of Canada. Beginning in the mid seventeenth century, the Roman Catholic church sponsored schools in urban centers of New France (later Lower Canada, now Quebec). Teaching orders dominated the field, including the Jesuits and *Récollects* for boys, and the Ursulines and sisters of *Mare Marie de l'Incarnation* for girls. By the eighteenth century, parish priests extended opportunities for schooling throughout rural New France. Church ventures continued among the Catholic population of Lower Canada following the British Conquest of 1759–1763, and were soon mirrored in Protestant communities by the Anglican-influenced Royal Institute for the Advancement of Learning.

Early in the nineteenth century, London-based church missionary groups such as the Society for the Propagation of the Gospel (SPG) began establishing schools in the English-speaking colonies of Nova Scotia, New Brunswick, Prince Edward Island, Newfoundland, and Upper Canada (now Ontario). At the same time, various community and private-venture schools sprang up and soon overshadowed these missionary endeavors. By the 1820s, loose networks of common schools, grammar schools, parish schools, academies, and colleges served rapidly growing populations in all the British North American colonies.

Pressured by growing industrialization and urbanization, and concerned with increasing "foreign" immigration and incipient democracy, colonial governments began systematizing education throughout British

North America. Provincial school superintendents were appointed, teacher-training institutes established, and funds made available for approved schools. Led by Upper Canada and Nova Scotia, most English-speaking provinces established publicly financed and publicly controlled school systems through the middle decades of the nineteenth century. Church control remained dominant, however, in Quebec and Newfoundland.

1867: PROVINCIAL CONTROL OF EDUCATION

Educational policy issues were important in constitutional debates when the Dominion of Canada was created. Delegates to both the Charlottetown, Prince Edward Island (1864), and Quebec conferences (1866) agreed that education should be a provincial rather than a federal responsibility. Section 93 of the British North America (BNA) Act of 1867 stated: "In and for each province the Legislature may exclusively make laws in relation to Education." This decision reflected the intense pride of each founding province (Ontario, Quebec, Nova Scotia, New Brunswick) in its emergent public education system. Quebec also saw provincial control as a guarantee of preserving its majority Catholic and francophone culture in a predominantly Protestant and anglophone nation.

Federal protection of religious minority rights in education, however, was the exception to exclusive provincial control. Quebec's Protestant and Ontario's Catholic minorities, benefiting from legislative protection in the earlier United Province of Canada (1841–1867), demanded constitutional protection in the new Confederation. Thus, the BNA Act Section 93 (1) stated: "Nothing in any such [future provincial] Law shall prejudicially affect any Right or Privilege with respect to Denominational Schools which any class of persons have in the Province at the [time of joining the] Union." Section 93 (3) allowed appeals to Ottawa for "remedial" legislation if provincial action threatened minority school rights.

The BNA Act Section 93 (1) also applied to later provinces with preunion minority religious rights in education (Alberta and Saskatchewan, 1905; Newfoundland, 1949), but not to new provinces without such laws (British Columbia, 1871; Prince Edward Island, 1873). BNA Act Section 93 (3) proved ineffective politically, as Ottawa refused to enact remedial legislation when Manitoba abolished public funding for Roman Catholic schools in 1891.

BNA Act Section 93 did not address linguistic and aboriginal school rights. French-speaking minorities in anglophone provinces and Quebec's English-language minority were left under provincial control and lacked federal protection. Aboriginal or Native education was assigned to Ottawa under a separate section of the British North America Act, although various Christian churches carried out Native schooling as missionary work.

EDUCATION POLICY DEVELOPMENT 1867–1918

Provincial education departments in late nineteenth century Canada enacted general regulations, determined curriculum, approved textbooks, set school-leaving examinations, and trained and certified teachers. Municipal school boards, elected by local resident taxpayers, provided classroom accommodation, hired teachers, and levied local property taxes. Although most school money was raised locally, provincial grants gradually increased through the late nineteenth and early twentieth centuries.

In the years after Confederation, the "common" schools of colonial days were reclassified as public elementary schools, educating 6- to 13-year-old children, grouped into grades 1 through 8. Pre-Confederation "grammar" schools were transformed into public high schools or secondary schools, although Quebec and Newfoundland proved the exceptions, with most secondary schools remaining under private, religious control until the mid twentieth century. Minimal provisions for compulsory school attendance were introduced during this period, again with Quebec lagging.

By the early twentieth century, issues of rural-urban discrepancy, socioeconomic class, and cultural diversity began to challenge provincial school authorities. Immigrant education proved a major issue in eastern cities (particularly Toronto, Ontario) and in the rapidly expanding school systems of the newer provinces of Alberta, Manitoba, and Saskatchewan. Patriotic exercises, culminating in annual Empire Day extravaganzas (the school day preceding Queen

Victoria's May 24 birthday) were introduced to assimilate continental European immigrant youth into Canada's mainstream anglophone culture.

Increased urbanization and industrialization, detected by the national census of 1911, produced demands that secondary schools extend their purposes to include technical or vocational education. Beginning in Ontario, and later spreading nationally, educational reformers worked with business and labor interests to reorganize public schooling to fit the needs of occupational selection for an industrial economy. They campaigned for technical education in either specialized vocational schools or through multilateral or composite high schools combining technical, commercial, and academic programs.

EDUCATION POLICY DEVELOPMENT 1918–1970

Much twentieth century curriculum reform spotlighted individual development. First came the turn-of-the-century new education movement (most active in Ontario), which promoted kindergartens; introduced new subjects such as manual training (industrial arts), domestic science (home economics), physical education, and school gardening; and harnessed schools to child-study and public-health concerns. The progressive education movement of the 1930s (strongest in Alberta) included a new social studies curriculum (combining history, geography, and civics), the "enterprise" system of inquiry-based learning, and the junior high school.

The greatest impact of this child-centered approach came with three later provincial education reports: Quebec's *Report of the Royal Commission of Inquiry* (Parent Report) of 1963–1966, Ontario's *Living and Learning* (Hall-Dennis Report) of 1968, and Alberta's *Report of the Commission on Educational Planning* (Worth Report) of 1972. These commissions recommended greater local autonomy in decision making, broadening curriculum through thematic and interdisciplinary approaches, and organizing learning through individual timetables and the abolition of grades.

Industrialization and urbanization depopulated rural areas and reinforced inequalities between city and country schools. Demand grew to reform rural school districts and for provincial educational funding. Beginning in Alberta in the late 1930s and culminating nationally in the early 1970s, rural school administration in Canada was transformed from small school districts based on school attendance to large regional or county school divisions. Between the 1930s and the 1960s, provincial governments assumed the main burden of financing elementary and secondary education by providing equalization grants.

From the 1960s through the 1980s, educational reforms also affected the school rights of religious and linguistic minorities. Even as secularization led to the demise of denominationally based school systems in Quebec and Newfoundland, Catholics in Ontario and Saskatchewan secured funding for separate schools through the end of secondary education (Catholics in Alberta had this since 1905) and religious groups in several provinces benefited from more generous financial assistance for private schools.

Linguistic choice for French-language minorities was promoted by the federal Royal Commission on Bilingualism and Biculturalism of the 1960s, enshrined in Section 23 of the Canadian Charter of Rights and Freedoms (1982) and sustained from the 1970s on through federal financial support for minority-language and second-language education programs. Quebec, however, never adopted Section 23 of the charter, placing English-minority schooling in a precarious position in an increasingly French-speaking political and cultural climate.

EDUCATION POLICY DEVELOPMENT 1980–2000

Curricular reforms of the 1960s and 1970s were scarcely started before complaints about lack of structure and standards and demands for "getting back to the basics" were heard from many parents and business interests. This opposition was persistent and effective. By the late 1980s and early 1990s, several official policy studies were published that forcefully articulated an alternative educational ideology to meet the challenges of a new global economy.

Provincial reports in Ontario (1987), British Columbia (1988), and New Brunswick (1992), together with the Economic Council of Canada's *A Lot to Learn* (1992), interpreted relatively high drop-out rates, widespread functional illiteracy, and mediocre results in international mathematics and science tests as evidence of the failure of public education. The authors of the reports believed these failures stemmed from muddled purposes, fragmented curricula, and inadequate accountability. These reports advocated a return to externally established curriculum and standards, with accountability mechanisms entrusted to provincial educational authorities.

Recent official policy studies substantially agree on basic principles: that educational policy should be redesigned to address the emergence of a global economy driven by technological change and international competition; that the purpose of elementary and secondary education is acquisition of basic knowledge and skills; and that public accountability should be restored to education.

Led by Alberta, Canadian provinces during the 1990s reformed their school systems through results-based provincial curricula, acquisition of basic skills, integration of special-needs students into regular classrooms, reorganization of local school districts to achieve greater economies of scale, and redistribution of provincial educational monies to promote greater equality of educational opportunity.

—*Robert M. Stamp*

See also Child Welfare Policy (Canada)

Primary Sources

The records of provincial departments (or ministries) of education are usually housed in the government archives of the respective provinces. Ontario's collection is among the richest, includes both manuscript and printed material, and is indexed as Record Group 2, Education Department Records, Archives of Ontario, Toronto (www.archives.gov.on.ca/); several major urban school boards, with the city of Toronto setting the pace, have established archive departments within their central administrative offices.

Current Comment

Miller, J. C. (1913). *Rural schools in Canada.* New York: Teachers College Press.
Provincial Committee on Aims and Objectives of Education in the Schools of Ontario. (1968). *Living and learning* [Hall-Dennis Report]. Toronto: Ontario Department of Education.
Sissons, C. B. (1917). *Bi-lingual schools in Canada.* Toronto, ON: J. M. Dent & Sons.
Weir, G. M. (1934). *The separate school question in Canada.* Toronto, ON: Ryerson.

Further Reading

Barman, J., Sutherland, N., & Wilson, J. D. (Eds.). (1995). *Children, teachers and schools in the history of British Columbia.* Calgary, AB: Detselig.
Gidney, R. D. (1999). *From Hope to Harris: The reshaping of Ontario's schools.* Toronto, ON: University of Toronto Press.
Henchey, N., & Burgess, D. (1987). *Between past and future: Quebec education in transition.* Calgary, AB: Detselig.
Manzer, R. (1994). *Public schools & political ideas: Canadian educational policy in historical perspective.* Toronto, ON: University of Toronto Press.
Wilson, J. D., Stamp, R. M., & Audet, L.-P. (Eds.). (1970). *Canadian education: A history.* Scarborough, ON: Prentice Hall.

EDUCATION POLICY (MEXICO)

Educational policy in Mexico has served to consolidate both a unifying national identity and the hegemony of the dominant groups. There have been four stages in the development of educational institutions and practices in Mexico: indigenous-colonial, independent, postrevolutionary, and contemporary.

INDIGENOUS AND COLONIAL EDUCATION

Prior to the arrival of the Spanish in 1519, indigenous educational institutions expressed and reproduced the social order sustained by the religious beliefs of the millennial culture developed by the peoples of Mesoamerica: *olmecas, mayas, teotihuacanos, toltecas, purépechas,* and so on. The Aztecs were the last dominant civilization prior to the Spanish Conquest of what is now Mexico and, thus, historians have provided clear accounts of what their educational institutions were like. Indigenous schooling corresponded to cultural practices rather than policy directives; hence, educational institutions were stratified. The offspring of nobles and priests were offered scientific, religious, and administrative instruction in the *Calmécac.* The *Telpochcalli* served as community schools where the children of the populace received agricultural, trades, and military instruction. Aztec youngsters attended the *Cuicacalli* to receive training in musical and literary arts.

After the Spanish Conquest in 1521, education during the colonial era was primarily a religious enterprise intended to evangelize the peoples of New Spain. The most important educational institutions developed during the colonial era included popular schools for indigenous peoples (literacy), popular schools for Spaniards (literacy), technical middle schools (trades), postsecondary institutions (arts and sciences), and, for the elite, the Royal and Pontifical University of Mexico (established in 1553). Yet the economic and political interests of landowners and other dominant groups clashed with the humanist spirit of Dominicans, Franciscans, Augustines, and, most important, Jesuits. In this context, during the first years of Spanish rule, the religious orders developed educational institutions that would help in the formation of a society where *criollos* (Spaniards born in the New World), *Mestizos,* and indigenous peoples could coexist: These took the form of the hospital-workshop-farm, convent-farm-school, and mission-pueblo. The humanist spirit of the friars who initiated the conversion of indigenous peoples soon faded away and religious dogmatism thwarted the intellect and the spirit of an emerging nation for nearly three centuries. In 1767, Spain expelled the Jesuits—who had developed the most important network of educational institutions in the Americas—because of their diffusion of Enlightenment ideas.

EDUCATION AFTER INDEPENDENCE

After the War of Independence, Mexico emerged as a federal republic. Article 50 of the 1824 Constitution established that the federal government would create educational institutions to provide instruction in military affairs, engineering, fine arts, and physical, political, and moral sciences. The article explicitly stated that the federal educational mandate should not preclude state governments from organizing public education within their territories. During the decade of instability and military struggle that followed the declaration of independence, numerous educational institutions opened, yet many had to be closed due to lack of funding. The emerging Mexican state posed its first challenge to the hegemony of the church over schooling in 1833 with a short-lived reform attempt by Vice President Valentín Gómez Farías. In 1842, a successful national network of institutions preparing teachers using the

methods of Bell and Lancaster was granted control over primary instruction throughout the country. In spite of the state's educational efforts, private educational institutions dominated schooling during this era. In education, the ideological, political, and military strife between conservatives (supporting the church and French imperialism) and liberals (supporting a secular, nationalist nation-state) centered on the issue of academic freedom.

The Constitution of 1857 established academic freedom and state control over licensing requirements for professional practice (credentials). Over the next two decades, a process of professionalization of pedagogy was initiated alongside the emerging bourgeoisie's embrace of positivist philosophical principles safeguarding free enterprise through social control by the state. Don Justo Sierra had engaged in a school improvement program (elementary, normal, arts, and preparatory schools) prior to becoming minister of public instruction and fine arts in 1905. As the head of this ministry, he supported the promulgation of the Elementary Education Law for the Federal District and Territories in 1908, the reestablishment of the National University of Mexico in 1910, and the work of intellectual circles such as *El Ateneo de la Juventud,* whose members would later contribute to define postrevolutionary educational institutions and, most important, national identity.

EDUCATION AFTER THE REVOLUTION

Article 3 of the 1917 Constitution established that public education would be secular and free—the two defining principles of schooling in Mexico. In 1921, José Vasconcelos became the first secretary of public education and his work set the standard for the state's postrevolutionary educational efforts: Federal and not municipal authorities would create and expand the Mexican educational system. He championed a national effort to educate the peasantry through his support of rural schools, public libraries, and rural community centers *(casas del pueblo)* where "cultural missionaries" would teach a range of subjects, from literacy to performing arts. Likewise, he stimulated the government's commitment to the teaching profession through its support of federal and provincial normal schools.

Moreover, secondary schools began to be established throughout the country in compliance with a 1925 mandate. The state's expansion of the educational system fueled the development of strong unions by federal teachers. By 1929, postrevolutionary efforts to secularize society through education were interpreted as a persecution of religious ideals and led to armed confrontation with Catholic groups. As public servants, teachers became primary actors in the struggle. Simultaneously, a general strike at the National University of Mexico (*Universidad Nacional de México*) resulted in a presidential decree granting partial autonomy to the institution—it was not until 1933, however, that its full autonomy was achieved (*Universidad Nacional Autónoma de México*). As part of a nationalist governmental program, a short-lived attempt to impose a "socialist education" model resulted in a 1934 constitutional amendment establishing the federal government's authority over educational content and accreditation of private institutions and congressional control over educational funding and legislation. President Lázaro Cárdenas created the National Polytechnic Institute in 1937 and welcomed exiled Spaniard intellectuals who created the *Colegio de México* in 1940.

In 1942, the Organic Education Law (*Ley Orgánica de Educación*) established a new regulatory framework for the educational system. Secretary Jaime Torres Bodet supported popular education through the National Literacy Campaign and the publication of millions of literacy texts both in Spanish and indigenous languages. He reinforced the professionalization of teachers, founding, in 1945, the Superior Normal School (*Escuela Normal Superior*) and strengthening the National Normal School. In 1946, Congress passed an amendment to Article 3 of the Constitution defining the postrevolutionary regime's commitment to compulsory, free, and secular education as a state effort to develop the individual's faculties, patriotism, and international solidarity based on independence and justice. In 1958, in his second term as secretary of education, Torres Bodet promoted the creation of administrative bodies responsible for educational planning and for publishing free textbooks for all elementary students. The following year, he developed the first systematic educational policy program in the nation. It was a directive that was expected to meet its (mostly quantitative) objectives over the course of two administrations; thus, it came to be known as the Eleven-Year Plan (*Plan de Once Años*).

The enactment of the Federal Education Law (*Ley Federal de Educación*) in 1973 provided the basis for subsequent educational planning efforts at both the federal and state levels. Over the course of the following decade, an increasingly specialized federal educational bureaucracy systematized the structure and operation of educational services nationwide. Yet, its excessive centralization, along with the politicized character of the massive teachers' union, hampered systemic efficiency. The debt crisis that began in the early 1980s intensified traditional qualitative concerns as well as pervasive educational inequities. Structural adjustment programs began to determine governmental priorities (efficient use of public funds and privatization of public enterprises). Thus, the emerging technocratic policy-making elite directed all subsequent policy directives to address qualitative problems through administrative reform efforts.

EDUCATIONAL POLICY TODAY

The principal features of contemporary educational policy were developed in the late 1970s. The state initiated a transfer of administrative authority over schooling from federal to state bureaucracies (creating new actors). The traditionally stable relationship between the teachers' union and policy elites was disrupted by the technocratic elite's reform program and by an emerging democratic faction within the union. Insurgent teachers challenged co-opted union leaders, who, in response, used their vast economic and political resources to gain greater influence over policy making. Democratic teachers also initiated national mobilizations demanding greater resources for education and opposing the antinationalist "modernization" governmental agenda.

The General Education Law (*Ley General de Educación*) enacted in 1993 defined the current legal framework of schooling in Mexico. It was the product of a national consensus-building strategy carried out by the federal government with traditional and new actors, and it was framed following the adoption of a constitutional amendment that made secondary education compulsory. Under the new scheme, federal authorities determine educational planning, content, evaluation, and funding; state authorities control administration and operations (including relations with the teachers' union); and municipal authorities are responsible for involving civil society in schooling though Social Participation Councils (*Consejos de Participación Social*). In 1994, Secretary of Education José Ángel Pescador appointed a representative in California in an effort to address a historic demand for educational support for immigrant children living in the United States.

Today, all the states of the Republic of Mexico have enacted or updated their local education laws; yet federal elites determine national educational priorities (including curricular content and teacher salaries). Congress appropriates resources for education but the executive sets funding allocation criteria. With the election of President Vicente Fox, a conservative administration took power in the year 2000, and it began to allow greater involvement of civil society in certain areas of schooling. Social participation (primarily by education scholars and insurgent teachers) has promoted the creation of administrative bodies that address the educational needs of indigenous children and provide accurate, objective, and comprehensive evaluation indicators for the educational system. Congress has also responded to social demands by increasing educational funding (particularly for higher education) and making preschool compulsory. Democratic governance guarantees that society's influence over educational policy will continue to grow, yet the ideological beliefs of executive elites will remain a crucial determinant of policy priorities, guiding the operation of a mostly urban educational system with over 30 million students evenly split by gender.

—*Octavio Augusto Pescador*

See also Economic Policy (Mexico); Rural Education (Mexico); Welfare Capitalism (Mexico)

Primary Sources

Archivo de la Secretaría de Educación Pública, Mexico City; *Boletín de la Secretaría de Educación Pública* (1922–1931); *Memoria relativa al estado que guarda el ramo de educación pública* (1932–1935); *Memoria de la Secretaría de Educación Pública* (1936–1951); *Acción educativa del gobierno federal.*

Current Comment

Observatorio Ciudadano de la Educación [On-line]. Available: www.observatorio.org/

Ramos, S. (1977). *Obras completas.* Mexico City: Universidad Nacional Autónoma de México.

Sánchez, G. I. (1936). *Mexico: A revolution by education.* New York: Viking.

Secretaría de Educación Pública [On-line]. Available: www.sep.gob.mx

Further Reading

Cárabes Pedroza, J., Reid Rodríguez, M., Pardo Zepeda, F., & Flores García, J. (1979). *Fundamentos político-jurídicos de la educación en México.* Mexico City: Editorial Progreso.

Latapí Sarre, P. (Ed.). (1998). *Un siglo de educación en México.* Mexico City: Consejo Nacional Para la Cultura y las Artes.

Morales-Gomez, D., & Torres, C. A. (1990). *The state, corporatist politics, and educational policy making in Mexico.* New York: Praeger.

Vaughn, M. K. (1982). *The state, education, and social class in Mexico, 1880–1928.* Dekalb: University of Northern Illinois Press.

EDUCATION POLICY (UNITED STATES)

Public education is the repository for the best hopes and worst fears of every generation and has been deeply influenced by shifting cultural values as well as by changing political, cultural, and economic realities. European settlers began enacting formal education and social welfare laws in the earliest years of the North American colonies. In 1642–1647, Puritans had barely arrived in Massachusetts when they began passing laws for schools and apprenticeships requiring the "ability to read and to understand religious principles and the laws of the colony." These laws reflected concern about a Christian vision, religious morality, and progress. Anxiety about education waned as settlements grew and it became clear Christian education was occurring, usually at home, directed by fathers or in schools, which opened a few months a year and taught boys and girls separately.

Education varied sharply by region and by the traditions of the settlers in the colonies. New Englanders and Protestant evangelicals were more likely to establish schools and be concerned with Bible reading and breaking the "evil will" of children. Southerners were more moderate and relied on families, tutors, and churches while schooling African American slaves for slavery only. More moderate colonial Americans focused on duty, industry, and the control of passion through cultivated reason. Low population concentrations often made formal schooling difficult, especially in the frontier regions.

Schooling became newly important with the establishment of the new nation in 1776, which required education appropriate for self-governing citizens. Curriculum materials such as Noah Webster's standardized American dictionary and special primers, the pledge of allegiance, and stories about national heroes were introduced to nurture national identity and pride. More profoundly, many Americans, like Thomas Jefferson, believed democracy required educated reason to preserve "a due degree of liberty." All attempts for government-legislated education, at the state or national level, however, failed. Americans were uneasy about giving either state or national government too much power, thinking education should be a local concern. As a result, in the early nineteenth century American schools varied widely by size, condition, funding, amount of time open, curriculum, and teacher quality. In general, local communities resisted taxing themselves to raise money for schools so user fees were common. Lack of oversight and consistent funding meant that the quality of schooling was often poor.

The increase of immigration from Ireland and Germany in the 1830s and 1840s created a change in the cultural climate that contributed to interest in a more organized system of education. After 1828, expanded suffrage to many immigrants increased fear among elites of the power of the uneducated mob, and immigrant cultures were seen as threatening to Protestant culture. In addition, an expanding economy and increased population mobility also heightened the perceived need for schooling since young adults less frequently lived lives in one community or served long apprenticeships. Thus, when Horace Mann led a common-school movement, states began to provide consistent funding, building and curriculum improvements, teacher training, and attendance laws. Common schools were supposed to teach a common curriculum of social and political values and were to be attended "in common" by children from diverse cultural and social-class backgrounds. Such schools, the "great

equalizer of the conditions of men," were envisioned to help alleviate poverty and crime and reduce ethnic and class tensions. They were favored both by Workingmen's parties, which argued that public education provided necessary knowledge for survival and success, as well as by reformers who viewed education as a means of disciplining the poor.

The actual diversity of common school children, however, was limited. The wealthiest and poorest children usually did not attend common schools. Children from wealthy families were privately tutored and many children of the poor remained unschooled. Black and other minority children were systematically segregated in separate schools. Later in the nineteenth century, children of Chinese workers in California faced similar segregation. The curriculum also did not accommodate diversity. Moral education was based on the King James Bible and the McGuffy Readers, textbooks that were widely used in the nineteenth century, which emphasized patriotism and heroism while presenting demeaning racial stereotypes of immigrants. School texts also described the poor as needing reform and regulation while extolling the moral virtues of the rich. Yet, in places like New York, nearly half of the residents were immigrants, including large numbers of Irish Catholics. In the tense atmosphere caused by urban rioting and church burnings, Catholics demanded funds for separate Catholic schools and created an alternative school system when their demands were ignored. African Americans also created schools. After emancipation, former slaves built schools all over the South. They were supported by the often meager contributions of freed slaves or by philanthropic aid societies and abolitionists. They laid the foundation for many of the historically African American colleges that exist today.

Although public education excluded most minorities, education for Native Americans involved a deliberate process of deculturalization that, as Carlisle Indian school founder Richard Henry Pratt believed, would "kill the Indian and save the man." Beginning in 1887, the federal government removed thousands of children from their extended families and tribal nations and placed them in boarding schools around the United States. Children were forced to take new names, forbidden to speak their languages, and had their hair cut, clothes removed, and sacred objects banned. After a long period of struggle, the Indian New Deal of the 1930s emphasized building community day schools, which Indian tribes struggle to control to the current day. In the early twentieth century, education policy was influenced by dramatic changes in population and by the rise of an industrial political economy. From 1866 to 1870, 98 percent of European immigrants came from northern and western Europe. By 1920, this shrank to 22 percent, with most immigrants then coming from southern and eastern Europe. This included Catholics from southern Italy and eastern Europe and Jews from Russia. Like Irish Catholics before them, these immigrants and their children were disdained and discriminated against, even though there were large numbers of immigrant children in the cities. Work and residence had changed as well. Earlier, the majority of Americans were self-employed in agriculture or industry and lived in rural areas, but most people now were employees, with many working in poor conditions in industrial production and living in large cities. After the Civil War, many workers fought against unsafe working conditions and joined labor unions. Some became active in socialist political organizations that called for a more equitable distribution of wealth. In the Progressive Era, state and federal governments grew increasingly active, regulating business, industry, labor, and education. During World War I, the government used schools to Americanize immigrants and to foster patriotism.

In 1900, only 11 percent of children attended secondary school; by 1930 more than half did and this period saw a fervent debate about the type of education American society required. Progressives believed that a curriculum of memorized classics, math, science, and history should be replaced and schools should consider the nature of the child as well as the needs of society in carrying out their mission. Progressive educators such as John Dewey believed that democracy required active participation by all citizens in social, political, and economic decisions and that curriculum should reflect the interests of both students and society. Other education reformers, the "social efficiency" progressives, felt children should be scientifically tested to determine their probable careers and then be tracked into segmented curricula. Placement and IQ testing became accepted. In retrospect, critics have argued that these measures were often biased and their use supported the interests of the dominant social class. In these modern, presumably meritocratic, schools, minorities were consistently tracked into vocational education whereas White middle-class Protestants populated college preparatory courses. Used for social control and to affirm existing class structures, education also provided opportunities for many.

During the depression of the 1930s, growing popular disillusionment with capitalism and industrialization contributed to the development of new democratic approaches to education. Educational reformers such as George Counts believed schools could "build a new social order." Harold Rugg's widely used social science textbook series, *Man and his Changing World*, reflected a vision of democratic citizenship, cross-cultural understanding, greater equality between sexes, and social justice. In actual practice, progressive education was most often simply added into the existing curriculum of tracked, social efficiency schools. In the 1940s, "life-adjustment education" was conceived to meet the needs of most students in "general tracks," and curriculum generally abandoned progressive approaches to education assuming "average" students were not suited to academic rigor.

After World War II, with increasing secondary enrollments, education policy again became hotly debated. Politicians and others denounced progressive education and called for a return to basics, more memorization, and teaching "the facts." During the cold war decade of the 1950s, the Russian launch of *Sputnik*, the first artificial satellite, sparked massive criticism of the nation's educational system as failing to teach the skills necessary for America's survival in an increasingly hostile world. The National Defense Education Act of 1958 emphasized education policy not to revitalize democracy but to fortify national defense, shifting attention to strengthening education in math, science, and foreign languages. Many schools were consolidated into large district high schools with a more differentiated curriculum and with advanced scientific courses.

In the 1960s and 1970s, curriculum policy was secondary to the issue of equity. Pushed by a growing civil rights movement and by the legal challenge of the National Association for the Advancement of Colored

People (NAACP), in 1954 the U.S. Supreme Court declared racial segregation in education to be unconstitutional in *Brown v. Board of Education.* The process of desegregation was generally slow and difficult in the American South. By 1964, less than one percent of African American children in the South attended desegregated schools. In 1965, the Elementary and Secondary Education Act allocated one billion dollars annually to schools with high concentrations of low-income children. Schools were pressured to accommodate diversity or they would lose funding. During the 1970s, after legal action and new legislation, schools recognized the educational rights of girls, the disabled, and non-English-speaking students.

In the late 1970s, public tolerance and government commitment to new educational programs declined even though by the 1980s schools were graduating more students than ever. The 1983 report to the secretary of education by the National Commission on Excellence in Education, *A Nation at Risk,* asserted that the poor performance of public schools was a national security threat and damaged the nation's capacity to compete economically. Rigorous standards and accountability were demanded of the nation's schools. Curricula, teaching, and learning were often homogenized. Minimum competency tests were commonly employed even though they often "dumbed down" curricula and reduced teacher autonomy. These tests continue to be used in contemporary education. The 1990s saw increased involvement by private schools in the nation's educational system. Their growth assumes that an education system based on competition and minimal regulation rather than expanded public provision will result in better-quality education at a lower cost. Hence, controversies regarding the "schools of choice" movement, charter schools, home schooling, and the weakening of

teacher certification and accreditation requirements are hallmarks of today's national debate on how best to prepare children for the needs of tomorrow.

—Elizabeth Heilman

See also Aboriginal People and Policy (United States); Rush, Benjamin

Primary Sources

Blackwell History of Education Museum, Northern Illinois University, DeKalb, can be accessed on-line (www.cedu.niu.edu/blackwell/). Many other primary sources are available on the World Wide Web. Visit the History of American Education Web Project (www.nd.edu/~rbarger/www7/). Digital versions of nineteenth-century schoolbooks and related texts can also be found on-line (http://digital.library.pitt.edu/nietz/).

Current Comment

Aikin, W. M. (1942). *The story of the eight-year study, with conclusions and recommendations.* New York: Harper & Brothers. Available: www.8yearstudy.org

Dewey, J. (1966). *Democracy and education: An introduction to the philosophy of education.* New York: Free Press. (Original work published 1916)

Mann, H. (1851). *Slavery: Letters and speeches.* Boston: B. B. Mussey.

Report of the superintendent of Indian schools. (1897/98–1903/04). Washington, DC: Government Printing Office.

Further Reading

Kaestle, C. F. (1983). Pillars of the republic: Common schools and American society, 1780–1860 (American Century Series). New York: Hill & Wang.

Kleibard, H. M. (2002). Changing course: American curriculum reform in the 20th century. New York: Teachers College Press.

McClellan, B. E. (2002). Moral education in America: Schools and the shaping of character since colonial times. New York: Teachers College Press.

Spring, J. (2000). The American school 1642–2000. New York: McGraw-Hill.

FAMILY ALLOWANCE/CHILD TAX BENEFIT (CANADA)

The Family Allowance program was a mainstay of the Canadian social welfare scene for almost 50 years, but in the past decade it has died and new programs with new meanings have been implemented. What follows here is a review of the creation of the Family Allowance program in Canada and its philosophical roots and how it has been transformed into a complex tax credit system that reflects very different beliefs and values.

From the last years of the Second World War until 1993, the federal government sent monthly checks for each child to each family across Canada. For Canadian families, the proverbial "baby bonus" became a way of life. The Family Allowance is now history and a new generation of families has little knowledge of its roots and the role it played in shaping the Canadian social welfare system. Its legacy, however, shaped the nation's current Canada Child Tax Benefit (CCTB), and the debates and arguments about the Family Allowance program are being echoed in the discussion of this new program. The CCTB is a tax-free monthly payment for families with children and it incorporates the various provincial programs. It is administered by the Canada Customs and Revenue Agency, the taxation department of the federal government.

Prior to the 1920s, a number of European countries boasted various family allowance schemes. These plans generated some interest in North America, but the general feeling was that, compared to the situation in Europe, wages in Canada and the United States were higher and therefore sufficient to support a family. This connection between the inadequacy of wages and family needs was central to the argument in support of the program. Some argued that it was unfair that a wage earner with a large family who earned a "working wage" was unable to meet the family's needs because the wage scale was based on the needs of a single individual. The supplementary support of a family allowance was intended to address this inequity. In Europe, however, there were also social reasons for family allowances. For example, it was believed that these programs could reverse a declining birth rate and prevent emigration of labor to neighboring countries where better wages or employment opportunities existed.

In Canada, one of the earliest proponents of family allowances was the Jesuit priest, Father Leon Lebel, known as the father of family allowances. In the 1920s, Lebel wrote a number of pamphlets about the financial difficulties that large families faced. He recognized that industrialization caused structural changes in the economic system resulting in the failure of the system to provide for large families. His arguments, based on the principles of justice and fairness, acknowledged the cost of raising children. Hence, family allowances were seen not as a disincentive to work but as an attempt to recognize reproduction costs, the service of raising children for society. Parenthood was a social service to the nation and should be supported by all.

At least part of the rationale for family allowances was their value in subsidizing worker wages to control the demand for increases in labor costs. During the Second World War, which followed the Great Depression, the Canadian economy heated up, creating a demand for labor as Canadian men enlisted in the military. After years of unemployment, many workers could find good-paying jobs. Although the federal government imposed wage controls, many feared that inflation would make the costs of war even higher.

As a new social welfare program, the Family Allowance was unique for a number of reasons. First, the recipients of the program never asked for it. Canadians were busy with the war and few had considered such a plan. Second, government departments whose mandate included social welfare were not involved in its conception. It was created in isolation of normal social program development, which usually involved commissions or inquiries. Third, the proponents were an "unlikely" group to create a national universal social program. The architects were senior bureaucrats, officers of the Departments of External Affairs and Finance and the governor of the Bank of Canada. These men, who had been extremely influential in managing the war economy, represented Canada's business elite.

With the end of the war in sight, labor pressed for lifting wage controls. From the perspective of its proponent, the equalizing effect of family allowances was not "social justice" or recognition of reproduction but to support wage controls, to maintain "industrial harmony" by discouraging collective bargaining, and to support Canada's economic competitiveness in the world (global) economy.

Family allowances, proponents expected, would assist in ensuring economic and political stability after the war. In a sense, the plan was the first proposed guaranteed income. Leonard Marsh, research adviser to the Dominion of Canada Committee on Reconstruction, had recommended a benefit of $7.50 per child per month. The 1944 Family Allowance Act,

however, failed where implemented as it provided for only some of the costs of raising a child. In 1946, the program provided an average benefit of $5.94 per child and $14.18 per family per month, far below Marsh's recommendation. Over the years, benefits steadily increased and, in 1993, the benefits averaged $31 per child per month. There were numerous minor changes over the life of the program and the provinces could change the pattern of benefits within limits. The province of Quebec, for example, established its own system in 1967.

In 1988, the federal government initiated a Child Tax Credit program replacing child deductions in income tax. For a few years, all eligible families continued to receive the Family Allowance of $31 per month per child, and low-income families could also receive a tax credit of $384 per year, giving them a total benefit of $750 per year per child. In 1993, the Child Tax Benefit and Work Income Supplement replaced the Family Allowance and the Child Tax Credit. The termination of the Family Allowance brought to an end the last social welfare program based on the principle of "universality."

By the late 1990s, the federal government found itself with an improving fiscal situation as a result of various program cuts and increasing tax revenues. Over 1.4 million children, however, still lived in poverty and the federal government's pledge to end child poverty became something of an albatross. Wanting to do something with the increasing revenues, the federal government set aside $850 million for a new child program, effective July 1, 1998, and a further $850 million as an election promise ($1.7 billion in all by the year 2000). These monies would be added to the existing $5.1 billion in the former Child Tax Credit program. The principal idea of the new National Child Benefit Initiative was to move 1.2 million children out of the welfare system, which is connected to the stigmatized means-tested "dole." It is estimated that 2.5 million children in low-income families, both working and on social assistance, would receive some benefits. The program would increase federal benefits for over 1.4 million families whose incomes were below the $25,921 threshold.

The National Child Benefit Initiative was meant to increase the financial resources of families with children and remove the barrier many poor families encountered attempting to enter the employment market. By accepting low-paying jobs, families on social assistance lose supplementary benefits such as noninsured health benefits like medications and dental services. The potential loss of these benefits has created a barrier for families on social assistance. It was intended that poor children would gradually move out of the means-tested "welfare" programs into a benefit system of support. The program was not designed to become an additional and separate program from provincial programs, but dovetail into these programs. The federal Child Tax Benefit, thus, was changed into the new Canada Child Tax Benefit, which saves the provinces about $510 million in social assistance. These "savings" are meant to be returned to support low-income families with children through special programs and services. The combination of the federal Canada Child Tax Benefit (CCTB) and provincial programs becomes the new National Child Benefit System (NCBS).

In July 2003, families with net incomes under the new threshold of $33,387 received a basic benefit of $1,169 a year for each child less than 18 years of age. There were additional benefits for the third and subsequent child ($82 each) and any child under the age of 7 years ($232). In addition to the basic benefit, the National Child Benefit Supplement (NCBS) is intended to support the working poor. The NCBS benefit was $1,463 for the first child and $1,254 for the second child and $1,176 for each additional child. Thus, a working poor family with three children would see an annual benefit of $7,482. As the parents move beyond the threshold family income of $21,529, their NCBS benefit is gradually reduced so that it is completely phased out and reduced to zero at a combined income of $80,000 with one child. Interestingly, a family with five children and an income of $150,000 would receive a monthly benefit that includes both the CCTB and NCBS of $22.11 ($265 per year). There are also special benefits for children with disabilities. The benefit calculations are complex and confusing and are calculated by taxation authorities based upon the family's income tax submission for the previous year. Most families simply accept their monthly benefit without question. For families with fluctuating incomes or suddenly out of employment, a prior tax report will not reflect their current situation or current

need. Also, many First Nations families have had to submit tax forms for the first time in order to receive benefits.

Each of the provinces operates a system of benefits (from $2,000 to $5,000 per year) mainly designed to support the working poor. Those families on social assistance, however, usually saw their checks cut by an amount equal to the child benefit; hence, social assistance recipients saw no increase in benefits, and it is alleged that this created an incentive to enter the employment market.

Today, the Canada Child Tax Benefit and other family benefits constitute a substantial portion of the family incomes of low-income people, which certainly includes the working poor. The refundable Child Tax Benefit is the largest and best known of the redistributive tax credits and provides a cash benefit for persons with dependent children through the income tax system. By its structure, it provides its benefits to low-income earners, who depend upon low-paying labor, part-time or seasonal labor, and social assistance.

Parents with direct expenses for child care, incurred for employment, also can deduct these expenses from their income. These deductions take advantage of the progressive nature of the income tax structure, benefiting higher-income earners over lower-income earners. Low-income earners are also eligible for the GST/HST credit (goods and services tax/harmonized sales tax), which is a tax-free payment to assist individuals and families offset the cost of the federal and provincial sales taxes.

After nearly 50 years, the Family Allowance program and its simple and direct universality had drawn to a close. It has been replaced by a complicated and confusing array of programs with income ceilings and selectivity requirements for each program in each province.

—Douglas Durst

See also Social Security (Canada); Social Welfare (Canada): Before the Marsh Report; Social Welfare (Canada): Since the Marsh Report

Primary Sources

Booke Claxton Fonds and Department of Finance Fonds, Library and Archives Canada, Ottawa, ON; Executive director's report. (1926). *Canadian Child Welfare News, 2*(2); Canada, House of Commons, Select Standing Committee on Industrial and International Relations. (1928). *Report.* Ottawa, ON: King's Printer.

Current Comment

King, M. [Prime minister]. (1943). *King diaries.* Ottawa, ON: King's Printer.

Lebel, L. (1928). *Le problème de la famille nombreuse: Sa solution, les allocations familiales.* Montreal, QC: Imprimé par Le Devoir.

Marsh, L. C. (1943). *Social Security for Canada.* Ottawa: ON: King's Printer.

Ursel, J. (1992). *Private lives, public policy: 100 years of state intervention in the family.* Toronto, ON: Women's Press.

Current federal and provincial program child tax benefit rates are available on-line (www.ccra-adrc.gc.ca/benefits/menu-e.html).

Further Reading

Durst, D. (Ed.). (1999). *Canada's national child benefit: Phoenix or fizzle?* Halifax, NS: Fernwood.

Hunter, G. (2002). Child poverty and the Saskatchewan child poverty initiatives. *Prairie Forum, 27,* 45–57.

Kitchen, B. (1987). The introduction of family allowances in Canada. In A. Moscovitch & J. Albert (Eds.), *The benevolent state: The growth of welfare in Canada.* Toronto, ON: Garamond.

McGilly, F. (1998). *An introduction to Canada's public social services.* Don Mills, ON: Oxford University Press.

FAMILY SERVICE ASSOCIATION OF AMERICA (UNITED STATES)

Under various names, the Family Service Association of America has been a leader in the development of social work practice since its founding in 1911. The association evolved within the community organization society (COS) movement. Initially called the National Association of Societies for Organizing Charity, the association had over 200 local COS members within a few years of its founding and was devoted to consulting with local charity organization societies and coordinating their activities. The Russell Sage Foundation provided funds to employ the first general secretary of the association, Francis H. McLean. McLean was an advocate of the social casework approach pioneered by Mary Richmond, a Russell Sage staff member and COS pioneer. In 1919, under McLean's leadership, the association changed its name to the American Association for Organizing Family Social Work to reflect its emphasis on services to families. In 1922, the association took over the Institute of Family Social Work that Richmond had developed for the training of social work practitioners. During the 1920s, many local COS groups changed their names to family welfare agencies.

The association was a strong proponent of the professionalization of social work practice. In the late 1920s, as more states were creating departments of public welfare and staffing them with political patronage appointees, the association, along with the American Association of Social Workers, struggled to have social and public welfare work defined as a professional activity requiring appropriate training. The association promoted a vision of social work using casework as the primary method, regardless of institutional setting. By pushing for standards of work that spanned different types of agencies (hospital, public welfare, child welfare, and others), the association was influential in the creation of the idea of generalist social work practice. This commitment to the casework approach is reflected in the journal published by the association over the past century: Originally titled *The Family* (1920–1946), the publication was retitled the *Journal of Social Casework* (1946–1949), then *Social Casework* (1950–1989), and is now familiar to readers as *Families in Society* (1990 to the present).

During the Great Depression, the association was active at the national level informing legislators of the hardships of unemployment for families. Along with other nascent social welfare organizations, the association advocated for federal assistance to unemployed workers and their families. This time period saw a shift in the historical focus of the community organization societies. With the decision of the Federal Emergency Relief Agency to channel all depression-era financial assistance funds solely to public agencies, the traditional role of the COS in the provision of relief to the poor was diminished. Responding to this changing landscape, in 1934 the association's General Director Linton Swift urged member organizations to turn away from relief work with the poor and to focus on the provision of social casework to "disorganized families" that were experiencing problems with adjustment.

The trend toward individually focused casework intensified in the 1940s as the association responded to the events of World War II. During the war, the association published a series of bulletins on *Family Welfare and the Home Front* and instituted new programs to maintain the quality of family life. Local affiliates provided assistance to families with service members and families in which the mother had entered the workforce as part of the war effort. In the postwar period, the association refocused its efforts on training of social workers to provide counseling services, particularly in the burgeoning area of marriage counseling.

In 1998, Family Service of America (a later name for the association) merged with the National Association of Homes and Services for Children to create the Alliance for Children and Families, based in Milwaukee, Wisconsin. This newest incarnation continues the association's tradition of providing leadership and coordination of local affiliates to deliver family counseling services. Current major activities include national advocacy for children and families, executive management training, information and funding resources, capacity building of local affiliates, education, and networking. The current organization continues a focus that began in the 1960s on strengthening communities to improve family life. Over 300 family counseling agencies in Canada and the United States are members of the Alliance for Children and Families.

In addition to its journal, the association has also been a prolific publisher of tracts related to social work practice, annual reports, newsletters, and proceedings from numerous conferences that it has hosted regionally and nationally. Now known as the Alliance for Children and Families, the association has changed names eight times since its founding (see Table F.1).

—*Taryn Lindhorst*

See also Charity Organization Societies (United States)

Primary Sources

Family Service Association of America Records, Social Welfare History Archives, University of Minnesota, Minneapolis; Florence Hollis and Rosemary Ross Reynolds Papers, Sophia Smith Collection, Smith College, Northampton, MA; Mary

Table F.1   Names Adopted by the Family Service Association of America, 1911–1998

Year	Name of Association
1911	National Association of Societies for Organizing Charity
1912	American Association of Societies for Organizing Charity
1917	American Association for Organizing Charity
1919	American Association for Organizing Family Social Work
1930	Family Welfare Association of America
1946	Family Service Association of America
1983	Family Service of America
1998	Alliance for Children and Families

Richmond Papers, Rare Books & Manuscript Library, Butler Library, Columbia University, New York; Russell Sage Foundation Records, Rockefeller Archive Center, Rockefeller University, Sleepy Hollow, NY.

Current Comment

Swift, L. (1934). *New alignments between public and private agencies in a community family welfare and relief program.* New York: Family Welfare Association of America.

Further Reading

Ormsby, R. (1969). *A man of vision: Francis H. McLean, 1869–1945.* New York: Family Service Association of America.

Rich, M. (1956). *A belief in people: A history of family social work.* New York: Family Service Association of America.

FAMILY VIOLENCE (CANADA)

In Canada, family violence as a field of study and as a site for social policy and action has developed remarkably since the early 1970s. The issue has emerged as a significant element in understanding family relations and as a hotly contested site of state intervention. Family violence is understood as intentional harm that is physical, sexual, emotional, psychological, or economic in nature and is inflicted on one family member by another member or members. Included in family membership are biological, adoptive, and stepfamily relations; common-law as well as legally recognized relations; heterosexual and gay and lesbian family arrangements; and immediate as well as extended family. Within this understanding, family violence encompasses such diverse topics as spouse abuse, marital rape, child abuse, neglect, incest, elder abuse, sibling abuse, and abuse of parents.

Instances of family violence have been documented in Canada since the earliest colonial times. Indeed, analysts have suggested that the European conquest of Native peoples introduced rationales, often religious, for wife abuse and child abuse to the indigenous peoples. Coincidental with similar events in the United States, societal attention to family violence as a social issue crystallized in the late 1800s. It was at this point that children's aid societies emerged to rescue children who were abandoned or maltreated by their families. The first children's aid society in Canada was founded in Toronto in 1891. It was also at this time that the temperance movement targeted wife abuse as evidence of the ills of alcohol use. A social-class perspective conditioned much of this early understanding of family violence. Working-class women and children were seen to be the primary victims of family violence and this violence was understood as evidence of class-based patterns of drunkenness, poor discipline, and immorality. Not surprisingly, relatively little attention was paid to the issue.

In the 1960s, family violence was radically reassessed. No longer dismissed as a problem that plagued only alcoholics, derelicts, and the rural and urban poor, violence among family members was reconstructed as a social ill that afflicted all classes of families, occurred frequently, affected the most powerless members of the family, and had long-term negative consequences.

First to emerge in this rethinking of the issue was child abuse. Once the notion of the "battered child syndrome" gained currency in medical communities, the seriousness and pervasiveness of child abuse was quickly established. Mary van Stolk's 1972 book on the battered child in Canada was followed by a 1980 Senate report providing the earliest estimates of child abuse rates. In 1984, Robin Badgley's monumental study on sexual offenses against Canadian young people firmly identified child abuse as an issue warranting investigation and action.

Wife abuse was soon also etched into the public consciousness. Fueled by the emergence of the contemporary women's movement, research into violence against women was given an enormous impetus. Almost immediately, women's rights advocates were mobilizing support for shelters for battered women and, by 1972, the first such shelters were established in British Columbia and Alberta. Reflecting the mushrooming concern over wife abuse, by the 1990s a network of more than 400 shelters had been established across Canada.

The establishment of woman abuse (a term identifying women in a variety of intimate relationships including legal marriage) as a central issue promoted research into the topic. The first important study in the area, completed by Linda MacLeod in 1980, was an interview survey of women living in shelters across Canada. Such early efforts were followed rapidly by a succession of increasingly rigorous and in-depth studies. Most notable was the 1993 survey on violence against women. This landmark research compiled a nationally representative sample of Canadian women and collected telephone interview data on their experiences of violence, including intimate violence. Putting to rest previous assertions that woman abuse was exceptional, this survey documented that upwards of one-quarter of women had experienced violence at the hands of a past or present intimate partner. Subsequent surveys, notably the 1999 General Social Survey on Victimization and recent national family violence profiles, continue to document the extent of woman abuse.

Simultaneously, there were important advances in child abuse research. Efforts were made to collate and analyze child abuse rates as reported by child protection agencies at both the provincial and national levels. Researchers provided more refined and in-depth examinations of child abuse experiences. Particular attention focused on the institutionalized child abuse that was recorded in government-created residential schools for aboriginal communities and various religious and training schools. This child abuse was found to often cascade into the surrounding communities as victims formed their own families and replicated patterns of victimization.

By the end of the twentieth century, family violence issues had assumed center stage in many social research and public discourses. A number of organizations played pivotal roles in these efforts. Notably, the Vanier Institute of the Family, established in 1965 as a national voluntary organization dedicated to promoting the well-being of Canada's families through education, research, and advocacy, helped disseminate information on family violence. In 1982, the federal government established the National Clearinghouse on Family Violence to provide information and consultation services for professionals as well as a base for public education. The clearinghouse's numerous family violence publications and website became a key resource for researchers and policymakers. The federal government also funded a variety of other important research and informational initiatives. In particular, in 1992 Health Canada, in collaboration with the Social Sciences and Humanities Research Council as well as other organizations, established five research centers on family violence and violence against women across Canada.

Various other groups and organizations also contributed to the effort. For example, organized labor groups supported research and education on family violence. Some research focused on specific segments of the population. The National Aboriginal Project (Proulx & Perrault, 2000) conducted interviews with aboriginal children and youth across Canada and focused on physical, sexual, and emotional abuse. Regional initiatives were also launched. In the Prairie provinces, a network called Research and Education for Solutions to Violence and Abuse (RESOLVE) funds and disseminates research on family violence.

In the course of these research efforts, the meaning of family violence was expanded. Senior abuse, the abuse of adult parents by teens, and violence among siblings all were revealed as important facets of family violence. Researchers also explored the ways in which diverse families experienced violence. Research examined gay and lesbian families; immigrant, rural, visible minority, and poor families; and families in which one or several members were disabled. Increasingly, family violence was approached as a complex and multifaceted issue.

Reflecting these advances in social research, changes were introduced in the criminal justice responses. The compulsory charging of violent spouses by the police, the increased provision of specialized domestic violence training for police, the introduction of increasing numbers of special family violence courts, along with the popularization of court-mandated anger management courses all speak to the search to refine responses to woman abuse. Similar efforts were made to assist child victims. Videotaped court testimony from child victims was permitted and restrictive time limitations on the laying of abuse charges by adults abused in their childhood years were lifted. In addition, more severe sentences were mandated for those convicted of child abuse.

Despite these enormous shifts in understanding and responding to family violence, it remains a contentious issue. For example, the dividing line between spanking, as appropriate discipline of children, and spanking, as child abuse, is hotly contested. Similarly, the failure of the criminal justice system to provide adequate protection to children who are at risk from their parents and to women who leave their abusive spouses has evoked considerable public debate. It is not yet clear how the rights of the assailant to the presumption of innocence and due process can be balanced against the victim's right to protection from often deadly attack.

The last three decades have been a dramatic and dynamic period for research into and responses to family violence in Canada. No longer dismissed as rare or harmless, the complexity and diversity of violence among intimates is now being fully explored. The mushrooming research record has, in turn, spawned a variety of new social policy initiatives. Improved understanding of the dynamics and contradictions within family violence are likely to result in increasingly nuanced social policy responses in the future.

—Ann Duffy

See also Women and Poverty (Canada)

Primary Sources

The Alliance of Five Research Centres on Violence (British Columbia/Yukon, Manitoba, Ontario, Quebec, New Brunswick) has links to each of its centers on its website (www.uwo.ca/violence/linked/alliance/english.htm); the National Clearinghouse on Family Violence (NCFV), Health Communities Division of

Health Canada, Ottawa, ON, can also be accessed on-line (www.hc-sc.gc.ca/hppb/familyviolence/).

Current Comment

Committee on Sexual Offences Against Children and Youth. (1984). Sexual offences against children [Badgley Report]. In *Proceedings of the Social Service Congress of 1914*. Ottawa, ON: Department of Supply and Services Canada.
National Clearinghouse on Family Violence [On-line]. Available: www.hc-sc.gc.ca/nc-cn
Van Stolk, M. (1972). *The battered child in Canada*. Toronto, ON: McClelland & Stewart.

Further Reading

Duffy, A. D., & Momirov, J. (1997). *Family violence: A Canadian introduction*. Toronto, ON: Lorimer.
Harrison, D. (2002). *The first casualty: Violence against women in Canadian military communities*. Toronto, ON: Lorimer.
Proulx, J., & Perrault, S. (Eds.). (2000). *No place for violence: Canadian aboriginal alternatives*. Halifax, NS: Fernwood.
Ristock, J. (2002). *No more secrets: Violence in lesbian relationships*. New York: Routledge.

FAMILY VIOLENCE (MEXICO)

Family violence, also known as domestic violence, can include acts of power, recurrent or cyclical, as well as acts of intentional omission directed against a family member. The main objectives are to cause harm, dominate, subjugate, control, and/or physically, verbally, or sexually abuse any member of the family whether in or out of the household. To consider such aggression as domestic violence, a connection between the aggressor and the victim needs to exist, whether by current or previous affinity, marriage, or partnership. It is important to mention that in international norms, no specific definition of domestic violence exists. On the other hand, for battered women, there is a specific definition. The United Nations *Convention on the Elimination of All Forms of Discrimination Against Women* (1979) defines all acts based on gender differences that damage or could damage women physically, sexually, or psychologically as violence against women.

Since the 1970s, feminists have actively attacked this worldwide problem, which exists among many different cultures, races, religions, and socioeconomic systems. It is generally manifested in male violence

directed against women, or in violence directed against children, the elderly, and the physically and mentally disabled. In many of these cases, it is an abuse of power over the most vulnerable people in the home.

Domestic violence is not only a social problem; it is also a public health problem. The World Bank has determined that violence directed against women, including domestic violence, is responsible for a 5 percent loss of a woman's health during her reproductive years in demographically developed countries. According to the World Health Organization, violence against women between the ages of 15 to 44 is responsible for more deaths and incapacitation than all other causes, including cancer, malaria, traffic accidents, and war.

Violence against women also has implications for sexual and reproductive health. It contributes to undesired pregnancies and therefore to abortions. Frequently, women living with violent spouses cannot make their own decisions regarding birth control, thus increasing the incidence of venereal diseases and HIV/AIDS.

Several international agreements clearly establish that violence against women and children constitutes a violation of human rights. These agreements include the *Convention on the Elimination of All Forms of Discrimination Against Women* (United Nations, 1979), the *Convention on the Rights of the Child* (United Nations, 1989), and the *Inter-American Convention on the Prevention, Punishment, and Eradication of Violence against Women, "Convention of Belém Do Pará"* (Organization of American States, 1994). As a result of these conventions, the Mexican government committed itself to oppose family violence.

In Mexico, one of the most recent advances in legislation was a 1997 revision of the civil and penal code that established that all family members have the right to have their physical and emotional integrity respected. In the legislation of many Mexican states, domestic violence is classified as a crime and offenders are sanctioned.

Domestic violence can be classified as physical, psychological, or patrimonial aggression. Physical violence refers to acts of intentional aggression where any part of the body is utilized, immobilized, or causes harm to another person using an object, a weapon, or a substance, including a range of behaviors from light hits to sexual abuse and mortal injuries. Frequently, women and children suffer this violence and, on occasion, the elderly too; yet it is unlikely to be reported. In the majority of the cases, the aggressor is someone close to the victim, usually a relative, member of the family, neighbor, or a friend of the family. Sexual abuse of children is defined as interactions between a minor and an adult or adolescent in which the minor is used for sexual gratification. This may be done through persuasion, threats, harassment, use of authority, or physical force. Other acts can be considered sexual abuse, for example, exhibitionism, pornography, genital manipulation, rape, and genital mutilation. In the case of adult women, sexual abuse is defined as actions that use physical force, blackmail, bribery, intimidation, or threats to obtain sexual relations or undesired sexual acts, prostitution, or genital mutilation. It is important to point out that in some countries violence in a marriage is typified as a crime, whereas in other countries coerced sexual relations are seen as a wife's obligation.

Psychological violence consists of acts or omissions that are repeated or expressed through verbal aggression, threats, prohibitions, intimidation, indifference, disdain, humiliation, abandonment, or lack of affection. Although these acts do not leave any physical injuries, the harm that is done is not minor because it affects mental health and self-esteem.

Material or patrimonial violence is defined as controlling, limiting, or denying economic resources. This is forbidding access to goods or services that threaten the well-being of any member of the family. Domestic violence also takes its toll when children witness violence between their parents. Some studies show that infants who are subjected to such exposure also are placed in danger.

—*Martha Alida Ramirez Solorzano*

See also Economic Crises, Family and Gender, 1980s to the Present (Mexico); Women and Social Welfare (Mexico)

Current Comment

Organization of American States. (1994). *Inter-American Convention on the Prevention, Punishment, and Eradication of Violence against Women, "Convention of Belém Do Pará"* [On-line]. Available: www.oas.org/main/main.asp? sLang= E&sLink=http://www.oas.org/documents/eng/documents.asp

United Nations Division for the Advancement of Women, Department of Economic and Social Affairs. (1979). *Convention on the Elimination of All Forms of Discrimination Against Women* [On-line]. Available: www.un.org/womenwatch/ daw/cedaw/cedaw.htm
United Nations Office of the High Commissioner for Human Rights. (1989). *Convention on the Rights of the Child* [On-line]. Available:www.unhchr.ch/html/menu3/b/k2crc.htm

Further Reading

Cámara de Diputados. (2001). *Violencia en casa.* Mexico City.
Ramírez Solórzano, M. A. (2002). *Hombres violentos. Un estudio antropológico de la violencia masculina.* Mexico City: Plaza y Valdés.
Torres Falcón, M. (2001). *La violencia en casa.* Mexico City: Croma Paidós.
World Bank. (1993). *World development report 1993: Investing in health.* New York: Oxford University Press.
World Health Organization. (1997). *Violence against women: A priority health issue* [On-line]. Available: www.who.int/ gender/violence/prioreng/en/

FAMILY VIOLENCE (UNITED STATES)

One of the distinctive characteristics of family violence is the difficulty researchers, clinicians, and policymakers have had in defining it. Family violence is often considered to be violent physical acts against a person with whom one lives, is related to, and/or with whom one has an intimate relationship; but it also includes nonviolent acts and/or omissions, such as psychological abuse and neglect. Most family violence policy, however, has focused on physical acts and neglect.

The literature on the development of family violence policy in the United States focuses on themes of family privacy, government interference in the family, and violence control. Key issues have included whether policy should focus on compassion in providing services to victims, or on maintaining social order by controlling violent perpetrators.

Historian Elizabeth Pleck has asserted that interest in family violence was connected to whether or not society has seen family privacy as more important than investigation into family problems. Family privacy in the nineteenth century was seen as secondary to ensuring the purity of the family. Family violence was seen as deviant; some communities punished wife beaters by tying them to whipping posts. Violent, lower-class, immigrant men were perceived as the primary perpetrators of family violence. In the 1870s, the Society for the Prevention of Cruelty to Children grew out of the Society for the Prevention of Cruelty to Animals. Society workers were concerned primarily with child abuse, but also dealt informally with wife abuse. Overall, family violence in the late nineteenth century was a problem addressed by charity organizations and moral reform movements. Some feminist reformers who spoke out against family violence were criticized for encouraging divorce and the breakup of the family.

Family breakup or disintegration of the family was thought to have negative consequences, especially in creating problems for children, such as delinquency. In the early twentieth century, one of the primary concerns in social welfare was to prevent child delinquency. The first White House Conference on Dependent Children was held in 1909 and the U.S. Children's Bureau was established in 1912, demonstrating government interest in child welfare issues. During the Progressive Era, states established mothers' aid programs to help children whose fathers had either died or deserted them, to keep them from becoming delinquents. During the 1920s, however, family violence "disputes" that showed up in domestic relations courts were most often referred for counseling and were not considered a violation of criminal law.

The Great Depression turned the attention of policymakers and social welfare advocates toward restoring employment, and interest in family violence waned. The New Deal's Social Security Act of 1935 redirected awareness toward child welfare. Title V of the act provided money for the states to develop child welfare services. After World War II, social welfare focused on promoting and encouraging the "ideal" family. Traditional ideas of what was expected of mothers coincided with the decline of feminism and a decreased focus on family violence until the 1960s.

The atmosphere of social reform of the 1960s brought family violence back to the attention of social welfare advocates. The civil rights movement and the women's movement encouraged the resurgence of feminist ideas that challenged the structure of the traditional, ideal family, and emphasized the danger

of policies that discouraged looking into family problems. This issue had been raised before; in 1946, for example, a pediatric radiologist had asserted that parents were the likely causes of children's bone fractures. It was not until 1962, however, that the issue of family violence became an issue of public concern. A paper published in the *Journal of the American Medical Association* on "battered child syndrome" included guidelines for pediatricians to recognize child abuse and noted the likelihood of parents causing such injury. As a result of this work, by 1971 every state had laws that mandated the reporting of child abuse. During this time, interest in all forms of family violence peaked, but child abuse was the focus of most attention.

The "discovery" of child abuse in the 1960s set off a flurry of legislation that has not ceased. In 1967, Congress added Title IV-B, the Child Welfare Services and Promoting Safe and Stable Families Program (formerly the Family Preservation and Support Services Program), to the Social Security Act, which focused on protecting and promoting the welfare of children, preventing situations that could lead to child abuse or neglect, averting family separation, and reuniting families. Interest in understanding the causes of child abuse became increasingly important in the 1970s. The passage of the Child Abuse Prevention and Treatment Act (CAPTA) of 1974 established research and demonstration projects, and the National Center on Child Abuse and Neglect (NCCAN) was created. Research surveys conducted during this time revealed that family violence was more common than previously thought, and affected more than just the lower classes. These findings sparked the interest of clinicians, researchers, policymakers, and activists, and thus the 1980s saw a plethora of studies and policy initiatives.

In 1980, weaknesses in the child welfare system were acknowledged, and Congress enacted the federal Adoption Assistance and Child Welfare Act to encourage family preservation. This act was amended in 1997 to recognize that family preservation was not always the best option for abused children. Movements were made toward prevention of abuse and compensation for abuse victims in 1984 with the passage of the Victims of Crime Act (VOCA). The

Office for Victims of Crime was established by VOCA to provide child abuse prevention and treatment grants; funds for victim compensation, advocacy, assistance, and emergency shelter; and counseling for abuse victims. Priority was given to victims of domestic violence, sexual abuse, and child abuse, marking the act as one of the landmarks of family violence policy.

The 1970s were also active years for domestic violence legislation. The first battered women's shelters opened in the early 1970s due to the efforts of advocates for battered women. They worked to establish state and federal funding for the creation and maintenance of shelters for victims of abuse and advocacy programs for battered women and their children. President Jimmy Carter's efforts to address domestic violence in the late 1970s were stymied when President Ronald Reagan did not support domestic violence bills. Although President Carter established the Office of Domestic Violence as an information clearinghouse, it was dismantled early in the Reagan administration because of advocacy by social conservatives who believed social welfare programs promoted dependency and the breakdown of the family. State rather than federal responsibility for some social welfare programs was preferred. Some conservative policy analysts suggested that focusing on family violence led to a weakening of basic family values and encouragement of family breakup.

Although there was a decline in interest in family violence in the 1980s, the 1970s Child Abuse Prevention and Treatment Act (CAPTA) was reauthorized. The Family Violence Prevention and Services Act (FVPSA), part of the 1984 amendments to the Child Abuse Prevention and Treatment Act of 1974, provided grants for shelters for abused women and children, counseling, and related services. Research and law-enforcement training were considered priorities for the FVPSA; the act was reauthorized in 1993. Four years later, CAPTA became part of the Child Abuse Prevention, Adoption, and Family Services Act of 1988. The Child Abuse, Domestic Violence, Adoption, and Family Services Act of 1992 (amended in 1992 and reauthorized in 1996) provided funding to states for assessment, prevention, prosecution of perpetrators, and treatment grants for nonprofit and public agencies.

In 1994, the Violent Crime Control and Law Enforcement Act was passed, and CAPTA was included under its auspices. This act was a significant step forward for family violence policy. Title IV of the act, the Violence Against Women Act (VAWA), was important acknowledgment of federal responsibility for preventing domestic violence. It called for improved coordination of law enforcement responses to domestic violence victims and encouraged the police to arrest perpetrators. VAWA was influenced in part by research findings that law enforcement and criminal justice personnel treated spousal assault cases less seriously than other assault cases, and by findings that suggested arrest deters perpetrators in spousal assault cases. Although these findings were later disputed, this research has had a profound effect on domestic violence policy. The Violence Against Women Act was reauthorized as the Victims of Trafficking and Violence Prevention Act of 2000, providing grants to assist states and Indian tribes in providing shelter and other types of assistance for victims of violence and their dependents, and for preventing several types of family violence, including elder abuse.

Federal family violence policy today emphasizes keeping victims safe from violence, often involving physical separation of the victim from the perpetrator. The emotional and financial ties between victims and perpetrators complicate keeping victims of abuse separated from their perpetrators. Future comprehensive family violence policies must involve a network of coordinated social systems that address family violence by balancing issues of compassion and control.

—Cyleste Cassandra Collins

Current Comment

Renzetti, C. M., Edelson, J. L., & Kennedy Bergen, R. (Eds.). (2001). *Sourcebook on violence against women.* Thousand Oaks, CA: Sage.

Further Reading

Daniels, C. R. (Ed.). (1997). *Feminists negotiate the state: The politics of domestic violence.* Lanham, MD: University Press of America.

Gordon, L. (1988). *Heroes of their own lives: The politics and history of family violence.* New York: Penguin.

Pleck, E. (1987). *Domestic tyranny: The making of social policy against family violence from colonial times to the present.* New York: Oxford University Press.

FEDERALISM AND SOCIAL WELFARE POLICY (CANADA)

Canada became a federation with the establishment of the British North American (BNA) Act of 1867, which was later incorporated into the Constitution Act of 1982. Embedded within the constitutional framework of the 1867 BNA Act is a recognition of two distinct jurisdictions and related separation of powers, whereby two orders of government are assigned particular authorities and responsibilities that neither order may unilaterally amend. The division of legislative powers between federal and provincial jurisdictions largely determines authority and responsibility for social welfare policy. Furthermore, the extent of social welfare services and programs available to citizens is driven by each government's political will and fiscal ability to finance social welfare initiatives. In general, social welfare policy is shaped by divergent and oftentimes conflicting dynamics within Canadian federalism.

Prior to the 1867 BNA Act, early political entities were established in Canada by French and English colonial authorities, and by First Nations peoples. For example, the Royal Proclamation of 1763 created the colony of Quebec, acknowledged First Nations' land rights, and partitioned land for hunting grounds and European settlements. Later, the 1840 Act of Union unified the colonies of Upper and Lower Canada, which were inhabited primarily by English- and French-speaking populations, respectively. Confederation was eventually achieved in 1867 by uniting the provinces of Ontario, Quebec, Nova Scotia, and New Brunswick.

CONSTITUTIONAL FRAMEWORK OF THE BNA ACT AND SOCIAL WELFARE POLICY

The 1867 BNA Act allocated exclusively federal, exclusively provincial, and concurrent legislative powers. The federal government was allocated powers over matters considered to be important to the economic performance of the nation, including taxation, trade and commerce, public debt, currency, and banking. Section 92 of the BNA Act assigned provinces with authority over areas such as justice, civil rights, provincial property rights, hospitals, charities, and any provincial matters considered to be local or private in nature. Section 93 of the Constitution gave the provinces exclusive jurisdiction over education. The BNA Act also gave provinces exclusive responsibility over social welfare matters not granted to the federal government. For example, the federal government was assigned jurisdiction over all matters related to First Nations peoples and the military, including authority over social welfare. In addition, whereas the majority of legislative powers were assigned exclusively to either order of government, jurisdiction over matters not identified in the Constitution, otherwise known as residual powers, were allocated to the federal government. Specifically, Section 91 of the Constitution assigned the federal government the power to make laws for the "peace, order and good government" of the country in areas not assigned exclusively to the provinces. Federal involvement in social welfare is often justified on the basis of this residual power and the constitutional right of the federal government to collect taxes and allocate financial resources.

EARLY SOCIAL WELFARE PROVISIONS

At the time of Confederation, although variation existed across regions, government involvement in poor relief was minimal, and social welfare was considered to be predominantly a personal and family responsibility. In Lower Canada, charity was mainly the domain of the church; and in Upper Canada, voluntary organizations played a major role in responding to social need. In Nova Scotia and New Brunswick, the approach to poverty was adopted from the 1601 English Poor Law and, accordingly, municipalities administered only rudimentary poor relief. In 1867, it was assumed that municipalities would eventually acquire primary responsibility for social welfare. The architects of the 1867 BNA Act foresaw neither the significant growth in federal and provincial social responsibilities witnessed in the twentieth century, nor the considerable increase in citizens' expectations pertaining to social welfare provision.

FEDERALISM AND POSTWAR SOCIAL WELFARE POLICY

As the twentieth century progressed, urbanization and the modernization of industrial society vastly increased the need for social welfare programs and services. Yet, controversy over the proper role of each order of government eluded consensus about how social welfare provision should be developed. Debate centered on divergent interpretations of the Constitution and both federal and provincial governments were protective of their jurisdictions.

Although the 1867 BNA Act designated social welfare largely as a provincial responsibility, it is a popular assumption that social policy is very closely tied to the federal role in Canada. The Great Depression altered the provisions set out in the 1867 BNA Act, as the country faced overflowing municipal welfare rolls and soaring unemployment. Provinces and municipalities struggled to provide relief to millions of jobless Canadians who could not control the economic downturns that led to unemployment. Prior to 1940, and as prescribed by the BNA Act, responsibility for matters related to unemployment fell under provincial authority. The challenges posed, however, by the lack of provincial and municipal capacity to respond to the tremendous hardships experienced during the Great Depression pointed to the need for a national social insurance program. The Employment and Social Insurance Act, introduced in Parliament in 1935, was defeated on constitutional grounds as it was alleged that the federal government was attempting to intrude in an area of provincial jurisdiction. Nevertheless, the Constitution was eventually amended to give the federal government the authority needed to pass the Unemployment Insurance Act in 1940.

In 1941, federal and provincial governments agreed on tax arrangements that permitted the federal government to collect taxes on behalf of the provinces. Consequently, federal control over postwar social welfare provision began to emerge. Canada, along with several other industrialized nations, entered into the Keynesian period of macroeconomic welfare state development. Both orders of government, federal and provincial, instituted a series of social programs over the next two decades, stimulated by federal conditional grants and cost-sharing programs. For example, in 1966 the Canada Assistance Plan (CAP) was introduced. Under CAP, federal and provincial governments shared costs on a 50-50 basis for health insurance, education, and welfare. In addition, in the 1960s the federal government introduced the Canada/Quebec Pension Plan.

FISCAL INSTABILITY AND SOCIAL WELFARE POLICY

Although the federal government played a pivotal role in establishing and maintaining social programs in Canada, this strong federal presence began to fade in the 1970s, when the Keynesian foundations of the postwar settlement started to destabilize. Productivity waned as government spending and ensuing debt climbed. Faced with economic recession in the early 1980s, governments chose to abandon full-employment policies and focus on curbing inflation. Not unlike many other countries in the Organisation for Economic Cooperation and Development (OECD), the burgeoning public debt in Canada added incentive to calls for social policy reform. Both federal and provincial governments exercised fiscal restraint that resulted in significant decreases in spending on social welfare policy. For example, the 1995 federal budget announced major changes to federal fiscal transfer programs to provinces. The federal government merged the Established Programs Financing (EPF) and the Canada Assistance Plan (CAP) into the Canada Health and Social Transfer (CHST). As part of the reform, federal conditions about how provinces could spend funds were reduced. Whereas CAP prescribed federal standards on social spending, the CHST removed all conditions with the exception of disallowing provinces to impose residency requirements for social assistance benefits. Moreover, the federal government made steep reductions in the amount of transfer funds received by provinces. In turn, reductions in federal transfers led to further decreases in social spending at the provincial level.

LATTER TWENTIETH CENTURY CONSTITUTIONAL DEBATE AND SOCIAL WELFARE

In addition to pressures stemming from fiscal concerns, federal and provincial governments were involved in constitutional deliberations during the 1980s and early 1990s. In part, what emerged from this debate was a concerted provincial challenge directed against the status quo division of roles and responsibilities between federal and provincial governments. Provinces, albeit for different reasons, demanded greater control and authority over social welfare policy. For example, to protect its cultural heritage and, indeed, its uniqueness in Canada, the province of Quebec demanded constitutional recognition of its distinctiveness as well as more autonomy over social welfare policy. Other provinces, provoked by federal fiscal restraint, also strived for greater responsibility and control over social policy. These debates, however, must be understood as having taken place among provinces with lesser and greater fiscal capacity. Motivated by different expectations of federalism, richer and poorer provinces asserted dissimilar priorities and positions about the appropriate federal-provincial division of responsibilities for social policy.

Quebec's longstanding dissatisfaction with federalism manifested itself in a number of positions, ranging from demands for greater devolution of federal powers, and recognition of its distinct position in Canada, to calls for sovereignty. Evidence of the discord between Quebec and the rest of Canada is its status as the only province not to sign the Constitution Act of 1982. The 1982 Constitution Act and the Charter of Rights and Freedoms entrenched in the act were strongly supported by then Canadian prime minister, Pierre Elliott Trudeau. Trudeau vied for Quebec nationalism, and he was reluctant to recognize Quebec as a distinct society for fear this would lead to special status for the province.

Constitutional debate continued to preoccupy federal-provincial relations into the 1990s. During this time, federal and provincial governments made two additional attempts to bring Quebec back into the fold, both of which resulted in failure. In 1987, the Meech Lake Accord initially expressed a consensus among the federal government and all 10 provinces. It was considered a historic achievement as it recognized Quebec as a distinct society. Because the Meech Lake Accord would revise the Constitution, it required the approval of all provincial legislatures before the ratification deadline of June 23, 1990. Two provincial governments, namely Manitoba and Newfoundland, did not pass the resolution within the specified time frame. Shortly thereafter, the premier of Quebec, Robert Bourassa, announced that the province would not participate in future intergovernmental meetings, and the Quebec National Assembly initiated plans for a referendum on sovereignty. Two years after the failure of the Meech Lake Accord, however, constitutional negotiations resumed. The provincial governments hammered out another agreement, known as the Charlottetown Accord, but it was rejected by Canadians, including the citizens of Quebec, in a national referendum in 1992. The unity crisis was extreme and pitched higher still when a sovereignty referendum in Quebec was defeated by only a few percentage points in October 1995.

CONTRASTING PROVINCIAL PERSPECTIVES: CALLS FOR AUTONOMY AND EQUITY

The severity of federal fiscal restraint fueled resentment and frustration in the provinces. As the 1990s progressed, provinces asserted their demands for increased financial resources and for more jurisdictional powers over social policy. At the Annual Premiers' Conference in 1994, concern was expressed over what was perceived as the lack of efficiency and effectiveness of national social programs. Premiers agreed to collaboratively pursue an agenda of social policy reform, and, at the 1995 Annual Premiers' Conference, the Ministerial Council on Social Policy Reform and Renewal was established. The ministerial council's *Report to Premiers* was released in early January 1996 and represents a consensus perspective among all provinces except for Quebec. Generally, the report is a reaction to several years of federal unilateral fiscal decision making that increased provincial costs pertaining to social policy. The report emphasizes the problem of high costs and loss of accountability associated with the overlap and duplication of federal and provincial programs, and points to the need for clarifying roles and responsibilities of both orders of government. Accordingly, the report calls for adequate levels of federal fiscal transfer payments to the provinces in order to fund social policy, and more cooperation and dialogue between the two orders of government prior to initiating major changes in social policy.

In addition to the challenges that stem from Quebec's unique history and its desire for greater autonomy, and the demands from other provinces for revised federal-provincial arrangements, Canadian federalism is marked by divisiveness between richer and poorer provinces. In the 1990s, calls for increased provincial autonomy contrasted with calls for greater equity among provinces. Conflicting provincial views that stem from disparities in provincial wealth serve to challenge consensus about the purpose of federalism in relation to social welfare policy. Although the federal government's fiscal support for social welfare policy has fluctuated with economic downturns and upswings and shifts in political ideology, there remains a strong reliance on federal mechanisms such as equalization payments to redistribute wealth among provinces. Challenges to national policy instruments that redistribute wealth undermine the goal of provincial equity and the provision of comparable levels of social welfare programs and services across the country.

At the end of the twentieth century, governments sought out collaborative solutions to renew and modernize social policy. In 1999, the federal government and all of the provinces and territories except for Quebec signed the Social Union Framework Agreement (SUFA). As part of the agreement and driven primarily by its renewed economic health, the federal government committed itself to significant increases in transfer payments. Moreover, the federal government agreed to consult with other governments about implementing major funding changes at least one year in advance of any changes. In shared areas of jurisdictional authority, a simple majority of the provinces must consent to new federal programs. Prior to this agreement such federal activity required the consent of seven provinces representing at least

50 percent of the population. SUFA commits both orders of government to work together to improve social welfare policy for Canadians. To this date, child poverty and disability are among the social policy issues selected as priorities to be addressed through intergovernmental collaboration.

—Erin Gray

See also Aboriginal People and Policy (Canada); The Marsh Report (Canada), Quebec Province Social Welfare Policy (Canada); Social Security (Canada); Social Welfare (Canada): Before the Marsh Report; Social Welfare (Canada): Since the Marsh Report

Primary Sources

British North America Act of 1867 and the Constitution Act of 1982; other pertinent documents include the Meech Lake and Charlottetown accords; reports and communiqués from Annual Premiers' Conferences, such as the Ministerial Council on Social Policy Reform and Renewal's *Report to Premiers* (1995); and *A Framework to Improve the Social Union for Canadians* (1999).

Current Comment

Banting, K. G. (1987). *The welfare state and Canadian federalism* (2nd ed.). Montreal, QC, and Kingston, ON: McGill-Queen's University Press.

Guest, D. (1985). *The emergence of Social Security in Canada* (2nd ed.). Vancouver: University of British Columbia.

Ismael, J. S. (Ed.). (1985). *Canadian social welfare policy: Federal and provincial dimensions* (Canadian Public Administration Series No. 12). Montreal, QC, and Kingston, ON: McGill-Queen's University Press.

Rice, J. J., & Prince, M. J. (2000). *Changing politics of Canadian social policy.* Toronto, ON: University of Toronto Press.

Further Reading

Assessing ACCESS (A Convention on the Canadian Economic and Social Systems): Towards a new social union. (1997). *Proceedings of the symposium on the Courchene proposal.* Kingston, ON: Queen's University, Institute of Intergovernmental Relations.

Bakvis, H., & Skogstad, G. (Eds.). (2002). *Canadian federalism: Performance, effectiveness, and legitimacy.* Don Mills, ON: Oxford University Press.

Gibbins, R., & Laforest, G. (Eds.). (1998). *Beyond the impasse: Toward reconciliation.* Montreal, QC: Institute for Research on Public Policy.

Young, R. (Ed.). (1999). *Stretching the federation: The art of the state in Canada.* Kingston, ON: Queen's University, Institute of Intergovernmental Relations.

FEDERALISM AND SOCIAL WELFARE POLICY (UNITED STATES)

The history of social welfare policy in the United States has been marked by great tension between states' demands for substantial control over assistance programs and federal urges to impose national standards. At stake for states are potentially troubling economic and moral implications posed by programs that provoke debates over lifestyle questions or that offer exit options from a low-wage labor market, among other concerns. Complicating these matters, cross-institution disagreements at the national level, typically though not always between Congress and the executive branch, have frequently aggravated the awkward balances of social policy struck in the context of a federalist system. Programs ranging from the Works Progress Administration to Aid to Families With Dependent Children (AFDC) and Medicaid have been at the crux of deep disagreements over state versus national control. Part of this difficulty is explained by the trade-off between competing goals—substantive and procedural—among policymakers. The well-worn argument about proximal government being good government, implying state dominance in designing solutions to state problems (an argument about process), has alternately been touted as a central principle or been quietly ignored in favor of advancing a set of substantive goals mandated by Congress.

Scholars have pointed to the frequent inability of the states and the national government to arrive at mutually agreeable and enduring compromises as a source of significant weakness in social programs. Problems ranging from the mundane, including fiscal inefficiency, to the severe, such as outright racial discrimination, have characterized the nation's chief cash assistance program for low-income families, AFDC (remade into Temporary Assistance for Needy Families, or TANF, in 1996).

Cash assistance to poor families with children and medical assistance to a somewhat wider clientele provide two examples of social policy that illustrate some of these cross-level tensions. Cash assistance, the nation's quintessential welfare program, began as Aid to Dependent Children, a federal-state shared program under the Social Security Act of 1935. Earlier aid programs, such as mothers' pensions, were operated entirely by states or cities during the early twentieth century. By the late 1980s, medical assistance, formalized in the Medicaid program legislated in 1965, grew into the second-most expensive program states administer, next to education. Both these programs illustrate successes and failures. States use the latitude provided by federal law to experiment, as U.S. Supreme Court Justice Louis Brandeis famously termed, making them "laboratories of democracy." The histories of other social welfare programs, including Unemployment Insurance and Food Stamps, also include both positive and negative by-products of American federalism.

The relative differences in financial abilities and geographic sizes of states versus the nation suggest more or less optimal divisions of authority across levels of government. Paul Peterson, a respected scholar on federalism, distinguishes between developmental and redistributive programs (the former geared to promote economic development, the latter public aid) and suggests states may choose to perform minimally at redistributive tasks that would shift money or assets to those in need. No state wants to be perceived as a welfare magnet, or one that attracts the poor. Conversely, states should excel at developmental programs, since their own economic futures lie at stake. Peterson's suggested division of labor—states leading on developmental programs and the federal government assuming a larger role in redistribution—has not always fit the actual allocation of responsibilities under American federalism. Arguably, programs under-perform as a result. One example is fiscal opportunism by states during the late 1980s and early 1990s under the Medicaid program. Many states took advantage of a loophole in federal Medicaid law to draw down tens of millions of federal dollars that Congress never intended them to receive.

When President Franklin Roosevelt's administration drafted Title IV of what would become the Social Security Act in the 1930s, it included language that would have mandated states to provide poor families with enough of a cash benefit to allow "a reasonable subsistence compatible with decency and health." Reacting to objections from southern Congress members fearful of an exodus of low-wage African American workers from the southern labor market, the bill was amended to require states to provide assistance only "as far as practicable under the circumstances of such state." This permitted states to pay benefits, subsidized with federal dollars, at whatever level they desired. As a legacy of this early decision, cash benefit levels differ dramatically across states, with the most generous of the 48 continental states paying more than four times that paid by the least generous. The Temporary Assistance for Needy Families (TANF) program that replaced AFDC in 1996 has no mandated state minimum payment to poor families. Jill Quadagno's study of old-age insurance under Social Security traces similar state concerns over eligibility. In the early years of Social Security, substantial state discretion prevailed regarding eligibility guidelines. Congress reduced that state discretion over time.

States have also used the latitude afforded them to discriminate along lines of class, race, and lifestyle. Winifred Bell's history of Aid to Dependent Children explains the use of suitable home and substitute parent provisions. Under these rules, states targeted mothers who bore children or who had sexual relationships outside of marriage for exclusion from the welfare rolls. In the agricultural South of the 1940s and 1950s, purges of public assistance rolls were common during planting and harvest seasons. These were based on the assumption that employment opportunities abounded, despite language in the Social Security Act mandating program access for all eligible individuals implicitly suggesting access at any time of the year. African Americans disproportionately bore the brunt of these actions. Not until the late 1960s did the U.S. Supreme Court intervene to preclude such state discrimination.

State experimentation with welfare and medical assistance has also led to some innovations deemed sufficiently successful that Congress has copied them in reforming federal law (though some critics remain unconvinced). Several state innovations from the 1980s and 1990s were incorporated into the federal welfare overhaul of 1996. Provisions barring benefits to minor mothers or to additional children born into welfare families provide two such examples. States also learned the value of enhanced flexibility in helping families ease their way off welfare and into the workforce. By increasing the amount of earned income disregarded or not counted when determining welfare eligibility, states smoothed the transition from welfare to work by minimizing the financial shock families experience as they gradually leave welfare for a low-wage job. Despite the financial investment this innovation represented for states, it was universally adopted by states in a variety of formats. These and other provisions were advocated by governors, along with more state discretion, generally, in the 1996 legislation. Perhaps the most significant change in this legislation was the elimination of the individual entitlement nature of welfare funding in exchange for greater state authority over welfare. States now receive a fixed block grant for welfare funding and may spend those funds largely as they see fit.

Medicaid has experienced a very different fate. As health care moves closer to being viewed as a human right by the public, state governments have invested, albeit reluctantly, much larger portions of their state budgets into this program than they would have imagined when first adopted in the 1960s. As of 2002, nearly 20 percent of the average state budget pays Medicaid expenses, mainly to long-term care providers such as nursing homes. Part of Medicaid's enduring political support relies on medical providers being major beneficiaries of the program. Although the Medicaid program pays less than what private insurance does for a given procedure, the availability of a reliable pool of funds supports many medical providers who treat recipients of public assistance. Intense fiscal pressure on states from this program has led directly to adoption of managed care systems, at first cautiously permitted by Congress and later strongly encouraged in an effort to slow rising costs through the 1990s. On the whole, the Medicaid debate has taken a much less ideological tone than that surrounding welfare. Recipients cannot readily abuse Medicaid benefits, as contrasted to arguably poor choices they might make with cash or Food Stamps.

The principle of federalism will continue to influence future social welfare policy as the federal government funds a large number of state programs with grants in aid. States undoubtedly will continue to experiment with social welfare programs and services that they see as meeting the needs of their residents.

—Greg M. Shaw

See also The New Deal (United States); Roosevelt, Franklin Delano; Social Security (United States)

Current Comment

Bell, W. (1965). *Aid to dependent children.* New York: Columbia University Press.

Coughlin, T., Ku, L., & Holahan, J. (1994). *Medicaid since 1980: Costs, coverage, and the shifting alliance between the federal government and the states.* Washington, DC: Urban Institute Press.

Soss, J., Schram, S., & Vartanian, T. (2001). Setting the terms of relief: Explaining state policy choices in the devolution revolution. *American Journal of Political Science, 45,* 378–395.

Thompson, F., & Dilulio, J., Jr. (Eds.). (1998). *Medicaid and devolution: A view from the states.* Washington, DC: Brookings Institution Press.

Weaver, R. K. (2000). *Ending welfare as we know it.* Washington, DC: Brookings Institution Press.

Further Reading

Lieberman, R. (1998). *Shifting the color line.* Cambridge, MA: Harvard University Press.

Melnick, R. S. (1994). *Between the lines: Interpreting welfare rights.* Washington, DC: Brookings Institution Press.

Peterson, P. (1995). *The price of federalism.* Washington, DC: Brookings Institution Press.

Skocpol, T. (1992). *Protecting soldiers and mothers: The political origins of social policy in the United States.* Cambridge, MA: Harvard University Press.

FOOD ASSISTANCE POLICY (CANADA)

Food assistance policy focuses attention on the sustainability of food systems as a whole and the relationship between food production, processing, distribution, and consumption in both local and global contexts. Tim Lang (1997), an international food policy expert, states that "food policy is about the decision-making processes [that] affect who eats what, when, where and on what conditions." He also observes that

> one of the joys and frustrations of food policy is that inevitably it ranges widely across the human and natural sciences. One moment we may be covering policy concerning the application of sciences. The next moment we are drawn to policies affecting whether people on low income can afford to eat adequately. Food policy thus weaves a complex picture from strands drawn from economics, politics,

science, nutrition, social policy, psychology and much more. (pp. 2–3)

From a social welfare perspective, key issues concern matters of food redistribution, including addressing hunger, advancing the human right to food, promoting nutritional well-being, and ensuring income security and the adequacy of the social safety net. It would be erroneous, however, to conclude that food policy has been integral to the development of social welfare in Canada.

Rod MacRae, a noted Canadian food policy analyst, argues that what passes for food policy in Canada was not consciously chosen but rather drifted into and comprises "many odd bits of policy, programming and regulations." It is "mechanistic, technocratic, incomplete, fragmentary and contrary" (Koc, MacRae, Mougeot, & Welsh, 1999, p. 182). Indeed, he claims that agribusiness has acted to prevent Canada from developing a coherent food policy and that today Canada "has nothing specifically labeled a food policy" (Koc et al., p. 185). Food policy is not regarded as a discrete policy envelope requiring comprehensive planning or decision making. Historically, and today, it falls between many stools: agriculture and fisheries; health and nutrition; trade and economic development; foreign aid; the environment; and social policy.

Historically, food policy has included agricultural policy, which, in the days since Confederation in 1867, was organized to meet the imperial food requirements of the United Kingdom and then the securing of national boundaries on the prairies. Trends since World War II have seen the decline of the family farm, the growth of farm organizations, and the dominance of agricultural corporations with a focus on the commodification of food rather than a concern with the food system as a whole and food nourishment as a primary public policy objective.

Nutrition policy, including nutrition labeling and the setting of dietary guidelines, is the responsibility of Health Canada. Early in the twentieth century, there was attention to food regulation with a focus on sanitation and food adulteration, but it was a fragmentary approach with little attention paid to relationships between food production systems, food quality, and health. In the 1970s, food policy briefly emerged on the federal public agenda, but Agriculture Canada's commitment to market-based approaches to agriculture prevailed and the links between production, processing, and distribution, including nutrition, were not pursued.

Since the early 1980s, however, different sectors within civil society—locally, nationally, and internationally—have directed increasing attention to food issues, and food security has received increasing public attention and also debate within the social welfare community. Contributory factors have included unresolved issues of global hunger; debates about Canada's policies of overseas aid and the role of the Canadian International Development Agency; the impact of structural adjustment policies on countries of the South and on Canadian agriculture and its consequences for farm families and rural communities; debates about the merits of industrial farming and genetically modified foods versus those of sustainable agriculture and organic and local production; food safety issues; and, of particular concern to social policy, growing domestic hunger and food inequality, fiscally conservative social spending, and the emergence of charitable food banks as an institutionalized second tier of the Canadian welfare system.

Since the mid 1970s, significant milestones in the debate about food security have been the ratification by Canada of the United Nations *International Covenant on Economic, Social and Cultural Rights* (1976), which guarantees the human right to food; the publication of *The Land of Milk and Money: The National Report of the People's Food Commission* (1980); the establishment of the Canadian Association of Food Banks (1988); the creation of the Toronto Food Policy Council within the Toronto Board of Health (1991) and a network of food policy organizations across the country; Canada's signing of the *World Declaration on Nutrition* (1992); the World Food Summit in Rome (1996) at which Canada's position paper was informed by international and local representatives of the country's fledgling food security movement; the release in 1998 of *Canada's Action Plan for Food Security* (CAPFS); and the creation of a national Food Security Bureau within Agriculture and Agri-Food Canada in 1999 charged with overseeing the implementation of the CAPFS recommendations and coordinating food security

activities at the federal, provincial, and civil society levels. The Centre for Food Security Studies at Ryerson University in Toronto, Ontario, established in 1995, has become an important focal point for advancing the academic study of food policy and promoting food security initiatives on a national and international basis and across different sectors.

In terms of the social welfare perspective, the emergence of food banking in Canada, following the establishment of the first food bank in the country in Edmonton, Alberta, in 1981, continues to raise critical questions about the adequacy of Canada's public safety net and the state's domestic compliance with its international obligations to "respect, protect, and advance" the human right to food. By 2002, 620 food banks and 2,192 affiliated agencies were feeding 747,665 people in an average month, a 90 percent increase over 1989, the year of the first national HungerCount survey. Forty percent of the recipients were children under the age of 18. The majority were social assistance beneficiaries. The recent National Population Health Survey (1998/1999) reported that an estimated 2.5 million Canadians, or 8.4 percent of the population, were experiencing compromised diets and living in food-insecure households. Such a high level of food poverty coupled with a weakened safety net explains the rapid growth of the charitable food bank industry.

Food banks form part of a growing web of community-based feeding programs, (e.g., school lunch programs, collective kitchens, soup kitchens). They are mainly organized by community- and/or faith-based organizations through cooperatives, unions, and educational institutions. Historically, the modern-day food banks hark back to earlier times and the Great Depression of the 1930s, when poor relief was provided under a patchwork of municipal, church, and charitable auspices.

In their origins, food banks in Canada have been strongly influenced by the food bank movement in the United States, dating back to 1967, and the Ronald Reagan and Bill Clinton administrations' attack on welfare entitlements and the shift to workfare and charitable giving. In Canada, the economic recession of the early 1980s, combined with an increasingly stringent social safety net (federal Unemployment Insurance and provincial social assistance), were critical factors in the rise of food banks north of the U.S. border. Welfare reform, the scrapping of the Canada Assistance Plan in 1996, and social spending cutbacks have resulted in stricter eligibility criteria and inadequate income benefits. The lack of affordable social housing, the high costs of rental accommodation in many Canadian communities, and utility costs have resulted in the depletion of household food budgets with the result that food banks have been meeting a basic need.

Food banks raise a number of important issues and debates for Canadian food policy and social welfare. They serve as a reminder that Canada at the start of the twenty-first century lacks a coherent national food policy that focuses on the food and nutritional needs of all its citizens and is based on a set of well articulated and coordinated agricultural, economic, environmental, health, and social policies. They are also a reminder that social welfare has a key contribution to make in the formation of food policy if it is to create a food system that addresses not only the requirements of production for an environmentally safe and sustainable system but also one that addresses the food needs of all Canadians, including the vulnerable.

—Graham Riches

See also Economic Policy (Canada); Social Security (Canada); Social Welfare (Canada): Since the Marsh Report

Current Comment

Canadian Association of Food Banks (CAFB). (2002). *Facts about food banks in Canada* [On-line]. Available: www8 .cpr.ca/cms/English/General+Public/Community/Holiday+ Train/Facts+About+Food+Banks+In+Canada.htm

Che, J., & Chen, J. (2001). Food insecurity in Canadian households. *Statistics Canada Health Reports, 12*(4), 11–22.

Further Reading

Koc, M., MacRae, R., Mougeot, L. J. A., & Welsh, J. (1999). *For hunger-proof cities: Sustainable urban food systems.* Ottawa, ON: International Development Research Centre.

Lang, T. (1997). *Food policy for the 21st century: Can it be both radical and reasonable?* (Discussion Paper No. 4). London: Thames Valley University, Centre for Food Policy.

Riches, G. (Ed.). (1997). *First world hunger: Food security and welfare politics.* New York: St. Martins.

Wilson, B., & Tsoa, E. (2002). *HungerCount 2002: Eating their words: Government failure on food security.* Toronto, ON: Canadian Association of Food Banks.

FOOD ASSISTANCE POLICY (MEXICO)

Food policies have undergone significant transformation throughout Mexican history. The Spanish Conquest of Mexico led to a change in land tenure policies, crops produced, and consumption. As capitalist development propelled Mexico from a rural to an urban society with significant inequality, vulnerability to food shortages, price hikes, and popular outcry demanded government intervention to alleviate shortages. Despite such demands, government intervention has been ad hoc and malnutrition has persisted.

CONQUEST, COLONIZATION, AND THE EARLY NATIONAL PERIOD

Prior to the Spanish Conquest (1519–1521), food variations abounded. In central and southern Mexico, maize was the primary staple for centuries. According to the *Popul Vuh*, the Mayan book of life, the gods created humans out of maize dough; hence, maize cultivation is intimately linked to the culture and identity of Mesoamericans. In addition to maize, from which tortillas and other dishes were made, squash, beans, *chiles*, and various meats formed the basis of the diet. In the North, where indigenous populations were more nomadic, diets consisted of various foods that could be hunted and gathered. Although natural disasters created temporary shortages, this mix of staples contributed to a balanced diet.

The Mexican food regime began to change with the Spanish Conquest. The Spanish introduced the staples of their diet, wheat and beef, and sought to de-emphasize maize. Throughout the colonial period (from 1521 to the 1820s), wheat was planted on better-quality land while maize was relegated to poorer rain-fed land. The change in the food regime disrupted traditional diets, weakening the indigenous population's immune systems and making them more susceptible to disease. Hence, shifts in the food regimen would be one factor contributing to the massive indigenous death rate in the years following the Conquest.

As the Spanish sought to make Mexico a more urban-oriented society, the countryside was used to supply cities with basic grains. To ensure a steady supply of foodstuffs, regulatory practices were implemented early on, including the appointment of an urban food officer to regulate weights and measures and to oversee the food distribution system. Nevertheless, maize prices were anarchic, creating instability and leading to food riots. By the 1590s, the Mexico City Council had created two regulatory institutions: the *alhóndiga* and the *pósito*. The *alhóndiga* was a public granary aimed at ensuring a steady supply of maize and wheat at a just price. Producers would bring grains to the *alhóndigas* to store and then sell the grains at the fixed price. The *pósito* was a grain reserve that was directly controlled by local city officials. *Alhóndiga* officials purchased grain when the price was low and stored it in the *pósito* to be released during periods of scarcity, in hopes of avoiding significant price hikes, panics, and riots. Although both institutions were initially established in Mexico City, they soon began to operate in many large cities and served as a buffer against famines and natural disasters; but they left rural Mexicans (approximately 90 percent of the population) subject to the whims of nature, market forces, and unscrupulous merchants.

Local regulation of food policy continued throughout the colonial period and well into the nineteenth century. Aside from the *alhóndiga* and the *pósito*, local jurisdictions regulated prices in the urban market to forestall potential grain shortages. Local regulatory policy unevenly benefited larger landowners and merchants at the expense of *campesinos* (farmworkers) and small producers. Nevertheless, by most accounts, significant grain scarcity occurred relatively infrequently.

THE ERA OF PORFIRIO DÍAZ

The first major federal intervention in food policy occurred during the presidency of Porfirio Diáz (1876–1911). During this period, Mexico experienced rapid economic growth and became more intricately linked to the world economy. The countryside was used to provide inexpensive foodstuffs to the city and to produce export crops such as coffee, sugar, and cotton. This policy demanded economies of scale, leading to the consolidation of large landholdings as peasants were evicted from their communal land. Food production became subject to the whims of an emerging national market in which supplies and price levels were precarious. A series of droughts and crop failures led to grain scarcities during the first decade of the twentieth century and forced a reluctant Díaz to establish a temporary regulatory agency and import grain.

Influenced by Social Darwinism, policies favoring European diets continued under the Díaz administration. Nutritional scientists and government officials studied the nutrition of the working classes. Scholars and policymakers argued that the poor nutritional content of maize was linked to Mexico's economic backwardness. One prominent scholar argued that centuries of a maize-based diet had created an inferior population, physically and mentally, unable to compete in the modern industrialized world. Ignoring questions of inequality, structural poverty, and the balanced pre-Conquest diet, government policies sought to substitute corn with wheat to create more productive workers.

THE MEXICAN REVOLUTION, FOOD, AND SOCIAL WELFARE

The outbreak of fighting during the Mexican Revolution in 1910 aggravated food shortages by disrupting food production and distribution networks. During the decade, crop production fell by approximately 70 percent for maize and 144 percent for wheat. During the most intense period of fighting, between 1913 and 1915, food prices soared. Food riots broke out in several cities and revolutionary leaders attempted to control prices and distribution. Such measures were generally palliatives but did signal some responsiveness on the part of local leaders.

Although the worst of the food shortages subsided by 1916, they had a lasting impact on popular memory and helped shape future food policy. The Constitution of 1917 included Article 28 to prevent monopolies and authorized the government to intervene in the economy to protect consumers from excessive increases in the price of basic foods. In addition, Article 27 gave the state the power to enact a land reform that the framers hoped would break the power of large landowners and create a class of small producers who would be more responsive to the needs of the majority. It was not until the presidency of Lázaro Cárdenas (1934–1940), however, that a centralized food policy was initiated. Cárdenas's aggressive land distribution policy led to the creation of the Regulating Committee of the Market for Basic Goods (*Comié Regulador del Mercado de Subsistencias*, or CRMS) in 1938 to purchase grains from small producers of maize, wheat, beans, and rice at a fixed price. While small producers were the agency's initial target, spiraling food prices during the late 1930s and throughout World War II caused the government to focus more on alleviating food prices for consumers and less on aiding producers. Panic purchasing and food crises in the cities led to riots in some cities and organized labor began to demand higher wages to offset the declining purchasing power. Women lined up early each morning to buy staple goods, only to see the stores run out of basic foods. Government responded with increased intervention in the grain markets, aimed at alleviating the prices of basic grains without disrupting business.

Beginning in 1939, the CRMS opened its first stores in Mexico. CRMS intended to provide low-cost staples to Mexico's working poor and serve as a hedge against inflation. As inflation continued, public outcry led to greater intervention beyond maize and wheat and into the milk market. By 1944, there were nearly 900 stores throughout Mexican cities that sold basic foods at approximately 10 to 25 percent of the price of the same goods in private stores. Price controls were implemented on all basic foods and a corps of inspectors was hired to enforce prices in both private and public markets.

From the later 1930s and on through the 1970s, as Mexico's leaders moved away from the social justice notions of the Revolution, food policy was used as a tool to subsidize capitalist industrialization and urbanization. During the 1940s and 1950s, real industrial wages declined, and workers increasingly organized to demand wage increases and a more responsive government. As part of the government's efforts to control unions and forge social peace, food policy was used to keep food prices down for urban consumers and to reduce wage pressures for employers. The state food agency, which underwent several name changes and

by 1961 would be known as the National Company of Popular Subsistence *(Compañía Nacional de Subsistencias Populares,* or CONASUPO), became a large bureaucracy operating throughout the country. It would, however, favor urban consumers over small farmers and *ejidatarios* (communal farmers). To keep prices of foodstuffs down in the city, government policy encouraged increased output in the countryside. Beginning in the 1940s, the Mexican government entered into an agreement with the United States and the Rockefeller Foundation to use the advances of modern agricultural science to increase the output and yield of Mexico's staple crops. Although the program worked with small farmers and *campesinos*, it favored large producers. Coupled with shifts in other rural programs, such as agricultural credit, irrigation policy, a weakening land reform effort, and declining guaranteed prices for farmers, a bifurcated agricultural system emerged that favored large producers over small producers. The production of basic crops rose throughout the late 1940s and 1950s, making Mexico self-sufficient. Nevertheless, by the late 1960s, Mexico was forced to import basic grains as government policy reduced production incentives and credit programs weakened.

Between the 1940s and the 1970s, small producers and peasants suffered from shifts in government policy. This contributed to rural poverty and was seen by many *campesinos* as a betrayal of the promises of the Revolution. Peasants organized to create more responsive organizations and some seized land. Others joined guerrilla organizations seeking to launch a popular war against the government. In urban areas, the increasing authoritarianism of the modern state led to efforts to break strikes and thwart popular organizing, culminating in a massacre of students in October 1968.

Subsequent governments responded to these challenges to political legitimacy with an aggressive campaign to reincorporate marginalized sectors. During the 1970s, Mexican presidents launched a renewed land reform program and rural extension programs. CONASUPO became more prominent, with the number of subsidized stores throughout the country expanding to 11,000 by 1982. The government had a significant presence in the countryside that, coupled with government repression of dissenters, worked to defuse popular complaints.

NEOLIBERALISM AND MARKET APPROACHES SINCE THE 1980S

Beginning in the early 1980s, Mexico suffered a profound economic crisis that led to the transformation of government policies away from an activist welfare state toward more market-driven policies. Precipitated by a drop in the price of oil and a profound debt crisis, Mexico followed the economic prescription of the world's financial institutions and began a policy of reducing tariffs, cutting public expenditures, and eliminating subsidies to various sectors of society. This resulted in rising unemployment, steep cuts in real wages, and significant rural poverty and migration.

CONASUPO expanded its operations at the outset of the economic crisis, but by 1988 the government had moved from a policy of general subsidies to one of targeting the "truly poor." In 1989, the government reorganized CONASUPO to eliminate costly and ineffective operations. CONASUPO closed or sold nine of its industrial plants, closed or transferred to unions thousands of its stores, and established warehouse stores to aid the rural poor. The number of crops that CONASUPO purchased at a guaranteed price from small producers fell from 12 to 2, with only maize and beans receiving some protection. Prices paid for these crops would decline in real terms throughout the 1990s until they were eliminated by the end of the decade. In lieu of general subsidies, targeted social welfare programs, such as the National Solidarity Program (*Programa Nacional de Solidaridad*, or PRONASOL), were created to aid the urban and rural poor. Such programs were criticized as thinly veiled attempts to buy political allegiance for an official party rapidly losing legitimacy. With the signing of the North American Free Trade Agreement (NAFTA), Mexico agreed to gradually end subsidies to producers and consumers and by the end of the millennium, subsidies on tortillas and milk were lifted and CONASUPO was liquidated.

The countryside has been transformed. Government programs that aided small producers, including low-interest loans, subsidized storage warehouses, and guaranteed purchase prices, were downsized. As a result, many peasant farmers were driven from their land because they could not compete with larger agribusinesses. Many rural dwellers had to migrate to other parts of Mexico or to the United States in search of work. These changes contributed to renewed social mobilization and were key factors in the Zapatista Army of National Liberation's (*Ejercito Zapatista de Liberación Nacional*, or EZLN) armed struggle for rights of self-determination against the national government that began in 1994 and continues today. Despite numerous efforts to increase food production and alleviate hunger, poverty and malnutrition remain at high levels in Mexico. Approximately 40 percent of the population lives in poverty. Poverty and malnutrition are especially high among Mexico's 12 million indigenous peoples, 90 percent of whom live in poverty and are at high risk for malnutrition. Recent studies indicate that two million Mexican children under the age of 5 suffer from malnutrition, a number that has been consistent for 30 years.

Throughout Mexican history, food policies have been intricately linked to capitalist development. Although there have been attempts to alleviate famine and poverty, basic issues of structural inequality have not been addressed and recent market reforms have exacerbated these historical patterns.

—*Enrique C. Ochoa*

See also Economic Policy (Mexico); Labor Movement and Social Welfare (Mexico); Land Reform (Mexico); Neoliberalism, Social Programs, and Social Movements (Mexico); Peasant Movements and Social Programs (Mexico); Poverty (Mexico)

Primary Sources

Ramo Presidenciales, Archivo General de la Nación, Mexico City; *Archivo Ramón Fernández y Fernández*, Zamora, Michoacán.

Current Comment

Barkin, D., & Suárez, B. (1985). *El fin de la autosuficiencia alimentaria mexicana.* Mexico City: Ediciones Océano.

Barry, T. (1995). *Zapata's revenge: Free trade and the farm crisis in Mexico.* Boston: South End Press.

Martínez Dominguez, G. (1950). *Intentos de control de precios en México.* Mexico City: Secretaría de Educación Pública.

Further Reading

Fox, J. (1992). *The politics of food in Mexico: State power and social mobilization.* Ithaca, NY: Cornell University Press.

Hewit de Alcántara, C. (1978). *La modernización de la agricultura Mexicana, 1940–1970.* Mexico City: Siglo XXI.

Ochoa, E. C. (2000). *Feeding Mexico: The political uses of food since 1910*. Wilmington, DE: Scholarly Resources.

Pilcher, J. M. (1998). *¡Qué vivàn los tamales! Food and the making of Mexican identity*. Albuquerque: University of New Mexico Press.

FOOD ASSISTANCE POLICY (UNITED STATES)

From the first moment of European settlement in the seventeenth century until the Great Depression of the 1930s, the fertile and virtually inexhaustible land of the American continent and its extraordinary bounty sustained the myth that anyone willing to work hard would never want for food. America as Garden of the World became the "master symbol" of the national collective enterprise. The growing productivity of American farms, particularly after the Civil War, bolstered a native optimism about the ability to convert the abundance of the environment to personal prosperity. By the late nineteenth century, the achievements of American agriculture not only provided the average household the most varied, generous, and lowest-cost diet in the world but also eventually gave rise to persistent agricultural surpluses that supported a robust export trade.

Although chronic privation on hardscrabble New England farms and frontier homesteads belied the myth of universal prosperity, providing food for the household through most of American history was a personal responsibility or in the most extreme cases a charitable obligation. Hunger entered the lexicon of public policy only on an episodic, temporary basis, and the response was invariably by local, not state or federal governments. After the panic of 1857, for example, the city of New York initiated a public works program for the unemployed in which compensation came in the form of potatoes, flour, and cornmeal. The city of Detroit addressed the ravages of the depression of 1893 by establishing municipal vegetable gardens on vacant lots, a program copied at the time by other cities and widely used again during the Great Depression of the 1930s. The first federal food assistance program to help the hungry did not appear until the early years of the Great Depression, when the Herbert Hoover administration distributed surplus

wheat through the Red Cross. President Franklin D. Roosevelt followed suit with the creation of the Federal Surplus Relief Corporation (FSRC) in 1933. The primary function of the FSRC was to dispose of price-depressing surplus commodities and incidentally to feed the needy.

The roots of the modern federal food assistance programs were laid with the creation of a Food Stamp program in 1939. The program, which lasted only until 1943, was designed as much to encourage people to purchase surplus food stocks that were depressing farm prices as to help the destitute. When World War II mobilization absorbed the surpluses, the program, which served about 4 million people at its peak, was terminated. Reform-minded legislators in the U.S. House of Representatives and the Senate, however, immediately began a long campaign to make Food Stamps a permanent part of the American social welfare system. In 1961, President John F. Kennedy, acting on a promise made in the Democratic party platform, ordered the U.S. Secretary of Agriculture to create a pilot Food Stamp program in the economically depressed Appalachian region and the iron ore ranges in the upper Midwest. After Kennedy's assassination, President Lyndon B. Johnson embraced a permanent national Food Stamp program as part of his War on Poverty, and Congress—following the lead of U.S. Representative Leonor Sullivan, a Democrat from Missouri and the program's most persistent advocate—acceded to the president's will in the late summer of 1964.

Food Stamps remain at the heart of a complex of federal food assistance programs in the United States. Available as an entitlement benefit to most individuals and households with net incomes at or below the official federal poverty line, Food Stamps provide on average of approximately $70 per person per month for the purchase of food. Participants in the program increasingly receive their allotment in the form of an electronic benefit card instead of the traditional Food Stamp coupons. After the welfare system was reformed in 1996, eligibility rules for Food Stamp participation were tightened, removing many legal immigrants from the rolls as well as placing time limits on the participation of able-bodied single adults without children. By 2003, however, the eligibility of certain categories of legal immigrants had been restored, and states had the option to waive the time limits for unemployed single adults. Participation in the program is still spotty, even among those households classified as "food insecure," the federal government's sliding measure of food deprivation. Approximately two-fifths of all eligible people do not enroll in the Food Stamp program for reasons that include the belief that benefits would not be worth the trouble, lack of information, fear of embarrassment, or language barriers. Nearly three-quarters of food insecure households are not enrolled. Nevertheless, the program is a large one: from a peak of 28 million recipients in 1994, Food Stamps in the twenty-first century enroll an average of about 19 million per month, nearly half of whom are children under 18, at an annual cost to the federal government of about $18 billion per year.

Besides the Food Stamp program, the U.S. Department of Agriculture funds an array of smaller programs targeted to particularly vulnerable groups, such as schoolchildren, pregnant women, newborn infants, and the elderly poor. The largest and oldest of these is the National School Lunch Program. The federal government began lunch aid in the Great Depression by distributing surplus commodities to schools, but it was not until 1946 that Congress established a permanent national lunch program, primarily as a response to the poor nutritional state of many World War II military draftees. The program now provides free or reduced-price meals to more than 15 million children from poor and low-income families. Another 11 million children pay full price for their lunches. In 1998, Congress expanded the lunch program to include funding for snacks for children enrolled in after-school educational enrichment programs.

On the recommendation of President Lyndon B. Johnson's Task Force on Agriculture and Rural Life, a pilot School Breakfast Program was established in 1966. Congress made it permanent in 1975. Much smaller than the lunch program, it serves free or reduced-price meals designed to provide at least a quarter of the daily recommended levels of key nutrients to slightly more than 6 million children a year. A third major childhood nutrition initiative, also from the Johnson era, is the Summer Food Service, established in 1968. This program targeted children from poor neighborhoods and distributed food during the summer vacation, primarily through day camp and various sponsored recreational programs. Currently, only about 2.1 million children receive food through this program. A fourth child nutrition initiative is the Child and Adult Care Food Program (CACFP), established at the same time as the summer program. CACFP pays for meals served in home and institutional day care centers and serves about 2.5 million children and a much smaller number of chronically impaired elderly adults.

The federal government also funds a supplemental nutrition program for pregnant and lactating women, newborn infants, and young children. Known as WIC, the Special Supplemental Nutrition Program for Women, Infants and Children began in 1972, first, like most other food assistance programs, as a pilot initiative. It was made permanent in 1974. WIC serves women and children in households with incomes within 185 percent of the federal poverty line—a larger pool of eligible recipients than any other federal food assistance program—and includes those who are deemed by a medical professional to be at nutritional risk. The program provides roughly $30 per month of dairy foods, cereals, eggs, and orange juice to about 7 million women and children.

The last major federal food assistance program was once called the Temporary Emergency Food Assistance Program (TEFAP). Established during the recession of 1981 under a different name, it first distributed surplus cheese and later a broader range of commodities directly to needy people. Almost a decade later in 1990, when it became apparent that the program was becoming a permanent fixture in the food safety net, Congress renamed it The Emergency Food Assistance Program, leaving its acronym unchanged. Today, TEFAP distributes commodities, mostly purchased on the market rather than drawn from diminishing surplus reserves, to states, which in turn distribute them to charitable food banks that give them to food pantries and soup kitchens, which set their own eligibility policies.

This network of private emergency food providers (EFPs) began to grow significantly only in the 1980s. A substantial majority are run by religious organizations, and their total, both faith-based and secular, may number as many as 100,000. Today the street-level organizations under the Second Harvest umbrella, the largest anti-hunger organization in the country, serve an estimated 23 million people at least once in any given year. Although these EFPs are not government organizations, they are critical institutions in the American food assistance system. About one-sixth of the food they distribute comes from the federal government, and they tend to serve population groups that fail to qualify for public food aid.

Despite the existence of an array of well-established public food assistance programs, including the means-tested, broadly available entitlement program of Food Stamps and the targeted smaller programs, as well as a vast population of charitable emergency food providers, the U.S. Department of Agriculture estimates on the basis of its annual food security survey that about 33 million Americans, of whom about 13 million are children, still suffer from hunger or live on its edge.

—*Peter Eisinger*

See also The New Deal (United States); Poverty (United States)

Primary Sources

Records of the Food and Consumer Services (Record Group 462) and Records of the Economic Research Service (Record Group 354), National Archives & Records Administration, College Park, MD.

Current Comment

Nord, M., Andrews, M., & Carlson, S. (2002, October). *Household food security in the United States, 2001* (Food Assistance and Nutrition Research Report No. FANRR29). Washington, DC: U.S. Department of Agriculture, Economic Research Service. Available: www.ers.usda.gov/publications/fanrr29/

Further Reading

America's Second Harvest. (2001, October). *Hunger in America 2001* [National Report]. Chicago: Author.
Eisinger, P. (1998). *Toward an end to hunger in America.* Washington, DC: Brookings Institution Press.
Poppendieck, J. (1986). *Breadlines knee-deep in wheat: Food assistance in the Great Depression.* New Brunswick, NJ: Rutgers University Press.

FRAZIER, E. FRANKLIN (1894–1962)

E. Franklin Frazier, the acclaimed sociologist, was closely associated with social work in the early years of his academic life. He served as director of the Atlanta University School of Social Work in the 1920s and later, with Inabel Lindsay, helped found the Howard University School of Social Work.

Born in 1894 to a race-conscious, working-class family in Baltimore, Frazier grew up acutely aware of the racial antagonisms and rising civil rights movement that dominated the first two decades of the twentieth century. He entered Howard University in 1916, and there became active in the student socialist society and the National Association for the Advancement of Colored People. Fiercely independent in his thinking, Frazier forged a lifelong political identity at Howard that embraced internationalism, class-consciousness, and the struggle for racial equality.

Graduating *cum laude* from Howard in 1916, Frazier taught at a number of African American schools in the South, where he often found himself at loggerheads with conservative administrators. As the United States edged toward entry into World War I, Frazier, unlike many of his generation, bitterly opposed it. He believed the war was a battle between rival imperialistic powers and that President Woodrow Wilson's claim that the war would make the world safe for democracy was hypocrisy given the treatment of Blacks in the United States.

In 1919, Frazier returned to graduate studies, first at Clark University in Massachusetts, where he explored rising African American radicalism, and later at the New York School of Philanthropy, one of the few schools of social work in the United States that accepted African American students. Frazier was interested in the lives of working people and in economic programs that would enhance their development. Supported by the Russell Sage Foundation and by mentors like Mary van Kleeck, who conducted research on labor issues, Frazier undertook a study of African American longshoremen. In this research, his abiding interest in the interaction between psychological processes and racial oppression first became apparent.

In 1921, Frazier won a scholarship from the American-Scandinavian Foundation to study rural cooperatives in Denmark. Frazier was fascinated by the strong cooperative movement in Scandinavia, which he felt offered important lessons in economic development for African Americans, and on his return wrote several articles about the benefits of economic cooperation.

In 1922, Frazier accepted a position at the fledgling Atlanta University School of Social Work and a year later became its director, a position he held until 1928. During his years at Atlanta, Frazier worked assiduously to strengthen the school. He traveled widely to raise funds for it and spread word of social work throughout the South. A prolific writer, he published 28 articles, many of them based on interviews with rural African Americans, work which would inform his later, well-known studies of the black family.

Frazier also spoke out courageously against the intense race hatred in the South during the 1920s, when membership in the Ku Klux Klan peaked and many lynchings of African Americans occurred. At one point, he advocated self-defense for black families whose homes were invaded, one of his many strong views that sometimes brought him into conflict with both White liberal supporters and moderate members of his own race. Racial segregation, which was practiced throughout the South and most of the North, was a frequent cause of this conflict. Frazier, who despised segregation, refused to attend meetings where Blacks and Whites were separated, and once walked out of a meeting of social workers in Atlanta, announcing: "I have told you White people not to invite me to any meeting where you are going to place the Negroes to themselves as if they were roaches or fleas and unfit for human association" (quoted in Platt, 1991, p. 75).

Frazier's years at the Atlanta University School of Social Work and his close association with social work came to an end in 1928 when he left Atlanta out of favor with both segregationists and liberal supporters of the Atlanta school who found him difficult to work with. Frazier tried to locate teaching jobs but could find none in either White or Black schools. It should be noted that no African Americans were hired as full-time faculty members in any U.S. institution of higher education other than segregated institutions for African Americans until 1942. He decided to return to full-time studies, this time at the University of Chicago's well-respected sociology department headed by Robert Park. By the mid 1930s, he had earned his doctorate. Soon after, he published *The Negro Family in America* (1939).

In 1935, Frazier took a position in sociology at Howard University and began his three-decade-long career there. His many books and articles, among them *Negro Youth at the Crossways* (1940), *Race and Culture Contacts in the Modern World* (1957), and *Black Bourgeoisie* (1957), earned him considerable recognition, and he became the first African American president of the American Sociological Association.

Out of daily contact with social work, he nevertheless was concerned that African American students be educated to fill the civil service jobs that were emerging in the 1930s and 1940s. Frazier taught courses in social work at Howard in the 1930s, and, with Inabel Lindsay, was instrumental in founding the Howard University School of Social Work in 1945. Frazier was also a regular and popular lecturer at the Columbia University School of Social Work in the 1940s and 1950s. He died of a heart attack in 1962.

—*Susan Kerr Chandler*

See also African Americans and Social Welfare (United States)

Primary Source

E. Franklin Frazier Papers, Moorland-Spingarn Research Center, Howard University, Washington, DC.

Current Comment

Edwards, G. F. (Ed.). (1968). *E. Franklin Frazier on race relations.* Chicago: University of Chicago Press.

Further Reading

Chandler, S. K. (2001). E. Franklin Frazier and social work: Unity and conflict. In I. Carlton-LaNey (Ed.), *African American leadership: An empowerment tradition in social welfare history* (pp. 189–202). Washington, DC: NASW Press.

Platt, A. M. (1991). *E. Franklin Frazier reconsidered.* New Brunswick, NJ: Rutgers University Press.

Platt, A., & Chandler, S. (1988). Constant struggle: E. Franklin Frazier and the African-American tradition in social work. *Social Work, 33,* 293–297.

FRENCH LANGUAGE AND IDENTITY (CANADA)

The origins of French Canada can be dated from 1604 (the foundation of Acadia) and 1608 (the founding of Quebec). Contrary to the situation in the English

North American colonies, where population growth was quite rapid, in New France it was very slow. This was due to an economy linked to the cod fisheries, where most of the fishermen returned to France each fall, and the fur trade that depended heavily on aboriginal expertise and labor. Furthermore, in the early years of settlement France showed limited interest in New France, due to its limited wealth potential, until about the 1660s, when active settlement was encouraged. In 1666, the population of New France was just 3,215. Most were single and male, but increasing numbers of settlers from France, especially women, established a community capable of sustaining itself through natural increase. It is estimated that only about 10,000 French settlers came to New France and remained, the others returning to France after a number of years in the colony. Today, most persons of French Canadian ancestry in Canada and the United States are descended from these early settlers.

In this article, the concept of identity is seen as the process by which French-speaking Canadians have defined themselves in relation to others and by the images that they have had of themselves. The first written indications of a unique sense of identity came in the late seventeenth century, when those born in Canada began to refer to themselves as *Canadiens.* They began to see themselves as different, more independent and more adapted to the Canadian social and economic environment than French people. Writings of French observers referred to the Canadians as being often insubordinate and insolent, at times in both manner and dress, resembling far too much the local Native population.

Some French Canadians married Natives, resulting in the creation of the *Métis* people. The Native cultures, however, influenced the *Canadiens* mainly in the ways of dressing, eating, and transportation; their spirit of independence; and their ways of waging war. This adoption of some aspects of Native culture, something that even today is little recognized, was an important factor in allowing the small but growing French-speaking population to survive and continue to develop in an often-hostile environment.

THE ACADIANS

The Acadians, centered in what is now Nova Scotia and parts of New Brunswick, evolved somewhat differently from the *Canadiens,* who settled along the St. Lawrence River between Kamouraska and Montreal. The Acadians came mostly from the western part of France, south of the Loire River Valley, whereas those who settled on the St. Lawrence came from the Parisian region, Normandy, Brittany, and Picardy. Acadian French, even today, is different from that of the rest of French-speaking Canada and is similar to that spoken by the descendants of the deported Acadians now living in Louisiana. The Acadians reclaimed land from the sea by building massive dikes, or *aboiteaux.* Their economic life was centered on farming and commercial links to New England.

In 1713, the Treaty of Utrecht conceded Acadia and all of Newfoundland to England, making the Acadians subjects of the British Empire. Though they refused to pledge allegiance to Britain, the Acadians were ready to take an oath of neutrality. The Acadians were seen as a threat to the English presence and their very fertile land was jealously eyed by New Englanders. As a consequence, between 1755 and 1763, over 10,000 Acadians, out of a total population of 14,000, were deported to other English colonies, to France, and to England.

Those who migrated back to Acadia and those who escaped deportation by hiding out with the Native population found that their rich farmland had been taken over by New England planters. They were forced to settle on far less fertile land in New Brunswick, Cape Breton Island, and coastal regions of eastern Quebec and Nova Scotia. After their return from exile, most Acadians turned to a mixed economy of multipurpose farming, lumbering, or coastal fishing to survive. Those who were unable to succeed economically often lived in the same area, resulting in pockets of poverty that often have persisted to the present day. Today, 280,000 Acadian descendants live in regions that are often referred to as *la nouvelle Acadie,* or New Acadia. In the past decades, even as they have become increasingly urbanized and made great strides in formal education, the Acadians continue to have a strong sense of their unique identity, which differs from that found elsewhere in French Canada. This sense of identity has been created in part out of a notion of belonging, with many different cultural reference points, and is related to their history of deportation, their long period of social and economic exploitation, their geographic isolation, and in many cases, their close ties to the sea. Out of this sense of identity, Acadians have developed a strong cooperative and relatively small private sector economic base, an autonomous school system, and distinctive literature and music. With official recognition from the province of New Brunswick, where the majority reside (they constitute 35 percent of the total population of the province), Acadians have developed greater political power there than in the other Atlantic provinces.

THE FRENCH CANADIANS

At the time of the English Conquest in 1763, nearly 60,000 French-speaking people lived along the St. Lawrence River; nearly 10,000 lived in the areas west of Montreal, notably in the Fort Detroit region, along the Mississippi River, and in parts of the present-day American Midwest. As the English-speaking population grew in the nineteenth century, the original Canadians, or *Canadiens,* began to refer to themselves as French Canadians to differentiate themselves from the Anglo-Celts who had settled both in Lower Canada (Quebec) and elsewhere in the British colonies. The French Canadian population, however, was not solely confined to Lower Canada. As the best land had already been taken up in Quebec, beginning in the 1840s over 500,000 French Canadians left for jobs in the cotton mills of New England. In the same period, others left for plentiful land available in eastern Ontario (in many ways an extension of Quebec) and existing French-speaking settlements in the Penetanguishene region near Georgian Bay and in southwestern Ontario. French Canadians from the lower St. Lawrence settled in the border regions of New Brunswick, intermingling with the existing Acadian population. In the 1880s, farmers and lumber workers left for northeastern Ontario, whereas others headed west to establish new settlements or join existing ones south and east of St. Boniface, across from Winnipeg, in present-day Manitoba. French-speaking villages with settlers from Quebec, France, and Belgium were established in Saskatchewan and Alberta. One of the most western French Canadian settlements, Maillardville, was a lumber town near New Westminster, British Columbia.

In many ways, these new settlements outside of the historic parishes of Quebec saw themselves as being part of a greater French Canada. French Canadian identity was based on historical links of family, descent, language, and religion. It was a society that extended from New England to British Columbia. Largely rural, many French Canadians worked in mixed agriculture and forestry economies. Others lived in the cotton mill cities of New England and Ontario, while thousands worked across the country in one-industry mining and lumbering towns where, at times, they formed the majority of the population. French Canadians managed to preserve many of their unique cultural forms. Seeing themselves as part of a greater French Canadian society, they recreated many of the social and economic practices they had known in Quebec. Their concentrated populations allowed them to establish new parishes, schools, and social institutions that would respond to their needs. In the early twentieth century, they founded credit unions (*caisses populaires*) and other cooperatives, similar to those established in Quebec and New Brunswick.

The geography of French Canada did not strictly follow provincial boundaries. Whereas large parts of western Quebec and the Eastern Townships of Quebec remained English speaking, much of eastern Ontario and parts of northeastern Ontario remained French speaking. Social life, centered on the French language and the Catholic church and built on a belief in social solidarity, assured the survival of French Canada, both within and outside Quebec.

A FRACTURED FRENCH CANADA

In the 1950s and 1960s, French Canada began to lose its historical common base. Quebec became increasingly secularized and undertook massive reforms in education and in the social and health fields under the direct control of the provincial state. In Quebec, where they made up 80.2 percent of the provincial population, French-speaking people began to identify themselves more with the territory of Quebec, as opposed to a greater French Canada. Rather than continuing to see themselves as French Canadians, they began to call themselves *Québécois,* referring to all those in the territory of Quebec, the geographic nation of all its citizens. This broader form of nationalism sought to include those of non–French Canadian descent who resided in Quebec. This process of changing identity was accentuated by the refusal of much of English Canada to recognize Canada as a country of two founding peoples, the French and the English, with language rights across all of Canada.

In Quebec, the French language has become the principal means for providing membership in the *Québécois* nation. It has become the main instrument for bringing together those of many different ethnic origins living in that society, within a French-speaking political state. There remain some aspects of the dual sense of belonging both to Canada and to Quebec on the part of the 5,805,000 (in 2001) *Québécois* whose first language is French. The sense of belonging to the Canadian side of the equation, however, has been decreasing in recent years. In the referendum of 1995, for example, about 60 percent of *Québécois* of French Canadian descent voted in favor of an independent Quebec, whereas most of those from anglophone and other ethnic communities voted against independence.

The development of a *Québécois* identity also meant breaking from those French Canadians in the other provinces, who were then forced to turn to their respective provincial governments for various services, often provided only in English. After the 1960s, religious institutions were no longer seen as the principal means for protecting both individual and collective identity. Nor were religious institutions critical for the development of new services in education, health, and social services. Much of the energy of French Canadians residing outside of Quebec would be focused on winning rights from the provinces where they resided. Many French Canadians outside of Quebec began to see themselves as national minorities, identifying themselves as Acadians, Franco-Ontarians, Franco-Albertans, and so on, although strong ties to the historical French Canada remain. Facing increasing urbanization, a mass media in which the English language is dominant, and frequent disrespect and lack of protection for French speakers, their communities have experienced great pressures for change.

Even though there is assimilation into the broader culture and society, especially in the regions farthest from Quebec, at least 926,400 (in 2001) French-speaking Canadians continue to live outside of the province of Quebec. Their numbers have been increased by new French-speaking immigrants from a multitude of countries in the French-speaking world and by interprovincial migration. The Canadian Constitution of 1982 protects French-language minority educational rights, and in New Brunswick their official language status is recognized. Other provinces with French-speaking populations have protected French-language rights. Ontario allows trials to be held in French, and, since 1986, the province's French Language Services Act (Bill 8) assures French-language provincial services in areas with a majority of Franco-Ontarians.

Even though the old French Canada no longer exists, there have been ongoing efforts in recent years to renew links between French-speaking Quebec residents and French-speaking minorities elsewhere in Canada, emphasizing common language and culture while respecting diversity. The French-speaking population continues to move throughout Canada as it has done throughout its history. It remains to be seen how the strong national feeling that sees Quebec as a national territory can be reconciled with the sense of national identity and resistance of the French-language minorities in the other provinces.

—David Welch

See also Quebec Province Social Welfare Policy (Canada)

Further Reading

Dumont, F. (1993). *Genèse de la societé québécoise.* Montreal, QC: Boréal.

Eccles, W. J. (1990). *France in America.* East Lansing: Michigan State University Press.

Silver, A. I. (1997). *The French-Canadian idea of Confederation, 1864–1900* (2nd ed.). Toronto, ON: University of Toronto Press.

Thériault, J. Y. (1999). *Francophonies minoritaires au Canada.* Moncton, NB: Éditions d'Acadie.

GAY, LESBIAN, BISEXUAL, TRANSGENDER POLICY ISSUES (CANADA)

Claims for greater public recognition of sexual diversity acquired modest visibility in Canada during the 1960s, a dramatically confrontational presence in the 1970s, and a foothold on the fringe of mainstream political processes in the 1980s. From the 1990s onward, such activism had a substantial impact on public policy and law on some issue fronts.

As it did elsewhere, the activist movement always contained both radical and reformist currents. Activists have debated the merits of seeking admission to existing institutions on equal terms or alternatively challenging established systems in transformative ways. Such differences have generally produced less polarizing conflict within the movement than in the United States and most European settings. Over the decades, the movement has been challenged to be more representative of the diversity of the constituency it claims to reflect—most forcibly at first by lesbians, then by people of color, and more recently by bisexual and transgendered people.

The Canadian movement has emerged in a context in which regionalism is profoundly important. The linguistic and cultural distinctiveness of Quebec has always set that province's activism apart, though not necessarily with an agenda or outlook categorically different from other regions. The distinctive histories and resource bases of British Columbia, Alberta, the other two Prairie provinces, and the Atlantic region all create activist groups and networks that are in many ways quite independent of one another, though the national group, Equality for Gays and Lesbians Everywhere (EGALE), has forged some cross-regional linkages. Outside the AIDS field, activist groups in Canada have modest resources, and usually no paid staff, creating impediments for effective linkage beyond the relatively localized. The substantial decentralization of the Canadian political system creates further incentives for recognizing regional differences and provincially specific challenges.

Despite the considerable importance of provincial and local jurisdiction, national developments in public policy and law since the late 1960s have resulted in significant public recognition of sexual diversity—more substantially and more uniformly so than in the United States. In 1969, the federal government partially decriminalized male homosexual activity (having never criminalized lesbian activity), though with continuing elements of discrimination in law (for example, in the age of consent) and policing. Raids directed at gay commercial establishments, including bathhouses, occurred in a number of Canadian cities during the 1970s and 1980s.

The 1982 enactment and constitutional entrenchment of the Charter of Rights and Freedoms marked an important threshold. Its major guarantee of equality was in Section 15, coming into effect only in 1985. The section's wording did not explicitly include sexual orientation, but courts were soon ruling that it did so implicitly. In part on that basis, several provinces added sexual orientation to their own human rights statutes (Quebec had been the first to do so, in 1977), formally prohibiting discrimination in both the public and private sectors.

By the late 1980s, in part as a result of the AIDS crisis, claims that same-sex relationships should be publicly recognized were proliferating. Some claims made their way to courts; others to workplace grievance processes and labor tribunals. Many cases were supported by a labor movement that was engaging issues of sexual diversity, however unevenly, ahead of other labor movements internationally. The Supreme Court of Canada delivered mixed rulings on relationship issues in the early and middle 1990s, but with increasingly clear messages that discriminating against same-sex couples was at least in principle unconstitutional. Through this decade, most of the successes won by advocates were won in the courts, though the New Democratic Party government in British Columbia had been moving to recognize same-sex couples from the early 1990s, and in 1995 became the first in the world to legislatively recognize adoption rights.

A Supreme Court ruling in 1999 (*M. v. H.*), which made any differentiation of same-sex couples and heterosexual couples unconstitutional, was a clear victory for equity advocates. Canadian law and policy had also moved as much as in any country to reduce the differences in rights and obligations associated with married couples and same-sex couples. A wave of legislation at the federal and provincial levels soon followed, eliminating or drastically reducing legal discrimination against same-sex couples in a wide range of policy areas. Increasingly, then, the major "relationship" issue remaining was marriage. In Canada, this issue has had more symbolic (as opposed to substantive) significance than in the United States, but nevertheless has been subject to hard-fought challenges in the courts.

Changes in employer policies have largely matched changes in public policy. In large corporations especially, benefit programs now routinely recognize same-sex partners as "families." In these and other institutions, the social acceptance of sexual diversity is often partial, and certainly uneven, but formally discriminatory policies would not survive a legal or union challenge.

Less clear-cut movement has been evident in some other policy areas. Censorship of gay and lesbian images by Canadian customs agents at border points remains a bone of political and legal contention. The acceptance of sexual diversity by police forces, evidenced in their personnel recruitment and their regulation of lesbian and gay establishments, is often halfhearted, and in some locales not even that.

Only a few school boards across Canada have even begun to address issues of sexual diversity among their students, teachers, and administrative staff. Even Toronto's public board, which has the longest history of developing inclusive policies, has not succeeded in ensuring implementation across its system. There and elsewhere, individual schools and teachers have taken up issues of sexuality; but in the secondary school sector, and even more at the elementary level, such matters are still regarded as controversial and risky. Transgendered issues have only barely been addressed in public policy and institutional practice, though modest steps have been taken in offering protections against discrimination in a few provinces.

The three provinces where most gains in law, public policy, and institutional practice have been made are British Columbia, Ontario, and Quebec. Their metropolitan centers—Vancouver, Toronto, and Montreal, respectively—are in their distinctive ways gay-friendly. Most of the path-breaking policy developments or court challenges have originated in those provinces, and the media coverage given to them has been largely positive. Public opinion on sexual orientation issues is more positive in those regions than in others, particularly in the more gay-friendly British Columbia and Quebec.

Quebec's population now regularly registers the most acceptance of gays in responses to surveys, in part because of low levels of religious practice in the province, and the relative weakness of religious voices in political debate. Popular support also reflects repeated suggestions by nationalist politicians that Quebec's distinctiveness is attributable in part to its supposedly more relaxed views of sexuality as compared with the rest of Canada. This has often not been reflected in public policy, with the provincial government being at least as hesitant to act as other provinces (for example in AIDS, policing, schooling, and relationship recognition). But with legislative steps taken in 1999 and 2002, Quebec has put into place a comprehensive "civil union" regime, open to same- and opposite-sex couples. In the rights and obligations extended to lesbian and gay couples, this system is not categorically different from those already in place, or being put into place, in other provinces (like Nova Scotia), but it does have the symbolic addition that comes with civil union registration.

Some regional and sub-regional variations in policy response to sexual diversity come from differences in the partisan balance in provincial politics; some also result from long-standing sociocultural differences. Levels of religious practice also vary significantly across regions, as does adherence to morally conservative spiritual traditions. Alberta is home to one of the country's most important concentrations of conservative Protestantism, and is fertile ground for antigay political mobilization. Such forms of Christian belief, however, are much less widespread in Canada than they are in the United States, and are more likely to be seen (by the media and the voting public) as extreme. The one political party in which religiously conservative views on abortion and gay rights are given assertive voice (the Canadian Alliance) has had recurrent difficulties portraying itself as a credible political voice outside pockets of the western provinces with concentrations of religious conservatism. Right-wing, neoliberal politics has become a forceful presence in the Canadian partisan landscape since the 1980s, but, unlike the United States, its reinvigoration has not been linked to moral or social conservatism.

Despite resource limits, and relative weakness of national organization, the activism deriving from sexual diversity has had significant political impact. This positions Canada alongside the Netherlands and Scandinavian countries in responsiveness to equity demands from sexual minorities, even if, as in such countries, unfriendliness and anxiety evoked by outward expressions of sexual diversity remain widespread.

—*David Rayside*

See also Human Rights (Canada)

Further Reading

Kinsman, G. (1996). *The regulation of desire: Homo and hetero sexualities* (Rev. ed.). Montreal, QC: Black Rose.

Rayside, D. (1998). *On the fringe: Gays and lesbians in politics.* Ithaca, NY: Cornell University Press.

Smith, M. (1999). *Lesbian and gay rights in Canada: Social movements and equality-seeking, 1971–1995.* Toronto, ON: University of Toronto Press.

Warner, T. (2002). *Never going back: A history of queer activism in Canada.* Toronto, ON: University of Toronto Press.

GAY, LESBIAN, BISEXUAL, TRANSGENDER POLICY ISSUES (MEXICO)

The concepts of homosexuality and bisexuality—defined in terms of object choice—arrived in Mexico soon after their emergence in European psychoanalysis and sexology. They accompanied other academic ideas brought by the Mexican educated elite, who at the time considered Europe as the source of cultural and scientific innovation. New interpretations of sexuality that emphasized object choice as the primary classificatory criterion contrasted sharply with understandings of sexual deviance that were prevalent in Mexico. Older interpretations in Mexico were based on expectations about gender roles and masculine/feminine demeanor. Individuals were transferred from the realm of normality into the realm of abnormality when their public demeanor suggested male effeminacy or female masculinity (or if they openly declared having same-sex attraction). In this classification system, individuals who were sexually attracted to their own sex could retain an identity as normal (*normales*) if their demeanor was consistent with social expectations of masculinity and femininity.

Over the course of the twentieth century, ideas about homosexuality spread and began to influence the formation of contemporary homosexual, lesbian, gay, and bisexual identities. Gender-based understandings of normality and deviance, however, did not disappear. Instead, they sometimes became combined with object-choice classifications in interpretations of sexual identity that are largely hybrid.

In the gender-based classificatory system in Mexico, masculine women typically have been assumed to reject men, or to want to be like men. This notion is captured in derogatory labels such as *machorra*. Other derogatory terms—*tortillera, chanclera*—denote the perception that "real" sex cannot happen in the absence of a penis. In the case of effeminate men, they have been assumed to play a sexual role similar to "that of a woman"—to seek sexual relations with masculine men who anally penetrate them. Derogatory labels commonly used to refer to effeminate men—*maricón, joto*—emphasize their being considered "less of a man" or, alternatively, their sexual availability (as in the term *puto*).

By contrast, more contemporary labels that are now common in Mexico, including *homosexual, gay,* and *lesbiana,* not only have been appropriated by those who wish to destigmatize homosexuality, but also contain no necessary connotations about gender roles or demeanor. These newer Mexican identities challenge the stereotype that exists among many in the United States that it is not possible to be gay or lesbian in Mexico. The notion of *transgénero*—understood in terms that go beyond the demeanor-based identities of transvestites (*vestidas* or *travestis*)—is of recent arrival in Mexico. It is important not to assume, however, that these contemporary terms mean exactly the same things in Mexico and the United States, since in Mexico their meanings have been influenced by local (often hybrid) interpretations.

CONTEMPORARY HOMOSEXUALITIES IN MEXICO

There is evidence of the existence of homosexual and lesbian social networks and gathering places in Mexican cities throughout the twentieth century. As demonstrated by Joseph Carrier's work, by the late 1960s several Mexican cities had homosexual bars and, later, U.S.-style dance clubs. These places were sometimes clandestine but tolerated by local authorities. Ian Lumsden has indicated that tolerance often meant that they were allowed to exist so long as owners paid bribes, and that they were often under threat of police raids and other forms of harassment by government officials. Despite these limitations, a fairly visible presence of homosexual men and lesbians developed in cities such as Mexico City, Guadalajara, Veracruz, and Acapulco. By the mid 1990s, homosexual gathering places were listed in weekly cultural

guides of newspapers in Guadalajara and Mexico City, as well as in gay magazines sold in newspaper stands.

Beginning in the early 1970s, influenced by the U.S. gay liberation movement, homosexual men and women formed small political and cultural groups. Collectively, these groups refer to themselves and their efforts as the Mexican gay and lesbian movement. Some of these groups emerged out of the 1960s student movement and were initially strongly linked to the political Left and, to some degree, to feminist organizing. In the late 1970s, the groups began to hold yearly gay and lesbian pride marches in Mexico City, which attracted several thousand participants. During the 1980s and 1990s, marches and other group activities took place in response to the changing political and economic climate. In 1991, Mexico hosted a meeting of the International Lesbian and Gay Association (ILGA), the first time it had met outside of Europe. It was held in Acapulco after social conservatives in Guadalajara prevented it from being held there. Since 2001, visible and well-attended gay and lesbian marches have occurred in Mexico City and Guadalajara.

During the 1980s, gay and lesbian groups were instrumental in initiating programs to combat AIDS, a shift in focus that curtailed, at least temporarily, emphasis on gay and lesbian organizing. Since then, the mass media have been used to present counterpoints to the antihomosexual attitudes of social conservatives. Gay and lesbian groups have questioned police repression of homosexuals as well as discrimination and violence against homosexuals. They organized events, such as an annual gay and lesbian cultural week in Mexico City, and have participated in international gay and lesbian conferences. In 1997, gay and lesbian activists were active in constructing the political platform that resulted in Patria Jiménez, a lesbian activist in Mexico City, being selected for a proportional representation position in the Chamber of Deputies representing the center-left Democratic Revolution party (*Partido de la Revolución Democrática,* or PRD).

Homosexuality is not illegal in Mexico but homosexuals have been prosecuted through the use of legal codes that regulate obscene or lurid behavior (*atentados a la moral*). Over the past two decades, there have been reports of violence against homosexual men, including the murders of openly gay men in Mexico City and of transvestites (*travesties*) in Chiapas. Local gay activists note that often these cases remain unsolved, blaming the police for lack of interest in investigating them and for assuming that homosexuals are responsible for the attacks against them.

Overall, however, men and women who self-identify as *homosexuales, gays,* or *lesbianas* in urban Mexico have created social networks and found public spaces for socialization without much social interference. Because of Mexican expectations that sexual differences be dealt with by "sexual silence" and fear of discrimination against homosexuals in the family, school, or workplace, it is common for gays and lesbians to be cautious in disclosing their sexual orientation. Mexican *homosexuales, gays,* and *lesbianas* frequently assume that those close to them know about their homosexuality. But leading "double lives" is often seen as necessary to ensure that one's connections with the nonhomosexual world remain intact. In the absence of legislation against discrimination, this strategy is perceived also as providing protection against being expelled from school or losing a job.

In recent years, there have been attempts to include homosexuality in Mexico City's antidiscrimination code. Today, young gays and lesbians often disclose their sexual orientation to families and heterosexual friends and in their workplaces. They assume that disclosing their sexual orientations will not produce extremely negative consequences.

MODERNIZATION AND CULTURAL CHANGE

Disclosure of one's homosexuality is facilitated by the ever-increasing visibility of homosexuals in the Mexican mass media. The onset of AIDS in the mid 1980s created considerable debate and public discussion about homosexuality. Many voices, both supportive and oppositional, such as the Roman Catholic church, have participated in public discussions that increased awareness and understanding of homosexuality. The popularity of gay tourism in Puerto Vallarta and elsewhere has also brought more national attention to the presence of homosexuality in Mexico.

Today, many Mexicans feel that acceptance of homosexuality is a sign of cultural modernity. Among some young, urban heterosexuals, it has become popular to attend gay dance clubs and to have gay friends. Overall, conservative voices, including those of the Catholic church, have not prevented the development of progressive and liberal attitudes about homosexuality.

In Mexican popular culture, it is now common to include gay characters on Mexican sitcoms and soap operas (*telenovelas*), and to discuss homosexuality on Mexican talk shows. But representations of male homosexuals in those shows vary widely. They include stereotypical versions of male effeminacy meant to provide comic relief as well as representations meant to increase social awareness and to generate greater acceptance of homosexuality. Similar efforts to represent *lesbianas* as television characters have not occurred. This absence might be related to the more general invisibility of lesbian lifestyles in Mexico. Over time, it is apparent that there is increasing acceptance of gays and lesbians in Mexican society.

—Héctor Carrillo

Current Comment

Lumsden, I. G. (1991). *Homosexuality, society and the state in Mexico.* Toronto, ON: Canadian Gay Archives.

Monsiváis, C. (1998). El mundo soslayado. Prologue of S. Novo, *La estatua de sal.* Mexico City: Consejo Nacional de Cultura.

Novo, S. (1979). Memoir. In W. Leyland (Ed.), *Now the volcano: An anthology of Latin American gay literature* (pp. 11–47). San Francisco: Gay Sunshine Press.

Taylor, C. L. (1978). *El ambiente: Male homosexual social life in Mexico City.* Unpublished doctoral dissertation, University of California, Berkeley.

Further Reading

Carrier, J. (1995). *De los otros: Intimacy and homosexuality among Mexican men.* New York: Columbia University Press.

Carrillo, H. (2002). *The night is young: Sexuality in Mexico in the time of AIDS.* Chicago: University of Chicago Press.

Mogrovejo, N. (2000). *Un amor que se atrevió a decir su nombre: La lucha de las lesbianas y su relación con los movimientos homosexual y feminista en América Latina.* Mexico City: Centro de Documentación y Archivo Histórico Lésbico.

Prieur, A. (1998). *Mema's house, Mexico City: On transvestites, queens, and machos.* Chicago: University of Chicago Press.

GAY, LESBIAN, BISEXUAL, TRANSGENDER POLICY ISSUES (UNITED STATES)

People who are attracted to others of the same gender have been known to exist for many centuries and popular attitudes toward them have changed over time. It was not until 1869 that the term "homosexual" was coined, a term that was initially framed by psychologists to create a category or label for such attractions, and to help them build their profession by creating diagnosable illnesses to treat, and to be recognized as professionals.

Since the beginning of the twentieth century, gay men and lesbians have come together to socialize and politicize, yet the emergence of the modern lesbian, gay, bisexual, and transgendered (LGBT) civil rights movement is widely recognized to have its roots in the aftermath of the 1969 Stonewall Riots, during which patrons of a local bar in New York turned on police during a raid. The rebellion was sparked in part by frustration with continuing police harassment and badgering of establishments that catered to the lesbian and gay communities. In addition to the harassment issues, gay men and lesbians charged the police with brutality and not responding to calls for help by gay men and lesbians for protection from beatings and harassment.

At the time of the Stonewall Riots, and for some time after, the movement was focused mainly on the rights of gay men, even though lesbians had long been involved in the quest for equal protection and recognition. Beginning in the early 1980s, lesbians became involved in a more activist way, and pushed for recognition of their status within the movement, rather than being rendered invisible under the guise of a "gay only" movement. Groups began renaming themselves to include lesbians as active participants in the movement. At the beginning of the 1990s, the same demands would be made by members of the bisexual and transgendered communities, resulting in the inclusion of these communities in the movement. There was clear recognition that sexual minorities were a very large group of people who had been largely ignored by the larger society and its social welfare policies.

The Stonewall Riots marked a significant change of belief and action for the members of the LGBT communities. Stonewall marked the beginnings of a more political movement, one in which members of the communities would no longer be pushed into hiding and living in fear. In the 1970s, the American Psychiatric Association voted to remove homosexuality from categorization as a mental disorder, a move that prompted activists to seek the decriminalization of their existence and to push for equal rights in the society.

Shortly after the Stonewall Riots, several organizations were formed to address the invisibility of gay and lesbian people. The National Gay Task Force (later to rename itself as the National Gay and Lesbian Task Force) and the Human Rights Campaign utilized mainstream political lobbying to achieve their objectives. Each organization had its explicit mission, but both focused on educating lesbian and gay communities as well as the general population. They lobbied at federal, state, and local levels for policy changes that would give LGBT communities adequate government protection. In 1974, California and New York moved to decriminalize homosexuality. Today, there are still 12 states that have not decriminalized homosexuality, even though there have been many attempts to do so by LGBT communities and their allies.

In the 1980s, the AIDS virus began to affect gay men in large cities, particularly New York and San Francisco. Gay men in New York, California, Illinois, and Florida were infected by the hundreds of thousands, with many of them facing death in a very short time. Much of the public saw AIDS as a virus that affected only gay men, and some blamed them for spreading the virus. Many social and political conservatives criticized gay lifestyles and continued to oppose the quest for gay and lesbian equal rights. Gay men grew increasingly frustrated by the unwillingness of government and the public at large to deal with the AIDS crisis. Throughout the 1980s, LGBT communities continued their fight for greater visibility and equal rights.

With the advent of the AIDS crisis, new groups, including Queer Nation and the AIDS Coalition to Unleash Power (ACT-UP), engaged in radical social and political action to argue for greater recognition of issues and concerns within the LGBT community. The failure of the federal government to take steps to prevent the spread of the AIDS virus, or to conduct research to find effective treatments, spurred increased political action and more public awareness of the AIDS crisis. A secondary effect was the increased awareness of the existence of LGBT communities in most metropolitan areas. By 1989, protest rallies and marches brought public attention to AIDS and the need for the health community to provide AIDS testing and treatment. In the 1990s, LGBT activism resulted in increased public concern as well as increased funding for AIDS research and treatment. The success of the AIDS movement motivated LGBT activists to pursue their quest for greater recognition and support of LGBT civil rights. In 1987, the March on Washington for Gay and Lesbian Civil Rights attracted more than 100,000 participants. Advocates presented a comprehensive list of demands to the federal government. They called for an end to discrimination in employment, housing, and education and demanded inheritance rights, partner benefits, and child custodial rights. Despite the large numbers of demonstrators, there was no response from the federal government, and by the end of the 1980s there was still virtually no inclusion of LGBT persons in civil rights protections.

By the beginning of the 1990s, the political environment was such that many political candidates running for office were seeking the endorsement of the LGBT communities. To gain votes and resources from the LGBT community, politicians at federal, state, and local levels made campaign promises that were difficult to fulfill. For example, in 1990, after winning the gubernatorial election in California, Governor Pete Wilson decided not to sign legislation prohibiting discrimination against gay men and lesbians even though he had pledged to do so if elected. This ignited outrage and anger in the LGBT community and riots broke out in San Francisco and Los Angeles. Protests were held at the state capitol in Sacramento, and a march on Washington was planned. The 1990s became a decade of increased visibility and recognition of the need for policies and laws that could assure a greater degree of equal treatment for the LGBT community.

Attempts to enact protective and supportive policies at the federal level were met with fierce opposition by an increasingly conservative Congress. In 1993, when President William J. Clinton promised to end discrimination against gay men and lesbians in the military, and introduced regulations to do so, he was faced with open and virulent hostility. Because of the fierce political backlash, he compromised and crafted the "Don't Ask, Don't Tell" policy, which was designed to stop the discharge from the military of men and women based solely on their sexual orientation. President Clinton did not foresee that the policy would result in an even larger number of forced military discharges of those who are, or are suspected of being, gay or lesbian. LGBT communities concluded that the president's broken promise was an act of betrayal. Growing frustration and concern over the government's unwillingness to address LGBT concerns resulted in the 1993 march on Washington, which drew an attendance of over 500,000 marchers and demonstrators.

Although little was accomplished at the federal level to assist the LGBT community, many positive changes were occurring at local levels and in the workplace. By the mid 1990s, many city governments, public employers, and businesses implemented policies prohibiting discrimination against anyone based on sexual orientation. Many began to offer domestic partner benefits. The LGBT community shifted its focus to change at the state and local levels and often succeeded, even as national political trends saw a shift toward a conservative agenda.

As the twentieth century came to a close, the conservative movement was able to impede or prevent efforts to end discrimination against persons because of their sexual orientation. In 1999, the supreme court of Hawaii ruled that marriage could not be denied to people based on their sexual orientation. The backlash resulted in the U.S. Congress enacting legislation prohibiting any state from recognizing any marriage not involving a man and a woman. This occurred when other countries were moving in the opposite direction, approving gay and lesbian marriage, gay and lesbian adoption, and other equal access policies. Within the United States, the more conservative environment has led the LGBT communities to focus on holding onto gains made, while still advocating for policies that will address threats to civil rights such as hate crimes.

—*Nancy M. Nystrom*

Primary Sources

Gay and Lesbian Studies Collection, Research Libraries, New York Public Library, NY (www.nypl.org/research/chss/grd/resguides/gay/index.html); GLBT Historical Society, San Francisco, CA (www. glbthistory.org/); Lesbian Legacy Collection Library & Archives, Los Angeles, CA (www-lib.usc.edu/~retter/one.html); Gay, Lesbian, Bisexual & Transgender Library/Archives of Philadelphia, PA (www.stevecap.com/libdraft/); Old Lesbians Organizing for Change (OLOC) Archives, Houston, TX (www.oloc.org/).

Further Reading

Cruikshank, M. (1992). *The gay and lesbian liberation movement.* New York: Routledge.

Kochman, A. (1997). Gay and lesbian elderly: Historical overview and implications for social work practice. In J. Quam (Ed.), *Social services for senior gay men and lesbians* (pp. 1–10). New York: Haworth.

Van Wormer, K., Wells, J., & Boes, M. (2000). *Social work with lesbians, gays, and bisexuals.* Needham Heights, MA: Allyn & Bacon.

Warner, M. (Ed.). (1993). *Fear of a queer planet: Queer politics and social theory.* Minneapolis: University of Minnesota Press.

GENERAL INSANE ASYLUM: *LA CASTAÑEDA* (MEXICO)

While the history of mental health care in Mexico dates back to colonial times—an era in which private parties, with the support of the Catholic church, established the *San Hipólito* and the *Divino Salvador* hospitals devoted to the care of mentally ill men and women, respectively—the emergence of the General Insane Asylum in 1910 represented the transition from custody and charity to therapy and correction in the history of mental health policy. The inception and planning of the "great hospital," as the General Insane Asylum project was called, grew at irregular intervals over a period of 24 years at the turn of the twentieth century in Mexico.

Analysis of confinement techniques and the role of state-funded insane asylums began as early as 1883, 7 years before classes on psychiatry were taught at the School of Medicine in Mexico City and only 6 years

after Porfirio Díaz became president of Mexico. Experts in a variety of fields—ranging from medicine to welfare, architecture to urban planning—began what was to become a long, at times stalled dialogue about the social, economic, and medical functions of large, state-funded insane asylums. As the project evolved, a diversity of perspectives and long-term goals came under scrutiny, yet they did not generate the vehement opposition that similar undertakings elicited in countries such as England. Indeed, most participants in the project agreed that "modern nations were measured by the extent of their public works," and most perceived state investment in an insane asylum as a clear sign of Mexico's growing modernity.

With this conviction in mind, Mexican experts identified and collected documents from foreign asylums, translated sources, evaluated existing institutions of mental health, drew blueprints, and elaborated budgets. Yet, an official committee did not emerge until 1894. Renewed state funds and increasing interest in the pathologies of the mind in the golden years of the Porfirian era led to the completion of the final asylum project in 1905. Still, deliberations continued. A new set of experts—criminologists and psychiatrists, engineers and welfare bureaucrats—studied the project carefully and made further suggestions regarding location, architectural design and decoration, medical treatments and technology, and even personnel issues.

It was not until 1908 that Porfirio Díaz, Jr., the son of the president, took charge of the construction works, which he completed in time for official inauguration on September 1, 1910—the first day of the month-long festivities organized for Mexico's centenary of independence. Sharing a relentless faith in the progressive nature of Porfirian society, most particularly modern medicine, and real anxieties caused by rapid change, the members of the different boards charged with the design of the asylum produced paradoxical views of institutions for the insane as both sites of control and places of refuge. Equally concerned with the improvement of psychiatric treatments and with the ordering of society at large, the ambivalence that permeated the Mexican asylum from beginning to end resulted in the construction of a massive establishment that, regardless of its unitary appearance, became various institutions over time.

The General Insane Asylum of Mexico City took shape imitating and challenging foreign architectural standards—especially those generated in the United States, known as the Kirkbride plan, and France, with the heavy influence from the urban redesign of Paris led by Haussmann. As expected, the asylum's appearance was spectacular. Surrounded by 32,925 square meters of gardens and forests, where authorities established the agricultural colony and the stables, the asylum also had 271 square meters of manicured lawns at the entrance of the institution. Structured in wards disseminated around a central building devoted to administrative affairs, the mental health institution soon became synonymous with Mixcoac, the peripheral village in which it was strategically located and, more pointedly, with *La Castañeda,* the original name of the hacienda acquired by the state to build the modern asylum. Organized according to a strict hierarchy, which placed doctors and administrators on the top, paying boarders over nonpaying ones, the institution, however, lacked professional vigilance. The professionals who created *La Castañeda* were well aware of the medical relevance of the insane asylum, but they never forgot the symbolic weight it conveyed. For this reason, those involved in the creation of the General Insane Asylum saw themselves not only as guardians of the mental health of affected individuals but also, and perhaps more important, as champions of the social order of the community and, by extension, of the entire nation. So *La Castañeda,* just as the general hospital and the penitentiary, became an eloquent reminder of the ascending level of modernization achieved by the regime of Porfirio Díaz.

While some still remember *La Castañeda* as a monumental complex "occupying nine blocks, almost 100,000 meters, with beautifully made wards, and each one destined to a different mental condition," the General Insane Asylum changed drastically, and at a rapid pace, after September 1910. The Mexican Revolution—a social upheaval that took over one million lives in the country—impacted the General Insane Asylum shortly after its official inauguration. Indeed, without the economic and political investment that gave it birth, the asylum soon faced mounting financial dilemmas, which affected both its administrative and medical branches, forcing a gradual redefinition of the institution as a whole. Rather than the medical and research institute envisioned by modernizing Porfirians, the establishment quickly reverted to its custodial functions. Although neglected, however, the asylum remained open throughout the early revolutionary era, fulfilling important welfare functions.

During the early postrevolutionary years, asylum authorities launched a sweeping medical and administrative reform that was intended to give new life to the institution. Although this asylum reform of 1929 brought much needed resources and attention to *La Castañeda,* it also represented, paradoxically, the beginning of the end. As asylum authorities had done in 1910, Samuel Ramírez Moreno and Manuel Guevara Oropeza, physician-directors of the institution between 1928 and 1932, depicted the 1930 reform as a breakthrough in the history of mental health in Mexico, but its glory was similarly short-lived. Authorities and psychiatrists incessantly fought to modernize the asylum, but old problems soon emerged again, namely overpopulation, lack of resources, and, eventually, social indifference. By 1940, the asylum, which had a capacity for 1,500 inmates, housed 3,139. Although the institution required 2.2 million *pesos* per year, it worked with only half of that budget.

In 1944, Edmundo Buentello became the new physician-director, and his plan of action reproduced concerns and solutions already tried in the past. In strongly supporting the system of work therapy, for example, he called for more resources to keep asylum workshops running. He also established classes for nurses and attendants to "increase the cultural and educational level of those who are under obligation, whether for bureaucratic or humanitarian concerns, to save inmates." He appointed "permanent committees" to analyze and find solutions for technical problems, such as feeding inmates, and for larger societal issues, such as the place of inmates in both penal and civil legislation. Buentello's plan, however, also featured innovative measures that included the creation of mental health facilities other than *La Castañeda.* Among them were, first, the construction of new asylums both in Mexico City and in the provinces; and second, the creation of *granjas para alienados* or, literally, farms for alienated individuals, devoted solely to the care of chronic patients who, while incurable, were still able to work. The first farm, located in San Pedro del Monte, near Leon, in the state of Guanajuato, was opened later that year. Lastly, Buentello recommended the creation of a system of external service, designed for inmates already integrated into society or mental health patients who did not need intensive psychiatric care.

These measures were intended to relieve the burdens of *La Castañeda,* but they were not intended to replace an institution most psychiatrists regarded as a center for scientific research of national relevance. This was, however, exactly what began in 1965. Under the title of *Operación Castañeda,* the Secretariat of Health and Welfare (*Secretaría de Salubridad y Asistencia*) mandated the final closing of the General Insane Asylum in 1968 and the creation of a series of hospitals designed to replace it, namely a hospital for acute mental patients with 600 beds, a pediatric hospital for 200 children, three country hospitals with 500 beds each, and two home-hospitals for incurable patients with 250 beds each. Then, brick by brick, the General Insane Asylum was dismantled, literally deconstructing a long saga of mental health care in Mexico.

—*Cristina Rivera-Garza*

See also Hygiene and Public Health Policy During the Porfiriato (Mexico)

Primary Sources

Records of the General Insane Asylum, *La Castañeda, Archivo Histórico de la Secretaría de Salubridad y Asistencia, Fondo Manicomio General,* Mexico City.

Current Comment

Moreno, S. R. (1940, September–November). Anexos psiquiátricos en los hospitales generales. *Revista Mexicana de Psiquiatría, Neurología y Medicina Legal, 8,* 75–76.
Narváez, G. C. (1966). Hospitales psiquiátricos de México: Desde la colonia hasta la actualidad. *Revista Mexicana de Neurología y Psiquiatría, 7*(3).

Further Reading

Berkstein Kanarek, C. B. (1981). *El hospital Divino Salvador.* Unpublished master's thesis, Universidad Nacional Autónoma de México, Mexico City.
Leiby, J. S. (1992). San Hipólito's treatment of the mentally ill in Mexico City, 1589–1650. *The Historian, 54*(3), 491–498.
Rivera-Garza, C. (2001). Dangerous minds: Changing psychiatric views of the mentally ill in Porfirian Mexico, 1876–1911. *Journal of the History of Medicine and Allied Sciences, 56*(1), 36–67.

Rivera-Garza, C. (2001). 'She neither respected nor obeyed anyone': Inmates and psychiatrists debate gender and class at the General Insane Asylum, La Castañeda, Mexico, 1910–1930. *Hispanic American Historical Review, 81,* 3–4.

GROUP WORK (CANADA)

Social group work in Canada arose out of the settlement movement that began in Great Britain in the 1870s as a response to the dramatic and dire social effects of the Industrial Revolution. The movement spread first to the United States, and later to Canada. The settlement movement provided a means to offer personal and community assistance to poor people and a vehicle for social action to address the new realities of the late nineteenth century. The period was characterized by developing industrialization: migration to cities, brutal working conditions and health-threatening living environments, poverty, and fractured family and community life. By the early years of the twentieth century, the effects of the Industrial Revolution were felt also in Canada. As Breton (1990, p. 22) observed, "The settlement movement chose to perceive people not only as individuals but as members of social groups and cultures affected by the social, economic, and political conditions in which they lived," calling for reforms to remedy unjust conditions, and acting on the belief that those affected should be involved in changing them. During this same era, social group work was born also out of the recreation and progressive education movements, both, like the settlement movement, based on a recognition of people as political entities and the value of social action to improve the circumstances of living.

Rooted in social gospel philosophy and purposes, but established under both religious and secular auspices, settlement houses appeared in Canadian cities, with Evangelia House in Toronto, Ontario, in 1902 as the first, an undertaking by Sara Libby Carson and Mary Lawson Bell and the Dominion Council of the YWCA. The Presbyterian church followed by setting up a chain of settlement houses: St. Christopher House in Toronto in 1912; Chalmers House in Montreal, Quebec, in 1912; Robertson Memorial House in Winnipeg, Manitoba, in 1913; St. Columba House in Point St. Charles in Montreal in 1917;

Vancouver Community House in Vancouver, British Columbia, in 1918; and Neighbourhood House in Hamilton, Ontario, in 1922.

Church-founded settlement houses provided a variety of activities to their neighbors, but tended not to be involved in the political action or social reform activities typical of settlements in Great Britain and the United States. University Settlement House and Central Neighbourhood House, however, both established as secular organizations in Toronto in 1911, introduced social activism into the work of the movement, laying the foundation for the development and recognition of social group work as a social work practice method in the 1930s. The settlement house heritage stamped social group work with its mission of community-based practice activity focused on meeting needs related to people's life issues and environmental conditions, inherently charged with concepts of empowerment, social justice, and action toward personal, community, and societal change.

During the early decades of social group work, Canadian experience paralleled, if it did not overlap, that of the United States. The American Association of Group Workers (AAGW) was an international organization with members in Canada and the United States. AAGW published a journal, *The Group*, from 1939 to 1955, an excellent resource with a wide readership in the United States and Canada. During the same period, another organization, the American Association for the Study of Group Work (AASGW), also had Canadian membership, and published periodic position papers. An interdisciplinary journal, the *Autonomous Groups Bulletin*, made a significant international contribution in the same time period.

Applying settlement concepts, social group work was evident in a myriad of neighborhood groups in community centers, Girls' and Boys' Clubs, YW- and YMCAs, YW- and YMHAs, Girl Guides and Boy Scouts, church youth groups, the camping movement, the co-op movement, *animation sociale* in Quebec, and community development work. Group workers regarded democratic group forms and democratic processes as essential to individual fulfillment and vital to a participatory citizenry. Accordingly, and reflecting the work of the secular settlements, social group workers served as providers of direct service to members and also as activists in areas of policy and social justice.

Social group work in Canada has been influenced and strengthened by its proximity to the United States, through the provision of educational resources, and by immigration. Social group work was taught at Canadian schools of social work as they became established in the early decades of the 1900s. Canadians also attended American universities for social group work training.

In current social work practice, the spirit of the settlement movement and early social group work can be seen in social work education and practice that speaks to issues of empowerment, anti-oppression, and social justice. Much group practice at present is problem-focused and specific to particular vulnerable and marginalized populations; it is also often time limited and structured in format. Components of social justice and social action, however, may be seen in many Canadian group work practices, an indication of the survival of the settlement movement's mission to provide personal assistance and a means for people to challenge and change communities and society to embrace full inclusion and social justice. An increase in the number of groups focused on various aspects of diversity and capacity-building holds hope that social group work in Canada is beginning to move back to its traditional mandate.

—Ellen Sue Mesbur and Nancy Sullivan

See also Community Development (Canada); Small Systems Social Work (Canada)

Further Reading

Breton, M. (1990). Learning from social group work traditions. *Social Work With Groups, 13*(3), 21–34.

Irving, A., Parsons, H., & Bellamy, D. (1995). *Neighbours: Three social settlements in downtown Toronto*. Toronto, ON: Canadian Scholars' Press.

Mesbur, E. S. (2002). Social group work practice: The Canadian experience. In F. J. Turner (Ed.), *Social work practice: A Canadian perspective* (pp. 282–300). Toronto, ON: Pearson Education Canada.

Ross, M. (1951). *The YMCA in Canada*. Toronto, ON: Ryerson.

Sullivan, N., & Mesbur, E. S. (in press). Groupwork practice. In F. J. Turner (Ed.), *Canadian encyclopedia of social work*. Waterloo, ON: Wilfrid Laurier University Press.

H

HAMILTON, ALICE (1869–1970)

Dr. Alice Hamilton is known for her pioneering work in industrial toxicology and occupational diseases and for her commitment to social reform. Born on February 27, 1869, in New York to Montgomery Hamilton and Gertrude Pond Hamilton, Alice was the second of five children—four girls and one boy. Hamilton grew up in relative social isolation, living on a large estate in Indiana with three houses inhabited by her family and her cousins. As a child, Hamilton's family was well-to-do, and siblings and cousins provided sufficient playmates and companions for one another, building attachments that were deep and endured through Hamilton's life. Hamilton's parents disapproved of the curriculum of public schools and educated their children at home. At 17, following a path set by her aunts and sister (classics scholar Edith Hamilton), Hamilton left Fort Wayne to study at Miss Porter's School for Young Ladies, an exclusive finishing school in Farmington, Connecticut.

The family's resources had dwindled significantly by the time Hamilton returned to Fort Wayne, thanks in large part to the failure of her father's business in 1885. Knowing that she would have to work for a living, Hamilton chose a career in medicine despite strong objections from her family. She began her medical training at Fort Wayne Medical College, and in 1892, enrolled in the Medical College of the University of Michigan—then one of the best medical schools in the country. In her last year at Michigan, she decided to become a bacteriologist and pathologist rather than a practicing physician. After completing internships in Minneapolis and Boston she spent a year in Germany, attending classes at the Universities of Leipzig and Munich, followed by another year of study at Johns Hopkins University.

In 1897, Hamilton accepted an offer to teach pathology at the Women's Medical College of Northwestern University in Chicago, an offer that allowed her to fulfill a long-held dream of living at the Hull House settlement. At the settlement, Hamilton quickly found her way to the inner circle that included strong women reformers such as Jane Addams, Florence Kelley, and Julia Lathrop. She remained in residence at the settlement for 22 years, and during that time assumed personal responsibility for safeguarding the health of Jane Addams. She left the settlement in 1919, but returned for a part of each year until the death of Addams in 1935.

Settlement work was transforming for Hamilton, bringing together the two major themes of her career: a dedication to science and a commitment to public service. Recalling her settlement years, she wrote, "To me, the life there satisfied every longing, for companionship, for the excitement of new experiences, for constant intellectual stimulation, and for the sense of being caught up in a big movement which enlisted my enthusiastic loyalty." Residence in the settlement opened to Hamilton the world of political thought and action, while life in Chicago's Nineteenth Ward exposed her to conditions of poverty and social need. She instituted some practical programs at Hull House, such as starting a well-baby clinic; but her real interests emerged in 1902 when Chicago faced a typhoid epidemic. Incidence of typhoid was much higher in the Nineteenth Ward, where Hamilton suspected that appalling sanitary conditions, particularly the hordes of flies, contributed to the spread of disease. Hamilton collected flies from the streets surrounding nearby tenements, and microscopic examination revealed the presence of typhoid. Her investigation and its results brought her recognition, but it was only later that she learned an even more valuable lesson. While disease-bearing insects increased the incidence of typhoid, a more significant factor in spreading the disease was a break in the pipes at a local pumping station. This resulted in raw sewage leaking into drinking water for a period of 3 days, a fact that the Chicago Board of Health kept from the public. Hamilton came to understand that although scientific knowledge was necessary for the protection of public health, political and social realities could not be ignored in gaining social reform and protective policies.

In 1908, Illinois Governor Charles S. Deneen appointed Hamilton to the Illinois Commission on Occupational Diseases, and in 1910 she became the supervisor of the state's survey of industrial poisons. The study focused on lead, the most widely used industrial poison, and combined lab experiments with field study to document nearly 600 cases of lead poisoning, an estimate Hamilton considered conservative. In response to the commission's findings, Illinois passed a law requiring safety measures for employees who worked with certain toxins, including lead and arsenic. In 1911, Charles O'Neill, the commissioner of the Bureau of Labor (the Bureau of Labor became the Department of Labor in 1912) invited Hamilton to replicate her survey at the federal level. She accepted the position, which provided no pay, and for the next 10 years investigated the health and social consequences that came from occupational exposure to toxic substances such as lead, arsenic, mercury, organic solvents, and radium. By 1916, she was the country's foremost expert on lead poisoning.

In 1919, Hamilton accepted a faculty position at Harvard Medical School—the first woman to hold a faculty appointment there—teaching in the area of industrial medicine. Because Harvard did not admit female students until World War II, all of her students were male. She continued doing industrial research while at Harvard, and from 1924 until 1930 served on the League of Nations Health Committee. She also wrote two major texts on industrial medicine, *Industrial Poisons in the United States* in 1925, and *Industrial Toxicology* in 1934 (revised in 1943).

Upon retiring from Harvard in 1935, Hamilton took a job as a consultant to the Department of Labor, Division of Labor Standards, and from 1944 until 1949 she served as president of the National Consumers League. In 1947, she received the Lasker Award from the U.S. Public Health Association, the first woman to have her work recognized with this award.

Throughout her life, Hamilton championed a range of social causes, including protective legislation for women and child laborers, birth control, and the protection of civil liberties for immigrants and aliens. She was deeply troubled by the conviction and death sentences of Nicola Sacco and Bartolomeo Vanzetti, and joined a group of citizens in a last-minute appeal to Massachusetts Governor Alvan Fuller for clemency. In the 1950s, she withdrew her opposition to the Equal Rights Amendment, which she had opposed because she feared it would undo some of the protective legislation in place for women workers. She also openly opposed McCarthyism, and in 1963 signed an open letter protesting American military involvement in Vietnam.

Deeply interested in international affairs, Hamilton devoted herself to the cause of peace. In 1915, she traveled with Jane Addams and Emily Balch to the International Congress of Women for a Permanent Peace at The Hague, and then toured the capitals of warring nations asking leaders to accept a mediated peace by a neutral party. She supported U.S. intervention in World War II, however, in part the result of having witnessed firsthand the Nazi stifling of dissent and persecution of the Jews during a visit to Germany in 1933.

She remained politically engaged well into her eighties, but in her nineties Alice Hamilton began to feel the infirmities that often accompany advancing age. She died of a stroke at her home in Hadlyme, Connecticut, on September 22, 1970, at the age of 101.

—*Megan Morrissey*

See also Addams, Jane; Hull House (United States); Settlement Houses (United States)

Primary Sources

The Alice Hamilton Papers and the Hamilton Family Papers are held by the Schlesinger Library on the History of Women in America, Radcliffe College, Cambridge, MA; Hamilton's letters from World War I are in the Swarthmore College Peace Collection, Swarthmore, PA.

Current Comment

Addams, J., Balch, E., & Hamilton, A. (1915). *Women at The Hague: The International Congress of Women and its results.* New York: Macmillan.
Hamilton, A. (1943). *Exploring the dangerous trades.* Boston: Little, Brown.

Further Reading

Sicherman, B. (1984). *Alice Hamilton: A life in letters.* Cambridge: Harvard University Press.

HEALTH POLICY (CANADA)

Canada's health care system is unique among industrialized countries: publicly financed hospital and medical care is delivered under uniform federal guidelines through 10 provincial and 3 territorial government systems by means of a mix of private and public services delivery (including public, not-for-profit, and for-profit services). This health care system has evolved slowly over the history of the country, and the national health insurance program (or "Medicare") has come to be perceived by Canadians as one of the country's defining social programs.

CONFEDERATION TO 1948

At the time of Confederation in 1867, health was considered a private rather than a public concern. Families and charitable and religious institutions provided the bulk of health services to community members.

Government's role was seen as largely restricted to epidemics and public health issues. Thus, under Canada's Constitution, the British North America Act (1867), where health care was mentioned, it was primarily a provincial responsibility. Provinces were given responsibility for the establishment, maintenance, and management of hospitals and asylums, whereas the federal government took on more limited responsibilities for marine hospitals and quarantine services for foreign entry. On the basis of early treaties, the federal government also took on responsibility for health services to aboriginal peoples.

Saskatchewan was the first province to experiment with a form of medical care insurance when, in 1914, a rural municipality offered physicians a retainer to practice in the area. The success of this plan led to the passage of an act in Saskatchewan to allow municipalities to levy property taxes to retain physicians and to develop many publicly supported plans across Saskatchewan. Communities in Manitoba and Alberta adopted similar plans. Also in Saskatchewan, in 1916 and 1917, acts were passed to allow municipalities to merge into hospital districts to build and maintain hospitals and to collect taxes for the financing of hospital care.

During the depression of the 1930s, managing costs of medical care became an issue. Hospitals were overwhelmed with the indigent, many municipalities went bankrupt, and people could not pay doctors' bills. Federally, the first attempt to develop national health insurance occurred in 1935, when the federal government passed the Employment and Social Insurance Act to collect taxes to provide Social Security benefits, including health benefits. The provinces challenged this act, however, as it trespassed on provincial jurisdiction. Other attempts by the federal government to establish a national health insurance program continued through the late 1930s and early 1940s, but these efforts failed because the provincial and federal governments could not agree on financial arrangements.

1948 TO 1977

With a role restricted to financing, the federal government still had considerable leverage in health care, as it could impose conditions under which it would provide funds to provinces. In 1948, the National Health Grants Act was passed, which included grants-in-aid to the provinces for hospital construction, laboratory services, and professional training for public health professionals. The Parliament enacted the Hospital Insurance and Diagnostic Services (HIDS) Act in 1957, and provided for 50 percent federal cost sharing of hospital services (excluding physician services) for provinces with a universal hospital insurance plan. Five provinces immediately joined, and, by 1961, HIDS was operating in all provinces and territories. HIDS ensured a basic uniformity of coverage for Canadians, but did not affect patterns of hospital care or ownership, nor did it affect provincial autonomy over health care delivery.

In terms of publicly funded physician services, Saskatchewan was once again the first to implement compulsory, government-sponsored medical insurance. The democratic socialist government of T. C. Douglas passed medical insurance legislation in 1961, despite a protracted and bitter physician's strike. Between 1963 and 1966, several other provinces, including Ontario, British Columbia, and Alberta, developed similar medical insurance programs. In 1965, the Royal Commission on Health Care (the Hall Commission, under Justice Emmett Hall) undertook a comprehensive review of health services in Canada and recommended strong federal leadership and financial support for medical care to ensure adequate coverage for all Canadians. As a result, discussions took place between the federal and provincial governments, and, in 1966, the federal government passed the Medical Care Act. It provided payments to provinces at a rate of half the average of the national per capita medical care cost multiplied by the number of insured in the province, and covered physicians' services and some dental and chiropractic services. For provinces to receive funding, services had to meet "four points": comprehensiveness (no dollar limits or exclusions, provided medical need was demonstrated), universality (at least 95 percent of eligible residents had to be covered), portability (from province to province, and to a lesser extent outside the country), and public administration (administered by a public agency accountable to the provincial government). By 1971, all provinces had programs that complied with the four points, and Canada's publicly funded hospital and medical care programs were in place.

1977 TO 1984

During the 1970s, the shared-cost programs became an issue for both provincial and federal governments, as inflation and rising costs of health care caused difficulties. Provinces also felt that the existing funding programs did not cover innovative services appropriately. As a result of negotiations, in 1977 the Federal-Provincial Fiscal Arrangements and Established Programs Financing Act (EPF Act) was passed. It provided for a financial contribution from the federal government for extended health care services (such as nursing homes, adult residential care, and ambulatory health care), but changed the funding formula for federal contributions so that contributions for hospital insurance and medical care (as well as postsecondary education) were no longer directly related to provincial costs. Instead, EPF was a block-funding system tied to economic growth under various formulas. Under EPF, cash and tax transfer points were provided to the provinces and territories.

Given the inflation that continued through the latter 1970s, federal contributions did not keep up with increasing costs, and provinces introduced cost containment measures such as restraints on physicians' fee-for-service schedules. Physicians in many provinces countered by "extra-billing" patients (charging patients directly for the portion above that provided by the fee schedule). In response, the federal government established a commission (again led by Justice Emmett Hall), which presented its findings in 1980. Where the previous Hall report had emphasized adequate coverage, the 1980 Hall report called attention to the issue of accessibility, suggesting that extra-billing was threatening accessibility of services for some people. A parliamentary task force also released a review of EPF financing in 1981. As a result of these two major reports, the Canada Health Act (CHA) was developed, and passed in 1984. The CHA replaced HIDS and the Medical Care Act, incorporated the hospital and medical care coverage included in these acts, and restated the principles and funding criteria of comprehensiveness, universality, portability, and public administration, and in addition, added accessibility (i.e., no obstructions to service such as extra-billing, and physical accessibility "where and as available"). Under the CHA, if provinces did not meet the criteria, cash portions of the federal contribution might be reduced.

1984 TO 2002

The CHA caused some conflict as several provincial governments enacted legislation to ban extra-billing. For example, in Ontario in 1986, many physicians went on a 25-day strike when legislation was introduced. By 1987, all five provinces that had allowed extra-billing had forbidden this practice.

Through the 1980s and 1990s, the federal level of financing for health care declined. In 1986, Bill C-96 was introduced, which reduced the annual per capita escalator under EPF to 2 percent below gross national product (GNP) growth. In 1996, Bill C-69 further reduced the escalator, and froze transfer payments for 2 years. As a result of these restrictions and as a result of concomitant cost-cutting efforts of provincial governments, cutbacks and restructuring of health services ensued. In response to a growing sense that one of Canada's most cherished social programs was under threat, in April 2001 the Commission on the Future of Health Care in Canada (the Romanow Commission) was established. The Romanow Commission report (November 2002) reaffirmed the commitment to publicly funded health care and the principles of the CHA and recommended new funding arrangements that would increase federal funding to provinces and add funding for new areas of service, including rural and remote access, home care, and catastrophic drug coverage. The current liberal federal government has endorsed the report, and at the time of writing has committed to implement the recommendations.

—Catherine A. Worthington

See also Mental Health Policy (Canada); Social Welfare (Canada): Before the Marsh Report; Social Welfare (Canada): Since the Marsh Report

Primary Sources

Tommy Douglas Fonds, Royal Commission on Health Services (1961–1967) Fonds, and Emmett Matthew Hall Fonds, Library and Archives Canada, Ottawa, ON (www.archives .ca/08/08_e.html).

Current Comment

Canadian Institute for Health Information. (2000–2002). *Health care in Canada: Something to talk about* [On-line]. Available: www.cihi.ca

Commission on the Future of Health Care in Canada (Romanow Commission report). (2002). Available www.hc-sc.gc.ca/ english/care/romanow/

Deber, R. B. (2000). Getting what we pay for: Myths and realities about financing Canada's health care system. *Health Law in Canada, 2,* 9–41.

Lomas, J., Woods, J., & Veenstra, G. (1997). Devolving authority for health care in Canada's provinces: 1. An introduction to the issues. *Canadian Medical Association Journal, 156,* 371–377.

Further Reading

Naylor, D. C. (1986). *Private practice, public payment: Canadian medicine and the politics of health insurance, 1911–1966.* Montreal, QC, and Kingston, ON: McGill-Queen's University Press.

Ostrey, A. (2001). The roots of North America's first comprehensive public health insurance system. *Hygiea Internationalis, 2,* 25–44.

Thomas, L. H. (Ed.). (1982). The making of a socialist: The recollections of T. C. Douglas. Edmonton: University of Alberta Press.

HEALTH POLICY (UNITED STATES)

Policymakers and policy intellectuals devised the concept of health policy in the mid twentieth century to describe collective action in the public and private sectors intended to maintain or improve the health of particular populations. It is, therefore, anachronistic to describe any history before the mid twentieth century as health policy. Asking retrospectively questions that are central to contemporary analysis of health policy, however, can increase understanding of collective action in the past to prevent and ameliorate the pain and suffering associated with illness and to maintain health.

Historical analysis of collective action about illness and health—what is now called health policy—explores questions about four interrelated subjects: ideas, illness, institutions, and interests. How people in authority in any society and those to whom they were accountable answered these questions, as well as their debates about alternative answers, helps to explain many decisions about collective action on behalf of health.

Questions about ideas examine the effects on collective action, in any place and at any time, of both broadly accepted and controversial assumptions about the causes and course of illness and its treatment and about maintaining health. For instance, which theories of the origin and transmission of particular illnesses prevailed (and which, if any, competed for legitimacy)? What interventions did these theories justify? In what circumstances did people in authority take collective action (e.g., at what level of risk of sickness or number of actual cases)?

The next set of questions is about illness: how people in a particular place at a particular time described their burden of pain, suffering, and premature death. What, for example, did contemporaries call their afflictions, and how did they classify them? How did they describe the amount and significance of disability and death that resulted from these afflictions?

Questions about institutions explore the details of collective action to prevent illness, to care for persons afflicted by it, and to promote a contemporary definition of health. For example, whom did contemporaries recognize as caregivers, and how were these people trained, legitimized, disciplined, and compensated? How did caregivers within and outside families relate to each other; under what circumstances was a sick person removed from home and to what kind of facility was he or she sent? What laws and regulations—enacted and enforced how and by whom—governed the prevention and treatment of illness and management of its socioeconomic effects? Who paid the costs of collective action and how did financial transactions occur?

Questions about interests explore the politics of collective action; that is, the behavior of organized groups whose members might gain or lose resources and authority as a result of particular collective decisions. How, for example, did members of the medical and other health-related professions define their self-interest and what did they do to protect and maximize it? How did the most powerful persons in economic and religious affairs define their interests in illness and health and what did they do to protect and maximize them?

Many changes in collective action to prevent and treat illness and maintain health have occurred since the seventeenth century in the territory that is now the United States. When illness appeared to threaten a community, its leaders usually supplemented or replaced the efforts of individuals and families. Epidemic infections, mental illness, natural disasters (floods, fires, or storms, for example), and violence (especially war and civic strife) were the most frequent causes of collective action on behalf of health.

Until the late nineteenth century, civic leaders in commerce and agriculture, the law, religion, and medicine frequently collaborated as peers in making most decisions about collective action to prevent or contain illness and maintain health. Since then, physicians have dominated key decisions about collective action for illness and health, especially decisions about interventions to prevent and treat illness, the organization and utilization of health services, and the priorities of biomedical research. Physicians have also had a strong and at times controlling influence on how personal health services are financed.

Medical dominance of collective action for health in the United States (and many other countries) since the late nineteenth century was mainly a result of widespread optimism generated by advances in science and technology. These advances stimulated confidence that, as a result of research, the causes of every disease would, eventually, be specified and that this knowledge of causation would lead to methods of prevention and cure.

The initial source of this confidence was research on the causes of and interventions in acute infectious diseases. During most of the twentieth century, government, civic, and medical leaders, and apparently most Americans as well, transferred this confidence to chronic diseases by hopeful analogy more than in response to science. Since the 1920s, these diseases have been the major, and increasing, burden of illness in industrial countries.

The prestige and authority of the medical profession in the United States increased, beginning early in the twentieth century, mainly because its leaders embraced the methods and findings of the rapidly developing basic health sciences and the application of this new knowledge in clinical and public health practice. Leading physicians, subsidized initially by major philanthropic foundations and then by government, precipitated collective action to infuse modern basic science into medical education, licensure requirements, and eventually practice. During the first half of the twentieth century, these leaders transformed hospitals, which had been residual institutions, into the central institutions of the health sector. Organized medicine became the dominant interest group in health affairs.

By the beginning of the twenty-first century, the health sector was the largest component of the American economy, almost 15 percent of the gross national product. As a result of health policy during the previous half-century, the public sector paid slightly more than 60 percent of the cost of personal health services and a larger but less precisely calculated share of the cost of population and public health services.

The amount and sources of expenditure are not, however, the best measures of the priority that people in a country or subunit of it accord to a particular set of policies. Many Americans had signaled for decades to the persons they elected to public office that they placed higher value on public spending for jobs, income, national security, and perhaps on education and home ownership than they did on spending for personal and population health services. A significant result of this prioritization has been the repeated failure of efforts to organize a coalition that could succeed in enacting policy to finance universal access to personal health services.

Because the priority that different groups in the United States accord policy to prevent disease and maintain health varies among different groups at any time and over historical time, there has frequently been considerable support for incremental changes in health policy. People who are sick and members of their families generally accord higher priority to health policy than anyone else. As a result, interest groups that advocate on behalf of persons with particular diseases, or of age cohorts that are particularly susceptible to disease, are significant participants in the politics of policy making for health. This advocacy has been most successful on behalf of financing services for the elderly and children and in increasing appropriations for biomedical research. Advocacy for substantial new spending for public health infrastructure was effective, for the first time in half a century, as part of the response to the events of September 11, 2001, and the subsequent cases of anthrax.

Toward the end of the twentieth century, a relatively new approach to analyzing and advocating alternative health policy, called population health, became fashionable among some researchers and public health officials in the United States and officials of the World Bank and the World Health Organization. Advocates of a population health approach to policy cite considerable evidence that personal and public health services are overrated as determinants of health status. Other significant determinants are income and social status, education, and the condition of the natural and built environments (the latter includes housing, workplaces, the organization of urban and suburban space, and modes of transportation). To the dismay of population health advocates, however, many policymakers for these determinants do not regard health as within their mission or conclude that explicit action to improve health would shift resources from other worthy purposes.

An increasing number of leaders in the public and private sectors take an alternative approach to population health policy. They observe that policy for population health varies among countries and their subunits because people in different places identify different sets of determinants of health and prioritize them differently. Examples of this variation in the contemporary United States include policies in different states to reduce environmental hazards to health (e.g., regulations to improve air and water quality and restrict tobacco use); to reduce the risk to health from the built environment (e.g., mass transportation, the redesign of urban space to encourage physical activity, even the abatement of lead paint); and to provide a safety net of health services (e.g., health insurance for workers whose employers do not provide it or subsidies for prescription drugs for persons with low incomes, or home- and community-based long-term care for frail elders). In sum, health policy in the United States remains what it has been historically: elusive and plastic.

—*Daniel M. Fox*

See also Child Welfare Policy (United States); Disability Policy (United States); Mental Health Policy (United States); Philanthropy (United States); Poverty (United States); Rush, Benjamin; Sanger, Margaret Higgins; Substance Abuse Policy (United States); Tax Expenditures (United States); Welfare Capitalism (United States)

Primary Sources

Records of the Public Health Service (Record Group 90), Records of the Agency for Health Care Policy and Research (Record Group 510), Records of the Health Resources and Services Administration (Record Group 512), National Archives & Records Administration, College Park, MD; the Manuscript Division of the Library of Congress, Washington, DC; the residential libraries of each president since Franklin D. Roosevelt.

Current Comment

Musto, D. F. (2002). *Drugs in America: A documentary history.* New York: New York University Press.

Further Reading

Fox, D. M. (1993). *Power and illness: The failure and future of American health policy.* Berkeley: University of California Press.

Gostin, L. O. (2000). *Public health law: Power, duty, restraint.* Berkeley: University of California Press; Milbank Memorial Fund.

Starr, P. (1982). *The social transformation of American medicine.* New York: Basic Books.

Stevens, R. (1998). *American medicine and the public interest: A history of specialization.* Berkeley: University of California Press.

HENDRY, CHARLES ERIC (1903–1979)

Charles Eric Hendry, who was born in the rural Ottawa Valley near Perth, Ontario, grew up in the Glebe area of Ottawa. "Chick," as he came to be known, was the son of a devout Baptist mother and a Presbyterian father who was employed as a moderately successful retail clothing and camping goods merchant. Chick became involved in community development at a young age. This participation began when he and several friends created a library loaning program out of his family home, which at its peak consisted of more than 700 books and a membership of well over 100 boys. As a teenager, Chick met Taylor Statten, who in 1919 was the boys' work secretary of the Canadian YMCA. Statten became a most influential mentor and for the rest of his life, Hendry was a devoted supporter of the YMCA movement. Hendry worked as a summertime leader in one of Statten's boys' camps, and later boarded with Statten's mother-in-law while pursuing undergraduate studies in political economy at McMaster University.

Statten helped Hendry secure his first job as provincial secretary of the Alberta Boys' Work Board. Moving to New York City in 1928, Hendry was awarded two master's degrees: one in religious education from Union Theological Seminary, and another in educational sociology from Teachers College, Columbia University. In 1931, he enrolled in the doctoral program at the University of Chicago's Department of Sociology, but he did not complete that degree.

Instead, Hendry began a 20-year-long professional career in the United States. At the Kenosha, Wisconsin, chapter of the YMCA, he was director of research and personnel (1928–1929), moving into a junior position in the Department of Sociology at the Y's George Williams College in Chicago (1929–1937). The director of the department, Hedley Dimock, gradually replaced Statten as Hendry's mentor. Hendry was the cofounder, and later national chairman, of the American Association for the Study of Group Work (1936–1940). With Dimock, he wrote a YMCA study entitled *Camping and Character* (1931). He authored a 1933 polemical on the embrace of technology and progress and a 1936 study on community development in Cleveland.

He returned to New York City in 1937, becoming director of programs and personnel training for the Boys Clubs of America (1937–1940). Other positions followed in series: national director of research and statistical services of the Boy Scouts of America (1940–1944); director of research for the American Jewish Congress National Commission on Community Inter-Relations (1942–1946); part-time lecturer at the New School for Social Research (1942–1944) and at Teachers College, Columbia University (1942–1946); and research associate at the Massachusetts Institute of Technology's newly founded Center for Group Dynamics (1944–1946).

In 1946, Hendry, along with his wife (Helen Isabel Bustard) and their two children, relocated to Toronto, where Harry Cassidy, director of the University of Toronto School of Social Work, had granted him a full professorship. Hendry was appointed the school's director 5 years later, following the death of Cassidy, and retained this position until his 1969 retirement. The school had increased in size fourfold during Cassidy's leadership and Hendry oversaw its continued postwar expansion and recruited some outstanding scholars. Many others departed during this phase of continent-wide university growth. Never a prolific author, one of his best-received efforts was a study written for the Anglican church regarding its relations with aboriginal peoples, *Beyond Traplines* (1969).

Hendry was profoundly influenced by Canadian Protestantism, the YMCA, American individualism, liberalism, positivism, and social science, as well as a social structure that favored the leadership advancement of men, even in professions dominated in numbers by women. He was recognized among Canada's corporate, political, and social elite, and functioned with great effortlessness and modest relative achievement in these environments. An advocate of action research and collaborative relationships, he was never strongly anchored to any one methodology; impatient with detail, freewheeling, and disorderly in thinking; a romantic, a poet, a dreamer, and full of charisma; always more of a doer than a philosopher; more an advocate than an academic.

His principal skills involved relationships and interaction, rather than academia. Through leadership and motivation, however, he compensated for what he might have lacked by way of single-minded, disciplined devotion to scholarly detail. By the time he returned to Canada, he had acquired a superb capability to network within and beyond academia; to identify, create, and sustain connections with people whose careers were clearly mounting; to initiate social advocacy efforts, to raise money, to persuade others to help support and campaign for social causes, to work crowds, and to bring attention to projects to which he was committed. Possessing a joyful disposition, an extremely influential personality, a far-reaching imagination, and that willing and confident spirit of enterprise that he had gathered from the YMCA, everything he did was infused with great and infectious enthusiasm. A skilled delegator, a risk taker, an outgoing, innovative, vivacious, and boldly ambitious behind-the-scenes operator, Hendry was eager to place his work beyond the limits of academia. He had a significant aptitude for traveling and a natural concern for the global village, and the demand for his expertise as a consultant in social policy, social work curricula, and professional development was not limited to within Canadian borders.

—*John R. Graham*

See also Bowers, Frank Swithun Barrington; Cassidy, Harry; Social Work Profession (Canada); Urwick, Edward Johns

Further Reading

Dimock, H. S., & Hendry, C. E. (1931). *Camping and character: A camp experiment in character education.* New York: Association Press.

Graham, J. R. (1994). Charles Eric Hendry (1903–1979): The pre-war formational origins of a leader of post–World War II Canadian social work education. *Canadian Social Work Review, 11*(2), 150–167.

Hendry, C. E. (1933). *Youth inspects the New World.* Chicago: Roy Sorenson.

Hendry, C. E. (1969). *Beyond traplines: Does the church really care? Towards an assessment of the work of the Anglican church of Canada with Canada's Native peoples.* Toronto, ON: Ryerson.

HISPANIC AMERICANS AND SOCIAL WELFARE (UNITED STATES)

Americans of Hispanic heritage have a varied ancestry that dates back hundreds of years. Spaniards explored territory that constitutes more than half of the present-day United States. In addition to colonizing more than half of that territory, Spain allied with the United States against its rival, Great Britain, during the American Revolution. The Hispanic influence on North America has been vast and far-reaching from the early 1500s to the present day. In fact, prior to the late 1800s, Spanish was the only collective language spoken in the southwestern United States and people immigrating to that region from western Europe in the 1800s learned the Spanish language in order to survive in this region.

Persons who are ethnically and culturally different have been disparaged by the dominant society throughout the history of the United States, and it has been pointed out that in the United States "American" often means "White." To understand the meaning of the social construction of race and the impact of changing social and economic situations on racial identity, political power and influence, and racial discourse, it is necessary to have a historical perspective on the Hispanic experience in the United States. Thus, to understand the life experiences and current needs of Hispanic Americans, it is necessary to have some understanding of the historical experiences of Hispanics in the United States.

Although many Hispanic people were living in territories when they became part of the United States, many other Hispanic people migrated to the United States from other countries, including Puerto Rico, Cuba, and Mexico. These nations have a long and arduous history with the United States. The following paragraphs discuss the relations between the United States and these three countries, each of which has been critical in the development of the Hispanic experience in the United States.

PUERTO RICO

Of all Spanish colonial possessions in the Americas, Puerto Rico is the only territory that never gained its independence. Internal and geopolitical dynamics during the last quarter of the nineteenth century, nevertheless, brought dramatic political, social, and economic changes to the island, setting the stage for the development of its national institutions and the transformation of its political system as a United States territory during the twentieth century.

After four centuries of Spanish colonial rule, the period between 1860 and 1898 witnessed a pro-independence rebellion, colonial reform, the establishment of the first national political parties, the abolition of slavery, and a short-lived experiment in autonomy under Spanish rule. The political and military strategies of a decaying Spanish Empire and the emerging regional power of the United States at the end of the nineteenth century, however, placed Puerto Rico, along with Cuba, at center stage in the Caribbean. The dynamics of this power imbalance culminated in the formal transfer of the island to the United States in 1898 at the end of the Spanish-American War.

The acquisition of Puerto Rico resulted from one of the more shameful acts in American history and one that is significant today when considering the history of Hispanics and social welfare. The continued possession of Puerto Rico is a throwback to a colonial era that should have been abandoned long ago as Puerto Rico's status as a "commonwealth" of the United States is one that has robbed Puerto Ricans of their dignity and honor.

Puerto Rico, impoverished and poor, became an American possession as compensation for expenses that the United States incurred fighting its war with Spain. This began a campaign of Americanization

that decimated a 400-year-old Spanish culture but did not succeed in turning Puerto Ricans into English-speaking Americans. As part of the Spanish Empire, Puerto Rico had voting representation in both chambers of the Spanish Parliament, whereas the United States denied Puerto Rico statehood, independence, or meaningful political participation in the federal government, although Puerto Rico does have a non-voting delegate in Congress. United States federal laws apply to Puerto Rico and they are enforced by federal agencies, yet Puerto Ricans have no say in the making of these laws.

Puerto Ricans have been leaving for the mainland since 1918, when the U.S. Labor Department set out plans for bringing more than 10,000 Puerto Rican laborers to the United States to work on war-related projects. Migration to the United States was slow and gradual in the period from 1900 to 1940. Although there was an increase in every decade, the migration rate for this period was modest when compared to the post–World War II period. During the Great Depression of the 1930s, the migration to the United States slowed dramatically and in some years many returned to Puerto Rico.

The "granting" of U.S. citizenship to all Puerto Ricans through the Jones Act of 1917 eliminated legal barriers to migration, as Puerto Ricans were now free to travel and settle anywhere in the United States or its possessions. As is true of most immigrant populations, Puerto Ricans left the island for the mainland to seek employment, not to take advantage of federal programs. The rate of migration fluctuated with the economic conditions of the island and the availability of economic opportunity on the mainland.

When the federal Food Stamp program was introduced in the 1960s, approximately 75 percent of the island's population became eligible. Puerto Rico received no less than 10 percent of all federal food stamp payments. The program brought billions of dollars to Puerto Rico. It fueled corruption, crime, drugs, and gang warfare, as well as a culture of dependency. Consequently, living on welfare was viewed, by many on the mainland, as lucrative and the greatest "export" became Puerto Rican citizens who went to the U.S. mainland where they could "take advantage" of U.S. federal programs. It was this perspective that became the norm and has been perpetuated onto the Hispanic culture along with the negative stereotypes that have been assigned to other Hispanic groups in the United States.

CUBA

The United States has had a long and volatile relationship with Cuba. Cuba struggled for over half a century to change its status from a theoretically independent state, dominated by American imperialism, into a truly independent country. In 1895, under the leadership of the writer and patriot José Martí, mounting discontent with the Spanish government culminated in a resumption of a Cuban Revolution. The U.S. government intervened on behalf of the revolutionists in 1898, precipitating the Spanish-American War. With the treaty signed terminating the conflict, Spain relinquished sovereignty over Cuba, resulting in American military rule that lasted until 1902.

From its earliest days of independence, the Cuban people have been plagued with corrupt government leaders. Using the strength of military power, these men have subverted and manipulated the democratic process to install themselves as presidents or to become the "strongmen" behind the appointment of a president.

Whereas United States immigration policy has traditionally reflected economic and xenophobic concerns, United States refugee policy has reflected foreign policy concerns. During the cold war, refugee policy was used as a tool to embarrass communist regimes. In the process of shaming communist countries, refugees from these states were evidence that the United States was winning its conflict with communism. A 1953 National Security Council memorandum cited the 1953 Refugee Act as a way to encourage defection from all communist nations and "key" personnel from Soviet satellite countries. In 1959, the United States was afforded the opportunity to implement the 1953 memorandum when Fidel Castro established a communist government in Cuba. Although Cubans had been immigrating to the United States before the 1960s, it was not until Cuba was deemed a communist regime that its people were seen as political refugees. After 1959, their status was not like that of other Hispanic immigrants. The United States, through several presidential administrations, tightened sanctions on Cuba. The sanctions ranged

from trade embargoes to restrictions on U.S. citizens' travel to the island. Although the restrictions were placed upon the Cuban government in an attempt to "oust" the communist regime, the most lasting effects have been on the Cuban people.

The U.S. sanctions led to increasing poverty in Cuba. Consequently, the sanctions led to greater numbers of Cubans attempting to flee the country for economic reasons rather than political ones. Recognizing this, the United States countered by ending automatic asylum to fleeing Cubans. They were no longer seen as welcomed exiles but as unwelcome immigrants. The crisis ended when, in 1994 and 1995, the United States, under bilateral accords, pledged to issue a minimum of 20,000 entry visas a year for Cubans to migrate permanently to the United States.

MEXICO

The expansion of the United States led to conflict with Mexico, even prior to the Mexican-American War (1846–1848). Because the entire southwestern region of the United States was originally part of Mexico, several historians have termed the period from 1848 to 1920 the "stage of forced acquiescence." In accordance with an ideology of Manifest Destiny, the United States was eager to acquire land and natural resources held by Mexico in what is now the southwestern United States. In 1848, the Treaty of Guadalupe Hidalgo accomplished the dual purpose of annexing Mexican territory and expanding the U.S. population by granting citizenship to Mexican nationals who were living within the ceded boundaries.

Thus, before the late twentieth century, the majority of Hispanic citizens acquired citizenship because of where they happened to live. Several scholars equate this with the case of the incorporation of Native American peoples and land into the newly emerging United States, although Indian citizenship was not universal until 1924. The Treaty of Guadalupe Hidalgo guaranteed the new citizens basic rights such as freedom of religion, the right to own property, and political liberty not generally guaranteed in Indian treaties. Federal and state governments, however, failed to adhere to the letter of the law. Unfortunately for the Hispanic population, the lack of enforcement of this treaty set the stage for disenfranchisement and political fragmentation of Americans of Mexican descent. In the aftermath of the Mexican-American War, policies set forth by the United States had the effect of displacing and dispossessing the Mexican American population, which now had to abide by the laws and regulations of the United States without any special consideration for their previous rights. Although the U.S. government negotiated the treaty, territorial and state governments provided the context for daily exercise of citizenship, especially before 1930. Thus, a second-class construction, although derived from treaties, legal judgments, and political ideologies, was imposed upon the former Mexican nationals who were now citizens of the United States. By the late nineteenth and early twentieth centuries, skin color had clearly become the primary identifier by which the second-class status of non-Whites would be assured and the legacy of the Hispanic culture and heritage would be distorted and misrepresented.

HISPANIC CIVIC ORGANIZATIONS

Hispanic civic organizations in the United States date back to 1894 when La Alianza Hispano Americana was founded. La Sociedad Progresista Mexicana y Recreativa, La Camara de Comercio Mexicana, and La Sociedad Mutualista Mexicana were organized around 1924. There were also hundreds of Catholic organizations that were founded in the early part of the twentieth century. As their Spanish names imply, these organizations linked Mexican Americans to Mexico. These organizations did not, however, attempt to represent other Hispanic people. Not until 1929, when the League of United Latin American Citizens (LULAC) was established, was there an organization that attempted to represent all of the Hispanic community in the United States. The founding of LULAC signaled the end of one era and the beginning of another. Today, LULAC represents not only Mexican Americans from the southwest, where it originated, but also Hispanics in most parts of the United States, including Puerto Ricans, Cubans, and even Hispanics from as far away as Guam. Membership has expanded to include all men and women of Hispanic origin who are legal residents of the United States or its territorial areas.

LULAC is the cornerstone of some of the most successful Hispanic national organizations to date, and stimulated the creation of the American GI Forum (AGIF) to address the rights of Hispanic veterans and the Mexican American Legal Defense and Education Fund (MALDEF), the legal arm of the Hispanic community. In addition, LULAC has developed thousands of low-income housing units through the Southwest. More important, LULAC has become an important influence in national policy making with a permanent national office in Washington, D.C.

THE CONTINUED LABELING OF HISPANIC PEOPLE

Due to political and social changes occurring in the United States after the 1960s, it became apparent that the Hispanic culture was far more diverse than prevailing stereotypes indicated. As Hispanics gradually acquired political influence, the U.S. government operationalized the concept of Hispanic in America in order to distribute resources more effectively. The term Hispanic was first introduced in 1978 by the Office of Management and Budget to describe and better "operationalize" the idea of persons of Mexican, Puerto Rican, Cuban, Central and South American, or other Spanish cultures of origin regardless of race.

As with any label used in demographic research, the label can mistakenly imply commonalities. It is important to realize, however, that Hispanic does not refer to a particular race, since Hispanics can be of any race. Most Hispanics consider themselves racially mixed as well as culturally different from one another, despite their common Spanish heritage.

HISPANICS AND SOCIAL SERVICES

Ethnically diverse groups have been subjected to dominance, oppression, and exploitation by White society. Thus, the history of the institutionalization of social services to culturally diverse populations reflects not only their historical oppression, but also suggests the need to create culturally competent delivery systems. The history of oppression of minority populations is further reflected in the existence of institutionalized discrimination toward culturally diverse populations in social service agencies. In the nineteenth and early twentieth centuries, for example, discrimination against Hispanics resulted in their exclusion from receiving social services. In addition, they have been denied equal access to land and civil rights and underpaid for their labor.

Although the status of the Hispanic population has improved, Hispanics still face the problem of diminished access to general social services due to multiple social and economic barriers. Although Hispanics have been found to be at greater risk for mental health disorders, for example, they are infrequent users of mental health services. Those who do form contacts with such services are likely to drop out of treatment prematurely. The mental health service system has historically responded more slowly to crises with culturally diverse families—Hispanic clients of social agencies typically receive less comprehensive service plans, and parents of color have been viewed as less able to profit from what the system has to offer.

—*Wesley T. Church II*

See also Immigration and Social Welfare Policy (United States)

Further Reading

Acuna, R. (1988). *Occupied America: A history of Chicanos* (3rd ed.). New York: Harper & Row.

Gann, L. H., & Dunnigan, P. J. (1986). *The Hispanics in the United States: A history.* Boulder, CO: Westview.

Garcia, F. C., & de la Garza, R. (1977). *The Chicano political experience: Three perspectives.* North Scituate, MA: Duxbury.

Rodriguez, C. E. (1997). *Latin looks: Images and Latinas and Latinos in the U.S. media.* Boulder, CO: Westview.

Takaki, R. (1993). *A different mirror: A history of multicultural America.* New York: Oxford University Press.

Takaki, R. (1994). *From different shores: Perspectives on race and ethnicity in America* (2nd ed.). New York: Oxford University Press.

HOMELESSNESS (UNITED STATES)

Since 1981, homelessness has emerged in the United States as the face of poverty, as well as a human rights issue. It looms as a persistent problem for the twenty-first century. This discussion presents a narrative history of homelessness in the United States as a basis for explaining and analyzing contemporary homelessness.

It identifies the major historical periods in which Americans experienced homelessness and explains how the character of homelessness and the homeless population has changed. It also describes social welfare responses to the problem during each historical period.

HOMELESSNESS IN THE COLONIAL ERA

The earliest colonial settlers brought the English poor laws with them and applied the principles of "indoor" and "outdoor" relief and residency in dispensing relief to beggars. Poor law distinctions between "neighbors" and "strangers" obligated communities to assist permanent residents, whereas poor strangers were deported to their place of origin. When the numbers of relief seekers remained small, these principles were adequate, but local responsibility proved to be inadequate to the demands of circulating strangers whose numbers grew with increased immigration. By the late seventeenth century, cities began to erect almshouses for emergency housing. Able-bodied poor were deemed eligible for temporary stays in the almshouses, but the unworthy poor, vagrants and runaway slaves, frequently occupied these facilities.

By the end of the eighteenth century, the perception developed that people in need of relief and shelter were indolent and lazy and not the proper objects of charity. Relief gave way to rehabilitation and almshouse residents were expected to work to obtain support. But many persons, including mothers with children, mentally ill poor, victims of illness, accident, or addiction, and the abandoned elderly could not comply with increasingly rigorous work requirements.

POST–CIVIL WAR, INDUSTRIALIZATION, AND URBANIZATION

Hundreds of thousands of vagrants or "tramps" appeared after the Civil War, mostly young men who were victims of wartime strife. Some were European immigrants who had not been able to find stable jobs. Others were dislocated by the economic depression of 1873, which forced agricultural workers to seek employment in cities. Urban crowding seemed to contribute to increasing poverty, crime, and moral disarray and fears that homeless vagrants threatened civilized society.

When prosperity and economic stability returned in the late 1870s, some of the wandering men found permanent jobs and homes, but hundreds of thousands remained migratory laborers. Many chose to work on their own terms, resisting the structure and demands of employment in factories and construction. These workers began to gather in neighborhoods that emerged in cities to accommodate them with transient housing and other basic services. These areas were the original "skid rows" as they came to be known by the 1930s. The name referred to the waterfront district of Seattle, where timber was skidded along sloping log roads to the water so it could be floated to sawmills. In addition to skid rows, makeshift temporary shelters were developed to house the homeless. Rooms were sometimes set aside in police stations for overnight transient lodging; but they could not accommodate the large numbers of transients who began to sleep in saloons, public waiting rooms, on the docks, the streets, and in garbage dumps. The federal government drafted many young homeless men into military service during World War I, when the elderly and disabled populated skid rows. Later in the twentieth century, skid rows diminished in size and character. Skid row residents were mostly older White male alcoholics and derelicts who were thought to be responsible for their own conditions. Some social welfare services were provided for them by private charities. Popular culture sometimes romanticized them as hoboes and the last of the free-spirited bohemians.

THE GREAT DEPRESSION

The Great Depression ushered in new waves of homelessness. Millions of Americans lost their jobs and homes after the stock market crash of 1929. The connection between the rise in homelessness and unemployment challenged earlier perceptions of dereliction as a correlate of homelessness. Private charities were sheltering up to 400,000 people each night. Those who could not find places in shelters began to hitchhike or ride the rails seeking work. "Shantytowns" consisting of flimsy shelters, built of almost any material that offered some protection from the elements, were built in cities across the nation.

President Franklin D. Roosevelt's "New Deal" responded to the problem of homelessness. The National Housing Acts of 1934 and 1937 established the Federal Housing Administration (FHA) and the United States Housing Authority (USHA) to insure loans by banks for housing construction and improvements and extend these to local agencies for slum clearance and public housing projects. In addition, the Federal Emergency Relief Administration (FERA) was established to dispense relief to the millions of unemployed Americans.

The programs of the New Deal did not end the Great Depression, but they did alleviate some of its worst aspects and homelessness was abated. The years of prosperity following the depression and World War II misled the American people to assume that poverty had been nearly eliminated. It was not until the 1960s that Americans would rediscover poverty in our supposed land of plenty. But poverty was not associated with homelessness, which was seen mainly as a problem of skid row derelicts.

HOMELESSNESS AT THE END OF THE TWENTIETH CENTURY

In the early 1980s, it was recognized that homelessness was a widespread social problem, not confined to urban skid rows. Homeless people were seen as victims of social forces, such as changing labor market demands, and not simply as immoral and lazy derelicts. But the combination of high unemployment and inflation in the late 1970s led to the erosion of the Democratic party's power in Congress that had prevailed since the Great Depression and to the rise of the antigovernment, neoconservative presidency of Ronald Reagan. From 1981 to 1988, federal funds for housing were cut by 69 percent. The number of low-income housing units dropped from 183,000 units in 1980 to 28,000 by 1985. Simultaneous cutbacks in social programs such as Aid to Families With Dependent Children (AFDC) and Social Security Disability Insurance (SSDI) frequently determined whether a poor family, a mentally ill person, or an otherwise disabled person could pay rent. In 1987, Congress passed the Stewart B. McKinney Homeless Assistance Act to provide emergency shelter, housing, education, and health care to homeless people. Two years later, however, the U.S. Conference of Mayors surveyed homelessness in 27 cities and found that none of the cities surveyed expected to be able to meet the housing needs of low-income households.

As increasingly visible numbers of people became homeless, social welfare responses retreated to earlier distinctions between the "deserving" and "undeserving" poor. Emergency shelters and soup kitchens, under the auspices of local charities and religious institutions, proliferated in lieu of more expensive federal programs for the homeless. Before long, a new system of homeless assistance services characterized by emergency responses emerged, with more limited approaches to the provision of transitional and long-term housing.

The public perception of the new homeless population combined elements of earlier views. Homeless advocates portrayed the homeless sympathetically as "deserving" victims of poverty, mental illness, substance abuse, and domestic violence and called for more emergency responses as well as more generous public entitlements. Others viewed the homeless as "undeserving" public nuisances and established local ordinances designed to "get tough" and drive them away. Interpretations of homelessness associated with disability remain controversial. Some analysts attribute homelessness to personal vulnerability, and cite high turnover rates in shelters and housing as evidence of chronic homelessness. Others interpret high turnover rates in shelters as indicative of successful efforts at re-housing.

A complex combination of poverty, lack of affordable housing, and personal vulnerability explains contemporary homelessness. Approximately one-half of people who experience homelessness over the course of a year are single adults. Another half are families. Most members of homeless families and single adults report a mismatch in service availability and service need. They report that they need assistance in finding affordable housing and financial help to pay for it. Instead, the assistance they most frequently receive is clothing, transportation, and help in obtaining public benefits. Whether as single persons or as members of families, today's homeless are nearly always sent to emergency homeless services, which often offer little other than shelter and perhaps a meal.

The homeless represent the harsh face of poverty at the beginning of the twenty-first century. Social welfare activists remain committed to bringing the plight of the homeless to the attention of politicians and policymakers. They feel the nation has a moral obligation to the homeless poor by providing them shelter as well as the means to escape from poverty. The National Coalition for the Homeless sees homelessness as an "unfinished" legacy of the civil rights movement and calls for social welfare activists to continue the fight to end homelessness and poverty.

—*Madeleine Stoner*

See also Housing Policy (United States); The New Deal (United States); Poor Law (United States)

Primary Source

General Records of the Department of Housing and Urban Development (Record Group 207), National Archives & Records Administration, College Park, MD.

Current Comment

Fantasia, R., & Isserman, M. (1994). *Homelessness: A sourcebook.* New York: Facts on File.

National Alliance to End Homelessness. (1998). *The ten year plan to end homelessness.* Washington, DC: Author. Available: www.endhomelessness.org/pub/tenyear/

Further Reading

Baumohl, J. (Ed.). (1996). *Homelessness in America.* Phoenix, AZ: Oryx.

Harrington, M. (1988). *The long distance runner: An autobiography.* New York: Holt.

Stoner, M. R. (2002). The globalization of urban homelessness. In M. J. Dear (Ed.), *From Chicago to L.A.* Thousand Oaks, CA: Sage.

HOMESTEAD ACT (UNITED STATES)

The Homestead Act, enacted by the United States Congress in 1862, provided a quarter section of land (160 acres) to actual settlers who were citizens or declared a desire to become citizens on payment of a fee. The act required that settlers occupy and improve the homestead for a period of 5 years before title would be granted. During this time, the land could not be encumbered and no taxes could be collected on it. The act also provided that settlers could purchase their land for $1.25 per acre before the end of the 5-year time period. This enabled settlers to participate in the market economy by borrowing funds using the land as collateral. Over two million persons filed homestead claims between 1863 and 1930; around half of the claims were proved up. Thus, the act represented the largest distribution of government assets to individuals in the history of the United States.

The provision of free land to settlers had been at the core of a land reform movement during the early nineteenth century. The theory of natural rights and the ideas of Thomas Jefferson and Thomas Paine had influenced these movements. The Homestead Act, enacted on May 20, 1862, came into effect on January 1, 1863. The act entitled any citizen or person who had filed a declaration to become a citizen and who was the head of a family or 21 years of age to enter 160 acres of free land. Women who were family heads and unmarried women were eligible to homestead, as were freedmen, immigrants, and Indians abandoning their tribal affiliations. The homesteader was required to pay a small filing fee to cover administrative costs related to surveying the land. After 6 months of residence, the settler could purchase the land at $1.25 an acre. Five years' residence on the land and cultivation were required before a title deed could be granted, in which case the homestead was free. The only payment required was the filing fee. An individual was only entitled to one homestead. The homesteader was required to swear that the land was intended for actual settlement and cultivation and that the entries were not being made for any other person.

The Homestead Act operated in "an incongruous land system," in the words of historian Paul Wallace Gates (1936). The states of Texas and California had their own land systems in force when they joined the Union. Other land legislation, in particular the Pacific Railroad and Morrill Land Grant College Acts, both also enacted in 1862, complicated implementation of the Homestead Act. Controlling speculation in western land proved to be difficult. The net effect was a shortage of adequate suitable land for homesteading.

For the advocates of land reform, homesteading was a panacea for the economic problems of the working class. It was expected to reduce the number of paupers and create a class of prosperous small farmers whose own prosperity would feed the economic development of the nation. It would be a "safety valve" for the growing population of the eastern states because it would draw off the surplus labor whenever industrial conditions were unsatisfactory. Thus, the homestead law was expected to stabilize the wages of employed workers.

Although much land was allocated to other uses, such as railroads, agricultural colleges, and land purchases, over 700,000 final homestead entries had been recorded by 1904. Homesteading continued to be important in the settlement of western states until the start of World War I. After 1900, Congress allowed enlarged homesteads in arid areas. Since little land available for homesteading was close to transportation, settlers purchased more western land than they obtained through the Homestead Act. The act emphasized crop production rather than other uses, such as grazing and mining.

The Homestead Act helped to open up a vast public domain to over 1.5 million people who acquired farmland in the western United States. Congress extended the principle of encouraging individual land ownership by enacting the Southern Homestead Act (1866), which made 80-acre farms in the southeastern states available to African American and White homesteaders. The act was not successful because most good farmland was already in private ownership; the public land available for homesteading in these states was, by and large, not good for farming. The General Allotment Act (1887) mandated the division of Indian reservations into 160-acre allotments, which would be distributed to individual Indian heads of households. This act resulted in the alienation of much reservation land, as Whites were able to acquire allotments through purchase or leasing arrangements.

Together with the Morrill Land Grant College and the Pacific Railroad Acts of 1862, the Homestead Act was responsible for shaping the development of much of the western United States. In Canada, the Dominion Lands Act (1872) was modeled on the Homestead Act. For a nominal fee, it provided 160 acres to any farmer who agreed to cultivate at least 30 acres and build a dwelling on the land within 3 years. Settlers could acquire another 160 acres upon payment of an additional fee.

—*Paul H. Stuart*

See also Social Welfare (United States): Before the Social Security Act

Further Reading

Gates, P. W. (1936, July). The homestead law in an incongruous land system. *American Historical Review, 41,* 652–681.

Gates, P. W. (1968). *History of public land law development.* Washington, DC: Government Printing Office.

Gates, P. W. (1996). *The Jeffersonian dream: Studies in the history of American land policy and development* (A. G. Bogue & M. Beattie Bogue, Eds.). Albuquerque: University of New Mexico Press.

Hyman, H. M. (1986). *American singularity: The 1787 Northwest Ordinance, the 1862 Homestead and Morrill Acts, and the 1944 G.I. Bill.* Athens: University of Georgia Press.

HOPKINS, HARRY LLOYD (1890–1946)

Harry Lloyd Hopkins, social worker, New Deal relief administrator, and President Franklin D. Roosevelt's emissary during World War II, played a key role in the formulation of the social policies that culminated in America's welfare system. Son of David Aldona Hopkins, a harness maker, and Anna Pickett Hopkins, a teacher, Hopkins was born in Sioux City, Iowa. His family later moved to Grinnell, Iowa, so their five children could attend Grinnell College. There, Hopkins's professors impressed upon him a dedication to democracy and public service. Soon after his graduation in 1912, Hopkins left rural Iowa to pursue a career as a social worker in New York City's Lower East Side, at Christodora Settlement House. There, he met and married his first wife, fellow settlement worker Ethel Gross. In 1913, Hopkins accepted a position with the Association for Improving the Condition of the Poor (AICP) as a friendly visitor. Having demonstrated his capabilities as an observant and efficient social worker, Hopkins was made superintendent of the association's employment bureau. Through this work, Hopkins saw firsthand the miseries attendant on poverty, a condition he saw as a problem of unemployment. He began to develop a set of convictions concerning poverty and unemployment that would define his relief programs in the 1930s. For Hopkins, it was merely a matter of finding jobs for those who wanted to work and, for whatever reason, could not find employment. For those unable to work, the government would provide assistance.

In 1915, Hopkins and a colleague, William Matthews, organized an early work relief program. Hopkins and Matthews discovered that the Bronx Zoological Park had received a gift of land that could not be utilized because of financial restrictions. The two social workers proposed that the AICP would provide workers to clear the land and pay their wages, if the zoo would supervise the work. The Bronx zoo project, although supported with private money, provided a prototype for future public works programs. That same year, the New York State Legislature passed the Mothers' Assistance Act, which established a program to support single mothers. New York City Mayor John Purroy Mitchel appointed Hopkins as head of the Board of Child Welfare (BCW) to administer this widows' pension program. From 1915 to 1917, Hopkins headed this locally funded and administered program to provide payment to poor, deserving mothers. The work of the BCW reflected some of the most important political issues of the era. It reinforced the value placed on home life articulated in the policy statement issued at the 1909 White House Conference on Dependent Children: No child should be removed from the home for reasons of poverty alone. Furthermore, the state laws that permitted funds to be allocated for these programs (called variously mothers' aid, mothers' pensions, widows' pensions) established the legitimacy of public outdoor relief, that is, using state money to assist the needy outside of institutions such as orphanages. For Hopkins, this was a period of growing political awareness as well as a continuation of his social work training. His experience in New York led him to believe that it was the responsibility of the government, through agencies such as the BCW, to provide programs to help the deserving needy.

With America's entrance into World War I, Hopkins (ineligible for the draft because of poor eyesight) worked for the Red Cross, Civilian Relief Division, in New Orleans and Atlanta. Also called Home Service, this division aided families of servicemen as well as wounded and demobilized soldiers and sailors. During this time, Hopkins had the opportunity to create a social welfare organization from the ground up and he built Civilian Relief into an important service agency for military families who experienced extreme hardships because of the war. In addition, he developed important educational programs for social work training. Through his work in the Red Cross, Hopkins entered into the upper ranks of the social work profession. He joined with other social workers to form an association to standardize social work standards and helped draft the charter for the American Association of Social Workers.

In 1922, Hopkins returned to New York City, where he became general director of the New York Tuberculosis Association (NYTBA) and directed his energies toward health issues. For him, illness as a result of an unfriendly and unhealthy environment was merely another form of social injustice. During his tenure at the NYTBA, Hopkins honed his administrative skills and became a nationally known figure in his profession.

When the Great Depression threw the nation into a downward economic spiral, Hopkins drew on his previous experiences to address the problems brought about by the high levels of unemployment. The crisis reinforced his belief that public works programs, federally funded and rationally planned, could be used to mitigate the effects of widespread unemployment and that it was in the interest of the nation to provide funds to support needy mothers.

In 1931, New York Governor Franklin D. Roosevelt called on Hopkins to run the first state relief organization, the Temporary Emergency Relief Administration (TERA), which provided both direct relief and work relief to the state's unemployed. After his inauguration as president, Roosevelt named Hopkins as New Deal relief administrator. Convinced that jobs were the antidote to poverty, Hopkins used his influence with the president to push for government-sponsored jobs programs. These included the Federal Emergency Relief Administration (FERA), the Civil Works Administration (CWA), and the Works Progress Administration (WPA). In late 1934, Roosevelt named Hopkins to the cabinet-level committee for economic security, which was directed to write legislation that would protect American citizens from what the president called "the hazards and vicissitudes of modern life." The Social Security Act, passed in August 1935, laid the foundations for the American welfare system by enacting legislation that established old-age pensions, unemployment insurance, and aid to children.

During World War II, Hopkins acted as Roosevelt's unofficial assistant and adviser. The worldwide attention that Hopkins received as the president's emissary to Winston Churchill and Joseph Stalin, as administrator of Lend-Lease, and as the shadowy figure behind Roosevelt at the war conferences has somewhat subsumed his role as an architect of American welfare policy. Yet Hopkins took great pride that he was able to marshal the resources of the federal government to champion the rights of the poorest one third of the nation.

Hopkins died in early 1946, as a result of long-term complications relating to stomach cancer.

—*June Hopkins*

See also Association for Improving the Condition of the Poor (United States); Lurie, Harry Lawrence; Mothers' Pensions (United States); The New Deal (United States); Perkins, Frances; Roosevelt, Anna Eleanor; Roosevelt, Franklin Delano; Social Security (United States); Work Relief (United States)

Further Reading

Adams, H. (1977). *Harry Hopkins.* New York: Putnam.
Charles, S. F. (1963). *Minister of relief: Harry Hopkins and the Depression.* Syracuse, NY: Syracuse University Press.
Hopkins, J. (1999). *Harry Hopkins: Sudden hero, brash reformer.* New York: St. Martin's.
McJimsey, G. (1987). *Harry Hopkins: Ally of the poor, defender of democracy.* Cambridge, MA: Harvard University Press.

HOUSING POLICY (MEXICO)

Public-sector interest in Mexico's housing problem can be dated to the late nineteenth century, when the national government developed plots to the north of Mexico City for worker housing. Previously, and for much of the early part of the twentieth century, formal housing construction for low-income groups involved ad hoc interventions by the church or industrialists who set up small, idealistic schemes, often with strict rules about moral behavior. Although Article 3 of the Mexican Constitution of 1917 obliged employers to provide their workers "with comfortable and hygienic housing," there was no enforcement, and, in 1921, it was estimated that about one quarter of the population of Mexico City lived in tenements (*vecindad*).

POLICY FORMATION AND CONSOLIDATION: 1925–1964

A rent strike in 1922 prompted the first serious attempts at public housing. In 1925, the *Dirección de Pensiones Civiles* was created for government employees and in 1932 the National Bank for Urban Mortgages and Public Works (*Banco Nacional Hipotecario Urbano y de Obras Públicas,* or BNHUOP) was established. The "arrival" of public housing, however, had to wait until the 1940s, when the BNHUOP inaugurated the *Conjunto Esperanza* with 200 units and the *Dirección de Pensiones Civiles* completed the *Centro Urbano Presidente Alemán* with 1,080 units. In 1953, the BNHUOP and the *Dirección de Pensiones Civiles* completed *Unidad Modelo* with 3,639 units, demonstrating the confidence in new industrial construction methods and architects such as Mario Pani, Enrique del Moral, and José Villagrán, who specialized in the design of public housing, schools, and hospitals. A host of public agencies and companies such as petroleum company PEMEX (*Petroleos Mexicanos*), the *Comisión Federal de Electricidad,* railway workers, and the military also began to provide some limited housing for affiliates and staff.

In 1954, it was decided to establish an agency dedicated to housing, the National Institute of Housing (*Instituto Nacional de Vivienda,* or INV). The INV was directed to conduct tenement rehabilitation, new construction, the provision of mortgage facilities, and the coordination of the activities of public agencies with interests in housing. The INV did attempt some innovation of project design, but, without a predictable source of funding and after 1965 a requirement to raise financing from domestic or international loans, the agency resorted to small projects, mostly for government employees. By the mid 1960s, housing policy seemed to be neither tackling the increasing number of squatter settlements nor the conditions in *vecindad.* Indeed, as Oscar Lewis illustrated in his widely read *The*

Children of Sanchez (1961), poor conditions in the tenements appeared to persist from generation to generation. Lewis attributed this persistence to a "culture of poverty," but housing experts suspected it was due to rent control and the difficulties of "renewal" in hotbeds of crime, promiscuity, and unemployment. Although such perceptions of the "pathologies" of poverty would be contested by subsequent research, they motivated a further extension in the scale of housing projects with the initiation in 1962 of *Conjunto Habitacional Tlatelolco,* which consisted of 11,916 units in 112 buildings, including schools, shopping centers, and sports facilities. Although legitimated as a response to a wider housing problem, *Tlatelolco,* as with over two thirds of public housing built from 1950 to 1964, was mostly dedicated to government employees.

POLICY EXPANDED AND DIVERSIFIED: 1964–1982

Concern for social unrest in the aftermath of the Cuban Revolution motivated an increased emphasis on housing policy. Primed with $100 million from the Alliance for Progress, the *Programa Financiera de Vivienda* from 1964 regarded the housing problem as fundamentally a question of finance. A number of new agencies were created of which the most important was the *Fondo de Operación y Financiamiento Bancario a la Vivienda* (FOVI). FOVI required commercial banks to allocate 30 percent of savings deposits to "social interest" housing, with the option of transferring funds to FOVI to provide mortgages to buyers of approved developer-initiated projects. Between 1964 and 1970, FOVI channeled $1.6 billion to housing, approximately four times more than all other agencies combined. But, the provision of capped interest rate mortgages to households earning over five minimum salaries and with the highest subsidies available to those able to repay loans over short periods meant that FOVI interventions were socially regressive.

In 1972, President Luis Echeverría removed the obligation on employers to provide housing and signaled that henceforth the state would take over responsibility. As Table H.1 indicates, the impact was dramatic. In 1971, Echeverría had already replaced the INV with the *Instituto Nacional Para el Desarollo de la Comunidad y la Vivienda* (INDECO) and in 1972 he created the National Institute of Housing for Workers (*Instituto Nacional de Fondo de Vivienda Para los Trabajadores,* or INFONAVIT). In an important shift of emphasis, INDECO adopted the use of "sites-and-services," often consisting of no more than a plot and "wet core" (a toilet, a faucet, and basic drainage) with the occupier given responsibility to complete a dwelling. By 1976, INDECO had begun 17 projects assisting 13,886 households. INFONAVIT operated through a mandatory payroll deduction of 5 percent, providing it with a stable source of funds. Both agencies, however, were subject to political manipulation. INFONAVIT involved the trade unions in its governance and as the organizers of housing developments, providing

opportunities for leader enrichment and repaying political loyalties. INDECO became Echeverría's troubleshooter to deal with politically organized land invasions and soon gained a reputation for cutting corners. In Puebla, the state planning agency protested that an INDECO sites-and-services project was located in an area destined for an urban park and the municipality refused to incorporate the settlement citing the poor quality of road surfaces and street lighting. In its defense, INDECO's budget was dictated by political expediency with annual variations of up to 400 percent and payment write-offs provoking default rates of 70 percent that meant operating deficits for all but 2 years from 1973 to 1982.

The 1970s witnessed reconsideration of the relationship between land and housing markets. Although public housing was able to meet about 10 percent of demand, an increasing number of

Table H.1   Public Housing Production (units completed) in Mexico, 1925–2000

Years (Presidential Administration)	*INFONAVIT*	*FOVI/SSSTE*	*FOVI*	*BANOBRAS*	*FONHAPO*	*OTHERS[1]*	*Total*
1925–1970	—	54,898	—	24,102	—	51,804	130,804
1964–1970 (Gustavo Díaz Ordaz)	—	1,302	92,016	16,662	—	9,798	119,778
1970–1976 (Luis Echeverría)	101,448	27,030	92,418	18,540	—	48,444	287,880
1976–1982 (José López Portillo)	262,890	56,628	209,316	6,192	—	115,530	650,556
1982–1988 (Miguel de la Madrid)	414,204	92,658	468,636	—	311,136[2]	105,462	1,392,096
1988–1994 (Carlos Salinas)	522,784	210,347	219,681	44,790	254,838	269,182	1,521,622
1994–2000 (Ernesto Zedillo)	856,255	141,927	268,915	59,965	78,472	586,420	1,991,954
Total	2,157,581	584,790	1,350,982	170,251	644,446	1,186,640	6,094,690

1. Includes INDECO and state-level housing agencies, and projects of PEMEX, CFE, and FOVIMI.
2. Includes 11,011 units for earthquake reconstruction through RHP.

Mexicans were acquiring land illegally upon which to build housing in a process known as *autoconstrucción.* Attempts by agencies such as INDECO after 1978 to acquire land reserves in order to sell at subsidized prices to low-income groups stalled due to inadequate budgets and resistance from affected landholders, especially the *ejidos* (agrarian communities), which accelerated illegal sales or even permitted invasions. The government response was to "regularize" land tenure. Within the Federal District, Echeverría set up the *Fideicomiso de Desarrollo Urbano* (FIDEURBE) to tackle tenure problems in highly politicized settlements. Unfortunately, FIDEURBE was embroiled in a battle with the treasury, which argued that the federal government should not fund a city agency, and with the mayor who in 1970 had set up the *Dirección General de Habitación Popular* (DGHP) as a competitor to FIDEURBE and INDECO. Ultimately, FIDEURBE delivered only a few thousand titles in a couple of settlements and often incorrectly identified recipients on poor-quality maps, prompting subsequent agencies to start from scratch. Fortunately, in 1973, Echeverría established the *Comisión Para la Regularización de la Tenencia de la Tierra* (CORETT) as a federal-level agency within, until 1999, the "agrarian" sector of government. CORETT operates in a nonpunitive manner, recognizing the right of occupancy as a "concession to the poor" and condoning *ejido* land sales. Between 1974 and 2000, CORETT issued 3.2 million titles to approximately 10 percent of Mexican households.

POLICY REAPPRAISED: 1982–2006

In 1982, President Miguel de la Madrid terminated INDECO, but with an eye to the forthcoming insertion of a "right to housing" clause in the Constitution; he also expanded the *Fideicomiso Fondo de Habitaciones Populares* (FONHAPO), established under his predecessor José López Portillo in 1981. FONHAPO has operated as Mexico's most decentralized housing agency in partnership with state governments and community groups earning less than 2.5 minimum wages. On the downside, some community organizations have been fronts for fraud and use FONHAPO as a means

to legitimate land occupations. On the upside, FONHAPO remains the exception to most housing agencies that promote massive and difficult-to-maintain units offering low-quality public space. The ability to work with communities gave it a vital role in the government's response to the 1985 Mexico City earthquake. After initial announcements that the displaced (*damnificados*) would receive temporary housing at the periphery of the city provoked a number of protests, the government created the short-lived *Renovación Habitacional Popular* (RHP) from within FONHAPO to rebuild or repair 49,000 units. RHP met its target in 2 years, providing housing to most households in situ, adopting imaginative housing designs, and contracting with smaller firms. Having provided no more than 4 percent of new construction in the 1980s, FONHAPO delivered 15 percent of public housing "starts" with only 9 percent of the federal housing budget by the 1990s, and with state-level agencies, FONHAPO has ensured that groups earning less than 2.5 minimum salaries now claim 25 percent of the housing budget.

Policy also revisited the theme of housing finance during the 1980s. In 1984, a dual interest mortgage was introduced to prevent loan amortization through inflation. This allowed the banks to charge market rates of interest but not threaten borrower affordability by pegging repayments to an index of the minimum salary. Shortfalls would be recapitalized or the loan term extended. Guided by World Bank advice and conditions on $750 million in loans, the forced-lending requirement imposed on the banks, said to be transferring $300 to $500 million per annum to middle-income groups, was removed and subsidies made more transparent. In 1992, President Carlos Salinas de Gortari sought to free up even more private sector capital with reforms to extend the secondary mortgage market (*bursatilización*). President Ernesto Zedillo encouraged the formation of locally based savings and credit organizations known as *Sociedades Financieras de Objeto Limitado* (SOFOLES), which President Vicente Fox has sought to institutionalize into housing policy through the oversight of the *Sociedad Hipotecaria Federal*. This is a means to reach the self-employed who are ineligible for affiliation-based schemes and whose incomes are above 2.5 but less than 5 minimum salaries through the *Programa Especial de Crédito y Subsidios a la Vivienda* (PROSAVI), which provides a subsidy determined by the size of deposit provided by the household.

In the past 50 years, the proportion of the Mexican population classified as urban has risen from under 30 percent to almost 80 percent, the proportion with access to domestic water has increased to over 50 percent, and the proportion of de facto owner-occupiers is approximately 60 percent. Yet, the "housing deficit" stands at 4.2 million units, including 756,000 households that lack housing altogether and one million units in need of immediate replacement. In the next 30 years, it is expected that the number of people over 20 years of age will increase from 57 to 97 million, adding to pressure to deliver affordable housing at scale.

—*Gareth A. Jones*

See also Economic Policy (Mexico); Labor Movement and Social Welfare (Mexico); Social Welfare (Mexico): Since 1867

Primary Sources

Information on the changing rationale for housing policy was collected from the national offices of INFONAVIT and CORETT, and from files held on the BNHUOP, INV, and INDECO at the library of the *Banco de México*, all in Mexico City. Data on housing supply are available from the *Secretaría de Desarrollo Social* (www.sedesol.gob.mx) and the *Sociedad Hipotecaria Federal* (www.shf.gob.mx).

Current Comment

Lewis, O. (1961). *The children of Sánchez: Autobiography of a Mexican family.* New York: Viking.
Villavicencio, J. (2000). La política habitacional en México: ¿Una política con contenido social? In R. Cordera & A. Ziccardi (Eds.), *Las políticas sociales en México al fin del milenio* (pp. 263–288). Mexico City: Universidad Nacional Autónoma de México; Miguel Ángel Porrúa.

Further Reading

Garza, G. (2003). *La urbanización de México en el siglo XX.* Mexico City: Colegio de México.
Pezzoli, K. (1998). *Human settlements and planning for ecological sustainability: The case of Mexico City.* Cambridge, MA: MIT Press.
Siembieda, W. J., & Moreno, E. L. (1999). From commercial banking systems to non-commercial banking systems in Mexico. In K. Datta & G. A. Jones (Eds.), *Housing and finance in developing countries* (pp. 75–88). London: Routledge.

HOUSING POLICY (UNITED STATES)

Living the American dream for many is the ability to afford and purchase a home. Home ownership is a symbol of success and marks for many the path to wealth and independence. U.S. federal policy since the late 1800s has supported the idea of home ownership. The vision of home ownership reflects a deep cultural and social value that has seen home ownership as a sign of personal success.

For many, however, the dream of home ownership is one that will never be realized. Many pay over 30 percent of their income toward housing costs, a figure considered affordable by the U.S. Department of Housing and Urban Development. Housing is often a major need that must be met before people can access other supportive services. But locating accessible housing is a challenge. The National Low Income Housing Coalition estimates that in 2000, 4.9 million additional affordable housing units were needed to meet the needs of very low-income persons.

The history of housing policy reflects the often-times contradictory objectives of home ownership and provision of affordable housing for those without the economic means to be homeowners. Many conservatives and others have seen the provision of affordable housing by the federal government as an intrusion into the free market. Nevertheless, government has often seen the provision of housing for marginal citizens as legitimate social policy.

FROM AGRICULTURE TO INDUSTRY

During the nineteenth century, America was in transition. Moving from its agrarian beginnings to the industrial age, America's transformation into a world power was just beginning. The provision of housing was seen as a personal responsibility. A person who could not provide housing for himself or herself looked first to friends and family and then to the community for housing support. Housing options were shaped by contemporary attitudes toward the provision of social welfare. The legacy of the Elizabethan Poor Laws in the United States and their focus on labeling the poor as "worthy" or "unworthy" justified using community resources to provide housing for those deemed worthy to receive assistance. Furthermore, ideas about personal responsibility supported a social system in which people were expected to care for themselves. Only those who were seen as having little ability to care for themselves merited any publicly supported housing.

Industrialization and urbanization brought new social problems to the attention of government at all levels. As people crowded cities looking for employment, more housing was needed. The provision of cheap, affordable tenement housing in cities helped meet that need. But tenement housing was often overcrowded, housing thousands in a single city block. With few building codes, tenement housing often lacked plumbing, ventilation, or other habitability and safety features that are required today.

With increasing urbanization, many urban residents began to seek housing options away from the noise, congestion, and pollution of inner cities. By the early 1800s, savings banks were developed to assist the middle class to escape the inner cities to achieve the American dream of home ownership in the suburbs. As the more affluent left the inner city, immigrants seeking work and housing replaced them. Often unable to afford homes, immigrant workers rented what was available and affordable—tenement housing.

For those unable to find work, local governments built almshouses, which began to replace traditional in-home care for the poor by the mid 1800s. In theory, almshouses provided employment, housing, and other services to help the able-bodied to move toward self-sufficiency. They were, however, often overcrowded and provided only custodial care.

By the late 1800s, the friendly visitors of the charity organization societies worked with people in their homes and began to advocate for tenement housing reform. By the end of the century, the industrial age had ushered in new progressive theories and proposals to provide support and housing for the poor.

PROGRESSIVE ERA

By the late 1890s, America's industrial economy was suffering from depression, job loss, increased immigration, and growing income inequality. The progressive movement saw new ideas about the causes of poverty. Instead of blaming persons for being poor by arguing that their own sloth or moral depravity had led them into poverty, progressive reformers, like Jane Addams, argued that social conditions, such as a lack of decent, affordable housing, contributed to poverty. Progressives saw urban slums and unsafe tenement housing as threats to the social order. Decent housing was seen as part of the solution to attacking poverty, crime, and delinquency.

The Progressive Era can be marked by three efforts intended to improve the housing conditions of the poor. First, the settlement house movement provided community-based service and education to build stronger neighborhoods. Advocating on behalf of the poor, settlement reformers worked at city and state levels to improve housing conditions. Additionally, reformers sought legislative reforms at all levels of government to improve the housing conditions for the poor. Finally, new "model" tenements were promoted as a means of compromising between the ideals of reformers and private real estate interests. They were supposed to demonstrate to real estate developers that safe housing could be profitable, but the idea was never very successful.

Prior to the Progressive Era, restrictive housing legislation that attempted to ensure adequate sanitation, lighting, and ventilation was not enforced and was largely ineffective. Early researchers and reformers, like Lawrence Veiller, advocated for restrictive legislation to prevent the development of slum tenements. In 1901, New York City enacted a Tenement House Law that placed restrictions on tenement construction to ensure proper lighting and ventilation. Other major cities followed suit and by 1910 most cities had enacted similar laws. Though these efforts improved housing conditions, they did not address housing affordability. Unfortunately, laws meant to provide for tenement safety increased construction costs and resulted in higher rents, forcing poorer tenants to seek other housing.

Even though progressive reformers argued for government intervention to provide social welfare benefits or services, housing programs continued to be limited to local and state efforts. Not until the Great Depression would the federal government take on a major role in the provision of housing.

DEPRESSION AND POSTWAR YEARS

The collapse of the banking industry in 1929 and America's decline into the Great Depression helped to rid American politics of its laissez-faire mentality. The housing strategy of President Franklin Delano Roosevelt's New Deal took a two-tiered approach that supported middle-class home ownership and subsidized rental housing for low-income persons impacted by the depression.

With the collapse of the banking industry, the administration's first response was to stabilize the housing market by reestablishing trust in the banking system. In 1932, the Federal Home Loan Bank was established, which created a home loan banking system to support provision of home mortgages, making home ownership possible for many. In 1934, the National Housing Act relieved unemployment and stimulated the housing market by making credit available for the repair and construction of housing. It created the Federal Housing Administration (FHA). The FHA insured mortgages, making them more available to prospective homeowners. Although these measures helped to spur housing development and rehabilitation, they did little to provide housing for lower-income, working families.

In response to this need, the Housing Act of 1937 (Wagner-Steagall Act) created the first public housing program by establishing the U.S. Public Housing Authority. This agency was authorized to loan funds to locally established public housing authorities for the development of public housing. Unemployed workers were hired to clear urban slum areas and to build affordable housing for the working class. Critics of the federal housing program included private developers, who spurred community opposition to public housing. Using scare tactics, they created adverse images of public housing and its occupants. Many public housing units used simple, rectangular, box-like designs with few amenities that were often seen as unattractive additions to the urban landscape.

From 1937 to 1949, labeled by some as the "happy years" for public housing, government housing programs effectively served the working poor and helped many obtain funding for private housing. From 1950 to 1960, public housing's aims and objectives changed again in response to several factors, including the development of modern highway systems and the availability of low-interest mortgages that enabled middle-class workers to move to suburbs. Unskilled and often uneducated workers from the South came to many northern cities seeking employment and housing, most often in public housing projects. Critics felt that public housing was becoming a ghetto for an emerging underclass living in poverty.

URBAN RENEWAL TO THE PRESENT

After the assassination of President John F. Kennedy, Lyndon B. Johnson initiated ambitious Great Society antipoverty programs, including urban renewal projects that cleared many urban slum areas. The Housing Act of 1965 created the first cabinet-level agency dealing with housing and urban renewal, the U.S. Department of Housing and Urban Development (HUD). Other legislation followed including in 1968 the Fair Housing Act, prohibiting housing discrimination, and legislation establishing the Government National Mortgage Association (Ginnie Mae) to expand availability of mortgage funds for moderate-income families. Six million new units of low- and moderate-income housing were planned over the next 10 years. Unlike the public housing programs of the 1930s, the Johnson administration promoted the privatization of low-income housing by providing subsidies to developers to build and manage multifamily housing for low-income families. The federal government ensured the success of the projects by providing low-interest loans for construction and guaranteed rent subsidies.

By the time of Richard Nixon's election in 1968, federal housing programs were being blamed for the decline in the working-class neighborhoods. This criticism caused President Nixon to declare a moratorium on federal public housing. In 1974, President Gerald Ford signed into law the Housing and Community Development Act, which created the Community Development Block Grant (CDBG) program. The CDBG program provided funds for housing that were to be administered by cities and states. The act also created the Section 8 program to provide low-income persons with rental assistance vouchers.

Since the administration of President Ronald Reagan (1981–1989), federal housing policy has supported home ownership for most Americans through the use of tax incentives, low interest loans, and loan insurance programs. U.S. housing policy for low- to moderate-income wage earners continued to support private market solutions to housing shortages. The Tax Reform Act of 1986 authorized a Low Income Housing Tax Credit that gave tax incentives to developers to build low-income housing. It is estimated that this has resulted in the construction of 800,000 units of rental housing.

In the 1980s and 1990s, renewed efforts to address the housing needs of specialized populations, including the homeless, the elderly, and persons with disabilities, resulted in new housing programs. The Stewart B. McKinney Act of 1987 provided community-level funding to address homelessness and the Cranston-Gonzalez National Affordable Housing Act of 1990 authorized housing for special needs populations, including persons with AIDS.

With the Republican victory in the 1994 congressional elections, housing policy moved further from subsidizing public housing toward increased use of tenant vouchers that are paid directly to landlords. State and local governments obtained block grants to provide housing that would be acceptable to local interests. Housing policy continues to be a private-public collaboration that emphasizes home ownership as the ultimate housing objective for Americans. Current policy emphasizes state and local development initiatives relying mostly on private real estate developers to provide accessible housing. The dilemma of how best to provide decent housing for poor and low-income persons remains unresolved.

—*Russell L. Bennett*

See also Charity Organization Societies (United States); Homelessness (United States); The New Deal (United States); Poor Law (United States)

Primary Sources

General Records of the Department of Housing and Urban Development (Record Group 207), National Archives & Records Administration, College Park, MD.

Current Comment

The National Low Income Housing Coalition (NLIHC) can be accessed on-line (www.nlihc.org/).

The Fannie Mae Foundation website hosts a series of on-line journals, including *Housing Policy Debate* and *Housing Facts*

and Findings (www.fanniemaefoundation.org/programs/journals.shtml).

The U.S. Department of Housing and Urban Development can be accessed on-line (www.hud.gov/).

Further Reading

Orlebeke, C. J. (n.d.). The evolution of low-income housing policy, 1949–1999. *Housing Policy Debate, 11*(2), 489–520.

Powers, M. E. (1979). *The pattern of emergence of social services in housing programs*. Unpublished doctoral dissertation, Brandeis University.

HULL HOUSE (UNITED STATES)

Hull House, once a hospital and a furniture store, became Chicago's first settlement house when Jane Addams and Ellen Gates Starr began residing there in 1889. Hull House was among the first of hundreds of settlements in the United States whose work heralded a new social movement that attempted to bridge the distance between social classes through fellowship, recreation, social reform, and political influence. Under the leadership of Jane Addams, Hull House served as an incubator for leaders of the Progressive and New Deal eras of social reform, whose efforts resulted in policies, community infrastructures, and social safeguards that remain fundamental to social welfare in the United States. Community institutions such as kindergartens and playgrounds, labor regulations such as the minimum wage, national social insurance policies, and the profession of social work all have foundations in the work of settlement houses and their activist residents.

Hull House and its mission were initially misunderstood by many who were more accustomed to the dominant model of charity as done by the charity organization societies. But the alternative approach and philosophy of the settlement house movement for serving the nation's recent immigrants who were poor made it attractive to its young, college-educated, and more privileged residents. Hull House itself was not a charity: The settlement house residents were not there to distribute goods or correct moral wrongs. Rather, Addams and Starr opened the doors of Hull House to bring people from different social classes together through the common bond of humanity and to foster greater understanding, enrichment, and social democracy for all involved. Appreciating the immigrants' efforts to maintain family and community amid urban poverty, the residents listened to their needs and partnered with their neighbors to secure better living and working conditions, richer quality of life, and more just representation. The activists embraced this new "way to serve and yet to avoid the cloying paternalism, the professional doing good of organized charity and mission societies" (Bryan & Davis, 1990, p. 4).

The activities at Hull House took three primary forms: social action, research, and recreational and educational club activities. For the new immigrants who were poor, the long hours of factory work and crowded tenement slums eroded community bonds, compromised children's development, and offered few healthy recreations. Although initial activities such as art exhibits and lectures could be considered esoteric, Starr and Addams were responsive to the needs of their neighbors and replaced these activities with programs addressing the more immediate needs of immigrants, including classes in basic English and American government. As the activities of Hull House grew, space was added for meetings, classes, and programs sponsored by such groups as ethnic groups, sports clubs, labor unions, and homemaker clubs. Off-site, the settlement house sponsored a summer camp.

As activities expanded, Hull House came to encompass as many as 13 buildings, including a coffeehouse, an art gallery, a branch of the public library, a gymnasium, a labor museum, a theater, a bookbindery, a children's nursery, a kindergarten, a music school, and a cooperative residence for working girls. Hull House was one of the first full-service community centers, complete with a bulletin of events and activities. Each bulletin began with a statement of Hull House objectives: "To provide a center for the higher civic and social life; to institute and maintain educational and philanthropic enterprises; and to investigate and improve the conditions in the industrial districts of Chicago" (quoted in Bryan & Davis, 1990, p. 85).

Besides Jane Addams, Hull House residents included many who became well-known activists and social reform leaders, such as Florence Kelley, Julia Lathrop, Frances Perkins, and Charles Beard, the noted historian, among others. Most residents paid rent and had outside jobs, devoting their spare time to settlement house activities. Short-term residents included future prime ministers, company presidents, and city planning experts. All were concerned with the emerging social problems in large industrialized cities and drawn to the intellectually stimulating arena of the Hull House dining room. Here, they discussed the problems of work hazards and poor living environments faced by vulnerable immigrant groups and factory laborers nationwide. As a result, residents worked not only for reform in their local neighborhoods and cities but also for national reform.

Disturbed by such practices as lack of workplace protections for children and women and inadequate housing for the poor (as well as seeking to enhance awareness of these issues among benefactors), residents became expert social investigators. Their research included studies of tenement conditions, wage rates, infant mortality, literacy rates, drug use, and truancy. With these studies, Hull House residents garnered the attention and financial support of many professional men, scholars, lawyers, and labor leaders, as well as wealthy Chicago women.

Some of these financial supporters did not approve of Hull House leaders' alignment with their neighbors or some of the more controversial campaigns of the Progressive Era. Prior to World War I, Hull House leaders were decried as anti-American and communists for their support of propositions safeguarding workers. During World War I, broad community and financial support for Hull House declined dramatically, in large part due to Jane Addams's outspoken pacifism. Hull House residents participated in battles for the regulation of child labor, women's suffrage, and the abolition of sweatshops. Later, these former residents played leading roles in advocating for state and federal reforms in labor law, protection of children, and the provisions of economic security programs. In 1931, Jane Addams received the Nobel Peace Prize, and during the Great Depression of the 1930s, many of the reforms proposed by Hull House residents were realized in the groundbreaking social legislation of the New Deal.

After World War II, Hull House hosted a pioneering program of citizen participation in urban renewal and helped to ease racially discriminatory housing policies. Despite a strong campaign of opposition, much of Hull House was razed to make way for a new campus of the University of Illinois in 1963. A few of the original buildings remained as a museum of Hull House, but a new organization was formed called the Hull House Association. The association administered social and community services at various locations and facilities around Chicago. Affiliate centers were staffed by human service professionals, and, without a single settlement facility, it was harder for Hull House to distinguish itself from other social service programs. The War on Poverty of the 1960s, which focused national attention on the poor, revived the organization. The Hull House Association benefited greatly from federal monies given to support anti-poverty programs, and many affiliate programs were able to double their services and add staff members. Programs varied widely and included child care, counseling and job referral, theater programs, art classes, and much more.

The Hull House Association, if not the settlement itself, endured through shifting national and public commitment to services for the poor and social justice for disenfranchised groups. The association continues to help Chicago residents strengthen their families and communities.

—*Bianca Genco-Morrison and Jan L. Hagen*

See also Abbott, Edith; Abbott, Grace; Addams, Jane; Hamilton, Alice; Lathrop, Julia Clifford; Settlement Houses (United States)

Further Reading

Addams, J. (1910). *Twenty years at Hull House.* New York: Macmillan.

Addams, J. (1930). *The second twenty years at Hull House.* New York: Macmillan.

Bryan, M. L. M., & Davis, A. F. (Eds.). (1990). *100 years at Hull House.* Bloomington: Indiana University Press.

HUMAN RIGHTS (CANADA)

Universal human rights are rights that belong to every human being solely by virtue of her or his membership in humankind. The history of human rights in Canada can only be fully understood in light of the international context in which it has taken place and of which it forms an integral part. The pivotal, internationally endorsed human rights principles of freedom, equality, and dignity of all human beings and all human groups are enshrined in the provisions of the United Nations (UN) Charter (1945), the *International Bill of Human Rights* (1978, 1988), and related covenants.

This conception of universal human rights is a twentieth century phenomenon: It should not be equated with the historical concept of natural rights because to do so would be to overlook the crucial fact that so-called natural rights were not rights held solely by virtue of one's humanity. Indeed, race, gender, and nationality were also relevant criteria. Natural rights, in reality, were the rights of dominant Westerners: White European men. Some 80 percent of all human beings were excluded.

Universal human rights represent international moral guidelines that are prior to law: Essentially, they serve to challenge states to revise laws in ways that offer guaranteed protections for the rights of citizens, especially members of minority groups, against abuses of state power. These principles are advocated by United Nations authoritative bodies as the universal human rights standards, to which all systems of justice should conform.

Although universal human rights are put forward as global moral standards, this is not to say that these principles are absolute or static: Indeed, human rights are continuously evolving as nations and concerned citizens within nations reconsider them and develop ever-newer covenants to protect more explicitly the human rights of persons and groups throughout the globe.

THE DEVELOPMENT OF INTERNATIONAL HUMAN RIGHTS COVENANTS

The bulk of the declarations advanced in current international human rights instruments have their roots in the *Universal Declaration of Human Rights* (UDHR, 1948). Elaborating on the mandate of the UN Charter (1945), the three guiding principles of the UDHR—freedom, equality, and dignity—address a common, threefold theme: the right of every human being to participate in the shaping of decisions affecting one's own life and that of one's society (freedom to decide/political rights); reasonable access to the economic resources that make that participation possible (equality of opportunity/economic rights); and affirmation of the essential human worth and dignity of every person, regardless of individual qualities and/or group membership (dignity of person/ social rights).

Under current UN human rights covenants, the three pivotal individual human rights principles—freedom to decide, equality, equivalence of opportunity, and dignity of person—are held to be inalienable. What this means is that all human beings can claim these fundamental human rights equally, regardless of demonstrated or assumed differences among individual persons in their talents, abilities, skills, and resources and regardless of their membership in different human groups.

Although fundamental human rights are held to be inalienable, they are not absolute: In the exercise of his or her fundamental rights, each human being must not violate, indeed must respect, the fundamental human rights of others. Human rights, then, are not unconditional: They are conditional on the exercise of social responsibilities or duties to others.

The fundamental principles of the interdependence of the individual and community and of the reciprocity of rights and duties, protected under the UDHR, provide the underpinnings for the moral justification of necessary restrictions on individual human rights. For, from a human rights view, any restriction or denial of the exercise of the fundamental human rights to freedom, equality, and dignity of any human being can be justified only in instances in which violations of the human rights of others can be fully substantiated. In such cases, appropriate restrictions may be imposed to prevent further violations of the rights of others. Canada's legal and justice systems impose restrictions on citizens to prevent, for example, murder, rape, theft, defamation of character, and group-level discrimination on the basis of race, sex, religion, ethnic origin, disability, and other grounds.

TWIN PRINCIPLES OF HUMAN RIGHTS: HUMAN UNITY AND CULTURAL DIVERSITY

Fundamental individual human rights are rooted in the distinctive biological attributes shared by all members of humankind as a single species, *Homo sapiens.* Recognition of the essential biological oneness of humankind provides the scientific basis for the universal principle of fundamental individual human rights. A primary assumption, then, behind international human rights covenants is that of the fundamental unity and kinship among all members of humankind.

Yet every human being is born not only into the human species but also into a particular human population and ethnocultural community. Collective, cultural rights represent the principle of cultural diversity, the differentness of unique ethnocultures, or blueprints for living developed by various ethnic populations of humankind. Taken together, individual and collective human rights represent the twin global principles of human unity and cultural diversity. Just as all human beings, as members of humankind, must respect the fundamental individual rights of all other human beings, so, also, all human beings as members of particular human cultures must respect all of the different ethnocultures shared by other human beings.

Since its proclamation, the UDHR has had international impact, influencing national constitutions and laws, as well as international declarations. Some countries sought a more forceful declaration that would establish binding obligations on the part of member states. As a result, two additional covenants were drawn up and came into force in 1976: the *International Covenant on Economic, Social and Cultural Rights* (ICESCR) and the *International Covenant on Civil and Political Rights* (ICCPR). Their provisions, however, apply only to those member states that have decided to ratify them. Less than half of the member states, including the United States, have not ratified either covenant. Canada, however, has ratified both.

Nations that ratify these covenants are expected to introduce laws that will reflect their provisions. Canada has taken measures to fulfill its commitment by enacting human rights legislation at both provincial and federal levels of jurisdiction and by entrenching a Charter of Rights and Freedoms in the Canadian Constitution (1982).

The Optional Protocol to the ICCPR provides individual citizens with direct recourse to the United Nations. Persons who believe that their rights as specified in the covenant have been violated can state their case before the UN Human Rights Committee. Such persons must first have exhausted all legal avenues within their own country. To date, Canada is one of only a small number of the nations signing the covenant that has ratified the Optional Protocol. In 1978, the UDHR and the two later covenants (ICCPR and ICESCR) were incorporated into the *International Bill of Human Rights* (IBHR).

THE DEVELOPMENT OF HUMAN RIGHTS IN CANADA

For almost a century after the British Emancipation Act of 1833, which marked the official demise of slavery in Canada, the trend at the federal, provincial, and municipal levels of Canadian government was to enact discriminatory legislation. Although there were isolated legislative attempts to overcome racial/ethnic discrimination in Canada as far back as the 1930s, it was not until the end of World War II, and the shocking revelations of Nazi genocide, that a real interest in antidiscrimination legislation developed. During the World War II period, Canadians bore witness to some of the most flagrant examples of racism in the country's history. In 1939, humanitarian petitions for Canadian acceptance of a fair quota of Jewish refugees fleeing the threat of extermination were ignored. In 1942, a policy of forceful evacuation of Japanese Canadians from west coastal areas led to the confiscation of their property and their confinement as "enemy aliens" in heavily guarded internment camps.

Following the war, Canadian public opinion became more sensitive to incidents of racial and ethnic discrimination. But, increasingly, other grounds of discrimination came to the fore, as various pressure groups began to lobby for antidiscrimination legislation and for more adequate means of implementation and enforcement of the laws. Thus, governments ventured slowly and carefully into the area of human rights legislation.

By 1975, all Canadian provinces had established human rights commissions to administer antidiscriminatory legislation and, 2 years later, the Canadian Human Rights Act established a federal Human Rights Commission. In 1982, Canada extended legal protection for its citizens' human rights to the constitutional level by entrenching the Charter of Rights and Freedoms in the Canadian Constitution—the highest law in the land.

International Human Rights as Legal Rights in Canada

When internationally endorsed human rights principles become incorporated into law, they become legal rights that can be invoked by persons or groups who perceive that their human rights have been violated and seek legal redress and recompense for the alleged violation. In Canada, the legal framework of human rights protection is based on a three-tiered system of standards governing human relations within the state. International human rights instruments (IBHR and related covenants) apply to relations between states and provide the global standards to which all state legislation should conform. In keeping with human rights tenets advanced by international instruments, Canada has enacted human rights legislation that prohibits discrimination on enumerated and sometimes, on more general grounds, at all jurisdictional levels—provincial, federal, and constitutional.

Constitutional rules apply to relations between governments within the state and provide the national standard to which all statutory laws should conform. To provide a national, constitutionally endorsed standard for human rights legislation throughout the country, Canada enacted a Charter of Rights and Freedoms in its amended (1982) Constitution. In keeping with the nondiscriminatory provisions of Articles 1 and 2 of the UDHR, Canada enacted the equality rights provisions of Section 15 of the charter under which discrimination on enumerated and analogous grounds is prohibited. Moreover, in keeping with the international principle of collective cultural rights under the provisions of Article 27 of the ICCPR, Canada enacted Section 27 of the charter affording ethnic minorities constitutional protection for their "multicultural" rights.

Statutory human rights legislation applies to relations between individuals and organizations within the state and should conform to the guarantees for human rights in the charter and related constitutional provisions. Since the enactment of the charter, Canada's provincial and federal human rights laws have been undergoing a process of amendment so as to bring their provisions into conformity with the charter standard. For example, the constitutional provision for affirmative action under Section 15(2) of the charter provided the catalyst for parallel, statutory legislation allowing affirmative remedies against the collective, adverse impact of systemic discrimination for disadvantaged groups in the society.

Canadian Legislation
Prohibiting Discrimination

There are significant differences in detail among current human rights statutes—in their enumerated grounds of discrimination, areas of application, and so forth. Statutes at the provincial and federal levels, however, share fundamental similarities in content and administration. All of the human rights statutes in Canada prohibit discrimination on the grounds of race, religion, color, nationality or national origin, gender, and disability. Most also include other grounds such as age and sexual orientation. All of the statutes are designed to ensure equality of access to places, activities, and opportunities. Accordingly, they all prohibit discrimination in hiring, terms and conditions of employment, job advertisements, job referrals by employment agencies, and membership in unions. Most also prohibit discrimination in professional, business, and trade associations.

Both federal and provincial statutes prohibit discrimination in the provision of accommodation, services, and facilities to which the public has access. The provinces and territories prohibit discrimination in residential property rentals and sales; many also cover commercial properties.

All jurisdictions have both administrative staff and citizen commissioners responsible to ministers of government, whose task is to administer the legislation, to enforce the acts, to carry out research on human rights, and to conduct public education programs.

The Charter of Rights and Freedoms

The Constitutional Debate

Since at least the mid 1950s, many legal scholars had advocated that Canada adopt an entrenched charter of rights. Entrenchment means the inclusion of a charter of rights as part of the Constitution. Scholars arguing for constitutional entrenchment of the Charter of Rights and Freedoms (CRF) contended that, as part of the supreme law of the land, the CRF would eliminate the many disparities among federal and provincial statutes by mandating that they be brought into conformity with CRF standards. Additionally, the CRF would override existing legislation, thus rendering all discriminatory laws inoperative. Because the charter provides a nationwide standard for all legislation, this means that once all laws have been brought into conformity with charter provisions, Canadians should be afforded the same protection for their human rights throughout the country, rather than differential protection from one jurisdiction to another.

During the constitutional debates of 1980–1981, and continuing until the present time, it has became increasingly clear that proponents and opponents of an entrenched charter look at its value from very different perspectives. One view is that a charter of rights diminishes the power of elected representatives in that all legislation enacted is subject to review by courts to ensure charter compliance. In 1982, to ensure that the notion of parliamentary supremacy would not be endangered, the drafters of the charter included two provisions to reinforce parliamentary sovereignty or parliamentary supremacy. One provision is Section 33 of the charter, which allows the Parliament of Canada and the legislatures of the provinces to opt out of certain sections as they apply to particular legislation. That is, Parliament or the legislatures may enact legislation that operates notwithstanding its conflict with Sections 2 and 7 through 15 of the charter. Secondly, Section 1 provides that even if a law is in violation of the charter, it may nonetheless be saved as a reasonable limit, demonstrably justified in a free and democratic society. A law will be found to be such if it is a rational, nondisproportionate, minimally intrusive means of achieving a pressing and substantial state objective.

Opponents continue to argue, however, that entrenchment of a charter of rights not only diminishes the notion of parliamentary sovereignty (in the sense that legislative enactments are now subject to review by the courts to ensure compliance with the charter), but it also, in effect, transfers authority from elected representatives to the nonelected judiciary. This, critics argue, is antidemocratic. On the other side of the debate, supporters of an entrenched charter take critical issue with both Sections 1 and 33 of the CRF, as undermining protection for the fundamental rights and freedoms of all Canadians, guaranteed in the other provisions of the charter.

Because the override clause (Section 33) in the CRF allows provinces to pass legislation that overrides the CRF in the areas of legal rights, equality rights, and fundamental freedoms, this clause, critics point out, thwarts the CRF's guarantees for human rights protection, and puts the most basic human rights and freedoms in jeopardy.

Similarly, critics argue, Section 1 of the charter (the "reasonable limits" clause) restricts charter rights in a number of ways. Under Section 1, limits must be "reasonable, prescribed by law, demonstrably justified, and in keeping with the standards of a free and democratic society." The problem with this articulation of limits on human rights is that it is subject to questionable, subjective interpretation by the courts. Three of the four criteria are open to judicial bias in interpretation because of their subjective nature; only the criterion "prescribed by law" is objective. Section 33 of the charter (the "opting out" clause) allows governments to exclude their laws from the requirements of the charter with regard to Section 2 (fundamental freedoms) and Sections 7 through 15 (legal and equality rights) for a period of 5 years at a time.

Application of the Charter

The charter primarily applies to actions of governments: As part of Canada's 1982 Constitution, its provisions override those of statutory law. Accordingly, federal and provincial governments must ensure that their laws conform to charter standards. The charter has an enforcement provision that authorizes courts to strike down laws that do not conform to its standards (Section 52) and to order appropriate and just remedies to complainants (Section 24).

The charter also provides private, nongovernmental bodies and individuals with a constitutional basis for challenging their federal and provincial governments when their laws or policies do not conform to charter standards. Prior to the enactment of the charter, private individuals and organizations could bring forward complaints alleging human rights violations against other private individuals or organizations only under the provisions of statutory human rights legislation at the federal and provincial levels. Claimants could not challenge any alleged discrimination in the laws themselves, or in government policies and practices under these laws.

—*Evelyn Kallen*

See also Gay, Lesbian, Bisexual, Transgender Policy Issues (Canada); Women and Social Welfare (Canada)

Primary Sources

United Nations Office of the High Commissioner for Human Rights (www.unhchr.ch/html/intlinst.htm); Human Rights Research and Education Centre, University Of Ottawa (www.uottawa.ca/hrrec/); Human Rights Program, Government of Canada (www.pch.gc.ca/progs/pdp-hrp/index_e.cfm).

Current Comment

Bryden, P. (1994). The Canadian Charter of Rights and Freedoms is antidemocratic and un-Canadian: An opposing point of view. In M. Charleton & P. Barker (Eds.), *Crosscurrents: Contemporary political issues* (2nd ed., p. 108). Scarborough, ON: Nelson.

Charleton, M., & Barker, P. (Eds.). (1994). *Crosscurrents: Contemporary political issues* (2nd ed.). Scarborough, ON: Nelson.

Martin, R. (1994). The Canadian Charter of Rights and Freedoms is antidemocratic and un-Canadian. In M. Charleton & P. Barker (Eds.), *Crosscurrents: Contemporary political issues* (2nd ed., p. 105). Scarborough, ON: Nelson.

Wilson, B. (1993). The institutional capacity of the court. In F. L. Morton (Ed.), *Law, politics and the judicial process in Canada* (2nd ed., p. 287). Calgary, AB: University of Calgary Press.

Further Reading

Beaudoin, G. A., & Mendes, E. (1995). *The Canadian Charter of Rights and Freedoms* (3rd ed.). Toronto, ON: Carswell.

Howe, R. B., & Johnson, D. (2001). *Restraining equality: Human rights commissions in Canada.* Toronto, ON: University of Toronto Press.

Kallen, E. (2003). *Ethnicity and human rights in Canada: A human rights perspective on ethnicity, racism and systemic inequality* (3rd ed.). Toronto, ON, Oxford University Press.

HYGIENE AND PUBLIC HEALTH POLICY DURING THE PORFIRIATO (MEXICO)

The period in Mexican history known as the Porfiriato (1876–1911) witnessed the expansion, consolidation, and professionalization of public health. During these years, a clear transition from simple sanitary reform to sophisticated state medicine occurred, as public health became one of the key issues of government and an indispensable requirement for the material progress of the nation. In addition, Mexican physicians and hygienists gained a position of power and authority without precedent, and they assumed with the state the shared responsibility to design and supervise health policies and programs that aimed to transform the country into a truly modern nation, and its inhabitants into hygienic and responsible citizens.

During the first National Congress of Physicians, held in Mexico City in 1876, public health officials, hygienists, and the state established that the high rate of infant mortality, the multiple diseases that impinged upon the laboring classes—both urban and rural—and the unsanitary conditions that prevailed in most cities, towns, ports, and borders, were issues that required an efficient, coordinated, and organized public health response. In addition, popular medical practices and traditions that predominated in a country as culturally heterogeneous as Mexico were regarded by licensed physicians as factors that contributed to the propagation of multiple diseases among the population.

The most formally organized and professional health authority during the final decades of the nineteenth century was the Superior Sanitation Council (SSC). When it was created in 1841, its jurisdiction had been circumscribed to the Federal District and its work had been seriously hampered because it had scant resources and only six members. In 1879, however, during the first presidency of Porfirio Díaz (1876–1880), a decree was issued making the Superior Sanitation Council answerable only to the Ministry of the Interior. This implied that the executive power through that governmental institution would supervise and guide all public health policies and programs, and that the state's involvement would cease to be limited to times of crisis. To this end, the Superior Sanitation Council was reorganized and subdivided into 12 permanent commissions responsible for separate surveillance of the sanitary and hygienic conditions found in hospitals, in jails, and in industrial establishments. The SSC also supervised the quality of medicines, food, and beverages produced and sold, as well as hygiene inside houses, tenements, churches, and any other site where people gathered.

From 1885 to 1914, when the SSC was directed by Dr. Eduardo Liceaga, it achieved primary jurisdiction over all matters of public health, and specific health and hygienic legislation was first formulated through the Sanitary Code of the United States of Mexico, approved by Congress in 1891. The sanitary code provided for the first time essential protection for Mexicans, since the 1857 Constitution did not include any provision relating to public health. The sanitary code was reformed in 1894 and 1903, and remained in force until 1926. It was divided into four books and included more than 353 articles that specified all possible issues that could have any effect on public health. It contained precise laws that had to be followed by the Federal District and in the territories of Baja California and Tepic, and public health legislation for all ports and borders. It established fines and penalties for all transgressions of the laws. The different states of the republic, however, had the constitutional right and freedom to adopt these laws or to create their own sanitary codes.

After 1891, additional health and sanitary regulations were issued that specified in further detail the obligations and attributions of the members who belonged to the SSC, among other topics. In addition, when Mexico hosted the Second International Congress of American States (January 1902), it was resolved that a general convention of representatives of the health organizations of the different American republics should convene. When the convention met in Washington, D.C., in December 1902, the International Sanitary Bureau was established. The convention resolved that the governments represented should employ similar measures to prevent the spread of yellow fever, bubonic plague, typhoid fever, and Asiatic cholera. Mexico was represented by Dr. Liceaga, who organized successful campaigns against bubonic plague in Mazatlan (1902–1903) and against yellow fever in Veracruz (1903), among others. In 1909, Mexico adhered to the International Treaty of Rome (1907), whereby the *Office International d'Higiène Publique* was established. On the eve of the 1910 Revolution, the country was in close communication with the main sanitary authorities of Europe and the Americas.

Even though public health legislation and internationally orchestrated sanitary reforms were of crucial importance, Porfirian Mexico displayed extremes of wealth and privilege that no legislation could possibly bridge. Mexico was, and remained, well into the twentieth century, a predominantly rural country. The contrast between the modes of living of the urban upper classes with that prevalent among the other millions of Mexicans was enormous, and endemic diseases, lack of proper clothing, unsanitary and badly constructed shelters, insufficient diets, lack of drinking water, and poor hygienic conditions were among the challenges health officials faced on a daily basis. From 1893 to 1907, more than 100,000 people died of typhus, and in 1905 typhus reached epidemic proportions in Mexico City. In 1910, the national census established that more than 50 percent of all registered houses fell under the category of huts: rooms without internal subdivision, drinking water, or sewers; with dirt floors and deficient ventilation; and where inhabitants lived in crowded conditions.

The focus of public health policies and programs during Porfirian Mexico was primarily urban. Their enactment represented an attempt to mitigate the effects of unplanned and unregulated growth in the cities that expanded primarily because of migration from rural areas. The need to foster national and international trade provided another motive. This meant that the capital of the country—Mexico City—the nation's largest, most populated, and important commercial city, enacted some of the most active and far-reaching health and sanitation reforms. Other important commercial cities, such as Puebla and Merida, were also noted for their health programs, but most cities and towns trailed far behind.

The number of licensed physicians was approximately 3,000 for a total population of 15 million inhabitants in 1910, and the majority of them were concentrated in urban centers. In 1895, for instance, Mexico City had 2,280 registered doctors for 329,000 people, whereas rural Mexico lacked physicians during the Porfirian era. During the 1880s and 1890s, the scarcity of physicians led the authorities of Guerrero and Jalisco to abandon their plans to

establish hospitals, and the number of hospitals throughout the country was inadequate and uneven. Mexico City housed the largest number, and when the General Hospital and *La Castañeda*, the first mental institution, opened their doors in 1905 and 1910, respectively, they were praised as the two most modern and efficient health institutions in the country.

Public health legislation was not, however, the only way the state and public health officials attempted to transform the nation into a safe and prosperous one. Health education came to be regarded as an instrument that would promote important changes in the lives, practices, customs, and behavior of the Mexican people, in particular of the indigenous populations and the slum-dwelling poor. Therefore, one of the most important activities of health officials was to foster public health education in a country marked by illiteracy. To this end, they organized conferences, lectures, and informal talks in markets, plazas, and schools throughout the country. The topics covered by physicians included the need to prevent alcoholism, in particular the consumption of *pulque*, and the negative effects of wet-nursing, as well as to encourage the urban and rural populations to abandon resorting to popular medical practices.

Physicians also believed it was indispensable to foster cleanliness and hygienic practices among the Mexican people. This was inexorably linked to the important breakthroughs in medical sciences of the period, when new understanding of the origin and prevention of disease and the gradual acceptance of the germ theory of disease causation led hygiene and cleanliness to be considered as indispensable requirements for the efficiency of health programs. How to dress, bathe, cook, and clean the home, as well as how to take care of infants, became important elements of public health education.

Health education also received much discussion during the national congresses on medicine and hygiene that took place during Porfirian Mexico, and led to the organization in Mexico City of the Popular Hygiene Exhibition in 1910. In addition, newspapers, magazines, and the penny press included articles on hygiene and domestic medicine for the country's limited literate public.

—Claudia Agostoni

See also General Insane Asylum: *La Castañeda* (Mexico); Social Welfare (Mexico): Since 1867

Primary Sources

Archivo Histórico de la Secretaría de Salubridad y Asistencia, Mexico City. Also see the following specialized journals of the period: *Gaceta Médica de México* (1864–1914); *Escuela de Medicina* (1879–1909; 1912; 1914); and *El Observador Médico* (1869–1883; 1886; 1901–1905; 1908).

Current Comment

Código Sanitario de los Estados Unidos Mexicanos. (1891). Mexico City: Imprenta del Gobierno Federal en el ex Arzobispado.

Ruiz, L. (1903). *Cartilla de Higiene. Profilaxis de las enfermedades transmisibles para la enseñanza primaria.* Paris: Viuda de Charles Bouret.

Ruiz, L. (1904). *Tratado elemental de higiene.* Mexico City: Oficina Tipográfica de la Secretaría de Fomento.

Silva, M. (1917). *Higiene popular. Colección de conocimientos y consejos indispensables para evitar las enfermedades y prolongar la vida, arreglado para uso de las familias.* Mexico City: Departamento de Talleres Gráficos.

Further Reading

Agostoni, C. (2002). Discurso médico, cultura higiénica y la mujer en la ciudad de México al cambio de siglo (XIX–XX). *Mexican Studies/Estudios Mexicanos, 18*(1), 1–22.

Agostoni, C. (2003). *Monuments of progress. Modernization and public health in Mexico City, 1876–1910.* Calgary, AB: University of Calgary Press; Boulder: University Press of Colorado; Mexico City: Instituto de Investigaciones Históricas.

Álvarez Amézquita, J., Bustamante, M., Picazos, A. L., & del Castillo, F. F. (1960). *Historia de la salubridad y de la asistencia en México.* Mexico City: Secretaría de Salubridad y Asistencia.

Carrillo, A. M. (2002). Economía, política y salud pública en el México porfiriano (1876–1910). *História, Ciências, Saúde—Manguinhos, 9,* 67–86.

I

IMMIGRATION AND SOCIAL WELFARE POLICY (CANADA)

The British North America Act of 1867 bestowed the federal government of Canada with wide-ranging powers over various domestic issues including immigration. In reviewing Canada's immigration policy since Confederation, a number of salient factors have shaped and influenced policy making in this area: the national and racial origins of prospective immigrants; the need for labor to fulfill specific job markets; the availability of relatives in Canada to act as official sponsors; internal economic growth, recession, or depression; international conditions affecting the number of people worldwide seeking to escape poverty, natural disaster, war or political unrest, and the number of countries willing to accept them; and the impact on both the French and English communities in the nation.

From 1867 to World War II, Canadian immigration policy was determined by the need to increase the population of the nation and by the desire to actively restrict specific groups from entering the country. Until the 1880s, when the Canadian government attempted to settle western Canada, the majority of immigrants came from Britain and France. But when it was discovered that their numbers were not significant enough to meet the potential and possibilities, the federal government looked beyond those two source

countries to actively recruit immigrants, primarily from other northern and eastern European countries. These immigrants, like their British and French counterparts, were attracted by the possibility of owning large amounts of land at a relatively low cost. It was during this period that Hutterites, Mennonites, and Doukhabors also ventured to Canada to escape religious persecution in their home countries. Through hard work and perseverance, these immigrants helped build and develop the agricultural economy in the Prairie provinces.

Although workers were recruited from China during the construction of the railway system in the 1880s, the Chinese Immigration Act was passed in 1885 after the completion of the railroad. The act made it more difficult to enter Canada with the introduction of the head tax system, and by 1923, immigration of the Chinese was completely banned. This was just one of several groups that encountered severe restrictions when attempting to immigrate to Canada. During the early part of the twentieth century, the Japanese and East Indians were targeted along with African Americans.

From a policy perspective, the most significant development occurred in 1910, when the federal government introduced the Immigration Act, which centered on the prospective newcomer's country of origin. A preference for immigrant workers from Great Britain, the United States, and northwestern

Europe was clearly stated, and individuals from racial groups that were deemed "unsuitable" because of the belief of their inability to adapt to the Canadian climate were not allowed to enter the country. The act was introduced to discourage groups such as the Black settlers from Oklahoma who expressed a desire to move to western Canada to become farmers.

Immigration to Canada was hindered during the Great Depression and World War II due to high unemployment. In 1931, the federal government enacted legislation that prohibited immigrants of all classes and occupations, with the exceptions of farmers with capital, British and Americans with sufficient means to maintain themselves until employment could be found, and those with financially secure relatives in Canada. These exceptions, however, did not apply to individuals of any Asian race.

The post–World War II period witnessed a renewed interest by the federal government in immigration matters, when the transition from an agrarian economy to one based on greater industrialization fueled the need for newcomers. Consistent with previous policy, immigrants from Europe were the preferred group. At this time, refugees housed in camps in war-torn Europe were trying to emigrate, as many were either unwilling or unable to return to their homelands, which, in many cases, were under the control of the Soviet Union. This group of refugees differed from other immigrants in that they were highly educated professionals and entrepreneurs, the majority settled in the urban centers, and their primary reasons for coming to Canada were political.

The need for skilled, trained workers dictated Canada's immigration policy from the mid 1950s to 1975. This period witnessed the growth of Canada as a consumer-based economy, but Canada faced challenges recruiting individuals from the United States and Great Britain as the economies in these countries were also expanding and this reduced the numbers of those wishing to relocate. During the late 1950s and early 1960s, when a number of colonies under British and French rule were gaining independence, Canada's immigration policies were criticized for being discriminatory and racist because of the continued preference for certain countries as primary sources of immigrants and refugees.

Canadian immigration policy underwent major changes in 1962, when criteria based on skills, education, and training were developed and decreased emphasis was placed on the long-held practice of preferential treatment of individuals from certain parts of the world. Despite the new policy, the new criteria still prevented individuals from Africa and certain parts of Asia from applying because they lacked the necessary education and skills.

In 1966, the White Paper on Immigration was published by the federal government. This report reaffirmed the position adopted 4 years earlier that the selection of immigrants should be based on an established set of criteria rather than designating certain countries as more favored over others. A year later, some of the recommendations in the White Paper were incorporated into a revised immigration policy. The major change was the introduction of the point system, in which individuals who applied to immigrate were assessed on their educational achievement, technical and professional training, labor market experience, and knowledge of one or both official languages. Each criterion was allocated a number of points and prospective immigrants required a minimum of 50 points to be eligible. One of the major reasons for this change was Canada's need to attract skilled immigrants from Africa, Asia, and South and Central America to support Canada's flourishing economy in the late 1960s.

The Immigration Act, amended in 1976, reaffirmed the principle that the selection of immigrants should not be based on race, nationality, or country of origin. It clearly identified three classes of immigrants who would be admitted to Canada: family, independent, and refugee. The family class provides individuals with family members living in Canada the opportunity to join their families. Independent class immigrants are those who are assessed using the point system. Refugees are individuals who fear for their lives or well-being and are allowed to enter Canada above the usual immigrant quota. Entry to Canada may be allowed if a refugee's circumstances are seen as part of Canada's humanitarian and legal obligations to the international community. A new class of immigrants was created with the 1976 amendment to the Immigration Act. Immigrants who have the financial resources to create employment opportunities for themselves and other Canadians would be given additional points. The rationale for this category was the belief that these immigrants would be in a position to make immediate contributions to the Canadian economy.

During the 1970s and early 1980s, the number of immigrants fluctuated based on the performance of the Canadian labor market and economy. Immigration decreased between the periods 1976–1978 and 1980–1986 but increased from 1978–1980. An important pattern that emerged during this time period was the increased number of immigrants that arrived from Africa, Asia, and Central and South America.

The declining fertility rate and the need to attract investment during the mid 1980s prompted the Canadian government to remove the prerequisite for arranged employment for independent applicants and to introduce the investor class. This group of immigrants would include those who agreed to invest in Canadian business. During the latter half of the 1980s, the annual intake increased and the federal government, under the leadership of Prime Minister Brian Mulroney, began to develop a 5-year plan for immigration. Necessitated by the need to sustain growth in the nation's population and economy, the plan was implemented in 1990. It advocated an increase in the annual number of immigrants to approximately 250,000 by the mid 1990s.

Since 1990, Canadian immigration policy has centered on addressing two primary concerns: (1) a commitment to humanitarian values by ensuring that appropriate numbers of newcomers are from the refugee and family categories (Fleras & Elliot, 2002), and (2) the need to attract individuals whose skills and fiscal resources will make an immediate impact from an economic perspective. In recent years, the emphasis on recruiting immigrants with job flexibility, entrepreneurial skills, and investment portfolios appears to be a high priority.

Despite the federal government's rationale for the need to increase the number of immigrants and refugees annually, Canada's immigration policy will continue to be controversial. Given the events of September 11, 2001, the debate will be centered on the number of newcomers that should be allowed into Canada as well as from what countries they should be accepted.

—*David Este*

See also Multiculturalism (Canada); Race and Ethnic Relations (Canada)

Primary Sources

Immigration Act, SC 1869; Immigration Act, RSC 1906; Immigration Act, SC 1910; Act to Amend the Immigration Act, 1919, C 25, S 15; Chinese Immigration Act, SC 1923, C 38, S 5; Immigration Act, SC 1976, C 52, S 3.

Current Comment

Kelly, N., & Trebilcock, M. (1998). *The making of the mosaic: A history of Canadian immigration policy.* Toronto, ON: University of Toronto Press.

Knowles, V. (1997). *Strangers at our gates: Canadian immigration and immigration policy, 1540–1995* (Rev. ed.). Toronto, ON: Dundurn.

Woodsworth, J. S. (1972). *Strangers within our gates.* Toronto, ON: University of Toronto Press. (Original work published 1909)

Further Reading

Abu-Laban, Y., & Gabriel, C. (2002). *Selling diversity: Immigration, multiculturalism, employment equity and globalization.* Peterborough, ON: Broadview.

Fleras, A., & Elliot, J. L. (2003). *Unequal relations: An introduction to race and ethnic dynamics in Canada* (4th ed.). Toronto, ON: Prentice Hall.

Hawkins, F. (1991). *Critical years in immigration: Canada and Australia compared.* Montreal, QC, and Kingston, ON: McGill-Queen's University Press.

Li, P. (Ed.). (1999). *Race and ethnic relations in Canada.* Don Mills, ON: Oxford University Press.

IMMIGRATION AND SOCIAL WELFARE POLICY (MEXICO)

Economic booms and busts, political debates, and world events have influenced Mexican immigration. The number of documented immigrants is relatively small compared to the United States, Argentina, and Brazil. But immigration policies mark much of Mexican history and reflect tensions between citizens and Mexican policymakers seeking to build a "modern" nation. Although immigration policies have been enacted, it is difficult to ascertain the degree of policy enforcement.

FROM COLONY TO NATION

After the Spanish and Aztec/Mexica encounter began in 1519, the Spanish Crown regulated who could come to the Americas. In principle, only Spanish subjects of "pure" blood (those not of Moorish or Jewish descent) were permitted to emigrate. Between 1504 and 1650, it is estimated that approximately 200,000 to 450,000 Spaniards migrated to the Americas, with the majority opting for New Spain (Mexico). Emigration was voluntary and regulated by the Spanish House of Trade and the Council of the Indies.

As the Spanish colonies grew in the sixteenth and seventeenth centuries, immigration became more difficult to trace. It is estimated that Portuguese, Dutch, Germans, Italians, and English constituted 2,000 members of the non-Spanish European community in Mexico during the colonial period. Scholars also estimate that Mexico received more than 200,000 African slaves during this time. Like these Africans, many Asians came to Mexico as slaves. In the seventeenth century, about 600 Asians entered Mexico per year.

Following independence from Spain in 1821, Mexico struggled to define the role of Spanish immigrants in Mexico. In 1824, Mexican officials asked Spaniards to leave the country and ordered the expulsion of Spaniards by 1828. Later, as Mexican liberals accused conservatives of being against immigration and unprogressive, some elites sought to reestablish ties to the Spanish Crown in 1836. The Mexican government, however, did not allow foreign immigration to Mexico until the 1850s.

THE PORFIRIATO, "PROGRESS," AND IMMIGRATION

President Porfirio Díaz (1876–1911) sought to stimulate the Mexican economy by giving preferences to foreigners, both as investors and settlers. In 1883, the Colonization and Naturalization Laws of the Republic were passed to encourage settlement in sparsely populated areas and to bring development to Mexico.

Immigrants from Italy were some of the first colonists in 1887. By 1896, the colonization program was abandoned as too costly and inefficient.

The Porfirian regime passed one of the first Mexican laws to acknowledge the presence of foreigners in Mexico. The Immigration and Naturalization Law of 1886 (*Ley de Extranjería y Naturalización de 1886*) conferred Mexican citizenship on certain foreigners almost by default; those who owned property were considered Mexican citizens if they did not express their intent to maintain their foreign nationality. In addition, the 1886 law deprived Mexican women of Mexican citizenship if they married foreigners. These Mexican women remained "foreign" even after becoming widows. Children born of such marriages were to be registered as "foreigners." The 1886 law was enforced until 1934.

Díaz's openness to immigration extended to Japan and China. After the U.S. Exclusion Act of 1882 terminated Chinese immigration to the United States, Mexico became an attractive alternative for Chinese immigrants. The 1888 Treaty of Friendship, Commerce, and Navigation between Mexico and Japan, the first "equal" treaty negotiated with a non-Asian country by Japan, facilitated the immigration of Japanese. Between 1891 and 1908, Japanese Emigration Companies sent thousands of Japanese emigrants abroad. In 1893, Mexico and China signed a Treaty of Amity and Commerce. When the Porfirian regime faced increasing economic difficulties in 1908, the policy of welcoming immigrants began to be reexamined. Immigrants who might become dependent on public sources for support were prohibited.

REVOLUTIONARY RESPONSES

During the Mexican Revolution (1910–1920), antiforeign rhetoric swept through the country. In May 1911, soldiers and civilians murdered over 300 Chinese in Torreon, Coahuila. Foreigners and immigrants, once the symbols of progress, became the scapegoats of the Mexican Revolution.

As a result, the new Mexican Constitution of 1917 specifically sought to compensate for the favoritism of early regimes toward foreign immigrants. Article 3 held that "the Federal Executive shall have the exclusive power to compel any foreigner whose remaining he may deem inexpedient to abandon the national territory immediately and without the necessity of previous legal action. Foreigners may not in any way participate in the political affairs of the country." The Constitution clearly states that Mexican nationality is acquired by birth (*jus sanguinis*, someone born of Mexican parents) or naturalization. Regardless of the nationality of the parents, someone born in Mexico has the right to Mexican citizenship (jus soli, birthplace determines one's nationality). A 1998 constitutional amendment recognizes Mexican nationality as transmitted by birth, but limits nationality to the first generation born abroad.

Following 10 years of violence and chaos, President Álvaro Obregón's administration (1920–1924) needed funds and began imposing a fee structure on incoming immigrants. On October 10, 1922, the U.S. consulate in Veracruz reported that all immigrants to Mexico were required to possess 50 *pesos* ($25) or the equivalent in other money, besides passage money to cover expenses to their destination in Mexico. Chinese and Blacks, however, were required to have 500 *pesos* ($250). This regulation illustrates how anti-immigrant discrimination was reflected in new social policy.

In 1926, medical reasons for excluding immigrants were added to the existing immigration restrictions. It was also mandated that official documents, such as birth certificates, had to be presented upon entering or leaving Mexico, along with proof of the possession of 10,000 *pesos* to satisfy basic necessities and living expenses as a means of regulating who could enter or leave the country.

On July 15, 1927, a legislative order to the Mexican migration department published in *Diario Oficial* stated that, "the immigration of persons of Syrian, Lebanese, Palestinian, Arabic and Turkish origin has reached a limit that makes itself felt in the national economy in an unfavorable manner on account of the conglomeration in urban centers." The law implied that whereas Mexican peddlers and merchants were acceptable, Arabs in the commercial sectors caused economic and social instability. In 1929, Mexico temporarily suspended the admission of all immigrant workers. The following year, the interior ministry decided to accept only those immigrants from nations with cultures similar to the Mexican culture, meaning those with Latin roots.

In June 1932, growing antiforeign sentiment and the severe economic depression led the Mexican government to establish a registry of foreigners over 15 years of age. Those on the registry were required to appear before authorities of the Mexican migration department and to show personal identification papers.

In 1934, President Abelardo L. Rodríguez (1932–1934) extended the ban on immigrants who had fewer than 10,000 *pesos,* except for those with technical skills that were approved by the Secretariat of Economy (*Secretaría de Economía Nacional*). Investors with capital of 20,000 *pesos* or more who were interested in agricultural and industrial businesses were allowed, but nobody interested in commerce was to be sanctioned. The popular administration of Lázaro Cárdenas (1934–1940) constructed an image of fulfilling many of the Revolution's promises, such as land distribution and the nationalization of the oil industry. But scholars debate the degree to which he challenged foreign investors and immigrant populations.

The General Population Law of 1936 aimed to resolve fundamental demographic problems by establishing and maintaining comprehensive records on the immigration and repatriation of foreigners. It prohibited the immigration of alcoholics, drug addicts, prostitutes, anarchists, and salaried foreign workers and banned commercial activities by foreigners, except when such activity was deemed necessary. Although the law did not explicitly mention particular ethnic groups, it clearly attempted to regain "Mexico for Mexicans."

Cárdenas also grappled with the question of how to deal with the Spanish Civil War and the rise of Gen. Francisco Franco. Fearing the spread of fascism, Cárdenas supported the Spanish Republic and in January 1939, the Mexican government officially welcomed Spanish refugees. Between 1939 and 1942, approximately 12,000 Spanish republicans resettled in Mexico; by 1943, 30 percent of them had acquired Mexican citizenship.

POST WORLD WAR II TO THE PRESENT

President Miguel Alemán (1946–1952) saw immigration as a form of international collaboration and a mechanism for national development. He offered hospitality to those foreign populations displaced by World War II, most notably Jewish refugees. Those admitted, however, had to be able to "ethnically fuse with national groups." This allowed Mexican policymakers latitude to interpret which ethnic groups were most useful to the Mexican economy and nation. According to Article 7 of the 1947 law (*Ley General de Población*), the Mexican government would facilitate the collective immigration of foreigners "who are easy to assimilate into our environment, with benefits to the race."

During the 1970s and 1980s, Chileans, Uruguayans, and Argentines fled military dictatorships to settle in Mexico. As of 1990, 356,400 refugees were settled in Mexico. Many Central American refugees, escaping civil wars at home, came to Mexico as well. While many Salvadorans have traveled to Mexican border towns to cross into the United States, many Guatemalan immigrants have taken refuge in Chiapas. Mexican government officials claim that nearly 25,000 Central American migrants were intercepted along the southern border of Mexico in the first 4 months of 2004. It has been estimated that 160,000 undocumented immigrants from Honduras, Guatemala, and El Salvador are detained and deported every year by Mexican police as they attempt to reach the United States.

Today, the Secretariat of Government (*Secretaría de Gobernación*) oversees immigration through the General Registry of Population and Personal Identification (*General del Registro de Población Identificación Personal*). The National Institute of Migration (*Instituto Nacional de Migración*) determines the admissibility of immigrants, considering whether the immigrants are professionals, investors, renters (lease-holders), scientists, artists, sports players, and/or family members. Based on Mexican census data, the foreign-born population has grown from four tenths of a percent in 1950, 1970, and 1990 to a half a percent in 2000, amounting to nearly half a million people in the total Mexican population of more than 97 million.

—*Theresa Alfaro Velcamp*

See also Aboriginal People and Policy (Mexico); Economic Policy (Mexico)

Primary Sources

Information on Mexican immigration policies can be found at the *Secretaría Relaciones Exteriores* and the *Archivo General de la Nación,* Mexico City. In the United States, the Records of the Department of State (Record Group 59), National Archives & Records Administration, College Park, MD, may also be of use.

Current Comment

González Navarro, M. (1994). *Los extranjeros en México y los mexicanos en el extranjero, 1821–1970* (Vols. 1-3). Mexico City: El Colegio de México.

Historias, 33. (1994, October–1995, March). Mexico City: Instituto Nacional de Antropología e Historia.

Information on recent immigration is posted on-line by the *Instituto Nacional de Migración.* Available: www.inami.gob .mx/paginas/212000.htm

Further Reading

Guillermo, M. B. B. (Ed.). (1993). *Simbiosis de culturas: Los inmigrantes y su cultura en México.* Mexico City: Fondo de Cultura Económica.

MacLachlan, C. M., & Rodríguez O., J. E. (1980). *The forging of the cosmic race: A reinterpretation of colonial Mexico.* Berkeley: University of California Press.

Mörner, M. (with Sims, H.). (1985). *Adventurers and proletarians: The story of migrants in Latin America.* Pittsburgh, PA: University of Pittsburgh Press.

Pla, D., Zárate, G., Palma, M., Gómez, J., Cardiel, R., & Salazar, D. (1994). *Extranjeros en México (1821–1990)* [Bibliography]. Mexico City: Instituto Nacional de Antropología e Historia.

IMMIGRATION AND SOCIAL WELFARE POLICY (UNITED STATES)

The history of the United States cannot be understood without acknowledging the millions of immigrants who have settled within its borders and who have shaped its culture. Popular belief holds that the United States is a refuge for the oppressed from across the globe, but history shows there have been confusing and complex immigration policies and practices in response to changing social needs and pressures. Theories have arisen to characterize the immigration experience. The "melting pot," or assimilation, theory contends that immigrants blend into the United States and eventually become Americans, often by ignoring or forgetting their roots. Another theory, that of the mosaic, holds that America is a land of many peoples from different cultures and ethnicities who adapt to the United States but also retain their cultural and ethnic identities. These theories can be used to help understand immigration history and how the nation has responded to the social welfare of immigrants.

In its early years and through the 1880s, the United States allowed nearly open immigration. Before American independence in the late eighteenth century, Great Britain encouraged immigrants to move to the colonies as a means of strengthening its power in North America. Many came to America looking for religious freedom and for opportunities to better themselves economically and socially. It must be remembered that slavery existed in the eighteenth and nineteenth centuries, indicating that freedom was limited by boundaries of race and social class. The importation of slaves into the United States was not outlawed until 1808. After the War for Independence, immigration to the United States increased dramatically. Between 1800 and the 1850s, nearly 5 million immigrants, mostly from northern and western Europe, came to the United States. Many were from Ireland and Germany. The potato famine in Ireland forced people off the land and they clamored to come to the United States to seek better living conditions. Many Germans immigrated to avoid political upheaval and turmoil in Europe. Immigration was never an easy process. In some places, the Irish were met by open hostility. Some Americans disliked the strong allegiance of many Irish to the Roman Catholic church. Others saw the Irish as tough opportunists who would compete for jobs. Still other Americans disliked German immigrants because of their language and customs. Many Irish settled in growing cities such as Boston and New York, where some entered local politics to gain the power to direct resources to their fellow immigrants. Many Germans settled in rural areas, where they became successful farmers.

Immigrant groups often created their own supportive charitable organizations to respond to their needs. In a time when there was little publicly supported charity available for needy immigrants, support was given by churches, fraternal and benevolent associations, and other private groups. In New York City, the Association for Improving the Condition of the Poor is an example of a private charity that tried to assist the needy, many of whom were recent immigrants.

After the Civil War, immigrants from other European areas, as well as China, joined the immigrant stream. Many Chinese laborers were recruited to help construct the railroads that were opening the American West to commerce and settlement. Their working conditions were often dangerous and demanding, yet, like other immigrants, they worked to obtain money to support families at home and to pursue opportunities for social betterment. Many settled in California, where they created communities that could support their cultural and social needs even though they often faced racist discrimination.

From the 1880s through the 1920s, although millions of immigrants came to the United States, Congress began to restrict immigration from certain parts of the world, especially Asia. Immigration from eastern and southern Europe increased. In some years, more than a million immigrants came to the United States. Some Americans resented new immigrants, seeing them as threats to their own social status and well-being. Some labor unions felt immigrant laborers threatened the job security of their members and they called for restrictions on immigration. Other Americans feared immigrants with few resources would become a burden on public as well as private resources if they needed financial or social support. Growing pressure to restrict and even exclude certain immigrants culminated in federal legislation to restrict immigration. The Chinese Exclusion Act of 1882 prohibited Chinese immigration for a decade. Restrictive immigration laws signaled growing animosity to certain immigrants based on bias and prejudice. Some Italian and Jewish immigrants faced harsh resentment from those who saw them as inferior to American Protestant "Yankee" citizens. New laws prohibited immigration by those who had been convicted of certain crimes, were mentally ill, or might not be able to support themselves and thus become dependent on society. Some influential Americans, including Senator Henry Cabot Lodge of Massachusetts, publicly argued against immigration by some southern Europeans because he believed they were inferior to northern Europeans. At the same time, private philanthropic and charitable groups, some of which were sponsored by religious denominations, assisted poor immigrants. Charity organization societies trained caseworkers to assist needy immigrants and other poor Americans and settlement houses sprang up in major cities and elsewhere to respond to their needy neighbors. Jane Addams's Hull House, a famous Chicago settlement house, raised funds from wealthy benefactors to offer a wide variety of services for its immigrant neighbors.

Despite federal laws restricting immigration, millions of immigrants came to the United States from 1880 to 1920. In the aftermath of World War I, the nation embarked on a period of renewed immigration restriction. Some powerful members of Congress feared that postwar turmoil in Europe would encourage millions of Europeans to flee to the United States and they worried about the ability of the nation to assimilate them. Some feared immigration by European political radicals, such as communist "Reds," who might threaten American institutions. The Ku Klux Klan, which saw itself protecting the White race and American Protestantism, attracted thousands of new members who supported its call for an end to immigration of "undesirables." The popularity of the Klan indicates that many Americans in the 1920s feared social interaction with "foreigners," which would be the result of liberal immigration policies. It should be noted that restrictive immigration policies were enacted during the 1920s, in a time of general economic expansion, a time when additional labor could conceivably have been welcomed. In 1921, Congress passed an immigration law that limited the number of allowable new immigrants to a percentage of the number of immigrants from that nation living in the United States as of 1910. This "quota system" became a hallmark for immigration policy until 1964. It is noteworthy that most Asian nations were not given immigration quotas because immigration from that part of the world had been prohibited earlier. Under the first year of the quota system, nearly 360,000 immigrants were allowed entry. Neither Mexican nor Canadian immigrants were affected by the quota system, which was meant primarily to regulate European immigration. Subsequent immigration laws tightened the quota system even more.

The Great Depression of the 1930s also discouraged immigration as unemployment in the United States made migration less advantageous. World War II brought new restrictions on immigration because of concerns about national security. These war years also saw the controversial detention of Japanese immigrants and more than 100,000 Japanese Americans in camps throughout the American West. Detention was justified by those who perceived Japanese Americans as wartime threats given the hostilities with Japan. World War II also saw some liberalization of immigration policies. Mexican farmworkers were encouraged to enter the United States to supply badly needed farm labor under the *bracero* program, which lasted until 1967.

Immigration policies after World War II continued the national quota system that had long been in force, but there was growing dissent against its restrictiveness by those who felt a more open and liberal policy was consistent with the nation's democratic and egalitarian ideals. Various religious advocacy groups, such as the National Catholic Welfare Conference as well as major labor unions, called for less restrictive policies and, in 1965, Congress, with the strong support of President Lyndon B. Johnson, enacted the Hart-Cellar Act, which eliminated the national origins quota system. Under a more liberal immigration policy, larger numbers of immigrants entered the United States from Asia, the Caribbean, South America, and other parts of the developing world while European immigration declined. Large numbers of legal as well as illegal immigrants entered the United States during the 1970s, 1980s, and 1990s. Debates over the impact of increasing immigration focused on the economic and social effects of the millions of new immigrants, many of whom did not speak English and had few marketable job skills. Some argued that these immigrants placed a heavy burden on social services, which increased the financial burden of the state and federal governments. Others saw unskilled immigrants as competitors for entry-level jobs that could be filled by Americans. Presidents Ronald Reagan, George H. W. Bush, and William J. Clinton seemed unable to deal effectively with the dilemmas posed by mass immigration. Increasingly, powerful immigrant advocacy groups, such as those started by Asian Americans, lobbied strenuously for liberal immigration policies that would allow more Asian Americans into the country. But opposition to liberal immigration policy continued. In 1994, Californians passed Proposition 187, which denied California social services to illegal immigrants, including many from Mexico. Eventually, the courts declared much of Proposition 187 null and void, but its enactment signaled widespread support in California for restrictive immigration policies. By the late 1990s, nearly 6.2 percent of California's population was made up of illegal, undocumented immigrants. Many Latino advocacy groups, including Roman Catholic church supporters, argued for liberal immigration policies as well as provision of sanctuary for Latinos who were persecuted by oppressive political regimes in Latin America. Others argued that the United States had a moral obligation to allow liberal access to refugees from political oppression across the world. Special-interest groups, such as farmers, have often supported liberal immigration policies given the need for relatively unskilled farmworkers in labor-intensive agricultural production. In 2004, President George W. Bush argued that undocumented illegal immigrants be given opportunities for residency that could culminate in citizenship. His proposal drew considerable criticism from members of groups who felt it demonstrated favoritism for illegal Hispanic immigrants, many of whom work in low-paying jobs throughout the country.

Immigration policy remains controversial and complex given the strength of opponents and supporters of liberalized immigration. In 1996, as part of federal welfare reform, public welfare benefits including Food Stamps and Supplemental Security Income under the Social Security Act were curtailed for legal immigrants, a controversial policy demonstrating once again the complexity of national attitudes toward immigration. In the future, the United States will continue to debate which immigration policies will contribute to national social welfare as well as how open it will be to those from around the world seeking a new homeland.

—*John M. Herrick*

See also Abbott, Edith; Asian Americans and Social Welfare (United States); Education Policy (United States); Hispanic Americans and Social Welfare (United States); Settlement Houses (United States)

Primary Sources

American Immigration and Citizenship Conference Records, 1932–1948, in the Social Welfare History Archives, University of Minnesota, Minneapolis; Immigration History Research Center, University of Minnesota, Minneapolis.

Current Comment

Abbott, G. (1917). *The immigrant and the community.* New York: Century.
Addams, J. (1990). *Twenty years at Hull House* [With autobiographical notes]. Urbana: University of Illinois Press. (Original work published 1910)
Morrison, J., & Zabusky, C. F. (1980). *American mosaic: The immigrant experience by those who lived it.* New York: Dutton.

Further Reading

Daniels, R. (1990). *Coming to America: A history of immigration and ethnicity in American life.* New York: HarperCollins.
Jones, M. (1992). *American immigration.* Chicago: University of Chicago Press.
Reed, U. (1994). *Postwar immigrant America: A social history.* New York: St. Martin's.

INFORMAL ECONOMY (MEXICO)

The informal economy can be considered a survival alternative in countries or sectors of the economy where there is an inadequate or nonexistent welfare system: This is the situation in Mexico. A 1972 International Labour Organization (ILO) report characterized the informal sector by ease of entry; smallness of scale; labor-intensiveness, with workers' skills acquired outside the formal educational system; simplicity of technology; and embeddedness in a competitive and unregulated market. This definition was endorsed for Latin America by the ILO's Regional Office for Latin America (*Programa Regional de Empleo Para América Latina e el Caribe,* or PREALC). More recently, informal labor, whether employed by informal- or formal-sector firms, has been included in the informal sector. The preferred term to describe both microenterprises and informal labor is the "informal economy." A widely endorsed definition of the informal economy is that it consists of those economic activities that escape state regulations, including taxation and protective labor laws, usually conformed to by formal-sector firms. It does not include criminal activities, since it provides legal goods and services; nor does it include use-values goods and services produced for family reproduction, as its goods and services are sold on the market. Informal economic activities in Mexico include both quasi-independent enterprises and informal work.

INFORMAL ECONOMIC ACTIVITIES

Included in the informal economy are self-employed persons working with or without the aid of family members; the owners of sweatshops (for the manufacture of shoes or garments, for example); other microenterprises (such as brick makers and other artisan work) that sometimes are in subcontracting relationships with larger, formal enterprises; and informalized workers who may be employed in microenterprises or by larger enterprises but who do not receive state-legislated benefits. In Mexico, subcontracted construction workers; casual and day laborers, whether urban or rural; domestic workers without contracts; and home workers (or outworkers) are some of those who fall into this last category. Also, in Mexico, it is the practice of both United States–based multinational (*maquiladora*) and domestic manufacturing companies to hire factory workers for a 3-month tryout period without benefits. Many of these workers are fired and rehired every 3 months; thus, they continue to work over long periods of time on a trial basis and without mandated benefits. Given the absence of a comprehensive welfare system or unemployment benefits in Mexico, the informal economy is the refuge of those unemployed or underemployed as formal labor in the formal economy. Nonetheless, some informal economy participants choose to work in the informal economy because they have greater autonomy and flexibility than they would in the formal economy.

Although modernization theorists once considered the informal economy a traditional sector that would eventually disappear as economic development progressed and Marxist and neo-Marxist theorists considered it a holding tank for the reserve army of labor, the informal economy has been reconceptualized over

time. One conceptualization holds that those involved in the informal sector (focusing on microenterprises rather than informalized labor) are incipient capitalist entrepreneurs and if overburdening regulations are removed, this labor can be an engine of economic growth. Another more structuralist view holds that the informal economy is subsumed by and supportive of the overarching, usually capitalist, economy. Once thought of as an independent sector, the myriad linkages the informal sector has had with the dominant economic system—in Mexico, capitalism—have been documented and have led to its relabeling as an economy. Thus, street vendors may be a "disguised proletariat," working for one or more formal-sector firms on a commission basis or distributing their products in places formal retailers would not select because they could not make acceptable profits. Garbage pickers recycle cardboard and metal used by domestic and multinational firms for which they are essentially outworkers. Women sewing garments, assembling plastic flowers or electronic components, or finishing shoes at home are also disguised workers for the companies that contract them. In each of these cases, companies that directly or indirectly hire these workers can pay lower prices per unit of labor than they would if the street vendor, garbage picker, or home worker were a full-time employee. By using "informal" workers, companies can avoid paying for legislated social welfare benefits, such as medical care provided by the Mexican Social Security Institute (*Instituto Mexicano del Seguro Social,* or IMSS) or subsidized housing provided by the National Institute of Housing for Workers (*Instituto Nacional de Fondo de Vivienda Para los Trabajadores,* or INFONAVIT). Informal economic activity, in effect, subsidizes formal-sector businesses as well as the national economy. It relies on exploitation of workers who work for low wages and receive few, if any, social welfare benefits. The phenomenon of informalized or casualized labor has also become common in the United States and Canada, where it receives much scholarly attention.

THE FUNCTIONAL SIGNIFICANCE OF THE INFORMAL ECONOMY

The informal economy in Mexico has had the welfare function of permitting the underemployed and unemployed to survive as well as absorbing those who lose their formal jobs during periods of economic crisis or structural adjustment. Thus, it expanded during the economic crisis that began in 1982 with the fall of oil prices on the world market, and again in the *peso* crisis of 1994–1995, when the Mexican government devalued the *peso* 11 months after the North American Free Trade Agreement (NAFTA) took effect. Neoliberal policies and the forces of globalization have led to the opening of Mexico's economy to foreign investors. Mexico entered into the General Agreement on Tariffs and Trade (GATT) in 1986 and NAFTA in 1994. Globalization and neoliberal restructuring have led to an increase in the informal economy in Mexico in three ways. First, in a globally competitive market, capital-intensive industry has been replacing labor-intensive industry, resulting in higher unemployment in the formal economy. Second, the introduction of high-technology industries has marginalized less educated and less skilled workers. Third, the desire to lower labor costs has encouraged traditional companies to subcontract labor and utilize home workers (outworkers who work on a piece-rate basis). There is little organization among home workers or domestic service workers due to their isolation from one another. Construction workers usually form small groups under the head of a subcontractor and are moved from one city to another, giving them little chance to unionize. Street vendors and artisanal workers, such as brick makers, may organize either in self-defense through grassroots efforts or through the top-down instigation of political parties or governmental dependencies.

MEASURING THE INFORMAL ECONOMY

It is difficult to measure the size of the informal economy since much of its activity is invisible. Measurement depends on how the informal economy is defined. Some researchers define microenterprises as any enterprise that employs fewer than 10 workers. Others define them as enterprises with fewer than 5 workers. Some measures ignore informalized agricultural day laborers, concentrating instead on urban laborers. It has been estimated that between the end of World War II and 1980, informal employment in Latin America constituted about 30 percent of the labor force. This percentage increased during the economic crisis of the 1980s, which strongly impacted the Mexican economy. A 2002 International Labour Organization (ILO) report suggests that the size of the urban-based informal economy is increasing: Whereas it employed 50 percent of the Latin American labor force in 1990, it employed 58 percent in 1997. This does not include agricultural day laborers, a largely informalized workforce. In 1998, the agricultural and urban-based informal economy provided 64 percent of Mexican employment, 19 percent of it agricultural laborers and 45 percent urban-based informal sector workers. In 2003, according to the National Institute of Statistics, Geography, and Information (*Instituto Nacional de Estadística, Geografía, Informática,* or INEGI), 49.3 percent of urban-based workers were employed in jobs without social welfare benefits even though they should have been covered as employees of formal-sector enterprises. This does not count informal economic activities, including intermittent garbage picking, vending, manufacturing activities, or women who sell processed foods door-to-door in their own and nearby neighborhoods (*colonias*) or who sew garments for friends and neighbors. According to the ILO (2002) report, twice as many men as women work in Mexico's informal economy: 16 million men as opposed to 7.7 million women or 58 percent of all female workers and 64 percent of all male workers. It has been estimated that the informal economy, including both urban and rural informalized labor and microenterprise labor, contributes between 30 and 33 percent of Mexico's gross domestic product (GDP).

POLICY PROPOSALS FOR THE INFORMAL ECONOMY

Policy proposals regarding the informal economy range from macroeconomic neoliberal proposals to remove what are seen as burdensome bureaucratic regulations that keep informal entrepreneurs from formalizing their microenterprises, to less extreme proposals that suggest training and credit packages to increase productivity (a suggestion also endorsed in some World Bank papers). Other suggestions include extending internationally recognized labor standards to informalized workers, and organizing those involved in the informal economy so that they could take collective action and pressure local and national governments to enact policies that would benefit them. In Mexico and elsewhere, the informal economy is a dynamic arena of economic activity whose existence is supported by the lack of adequate national welfare systems that could support workers in times of need.

—*Tamar Diana Wilson*

See also Economic Crises, Family and Gender, 1980s to the Present (Mexico); Economic Policy (Mexico); Poverty (Mexico); Social Security (Mexico)

Primary Source

International Labour Organization (ILO) working papers are available on the ILO website (www.ilo.org).

Current Comment

Carr, M., & Chen, M. A. (2002). *Globalization and the informal economy: How global trade and investment impact on the working poor* (Working Paper). Geneva, Switzerland: International Labour Office, Employment Sector.

Heath, J. (1998). The impact of Mexico's trade liberalization: Jobs, productivity, and structural change. In C. Wise (Ed.), *The post-NAFTA political economy: Mexico and the Western Hemisphere* (pp. 171–200). University Park: Pennsylvania State University Press.

International Labour Organization. (2002). *Women and men in the informal economy: A statistical picture.* Geneva, Switzerland: International Labour Office, Employment Sector.

Portes, A., & Sassen, S. (1987). Making it underground: Comparative material on the informal sector in Western market economies. *American Journal of Sociology, 93,* 30–61.

Further Reading

Portes, A., Castells, M., & Benton, L. A. (Eds.). (1989). *The informal economy: Studies in advanced and less developed countries.* Baltimore: Johns Hopkins University Press.

Rakowski, C. A. (Ed.). (1994). *Contrapunto: The informal sector debate in Latin America.* Albany: State University of New York Press.

Tokman, V. E. (Ed.). (1992). *Beyond regulation: The informal economy in Latin America.* Boulder, CO: Lynne Rienner.

Wilson, T. D. (Ed.). (1998). The urban informal sector [Special issue]. *Latin American Perspectives, 25*(2).

INTERNATIONAL SOCIAL WELFARE

The current popularity of the concept of globalization has erroneously created the impression that international contacts, world trade, and global integration are of recent historical origin. Although it is true that international economic exchanges, communications, cultural diffusion, and diplomacy have intensified to an unprecedented degree in recent years, exchanges of this kind are hardly new. It has been over the course of the last 400 years, ever since international affairs were dominated by European imperialism, that communications, commerce, migration, and political activities assumed a global rather than a local or regional character.

Historians have focused primarily on indigenous factors when seeking to explain the development of social welfare institutions in different parts of the world, but there is a good deal of historical evidence to show that social welfare ideas and practices diffused internationally to influence the emergence of local welfare institutions. Neglect of international influences has resulted in partial explanations that do not pay sufficient attention to the complex role that both domestic and international factors play in the genesis of welfare institutions. The contribution of international factors needs to be more systematically incorporated into accounts of the historical emergence of social welfare policies and programs. To understand current social welfare practices, it is not enough to understand their history; historical accounts that incorporate international developments are also needed.

INTERNATIONAL INFLUENCES ON SOCIAL WELFARE IN THE UNITED STATES

The development of social welfare policies and programs in the United States owes a great deal to European influences, particularly as a result of colonialism. In the early colonial era, American social welfare mirrored established practices in Europe, particularly in Britain, where individual philanthropy, church-sponsored charities, and the government all contributed to meet welfare needs. With the enactment of the English Poor Law in 1601, the role of government in England became more extensive than elsewhere. Social welfare provision in England involved a degree of centralized state involvement that did not exist in continental Europe, where religious charity and, to a lesser extent, municipal programs predominated.

The replication of the poor laws in the English colonies of North America laid the foundations for the subsequent expansion of government involvement and the eventual emergence of the so-called "welfare state" in the twentieth century. The Elizabethan poor laws were first introduced in the American colonies in Virginia in 1646, although legislation providing for the punishment and deportation of vagrants and the destitute had been enacted earlier not only in the British colonies but in the Dutch colony of New Amsterdam. As in other colonies, the statutes applied only to indigent European settlers. On the other hand, continental European and, in particular, Latin approaches to social welfare were adopted in colonies such as Louisiana, reflecting similar developments in Central and South America and the French Caribbean. In these territories, social welfare was regarded as the proper domain of the parishes, monasteries, *confraternia* (voluntary associations of laypeople), and other sectarian organizations, whereas in the English-speaking North, state involvement designed to supplement voluntary effort was expected.

Colonial practices continued to influence social welfare policies and programs long after independence from European rule. Although Louisiana was absorbed into the United States in 1803, the state's welfare system continued to reflect the influence of the Latin tradition well into the twentieth century. This was also true of the English North, where the poor laws survived in the guise of the general assistance programs operated by the states, and the federal government's Aid to Dependent Children program. During the late nineteenth century, formative colonial approaches were often augmented by new ideas emanating from Europe and often they were modified and adapted by American social welfare pioneers. Some of these adaptations, such as charity organization societies and settlement houses, subsequently became an integral part of the American social welfare system.

The emergence of social insurance in Germany in the last decades of the twentieth century also influenced American welfare policy. Following the introduction, for electoral reasons, of a state-managed work accident and sickness program for industrial workers by the chancellor, Count Otto von Bismarck, in the 1880s, American social reformers began to campaign for the introduction of similar programs in the United States. These efforts culminated in the enactment of Unemployment Insurance and in 1935 of the historic Social Security Act by the Franklin D. Roosevelt administration.

The adoption and adaptation of these innovations helped shape modern-day social welfare institutions in the United States. The syncretic approaches that emerged in the United States translated European innovations in ways that were compatible with local social, cultural, and economic realities. These became more common in the twentieth century, and formed the basis for new approaches that were uniquely American. For example, the adaptation of the English charity organizing and settlement approaches made a vital contribution to the subsequent emergence of professional social work. Whereas the English charity visiting idea extolled the virtues of vocationalism and voluntarism, American social work pioneers committed themselves to promoting professionalization. Although social work subsequently acquired professional status in Europe and elsewhere, it was in the United States that its professionalization was most ardently and effectively pursued. Consequently, by the mid twentieth century, international professional standards in social work were largely defined by American social workers and American theories and practice approaches were internationally admired. Another example of the ability of American social welfare pioneers to adapt European developments to local social and cultural realities is the way Jane Addams and her followers transcended the original settlement house concept and successfully linked community-based service provision with neighborhood activism and a wider commitment to social reform. The American settlements, and Hull House in particular, were far more successful than the British settlements in promoting social reform, and particularly in subsuming the collectivism of European socialism under a culturally more acceptable reformist populism. American populism also played an important role in legitimating the introduction of social insurance, which was attacked for being ideologically linked to European socialism. The rhetoric of populism helped to counter these criticisms and facilitate the adoption of European-style social insurance.

American syncretic innovations gradually attracted international attention and were subsequently reexported to Europe and elsewhere. In some cases, they had a particularly strong international impact. A good example is the infusion of Freudian psychoanalysis into American social work. American social workers were dazzled by psychoanalysis after Freud made his North American debut in 1911 and, as his work became better known among social work educators, social casework was infused with psychoanalytic ideas. Psychoanalysis also facilitated the emergence of psychiatric social work, which evolved as a high-status professional specialization in the early decades of the twentieth century. It was soon exported to Europe and other parts of the world. One of the first social work training programs in England, which had been established by the politically active and reform-minded Webbs at the London School of Economics in 1911, embraced American-style psychiatric social work in 1927, and continued faithfully to train students for psychoanalytic practice for many subsequent decades. During the post–Second World War decades, American psychoanalytic social work was emulated in many parts of the world, including the low-income developing countries where, critics charged, a preoccupation with psychotherapeutic counseling did little to address the pervasive problem of poverty and deprivation.

UNITED STATES INFLUENCES ON INTERNATIONAL SOCIAL WELFARE

The growing political and economic influence of the United States after the Second World War facilitated the pervasive diffusion of American social welfare approaches to different parts of the world. The work of American social workers, social policymakers, and social welfare scholars attracted growing international attention, and their innovations were increasingly emulated. Despite being rooted in the American cultural milieu, American social welfare approaches now exert a strong influence on social welfare policy and practice in many different parts of the world.

Before attaining its current position of international influence in social welfare, the United States had previously exported its welfare policies and programs to other nations over which it had direct colonial or military control. The most obvious example is the Philippines, which was under American colonial rule

from the end of the nineteenth to the mid twentieth century. During this time, various American welfare approaches were introduced. For example, American administrators encouraged the creation of the Associated Charities of Manila in 1917, based on the charity organization society model. Child welfare innovations in the United States were also emulated and, in 1941, a public assistance program for poor women with children, based on the Aid to Dependent Children program, was established.

After World War II, the United States exerted growing influence in the international arena through its engagement in the new international organizations that had been created in the wake of the founding of the United Nations (UN). The government of the United States has, in particular, played a key role in funding and thus influencing policy at the International Monetary Fund, the World Bank, and other international organizations. Its role in the United Nations has been somewhat more ambiguous as congressional support for the organization and some of its affiliated agencies has wavered, particularly in recent years. This was not always the case, however, and in the years following the creation of the United Nations, the American contribution was universally applauded. The United States had also played a critical and much admired role in the creation of the UN's precursor, the League of Nations, and has been active in the International Labour Organization since its founding in the 1920s. Although it has also participated in other organizations with a clear social welfare mandate, such as the United Nations Children's Fund (UNICEF), the World Health Organization (WHO), and the United Nations High Commission for Refugees, the United States does not exercise the kind of leadership in these organizations that its global status might suggest. This is partly because of ideological differences between the government of the United States and key personnel at these organizations as well as representatives of these organization's other member states.

In addition to contributing to the multilateral organizations, the United States also engages in bilateral social welfare exchanges with numerous countries, particularly through its international aid (or official development assistance) programs. Although the volume of aid provided by the federal government is smaller than that of many European nations, and is focused on military and diplomatic initiatives, particularly in the Middle East, many developing countries receive aid for social development purposes. Much of this is channeled through the federal government's International Development Agency, which is administratively located within the state department. The organization has historically been engaged in promoting social welfare, and one of its earliest initiatives, dating from 1939, was to sponsor the professional education of Latin American social work educators in the United States. Although the emphasis subsequently shifted from funding traditional welfare programs to the promotion of community and private sector development, the organization has continued to promote a variety of programs with a social component; these include rural community development, child health, AIDS treatment and prevention, and basic education programs. In addition, the Peace Corps, created in 1961, also places a strong emphasis on programs of this kind, involving its volunteers in a variety of educational, health, and community development activities. Mainstream federal agencies that are primarily responsible for domestic programs, such as the Departments of Health and Human Services, Labor, and Agriculture, also have international interests and actively engage in international social welfare activities.

The federal government also provides funds to assist nonprofit organizations engaged in social programs. In keeping with international trends, a higher proportion of bilateral aid is now funneled through organizations of this kind. The emphasis on the nongovernmental sector is intended not only to bypass what many aid administrators regard as endemic governmental inefficiency but also to strengthen civil society institutions in regions of the world where the voluntary sector remains undeveloped. Of course, many nonprofit organizations in the United States also have international linkages and some are able to raise substantial domestic resources from private and corporate donors to fund their activities. They range from large organizations such as Cooperation for American Relief Everywhere (CARE) to small but highly committed organizations such as the American Friends Service Committee.

Many nonprofit organizations also engage in international activities through national bodies that are linked to worldwide organizations such as the International Council on Social Welfare (ICSW). Founded in 1928, ICSW has national member organizations in more than 70 countries. The organization is committed to promoting social welfare and social development around the world, and it has been particularly active in lobbying governments and official development organizations such as the United Nations. In recent years, ICSW has played a key role in promoting the implementation of the Declaration on Social Development, which was published following the 1995 World Summit on Social Development.

Professional social workers in the United States are, it seems, participating in international activities to a greater extent than ever before. The National Association of Social Workers (NASW) and the Council on Social Work Education (CSWE) are active members of international bodies such as the International Federation of Social Workers (IFSW) and the International Association of Schools of Social Work (IASSW). These organizations also provide opportunities for their members to participate in international activities. The IASSW has been active in fostering international collaboration in social work education since it was founded in 1928. IFSW was established in 1956. Another organization that has growing support among social workers in the United States is the Inter-University Consortium for International Social Development (IUCISD). This organization was funded by a group of American schools of social work in the 1970s and has actively promoted the adoption of an international development perspective in the profession. Of course, as in other countries, social workers in the United States utilize many other opportunities for engaging in international social welfare, such as attending international conferences and meetings, participating in exchange programs, and visiting other countries for the purpose of studying their welfare systems.

POWER, IDEOLOGY, AND INTERNATIONAL SOCIAL WELFARE

International exchanges in social welfare have historically reflected differentials in power and status between nations. This is not to suggest that these exchanges can be reduced to a simple process in which powerful nations impose their welfare institutions on passive recipient states. Obviously, the idea that the history of a country's social welfare system can be analyzed only in terms of unidirectional international forces offers only a crude and partial explanation of very complex processes. Nevertheless, it has been shown that influences emanating from the centers of world power have contributed significantly to the way domestic welfare systems in many parts of the world evolved.

Direct transfers introduced through government action in the form of either colonialism or international aid can shape international exchanges. But equally important is the role of indirect influences resulting from interpersonal contacts and a cultural and intellectual climate that facilitates the spread of ideas. As the United States became more influential in the world in the post–World War II decades, American social welfare approaches have been increasingly adopted in other countries as a result of both official government intervention and less formal interactions.

Nonformal influences operating through interpersonal contacts have been very important in promoting the diffusion of American welfare approaches. Intellectual exchanges through the scientific literature, conferences and meetings, and personal contacts have been an important source of diffusion. These exchanges have been facilitated by the prestige and influence of American scholars and policymakers. In the same way that American welfare pioneers admired European innovations in the late nineteenth century, social policymakers, administrators, and social workers in many other countries have viewed developments in the United States favorably. This explains the adoption of American ideas in other economically developed countries such as Britain, where American social work theories and practice approaches were emulated and where urban community programs based on President Lyndon B. Johnson administration's War on Poverty programs were implemented. The process continues today as American approaches to social welfare diffuse through academic and other nonformal linkages. Policy approaches for addressing underclass poverty, welfare-to-work programs, and, more recently, the idea of faith-based social welfare, have all exerted influence in other countries through mechanisms of this kind.

The diffusion of American social welfare has also been facilitated by government action. American colonialism facilitated the replication of domestic practices in the Philippines. During the cold war years, when the United States competed with the Soviet Union to exert international influence, government support for international social welfare projects was fairly common. This support often formed a part of wider economic, military, diplomatic, and geopolitical initiatives. American academics have often been involved in these initiatives. This was the case with American support for the Augusto Pinochet regime in Chile, when academics from the University of Chicago played a key role in reshaping the country's economic and social policies. The abolition of the country's venerable social insurance system, and the introduction of commercially managed individual retirement accounts in 1981, did not replicate existing practices in the United States, but clearly reflected the growing influence of neoliberal ideology in American economic and social welfare thinking. As this ideology has become ascendant, it is being increasingly diffused to nations over which the United States exerts influence or seeks to exert influence.

Ideology and power relations play a significant role in international social welfare, and it is clear that historical accounts of the development of social welfare systems should pay attention to these factors. But again, the complexity of these relations must be stressed. Despite its global influence, the United States does not have hegemonic control over social welfare in other countries, and its influence is often challenged not only in academic but in official circles as well. Many critics, as well as street protestors, have condemned the role of the United States in promoting neoliberal ideas through the agency of the International Monetary Fund and World Bank.

Other international social welfare organizations, such as the International Labour Organization and UNICEF, have been much more resistant to the influence of ideas from the United States and have been critical of the way that international organizations dominated by the United States have exported neoliberal economic and social policy to many poor countries. The refusal of the government of the United States to ratify international social welfare treaties, such as the Declaration on the Rights of the Child, has further weakened its influence. U.S. efforts to undermine international family planning programs have also harmed its reputation. Its current engagement in the Middle East has alienated many in the Islamic world who previously had a much more positive view of American innovation and leadership. Whether the United States will be able to address these challenges and use its unique global position as well as its considerable economic and political power to promote the welfare of all the world's citizens remains to be seen.

—James Midgley

See also Economic Crises, Family and Gender, 1980s to the Present (Mexico); Economic Policy (Mexico); Neoliberalism, Social Programs, and Social Movements (Mexico); The Rockefeller Foundation and Public Health (Mexico); Roosevelt, Anna Eleanor

Primary Sources

Records of the International Association of Schools of Social Work and the International Conference on Social Work, Social Welfare History Archives, University of Minnesota, Minneapolis; Records of the Agency for International Development and predecessor agencies (Record Group 286), National Archives & Records Administration, Washington, DC, and College Park, MD; Archives of the International Monetary Fund, Washington, DC; United Nations Archives and Records Centre, Archives and Records Management Section, United Nations, New York.

Current Comment

Broughton, J. (2001). *Silent revolution: The International Monetary Fund, 1979–1989.* Washington, DC: International Monetary Fund.

Roosevelt, E. (1948, April). The promise of human rights. *Foreign Affairs, 26,* 470–477.

United Nations, Office of the High Commissioner for Human Rights. (1959). *Declaration of the rights of the child.* Available: www.unhchr.ch/html/menu3/b/25.htm

Further Reading

Deacon, B., Hulse, M., & Stubbs, P. (1997). *Global social policy: International organizations and the future of welfare.* London: Sage.

Healy, L. M. (2001). *International social work: Professional action in an interdependent world.* New York: Oxford University Press.

Midgley, J. (1997). *Social welfare in global context.* Thousand Oaks, CA, and London: Sage.

J

JUVENILE JUSTICE POLICY (UNITED STATES)

For most of recorded history, juveniles who committed crimes were ignored, handled informally, or processed as "little criminals" in the same courts as adults and sentenced to the same dispositions as adults. Even though there was a common belief since the early 1800s that children who violated a law should not be confined with adult criminals, a separate juvenile court to separate and individualize juvenile cases was not created in the United States until 1899.

The foundation for the creation of the juvenile court was also English common law, but civil rather than criminal law. Before the creation of separate juvenile courts in the United States, courts of chancery, sometimes known as equity courts, frequently handled legal functions involving juveniles. Even today, juvenile matters are sometimes handled by probate courts, courts that are tightly circumscribed by the principles of equity jurisprudence. Equity courts were established as chancery courts in England in 1474. They operated not only to meet legal requirements, but also to achieve fairness in settling disputes and correcting wrongs. This philosophy was carried over into the juvenile court.

The movement toward a separate juvenile justice system in America can be traced to 1825, when the first house of refuge was created in New York. In 1841, a Boston boot maker, John Augustus, began asking the police court to release convicted juveniles (and adults) into his custody as an alternative to incarceration, a system we now call probation. Massachusetts law in 1870 required that juvenile offenders under the age of 16 have their cases heard "separate from the general and ordinary criminal business," but they were still handled in adult courts.

The first juvenile court was the culmination of a reform effort in Illinois in 1899. Within a few years, all the states provided for separate courts to process juvenile offenders. Unlike adult criminal courts, juvenile courts had jurisdiction over other matters, such as dependency and neglect, in which the welfare of the child was at stake. Using the concept of *parens patriae,* a legal doctrine that the courts can make decisions for persons who are incapable of making decisions for themselves, the emphasis was on rehabilitation rather than punishment. Also, unlike adult courts, juveniles had few constitutional rights. Probation supervision was the most common disposition for a juvenile offender. Volunteers originally served as probation officers, but social workers quickly came to staff probation services.

Beginning with the decision in *Kent v. United States* in 1966 (383 U.S. 541), the U.S. Supreme Court has granted juveniles some of the due process guarantees that are afforded to adults, but it has stopped short of granting them the same constitutional rights. The next year, the Court expanded juvenile rights in *In Re Gault* (387 U.S. 1), by extending the right to counsel, the right to confront witnesses, the right to confront accusers, and the right to timely notice of charges to all juveniles. From the beginning of the juvenile court movement, some were concerned that the court's unchecked rehabilitative powers could pose a serious threat to juveniles; harm could be done under the guise of looking after the child's "best interests." For example, indeterminate sentencing was common practice in the juvenile court, and it could (and sometimes still does) result in a juvenile being incarcerated longer than an adult for committing the same crime.

There have been three major policy shifts in federal juvenile justice policy since the 1960s. In the early 1960s, community organization models were used to foster local responsibility for juvenile misbehavior, but they were generally not successful. A second shift came as a result of a number of presidential commissions studying crime and violence. In 1967, the President's Commission on Law Enforcement and the Administration of Justice recommended the decriminalization of status offenses, the diversion of juvenile offenders from official court processing, and the deinstitutionalization of juvenile offenders. The culmination of this policy shift was the Juvenile Justice and Delinquency Prevention Act (JJDPA) of 1974.

A third major shift occurred in the mid 1970s, with a new "law and order" philosophy gaining momentum, partly as a spillover from a similar change in attitude about adult offenders. Although JJDPA was intended to prevent delinquency and remove children from adult jails and lockups, it was amended in 1977 to make it more controlling of juvenile behavior. In 1981, the administration of President Ronald Reagan targeted serious juvenile offenders for special attention. In 1984, a committee recommended that the deinstitutionalization grants to the states be suspended, and the Comprehensive Crime Control Act of 1984 contained other "get tough" measures.

Since 1992, the "law and order" trend has gained momentum, with 45 of the states adopting laws making it easier to prosecute juveniles in adult court. As many as 200,000 juveniles under the age of 18 are processed annually in adult criminal courts. Only a fraction of these children are waived from juvenile to adult courts; most are charged as adults because of prosecutorial discretion or statutory exclusions. In recent years, the proportion of juvenile cases handled formally, rather than informally, in juvenile court has also increased, another indication of a more punitive policy toward juvenile offenders. At each stage of processing in the juvenile system, members of minority groups are treated more harshly.

It appears that as juveniles have gained more due process rights over the last four decades, they have also been treated more like adult criminals. The rehabilitative ideal of the original juvenile court movement has evolved into a policy of retribution; making the punishment fit the crime has become more important than the well-being of the juvenile offender. The current "get tough" philosophy has also resulted in more children being processed as adult criminals.

—*C. Aaron McNeece*

See also Child Welfare Policy (United States); Criminal Justice Policy (United States); Progressive Era (United States)

Current Comment

National Advisory Commission on Criminal Justice Standards and Goals. (1976). *Report of the Task Force on Juvenile Justice and Delinquency Prevention.* Washington, DC: Government Printing Office.

President's Commission on Law Enforcement and the Administration of Justice. (1967). *The challenge of crime in a free society.* Washington, DC: Government Printing Office.

Further Reading

McShane, M. D., & Williams, F. P., III. (Eds.). (2003). *Encyclopedia of juvenile justice.* Thousand Oaks, CA: Sage.

Mennel, R. M. (1973). *Thorns and thistles: Juvenile delinquents in the United States, 1825–1940.* Hanover, NH: University Press of New England.

Platt, A. M. (1977). *The child savers: The invention of delinquency* (2nd ed., enl.). Chicago: University of Chicago Press.

K

KELSO, JOHN JOSEPH (1864–1935)

J. J. Kelso holds an important place in the history of social reform in Canada and is regarded as a most influential figure in the development of Canadian child welfare. He was directly involved in the development of the Toronto Humane Society, the Children's Fresh Air Fund, the Children's Aid Society of Toronto, and the first children's protection act, which served as the foundation for the development of children's aid societies in Ontario. At the age of 29, he was appointed Ontario's first superintendent of neglected and dependent children. In this position, he was responsible for the implementation of Canada's first child welfare legislation. Kelso continued in this position for the next 41 years.

J. J. Kelso was born in Dundalk, Ireland, in 1864, the eighth of ten children born to George Kelso and Anna MacMurray Kelso. His family owned a large starch mill, which provided a good standard of living for that time and location. A fire destroyed this uninsured manufacturing plant at the end of the 1860s and this financial setback prompted the family's migration to Toronto, Ontario, when J. J. was 10 years of age. Kelso put his education on hold during his teenage years, and he worked at a series of part-time jobs to financially support his family. Employment during his teens included positions as a street bookseller, telegraph messenger, sales assistant, and an apprentice printer. At the age of 21, Kelso became a reporter for a Toronto daily newspaper and began to use this public position to highlight the need for social reform in Toronto.

Kelso prepared a series of newspaper articles in 1887 about neglected children in Toronto. This series was primarily based on a chance encounter with two children he found panhandling on the street late one night, and it described his personal struggle to find safe accommodations for the children for that night. Later that same year, he was instrumental in the development of the Toronto Humane Society, a voluntary, nondenominational organization designed to protect women, children, and animals. He was nominated to the volunteer position of secretary of the humane society and worked collaboratively with Toronto institutions and the general public to protect individuals and animals at risk. In this position, Kelso developed a series of new initiatives to support Toronto children who were affected by poverty and neglect. He started the Children's Fresh Air Fund to provide community activities and excursions for urban youth, and later developed the Santa Claus Fund. The initiatives were later taken over by the Toronto *Star* newspaper.

In 1888, Kelso collaborated in the preparation of draft legislation for the protection of neglected and at-risk children that was subsequently submitted to Sir Oliver Mowat, the premier and attorney general of Ontario. The act was designed to provide legal authority to intervene when a child was being harmed by neglect, or had been orphaned or abandoned. This new legislation was known as the Act for the Protection and Reformation of Neglected Children of 1888. It was the first indication that social welfare was considered paramount to the rights and privileges of individuals. The act served as the foundation for subsequent legislation for the protection and safety of children in Ontario.

In 1889, the Prison Reform Commission prepared a report on the relationship between crime and intervention. It concluded that the care of young children at risk was critical for the prevention of adult crime, and that children at risk were better served in family foster homes than in larger institutions. Kelso at first proposed that the Toronto Humane Society would be the best organization to coordinate the placement of children in foster care. This agency, however, was consistently being challenged in meeting the needs of both children and animals in the same organizational setting. Kelso proposed developing a children's aid society modeled on the New York Children's Aid Society (CAS), which had been established in 1854. In 1891, the Children's Aid Society of Toronto was officially founded with Kelso in the volunteer position of president.

In March 1892, the Toronto CAS opened the first children's shelter to provide temporary room and board for destitute and neglected youth. This shelter provided temporary placements for youth, but the CAS did not have legislative approval to establish foster homes for the long-term placement of children who were homeless or extremely at risk in their homes. Soon after, Kelso began to lobby the Ontario government for legislation to address this issue, and J. M. Gibson, the provincial secretary, was subsequently commissioned to draft the act. Relying heavily on legislation from Australia and England, and the findings of the Prison Reform Commission, Gibson composed an Act for the Prevention of Cruelty to and Better Protection of Children that was approved by the legislature in May of 1893. This children's act consisted of 31 clauses outlining Ontario's new approach to child welfare and established the position of superintendent of neglected and dependent children, which Kelso held for 41 years. In this role, he was actively involved in the further development of the Children's Protective

Association of Ontario, a federation of child-saving agencies from across the province, and the further development of other Ontario children's aid societies, in Ottawa and Peterborough in 1893 and in Hamilton in 1894. The number of children's aid societies in Ontario continued to grow from 29 in 1896 to 55 in 1906, a number that has remained fairly stable to the present day. Kelso died in Toronto in 1935.

J. J. Kelso was a leader in the development of child welfare services in Canada during the latter part of the nineteenth century and the first part of the twentieth century. He contributed significantly to the promotion and acceptance of legislation, public policy, and program development that served as the foundation for child welfare in Ontario and most other provinces in Canada.

—*Bruce MacLaurin*

See also Child Welfare Policy (Canada)

Primary Source

J. J. Kelso Papers, Library and Archives Canada, Ottawa, ON.

Further Reading

Bullen, J. (1991). J. J. Kelso and the "new" child-savers: The genesis of the children's aid movement in Ontario. In R. Smandych, G. Dodds, & A. Esau (Eds.), *Dimensions of childhood: Essays on the history of children and youth in Canada.* Winnipeg: University of Manitoba, Legal Research Institute.
Jones, A., & Rutman, L. (1981). *In the children's aid: J. J. Kelso and child welfare in Ontario.* Toronto, ON: University of Toronto Press.
McCullagh, J. (2002). *A legacy of caring: A history of the Children's Aid Society of Toronto.* Toronto, ON: Dundurn.
Rooke, P. T., & Schnell, R. L. (1983). *Discarding the asylum: From child rescue to the welfare state in English-Canada (1800–1950).* Lanham, MD: University Press of America.

KING, MARTIN LUTHER, JR. (1929–1968)

Martin Luther King, Jr., was born on January 15, 1929, in Atlanta, Georgia. He was the second of three children of the Reverend Michael (later Martin) King and Alberta Williams King. He attended racially segregated public elementary and high schools, and the private Laboratory High School of Atlanta University.

In September 1944, at the age of 15, he began undergraduate study at Morehouse College. After completing the curriculum in 3 years, he received a BA in sociology in 1948. At the age of 18, he was ordained a Baptist minister in the Ebenezer Baptist Church in Atlanta, where his father was pastor. Subsequently, he entered Crozer Theological Seminary in Chester, Pennsylvania, and was awarded a BD degree in 1951. In recognition of his exceptional intellect, he won the Plafker Award as the outstanding student of the 1951 graduating class. He also was awarded the J. Lewis Crozer Fellowship, to help him finance graduate school. That same year, King began doctoral study at Boston University, where he earned his PhD in systematic theology in 1955. While pursuing his doctorate, he married Coretta Scott in 1953. They had four children.

King's speaking skills were extraordinary. The way he used his voice to preach to his parishioners and speak to other audiences was superlative. As he did in his famous "How Long? Not Long" speech delivered in 1965 on the Selma-to-Montgomery March, a significant event in the African American struggle for recognition of their civil rights, King always masterfully combined biblical passages that assured everyone that God was on the side of justice with deliberate speaking cadence and pointed gestures. For many people, his words alone inspired passionate involvement in the fight for civil rights. After King delivered his famous "I Have A Dream" speech at the March on Washington for civil rights and jobs in 1963, *Time* magazine designated him the "Man of the Year." Four months later, he was honored as the recipient of the 1964 Nobel Peace Prize.

King is readily credited as a driving force behind Black Americans' struggle against racial discrimination, especially from 1955 to 1965, when the civil rights movement used nonviolent direct action to achieve its goals. During this decade, his philosophy of peaceful protest for social change grounded in spiritual love (*agape*) was epitomized by such events as the Montgomery Bus Boycott (1955–1956), the Birmingham Campaign (1963), the March on Washington (1963), and the Selma-to-Montgomery March (1965). These widely publicized events brought attention to African American efforts to end racial segregation in the South. They contributed to the enactment of the federal Civil Rights Act of 1964 and the Voting Rights Act of 1965. King was a founder and served as president of the Southern Christian Leadership Conference (SCLC). Its original mission was to end segregation in the South, but in the mid 1960s its goals changed in an effort to attack racial discrimination in the North as well.

From 1956 to 1965, King became increasingly concerned with the problems in the northern cities. He believed that northern urban slums and widespread segregation in northern schools contributed to poverty and social dysfunction in Black communities. The SCLC and King worked with community organizations to desegregate schools and housing in Chicago. This became known as the Chicago Movement.

The Chicago Movement was not successful in forcing Chicago's Mayor Richard M. Dailey and the city's realtors to support open occupancy in housing without regard to race. Nevertheless, for the first time the White power structure in a northern city was compelled to sit in a room with Blacks and agree on a fair housing ordinance.

The final phase of King's career occurred in the period from 1966 to 1968, when King began to pursue social welfare goals. His activities were intended to obtain economic justice not only for impoverished Blacks but also for all poor Americans. This was to be achieved by forcing the federal government to enact antipoverty programs that would make more financial support and social welfare services available for the poor. Although King believed President Lyndon Johnson sincerely wanted to eliminate poverty, he protested what he saw as the inadequacies of the president's War on Poverty. The many antipoverty programs that were part of Johnson's Great Society initiative were unsuccessful, King argued, because the financial resources needed to lift the needy above the poverty line were diverted to pay for the Vietnam War. Equally important was King's belief that economic, racial, and class inequality in America was attributable to capitalism. This pointed to the need for a revolutionary way of redistributing income, a democratic form of socialism as an alternative to capitalism that had resulted in glaring social inequalities. King felt that social inequality related to social class as well as race and needed to be considered by the civil rights movement.

He enthusiastically responded to suggestions to bring poor people to the nation's capital to demand a "real war on poverty." The Poor People's Campaign, unlike the March on Washington, which had lasted for one day, was intended to bring protesters to Washington, D.C., for several days of sit-ins, to interrupt congressional proceedings and the daily routines of the city, and to get the government to respond to the plight of the poor.

Without the full support of SCLC and other allies, King planted the seeds for his "last, greatest dream," a march of 3,000 people—the unemployed, welfare recipients, sharecroppers, Appalachian Whites, Mexican Americans, and Puerto Ricans—who would demand, among other things, financial support for a $12 billion "Economic Bill of Rights." It called for a guaranteed annual income, jobs for anyone who wanted to work, and the elimination of slums. The march was scheduled for late April 1968.

King's decision to interrupt his planning of the Poor People's Campaign in order to go to Memphis, Tennessee, to support striking sanitation workers was another illustration of his social welfare agenda. Speaking and marching on their behalf was yet another opportunity to highlight nonviolence as the most effective avenue to radical social change and to focus national attention on the poor. On April 3, King delivered his last speech at the Bishop Charles J. Mason Temple. He was assassinated by James Earl Ray at the Lorraine Hotel in Memphis on April 4, 1968.

King's progressive social welfare proposals are relevant today. The problems—poverty, homelessness, and racism—that prompted him to advocate enactment of a guaranteed income and legislation to eradicate slums exist today. Poor urban and rural communities still experience many social problems.

Today, as a result of economic processes such as globalization, the divide between the "haves" and the "have-nots" grows in the United States and globally. One of King's insights—"what happens to one impacts the other"—should not be ignored. Though America has developed into an economic and military power, King's words, "True compassion is more than flinging a coin to a beggar; it understands that an edifice which produces beggars needs restructuring," serve as an inspiration for those who are concerned about social injustice and poverty.

—Marlene Anita Saunders

See also African Americans and Social Welfare (United States); Social Reform Movements (United States)

Primary Sources

Martin Luther King, Jr., Papers, Special Collections Department, Mugar Library, Boston University, Boston, MA; Martin Luther King, Jr., Papers, Center for Non-Violent Social Change, Atlanta, GA.

Current Comment

King, M. L., Jr. (1958). *Stride toward freedom: The Montgomery story.* New York: Harper & Row.

King, M. L., Jr. (1964). *Why we can't wait.* New York: New American Library.

King, M. L., Jr. (1967). *Where do we go from here: Chaos or community?* New York: Harper & Row.

Further Reading

Branch, T. (1988). *Parting the waters: America in the King years 1954–63.* New York: Simon & Schuster.

Dyson, M. E. (2002). *I may not get there with you: The true Martin Luther King, Jr.* New York: Free Press.

Garrow, D. J. (1986). *Bearing the Cross: Martin Luther King, Jr. and the Southern Leadership Conference, 1955-1968.* New York: Morrow.

Ling, P. (1988). *Martin Luther King, Jr.* New York: Routledge.

LABOR MOVEMENT AND SOCIAL WELFARE (MEXICO)

An alliance with Mexico's labor movement motivated Mexico's postrevolutionary government to initiate worker-oriented social policies following the Revolution of 1910. These included policies that benefited all wage earners and poverty relief programs that targeted working-class neighborhoods, often disproportionately benefiting union members. After 1982, however, the labor movement lost political influence and urban workers suffered a precipitous decline in their standard of living.

ORIGINS OF THE STATE-LABOR ALLIANCE

Fear of labor unrest initially motivated the Mexican government to address the concerns of urban workers. The first revolutionary president, Francisco Madero (1911–1913), actively sought to resolve rising industrial conflict. Although unions represented only a small portion of Mexican workers at that time, unionized workers were concentrated in Mexico's most strategic industries. With the violent strike at the Cananea Copper Company in 1906 in mind, Madero facilitated labor-management negotiations in the strategically important textile, mining, and railroad industries. As a result, in 1912, textile workers won a 10-hour workday, holidays, and uniform wages across the industry.

Later revolutionary presidents built a state-labor alliance not only to contain labor conflict but also to use workers as a base of political support. In the 1920s, Presidents Álvaro Obregón and Plutarco Calles convinced some union leaders to provide political and military support in exchange for access to political power. The 1931 labor code facilitated the growth and predominance of unions allied with the government rather than the labor movement through state regulation of unions and labor conflicts. President Lázaro Cárdenas (1934–1940) institutionalized an enduring state-labor alliance not only by implementing worker-oriented social policies but also by fostering a new union confederation, integrating some unions within the political decision-making process and giving some unions a financial stake in nationalized industries. The Confederation of Mexican Workers (CTM) quickly became the largest union confederation after Cárdenas gave the CTM control over the institution conferring official recognition on unions (the Conciliation and Arbitration Boards). By 1938, 2 years after the confederation's formation, three quarters of all unions were affiliated with the CTM, including the powerful unions representing miners, oil workers, and railroad workers. Cárdenas made the CTM one of four organizations that officially represented Mexican society within his political party, which later became known as the Institutional Revolutionary party (*Partido Revolucionario Institucional,* or PRI). Cárdenas cemented his relationship with organized labor by expropriating foreign-owned companies in the oil and railroad industries and granting CTM unions some control over their management.

WORKER-ORIENTED SOCIAL POLICIES

The state-labor alliance improved the quality of life for Mexico's urban workers and their families. All workers enjoyed the steady increase in purchasing power driven by the 25-year ascent in the minimum wage that began in 1951. Workers secured the right to a minimum wage, set by minimum wage commissions that included unions, in 1934. In 1937, the government initiated a food policy that included selling subsidized food in stores concentrated in Mexico City's working-class neighborhoods. Workers employed by legally recognized companies gained access to state-run hospitals and to old-age pensions when President Manuel Ávila Camacho (1940–1946) implemented the Mexican Social Security Institute (*Instituto Mexicano del Seguro Social,* or IMSS) in 1943. President Luis Echeverría (1970–1976) created the National Institute of Housing for Workers (*Instituto Nacional de Fondo de Vivienda Para los Trabajadores,* or INFONAVIT), a program to build houses for workers, and the National Workers Credit Fund (*Fondo de Fomento y Garantía Para el Consumo de los Trabajadores,* or FONACOT), a program extending credit to workers. Union members gained privileged access to subsidized food, public housing, and bank credits as unions gained control over program resources.

DECLINING WORKER SOCIAL WELFARE

Over the past three decades, the social welfare of the urban poor has declined, widening the gap between rich and poor. Despite rising worker productivity, the real value of manufacturing wages fell by a quarter in the 1980s. The minimum wage is currently about half of what it was in 1982. Deep cuts in social spending, particularly in the 1980s, and lax regulation on food prices further eroded working-class quality of life. The partial privatization of retirement pensions has made old age more precarious and the quality of IMSS health care has declined.

SOURCES OF LABOR'S DECLINE

Although labor militancy surged in the mid 1980s, the CTM subsequently acquiesced to wage constraints and social spending cuts. The quiescence of the CTM can be traced to labor's historical dependence on the government. Not only did the official unions depend on the government to ensure their dominance over the labor movement, but union leaders also profited from the state-labor alliance. Through the PRI, unionists launched political careers, and on average represented 15 percent of the national legislature. Labor leaders used their access to management over state-owned enterprises to secure lucrative contracting arrangements. Moreover, the early demise of the CTM's precursor taught CTM leaders that opposing the PRI could be fatal. Thus, longtime CTM leader Fidel Velásquez sought to preserve labor's organizational strength, access to political leadership, and financial security when, in 1987, he signed the first in a series of "social pacts" with government and business that constrained wages.

A hostile political and economic climate placed additional pressure on Velásquez. An economic crisis, a new economic development strategy, and a shift in government orientation to labor instigated labor's declining influence in the 1980s. Mexico's economic crisis, triggered by the declaration that Mexico would not make its foreign debt payment in 1982 and Mexico's stagnant economy since then, has weakened labor's bargaining position. Mexico's new neoliberal development strategy, in particular the policy to privatize state-owned enterprises, undermined the official labor movement. Unions in state-owned enterprises constituted some of the official labor movement's most influential unions. Steps designed to prepare enterprises for privatization, such as drastic cuts in the workforce and the elimination of union contract clauses that regulated pay, gutted unions in state-owned airline, steel, and automobile enterprises. The government disbanded other state-owned industries, including nuclear power, eliminating unions altogether.

After 1982, Mexican presidents continued to work largely within the postrevolutionary state-labor institutions, but undermined the legitimacy of official unions. Presidents still employ tripartite (labor, business, and government) negotiations and, despite repeated threats, have not dismantled legal protections for unions, protections that work to the advantage of official unions. Thus, even though several high-profile defections and the proliferation of secret union contracts have diluted the monopoly of the labor movement's umbrella organization, the Labor Congress, most unions (78 percent) still affiliate with the Labor Congress, and the unionization rate remains about 15 percent.

Post-1982 presidents, however, undermined union legitimacy by redirecting social spending away from union-controlled programs and by promoting non-CTM union leaders. The proportion of the housing budget allocated to INFONAVIT, a union-controlled social program, declined from half to a quarter during the 1980s. President Carlos Salinas de Gortari (1988–1994) rewarded union leaders who were amenable to his economic policies, such as the renegade leader of the telephone workers, Francisco Hernández Juárez. Gortari punished union leaders who opposed his economic agenda, such as the prominent CTM leader of the oil workers, Joaquín Hernández Galicia, with jail time. As a result, Velásquez only managed to leverage some control over distributing subsidized food in exchange for agreeing to wage constraints in the "social pacts."

LABOR'S UNCERTAIN FUTURE

Political leaders will probably continue to engage the official labor movement, mostly because official unions contain worker militancy. Without labor militancy and more strategic political allies, however, it seems unlikely that the urban working class will regain its former quality of life. Independent unions (unions not affiliated with the PRI) have led marches, organized new unions, formed new union centrals, and developed international labor strategies to challenge the predominance of official unions. Nevertheless, effective CTM control over strikes and union registration has stymied independent union drives. Continued CTM privilege at the presidential palace has diluted the efficacy of new independent union centrals. More promising may be the democratic movements emerging within the official teacher's, textile, and some *maquiladora* unions that represent

workers in foreign-owned multinationals. Shielded from immediate political opposition, these movements may rebuild union capacity to mobilize workers. The future social welfare of urban workers and their families depends on the success of these varied strategies to reinvigorate Mexico's labor movement.

—*Leslie Gates*

See also Food Assistance Policy (Mexico); Housing Policy (Mexico); Neoliberalism; Social Programs and Social Movements (Mexico); Social Reform and State-Building (Mexico); Welfare Capitalism (Mexico)

Primary Sources

Junta Federal de Conciliación y Arbitraje (JFCA) and *Tribunal Federal de Concilición y Arbitraje* (TFCA); *Secretaría del Trabajo y Previsión Social* (STPS); and the presidential collections in the *Archivo General de la Nación* (AGN), Mexico City.

Current Comment

El Cotidiano. Mexico City: Universidad Autónoma Metropolitana, Itztapalapa. Available: http://dcsh.azc.uam.mx/cotidiano/

De la Garza Toledo, E. (1994). The restructuring of state-labor relations in Mexico. In M. L. Cook, K. J. Middlebrook, & J. M. Horcasitas (Eds.). *The politics of economic restructuring* (pp. 195–217). La Jolla: University of California, San Diego, Center for U.S.-Mexican Studies.

La Botz, D. (Ed.). *Mexican Labor News and Analysis* [On-line serial]. Available: www.ueinternational.org/

Further Reading

Cook, M. L. (1996). *Organizing dissent: Unions, the state, and the democratic teachers' movement in Mexico.* University Park: Pennsylvania State University Press.

Middlebrook, K. (Ed.). (1991). *Unions, workers and the state in Mexico.* La Jolla: University of California, San Diego, Center for U.S.-Mexican Studies.

Middlebrook, K. (1995). *The paradox of revolution: Labor, the state and authoritarianism in Mexico.* Baltimore: Johns Hopkins University Press.

LABOR MOVEMENT AND SOCIAL WELFARE (UNITED STATES)

Labor unions have played a key role in contributing to the social welfare in the United States since they emerged over 200 years ago. Control of production was shifting quickly away from the individual skilled craft worker to wholesale-order shopkeepers who, in order to compete successfully, strove to reduce costs by turning out work more inexpensively than they could under the craft system. Workers formed unions primarily to secure or maintain a decent wage for their members within this new production system. At times, workers withheld their labor and went on strike in order to reach agreement with their employers. When this occurred, they shared funds, set aside from their union dues, to ease the financial burden on union members and their families during long work stoppages.

The primary function of unions has been constant from the founding of the first union (the Cordwainers in Philadelphia) in the United States in 1792 to the formation of the first national federations (the Knights of Labor in 1869 and the American Federation of Labor, or AFL, in 1886) to the present day: to achieve better wages, benefits, and working conditions for their members. Mostly, this has been achieved through collective bargaining, though union-driven legislative initiatives have helped to solidify gains achieved at the bargaining table and make them more widely available to all workers. Lawrence Mishel and Matthew Walters of the Economic Policy Institute conclude that unionized workers have higher wages, suffer less wage inequality, and are more likely to receive paid leave, employer-provided health insurance, and to participate in employer-provided pension plans than nonunionized workers.

Economic benefits of unionization extend to the unorganized, as well, especially those employed in industries with strong union representation. Data from the Mishel and Walters (2002) study support the conclusion that strong unions within an industry set a pay standard that nonunion employers follow and that the impact of unions on total nonunion wages is almost as large as the impact on total union wages.

Contributions to the social welfare go beyond higher wages and better benefits, as important as those are to the well-being of families and communities. Unions have been the driving force behind numerous workplace initiatives that protect or enhance the safety, security, and quality of life of working people. Many of the battles to secure these rights and benefits occurred years ago with the result that the role unions played in their achievement goes unrecognized and employer good will is assumed to be the force behind their widespread availability. Such is not often the case.

For example, the regular workday for most full-time employees today is 8 hours. The 8-hour day is, however, the result of a decades-long, union-led struggle that began in the 1850s and culminated in widespread adoption of the standard in cities across the country in the 1890s and early 1900s. Likewise, first a 6- then a 5-day, 40-hour workweek, now widely accepted as the norm, came about through union-led collective action that was ultimately codified into law in the Fair Labor Standards Act (FLSA) of 1938. In addition to a standard 40-hour workweek, the FLSA also established a minimum wage and required payment of time-and-a-half for any hours worked in excess of 40 hours per week. This union-led legislation helped provide increased economic security for working people and the potential for more time to engage in family life and participate in the social and civic life of their communities. Shorter workdays and weeks also helped to reduce workplace fatigue, which can adversely affect work quality, safety and health, attendance, and productivity.

It should be noted that the FLSA was passed during a time in which union membership grew dramatically and Congress and the courts viewed unions much more favorably than they had during previous years. In 1932, Congress passed the Norris-LaGuardia Act, which denied the federal courts the right to forbid strikes, peaceful picketing, and other actions not illegal in themselves that unions employed in their dealings with employers. From the early 1800s, courts had impeded collective union activity by ruling that such activity, though legal if it involved only one person, constituted a "conspiracy" if it involved more than one and was therefore illegal. Injunctions to restrain union strike activity were also frequently employed by judges at the request of employers.

In 1935, Congress passed the landmark Wagner or National Labor Relations Act (NLRA), which gave to employees the "right to self-organization, to form, join or assist labor organizations to bargain collectively through representatives of their own choosing, and to engage in concerted activities, for the purpose of collective bargaining or other mutual aid or protection." Passage of the Wagner and Norris-LaGuardia acts removed significant barriers to union organizing attempts, which helped the Steelworkers Organizing Committee (later the United Steel Workers of

America) and the United Auto Workers—two of the emerging industrial unions—to gain recognition and strength during the mid-to-late 1930s. Union membership grew from 4 million in 1935 to roughly 16 million by 1948.

Problems with labor practices that employers regarded as unfavorable and that the NLRA did not address led to the passage of the Taft-Hartley Act in 1947. These changes as well as the countervailing protection given by Taft-Hartley to the right of individuals to refrain from engaging in collective activity has served to dilute the influence of the NLRA, sometimes considerably. Nonetheless, union membership increased for a time as a percentage of the labor force to 27 percent (16.9 million members) in 1953, and in total membership with 22.2 million members (23 percent of the civilian labor force) in 1975. Union membership has declined in total numbers and as a percentage of the labor force ever since.

Numerous other workplace benefits, now widely available to nonunion workers as well, can be traced to gains first achieved through collective bargaining. Paid leave time—as vacation days, personal days, holidays, bereavement days, and sick leave—are critically important to the well-being of individuals and families, not just to be able to respond appropriately in times of crisis but also to strengthen and celebrate the family ties that are essential for solid communities. Employer-paid insurances—health, dental, vision, life, disability, and legal—help to moderate the effects of situations that could have profoundly negative effects on workers and their families. Pensions, profit sharing, stock ownership, and other retirement funds allow working people to retire with dignity without becoming a financial burden on their families or their communities. Apprenticeship, training and upgrading, tuition assistance, and other educational programs strengthen the capabilities that people can apply to their workplace as well as to the vitality of their communities and the economy at large. Workplace health and safety programs save lives in the short run and in the long term. Federal occupational safety and health programs, underfunded as they currently might be, owe their very existence to union-led initiatives. Employee assistance programs offer a lifeline to workers whose employment, family life, and health are threatened by addictions or other disabling conditions.

For a number of reasons that include deterring unionization as well as rewarding, motivating, or retaining employees, many nonunion workplaces provide some or all of these benefits, extending the gains to far more than households with union members.

Unions have contributed in other unique ways over the years. For example, unions representing low- or moderate-wage workers built and managed apartment buildings in East Coast cities, where they had a large membership, to provide affordable housing to their members. Other unions, such as those representing garment and autoworkers, acquired educational facilities with modest, resort-type amenities, and made them available to their members and families who might not have had a chance for that type of vacation otherwise. In addition, unions play a prominent role in promoting contributions to the United Way, blood and disaster-relief drives, and other community activities.

Union growth and effectiveness in advocating for a social welfare agenda have been hindered by several factors over the years. Employer resistance, supported by "employer-friendly" judicial and legislative actions, has done much to make the organizing process difficult. Union leaders' reluctance to bring industrial workers into their fold—workers who were often female, recent immigrants, or members of minority groups—created unnecessary divisions within the labor movement, such as the creation of the Congress of Industrial Organizations (CIO) in the 1930s, and diverted energy from the task of advancing a common agenda. Fortunately for workers, the labor movement, and U.S. social welfare, the AFL and CIO resolved their differences and merged in 1955. The loss of manufacturing jobs to low-wage, developing countries has contributed greatly to the decline in union membership that has also weakened unions' political influence. Today, the continuing decline in membership presents perhaps the greatest challenge to unions and their ability to enhance U.S. social welfare. Nonetheless, the mere presence of unions contributes significantly to higher quality of life for union and nonunion workers alike and serves as a check to a corporate-employer-driven social policy agenda.

That said, it is important to look beyond these tangible contributions to social welfare and look at the equally important, but less than tangible, contributions unions continue to make in helping people to find and strengthen their "civic voice" in the ongoing struggle for economic and social justice. Union-negotiated grievance procedures protect individual workers from reprisal when giving voice to concerns in the workplace. Union-led civic actions and campaigns provide strong examples of how social change can be achieved through the collective voice and action of ordinary people. Both help to strengthen the capability of individuals to contribute to social improvements.

Workplaces are typically not democratic. In most cases, they do not even assure workers the right to provide input on matters under discussion or review. The practice of reporting only information that management wants to hear may result. In unionized workplaces, an employee's individual voice is protected. Employers must show "just cause" to support termination, and articulating an unpopular viewpoint is not usually a justifiable reason for discipline or termination. Thus, giving voice to a concern is protected by union representation.

Unions as organizations are democratic. Leaders are elected by and from the rank and file and, ultimately, must answer to the members. Many decisions or questions are put before the members—or at least the union's elected representatives—before they are acted upon. This practice pertains to matters of collective bargaining, as well as such things as endorsing political candidates, supporting or challenging public policy initiatives, agreeing to sponsor various events, or initiating legislation. Through interacting in union discussions and actions, as well as through collective bargaining, union leaders and members come to understand that gain is achieved only by giving voice to their questions and concerns, struggling together to come up with appropriate solutions, and acting collectively and in concert with other groups to achieve them. Not only does the process of engagement often lead to positive outcomes—in itself providing an important example to working people— it also helps individuals to develop the skills necessary to act on those issues that are important to them.

Union contributions to the civic culture are of great value because unions struggle not only on behalf of their members but also on behalf of all working people. This is the way that unions achieve widespread support for the initiatives that will provide justice and security for their members as well as stability for the communities in which they live and work.

—Michael J. Polzin

See also Van Kleeck, Mary

Primary Sources

George Meany Memorial Archives, George Meany Center for Labor Studies, National Labor College, Silver Spring, MD (www.georgemeany.org/archives/home.html); Tamiment Library & Robert F. Wagner Labor Archives, New York University, New York (www.nyu.edu/library/bobst/research/tam/); Archives of Labor and Urban Affairs, Walter P. Reuther Library, College of Urban, Labor and Metropolitan Affairs, Wayne State University, Detroit, MI (www.reuther.wayne.edu/).

Current Comment

Kaufman, S. B. (Ed.). (1986). *The Samuel Gompers papers* (Vols. 1–4). Urbana: University of Illinois Press.

Levine, P. (2001). The legitimacy of labor unions. *Hofstra Labor & Employment Law Journal, 18,* 527–571.

Mishel, L., & Walters, M. (2003, August). *How unions help all workers* (Economic Policy Institute Briefing Paper No. 143 [On-line]). Available: www.epinet.org

Further Reading

Foner, P. S. (1975). *The history of the labor movement in the United States* (2nd ed., Vols. 1–8). New York: International Publishers.

Herman, E. E. (1998). *Collective bargaining and labor relations* (4th ed.). Upper Saddle River, NJ: Prentice Hall.

Rayback, J. G. (1966). *A history of American labor.* New York: Free Press.

Robinson, A. (1981). *George Meany and his times.* New York: Simon & Schuster.

LABOUR MOVEMENT AND SOCIAL WELFARE (CANADA)

Organized labour has played a significant part in Canadian history from the beginning of the nineteenth century, when workers in particular trades and local communities formed unions to influence employers, governments, and the public in matters affecting their working and living conditions. The earliest organizations were usually founded by workers in the skilled trades and often presented themselves as benefit associations designed to protect members and their families from the consequences of illness, injury, and unemployment. Although many workers engaged in protests, only a small number were successful in forming permanent labour organizations, especially in the era before the Trade Union Act (1872) confirmed the legality of unions in Canada.

The emergence of a broader labour movement was the result of local, regional, and national solidarities that demonstrated the common interests of workers in varied occupations and different locations. Among the more successful of these local labour movements was the Toronto Trades Assembly (1871), which helped launch two other groups. The Nine Hours League, established in 1872, campaigned for a reduction in the working day, and the Canadian Labour Union, formed in 1873, attracted support for a program of labour reform in the industrial towns of southern Ontario. Examples of other regional labour movements included the Provincial Workmen's Association (1879) in Nova Scotia and the Miners' Mutual Protective Association (1881) in British Columbia.

The Knights of Labor entered Canada from the United States in the 1880s and organized workers from many trades into 450 assemblies, mainly in Ontario, Quebec, and British Columbia; unlike the unions in the skilled trades, the Knights opened their ranks to workers of all kinds, including women, but with the significant exception of workers of Asian origin. The Trades and Labour Congress (TLC) of Canada (1883) aimed to become an inclusive national organization of labour, but did not establish a strong presence across the country until after 1902, when it defined itself primarily as a federation of the Canadian branches of unions affiliated with the American Federation of Labor (AFL) in the United States.

Until the 1950s, the Canadian labour movement remained divided in significant ways. Radicals and revolutionaries joined Canadian branches of the Industrial Workers of the World (1905) and later established the One Big Union (OBU, 1919) and the Workers' Unity League (1929–1936). More conservative and nationalist principles were represented in Quebec by the *Confederation des Travailleurs Catholiques du Canada* (1921), reorganized on a more secular basis in 1960 as the *Confederation des Syndicats Nationaux*, and by the All-Canadian Congress of Labour (ACCL, 1927–1940) elsewhere.

In the 1930s, Canadian branches of the Committee for Industrial Organization (CIO) were expelled from the TLC and formed the Canadian Congress of Labour (CCL; 1940). By absorbing the ACCL membership as well, the CCL anticipated the mergers that would later unite the TLC unions and the remnants of the OBU in a new labour organization, the Canadian Labour Congress (CLC, 1956).

By this time, the face of labour in Canada had changed significantly. A wave of unrest at the end of World War I broadened the agenda for labour organization and social reform, a moment symbolized by the Winnipeg General Strike (1919) and the labour wars in the coalfields of eastern and western Canada in the 1920s. Protests against unemployment in the Great Depression culminated in the famous On to Ottawa Trek (1935). These were followed by a wave of union organizing among workers in the new mass production industries neglected by older unions. The automobile workers' strike in Oshawa, Ontario, against General Motors (1937) was an early breakthrough for the cause of industrial unionism.

Union membership rose rapidly during and after the Second World War. New laws, such as the federal Industrial Relations Disputes Investigation Act (1948) and equivalent provincial laws, established the worker's right to representation and recognition in collective bargaining. Public employees secured similar rights in the 1960s and 1970s. These laws established a regime of industrial legality under which unions benefited from legal certification as bargaining agents while also accepting limits on their freedom of action. In Quebec, strikes such as the Asbestos Strike (1949) and the Common Front (1972) were major events in the development of a modern social democracy in that province. Meanwhile, at a time when women were entering the labour force at an unprecedented rate, the rise of public sector unionism among nurses, teachers, and civil servants strengthened the presence of women in organized labour. The Canadianization of the labour movement was also reinforced when districts of some international unions, such as the United Auto Workers, separated from their American partners. Despite structural changes in the labour force that undermined traditional sources of union strength, union membership in Canada has remained at levels in excess of 30 percent since the 1950s (31.2 percent in 2002). This is a marked contrast to the relative decline of organized labour in the United States during the same period.

At the beginning of the twenty-first century, the Canadian labour movement had a strong institutional presence in the form of the Canadian Labour Congress, whose affiliated unions represented 72.8 percent of the more than four million union members in Canada in 2002. In addition, the largest unions, such as the Canadian Union of Public Employees, the National Union of Public and General Employees, the Canadian Auto Workers, the United Steel Workers of America, and the United Food and Commercial Workers, had come to represent large and diverse groups of workers across the country. Local labour councils and provincial federations of labour remained significant in their own communities and regions, especially in the promotion of labour and social reform policies at the provincial level. Although most workers have not belonged to unions, the labour movement has campaigned not only for enhanced contract provisions for union members but also for social reforms that have benefited all workers. Historically, union campaigns focused on themes such as the regulation of child labour, fair wages on government contracts, worker's compensation, and minimum wages for women (and later all workers). In recent decades, unions have advocated the enactment of human rights, health, safety, and pay equity legislation and taken strong positions on social justice issues such as child poverty, education, literacy, and the rights of minorities. Landmark social reforms, such as unemployment insurance, old-age pensions, and universal medical care, have been among the causes that organized labour succeeded in elevating to the level of national priorities. Since the 1980s, the labour movement has been prominent in defending these social programs and other public services against radical downsizing, restructuring, and privatization. They have also demonstrated support for international solidarity among workers in an age of increased trade and economic integration. The extension of the union presence in the workplace has remained a challenge, especially in respect to nontraditional workers and rapidly changing sectors of the economy and the need for first-contract legislation and anti-strikebreaking laws. Although the most

significant historical achievements of organized labour have been in the realm of securing and defending the right to union membership and collective bargaining, support for a broader form of social unionism has also remained one of the hallmarks of the Canadian labour movement.

—David Frank

See also Economic Policy (Canada); Social Welfare (Canada): Before the Marsh Report; Social Welfare (Canada): Since the Marsh Report

Primary Source

Guide to Canadian Labour History Resources, Library and Archives Canada (www.collectionscanada.ca/2/26/h26-201-e.html).

Current Comment

Hobbs, M., & Sangster, J. (Eds.). (1999). *The woman worker, 1926–1929.* St. John's, NL: Canadian Committee on Labour History.
Kealey, G. S. (Ed.). (1973). *Canada investigates industrialism: The Royal Commission on the Relations of Labour and Capital.* Toronto, ON: University of Toronto Press. (Original work published 1889)
McKay, I., & Jackson, L. (Eds.). (1996). *For a working-class culture in Canada: A selection of Colin McKay's writings on sociology and political economy, 1897–1939.* St. John's, NL: Canadian Committee on Labour History.
Penner, N. (Ed.). (1973). *Winnipeg 1919: The strikers' own history of the Winnipeg General Strike.* Toronto, ON: Lorimer.

Further Reading

Forsey, E. (1982). *Trade unions in Canada, 1812–1902.* Toronto, ON: University of Toronto Press.
Heron, C. (1996). *The Canadian labour movement: A short history.* Toronto, ON: Lorimer.
Morton, D. (1998). *Working people: An illustrated history of the Canadian labour movement.* Montreal, QC, and Kingston, ON: McGill-Queen's University Press.
Palmer, B. D. (1992). *Working–class experience: Rethinking the history of Canadian labour, 1800–1991.* Toronto, ON: McClelland & Stewart.

LAND REFORM (MEXICO)

Although land reform began after the 1910 Mexican Revolution, the major part of the land was distributed during or after the government of Lázaro Cárdenas (1934–1940). The last major redefinition of the reform was in 1992, when the administration of President Carlos Salinas introduced constitutional changes to end land redistribution and allow market mechanisms to drive reconfiguration of land ownership. Mexico thus remains at the center of debate about the contributions of land reform to social welfare and the best means of broadening access to land.

Agrarian communities are heterogeneous in Mexico, which is a highly regionalized country. They differ in the quantity and quality of resources they possess and types of economic activities they can pursue—on and off the farm, for few households subsist on farm income alone. How they organize themselves also varies in ways best understood by qualitative historical and ethnographic studies at the local level. The political and economic objectives of the national state have been central to shaping land reform, but so has peasant mobilization. Demands "from below" do not necessarily reflect simple economic motivations. The indigenous movement's demand for autonomous control over a "territory" as a basis for collective cultural survival and self-determination is an important countercurrent to neoliberal "reform of the reform."

BEGINNINGS

One aim of postrevolutionary land reform was to calm conflicts rooted in the disentailment of the corporate landholdings of indigenous communities in the nineteenth century. Peasants opposed to the liberal reform laws of the 1850s seldom objected to individualized private land titles as such. Farmland was often possessed and inherited by individual families and only woodlands and pastures were actually used in common. But once communities were no longer legally recognized entities, the reform broke down their defenses against loss of land to outsiders. The power relationships of the era provoked widespread dispossession even where no great estates coveted the former commoners' assets. In extreme cases, indigenous communities were completely displaced by invading ranchers of the *Mestizo* (mixed-race) ethnic category that became the foundation for a new national identity, based on the idea that "modern" Mexico should turn its back on its indigenous past.

This strategy of "Mexicanization of the Indian" (or assimilation) influenced the type of land reform favored by postrevolutionary state-builders, within a new political order geared to demobilizing regional peasant movements. Although the new agrarian laws allowed for restitution of land taken away from former indigenous communities that could produce colonial titles, the state preferred to make land grants (*dotaciones*) to create a new kind of agrarian community, the *ejido*. This strategy turned the beneficiaries into dependent political clients of the regime. In some cases, claimants from former indigenous communities split into agrarian (*agrarista*) factions that favored the creation of an *ejido,* and commoner (*comunero*) factions that demanded restitution with restoration of a common property regime. Government preferences left the *agraristas* in the dominant position until changes in the 1980s allowed a resurgence of *comunero* activism.

Ejido land remained state property. Beneficiaries enjoyed permanent rights of use, inherited by a nominated successor subject to ratification by the *ejido* assembly. Legally, the land could not be divided on the death of the holder, nor be sold or rented in the long term. Although these restrictions were widely violated, they remained significant. When *ejido* land was sold, its value was lower than in a free market, and it could not be used as security for a bank loan.

Each *ejido* is administrated by an elected president (*comisariado ejidal*) with a team of treasurer, secretary, and other functionaries. A parallel "vigilance council" supervises the performance of these officeholders. Although these groups might correspond to rival factions, it is not unusual for the vigilance council to be elected on the same slate as the *comisariado ejidal,* for local agrarian communities possess some de facto autonomy in organization. Another example involves local residents who are not landholding members of the agrarian community (*ejidatarios*), but enjoy informal access to its resources.

But under Mexico's Institutional Revolutionary party (*Partido Revolucionario Institucional,* or PRI), which monopolized the national government for 70 years until 2000, top-down control prevailed in appointments to regional and national positions in state-recognized peasant organizations. This "system" underlay a prevalence of "boss rule," administrative corruption, and development project failure within the *ejidos* themselves, despite continuous struggles to resist impositions and create peasant organizations independent of state control.

In the first phase of postrevolutionary land reform, large-scale capitalist farms and agro-industries were assumed more productive and the reform was a political tranquilizer. In central Mexico, small plots were distributed to provide supplementary income to rural workers, while revolutionary leaders acquired their own estates in northern Mexico.

REFORM RETHOUGHT AND EXTENDED

The number of land reform beneficiaries doubled from 801,392, organized in 4,189 communities, or *núcleos agrarios,* in 1930 to 1,601,392, organized in 14,683 *núcleos agrarios* by 1940. By this stage, 28,922,808 hectares had been distributed, more than three times the total up to 1930. This reflected a radical reorientation. President Cárdenas allowed the workers on large estates to claim the land. He moved the *ejido* to center stage in rural development; the state would provide technical assistance and credits for the development of commercial peasant farming.

Yet older thinking was not abandoned completely. "Mexicanization of the Indian" remained a goal and Cárdenas favored collective organization of farming to preserve the productivity of capitalist agro-industry. Some cooperatives were created to manage processing and marketing, but these activities generally remained in private hands. This could lead to serious conflicts, but Cárdenas sought to develop the land reform sector without alienating the private sector completely.

COUNTERREFORM, CRISIS, AND RESPONSE

Cárdenas's successors drastically reduced state support for the land reform sector. Where *ejidatarios* found themselves unable to work high-quality land due to lack of credit, they rented it to local entrepreneurs and migrated to the United States or worked as day laborers. Corn farmers sowing more marginal land intensified inputs of household labor in the face of declining income from falling prices, thereby helping to maintain the flow of cheap food toward rapidly expanding cities.

By the end of the 1960s, however, further adjustment was impossible and growing agrarian militancy menaced political stability. The government of Luis Echeverría (1970–1976) responded with a more technocratic version of the Cárdenas model. New land expropriations included foreign-owned capitalist farms in northern states, turned into collective *ejidos.* More collective *ejidos* were formed in tropical lowland regions whose colonization had been energetically promoted as an alternative to land redistribution. The state also restored credits and technical assistance to the much more numerous individual peasant farms, deepening its intervention by creating new *ejido* agro-industries.

This approach continued under President José López Portillo (1976–1982) and had a positive impact on rural incomes and social welfare. But pervasive corruption still limited the gains of individual farmers and brought many of the new state enterprises to insolvency. Mexico also became increasingly subordinate in an international agro-food system dominated by U.S. interests. The contradictions of this pattern of development proved insuperable as the country was impelled by debt crisis into a decade of structural adjustment.

REFORMING THE REFORM

According to Salinas's neoliberal model, once *ejidatarios* became full owners of their land, private credit would reinvigorate production for those farmers able to survive in a competitive environment, and the burden of corruption would be removed with the end of "state paternalism." The reform was a two-stage process. A new department (the *Procuraduría Agraria*) would regularize the tenure of what were now 3.5 million beneficiaries, providing the *ejido* assembly agreed that the process should begin. Once rights were certified, assemblies were empowered but not compelled to fully privatize the land. By December 2001, 77 percent of agrarian units had been regularized, and nearly 60 million hectares certified or titled. But since land reform communities occupied 103 million hectares in 1990, these figures reveal the existence of many intra- and inter-community land conflicts that defied consensual resolution.

Deepening crisis in the whole farm economy following implementation of the North American Free Trade Agreement (NAFTA) in 1994, reinforced by continuing neoliberal policies after President Vicente Fox's defeat of the PRI in 2000, makes it difficult to identify any clear gains from the Salinas reform. Most *ejidos* have not proceeded to full privatization, so land transferred solely on the basis of certification retains a lower market price.

COUNTERCURRENTS

The 1994 rebellion of the Zapatista Army of National Liberation prompted a wave of land invasions in Chiapas, but new official land reform was mainly "market-assisted": Groups of "co-proprietors" received land purchased by the state and were not granted *ejidos*. Nevertheless, the *Zapatistas'* indigenous autonomy demands reflected a movement far broader than themselves or Chiapas.

Despite the antagonism of the victors of the revolution, the communal-property-holding indigenous community survived alongside the *ejido*. Global developments, such as the International Labour Organization (ILO) Convention 169 on Indigenous and Tribal Peoples (1989), increased the pressure on states to grant special rights to indigenous groups during the 1980s and 1990s. Indigenous leaders, frequently drawn from the ranks of bilingual school-teachers, originally trained to promote the dissemination of "national" (*Mestizo*) culture, were not new figures on the political stage. Their politics have been and remain varied. But an increasing self-assertion on the part of indigenous people, including those of Chiapas, was already visible before the 1990s. Although legislation sought to encourage concessions of communal resources such as woodlands to private capital, indigenous communities increasingly demanded support for their own self-managed enterprises. The results of efforts by communities to organize the exploitation of their own resources have been mixed, but the stakes in struggles for self-determination are high and support forthcoming from transnational nongovernmental organizations. Many of Mexico's indigenous peoples live in tropical regions in the front line of transnational corporations' new interests in biodiversity alongside mining, logging, and ecotourism.

Indigenous demands for autonomous territories governed according to their own cultural norms go beyond control of economic resources and challenge all previous conceptualizations of land reform. But machete-wielding *ejidatarios* also delivered a surprise to national society in 2002, defeating a plan backed by exceptionally powerful elite interests to build a new Mexico City airport on their land. This revealed the continuing meaningfulness of the popular symbols of the revolutionary struggle for land and the collective historical memory they embody for a broad spectrum of the 28 percent of Mexicans who still live in rural areas. The noneconomic value of land, as a measure of social worth and anchor for place-based identities, is also important in the behavior of land markets. Peasants transacting (or refusing to transact) in land do so according to local social and cultural logics that still require elucidation even in the era of globalization.

—John Gledhill

See also Aboriginal People and Policy (Mexico); Food Assistance Policy (Mexico); Neoliberalism, Social Programs, and Social Movements (Mexico); Peasant Movements and Social Programs (Mexico); Rural Education (Mexico)

Primary Sources

The *Archivo General Agrario*, housed in the offices of the *Secretaría de la Reforma Agraria* in Mexico City, is now under the purview of the *Registro Agrario Nacional*, (RAN). The *Centro de Investigaciones y Estudios Superiores en Antropología Social* (CIESAS) signed an agreement with RAN in 1996 to catalogue and facilitate research on the collection, which can be accessed on-line (www.ran.gob.mx/archivos/AGA/index.html). Additional documentation can be found in the archives of regional offices of government departments, court records, and individual agrarian communities.

Current Comment

Cornelius, W. A., & Myhre, D. (Eds.). (1998). *The transformation of rural Mexico: Reforming the* ejido *sector*. La Jolla: University of California, San Diego, Center for U.S.-Mexican Studies.

Snyder, R., & Torres, G. (Eds.). (1998). *The future role of the* ejido *in rural Mexico*. La Jolla: University of California, San Diego, Center for U.S.-Mexican Studies.

Stephen, L. (2002). *Zapata lives! Histories and cultural politics in southern Mexico*. Berkeley: University of California Press.

Further Reading

Gledhill, J. (1991). *Casi nada: A study of agrarian reform in the homeland of cardenismo.* Albany: State University of New York, Institute for Mesoamerican Studies.

Rello, F. (1986). *El campo en la encrucijada nacional.* Mexico City: Secretaría de Educación Pública.

Ronfeldt, D. (1973). *Atencingo: The politics of agrarian struggle in a Mexican* ejido. Stanford, CA: Stanford University Press.

Villafuerte Solis, D., Díaz, S. M., Franco, G. A., del Carmen García Aguilar, M., Rivera Farfán, C., Lisbona Guillén, M., & Morales Bermúdez, J. (1999). *La tierra en Chiapas: Viejos problemas nuevos.* Mexico City: Plaza y Valdés.

LATHROP, JULIA CLIFFORD
(1858–1932)

Julia Clifford Lathrop emerged as a leading activist for social welfare programs in the United States and around the world in the early decades of the twentieth century. Among her activist associates, Lathrop was distinctive in stressing openness to the values and practices of many cultures, though strongly rooted in the tradition of humanistic Western social science. Lathrop was a respected leader at Hull House, the famous Chicago settlement house founded by Jane Addams. She was a close friend of Addams and her involvement in the influential Hull House social and political network would sustain her work as a social reformer. From Hull House, she went to Washington, D.C., in 1912 to become the first woman to head a federal bureau, the U.S. Children's Bureau. Lathrop extended the vision of the Hull House reformers to the federal level by creating a space for female activists to develop policies and programs that addressed the needs of children and families. Lathrop emerged as a leading child welfare expert and innovator in not only the United States but also in many other parts of the world.

Lathrop was born in Rockford, Illinois, in 1858. Her parents were active in Republican party politics and fought for women's suffrage. Her father played a leading role in the passage of the Illinois' women's suffrage law. Julia Lathrop attended Rockford Female Seminary for one year and finished her education at Vassar College in 1880. After college, she went home and for 10 years worked as a secretary in her father's law office; for some of that time she studied the law.

Restless and wanting more out of life, Lathrop joined Jane Addams at Hull House in 1890, a year after its opening. Lathrop organized and led one of the first educational groups at the settlement, called the Plato Club, which met on Sunday afternoons to discuss and debate the meaning of Plato's work. Early on, Julia Lathrop became part of Jane Addams's inner circle. She mentored many of the youngest residents, who found her accessible, charming, and a great listener.

In 1892, the governor of Illinois appointed Julia Lathrop to the Illinois Board of Charities, a commission that supervised county institutions. She began her public career in social welfare by visiting facilities for the insane, where she found despicable conditions. She searched for models of good patient care from other parts of the world and learned of a model of "family care" for the mentally ill as used in Europe and visited Belgium, Scotland, and France to observe them. Impressed with the positive impact of these programs on patients, she advocated for their adoption in the United States.

Lathrop shared opposition with other Progressive Era reformers to the practice of political patronage in public institutions. In 1901, after 8 years of service, she resigned from the Illinois State Board of Charities to protest the Illinois governor's awarding of jobs in public institutions to his political supporters. Two years later, she regained her position under another governor and remained in the post until 1909.

During this period, Lathrop became a leading voice in the campaign to create a juvenile court in Chicago. Progressive reformers studied children and their developmental needs and understood that the general court system did not provide children and young offenders with appropriate judicial hearings. Lathrop argued that a special juvenile court could assess a child's circumstances and prescribe suitable rehabilitative services to prevent further delinquency or antisocial behavior. In 1899, Chicago established the nation's first juvenile court, which became a model for other states.

In 1912, Julia Lathrop went to Washington, as the appointed chief of the newly created U.S. Children's Bureau. The Children's Bureau was given the mandate to "gather information on all matters concerning the welfare of children." Lathrop's wit, diplomacy, brilliance, and support from her network of female social reformers spanning many nations secured her new position.

As bureau chief, Lathrop demonstrated strategic skills early in her tenure. Seeking a noncontroversial focus, she chose birth registrations as the bureau's first campaign. She understood that accurate birth records were necessary to document climbing infant mortality rates in the United States. The bureau organized women's groups to collect statistics in their neighborhoods and compare those numbers with those collected by local governments. Her focus on infant mortality ultimately culminated in the Sheppard-Towner Maternity and Infancy Act of 1921, which provided health education and services through federal grants-in-aid to the states.

In addition to her emphasis on maternal and child health, Lathrop focused on child labor and lobbied for a federal child labor law. Under Lathrop's leadership, the bureau supported mothers' pensions to financially support widows and some single mothers so they could stay home to raise their children. Lathrop and other reformers wanted to reform the administration of mothers' pensions to increase funding and to ensure equitable payments for women from rural and urban areas. She argued for improving the quality of services and widening eligibility criteria.

The Children's Bureau worked with reformers, government officials, and individuals from around the world to learn how children's needs were being addressed. It organized conferences where child welfare reformers could share ideas and it became an international clearinghouse for information on the health and welfare of mothers and children.

After her retirement from the Children's Bureau in 1921, Lathrop continued her activist career. She took trips to Latin America, Europe, and the Soviet Union. Her international repute as a child welfare expert was recognized in 1925, when she was appointed to the League of Nations Advisory Child Welfare Committee. Lathrop believed that the creation of the committee signaled that the world was alert as never before to the needs and rights of children.

Julia Clifford Lathrop, an early and influential resident of Hull House, was one of the most important female reformers of the early twentieth century. Her brilliant leadership helped develop some of the first federal health and welfare programs for women and children. When she died in 1932, many of the world's social welfare leaders took note of the loss of this humble and influential citizen of the world.

—Barbara Machtinger

See also Child Welfare Policy (United States); Hull House (United States); Mothers' Pensions (United States); Settlement Houses (United States)

Current Comment

Addams, J. (1974). *My friend, Julia Lathrop.* New York: Arno. (Original work published 1935)

Lathrop, J. (1918). *Provision for the care of families and dependents of soldiers and sailors.* New York: Academy of Political Science.

Further Reading

Muncy, R. (1991). *Creating a female dominion in American reform, 1890–1935.* New York: Oxford University Press.

Skocpol, T. (1992). *Protecting soldiers and mothers: The political origins of social policy in the United States.* Cambridge, MA: Harvard University Press, Belknap Press.

LOWELL, JOSEPHINE SHAW (1843–1905)

Philanthropist, social reformer, and a leader of the American scientific charity movement, Josephine Shaw was born into a wealthy and prominent abolitionist Boston family that in the 1850s resettled in Staten Island, New York. During the Civil War, the teenaged Josephine volunteered her services to the U.S. Sanitary Commission. "The Sanitary" taught Josephine the virtues of organization and efficiency in dispensing aid to the Northern soldiers. A brief marriage to Colonel Charles Russell Lowell, Jr., ended with his death in battle. A young widow with a daughter, Lowell volunteered her services to the fledging New York State Charities Aid Association in 1871. There she specialized in studies analyzing the rise of pauperism, considered a massive social problem throughout the 1870s. In 1876, Governor Samuel Tilden, impressed with Lowell's influential reports on pauperism, appointed her to fill a vacant spot on the New York State Board of Charities (SBC), a regulatory agency established in 1867.

Commissioner Lowell, the first woman to occupy a state office in New York, became a well-known specialist on charity and welfare concerns. During her 13-year tenure on the SBC, Lowell inspected, reported on, and recommended changes for many different kinds of institutions for dependent populations. Her major concerns included advocating separate asylums and reformatories for poor women. She worked closely and successfully with various interest groups and state legislators in an attempt to make social welfare services and institutions operate more efficiently in New York. In the late 1870s, along with civil service reformers, Lowell led a campaign against the strong New York City political machine, which she saw as administering "outdoor relief" ineffectively and to support a political agenda.

A few years after she was appointed a commissioner of the New York State Board of Charities, Lowell felt her work was unable to address the problems found among "private" charities. She believed too many private charities in New York City were giving what she saw as "indiscriminate relief" that might do more harm than good. She believed that the charity organization movement, which advocated welfare based on scientific and business principles, offered an important solution to reining in the social chaos unleashed as the forces of industrialization, urbanization, and immigration disrupted social harmony in the Gilded Age.

Based on her beliefs, the 38-year-old Lowell founded the Charity Organization Society of the City of New York (COSCNY) in 1882. The organization quickly became a major part of New York City's governing structure and a trendsetter in social welfare policy. Under Lowell's guidance and leadership, the COSCNY pioneered important research on poverty, developed and refined the "casework" approach to social welfare, and promoted the professionalization of social work. A social activist, Lowell worked hard for labor arbitration, founded the Consumer's League of the City of New York in 1892, and played a prominent role in the anti-imperialist movement of the early twentieth century.

Josephine Shaw Lowell died in New York City on October 12, 1905. Lowell's legacy is mixed. She is remembered more for her advocacy of harsh policies toward the poor than for her solid record of developing

modern preventive programs addressing the roots of poverty. Any fair assessment of Lowell's career, however, would acknowledge her flexible and innovative approaches to solving the problems of the new industrial era.

—Joan Waugh

See also Charity Organization Societies (United States)

Current Comment

Lowell, J. S. (1884). *Public relief and private charity.* New York: Putnam.
Stewart, W. R. (1974). *The philanthropic work of Josephine Shaw Lowell.* Montclair, NJ: Patterson Smith. (Original work published 1911)

Further Reading

Waugh J. (1997). *Unsentimental reformer: The life of Josephine Shaw Lowell.* Cambridge, MA: Harvard University Press.

LURIE, HARRY LAWRENCE (1892–1973)

Harry Lawrence Lurie provided leadership and direction in social work from the 1920s until the 1960s. Lurie contributed to the development of social work in the areas of practice, education, and research. A thread woven through these contributions was a continuing call for social workers to recognize their dual responsibilities for both individual casework and social change. Lurie was among the first to argue that social workers needed to recognize the importance of both individual human behavior and the larger social environmental systems that directly affected the well-being of individuals, families, groups, and communities. Lurie's career spanned many of the vacillations and uncertainties encountered in defining the social work profession, including whether its primary focus should be individual and internal issues or social and external issues. Lurie was able to serve as a bridge in the profession, especially during the 1930s and 1940s, between many mainstream social workers who aligned themselves primarily with individual-focused casework and a rank and file movement much more committed to social-environmental and social-change orientations.

Lurie was born in Latvia in 1892 and immigrated to the United States in 1898, settling in Buffalo, New York, as a result of the family's persecution (the family was Jewish) and its search for economic prosperity. These roots in persecution and poverty became hallmarks in his development as a social worker and his lifelong commitment to the social and economic justice ideals of the social work profession.

As a student at the University of Michigan, Lurie was introduced to the philosophy and activism of the progressive movement as well as a scientific approach to assessing and addressing social concerns. After completing his education, in 1925 Lurie became superintendent of the Jewish Social Service Bureau in Chicago and taught courses at the University of Chicago School of Social Service Administration. In Chicago, Lurie was influenced heavily by the work and philosophy of Jane Addams and the settlement house movement. While he was teaching at the School of Social Service Administration, the school's leaders, including Edith and Grace Abbott and Sophinisba Breckinridge, reinforced Lurie's progressive ideas. During the 1920s, as an increasing number of social workers began to align themselves with the theories and practices of individual, psychoanalytically driven casework, Lurie became a model for social workers to adhere to their roots in social and economic justice.

Following his time in Chicago, Lurie moved increasingly into social work leadership positions. In 1930, Lurie returned to New York as executive director of the Bureau of Jewish Social Research in New York City. In 1935, the bureau merged with the Council of Jewish Federations and Welfare Funds (CJFWF), a federated fund-raising organization somewhat like the United Way. After the merger, Lurie became the CJFWF executive director. This position provided Lurie with a national platform to advocate his views on social work but, at the same time, placed him squarely in the mainstream of the social work profession.

Throughout the 1930s, largely as a result of the Great Depression, Lurie witnessed and vigorously supported the return of many social workers to recognition of the importance of addressing social environmental, economic, and political realities. During this period, Lurie became a bridge between the social work mainstream and the emerging more radically oriented social work rank and file movement. This radicalism was most intensely reflected in the call by movement members for social workers to adhere to their social change roots. Most notably, movement members called for protection of worker rights, employment security for all workers, unionism, and a redistribution of wealth and resources from the wealthiest to the most needy. The rank and filers were often at odds with the social work mainstream. It was in this context that Lurie functioned as a conduit between the more conservative social work mainstream and this nascent more radical wing of the profession. Within the mainstream, Lurie participated in and provided leadership for the National Conference of Social Work and the American Association of Social Workers. His close affiliation with the rank and filers included serving on the editorial board of their journal, *Social Work Today,* and addressing numerous conferences and meetings organized by members of the movement. Lurie also employed such notable leftists as Jacob Fisher while executive director of CJFWF.

The election of Franklin Roosevelt as president and the bold, though short-lived, New Deal, led by social worker Harry Hopkins, provided Lurie with hope that social workers were shifting their focus toward assuming responsibility for social and environmental responses to human need. His optimism, however, subsided when New Deal programs that Lurie and rank and filers believed should be permanent solutions to unemployment and destitution began to be dismantled in the mid 1930s and early 1940s.

With the coming of World War II, Lurie's focus increasingly shifted to the global arena, while retaining a commitment to social and economic justice that Lurie believed was so central to social work. Lurie's focus on the global scene, however, was also reflected clearly in his continuing concerns domestically for workers' and immigrants' rights, as well as the need for tolerance of human differences and recognition of the strengths of cultural diversity.

Lurie's later years during the 1950s and 1960s reflected his position as senior leader as well as constructive critic of social work. His continuing efforts to find a balance in the profession for social as well as individual interventions included his service as a project consultant for the "community organization" component of Werner Boehm's landmark 1959 curriculum study of social work education. In 1962, the Council on Social Work Education formally accepted community organization as a major social work method along with individual and group practice. Lurie also served as editor of the 1965 edition of the *Encyclopedia of Social Work.*

Lurie's 40-year career in social work serves as an exemplar of the social work profession's struggle to find a true balance between concern for individuals and attention to the social and economic roots that result in the growth of individual problems. This struggle remains critical to social work today.

—Joe M. Schriver

See also Abbott, Edith; Abbott, Grace; Hopkins, Harry Lloyd; Rank and File Movement (United States); Settlement Houses (United States)

Primary Sources

The Harry Lawrence Lurie Papers are located at the Social Welfare History Archives, University of Minnesota, Minneapolis.

Other primary source materials are in the author's personal collection.

Current Comment

Lurie, H. L. (1932). Spreading relief thin. *Social Service Review, 5,* 223–234.
Lurie, H. L. (1935). The dilemma of the case worker. *Social Work Today, 3,* 13–15.
Lurie, H. L. (1931). [Review of the book *A changing psychology in social case work by V. Robinson*]. *Social Service Review, 5,* 488.

Further Reading

Fisher, J. (1980). *The response of social work to the Depression.* Cambridge, MA: Schenkman.
Leighninger, L. (1987). *Social work: Search for identity.* Westport, CT: Greenwood.
Schriver, J. M. (1987). Harry Lurie's assessment and prescription: An early view of social workers' roles and responsibilities regarding political action. *Journal of Sociology and Social Welfare, 14,* 111–127.
Schriver, J. M. (1987). Harry Lurie's critique: Person and environment in early casework practice. *Social Service Review, 61,* 514–532.

M

THE MARSH REPORT (CANADA)

The *Report on Social Security for Canada,* more commonly known as the "Marsh Report," was presented to the Advisory Committee on Reconstruction in February 1943 and forwarded to the Canadian House of Commons in the following month. Named after the principal author and research adviser, Leonard Charles Marsh (1906–1982), the report offered a broad overview of existing Social Security legislation and practice at both the dominion (federal) and provincial levels of government, made suggestions for improvement and expansion of these programs, and argued for the creation of a planned, integrated, and comprehensive system of Social Security.

The Marsh Report reflected the social-democratic values of its author, Leonard Marsh, a graduate of the London School of Economics (1928). Marsh had been an associate of Sir William Beveridge, who went on to write *Social Insurance and Allied Services* (1942), the famous "Beveridge Report" that outlined the future British welfare state. Marsh immigrated to Canada in 1930, when he became director of social research at Ontario's McGill University.

The Marsh Report covered a wide variety of subjects including unemployment and health insurance, pensions, and supports for widows and orphans; outlined interprovincial and municipal differences in the scope and extent of social services; and illustrated the stark differences between urban and rural Canada. The central theme was the need to provide for organized and collective provision against individual risks—such as unemployment, sickness, old age, and premature death. This was underscored by the imperative to establish a "national minimum" that, it was believed, would lead to the "direct elimination of poverty." Of considerable importance, the report suggested that the majority of supports be funded largely on a contributory insurance basis, as opposed to being financed solely from general taxation revenues. Yet even with this bifurcated approach, the estimated cost of the proposals amounted to more than a billion dollars.

The report was very much a product of the times, being closely linked to the bitter legacy of the Great Depression, the generally positive experiences with wartime collective planning and increased government involvement in the economy, and, finally, the aspirations of postwar reconstruction, economic growth, and full employment. The contemporary experiences of other countries in the British Empire—particularly New Zealand—together with the broad ideological and popular influence of the United Kingdom's Beveridge Report (1942) also had a direct impact on the creation, content, and direction of the Marsh Report. In many ways, with its emphasis on planning in both economic and social spheres, the Marsh Report was an important precursor of what came to be known as the Keynesian welfare state.

For a variety of reasons, the suggestions were not implemented in a comprehensive and integrated manner. Cost was certainly a factor. Ideology was another. And given the division of powers between the dominion and provincial levels of government, there was a lack of constitutional clarity as to which level of government would have responsibility (and financial liability) for the implementation of the suggestions. Nevertheless, important elements and themes of the report were eventually adopted, albeit in a largely piecemeal fashion.

—*Timothy Wild*

See also Federalism and Social Welfare Policy (Canada); Social Welfare (Canada): Since the Marsh Report

Primary Source

Marsh, L. C. (1975). *Report on Social Security for Canada.* Toronto, ON: University of Toronto Press. (Original work published 1943)

Further Reading

Guest, D. T. (1997). *The emergence of Social Security in Canada* (3rd ed.). Vancouver: University of British Columbia Press.

Horn, M. (1976). Leonard Marsh and the coming of a welfare state in Canada: A review article. *Histoire Sociale, 9*(17), 197–204.

Kitchen, B. (1986). The Marsh Report revisited. *Journal of Canadian Studies, 21*(2), 38–48.

MEDICINE AND POPULAR HEALING PRACTICES IN COLONIAL MEXICO

There is no doubt that "unofficial" medicine was practiced continually outside of official circles in colonial Mexico, but that story is difficult to unearth given the limitations of documentation. The history of medicine in colonial contexts is a relatively new and growing field. Historians of such diverse areas and eras as nineteenth century Australia, British India, and colonial New England, New France, and New Spain have only begun to tap the richness of colonial medicine for explaining imperial power relations, and for that reason any attempt at a comprehensive study of colonial Mexican medicine and medical practices is by necessity a preliminary one. Though important works have appeared over the last three decades, they have remained relatively isolated from one another, and tend to concentrate on official practices in urban areas. A growing body of evidence and a growing number of historians interested in such matters will no doubt enhance this field.

"OFFICIAL" MEDICINE IN COLONIAL MEXICO

Despite problems of gaps in investigation and evidence, it is possible to trace the main outlines of official and popular medical practices in colonial Mexico. Official medical practice mirrored that of Spain, from the range and responsibilities of different practitioners to the methods of medical regulation. As in Spain, the medical profession employed a number of different practitioners, including physicians, surgeons, apothecaries, phlebotomists, nurses, and midwives. Although their training and duties varied widely, all medical practitioners shared certain common characteristics. First, they were part of the colonial bureaucratic structure and as such, it could be argued, served to support Spanish imperial power and promote Hispanization, social control, and patriarchy through the spread of Western medical concepts. "Colonial" medicine meant European medicine, and indigenous people and women in general were legally forbidden to practice. Indigenous medicine was, in theory, to have no place in colonial Mexico, though as we shall see, it did have a significant influence on certain practices, and it by no means ended with the imposition of the colonial power structure. Second, following Western medical tradition, the theory guiding practitioners' actions derived mainly from the writing of ancient Greek and Roman authors, particularly that of Hippocrates and Galen. These authors taught that disease resulted from an imbalance in the body's fluids, which consisted of "four humors": black bile, yellow bile, blood, and phlegm. Most treatments, therefore, aimed at reestablishing a harmonious balance within the body by employing techniques that altered the body's fluids, including bloodletting, administering enemas, raising blisters, or prescribing medicines that would induce the patient to vomit, sweat, or urinate.

Medical professionals in colonial Mexico were also subject to certain moral and ethical standards that reflected values peculiar to the multiracial, largely Catholic culture of colonial Mexico. Within the higher echelons of the medical profession, practitioners had to prove their "blood purity" (*limpieza de sangre*), a concept developed during the Christian "reconquest" of the Iberian Peninsula after seven centuries of Moorish rule. In order to establish their *limpieza*, potential practitioners had to present a certificate issued by the Inquisition that stated that their family and their ancestors were not "tainted" by the blood of "Indians," Jews, or Moors, or by denouncement of the Inquisition. Only those of pure blood, it was argued, were capable of true morality and therefore to be trusted with such delicate matters as the diagnosis and treatment of disease. Morality was also proven by the practitioners' demonstrated commitment to charity. In the Catholic context of colonial Mexico, acts of charity were thought to be among the most fundamental ways to show religious faith, for they constituted the "good works" necessary to gain salvation. Curing the sick, considered one of these acts, thus had moral and religious connotations: It was a duty to be provided to the less fortunate, and it held the promise of eternal salvation for the caregiver. In order to establish and maintain a respectable place in the medical hierarchy, practitioners often treated the "poor sick" (*los pobres enfermos, los miserables*) free of charge, and sometimes donated thousands of *pesos*' worth of medicines to the poor as well as to charitable and religious institutions, including hospitals, convents, monasteries, orphanages, and homeless shelters. This context helps to explain the relatively extensive network of at least 128 colonial hospitals that were spread throughout Mexico and that treated all variety of physical and even mental illness. Many of these hospitals had been established through charitable funds and were run by religious orders, and provided an important stabilizing influence in colonial society.

THE MEDICAL PROFESSIONS

In the official medical hierarchy, physicians occupied the highest position, for they were the most educated of all practitioners, and their work was considered more an intellectual than a manual labor. Beginning in 1252, medical doctors in Spain were required to have university degrees, and had to pass a series of complicated and expensive examinations before receiving their medical license. Their education required little in the way of clinical knowledge but consisted mainly of reading and analyzing ancient medical texts, and this curriculum continued with little modification in Mexico after the first chair of medicine was established at the University of Mexico in 1578. For the most part, physicians' work consisted largely of examining patients and writing prescriptions, diagnoses, and descriptions of cases, with little in the way of hands-on treatment.

That treatment was applied by other medical professionals: surgeons, apothecaries, phlebotomists, midwives, and nurses, who carried out the more practical duties of administering medicine to the populace. Surgeons had no formal education but underwent a 4- to 5-year apprenticeship in which they learned to make incisions, to puncture abscesses, to remove tumors, organs, and gangrenous limbs and, for the less specialized, to cut hair and shave beards. Phlebotomists, or those specialized in bloodletting, could receive a license after a 3-year apprenticeship, while nurses and midwives had no formal requirement for education or training. Rather, they learned their trade either in hospitals or informally from other practitioners. Their low-status position meant that general regulations among these professions were rarely enforced, and practitioners themselves tended to reflect the racial diversity of colonial Mexican society.

Apothecaries, in contrast, occupied a middling status: they gained licenses after a 4-year apprenticeship, but they had to be able to read Latin, which implied some formal educational training and a certain level of literacy. Apothecaries' main duties revolved around the preparation and dispatch of medicine. Although historians often dismiss pre-modern therapies as backward and ineffective, the making of medicines was in fact a complex and laborious process, which grew more precise over the centuries due to increasing use of chemical laboratory equipment. The materials contained in apothecary shops also attest to the complexity of colonial medicine. Apothecary shops throughout Mexico carried over 1,500 different types of medicines drawn from the plant, animal, and mineral kingdoms. Most of the medicines followed the standard European pharmacopoeia and had to be imported from Europe, Asia, or the Middle East. However, pharmacists also made use of locally grown herbs, many of which were indigenous to Mexico. These herbs had been part of Aztec and other indigenous medical traditions, and sixteenth century Spanish doctors and friars such as Bernardino de Sahagun, Francisco Hernandez, and Nicolas Monardes made concerted efforts to learn about and record them. Beginning in the seventeenth century, pharmacists were also able to take advantage of a growing internal economy and interregional transport to use these local products, which included herbs such as Yerba Buena for intestinal parasites, Taray bark for dropsy, Tacamahaca resin for colds and rheumatism, Liquidambar balsam for head- and stomachaches, and Mechoacán root, which was said to cure no less than eight major diseases, including bubonic plague, scrofula, dropsy, jaundice, and malaria. In this way, some indigenous medical knowledge was able to survive by being incorporated into the official colonial pharmacopoeia.

REGULATION OF MEDICINE: THE *PROTOMEDICATO*

Medical practice in colonial Mexico was thus regulated by a host of laws and stipulations that in theory provided standards for practitioners' education and training, the ethics of their practice, and their social and racial standing. Yet how did the system function in practice, and how were these laws to be enforced? That job fell to a medical board called the *Protomedicato*, a medieval Spanish institution composed of three appointed doctors, whose duty it was to root out "ignorant" practitioners and ensure the "dignity and honor" of the medical profession. The first formal office of the *Protomedicato* in the New World was set up in Santo Domingo in 1517, and a full tribunal was set up in Mexico City in 1646. The *Protomedicato* was highly centralized: It resided in the capital, and it combined both executive and juridical power. It was the only institution allowed to issue medical licenses, which occurred only after a practitioner had traveled to Mexico City and passed a formal examination. The *Protomedicato* was also charged with organizing

"inspections" of medical practitioners and their premises on a regular basis. In this way, the *Protomedicato* served as a microcosm of colonial authority to buttress the stability of the Spanish Empire.

POPULAR HEALING IN COLONIAL MEXICO

Despite the *Protomedicato*'s power, however, there is clear evidence that the medical establishment rarely functioned as it was supposed to. Logistical difficulties and corruption led to many problems within the medical establishment, not least of which was the fact that there were not nearly enough licensed practitioners to serve the population of Mexico, and this was true throughout the entire colonial period. Despite the early establishment of medical chairs, the University of Mexico graduated relatively few students, and even fewer doctors, surgeons, or pharmacists ever gained a *Protomedicato* license. In 1812, in Mexico City (where licensed practitioners would have been most numerous) there were only two licensed physicians, one surgeon, and three pharmacists per 10,000 people.

Clearly, licensed practitioners could not possibly meet population demand, and although several sixteenth century physicians wrote medical treatises of "folk medicine" geared for the nonspecialist, a number of "unofficial" or illicit practitioners stepped in to fill the need for medical treatment. The most prominent of these were the local *curanderos*, or healers, both male and female, who combined a variety of indigenous, African, and European techniques, materials, and symbols in their practice, and often drew from religious and mystical traditions as well. Though labeled by many historians as "superstitious quacks," these practitioners were crucial members of colonial Mexican society. Not only did they bring medical care and solace to the majority of Mexico's population, they also were important conduits for the preservation of both indigenous and African medicoreligious traditions. More work remains to be done in studying the practices of these *curanderos*, but preliminary evidence indicates their extreme importance.

—*Paula De Vos*

See also Social Welfare (Mexico): Before 1867; Substance Abuse Policy (Mexico)

Further Reading

De Vos, P. (2001). *The art of pharmacy in seventeenth- and eighteenth-century Mexico.* Unpublished doctoral dissertation, University of California, Berkeley.

Hernández Saénz, L. M. (1997). *Learning to heal: The medical profession in colonial Mexico, 1767–1831.* New York: Peter Lang.

Lanning, J. T. (1985). *The royal Protomedicato: The regulation of the medical professions in the Spanish Empire* (J. J. TePaske, Ed.). Durham, NC: Duke University Press.

Risse, G. (1987), Medicine in New Spain. In R. L. Numbers (Ed.), *Medicine in the New World: New Spain, New France, and New England* (pp. 12–63). Knoxville: University of Tennessee Press.

MENTAL HEALTH POLICY (CANADA)

The history of the development of mental health services in Canada parallels that of Great Britain, France, and to a lesser extent, the United States of America. Beginning in the 1830s, when county asylums were built in Great Britain, many jurisdictions in British North America, which was to become the Dominion of Canada, were starting to build their own places of refuge or "asylums" for the mentally ill. As "asylums" grew, they could not keep pace with the flood of admissions. Eventually, overcrowding and the deteriorating conditions in the asylums made it difficult to use "moral therapy," an influential, benign treatment modality for the mentally ill popularized by Quakers. Crumbling, overcrowded, and understaffed asylums became scarcely better than the infamous "madhouses" of Europe.

NINETEENTH CENTURY

Canada in the nineteenth century was segregated according to ethnic, religious, and language origins. English Canada at that time was basically agrarian, rural, and underdeveloped. Temporary quarters in condemned or outdated buildings, such as prisons or cholera "fever" hospitals, served as mixed-use institutions for the mentally ill, the physically ill, and as temporary and permanent penal placements. The first true asylums in English Canada were the New Brunswick Lunatic Asylum, built in 1847, and the

Toronto Lunatic Asylum, established in 1850. In French Canada, Quebec was influenced by France and its unique colonial administration. A general hospital, the Hotel Dieu, began as early as 1639. The Hotel Dieu Hospital provided care for "indigents, the crippled, idiots, and lunatics." In 1845, Beauport, or the Quebec Lunatic Asylum, opened its doors to the mentally ill as a separate and permanent institution.

In 1864, 3 years before the confederation of Canada, a British Colonial Office report stated that "in the North American colonies of Great Britain insanity almost engrosses public attention and care." This was a reference to the care given to over 1,500 insane persons then confined to Crown-supported asylums established in Quebec and Ontario, which were under the supervision of the Board of Inspectors of Prisons, Asylums, and Public Charities.

It is most notable that, even before Canada became a nation, a policy shift toward the mentally ill occurred, which was characterized by a sense of responsibility for them. The care, protection, and treatment of the mentally ill would take place in asylums. The 1830s and 1840s already had seen the beginnings of asylum construction in Ontario, Quebec, and New Brunswick. Prior to the construction of these asylums, the mentally ill in Canada and elsewhere in the civilized world, if considered harmless, were often left to wander at will as beggars. They were stigmatized as public nuisances at best. At worst, they were often detained and incarcerated in restrictive environments such as jails and poorhouses, where they were subject to deficient diets and substandard shelter, and where no attempts at "rehabilitation" were made. In French Canada the religious orders of the Roman Catholic church provided the same function of containment of the mentally ill. Only a few privileged mentally ill persons were cared for at home or domiciled in privately run rest homes.

Toward the middle of the nineteenth century, social movements for the mentally ill, of clerical, philanthropic and humanitarian, political, and journalistic dimensions, were very much apparent. Under the influence of the moral therapy philosophy of the Quakers in Great Britain, the Tuke brothers, Quakers in the English city of York, began the York Retreat for the mentally ill. It treated the mentally ill in a humanitarian manner, creating therapeutic surroundings of a noncustodial and noncoercive nature. Treatment sometimes had an evangelical fervor and life in the asylum was similar to what one would find in a typical middle-class English family of the time.

The use of moral therapy for the mentally ill in Canada was influenced by the Tuke brothers and by Dorothea Dix, a strong advocate for humane treatment of the mentally ill in the United States. Reforms in the care and treatment of the mentally ill in Canada and elsewhere had grown up in the wake of the European Enlightenment and a wave of new ideas about social responsibility in Canada. It was influenced by British thought as well as by the creation of asylums in the United States.

TWENTIETH CENTURY

By 1900, the prospects for the care of the mentally disordered in Canada were especially bleak. Within a few decades, treatment of the mentally ill had turned almost full circle. The process began with the introduction of positive and humane reforms in care and treatment, which were sufficiently successful to convince specialists of their merit. But often, within months, new admissions poured into the asylums until overcrowding and inadequate financial support became a stifling affront to any sincere attempt to apply the ideal of caring and treatment as characterized by moral therapy. The inevitable consequence was to offer custodial care in the absence of any alternatives. The ambitious vogue of reforming conditions for the mentally disordered had quietly subsided. Many of the new asylums in Canada became so large that good treatment was nearly impossible. The Hospital St. Jean de Dieu in Montreal, for example, housed nearly 6,000 patients in the 1950s. The principles of moral therapy could no longer be applied. The period from 1900 to 1945 could be characterized as a time of nihilism as well as hope in the treatment of the mentally ill. Nihilism was reflected in the asylum superintendents' annual reports, which emphasized budgetary, accounting, and administrative details. In previous decades, therapy, humanitarian and rehabilitative efforts, and positive outcomes had been stressed. Hyperbolic references to cure rates of 80 to 90 percent were common in earlier reports.

The twentieth century saw dramatic changes in the treatment of the mentally ill. First, moral therapy was abandoned. Then biological or neuropathological explanations of mental illness became prominent, bringing psychiatry closer to mainstream medicine. The First World War (1914 to 1918) had a strong impact on psychiatric thinking. Unlike previous conflicts fought by professional soldiers, large numbers of civilians were recruited into the military and many of them were incapacitated by "shell shock," a condition we now realize and recognize as a form of "posttraumatic stress disorder." Hospital and other mental health services that had focused on chronic psychosis and dementias now were called upon to treat "normal" people back from the war. An example of this would be the Hospital for the Insane, in Whitby, Ontario. While still under construction in 1918, it was converted to a military hospital to treat mentally ill military personnel returning to Canada from World War I. A voluntary movement, the Canadian Mental Health Association (CMHA), began in 1918. The CMHA educated the public about mental illness and its causes.

In 1930, a Canadian Royal Commission on Health Services Report concluded that although provincial psychiatric hospitals were somewhat better than jails or county poorhouses in treating the mentally ill, they were found wanting from therapeutic or humane accommodation perspectives. By the 1930s, provincial psychiatric institutions were deteriorating due to overcrowding and a corresponding lack of resources. The Royal Commission Report of 1930 recommended $20 million of capital expenditures to upgrade existing facilities, a sum that was unrealistic owing to the economic distress resulting from the worldwide economic depression. From the decade of the 1930s through the end of World War II, Canadian mental health services can be characterized as years of neglect of the mentally ill. Moral therapy and humane care shifted to an emphasis on social control of patients. Keeping the mentally ill away from the public in segregated geographic sites became a social objective.

THE GROWING INFLUENCE OF THE FEDERAL GOVERNMENT

The Second World War saw increased awareness of the mental health needs of the Canadian people and increased funding for services and treatment. Constitutional considerations and federal involvement were paramount in this transformation of thought, attitude, and action. In 1945, the Canadian Department of National Health and Welfare became more involved in mental health. The Canadian government offered National Health Grants (Mental Health Grants) in 1948 whereby amounts up to $7 million ($4 million the first year, $5 million the second year, and $7 million for the third and subsequent years) were provided to the provinces. Priority was given to training of mental health professionals. This had the effect of raising care and treatment standards in mental hospitals as well as increasing the existing pool of mental health professionals throughout the entire Dominion of Canada.

THE MOVE INTO THE COMMUNITY

The province of Saskatchewan, which pioneered universal Medicare in Canada, also pioneered the move to community psychiatry, regionalization, and the deinstitutionalization of the mentally ill. The innovative 1957 Saskatchewan Plan was a forerunner of the CMHA's and the federal government's ambitious mental health policy, More for the Mind, which was developed in 1965. The main recommendations included, first, regionalization of personnel and facilities for the mentally ill, and second, comprehensive care of the mentally ill within the community. More for the Mind advocated the treatment of mental illness on the same basis as physical illness and demanded that standards of care and facilities for anyone with any illness should be equal. It highlighted the grossly inadequate services for the mentally ill and the appallingly bad conditions in mental hospitals. At this time, a Royal Commission on Health Services, chaired by Justice Emmett Hall, which had been created under the Progressive Conservative party administration of John Diefenbaker, issued a report that recommended sweeping reforms in mental health treatment and services. It proclaimed, "that henceforth all discrimination on the distinction between physical and mental illness, and the organization and provision of services for the treatment and attitudes upon which these discriminations are based, be disavowed for all time as unworthy and unscientific." Reformers argued that the mental hospitals should not be seen as institutions for custodial care and that

sound treatment, however protracted, should be their main purpose.

By 1970, 86 general hospitals offered services to 3,000 patients needing mental health care. It soon became apparent that general hospital psychiatric units did not provide good treatment for those suffering from severe and chronic mental illnesses. In 1978, McKenzie and Company stated that provincial psychiatric hospitals and general hospital psychiatric units were serving different patient populations. Although this two-tiered system was and still is a reality in Canada, the number of patients discharged from general hospitals with a diagnosis of functional psychosis increased from approximately 28 percent to 40 percent from 1971 to 1986.

In short, the overlap between the two types of hospital patients is increasing as general hospitals accept more severe cases. In other words, what started as an encouraging drop in hospital bed numbers brought about by the success of new treatments begun in the 1960s has brought a reduction in services offered to those most in need of full-time hospitalization along with a sharp decline in outpatient services. By 1976, there were 15,000 patients in provincial psychiatric hospitals and close to 6,000 in general hospitals. Community care had very much become a feature of the mental health system in Canada. In the mid twentieth century, the largely provincially funded institutions made up almost all of the mental health services in Canada. Over the four decades from 1960 to 2000, the psychiatric hospitals almost completely disappeared.

At the start of the twenty-first century, remaining psychiatric hospitals are shells of their former selves, often poorly funded appendages of other facilities such as general hospitals. The seriously mentally ill are still not welcome at the general hospitals and the inadequacy of mental health facilities resources harkens back to the days of Dorothea Dix in the nineteenth century. Her proselytizing efforts on behalf of the mentally ill influenced significantly the development of mental health services in Canada in the form of psychiatric hospitals. The closing of such institutions has resulted in seriously mentally ill patients filling jails or living on the streets. In Canada, as elsewhere, it has become impossible to provide equivalent services in an era of deinstitutionalization, which can more accurately be described as dehospitalization.

The costs of the new "system," community care, and psychiatric inpatient facilities, increased rather than decreased as promised by advocates for change. Soon rising costs became a political consideration. Operational principles based on government parsimony articulated that if jurisdictions in Canada could get by with half as many beds, why not a quarter or even less. In fact, the number of psychiatric beds per 100,000 people in Canada was reduced from about 430 in 1959 to about 50 today, an eight-fold decrease, with targets of 30 beds per 100,000 persons. Increasing community-based services has been significant but it has been clearly unable to provide community care equal to care received by the general medical care consumers. Inadequate funding for the mentally ill, a disadvantaged social group, has become an integral feature of the landscape created by all provincial governments in the Dominion of Canada.

Psychiatry in Canada, as elsewhere, has emphasized genetics, biochemical disorders, and complex physiological processes in the treatment of mental illness. But other Canadian mental health professionals see mental illness as a social rather than a medical problem.

Recognition of the complex nature of mental illness and its bio-psycho-social dimensions is beginning to result in important changes in Canadian mental health policy. Mental illness is seen as an inextricably interrelated psychological, social, and biological phenomenon requiring new treatment approaches. But politics will determine funding and ultimately the effectiveness of the community-care system for the mentally ill and whether or not adequate inpatient care will be created for this vulnerable population.

—*Sam Sussman*

See also Health Policy (Canada)

Current Comment

Canadian Mental Health Association, (1963). *More for the mind.* Toronto, ON: Author.

Hurd, H. M. (1916). *The institutional care of the insane in the United States and Canada.* Baltimore: Johns Hopkins University Press.

Colonial Office. (1864). *Report No. 885/3.* London: Her Majesty's Stationery Office.

Royal Commission on Health Services report. (1963). Ottawa, ON: Queen's Printer. (Original work published 1930)

Further Reading

Blom, D., & Sussman, S. (1989). *Pioneers of mental health and social change, 1930–1989.* London, ON: Third Eye.

Shortt, S. E. D. (1986). *Victorian Lunacy: Richard M. Bucke and the practice of late nineteenth-century psychiatry.* Cambridge, UK: Cambridge University Press.

Simmons, H. G. (1989). *Unbalanced mental health policy in Ontario, 1930–1989.* Toronto, ON: Wall and Thompson.

Sussman, S. (1998). The first asylums in Canada: A response to neglectful community care and current themes. *Canadian Journal of Psychiatry, 43,* 260–264.

MENTAL HEALTH POLICY (UNITED STATES)

Before 1800, the problems posed by mental illnesses were relatively minor and generally of little public concern. The number of mentally ill persons was small, and such individuals were generally cared for by their families or by local officials who assumed responsibility for their welfare. Confinement in institutions was rare. Insane persons without families or resources received the same treatment as sane paupers; they were either boarded out with families or kept in public almshouses. Insanity became an issue of public concern only when persons with mental illnesses did not have access to the basic necessities of life, or when their violent behavior threatened others. At that time, the concept of "social policy," involving the creation of systematic structures to deal with individual and group distress and dependency, was largely absent.

After 1800, however, new circumstances ultimately led to reliance on some form of institutional care. Demographic changes, including immigration, urbanization, and population growth, helped to undermine older informal mechanisms to care for mentally ill persons. In 1820, only one state hospital for the mentally ill existed in the United States; by the Civil War virtually every state had established one or more public institutions.

The creation of institutions reflected an extraordinarily optimistic view of the nature and prognosis of mental illnesses. Early nineteenth century American psychiatrists, following such figures as Philippe Pinel in France and William Tuke in England, maintained that insanity followed the violation of the natural laws that governed human behavior and was linked as well with immorality, improper living conditions, or other stresses that upset the natural balance. Since insanity followed improper behavioral patterns associated with a defective environment, therapy had to begin with the creation of a new and presumably more appropriate environment. Institutionalization was a sine qua non because it shattered the link between the patient and the environment that had precipitated the disorder. In an asylum or mental hospital, patients could be exposed to a judicious amalgam of medical and moral (i.e., psychological) therapy. From this model, asylum physicians drew an obvious conclusion; insanity was as curable as, if not more curable than, most somatic illnesses.

Early nineteenth century psychiatrists claimed that nearly 90 percent of cases of recent insanity (defined as insane for a year or less) were cured. Chronicity was neither inherent nor inevitable, but followed the failure to provide acute cases with the benefit of moral therapy. There was some evidence that individuals benefited from hospitalization. In a follow-up study of slightly over 1,000 patients discharged as recovered on their only or last admission, 58 percent never again were hospitalized. In general, early and mid nineteenth century hospitals, most of which remained relatively modest in size, did not have a large long-stay population; most patients were institutionalized for only brief periods lasting from 3 to 9 months.

The low proportion of institutionalized chronic patients was due in part to the pattern of funding and, to a lesser extent, the exclusion of senility from psychiatric diagnostic categories. Because local communities were required to pay for the upkeep of their residents in state hospitals, many of them preferred to retain mentally ill and aged senile persons in local almshouses. Hence, for much of the nineteenth century a significant proportion of mentally ill persons lived either in the community or in municipal almshouses.

Disillusioned by a system that divided authority and left many mentally ill persons in poorhouses, states—led by New York and Massachusetts—adopted legislation that made all such persons wards of the state. These laws, however, had unanticipated consequences. Local officials redefined senility in psychiatric terms and began to transfer aged senile persons from almshouses (which in the nineteenth century served in part as old-age homes) to state hospitals. During the first half of the twentieth century, the proportion of long-stay patients increased dramatically as hospitals increasingly functioned as old-age homes. The aging of the hospital population mirrored a different but related characteristic of the institutionalized, namely, the presence of large numbers of patients whose abnormal behavior reflected an underlying somatic pathology. Both factors contributed to a dramatic increase in hospital populations, a development that tended to weaken their therapeutic functions. Nevertheless, release rates for nonelderly patients tended to improve between the two world wars. Thus, mental hospitals developed a dual character that included both custodial and therapeutic functions.

By 1940, the daily census at public mental hospitals exceeded 400,000; the peak of nearly 560,000 would be reached in the mid 1950s. Despite its size, this vast hospital system was in disarray. A decade and a half of financial neglect, due largely to the impact of the Great Depression of the 1930s and the global conflict of the 1940s, simply exacerbated already severe problems. The stage was set for fundamental change.

After 1945, public mental hospitals—institutions that had been the cornerstone of public policy since the early nineteenth century—began to lose their social and medical legitimacy. This was hardly surprising. Indeed, after World War II the prevailing consensus on mental health policy slowly began to dissolve. Developments converged to reshape public policy during these years. First, a series of journalistic exposés seemed to reveal fundamental defects in the nation's mental health system. Second, there was a shift in psychiatric thinking toward a psychodynamic and psychoanalytic model emphasizing life experiences and the role of socioenvironmental factors. Third, the experiences of World War II appeared to demonstrate the efficacy of community and outpatient treatment of disturbed persons. Fourth, the belief that early intervention in the community would be effective in preventing subsequent hospitalization became popular. Fifth, a faith developed that psychiatry could promote prevention by contributing to the amelioration of social problems that allegedly fostered mental diseases. Sixth, the introduction of psychological and somatic therapies (including, but not limited to, psychotropic drugs) held out the promise of a more normal existence for patients outside of mental institutions. Finally, the federal government began to assume an enhanced social welfare role. The passage of the National Mental Health Act of 1946 and subsequent creation of the National Institute of Mental Health not only began to diminish the authority of state governments, but also hastened the transition from an institutionally based to a community-oriented policy.

During the 1950s, support for a community-based policy steadily increased. By 1959, there were more than 1,400 clinics serving over half a million individuals, most of whom were not severely mentally ill. Indeed, claims about the efficacy of community care rested on shaky foundations. A community-based policy assumed that severely mentally ill patients had homes and families to care for them. In 1960, however, 48 percent of hospitalized patients were unmarried, 12 percent were widowed, and 13 percent were divorced or separated. Hence, the assumption that patients would reside in the community with their families while undergoing rehabilitation was hardly realistic.

The rhetoric of community care and treatment carried the day in the 1950s and after. From the creation of the Joint Commission on Mental Health and Illness in 1955 and the publication of its influential *Action for Mental Health* (1961) to the passage of the Community Mental Health Centers Act of 1963, the advocates of a community-oriented policy succeeded in forging a consensus regarding the desirability of diminishing the legitimacy of mental hospitals and strengthening community facilities. Yet, the growth in the number of community mental health centers did little to help the severely mentally ill. Most centers made little effort to provide aftercare services and continuing assistance to persons with severe and long-term mental illnesses. They preferred instead to emphasize psychotherapy, an intervention especially adapted to individuals with emotional and personal problems.

During the 1960s, the attack on institutional care began to bear fruit, and hospital populations declined rapidly after 1965. Nevertheless, what subsequently became known as deinstitutionalization was largely the result of serendipity rather than conscious policy choices. The passage of Medicare and Medicaid hastened the exodus of elderly patients from mental hospitals to chronic nursing homes as states shifted expenditures to the federal government. Similarly, Social Security Disability Insurance (SSDI), Supplemental Security Income for the Aged, the Disabled, and the Blind (SSI), Food Stamps, and public housing programs provided resources to discharged patients to live in the community, and states hastened to take advantage of these federal entitlements.

Deinstitutionalization had positive consequences for some of the nation's population with severe and persistent mental illnesses. Under the best of circumstances, however, deinstitutionalization also created difficult problems. The diminished federal role and decline in funding during and after the Ronald Reagan presidency, the fact that the shrinkage of institutional populations and the closing of state hospitals did not result in the transfer of funds to community support programs, the appearance of a new group of young adult chronic patients with a dual diagnosis of severe mental illness and substance abuse, and the multiplication of programs and absence of formal integrated linkages complicated the lives of the severely mentally ill as well as those responsible for providing care and treatment.

In the closing decades of the twentieth century, policy fragmentation was evident. Severely mentally ill persons require a variety of support services as well as psychiatric and medical care. The decentralized nature of the American political system encouraged competing rivalries between local, state, and national governments; each level of government sought to shift costs and expenditures to other levels. The result was an inability to define and implement a policy that would meet the needs of a population whose illness often led to disability.

—*Gerald N. Grob*

See also Health Policy (United States); Rush, Benjamin; Substance Abuse Policy (United States), Supplemental Security Income (United States)

Primary Sources

Records of the Alcohol, Drug Abuse, and Mental Health Administration (Record Group 511), National Archives & Records Administration, College Park, MD; Washington National Records Center, Suitland, MD; John F. Kennedy Papers, John F. Kennedy Library, Boston; Records of the American Psychiatric Association, Archives of the American Psychiatric Association, Washington,

DC; American Foundation for Mental Hygiene Papers, Institute for the History of Psychiatry, Weir Medical College of Cornell University, New York; Adolf Meyer Papers, Chesney Medical Archives, Johns Hopkins Medical Institutions, Baltimore.

Current Comment

Beers, C. W. (1908). *A mind that found itself.* New York: Longmans, Green.

Bucknill, J. C. (1876). *Notes on asylums for the insane in America.* London: J. & A. Churchill.

Deutsch, A. (1948). *The shame of the states.* New York: Harcourt, Brace.

Mechanic, D. (1999). *Mental health and social policy: The emergence of managed care.* Boston: Allyn & Bacon.

Further Reading

Grob, G. N. (1994). *The mad among us: A history of the care of America's mentally ill.* New York: Free Press.

Tomes, N. (1984). *A generous confidence: Thomas Story Kirkbride and the art of asylum-keeping, 1840–1883.* New York: Cambridge University Press.

Torrey, E. F. (1988). *Nowhere to go: The tragic odyssey of the homeless mentally ill.* New York: Harper & Row.

MEXICO CITY POOR HOUSE

Latin America's largest welfare institution, the *Hospicio de Pobres*, was founded in 1774 as the centerpiece of a bold experiment to eliminate begging and reform the poor. Reflecting contemporary European attempts to discipline the poor, the Mexico City Poor House was designed to confine the disorderly street people of the huge capital and transform them into pious Christians and productive workers. Yet the experiment never worked in practice as originally conceived. Gradually shifting its focus from forcibly enclosing a mixed-race, adult population to sheltering an increasingly White, female, young, and voluntary clientele, the asylum had minimal impact on the urban poor. The gap between the poorhouse mission and its implementation points to the unreliability of depending on policy statements to understand the nature of welfare institutions. It also suggests some peculiarities of poor relief in a multiracial Hispanic environment.

PHILOSOPHY

The poorhouse experiment embodied new ideas about poor relief that were sweeping the Catholic as well as the Protestant world. The vice-regal decree that founded the asylum in 1774 criminalized begging, a significant break from the Christian tradition that sanctified poverty and considered almsgiving a means of salvation. This decree was not an attack on religion; on the contrary, the poorhouse proposal originated with Mexican priests and, in its early years, the institution was jointly administered by the church and the state. Because both secular and religious reformers believed that indiscriminate handouts encouraged idleness, they sought to channel alms to a central establishment that could rationalize the distribution of aid and shape the recipients to serve a larger utilitarian project. Ineligible for assistance were robust youth (labeled vagrants), who were to be immediately placed in the military, public works, or domestic service. Other indigents, although considered deserving of help, needed to be institutionalized until they could be "rehabilitated." Combining social services with correction, the poorhouse was supposed to serve simultaneously as a homeless shelter and nursing home; as a school for manners, religious indoctrination, and vocational training; and as a workhouse, reformatory, job placement agency, and prison.

THE EXPERIMENT IN PRACTICE (1774–1806)

This plan proved difficult to implement. During its first two decades, the poorhouse did confine many of Mexico City's bothersome beggars. It contained nearly 1,000 inmates during its heyday in the late eighteenth century. Reflecting the city's multiracial population of street people (and unlike the many racially segregated institutions in the United States), it integrated Indians, Mestizos, and Whites under one roof. But the asylum also sheltered paupers who were not part of the original target population. From the start, city residents used the institution for their own ends. Propertied citizens and authorities turned to it for help in correcting unruly youth or subordinates, and the destitute incorporated it into their survival strategies. Orphans, single mothers, and homeless families welcomed temporary refuge, and the "shamefaced" poor (genteel Whites who had fallen on hard times) demanded preferential housing in upstairs rooms separated from the common dormitories. Under pressure from its willing clients, the poorhouse admitted people who had never begged on the streets, among them healthy unemployed men and women who should have been excluded as vagrants. Whether they came by force or voluntarily, few inmates stayed long. Those that did were often genteel ladies who viewed the poorhouse as their home. If some inmates were disciplined through labor in the asylum's workshops or placement as apprentices and servants, these were more often young people than adults. The vocational training offered by the institution was quite weak. So was the "moral correction" of inmates, for popular culture proved stubbornly resilient. The utopianism of the poorhouse founders soon gave way to the realization that it was easier—albeit prohibitively expensive, given the high level of demand—to provide lodging, food, and medical care than to reform adults.

As the years passed, the poor house barely tried to discipline its inmates. As the capital's street people resisted internment and as dwindling resources forced the staff to focus on the city's "worthiest" poor, the asylum catered to those who entered voluntarily. Showing little enthusiasm for its original goal of social control, the staff instead considered institutional aid as a privilege best reserved for unprotected women and orphaned children, the elderly and disabled, and the "shamefaced" poor. Although poverty in Mexico particularly afflicted people of Indian descent, the inmates were disproportionately Whites. Thus, centuries-old notions about who deserved aid reasserted themselves to distort the asylum's stated mission. So did contemporary concerns. As they saw the caste system crumbling around them, the institution's board members and staff were less interested in reforming the multiracial populace that thronged the streets of the capital city than in preventing the downward mobility and public begging of Whites. Far from seeking to reduce social inequalities, the poorhouse thus reinforced the racial hierarchies and prejudices of Mexican society.

TRANSFORMATION (1806–1906)

The institution's transformation was hastened by its opening of a boarding school for orphans, known as the Patriotic School, in 1806. Even as the poorhouse suffered from the financial crises that accompanied

Mexican independence in 1821, its elementary school grew to become the core of the institution. Although republican leaders repeatedly tried to revive the goals of suppressing mendicity and deterring vagrancy, the persecution of beggars did not strike a responsive chord among many residents of Mexico City. By tolerating its street people and continuing to give alms, they showed the persistence of the customary "moral economy" that shaped the relations between rich and poor. The original plan folded in the face of resistance by beggars, donors, the asylum's personnel, penurious Whites, and even the capital's police, who rarely arrested those who solicited alms. Thus, modern, utilitarian notions of poor relief did not set deep roots in Mexico. In contrast, the school for orphans flourished because it built upon the charitable tradition of caring for abandoned children, and appealed both to the growing sentimentalization of childhood and to the enlightened view that education was necessary to avert future pauperism.

Recognizing the failure of the poorhouse experiment, Mexico City authorities re-legalized begging in 1871. In 1884, a new set of bylaws defined the asylum as a boarding school for orphans from ages 2 to 10 for boys and 2 to 14 for girls. Now known as the House of Children (*Hospicio de Niños*), it provided elementary schooling and vocational training for some 500 mostly White children until its demolition in 1906 as part of a plan to beautify the center of Mexico City. According to Ann Blum, these students became the city's "welfare elite." They received the latest equipment for training in industrial arts such as photography and weaving. They were paraded at public festivities as a symbol of governmental benevolence. Upon graduation, they found jobs in the city's factories, printing presses, and offices.

EVALUATION

Despite some well-known success stories, inspection reports continued to reveal that the institution often fell short of the prescribed orderly regime and high level of instruction. Notwithstanding the good intentions of many dedicated staff members, neglect, harsh punishment, and occasional scandals plagued the perennially underfunded and understaffed institution, where children were often warehoused rather than nurtured. Waste and corruption also undermined the dream of achieving efficiency and savings through centralization. The institutionalization of paupers, whether adults in the asylum's early years or children in its later years, was far from an ideal solution to Mexico's social problems.

Over the century and a quarter of its existence, the Mexico City Poor House also manifested other trends shared by asylums throughout the Western world. For example, its employees quickly became an entrenched bureaucracy that took up an increasing portion of the poorhouse rooms and revenues, thereby diverting resources away from its intended clientele. Its staff and governing board became increasingly feminized as the nineteenth century progressed. The involvement of the church with the institution decreased, and the teaching of religion declined. Yet liberal rhetoric about the benefits of having the government assume control for public assistance did not always translate into visible improvements for the institution's inmates. Indeed, the poorhouse experiment demonstrates the limited power of the state to implement social reforms.

—*Silvia Marina Arrom*

See also Philanthropy (Mexico); Social Welfare (Mexico): Before 1867

Further Reading

Arrom, S. M. (2000). *Containing the poor: The Mexico City Poor House, 1774–1871.* Durham, NC: Duke University Press.

Blum, A. S. (2001, July). Conspicuous benevolence: Liberalism, public welfare, and private charity in Porfirian Mexico City, 1877–1910. *The Americas, 58*(4), 7–38.

Haslip-Viera, G. (1986). The underclass. In L. S. Hoberman & S. M. Socolow (Eds.), *Cities and society in colonial Latin America* (pp. 285–312). Albuquerque: University of New Mexico Press.

MOTHER AND FAMILY PROGRAMS (MEXICO)

The health and welfare of mothers and children has always been of central importance to both reformers and the Mexican government throughout the twentieth century. The ideology of republican motherhood, coming out of the late eighteenth century Enlightenment, effectively linked political and social reform to the status of mothers and children. It would not be until a liberal reform government took power in 1856, however, that the Mexican state officially took responsibility for their health and welfare, declaring them to be duties of the state. The centrality of women through their role as mothers would increase in political significance in the late nineteenth century. Twentieth century programs had their origins in nineteenth century reforms. Because children were viewed as the wealth of Mexico, government and private reformers alike believed that this resource could only be protected through the proper training of mothers. Child welfare, and by extension, maternal-child welfare, were important symbols of national progress throughout the twentieth century.

PORFIRIAN WELFARE

Porfirio Díaz, president of Mexico from 1876 to 1911, continued the centralizing process of state welfare begun earlier in the nineteenth century. An 1881 law grouped beneficence centers into three categories: hospitals, orphanages, and educational/correctional facilities. Catholic charities remained active in welfare work and it was private Catholic charity organizations, administered and staffed predominantly by elite women, that would shift the focus of welfare work to poor mothers and their children. Female reformers, such as Carmen Romero Rubio de Díaz, wife of the president, founded schools, including the *Casa Amiga de la Obrera,* an educational facility for the children of working mothers. Other groups organized day care centers, mothers' clubs, and cooperatives. Charity organizations, focusing on children as the future wealth of the nation, targeted mothers to ensure that they had "proper" mothering techniques. Public welfare run by the state coexisted with private, often religious, charitable activity as well.

THE REVOLUTION

The Mexican Revolution (1910–1920) created conditions that made more broad-scale public aid necessary. In 1914, Mexico City's Department of Public Beneficence established Sanitary Brigades to tend to those wounded in fighting. In 1915, a newly formed Department of Aid built shelters and educational centers for the homeless and for children orphaned by the violence of the war. Because the middle class was affected by the upheaval, the city agency set up aid centers and public dining halls. In 1917, the new Constitution officially mandated that all charity and welfare organizations were under state control, thereby officially coordinating all beneficent activities.

After the upheaval of the Revolution, welfare activities refocused attention on mothers and children. Revolutionary reformers, like their Porfirian predecessors, believed that children were the wealth of the nation, and believed that this resource could be harnessed only through the proper training of mothers. In 1921, reformers convened the First National Child Congress to discuss the role the state should play in training "fit" mothers and educating children. The congress greatly influenced policymakers, who in 1922 created the School Hygiene Service and in 1923, two hygiene centers for children. These programs focused on health care and instituted vaccination programs for children. In 1927, the Mexico City Department of Public Beneficence constructed a shelter for homeless children.

In addition to public-sector programs, private women's societies organized on behalf of maternal and child welfare. In 1929, the Association for the Protection of Childhood, established by female reformers, focused on distributing school breakfasts and creating centers for the prenatal care of pregnant women. Their activities would become models for future state-operated welfare programs.

The year 1929 also saw the creation of the Mexico City Child Hygiene Service, a precursor of the federal Secretariat of Public Assistance (*Secretaría de Asistencia Pública,* or SAP), created by President Lázaro Cárdenas in 1937. SAP's mission was to combat poverty by integrating the poor as a class, rather than just mothers and children, into an industrializing Mexico, an ambitious goal. By the 1940s, given political realities, SAP shifted its focus back to the welfare of poor mothers and children.

MOTHERS AND THE MODERNIZATION PROJECT

In 1943, President Manuel Avila Camacho merged the Secretariat of Public Assistance with the Secretariat of

Health to form the Secretariat of Health and Welfare (*Secretaría de Salud y Asistencia,* or SSA) at the same time the government was beginning the Mexican Social Security system. Social Security protected male workers for the most part, following European models that paid little attention to the needs of workingwomen. SSA provided assistance to those not covered under Social Security—mothers, children, adolescents, the elderly, and the unemployed. It built hospitals, education centers, and shelters for the poor and homeless, the majority of which were located in Mexico City.

Social welfare reformers once again sought to train mothers to educate their children in ways that would make them hardworking and productive modern citizens. Mother-child centers taught poor women proper hygiene and how to care for their children. Family dining halls were established to provide poor families with nutritious meals at which proper hygiene and cleanliness were discussed. In addition to maternal care programs, SSA also maintained schools and day care centers for the children of working mothers, which provided safe places for workingwomen to leave their children during the day. Young girls were taught vocational skills, such as sewing and hairstyling. These services provided women with the means to earn money and gave their children safe schools and day care. Children learned skills needed to participate in a modern economy.

SSA also organized mothers' clubs through the mother-child centers to teach mothers vocational skills. Volunteers staffed the mothers' clubs, effectively bringing private philanthropic activity under the aegis of the state. Although this training did not provide women with skills needed for industrial labor, it did enable them to work from their homes. They learned various small industries or skills (*pequeñas industrias*) such as sewing and candy making that would allow them to earn money yet still stay at home and care for their children. Policymakers acknowledged the need for poor mothers to work, so they sought to train women to work in ways that did not fundamentally challenge what policymakers considered to be women's primary role: being mothers.

In 1961, the government reorganized maternal-child welfare programs under the National Institute for Child Protection (*Institut Nacional de la Protección*

Infantil Propriété Industrielle, or INPI). It reaffirmed the state's dedication to the protection of children, but refocused policy to support families rather than mothers and children. In 1968, the Mexican National Institute for the Attention of Children (*Institución Mexicana de Asistencia a la Niñez,* or IMAN) was established to organize and direct all welfare activities for children. Both the INPI and the IMAN were dedicated to the protection of children, but the INPI now concentrated on child nutrition programs. In 1974, all welfare activities were recentralized under INPI, which again rededicated activities to children, families, and communities. It was the precursor to the National System for the Integrated Development of the Family (*Sistema Para el Desarrollo Integral de la Familia,* or DIF), the current state agency serving mothers, children, and families.

DIF AND THE ECONOMIC CRISIS

Beginning in the 1970s, Mexico's economic miracle began to crumble. Poverty levels increased as the economy faltered. The government moved to restructure public assistance once again. DIF was created to coordinate government and private welfare initiatives focused on the family rather than just on mothers and children. DIF focused on the prevention of poverty. Many of its initiatives were linked to private and international aid programs. For example, since 1954, the United Nations Children's Fund, UNICEF, has sponsored public health initiatives such as vaccination and sanitation programs and clinics for pregnant and lactating women, which today work with DIF. In the 1980s and 1990s, child nutrition programs were expanded and efforts have been made to assist the homeless, especially homeless children. DIF began to ask for greater community input into its planning processes.

Throughout the twentieth century, the health and welfare of mothers and children has been of paramount importance to reformers and to the Mexican government. Policymakers have seen children as the wealth of the nation and believed that their health and well-being was an important marker of national progress. Although the balance between public and private support for mothers, children, and families has shifted throughout the twentieth century, Mexico's

goal of supporting its vulnerable citizens has been consistent.

—*Nichole Sanders*

See also Child Welfare Policy (Mexico); Social Reform and State-Building (Mexico); Social Welfare (Mexico): Since 1867; Women and Social Welfare (Mexico)

Primary Sources

Archivo Histórico de la Secretaría de Salubridad y Asistencia (AHSSA), *Archivo de la Secretaría de Salubridad y Asistencia* (SSA), and *Ramos Presidenciales,* all located in the *Archivo General de la Nación*, Mexico City.

Current Comment

Asistencia, the official journal of the *Secretaría de Asistencia Pública.*

Further Reading

Bliss, K. (2001). *Compromised positions: Prostitution, public health and gender politics in revolutionary Mexico City.* University Park: Pennsylvania State University Press.

Blum, A. S. (2001, July). Conspicuous benevolence: Liberalism, public welfare, and private charity in Porfirian Mexico City, 1877–1910. *The Americas, 58*(1), 7–38.

Fuentes, M. L. (1998). *La asistencia social en México: Historia y perspectivas.* Mexico City: Ediciones del Milenio.

Schell, P. (1999, Winter). An honorable avocation for ladies: The work of the Mexico City Union de Damas Catolicas Mexicanas, 1912–1926. *Journal of Women's History, 10*(4), 78.

MOTHERS' PENSIONS (UNITED STATES)

Mothers' pensions (also called mothers' aid or widows' pensions) provided public funds to mother-only families to prevent the breakup of families as a result of poverty. State legislatures passed enabling laws for mothers' pensions as early as 1911; but it remained the local county's responsibility to implement and pay for this groundbreaking social welfare policy. Few examples of public aid to mother-only families existed before 1911. Its rapid spread across the states has been attributed to the combined efforts of juvenile justice reforms, the political involvement of organized women, and the awakened social conscience of Americans, shocked at the social injustice that accompanied industrialization. The mothers' pension model was adapted in the Social Security Act of 1935 and renamed Aid to Dependent Children.

Rapid industrialization, immigration, and the tremendous increase in population within the nation's cities expanded the numbers of the poor. In addition, the support networks that a family might have relied upon "back home" did not exist in the new cities. In this context, the economic dependency of mother-only families caused by the death, desertion, or disability of the husband became more common and visible to the urban middle class at the end of the 1800s. Children quit school to take jobs to help support their families. Mothers worked long hours away from home to earn what they could. The poor working conditions and unsanitary tenements created conditions for disease and more dependency. These problems existed before, notably during times of war. By the turn of the century, however, the causes of poverty arose from aspects of American economic development. Furthermore, they were not isolated local issues, but often regional or national. New causes demanded new solutions.

American reformers believed that, if ignored, these problems would threaten democratic principles, economic justice, standards of living, and social justice for women, children, and racial minorities. Organized women emphasized the threat to home preservation, child development, and child welfare. The campaigns for women's suffrage, employment opportunities, and better wages sought not only to provide more humane care to young children, but also to examine how the mothers of those children might be better able to support their families without the wages of an adult male.

Discussions about dependent mothers and aid to dependent children became more frequent within the National Conference of Charities and Corrections, a national organization of judges, charity workers, educators, and justice officers. Members saw firsthand the negative impact of a father's death or desertion on the entire family. Similarly, at the 1909 White House Conference on Dependent Children, participants discussed the need to provide aid to these families. An early consensus emerged to keep social welfare programs privately funded and administered locally despite the knowledge that the local solutions were increasingly inadequate. Traditionalist women's organizations, such as the National Congress of Mothers

(NCM), raised a new perspective—one that emphasized women's duties and rights within marriage. Impoverished mothers had trusted in the tenets of marriage and family, yet those institutions failed them when they lost their husbands. Drawing parallels between soldiers' pensions and mothers' pensions, the NCM argued that women provided a service to the nation by raising healthy and productive citizens, and the government should aid them in doing so. A third group of proponents for mothers' pensions blended the concerns of child welfare with a women's rights perspective. Single mothers were being asked to take on the roles of both breadwinning and child rearing. Furthermore, they were doing so without a safety net, nor an equitable wage system. Unskilled and generally untrained, the earning power of these mothers was poor. In numerous case records, the recurring illnesses of working mothers contributed to their inability to properly care for children at home. As the debate over maternal dependency continued into the early 1900s, the program remained lodged between charity and social insurance.

Two states, Illinois and Missouri, adopted the first publicly funded mothers' pension programs in 1911. Kansas City enacted local rules first and Illinois passed the first statewide legislation that spring. Within the next decade, a majority of states passed some form of comparable legislation. The states' landmark laws, however, carried no funding or administrative guidance. They were strictly enabling laws. Each county decided whether or not to implement the law, raised funds to pay the pensions, and determined how the program would be administered. Often the program was administered by the county juvenile court, if the county had established one. Smaller counties or those with no structure for juvenile justice relied on the poor relief system. Chicago had a juvenile court and an extensive private and public relief system. Yet even in Chicago, the rules governing mothers' pensions needed to be created from the ground up. This localism threatened the goals of the policy and led advocates to push for centralized administration and funding of the program.

The U. S. Children's Bureau filled the policy vacuum that surrounded mothers' pensions by supplying research and information as well as a network of social workers. The bureau produced major studies on mothers' pensions as they existed in other countries and as they began in the United States. The bureau supplied prototype bills and progress reports to states that were planning to pass similar legislation. The reports surveyed wage earning by mothers receiving pensions, standards of living relative to pension stipends, and administration of the state laws. These studies offered a composite portrait of pension recipients as widows with four or five children under the age of 16. Urban areas had a majority of immigrant recipients, yet across the states, White, native-born women received the majority of pension grants. Finally, the reports documented that a majority of women who received pensions were encouraged to earn wages. This finding contradicted an early premise of the program that mothers would be supported to stay home and raise their children. Rather, the pension allowed children to remain in school longer, while the mother went to work.

This experiment in paid motherhood never became universally accepted. The rhetoric proclaiming the value of a mother's work raising children did not overcome the legacy of limited government or the resistance of politicians opposed to any form of social subsidy. A handful of states never passed the legislation. Similarly, numerous counties never set up the apparatus to provide the aid. These limitations of the mothers' pension program paled, however, in comparison to the devastation experienced during the depression of the 1930s.

As the economic crises of the Great Depression diminished state and county revenues, funds for mothers' pension programs disappeared. Public and private charities had difficulty raising funds to meet the increased need of unemployed families, let alone the long-term demands of mother-only families. The Children's Bureau reported on three methods used by counties to deal with the emergency: they closed the program entirely, added additional restrictions on eligibility, or reduced the amounts of grants to families. As the Franklin D. Roosevelt administration made plans to establish a national Social Security system, attention focused primarily on the workingman and his family. Plans for aid to dependent children in mother-only families would have disappeared if not for the timely efforts of Children's Bureau directors.

Title IV of the Social Security Act (1935) included provisions for the Aid to Dependent Children program. The legislation drew upon state mothers' pension programs and made two improvements. A state that accepted federal funds agreed to implement the program in every county, share costs with counties, and provide for a central state administration. Secondly, the eligibility expanded to include mothers who had been divorced, deserted, or never married. These extensions of the earlier programs were frequently muted by the states, however, because they retained the authority to limit eligibility in relation to their revenue resources. This loophole allowed for significant disparity between the races in many localities during the subsequent decades.

Mothers' pensions left a mixed legacy. The advocates of the policy won an extraordinary political battle. In an era of limited government and virtually no social insurance, they convinced state legislatures to pass this early form of social provision to mother-only families. Even more remarkable, they legitimated the new entitlement on the basis of the value of a mother's work in child rearing. Local governments never truly embraced this policy, however, and it remained poorly funded, inequitably distributed, and available in only some areas. The tension surrounding public aid to mother-only families continued in the Aid to Dependent Children provisions of the Social Security Act (1935).

—*Joanne L. Goodwin*

See also Abbott, Edith; Abbott, Grace; Aid to Dependent Children/Aid to Families With Dependent Children (United States); Child Welfare Policy (United States); Hopkins, Harry Lloyd; Lathrop, Julia Clifford; Poor Law (United States); Social Security (United States)

Primary Sources

Papers of Grace and Edith Abbott, Regenstein Library, University of Chicago; Records of the U.S. Children's Bureau (Record Group 102), National Archives & Records Administration, College Park, MD.

Current Comment

Abbott, E., & Breckinridge, S. (1921). *Administration of mothers' aid law in Illinois* (U.S. Children's Bureau Publication No. 82). Washington, DC: Government Printing Office.

Laws relating to "mothers' pensions" in the United States, Denmark, and New Zealand (U.S. Children's Bureau Publication No. 7). (1914). Washington, DC: Government Printing Office.

Lundberg, E. O. (1928). *Public aid to mothers with dependent children* (U.S. Children's Bureau Publication No. 162). Washington, DC: Government Printing Office.

Nesbitt, F. (1923). *Standards of public aid to children in their own homes* (U.S. Children's Bureau Publication No. 118). Washington, DC: Government Printing Office.

Further Reading

Abbott, G. (1941). *From relief to Social Security: The development of the new public welfare services and their administration.* Chicago: University of Chicago Press.

Goodwin, J. L. (1997). *Gender and the politics of welfare reform: Mothers' pensions in Chicago, 1911–1929.* Chicago: University of Chicago Press.

Gordon, L. (1994). *Pitied but not entitled: Single mothers and the history of welfare, 1890–1935.* New York: Free Press.

MULTICULTURALISM (CANADA)

Multiculturalism, as it has evolved in Canada during the past 30 years, is now regarded as a distinctive feature of Canada as a national state. Successive federal governments have promoted multiculturalism as a model for how Canadians from diverse backgrounds should relate and live together. The dominant theme of Canadian multiculturalism is that all citizens should enjoy the same rights, duties, and entitlements regardless of differences related to color, country of origin, or religion.

Multiculturalism can be defined in a number of ways. It can refer to the empirical fact that the Canadian population is diverse in its composition. Viewed as an ideology, multiculturalism encompasses an established set of ideas and ideals that influence how Canadian society should be organized or how people ought to behave. For others, multiculturalism is an explicit government policy that is actualized through the provision of programs and services. Finally, multiculturalism can be defined as a set of practices that promote political and minority group interests or as a set of ideas and practices for engaging diversity as different yet equal for the purpose of living together with differences.

Specific support for multiculturalism began in 1971, when Prime Minister Pierre Elliott Trudeau announced Canada's first official policy on multiculturalism. He envisioned a society where all Canadians, including minorities, would have the opportunity to participate and contribute to the development of Canada as a nation. A major catalyst for the adoption of multiculturalism as a policy stemmed from the Report of the Royal Commission on Bilingualism and Biculturalism, released in 1969. Appointed by Prime Minister Lester Pearson in 1963, the commission's mandate was to examine the state of bilingualism and biculturalism in relation to the various ethnic groups in Canada. It recognized that Canadian society consisted of ethnic groups other than the French and English and that it was imperative for the federal government to pay attention to the needs, issues, and aspirations of these groups. In its recommendations, the commission focused on ways in which major Canadian institutions could protect the rights of ethnic minorities and allow them to maintain their languages and cultures.

In 1967, the federal government introduced a point system that was used to assess individuals applying to immigrate to Canada. Points were awarded for personal suitability, education, specific vocational preparation, occupational demands, arranged employment, language, relatives, and specific destination in Canada. The point system resulted in a major shift in the countries of origin of immigrants, increasing the numbers of immigrants from Asia, Latin America, and Africa, which resulted in a more diverse population.

Pressure from ethnic communities, such as the Ukrainians and Germans, also influenced the government in adopting multiculturalism as an official policy. They challenged the belief that Canada consisted of the two large groups—the English and the French—by strongly proclaiming that other cultural groups made major contributions to the development of Canadian society.

Multiculturalism, as introduced by Prime Minister Trudeau, was intended to serve as a mechanism to unite Canada by enabling all Canadians to participate without discrimination in defining and building the country's future. Multicultural policy consisted of four major elements. First, resources would be provided to assist all cultural groups in Canada who displayed the desire to develop and contribute to Canada. In particular, assistance would be available to those groups that demonstrated the need for financial assistance. Second, government would support members of all cultural groups in their efforts to overcome cultural barriers. Third, interactive encounters and exchange among all Canadians was promoted to enhance national unity. Finally, the government pledged to provide assistance to immigrants to learn either English or French, Canada's official languages, so that they could become full participants in Canadian society.

In 1972, the federal government established the Multicultural Directorate within the Department of Secretary of State, whose mandate was to assist ethnic and cultural groups in dealing with issues surrounding racism, human rights, citizen involvement, and immigrant services. The Canadian Consultative Council on Multiculturalism was introduced the following year to monitor implementation of the federal government's initiative on multiculturalism.

As immigration trends in the late 1970s and early 1980s altered the composition of Canada's population, other racial and ethnic groups criticized the federal government for its promotion of multiculturalism. Some felt their cultures and contributions to Canadian society were devalued in comparison to those of the English and French. Multiculturalism also came under attack for not dealing with systemic forms of racism and discrimination associated with employment, education, and housing, which became more common as the population became more diverse. Critics argued that multicultural policy as enacted maintained the status quo regarding those holding power in Canada. They also criticized the government for what was perceived to be a lack of sufficient resources to deal with systemic and structural barriers that precluded all Canadians from contributing to and benefiting from participation in Canadian society. The government's focus on celebrating differences and the practice of cultural sharing was regarded by critics as a mechanism to ignore the concerns of non-French and non-English communities. In response to criticism, the federal government shifted its focus to improving race relations across Canada. Policies and programs were introduced that were intended to eradicate racial discrimination at both personal and institutional levels. Institutions became targets for programs meant to deal with structural and systemic barriers that reduced employment opportunities for certain groups.

The most significant multicultural development occurred in 1986, when the Employment Equity Act was enacted to address the exclusion of particular groups from the Canadian workforce. The findings of the Royal Commission on Equality in Employment, chaired by Rosalie Abella, provided a major impetus for this legislation. Its mandate was to investigate the most effective way to integrate marginalized groups into the Canadian labor force. It concluded that four groups—Native people, visible minorities, persons with disabilities, and women—experienced strong barriers in their attempts to enter and advance in the Canadian workforce. The Employment Equity Act aimed to provide equitable employment opportunities for all Canadians through the removal of discriminatory barriers and implementation of protective measures to accommodate differences. From a legal perspective, the ideals of multiculturalism were established in the Constitution Act (1982) and the Charter of Rights and Freedoms, which came into effect in 1985. Section 27 of the charter is clear in making multiculturalism a prominent part of the national agenda at the highest levels, when it states, "the Charter shall be interpreted in a manner consistent with the preservation and enhancement of the multicultural heritage of Canadians."

Another milestone in the development of multiculturalism was the Canadian Multiculturalism Act of 1988, which made Canada the first country in the world to enforce multiculturalism as a federal law. It acknowledged multiculturalism as a fundamental characteristic of Canadian society and called for full and equitable participation of individuals and communities of all origins in all Canadian social, political, and economic activities. Building on Trudeau's 1971 multicultural objectives, the 1988 act focused on the elimination of racism and discriminatory barriers based on national or ethnic origin, color, and religion; the preservation and enhancement of language and cultural heritage; and promotion of programs that would be accessible and well-suited to all Canadians. It reaffirmed one of the main pillars of multiculturalism as an official government policy in asserting "the right of all [individuals] to identify with the cultural heritage of their choice yet retain full and equal participation . . . in all aspects of Canadian society."

The Multiculturalism Act requires the federal government to present annual reports to Parliament that describe progress toward the goal of integrating multiculturalism at the national level. It also endorses strategies to connect Canadians with their communities to "promote understanding and creativity that arises from the interaction between individuals and communities of different origins." Multicultural social change is the responsibility of the entire population.

Since the 1990s, the primary goal of federal multiculturalism policy has centered on enhancing Canada as a national state by promoting the ideal of a commonly shared citizenship. Described as civic multiculturalism, the emphasis is on creating a sense of belonging and a shared awareness of Canadian identity that does not deny or downplay differences that enhance Canada as a nation-state. Its goals are to create a society with a unique identity that recognizes and reflects a diversity of cultures, to instill a sense of belonging and attachment to Canada, and to create an environment in which all Canadians have the opportunity and capacity to participate in the development of their own communities as well as the nation. The policy is built on principles of social justice whereby all Canadians, regardless of origins or culture, are treated in an equitable manner. To achieve the objectives of the Multiculturalism Act, the federal government created a separate Department of Multiculturalism. Over time, as the government has become preoccupied with reducing government expenditures, funding allocated to the department has declined. The election of the Liberal government in 1993 resulted in the reorganization of federal departments and the activities of the multiculturalism department were distributed to the Departments of Canadian Heritage and Citizenship and Immigration.

When one reviews Canada's multiculturalism policy, the objective of creating a society that promotes social integration has been consistent since it began in 1971. Although individuals and cultural groups are encouraged to maintain important aspects of their heritage, it is important to stress that multiculturalism promotes a society in which all Canadians have opportunities to participate and contribute to the country. The ongoing challenge is to actualize the ideals of multiculturalism so that all Canadians feel valued and respected.

—*David Este*

See also Immigration and Social Welfare Policy (Canada); Race and Ethnic Relations (Canada)

Primary Sources

Canadian Multiculturalism Act (RS 1985, c. 24 [4th Supp.]), (c. 31, assented 21st July, 1988). The Constitution Act, 1982, Part I, Canadian Charter of Rights and Freedoms, assented to July 1, 1982. Canada: House of Commons, 1971 House of Commons Debate, 8 October, and Statutes of Canada. Minutes of proceedings and evidence of the Legislative Committee on Bill C-93, an Act for the Preservation and Enhancement of Multiculturalism.

Current Comment

Abu-Laban Y., & Gabriel, C. (2002). *Selling diversity: Immigration, multiculturalism, employment equity and globalization.* Peterborough, ON: Broadview Press.

Day, R. (2000). *Multiculturalism and the history of Canadian diversity.* Toronto, ON: University of Toronto Press.

Fleras A., & Elliot, J. L. (1992). *Multiculturalism in Canada: The challenge of diversity.* Scarborough, ON: Nelson.

Further Reading

Bissondath, N. (2002). *The selling of illusions: The cult of multiculturalism* (Rev. ed.). Toronto, ON: Penguin.

Fleras A., & Elliot, J. L. (2002). *Engaging diversity: Multiculturalism in Canada.* Toronto, ON: Thomson Nelson.

Fleras A., & Elliot, J. L. (2003). *Unequal relations: An introduction to race and ethnic dynamics in Canada* (4th ed.). Toronto, ON: Prentice Hall.

Mensah, J. (2002). *Black Canadians: History, experience and social conditions.* Halifax, NS: Fernwood.

MUTUAL AID (UNITED STATES)

During the nineteenth and early twentieth centuries, Americans relied on a wide variety of mutual aid arrangements for social welfare. Some of the most important of these were fraternal societies. A few were the Knights of Pythias, the Sons of Italy, the Polish National Alliance, B'nai B'rith, the Independent Order of Odd Fellows, the Mexican *mutualistas,* and the Jewish *landsmanshaftn.*

The defining characteristics of most fraternal societies included an autonomous system of lodges, a democratic form of government, a ritual, and the provision of mutual aid, such as sickness and death benefits for members and their families. Women's groups that met these criteria generally embraced the term "fraternal" rather than "sororal." In contrast to the hierarchical methods of governmental welfare and organized charities, fraternal aid more often rested on a principle of reciprocity.

In 1920, there were 10,000 fraternal societies in the United States with 100,000 separate lodges. That year, about 18 million Americans (many of them working class) were members. This was about 30 percent of all adult men in the United States. By contrast, about 10 percent of wage earners belonged to labor unions prior to the 1930s.

Most historians agree that Freemasonry, the first and most prestigious of all modern fraternal orders, arose at the very end of the seventeenth century in either England or Scotland. It seems to have developed out of the craft guild for stone (or operative) masons. The first Masonic lodge in the American colonies opened in Boston in 1733. At first, barely a pretense of centralization existed as each lodge was responsible only for its own members. By the 1780s, however, state grand lodges established charity committees to supplement (although never supplant) the local lodges. Between 1798 and 1800, the Masons in Pennsylvania disbursed over $6,000 to needy members, an amount higher than any other private charity in Philadelphia.

Freemasonry was primarily for professionals and the middle class. Those lower on the income scale generally relied on small locally based mutual benefit societies. The 1810s and 1820s brought the emergence of affiliated orders with multiple lodges that were more open to the working class. The largest was the Independent Order of Odd Fellows, originally a British society, which established its first lodge in the United States in 1819.

The Odd Fellows was a fraternal trendsetter. It initiated the first major departure from the haphazard grants of previous societies by using a clear schedule of guaranteed benefits. Each member when taken sick could claim a regular stipend per week (usually $3 to $6) to compensate for working days lost. The decades before and after the Civil War were ones of sustained expansion for the Odd Fellows. Between 1830 and 1877, the membership rose from 3,000 to 456,000 and total aid reached $69 million. Lodges also devoted substantial sums to purposes other than sickness and burial benefits. In 1855, the Grand Lodge of Maryland gave aid to 900 orphans of deceased members.

Fraternalism was not an exclusively White phenomenon. In 1775, a British army lodge of Masons initiated 15 free Blacks. One of them was Prince Hall from Barbados. After the White Masons spurned them, the Black Masons obtained a charter from the grand lodge in England and formed a separate organization. By the 1840s, Prince Hall Freemasonry had spread across much of the Eastern Seaboard. Throughout its history, its membership was almost a "who's who" of well-known Blacks including Booker T. Washington, W. E. B. DuBois, Thurgood Marshall, and Martin Luther King, Jr.

Blacks also founded a separate version of the Odd Fellows under Peter Ogden. Like Prince Hall, he secured a charter from the home lodge in Britain after Whites barred him from membership. By 1867, the Black Odd Fellows had 3,000 members and 50 lodges and disbursed several thousands of dollars in benefits during a typical year. It had over 300,000 members by 1916, making it by far the largest Black voluntary association in the United States.

The formation of the Ancient Order of United Workmen in 1868 signaled the onset of a new phase of American fraternal development, the national life insurance order. The life insurance plan was originally an incidental feature but quickly moved to center stage. It guaranteed a death benefit of $1,000 (later raised to $2,000). Funding came from a per capita assessment. The Ancient Order centralized the authority for raising and dispersing death benefits into state (and later national) organizations. Because of the attraction of the death benefit feature, the membership skyrocketed, cresting at 450,000 in 1902.

The next three decades brought a flowering of similar life insurance orders, including the Royal Arcanum, the Knights of Honor, and the Modern Woodmen of America. By 1908, the hundred leading societies had paid well over one billion dollars in death benefits. Because many did not charge premiums that were sufficient for adequate reserves, they were forced into a painful period of readjustment between the 1890s and the 1910s. Many had to raise rates to better reflect risks based on age and occupation. While fraternalism was primarily a male phenomenon, women also formed life insurance orders, most notably the Woman's Benefit Association.

Fraternal societies contributed to high rates of insurance ownership among Blacks and immigrants. A government survey of wage earners in Chicago in 1919 revealed that 93 percent of Black families had at least one member with life insurance, followed by Bohemians, Poles, and Irish (at 88 percent each), and native Whites and Germans (both at 85 percent).

By this time, fraternal societies had rapidly expanded their range of services to include tuberculosis sanitariums, youth camps, and homes for the elderly. They founded 71 orphanages between 1890 and 1922, most without government subsidy. Two sponsors stood out: the Independent Order of Odd Fellows and the Masons. Between them, they controlled 64 orphanages in 1933. Probably the largest single facility was Mooseheart. Operated by the Loyal Order of Moose, now Moose International, it was home to over 1,000 children of deceased members during the Great Depression.

Just after 1900, many societies added treatment by a physician to their menu of services. The favored method was for an individual lodge to contract with a general practitioner to treat members and their families on a per capita basis. Two of the most prominent organizations to rely on this system, known as lodge practice, were the Foresters and the Fraternal Order of Eagles. The typical annual cost per member was from one to two dollars.

Lodge practice established a particularly strong foothold in urban areas. In the Lower East Side of New York City, 500 doctors had contracts with Jewish lodges alone. During the 1920s, Blacks belonged to an estimated 600 fraternal societies in New Orleans that offered the services of a physician. In most cases, lodge practice entailed nothing more extensive than basic primary care. Some societies experimented with hospitalization.

The Security Benefit Association, based in Topeka, Kansas, had one of the most ambitious programs. It opened a 300-bed hospital that was part of an effort to protect members "from the cradle to the grave." The association also provided an orphanage, school, and home for the elderly. The hospital enjoyed extensive use and over 1,200 operations were performed there in

1933. Each patient paid in total charges a $10 entrance fee and one dollar a day. Although the hospital itself lost money, it was initially considered a profitable venture because it attracted new customers for life insurance, which was always the mainstay of the association.

The Taborian Hospital of the all-Black Knights and Daughters of Tabor offered one of the more fascinating examples of fraternal hospitalization. The hospital was located in the small town of Mound Bayou in the heart of the Mississippi Delta. When it opened in 1942, the final cost of construction had been over $100,000. Taborian Hospital offered a wide range of services, including major and minor surgery and obstetrics. The facilities included two major operating rooms, an X-ray room, sterilizer, incubators, electrocardiograph, blood bank, and laboratory. The hospital usually had two or three doctors on the staff; all were Black. Because of the hospital, the membership of the Knights and Daughters of Tabor in Mississippi increased to 50,000 by 1945. Between 1942 and 1964, the hospital cared for over 135,000 outpatients and an average of 1,400 inpatients annually.

For the most part, however, fraternal societies had already entered a period of decline by the 1930s. Historians have pointed to several possible explanations, including the spread of reliable commercial insurance among the working class and the lure of competing forms of entertainment, such as the radio and movies. Another factor was pressure exerted by organized medicine. By 1910, the profession had launched an all-out war against lodge practice as medical societies imposed sanctions against doctors who accepted these contracts. Today, most fraternal societies have abandoned their roles as mutual aid organizations though many still dispense charity for nonmembers.

—David T. Beito

See also Voluntarism (United States)

Primary Sources

The Immigration Research Center, University of Minnesota, Minneapolis (for records related to eastern and southern European fraternal societies); the Schomburg Center for Research in Black Culture, New York Public Library (for records related to Black fraternal societies, including the Prince Hall Masons); Moose International, Mooseheart, IL.

Current Comment

Connecticut Bureau of Labor Statistics. (1892). *Annual report.* New Haven: CT: Author.

Illinois Health Insurance Commission. (1919) *Report.* Springfield, IL: Illinois State Journal.

U.S. Department of Commerce, Bureau of the Census. (1913). *Benevolent institutions.* Washington, DC: Government Printing Office.

Further Reading

Beito, D. T. (2000). *From mutual aid to the welfare state: Fraternal societies and social services, 1890–1967.* Chapel Hill: University of North Carolina Press.

Kaufman, J. (2002). *For the common good? American civic life and the golden age of fraternity.* New York: Oxford University Press.

Wright, C. E. (1992). *The transformation of charity in postrevolutionary New England.* Boston: Northeastern University Press.

N

NATIONAL ASSOCIATION OF SOCIAL WORKERS (UNITED STATES)

In October 1955, five specialist organizations merged with the American Association of Social Workers to create one voice for the social work profession: the National Association of Social Workers (NASW). The new organization sought to solidify social work's identity and recognition as a profession, to increase social work's impact on national social policy, and to attend to basic professional issues, such as defining the skills and scope of social work practice, credentialing members of the profession, ensuring ethical practice, and planning for adequate and appropriate staffing of social agencies. Pursuing all these goals within a diverse profession was a major challenge for the new organization and remains so for NASW today. Currently, the association has over 100,000 members, representing about 20 percent of social workers in the United States.

The NASW brought together a variety of social work organizations. One grouping consisted of associations reflecting particular fields of practice: medical, psychiatric, and school social work. Social caseworkers in medical settings were the first to organize, establishing the American Association of Medical Social Workers (AAMSW) in 1918. By the 1940s, membership standards were high, requiring a 2-year graduate degree in social work, including an approved medical social work curriculum. Membership requirements based on graduate education were often seen as a way to promote high standards in the profession. Psychiatric social workers formed a separate organization, the American Association of Psychiatric Social Workers (AAPSW), in 1926. It, too, had high membership standards. The National Association of School Social Workers (NASSW) organized in 1919. The group developed specialized educational requirements, but, because of state and local certification standards, NASSW was less stringent regarding required educational preparation.

The other specialist groups were of a different nature. The American Association of Group Workers (AAGW), formed in 1936, constituted a methods specialization. Emerging from the settlement house movement, group workers had a strong identity, were less interested in professionalization, and were not always welcomed by other social workers. As a sign of the group's breadth, the graduate education required for membership could be in social work, education, or recreation. The Social Work Research Group (SWRG) was formed in 1949 by persons doing research on social work and social services. Membership did not require professional social work education. Finally, community organization practitioners developed the Association for the Study of Community Organization (ASCO) in 1946. ASCO was open to all those interested in community organization, although by the 1950s, 80 percent of its members were social workers.

Only one organization purported to speak for all of social work. The American Association of Social Workers (AASW) had been founded in 1921 by social work leaders hoping to establish professional standards in training and practice and to bring a common identity and high standards to a broad group of practitioners. These standards were maintained through specific membership requirements. The organization's goals also included interpreting social work's goals and methods to the broader society and influencing national social policy. In the early years of the Great Depression, AASW leaders testified before congressional committees on the need for federal relief measures; later, the organization called for national social and economic planning. In the 1950s, AASW hired a lobbyist and established a branch office in Washington, D.C.

Despite the existence of an umbrella professional group, specialized social work groups continued to flourish. In the late 1940s, only about 16 percent of the country's social workers belonged to AASW. As social work's numbers increased and the profession matured, the feeling grew that social work needed a larger, more unified voice to influence policy and practice. The AASW began to reach out to other social work groups, suggesting exploration of consolidation into a broader organization. Although the more selective bodies worried about the erosion of high membership standards, others saw the advantages of a large group in the policy arena and in the creation of a stronger professional identity.

The mechanism for consolidation was a Temporary Inter-Association Council, or TIAC. It included AASW, the medical, psychiatric, and school social work associations, and the group workers and researchers (the community organization body was initially excluded because its membership was thought to be too broad). Deliberations about a common group were marked by tensions between a commitment to specialized practice and a desire for a common professional identity. In addition, the goal of promoting high standards through exclusion of "non-professionals" had to be weighed against the potential power of a more inclusive and larger group in the

social policy arena. After protracted debate and compromise, a new organization, the National Association of Social Workers, emerged in 1955. It established divisions for the specialties, six commissions on professional and social policy issues, state chapters, and a delegate assembly responsible for setting the broad policies of the association. Proponents of high membership standards prevailed; the new organization was open only to those with a 2-year graduate degree in social work.

The goals of NASW included defining social work practice, creating a code of ethics, developing personnel standards, and influencing legislative and federal agency policy. Its Commission on Social Work Practice developed a working definition of social work practice, but an anticipated study of practice never materialized. Thus, a major expectation of many of the specialist groups—the attention of the profession as a whole to issues of practice—was not fulfilled. The organization did, however, develop a code of ethics and begin work toward establishing certification and licensing. In 1961, the NASW created an internal certification program, the Academy of Certified Social Workers, based on graduate education and practice experience. It did not get involved in licensing issues until a decade later when individual state chapters lobbied for state licensing of social workers.

The organization also grappled for years over the legitimacy of undergraduate social work education and practice. Debate over this issue had torn the social work education community apart and was one reason why TIAC did not include the American Association of Schools of Social Work (a predecessor of the Council on Social Work Education) in the new association. Debate was heated, but awareness of staffing shortages and strong lobbying by champions of baccalaureate social work helped lead to NASW's 1969 decision to extend membership to persons who had undergraduate degrees in social work.

NASW was arguably most successful in meeting its goal of influencing social policy. It has maintained a policy infrastructure throughout its history. Upon its creation, NASW took over the Washington, D.C., office of AASW. The Commission on Social Policy and Action formulated policy statements on social and economic issues. Once adopted by the delegate assembly, these became a blueprint for the organization's legislative positions. The Washington office staff then lobbied members of Congress, testified at hearings, and facilitated chapter contacts with federal legislators. In 1957, the organization also attempted to influence federal officials by creating a NASW-HEW (U.S. Department of Health, Education and Welfare) liaison committee, which met with the departmental secretary to express NASW's views on HEW programs and policies. In the 1960s, NASW joined other groups in lobbying for the 1962 "social service amendments" to the Social Security Act and created a Commission on Civil Rights, which supported passage of the 1964 Civil Rights Act. At the end of the decade, the association campaigned for a guaranteed income system, such as a negative income tax. To have a greater effect on national policy making, NASW moved its headquarters to Washington, D.C., in 1972. During the 1980s, the association fought cuts in federal funding for social services and in the 1990s it championed a single-payer national health care system and tried to mitigate some of the negative effects of welfare reform.

NASW increased its concentration on electoral politics in 1976, when it created the Political Action for Candidate Election (PACE) to endorse candidates for office and contribute to their campaigns. In recent years, increasing numbers of social workers have themselves been elected to public office on the local, state, and national levels.

In the last few decades, NASW has increased its lobbying on professional issues, such as recognition of social workers as reimbursable providers of mental health care services under Medicare. Some see this as self-serving, and a departure from a commitment to improving the country's health and social welfare systems. This concern reflects ongoing tensions between policy goals and "inner-directed" professional goals within NASW. The recent growth of specialty sections such as private practice and aging constitutes another familiar strain between specialization and a broad-based organization. Finally, debates over professional standards, including the scope of social work licensing and the appropriate roles of MSW and BSW practitioners, have not been completely resolved. All of these debates affect the profession as a whole; NASW provides an arena for attempts to resolve them.

—*Leslie Leighninger*

See also National Conference on Social Welfare (United States); Social Work Profession (United States)

Primary Sources

National Association of Social Workers Records and Council on Social Work Education Records, Social Welfare History Archives, University of Minnesota, Minneapolis.

Further Reading

Leighninger, L. (1987). *Social work: Search for identity.* Westport, CT: Greenwood.

Leighninger, L. (1999). The service trap: Social work and public welfare policy in the 1960s. In G. R. Lowe & P. N. Reid (Eds.), *The professionalization of poverty: Social work and the poor in the twentieth century* (pp. 63–88). New York: Aldine de Gruyter.

Lubove, R. (1969). *The professional altruist: The emergence of social work as a career, 1880–1930.* New York: Athaneum.

Weismiller, T., & Rome, S. H. (1995). Social workers in politics. In R. L. Edwards & J. G. Hopps (Eds.), *Encyclopedia of social work* (19th ed., Vol. 3). Washington, DC: NASW Press.

NATIONAL CONFERENCE ON SOCIAL WELFARE (UNITED STATES)

Before the United States had the complete network of helping services we know today, much of the work of providing human services was done on a local and voluntary basis. This changed when states began organizing bodies of knowledge and expertise in social services. Soon, members of these state boards of charities and correction realized the strategic advantage of sharing their information with other states. Representatives of state boards first met in the early 1870s to share perspectives and exchange information and resources regarding the advancement of services in "charities and corrections." Soon, however, this networking between a few state boards evolved into the most important gathering in the United States for the exchange of information, techniques, and advances in social work and social service practice and theory.

The National Conference on Social Welfare began as an idea exchange in 1872, when members of the Wisconsin State Board of Charities and Reform invited Frederick Wines, secretary of the Illinois Board of State Commissioners of Public Charities, to observe their methods and institutions. The participating

Table N.1   Names of the National Conference on Social Welfare, 1874 to 1984

Year(s)	Name of Association
1874	Conference of Boards of Public Charities
1875–1879	Conference of Charities
1880–1881	Conference of Charities and Correction
1882–1916	National Conference of Charities and Correction
1917–1956	National Conference of Social Work
1957–1984	National Conference on Social Welfare

individuals considered the event such a success that invitations were extended to other nearby states. The following year, another informal gathering took place involving three states. The national conference began to take shape in 1874 as a section of the annual meeting of the American Social Science Association (ASSA). This joint venture did not last long. In 1879, state board delegates voted to break away from the ASSA and hold their own yearly conference.

The conference went through several name changes during its 110 years, reflecting the dynamic history of social work. It began in 1874 as the Conference of Boards of Public Charities. Although representatives of private charities attended (hence the "Conference of Charities" years), the organizing impetus was from the public sector. Corrections officials also participated, and the name change to the Conference of Charities and Correction reflected their inclusion. In 1917, the conference became the National Conference of Social Work to reflect its support for the professionalization of social work. That change lasted until 1956, when the membership voted to change the name to the National Conference on Social Welfare to reflect a shift in its purposes and functions. Contextually, this name change reflected the merger of seven social work membership organizations to form the National Association of Social Workers (NASW) on October 1, 1955. Conferees were delighted, and gave their "National Conference of Social Work Award" to the committee that spearheaded the creation of NASW. This development, however, would undermine the conference's claim to be the "central place" where all social work organizations could come together, and the meetings stopped in 1984.

The conference met most frequently in the East and the midwestern portions of the United States. Despite

the inclusion of "national" in many variants of the conference's name, organizers did acknowledge the international nature of social work and social welfare and included many foreign social workers. The conference also met three times outside of the United States, twice in Toronto, Ontario, and once in Montreal, Quebec. Because of travel difficulties during World War II, the conference was held in three different locations in 1943, and there was no meeting in 1945, although contributions from individuals who would have spoken were published.

Each year, the conference published a volume commemorating the meeting. In the early years, the complete proceedings and all papers were included. As the conference grew in strength and attendance, however, fewer papers and presentations were selected for publication. Although the majority of social workers in the United States have historically been women, men dominated the printed works in the conference proceedings. Roughly 70 percent of the papers and presentations published in the proceedings were written in whole or in part by men, whereas 30 percent were written in whole or in part by women. The papers are difficult to categorize because of the vast scope of the conference, both in years and in changing foci for inclusion. Nonetheless, many of the common problems that have concerned social work and other social welfare professionals are present, including mental illness, broken families, substance abuse, criminal justice, child welfare, social justice, the elderly, and social planning, among others. On the other hand, one is struck by some omissions, such as issues of racism and prejudice that were not extensively discussed. Despite the difficulty in categorizing the enormous body of works collected in the proceedings, they represent the distance that social work has traveled in pursuit of improved services and a better understanding of social conditions. Part of the reason categorization is difficult is that little research has been done on the collection as a whole. The logistical enormity of collecting and reading over 100 volumes is indeed daunting. Through the efforts of the authors and the University of Michigan's School of Social Work and Library (the Digital Library Project), the complete set of volumes is now available in searchable format on-line.

One of the traditions of the National Conference on Social Welfare was an opening speech, delivered each year by the conference president, which would set the tone or theme (when one was specified). The presidency gave individual social workers the ability to address the nation's social work community when there were few other opportunities available. Diversity in presidents, however, was somewhat limited: 22 were women, the first of whom was Jane Addams in 1910, and five were African American, beginning with Lester Granger in 1951. What the presidents lacked in racial and gender diversity may have been balanced occupationally. Besides prominent social workers, presidents were also volunteers in social service agencies, lawyers, public health practitioners, nurses, doctors, and priests. Looked at in totality, the presidential addresses represent the thoughts of a group of men and women, who sought to appreciate, reinforce, inspire, and justify social work to an audience of their peers as well as distant readers.

Though no longer active in the field of social work and social welfare, the National Conference on Social Welfare served to unite local social services into a greater body of national and international social work. With its demise in 1984, the social work/social welfare community lost an important forum for discussion and action. Through the efforts of the conference, social workers could share their successes, as well as failures, and influence the entire nation's social service delivery system. Many of the debates that plague social work and social welfare today are reflected in the sage words of the men and women who gathered from across the country, united in their desire to help others and craft a space for social work in the social sphere. The conference reminds us how far social work has come, but also the distance left to travel.

—John E. Tropman and Rebecca L. Stotzer

See also National Association of Social Workers (United States); Settlement Houses (United States); Social Work Profession (United States); State Boards of Charities (United States)

Primary Sources

Records of the National Conference on Social Welfare, Social Welfare History Archives, University of Minnesota, Minneapolis; proceedings of the National Conference on Social Welfare and its predecessor organizations, University of Michigan Digital Library (www.hti.umich.edu/n/ncosw/); another useful resource is Alexander Johnson's *A Guide to the Proceedings of the National*

Conference of Charities and Correction, 1874–1907, published by the conference in Indianapolis, IN, in 1908.

Further Reading

Bruno, F. J. (1957). *Trends in social work, 1874–1956* (2nd ed.). New York: Columbia University Press.

NATIONAL COUNCIL OF WOMEN OF CANADA

The National Council of Women of Canada (NCWC) has demonstrated for over 100 years the ability of concerned women to reach a national consensus on a broad range of social issues. The NCWC was formed following the attendance of at least 22 Canadian women at the International Council of Women (ICW) meeting in Chicago in May 1893. On October 27, 1893, about 1,500 women representing missionary societies, academic groups, professional associations, social and political reform groups, and cultural organizations at the local, provincial, and national levels gathered in Toronto. The NCWC was created that day as an affiliate of the ICW—an association of associations, with membership including local and provincial councils of women and national women's organizations. The first members were seven local councils from Manitoba, Ontario, and Quebec, and three national societies: the Woman's Art Association, the Girls' Friendly Society in Canada, and the Dominion Women's Enfranchisement Association.

The goal of the council was to bring women together in a united front to provide leadership on social issues affecting women and families. The preamble to the constitution, adopted in 1894, states

> We, Women of Canada, sincerely believing that the best good of our homes and nation will be advanced by our own greater unity of thought, sympathy and purpose, and that an organized movement of women will best conserve the highest good of the Family and State, do hereby band ourselves together to further the application of the Golden Rule to society, custom and law.

By 1914, the NCWC membership included 20 affiliated associations at the national level and 32 local councils. The NCWC was legally incorporated that year by an act of Parliament.

From the start, the NCWC was involved in organized charity. Early interests were in supporting the unemployed, female prisoners, and women and children working in factories. Achievements of the council over the years included the founding of the Victorian Order of Nurses and the Canadian Consumers Association, successful lobbying for the development of federal offices for women and seniors, and support for the development of children's aid societies in Ontario and elsewhere. Perhaps one of its most important roles was in supporting the five Alberta women, all council members, who appealed to the British Privy Council, before it was decided on October 18, 1929, to have the word "person" in the British North America Act (1867) interpreted to include women.

The interests of the NCWC have varied over the past 110 years, but the focus has always been on identifying and finding consensus on issues significant to Canadian women and families. Each year, key issues have been addressed through resolutions calling for action by the federal government. The NCWC has taken positions on matters including the need for female matrons in prisons for women; the plight of poor senior citizens; decriminalizing dissemination of birth control information, and, several years later, decriminalizing abortion; aboriginal rights; air and food quality; prevention of violence against women, children, and the elderly; third world development; and guidelines for stem cell research. The council also remains a member of the ICW, addressing similar issues through the United Nations. Although the organization has never been radical in action or position, the NCWC continues to provide an opportunity for Canadian women to share a vision and speak with a united voice.

—Alison B. MacDonald

See also Human Rights (Canada); Women and Social Welfare (Canada)

Further Reading

Griffiths, N. E. S. (1993). *The splendid vision: Centennial history of the National Council of Women of Canada, 1893–1993.* Ottawa, ON: Carleton University Press.

National Council of Women of Canada. (1894). *Yearbook.* Ottawa, ON: Author. Available: www.ncwc.ca

Shaw, R. L. (1957). *Proud heritage.* Toronto, ON: Ryerson.

NEOLIBERALISM, SOCIAL PROGRAMS, AND SOCIAL MOVEMENTS (MEXICO)

Neoliberalism is a term popularly understood in Mexico and in many developing world regions as a shift in development policy of third world states and their international creditors. Beginning in the early 1980s, architects of neoliberal policies aimed to reduce the role of the government in the economy and emphasize the role of domestic and international private sector actors in producing national growth and development. Programs of market-oriented economic policy were deemed "neo" liberal because of their similarities to nineteenth and early twentieth century classical liberal economic practices in Latin America in which countries depended heavily on revenues from mining and agricultural exports to purchase manufactured goods. This marked a turnaround from mid twentieth century statecraft in which governments in Latin America sought to diversify their economies through import substitution industrialization.

Mexico's shift from inward-oriented development to market-driven development began sporadically following rapid reversals in global financial and energy markets in the early 1980s. Unable to service an $80 billion external debt in 1982, the Mexican government began implementing fiscal and structural adjustments to reestablish its international credit line. Adjustments included privatization of state-owned enterprises, cuts in public sector spending and employment, termination of many subsidies, and the phasing out of tariffs on many goods and services. During the 1980s and 1990s, the government also eased restrictions on foreign ownership and repatriation of profits to expand foreign investment in manufacturing, financial markets, and services.

Neoliberal policies represented a sharp break with previous policies of inward-oriented economic development. They provoked strong political reactions from labor unions, peasants, and groups representing public sector employees, students, and informal sector workers. Mass protests over job losses, wage freezes, cuts to popular social programs, and eventually a flood of foreign imports that undercut many domestic industries created a broad crisis of legitimacy for the Mexican government by the late 1980s and contributed directly and indirectly to political democratization in the late 1990s.

DISTRIBUTIVE PROTEST AND THE RULING PARTY IN MEXICO

The extent to which transformative social movements are linked to the termination of social programs in Mexico or anywhere else is a matter of debate. The formation of social movements cannot be viewed as a direct result of popular anger over the termination of basic subsidies and welfare programs. Rather, neoliberalism set in motion a set of social and political processes that made it increasingly difficult for governing elites to maintain power through a single governing political party, the Institutional Revolutionary party (*Partido Revolucionario Institucional,* or PRI). Dominating federal, state, and local elections since its inception in the late 1920s, the PRI preempted political competition through control of mass media, co-optation of political rivals, as well as through violence and bribery. The Mexican regime differed from various authoritarian regimes in other Latin American countries, however, in two critical ways: First, the Mexican military remained subordinate to civilian leaders, and second, presidential successions were uniformly peaceful and uncontested after the consolidation of the state following Mexico's Revolution of the early twentieth century.

This degree of social and political order depended increasingly after 1930 on the expansion of programs meeting certain basic social demands while refraining from heavy taxation of private sector businesses. The result was a political system in which government legitimacy hinged on the ability of the state to incorporate large portions of the populace into a political order through mass organizations and to maintain a number of limited but visible distributive programs and universal subsidies. By the 1970s, government spending was financed by massive loans from foreign banks. Notably, subsidies and state-led industrialization did little to reduce levels of income inequality but did at certain points increase the purchasing power of the working class and the rural poor. Access to many popular programs depended on individuals' and groups' allegiance to the PRI.

The fiscal and monetary crises of the 1980s hampered governing elites' power to quell social conflict through distributive channels. Between 1985 and 1995, government spending declined by 61 percent in agriculture and by 50 percent in urban development. Spending on industry outside the energy sector declined to near zero as government enterprises were sold to the private sector. Privatization, market and trade liberalization, and fiscal retrenchment undertaken as a means of restoring the government's access to foreign credit challenged the basic organizational logic of the ruling party.

Although leaders of labor and peasant organizations remained loyal to the ruling party as the buying power of significant portions of the population declined, contention around specific shortfalls rose and some temporary alliances emerged. Mass campaigns in the early 1980s against austerity measures were organized by *coordinadoras*, or loose national associations representing labor unions, neighborhood groups, and peasants both inside and outside the ruling party. In 1983 and 1984, a group of *coordinadoras* mounted two massive civil strikes with an estimated two million people taking part, paralyzing traffic and commerce in the capital and several major cities. The government responded by loosening austerity policies; a new wave of inflation and capital flight, however, rendered any temporary gains nil.

Alongside the bread-and-butter campaigns of the *coordinadoras*, groups representing many of the same constituencies also began to identify government corruption and a lack of democracy as culprits in ongoing national crises. Dating roughly from the 1970s, latter-day movements for trade union democracy were important in the field of public protest in the 1980s. Dissident currents of miners, steelworkers, teachers, electricians, autoworkers, textile workers, and university employees challenged the government's monopoly over workplace representation, claiming that drastic cutbacks, mass dismissals, and wage freezes placed an unfair burden on the poor for national recovery. As a result, movements for union democracy, organized around campaigns for clean union elections, better wages, workplace health and safety, and enforcement of labor law, were clear precursors to national-level campaigns for democracy in the 1990s. Considerably prior to the emergence of competitive elections at the national level, dissident union groups such as the teachers' National Coordinator of Education Workers

(*Coordinaroa Nacional de Trabajadores de la Educación,* or CNTE) in Oaxaca or Miners' and Steel-workers' Local 271 in Michoacán organized regional networks of support and were able to muster sizable blocs of votes against the PRI in municipal and state races.

Meanwhile, in rural areas, protest flared over access to land and markets. Many groups also sought to reform the government's role in agriculture and rural administration. Some protest was also linked to the availability of food and basic services in rural areas, particularly for the increasing number of peasants whose harvest did not cover year-round food needs and who relied on wage labor to bridge the deficit. Notably, many of these protests in the early 1980s were supported by employees of government agencies, reflecting division inside the ranks of the government over fiscal policy and administrative priorities in the food sector.

In a manner parallel to urban movements for trade union democracy, networks of small farmers challenged the monopoly of the PRI over agricultural cooperatives and marketing associations. Independent farm groups denounced political manipulation of the agricultural sector whereby party loyalists controlled the distribution of finance, inputs, and machinery to the *ejido,* or land reform sector. Land reform beneficiaries had little control over production and met serious obstacles when seeking alternative markets for grain or produce. Groups such as the Independent Central of Agricultural Workers and *Campesinos* (CIOAC), the *Plan de Ayala National Coordinator* (CNPA), and the National Union of Autonomous Regional *Campesinos* (UNORCA) denounced the monopoly of the PRI-affiliated National Confederation of *Campesinos* over fiscal resources in the small farm sector and pressed for autonomy and better access to markets for small-scale producers. As with trade union activists, rising poverty and crises of household consumption were effectively linked to calls for greater democracy.

PROTEST AND SYSTEMIC POLITICAL CRISIS

Public fury over shortages amid calls for democratization expanded significantly after 1988, when fraudulent presidential elections resulted in an unprecedented succession crisis. The ruling party's candidate, Carlos Salinas de Gortari, assumed office amid scandal and significant protest following the election. Many believed that his competitor, Cuauhtemoc Cardenas, a senator who left the PRI to run for office, had in fact won the election. Salinas was viewed suspiciously by many inside the ruling party as a Harvard-trained technocrat with few political skills, but he made promises of national economic recovery through a deepening of neoliberal reforms. He achieved reforms rapidly and sidelined portions of the ruling party associated with organized labor, agriculture, and human services. He gave prominent new roles to the ministry of the treasury and the ministry of trade and commerce. While restoring Mexico's creditworthiness, diversifying its export portfolio, restoring inflows of foreign investment, and reducing the fiscal drag of unprofitable government-owned enterprises, the Salinas reforms also threatened some new constituencies formerly tied to the ruling party. Deliberate over-valuation of the *peso* against the U.S. dollar, for example, attracted foreign investment in stocks and government bonds and kept the price of imported food low, but it also rendered domestic manufactures and food grains uncompetitive. Debt loads and bankruptcies among mid-sized farmers and small business owners grew precipitously. Meanwhile, the Salinas administration's termination of land reform in 1991 also stirred conflict. Though publicly intended to give small producers better access to finance and markets, the changes allowing for the privatization of *ejido* land exacerbated many regional and local feuds over land tenure, particularly in the poorer south of the country.

These liabilities fueled new popular movements of unprecedented size and visibility. On January 1, 1994, armed peasant insurgents in the southern state of Chiapas launched an attack on the state capital, San Cristobal de las Casas, and town halls in six other municipalities. A largely Mayan indigenous army drawing combatants from hundreds of settlements throughout the Chiapan highlands, the Zapatista Army of National Liberation (*Ejército Zapatista de Liberación Nacional,* or EZLN, which drew its name from Revolution-era general Emiliano Zapata) issued broad calls for solidarity and accordingly generated well-attended protests across Mexico and abroad.

Paradoxically, while decrying the specter of those left behind by Mexico's neoliberal economic policies, the EZLN assumed a vanguard position of sorts in including in its demands calls for democratization and free and fair elections, in addition to demands for the reinstitution of land reform, rural health care, bilingual education, and basic social services.

Within a year of the Zapatista uprising, other mass movements calling for economic and political changes emerged. In sheer numbers, the most significant was a mass movement of working- and middle-class debtors known as the *Barzón* movement. Beginning in the countryside among bankrupt farmers and expanding in size in the months after a disastrous devaluation crisis in December 1994, this movement denounced corruption in the government and the banking system as well as the economic recovery measures undertaken by President Ernesto Zedillo Ponce de Leon. Maintaining that such measures favored large banks at the expense of debtors, many of whom were forced into bankruptcy as annual interest rates soared over 100 percent, *Barzonistas* not only called for a suspension of bank repossessions of debtors' properties, but also called for the renegotiation of the National American Free Trade Agreement (NAFTA), investigations of banks and government officials, and attention to the demands of the EZLN in Chiapas. The *Barzón* movement drew hundreds of thousands of urban protesters but emphasized its roots in the countryside. Members often rode on tractors and horses, and frequently staged nonviolent but highly disruptive actions to highlight their cause.

THE END OF ONE-PARTY GOVERNANCE

Pressed by popular organization and public protest, the PRI-led government acceded to calls for electoral democratization by the late 1990s. Elections at the national level were considered genuinely competitive by 1997, and in 2000 the PRI candidate for the presidency lost to opposition party member Vicente Fox Quesada. Ironically, however, the bulk of the neoliberal policies that had generated protest and popular calls for economic reform remained in force. Importantly, the transition to a competitive multiparty political system has produced new freedoms of association and speech for popular movements and left-of-center parties, which have continued to pressure government with some limited success on issues pertaining to housing, taxes, government transparency, policing, education, migration, and agriculture.

—Heather Williams

See also Economic Crises, Family and Gender, 1980s to the Present (Mexico); International Social Welfare; Labor Movement and Social Welfare (Mexico); Land Reform (Mexico); Peasant Movements and Social Programs (Mexico); Poverty (Mexico); Poverty Policy (Mexico); Welfare Capitalism (Mexico)

Current Comment

Collier, G. (1999). *Basta! Land and the Zapatista rebellion in Chiapas.* San Francisco: Food First Books.

Gilly A. (1997). *Chiapas: La razon ardiente.* Mexico City: Era Press.

Ramirez, J. M., & Regalado, J. (Eds.). (1997). Los cuatro actores socials: *El debate nacional.* Mexico City: Diana Press.

Ongoing writing and debate in the Mexico City daily, *La Jornada;* the quadrennial journal *Sociedad Civil.*

Further Reading

Ochoa, E. (2000). *Feeding Mexico: The political uses of food since 1910.* Wilmington, DE: Scholarly Resources.

Peters, E. D. (2000). *Polarizing Mexico: The impact of liberalization strategy.* Boulder, CO: Lynne Rienner.

Williams, H. (1996). *Planting trouble: The* Barzón *debtors' movement in Mexico.* La Jolla: University of California, San Diego, Center for U.S.-Mexican Studies.

Williams, H. (2001). *Social movements and economic transition: Markets and distributive protest in Mexico.* New York: Cambridge University Press.

THE NEW DEAL (UNITED STATES)

The New Deal was the domestic program of President Franklin Delano Roosevelt. A watershed event in American history, it altered the balance of power between national and state government and the branches of the federal government. During the New Deal, Washington began to play a dominant role in setting the nation's economic agenda and sustaining a level of authority heretofore used only during wartime. The presidency also grew in power as Roosevelt created the Executive Office of the President (EOP) and began to formulate domestic policies and legislation that would be sent to Congress for passage. Although previous presidents had cabinets and informal advisers, Roosevelt created several new administrative agencies that came under the president's authority. The changes wrought by the New Deal created the modern government of the United States. Whereas many of these changes had been sought by social workers and others after the Progressive Era, it took a serious economic depression to cause their enactment.

The Great Depression, which began with the stock market crash in October 1929, caused widespread business failures and joblessness for millions of Americans. By the fall of 1932, more than one fourth of America's workforce was unemployed. Local community chests and other private charities expended all of their resources trying to provide assistance to the jobless. Several state governments were facing bankruptcy. Although economic depressions had been considered normal, cyclical occurrences in a capitalist economy, the severity and duration of this depression led many to doubt long-held assumptions about the ability of financial markets to be self-correcting. Social workers and charity executives began to question prevailing theories about the root causes of poverty. Many began to demand that the federal government take more direct actions to stimulate economic recovery. President Herbert Hoover took some limited actions, most notably signing legislation to provide loans to states to finance relief programs through the Reconstruction Finance Corporation, but he remained convinced that prosperity would return if Americans would only demonstrate confidence in their economic institutions. Dissatisfied with Hoover's timid actions, Americans elevated New York Governor Franklin Delano Roosevelt to the presidency in November of 1932.

Following his inauguration in March 1933, Roosevelt immediately began to transform the federal role in directing an economic recovery. Previous presidents had generally accepted the laissez-faire doctrine that government should refrain from interfering with business matters and allow the capitalist system to correct itself during periods of economic depression. Roosevelt believed instead that the resources of Washington must be harnessed to help those left destitute by hard times. The shutdown of the nation's

banking system the week of his inauguration left the new president with little recourse other than to take quick, decisive action. As a result, the first hundred days of the New Deal witnessed the passage of a vast amount of legislation intended to stimulate the economy and provide assistance to the unemployed. The swiftness with which Roosevelt responded set a new standard and all presidents since have been judged on their ability to implement their agendas during the first hundred days of their administrations.

There have been various interpretations of the New Deal. Some contend that Roosevelt's program differed little from what Hoover had done and that Roosevelt was intent upon preserving traditional financial institutions. Some critics pointed to Roosevelt's refusal to embrace a more radical economic reconstruction or to push an aggressive agenda of civil rights for African Americans. Others have charged that Roosevelt ushered in an era of federal largesse that resulted in welfare dependency, an erosion of the family structure, and massive deficits. Some view the New Deal as a loosely constructed program lacking specific allegiance to either conservative or liberal doctrines. They argue that the president simply experimented with different remedies, hoping to spark a recovery.

Many historians agree that there were actually two new deals, although they differ on which was the more radical. The first lasted from 1933 to 1935. Programs such as the Federal Emergency Relief Administration (FERA) and the Public Works Administration (PWA) were created during this period in an effort to bring immediate relief to the nation's unemployed. There were also efforts to restructure the nation's economic institutions during this period typified by the National Industrial Recovery Act and the Agricultural Administration Act. The Supreme Court declared the National Industrial Recovery Act unconstitutional in 1936.

The second new deal began in 1935. The Social Security Act was the most notable legislative accomplishment during this period. Earlier historians argued that the second new deal was more radical and created more permanent changes. More recent scholars contend instead that the most radical movement for a planned economy had ended by 1935, and that Roosevelt grew more conservative in his approach. They also argue that the New Deal was effectively over after the 1938 midterm elections, when a sufficient coalition of Republicans and conservative Democrats emerged in the Congress to thwart any new social legislation.

One of the most significant accomplishments of the New Deal was the creation of a permanent national welfare structure. This was achieved through passage of the Social Security Act. The major intent of this legislation was to protect different groups of poor persons through a combination of social insurance and categorical public assistance programs. Old Age Assistance was crafted for persons who were retired from the labor force; Unemployment Insurance was added to protect persons from temporary job losses. Mothers and children received assistance through services such as Aid to Dependent Children, Maternal and Child Health Services, and Services for Crippled Children. The Social Security Act also provided assistance for persons who were unemployed because of blindness. Federal grants were provided to the states to administer these programs.

Before the New Deal, public relief for unemployed and other categories of poor was the responsibility of state and local governments. This arrangement had existed since the nation's founding. The effects of the Great Depression, coupled with the emergence of a more urban and modern nation, rendered many state governments unable to meet the challenges brought by such widespread and long-lasting destitution. Several governors and congressmen began to demand help from Washington to finance relief programs. The result was a shift in the federalist arrangement that saw the federal government become more directly involved in funding and directing public assistance programs at state levels. The Social Security Act was the central piece of legislation that brought about the transformation. It would be the foundation of America' public assistance system for the next 60 years.

The incursion of the federal government into relief also brought about profound changes in public welfare and the profession of social work. Before the New Deal, most relief work carried out by social workers was done through private agencies. A few states had public welfare offices, but most relied upon existing poor law statutes to provide care for their destitute. These laws typically authorized such care to be funded and provided at the county or municipal levels. Some states had constitutional prohibitions against state-level funding of relief.

An earlier generation of social workers tended to view poverty as the result of personal failings such as drunkenness, immorality, or laziness. Relief, they argued, was best provided by trained social workers who could recognize and correct the causes of poverty in the individual. They also distrusted public welfare, believing that it too easily became a tool of patronage in the hands of corrupt elected officials. By the 1920s, a group of younger, more pragmatic social workers emerged. Heirs of the Progressive Era, they viewed relief as much a proper role for government as public health.

The scope of unemployment during the Great Depression bolstered the conviction of the newer generation of social workers that poverty was very often caused by conditions outside the control of individuals. The problems experienced by most families, they argued, were the result of a lack of money and that a provision of relief alone could help them regain adequate functioning. They also felt that federally funded relief should become the sole province of public agencies.

Harry Hopkins was one of this newer generation of social workers who wanted relief to become a public enterprise. He had directed Roosevelt's relief program in New York State and was brought to Washington to do the same job on a national level. With the passage of the Federal Emergency Relief Act in May of 1933, Hopkins was named director of the Federal Emergency Relief Administration (FERA). He was given $500 million to distribute to states in relief and wide latitude to determine how the agency should operate. The funds were to be distributed as grants-in-aid, rather than as a loan system, such as the one operated under the Reconstruction Finance Corporation the previous year.

The first published regulation of FERA mandated that as of August 1, 1933, only public agencies would be allowed to distribute federal relief funds. States were thus required to establish emergency relief offices, if state welfare agencies did not already exist, to receive grants-in-aid. Some private agencies turned public so they could continue to distribute relief, while others discontinued relief-giving activities and turned their attentions more toward the provision of casework and other services.

This FERA regulation had an impact upon both the social work profession and public welfare that is still being felt. It drove a wedge between public and private models of social work practice. Many have questioned whether it actually led the social work profession away from work with the poor. Critics continue to charge that on the whole a bifurcated system of public assistance developed under the New Deal whereby the elderly, temporarily unemployed, and other categories of nonchronically poor receive help under a nonstigmatizing social insurance program. The chronically poor, in contrast, are those perceived in the popular imagination to be America's welfare class. Still, the current public assistance structure in America remains largely the result of the Roosevelt administration. Although the Personal Responsibility and Work Opportunity Reconciliation Act of 1996 structurally altered much of the welfare system, it did not succeed in a repeal of the New Deal as some had hoped.

The New Deal remains the benchmark by which current social and economic policies are judged. Contemporary attempts at curtailing welfare are seen as a referendum on the New Deal. So too is the "new federalism," which proponents argue returns to the states the autonomy they should rightfully retain. The power wielded by the president over domestic policies and the vast number of agencies under his authority that set economic and welfare policies remain, perhaps, the most lasting legacy of the New Deal.

—*Vincent J. Venturini*

See also Federalism and Social Welfare Policy (United States); Homelessness (United States); Hopkins, Harry Lloyd; Housing Policy (United States); Perkins, Frances; Rank and File Movement (United States); Roosevelt, Anna Eleanor; Roosevelt, Franklin Delano; Social Security (United States); Van Kleeck, Mary; Work Relief (United States)

Primary Sources

Franklin D. Roosevelt Papers and Harry Hopkins Papers, Franklin D. Roosevelt Presidential Library, Hyde Park, NY; Records of New Deal agencies, National Archives & Records Administration, College Park, MD; Frances Perkins Oral History Interview, Oral History Research Office, Butler Library, Columbia University, New York.

Current Comment

Alsop, J., & Kintner, R. (1971). *Men around the president.* Lincoln: University of Nebraska Press. (Original work published 1939)
Hoover, H. (1934). *The challenge to liberty.* New York: Scribner.
Moley, R. (1939). *After seven years.* New York: Harper & Row.

Further Reading

Amenta, E. (1998). *Bold relief: Institutional politics and the origins of modern American social policy.* Princeton, NJ: Princeton University Press.
Brinkley, A. (1995). *The end of reform: New Deal liberalism in recession and war.* New York: Vintage.
Leuchtenberg, W. E. (1963). *Franklin D. Roosevelt and the New Deal.* New York: Harper & Row.
Leuchtenberg, W. E. (1993). *In the shadow of FDR: From Harry Truman to Bill Clinton* (2nd ed.). Ithaca, NY: Cornell University Press.

P

PEASANT MOVEMENTS AND SOCIAL PROGRAMS (MEXICO)

Peasant movements and social programs in Mexico are inextricably linked to the outcome of the Mexican Revolution (1910–1920). Primarily an agrarian rebellion, the decade-long popular uprising resulted from increased land concentration, a closed political system, and the general deterioration of labor conditions during the dictatorship of Porfirio Díaz (1876–1911). The resulting Constitution represented a series of compromises between the different revolutionary factions, and peasants' right to land became enshrined in Article 27. The rural poor received land titles in the 1920s—especially in Morelos, where rural dwellers led by Emiliano Zapata (1879–1919) mounted an especially tenacious struggle to protect their land and local autonomy—but a real agrarian distribution did not occur until the late 1930s, when President Lázaro Cárdenas (1934–1940) distributed 18.4 million hectares of land to peasants throughout Mexico. The government partitioned much of the land as *ejidos,* collective landholdings that could not be bought or sold, only passed on through inheritance. The state also created hierarchical agencies to deliver credit, fertilizers, and irrigation projects to small farmers. Cárdenas's reforms made him Mexico's most popular president, especially in the countryside. His administration, however, also marked the consolidation of the modern Mexican state and its official party. Originally the National Revolution party (*Partido Nacional Revolucionario,* or PNR) in 1929, Cárdenas changed its name to the Mexican Revolution party (*Partido de la Revolución Mexican,* or PRM) in 1938. In 1946, it was renamed the Institutional Revolutionary party (*Partido Revolucionario Insitucional* or PRI). By implementing massive social reforms, Cárdenas linked the notion of revolutionary justice to the official party and for decades to come the PRI legitimized itself through claims over the Revolution. Whereas Cárdenas had conceived of the state, and especially the office of the president, as the entity responsible for keeping the abuses of a capitalist system in check, subsequent administrations would increasingly ally themselves with the business class, foreign and national. Although the PRI used the language of agrarian reform and appropriated the figure of Emiliano Zapata, the quantity and quality of land distribution diminished significantly after the Cárdenas administration.

Cárdenas's reforms involved a mass mobilization of the popular sectors in separate associations and under state tutelage. For the countryside, he created the National Peasant Confederation (*Confederación Nacional Campesina*, or CNC) representing peasants, agricultural workers, small landowners, and landless peons. The CNC stood as a channel to officiate land reforms but did so increasingly in exchange for PRI votes. Social welfare agencies functioned in a similar manner. The National Agricultural Credit Bank, established in 1926, was one of the first institutions created to ensure the viability of the peasant economy. Other credit institutions included the National Bank for Ejidal Credit (*Banco Nacional de Crédtio Ejidal,* or BNCE), created in 1936 to support new land recipients. In 1975, the National Bank for Rural Credit (*Banco Nacional de Credito Rural,* or BANRURAL) was created from the mergers of previous credit institutions. This agency was designed to finance the agricultural production of small farmers and prevent abuses of private entrepreneurs charging usurious fees for their loans. Although BANRURAL provided much-needed resources, it was substantially underfunded, plagued by corruption, and used for purposes of political control. Land distribution, credit, and access to water became instruments of control and political reward for peasants loyal to the regime.

RURAL MOBILIZATIONS

Because the government appointed CNC leaders to ensure their institutional loyalty, one of the major battles waged by peasant groups was for political independence. By organizing autonomously, rural dwellers sought to force concessions through direct action, such as land takeovers, protests, or marches to state and national capitals. The General Union of Workers and Peasants of Mexico (*Unión General de Obreros y Campesinos de México,* or UGOCM), for example, formed in 1949 to mobilize peasants independently of the state. The UGOCM grouped peasants and rural laborers throughout Mexico demanding the partition of *latifundios* (large landholdings). It exerted the strongest presence in the northern states of Sinaloa, Chihuahua, Baja California, and Sonora, where, in the late 1950s and early 1960s, it led massive land takeovers. The government recognized the potential threat of the UGOCM and moved to dismantle it through a combination of co-option and repression. It isolated the radical sectors and offered enticing concessions to the more moderate groups causing drastic divisions in the organization that severely limited its impact.

The fate of groups like the UGOCM—but especially the repression that prevailed in the countryside carried out by hired gunmen, judicial police, local authorities, large landowners, or the army—convinced some agrarian leaders that the only way to defend the rights of the rural population was through armed struggle. One important group rose up in Morelos. Led by Rubén Jaramillo, a peasant who had fought in the Zapatista army during the Revolution, the *Jaramillistas* fought for the implementation of rural reforms mandated by the Constitution. They initially organized through legal channels, even running Jaramillo for governor of the state in 1946 and 1952 with a political platform advocating the protection of peasant and worker rights. But when local authorities responded with persecution, Jaramillo took up arms and formed a small guerrilla group. He received a presidential pardon in 1958, but in 1962 army troops killed him, his wife, and his three stepsons. Peasant guerrilla groups also arose in other states. In Guerrero, Lucio Cabañas was persecuted by the state's judicial police for speaking in defense of local copra farmers. To avoid being killed, he went into hiding in 1967 and formed a small guerrilla group known as the Poor party (*Partido de los Pobres*). Cabañas's group attempted to raise consciousness among the population of Guerrero and carried out several attacks on the army. The government sent 24,000 troops to Guerrero and launched a campaign of terror against the state's population and eventually killed Cabañas in an ambush. Both Jaramillo and Cabañas are remembered as agrarian leaders who defended the rights of rural people. The PRI's violent campaigns against them were typical of the regime's repressive treatment of dissenting groups.

In spite of repression inflicted on *campesinos* in Guerrero, Morelos, and throughout Mexico, and despite the radicalization of these groups during the 1960s and 1970s, by 1979 rural organizations came together in a legal movement. Seeking once again to organize independently of the state, peasant groups across the country formed the National Coordinator Plan of Ayala (*Coordinadora Nacional Plan de Ayala,* or CNPA). Land continued to be the central issue for the CNPA and the organization represented rural dwellers' efforts to regroup after suffering so many setbacks. Some 1,500 delegates representing 40 organizations arrived at the constituting congress. The ranks of the CNPA continued to swell as it mobilized throughout the country and marched on the capital against President José López Portillo's (1976–1982) official declaration to end land redistribution. Despite the CNPA's large numbers, continuous appeals, and powerful presence, the Department of Agrarian Affairs (*Departamento de Asuntos Agrarios*) consistently blocked its land petitions. In addition, the CNPA had to devote much of its efforts and energy to combat government repression in the countryside. Thus, many mobilizations demanded the freedom of peasants incarcerated because of their fight for land and protested the political assassinations that occurred with such frequency in rural Mexico. Overall, the CNPA's real significance lay in the political realm: It represented the ascendancy of peasant political initiatives, a refusal to be ignored by a regime whose policies increasingly abandoned the countryside, and a national coordinated body that would continue to speak in the interest of Mexican peasants.

GOVERNMENT PROGRAMS

Despite a return to agrarian language during the regimes of Adolfo López Mateos (1958–1964) and Luis Echeverría (1970–1976), post-Cardenista administrations never implemented far-reaching land reform. Instead, they dealt with discontent in the countryside by implementing food and social welfare programs. Examples of such policy included the establishment of the National Company of Popular Subsistence (*Compañía Nacional de Subsistencias Populares*, or CONASUPO) in 1965, which was charged with the distribution, storage, price control, and sales of rural products. CONASUPO stores were especially important in isolated areas where peasants would otherwise have to depend on middlemen who siphoned off most of the profits in transportation costs. Peasants also relied on CONASUPO to purchase basic household items at reasonable prices. But this agency was not far-reaching enough and accounted for only a miniscule percentage of total retail food purchases. Still, although limited in its scope and severely underfinanced, for a vast number of rural dwellers CONASUPO meant the difference between poverty and indigence. President López Portillo created a more ambitious program in 1980. The Mexican Food System (*Sistema Alimentario Mexicano,* or SAM) was meant to provide credit, fertilizers, improved seeds, and crop insurance to small-scale rural producers. By 1970, Mexico had lost its food self-sufficiency and SAM represented an attempt to deal with what had become a crisis in the countryside. The government planned to invest the country's oil revenues to reinvigorate grain production throughout Mexico. SAM's accomplishments included an increase in guaranteed prices to counterbalance inflation and a substantial growth of storage capabilities for peasant warehouses around the country. The program's top-down nature, competing policy priorities, and its replication of extant rural power relations, however, prevented it from taking root in the countryside. It was short-lived and ended with López Portillo's term in office.

NEOLIBERALISM AND PEASANTS' RESPONSE

The 1980s and 1990s saw a worsening of conditions in the countryside. In 1982, Mexico entered a deep financial crisis leading it to devalue the *peso*, default on its foreign debt, and dramatically reduce social spending. Coupled with the neoliberal reforms implemented in the late 1980s and throughout the 1990s, poverty reached unprecedented levels. In preparation for Mexico's entry into the North American Free Trade Agreement (NAFTA), President Carlos Salinas de Gortari (1988–1994) amended Article 27 of the Constitution, allowing for the sale of the *ejidos* and declaring all pending land petitions null and void. Other austerity measures included the eventual abolishment of CONASUPO.

On the eve of January 1, 1994, the day NAFTA went into effect, indigenous rebels in the southern state of Chiapas took over several municipalities. Proclaiming themselves in open rebellion against the Salinas government, they demanded land, schools, food, shelter, health care, and democracy. The Zapatista Army of National Liberation (*Ejército Zapatista de Liberación Nacional,* or EZLN) cited Salinas's reform of Article 27 as the final straw leading them to take up arms. The rebels' call for indigenous rights—deeply rooted in their historic ties to the land and its cultivation—elicited national and international support, forcing the government to a cease-fire within a few days of the uprising. The army and paramilitary groups, however, continued to wage a low-intensity warfare in Chiapas. The triumph of the National Action party (*Partido de Acción Nacional,* or PAN) in 2000 ended the 71-year PRI rule, but President Vicente Fox (2000–2006) remained committed to the neoliberal policies, eliciting militant peasant protests demanding major revisions of NAFTA. Although Mexico entered the twenty-first century as a primarily urban nation, peasant movements showed no signs of abating and continued to force issues of land onto the national agenda.

—Tanalís Padilla

See also Land Reform (Mexico); Neoliberalism, Social Programs, and Social Movements (Mexico)

Primary Sources

Presidentes and *Dirección General de Gobierno* Collection, *Archivo General de la Nación,* Mexico City; peasant land petitions, *Archivo General Agrario,* Mexico City.

Current Comment

Jaramillo, R. (1967). *Autobiografía.* Mexico City: Editorial Nuestro Tiempo.
Simpson, E. N. (1937). *The ejido; Mexico's way out.* Chapel Hill: University of North Carolina Press.
Suárez, L. (1984). *Lucio Cabañas. El guerrillero sin esperanza.* Mexico City: Grijalbo.

Further Reading

Harvey, N. (1998). *The Chiapas rebellion.* Durham, NC: Duke University Press.
Hodges, D. (1995). *Mexican anarchism after the Revolution.* Austin: University of Texas Press.
Ochoa, E. (2000). *Feeding Mexico: The political uses of food since 1910.* Wilmington, DE: Scholarly Resources.
Sanderson, S. E. (1981). *Agrarian populism and the Mexican state.* Berkeley: University of California Press.

PERKINS, FRANCES (1882–1965)

Frances Perkins, the first woman appointed to a U.S. president's cabinet, served as secretary of labor under President Franklin D. Roosevelt. Perkins, who played a central role in establishing U.S. social welfare

policy, worked for passage of the historic Social Security Act of 1935, the landmark social legislation of the New Deal era, and the foundation of U.S. federal social welfare policy. Lecturing until 2 weeks before her death in 1965, Perkins's lifework was devoted to improving conditions for the working poor and promoting the welfare of all Americans. Overcoming prejudices and biases, Perkins pursued her mission in arenas then dominated by men. Practical by nature, she contributed her capacities as an author, teacher, lobbyist, and public official to develop policies that drastically altered the federal government's role in promoting and safeguarding public welfare. These policies included the minimum wage, Unemployment Insurance, and Social Security benefits—policies that continue to provide economic security for citizens vulnerable to the inequities and hardships of a capitalist economy.

Born in 1880, Fannie Coralie Perkins was the daughter of Fred and Susie Perkins of Boston. (She changed her name to Frances in 1905.) Perkins attended Mount Holyoke College, graduating in 1902. While at Holyoke, her studies included outings to local factories. These initial encounters with working people who were poor marked the beginning of her interest in and compassion for the less fortunate. Like many of her well-educated, socially conscious contemporaries, Perkins affiliated with settlement houses in Chicago and Philadelphia, teaching and working for better living conditions for her poor neighbors.

In 1907, as secretary of the Philadelphia Research and Protective Association, she authored a comprehensive report on the living and working conditions of working girls. This report later aided her lobbying effort for stricter standards in the licensing of rooming houses. Perkins then continued her education by pursuing a master's degree at Columbia University, graduating in 1910 after completing a major essay on malnutrition among schoolchildren.

Working as executive secretary of the Consumer's League in New York City between 1910 and 1912, Perkins lobbied for a 54-hour workweek for women. Having witnessed the 1911 Triangle Shirtwaist Factory fire, in which 600 workers were trapped and 146 died, Perkins intensified her efforts in the area of factory and workplace safety. She became well-known for her social action and dedication to legislative reforms during the Progressive Era preceding World War I. In the following years, her commitment and abilities propelled her to positions in which she was able to aid and influence increasingly powerful political figures.

While lobbying with the New York Committee on Safety, Perkins met then New York Assemblyman Al Smith. Working later on his campaign for governor, Perkins urged Smith to take women voters seriously and organized women to care about politics. After Smith became governor, he appointed her as member (1919–1921) and then chair (1923–1926) of the New York State Industrial Commission, which administered the state's labor legislation.

When Franklin Delano Roosevelt became governor of New York in 1929, he appointed Perkins as state industrial commissioner, the state's chief labor officer. Some who believed that men would not work for a woman criticized this appointment. Roosevelt would continue to defy this and similar criticisms of his appointments for Perkins. The working relationship between Roosevelt and Perkins lasted through his presidency, a relationship Perkins chronicled in her book, *The Roosevelt I Knew* (1946).

Upon winning the presidency in 1933, President Roosevelt appointed Perkins to his cabinet as secretary of labor, giving her a formal venue to propose new social programs. Roosevelt also appointed her chair of the Committee on Economic Security, a committee formed to investigate social insurance and make recommendations for its implementation in the United States. Under Perkins's leadership, the committee fulfilled Roosevelt's campaign promises for state unemployment insurance and assistance to the elderly and proposed a far-reaching, comprehensive system of Social Security. The resulting Report of the Committee on Economic Security, issued in January 1935, was the foundation for the landmark Social Security Act, signed by President Roosevelt in August 1935. Passed in 1935, the Social Security Act included 11 titles that addressed not only Unemployment and Old-Age Insurance but also new protections and programs for maternal and child health, crippled children, vocational rehabilitation, Old-Age Assistance, Aid to Dependent Children, and Aid to the Blind.

Perkins served as the secretary of labor from 1933 to 1945, the longest period anyone has held that position. This was a particularly significant accomplishment for Perkins who, like many other women activists of the era, was labeled as a communist by opponents of her work and criticized for being more of a social worker than a political official. Though not trained as many of her peers were in the burgeoning profession of social work, her activism reflected her settlement house background. Her speeches, writings, and campaigns were rooted in the belief that poverty was not solely a reflection of the individual but of larger social and economic conditions that made anyone vulnerable to the shifts and imperfections in the market system. Before the Great Depression, government interventions to safeguard individuals vulnerable to financial hardship were often characterized as un-American, socialist, and radical. After surviving the depression, more Americans were amenable to the idea of governmental interventions, not only on humanitarian grounds but also, as Perkins presented it, in the interest of the national economy.

After resigning her post as labor secretary in 1945, Perkins served from 1946 to 1952 on the U.S. Civil Service Commission, resigning after her husband's death. (When she married Paul Wilson in 1913, Perkins chose not to take his name, an act of feminism that garnered Miss Perkins much criticism.) She remained active as a teacher and lecturer until her death at age 85 in 1965, and was survived by her daughter.

—Bianca Genco-Morrison and Jan L. Hagen

See also Hopkins, Harry Lloyd; The New Deal (United States); Roosevelt, Franklin Delano; Settlement Houses (United States); Social Security (United States)

Further Reading

Martin, G. W. (1976). *Madam secretary, Frances Perkins.* Boston: Houghton Mifflin.

National Conference on Social Welfare. (1985). *The report of the Committee on Economic Security of 1935 and other basic documents relating to the development of the Social Security Act.* Washington, DC: Author. Available: www.ssa.gov/history/reports/ces/ces5.html

Sicherman, B., & Green, C. H. (Eds.). (1980). *Notable American women, The modern period: A biographical dictionary.* Cambridge, MA: Harvard University Press.

PHILANTHROPY (CANADA)

Philanthropy is most commonly associated with upper- or middle-class citizens providing aid to the poor, the sick, or the otherwise needy by donating money, organizing charities or voluntary associations, or creating foundations. The range of philanthropic activities is much larger than the relief of poverty, however, and has included hospitals, educational institutions, cultural institutions, projects connected to housing reform and public health, as well as humanitarian/reform movements such as antislavery and temperance.

The early British settlers to Canada brought with them a long tradition of philanthropy and the private provision of social services was well established by the early nineteenth century. The respective role of philanthropy and state aid in early Canada varied by region. Poor law legislation in the Maritime colonies meant philanthropy existed alongside some publicly supported rate-based relief structures such as poorhouses. Neither Quebec nor Ontario enacted poor law legislation during the colonial period, leaving more scope and more power for private philanthropy, which, for the most part, determined the forms of services available. Catholic Quebec had the further distinction that the Catholic church and its religious orders controlled social services. Thus, Catholic philanthropists like Olivier Berthelet, a French-speaking businessman who was one of Montreal's leading philanthropists, carried out their philanthropic work by providing money or real estate for church efforts. The Protestant elite in cities like Montreal and Quebec, however, established a wide range of welfare, social, and cultural institutions.

A coexistence of state efforts and private philanthropy developed in Canada as, even in areas without a poor law, the state subsidized private efforts and gradually assumed a more directive role in some areas. This "mixed social economy" remained in effect after the development of state welfare services in the mid twentieth century.

Canadian philanthropy in the nineteenth century had several defining characteristics. Much philanthropic work was carried out in connection with individual churches and almost every ethnic group provided for the needs of its own community and immigrants. One of the most common forms of philanthropy was the subscription-based voluntary society to which members paid annual fees to a privately administered association. This enabled individuals without large private fortunes to undertake philanthropic work collectively and substantially increased the volume of philanthropy. Institutions were the physical representation of philanthropy, but personal involvement was another key aspect and was central to efforts like visiting societies and the Society of St. Vincent de Paul as well as to fund-raising and the day-to-day supervision of institutional regimes. Women did much of this charitable work.

The philanthropic landmarks from the past are remarkable and highlight the myriad causes philanthropists advanced: charities of all sorts (orphanages, reform schools, old-age homes, poorhouses, workshops, immigrant reception homes, insane asylums, institutions for "fallen women," known as Magdalen asylums, women's refuges, boys homes, and so on), hospitals, universities, art museums, and housing projects, to name a few. Many of these, like the Royal Victoria Hospital in Montreal, paid for by George Stevens and Donald Smith, represent the efforts of a few individuals; but others like McGill University, the Montreal General Hospital, the Montreal Protestant House of Industry and Refuge, the Montreal Museum of Fine Arts, the Toronto General Hospital, the Toronto House of Industry, and the Art Gallery of Toronto, among others, represented numerous donations.

Philanthropy was closely linked with nineteenth century elite culture and the role the elite hoped to play in society. Individuals had many motives for their philanthropy, not the least of which was the basic human instinct of kindness or the desire to make a difference. Religious motivations are not to be underestimated; charity was a precept in every major religion and the evangelical urge to save souls was very strong in the nineteenth century. The rise of humanitarianism and the idea of progress were other important factors. Philanthropic involvement, however, was also a way for families to acquire or confirm social status in the community and to be accepted as part of the elite. Further, contemporaries believed that social service efforts helped to build bridges between the classes, relieve urban disorder, and establish elite control over public space. Many were also convinced that the elite had a civic and social responsibility to address problems like poverty, substandard housing, inadequate sanitation, and public health in the new industrial city and to establish social and cultural institutions that would make their city proud. Finally, some philanthropy had financial benefits.

Much of the philanthropic work connected to poor relief had clear overtones of moral reform and was driven by the conviction that prolonged poverty was a result of individual moral defect. The rhetoric, however, was often more severe than actual practice and many philanthropists came to recognize the socioeconomic causes underlying poverty. Throughout the nineteenth century, there were those who argued that charity encouraged dependence in the poor. This movement took more concrete form with the charity organisation societies (COS) that formed in England in 1869 and began in Canada around 1880. The "scientific" charity advocated by the COS was based on the investigation of applications to reduce unnecessary giving, the establishment of a more systematic approach to relief, the coordination of different organizations to increase efficiency, and the attempt to teach self-reliance to the poor rather than distribute relief. Many distinguished between scientific charity, which they called philanthropy, and old-fashioned benevolence, or "charity."

Philanthropy as a larger movement was not limited to the wealthy helping the less fortunate. Kin or family support, neighborhood sharing, and forms of working-class mutual aid were all crucial in helping many of the impoverished or sick overcome their difficulties and either avoid or postpone the need to request aid from others. These forms of philanthropy are much harder to measure than the activities of foundations or charitable subscriptions but are nonetheless important to a broader understanding of philanthropy.

The thrust for change represented by the COS grew in the early twentieth century. Part of this "scientific" approach involved the shift to professional workers instead of volunteers and a decreased emphasis on moralizing attitudes, although these proved remarkably persistent. The role of the state in financing and controlling the social services sector increased dramatically during the depression of the 1930s and during the interwar years as a welfare state and social insurance programs were slowly put in place. Philanthropy, however, remained a central part of the Canadian reality. Some private charities and social service organizations kept on with the same services alongside or under the supervision of state services; others altered their role to fill the gaps left by the state. The importance of the voluntary sector as it is now often called has increased in recent years with the contraction of state welfare. In the year 2000, there were 77,000 registered charities in Canada.

Other than its place in a welfare state, twentieth century Canadian philanthropy has several features that distinguish it from its nineteenth century roots. For the most part, the scale is no longer local. National medical research organizations have multiplied alongside other national associations working on social or cultural causes in Canada or in international relief. With recent cuts to social programs, a myriad of small local private charities have indeed emerged, but these tend to be very small scale by comparison.

Much of the money for philanthropic causes still comes from individuals, but both corporate donations and private foundations have become important sources of funding. The latter includes Canadian foundations (estimated at 1,700 in 2000) but also American foundations such as Carnegie and Rockefeller and international foundations such as the Baron de Hirsch Fund. Furthermore, fund-raising methods have changed. The charity bazaar has been superseded by sophisticated telethons and telephone/mail solicitation. Payroll deduction, income tax credits, and the sale of goods and services make donations more convenient than ever.

And Canadians do respond. Besides the money provided by foundations and corporations, 78 percent of Canadians (more than 19 million people) recorded charitable donations on their income tax returns in 2000. Average donations increase with household income, but the poor give a larger proportion of their income. Voluntarism is also important. Approximately 6.5 million Canadians did volunteer work of some sort in 2000. Clearly, philanthropy is still an integral part of the Canadian social reality.

—Janice Harvey

See also Charity Organization Societies (United States); Social Welfare (Canada): Before the Marsh Report

Primary Sources

The records of many private charities or associations are available at the Library and Archives Canada, Ottawa, ON, and in regional and provincial archives. The debates in the *Proceedings of the Canadian Conference of Charities and Corrections* (1899–1912) are also of interest.

Current Comment

Canadian Centre for Philanthropy [On-line]. Available: www
.ccp.ca/

Drummond, J. (1894). Co-operation as shown in associated charities. In *Women workers of Canada: Being a report of the proceedings of the first annual meeting and conference of the National Council of Women of Canada*. Ottawa, ON: Library and Archives Canada.

McLean, F. (1901). Effects upon private charity of the absence of all public relief. *Proceedings of the 28th National Conference of Charities and Correction, 28,* 139–146.

Minville, E. (1939). *La législation ouvrière et le régime social dans la province de Québec.* Ottawa, ON: J.-O. Patenaude.

Further Reading

Adams, T. (2001). Philanthropic landmarks: The Toronto Trail from a comparative perspective, 1870s to the 1930s. *Urban History Review, 30*(1), 3–21.

Harvey, J. (2001). Dealing with the "destitute and the wretched": The Protestant House of Industry and Refuge in nineteenth-century Montreal. *Journal of the Canadian Historical Association*, New Series, *12,* 73–94.

Reid, J. G. (1984). Health, education, economy: Philanthropic foundations in the Atlantic region in the 1920s and 1930s. *Acadiensis, 14*(1), 64–83.

Speisman, S. (1973). Munificent parsons and municipal parsimony: Voluntary vs. public relief in nineteenth century Toronto. *Ontario History, 65,* 33–50.

PHILANTHROPY (MEXICO)

Philanthropy, charitable giving, and voluntary service for the collective good has a long history in Mexico. Throughout much of Mexican history, philanthropy was closely associated with the Catholic church. When the state came to dominate social welfare activities, in the nineteenth and twentieth centuries, it overshadowed most volunteer and philanthropic efforts. During the past few decades, there has been a boom in philanthropic organizations and a concerted effort to transform philanthropy and corporatist state policy away from charitable giving and toward solidarity and alliance building. The process of economic underdevelopment, however, has served to create significant economic inequality and poverty that has yet to be fully addressed.

Long before the Spanish Conquest of Mexico (1521), notions of collective responsibility were widely practiced. Although conceptions of collective responsibility varied over time and space, indigenous communities often worked land cooperatively and had numerous forms of community service built into their societies. The Spanish viewed these indigenous relationships to the land and to each other as backward and sought to instill Christian notions of civilization and service. But indigenous communities resisted efforts to transform their ways of life; many were able to retain their ideas of community and either adapt it to Spanish and Catholic concepts or maintain traditional practices covertly. Beginning in the colonial period, charitable organizations linked to the church were established to provide services, including hospitals and education. Operated by volunteer societies, such as the Society of St. Vincent de Paul and the Ladies of Charity, founded in 1845 and 1863, respectively, these societies had thousands of members in a number of states and operated until the end of the century.

With the rise of modern liberalism in the nineteenth century and the Mexican Revolution of 1910, the state usurped the role of the church in social welfare, stressing the relationship of the individual to the nation-state. During the 1860s, the state assumed responsibility for education, the establishment of hospitals, and other social programs. This was both a nation-building exercise as well as an effort to rationalize and systemize social welfare policy. Following the Revolution of 1910, elites used the state to create social peace and maintain political control by creating a number of social programs. Small-scale volunteer programs run by the state were created to instill notions of civic responsibility. In 1945, 480 hours of social service were incorporated into college graduation requirements and from 1977 to 1995 the nation's first ladies established the National Patronage of Voluntary Promoters.

Despite the dominance of the state, private philanthropic organizations continued to exist and gradually expanded. Before 1940, these institutions were created by the Catholic church or its wealthy benefactors and donated funds to organizations that provided charity services to the poor. Between 1940 and 1960, a number of organizations emerged, dominated by faith-based groups, that funded self-sustaining development projects in the countryside. From 1960 to 1984, the modest growth of philanthropic institutions continued and became more professionalized. Some organizations began to work in areas of human rights and social justice.

Sparked by the erosion of government legitimacy, the 1980s witnessed renewed popular initiative and the reawakening of civil society. Mexico's economic crisis, characterized by rapid inflation, growth in unemployment, and declining real wages, was coupled with reductions in social programs. The devastating 1985 Mexico City earthquake led to the loss of thousands of lives, but was met with little government response. Thousands of Mexicans formed volunteer rescue brigades in response to government inaction. These factors fueled a growing civil society that saw the weaknesses and unresponsiveness of the authoritarian government.

Since the 1990s, the nonprofit sector has grown significantly. Several organizations emerged to address issues of social welfare and community development as well as human rights, the environment, and women's rights, long considered taboo issues. As of 2002, there were approximately 20,000 nonprofit civil society organizations in Mexico, including religious organizations, mutual associations, political parties, and service-providing organizations.

Community foundations also expanded rapidly during the 1990s. These entities emerged to deal with local problems of poverty and inequality. It is estimated that between 15 and 20 community foundations currently operate in cities such as Tijuana, Cozumel, Oaxaca, Puebla, San Luis Potosi, and in the Bajio regions of North-Central Mexico. The more successful of these foundations work to convene a broad range of interests and community leaders to assess the needs and priorities of the community and implement targeted programs, including nutrition programs, schools, and water treatment plants.

A recent source of community development funds has been Mexicans residing in the United States. Since the 1980s, Mexican migrants in the United States, working with local consulates and community leaders in their hometowns, have sent funds to their communities for the development of specific projects, such as recreation centers and medical clinics. Although the amount of these funds is growing, it is still relatively small when compared to the total amount that migrants send home, one of Mexico's leading sources of foreign exchange.

To give direction to Mexico's emerging nonprofit sector, the Mexican Center for Philanthropy (*Centro Mexicano Para la Filantropía,* or CEMEFI) was established in 1988 as an umbrella organization of several foundations and nonprofits. CEMEFI sought to promote a culture of philanthropy that would contribute to an integral development of the nation. CEMEFI has been successful at raising the profile of the nonprofit sector. The organization made important contacts with research centers in the United States and in Europe and has collaborated with U.S-based foundations.

Private U.S. and European foundations have been active in Mexico since the mid twentieth century. The Rockefeller and Ford foundations have been joined in recent decades by the MacArthur, Hewlett, Packard, and AVINA foundations. In some cases, these foundations have full-time staffs, including Mexican nationals, in Mexico City to develop and implement their programs. Foundation programs have tended to focus on environmental and social policy issues and have made only tepid forays into the area of human rights, political organization, and judicial reform. Mexico does not have tax incentives for donations to nonprofit organizations and thus few large private foundations have emerged.

There remain several obstacles to the growth of philanthropy and the nonprofit sector in Mexico. The authoritarian character of the Mexican state has limited independent organizing and autonomous activities. There has been significant work by CEMEFI and other groups to change this through the 1990s, but a congressional bill that would create tax exemptions and other incentives and clarify the relationship between the nonprofit organizations and the Mexican government has yet to be passed. Although philanthropy has developed considerably over the past few decades, it has done so as the government has retreated from funding social programs. In addition, there has been growing inequality and poverty in Mexico over the past several decades. A comprehensive approach to poverty eradication is beyond the reach of all but a few foundations.

—*Enrique C. Ochoa*

See also Mexico City Poor House; Poverty (Mexico); The Rockefeller Foundation and Public Health (Mexico); Social Welfare (Mexico): Before 1867; Social Welfare (Mexico): Since 1867; Social Work Profession (Mexico); Women and Social Welfare (Mexico)

Primary Source

Centro Mexicano Para la Filantropía can be accessed on-line (www.cemefi.org).

Current Comment

Arango, M. (2002, Spring). Philanthropy in Mexico: Challenges and opportunities. *ReVista: Harvard Review of Latin America*, 33–37. Available: http://drclas.fas.harvard.edu/publications/revista/Volunteering/tcontents.html

Further Reading

Arrom, S. M. (2002, Spring). Philanthropy and its roots: The societies of St. Vincent de Paul in Mexico. *ReVista: Harvard Review of Latin America*, 57–59. Available: http://drclas.fas.harvard.edu/publications/revista/Volunteering/tcontents.html

Morales Camarena, F. J. (2004). Volunteerism in Mexico. ServiceLeader.org: International [On-line]. Available: www.serviceleader.org/new/international/articles

Winder, D. (2001, Fall). Mexican philanthropy breaking new ground: The Bajio Foundation. *ReVista: Harvard Review of Latin America*, 24–25. Available: http://drclas.fas.harvard.edu/publications/revista/mexico/tcontents.html

Winder, D. (2004). Innovations in strategic philanthropy: The case of Mexico (Paper prepared for the International Network on Strategic Philanthropy). New York: Synergos Institute. Available: www.synergos.org/globalphilanthropy/04/inspmexico.pdf

PHILANTHROPY (UNITED STATES)

Originally a term connoting a generalized love of humanity usually expressed in the form of charity toward individuals, since the late nineteenth century philanthropy has come to refer to grant-making charitable foundations and activities by wealthy individuals to establish or support charitable institutions and causes.

The distinction between charity and philanthropy began to emerge in the late 1860s, when upper-class reformers, challenged by rising urban poverty and disorder, sought to develop scientific approaches to social problems. Working through state charity commissions and voluntary associations like the American Association for the Advancement of Science and the charity organization societies, reformers classified and quantified the dimensions of poverty. Arguing that spontaneous and "sentimental"—often religiously mediated—responses to suffering both caused and perpetuated poverty, these reformers worked both to secularize and professionalize charity and poor relief.

Additional impetus to these efforts came from millionaire industrialists like Andrew Carnegie (1835–1919). An ardent social Darwinist, Carnegie believed that the progress of the human race was impeded by almsgiving that rewarded the poor for their poverty. The better solution, he argued in his famous 1889 essay, *Wealth,* was for millionaires to use their wealth "to place ladders within the reach of those who would rise." Carnegie believed that philanthropy should address the causes of poverty and other social problems rather than trying to mitigate their symptoms. In the early twentieth century, Carnegie established several foundations: the Carnegie Corporation of New York, the Carnegie Foundation for the Advancement of Teaching, and the Carnegie Endowment for International Peace.

The first true philanthropic foundation was established by Olivia Slocum Sage (1828–1918), widow of financier Russell Sage. Olivia Sage, who had long been active in the charity organization movement in New York City, created the Russell Sage Foundation in 1901. The foundation sought to consolidate knowledge about social problems and their solutions and to support organizations that addressed these issues.

Oil magnate John D. Rockefeller (1839–1937), though inspired by his religious beliefs rather than social science, shared many of Carnegie's ideas. His early philanthropies—the General Education Board and the Rockefeller Institute—focused on medicine and higher education. In 1913, he gave $100 million to establish the Rockefeller Foundation, which, with the broad mandate of "serving mankind," made grants for a wide range of purposes under the guidance of experts and professionals. Rockefeller's son,

John D. Rockefeller, Jr., (1874–1960) and grandsons, John D. Rockefeller III, Nelson, Laurence, and David, would set the pace for foundation philanthropy for much of the twentieth century.

Through most of the twentieth century, grant-making foundations would make vitally important contributions to American public life. Before the advent of large-scale government support, foundations were virtually the only source of funding for the development of the social sciences, the framing of public policy, the modernization of university curricula, and the sustaining of arts and culture institutions.

In addition to grant-making foundations, like those established by Rockefeller and Carnegie, and operating foundations like Russell Sage, the early decades of the twentieth century produced other forms of institutionalized philanthropy. In 1913, the Cleveland Chamber of Commerce established the first Community Chest, an organization that consolidated the many annual fund drives conducted by the city's charities into a single annual appeal and, by vetting recipient charities in advance, assured that donated dollars were put to the best and most efficient use. By the 1930s, such organizations existed throughout America. The Community Chest is the organizational ancestor of today's United Way.

Another Cleveland contribution was the community foundation, the first of which was established in 1914. Intended to broaden philanthropy's donor base, the community foundation encouraged donors large and small to create endowment funds and place them under common management. Usually governed by quasi-public boards, community foundations exemplified the democratic possibilities of philanthropy, showing that charitable giving was not just for the rich.

During the 1920s, colleges, universities, hospitals, and organizations like the Red Cross helped to create a flourishing professional fund-raising industry, carried out by experts in the use of new advertising and marketing techniques.

The steeply progressive income and estate taxes of the 1930s and the universalization of income taxation during the Second World War fueled the rapid growth in the number and size of foundations and other forms of institutional philanthropy. In the early 1950s, court rulings permitting philanthropic giving by business

corporations stimulated a proliferation of company foundations and corporate contributions programs.

In the 1950s and 1960s, the growing number and wealth of foundations and other exempt entities fueled congressional concern about the use of philanthropic giving as a method of tax avoidance and the possibility that some foundations were supporting subversive causes. A succession of congressional investigations in the 1950s and 1960s led to the passage of the Tax Reform Act of 1969, legislation intended to ensure that organized philanthropy was more responsive to the public interest.

Following the passage of the Tax Reform Act of 1969, foundation leaders sought to convince the public and its elected representatives that philanthropy was an important and valuable part of American public life: a vital source of social innovation and democratic pluralism. By subsidizing scholarship and energetic public relations activities through trade associations, philanthropy was redefined as part of a broad and inclusive "nonprofit sector" that embraced not only grant-making foundations but charities of every kind as "private initiatives in the public interest."

Through most of the twentieth century, philanthropy, however defined, tended to be tied to agendas of liberal reform, concerned largely with the redistribution of wealth and opportunities. Generally, political conservatives had been hostile to philanthropy and had resisted establishing foundations and other nonprofits to advance their causes. Following the defeat of conservative Republican Barry Goldwater in 1964, the American Right began to reassess philanthropy, coming to recognize how vital it had been to producing the liberal policy agenda and propagating it through the universities, government, and other institutions. After 1970, conservatives began establishing foundations and supporting think tanks, colleges and universities, and social movement organizations favorable to their views. Conservative philanthropy played a key role in the success of the conservative revolution that dominated American public life in the last two decades of the twentieth century.

With the globalization of the world's economy at the end of the twentieth century, philanthropy has followed the interests of global economic actors into new domains of transnational activity. Older philanthropies like Ford and Rockefeller have been joined by new foundations, notably the Bill and Melinda Gates Foundation, in supporting economic development, medical care, and the growth of civil society throughout the world.

—*Peter Dobkin Hall*

See also Health Policy (United States); Voluntarism (United States)

Primary Sources

Rockefeller Foundation Archives and Russell Sage Foundation Records, both at Rockefeller Archive Center, Sleepy Hollow, NY.

Current Comment

Carnegie, A. (1889). Wealth. *North American Review, 148,* 653–664; *149,* 682–698.

Glenn, J. M., Brandt, L., & Andrews, F. E. (1947). *The Russell Sage Foundation, 1907–1947.* New York: Russell Sage Foundation.

Warner, A. G. (1894). *American charities: A study in philanthropy and economics.* New York: Thomas Y. Crowell.

Watson, F. D. (1922). *The charity organization movement in the United States: A study in American philanthropy.* New York: Macmillan.

Further Reading

Brilliant, E. L. (1990). *The United Way: Dilemmas of organized charity.* New York: Columbia University Press.

Friedman, L. J., & McGarvie, M. D. (Eds.). (2003). *Charity, philanthropy, and civility in American history.* New York: Cambridge University Press.

Magat, R. (Ed.). (1989). *An agile servant: Community leadership by community foundations.* New York: Foundation Center.

Sealander, J. (1997). *Private wealth and public life: Foundation philanthropy and the reshaping of American social policy from the Progressive Era to the New Deal.* Baltimore: Johns Hopkins University Press.

POOR LAW (UNITED STATES)

Popular accounts suggest that the origin of public assistance to the poor was borne of the deep and persistent unemployment of the Great Depression and that its first cry was President Franklin D. Roosevelt's signing of the Social Security Act in 1935. The "poor laws"—the compulsory tax on property providing for the "indoor" and "outdoor" relief of the poor—can in fact be traced without interruption to the colonial era of the seventeenth century. From colonial times to the 1920s, "outdoor relief" referred to relief in cash and in-kind assistance such as food consumed at home or in transit; "indoor relief" was a generic term referring to relief given literally "indoors": in the poorhouse, say, or in a home for the feebleminded. Public assistance, in other words, indoor and outdoor, begins with the poor laws of the early seventeenth century.

The first poor laws in the New World were influenced mainly by British examples, the legal and financial responsibility for the poor being assumed by the town, the parish, or the county, when self or relatives were not sufficient. The British colonies in America stayed close to the spirit of England's "43rd of Elizabeth," the so-called Elizabethan Poor Law of 1601. The Elizabethan Poor Law established in England the first secure basis for public assistance to the poor and soon after it found a ready export market. The colony of Rhode Island adopted the Elizabethan Poor Law with hardly a revision and other colonies changed it only slightly.

The poor law required each town or parish to provide for the poor by levying a rate on property held within the jurisdiction. The law set in motion the idea in the United States that public provision for the poor is guaranteed. It enabled various means of providing tax-financed relief, including but not limited to outdoor relief for the aged and infirm poor, apprenticing of pauper children to farmers, and construction of poorhouses or "almshouses." Administrative duties were the responsibility of selectmen or of an unpaid "overseer of the poor." There were exceptions to the British pattern. New Mexico and Louisiana were deeply shaped by the concept of charity or *caritas* of the Catholic church. And in the colony of New Netherlands (1609–1664), the ecclesiastical practice of the Dutch Reformed church had put a profound mark on care for the poor, a set of practices that would be only gradually replaced by the English poor law in developing New York.

More so than would Britain, the American colonies, and then later the states, would adjust the poor laws to facilitate difference in local or regional economic conditions and culture. Thus, for example, the municipal practice of "auctioning" the poor—providing a contract for the care of a poor person to the lowest bidder—had faded from much of New England by the late 1820s and yet auctioning did not leave a less-settled Indiana until the 1840s. Indeed, ridding a burdened house of its children at auction to the lowest bidder (lowest, because the tax would subsidize the taker) was a legal form of assistance in Arkansas as late as 1903. And whereas almshouses could be found in New England in the late seventeenth century, the old Northwest Territory would not see the almshouse as common until the 1830s.

American struggles with poverty, and collective strategies to deal with it, came early. Even as the Continental Congress was debating independence, the managers of the Philadelphia almshouse, eight blocks away, were writing a sad report on the care of the poor. They felt they could not cope with the rising numbers of the poor. They wrote that "of the 147 Men, 178 Women, and 85 Children [admitted to the almshouse during the previous year] most of them [are] naked, helpless and emaciated with Poverty and Disease to such a Degree, that some have died in a few Days after their Admission." The almshouse in colonial Philadelphia, like most almshouses throughout the pre–Civil War period, was a miscellaneous receptacle for human distress. A single almshouse could serve as a hostel, a hospice, a prison, and a home for the physically disabled. The common laborer and the immigrant widow often shared quarters with the insane, the helpless, and the emaciated, as they did in colonial Philadelphia.

From colonial times to the present, the history of public assistance is in part a history of increasingly specialized goods and services being redistributed to increasingly diverse populations. Taking the long view, it is a history of an increasingly centralized system of finance and administration, evolving from the township trustee to the federal government, from local property taxes to the federal income tax. But when seen in closer range, the history of public assistance is a "nonlinear" history, a story filled with switchbacks and sometimes-radical social policy reversals, such as those put forward by Presidents Richard Nixon and William Clinton.

The history of public assistance, when viewed from a long-run perspective, is also a history of withdrawal—though never complete—from the explicitly punitive, correctional, and mental health institutions.

Most Americans nowadays would not consider the auctioning system of the 1800s or the public whippings of the 1700s a "good" or "service"; the practices hardly deserve the word "assistance" or "relief." Likewise, most Americans in the Victorian period would have shuddered at the very idea of the 1970s "welfare rights."

The separation of spheres, and its division of labor, would come slowly and unevenly. In his study of the poor law in New York in 1823, John Yates, New York's secretary of state still included pauper auctions as part of New York's public assistance programs. And state departments of public welfare, formed as recently as the 1920s, were preceded for 60 years by "state boards of charities and corrections" and by "state boards of charities, corrections, and lunacy."

The evolution of the poor law in nineteenth century New York can probably be regarded as fairly typical of northern states, although sometimes ahead of its time. New York State was a leading participant in each major reform movement and the state's poor law often served as a model for other states. Prior to 1824, public relief in New York State was the responsibility of town governments, and the forms of relief varied from town to town. Under its 1824 poor law, as revised in 1827, New York State transferred primary responsibility to county governments (though towns in many counties continued to assume responsibility for temporary outdoor relief). The 1824 law required that each county establish a poorhouse; and although many counties were exempted from this provision, by 1840 almost every county operated a poorhouse. All public relief recipients, except those deemed to be in need of only temporary assistance not to exceed $10 during the year, were to be supported in a county poorhouse. Public assistance evolved similarly in Pennsylvania and in the states of the old Northwest Territory.

The almshouses erected during the antebellum period remained central to the administrative structure of relief systems and in New York they absorbed well over half of the funds of local public relief for the remainder of the century. Across the northern states, almshouse administration budgets expanded. Yet, nationwide, the percentage of the population living in almshouses was not particularly large. Between 1850 and the 1920s, the fraction of the population living in almshouses peaked at 2.7 persons per 1,000. From its peak (in 1860), the fraction of the population living in almshouses fell at each census enumeration and to a low of 0.08 percent in 1923. During the same period, local officials provided outdoor relief to an increasing share of all public relief recipients.

The poorhouse of the early republic was seen to be inhumane by the standards of the late nineteenth century. From New York to California, the miscellaneous poorhouse evolved into an "old folks home," a home for aged, unskilled, "feebleminded," and physically disabled men and women; more natives than immigrants, more Whites than African Americans. Most almshouse dwellers had never been married and had no children alive or able and willing to care for them. By 1915, just 0.1 percent of all paupers or poor persons in almshouses were, like Charles Dickens's Oliver Twist, children with neither parent living.

Like indoor relief, outdoor relief had its fashions, too. The mid-century expansion of outdoor relief was rather abruptly halted when economic downturns of the 1870s and the 1880s swelled the need for assistance to the poor. In response to crippled municipal budgets and a rising fear of pauperism or of encouraging an increase in the number of the dependent poor by giving relief, charity organization societies launched a crusade against public outdoor relief. Ten of the nation's largest cities abolished public outdoor relief and many others sharply reduced it.

Alternatives to local relief in the late nineteenth and early twentieth centuries included federal pensions for veterans of the Civil War and, after 1911 in many states, mothers' pensions on which the Aid to Dependent Children (ADC) program of the Social Security Act was later modeled. By 1910, 28 percent of all American men aged 65 and over, and some 300,000 widows, orphans, and others were receiving benefits under the veterans' benefits programs (four times the number living in almshouses). By 1920, 40 states had enacted mothers' pension programs that provided regular payments to impoverished mothers of dependent children funded and administered by local governments. Still, the U.S. Bureau of the Census conducted enumerations of paupers in almshouses until the 1930s, attesting to the continuing

symbolic importance of the county poorhouse to middle-class imaginations.

The separation of public assistance from matters of crime and mental illness is a process that parallels the great twentieth century expansions of criteria for eligibility for relief and of the sovereignty of the poor as consumers. Throughout the nineteenth century, there were moments when those who worked most closely with the poor had acknowledged transpersonal social and economic causes of poverty. But the belief that the roots of poverty reside in the character of the poor themselves and the fervent faith that public relief "causes" poverty remained dominant forces in the shaping of public policy. In the twentieth century, the separation from crime and "lunacy" was a slow process of conceding ground to causes of poverty that lay outside the domain of personal responsibility. Perhaps most important, these causes included recognition of the uncertain and sometimes volatile breakdown of markets and of marriage, and recognition of the facts of institutional racism, patriarchy, and mental and physical difference.

Between the early 1960s and the early 1980s, public assistance was relatively divorced from corrections and mental health. And as an expanding state and federal apparatus diminished the power of local self-government, the sovereignty of the poor was also expanding. Legal challenges and legislation gave the poor more rights to assistance. The Personal Responsibility and Work Opportunity Reconciliation Act of 1996—signed into law by President William Clinton—made way for a substantial reversal of these developments.

The history of public assistance can of course be seen as a history of race, of class, and of gender struggles to define work, home, and the American Dream. From early nineteenth century lists of the "causes of pauperism," on which immigration occupied the number one spot, through the Americanization efforts of early social workers, to restrictions on Food Stamps imposed by the 1996 reform, the immigrant poor have often been subjected to a medieval distinction of "deservingness." Similarly, from gender and racial segregation of nineteenth century poorhouse residents, through the fight for mothers' pensions and federal funds for Aid to Families with Dependent Children (AFDC), to contemporary provisions that allow states to deny benefits to unmarried teen mothers and to impose limits on the number of family members receiving assistance or "family caps," the history of welfare policy is linked integrally with the politics of race, gender, and the American family. To take just one more example, in the first half of the nineteenth century a free "Negro or mulatto" could enter the state of Ohio only "by giving to the clerk of the common pleas court a freehold security to the amount of five hundred dollars, which was later used for his support in case he became a pauper." In the first half of the nineteenth century, $500 exceeded the annual income of a comfortable White male, giving some indication of common attitudes toward race and poverty in poor law history.

—*Stephen T. Ziliak*

See also Aid to Dependent Children/Aid to Families With Dependent Children (United States); Charity Organization Societies (United States); Homelessness (United States); Housing Policy (United States); Mothers' Pensions (United States); Poverty (United States); Religion and Social Welfare (United States); State Boards of Charities (United States)

Primary Sources

Detailed information on the administration of the poor law at the local level tends to be located in the special, governmental, or archival collections of local courthouses, town halls, public libraries, private charitable organizations, universities, and historical libraries. In some cities and towns, the local newspapers remain an invaluable resource for poor law history. Still, one can find considerable collections on the poor laws, some of them with local, state, national, and even international scope. Primary documents are available at the Disability History Museum website (www.disabilitymuseum.org); Indiana Historical Society Library, Indianapolis; Library of the London School of Economics and Political Science; Social Welfare History Archives, University of Minnesota, Minneapolis.

Current Comment

Kennedy, A. E. (1934). *The Ohio Poor Law and its administration*. Chicago: University of Chicago Press.
Schneider, D. M. (1938). *The history of public welfare in New York State, 1609–1866*. Chicago: University of Chicago Press.
Warner, A. G. (1894). *American charities: A study in philanthropy and economics*. New York: Thomas Y. Crowell.
Webb, S., & Webb, B. (1927). The old poor law. Part I of *English local government: English Poor Law history*. London: Longmans, Green.

Further Reading

Hannon, J. U. (1984, January). Poor relief policy in antebellum New York State: The rise and decline of the poorhouse. *Explorations in Economic History, 22*, 243–247.
Katz, M. B. (1986). *In the shadow of the poorhouse*. New York: Basic Books.
Ziliak, S. T. (2002, June). Pauper fiction in economic science: "Paupers in almshouses" and the odd fit of *Oliver Twist*. *Review of Social Economy, 60*(2), 159–181.
Ziliak, S. T. (2004). Self-reliance before the welfare state: Evidence from the charity organization movement in the United States. *Journal of Economic History, 64*(2), 433–461.

POVERTY (CANADA)

Concern about poverty has a long tradition. The Bible notes, "The poor will always be with us." Yet no consensus exists on what poverty is, or how to measure it. One perspective equates poverty with the inability to participate in society with dignity. According to classical economist Adam Smith, "poverty is a lack of those necessities that the custom of the country renders it indecent for creditable people, even of the lowest order, to be without." For the Nobel laureate Amartya Sen, the poor "cannot participate adequately in communal activities, or be free of public shame from failure to satisfy conventions."

ATTITUDES TOWARD THE POOR AND SOCIAL SERVICES

Attitudes toward the poor are shaped by stereotypes. They are important because they shape social support programs. There has always been a distinction in the public mind between the "deserving poor," those unable to work due to age, disability, or sickness and the "undeserving poor," able-bodied individuals without employment. The circumscribed compassion for the able-bodied belies suspicion that unemployment is due to laziness or substance (drug or alcohol) abuse. These attitudes establish conflicting objectives for most social support programs: to provide the resources for a decent standard for those "truly in need," while minimizing the opportunities for abuse by those who should be more self-reliant. Society has been much quicker to support the "deserving poor," often without conditions. Support for the able-bodied is much more circumspect, limited, residential, more likely to be "in-kind" rather than cash, and conditional on participation in make-work projects.

Governments create social welfare against a background of economic conditions. During very hard economic times (like the depression years of the 1930s), it was more difficult to see all the poor as lazy or drunkards and there was some incentive to develop government responses. In good times, it is easier to portray poor Canadians as authors of their own demise.

Pre-Confederation

Early legislation in British North America reflected many of the practices of the British Isles. Charitable and religious groups provided much relief. England's Poor Law was not adopted in Upper Canada because it was thought impractical to impose a local tax on a principally agrarian nonmonetary economy. But the poor laws were adopted more faithfully in New Brunswick and Nova Scotia. As well, support for the able-bodied was thought unneeded because with the limitless opportunities in Canada, all able-bodied were thought capable of supporting themselves.

The houses of industry (or workhouses) for those "unable to care for themselves" were run such that no one with any alternative means of support would enter. Where such houses were unavailable, the poor could be jailed. Concern that relief encouraged sloth and abuse of society's benevolence sparked debates between proponents of "indoor relief," where recipients would live within institutions, such as houses of industry, and outdoor relief, where recipients could receive relief in their own homes.

Post World War I

The support by governments of disabled soldiers and their wives and children, together with widows and orphans, led many to see the possibility of government playing a more supportive role. Public cash support, in their homes, was provided to two of the most worthy groups: children without fathers and the elderly. Mothers' allowance began for the support of single mothers and their children (whether divorced, deserted, or widowed). At the same time, Old Age Security was introduced to the poor who were unreservedly deserving, seniors. Also at this time, some initial, yet very modest, minimum wage legislation was introduced.

The Great Depression

The Great Depression of the 1930s shaped attitudes toward the poor. Unemployment was no longer exclusive to "others" presumed to be "at fault." In a nonagrarian economy, unemployment could affect anyone. Also, safety valves that operated during previous economic downturns were absent during the Great Depression. Fewer unemployed could return to the family farm, or move to unsettled areas of the West or the United States. The depression era saw some expansion in social welfare programs, an allowance for blind people, and federal cost sharing with the provinces.

World War II and After

The acceptance of public responsibility for social supports opened the doors for a variety of programs in the decades of the 1940s to the 1970s. A national Unemployment Insurance program adopted in 1941 recognized the need for temporary support for those who had lost jobs. This development demonstrated some acceptance of societal responsibility for the unemployed. As well, the family allowance program, better known as the baby bonus, began in 1944 and was noteworthy for being a universal entitlement not based on need. Federal-provincial cost sharing expanded in the breadth and generosity of various programs with the Canada/Quebec Pension Plans. The Canada/Quebec Pension Plans were introduced in 1967 to provide a public pension based on contributions related to earnings throughout one's lifetime. These efforts later resulted in significant declines in poverty rates for seniors.

Recent Decades

Economic conditions affected income inequality, which grew substantially in the 1980s and 1990s. For much of this period, increased social spending offset this trend so that relative poverty, measured using total income (which included such government transfers as Unemployment Insurance and social assistance) did not appreciably increase.

The 1995 federal budget introduced changes in cost sharing with the provincial governments for health and social programs that led to changes in welfare policy in the late 1990s. Under the Canada Assistance Plan, the federal government shared half the cost of provincial welfare services, subject to conditions including the principle that "provinces meet identified needs regardless of cause." The new Canada Health and Social Transfer dropped this condition and introduced the requirement that recipients of social assistance must work if able to so—"workfare." Some provinces introduced lifetime bans from welfare eligibility for those convicted of welfare fraud.

Support for families with children also underwent significant changes. Canada's family support system was once made up of the family allowance (the baby bonus), a universal and taxable payment to mothers, a child tax deduction, and a child tax credit. In 2000, these programs were combined to create a Child Tax Benefit, which increased support for low-income families who were not receiving welfare support.

SETTING A POVERTY LINE

Establishing a poverty line and measuring trends over time is important for tracking social and economic progress and assessing the effectiveness of government programs. A poverty line suggests a living standard that social norms would find unacceptable. As such, it changes over time and place. Regardless, debates between absolute or relative concepts of poverty recur. The absolute approach argues that the poor are those who cannot purchase the "basket of commodities" required for survival. The relative approach sets a poverty line relative to the accepted norms of society. The debate is confused when many proponents of the absolute approach acknowledge that poverty standards require periodic adjustments according to changing notions of what is a minimally acceptable standard of living. At its heart, the debate is not about absolute or relative poverty but whether the adjustments to

a poverty line for community standards should be automatic, as under relative measures, or ad-hoc and discretionary, as with absolute measures.

Identification of the Poor

In 1896, Herbert Ames, a Canadian pioneer in the measurement of poverty, studied a square mile of downtown Montreal and concluded "want of employment was believed to be the cause of distress in as many cases as sickness, intemperance and shiftlessness combined." His research determined that $5 per week for a family was the minimum income necessary to keep a family out of poverty. He estimated that about 12 percent of families in Montreal lived in poverty.

Until 1992, the only poverty measures commonly used in Canada employed relative definitions of poverty. They included Statistics Canada's Low-Income Cut-Off, and the Senate and Canadian Council on Social Development (CCSD) poverty lines, which determined poverty by looking at the basic income needed by Canadian families.

The Low-Income Cut-Off (LICO) was developed and published by Statistics Canada. It is the most commonly used measure of poverty. Statistics Canada does not sanction the interpretation of LICOs as measures of poverty but instead as conceptions of poverty that the federal government does not officially sanction. The LICO sets a cutoff at the income level where, on average, families are spending 20 percent more on necessities than the average families does.

Some objected to the LICO during the 1990s because they rejected the notion of a relative poverty measure and others did so because it did not adequately account for differences in the cost of living between cities, overstating the extent of poverty in some urban areas and understating it in others. Some Canadian cities developed local poverty measures, such as the Market Basket, developed by the Social Planning Council of Metropolitan Toronto in Ontario, but these are not widely used.

The Fraser Institute introduced a "Basic Needs" measure in 1992, arguing that poverty as understood by the public related solely to basic needs. True to the "Basic Needs" nature of this measure, it included funds for shelter, food, and clothing but excluded books, magazines, toys, or a television. By this measure, only about 8 percent of Canadians were poor.

In the late 1990s, the provincial ministers of social services asked federal officials to develop a Market Basket measure of poverty, which would better account for regional differences. At the time of this writing, the measure is about to be published; but two factors are causing concern among antipoverty groups. First, officials were directed to index the poverty measure over time for changes in prices, not living standards. Second, the composition of the Market Basket would be reviewed by experts but would ultimately be subject to the approval of the provincial ministers. Ultimately, assessing the adequacy of welfare benefits will be difficult because the same provincial ministers who set welfare rates will also control the government-endorsed poverty line.

With these new poverty measures, Canada has moved in 10 short years from the LICO being the poverty measure of choice to having competing measures supported by conservative voices, including additional absolute measures of poverty, such as the Fraser Institute's Basic Needs measure.

Trends in Poverty

The trends and poverty rates in the section below are based on the Low-Income Cut-Off (before income taxes) published by Statistics Canada. This is the poverty measure that has been most often used by those conducting research in this field. Unless stated otherwise, the poverty data are for the year 1997. The overall poverty rate measured in this fashion has remained remarkably constant over recent decades, between 16 percent in 1973 and 18 percent in 1997. Since the LICO is a relative measure of poverty, it increases as living standards rise. This constant trend implies that although the absolute standard of living of the poor may have improved, no progress has been made in addressing the gap between the poor and the rest of society.

Whereas the overall rate of poverty may be relatively constant, the composition of the poor has changed dramatically. Younger single people, aboriginal people, persons with disabilities, women, and children are more likely to be poor than other Canadians. Although the poverty rate for seniors has fallen, unattached seniors, particularly women, have very high rates of poverty.

The average earnings of young single people under 25 have been falling when adjusted for inflation. The poverty rate for young single people increased from 39 percent in 1981 to 61 percent in 1997, reflecting this trend. For those aged 25 to 34, the poverty rate increased from 18 percent to 31 percent in the same time period.

The living conditions of Canada's aboriginal persons are usually far below Canadian norms and often mimic third world conditions. Poverty lines using money income cloud the measurement here because they ignore the nonmonetary income (hunting, fishing, or trapping) of many aboriginals. Regardless, the poverty rate of aboriginals at about 43 percent in 1995 far exceeds the 19 percent for non-aboriginals.

Persons with disabilities are disadvantaged by very high unemployment rates. Income supports for those persons with disabilities without other means tend to be modeled on welfare albeit at slightly higher benefit levels. The poverty rate for persons with disabilities was 31 percent in 1995 compared to 18 percent for other Canadians.

The poverty rate of women tends to be high when they are not in a family and not pooling their income with a man. Single women under age 65 have higher poverty rates than men, 41 percent compared to 35 percent. Female single parents had the highest poverty rate of all family types at 56 percent in 1997.

Child poverty remains a particular concern to Canadians because children are unambiguously not to blame for their situation. Also, raising children in poverty limits their career opportunities, which hampers Canada's economic future. Despite a 1989 unanimous House of Commons resolution to eliminate child poverty by the year 2000, child poverty increased from 964,000 (or 15 percent) in 1981 to 1.4 million (or 20 percent) in 1997, mostly because of the increasing poverty rate of working-age families and the increasing numbers of female-headed, one-parent families.

Seniors no longer constitute the largest share of poor Canadians. Their overall poverty rate declined from 41 percent in 1973 to 24 percent in 1997. Despite some improvement, the poverty rate for unattached seniors remains very high at 45 percent; and higher still at 49 percent for unmarried female seniors.

—Richard Shillington

See also Economic Policy (Canada); Social Security (Canada); Social Welfare (Canada): Before the Marsh Report; Social Welfare (Canada): Since the Marsh Report; Women and Poverty (Canada)

Current Comment

Ames, H. B. (1972). *The city below the hill.* Toronto: University of Toronto Press. (Original work published 1897)

Canadian Council on Social Development. (2000). *The Canadian fact book on poverty.* Ottawa, ON: Author. Available: www.ccsd.ca/pubs/2000/fbpov00/index.htm

Poverty in Canada: Report of the Special Senate Committee. (1971). Ottawa, ON: Information Canada.

Further Reading

Canadian Council on Social Development. (1984). *Not enough: The meaning and measurement of poverty in Canada.* Ottawa, ON: Author.

Graham, J. R., Swift, K., & Delaney, R. (2003). *Canadian social policy: An introduction* (2nd ed.). Toronto, ON: Prentice Hall.

Sarlo, C. A. (1996). *Poverty in Canada.* Vancouver, BC: Fraser Institute.

Sen, A. (1997). *Resources, values and development.* Cambridge, MA: Harvard University Press.

POVERTY (MEXICO)

Although Mexico's economy has risen to be the 10th largest in the world, and although it joined the Organisation for Economic Cooperation and Development (OECD) in 1994—an indicator to some that Mexico would soon be a member of the highly industrialized or "advanced" nations—the pervasiveness of poverty has continued to define Mexico. Yet, the precise magnitude and trends in the poverty level remain important, contested issues. Different methods are used to define poverty: The United Nations' research center in Santiago, Chile—the Economic Commission for Latin America (*Comisión Económica Para América Latina y el Caribe,* or CEPAL—utilizes two basic definitions: extreme poverty, or "indigence," and the "poverty line."

DEFINING POVERTY IN MEXICO

This distinction was adopted by the Mexican government, with "extreme poverty" being defined as the inability to obtain sufficient food to meet basic nutritional requirements—quite similar to CEPAL's concept of indigence. In 1989, the Mexican government set this level at $25 per person per month. The "poverty line" was set at a level at which an individual would have a minimally adequate level of food, housing, health care, education, culture, and public transportation. This was very distinct from CEPAL's poverty line—defined as two times the minimal food budget in urban areas and 1.75 times this budget in rural areas. To buy an "adequate" amount of the above items, Mexico's poverty line was set at the equivalent of $98 per person per month, based on 1989 purchasing power. These indexes of poverty indicators are adjusted to inflation.

HISTORICAL BACKGROUND

Using the CEPAL standard, overall poverty declined during Mexico's long economic boom period—from 1950 to 1980—when average annual real economic growth exceeded 6 percent. Since then per capita growth has been low or negative and poverty has been very high, with periods of decline inevitably followed by increases. In 1968, 43 percent of Mexico's population was below the poverty line. The economic boom of the 1970s pushed the poverty line (in spite of relatively high population growth) down to 36 percent by 1981. Since 1981, Mexico has not been able to reattain this rate. By 1989, 47 percent of the population was below the poverty line, and at the bottom of the devastating recession of 1994–1996, 53 percent had fallen below the line.

Mexican researchers, including Julio Boltvinik, whose work is recognized as authoritative, do not base their analyses on CEPAL's categories. Rather, there has long been a concerted effort by Mexican researchers to offer a much more detailed and nuanced measure of poverty. CEPAL's work measures only "income poverty," whereas Mexican specialists have developed a creative range of concepts including "food poverty," "capability poverty" (insufficient access to food, health care, and education), and "comprehensive poverty" (insufficient access to food, housing, clothing, health care, education, and public transportation). By these measures, 24 percent of the population suffered from extreme poverty in 2000, whereas CEPAL's measure showed 15 percent of the population below the "indigence" line. (Note that the rate for 2000 is very high by historical standards: Extreme poverty affected "only" 14 percent of the population in 1984—after the devastating economic crisis of 1982–1984.)

CURRENT CONDITIONS

In 2000, according to official estimates, 53.7 percent fell below Mexico's "comprehensive" poverty line, but CEPAL's poverty line number—41 percent—showed major improvement since 1996. Since another economic slowdown began in 2000—lasting into 2003—there has been much debate in Mexico over poverty trends. The government, after many delays, issued a report showing further declines in poverty, but Boltvinik has demonstrated that these "findings" were the result of new techniques of measurement and dubious assumptions. He found, for example, that the percentage of the population suffering from "food poverty" had risen to 26 percent—a substantial increase over the 24 percent in 2000.

Mexico's worst poverty is in rural areas. In 2000, 42 percent of the rural population, according to official estimates, was unable to have access, via their income, to a minimal diet. Mexico's Indian population, 12 million *indigenistas,* is heavily concentrated in rural areas and 92 percent live below the government-designated "comprehensive" poverty line. One careful estimate examining data from 1994 concluded that 94 percent of all rural families lived below the "comprehensive" poverty line with 43 percent in extreme poverty.

By any measure, Mexico's ability to confront poverty via income growth has been dismal. Part of the reason is that overall economic growth has been much slower since the crisis of 1982. Equally important has been the pattern or style of growth—Mexico has relied since 1982 on a neoliberal "model" of

market-driven policies. Touted by Presidents Carlos Salinas (1988–1994) and Ernesto Zedillo (1994–2000), the model has been widely described as "exclusive." Clearly, the alarmingly high levels of poverty experienced since the early 1980s, and the inability to drive those rates downward for any sustained period, indicates that the model has been exclusive. Mexico's development prior to the 1982 crisis indicated a pattern of social development inspired by a desire for social justice. Through its import substitution policies, Mexico had built a complex web of institutions that permitted all social classes to move upward when the economy expanded. Relatively strong unions, encompassing labor laws and a socially committed government, tended to ensure that growth was to some degree "shared" across class lines. But since 1982, Mexico's economic growth has been led by low-wage *maquiladora* export firms. At the same time, the "informal" sector of the economy has grown at a rapid rate—approximately 63 percent of the labor force works in the "informal" sector, generally as "self-employed" workers, without the protection of job benefits or labor standards.

Since 1982, the economy has grown very little and the benefits of what growth has been achieved have generally gone to the top 10 percent of the population. Wages have fallen substantially in virtually every category. In addition, the support network for small farmers has steadily been reduced, thereby exacerbating rural poverty while pushing up the poverty rates.

GOVERNMENT POLICIES

Income poverty can be addressed, at least to some degree, through social antipoverty programs. Including the impact of these programs pushes the poverty rate downward, or prevents it from rising even higher. Here the focus turns from income (primarily attained through the market for labor) to income plus social transfers. Social transfers are sometimes called the social wage and include, for example, school subsidies, housing and food subsidies, and cash transfers. Analyzing forms of "specific poverties," Boltvinik shows that the incidence of educational poverty—the portion of the population with zero or low levels of education—went down from 53 percent in 1970 to 19 percent in 2000. His "equivalent incidence of living space and housing services poverty" (which includes access to piped water, sewage lines, and electricity) fell from 49 percent in 1970 to 21 percent in 2000. Likewise, his "equivalent incidence of health care and social security poverty" fell from 67 percent in 1970 to 35 percent in 1999.

A wide range of government policies designed to offer a limited and selective social safety net has continued to reduce "specific poverties." When Boltvinik took into account the improvements in access to basic needs (water, sewage, housing size, electricity, and health care), all provided via the public sector, with the decline in living standards measure by income received in the private sector, the net effect continued to be one of decline. His "integrated equivalence incidence of poverty" increased by 35 percent in the 1984–1998 period.

The "intensity" of poverty can be measured by the degree to which the average poor individual falls below a given poverty measure or norm. For those left in the poverty categories, be they measures of income or "specific" poverties, the intensity of poverty increased—overall by 23 percent in the 1984–1998 period.

During President Salinas's term, the National Solidarity Program (*Programa Nacional de Solidaridad,* or PRONASOL) began as a "targeted" program for the poor. Rather than aiding the poor through entitlements or subsidies that could also be accessed by the nonpoor, PRONASOL, or *Solidaridad,* was viewed as an innovative program that would complement Salinas's neoliberal economic policies. In fact, PRONASOL had a very poor record of accomplishment and subsequent research has demonstrated that the underlying motive of the program was to gain clients and political support for Salinas's policies.

President Zedillo ended PRONASOL and set up the Program for Education, Health and Food (*Programa de Educación, Salud y Alimentación,* or PROGRESA)—a support program for the rural poor. In the late 1990s, PROGRESA brought food subsidies to 2.3 million families and 2.2 million rural children received educational scholarships designed to encourage families to send their children to school by offering the amount of money the child would have added to family income from working. PROGRESA funds have gone to the more able and agile of the poor—80 percent of rural families that the government defined as indigent or below the "food poverty" line did not receive aid.

It is probably accurate, as a broad generalization, to state that the majority of Mexicans continue to suffer the indignity of poverty. Alleviation or serious reduction of poverty can come only through a constructive combination of (1) redistribution of income (as the result of social justice in the workplace), (2) new policies toward inclusive economic growth, and (3) dynamic, functional public-sector programs that are broadly effective and sustainable.

—James M. Cypher

See also Economic Policy (Mexico); Food Assistance Policy (Mexico); Informal Economy (Mexico); Neoliberalism, Social Programs, and Social Movements (Mexico); Philanthropy (Mexico); Poverty Policy (Mexico); Social Welfare (Mexico): Since 1867

Primary Source

Comisión Económica Para América Latina y el Caribe (CEPAL). (2003). *Panorama social de América Latina, 2002–2003.* Santiago, Chile: Naciónes Unidas. Available: www.eclac.cl/

Current Comment

Boltvinik, J. (2003). Welfare, inequality and poverty. In K. Middlebrook & E. Zepeda (Eds.), *Confronting development* (pp. 385–446). Stanford, CA: Stanford University Press.

Ramírez de Aguilar, F. (2002, August 14). En la decimal economía del mundo, 53.7% de la población vive en la pobreza. *El Financiero,* p. 44.

Further Reading

Cypher, J. (1990). *State and capital in Mexico.* Boulder, CO: Westview.

Cypher, J., & Dietz, J. (2004). *The process of economic development* (2nd ed.). London: Routledge.

Kopinak, K. (2004). *The social costs of industrial growth in northern Mexico.* La Jolla: University of California, San Diego, Center for U.S.-Mexican Studies.

Middlebrook, K., & Zepeda, E. (Eds.). (2004). *Confronting development: Assessing Mexico's economic and social policy challenges.* Stanford. CA: Stanford University Press.

POVERTY POLICY (MEXICO)

PRONASOL, PROGRESA, and OPORTUNIDADES constitute three successive antipoverty programs in Mexico. They were introduced respectively by the administrations of Presidents Carlos Salinas de Gortari (1988–1994), Ernesto Zedillo (1994–2000) and Vicente Fox (2000–2006). Operating in an era of repeated crises and economic restructuring programs, all three presidential administrations have been involved in reforming the institutional forms and policy content of Mexican social policy. Integral to this process has been the establishment of the three antipoverty programs to stem the deleterious social consequences of economic crises while providing new political tools for ensuring social stability and disarming political opposition.

PRONASOL

Following the 1982 debt crisis, and again after the 1994–1995 Mexican *peso* crisis, Mexican real wages fell significantly and the incidence of poverty and social inequality rose in a sustained fashion. Concurrently, neoliberal reforms imposed a new fiscal discipline upon the state and undermined many of the corporatist institutions through which resources had previously been distributed to worker and peasant groups. Within these circumstances, President Carlos Salinas initiated in 1989 a systematic reform of social policy. This was achieved primarily through the establishment of a flagship antipoverty effort called the National Solidarity Program (*Programa Nacional de Solidaridad,* or PRONASOL). Several disparate government agencies were replaced by a new ministry to implement and manage social development policies. It was named the Secretariat for Social Development (*Secretaría de Desarrollo Social*, or SEDESOL).

Both these initiatives were manifestations of what Salinas labeled as a new philosophy of "social liberalism" that sought to support neoliberal restructuring with a stronger social safety net. As a mark of Salinas's commitment to the new project, the resources involved in PRONASOL were substantial. By 1993, the annual budget had grown from an initial $680 million to $2.5 billion, with the expenditure covered primarily by tax revenues, resources generated by the government's large-scale privatization program, and World Bank loans. PRONASOL, therefore, accounted for a significant proportion of the increases in social welfare expenditure in the Salinas period that reversed the post-debt crisis trend toward retrenchment.

Whereas previous antipoverty policies depended heavily upon universal subsidization of staple foods, PRONASOL introduced a system of credit funds for development projects alongside the targeted distribution of consumption subsidies in rural areas, a system known as the Program to Support the Countryside (*El Programa de Apoyos Directos al Campo,* or PRO-CAMPO). The credit funds operated on the principle of participatory social-development practices that engaged communities in the design and implementation of local antipoverty projects. Communities that wanted to receive PRONASOL funding were obliged to form a committee to plan and oversee a small-to-medium-sized social development project, commonly infrastructural in nature. Additionally, communities were required to contribute toward total costs and provide much of the labor necessary to implement the project. Active participation in this manner was extolled on grounds of the increased efficiency of projects as well as the formation of social solidarity and cohesion.

Resources were controlled in a highly centralized manner, with the program run by SEDESOL in close conjunction with the president's office. In bypassing the traditional forms of resource disbursement and fostering the active participation of target communities, the initiative was suggested to represent a new form of state-society relations in Mexico, an attempt to engineer a stronger civil society in a top-down fashion.

Given the extent of poverty in Mexico and its exacerbation following the 1982 crisis and subsequent austerity measures, PRONASOL had a limited effect. United Nations statistics show a slight decrease from 39 to 36 percent of households in poverty between 1989 and 1994. Within selected communities, PRONASOL-funded projects played an important role in providing basic infrastructure to aid social reproduction and stimulate productive activity (e.g., provision of water supply, electricity, drainage systems, road paving, and housing). Other projects also contributed to the formation of human capital, such as school and clinic construction.

Recipient communities, however, were not necessarily the poorest and, likewise, the majority of PRONASOL expenditure was not targeted for the poorest states but rather the most politically sensitive ones. Indeed, the overt manipulation of PRONASOL as a tool for engendering political support for both the president and the ruling PRI Party induced repeated criticism. The disproportionate amount of PRONASOL resources, estimated at 12 percent, spent in the small but politically key state of Michoacán is testimony to the explicit political dimension of the program. The eruption of the *Zapatista* rebellion in the state of Chiapas in 1994 and continued guerrilla struggles in other southern states, however, challenged the effectiveness of the PRONASOL and other initiatives in ensuring social cohesion in the countryside.

PROGRESA

The change of administration in 1994 and the economically and socially devastating Mexican *peso* crisis of 1994–1995 led to a further reformulation of social policy by the administration of President Ernesto Zedillo. In 1997, the Program for Education, Health and Food (*Programa de Educación, Salud y Alimentación,* or PROGRESA) replaced PRONASOL. Institutionally, PROGRESA represented a break with PRONASOL by introducing a broad decentralization of responsibility and resources from federal to state levels. Moreover, the program also downscaled credit funds and accentuated the trend toward targeted subsidies. PROGRESA, therefore, involved extensive processes of social profiling to delineate with greater precision the population in conditions of extreme poverty. Once identified, households under the stipulated threshold received direct benefit transfers for a period of 3 years, renewable for a further 3, including income subsidies, nutritional support, and provision of health and education services. In return, households would assume certain responsibilities, such as the enrollment and attendance of children in

schools and the maintenance of a regular schedule of health clinic visits. In this respect, the program presented itself as a targeted intervention to build the human capital of the poorest sectors of society.

PROGRESA has been acclaimed as a model program, championed by the World Bank and deemed worthy of promulgation in other areas of Latin America, particularly Central America. Given the technocratic nature of identifying poverty-stricken households and disbursing demand subsidies, there is considerably less room for the overt manipulation of funds for political ends as compared to PRONASOL. This facet of PROGRESA dovetails with the new internationally extolled development paradigm of "good governance." Econometric studies have nonetheless indicated that politically important regions continued to receive a relatively greater amount of PROGESA funds during the Zedillo era.

At a more technical level, questions have been raised concerning the methods used to identify the target population. At one level, given the stipulation of school and health clinic attendance as prerequisites for participation, PROGRESA often overlooked communities where no or limited education or health services were available. At another level, the selection of recipient households was based on a screening process that first highlighted areas of dense poverty, followed by the comprehensive delineation of the most impoverished households within these localities. Given these targeting specifications, PROGRESA was oriented primarily toward rural areas, which had higher and more compact incidences of poverty. Urban areas, however, display more heterogeneous income levels and, therefore, were largely bypassed by the initial PROGRESA screening process even though 7 percent of the urban population lived in poverty in 1998.

The overall effectiveness of PROGRESA is still debated. Recipient families numbered 2.3 million by 2000 and received subsidies worth up to 25 percent of their incomes. Critics suggested that the program was insignificant compared to the extent of the problem as it benefited only one fifth of impoverished households. In the late 1990s, poverty levels did decrease, returning to just below the 1984 level of 34 percent of households. Separating the contribution of PROGRESA to this trend from that of several years of rapid economic expansion, however, is problematic.

OPORTUNIDADES

OPORTUNIDADES (Opportunities) is the latest permutation of antipoverty policy, established under the administration of Vicente Fox in 2001. Although the myriad of subprojects supported broach some new areas, substantive changes are few, and the program does not differ greatly from the tenets established by the PROGRESA template. The publication of *Mexico—A Comprehensive Development Agenda for the New Era* in 2003, a 5-year blueprint for social policy based on the World Bank's *Comprehensive Development Framework,* solidifies Mexico's adoption of these decentralized, targeted, and compensatory antipoverty and social policy principles. The program outlined in the document, which provides the macro-framework in which programs such as OPORTUNIDADES operate, will receive $1.5 billion per year from the World Bank.

—Marcus Taylor

See also Economic Policy (Mexico); Neoliberalism, Social Programs, and Social Movements (Mexico); Philanthropy (Mexico); Poverty (Mexico)

Primary Sources

The SEDESOL web page, outlining all current antipoverty and social policy initiatives can be found at www.sedesol.gob.mx; information on OPORTUNIDADES is available on the official website at www.oportunidades.gob.mx; information on the World Bank's *Comprehensive Development Framework* is also available on-line (www.worldbank.org/).

Current Comment

Giugale, M. M., Lafourcade, O., & Nguyen, V. H. (2001). *Mexico: A comprehensive development agenda for the new era.* Washington, DC: World Bank.

Further Reading

A La Pobreza, A. (1998). *Análisis del programa de educación, salud y alimentación en la política social.* Mexico City: Programa de Educación, Salud y Alimentación; Centro de Investigaciones y Estudios Superiores en Antropología Social.
Cornelius, W., Craig, A., & Fox, J. (Eds.). (1994). *Transforming state-society relations in Mexico: The national solidarity strategy.* San Diego: University of California Press.

Lomelí, E. V., Gendreau, M., & Tepichín, A. M. (Eds.). (2000). *Los dilemas de la política social: Como combatir la pobreza?* Mexico City: Universidad Iberoamericana.
Soederberg, S. (2001). From neoliberalism to social liberalism: Situating the National Solidarity Program within Mexico's passive revolutions. *Latin American Perspectives, 28*(3), 104–123.

POVERTY (UNITED STATES)

Poverty is generally understood as deprivation in some dimensions of human well-being. There are, however, varied conceptions of deprivation and well-being that influence how the poor are identified and the actions taken by the government to alleviate or eradicate poverty. Government actions to alleviate poverty are elements of a nation's social welfare system, which reflect how a particular society takes care of its members in reduced circumstances. The conceptions of poverty and social welfare systems are usually influenced by assumptions regarding the nature and causes of poverty, dominant ideological values, and historical background of a particular country. In the United States of America, conceptions of poverty and policy measures have historical roots in European traditions, particularly those of the English during the seventeenth century.

CONCEPTIONS OF POVERTY

There are two widely used conceptions of poverty: relative deprivation and absolute deprivation. In the case of relative deprivation, one is poor in contrast to others who are not poor with respect to the prevailing living standard in a particular country or society. Specifically, one is assumed to be poor if one cannot obtain, at all or sufficiently, the conditions of life including diets, amenities, standards, and services that allow one to play the roles, participate in relationships, and follow the customs expected of one by virtue of one's membership in society. This notion of poverty is usually analyzed from the perspective of inequalities in income distribution.

Absolute deprivation focuses on nonfulfillment of basic material or biological needs reflected in inadequate nutrition, clothing, housing, and transportation.

Basically, one is assumed to be poor if, and only if, one's access to economic resources is insufficient for a reasonable expectation that one will acquire enough commodities to meet basic material needs adequately to ensure physical efficiency. Historically, this notion of poverty is associated with the English reformer Joseph Rowntree, who developed a measure of poverty based on absolute deprivation in 1901. This is the conception of poverty often used by the U.S. government in poverty analysis and policy formulation.

MEASURING POVERTY

The method used by the U.S. government to identify the poor is based on the absolute deprivation notion of poverty. It involves estimating an income threshold that is required to obtain the minimum acceptable standard of living. A household with income below that threshold is considered poor. In the United States, the first income threshold based on this method was developed by Mollie Orshansky in 1965 and adopted by the U.S. Bureau of the Budget in 1968 as the official measure of poverty.

Orshansky's poverty line was based on the cost of predetermined minimum food items recommended by the U.S. Department of Agriculture as essential to provide necessary calories to ensure normal functioning. The cost of food was then multiplied by a factor of three to cover the cost of basic nonfood items such as housing, clothing, and transportation. Using equivalent scales, various income thresholds were then developed to account for differences in family size and composition. Income surveys were used to determine the actual incomes of households. Families whose incomes were below predetermined income thresholds were counted as poor. Also, thresholds were used to determine the incidence of poverty or the percentage of population with income below the poverty line and the depth of poverty or extent to which the average income of poor households differed from the established income threshold.

This method does not necessarily provide a realistic assessment of poverty. It tends to overestimate the incidence of poverty because much of the in-kind benefits received by the poor, such as food coupons, housing subsidies, medical assistance, and tax rebates are not factored in household income assessment. On the other hand, the method may underestimate poverty because income thresholds are based on a narrow range of prescribed basic material needs, excluding other human needs equally valued by the poor such as personal security and employment.

EUROPEAN HERITAGE

Before 1900, the role of the federal government in poverty alleviation was minimal. Individual states, private charities, and families were responsible for assisting the poor. During this time, the policies and programs for poverty alleviation were, by and large, a replica of provisions of the English Poor Law of 1601. Among the provisions were recognition of a resident individual's right to public assistance, based on a categorization of the poor as children, able-bodied adults, and the elderly or disabled, often considered the "worthy poor." The prescribed types of assistance for each category of dependents were skills training for children, employment for able-bodied adults, and relief for the incapacitated. These provisions provided the philosophical foundation and structure of federal welfare provision in the twentieth century.

ROLE OF THE FEDERAL GOVERNMENT

Not until the economic depression of the 1930s did the federal government become directly involved in poverty alleviation, with the passage of the Federal Emergency Relief Act of 1933 and the Social Security Act of 1935. These were the first major attempts by the federal government to institute a comprehensive system of care for the poor; they laid the foundation for the development of the U.S. welfare state. The Social Security legislation embraced the principles of individual entitlement to public assistance and the means test. The former ensured that public assistance was provided to the most deserving poor.

The 1935 legislation covered a wide range of contingencies of life that predispose individuals to poverty, including old age, physical disabilities, unemployment, widowhood, and dependent children. In addition, several poverty prevention and relief programs and services were introduced during the 1930s.

Relief programs for unemployed adults included the provision of public work schemes, vocational training, and food coupons. Following President Lyndon Johnson's declaration of a War on Poverty in the mid 1960s, there was another expansion of federal government-supported programs and services that continued through the 1970s. Most of these focused on education, health programs, and employment-related measures, including work training and work incentives.

The last two decades of the twentieth century witnessed a reconceptualization of poverty policies and a rolling back of the U.S. welfare state. This was triggered in part by the rise to prominence of neoconservative socioeconomic thought, and partly by increasing welfare expenditures amid economic problems. The period was characterized by strategic withdrawal of the federal government from direct provision of welfare services through devolution of responsibilities to states, increasing reliance on the private market and the family as primary mechanisms for poverty alleviation, and negation of the principle of welfare entitlement for unemployed, able-bodied adults and parents with dependent children.

These developments culminated in the passage of the Personal Responsibility and Work Opportunity Reconciliation Act (PRWORA) in 1996. The nation's poverty alleviation strategy is now anchored on labor-force participation, designed to reduce dependency on public assistance by promoting economic self-sufficiency. The 1996 legislation established the Temporary Assistance for Needy Families (TANF) program to aid poor families. Receipt of TANF benefits is limited to 5 years. During this period, access to public assistance is conditional upon fulfillment of prescribed job-related training activities. In addition, a package of job-retention incentives is provided for low-income labor-force participants including the Earned Income Tax Credit, child support services, and medical insurance. The basic idea of this policy strategy was to use public assistance to try to integrate the poor into the labor force.

LIMITATIONS AND EMERGING TRENDS

Although an employment-based poverty alleviation strategy is consonant with dominant neoconservative market ideology, its effectiveness was the subject of intensive debate among academics and policymakers as the twentieth century came to a close. Skepticism about the strategy results from the perception of unrealistic assumptions regarding the capacity of the private market to generate living-wage jobs for the poor. Labor market trends and economic fortunes are highly unpredictable. The last decade of the twentieth century had been a period of relative economic prosperity in the United States. Since the beginning of the 21st century, however, the country has undergone an economic recession with diminishing employment opportunities for the poor. Similarly, most of the poor do not have the capacity to compete effectively for good-paying jobs partly because workforce training programs have not reflected the realities of a postindustrial, high technology economy. The poor seldom have the skills to readily compete for high-paying jobs in the emerging economy, leaving them with few opportunities for employment other than in low-skilled jobs, often in the service sector—jobs that offer few benefits or long-term job security.

The intractable nature of poverty and limitations of wage employment strategies continue to suggest the need for more effective approaches to poverty alleviation. One strategy, with strong appeal among academics, practitioners, and policymakers alike, is promoting capital or asset formation among the poor through individual development accounts and ownership of microenterprises. The effectiveness of asset-based poverty alleviation strategies, however, is yet to be documented.

—Benson Chisanga

See also Association for Improving the Condition of the Poor (United States); Charity Organization Societies (United States); Health Policy (United States); Poor Law (United States); Scientific Philanthropy (United States); Social Security (United States); Social Welfare (United States): Before the Social Security Act; Social Welfare (United States): Since the Social Security Act; Welfare Capitalism (United States); Work Relief (United States)

Primary Sources

Records of the Community Services Administration (Record Group 381), National Archives & Records Administration,

College Park, MD; Social Security Administration History Archives, Social Security Administration Headquarters, Baltimore, MD.

Current Comment

Harrington, M. (1962). *The other America: Poverty in the United States.* New York: Macmillan.

Moynihan, D. P. (Ed.). (1969). *On understanding poverty: Perspectives from the social sciences.* New York: Basic Books.

Orshansky, M. (1965). Counting the poor: Another look at poverty profile. *Social Security Bulletin, 28,* 3–29.

Further Reading

Gilbert, N. (1995). *Welfare justice: Restoring social equity.* New Haven, CT: Yale University Press.

Trattner, W. I. (1999). *From poor law to welfare state: A history of social welfare in America* (6th ed.). New York: Free Press.

Wilensky, H. L., & Lebeaux, C. N. (1958). *Industrial society and social welfare.* New York: Russell Sage Foundation.

PROGRESSIVE ERA (UNITED STATES)

The Progressive Era occurred during the late nineteenth and early twentieth centuries at a time of rapid urbanization, industrialization, and economic growth. Millions of immigrants from Europe and elsewhere came to the United States seeking opportunities for better lives. The era was termed "progressive" since it was characterized by social and political reform and moderate social change in response to changing social conditions. Progressive social reformers came from all parts of the nation and they were often from middle-class or upper-middle-class backgrounds. Generally, they argued that government should actively support efforts to achieve social welfare, which they defined broadly. They affiliated with both dominant political parties, the Republicans and the Democrats.

In the election of 1912, the new Progressive Party nominated Theodore Roosevelt—who had previously served as a Republican president—as its presidential candidate. He spoke for "New Nationalist" progressivism that would use the regulatory powers of the national government to promote social welfare. Roosevelt relied on progressive social reformers for

ideas about new social welfare policies. Jane Addams, a prominent social reformer from Chicago and an active leader in the settlement house movement, was one of his policy advisers. The Progressive party platform called for regulation of child labor and for protection of women working in hazardous occupations.

Woodrow Wilson, the Democratic party candidate for the presidency in 1912, accused Roosevelt of using too many experts to develop his policy proposals. Wilson's progressive vision advocated for a "New Freedom." He saw open competition, not government regulation, as the key to social progress.

Historians have studied progressive reformers and concluded that at various times and on various issues, progressives included labor union members; farmers; businessmen; social workers; professionals such as lawyers, physicians, teachers, and university-based academics; and politicians who advocated for reform of public administration to eliminate graft, corruption, and political patronage. Some progressives wanted improvements in sanitation and new laws and regulations to promote public health. Others saw public education as a key element in progressive reform. John Dewey, a progressive educator, urged reform in public education and argued that children needed to be educated to be effective citizens. Toward the end of the Progressive Era around 1920, the number of public school graduates had nearly tripled from the 1890s. As public education expanded, it required more public funds for its support. Calling for more taxes for education could be unpopular politically. Reformers learned their proposals were sometimes unpopular. For example, promotion of public health required better sanitation systems that were very expensive and required considerable public investment, which could be opposed by business and the general public.

During the Progressive Era, universities expanded programs in education, economics, sociology, and other social sciences. The new social scientists conducted research on social welfare problems and offered suggestions for ways to improve general social welfare. Progressives attacked large business monopolies for preventing competition in the marketplace. Competition, they believed, would result in better and safer products for consumers. There were rural as well as urban progressives. Some reformers promoted conservation of natural resources by applying principles of scientific management to protect forests and waterways. Other progressives attacked racial inequality as unfair and argued for harmonious race relations. Some progressives came from organized religious groups and argued for social justice and social welfare on religious grounds.

Progressives could disagree on issues and reform measures could create ambivalent responses. Shifting coalitions of interest groups responded to issues on the basis of self-interest as well as differing assumptions about how to reform society to produce social betterment. Some reformers were influenced by reforms occurring in Europe as nations such as Great Britain and Germany used government to deal with social problems resulting from urbanization and industrialization.

To understand the Progressive Era, it is important to understand how social change influenced progressive reformers. The era saw large increases in the numbers of immigrants, the rise of large cities, and the emergence of large industrial corporations. Advances in technology and manufacturing made it possible to produce goods for mass consumer markets. People were becoming more mobile. Automobile production made it possible for consumers to engage in business and personal travel. Electric lights illuminated homes and cities. Telephones made communication much easier.

Changes were occurring in the culture of the United States as well. Popular magazines appealed to readers eager to learn about the latest fads. People flocked to movie houses to see films that reflected changing social values. An emerging consumer culture was influenced by literature and advertising. Novelists such as Upton Sinclair, whose fictionalized account of the Chicago stockyards, *The Jungle* (1906), graphically described how spoiled meat was marketed to consumers, drew the public's attention to social problems that threatened public health and welfare. This resulted in popular calls for government regulations to improve both food and worker safety, and in 1906, Congress passed the Meat Inspection Act.

The Progressive Era saw changes in the roles and status of women. Many social reformers were women who were first-generation college graduates. Jane Addams, daughter of a prominent Illinois family, traveled to Europe, where she learned about the settlement house movement in England. Returning to

the United States, she and a group of young and idealistic women established Hull House, one of the first settlement houses in the United States, on the near West Side of Chicago. Hull House was located in a working-class neighborhood filled with immigrants striving to adjust to a new homeland and to succeed in providing decent and healthy lives for their families. Settlement house residents, many of whom were educated women dedicated to lives of service to others, worked to improve the neighborhood and the lives of their neighbors by offering English-language classes, recreational opportunities, health classes, nursery schools, and opportunities to learn about the obligations and responsibilities of citizenship as well as practical ways to engage in social and political action. Jane Addams and her colleagues, working in settlements throughout the nation, were instrumental in creating the modern social welfare system and were involved in the creation of social work, a female-dominated profession.

Women reformers were active in the Women's Trade Union League, which protested the exploitation of women and children workers in sweatshops and worked for better working conditions and fair wages. Progressive reformers worked in state legislatures for shorter working hours and safer working conditions for women. By 1917, 41 states had passed laws to protect women workers. While these reforms brought benefits, they also prohibited women from working in occupations considered to be unsafe, thereby limiting women's occupational choices. In 1909, the federal government sponsored the White House Conference on Dependent Children at which progressives argued that government should protect families and home life since they were critical for producing healthy and productive children. Reformers lobbied state legislatures to enact mothers' pension laws to provide public support for needy families. By 1921, most states had enacted mothers' pensions, recognition that state governments had important public welfare obligations to children and families. The White House Conference also recommended creation of the federal Children's Bureau, which was established in 1912. The Children's Bureau conducted research on the welfare of women and children and supported the Sheppard-Towner Maternity and Infancy Act that provided federal funding for maternal health information clinics.

Progressives worked for women's suffrage and in 1920 they achieved success when the Twentieth Amendment to the U.S. Constitution gave women the right to vote. Others called for the elimination of child labor in dangerous industries such as coal mining and textile mills. Although many middle-class progressives supported these reforms, working-class men and women sometimes resented them since they depended on the wages of women and children for family support. Other progressives encouraged divorce for women in abusive family situations and divorces increased in the Progressive Era, signaling changing public attitudes about women's roles. Progressive reformers were active in international social reform activities, such as the Women's International League for Peace and Freedom. During World War I, some women reformers argued against the entry of the United States into the war in 1916 because they felt war threatened the reforms they were struggling to achieve. Jane Addams was called unpatriotic because of her opposition to the war.

Many municipal and state governments enacted progressive laws and regulations. In Wisconsin, progressives such as Robert LaFollette succeeded in passing legislation to provide worker's compensation after a protracted struggle that pitted those who felt the state had an obligation to protect workers from workplace hazards against those who believed the state had no such obligation. The opponents argued that workers had remedies in the courts if the actions of others contributed to their injuries. State reforms were not always successful. The supreme court of Illinois overturned a state child labor law, leading reformers to call for national child labor laws. Progressives were concerned about the exploitation of women and children in the workplace and in 1912, Massachusetts enacted a minimum wage law for women and children in private industry.

In 1906, the federal government enacted the Pure Food and Drug Act. Prior to its passage, it was possible for nearly anyone to purchase dangerous narcotics. Many privately manufactured medicines contained opium and its derivatives and they were widely available to the public. Cocaine was an ingredient of some popular soft drinks. Proponents of regulation argued that consumers should be protected from impure as well as dangerously addictive drugs. Some reformers saw alcohol consumption as a threat to morality and family life because it seemed to be chronically abused by many male heads of households, resulting in family abuse, loss of employment, and health problems. Those opposed to the easy availability of alcoholic beverages joined temperance organizations that protested against taverns and saloons. Those who favored prohibition of the manufacture and sale of alcoholic beverages worked successfully to add the Nineteenth Amendment to the U.S. Constitution in 1919. Even though prohibition became law, it was very difficult to enforce as illegal alcoholic beverages were smuggled into the country from Canada and elsewhere to satisfy public demand. Other reformers worked to prohibit prostitution, which they saw as immoral and a threat to young women. Still others lobbied for less popular, often-controversial reforms. Margaret Sanger, a physician and advocate for women's health, argued for legalized birth control as a way to improve the lives of women and opened a birth control clinic in 1916. She was opposed by powerful physicians and others who felt that legalizing birth control would result in less reproduction by the elite and racially pure classes of American society in the face of growing numbers of the racially and socially "inferior" lower-class immigrants. Reformers, including newly trained women physicians, challenged these attitudes.

The Progressive Era took place in a period when the United States still practiced widespread racial discrimination. In 1894, the Supreme Court of the United States upheld the practice of racial segregation in the case of *Plessy v. Ferguson*. The Court held that separate but equal facilities were constitutional, thereby upholding Jim Crow practices of racial discrimination in much of the South. Mob violence and lynchings of African Americans galvanized reformers who formed the National Association for the Advancement of Colored People (NAACP). W. E. B. DuBois, an African American Harvard-educated social scientist and reformer, shared the views of the NAACP that the problems of African Americans should be addressed by the same reformist idealism that characterized the Progressive Era. Racist beliefs were widely held during the Progressive Era. At the St. Louis World's Fair in 1904, visitors could visit an exhibit of Philippine natives who posed for pictures with mostly White fairgoers. The U.S. military occupied the Philippines after the Spanish-American War of 1898 and the exhibit was supposed to show fairgoers how the superior civilization of the United States was benefiting uncivilized native people. Toward the end of the Progressive Era, the Ku Klux Klan (KKK) became very popular. It appealed to White Americans who were fearful of social change. Its members disliked African Americans and other people of color, as well as Jews and Catholics, many of whom were new immigrants whose loyalty and patriotism were suspect. The KKK felt Roman Catholics owed their allegiance to the Pope in Rome and were un-American.

Historians have written conflicting interpretations of the Progressive Era. In the 1960s, some concluded that the Progressive Era was dominated by conservative interests whose reforms were meant to preserve the status quo. Reform meant conforming to the ideals of an emerging business culture. Others argued that progressivism shared liberal, democratic ideals with earlier reform movements and that the Progressive Era was best understood as a time of democratic reform against regressive and conservative social and business interests concerned only with profits and not the social welfare of the American people. Recent studies argue that the Progressive Era cannot be understood apart from the dynamic moral idealism that characterized so much of the period. Progressives had a democratic vision that informed their call for reform, a vision they felt would create a better and more prosperous America. Progressive reforms and reformist idealism were manifested in drives for better wages and safer working conditions, for public health measures, and for calls to use government to promote social welfare. The Progressive Era was a time of social change, of changing gender roles and social tensions. Even though the progressive legacy suggests the ambivalence of reform, it produced new social welfare policies and articulate reformers whose actions would influence the future of American social welfare.

—John M. Herrick

See also African Americans and Social Welfare (United States); Child Welfare Policy (United States); DuBois, W. E. B.; Juvenile Justice Policy (United States); Sanger, Margaret Higgins; Settlement Houses (United States)

Primary Sources

Jane Addams Papers, Swarthmore College Peace Collection, Swarthmore, PA; Hull House Papers, University of Illinois Archives, Chicago; Survey Papers, Social Welfare History Archives, University of Minnesota, Minneapolis.

Current Comment

Addams, J. (1930). *The second twenty years at Hull House.* New York: Macmillan.
Sinclair, U. (1906). *The jungle.* New York: Jungle Publishing.

Further Reading

Chambers, J. W. (2000). *The tyranny of change: America in the Progressive Era, 1890–1920.* New Brunswick, NJ: Rutgers University Press.
Dawley, A. (1991). *Struggles for justice: Social responsibility and the liberal state.* Cambridge, MA: Harvard University Press.
Koven, S., & Michel, S. (Eds.). (1993). *Mothers of a new world: Maternalist politics and the origins of welfare states.* New York: Routledge.

QUEBEC PROVINCE SOCIAL WELFARE POLICY (CANADA)

Even a brief sketch of the development of social welfare in Quebec must be more than the history of the exercise of an important item of legislative jurisdiction by one member unit of a federal state. It is also an account of the (eminently successful) struggle for cultural survival on the part of the French of Quebec—an ethnic minority present on the soil far longer than any of the ethnic groups that constitute the majority—in a nation and in a struggle in which the role of the institutions of social welfare has been crucial. It must also bear witness to a social change of revolutionary dimensions in the second half of the twentieth century, notably in the precipitous decline in the social influence of organized religion; in this process, too, the institutions of social welfare have been central.

The roots of a distinct social welfare policy in Quebec go back to the century and a half (1608–1760) when Quebec was a French colony, part of the extensive French possessions in North America. The colonial government, with limited sources of revenue, implemented measures for the relief of the poor at times of agricultural failure or other hardship. Almost all the care of the poor and the sick was, however, in the hands of institutions operated by Catholic missionary priests and nursing sisters, and the faithful laity, the latter providing assistance in the home through *Bureaux des Pauvres*.

For nearly 200 years after the British conquest, social welfare in what is now Quebec remained to a great extent in private, primarily religious hands. The terms of the Treaty of Paris (1763) and, more explicitly, the Quebec Act (1774) left untouched much of the social fabric of French Canada; the "Canadiens" were free to use the French language in local (and eventually in provincial) government, in their schools and in business, to retain their system of civil law, and to practice their religion. The population was overwhelmingly French (as it is today, though much less so). Still, substantial numbers of English-speaking people settled in Quebec, nearly all British, and nearly all Protestant, the Irish excepted. Their accustomed pattern of welfare provision, based on the English Poor Law tradition, involved a significant role for the state, but they fell in with the prevailing Quebec model, creating their own sectarian philanthropic institutions.

In 1867, the British Parliament enacted the British North America Act, creating the Dominion of Canada, a federation of, at first, four existing colonies, thereafter called "provinces," including Quebec (the "Quebec" of the Quebec Act of 1744 extended westward as far as the Ohio River; the western boundary of the Quebec of 1867 was much as it is today). The necessity to accommodate Quebec's cultural uniqueness weighed heavily in the distribution of sovereign powers between the federal and provincial levels of government. Left to the provinces, among other things, were education, health (other than matters with international implications), and what we now think of as "welfare." The relationship between the federal government and the provinces must be kept in mind when discussing welfare policy. This is especially important with regard to Quebec; later, when the federal government put in place arrangements to share with the provinces the costs of certain welfare programs, Quebec was always reluctant to participate. Quebec's elite spokesmen insisted that the best foundation for the care of the needy was the bond of Christian charity; public intervention risked corrupting both giver and receiver.

As time passed, the cities and towns of Quebec took on some responsibility for relief of the indigent, so authorized by the provincial Municipal Code of 1871. They did so largely by granting ad hoc subsidies to existing institutions; this they did sporadically and unevenly, for their tax resources and their willingness to spend varied considerably.

Quebec, substantially industrial by the early 1900s, did not escape those effects of industrialization and urbanization that brought on increasing public intervention in welfare elsewhere. The vagaries of unemployment, the consequences of illness and incapacity to work, and the situation of the dependent elderly were of a different order than in the rural/agricultural past; in the urban setting, the typical family could not bear the burdens of indigence and illness. The efforts of such noninstitutional volunteer organizations as the Societe de St. Vincent de Paul, with its emphasis upon giving assistance in the homes of the poor, could go only so far. Still, well into the industrial era, primary reliance upon institutions—hospitals, shelters, and orphanages, mostly religious—and upon private charity, especially among the English speaking, remained the hallmark of Quebec's welfare "system." Its defenders buttressed their case by pointing out that the services of the religious orders, principally nuns, that staffed the institutions were exceedingly inexpensive, as indeed they were in the accounting sense.

Inevitably, the obsolescence of this approach began to show. To evade the constraints of the formal system,

subterfuges became common. If, in order to get help, a needy person had to be enrolled in an institution, then that person, or that person's family, or a sympathetic dispenser of aid would look for a way to get the person into an institution, whether or not such an admission was entirely justified. The first overt acknowledgement of provincial responsibility was the enactment in 1920, over considerable opposition, of the Public Charities Act, committing the government of the province to a measure of financial support to persons in need; the act still authorized the provincial government, and the municipalities, only to subsidize, on a regular basis, institutions whose programs provided defined services to needy individuals, and within whose walls they would reside. But the typical poor families served by many charitable organizations were living in their homes, and wanted to stay there. In time, this obstacle was circumvented by the recognition, in the law, of so-called "institutions without walls." Even so, public funds were still directed to organizations, and only through them to individuals and families.

In the course of time, measures of direct public assistance to individuals were introduced, all, however, following the standard pattern of "categorical" programs. In Quebec, the first was the Needy Mothers Assistance Act in 1937. The necessities of the Great Depression obliged the province to contribute to relief measures, though in a manner not well described as systematic; there was some jockeying between the provincial government and the municipalities of Quebec over responsibility for the financing and administration of relief; as elsewhere, this resulted in very uneven performance.

In another realm related to social welfare, Quebec became in 1931 the last but one of the provinces to legislate a program of Workers' Compensation; basically an insurance program, Workers' Compensation is financed almost wholly by employers and employees, with only a small government contribution.

In 1927, the federal government entered the field of welfare with the enactment of the Old Age Assistance Act, whereby it undertook to pay half the costs of programs created by willing provinces to provide income-tested "pensions" to elderly persons (the British North America Act was understood to prohibit the federal government from administering a welfare program itself). Quebec was the last province to enter into the necessary agreement with the federal government, joining the program in 1936. After World War II, the federal government similarly undertook to share the costs of assistance to needy blind persons, needy elderly, the disabled, and, finally, needy unemployed not eligible to receive Unemployment Insurance benefits. In every case, Quebec was the last, or nearly the last, province to come on board. This reluctance was no doubt due in part to the expected costs, but the avowed reasons were invariably (1) resistance to federal intervention, however benign, into a policy field within provincial jurisdiction, and (2) fear of the intrusion of the state into the domain of Quebec's traditional institutions, be the "state" federal or provincial. (Quebec did not have a government department devoted to welfare until the 1960s; the province's limited welfare programs were administered by a bureau in the department of public health.)

To understand the social welfare programs of Quebec, it is necessary to take account of the federal presence in the welfare field. In addition to the cost-sharing programs mentioned, Canada initiated a nationwide contributory program of Unemployment Insurance in 1941, having obtained the required constitutional amendment with unanimous consent of the provinces. In 1944 came a universal federal program, called the Family Allowance, subsequently converted into a more selective, and progressive, Child Tax Benefit (1998). Having paved the way with another constitutional amendment, Canada adopted a universal Old Age Security program in 1951, to which was added later (1966) an income-tested supplemental program that amounts to a guaranteed minimum income for all Canadians over 65. The mechanism for cost sharing has been changed over time from sharing of the costs of specific programs to a generalized health and social services grant from the federal government to the provinces based on each province's measured tax-collecting capacity. Although the provinces' primary jurisdiction in welfare is respected, welfare programs created by provinces had to fit themselves around the strictly federal programs and around the

conditions attached to the federal contributions to the cost-shared programs.

Quebec maintained its conservative stance in welfare matters until the 1960s. An ultraconservative political party, the *Union Nationale*, was in power in Quebec from 1937 until 1960, with a brief interruption during World War II. The party appealed to the nationalist sentiments of the French of Quebec, and to the uniqueness of Quebec's established ways of doing things, which, as noted, gave a dominant position to the Catholic church. At the same time, the party was openly hospitable to outside industrial investment, thus encouraging social change while resisting adaptations to social policy.

Quebec nationalist feeling has continued to shape social welfare policy. The French of Quebec have had ample reason, since 1763, to be concerned about the preservation of their culture and their collective identity. A minority in Canada, and much more so in North America, they adhered to their social structure and its characteristic institutions; and since religion was an important element of that structure, the church's long domination of charitable institutions and hospitals, as well as of schools and French-language universities, and even, for a time, of labor unions, contributed to Quebec's social and cultural survival. This point of view is unambiguously, even proudly, expressed in official documents, such as the expositions of Quebec's welfare system in the annexes to the federal Royal Commission on Dominion-Provincial Relations (1939) and the Quebec Royal Commission on Constitutional Problems (1957). The position of the church did not go unchallenged; there was always a vigorous red (*rouge*) tendency in intellectual and political life, still nationalistic, anticlerical only at the margins, but rooted in classical liberalism; but even when politically successful, its adherents left substantially untouched the institutional basis of care of the needy and the sick.

The traditional system was undoubtedly doomed to give way eventually. The turning point came with the sudden death in 1959 of Maurice Duplessis, founder and leader of the *Union Nationale*. His party was defeated by the Liberal party of Quebec in the provincial election of 1960. The era thus terminated has become known in Quebec as the great darkness (*la grand noirceur*). It was brusquely followed by the historic process known as the Quiet Revolution (*la Revolution Tranquille*).

There have been few if any instances anywhere of such deep, broad, rapid, yet totally peaceful social change on the scale of the changes in Quebec in the 1960s and 1970s (the population of Quebec exceeds that of many countries readily recognized as "societies," e.g., Norway, Ireland, Israel). To point to only one striking illustration, the birth rate in Catholic Quebec until the 1950s was among the highest, if not the highest, of all population units in the developed world for which statistics are available; by the 1970s, it was among the lowest. Among the provinces of Canada, Quebec now records by far the highest proportion of common-law marriages and the highest rate of abortions. This rapid secularization has shown itself markedly in the provision under governmental auspices of broad health care, social services, and social welfare programs. The process has gone hand in hand with a shift in the institutional allegiance of Quebec nationalism from the church to the state, that is, the province, whatever the political banner of the party in power. This recognition of the state as the embodiment of the *Québécois* collective identity helps to explain why Quebec has been more ready than some of its neighbors to adopt collective solutions to social problems.

In the field of social welfare, it was indicative of change that Quebec created its first-ever department of welfare (actually, Department of the Family and Social Welfare) in 1961. Then, acting upon the findings of a remarkably candid 1963 Report of the Study Committee on Public Assistance, known as the Boucher Report, which recommended a liberal public assistance program for the province, Quebec radically revised its public assistance program with the Social Aid Act of 1969. This act integrated the preexisting categorical welfare programs (aged, long-term unemployed, needy mothers, etc.) into a single needs-based program. In 1967, the federal government had replaced its several acts in support of provincial categorical programs with the Canada Assistance Plan, which encouraged the shift away from categorical to generalized means- and income-tested programs. When the federal government offered a new mode of subsidization less restrictively tied to the content of

programs, Quebec characteristically was the first to opt for it. By the 1990s, under the terms of the still-later subsidization formula called the Canadian Health and Social Transfer, which applies to all provinces, the conditions attached had become very lenient. Other Quebec legislation, in areas not subsidized by the federal government, followed rapidly through the 1960s and 1970s: an act concerning Health and Safety at Work, revising and greatly expanding the previous Workers' Compensation Act and including much-enriched programs in work safety; the Quebec Pension Plan Act, creating a contributory old age and disability pension program managed entirely within Quebec, parallel to the Canada Pension Plan that is in effect in the rest of Canada; an Act respecting Health and Social Services, which brought into being a provincewide network of linked agencies providing quite comprehensive services in both fields; a subsidized day care program, promising daytime care for young children for $5 per day; a Family Assistance Act, supplemental to the above-mentioned federal Family Allowance program, but sharply skewed in favor of families with more than three children; a Parental Wage Assistance Act, to assist parents with low and/or precarious earned incomes, encouraging them to stay in the labor force rather than fall back on public assistance. Since 1988, public assistance benefit levels in Quebec have been based, not on assessments of the needs of recipients, but on the actual consumption spending of families with incomes in the low decile of earned incomes.

These social programs have operated alongside very comprehensive medical care and hospital care insurance, also federally subsidized, though in decreasing proportion as time has passed. Families and individuals are also covered by a program of medication insurance, blunting the edge of a contingency that can be catastrophically expensive even for those with average incomes. The programs of the Quebec government are financed by a tax structure among the most highly progressive in existence (provinces collect income taxes of their own, alongside the federal income tax). Quebec is the first jurisdiction in North America in which political parties contending for office (in 2003) have seriously proposed to legislate a 4-day working week, albeit not immediately.

No broad welfare program can operate without difficulties. Health and welfare expenditures have contributed to Quebec being regularly the most highly taxed jurisdiction in North America, though there has been less political backlash over this than might be expected. Experiencing the same economic climate as the rest of North America, Quebec seriously modified its public assistance program in 1988 to incorporate controversial features that sharply relate eligibility for assistance to fitness and readiness to work, similar to so-called "workfare" programs, familiar elsewhere, that reduce benefits for single persons fit to work, and that also impose upon families financial responsibility for (principally young adult) family members. The reductions in benefits for employable persons prompted a lawsuit against the province alleging that the low benefits constituted discrimination as defined by the Canadian Charter of Rights and Freedoms (the case went to the Supreme Court of Canada, which decided against the plaintiff). The demand upon day care places generated by the $5-a-day fee not surprisingly swamped available facilities, raising concerns about the quality of service. The Quebec Pension Plan was given two mandates: (1) to provide pensions to contributors, and (2) to support the economic development of Quebec; certain investments of the accumulated funds made in pursuit of the second mandate have appeared to put at some risk the secure achievement of the first, bringing about a reorganization of the plan's administration in 2002–2003. In all fairness, such shortfalls from perfection have been no more drastic than elsewhere.

Looking ahead, Quebec provided itself in 2002 with a design for a renewed "welfare state," an act respecting Social Security and Exclusion. This act was passed unanimously by the Quebec National Assembly (as the legislature is called, reflecting Quebec's sense of itself as a distinct "nation" within Canada). Admittedly, for the most part, the act proclaims objectives; skeptics await its concrete implementation. It creates no new programs, nor does it revise old ones. All the same, this act is unique in its emphasis upon social "exclusion" as well as material "insecurity" as the business of social welfare. It is well understood in social science that the social and the material are intertwined, that deprivation is not compatible with positive participation in social life and with the exercise of acknowledged human rights; it is rarely stated in law. And it is no small thing for a state to commit itself explicitly in legislation to the reduction of poverty, according to internationally recognized measures, to practically the lowest level achieved anywhere. And some process has been put in place to monitor achievement. For instance, every government proposal for new legislation must be accompanied by an assessment of its impact upon the poor and excluded, and Quebec will create an *"Observatoire"* of independent citizens, served by the provincial statistical agency, that will report at regular intervals on progress toward the elimination of poverty and social exclusion in Quebec. If these are as yet aspirations, they are interesting ones.

—*Frank McGilly*

See also Federalism and Social Welfare Policy (Canada); French Language and Identity (Canada); Social Welfare (Canada): Before the Marsh Report; Social Welfare (Canada): Since the Marsh Report

Primary Sources

Archives of the Province of Quebec, notably successive issues of the *Rapport de l'Archiviste de la Province du Quebec*; Archives *Judiciaries de Montreal*, Library and Archives Canada.

Current Comment

Angers, F. A. (1955). *La sécurité sociale et les problèmes constitutionnels*. Quebec: Commission Royale d'Enquête sur les Problèmes Constitutionnels.

Minville, E. (1939). *Labor legislation and the social regime in the province of Quebec* (Annex to the Report of the Royal Commission on Dominion-Provincial Relations). Ottawa, ON: J.-O. Patenaude, Printer to the King.

Province of Quebec, Comité d'Étude sur l'Assistance Publique. (1963). *Report of the Study Committee on Public Assistance*. Montreal, QC: Author.

Further Reading

Vaillancourt, Y. (1988). *L'evolution des politiques sociales au Quebec, 1940–1960* Montreal, QC: Presses de l'Université de Montréal.

Mongeau, S. (1967). *L'evolution de l'assistance au Quebec*. Montreal, QC: Montréal Éditions du Jour.

Poulin, G. (1955). *L'assistance sociale dans la province de Québec, 1608–1951* (Memoir). Quebec: Commission royale d'enquête sur les problèmes constitutionnels.

R

RACE AND ETHNIC RELATIONS (CANADA)

The field of race and ethnic relations is often defined from the perspective of academics, such as sociologists, historians, and political scientists. Of interest is identifying some of the government and public's response to understanding racial difference and ethnic tension and conflict. This particular approach to race and ethnic relations involves examining the power differentials embedded within dominant and subordinate relationships socially constructed from fixed understandings about race and ethnicity. Definitions of race and ethnicity affect the evolution of Canadian social and institutional arrangements, for example, how social interactions are organized. Furthermore, recognizing Canada as a nation-state within the context of European colonialism raises questions about how social problems are defined, the explanation of the problem, the individual and organizational level solutions to the problem, and, finally, the effectiveness of the solutions.

The concept of race, as a modern definition, developed between the end of the eighteenth and middle of the nineteenth centuries. Generally, race refers to people of common ancestry or descent and is primarily based on physical characteristics such as color of skin, eyes, and hair. This definition of race fits well with the precepts of science and people's tendency to want to classify and order the social world, and to resort to generalizations when making sense of behaviors different from their own. Few would reject the reification of the concept of race as a valid biological entity as evidenced by the commonly held view that present-day social, political, and economic arrangements are fair and neutral and do not hold biases toward the dominant/majority group. People's unawareness of society's social relations never comes to the fore because processes of racialization must operate on the basis of myth and illusion and, therefore, are hidden from conscious awareness. For example, the notion that racism does not exist prevents any possibility of its elimination and a further taken-for-granted acceptance that this is the way things are and should be.

Ethnicity can be defined as how people would self-identify themselves in terms of their cultural heritage and tradition as part of a common group. Interestingly, in everyday Canadian discourse the common usage of the term ethnic by itself can mean the less dominant cultural identity to that of the dominant/majority group. This is inaccurate, however, because many people whose skin color is White do have an ethnicity that is known to be a part of the dominant/majority group. Therefore, subordinate groups such as Black, East Indian, South Asian, Southeast Asian, and West Asian may be referred to as ethno-racial minority groups. In sociological studies, the focus on ethnic relations refers to the different approaches taken to foster a harmonious and unified set of social relations in Canadian society, while recognizing that there may be tensions and conflicts among different groups of people. To deal with these differences, practices of assimilation are encouraged because they focus on how various ethnicities may be weakened to increase their absorption into the dominant/majority group. In contrast, pluralism recognizes that various ethnicities may want to maintain their cultural heritage and distinctiveness and, consequently, policies such as multi-culturalism successfully promote the coexistence of ethnically and racially diverse groups in society. The problem of structural inequality and racism are not issues of importance within the assimilation and pluralism approaches.

The role of the British and French as colonizers of the aboriginal people has also profoundly influenced and shaped current understandings about race and ethnic relations. The British and French people fought not only the indigenous people but also each other for aboriginal land known to its inhabitants as Turtle Island. The Europeans conquered and colonized the civilizations of Turtle Island. The British and French gained control of the territories belonging to the aboriginal people living in the North and renamed that land "Canada." Several aboriginal nations refer to the land called "Canada" as Turtle Island because the word is a mythic reference by and for aboriginal nations. From a legal standpoint, the British and French are considered "charter groups" because they were the first immigrants who shaped Canada's political and social agenda.

Given that aboriginal people were the first inhabitants of the continent of North America, a vision of Canada based on British and French hegemony has come under question by ethno-racial minorities. Furthermore, state policies and actions determined by the founding people have clearly shaped and influenced the role and place of aboriginal people and various racial and ethnic groups, especially in relation to British and French relations. For instance, the Indian Act of 1876 was a significant policy statement that determined how aboriginals were to be treated in Canada and, more important, shaped the relationship between natives and White Canadians, in the present as well as in the past. Up to the present time, the

Indian Act carries vestiges of processes of colonization as shown by the institutionalized restrictions placed upon aboriginals throughout Canadian history.

Another example includes the numerous bills passed between the years 1885 and 1967 and restrict the legal rights of the Chinese from permanently settling as citizens in Canada. These state policies not only marginalized the Chinese population but also affected the way other Canadians perceived and treated them. The Chinese had to endure restricted labor market opportunities, which, in turn, allowed dominant or majority groups to racialize and stereotype Chinese communities into various occupations. The establishment of multigenerational family building in Canada without family members returning back to the country they left is a more recent occurrence given the historical mistreatment of the Chinese.

Patterns of Canadian immigration regulated and controlled by the government also shaped the growth and size of various ethnic communities. Immigrants from European countries, such as the United Kingdom and northern Europe, were readily accepted into Canada, whereras immigrants from Asia and non-European countries did not gain favorable access to the country. Canada's immigration policies since 1867 helped reinforce the negative racialization of various ethnic groups. For example, Canadian policy attempted to increase population growth. A deliberate policy of settling the West resulted in a population increase from 400,000 in 1897 to 2.4 million in 1930, yet ethnic groups from eastern Europe were favored, whereas Jews and Mediterranean populations required special permits to enter the country. Another example is the way that Chinese and Indians were reluctantly accepted into the country to serve the expansion of the Canadian capitalist economy. The Chinese were the only ethnic group required to pay a "head" tax to enter the country. The head tax amount increased from $100 in 1900 to $500 in 1903 and, thus, resulted in a dramatic decrease in Chinese migration to Canada. This discriminatory legislation was not repealed until 1947. Similarly, it was not until 1962 and later, in 1967, that Canada changed its immigration policy, in general, by eliminating the practice of favoring particular countries, nationalities, ethnicities, and races for admission to Canada. Instead, a point system was developed and people were chosen for their potential capacity to contribute to Canadian society.

Many ethnic groups other than the British and French contributed to the making of the Canadian nation but are given only cursory mention in most accounts. In fact, in many historical accounts aboriginal people and ethnic groups are discriminatorily portrayed from the vantage point of the White settlers. At center stage rests much documentation on the European settlers' encounter with the indigenous people of Turtle Island and other various ethnic groups in ways that demonstrate how they are not accepted and included in Canadian society. Henceforth, an understanding about race and ethnic relations cannot be seen out of its historical and political context of the formation of the Canadian nation. In so doing, the concept of racism as an important feature of the political history of Canada shifts the interpretation of race and ethnic relations to understandings about colonialism and oppression. Social problems must be framed with attention to an analysis of how inequality and common sense understandings about race produce differential outcomes for various groups. In turn, the individual and organizational level solutions must focus on the historical development of various ethnic groups for the explicit purpose of making conscious deep-rooted ideologies that have shaped, informed, and dictated institutional policies and practices. These analyses allow for a multiplicity of perspectives to be explored and applied to an understanding of race and ethnic relations in Canada.

—June Ying Yee

See also Immigration and Social Welfare Policy (Canada); Multiculturalism (Canada)

Primary Sources

Multiculturalism Act, 1988; Charter of Rights and Freedom, 1985; Employment Equity Act of 1986.

Current Comment

Chao, L. (1997). *Beyond silence: Chinese literature in English.* Toronto, ON: TSAR Publications.
King, T. (2003). *The truth about stories: A native narrative.* Toronto, ON: House of Anansi.

Further Reading

Stanley, T. J. (2000). Why I killed Canadian history: Towards an anti-racist history in Canada. *Histoire Sociale/Social History, 33*(65), 79–103.
Steinberg, S. (2001). Race relations: The problem with the wrong name. *New Politics, 8, 2*(30) 57–61.
Ward, P. W. (2002). *White Canada forever: Popular attitudes and public policy toward Orientals in British Columbia* (3rd ed.). Montreal, QC: McGill University Press.
Winks, R. W. (1997). *The Blacks in Canada: A history* (2nd ed.). Montreal, QC: McGill University Press.

RANK AND FILE MOVEMENT (UNITED STATES)

The social work rank and file movement was formed in response to the political and economic conditions of the Great Depression. From 1926, when social workers organized the Association of Federated Social Workers in New York City, to 1934, when the journal *Social Work Today* was launched, the rank and file movement grew from a small group of dissident workers in New York City into a social movement that spanned the country. From the beginning, the movement attracted young, radical social workers who fought to improve their own working conditions so that they could better serve their clients. They argued for using collective bargaining rather than the dominant social work association, the American Association of Social Workers (AASW), as a framework for organizing because they did not believe that AASW was addressing the pressing issues of the times. They formed discussion clubs, practitioners' groups, and social work unions. For rank and filers, the major threat to American democracy was concentrated wealth. If the widening gap between the haves and the have-nots continued, they believed, both social work standards and labor standards would be destroyed.

Their ideology was rooted in a Marxian class analysis with a commitment to class struggle. Although some of the discussion clubs had close ties to the Communist party, most rank and filers supported a radical ideology absent of any specific political party affiliation. As a group, they were dissatisfied with social work's increasing emphasis on "function" rather than "cause." They saw social workers as white-collar proletarians whose mission was to strengthen alliances between themselves and other workers. They argued that control must be in the hands of workers who would join together to oppose the partnership of government and industry.

Social Work Today, begun in 1934 and edited by Jacob Fisher, an active rank and filer, gave the movement its voice. The journal raised the political consciousness of social workers in a number of areas including the oppressive economic system and political order, the importance of alliances with the labor movement, the inadequacy of public relief programs, and the need for nondiscrimination. Through the journal, rank and filers focused on advocating for a federal job program paying union wages and a social insurance system financed out of general revenues as well as fair hearings of grievances for those receiving assistance. They wrote about urban renewal, private philanthropy, social work education, war and peace. They promoted an awareness of—as well as ways to respond to—the growing fascism in Europe. Rather than accepting the standard social work education, where students were taught that individuals must be adjusted to the environment, they supported social work education in which the fundamentally oppressive economic and political order was challenged.

Other social work journals also carried articles by rank and filers. The *Journal of Jewish Communal Service* carried reprints of several papers given by rank and filers at various meetings of the National Conference of Jewish Social Services in the 1930s. *The Survey* also published a number of articles on the rank and file movement. Some of those articles are written by leading rank and filers, explaining the positions of the movement. The *Compass,* the official journal of the American Association of Social Workers, carried many articles about the movement.

In 1934, Mary van Kleeck, an active rank and filer, presented a paper at the National Conference of Social Work that questioned the underlying assumptions of the New Deal. Her pointed words strongly suggested that, rather than helping poor people, the New Deal actually strengthened corporate America. She reminded social workers that their allegiance was to their clients and that a socialized economy might best raise the standards of living for all people.

Yet, by 1935, with a membership of more than 15,000, almost twice the size of the AASW, the movement began a shift from criticism directed at New Deal programs to an emphasis on the need to expand and increase the benefits provided in these programs. After 1936, *Social Work Today* published an increasing number of articles on professional issues. By 1938, with many members of the rank and file movement now working in the New Deal programs, the movement was fighting those who were trying to dismantle the New Deal. They were becoming less cause focused and more reform oriented. In 1939, with the signing of the Nazi-Soviet Pact, many social workers left radical organizations, including the rank and file movement. Articles in *Social Work Today* continued to support peace until 1941, when the journal's position shifted dramatically toward support of those opposed to the Nazis. The movement ultimately supported the U.S. entry into World War II. The journal continued irregularly until it ceased publication in June 1942. This effectively brought to a close the rank and file movement.

—*Janice Andrews*

See also Lurie, Harry Lawrence; The New Deal (United States); Social Work Profession (United States); Van Kleeck, Mary

Primary Sources

The Jacob Fisher Papers, a complete set of the journal *Social Work Today,* the Harry Lurie Papers, and the Verne Weed Papers, are all held by the Social Welfare History Archives, University of Minnesota, Minneapolis.

Current Comment

Fisher, J. (1936). Rank and file movement, 1931–1936. *Social Work Today, 2,* 5–6.
Van Kleeck, M. (1934). Our illusions regarding government. *Proceedings of the National Conference of Social Work, 61,* 473–485.

Further Reading

Fisher, J. (1980). *The response of social work to the Depression.* Cambridge, MA: Schenkman.
Reisch, M., & Andrews, J. (2001). *The road not taken: A history of radical social work in the United States.* Philadelphia: Brunner-Routledge.
Spano, R. (1982). *The rank and file movement in social work.* Lanham, MD: University Press of America.

Wenocur, S., & Reisch, M. (1988). *From charity to enterprise: The development of American social work in a market economy.* Urbana: University of Illinois Press.

RANKIN, JEANNETTE PICKERING
(1880–1973)

In 1916, prior to universal suffrage for women in the United States, Jeannette Pickering Rankin was elected as the first woman to serve in the U.S. Congress, representing Montana in the House of Representatives. Rankin, who worked initially as a teacher and social worker, joined the women's suffrage movement in 1909 and served as a field secretary for the National Women's Suffrage Association. In this capacity, she worked on behalf of campaigns that granted women the right to vote in the state of Washington in 1910 and in Montana in 1914. These successes and her commitment to women's suffrage prompted her to run for Congress so she could pursue the passage of a constitutional amendment granting women the right to vote. In addition to women's suffrage, Rankin's work throughout her life focused on social reforms on behalf of women and children and international peace.

The oldest of seven children, Rankin was born in 1880 to Olive Pickering and John Rankin at Grant Creek Ranch, Montana. Growing up in an upper-middle-class frontier family allowed Rankin to pursue opportunities often not open to women of that era, including higher education. She received a degree in biology from the University of Montana in 1902. In 1908, Rankin decided to attend the New York School of Philanthropy. She then practiced briefly as a social worker in Montana and Washington State.

In 1909, Rankin began work for the National Women's Suffrage Association. After traveling the country as a field organizer for the National Women's Suffrage Association, she entered electoral politics in Montana, campaigning as a Republican on a platform calling for women's suffrage, prohibition, and protective legislation for children. During her first term in the House of Representatives, Rankin joined 56 others in Congress in opposing U.S. entry into World War I. This public act of pacifism contributed significantly to her unsuccessful bid to run for the Senate in 1918.

Rankin remained in the nation's capital working as a lobbyist for several pacifist organizations, including the Women's International League for Peace and Freedom. She also campaigned for the passage of the Sheppard-Towner Act, landmark legislation authorizing federal-state cooperation in addressing maternal and infant mortality through preventive public health initiatives.

In 1940, Rankin successfully won a seat in Congress, serving again as a Republican representative for Montana. With Europe already engaged in armed conflict, Rankin continued her crusade against war, arguing against both the military draft and the repeal of the neutrality legislation passed in the 1930s. Rankin's most notable pacifist statement was her casting the lone vote against U.S. entry into World War II on December 8, 1941, the day following the attack on Pearl Harbor.

This act of pacifism doomed her political career but did not hamper her commitment to pacifism. Between 1946 and 1971, she traveled and studied antiviolence methods in other countries, including Gandhi's India seven times. During the Vietnam War, Rankin allowed a group of protesters to call themselves the Jeannette Rankin Brigade, which demonstrated against the war in Washington, D.C., in 1968. Rankin died in 1973 at the age of 93.

—Bianca Genco-Morrison and Jan L. Hagen

See also Women and Social Welfare (United States)

Further Reading

Giles, K. S. (1980). *Flight of the dove: The story of Jeannette Rankin.* Beaverton, OR: Touchstone.

Josephson, H. (1974). *Jeannette Rankin, first lady in Congress: A biography.* Indianapolis, IN: Bobbs-Merrill.

Sicherman, B., & Green, C. H. (Eds.). (1980). *Notable American women, The modern period: A biographical dictionary.* Cambridge, MA: Harvard University Press, Belknap Press.

RELIGION AND SOCIAL WELFARE (CANADA)

In Canada, social reform and welfare policy evolved, until World War II, within an institutional culture framed by Protestant churches that defined social service in explicitly Christian terms. This evolution stands in contrast to the model of social welfare development that characterized the United States. In the latter country, some components of social scientific investigation and the practice of social work developed largely within university environments, and the intellectual discourse was founded, at least in part, upon scientific models.

At the turn of the twentieth century, the mainstream Protestant denominations in Canada rejected the elitism and narrowness of traditional theology as the intellectual touchstone of Christian teaching. In an effort to make Christianity more relevant to an emerging industrial society, they reoriented traditional evangelicalism, which focused solely upon the reform of individual character, outwards toward what they conceived of as a more modern and inclusive notion of social or practical Christianity. This intellectual reconceptualization of the role of the church and its clergy, which saw the reform of all society as building the spiritual Kingdom of God on earth, greatly expanded the purview of Christian culture far beyond the confines of the traditional institutional church. By defining the ideal clergyman in terms of community activism and political leadership, Protestant denominations hoped to make their churches more appealing to a working-class constituency and by so increasing their membership, they hoped to preserve the cultural authority of Protestantism in a rapidly changing, modern industrial society.

To this end, in 1902 the Methodist church established the Department of Temperance and Moral Reform, renamed in 1907 as the Department of Evangelism and Social Service, which was intended to symbolize the degree to which the churches had reinvented themselves as an arm of social reform. In a similar manner, in 1908 the Presbyterian church founded the Board of Moral and Social Reform. These bodies took as their focus issues of protective labor legislation, such as minimum wage laws, child welfare measures, the creation of urban and rural social surveys and the collection of data for government policy creation, and the establishment of a wide range of institutions of reform, including urban settlement houses, maternity homes for unwed women, and old-age homes By 1914, interdenominational cooperation led to the creation of a network of provincial social service councils. These organizations, in turn, united to form the Social Service Council of Canada, which remained until 1940 one of the premier forums for the formulation of social welfare initiatives. So dynamic was the church leadership during this period that the Social Service Council effectively integrated a range of previously disconnected social reform groups such as the Trades and Labour Congress (which was the first to join in 1914), the National Council of Women, the Dominion Grange, the Prison Reform Association, and the Women's Christian Temperance Union. The research focus of the Social Service Council of Canada was wide-ranging, incorporating both agricultural and urban advocacy groups, and, prior to World War II, it lobbied for legislation in the realms of immigration, divorce, mothers' pensions, unemployment insurance, old-age pensions, reform of labor relations, hospital insurance, and child welfare protection, measures that formed the backbone of modern social welfare legislation. But because Protestant church leaders continued to conceive of social reform both in terms of altering the social environment as well as spiritually saving the individual, their impact upon the development of a social welfare perspective was a key factor in slowing the expansion of a state welfare bureaucracy and in making those welfare provisions that were erected largely residual in nature.

As part of the Protestant initiative to expand the purview of the church into the broad realm of social welfare, the churches were instrumental in establishing the discipline of social work in Canada. As part of their broad campaign to inculcate young clergyman in the tenets of practical social Christianity, both the Methodist and Presbyterian churches created informal reading courses in social work, sociology, and psychology, and, by 1918, formal courses were established within the leading theological colleges. The first chair of Christian sociology was established in 1919 at Victoria College, where sociology was taught as a corollary to theology. In this period, clerical advocates of sociology proffered a synergy between science and religion founded upon the belief that social science could service the ends of religion by conceiving of ideal social relations in terms of the higher spiritual good. Needless to say, harnessing sociology and social work to distinctly Christian ends meant rejecting specialized and objective social science in favor of a form of social science that depended heavily upon the interconnection between empirical investigation and idealist social philosophy. Because professional social work in Canada was founded by church denominations, there was little fertile intellectual ground for the development of positivistic claims of the natural sciences as had occurred in the United States by the end of World War I. Indeed, in Canada the professionalization of social work remained channeled into overtly Christian reformist ends that prevented its intellectual grounding in a culture of scientific empiricism.

McGill University's Department of Social Study and Training was founded in 1918 explicitly to educate aspiring male clergymen in the tenets of modern social work theory and practice, and indeed it survived only as long as the financial contribution of the theological colleges remained intact. Hence, its doors closed in 1931 because the school had become, from the point of view of the churches, overrun with female social workers (some of whom were Jewish), and thus no longer served the recruiting needs of Protestantism. The department's first director was J. Howard Toynbee Falk, who adhered to the view that social work was but the handmaiden of Christianity because its central role was "the transfusion of the spirit and power of God" to the underprivileged in society. His successor, Carl Dawson, best known for his later contribution to the McGill Social Science Research Project, had long advocated the seamless fusion of social investigation and Christian social reform, having trained as a Baptist minister in the Department of Practical Sociology at the University of Chicago. The School of Social Service at the University of Toronto was likewise animated by the ideals of Christian social service. In 1914, the university's president, the Reverend Robert Falconer, a member of the Presbyterian Board of Moral and Social Reform, advocated the creation of academic courses in social work. The strong links between church and academy, and the forging of professional social work within the culture of social evangelism was further enhanced by the appointment in 1927 of a leading British social philosopher, E. J. Urwick, as director of the school.

A Congregationalist, Urwick had dedicated himself to the view that society was at root a spiritual organization and he thus rejected the shibboleth of positivistic social science because in his view all social facts were created by individual spirituality.

It was with the aim of establishing the Kingdom of God on earth through the application of Christian values to modern social work that the Canadian Association of Social Workers was established in 1926. In addition, the Protestant churches were responsible for establishing the Conference on Charities and Corrections and the Canadian Conference on Public Welfare, both of which functioned under the aegis of the church-dominated Social Service Council of Canada. All of these organizations dedicated to the creation of welfare reform remained closely tethered to the concept of Christian reform and indeed all the social workers associated with these movements used the periodical *Social Welfare*, the publication of the social evangelistic wings of the Methodist and Presbyterian churches, as their organ. The first cracks in this Christian reform nexus began to appear in the mid 1930s, when professional social workers, made up increasingly of women, symbolically rejected the leadership of male clergyman by establishing their own separate professional journal, *Canadian Welfare*. This eviscerating of a Christian tincture from social work forced clerical social workers to meet for the first time in 1935 as the Church Conference of Social Work, thus identifying professionalization irrevocably with more narrowly "secular" imperatives. By 1939, the head of the Social Service Council of Canada, the Reverend Claris Edwin Silcox, began to express concern about the alliance between the churches and social work, fearing that as social work became increasingly dominated by nonclerical practitioners, its Christian foundation would be eroded. Since many of these male and female social workers remained wedded to a distinctly Christian worldview, Silcox's supposed restiveness with "modern" social work reflected a fundamental concern about the cultural authority of the Protestant churches.

The rupture of the alliance between the churches and social work marked by the creation of separate secular and Christian organizations of social welfare reflected deeper transformations within the concept of social Christianity itself. By 1940, church leaders were no longer invited to join in government projects for wartime social welfare planning. Conservatives within the mainline Protestant denominations began to conceive of culture as bifurcated between the secular and sacred. The churches thus officially rejected the holistic conception of Christian society promulgated by an earlier, more optimistic group of reformist clergymen, and church organizations began to withdraw significantly from the field of social welfare, which they and others now defined as a peculiarly secular terrain.

—Nancy Christie

See also Settlement Houses (Canada); Social Reform Movements (Canada); Social Welfare (Canada): Before the Marsh Report

Primary Sources

United Church of Canada/Victoria University Archives, Toronto, ON (http://vicu.utoronto.ca/archives/archives.htm); Canadian Council of Churches Fonds, Library and Archives Canada, Ottawa, ON (www.collectionscanada.ca/index-e.html); Ontario Welfare Council Fonds, Archives of Ontario, Toronto (www.archives.gov.on.ca).

Further Reading

Allen, R. (1990). *The social passion: Religion and social reform in Canada, 1914–1928* (2nd ed.). Toronto, ON: University of Toronto Press.

Christie, N., & Gauvreau, M. (1996). *A full-orbed Christianity: The Protestant churches and social welfare in Canada, 1900–1940*. Montreal, QC, and Kingston, ON: McGill-Queen's University Press.

RELIGION AND SOCIAL WELFARE (UNITED STATES)

Religions in the United States are major sources of the values that have shaped our thinking on social issues and provided the moral fervor necessary for the provision of social welfare. Less well understood is the role of religion in creating institutions and organizational strategies that have guided movements for reform and influenced public policy.

The great faith communities of the United States—Protestant, Catholic, Jewish, and Muslim—exemplify our heritage of religious freedom and the diversity of belief and ethnicity that has emerged from the two previous centuries. These groups share not only some fundamental values but also a set of sacred texts; both Christianity and Islam affirm the essential teachings of the Hebrew scriptures while adding new revelations of Jesus and Mohammed. The interpretive key to the Old Testament is God's revelation to the leader of an oppressed people. Successive prophets denounced injustice as the source of poverty.

The core ethical principle of Christians, Jews, and Muslims is the spiritual equality of all humans because all are created by God. In Christian teaching, for example, God's incarnation is present in the poor and the imprisoned so that acts of charity toward them are the highest form of piety. This central tenet is also expressed in the moral imperative of empathy common to all faiths: that we should provide for others what we would wish for ourselves. "None of you," reads the Islamic version, "is a believer as long as he does not wish his brother what he wishes himself."

The prophetic tradition of the Hebrew scriptures also demands that civil and religious authority be accountable to the judgment of a God who will punish nations that break their covenant with Him, a sentiment echoed in Abraham Lincoln's Second Inaugural Address: "If God wills that . . . every drop of blood drawn with the lash shall be paid by another drawn with the sword . . . so still it must be said 'the judgments of the Lord are true and righteous altogether.'"

Though Catholic Spain and France had first explored the Southwest and Canada, it was the English, Anglican, and Puritan, who, with Dutch Protestants, brought the first religious ideas and institutions to what would become the United States. In the first colonies of Virginia and Massachusetts, these included adaptations of the English Poor Law, codified in 1601, which assigned responsibility for the needy—in America, mostly widows and orphans—to local parishes. Thus, the principle of public provision for the poor was introduced by the first settlers as part of the collective responsibility of a religious community.

In New England, this duty was shaped by the ethical principles of Protestantism, specifically the version of Calvinism practiced by English Puritans. God had chosen some, they believed, but not all, to be saved. And to the fortunate elect, God often imparted gifts of industry, prudence, and thrift that tended naturally to greater prosperity and happiness. Thus were sown those suspicions that the poor, though we are obligated to care for them, may deserve their lot because they lack the virtues necessary for even modest wealth. Max Weber, who analyzed these relationships in *The Protestant Ethic and the Spirit of Capitalism,* thought that Benjamin Franklin best exemplified the Puritan virtues even as he secularized them, making wealth itself, rather than salvation, the ultimate reward: "Early to bed, early to rise; makes a man healthy, wealthy, and wise."

Until the revolutionary war, American religious polity was that of the previous 15 centuries, the state church. Even the degree of religious tolerance that existed in England by 1789 still presupposed an established church, its faith defended by the king himself, supported with taxes, represented in Parliament by its bishops, with civil penalties for dissenters. A weakened version of this pattern persisted in New England even after the Revolution, but the advance of religious diversity in the colonies taken as a whole was such that no one religion could be accorded preference. The terse language of the Constitution—no religious test, no establishment of religion—brought about a new principle of religious organization, that of voluntary association. Churches were now to be supported entirely by the free participation and gifts of their members who could also ordain, employ, or dismiss their clergy, or break away to create an entirely new congregation.

The possibilities of this "voluntary system"—now called "denominationalism"—were exploited first and most effectively by Methodists and Baptists who were thus able to keep pace with a growing, westward-moving population and become the nation's largest religious bodies by mid century. But the model was soon extended to interdenominational associations for missionary work and social reform. Periods of voluntary group formation on behalf of social welfare and reform in the nineteenth century coincided with the Second Great Awakening, a religious revival of the early nineteenth century, and post–Civil War urban revivalism. These associations, which promoted the abolition of slavery, temperance, women's suffrage, and other causes with their grassroots organization,

moral fervor, and multitiered federal structure were, in Theda Skocpol's phrase, "the quintessential form of translocal U.S. voluntarism well into the twentieth century." Many associations fit this model; the latest examples include the American Association of Retired Persons (AARP) and Mothers Against Drunk Driving (MADD).

The denominational model was both a consequence of the constitutional disposition of religion and an invention of the nation's first Protestant groups. It was adapted by Catholic and Jewish communities as their numbers in the population increased.

First Germans and Irish and, later, Italian and Polish Catholics crowded into eastern cities to face the lot of new immigrants: poor wages, harsh living conditions, and often outright hostility and violence. The Knights of Columbus, founded by Catholic laity in response to these conditions, asserted by its name the essential harmony of Catholic teaching and American democracy. The Knights of Labor, founded in 1869, attracted many working-class Catholics, including Terence Powderly, its leader in the successful strike against Jay Gould's railroad combine in 1885. The Knights' superficial similarities to secret societies like the Freemasons sparked a controversy in the American Roman Catholic hierarchy that was settled in Rome after Archbishop James Gibbon's defense of Catholic participation in the Knights of Labor. The workers' grievances were real, he argued, and the church must not abandon them to greedy owners and monopolistic corporations. American Catholic experience was guided and interpreted in the light of several encyclicals on social issues, including *Rerum Novarum* of Leo XIII in 1891 and, in 1963, John XXIII's *Pacem in Terris.*

For American Jews, the forms of voluntary association available in the United States were familiar since the synagogue had always been a community center as well as a place for worship and instruction. In every major Jewish community, there were hospitals, orphanages, and social agencies for the poor. The prophetic tradition and the marginal status of Jews in Germany and eastern Europe may explain the extraordinary contributions of American Jews in labor unions, civil rights, and social welfare professions.

—Milton Powell

See also Brace, Charles Loring; Charity Organization Societies (United States); Children's Aid Society (United States); Poor Law (United States); Settlement Houses (United States); Social Gospel (United States)

Further Reading

Bane, M. J., Coffin, B., & Thiemann, R. F. (2000). (Eds.). *Who will provide? The changing role of religion in American social welfare.* Boulder, CO: Westview.

Leiby, J. (1978). *A history of social welfare and social work in the United States.* New York: Columbia University Press.

Smith, T. L. (1958). *Revivalism and social reform in mid-nineteenth-century America.* New York: Abingdon.

THE ROCKEFELLER FOUNDATION AND PUBLIC HEALTH (MEXICO)

The Rockefeller Foundation (RF)—launched in the United States in 1913 with a $50 million endowment from oil baron John D. Rockefeller—invested 30 years and approximately $15 million in current (2000) dollars to help institutionalize Mexico's commitment to public health. From 1921 to 1951, the RF's International Health Board (IHB; renamed the International Health Division, or IHD, in 1927) worked with Mexico's Department of Public Health (*Departamento de Salubridad Pública*, or DSP) through a series of cooperative programs, including campaigns against yellow fever and hookworm, the establishment of permanent health units, field research, and the advanced education of public health personnel in North American institutions and Mexican training stations.

Although the RF sponsored disease campaigns and advocated public health organization and education in more than 90 countries, the IHB's relationship with Mexico was special on several levels: It was one of the longest ongoing relationships the RF maintained, it involved a very wide range of activities, and the Mexican public health sector proved a formidable partner and rival to the IHB.

EARLY YEARS

In the wake of the Mexican Revolution (1910–1920), the country was faced with enormous challenges of institution (re)building and rising public expectations for state services, such as health and education. Around the same time, the Rockefeller Foundation was seeking to initiate public health activities in Mexico and displace existing continental influences. Given the long-standing geopolitical hostilities between the United States and Mexico, the RF was initially unable to convince Mexican authorities of the value of cooperation, particularly since the DSP—having acquired a larger purview through the 1917 Constitution—was developing its own plans for expansion based on national needs. But in late 1920, the situation changed. General Álvaro Obregón's accession to the presidency coincided with a deadly outbreak of yellow fever, after a hiatus of some 15 years, threatening trade in the oil-rich port of Veracruz. That Veracruz was the home of an important antigovernment rebel movement and the RF was so keen to control yellow fever in Mexico that it was footing the entire bill sweetened the deal considerably.

In January 1921, the Special Commission for the Eradication of Yellow Fever in Mexico dispatched 10 IHB officers, 11 DSP officials, and numerous military doctors from forces loyal to Obregón to Mexico's Gulf Coast. The commission also hired hundreds of local laborers. Over the course of 3 years, organized teams pursued the *Aedes aegypti* mosquito that transmits yellow fever by inspecting tens of thousands of houses, treating several million water receptacles and stagnant water sources, and depositing countless larvicidal fish into mosquito breeding sites.

The successful eradication of yellow fever in late 1923 was accompanied by enormous popular support for omnipresent public health personnel and the reduction of household insects. Obregón, recognizing the economic, political, and social usefulness of the IHB, invited it to stay on. The IHB proffered its standard campaign against hookworm, characterized by IHB founding director Wickliffe Rose as an "entering wedge" designed to convince the public and government authorities of the value of public health. Known as the "germ of laziness" because of the anemia it provokes, hookworm is spread through small worms that live in the moist soil of tropical zones. Worms typically enter the body through tender skin in bare feet, make their way into the digestive track, feed off the stomach lining, and are expelled through the feces. Promoting shoe wearing and the building of latrines—together with house-to-house administration of the worm-killing drug chenopodium—made for rapid, dramatic, and low-cost RF hookworm campaigns beginning in the southern United States in 1910.

Given the financial and administrative obstacles faced by the DSP as it sought to expand its reach in the 1920s, the campaign was much favored. But there was a catch: Unlike the high-profile yellow fever effort, the 5-year hookworm campaign required DSP cofinancing, beginning with 20 percent of costs the first year and reaching 100 percent the last. This arrangement turned hookworm—estimated by the IHB's own survey as a far smaller burden than malaria, diarrhea, and respiratory diseases—into a funding priority for the DSP, and it gave considerable administrative latitude to the IHB officer (who was also appointed to the DSP). Given that hookworm-induced anemia was not a popularly recognized health problem in Mexico, initial attempts to convince the public to spend money on shoes and latrines proved difficult—until the brigades themselves began to build latrines. By 1928, over 400,000 treatments had been administered and more than 15,000 latrines constructed in a band of small towns across the states of Veracruz, Oaxaca, and Chiapas.

CRISIS AND INSTITUTIONALIZATION

The hookworm campaign served as effective public health propaganda, and the DSP's annual reports highlighted its scope and impact. At the same time, there was mounting pressure both at the community level and within the DSP to establish permanent, comprehensive health services throughout the country. In 1926, Mexico's sanitary code was revised to enhance federal authority in public health matters, and the following year the DSP appealed to localities to establish permanent health units; because no financing was provided, the call met with little response. The IHD jumped in, inaugurating a local health unit in the coastal Veracruz towns of Minatitlán and Puerto México in late 1927, even before it had reached an agreement for continued cooperation with the DSP. Because of tensions over financing and administrative

control, this initial RF health unit received state and municipal support but no DSP monies in its first 2 years of operation.

Meanwhile, a more comprehensive plan for coordinated state health services was being forged by the DSP's Miguel Bustamante, an Oaxacan doctor who had just returned from doctoral studies in public health at Johns Hopkins University as a Rockefeller Foundation fellow. In 1929, Bustamante was named the director of a new health unit in the port of Veracruz. He pursued an ambitious agenda of communicable disease control, child hygiene, sanitation, milk and food inspection, health education, and other measures. Heavily supported by the DSP, the Veracruz unit served as a model health department that showed up the modest efforts of the first IHD unit, which had remained heavily focused on hookworm control. Notwithstanding tensions between Bustamante and IHD representative Henry Carr, Bustamante was promoted in 1931 to the helm of the DSP's new Rural Hygiene Service, which received RF support to expand the network of health units. By 1932, there were four Rockefeller Foundation–supported units in Veracruz and one in the state of Morelos offering a range of services, including maternal and infant care, midwifery training, school health, vaccinations, oral hygiene, sanitary engineering, food hygiene, and compilation of vital statistics.

The organization of local health units generated both rivalry and mutual imitation, with the RF and the DSP seeking to outshine one another while they continued to cooperate. Local health units also reflected competing models of public health practice with the RF promoting technically oriented and medicalized services while the DSP favored more socially oriented, comprehensive delivery of services, even if this meant relying temporarily on teachers and part-time staff.

In 1934, the political stability engineered under the continued power brokering of former President Plutarco Elías Calles began to unravel. Official party candidate Lázaro Cárdenas espoused radical populist politics in his presidential platform, while peasants, workers, and other sectors articulated increasing claims on the state. The Rockefeller Foundation was sufficiently concerned that its president, Max Mason, dispatched a personal envoy to survey the political situation, and the IHD continued to watch and wait until late 1935. After being pressed repeatedly by both Cárdenas's DSP chief, General José Siurob, and its own Mexico officer, Charles Bailey, the IHD finally agreed to support a limited demonstration area of health units in Morelos.

With the growing capacity and reach of the DSP, by 1936 the system of Coordinated Health Services in the states had expanded to cover 23 of Mexico's 30 states with some 140 health units. The system was soon complemented by a network of medical units in *ejidos,* small communal villages in rural areas. As the DSP expanded, the IHD appeared to be scaling back its efforts in Mexico as redundant. But instead, the IHD had subtly changed its emphasis to public health training, reflecting both internal RF priorities and the new needs of Cardenista Mexico. Beginning in 1936, the number of RF fellowships granted to doctors, nurses, and sanitary engineers to pursue graduate degrees in the United States accelerated, while the IHD also helped to found a series of training stations in Morelos, the Mexico City region, and other states. Between 1920 and 1951, the RF sponsored 68 public health fellows, organized public health tours to the United States for 36 high-level DSP officials, and helped prepare almost 2,000 Mexican health workers, including doctors, sanitary engineers, technicians, nurses, and midwives in regional training stations. These efforts were only reinforced after Cárdenas nationalized foreign oil holdings in March 1938, and the RF helped to assure U.S.-Mexican "good neighborliness" in the buildup to World War II.

The 1940s marked the IHD's denouement in Mexico. Three developments—all launched in 1943—reflected the influence of the IHD even as they overshadowed it. First, the Mexican government expanded its institutional commitment to public health through the elevation of the DSP to the ministerial level and the founding of the Mexican Social Security Institute (*Instituto Mexicano del Seguro Social,* or IMSS). Second, the RF invested in an enormous new venture—the Mexican Agricultural Program—designed to increase food production through the use of new agricultural biotechnologies. Finally, the U.S. State Department's Office of the Coordinator of Inter-American Affairs undertook a massive health and

sanitation program in Mexico—the likes of which the Rockefeller Foundation would not have favored and could not afford—as part of President Franklin D. Roosevelt's campaign to ensure the region's support for the Allies in World War II. As a result, the IHD's efforts were confined to small-scale nutrition and malaria studies, as well as the world's first trials of DDT to control louse-borne typhus.

Since the IHD's departure from Mexico in 1951 (the same year the IHD was collapsed into the RF's Division of Medicine and Public Health), the Rockefeller Foundation has continued to fund Mexican fellows and research projects but never again on the scale of the postrevolutionary period. Its long presence and varied activities in Mexico made the IHD an influential but not a dominant player in the development of public health institutions, policies, and practices. The RF interacted with an array of actors that included government authorities, medical elites, public health professionals, traditional healers, townsfolk, and local power brokers, all of whom were shaped and reshaped by their dealings with one another. Through moments of productive cooperation, appropriation, disdain, rejection, outright hostility, and bona fide accomplishment, public health ideas—some homegrown, some imported, some local, some international, some traversing back and forth—bloomed, many of which have continued to shape Mexican public health to the present.

—*Anne-Emanuelle Birn*

See also International Social Welfare; Philanthropy (Mexico); Social Reform and State-Building (Mexico); Social Welfare (Mexico): Since 1867

Primary Sources

Rockefeller Foundation Archives, Rockefeller Archive Center, Rockefeller University, Sleepy Hollow, NY; *Departamento de Archivos de Concentración e Histórico de la Secretaría de Salud* and the *Archivo General de la Nación,* both in Mexico City.

Current Comment

Bustamante, M. (1931). Local public health work in Mexico. *American Journal of Public Health, 21,* 725–736.
Carr, H. P. (1926, July). Observations upon hookworm disease in Mexico. *American Journal of Hygiene, 6*(Suppl.), 42–61.

Siurob, J. (1936, December). La sanidad en México. *Boletín de la Oficina Sanitaria Panamericana, 15*(12), 1148–1153.

Trabajos especiales del servicio de higiene rural, a cargo del Señor Dr. Henry P. Carr. (1932). *Salubridad, 3*(2), 443–445.

Further Reading

Birn, A.-E. (1998). A revolution in rural health? The struggle over local health units in Mexico, 1928–1940. *Journal of the History of Medicine and Allied Sciences, 53*(1), 43–76.

Birn, A.-E. (2003). Revolution, the scatological way: The Rockefeller Foundation's hookworm campaign in 1920s Mexico. In D. Armus (Ed.), *Disease in the history of modern Latin America: From malaria to AIDS* (pp. 158–182). Durham, NC: Duke University Press.

Cueto, M. (Ed.). (1994). *Missionaries of science: The Rockefeller Foundation and Latin America.* Bloomington: Indiana University Press.

Solórzano Ramos, A. (1997). *¿Fiebre dorada o fiebre amarilla? La Fundación Rockefeller en México, 1911–1924.* Guadalajara, Mexico: Universidad de Guadalajara.

ROOSEVELT, ANNA ELEANOR
(1884–1962)

Throughout her career—as settlement worker, teacher, party activist, first lady, journalist, fundraiser, and diplomat—Eleanor Roosevelt made social welfare issues the focus of her considerable energy. As she aged, her interpretation of social welfare issues surpassed the traditional Progressive Era notions of protective social legislation to encompass a broader human rights–based commitment to social, political, and economic equality. This transition was not smooth. As the niece of Theodore Roosevelt and the wife of Franklin D. Roosevelt, Eleanor Roosevelt had to balance her increasingly independent views with those of her relatives, two of the most dominant political leaders of the twentieth century.

Her father, Elliott, and her great mentor, Allenswood Academy headmistress Marie Souvestre, instilled a strong sense of duty and social responsibility in the young Eleanor. In her late teens, she volunteered at New York's Rivington Street Settlement, where she experienced the hardships extreme poverty and unsafe working conditions imposed on families. In 1903, she joined the National Consumers League, where she began her lifelong advocacy for the living

wage, child labor regulation, the 10-hour day, safe affordable housing, the right to join a trade union, and protective labor legislation for women. In the 1920s, she worked closely with Rose Schneiderman and Maud Schwartz to help the Women's Trade Union League secure safe, nonexploitative working and living conditions for women as well as monitoring social welfare and housing policies for the League of Women Voters and the Women's Civic League. During Franklin D. Roosevelt's governorship, she traveled throughout New York State inspecting prisons, juvenile facilities, hospitals, and Temporary Emergency Relief Administration programs and reporting on the social conditions she observed. She began to depart from a traditional progressive philosophy, which emphasized a limited role for government, to argue that the government had a responsibility to ensure a minimum standard of life for all its citizens.

As the New Deal began, Eleanor worked to ensure that workingwomen, young people, and African Americans were included in Works Progress Administration, Federal Emergency Relief Administration (FERA), and Social Security Administration programs. With Ellen Woodward and Florence Kerr, she worked to establish regional directors for women's relief programs and helped establish the Federal One Programs for unemployed artists and writers. She played a key role in establishing the National Youth Administration (NYA) to offer work relief and education benefits to high school- and college-age youth and secured Mary McLeod Bethune's appointment as NYA's director of minority affairs. Worried that the FERA programs did not meet enough of people's needs, she pressured FERA administrator Harry Hopkins to hire Lorena Hickok to tour different parts of the nation, observe FERA programs, and report on the programs' effectiveness. She then worked with Hilda Worthington Smith to establish the "she-she-she" camps for workingwomen, modeled after the successful Civilian Conservation Corps (CCC) camps that provided employment to unemployed young men.

Determined to make the New Deal as much reform as relief, Eleanor pressured Hopkins and Secretary of the Interior Harold Ickes to address those most marginalized by Franklin D. Roosevelt's policies. She criticized the Economy Act for penalizing married federally employed women; urged the Civil Works Administration to hire unemployed women and raise the wages of African American workers; and carefully monitored the construction of the Arthurdale subsistence homestead at Morgantown, West Virginia. She held White House conferences on the emergency needs of unemployed women (1933), the "she-she-she" camps (1934), and the specific needs of African American women and children (1938). She worked to expand both the public's knowledge of Social Security and the program itself, lobbying for the inclusion of servicemen's wives and children, women working in professions excluded from coverage, and health insurance. Working closely with Lucy Randolph Mason, Aubrey Williams, and other southern liberals, she gave consistent, strong support to the multiracial, multiclass Southern Conference on Human Welfare (SCHW) and the Southern Conference Education Fund's campaigns to challenge conventional segregation and to promote equal access to health, education, and political institutions, telling those attending the 1938 SCHW conference that "justice begins at home."

During World War II, Eleanor Roosevelt argued that America should not repeat the mistakes of World War I and, thus, should focus on winning both the war and "the peace." Unwilling to accept a return to high levels of unemployment, she goaded her husband, much to his irritation, to address postwar economic plans and full employment proposals. She also argued, unsuccessfully, that housing built for military personnel should be designed to meet postwar housing needs, rather than serve as temporary shelters. She worked to prod Congress to provide on-site day care for women working in the defense industries and to encourage the president to establish the Fair Employment Practices Commission. When she equated Hitler's discussions of a master race with American racism, attacks on her increased. National media declared "it's blood on your head, Mrs. Roosevelt," when race riots erupted in Detroit in 1943, and when she returned from visiting troops in the Pacific and was photographed holding the hands of wounded African American soldiers, segregationist newspapers printed special editions highlighting her conduct and calling for her "removal" from America.

After leaving the White House in 1945, Eleanor rejected calls to run for elective office, arguing instead that she could be more effective working with reform organizations, writing and speaking on social justice issues, and that any other position would require her to temper her language in ways she no longer wanted to do. She did, however, accept a position on the first American delegation to the United Nations, where she served as chair of the Committee on Social, Cultural, and Humanitarian Concerns as well as chair of the subcommittee charged with drafting the Universal Declaration of Human Rights. She moved the American delegation to recognize that human rights include social and economic rights as well as political and civil rights. Outside the United Nations, she supported the National Association for the Advancement of Colored People's attack on segregation, the National Consumers League's efforts to assist migrant workers, and labor unions' right to organize and to provide quality low-income housing to their members. In 1961, John F. Kennedy appointed her chair of his Presidential Commission on the Status of Women, a position she held until her death in 1962.

—*Allida Black*

See also African Americans and Social Welfare (United States); Hopkins, Harry Lloyd; International Social Welfare; The New Deal (United States); Roosevelt, Franklin Delano; Women and Social Welfare (United States)

Further Reading

Black, A. (1996). *Casting her own shadow: Eleanor Roosevelt and the shaping of postwar liberalism.* New York: Columbia University Press.

Black, A. (Ed.). (1999). *Courage in a dangerous world: The political writings of Eleanor Roosevelt.* New York: Columbia University Press.

Cook, B. W. (1992). *Eleanor Roosevelt: A life.* New York: Viking.

Ware, S. (1981). *Beyond suffrage: Women in the New Deal.* Cambridge, MA: Harvard University Press.

ROOSEVELT, FRANKLIN DELANO (1882–1945)

Franklin Delano Roosevelt, the 32nd president of the United States, sponsored many programs that are important in the history of social welfare policy. He became president in March 1933, a time when the people of the United States were experiencing many hardships because of the Great Depression.

Roosevelt was born into a wealthy New York family of Dutch ancestry in 1882. His birthplace, an estate in Hyde Park, is today the home of the Franklin D. Roosevelt Presidential Library and Museum. President Theodore Roosevelt, Franklin's third cousin, was a member of his extended family. As a child, Roosevelt lived as the son of a wealthy family, was privately tutored, and enjoyed a life of privilege. In 1896, he was sent to Groton, a private boarding school. After graduation in 1900, he entered Harvard and earned an undergraduate degree in 1903. In 1905, he married his distant cousin, Eleanor Roosevelt, whose uncle was Theodore Roosevelt. He studied law and later was elected as a Democrat to two terms in the New York state senate. He supported progressive causes as a state senator, including women's suffrage, worker's compensation, and legislation limiting the number of hours that could be worked in a week. From 1913 to 1920, Roosevelt served in the federal government as assistant secretary of the navy. Roosevelt's talents were recognized and he became the Democratic party vice presidential candidate in 1920, running with the presidential candidate, James M. Cox. The Democrats lost the 1920 election to the Republican candidate, Warren G. Harding of Ohio. In 1921, Roosevelt contracted polio, which left him with paralysis in his legs. Roosevelt remained active in Democratic party politics and, in 1928, he was elected governor of New York. The Great Depression began in 1929 after the stock market crash and Roosevelt used his skills to craft programs that would assist New Yorkers affected by the economic downturn. States were challenged to provide support for unemployed workers and their families since the Republican president, Herbert Hoover, did not believe the federal government should supply relief or welfare to individuals. Hoover felt that if charity or welfare support was to be given to the needy, it should be done by local governments or by private charities. But, as history demonstrated, there simply was not enough private charity or money available from the states to care for the millions of Americans who were unemployed and in need. During Roosevelt's second term as governor,

Harry Hopkins, a social worker, headed New York's relief program, which aimed to provide jobs and support for the unemployed.

Roosevelt's record as governor of New York made him a strong Democratic candidate for the presidency in 1932, an election he won with a large electoral margin. He used his political and social skills to explain to the people of the United States that they should remain confident in the ability of the federal government to respond to their needs in the midst of the chaos and fear resulting from the Great Depression. In early 1933, there were more than 12 million people out of work. To carry out the task of healing the nation, Roosevelt surrounded himself with energetic and enthusiastic supporters whose expertise in law, economics, social work, and other fields was used to craft new federal policies and programs that aimed to lift the country out of the depression. The Federal Emergency Relief Act of 1933 gave federal funds to public welfare agencies across the United States to distribute to those in need. This was important in the history of American social welfare because it made the administration of welfare a public responsibility. Professional social workers were employed in many public welfare agencies. Later, the Works Progress Administration (WPA) offered employment to many on public works projects, such as the construction of government office buildings across the United States. Subsequent federal social welfare policy and programs, all part of Roosevelt's New Deal (including the Social Security Act enacted in 1935) established modern social welfare programs that were meant to provide a "safety net" for workers against the vicissitudes of old age, illness, disability, and unemployment. This marked the beginning of America's "welfare state," which has always been controversial. Critics of Roosevelt's New Deal felt the federal government should not provide social welfare programs because they believed they were the responsibility of local governments or private charities. Others argued that provision of relief or welfare should only be given to those who were worthy to receive it. Still others felt government had a responsibility to provide for those in need and that their worthiness or suitability should not be considered in providing welfare assistance. During the Great Depression, there were not enough resources available locally to provide for those in need. Challenged in the courts, much New Deal legislation survived and supported the creation of federal government social welfare programs that provided welfare and services directly and through grants in aid to the states. Some New Deal programs remained controversial throughout the rest of the twentieth century. Aid to Dependent Children (ADC), enacted to provide support for needy children and to attack poverty, became one of the most controversial programs because some felt it provided support to women and children who were not worthy or "moral" enough to receive it. ADC and its successor, Aid to Families With Dependent Children (AFDC), provided monetary support for many of America's poor until they were replaced by the Personal Responsibility and Work Opportunity Reconciliation Act of 1996.

Franklin D. Roosevelt served four terms as president of the United States. He guided the nation into World War II in 1941 and died in office before the war ended. His successor, President Harry S Truman, saw the end of the war in 1945. President Roosevelt is remembered for his strong leadership during a period of national crisis. He used the radio to communicate with millions of Americans at the height of the depression and asked them to have faith in their national government and in their national leaders. Under his leadership, the federal government used its resources to provide social welfare services and financial support for millions of Americans who would otherwise have remained in poverty.

—*John M. Herrick*

See also Aid to Dependent Children/Aid to Families With Dependent Children (United States); Federalism and Social Welfare Policy (United States); Hopkins, Harry Lloyd; The New Deal (United States); Roosevelt, Anna Eleanor; Social Security (United States); Work Relief (United States)

Primary Source

The Franklin D. Roosevelt Papers are located at the Franklin D. Roosevelt Presidential Library, Hyde Park, NY.

Current Comment

Brown, J. C. (1940). *Public relief, 1929–1940*. New York: Henry Holt.

Lowitt, R., & Beasley, M. (Eds.). (2000). *One third of a nation: Lorena Hickok reports on the Great Depression*. Urbana: University of Illinois Press.

Perkins, F. (1946). *The Roosevelt I knew*. New York: Viking.

Further Reading

Greer, T. H. (2000). *What Roosevelt thought: The social and political ideas of Franklin D. Roosevelt*. East Lansing: Michigan State University Press.

Leuchtenburg, W. E. (1963). *Franklin D. Roosevelt and the New Deal*. New York: Harper & Row.

Schlesinger, A. M., Jr. (1957–1960). *The age of Roosevelt* (Vols. 1–3). Boston: Houghton Mifflin.

RURAL EDUCATION (MEXICO)

When scholars today speak of rural education in Mexico, they are invariably referring to the programs and legacies of the federal Secretariat of Public Education (*Secretaría de Educación Pública*, or SEP). The SEP was founded in 1921 on the heels of the Mexican Revolution (1910–1920). This bloody civil war cost over one million lives and wrought devastation on most of the country. The victorious faction was anxious to create a cultural and social institution to legitimate the triumph that it had achieved through violence. The SEP was given an extraordinarily broad mandate to transform rural Mexico. It built schools and libraries, as might be expected, but it also stimulated local development, introduced modern health care practices, promoted the arts, and tried to forge a cohesive nation out of people endlessly divided along ethnic, linguistic, geographic, and class lines. It is, arguably, the most important and enduring institution of the Mexican Revolution.

HUMBLE BEGINNINGS

It is actually incorrect to assert that rural education in Mexico started with the SEP. During Mexico's colonial period, the Spanish Crown, various religious orders, and villages themselves provided schooling on a sporadic basis. Rural education was again made available in parts of Mexico during the dictatorship of Porfirio Díaz (1876–1911). The regime recommended a pedagogy that was largely influenced by French positivist thinking and tended to place great emphasis on discipline and the emulation of French and Anglo-Saxon cultural norms. Actual implementation of this pedagogy, however, was in the hands of local education officials and teachers.

The decentralized nature of the Porfirian education system also meant that financial support for schooling varied dramatically. In the wealthier northern states or in states enjoying export booms, there was generally enough money to build schools in cities, towns, and the countryside. The poorer states, though, had great difficulty extending their school networks into rural areas. With the creation of the SEP, Mexico at last had a federal institution with a budget to build and maintain schools throughout the country.

THE UTOPIAN 1920s

In 1922, SEP director José Vasconcelos sowed the seeds of the new federal schooling circuit. He sent normal school graduates, whom he dubbed "missionaries," to rural areas to interest community members in education, to recruit prospective teachers, and to establish schools. Their results were mixed. Schools took root in communities that already had a tradition of rural schooling, but often failed in communities that did not. Educators and reformers searched for new ways to bring education to the countryside and to train teachers, impose high standards, and impart a new pedagogical vision. They found two solutions. The first was the "school of action" inspired by the North American pedagogue John Dewey. Teachers were implored to stimulate small-scale industry, provide technical training in agriculture and animal husbandry, facilitate the sale and consumption of locally produced products, and coordinate civic festivals. In a country still struggling to feed itself, teachers "inculcated the love of the soil" and encouraged peasants to stay rooted to the land, planting and harvesting grains.

The second solution, the cultural mission, targeted primarily indigenous communities. Part traveling normal school, part anthropological survey team, part home economics workshop, and part country fair, the cultural missions organized brief but intensive seminars. The ideal mission consisted of a doctor, an agronomist, an instructor in aesthetic (primarily European) culture, a carpenter, an ironworker, a potter, a master tanner, a soap maker, and a cook who would introduce new dishes and teach rural Mexico's corn tortilla eaters to make bread. The Eurocentric bias of the missions was clear.

Although the cultural missions were intended to address the shortcomings of Vasconcelos's missionary program, in many respects they suffered from the same constraints. All instruction was conducted in Spanish by *Mestizos* regardless of the language of the community in question. In some parts of Mexico, missions could not physically reach their target population. Often there were no roads into the hinterland, or locals did not produce enough surplus food to provision seminars that lasted several weeks. Some missions enjoyed the support of local authorities; others did not. Nonetheless, in states where the SEP did not build teacher training schools until the 1930s, the cultural mission was the closest many teachers would get to formal pedagogical training.

"SOCIALIST" EDUCATION

The SEP's populist pedagogy took a radical turn in 1931, when Narciso Bassols became director. The first avowed Marxist to hold a cabinet position in the Mexican government, Bassols supported collectivized agriculture and a blatantly antireligious curriculum. These and other tendencies eventually produced "socialist" education, which became the SEP's official operating philosophy beginning in late 1934.

Although much Marxist rhetoric was bandied about, socialist education was first and foremost a nationalist, rationalist pedagogy. It was an integral part of the presidency of Lázaro Cárdenas (1934–1940), whose great contribution to rural Mexico was the redistribution of close to 50 million acres of land and the creation of rural credit banks. Socialist education gave federal rural teachers an enormously broad mandate. For the duration of the 1930s, federal teachers helped peasants apply for land reform. They also became labor inspectors, union organizers, immigration officials, agronomists, and agents of Mexicanization. As in the 1920s, their schools were still expected to keep chickens, rabbits, pigeons, sheep, pigs, and bees, and feature a garden plot, including a greenhouse, an orchard, and a vegetable garden. Little emphasis was placed on teaching the three Rs—reading, writing, and arithmetic.

"Socialist" teachers also performed a dizzying amount of social work. They campaigned against dysentery, malaria, smallpox, measles, and onchocerciasis, and they conducted hygiene campaigns against lice and local diseases. They encouraged villagers to drain swamplands, protect sources of drinking water, and burn their trash. Finally, teachers (particularly female teachers) tried to modernize the peasant household. They attempted to convince peasants to leave their animals outside, to build waist-level hearths, and to increase ventilation in their homes.

Arguably, socialist education represented the most ambitious attempt to change the Mexican *mentalité* since the mass religious conversions of the sixteenth century. The SEP attempted nothing less than the creation of a new Mexican—sober, secular, clean, disciplined, hard working, and patriotic. It hoped to replace the cult of the saints with the cult of the state and to replace the religious calendar with a secular one. Patriotic celebrations, "cultural Sundays," and sporting competitions were used to instill a Mexican national identity, to "de-fanaticize" the population and distract youth from the lure of alcohol. Resistance to this new curriculum was especially fierce in western Mexico and in other places where the Catholic church was historically strong. Some rural schoolteachers paid with their lives for initiating land reform, organizing land invasions, implementing sobriety laws, and unionizing workers, whereas others were targeted for being the agents of an anticlerical federal government.

RURAL EDUCATION SINCE 1940

President Cárdenas's successors shifted their attention away from the rural sector as Mexico entered a period of rapid industrialization and modernization. The pace of land reform slowed, and teachers were told to tone down their rhetoric and their activism. Education (rural and urban) saw its share of the federal budget fall to 7.1 percent in 1952, down from a high of 13.6 percent in 1937. To a certain degree, the SEP's relative neglect of the countryside since 1940 has been warranted. Mexico has become increasingly urban. While 65 percent of the workforce was engaged in agriculture in 1940, that number fell to 54 percent in 1960 and 35 percent in 1970. No longer was the rural school regarded as the first and most critical site of state- and nation-building.

During the 1920s and 1930s, SEP schools largely failed to educate Mexico's indigenous populations and "incorporate" them into the *Mestizo* mainstream. In tacit recognition of the SEP's shortcomings, a new federal institution, the National Indigenous Institute (*Instituto Nacional Indigenista,* or INI), was created in 1948. The INI's "coordinating centers" were built in dozens of isolated indigenous regions and promoted the economic development of indigenous people without directly threatening their cultural integrity. In INI's schools, indigenous teachers used a bilingual-bicultural curriculum. In the middle 1960s, the SEP absorbed the INI's schools and adopted their bilingual-bicultural methodology, although it must be said that indigenous education today is still plagued by an array of problems. In many communities, schooling is not offered beyond the fourth grade. Bilingual texts do not arrive in sufficient quantities. Teachers often lack proper training and their absentee rates are high, in part because they cannot survive on their miserable salaries.

By the early 1980s, it had become clear that Mexican rural education—and the Mexican countryside itself—was in severe crisis. Following Mexico's economic meltdown in 1982, the international banking community forced the government to cut social spending. Federal support for education and agriculture began to dry up. Throughout the 1980s and 1990s, succeeding waves of free-market (or neoliberal) reforms and budget cuts stripped farmers of the credit and price supports that they needed to compete in the NAFTA free-trade zone. As Mexico increasingly imported its food, millions of acres of land went uncultivated, and Mexican peasants migrated to the cities (and the United States) in droves. By 1995, only 15.7 percent of the Mexican workforce engaged in agriculture.

At the dawn of the twenty-first century, the Mexican countryside was in its worst crisis since the Revolution of 1910, and rural education was not far behind. The SEP's rural school system has been largely decentralized and dismantled and its rural normal schools are anachronistic bastions of 1970s radicalism. Since 2000, the administration of President Vicente Fox has done little to make rural education a national priority.

—Stephen E. Lewis

See also Aboriginal People and Policy (Mexico); Education Policy (Mexico); Land Reform (Mexico); Peasant Movements and Social Programs (Mexico)

Primary Sources

Information on rural education in Mexico can be found in the *Secretaría de Educación Pública* (SEP) historical archive in downtown Mexico City. The archive is especially rich in holdings from the 1920s to the 1970s. Since its inception, the SEP has published a bulletin of its activities. Its name has changed over the years: see *Boletín de la Secretaría de Educación Pública* (1922–1931); *Memoria Relativa al Estado que Guarda el Ramo de Educación Pública* (1932–1935); *Memoria de la Secretaría de Educación Pública* (1936–1951); then *Acción Educativa del Gobierno Federal.*

Current Comment

El sistema de escuelas rurales en México. (1927). Mexico City: Talleres Gráficos de la Nación.

Ruiz, R. E. (1963). *Mexico: The challenge of poverty and illiteracy.* San Marino, CA: Huntington Library.

Vasconcelos, J. (1982). *The memoirs of José Vasconcelos: Vol 2. El desastre* in *Memorias.* Mexico City: Fondo de Cultura Económica.

Further Reading

Lewis, S. E. (2002). Ghosts and the machine: Teaching Emiliano Zapata and the Mexican Revolution since 1921. In J. Marten (Ed.), *Children and war: An historical anthology* (pp. 147–159). New York: New York University Press.

Meneses Morales, E. (1988). *Tendencias educativas oficiales en México, 1934–1964.* Mexico City: Centro de Estudios Educativos and Universidad Iberoamericana.

Vaughan, M. K. (1996). *Cultural politics in revolution: Teachers, peasants, and schools in Mexico, 1930–1940.* Tucson: University of Arizona Press.

RURAL/NORTHERN SOCIAL WELFARE (CANADA)

When New Brunswick, Nova Scotia, Ontario, and Quebec joined together to form the Canadian Confederation in 1867, a new era of economic and social reform was unleashed that would extend Canadian sovereignty across the West to Manitoba (1870), British Columbia (1871), and to Alberta and Saskatchewan in 1905. Canada's interest in the Far North resulted in the Northwest Territories joining the Confederation in 1870 and the Yukon Territory in 1898. Nunavut would be formed in 1999.

From the earliest years of Confederation, economic and political power became centralized in areas of high population density, which also promoted the development of industrial Canada. Moreover, social welfare, including education and health, was underdeveloped at the time of Confederation and was designated a provincial jurisdiction. The English poor laws were firmly established in all of the founding provinces except Quebec, where social welfare tended to follow a Roman Catholic religious rather than secular tradition. This combination of centralized power in Canada's southern areas and a lack of social welfare standards would have a profound effect on Canada's rural and northern areas.

In Canada today, approximately one percent of the Canadian population occupies the northern 80 percent of the country's landmass whereas 90 percent of the population lives within 200 miles of the border with the United States. Six out of 10 Canadians live in a narrow, largely urban, corridor between Quebec City and Windsor, Ontario.

This population and power concentration has created two Canadian "norths." The first north is the vast region contained in Canada's three territories, the Northwest Territory, the Yukon Territory, and Nunavut. The second north consists of the provincial norths in all but the Maritime provinces of Nova Scotia, New Brunswick, and Prince Edward Island. The northern area of the non-Maritime provinces consists of 61.6 percent of the total area of the provinces. In terms of social policy, these vast areas of Canada's two norths will be treated as hinterland. Because of the population concentrations, political power lies in the hands of politicians from the South who have little or no knowledge of the norths and who essentially see the norths as trees, minerals, oil, animals, and water waiting to be exploited. This attitude quickly leads to the impoverishment of the indigenous population, an emphasis on rapid, profit-oriented development, and the inability of local residents to control their destiny. The populating of Canada's North has been referred to as settler colonialism.

The hinterland mentality also allowed the government of Canada to create some of the 200 communities in the vast regions of northern Canada to establish its sovereignty in the High Arctic when this land was threatened by foreign takeover. Inuit were relocated to very remote isolated areas away from family, kinship, and the familiarity of the land necessary for their very survival. Many of these communities would never recover from such changes. This same hinterland attitude would impact the people of Newfoundland and Labrador who experienced relocation for different reasons. Tiny family and kinship communities were relocated from coastal islands and remote parts of the region to add to the population of other rural communities. Again, the result was mixed, with many communities suffering as a result.

With the establishment of the Department of National Health and Welfare (DNHW) in 1944 came an important development for Canada's rural and northern areas. In 1945, Native health was transferred to the DNHW, leading to the establishment of the Medical Services Board (MSB) in 1954. Although MSB had a significant impact in ensuring health care standards across all of Canada, its impact was particularly felt in Canada's rural and northern areas, which were tragically underdeveloped.

For many rural and provincial north communities, however, the politics of handouts dominated much of the 1940 to 1980 era. The politics of handouts include the delivery of social services that are viewed by local residents as bribes but are usually presented as incentive money; the provision of essential services as if they were gifts; and the appointment of local politicians to cabinet posts of relatively little importance. Essentially, the provincial norths and rural communities have been unable to voice their issues in parliaments, where hinterland issues are perceived as being not only of little importance, but more important, of little political value.

In an effort to address this power imbalance and to inform Canadians and helping professionals, the Canadian Social Work Forum was established. In 1976, the conference met in Winnipeg, Manitoba, to discuss rural social work education. Subsequent Canadian meetings in Fort-Qu'Appelle, Saskatchewan (1978), Victoria, British Columbia (1979), and Thunder Bay, Ontario (1981), as well as similar rural meetings in the United States, gave voice to rural and northern social welfare issues and brought these issues to the public and professional consciousness. Moreover, the mid 1970s also stimulated a growth in rural social work publications and a number of important texts were written over the next 10 years. In the early 1990s, M. Kim Zapf and Brian Wharf began to deconstruct earlier views about Canada's Far North and to promote the notion of homeland to replace hinterland as the cornerstone for social welfare policies and practices.

—*Roger Delaney and Keith Brownlee*

See also Aboriginal People and Policy (Canada)

Further Reading

Coates, K., & Morrison, W. (1992). *The forgotten North: A history of Canada's provincial norths.* Toronto, ON: Lorimer.

Dacks, G. (Ed.). (1990). *Devolution and constitutional development in the Canadian North.* Ottawa, ON: Carleton University Press.

Tester, F., & Kulchyski, P. (1994). *Tammarniit: Inuit relocation in the eastern Arctic.* Vancouver: University of British Columbia Press.

Weller, G. (1993). Hinterland politics: The case of northwestern Ontario. In C. Southcott (Ed.), *Provincial hinterland: Social inequality in northwestern Ontario* (pp. 5–28). Halifax, NS: Fernwood.

RUSH, BENJAMIN (1745–1813)

Even if there had not been an American Revolution, Dr. Benjamin Rush would have been one of America's leading social reformers. But the "Revolution," which he insisted was programmatically different from the War of American Independence, was for Rush the unifying conception for all his thought about changing America and the world for the better.

The descendant of English Quakers and Baptists who settled in Byberry (now Philadelphia), Pennsylvania, in 1683 in search of religious freedom, Rush was, like William Penn himself, a deeply religious thinker whose understanding of reality, especially social reality, was theological rather than "scientific" in any modern sense. Byberry, he wrote, was the

place where I drew my first breath. It has been and I hope will always be dear to me on that account, for I consider existence or life in any shape or form a blessing, but to exist as a rational creature, to be made capable of knowing the great I AM, and above all to be interested in the prospects of life and immortality which the Gospel opens beyond the grave, are blessings which no expressions of thankfulness will ever be able to exhaust. (Butterfield, 1951, Vol. 1, p. 621)

Fatherless at an early age, his mother left struggling to raise her family, Rush and his brother were placed in West Nottingham Academy, an evangelical "New Light" Presbyterian boarding school whose principal was the Reverend Samuel Finley (1715–1766), his maternal uncle and a leader of the Great Awakening in the colonies. At Nottingham and later at the College of New Jersey (now Princeton University), Rush matured in the evangelical faith of his teachers who included not only Finley but also the Reverends Gilbert Tennent (1703–1764) and Samuel Davies (1723–1761), prominent ministers in the great religious revival. In these "Schools of the Prophets," as they were called at the time, the young man's Great Awakening, theocentric worldview was formed for a lifetime.

Rush believed that he was not called by God to the Presbyterian ministry, his first love. So, after graduating from the College of New Jersey in 1759, he decided on a medical apprenticeship in Philadelphia and later matriculated at the University of Edinburgh School of Medicine. In his study of natural philosophy at Princeton and Edinburgh, which included medicine—not yet autonomous—Rush was introduced to Enlightenment philosophy, especially while in Scotland in the thought of the celebrated medical thinker and Newtonian, Dr. William Cullen (1710–1790). Even more influential was the work of the English associationist psychologist, David Hartley (1705–1757). Hartley, in his doctrine of associationism, would later provide Rush with a physics or mechanism of social reform by showing what John Locke had failed to demonstrate, that is, the very physiological process by which ideas are associated in the mind.

In his *Observations on Man* (1749), Hartley for the first time combined Locke's theory of the association of ideas with Sir Isaac Newton's theory of vibrations. All mental phenomena, the English physician and philosopher argued in agreement with Locke, are derived from sense experience. According to Hartley, external objects cause vibrations of the white

medullary substance of the brain and spinal cord. Hence, all consciousness is ultimately formed by the physical environment.

Man and society, Rush believed in his utopianism, could be perfected in a revolutionary program of social education and reform if only man would cooperate with the all-benevolent God in producing morally correct associations of ideas to replace the perverted ones of prerevolutionary times.

In his *Inquiry Into the Influence of Physical Causes Upon the Moral Faculty,* read before the American Philosophical Society in 1786, Rush argued from Hartley's system of physiological psychology and proposed "the moral education of youth upon *new and mechanical principles*" [italics added]. Physical causes, impressions upon the body, could be scientifically and mechanically arranged in a program of moral education to produce correct associations of ideas. A "temperate and vegetable diet," water in place of "spirituous liquors," moderate labor and sleep, cleanliness, and music—for example—were essential physical and environmental causes that together would restore to man his long-lost direct perception of truth and virtue that God had blessed man and woman with before the sin of Adam and Eve.

Rush began his scientific program of social reform in 1772 with his *Sermons to Gentlemen Upon Temperance and Exercise.* To the very end of his life, he was a vigorous crusader against distilled spirits. The organizers of the first temperance society founded in the country at Moreau, New York, in 1808, acknowledged his influence, especially in his much-read *Enquiry Into the Effects of Spirituous Liquors Upon the Human Body, and Their Influence Upon the Happiness of Society* (1784).

Rush's *An Address to Inhabitants of the British Settlements in America, Upon Slave-Keeping* (1773) was inspired by Quaker abolitionists Anthony Benezet (1713–1784) and John Woolman (1720–1772), and dedicated to the former. The following year, Rush was cofounder of the Pennsylvania Society for Promoting the Abolition of Slavery and the Relief of Free Negroes Unlawfully Held in Bondage. When he signed the Declaration of Independence, it is clear he understood Jefferson's "self-evident Truths" to include equality and liberty for African Americans as well as other men. In 1794, Rush donated 5,200 acres of land in western Pennsylvania for the use of Black farmers. He named the farm colony "Benezet" in honor of the Quaker reformer.

But Rush's reforms were many and diverse. In politics, in education, for both men and—radically for the times—women; in college-founding, medicine, penology, religion, and in so many other fields, he was a reformer of great courage and imagination. He was not a meliorist or pragmatist, but a systematic thinker, a Newtonian, a man of *esprit de systeme* whose bedrock principle was the Judeo-Christian belief in the infinite value of the human person created in the image and likeness of God and called to the higher life in society that he deserves.

—Donald J. D'Elia

See also African Americans and Social Welfare (United States); Criminal Justice Policy (United States); Education Policy (United States); Health Policy (United States); Mental Health Policy (United States); Substance Abuse Policy (United States)

Primary Source

Butterfield, L. H. (Ed.). (1951). *Letters of Benjamin Rush* (Vols. 1–2). Princeton, NJ: Published for the American Philosophical Society by Princeton University Press.

Further Reading

D'Elia, D. J. (1974). *Benjamin Rush: Philosopher of the American Revolution.* Philadelphia: American Philosophical Society.

Goodman, N. G. (1934). *Benjamin Rush: Physician and citizen, 1746–1813.* Philadelphia: University of Pennsylvania Press.

Hawke, D. F. (1971). *Benjamin Rush: Revolutionary gadfly.* Indianapolis, IN: Bobbs-Merrill.

S

SANGER, MARGARET HIGGINS (1879–1966)

Margaret Sanger, feminist and activist, has been identified as the founder of the birth control movement. Sanger believed that women needed accurate information and knowledge about their own bodies. She defied obscenity laws that made distribution of birth control information through the U.S. mail a punishable offense. Her political and social activism was centered on the belief that women had the right to control their bodies and limit family size. Margaret Sanger emerged as the leading advocate in the struggle for reproductive freedom for women.

Margaret Louise Higgins was born into an Irish American family on September 14, 1879, in Corning, New York. She was the sixth of 11 children of Michael Hennessey Higgins and Anne Purcell Higgins. Her father was a stonemason and an outspoken atheist whereas her mother maintained her Roman Catholic faith. Her family's inadequate household income was often supplemented by the financial contributions of the two oldest Higgins daughters.

Michael Higgins often engaged in political discussions and encouraged his children to challenge authority and think independently. Anne Higgins suffered from tuberculosis. Her health was undermined both by the disease and by Anne Higgins's frequent pregnancies. Margaret Sanger's family influenced her social activism as well as her ideas on reproductive freedom for women. Her father's candid and forthright positions combined with her intimate familial experiences as her mother struggled to raise 11 children with limited financial resources catalyzed her activism. Her belief that women needed to control their reproduction was formed as she witnessed her mother's weakened physical condition.

Margaret Higgins attended St. Mary's Parish School in Corning until a teacher humiliated her for being tardy and for wearing a pair of fancy white gloves to school. The gloves were a gift from one of her older sisters and she was so upset that she adamantly refused to attend further classes at the school. Her two older sisters, Mary and Nan, paid her tuition and helped her attend Claverack College and Hudson River Institute, a private boarding preparatory school. She worked in the school's kitchen to defray the cost of room and board. She was generally quite happy with her studies and her time at the school. Her leadership skills were enhanced during her enrollment at the boarding school. Although she continued to challenge authority at the school, she also learned that responsibilities were intricately linked with leadership activities.

Margaret Higgins was called home in 1898 to help care for her ailing mother and, as a result, failed to complete her final year of studies at Claverack. Her mother died as a result of tuberculosis in 1899 and, in

1900, Margaret Higgins enrolled in a nursing training program at White Plains Hospital. Her nursing studies were interrupted by her own treatment for tuberculosis.

Margaret Higgins's plans to become a registered nurse were derailed after she met and subsequently married William Sanger, an architect and aspiring artist, in August 1902. William was 10 years her senior and did not want to postpone marriage to allow her to complete her nursing studies. Once married, she was dismissed from the nursing program at White Plains Hospital because married women were not allowed to participate.

After their marriage, the couple moved to Hastings-on-Hudson, a New York City suburb. Six months later, Sanger was pregnant with her first child. She spent much of her pregnancy with her first-born son, Stuart, in a sanatorium. The pregnancy aggravated her tuberculosis and she returned to the sanatorium after the birth to restore her health. Her son Grant was born in 1908 and a daughter, Margaret (Peggy), was born in 1910.

Sanger was unfulfilled playing the roles of wife and mother and her relationship with her husband was weakened during these years in the suburbs. The Sangers decided in 1910 to return to New York City, where they became engaged in socialist politics and labor organization activities for the International Workers of the World (IWW). Sanger published articles on women's health, venereal disease, and sexuality in *The Call,* a socialist newspaper and was involved in the textile worker strikes in 1912 and 1913.

Margaret Sanger's nursing skills were utilized when she worked as a home nurse specializing in obstetrical cases as she cared for lower-income women in the city's Lower East Side. One of her patients, Sadie Sachs, died from a self-induced abortion in 1912. This tragic event synthesized many of her prior personal experiences with women and families living in poverty and struggling to survive without adequate information on preventing unwanted pregnancies.

Thus galvanized, Margaret Sanger launched her campaign for reproductive freedom for women. She coined the term birth control and began publishing *The Woman Rebel,* a monthly militant feminist journal, in 1914. The publication of *The Woman Rebel* and

an even more explicit pamphlet on contraception, *Family Limitation* (1914), entangled Sanger in legal difficulties related to the Comstock laws. The 1873 Comstock Act was named for Anthony Comstock, secretary of the New York Society for the Suppression of Vice, who personally lobbied Congress to pass the law defining the dissemination of contraception and birth control information as "obscene" and therefore illegal. After she had published just six issues of *The Woman Rebel,* Sanger was arrested.

In October 1914, Sanger left the United States to avoid prosecution. In Europe, she studied alternative methods to limit family size and birth control methods. She visited birth control clinics in the Netherlands and had an opportunity to see how the "Dutch Cap" diaphragm was being used there.

Sanger returned to the United States in 1915 and learned that public attitudes toward the dissemination of birth control information had become more favorable during her absence. The unfortunate illness and death of Sanger's only daughter, Peggy, swayed public support in her favor as she faced indictment for her 1914 arrest. Hundreds of women who were grateful for the help they received because of Sanger's efforts, together with feminists from the United States and Europe, wrote letters to the judge. The prosecutor tried to settle the case out of court but Sanger refused, determined to win and undermine the influence of the Comstock Act. The prosecutor finally dropped all charges against her in February 1916.

Sanger and her sister Ethel Byrne opened the first birth control clinic in the United States in October 1916. This clinic, in Brownsville, Brooklyn, had women waiting in long lines to receive birth control information. The clinic was raided and closed shortly after it opened and both Sanger and her sister were arrested and jailed. Sanger was found guilty of circulating birth control information and sentenced to 30 days in jail.

After receiving financial help from friends, in 1917 Sanger founded, edited, and published the first issue of the monthly *Birth Control Review.* She also authored a book, *Women and the New Race* (1920). With the support of her friends, in 1921 Sanger founded the American Birth Control League and served as the organization's first president.

Margaret Sanger's activism and her personal belief that women should have sexual freedom strained the Sanger marriage. The Sangers separated in 1914 and were quietly divorced in 1920. Two years later, Margaret Sanger married J. Noah Slee, a wealthy oil magnate. The marriage gave Sanger increased access to influential people, and Slee was willing to use his considerable financial resources to support Sanger's efforts to promote birth control in America and abroad. Sanger, with the help of Slee, smuggled diaphragms into the United States from Europe and distributed them to birth control clinics throughout the United States.

She organized birth control clinics in Hawaii, China, and Japan and lectured in various European cities in 1922. In 1923, she opened the Birth Control Clinical Research Bureau in New York, the first birth control clinic in the United States staffed by physicians. Sanger was involved in the Birth Control Conference (1925) held in New York City and helped to organize the World Population Conference (1927) in Geneva, Switzerland.

Sanger and others continued their fight to mandate a legal right for women to obtain birth control information. She led the National Committee on Federal Legislation for Birth Control from 1929 to 1935. This effort led to a breakthrough in *United States v. One Package* (1936). The case centered on Hannah Stone, a physician who had been arrested for receiving a package of contraceptive materials through the U.S. mail. The decision in favor of Stone, who was employed by Sanger's New York Birth Control Clinical Research Bureau, was a major victory for the birth control movement in the United States. The decision paved the way for the repeal of the repressive Comstock laws. Another victory came in 1937, when the American Medical Association (AMA) allowed contraception to be included in medical school curricula.

Sanger wrote two autobiographies, *My Fight for Birth Control* (1931) and *Margaret Sanger: An Autobiography* (1938). The American Birth Control League and the Birth Control Clinical Research Bureau merged in 1939 to become the Birth Control Federation of America. In 1942, the Birth Control Federation became the Planned Parenthood Federation of America with Sanger as its honorary chair.

Sanger continued to travel. She frequently lectured in Europe and Asia to promote the availability of birth control information internationally. She found very receptive audiences in India and Japan, where there was concern about high fertility rates. After World War II, both nations initiated state-supported birth control clinics based upon Sanger's approach. Sanger was the first president of the International Committee on Planned Parenthood (1946) and she sponsored the Cheltenham Congress on World Population and World Resources in Relation to the Family (1948). These efforts culminated in the creation of the International Planned Parenthood Federation (IPPF) in 1952. The IPPF became the largest organization promoting and disseminating birth control information throughout the world.

Sanger was also involved in the creation of the first oral contraceptive through her association with Katherine McCormick. As an heiress to the fortune of the International Harvester Company, McCormick subsidized the work of biologist Gregory Pincus. He and his team of scientists had been experimenting with synthetic hormones and, following clinical testing, produced the first biochemical contraceptive. In 1960, "the pill" was first offered to women as an innovative birth control method.

Sanger received an honorary LLD degree from Smith College in 1949, the 3rd class Order of the Precious Crown—the highest honor accorded to women in Japan—in 1965, and an honorary LLD degree from the University of Arizona in 1966. The Planned Parenthood Federation of America in 1965 created the Margaret Sanger Award to honor people who demonstrate a commitment to social justice and the Margaret Sanger Medallion to recognize contributions in community work.

Margaret Sanger died of congestive heart failure in 1966 in Tucson, Arizona, shortly before her 87th birthday. Sanger was a feminist and her unwavering conviction that every woman should own and control her own body was the motivation for her continuing fight for reproductive freedom for women.

—*Joan E. Esser-Stuart*

See also Health Policy (United States); Progressive Era (United States); Women and Social Welfare (United States)

Primary Sources

Margaret Sanger Papers, Sophia Smith Collection, Smith College, Northampton, MA; Margaret Sanger Papers Project, Department of History, New York University, New York (www.nyu.edu/projects/sanger/index.html).

Current Comment

Sanger, M. (1920). *Women and the new race.* New York: Truth Publishing.
Sanger, M. (1969). *My fight for birth control.* New York: Maxwell Reprint. (Original work published 1931)
Sanger, M. (1971). *Margaret Sanger: An autobiography.* New York: Dover. (Original work published 1938)

Further Reading

Chesler, E. (1992). *Women of valor: Margaret Sanger and the birth control movement in America.* New York: Simon & Schuster.
Gordon, L. (1976). *Woman's body, woman's right: Birth control in America.* New York: Viking.
Kennedy, D. M. (1970). *Birth control in America: The career of Margaret Sanger.* New Haven, CT: Yale University Press.
Lader, L. (1955). *The Margaret Sanger story: And the fight for birth control.* Westport, CT: Greenwood.

SCIENTIFIC PHILANTHROPY (UNITED STATES)

Scientific philanthropy was a movement first begun by members of Protestant social and economic elites to curtail urban poverty and begging in England in the 1860s. Between 1877 and 1920, scientific charity spread rapidly to most northeastern and midwestern large- and medium-sized cities of the United States. The vehicle for anchoring and institutionalizing the movement for bringing greater efficiency, professionalism, and dispassionate inquiry to bear on philanthropy, pauperism, and poverty was the charity organization society. Minimizing the economic dependency of poor individuals and families and maximizing their self-sufficiency were the overarching aims of scientific charities.

The charity organization society, founded in the United States by Protestant clergymen and their wealthy and near-wealthy male and female congregants, sought the creation of a rational, systematic, and efficient charitable enterprise rooted not in sentiment but in facts derived from social science inquiry. If emergent social science principles could be brought to bear on making the pivotal distinction between the worthy and unworthy poor, then the former could be assigned suitable and temporary assistance (whether a job, medicine, counseling, or a referral to better housing), while the latter could be sent packing. Assessment of each individual through careful one-on-one investigation and casework, guided by the theories and methods of economics, sociology, political science, anthropology, and psychology, became the core activity of the charity organization volunteer.

Beginning in 1898 with the summer school of the New York City Charity Organization Society, professional training became a prerequisite of paid charity work in the realm of scientific philanthropy. Mary Richmond, who later authored the classic work, *Social Diagnosis* (1917), perfected her conception of case-by-case assessment and casework while coming up through the ranks of the Baltimore and Philadelphia charity organization societies.

Leaders of scientific philanthropies not only crafted the casework methodology used by its line workers but also took active and influential parts in urban environmental reforms in the early twentieth century. They launched model housing projects, tenement reform lobbying initiatives, and tuberculosis clinics in conjunction with older charities, such as New York City's Association for Improving the Condition of the Poor. Charity organization society officials created a formal job bank for unemployed clients in New York City in 1916 (the Social Service Exchange), piloted one-stop multiservice centers in the 1920s, and helped launch the community chest movement (known now as United Way) after World War I.

On the explosive topic of the wisdom of distributing public welfare, the leaders of the charity organization society movement, at two critical historical moments, reversed their original course. Scientific philanthropists bitterly opposed public alms in the late nineteenth century and during the mothers' or widows' pension movement in the second decade of the twentieth century. During the economic depression of 1893–1896, however, and in the late 1920s, the spiraling economic situation and rates of joblessness in the urban United States motivated overwhelmed caseworkers and spokespersons of the charity organization societies, by now often called family welfare societies, to join the fight to expand public welfare. In testimony before the U.S. Congress and state legislatures between 1929 and 1933, they helped document the hunger, homelessness, migrations, and joblessness of every state and region of the nation.

Antipathy to political displacement, fear of huge immigration surges from southern and eastern Europe, public-spiritedness, and a passion for modernity together fueled the pursuit and popularity of American scientific philanthropy. A tangled web of contradictory impulses—some backward-looking, some forward-looking—moved scientific philanthropists to devote a significant portion of their lives to the work of charity organization societies.

Profound opposition on the part of urban upper and upper-middle classes to public outdoor relief (public relief for people living in their own residences, rather than in almshouses) was one inspiration for the rise of scientific philanthropy. Receipt of public charity, they believed, eroded urban dwellers' economic self-reliance and corroded their character through fostering dependency on public alms through the mechanism of political patronage. Similarly, founders and supporters of the charity organization societies despised private "indiscriminate" giving as damaging to the moral fiber of the city and the poor.

After the Civil War, scions of old Protestant families that launched scientific charity harbored fear and resentment of big-city Democratic party bosses, like Boss Tweed of Tammany Hall in New York City, who had supplanted Republican elites' preeminence in city governance. Also frightening to Protestant gentry and the wealthy were the hundreds of thousands of impoverished immigrants from southern and eastern Europe of Catholic, Eastern Orthodox, and Jewish faith communities who were the chief constituents of the patronage machines.

Equally terrifying to Republican and Protestant urban leaders was the prospect of bloody social class warfare that had been foreshadowed in Great Britain and Europe in the 1840s and in the United States of the 1870s and 1880s. Schisms—be they economic, regional, ethnic, ideological, theological, social, racial, or political—raised the specter of recurring and widespread death and destruction. The prospect of open conflict was anathema to a generation of urban reformers who, like Josephine Shaw Lowell, the founder of the New York City Charity Organization Society, had lost a husband and brother in the carnage of the Civil War. For a group of people so directly knowledgeable about the incalculable losses associated with the passions of regional fratricide, science, not ardor or physical might, would make right.

Urban epidemic and endemic diseases, such as cholera, typhus, and tuberculosis, evoked among scientific philanthropists both fear of and compassion for those who were sick and impoverished. Knowing that epidemics proved most deadly in poor neighborhoods, but spread quickly into adjacent blocks of the better-off, members of the charity organization societies joined public health and settlement house workers in battling the environmental correlates of disease, such as impure water, filthy tenements, and open sewers.

Finally, scientific philanthropists were mid-Victorian men and women who sought to enter and shape a more modern world than that of their parents' generation. Inspired by Darwinian thought, the bacterial revolution, and the rise of social sciences, scientific charity leaders, volunteers, and paid staff hoped to employ expertise to make the urban United States a more efficient, orderly, and peaceful place.

—Barbara Levy Simon

See also Charity Organization Societies (United States); Lowell, Josephine Shaw; Poverty (United States); Social Work Profession (United States); State Boards of Charities (United States)

Primary Sources

Community Service Society Records and the Mary E. Richmond Archives, Rare Book & Manuscript Library, Butler Library, Columbia University, New York.

Current Comment

Devine, E. (1904). *Principles of relief.* New York: Macmillan.

Gurteen, S. H. (1882). *A handbook of charity organization.* Buffalo, NY: Author.

Lowell, J. S. (1884). *Public relief and private charity.* New York: Putnam.

Richmond, M. (1917). *Social diagnosis.* New York: Russell Sage Foundation.

Richmond, M. (1922). *What is social case work?* New York: Russell Sage Foundation.

Further Reading

Fitzpatrick, E. (2003). Social welfare. In T. M. Porter & D. Ross (Eds.), *The Cambridge history of science: Vol. 7. The modern social sciences* (pp. 608–620). New York: Cambridge University Press.

Greeley, D. (1995). *Beyond benevolence: Gender, class and the development of scientific charity in New York City, 1882–1935.* Unpublished doctoral dissertation, State University of New York at Stony Brook.

Rosenberg, C. E. (1997). Science, society, and social thought [Introduction]. In C. E. Rosenberg (Ed.), *No other gods: On science and American social thought* (2nd ed., rev. and enl.; pp. 1–21). Baltimore: Johns Hopkins University Press.

SETTLEMENT HOUSES (CANADA)

Most but not all of Canada's population lived on farms or in small towns and villages in the nineteenth century. Montreal, Quebec, was an important commercial center that retained its French language, culture, and Roman Catholic institutions for the poor and sick. Toronto, Ontario, was a rapidly growing center of finance and industry where most people had British roots. Numerous Protestant churches dominated its religious life. Compared with cities in Britain and the United States, Toronto's population was miniscule: in 1890, about 100,000 people or roughly a tenth of the number in New York City. European immigration to Canada had barely started by the end of the nineteenth century and most Canadian cities were in the earliest stages of development. Toronto's history made it the most active among Canadian cities in establishing settlement houses.

As a thriving industrial center, Toronto's sizeable low-income population lived in overcrowded slums. The Protestant churches, most of them Presbyterian, were imbued with the social gospel; toward the end of the century they slowly took the initiative to establish missions for the sick, the impoverished, and the uneducated and to spread Christianity. The church missions they established had the financial support of wealthy businessmen. In fact, the Christian institutional churches and missions took the place of settlement houses until the early twentieth century. Most of them ran settlement-type programs, and sometimes were referred to as "settlements."

Preceding London's Toynbee Hall, an early English settlement house, by several years, Toronto's Dorset Mission, later the St. Andrews Institute, was established in 1870 by St. Andrews Presbyterian Church. The minister in charge introduced programs of night school, gymnasium, swimming, and other recreation activities. The Memorial Institute, referred to as a church settlement, was established in Toronto by Plymouth Brethren in 1873 and continued to provide services until World War II. Another Toronto mission dating from 1883 was later transformed into the Fred Victor Mission with the support of wealthy farm implement manufacturer and philanthropist Hart Massey. Its primary activity was in temperance work carried out alongside a night school. To this day, Toronto's early Protestant missions, along with Catholic and other religious institutions, serve vagrant and homeless people. Similar ones exist in other Canadian cities.

Jewish immigration from eastern Europe started to pick up only at the close of the nineteenth century. By 1908, there were 15,000 Jewish people in Toronto and a number of synagogues. The evangelical churches established special programs to proselytize among Jews and other European immigrants. The Toronto Jewish Mission began in 1894 under interdenominational leadership. It was followed in 1908 by the Presbyterian Mission to the Jews in Toronto with the aim "to Christianize and Canadianize the Jews." Similar Presbyterian missions were formed in Winnipeg, Manitoba (1911), and Montreal (1915). In 1912, the Church of England established a Jewish mission in Toronto. Then, the Christian Synagogue in Toronto opened in 1913 adjacent to a public school with the aim of attracting Jewish children. The Christian Synagogue became an all-people's mission in 1922, called the Scott Institute, which was later renamed the Scott Mission. A number of theologians who had converted to Judaism provided the leadership in these evangelical organizations. In time, their very modest success was combined with sometimes-hostile protests, and the efforts were generally deemed futile. The development of Jewish institutions by the growing Jewish community itself was a significant outcome.

It was the turn of the nineteenth century before social conditions in Canada justified having settlement houses like those in British and American cities. The pioneer who gave leadership to the movement was an American, Sara Libby Carson. She had established Christadora House in 1897 in New York City to serve a diverse neighborhood of immigrants. In 1902, after being invited to Toronto, Carson and her coleader Mary Lawson Bell set up Canada's first settlement, Evangelia House, with initial support from the YWCA. When it opened, the pair, along with 12 staff members in residence and student volunteers, launched a successful program with a strong Christian focus. Among the early initiatives at Evangelia House were Toronto's first nursery school, a neighborhood playground, and a medical clinic. Carson returned to New York and remained there for some years until the Presbyterian church asked her to return to Canada in 1912 and set up a chain of six settlements across the country. The interest generated undoubtedly influenced the opening of a University Settlement in Montreal at that time.

As a result of Carson's new mandate and leadership, St. Christopher House in Toronto opened in 1912. Chalmers House began in Montreal the same year, but closed due to a lack of financial support after church union in 1925. In Winnipeg, Robertson Memorial House began in 1913 and was followed during World War I by St. Columbia House in Montreal. Vancouver Community House in British Columbia became an institutional church before closing in the 1930s. Neighbourhood House in Hamilton, Ontario, began in 1922, but closed for financial reasons during World War II.

From the outset, Toronto's St. Christopher House was a full-fledged social settlement and kept a long association with the Presbyterian church. It had a strong board and the financial support of wealthy local patrons, notably Sir James and Lady Woods. The settlement rapidly gained influence in the community through services that included home visiting, counseling, public health clinics, summer camps, language teaching, and help to immigrants.

Around the same time, leading social reformers had key roles in developing the University Settlement and Central Neighbourhood House. The most notable were highly placed citizens: John Shearer, initially a pastor and moral reformer, who headed the Moral and Social Reform Council of Canada (later the Social Service Council of Canada); Robert Falconer, head of the Presbyterian Theological College in Halifax, Nova Scotia, before his appointment as president of the University of Toronto; and J. J. Kelso, the passionate founder of Ontario's child protection services and the superintendent of neglected and dependent children.

The energy and commitment of Shearer, Falconer, and Kelso over several years lay behind Toronto's leadership in generating the settlement house movement across Canada. These three men had been strongly influenced over the years by social workers in the United States. One source of their enthusiasm was their participation in the National Conference of Charities and Correction in the United States. In addition, they were personally acquainted with the leaders and programs of New York and Chicago settlement houses. Another impetus for change came from theology students at Victoria College in Toronto, who conducted an extensive social survey in 1909 and 1910. The superintendent of Toronto's Fred Victor Mission, supported strongly by the Methodist City Mission Board, led the study. Arthur Burnett, one of the theology students, had worked in downtown London. Another, George Bryce, had spent a year at the New York School of Philanthropy (now the Columbia University School of Social Work). A third student, James Shaver, had an active career in social reform. Their shocking revelations of slum conditions in downtown Toronto, comparable to those in other major cities, had immediate results.

Shaver and members of the University of Toronto YMCA were active in starting the University Settlement. It opened in 1910 with its own board independent of the YMCA. This settlement took a secular approach to attract university-wide participation and encourage work with diverse immigrant populations. Initially led by a head social worker and his wife with two student residents, the program was intended for men and boys. It was an immediate success. A new head social worker, recruited from Hull House in Chicago soon afterward, redesigned the program to include women and girls and offered health care for babies. What followed was formal cooperation with the Toronto General Hospital, welfare visitors, and playground authorities, all of which improved neighborhood services around the University Settlement. Case conferencing with the other settlements eventually led to the establishment of the Toronto Neighbourhood Worker's Association (later the city's Family Service Association). City public health nurses were located in University Settlement by 1914, a year when terrible slum conditions in its downtown neighborhood were revealed in another survey, this one by the Bureau of Municipal Research in conjunction with University Settlement. Very soon, serious labor problems and financial stringency induced Sara Libby Carson to return and reorganize the settlement.

Central Neighbourhood House was quick to follow the University Settlement and opened in 1911. A Jewish head worker, Elizabeth Neufeld, a graduate of the Columbia University School of Social Work, was put in charge. As with the other settlements, student volunteers came from the nearby university. To allay anxiety about proselytizing activity among the children of Jewish immigrant families living in the area, Neufeld ensured that Jewish traditions, religious beliefs, and dietary laws were respected.

The development of a boy's parliament was a unique project in citizenship education at Central Neighbourhood House. One outcome of the interest in civic affairs was advocacy for better utilities, including improved garbage collection, street lighting, and safe streets. An early proposal to build low-cost housing was set aside for years, but leaders at this settlement never lost interest in preserving and improving housing in the area. Neufeld's vast energy also led to the start of a national Conference on Charities and Corrections in Canada that was aimed at discussing the main welfare issues of the day.

The Toronto Federation of Settlements, established in 1918, provided a national forum for settlements in Canada. Much later, this body was renamed the Toronto Association of Neighbourhood Services (TANS), and was followed by the National Federation of Settlements (later the Canadian Association of Neighbourhood Services, or CANS). Both organizations continue to be based in Toronto, thus accounting for the significant historical role of Toronto in settlements across Canada.

Generous philanthropic contributions to the settlements were not always sustained. In the case of St. Christopher House, the sponsoring Presbyterian church cut its financial support when secular programming became pronounced. Successful fund-raising by the Toronto Federation of Community Service after World War I led to secure funding and a stable future for all of the settlements.

During the depression of the 1930s, when a third of the population was unemployed, Canadian settlement houses gave what relief in kind they could manage

while also offering their traditional programs. In 1929, when the economic crisis began, new organizations also sprang up, such as Dixon Hall, which operated a soup kitchen near downtown Toronto and eventually was recognized as a major member of the Canadian settlement movement. During World War II, the settlements were lively recreation centers for men and women in the services.

At times, radical politics and episodes of racial conflict would surface and gain the attention of the larger community. Changing legal and social norms and values were at times also an issue. In 1936, an industrialist donated supplies and paid a nurse to staff a birth control clinic at the University Settlement. This program caused conflict between members of the board of directors until the program closed after World War II. Movies deemed unsuitable for children and Sunday dances were other sources of alarm at this settlement. Demographic changes were increasingly rapid as an influx of non-English-speaking immigrants from Europe set the stage for truly multicultural neighborhoods. The long-standing Presbyterian affiliation of St. Christopher House led to a strain between the church authorities and demands for secular programs. The result was weakened financial support from the church, which the Toronto Federation of Community Service had to deal with.

The antipoverty movements in Canada of the 1960s and 1970s spurred Canadian and provincial governments to undertake major programs such as "New Horizons," which made financial grants available to local community service organizations. Although the settlement houses were major beneficiaries, even more far-reaching was the establishment of numerous neighborhood services including health centers and multiservice centers across the country, and about 30 multiservice centers in Toronto. Similar developments occurred in other Canadian cities. Publicly funded local community service centers throughout Quebec provide an example. In recent decades, a changing organizational environment resulted in corporate forms of administration that have replaced the head settlement worker-in-residence with skilled social service managers.

Toronto's original settlement houses have kept their identities but have enlarged their programs to meet growing needs, especially those brought about by immigration and the need for multicultural programs. In doing so, they have far outgrown their building facilities for which they have compensated by working from five or six neighborhood locations. Their funding is no longer hand-to-mouth as in former days. Their budgets of around $5 million (in Canadian dollars) are now met by many newly emerged family foundations, other generous donors, corporations, project grants, and federal funding.

—Donald F. Bellamy

See also Religion and Social Welfare (Canada); Social Welfare (Canada): Before the Marsh Report

Primary Sources

Records of the Toronto Federation of Settlements, the National Federation of Settlements, University Settlement, Central Neighbourhood House, and St. Christopher House, City of Toronto Archives, Toronto, ON; Records of the Wesley Institute (Fort William), Fred Victor Mission (Toronto), and Italian Methodist House (Toronto), Archives of the United Church of Canada, Toronto, ON; Records of the Presbyterian Mission to the Jews (Toronto), Presbyterian Church Archives, Toronto, ON; Papers of J. J. Kelso, Library and Archives Canada, Ottawa, ON.

Further Reading

Irving, A., Parsons, H., & Bellamy, D. (1995). *Neighbours: Three social settlements in downtown Toronto.* Toronto: Canadian Scholars' Press.
Masters, D. C. (1947). *The rise of Toronto, 1850–1890.* Toronto, ON: University of Toronto Press.
Speisman, S. A. (1979). *The Jews of Toronto: A history to 1937.* Toronto: McClelland & Stewart.

SETTLEMENT HOUSES (UNITED STATES)

In the late nineteenth and early twentieth centuries, middle-class social reformers committed themselves to ameliorating social problems such as poverty by taking up residence in the neighborhoods of those they wanted to help. They resided in houses called settlements that often became complexes of buildings offering a variety of services and programs for those in settlement neighborhoods.

The idea for American settlements came from Samuel Barnett in London, England. In 1884, he established Toynbee Hall in the East End of London, an area characterized by poverty and social inequality resulting from the social change brought about by the Industrial Revolution. His motivation was to actualize the Christian Gospel by taking up residence with the poor to share with them the finer aspects of culture and manners, which he and his followers who took up residence in the slums thought would help bridge the gap between the rich and the poor and improve the lives of the poor.

Barnett's settlement house idea had great appeal for several idealistic young Americans who traveled to London, saw Toynbee Hall, and returned to America determined to do something similar. For many of these settlement house leaders, the settlements offered the opportunity to do something meaningful with their lives as social reformers and social workers. Many of the early social settlement leaders and residents were middle- and upper-class college-educated women who saw the settlements as places where they could lead meaningful lives devoted to social service and social reform. The first American settlements began in American cities such as New York, Boston, and Chicago. Led by idealistic and committed young reformers—like Jane Addams at Chicago's Hull House; Lillian Wald at the Nurses' Settlement, which would become the Henry Street Settlement in New York City's Lower East Side; and Robert A. Woods at Boston's South End House—the settlement idea took hold.

Settlement residents understood the problems of their urban neighbors because they lived among them. Settlement neighborhoods were often filled with immigrants who needed to learn the English language and how to cope with the demands of their new environments. Settlement residents learned that there were needs for public baths and for playgrounds and recreational facilities for neighborhood youth. Sometimes older persons needed a place to socialize outside of the stifling confines of tenement apartments and the settlements gave them opportunities to do so. Neighborhood mothers joined settlement mothers' clubs that offered cooking classes and speakers on well-baby care as well as many opportunities for relaxation. In the summer, settlements took neighborhood women and children away from hot city streets into the countryside for enjoyable events, including recreation and camping. Public health education offered advice on hygiene and how best to protect against influenza and other communicable diseases.

Settlements often opened their doors to those with ideas about how to respond to the plight of the poor and political discussion was common. This often led to social and political action to improve the lives of settlement neighbors. Settlement workers tried to listen to their neighbors so they could respond to their needs. Jane Addams wrote about the lives of her Hull House neighbors and the effects of poverty and hardship. She brought the plight of her neighbors to the attention of Chicago's city hall and demanded that the city improve garbage pickup in her neighborhood. She worked with sociologists from the University of Chicago to study Chicago's neighborhoods and their social problems. Jane Addams and many of her colleagues were in the vanguard of Progressive Era social reform activities prior to World War I. From a modern perspective, it is clear that settlements functioned as early community centers as they tried to respond to the needs of urban America.

Those who used the services of settlements most often came from neighborhoods adjacent to the settlement houses. As neighborhoods changed, some newer residents, particularly those of color, might find settlement houses that did not serve newcomers. Furthermore, given patterns of racial discrimination at different times in American history, people of color, primarily African Americans, developed settlement houses to respond to the needs of African Americans because these were at times ignored by the mainstream settlement movement. Settlements were also active in rural areas, most notably in the southeast and Appalachia. Some settlements had specific religious goals.

Financing the settlements was never easy. For the most part, they depended on the generosity of wealthy benefactors, which required settlement leaders to be effective fund-raisers. Sometimes, this produced conflict when benefactors disagreed with the actions or programs of a settlement. By the 1920s, community chests were funding some settlement activities. In the 1930s, in response to the Great Depression, settlements worked with the state and federal governments to assist the poor and the unemployed by providing relief programs. By mid century,

the settlement movement had changed from its early days. Some settlements disappeared as old residents left for the suburbs and new neighbors, who demanded new kinds of services, turned elsewhere. Other settlements changed their missions to accommodate new neighbors, many of whom were people of color. Settlement work no longer attracted young persons interested in living in settlement neighborhoods. Professionally educated social workers and other human service workers took over the operation and administration of settlements, which functioned mainly as community centers. Most funding now came from the United Way or from government programs rather than the wealthy.

Settlements are still active today. Henry Street Settlement in New York City continues to provide an array of services and programs for those in its urban neighborhood. The settlements contributed to the development of professional social work. Settlement workers' emphases on working with neighbors to solve personal and social problems and engaging in social and political action when necessary are important legacies in the history of social work.

—*John M. Herrick*

See also Addams, Jane; Hamilton, Alice; Hull House (United States); Immigration and Social Welfare Policy (United States); Lathrop, Julia Clifford; Lurie, Harry Lawrence; National Conference on Social Welfare (United States); Perkins, Frances; Progressive Era (United States); Religion and Social Welfare (United States); Social Work Profession (United States); Wald, Lillian D.

Primary Sources

Information on the history of the settlements can be found in the Records of the National Federation of Settlements and Neighborhood Centers, the United Neighborhood Houses of New York City, and the National Conference on Social Welfare, as well as the records of individual settlement houses, all located at the Social Welfare History Archives, University of Minnesota, Minneapolis. The largest collection of Jane Addams Papers are in the Jane Addams Memorial Collection in the University Library, University of Illinois at Chicago; Lillian D. Wald Papers are in the New York Public Library, New York, and the Rare Book & Manuscript Library, Butler Library, Columbia University, New York.

Current Comment

Addams, J. (1990). *Twenty years at Hull House* [With autobiographical notes]. Urbana: University of Illinois Press.

Simkhovitch, M. K. (1926). *The settlement primer.* Boston: National Federation of Settlements.

Wald, L. (1915). *The house on Henry Street.* New York: Henry Holt.

Further Reading

Carson, M. (1990). *Settlement folk: Social thought and the American settlement movement, 1885–1930.* Chicago: University of Chicago Press.

Davis, A. F. (1984). *Spearheads for reform: The social settlements and the progressive movement 1890–1914* (2nd ed., with a new introduction by the author). New Brunswick, NJ: Rutgers University Press.

Lasch-Quinn, E. (1993). *Black neighbors: Race and the limits of reform in the American settlement movement, 1890–1945.* Chapel Hill: University of North Carolina Press.

SMALL SYSTEMS SOCIAL WORK (CANADA)

An initial challenge in addressing this topic is a question of definition. Just what is meant by small systems social work in Canada? Immediately, one is plunged into issues of the history and sociology of the profession. Although still far from precise, from the perspective of the present, the meaning is clearer than in an earlier day. But to fully understand it, one needs to begin with a historical perspective.

In contemporary terms, small systems social work is the term used to identify the micro terminus of the macro-micro spectrum, which for over a century has been the identifying commitment and challenge for Canadian social work. In this sense, the concept refers to that use of values, knowledge, skills, and resources of social work to bring about sought-for psychosocial change in individuals, dyads, families, and small groups. In this mode of practice, an identified person(s), the client, is the direct target of the social worker's intervention. But even this is not a precise concept, for in this component of Canadian social work practice there has been and still is a further terminological subdivision, a distinction also a part of the thinking in United States practice. Here we speak of a perceived division between "direct work" and "indirect work" in small systems practice.

The concept of direct work is easy to comprehend in a discussion of small systems work. It refers to the activities of the social worker in face-to-face interactions with the client, be it an individual, dyad, group, or family.

The term indirect work refers to those activities of the social worker involving work with significant persons or systems in a client's life, where change or resources are sought that are deemed to be of assistance in helping the client achieve particular identified life goals. Since the term "person in situation" has been and continues to be an anchoring concept of Canadian social work practice, the distinction between what is large systems work and what is indirect work from a small systems perspective is not a clear or distinct one. Neither should it be, because an ongoing historical thrust of Canadian social work practice has been to avoid letting practice be divided precisely along a small-large dichotomy, or in more current terms, micro-macro dichotomy. Rather, the wish is to see these two foci of practice be the end points of a continuum with the awareness that there will be considerable overlap in the activities of many social workers. Thus, social workers who identify themselves as small systems practitioners may well find themselves advocating for a client before the city council just as large systems practitioners may quite appropriately need to deal therapeutically with very upset individuals as part of a neighborhood project.

Clearly, there are Canadian social workers whose interests, skills, commitments, and activities are in the large systems arena, where their professional efforts are aimed at bringing about systemic change, such as national social policies. Such practitioners may never see an individual client directly. (The word client here is used in the traditional sense of describing someone in society with whom a social worker has engaged in a professional relationship related to the psychosocial goals of that person.)

In the same way, there are social workers in Canada whose interests, skills, commitments, and activities are focused on direct work with clients who clearly could and would be identified as practicing in the small systems component of the profession. Even though in some professional circles, dialogue and debate continue as to which ends of the spectrum are to be favored, and by whom, the nature of the Canadian geography, demographics, and values of the profession have helped to maintain a balance that gives equal interest to these two essential components of the profession and the strong wish to see the distinction as a part of a spectrum rather than a dichotomy. Nevertheless, there is a significant component of Canadian social work practice that clearly can be called small systems work and can be looked at as a specific entity with its own qualities and characteristics.

As mentioned above, to understand small systems social work in Canada it is important to view it from a historical perspective, beginning with the end of the nineteenth century. At this time, as the profession began to emerge as a distinct entity among the group of human service professions in Canada, particularly in large urban settings, there was an understanding of the need to individualize efforts to respond to persons in need as well as to seek to address systemic issues. Originally, this was done from a moralistic and probably a sense of charitably colored social responsibility. As happened in many countries in Europe and North America, however, from this need to understand each client as a unique person there emerged the need for specialized professional knowledge and training to deal appropriately and sensitively to individual cases. The term that emerged to categorize this specialized knowledge and its application was casework. Initially, the majority of the first cluster of persons in Canada seeking professional training in casework sought it in the United States, where the concept of casework was very much to the fore. In those universities where social work was housed, although there was a stated commitment to societal change, the theory base of the profession was largely being developed around work with individuals and to some extent small groups.

One factor that is different about the way the profession developed in Canada, however, was that in addition to the number of persons who sought professional training in the United States, a number of Canadians went to England for this training. In England, systems change, societal change, and neighborhood development were much more emphasized than casework. Those who studied in England returned to Canada with a less clearly divided either/or approach to practice.

In addition to the development of a cadre of trained personnel, there had developed a large network of services, institutions, and resources for various categories of need even in the most remote regions of the county as well as in the many isolated rural areas. It was in this network of services and institutions that this first group of professional social workers found their practice base. For the most part, various religious groups sponsored these settings, but there were also a significant number sponsored by the pubic purse. Many of these institutions and services, in addition to providing resources for individuals in various categories of need, had a commitment to large systems change as the persons in charge saw the interconnections between private problems and public issues. Thus, many social workers who viewed themselves as caseworkers understood that a part of their responsibility was to address large systems issues and indeed saw this as a part of their casework identity.

As the number of persons seeking professional training increased, Canada developed its own network of schools of social work. These, for the most part, reflected the professional issues and conceptual and theoretical struggles taking place in the United States. So close was this relationship that well on into the 1960s the American-based Council on Social Work Education accredited Canadian schools and faculties of social work. In these schools, casework was the predominant and popular thrust of the curricula, although, of course, other large systems issues and methods were considered.

But because, for the most part, the early theoretical base of casework was strongly influenced by psychodynamic thinking, a very high-status theory in the sociology of the profession, casework tended to be viewed from a narrow small systems framework moving it away from larger systems work. Throughout most of the profession's history, the term "caseworker" gave a type of status to those so identified. This influenced the extent to which persons within the profession proudly identified themselves as caseworkers rather than social workers, as a perceived status symbol. Canada played an important role in this matter in that Frank Swithun Bowers, of St. Patrick's College School of Social Work of the University of Ottawa, wrote a definition of casework—one that stood for many decades in North America as the authoritative statement for the profession.

One of the several problems with the term and concept of casework from the Canadian small systems perspective was the uncertainty of its scope. Although never defined as a methodology that focused only on direct work with individuals, that is, small systems work, this certainly was implied in its mores and projected image. Indeed, when a student entered a school of social work well into the 1970s, one of the decisions that he/she had to make was whether to elect the casework stream, group work stream, or that of community development in its various designations.

The emergence of group work as a separate methodology also needs to be considered in seeking to understand the small systems component of contemporary practice. For much of its early history, group work belonged neither to large systems work nor to casework but to both, standing somewhere in the middle of the spectrum. Caseworkers were unsure as to how to respond to this format of practice. Out of this uncertainty, conceptual and operational struggles emerged, struggles that were much more intense in the United States, where at one time it appeared as if the profession was going to divide itself into separate entities. It is important to remember that, for the most part, this division was one resting in the halls of academe rather than in practice.

In Canada, and, indeed, in most other parts of the world, social workers found that it was difficult to practice in an agency without needing both group and individual skills. It is interesting that in this process little attention was given to work with couples and with families as separate professional functions although many practitioners found themselves involved in both couples and family situations but lacking a conceptual base into which to place these activities. Thus, somewhat apologetically they were seen as a part of casework. Thus, the term casework, although theoretically based on an individualist theory, in practice included work with couples, groups, and families. Frequently, to preserve the importance of a focus on the individual client, these activities were viewed as "collateral work" and implicitly given a lesser status than pure casework, which was with individuals.

Thus, the concept of small systems work was in practice a multimethod form of practice and, indeed, less evidently a multitheoretical one, although this latter point was not acknowledged as such. In Canada, the term casework still was enthroned as the predominant title for what social workers did in working with small systems. At this time, the term small systems was not as yet in the professional lexicon; rather this range of activities remained under the

terminological umbrella of casework. Caseworkers and group workers still identified themselves by these titles, although in practice there was little difference in what they did apart from highly specialized services—caseworkers worked with groups and vice versa.

One of the factors that helped strengthen the concept of a small systems practice as being a multimethod one with all methods being interconnected was the advent of family therapy, which took place in the latter part of the 1960s. This phenomenon, which swept North American small systems practice, required a major adjustment in all small systems thinking. As this family focus took on a high status, within and among the human service professions, both Canadian caseworkers and group workers found themselves eagerly involved in working with the family as a unit from one or more of the several extant high-profile theoretical perspectives. Apart from its important addition to the armamentarium of small systems practitioners, this development contributed greatly to the emergence of a perception of a small systems practitioner as a person requiring a range of methodological skills. For a brief period, there was an effort to maintain the co-identification of casework and small systems practitioners. Thus, in the literature, one can find articles in this period that talked about "casework with families" as being different from family therapy as well as "casework with groups" as being different from group work. This trend, however, was short-lived and in some ways was the final effort to retain the term casework as the descriptor of small systems practice.

This was only a brief phenomenon, however, and by the 1970s there could be seen in Canadian schools the development of a concept of the multimethod practitioner in small systems work, requiring individual, group, and family skills in addition to an ability to work within the client's significant social systems. Interestingly, work with dyads had not as yet been recognized as a distinct method of intervention in most Canadian schools, and although most small system practitioners work with a variety of dyads, conceptually, this form of intervention is seen as some type of combination of group and individual skills.

Two further factors contributed to the decline of the casework concept as coterminus with small systems work in Canadian practice. The first, the reality that the term casework, once an identifying concept of a particular form of small systems social work practice, began to be used by a broad spectrum of other disciplines as a generic term to describe a broad range of person-directed activities in the human services. This trend thus diminished its being understood as being an integral part of the social work lexicon with a specific meaning. Second, from its earliest days, the term casework had been identified principally but not entirely with psychodynamic theory. Again in the 1960s, however, on a worldwide basis, social work theory was marked by an explosion of its theoretical base so that in a few years it moved from a single theoretical basis to the some 30 bodies of theory that currently drive it.

Hence, the term casework is no longer the important term in Canadian social work practice that it once was. Rather, it has been replaced by a number of new terminologies, which bring with them new and different conundrums or choices. Thus, in Canadian small systems practice issues around the use of terms such as treatment, therapy, counseling, and psychotherapy are still the basis of discussion both within and without academe. A term that seems to be growing in acceptance to describe these multimethod practitioners is that of the clinical practitioner. But this is also not a clearly understood term, as some would restrict its meaning to direct work with a client in reference to some aspect of their person or functioning, and this is viewed as a more demanding and status-bearing type of practice than working with the client's significant systems, while others see it as a much more general term that has virtually the same meaning as small systems.

Although such terminological issues serve to fuel the fires of academic discourse and meetings of professional organizations, they do have implications for contemporary social work practice. This stands in relation to such things as recognition in various pieces of legislation, access to insurance payments for clients, recognized titles, acceptance as expert witnesses, status among other professions, and eligibility to memberships in some professional associations. Thus, their resolution for Canadian practitioners is important.

This latter point relates partially to the rapidly growing trend in Canadian social work practice of the emergence of the private practitioner. Although the debate as to whether this form of practice is an abandonment of the profession's values or not, as once was argued, is long since over, questions of accountability, recognition, and titles are still extant. For the most part, private practitioners are clearly in small systems work, although this is not an absolute. Such practitioners offer a wide range of quality psychosocial services and are much sought after by members of the public. How they identify their services and their professional identity, however, greatly influences their viewed position as a sought-after source of help. This, of course, affects one's income.

In the world of education, schools and faculties of social work have moved away from the concept of methods, such as work with individuals, groups, and families as separate curricular streams but rather as separate methods within small systems or clinical streams and courses. Indeed, the concept of the generalist, a person who has beginning competence in all methods, is the sought-after hallmark of many social work programs at the university level.

In looking back at what has been written thus far, at first blush it would appear that the development and emergence of small systems social work practice in Canada is identical to that of the United States. Although there is much in common, it would be in error to overgeneralize, for there are clear differences that need to be noted.

The move to a multitheory orientation to practice has occurred much more rapidly in Canada than elsewhere. Indeed, some of the texts on this topic and leading writers on various theories are Canadian. Small systems practice in Canada has given much more attention to the reality of geographic remoteness as an important factor in the development of theory, practice, and the service delivery of small systems social work. Although much of the contemporary Canadian social work literature still has a heavy urban flavor to it, to an increasing extent there is a developing body of knowledge related to the special features of the delivery of services to small groups of persons widely separated by vast distances.

It is also clear that small systems work in Canada has responded imaginatively, conceptually, and operationally to the realities of an ever-expanding component of diversity of population. Unlike an earlier day, there is now a much richer understanding of the resources and challenges that diversity brings and of the multifaceted components of this variable in all areas of practice. Although for a long time Canada was virtually totally dependent on social work texts and periodical literature from the United States, and to a lesser extent England, in recent years the roles have shifted and there is emerging a rapidly developing Canadian small systems literature that is being used not only in Canadian schools and thus more precisely shaping Canadian practice, but in other countries as well.

Two factors that have contributed to the incorporation of diversity issues into the conceptual base of all practice, especially small systems work and to the understanding of and sensitive response to clients, are Canada's bicultural heritage and its "open door" immigration policies. From its conception as a country, Canada has been a bilingual, bicultural nation with a less clearly defined understanding that First Nations people are also a part of Canadian national identity. Although small systems social work did not and has not fully appreciated or tapped the significance of this for practice, it is rapidly doing so, and the challenge for the profession is not should it but how should it. There is yet a distance to cover before the Canadian social work establishment fully appreciates the significance of the tricultural origins of the country, but much progress has been made in Canadian social work teaching and practice. Throughout most of Canadian history, apart from a few less-than-noble episodes, Canada has welcomed people from all over the world as fellow citizens. Today, most of Canada's large cities are richly multicultural. In Toronto, Ontario, there are over 150 different languages spoken by Canadian citizens. Such diversity is reflected in most parts of the country. This reality has moved social workers to create differential responses that enrich practice and the nature and structure of services.

SUMMARY

Overall, small systems social work has been and is an integral part of social work practice in Canada. Historically, it reflects the development of this component of practice in other countries, although in recent years it has begun to take on its own idiosyncratic qualities and to contribute to the profession in other parts of the world. Perhaps its greatest contribution in recent years has been the achievement of comfort with the need to bring precision to the conceptual bases of practice, but from a spectrum viewpoint rather than seeking absolute differences. Thus, in Canada, there are many social work professionals whose day-to-day activities and whose skills lie in bringing the rich range of knowledge, skills, and resources to bear on individuals, couples, families, and groups but who do so with a strong and unwavering commitment to bring about societal changes that will enhance the abilities of all persons to develop to their optimum potential.

Small systems practice is not a single-concept term. Rather, it describes an increasingly complex mélange of values, theories, methods, techniques, resources, and skills, which, when skillfully applied, manifest a powerful medium of help to the citizens of Canada.

—*Francis J. Turner*

See also Bowers, Frank Swithun Barrington; Social Work Profession (Canada)

Current Comment

Bowers, S. (1950). Nature and definition of social casework. In *Principles and techniques in social casework* (pp. 97–126). New York: Family Service Association of America.

Further Reading

Armitage, A. (1988). *Social welfare in Canada* (2nd ed.). Toronto, ON: McClelland & Stewart.

Turner, F. J. (1996). *Social work treatment* (4th ed.). New York: Free Press.

Turner, F. J. (2002). *Social work practice: A Canadian perspective* (2nd ed.). Toronto, ON: Prentice Hall.

Yelaja, S. A. (1985). *An introduction to social work practice in Canada.* Toronto, ON: Prentice Hall.

SOCIAL DEMOCRACY (CANADA)

Social democracy is a philosophical and political belief system concerned with the development of a welfare state based upon social justice, distributive justice, egalitarianism, and respect for all sectors of society. Philosophically, social democracy finds its roots in Marxism and socialism. Social democracy shares with other socialist forces a belief in the following principles: a planned economy, where the state coordinates the economy to benefit all people; public ownership of productive property so that production benefits society as a whole; equality of condition to reduce as much as possible inequalities in wealth, status, political control, and income; and last, a historically determined value of human nature that considers equality, collectivism, and community to be universal human characteristics.

The main difference between social democrats and other socialists is found among the strategies proposed to achieve their objectives. For socialists, acceptable and necessary tactics to bring an end to capitalism include civil disobedience, insurrection, and other forms of armed struggle. On the other hand, social democrats believe in evolutionary capitalism—that capitalism can be reformed from within through legislative initiatives that have the support of the working people.

Social democrats in their political action pursue three fundamental beliefs: equality, freedom, and community/collectivism. These are essential ingredients to foster democratic participation and humanitarianism. Social democrats believe in equality because it reduces alienation and creates a greater sense of social belonging. Moreover, equality increases economic efficiency, natural rights, and human dignity. According to social democrats, within a capitalist society, talented people who are not born into the upper classes are prevented from achieving their full potential, limiting their contribution to society and reducing human dignity. Social democrats regard equality as a crucial factor in the level of freedom people enjoy—the greater the equality, the more freedom that exists. Freedom is associated with the amount of resources people have. The more resources, the greater the freedom people have to choose what they need to live a fulfilling life. According to social democrats, the government has a role in increasing freedom by intervening to provide all citizens with the resources required to make good life choices. The state has a responsibility to redistribute wealth through social programs and transfer payments. Social democrats believe in collectivism as they emphasize cooperation over competition and the preeminence of society, rather than individual rights.

In the economic realm, social democrats hold that government intervention through public ownership of industry and redistribution of income and opportunities is needed to ensure a democratic, just, and humanitarian society. Social democrats criticize free market capitalism because they claim that the collective purpose of a society is lost when individuals pursue their own private interests. They consider the free market system as fundamentally unjust because the distribution of rewards is solely based on a principle that allows people to extract all that they can from their fellow citizens without breaking the law. Social democrats view the market system as essentially undemocratic because a few powerful individuals make decisions without considering the needs of the majority. They consider that without government regulations the market system is inefficient, causing environmental disasters, economic recession, uneven economic regional development, and the overproduction of less useful goods and the underproduction of socially needed goods. Finally, social democrats claim that left on its own, a free market system discriminates against the disadvantaged and dependent in society because it will not produce the goods and services needed by these populations.

As such, social democrats believe that the state should control the economy through rational social and economic planning. Planning should organize economic activity to take into account the needs of all members of society. According to social democrats, nationalizing some industries, regulating private industry, and developing worker-controlled industries would gain control over the economy.

The most important social democratic political belief is that of the social welfare state. Accordingly, the state can and should be used to protect the less powerful members of society. In contraposition to neoconservatives, social democrats believe that the state should promote the well-being of all people and not just those who are rich or politically powerful. Unlike some Marxists, who believe that a welfare state would only prevent workers from developing a revolutionary conscience, social democrats believe that the state can be a positive force to assist all people in society. Capitalism can be transformed into socialism through democratic means. Thus, the welfare state ensures the well-being of all people in society and at the same time increases democracy by seeking the participation of all citizens concerning decision-making processes in all spheres of their lives (economic, political, social, etc.).

Social inequality is the main source of conflict in capitalist society and social problems result from a societal structure that relegates people into two categories, the haves and the have-nots. Through its political praxis, social democracy attempts to transform capitalist-based societies to social democratic (welfare) states associated with national or universal coverage of Social Security programs. In Canada, social democracy subscribes to the social conflict school, which believes that universal disbursement of benefits will create a sense of community solidarity that will reduce unnecessary divisions and conflict between diverse members of society. Social democrats in Canada pursue an ideal socialist model of state welfare, including equal distribution of societal resources, collective consumption, and universal, comprehensive, and free social services such as health care and education. In theory, social democrats lodge significant criticisms against neoliberal and neoconservative agendas that argue for free market economics, minimal government involvement in both the market and civil society, and a residual social welfare safety net.

The New Democratic party (NDP) is associated with social democratic values in Canada. The NDP is considered the "third party" and has never been elected federally. It has experienced some success provincially, and is currently the elected party in two western Canadian provinces—Saskatchewan and Manitoba. The NDP finds its roots in the Co-operative Commonwealth Federation (CCF), a political party founded in Saskatchewan during the Great Depression year of 1932. The CCF made political history by calling for the eradication of capitalism. The NDP's ideological roots are found in British socialism and its opposition to the hierarchical conception of society espoused by Conservatives. Sustaining collectivist and equality principles, New Democrats advance equality of opportunity as an important objective. As such, its social welfare policies espouse universal access and uniform distribution of services and benefits across Canada.

Much more than any other federal or provincial political party, the NDP has historically defined itself through the development of social welfare programs. The NDP has been the clearest and most consistent

proponent of social welfare in the Canadian political spectrum—signaling a strong commitment to the socialist ideal of the redistribution of income, wealth, and power. Particularly, CCF-NDP (renamed NDP after 1961) governments in the province of Saskatchewan (1944–1964 and 1971–1982) left a legacy of social welfare programs (e.g., hospital insurance and advanced trade union legislation) that became benchmarks in Canada and elsewhere in North America. The CCF-NDP governments in Saskatchewan creatively and determinedly developed and expanded public ownership in a province where historically most large corporations were owned by outside interests. Such social democratic activities allowed a relatively poor province to afford Medicare and to introduce other programs to improve the quality of life of Saskatchewan citizens.

The NDP has generally differentiated itself from other Canadian political parties by advocating for full employment, the creation of long-term quality jobs, a progressive taxation system, social programs to support the raising of children (a universal child care program), elimination of child poverty, some form of subsidized housing, universal programs of health and income security, and a comprehensive social welfare system. These policy initiatives have consistently been included in NDP platforms, making it, in the eyes of many Canadians, the party of the "Left."

—Miguel Sanchez
and Jeff Karabanow

See also Social Welfare (Canada): Before the Marsh Report; Social Welfare (Canada): Since the Marsh Report; Structural Social Work (Canada); Welfare Capitalism (Canada)

Primary Sources

Co-operative Commonwealth Federation and New Democratic party Fonds (1905–1983), Co-operative Commonwealth Federation and New Democratic party election literature and other material (1948–1964), Co-operative Press Association Collection (1944–1980), and CCF-NDP Subject Files (1926–1981), Library and Archives Canada, Ottawa, ON.

Current Comment

Godfrey, D., & Watkins, M. (Eds.). (1970). *Gordon to Watkins to you, a documentary: The battle for control of our economy.* Toronto, ON: New Press.

Layton, J. (2004). *Speaking out: Ideas that work for Canadians.* Toronto, ON: Key Porter.

Woodsworth, J. S. (1911). *My neighbour: A study of human conditions, a plea for social service.* Toronto, ON: Missionary Society of the Methodist Church.

Young People's Forward Movement Department, Research Committee of the League for Social Reconstruction. (1935). *Social planning for Canada.* Toronto, ON: Thomas Nelson.

Further Reading

Brown, L., Roberts, J., & Warnock, J. (1999). *Saskatchewan politics: From Left to Right '44–'99.* Regina, SK: Hinterland.

Mullaly, R. (1993). *Structural social work: Ideology, theory and practice.* Toronto, ON: McClelland & Stewart.

Swanson, J. (2001). *Poor bashing: The politics of exclusion.* Toronto, ON: Between the Lines.

Teeple, G. (1995). *Globalization and the decline of social reform.* Toronto, ON: Garamond.

SOCIAL GOSPEL (UNITED STATES)

The social gospel, a movement within North American Protestant churches that sought to ameliorate the problems of people living in industrialized cities, occurred in the years between the Civil War and World War I with the peak of activity in the early twentieth century. Since 1960, similar ideas have surfaced in Protestantism and, to a lesser extent, Roman Catholicism. Those following the social gospel shifted the focus of activity from the concerns of evangelicals, such as personal sin and individual salvation, to the problems of industrial society. Actions, not beliefs, defined the Christian; community, not the individual, was the focus.

BACKGROUND

The background against which the social gospel, a term not commonly used until 1900, emerged included social developments, intellectual issues, and status concerns. Scholars dispute whether the movement responded to new developments in North American society or resulted from an internal dynamic in Christianity, a moment in history or a social consciousness.

The social gospel focused on cities as urbanization after the Civil War produced masses of people living in conditions that shocked middle-class ministers. That prostitution and drinking thrived in such areas contributed to Christian concerns. The influx of immigrants added the problem of language. Industrialization, which supported the cities' population, brought long working hours, uncertain employment, and disease-ridden slums.

In the world of ideas, Darwinian evolution and German biblical criticism challenged beliefs in biblical literalism. Although intellectuals, including ministers of major denominations, sought to reconcile the findings of science and history with the Bible, many Christians retreated into individualistic concern with personal salvation. For others, however, the declining acceptance of the notion of hell and the questioning of heaven contributed to the shift away from revivalism and individual salvation. When the hereafter ceased to be important, the here and now became more so.

The social gospel movement, led by ministers, has been interpreted as an effort by them to reclaim symbolic leadership and status in a society increasingly dominated by big business. Although educators, newspaper editors, and others were active in promulgating the agenda of the social gospel, the bulk of the writing came from ministers. Some scholars believe ministers moved from Christianizing the people by revivals to the social gospel, whereas others see the movement as a continuation of the thrusts that earlier focused on abolition, Sabbatarianism, temperance, and feminism.

Finally, the new ideas of social science presented advocates for the social gospel with techniques and categories to analyze the problems of society. Also, social science promoted the belief that society could be progressively improved, a belief furthered by the successes of abolition and the gains of temperance.

ASPECTS

Promoters of the social gospel set goals of increasing wages, reducing working hours, improving the conditions of labor, attacking tenement crowding, creating old-age pensions, facilitating unionization, regulating liquor traffic, eliminating municipal corruption, and abolishing monopolies. Not an organized or unified movement, though its leaders were clearly the ministers, the social gospel never emerged as a political party in either the United States or Canada. Proponents of the social gospel could be found in other reforming groups and representatives of various movements, such as progressives, socialists, and trade unionists, often joined them to pursue common goals such as government ownership of utilities and minimum wage laws. Scholars debate how much public attention the social gospel positions on race, women's rights, and imperialism attracted. Temperance was the rare issue that united supporters of the social gospel and evangelicals. Similarly, settlement houses, sometimes run by university students with no religious interests, were common by 1900 and worked with churches to pursue common goals.

Many of the urban churches took an expansive view of their mission to include soup kitchens, employment agencies, recreational activities, visiting nurses, and dispensaries. Some churches featured classes for "Americanization" or "Canadianization." Governments—local, state or provincial, and federal—gradually superseded these churches as social service agencies after World War I.

Although the social gospel was not limited to one denomination, it was chiefly found among Protestants and, within that tradition, among Methodists, Congregationalists, Episcopalians, Presbyterians, and Baptists. With so many Protestants espousing the same views, efforts at ecumenical union occurred. In the United States, this led to the foundation in 1908 of the Federal Council of Churches, the forerunner of today's National Council of Churches. In Canada, Methodists, Congregationalists, and some Presbyterians joined in the United Church in 1925.

Prominent individuals, their sermons and writings, not social service in action, have been the object of most scholarship. Washington Gladden, longtime Congregational minister in Columbus, Ohio, and often called the father of the social gospel, was the leading early proponent of social gospel ideas. Walter Rauschenbusch, a Baptist minister who, while serving in Hell's Kitchen in New York City, came to the social gospel, became the leading writer setting forth the social gospel most clearly in works such as *Christianity and the Social Crisis* (1907), *For God and the People* (1912), *Christianizing the Social Order* (1912), and *The Social Principles of Jesus* (1916). Professors such as Richard T. Ely of Johns Hopkins University and later the University of Wisconsin, college presidents such as George A. Gates of Iowa (now Grinnell) College, seminarians such as William Jewett of Andover Theological Seminary, and countless newspaper editors promulgated the social gospel in writing.

Theology received little attention despite a call in 1917 by Rauschenbusch for such work because action, not ideas, was the motif of the social gospel. Just as Old Testament prophets decried the injustices of a newly aristocratic society, preachers of the social gospel inveighed against the industrial world and applied the life and teachings of Jesus to society. As the goal was not individual salvation but the improvement of society into Jesus's Kingdom of God, sanctification led to action. The immanence of God meant divine presence in society leading to a world dominated by peace, brotherhood, and an equitable distribution of wealth. Since the social gospel preachers believed the incarnation of Christ could be found in everyone, the Second Coming was at hand. As sin was both individual and social, so was salvation. The Kingdom of God could be here and now, on earth.

Criticism of the social gospel came from two sources. Some thought religion and especially ministers had little business in government. Washington Gladden sought and won elective office in Columbus, Ohio, which concerned some critics about church-state issues and the purpose of the church generally. Within Christianity, opposition to the social gospel came from evangelicals, who thought the social gospel ignored the transcendence of God and the reality of sin and evil. With the publication of *The Fundamentals: A Testimony to the Truth* between 1909 and 1912, this group found its identification, and the word "fundamentalism" became attached to them. Today, still, Protestant Christianity in North America remains divided about the role of religion in society, the social gospel.

—Allen Horstman

See also Religion and Social Welfare (United States); Settlement Houses (United States); Social Justice (United States); Social Work Profession (United States)

Primary Sources

Walter Rauschenbusch Papers, American Baptist-Samuel Colgate Historical Library, American Baptist Historical Society, Rochester, NY; Washington Gladden Papers, Ohio Historical Society, Columbus, OH; Methodist Archives and History Center of the United Methodist Church, Drew University, Madison, NJ.

Current Comment

Gladden, W. (1892). *Applied Christianity: Moral aspects of social questions.* New York: Houghton Mifflin.

Rauschenbusch, W. (1912). *Christianizing the social order.* New York: Macmillan.

Rauschenbusch, W. (1917). *Christianity and the social crisis.* New York: Macmillan.

Further Reading

Deichmann Edwards, W. J., & De Swarte Gifford, C. (Eds.). (2003). *Gender and the social gospel.* Urbana: University of Illinois Press.

Handy, R. T. (1966). *The social gospel in America, 1870–1920: Gladden, Ely, Rauschenbusch.* New York: Oxford University Press.

Herron, G. D. (1968). *Social meanings of religious experience.* New York: Johnson.

White, R. C., Jr., & Hopkins, C. H. (1976). *The social gospel: Religion and reform in changing America.* Philadelphia: Temple University Press.

SOCIAL JUSTICE (UNITED STATES)

Since the early twentieth century, the pursuit of social justice provided an alternative to the concept of social welfare as charity in the United States. It became a core value of the social work profession and has shaped the evolution of social policy in the United States by forging an awkward synthesis of individualistic and collectivist orientations to society and its problems. In the 1990s, two major social work organizations, the National Association of Social Workers and the Council on Social Work Education, declared social justice to be an imperative of social work practice and education.

BACKGROUND

The concept of social justice emerged in the United States through a synthesis of religious movements, like Quakerism and the social gospel, and secular ideas, as far ranging as pragmatism and Marxism. Among social workers, it was first expressed through the political activities and writings of settlement house leaders such as Jane Addams, Florence Kelley, Ellen Gates Starr, and Lillian Wald on behalf of workers' rights, women's suffrage, racial justice, and peace. They forged alliances with feminist organizations, trade unions, neighborhood-based community associations, civil rights groups, and radicals outside of social work to advocate for reforms in child welfare, housing, income support, juvenile justice, education, and public health.

By the 1920s and 1930s, proponents of social justice came to regard the establishment of welfare state policies as a primary means of ameliorating the impact of structural inequalities in a market-driven economy. Their efforts helped produce the modest reforms embodied in the New Deal, particularly the Social Security Act (1935) and the Fair Labor Standards Act (1938). They also sought to apply social justice principles to social work practice. For example, at the height of the Great Depression, the radical rank and file movement, which had over 15,000 members and was larger than the American Association of Social Workers, articulated "five simple principles" as the basis for developing a justice-centered social work profession. These principles emphasized class-consciousness, individual and community self-determination and empowerment, worker-client mutuality, the linkage of social work with other movements for social justice, and nonhierarchical forms of practice.

For nearly half a century after the New Deal, this focus helped produce a broad range of legal entitlements and a variety of forms of institutionalized compensation or redress in the policy arena. It shaped the conceptual frameworks of social work practice and social work education in the United States. Since the early 1980s, however, political and ideological attacks on social welfare have undermined its utility as an instrument for achieving social justice and challenged many of its basic assumptions. These attacks culminated with the passage of the Personal Responsibility and Work Opportunity Reconciliation Act (1996) and have continued in proposals to cut back or privatize Social Security, Medicare, and other social and health care services.

CONTEMPORARY
VIEWS OF SOCIAL JUSTICE

During this era of social welfare retrenchment, social welfare advocates in the United States have sought to focus an abstract commitment to social justice principles on specific policy changes. They have adopted such causes as peace and nuclear disarmament;

opposition to intervention abroad; support for the rights of women, gays, and lesbians; defense of affirmative action; and the promotion of multiculturalism. In recent years, however, differing definitions of social justice—applying concepts from libertarian, utilitarian, communitarian, and egalitarian theories—guided social welfare advocates. The work of Rawls (1999) has been particularly influential because it attempts to resolve historic tensions such as individual liberty and social equality, self-determination and social justice.

Influenced by postmodern ideas, some have linked social justice with diversity or multiculturalism and with challenges to the normative power structure. Building on the ideas of Reynolds (1951) and Freire (1972), others have focused on human transformation or on ways of integrating the role of narrative into a social justice framework. They have emphasized clients' strengths, an awareness of the role of power in professional relationships, and a focus on positionality. In the macro arena, social justice has been connected to issues like affirmative action and sexual harassment, values such as human worth and dignity, and such principles as social responsibility, opposition to oppression and domination, and the eradication of racism and poverty.

One contemporary definition of social justice focuses on rewarding individuals for past services or contributions, or redressing injuries or losses inflicted unjustly on individuals or groups. Another proposes to use the social welfare system to meet basic human needs equally, while allowing the market to reward people for their efforts by providing them with benefits beyond these needs. A communitarian perspective on social justice seeks to balance individual rights and responsibilities to the community.

Despite such differences, many continue to view social justice as an alternative to charity, with an emphasis on egalitarianism and mutuality instead of dominance and hierarchy. At one end of the ideological spectrum, a Marxist view of social justice recognizes that neither the human condition nor social reality is fixed, but are the consequences of socioeconomic relationships and cultural patterns, including the ideological frameworks that rationalize them. A liberal view focuses on the distribution of benefits and burdens and the protection of persons' rights, particularly at the level of individuals. It also involves the assignment of fundamental rights and duties,

economic opportunities and social conditions, and incorporates a principle of compensation or redress.

Conservatives differ from liberals in four important ways. First, they would assign these rights solely to individuals and not to groups or classes of persons. Second, they would limit these rights to the political sphere and exclude the redistribution of resources and status. Third, they would regard the protection of property rights as of equal or greater importance. Finally, they would assert that social justice requires a balancing of rights with responsibilities or obligations.

In contrast, Held (1995) and Gil (1998) maintain that the pursuit of social justice complements rather than competes with the pursuit of human rights. Both are products of social cooperation, trust, and mutuality. Postmodern scholars propose an expansion of modern visions of social justice to include groups traditionally omitted from justice-oriented debates, an examination of justice and injustice in the sociocultural as well as the political-economic spheres of society, and a focus on societal processes as well as societal goals and outcomes.

Each of these contrasting definitions of social justice attempts to balance two important social functions—fair distribution of goods and social and political stability. The synthesis each society creates reflects the course of its development, its culture, and the particular array of internal and external forces it confronts in a specific historical context.

For example, in recent discussions of social justice, scholars have confronted the dilemma of how social justice could be achieved in a political-economic environment in which market forces are ascendant. Some authors have suggested that the solution to this dilemma could be found by a return to universalist approaches to social welfare. Others have postulated a synthesis of justice perspectives that combine social work's ongoing concern about human dignity and self-determination with a distributive justice approach. This would expand the idea of social justice beyond its traditional aspirations of satisfying basic human needs to produce outcomes that would enable individuals to realize their full human potential.

The complex environment of the twenty-first century has created new questions about the meaning of social justice for social welfare. For example, are the egalitarian and libertarian goals of social justice compatible? What would social justice look like in a multicultural society? Can social justice be legislated? If so, how? Can social justice be achieved in one country or must its attainment be global?

A social justice approach to social policy would acknowledge the connection in the design and delivery of social services between peoples' needs for economic assistance and the supports agencies provide. This would reflect the goals of empowerment as originally articulated by Solomon (1976) and developed by social work scholars over the past quarter century. Some principles for policy development derived from a justice-centered approach could include the following:

1. Policies and services should hold the most vulnerable populations harmless in the distribution of societal resources. Based upon the notion of redress, unequal distribution of resources would be justified only if such inequalities served to advance the least advantaged groups in the community.

2. Reflecting principles of worker-client mutuality, the construction of social services would embody the idea that such services are the expression of collective responsibility for people's needs.

3. To achieve the long-range goals of social justice, when scarce resources make such choices necessary, social policies and services should emphasize prevention rather than correction, amelioration, or remediation.

4. To incorporate ideas developed both by multiculturalists and postmodernists, social services should stress multiple forms of helping and multiple means of providing access to services and benefits to recognize that needs and helping are defined differently by different groups in a multicultural society.

5. Finally, social policies and services should be developed so as to enable clients and constituents to define their own situations and contribute to the development and evaluation of solutions as much as possible.

—Michael Reisch

See also Addams, Jane; The New Deal (United States); Rank and File Movement (United States); Social Gospel (United States); Social Work Profession (United States); Wald, Lillian D.

Current Comment

Freire, P. (1972) *Pedagogy of the oppressed.* Harmondsworth, UK: Penguin.

Hayek, F. A. (1976). *The mirage of social justice.* Chicago: University of Chicago Press.

Rawls, J. (1999). *A theory of justice* (Rev. ed.). Cambridge, MA: Harvard University Press, Belknap Press.

Reynolds, B. (1951). *Social work and social living: Explorations in philosophy and practice.* New York: Citadel.

Solomon, B. B. (1976). *Black empowerment: Social work in oppressed communities.* New York: Columbia University Press.

Further Reading

Gil, D. (1998). *Confronting injustice and oppression: Concepts and strategies for social workers.* New York: Columbia University Press.

Gilbert, N. (1995). *Welfare justice: Restoring social equity.* New Haven, CT: Yale University Press.

Held, V. (1995). *Justice and care: Essential readings in feminist ethics.* Boulder, CO: Westview.

White, J. E. (2000). *Democracy, justice, and the welfare state: Reconstructing public care.* University Park: Pennsylvania State University Press.

SOCIAL REFORM AND STATE-BUILDING (MEXICO)

The armed (1910–1920) and reconstruction (1920–1940) phases of the Mexican Revolution stimulated significant processes of state-building and social reform in Mexico. Although the dictatorship of Porfirio Díaz (1876–1911) can be credited with emphasizing industrialization, modernization, and social progress, the revolutionaries who toppled the Díaz government rejected many of the Porfiriato ideologies as elitist and sought to imprint the new regime with an emphasis on the rights of the popular classes. Many of the formal state institutions responsible for implementing progressive policies under Díaz had been destroyed in the course of revolutionary fighting. Others came under attack in the context of debates over crafting the 1917 Constitution, which authorized federal oversight of education, labor, health, welfare, and judicial reform processes. The revolutionary Constitution provided the blueprint for social change in the heyday of revolutionary reconstruction from 1920 to 1940. Reformism in early twentieth century Mexico, however, was not a strictly revolutionary endeavor. Social reform went hand in hand with domestic state-building and reconstruction. It responded to international trends in social activism and reflected the regional influence of social movements related to hygiene, eugenics, and child development.

REVOLUTION AND REFORMISM

In discussions about revolutionary Mexico, two distinct definitions of state-building emerge. The first refers to the creation or renovation of public bureaucracies and institutions that carry out the business of state. As part of a broader societal rejection of the *Porfiriato*, the revolutionary nation witnessed the destruction and renovation of significant social sector offices. Revolutionaries sought to guarantee access to social services as a right of the Mexican people. They also envisioned reformism as a way to promote economic development and foster support for government and revolutionary programs. But the concept of state-building, insofar as it refers to state-formation, also carries a second definition in Mexican historiography. Many scholars discuss state-formation as a process of negotiating rules. In this definition, state-formation is a dynamic exchange of proposals and ideas by officials and members of the popular classes regarding the uses of state institutions. In revolutionary Mexico, many of the debates over the role of the state centered on how the new institutions would be used to implement reformist-revolutionary ideology.

Reformers included men and women from all social classes who sought to use government to change the social, economic, and political direction of Mexico. Although some reformers did, in fact, participate in revolutionary events as soldiers or policymakers, many others were lawyers, doctors, teachers, and social critics who became committed to social change during the reconstruction efforts of the 1920s and 1930s. Legislators, physicians, and intellectuals were prominent among reformers, but their ranks also included nurses, social workers, union activists, and members of religious lay organizations who had daily contact with Mexico's poorest citizens. Reformers organized such religious and civil associations as the Catholic Women (*Damas Católicas*), the Mexican Eugenics Society (*Sociedad de Eugenesia Mexicana*), and the women's rights group *Frente Unico pro-Derechos de la Mujer*. They joined antialcohol leagues and associations to abolish prostitution and white slavery. Many supported political parties such as the Mexican Communist party (*Partido Comunista Mexicana*, or PCM) and the National Revolution party (*Partido Nacional Revolucionario*, or PNR). Some reformers, such as Dr. Mathilde Rodríguez Cabo, played multiple roles. A psychiatrist who translated the work of Sigmund Freud into Spanish and headed the Department of Social Prevention (*Departamento de Prevención Social*), Rodríguez Cabo was a member of the eugenics society and gave speeches about child welfare, feminism, and birth control to such groups as the Union of Socialist Lawyers. Others, like former *Zapatista* (agrarian revolutionary) and anarchist Antonio Díaz Soto y Gama, used their positions as elected federal legislators to advocate reformist positions regarding women's labor rights. Yucatan doctor and revolutionary General José Siurob served first as director of the Department of Public Health (*Departamento de Salubridad Publica*) and then as governor of the Federal District under reformist President Lázaro Cárdenas. Despite their diverse backgrounds, Mexican reformers confronted similar realities as they sought to implement new cultural practices in Mexico. Their goals frequently brought them into contact—and often into conflict—with the people they intended to reform.

INSTITUTIONALIZING REVOLUTIONARY REFORM

The Department of Public Health (*Departamento de Salubridad Pública*), the Board of Public Charity (*Junta de Beneficencia Pública*), and the Secretariat of Public Education (*Secretaría de Educación Pública*) as well as the reformatories and prisons dedicated to adult and juvenile justice were among the most important institutional bases of social reform during the revolutionary period. The *Departamento de Salubridad Pública* (DSP) was created in 1924 under the auspices of the Constitution, which authorized the federal government to take measures to ensure the well-being of the "Mexican race." Based on the older and largely municipal Porfirian Health Council (*Consejo Superior de Salubridad*), the new *departamento* had federal status. Dependencies of the *departamento*, including the *Hospital General*, the *Hospital Morelos*, and the mental health hospital, *La Castañeda*, reflected revolutionary ideologies that the public had a right to enjoy good health. In accordance with the sanitary code of 1926, the DSP implemented a variety of new community-based programs including prenatal and venereal disease treatment clinics. These efforts incorporated older goals of disease treatment with new concepts of prevention and employed visiting nurses who spread the message of good health to poor urban and rural communities. The DSP oversaw projects dedicated to raising levels of public sanitation, such as the regulation of markets and venues that sold prepared food. In Mexico City, the DSP offered vaccinations and sponsored campaigns against alcoholism, syphilis, and tuberculosis. New policies required couples planning to marry to produce proof that they were not infected with syphilis, a disease associated with miscarriage and birth defects. The intrusive nature of such reforms was frequently countered by a population resistant to public interference in its private activities. The prenuptial certificate, for example, earned the *departamento* criticism that it was creating a "dangerous sanitary dictatorship."

Programs dedicated to public welfare similarly served as an institutional base for reformism and social change. In the 1920s, revolutionaries eager to consolidate the anticlerical policies of the new regime sought to replace the Porfirian notion of charity or benevolence with "revolutionary" concepts of public welfare and social assistance to underscore the state's duty to protect Mexico's most vulnerable populations: women, children, the poor, the elderly, and the physically disabled. By the 1930s, a new federal Department of Public Welfare *(Departamento de Asistencia Pública)* had replaced the older, municipal *Junta de Beneficencia Pública* and assumed responsibility for promoting antialcoholism campaigns, disease prevention, and the well-being of infants and single mothers. Like the work of the *Departamento de Salubridad Pública*, social assistance efforts under the auspices of the *Departamento de Asistencia Pública* centered around the idea that promoting individual and family well-being was a way to ensure the progress and health of the nation. Social workers, usually young women or older widows, did most of the work of this new department. They traveled to poor neighborhoods and interviewed family members to gather information about the extent and experience of

poverty in the nation's largest cities. In addition to linking health, welfare, and judicial agencies, social workers were often the only contact some families had with the growing revolutionary state. By the late 1930s, the *Departamento de Asistencia Pública* was elevated in federal status and reconfigured as the Secretariat of Social Welfare *(Secretaría de Asistencia Social)*. In 1943, this secretariat merged with the *Departamento de Salubridad Pública* to form a new entity, the Secretariat of Health and Welfare *(Secretaría de Salubridad y Asistencia)*.

The revolutionary Secretariat of Public Education *(Secretaría de Educación Pública,* or SEP) had a constitutional mandate to transform Mexican society. It was created in 1921 from the older Porfirian Secretariat of Public Instruction *(Secretaría de Instrucción Pública)*. In addition to bolstering the goal of promoting national economic development through enhanced literacy and vocational skills, revolutionary socialist educators sought to reduce the Catholic church's influence in education matters in accordance with the Constitution's Article 3. Under such leaders as Félix Palavicini and José Vasconcelos, the SEP supported anticlericalism, antialcoholism efforts, and hygiene awareness for people in remote communities. It also supported public arts projects. Artists including Diego Rivera, José Clemente Orozco, and David Alfaro Siqueiros brought graphic depictions of Mexican life to an often-illiterate public by covering the walls of public buildings with colorful murals that depicted Mexican political history. By the 1930s, radical education reform included mandatory sex education and socialist instruction in public schools. In such states as Sonora, teachers taught students about Marxism and limited the influence of the clergy by encouraging students to burn religious artifacts. Widespread popular discontent with the socialist nature of school policies in the early 1930s led public officials to back away from the more radical aspects of reform and to focus on building schools and bringing teachers to new communities.

Judicial reform was also a key component of state-building and social change in the early part of the twentieth century. Revolutionary leaders released prisoners confined during Porfirian times, tore down old prisons, and drafted new penal codes in 1929 and 1931. A sense that crime was related to social and environmental factors as opposed to personal hereditary traits led to transformations in criminology and judicial practice. Social workers, police, psychologists, and lawyers sought to shift emphasis from crimes to the world of the criminal, allowing judges considerable discretion in sentencing and determining rehabilitation schemes. Recognizing developments in adolescent psychology, the concept of juvenile offenders as distinct from adult offenders influenced the criminal justice system. In the Porfiriato, correctional facilities (*casas de corrección*) for children and teenagers had functioned largely to segregate and discipline young offenders, who in many cases were eventually transferred to adult facilities. In 1926, the Federal District established a council to deal with underage offenders, the *Consejo Tutelar Para Menores Infractores*, which oversaw juvenile courts (*Tribunal Para Menores*) and which was linked to the *Departamento de Prevención Social* in the capital. Rejecting the notion that boys and girls under the age of 18 should be tried and incarcerated in the same manner as adults, the *consejo* and the *Tribunal Para Menores* (and its reform schools) sought to rehabilitate children and to inculcate in them values of progress and patriotism.

Whereas health, welfare, and education reforms centralized reformist institutions, revolutionary rejection of Porfirian judicial practices resulted in the decentralization of the Mexican justice system in the revolutionary period. By the 1940s, the passage and implementation of Social Security legislation and the creation of such national Social Security agencies as the *Instituto Mexicano del Seguro Social* set the stage for a new phase of institutional reform and state-building.

—*Katherine Elaine Bliss*

See also Constitution of 1917 (Mexico); Labor Movement and Social Welfare (Mexico); Mother and Family Programs (Mexico); The Rockefeller Foundation and Public Health (Mexico); Rural Education (Mexico); Social Welfare (Mexico): Since 1867; Welfare Capitalism (Mexico); Welfare Ministries in the Twentieth Century (Mexico)

Primary Sources

Consejo Tutelar Para Menores Infractores, Gobernación, and the *Presidencia de la República* Collections, *Archivo General de la Nación*; *Archivo Histórico de la Secretaría de Salubridad y*

Asistencia; the *Sanidad, Cárceles,* and *Diversiones Públicas* Collections, *Archivo Histórico del Ex-Ayuntamiento de la Ciudad de México*; *Archivo Histórico de la Secretaría de Educación Pública,* all in Mexico City.

Current Comment

Gastelum, B. J. (1926). La persecucion de la sifilis desde el punto de vista de la garantia social. *Boletin del Departamento de Salubridad Publica, 4*(8).

El Primer Congreso Femenista de Yucatan, convocado por el C. Gobernador y Comandante Militar del Estado de Yucatan, General D. Salvador Alvarado, y reunido en el Teatro "Peon Contreras" de esta Ciudad del 13 al 16 de enero de 1916. Merida, Yucatan: Talleres Tipograficos del Ateneo Peninsular.

Rodriguez Cabo, M. (1931). *Estudios sobre la delicuencia e infancia abandonada.* Mexico City: Imp. Compania editora "La Razon."

Further Reading

Blum, A. S. (2004). Cleaning the revolutionary household: Domestic servants and public welfare in Mexico City, 1930–1950. *Journal of Women's History, 15*(4), 67–90.

Buffington, R., & Aguirre, C. (Eds.). (2000). *Reconstructing criminality in Latin America.* Wilmington: DE: Scholarly Resources. (Especially articles by Pablo Piccato, Katherine Elaine Bliss, and Enrique Ochoa)

Ochoa, E. C. (2001). Coercion, reform and the welfare state: The campaign against begging in Mexico City during the 1930s. *The Americas. 58*(1), 39–64.

Stern, A. M. (1999). Responsible mothers and normal children: Eugenics, nationalism and welfare in post-revolutionary Mexico, 1920–1940. *Journal of Historical Sociology, 12*(4), 369–397.

Vaughan, M. K. (1997). *Cultural politics in revolution: Teachers, peasants and schools in Mexico, 1930–1940.* Tucson: University of Arizona Press.

SOCIAL REFORM MOVEMENTS (CANADA)

Between 1890 and 1939, a vast network of social and moral reform movements swept the country in an effort to reshape Canadian society. This reform spirit was promoted by an eclectic mix of groups, including, among others, labor unions, voluntary organizations, temperance organizations, prohibitionists, child welfare activists, academics, medical professionals, urban reformers, social workers, liberal and Left-leaning activists, early feminists, and church organizations that embraced the social gospel movement. It was advanced by the likes of J. S. Woodsworth, the first leader of the Co-operative Commonwealth Federation (CCF); Montreal businessman Sir Herbert Brown Ames, who pioneered the Canadian social survey movement; Charlotte Whitton, executive director for the Canadian Council on Child and Family Welfare, and J. J. Kelso of the Child Savers Movement, among others. While often-disparate groups with competing agendas, they shared a common goal to reshape and "regenerate" both society and the human soul. Their efforts transformed Canada from a country lacking social-legal protections to an advanced social welfare state.

In a country grappling with economic crises, urban expansion, rapid industrialization, and mass immigration, the social reform impulse sparked a widespread campaign to raise public consciousness over the perceived growth of moral and social problems. The depression of the early 1890s highlighted the limitations of and exploitation inherent in laissez-faire capitalism. This, together with the emergence and expansion of urban slums and reports of deplorable factory working conditions, as well as fears about the number of foreigners in Canada, gave rise to a general concern over the social cohesion of society. The growing number of paupers, the perceived breakdown of the family, and the perception of rising crime and vice were attributed to these pressures. Within this context, social reformers promoted a new approach to resolving "social problems," one that emphasized collective action and greater public responsibility, particularly in the areas of economic and social welfare.

Reformers encouraged government responsibility and legislative reforms in the areas of labor, public health, social welfare, housing, city planning, child welfare, corrections, civic politics, sanitation, recreation, and education. They lobbied for the nationalization of basic natural resources, such as minerals, oil, timber, electric power, and transportation, and for agricultural reforms like the creation of cooperative marketing structures. Canadian labor unions grew in strength and militancy and pressed for protective legislation, including minimum wages, better working conditions, and unemployment insurance. Indeed, many attempts to address issues of poverty, vice, crime, and exploitation were attributed to the efforts of social reformers. They pressed for social security programs including family allowances and old age

security and were primarily responsible for fostering public responsibility and expenditures on social services.

The theoretical and practical underpinnings of Canadian social reform movements were stimulated by intellectual currents and developments spreading throughout North America, Britain, and elsewhere. Reform Darwinism, biblical criticism, and leftist critiques of industrial capitalism brought to light new social understandings of societal problems. Advances in the social sciences, particularly in the disciplines of sociology, social work, psychology, and political economy introduced social scientific methods of investigation, like social casework and social surveys, that generated new approaches for the study of poverty, vice, and crime. Social reformers readily adopted these theoretical and social scientific developments in their efforts to grapple with societal problems. These approaches redefined the causes of poverty by drawing attention to the importance of social and economic relations and the environment rather than narrowly focusing on the individual. The view that unemployment was rooted in individual behavior was no longer tenable.

These intellectual currents also animated new forms of religious practice. Many of the same people advocating social reform belonged to the Protestant social gospel movement. The movement advanced a new evangelical spirituality in which salvation was to be realized through social action and not simply inner piety. This "social evangelism" advanced by Protestant ministers, such as J. S. Woodsworth, W. Ivens, S. Bland, H. Dobson, and S. D. Chown, emphasized the importance of social obligation and political responsibility. They called for a new Christian social order in which the churches would become the main agents of social change. The Protestant-led Moral and Social Reform Council of Canada, formed in 1907 and renamed the Social Service Council of Canada in 1914, emerged as the most powerful vehicle for social reform. The council, while spearheaded by the Protestant churches, brought together a number of religious groups, including Catholic and Jewish organizations, along with other social groups in an effort to lobby government for social betterment.

Although Protestants figured prominently in reform movements, other religions, including Catholicism and Judaism, were influenced by similar theological transitions and actively participated in social reform. Jewish groups were particularly prominent in labor and radical political organizations. Within the Catholic church, a new social action movement emerged that paralleled the Protestant social gospel in its demand for political, social, and economic reforms. Catholic social action was largely a response to the 1891 Papal encyclical, *Rerum Novarum*, which attacked both socialism and the vicissitudes of laissez-faire capitalism and encouraged Catholics to join forces with other religions to demand social legislation. Social provisions were identified as the best means of combating the spread of communism, particularly among the poor and immigrants.

Church groups were able to dominate much of the social and moral reform agenda because they actively promoted workers' rights. In championing the rights of workers, they were able to garner the support of labor and other social reformers. Both church and labor organizations came to construe social problems in similar ways and saw their interdependence as crucial to achieving their goals. This coalition, however, did not lend support to extreme Left forms of socialism or feminism. The reform agenda was largely set by anglophone middle-class reformers who sought to strengthen the fabric of Canadian society, not undermine it. Radical or militant action that could disrupt social stability was rarely tolerated.

Raising the moral tone of Canadian society underlay most reform efforts. The scope of reformers encompassed a project much larger than social and economic change; they sought to reshape the moral fiber of Canadian citizens. Many of the same organizations lobbying government for social change overlapped with those calling for sexual purity, temperance, Sunday observance, and the suppression of prostitution, drugs, gambling, and other vices. Immigrants, racial minorities, and the poor were the main targets of this reform agenda. These minorities lacked the proper middle-class values deemed necessary for civic responsibility in a modern democratic state. Reformers sought to inculcate a new moral subjectivity through a number of strategies, including philanthropic societies and settlement houses. The goal was not to erase class distinctions, or all cultural diversity, but to ensure the dominance of the

anglophone middle-class by having others inculcate their beliefs and values. In contrast to the United States, Canada tolerated a modicum of cultural diversity. Private displays of cultural preservation were to some degree ignored so long as middle-class moral boundaries were not transgressed.

The social reform movement is often characterized as having progressed from an initial period dominated by religious moralism to a post-1920 progressive secular movement in which a new breed of professionals came to dominate the movement, replacing church leaders. The adoption of Darwinian and other social scientific principles by social reformers is said to have laid the groundwork for this process of secularization. Indeed, the scientific impulse that infused the reform movement may have provided the "vehicle" for its secularization.

Some historians have argued that social investigations conducted by prominent academics and social reformers supplanted moral and religious approaches. The Moral and Social Reform Council became the Social Service Council of Canada in 1914, signaling the shift from a religious to a secular orientation. A growing body of research, however, has begun to challenge this conventional wisdom. Secularization was undeniably a significant trend during the interwar period, but some argue that its comprehensiveness is overstated. The secularization approach oversimplifies the complexity of church and state relations by presenting a unified linear progression from religious dominance to a secular modernity that traverses diverse institutions and religions in much the same way. In their study of Protestant social welfare, Nancy Christie and Michael Gauvreau suggest that the Protestant churches continued to be at the forefront of social reform, social investigation, and the expansion of the welfare state. Unlike the United States and Britain, where professional schools of social work and social service had emerged earlier and had distanced themselves from religious institutions, in Canada, academic social work developed much later and maintained its religious affiliations during the interwar period. Religious organizations during this period embraced social scientific methods and began to replace their clerical and lay leadership with professionally trained administrators. Paula Maurutto's work, likewise, documents the continued prominence of the Catholic church in moral and social reform well into the 1940s. Many Canadian historians may have too readily adopted trends in the United States and Britain to explain events in Canada and in the process may have obscured the continuing influence of religion, particularly in the area of social reform.

—*Paula Maurutto*

See also Human Rights (Canada); Kelso, J. J.; Religion and Social Welfare (Canada); Social Gospel (United States); Whitton, Charlotte; Women and Social Welfare (Canada)

Primary Sources

Records of the Canadian Council of Churches and John Joseph Kelso Papers, Library and Archives Canada, Ottawa, ON; Methodist Church of Canada and Hugh Dobson Papers, both in United Church Archives, Victoria College, University of Toronto, ON.

Current Comment

Allen, R. (1973). *The social passion: Religion and social reform in Canada, 1914–1928*. Toronto, ON: University of Toronto Press.
Cook, R. (1985). *The regenerators: Social criticism in late Victorian Canada*. Toronto, ON: University of Toronto Press.
Marshall, D. B. (1992). *Secularizing the faith: Canadian Protestant clergy and the crisis of belief, 1850–1940*. Toronto, ON: University of Toronto Press.
Valverde, M. (1991). *The age of light, soap, and water: Moral reform in English Canada, 1885–1925*. Toronto, ON: McClelland & Stewart.

Further Reading

Bruce, S. (Ed.). (1992). *Religion and modernization: Sociologists and historians debate the secularization thesis*. Oxford, UK: Clarendon.
Christie, N., & Gauvreau, M. (1996). *A full-orbed Christianity: The Protestant churches and social welfare in Canada, 1900–1940*. Montreal, QC, and Kingston, ON: McGill-Queen's University Press.
Lyon, D., & Van Die, M. (Eds.). (2000). *Rethinking church, state, and modernity: Canada between Europe and America*. Toronto, ON: University of Toronto Press.
Maurutto, P. (2003). *Governing charities: Church and state in Toronto's Catholic archdiocese, 1850–1950*. Montreal, QC, and Kingston, ON: McGill-Queen's University Press.

SOCIAL REFORM MOVEMENTS (UNITED STATES)

Social reform movements have been defined by Ash (1972, p. 1) as "self-conscious action on the part of a group of people directed toward change in the social structure and/or ideology of a society and carried on outside of ideologically legitimated channels or which uses these channels in innovative ways." Social welfare reform movements are a subcategory of social movements that seek changes related to the position of poor and oppressed people in society. The history of the United States has been characterized by a steady sequence of social reform movements aimed at correcting conditions perceived to be unjust or problematic by various social groups. These conditions have stemmed from two basic sources. The first is the problems and inequities that were built into American society at its beginning. The second is problems that have resulted from more than 200 years of increasingly rapid social changes.

When the United States emerged from the American Revolution as an independent nation, the resulting society was a brilliant experiment in liberty and democracy, but also one that was fraught with peril for individuals and minority groups. The frontier mentality and the emerging influence of laissez-faire capitalism resulted in a country with little sympathy for individuals experiencing problems, particularly any problem with a cause that was not obvious. Then there was what Tocqueville referred to as the "tyranny of the majority," meaning that in a society where the majority rules, the consequences for people in minority groups can be very harsh. The phrase "all men are created equal" literally meant men, and more so meant White, Anglo-Saxon, Protestant men. The further one was from this standard in terms of gender, religion, ethnicity, or race, the less the principles of liberty and equality applied. Thus, one of the primary themes of social reform movements in the United States has been extending full rights to all individuals and groups in society.

The other general source of social reform movements has been the rapid pace of social change that has accelerated since the founding of this country. When the country was formed, it was rural, the economy was agricultural, and the population was fairly homogeneous. Beginning in the nineteenth century and becoming even more pronounced in the twentieth century, the country rapidly became urban, the economy industrial, and rapid immigration created a very heterogeneous population. These changes brought about many actual problems (cities had problems in sanitation, housing, and the like; an industrial economy had problems of unemployment, worker disability, etc.), and also problems that were not so much actual as perceived (immigrants brought strange customs and religions that were viewed as threats to the "American way").

The social welfare reform movements that resulted from these sources can be categorized into two loose, overlapping groups. The first is a series of movements that have had as their aim liberation of various groups that had been excluded from full participation in American society. Women (especially married women) were initially denied many rights as citizens, including the vote and the right to own property. In 1776, New Jersey granted suffrage to single women and widows, but this was an isolated event as women made little progress for the next 100 years. At the beginning of the twentieth century, women became involved in reform organizations, notably the General Federation of Women's Clubs, the National Congress of Mothers, the National Consumers League, and the Women's Trade Union League. These groups focused on issues of special concern to women, mainly children, families, and women in the workplace. Led by the two-million member National American Woman Suffrage Association, the cause of granting the vote to women gained momentum until the Nineteenth Amendment to the Constitution was passed in 1920. The women's movement reemerged in the 1960s with the Presidential Commission on the Status of Women in 1961, the inclusion of gender as a protected category in the Civil Rights Act of 1964, and the founding of the National Organization for Women in 1966. This movement reached its zenith in 1972, when Congress passed the Equal Rights Amendment, which read, "Equal rights under the law shall not be denied or abridged by the United States or by any state on account of sex." This amendment met with a strong reaction and fell three states short of the required 35 for ratification when the time limit expired in 1982.

Treated even more unjustly than women were racial and ethnic minorities such as African Americans and American Indians, who were initially granted almost no civil rights. African Americans were brought to this country as slaves and this resulted in the first massive social welfare reform movement, the abolition movement. The Civil War of 1861–1865 probably was not caused by slavery, but certainly brought it to an end. The war left African Americans with a freedom that was accompanied by few rights and fewer resources. Following Reconstruction, southern Whites engaged in a successful campaign that resulted in segregation statutes, known collectively as Jim Crow laws, that denied Blacks access to most resources, and passed laws such as the poll tax and grandfather clauses that effectively denied them the vote. These injustices led to a century-long struggle for civil rights that began with the founding of advocacy organizations such as the National Association of Colored Women (1900) and the National Association for the Advancement of Colored People (NAACP, 1910). With the leadership of the NAACP, and support from later-formed civil rights groups such as the Southern Christian Leadership Conference, the Student Nonviolent Coordinating Committee, and the Congress of Racial Equality, the Civil Rights Act of 1964 was passed. The law prohibited segregation in public accommodations such as hotels, restaurants, gas stations, theaters, and parks, and outlawed employment discrimination on federally assisted projects. It also created the Equal Employment Opportunity Commission to protect minority groups against job discrimination.

Inspired by the success of the civil rights movement, a number of other movements for the liberation of oppressed groups emerged during the 1960s. Among these was the American Indian Movement that began in 1968 and sought to increase economic opportunity for Indians and to stop police mistreatment; gay and lesbian activism that began when police raided Manhattan's Stonewall Inn in June 1969 and patrons fought back, resulting in a weekend of disorder; the beginning of a movement that appears to still be gaining strength—advocacy for older citizens promoted by the radical Gray Panthers, and the mainstream and very effective lobbying group the American Association of Retired Persons, that resulted in the 1965 Older Americans Act; and the "brown power" movement by Latinos that demanded bilingual education, immigration reform, and organized the United Farm Workers, a union that advocated for better pay and conditions for the largely

Latino agricultural workforce in Southern California and Texas.

Other types of social welfare reform movements were those that addressed poverty and economic inequality. When this country was founded, poverty was not a major social issue because most people were what passed for middle class at the time. There were few truly rich citizens, and those that were poor were in this condition for obvious reasons such as illness or old age. As the country grew and became more industrial, the number of people who were poor simply because they were out of work grew at a corresponding rate. This problem has given rise to a never-ending series of movements seeking to get the problem under control. These movements have been like a pendulum swinging from those that are sympathetic to the poor and want to make their lives better, to those that view the poor as leeches on the body politic and want to make their lives on welfare so unpleasant that they will be forced to go to work and become self-supporting. The first major movement was the poorhouse movement that began in 1824 when the state of New York appointed a commission to study poor relief in that state. This commission recommended that all public relief granted to people in their own homes be discontinued and be replaced by a system of county poorhouses. This movement caught on to the extent that by 1860 four out of every five recipients of public aid were receiving it within the walls of an institution. This movement was followed by the charity organization society movement (also known as scientific charity) that began in New York in 1877, the widows' or mothers' pension movement that began at the White House Conference on Dependent Children in 1909, the movement for social security that culminated with the Social Security Act of 1935, and finally the welfare reform movement that resulted in the passage of the 1996 Personal Responsibility and Work Opportunity Reconciliation Act. This last reform is of the variety that seeks to force people off of public assistance and into the job market at almost any price. It has long been anticipated that this act will be followed by a movement to once again liberalize public assistance policy in the United States, but so far no such movement is evident.

There have also been a number of social movements that, while not social welfare reform movements, relate to and support them. Notable among these have been movements aimed at the moral uplift of the American people such as the Second Great Awakening, and the network of church-affiliated reform organizations known collectively as the Benevolent Empire. Of special relevance was the social gospel movement, begun by Congregational minister Washington Gladden in 1884, which exhorted Christians to support social reform to alleviate poverty, slums, and labor exploitation. A faint echo of this movement can be heard in the currently popular question of young people "what would Jesus do?" There have also been periodic movements promoting more efficient ways of doing things such as the late eighteenth century movement for civil service reform and the early twentieth century scientific management movement. Because Americans consider social welfare to be inherently inefficient, these movements generally have components calling for the reform of social welfare programs. Two of the most significant social welfare reform movements, the late nineteenth century Charity Organization Society Movement, and the recent welfare reform movement that culminated in the Personal Responsibility and Work Opportunity Reconciliation Act (1996), were both based on calls to make the delivery of assistance to the poor more efficient.

—Philip R. Popple

See also African Americans and Social Welfare (United States); King, Martin Luther, Jr.; Sanger, Margaret Higgins; Women and Social Welfare (United States)

Primary Sources

Information on the role of women in social welfare reform can be found in the Schlesinger Library on the History of Women in America, Radcliffe College, Cambridge, MA. Subject areas of note in this collection are women's rights and suffrage, social and labor reform, family history, and women in the professions, government service, and political movements. The papers of Dr. Martin Luther King, Jr., and information on the U.S. civil rights movement are at the King Center's Library and Archives in Atlanta, GA. Significant collections are the Papers of the Congress of Racial Equality, the Southern Christian Leadership Conference, and the Student Nonviolent Co-ordinating Committee. The holdings also include the papers of a number of individuals with important roles in the civil rights movement, including those of Julian Bond and Fred Shuttlesworth, in addition to Dr. King. The Social Welfare History Archives (SWHA) at the University of Minnesota, Minneapolis, contain the records of a number of organizations and individuals central to social welfare reform movements in the United States. Significant collections include those of the National Conference on Social Welfare, the United Neighborhood Centers of America, and the American Public Welfare Association. The SWHA also includes the papers of a number of individuals who had significant impact upon social welfare reform efforts, including those of Helen Hall, Paul Kellogg, Alvin Schorr, and Ernest Witte.

Current Comment

Abbott, E. (1940). *Public assistance.* Chicago: University of Chicago Press.

Addams, J. (1910). *Twenty Years at Hull House.* New York: Macmillan.

Riis, J. (1890). *How the other half lives.* New York: Scribner.

Rubinow, I. M. (1934). *The quest for Social Security.* New York: Arno.

Further Reading

Ash, R. (1972). *Social movements in America.* Chicago: Markham.

Evans, S. (1979). *Personal politics: The roots of women's liberation in the civil rights movement and the New Left.* New York: Knopf.

Lubove, R. (1968). *The struggle for Social Security, 1900–1935.* Cambridge, MA: Harvard University Press.

Piven, F. F., & Cloward, R. A. (1977). *Poor people's movements: Why they succeed, how they fail.* New York: Pantheon.

SOCIAL SECURITY (CANADA)

Generally, the purpose of Social Security programs is to protect citizens against the major adversities of life, such as unemployment, disability, poor health, death or injury of a wage earner, old age, or dependency, generally, through a cash entitlement. William Beveridge, one of the United Kingdom's principal architects of the World War II-era welfare state, referred to a Ministry of Social Security that would be responsible for social insurance and national and voluntary assistance in all national and local systems. In the United States, following the tradition of the New Deal, definitions of Social Security tend to be limited to particular forms of income security—most narrowly defined as social insurance. In Canadian usage, Social Security has been more broadly defined to include social services as well as income programs, where "social services" include such varied non-income services as adoption, protection, day care, and

probation. Within the Canadian context, there are three types of income security programs. Income- or means-tested programs constitute the first type of income security programs in which individuals or families with incomes below a given threshold (i.e., meeting an eligibility requirement) receive assistance. These include such programs as Social Assistance, Guaranteed Income Supplements, Spouse's Allowances, and Child Tax Benefits. The second type of income security is provided through programs such as the Employment Insurance Program and the Canada/Quebec Pension Plans. These programs are predicated on contributions made from workplace earnings such that benefits and premiums rise in proportion to a worker's earnings within a defined income ceiling. The third type of income security is provided through universal programs. In universal programs, everyone within a specific category (e.g., being over or under a certain age: the elderly and children) receives payments from the program. Historic examples of universal programs include the Family Allowance (FA, 1944–1992) and Old Age Security (OAS, 1951–). In 1992, the FA was replaced by a system of selective Child Tax Benefits. The OAS program has also undergone changes. Since 1989, the tax system has been used to "claw back" some, or all, of the OAS benefits received by a number of high- and middle-income earners. This calls into question whether the OAS can continue to be classified as a universal program.

HISTORICAL CONTEXT

The welfare state, and with it Social Security programs, came to prominence in Canada during the twentieth century as a transplant from Europe. Before the twentieth century, the care of the elderly, sick, and orphaned in the province of Quebec was the responsibility of the Roman Catholic church, whereas in the provinces of Nova Scotia and New Brunswick, local jurisdictions took control of care for the poor under the English Poor Law. Other provinces, for example Ontario, did not enact a poor law, making voluntary charities of the utmost importance. Thus, Social Assistance (i.e., Unemployment Relief until the end of the Great Depression in the late 1930s) has important municipal and local roots in Canada.

CANADIAN DEVELOPMENT OF SOCIAL SECURITY

As assigned by the Canadian Constitution, social welfare is a provincial responsibility. Both the provincial and federal levels of Canadian government, however, have supported a number of major income security programs throughout the twentieth century. Examples of these programs include Worker's Compensation, (first established in Ontario in 1914), Mothers' Allowances (first established in Manitoba in 1916), Old Age Security (federal-provincial cost shared and selective, 1927), Unemployment Insurance (federal, 1940), Family Allowance (federal, 1944), and Old Age Security as a universal program (federal, 1951). In the era of welfare state expansion, these programs grew to include the Canada/Quebec Pension Plan (1966), Guaranteed Income Supplements for Canada/Quebec Pension Plan recipients (1967), and OAS Spouse's Allowances (1975). New provisions under the Unemployment Insurance program were instituted in 1971 that include some previously excluded workers (e.g., fishing industry) as well as work leave for illness and maternity. Funding for Social Security programs found new stability through the Canada Assistance Plan (CAP, 1966–1996). This federal transfer payment program provided to the provinces, on a cost-share basis, monies for the delivery of health, education, and social services. From the mid 1970s, transfer payments were gradually reduced, and in 1996 a less robust Canada Health and Social Transfer program replaced CAP. Hand in hand with this came the erosion of the federal government's ability to enforce national government standards. The tax system over this same time period has increasingly become the preferred instrument of income redistribution through a system of tax credits and benefits.

TRANSFORMATION OF SOCIAL SECURITY

A radical transformation of income security programs in Canada began during the mid 1970s, and accelerated throughout the late 1980s and the 1990s. As a cost-cutting measure, governments curtailed social program spending in relative terms to the rates of inflation and population growth, and in many instances in absolute terms as well. The result was that federal government transfers to the provinces did not keep pace with inflation. The result was a domino effect— severe cutbacks by the provinces in Unemployment Insurance, Social Assistance, Worker's Compensation, and other social spending that produced programs with reduced levels of entitlement and restricted access. Some programs, such as the Family Allowance, were eliminated entirely. During the 1980s, the slack in government assistance required the voluntary sector to take up a greater portion of the burden of helping. For example, the 1980s witnessed the rise of new institutions, such as food banks, that had become firmly ensconced in the Canadian social welfare landscape by the 1990s. At the beginning of the new millennium, a number of important factors merge within the Canadian social scene: Child poverty remains especially pronounced; universality is all but dead; a liberal ideology and the political economy of globalization are exceptionally influential; and community care, the marketplace, and privatized social service have been trumpeted as increasingly important to social policy. The ability of Social Security programs to respond effectively and efficiently to social problems has been commensurately diminished.

—John R. Graham

See also Federalism and Social Welfare Policy (Canada); Poverty (Canada); Social Welfare (Canada): Before the Marsh Report; Social Welfare (Canada): Since the Marsh Report; Welfare Capitalism (Canada)

Further Reading

Armitage, A. (1996). *Social welfare in Canada revisited: Facing up to the future*. Toronto, ON: Oxford University Press.

Beveridge, W. H. (1943). *The pillars of security and other wartime essays and addresses*. New York: Macmillan.

Graham, J. R., Swift, K. J., & Delaney, R. (2003). *Canadian social policy: An introduction* (2nd ed.). Toronto, ON: Prentice Hall.

Ross, D. P., Scott, K. J., & Smith, P. J. (2001). *The Canadian fact book on poverty—2000*. Ottawa, ON: Canadian Council on Social Development.

SOCIAL SECURITY (MEXICO)

The Mexican Social Security system is a complex entity that includes several institutions, yet its coverage is limited. According to the 2000 census,

Social Security covered only 40 percent of the total population. The Social Security system is shaped by the Mexican Social Security Institute (*Instituto Mexicano del Seguro Social*, or IMSS), the Social Security Institute for Government Workers (*Instituto de Seguridad y Servicios Sociales de los Trabajadores del Estado*, or ISSSTE), and other small institutes for oil, military, and local state workers. Only workers in formal labor markets and their families are affiliated with Social Security pension and health systems. Workers in the informal labor market and the unemployed have no pension rights or health rights in the Social Security system, but they do have access to other health services: 22 percent of the population use the services of the Health Ministry (*Secretaría de Salud*) and 33 percent use private services. These percentages are different in rural and urban areas and in labor market sectors: Rates of affiliation with different institutes vary from 10 to 37 percent of private-sector workers, and from 8 to 30 percent for government workers. This pattern emerges from a complex historic process: The Mexican Social Security system was created in the early twentieth century as several corporate insurance or saving societies. The first Social Security benefits were provided under the Laws for Work Accidents, established in 1904 and 1906 by local governments in the states of México and Nuevo León. These state laws provided rights for workers in the case of illness, accident, or death. In 1905, the federal government created the General Hospital of México. After the 1910 Revolution, the Mexican government promulgated a law for work-related accidents, and the 1917 Constitution created pension funds with voluntary contributions from groups of workers that were economically stable, beginning in 1921. As this Constitution did not permit the government to unify these scattered programs and create an integral system, only local governments could establish programs to provide workers with benefits such as rights to housing, regulation of the workday, and Social Security. Some of these laws still exist, making the Mexican Social Security system very complex. Some institutes offer housing credits and nursery schools, for example, whereas others do not. The most highly organized groups of workers developed their own specific funds, which were progressively centralized by government in different periods.

In 1925, the Law of Civil Pensions and Retirement established pensions for disability, death, and retirement at age 65 for government workers and veterans of the recent Revolution. In 1947, the age of retirement eligibility for these groups was reduced to 55 years. In 1959, the federal government created the Social Security Institute for Government Workers (ISSSTE), which centralized pensions and health services for federal government workers and their families. In 2000, ISSSTE covered 6 percent of the total population, or 15 percent of formal workers. Today, some groups have corporate Social Security systems: workers in the national oil company *Petróleos Mexicanos* (PEMEX), members of the military, local government employees, and others, covering up to 2 percent of the total population.

Workers in the formal labor market and private companies had their savings and health societies centralized by the government in 1943 as the Mexican Social Security Institute (*Instituto Mexicano del Seguro Social*, or IMSS). In 2000, the IMSS covered 32 percent of the total population, or 81 percent of formal workers. In addition, several private companies offered prepaid health plans.

Workers in the informal labor market and the unemployed cannot affiliate with these institutes to get pension and health benefits. They have, however, received health care from social assistance, similar to poor relief in the United States, since the nineteenth century. In 1917, the government created a national health service, later centralized in the Health Ministry, which offered accessible health services through small taxes, similar to a fee-for-service program.

ECONOMIC AND DEMOGRAPHIC TRENDS

In the 1940s, life expectancy in Mexico was nearly 40 years. Life expectancy increased steadily over the next three decades. Improvements in sanitation and health care, and the introduction of antibiotics and immunization contributed to increases of nearly 15 years in life expectancy and increases in the economically active population. At the same time, the government's policy of import substitution industrialization (protected industrial development from the

1940s to 1970s) promoted increases in the rates of formal employment, absorbing these numerous cohorts of new workers in urban areas. These trends increased the number of taxpayers and increased revenues for the Social Security system. Taxpayers of working age were more numerous than those receiving pensions. These resources were accumulated in the collective Social Security funds managed by the government and used to promote industrialization, employment, and welfare through social policies that provided education, health care, social assistance, Social Security, and housing. Most Mexican private hospitals, laboratories, and surgical centers were built with resources of the IMSS, ISSSTE, and the Health Ministry.

Between 1970 and 1980, life expectancy increased by another 5 years; health improvements and increases in income, education, and nutrition all contributed to decreases in mortality. During the 1990s, however, an opposite scenario took hold: the economy experienced an acute crisis, with decreases in formal employment and numbers of taxpayers. A large number of taxpayers survived to the age of 65 years, retired, and began to receive pensions. As a result, demands on the Social Security system increased.

The number of taxpayers contributing to the IMSS increased from 137,000 in 1944 to 1.2 million in 1960, 4.8 million in 1980, and 10.6 million in 1996. The number of family dependents, including children, however, increased much more rapidly, from 219,000 to 29.4 million between 1944 and 1990. The number of family dependents per taxpayer was 1.6 in 1944 and reached its maximum of 4.1 in 1978. The increasing number of taxpayers and dependents resulted in increases in expenses for health services. The number of dependents per taxpayer diminished to 2.5 dependents per taxpayer in 1996 (see Figure S.1).

A large number of previously covered individuals who survived beyond 65 years of age and were retired received pensions. The number of pensioned persons increased from 36,000 in 1973 to near 3 million in 1996, multiplying expenses and placing extreme financial burdens on the system. In 1973, there were 8.4 contributors per pensioner

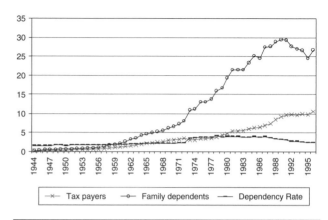

Figure S.1   *Number of Taxpayers, Family Dependents, and Dependency Rate (in millions), IMSS, 1944–2000*

Source: *Memoria Estadística,* 2000, IMSS

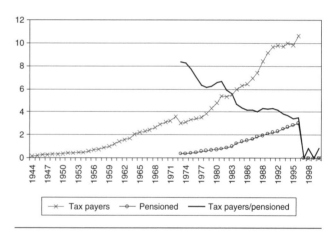

Figure S.2   *Number of Taxpayers, the Pensioned (including Family Dependents), and Ratio of Taxpayers to Pensioners (in millions), IMSS, 1944–2000*

Source: *Memoria Estadística,* 2000, IMSS

affiliated with the IMSS, but by 1996 this number had decreased to 4.5 contributors per pensioner (see Figure S.2). This trend is related to the aging of the affiliated population, but also it is due to decreases in formal employment and consequently in contributors. As a result of these changes, the Social Security system underwent several political and institutional reforms.

REFORMS

In 1982, the federal government initiated reform and decentralization of the health system, which reproduced inequalities in power relationships among states and social groups. Successive federal administrations attempted to address these inequalities.

According to the census of 2000, nearly 30 percent of the population used the IMSS health services and 3.5 percent used the IMSS Solidarity health services (for poorer rural populations); 6 percent used the ISSSTE and one other government health service; 22 percent used the Health Ministry; and 33 percent used private services. Children and adults tended to make more use of the Health Ministry's facilities, whereas the elderly tended to use private services and the services of the Social Security system (IMSS and ISSSTE).

In 1994, the federal government created the Savings for Retirement system (SAR), increased the percentage of worker's wages taxed to save for retirement from 6 to 8.5 percent, and separated definitively pension and health care funds. In 1997, the public and Solidarity funds of contributions were also transformed. First, taxes paid to IMSS to finance the health system were placed in a separate health fund. Second, taxes paid for pensions for retirement and housing costs were transferred to individual savings accounts in private banks.

The new Social Security Law of 1997 also created 14 Administrators of Retirement Funds (*Administradoras de Fondos Para el Retiro,* or AFOREs) to manage contributions for pensions for work injury, disability, age, and death. The funds accumulated by workers were transferred from the collective Social Security fund to new individual accounts, as part of a capitalization system managed by banks. The ratio between Social Security taxes paid by employers and workers (80 percent) and government (20 percent) continued after the reform. The new law established that, in any case of imbalance in the accounts or bank failure, the government would assume the responsibility to cover deficits and pay pensions. The criterion to receive a pension is still reaching the age of 65 years for both sexes, and 80 percent of IMSS pensions give retirees approximately the minimum wage. In order to receive benefits, workers must have 24 years of payments into the system. In 1996, the IMSS had almost 12 million contributors, while 13 million people collected pensions After 1997, the number of IMSS contributors decreased, and the number of pensioners increased. In addition, the new system of AFOREs received 17.5 million transferred contributors from IMSS.

Some basic problems of the older system persist—high administrative costs, limited control that contributors have over their accounts, and lack of coverage, especially for workers in the informal labor market and for rural and low-income workers. Despite these limitations, the pensioned elderly are less likely to be in extreme poverty as a result of the Social Security system.

—Gomes Da Conceicao, Maria Cristina

See also Aging Policy (Mexico); Informal Economy (Mexico); Social Welfare (Mexico): Since 1867

Primary Source

Ramo Presidenciales, Archivo General de la Nación, Mexico City.

Current Comment

García Cruz, M. (1961). La seguridad social. In *México, cincuenta años de revolución: Vol. 2: La vida social.* Mexico City: Fondo de Cultura Económica.

Further Reading

Abel, C., & Lewis, C. M. (Eds.). (2002). *Exclusion & engagement: Social policy in Latin America.* London: Institute of Latin American Studies.

Mesa-Lago, C. (1978). *Social Security in Latin America: Pressure groups, stratification, and inequality.* Pittsburgh, PA: University of Pittsburgh Press.

Montes de Oca, V., & Gomes, C. (2003). *Envejecimineto y politicas públicas para adultos mayores: México y Iberoamerica ante un nuevo siglo.* Mexico City: Universidad Nacional Autónoma de México, Coordinación de Humanidades, Instituto de Investigaciones Sociales.

Scherlock, P. L. (Ed.). (2003). *Aging, development and social protection.* Thousand Oaks, CA: Sage.

SOCIAL SECURITY (UNITED STATES)

Central to the history of the American social welfare state is passage of the 1935 Social Security Act, which created two social insurance programs (federal Old Age Insurance and federal-state Unemployment Insurance), three federal-state public assistance programs (Old Age Assistance, Aid to the Blind, and Aid to Dependent Children), as well as grants to states for five social service and health programs (child welfare, crippled children's programs, maternal and child health, public health work, and vocational rehabilitation). By the end of the twentieth century, social insurance and public assistance programs had expanded to touch the lives of most Americans, transforming social welfare provision since the days of the Great Depression and providing an unprecedented level of economic security for the country's aged. In the six and a half decades since the original act, a once highly limited old-age social insurance system grew to include survivor benefits (added in 1939), disability insurance (1956), and health insurance for the aged (Medicare, 1965). Automatic cost-of-living benefits increases were added (1972) and a vast broadening of employee coverage had taken place. The inflow of payroll taxes used to finance social insurance had become huge, being the second-largest source of federal revenues (larger than corporate income tax receipts but smaller than individual income tax revenues). The size of this revenue stream and the projected outflow of benefits established Social Security as a crucial feature of national budget debates.

In 1935, the phrase "social security" was used for both social insurance and public assistance programs. They were seen as complementary parts of a unified whole. In this view, social insurance was to be dominant, and public assistance was to perform a supportive, and, it was hoped, temporary, role—withering away, for the most part, as social insurance matured. Over time, however, and in large part through the efforts of Social Security leaders, the phrase "social security" has come to mean only the social insurance programs. In part, this shift in terminology was caused by the failure of public assistance to fade away. In fact, given the slowness with which the early social insurance system was developing and the early popularity of old-age public assistance, Social Security leaders throughout the 1930s were worried that assistance might outpace social insurance as the nation's preferred policy and they struggled to prevent that. As late as the 1940s, the number of people relying on old-age public assistance

exceeded those receiving old-age social insurance, and nonsocial insurance approaches to old-age security had continuing pockets of political strength. Amendments to the act in the 1950s raised benefit levels and significantly expanded workforce coverage. President Dwight D. Eisenhower's subsequent endorsement of Social Security finally removed concerns about the system's permanency. Over the following decades, Social Security became one of the most strongly supported of all public programs.

The changing meaning of the phrase, "social security," was part of an evolving system of social security ideology that emphasized differentiating social insurance from public assistance. This ideology has played an important role in legitimating social insurance, in terms of the argument that social insurance has a unique congruence with American values and public assistance does not. It has characterized American social insurance as (1) contributory and with earned benefits: Workers and employers pay earmarked payroll taxes to finance the system; (2) wage-related: an individual's level of benefits is tied, within limits, to prior earnings level, thus rewarding work; and (3) universal: Poor and nonpoor alike participate with no means testing and with benefits going to the wealthy as well as the poor. This contrasts with welfare, which is characterized as (1) not contributory and thus unearned because it is financed through general revenues; (2) not wage-related and thus out of step with the work ethic: Benefits are not conditional on the recipient's participation in the workforce; and (3) selective: Welfare targets the poor, splitting them away from a politically powerful alliance with the nonpoor as found in social insurance. In the early years, these conceptualizations were expressed in a frequently used private insurance metaphor. Social Security benefits were explicitly compared to private insurance policies. Payroll taxes were said to be not taxes but "premiums" on a social security "policy" held by workers and the resulting benefits had connotations of private property. This was contrasted with the "charity" quality of public assistance and its association with dependency. Over the years, the use of explicit private insurance imagery has moderated and although social insurance terminology is still in use, few today would compare Social Security to a private insurance policy or deny that payroll deductions are taxes as was done in the early days.

These conceptualizations flag what many observers call the split-level nature of the American welfare state: a politically very strong social insurance realm, stigma-free and with connotations of benefits as rights and, in contrast, a welfare realm marked by political volatility and at times demeaning conditions for recipients and less generous benefits. This duality both reflects the long-standing American suspicion of welfare and speaks to the successful efforts of Social Security leadership to establish social insurance as something apart from and superior to welfare. The split-level nature of the American social welfare state was aggravated by the failure of the 1935 Social Security Act to address the needs of African Americans. The original social insurances did not cover agricultural and other employment sites where most African Americans worked at the time. Further, the state-controlled public assistance programs meant as a backup system were often implemented in an overtly discriminatory fashion. Although Social Security coverage eventually expanded to include agricultural labor and African Americans became a primarily urban population, the impact of historical and continuing racial discrimination in the workplace has meant that African Americans are disproportionately represented in the lower, public assistance level of the social welfare state.

At times, Social Security has been subjected to redistributional critiques. The payroll tax is a highly regressive one. Although the benefit formula contains a weighting element in favor of low-wage earners, it remains the case that benefits flow to the very wealthy and, in large part, the program reflects the inequalities in the pre-retirement distribution of income. Social Security supporters reject the critiques, arguing Social Security has been crafted to avoid class conflict, joining poor and nonpoor alike in a politically powerful coalition. They point to the unequivocal political strength of Social Security and its record of expansion as evidence of the success of the Social Security approach.

A challenge for contemporary Social Security is how to finance future benefits—a problem that has been emerging since the late 1970s and is now full-blown. The original retirement system was highly conservative, designed to operate on a full reserve basis. Projected benefits could not exceed actual payroll taxes on hand. This proved to be a political liability because

it meant benefit levels then had to be so low as to be unresponsive to the actual needs of the elderly. In the 1939 amendments, the full reserve model was abandoned, and the system has been on a modified reserve basis since. Benefit levels have been limited not by funds on hand but by projections of future funding. At the time, Social Security staff predicted the 1939 abandonment of full reserves meant, over the long run, payroll taxes alone would be insufficient to finance benefits and that eventually (some predicted by the 1990s) additional sources of revenues from general taxation would have to be used. That long-ago prediction now resonates with the contemporary funding challenge facing Social Security. With the imminent retirement of the large baby-boom generation, the current payroll tax structure cannot sustain benefit levels in either the retirement or Medicare program over the coming decades. Policy leaders and Congress are faced with difficult choices to resolve the problem and options under consideration include cutting benefits, postponing retirement age, raising payroll taxes, using general revenues, and privatizing portions of Social Security.

—Jerry R. Cates

See also Aid to Dependent Children/Aid to Families With Dependent Children (United States); Altmeyer, Arthur Joseph; Ball, Robert Myers; Cohen, Wilbur Joseph; Federalism and Social Welfare Policy (United States); Hopkins, Harry Lloyd; Mothers' Pensions (United States); Perkins, Frances; Poverty (United States); Roosevelt, Franklin Delano; Social Welfare (United States): Since the Social Security Act; Social Work Profession (United States); Supplemental Security Income (United States)

Primary Sources

Records of the Social Security Administration (Record Group 47), National Archives & Records Administration, Washington, DC, and College Park, MD; Social Security Administration History Archives, Social Security Administration Headquarters, Baltimore, MD; Arthur J. Altmeyer Papers and Wilbur J. Cohen Papers, Wisconsin Historical Society, Madison.

Current Comment

Altmeyer, A. J. (1966). *The formative years of Social Security.* Madison: University of Wisconsin Press.
Burns, E. M. (1956). *Social Security and public policy.* New York: McGraw-Hill.
Witte, E. E. (1962). *The development of the Social Security Act.* Madison: University of Wisconsin Press.

Further Reading

Cates, J. R. (1983). *Insuring inequality: Administrative leadership in Social Security, 1935–1954.* Ann Arbor: University of Michigan Press.

Derthick, M. (1979). *Policymaking for Social Security.* Washington, DC: Brookings Institution Press.

Skocpol, T. (1988). *The politics of social policy in the United States.* Princeton, NJ: Princeton University Press.

SOCIAL WELFARE (CANADA): BEFORE THE MARSH REPORT

North America was forever changed by European contact. Sporadic attempts at tenth century Viking settlement along the northeast coast were followed by permanent settlement of French habitants in the sixteenth century, largely along the St. Lawrence River, in a land they named New France. The French, and, after the 1759 conquest of New France, the British, brought myriad precepts of European life to the New World, principal among them what is now understood to be the political, economic, social, and cultural machinations of "colonialism." The tragic experiences of the country's native populations are beyond the scope of the present article. At first pillaged by disease and war, aboriginal peoples in Canada were forced in the latter half of the nineteenth and early twentieth centuries onto reserves of land where they were subject to further colonialism and economic and political marginalization.

Social welfare in pre-1943 Canada emerged in five phases, each reflecting the demographic, political, and economic currents of the day. The first of these, pre-European contact, also requires greater attention beyond the scope of the present effort. The next, the period of New France, saw the emergence of a Roman Catholic tradition of community concern, as orders of nuns, monks, and priests provided educational, hospital, and charitable services for a small population. Thus, for example, we see the establishment of Hotel Dieu, founded in 1639, and one of the earliest relief initiatives in 1688, both in Quebec City.

European settlement had been based first on the cod fishery and later on the fur trade. New France's population at the time of the 1759 British Conquest was about 65,000. The British Conquest initiated a third phase of social welfare. Settlement, largely from Britain and the United States, swelled the population of British North America to 2.4 million in 1851. Farming and the timber trade were the colonies' major economic activities. A long-standing European custom of local responsibility for social welfare was adapted haphazardly to the dispersed, sparsely inhabited patterns of colonial settlement. In the maritime region, there were poor laws; in Quebec, a Roman Catholic eleemosynary tradition; and in Ontario, in the absence of either, spontaneous forms of community concern prevailed. The House of Industry, a Toronto poorhouse, was created in 1837; the Halifax Poor Man's Friend Society had opened a decade earlier; numerous Roman Catholic orders emerged alongside Protestant charities to respond to social problems.

The latter half of the nineteenth century saw a fourth phase of social welfare that was transformed by the combined effects of a more diverse European migration, urban growth, the Industrial Revolution, and Canadian Confederation (1867). At the time of Confederation, Canada's population had risen to 3.3 million. It increased to a startling 7.2 million by 1901 and those living in urban areas grew from 13 percent of the population in 1851, to 35 percent in 1901. The increasing complexity of social problems saw the proliferation in kind and function of charitable organizations: houses of industry and providence, boys' and girls' homes, city missions, Protestant and Roman Catholic orphanages, Jewish philanthropic activities, hospitals for the sick, refuges for the old, settlement houses for the poor. More systematic ways of helping developed: the actual process of helping, the manner in which social services were organized, and the way that they were evaluated. In Toronto, the position of a municipal relief officer was created. There, and in other major cities, charity organization societies promoted expert forms of charity work, and systematic investigations were intended to replace the simple provision of relief. The emergence of a social gospel movement in the latter half of the nineteenth century, the rise of a coalition of concerned citizens dedicated to social research and social betterment, a women's movement, trades and labor organizations—these and other groups formed a loosely affiliated alliance committed to improvements in social welfare.

Free public education systems were introduced in the provinces of Prince Edward Island in the 1850s and Nova Scotia in the 1860s. By the 1870s, free primary public education was introduced in the provinces of British Columbia, Manitoba, and Ontario. Various pieces of legislation were introduced to limit, and ultimately end, child labor. The first federal legislation regulating child labor in factories and mines was passed in the 1870s and 1880s.

Ontario's first children's aid society was established in Toronto in 1891, and the province's first Child Protection Act was passed in 1893. The Ontario Child Protection Act made the abuse of children an indictable offense for the first time, promoted foster care and children's aid societies, and established the early machinations of what was to become a growing child welfare social service system.

More stringent legislation emerged in the twentieth century, and by 1929 children under 14 had been legally excluded from factory and mine employment in most provinces. The women's movement was extremely important to social welfare, providing a broad constituency to advocate for improved conditions for women and children, for the right to vote for women, and constituting leadership for much of the country's emergent social services, whose personnel were overwhelmingly female. The last quarter of the nineteenth century saw the passage of various laws on workplace conditions, trades and unions, as well as the ad hoc emergence of municipal and provincial sources of funding for local social services and the gradual creation of provincial offices to oversee these activities. Lower levels of Canadian government remained essential to social welfare, and under terms of the British North America Act of 1867, provinces were delegated responsibilities for health, education, and social welfare services—although local jurisdictions continued the longstanding practice of being involved in their funding and delivery. The federal government, however, retained the most robust capacities to generate revenues.

At the local level, considerable efforts were made in public health legislation. Sanitation campaigns in the latter half of the nineteenth and early twentieth centuries were led by an urban reform movement committed to reducing overcrowding, high infant and childhood mortality rates, poverty, and sickness.

Water and milk supplies were sanitized; pasteurized milk, which curtailed the spread of bovine tuberculosis, was introduced in major cities after 1900; immunization programs were initiated to combat such diseases as smallpox and diphtheria; improved standards of meat inspection, sanitation, and other aspects now taken for granted, were developed. Municipal departments of health also tended to be the loci wherein local departments of social welfare emerged during the early decades of the twentieth century. All three levels of government created a growing number of libraries and parks to complement the country's social infrastructures. We also see the rise of the public school system. Whereas few children attended school around 1800, by 1900 most had at least some formal education. Many had attended school for several years, and some up to the age of 16 and beyond. Indeed, by 1911 about 85 percent of all Canadian children from 10 to 12 years of age were in school.

A fifth and final stage of social welfare, during the first four decades of the twentieth century, saw the gradual maturing of those structures upon which a comprehensive welfare state evolved after 1943. Canada's population between 1901 and 1941 grew from to 7.2 million to 11.5 million, and the proportion of the total population living in cities from 35 to 52 percent, although settlement was concentrated along a narrow ribbon of geography closest to the border with the United States. Schools of social work were established at the Universities of Toronto (1914), McGill (1918), and British Columbia (1928). Other organizations provided lobbying, research, and further impetus to social welfare measures. Among them were the Canadian Association of Social Workers (1926), what became the Canadian Council of Social Development (1920), the Social Service Council of Canada (1913), and what ultimately became social planning councils in major urban centers.

Local jurisdictions provided an increasing amount of money toward the funding and delivery of social services between 1900 and 1930. But various pieces of provincial legislation also paved the way for a more socially responsive state: worker's compensation (first in Ontario, 1914), mothers' pensions (first in Manitoba, 1916), and a federal Old Age Pension Act (1927), which was the first instance of a major social program that was cost shared on a 50-50 basis between provinces and the federal government. The mothers' pension and old-age pension programs were selective, and all three were restrictive in entitlement. Various programs that emerged in other industrialized nations were forestalled in Canada. As early as 1919, the federal government had furtively considered national systems of health and unemployment insurance; but they did not come into being on a national scale until the early 1940s and mid 1960s, respectively.

The Great Depression of the 1930s massively transformed Canadian social welfare. Local governments, under the Constitution, were creatures of the provinces. They could be created or disbanded by provincial writ, possessed no constitutional authority, and had a limited tax base. The country's unemployment rate hit upwards of 25 percent in 1933, and local governments over the course of this decade could not withstand the financial and administrative commitments of unemployment relief, among other social programs for which they had always been held responsible. On a yearly basis, provincial and federal governments had to assume the responsibility for funding unemployment relief programs as an increasing number of municipal jurisdictions went bankrupt. But, by then, a new consensus was emerging in Canada.

World War I had been extremely significant to Canadian social welfare. It expanded the scope of state activity into the domestic economy, introduced an income tax, and launched various services for soldiers returning home from war—such as health, housing, veterans' allowances, and soldier settlement schemes. It also provided policymakers with evidence that the domestic health and welfare of the population might not be sufficiently high if recruitment efforts for wars of this scale were to ever reoccur. World War II, in like manner, was massively transforming. The country had embarked upon a Royal Commission on Dominion-Provincial Relations (1937–1940), whose numerous reports provided policymakers with data and analysis that could help forge the contours of a more comprehensive welfare state. In 1940, a national system of Unemployment Insurance was proposed in the House of Commons, following a change to the British North America Act (as the Canadian Constitution had been called), allowing for federal participation in what was otherwise

a provincial prerogative. A scholar at McGill University, Leonard Marsh, was given the task of writing a report on health, unemployment, housing, and income, which ultimately echoed much of what had been written in the United Kingdom's Beveridge Report (1942). Canada was at the precipice of moving from a strongly residual basis of social welfare, where responsibility for individual welfare had rested with the individual, the family, and the community, and where recourse to private and public programs of a characteristically temporary and minimal nature were considered the last resort. In its stead, an institutional framework would appear in which governments would respond to peoples' social needs as a reflection of their collective citizenship.

Canada's welfare state would be more comprehensive and universal than the one developed in the United States. In part, this was associated with the social democratic traditions that the country had nurtured, in part, to the more Tory and pragmatic sensibilities that had characterized the country's conservative traditions. The state, after all, had interceded to create a fledgling country, from sea to sea, out of an original composite of four sparsely populated former British colonies located in eastern and central North America. A national policy of the ruling Conservative party in the late 1870s and 1880s had promoted the westward settlement of peoples, the construction of a railway, and a tariff to finance both. Canadians may have instinctively appreciated the need for the state to have some influence upon national life, and so avert the seemingly powerful forces of American Manifest Destiny. The emerging welfare state of the 1940s in some ways continued that tradition. But in our own time, where globalization, cultural and economic convergence with the United States, and multilateral trade agreements with the United States and other countries all reign supreme, will Canadians be able to assert comparable collective efforts of national expression?

—*John R. Graham*

See also Federalism and Social Welfare Policy (Canada); The Marsh Report (Canada); Poverty (Canada); Social Security (Canada); Social Welfare (Canada): Since the Marsh Report; Welfare Capitalism (Canada); Women and Poverty (Canada); Women and Social Welfare (Canada)

Primary Sources

Canadian Association of Social Workers Fonds, 1922–1977; Canadian Welfare Council Records, 1918–1959; Department of National Health and Welfare Fonds, 1815–1993; Unemployment Insurance Commission Fonds, 1900–1982; Charlotte Elizabeth Whitton Fonds, 1850–1977; all in Library and Archives Canada, Ottawa, ON.

Current Comment

Ames, H. (1972). *The city below the hill.* Toronto: University of Toronto Press. (Original work published 1897)

Marsh, L. C. (1975). *Report on Social Security for Canada.* Toronto: University of Toronto Press. (Original work published 1943)

Research Committee of the League for Social Reconstruction. (1935). *Social planning for Canada.* Toronto, ON: Thomas Nelson.

Whitton, C. (1943). *The dawn of ampler life.* Toronto, ON: Macmillan.

Further Reading

Armitage, A. (2003). *Social welfare in Canada* (4th ed.). Toronto, ON: Oxford University Press.

Graham, J. R., Swift, K., & Delaney, R. (2003). *Canadian social policy: An introduction.* (2nd ed.). Toronto, ON: Prentice Hall.

Lightman, E. (2003). *Social policy in Canada.* Toronto, ON: Oxford University Press.

Rice, J. J., & Prince, M. J. (2000). *Changing politics of Canadian social policy.* Toronto, ON: University of Toronto Press.

SOCIAL WELFARE (CANADA): SINCE THE MARSH REPORT

Social welfare programs are designed to help citizens meet risks created by economic and social change. Before the Depression of the 1930s, social welfare generally involved a local charity assessing a family's level of poverty and, when needed, providing limited relief. After the 1930s and the Second World War, social welfare was transformed into a wide variety of government programs and services allocated on the bases of social rights reflected in the principles of universal entitlement, social insurance, and social assistance. These new programs and services provided support for families, the elderly, employees, and those unable to work because of family or health reasons.

Over 30 years, from the 1940s to the 1970s, the Canadian welfare state slowly emerged as an important array of programs and services meeting the needs of many people. The process began with the conservative growth of Unemployment Insurance and Family Allowance programs in the 1940s, the development of Old Age Security in the 1950s, and the consolidation of the welfare system in the 1960s with the development of the Canada Pension Plan, Medicare, and the Canada Assistance Plan. No sooner had the programs been put in place than the ideas supporting welfare came under attack from all sides. By the 1980s, political critics from the Right and the Left attacked the "principles" of the programs claiming they undermined the "freedom" of the market, or limited peoples' liberty. Feminists found the system patriarchal and demeaning; recipients felt the programs to be constraining and stigmatizing; and service providers demanded more resources to meet growing needs. The most influential group of critics claimed spending on social programs contributed to the nation's debts and deficits of the 1970s and 1980s. The criticisms weakened the social consensus that held the welfare system together. During the 1980s and 1990s, many programs were altered to make the social welfare system more stringent, more targeted, and less supportive.

ENVISAGING A WELFARE SYSTEM

The basic ideas for Canadian welfare programs were developed during the first half of the twentieth century as Canada changed from an agricultural society into a modern industrial state. It was during this time that people found their lives disrupted and dislocated by the processes of urbanization and industrialization, intermixed with waves of immigration. Although these developments created many opportunities, people found that they also engendered increased economic uncertainty and social disruption. Moving from the farm to the city, or from one job to another, often meant people could no longer rely on their families, friends, or communities for help when things went wrong. As the depression of the 1930s developed, people saw others living in slums, walking bread lines, and being forced to take any kind of employment. They heard stories of elderly people living in hovels, children working in factories, and women raising large families on little income. People wanted protection against the problems of the modern world.

The political struggles of the 1930s and the search for a better future following the Second World War encouraged governments to think about comprehensive welfare programs. Writers were crafting a new set of ideas as they explored how the nation could create "social security" programs that provided protection for citizens. This idea of "social security" was expressed in five great Canadian reports written in the 1940s: The Marsh Report (1943) on income security argued in favor of greater use of social insurance and provided important arguments for the development of comprehensive Social Security; the Haggerty Report (1943) presented plans for a joint federal-provincial health and medical insurance scheme, recommending the population be covered for medical, dental, pharmaceutical, hospital, and nursing services; the Curtis Report (1944) described how the government could support the building of new homes and encourage the process of community planning; the White Paper (1944) examined how governments could prevent unemployment after the war by making a commitment to full employment through economic stimulation; and the Green Books (1945) described how the national and provincial governments could work together to ensure economic stability. Running through these reports were a number of themes reflecting the shifting beliefs and values regarding social welfare. First, they all made reference to the idea that the economy was not self-regulating and if left unattended would collapse, leading to social upheaval. Second, they argued that the possibility for individual self-reliance had been dramatically altered by urbanization and industrialization, and in dire economic circumstances people could no longer count on family members, charity, or the market to meet their needs. Finally, they recognized that the federal and provincial governments separately and cooperatively would have to become dominant actors in providing protection against income disruption. Each paper described how social interventions could address particular problems, and together they suggested a blueprint for how Canada could develop social welfare programs.

After the Second World War, the public wanted government to take a more active role in managing the economy in the hopes of achieving high and stable levels of income and employment. Many people believed governments should organize, finance, and deliver programs providing education, health care, housing, income support, and social services. Although social welfare had been essentially a provincial responsibility, the federal government now moved to the fore and began providing leadership in developing a comprehensive, national Social Security system. Powerful forces encouraged the development of welfare programs. The quiet, then less-than-quiet revolution in Quebec, the split between the have and have-not provinces, and the divisions between the central part and the rest of Canada all put enormous pressure on the federal government to hold the country together. At the same time, income and employment disparities created class divisions while differences in wages between men and women created social divisions that needed to be addressed. The federal government used welfare programs as important mechanisms for sharing political power between the federal and provincial governments, shifting and redistributing resources between the provinces, and increasing the positive feelings people had about being Canadian by providing universal benefits.

Looking back from today's vantage, we see how the Canadian network of social programs was incrementally built over a 30-year period. The system was created program-by-program in response to political demands for meeting social needs and conditioned by the politics of federalism, including at times provincial pressures for federal action. Yet, if there was no articulate philosophy or underlying unifying goal upon which the system was built, there was a set of ideas, expounded in the five reports, about a new economic and social role for the state. These ideas reflected the growing belief that governments could develop social policies that protected most Canadians from the risks of economic and social insecurity. They were based on new economic theories proposed by John Maynard Keynes asserting that government spending for social programs could be used to stabilize the economy while helping those who needed assistance in meeting the demands of daily living. Keynes's theories provided the foundation upon which governments began to create a mixed economy in which private ownership and production are combined with state intervention and regulation to develop a broad-based welfare system.

Over time, the federal and provincial governments developed a series of programs and services that provided an important "social safety net" that stopped most people from falling into destitution when social problems arose. Part of this safety net provided universal benefits through national social programs such as Old Age Security, Family Allowance, and Medicare. Another part provided income protection for those who paid social insurance through Unemployment Insurance, and the Canada and Quebec Pension Plans. And equally important were those programs that provided income support through means-testing devices offering programs such as social assistance for families and Guaranteed Income Support for the elderly. These wide-ranging programs, originally envisioned in one form or another in the five great reports, are the foundation of the Canadian welfare system.

THE SIX MOST IMPORTANT SOCIAL WELFARE PROGRAMS

Unemployment/Employment Insurance

The Unemployment Insurance program began in 1940 and was the first large-scale income mainte-nance program in the country. The purpose of (un)employment insurance is to protect those workers who pay into the insurance fund from job loss due to no fault of their own. The early program protected three-quarters of the working population and was slowly expanded to cover all workers who are in an employee-employer relationship. Although there have been many changes in the way the program is administered, the basic principles have remained the same. Eligible workers and their employers must pay into an employment insurance fund. Workers must have worked for a certain period of time, nowadays, between 420 and 700 hours over a qualifying period, usually the previous 52 weeks. The number of insur-able hours required depends on where the worker lives in Canada and the unemployment rate for that region. Workers must wait 2 weeks before benefits are paid, and if they earn income during this period it is deducted from their benefits. To receive benefits,

workers must be actively seeking employment, able and willing to go to work, keep records of employers they have contacted in looking for work, and report any income they earn. Workers are eligible to receive between 14 and 52 weeks of benefits, depending upon how long they have worked and the unemployment rate in their area.

The employment program also came to provide benefits to employees who must leave work due to pregnancy, illness, or injury. To be eligible for this program, workers must show they have worked for 600 hours in the last 52 weeks and that their earnings have decreased by more than 40 percent. Mothers and surrogate mothers as well as injured workers can receive benefits for 15 weeks, while those on parental leave can receive benefits for 35 weeks.

Family Allowance/Canada Child Tax Benefit

The federal government introduced the Family Allowance Act in 1944. This program was meant to provide financial assistance to all families with children up to the age of 16. The only condition was that the children who were old enough had to be attending school. This was Canada's first "universal" program, meaning that every family was eligible for the benefits no matter what their income level. The great advantage of universal programs is that since everyone gets the benefit, there is no stigma in receiv-ing the money. By providing money to all families, the government achieved two important goals. First, it supported low-income families without undermining their social status and second, it stimulated the econ-omy by putting cash into the hands of people who would spend it on necessities.

Starting in the late 1970s, the Family Allowance program was slowly altered as the government moved it from a universal to a selective program. First, the government introduced a refundable child tax credit, next they taxed back the benefits of those earning over a certain level of income, then finally they introduced an income-tested child tax benefit that provided monthly benefits based on the number of children and the level of family income. By the 2000s, this Canada Child Tax Benefit had been increased and fully indexed to the cost of living. The federal government claimed it wanted to recognize the cost of raising children and the value of parenting. The federal government also claimed the new program was an important tool in fighting poverty, but it allowed the provincial governments to deduct this same amount from their social assistance programs so that very poor families were no better off.

Old Age Security

The Old Age Security (OAS) program began in 1951. When first developed, it provided non-taxed modest monthly universal benefits to all eligible Canadians over the age of 70 (now 65). Every Canadian who had lived in the country for at least 20 years was eligible for the benefits and they were paid until the person died. For many Canadians, this benefit was a kind of "social glue" that made them feel "part" of Canada. In 1966, a Guaranteed Income Supplement (GIS) was added to Old Age Security so that Canadians with little or no other source of income would have enough income to live on in their old age. The amount of the benefit from the GIS is determined by an income test on the basis of a couple's combined yearly income. There is also a Spouse's Allowance program that provides income support for people who are between 60 and 64 and who have a spouse receiving Old Age Security. Benefits for OAS, GIS, and the Spouse's Allowance are paid out of general tax revenues. Some provinces and territories also provide income supplements to low-income seniors.

The most important change in Old Age Security took place in 1989, when the federal government decided to recover through taxation some of the benefits of OAS from people with incomes of more than $50,000. This meant it was no longer a universal program and people earning over a certain amount ($55,309 in 2001) have a portion of their Old Age Security taxed back.

Health Care

Canada has a universal health care system that provides for most health care services. The health care initiative began in 1957 with the introduction of the Hospital Insurance and Diagnostic Services Act, which provided comprehensive coverage for in-hospital care. Although health care is primarily within the jurisdiction of the provinces, this legislation required the federal government to pay the provincial costs of hospital insurance, laboratory, and other diagnostic services.

In 1966, the federal government introduced Medicare, a program that extended health coverage to include physicians' services outside hospitals. Canadian programs providing health care are expected to reflect five principles: The services must be administered by a public authority; all medically necessary services provided by hospitals and doctors must be insured; the services must be universal; insured services must be portable so people are covered when they move or travel within Canada; and services must be accessible and unimpeded by financial or other barriers.

The health care system has just come through a major review by the Commission on the Future of Health Care in Canada, which recommended that the federal government expand Medicare with an infusion of 15 billion dollars by 2005–2006; improve services to rural communities, diagnostic services, and services to aboriginal Canadians; help people who require expensive drugs; and start developing a national home care program.

Canada Pension Plan

The Canada Pension Plan was introduced in 1966 and provides a monthly retirement income for people who have contributed to the system through their place of employment. It also provides disability pensions, payments to surviving spouses, and a one-time death benefit. The pension is based on work-related contributions made by both the employee and the employer. Each party contributes a set percentage of income into the plan and receives benefits in relationship to his or her contributions up to a maximum level. Depending upon when a person retires and how old he or she is, the plan replaces about 25 percent of eligible earnings. The benefits of the program are fully indexed to the Consumer Price Index. To meet the increasing demands created by an aging population, the federal government has been increasing the percentage of income that must be contributed into the plan.

The Canada Assistance Plan/Health and Social Transfer

The Canada Assistance Plan (CAP), introduced in 1966, was meant to be the social safety net of last resort. The program replaced the conditional grants the federal government provided to the provinces to help them pay for social assistance programs. The new program helped pay half the costs of provincial and territorial government social assistance programs designed to support persons in need, single-parent families, and people who are unable to find employment, or who have disabilities. The program also provided for half the costs of a range of social services such as day care, in-home care, and family counseling to Canadians on low or modest incomes. This program was replaced in 1996 by the Canada Health and Social Transfer (CHST) program, which switched from a cost-sharing formula (50 percent each from the federal and provincial governments) to a block-funding process. The new CHST dramatically altered the relationship between the federal government and the provinces. Provincial governments now receive one block grant covering not only the social assistance and social services but also health care and post-secondary education program costs. This means that provinces are now in a position to alter their commitments in any of these three areas without federal government review. The CHST is provided through cash payments and tax transfers.

SUMMARY

The social welfare programs developed between the 1940s and the 1970s created the foundations of a comprehensive system for helping people deal with the risks created by economic and social change. It reflected a broadly shared set of beliefs about Canadians caring for Canadians. All the categories of social need and risk enumerated by the reports written in the 1940s were provided for in some way by federal, provincial, and intergovernmental social programs. These programs reflected the social consensus forged in the Great Depression and the Second World War and expressed the experiences and aspirations of many Canadians. The public expected that social policy measures would significantly reduce insecurity and poverty, solve social problems, and create economic stability. The welfare programs produced a safety net that protected most citizens from the ravages of changing economies. For many people, the development of social welfare created a sense of

what it is to be Canadian. In the last few years, many questions have been raised about the effectiveness of social welfare programs. Even as they have provided important protection against some of the risks present in our modern society, they have not solved the problems of poverty, and in many ways governments have altered the eligibility and benefits of the programs so that they no longer provide the safety net on which people have come to count. In the next few years, we can expect to see governments increase their commitment to social welfare programs. Although the system may be more selective than before, it is clear that there are people who will need to be supported because they cannot find employment in the existing market structure.

—*James J. Rice*

See also Federalism and Social Welfare Policy (Canada); The Marsh Report (Canada); Poverty (Canada); Social Security (Canada); Social Welfare (Canada): Before the Marsh Report; Welfare Capitalism (Canada); Women and Poverty (Canada); Women and Social Welfare (Canada)

Primary Sources

Canadian Association of Social Workers Fonds, 1922–1977; Canadian Welfare Council Records, 1918–1959; Department of National Health and Welfare Fonds, 1815–1993; Unemployment Insurance Commission Fonds, 1900–1982; Charlotte Elizabeth Whitton Fonds, 1850–1977; all in Library and Archives Canada, Ottawa, ON.

Current Comment

Adams, I. (1971). *The real poverty report.* Edmonton, AB: M. G. Hurtig.

Commission on the Future of Health Care in Canada. (2002). *Building on values: The future of health care in Canada* (Final Report to Canadians). Ottawa, ON: Author. Available: www.hc-sc.gc.ca/english/care/romanow/index1.html

Lalonde, M. (1973). *Working paper on Social Security in Canada* (2nd ed.). Ottawa, ON: Department of National Health and Welfare.

Marsh, L. C. (1975). *Report on Social Security for Canada.* Toronto, ON: University of Toronto Press. (Original work published 1943)

Further Reading

Armitage, A. (2003). *Social welfare in Canada* (4th ed.). Toronto, ON: Oxford University Press.

Graham, J. R., Swift, K., & Delaney, R. (2003). *Canadian social policy: An introduction* (2nd ed.). Toronto, ON: Prentice Hall.

Lightman, E. (2003). *Social policy in Canada.* Toronto, ON: Oxford University Press.

Rice, J. J., & Prince, M. J. (2000). *Changing politics of Canadian social policy.* Toronto, ON: University of Toronto Press.

SOCIAL WELFARE (MEXICO): BEFORE 1867

The role of the Catholic church (the only recognized religion in colonial Mexico) in the history of social welfare in Mexico dates prior to the conquest and the evangelization of indigenous societies. The papal bulls issued by Pope Alexander VI in 1493 and Pope Julius II in 1501 and 1508 gave the Spanish kings of Castile and Aragon control over the collection and distribution of ecclesiastical taxation, over the appointment and number of religious personnel, and over the creation of new dioceses, among other things. For all intents and purposes, the Catholic church became an extension of royal government and as such enjoyed a monopoly in providing for the spiritual, medical, and educational needs of the society. In short, religion and social welfare became inseparable during the colonial period.

FIRST CATHOLIC WELFARE INSTITUTIONS IN MEXICO

The first social welfare institutions established in Mexico were hospitals, and throughout the colonial period this activity became one of the most prominent of the Catholic church. The earliest medical facilities in Mexico appeared soon after the military conquest of Tenotchtitlán in 1521. The first hospital in Mexico, the Immaculate Conception, was established by the confraternity of Our Lady, whose most prominent member was the *Conquistador* Hernán Cortés. Because Immaculate Conception refused to treat those with contagious diseases, the Bishop of Mexico, Fray Juan de Zumárraga, established the Hospital of the Love of God (*Hospital del Amor de Dios*) between 1535 and 1540. The precipitous decline of an indigenous population decimated by war, slavery, and pandemics such as smallpox, measles, and typhus created a humanitarian crisis and in 1555 the first Mexican Council ordered that hospitals be established in every parish and mission church in Mexico.

The growth and spread of religious orders after the conquest, coupled with the rapid decline of the native population, created a large infrastructure that provided a wide variety of social services. Missionaries established medical and other social services to assist and convert the indigenous population. By 1574, more than 200 religious houses had been established in New Spain, as the territory that became Mexico was known. Many of these religious houses provided medical and economic assistance. Many convents provided medical care for the local population, accepted abandoned or orphaned girls, or *expuestas,* provided shelter for destitute or abused women, and operated schools for girls, many of which charged fees for education.

THE FINANCE AND OPERATION OF CATHOLIC WELFARE INSTITUTIONS IN MEXICO

The expense of establishing and operating institutions of social welfare was met from multiple sources, all tied to the Catholic church. Groups providing most funding and staffing of social welfare institutions in colonial Mexico were the regular and secular religious orders, pious foundations established by the laity, confraternities, and religious brotherhoods. Confraternities were one of the church's most socially active institutions. These lay organizations were major, if not the main, sources of funding for the many social welfare activities established in their communities. The obligations of confraternity membership included veneration of the confraternity's patron saint, upkeep of the patron saint's image, support of a school and/or hospital, provision of appropriate funeral arrangements for members, and, in the case of Spanish confraternities, providing dowries for orphaned Spanish women. The Franciscan and Augustinian religious orders were particularly active in the establishment of small hospitals in indigenous villages, mostly funded by indigenous *cofradias,* or confraternities, whose members also volunteered to take care of the ill. These facilities, or *hospitales de naturales,* catering to the indigenous population, were some of the first to blend New World and European medical traditions.

Less active but also significant were the activities of the third orders and *beatas. Beatas* and individuals belonging to third orders took less formal religious vows than priests and nuns and remained part of the laity. These groups were active in volunteering and supporting hospitals, orphanages, and asylums for the mentally ill. *Beatas* lived together in a *beatario or recogimiento* and provided shelter for women who were abused by their husbands and to unwed mothers, and ran schools for girls.

Wealthy Spaniards established many of the hospitals administered by the church. Following the Catholic belief that salvation is tied to actions and deeds, many devout Catholics sought to ingratiate themselves with the Lord by building churches or establishing hospitals and foundations. A prominent colonial philanthropist, Bernardino Alvarez, a Spaniard and a gambler who made a fortune in Peru, founded his first hospital in Mexico in 1566. Alvarez's pious works led to the founding of many hospitals, including one devoted to the care of convalescents. He created a religious order that ran 10 hospitals in New Spain. Other well-known philanthropists included the physician, Pedro López, who, in 1572, founded the *Hospital San Lazarus* for the care of lepers, and, in 1582, supported by the confraternity of Our Lady of the Forsaken, built the Hospital of the Epiphany for the care of Blacks, Mestizos, and mulattoes.

SERVICES PROVIDED BY CATHOLIC WELFARE INSTITUTIONS IN COLONIAL MEXICO

Hospitals offered a number of social welfare services in addition to caring for the sick. They served as temporary shelters for travelers and as poorhouses where the aged, blind, maimed, and poor were fed, sheltered, and given financial support. The most innovative effort to blend medical assistances with a larger social welfare project came from the future Archbishop of Michoacán, Vasco de Quiroga (1470–1565). In 1532, influenced by Thomas Moore's *Utopia*, Quiroga established on the outskirts of Mexico City and in western Mexico two experimental hospitals or hospital-*pueblos* both named *Santa Fe de los Altos*. Quiroga's hospital-*pueblos* included wings for contagious and noncontagious diseases, dispensaries, workshops, storehouses, tool banks, and a school where Natives would learn the Catholic catechism, reading, writing, and farming techniques. Quiroga's

hospital-*pueblo* model would influence religious missions established throughout Mexico's northern frontier, the present-day western United States. Besides founding and administering hospitals, the Catholic church spent much of its energies and resources on schools. Primary schools were an integral component of the missionary activity of the church because education and religious-moral instruction went hand in hand in colonial Mexico. The Franciscan, Jesuit, Augustinian, and Dominican religious orders were especially active in the formation of primary schools. Usually attached to a monastery or parish church, schools provided boys with daily mass, religious instruction, reading, writing, singing, and, if possible, lessons in playing musical instruments. Although the initial educational impetus was directed at the children of the native nobility, schools later were opened to boys of all social classes. Although schools for girls were established soon after the conquest, their numbers were much smaller than those for boys and education for girls was more limited. Originally started by Franciscans and other male orders, schools for girls soon became the responsibility of cloistered nuns and *beatas*. Enrolled girls were usually boarded and the education received was geared toward basic literacy, religious instruction, and household tasks.

Technical schools were also established by the church in colonial Mexico. Manual labor was seen as a way to combat idleness and vice while providing moral and economic uplift. Technical schools trained adults to be blacksmiths, masons, carpenters, sculptors, embroiderers, and ceramicists. The most famous technical schools were Quiroga's hospital-*pueblos*, but all the major religious orders established their own schools. The Franciscan technical schools in western Mexico were known for teaching students how to build furniture and chests. Religious orders often hired Spanish artisans to instruct students and used their labor in the building of churches.

Despite these efforts, hospitals, orphanages, asylums, and schools were always in short supply in colonial Mexico and the resources they commanded were never large. It was not uncommon that hospitals were in disrepair, with leaking roofs and shaky foundations, or lacking basic necessities, such as mattresses, food, and medicines. Some hospitals, especially those caring for lepers, allowed their patients to wander the streets begging for food. These conditions would worsen by the second half of the eighteenth century.

DECLINE OF CATHOLIC CHARITIES AND THE SECULARIZATION OF WELFARE

By the end of the eighteenth century, the Spanish Crown had expelled the Jesuits from the empire, taken steps to secularize parishes belonging to monastic orders, and passed laws curtailing fund-raising by the church. The Spanish monarchy, influenced by Enlightenment ideas, began to build a more secular welfare system that was removed from the administrative and financial control of the Catholic church. The trend toward the secularization of welfare increased after Mexican independence.

In 1833, 12 years after independence, the Mexican government attempted to secularize public education, until then an activity dominated by the Catholic church, by ordering curriculum changes for all parish schools, by ending state subsidies of church-run schools, and by establishing a public school system. Despite these changes, the Mexican government, politically unstable and financially bankrupt, was unable to invest the resources necessary to achieve its ambitious educational reforms. By 1849, it had established only two public schools in Mexico City. The Catholic church continued to exercise a dominant influence in the education of Mexicans, operating nearly 1,310 registered primary schools (a number the ministry of education calculated was three times the figure if unregistered schools were included).

In 1856 and 1861, legislation was enacted that deeply impacted the role of the church in providing welfare services. In 1856, the Mexican government passed the *Ley Lerdo,* a law for the disentailment of corporate property, ordering institutions such as the Catholic church to sell off all properties not directly related to supporting its essential religious functions. The *Ley Lerdo* eventually led to the forced sale or confiscation of income-producing properties belonging to the clergy, confraternities, pious foundations, and monastic orders that were one of the principal sources of funds for the church's welfare operations. The other major reform was a series of laws put forward by President Benito Juarez in 1861 that decreed the secularization of welfare institutions and created a central government administration that would fund and manage all welfare activities. These laws dealt a serious blow to Catholic charitable activities by making social welfare the responsibility of the state. Catholic welfare organizations experienced a rapid decline in the quality and quantity of services they provided as they lost funding from the Catholic church and Catholic philanthropists. Private donations to the Mexico City Poor House dropped 74 percent after the passing of the *Ley Lerdo.*

While the role of the Catholic church as a principal provider of charitable activities was being challenged by liberal legislation, the French occupation of Mexico and the arrival of Emporer Maximilian and Empress Charlotte of Mexico (1863–1867) led to a new model for Catholic welfare activities. In her efforts to rebuild a shattered welfare system, Empress Charlotte recruited upper-class Mexican women into the Association of Ladies of Charity, an organization devoted to funding, administering, and establishing welfare institutions. Independent of any government organization, centered around parish churches and under the guidance of the clergy, these independent voluntary organizations of upper-class women became the model the Catholic church would use to rebuild its social welfare institutions. By the end of the nineteenth century, Catholic lay organizations existed throughout the Mexican Republic, running schools, vocational training facilities, hospitals, and many other welfare institutions. Even though the Catholic church would never reach the overwhelming influence it exercised during the colonial period, it continued to offer important social welfare services. In the future, secular government agencies would slowly come to replace the Catholic church as the main provider of social welfare services.

—*Rodney R. Alvarez*

See also Medicine and Popular Healing Practices in Colonial Mexico; Mexico City Poor House

Primary Sources

Archivo de Templos y Conventos; Archivo del Clero Regular y Secular; Archivo de Obras Pias, Derechos Parroquiales, Cultos Religiosos e Iglesias; Archivo de Cofradias y Archicofradias; all housed in the *Archivo General de la Nacion,* Mexico City.

Current Comment

Aguayo Spencer, R. (Ed.). (1939). *Don Vasco de Quiroga: Documentos: Biografia de Juan Jose Moreno, Ordenanzas de los hospitals, testamento, informacion en derecho, juicio de residencia, litigio por la isla de Tultepec*. Mexico City: Editorial Polis.

Chauvet, F. de J. (Ed.). (1951) *Cartas de Fray, Pedro de Gante*. Mexico City: Fray Junipero Serra.

Mendieta, G. de. (1993). *Historia eclesiastica indiana: Obra escrita a fines del siglo XVI* (4th ed). Mexico City: Editorial Porrua.

Further Reading

Arrom, S. M. (2000). *Containing the poor: The Mexico City Poor House, 1774–1871*. Durham, NC: Duke University Press.

Dussel, E. (1984). *Historia de la iglesia en America Latina: Vol. 5. México*. Mexico City: Ediciones Paulistas.

Gutierrez Casillas, J. (1984). *Historia de la iglesia en México* (2nd ed.). Mexico City: Editorial Porrua.

Muriel, J. (1956). *Hospitales en la Nueva Espana*. Mexico City: Universidad Nacional Autónoma de México, Instituto de Investigaciones Historicas.

SOCIAL WELFARE (MEXICO): SINCE 1867

Until the middle of the nineteenth century, Mexico's economic performance and social conditions were comparable to those found in the United States. Yet, its social hierarchies and institutions portended a future of sharp contrasts between rich and poor that post-independence governments would approach with different ideologies and policy instruments. Rather than a continuous, slow and imperfect, yet progressive, accumulation of welfare entitlements for the population, the result has been a discontinuous historical process of alternating construction and destruction closely associated with the crucial processes and events that have marked the creation and evolution of Mexico's modern state.

The early postindependence period (1823–1867) left colonial institutions relatively untouched (yet steadily deteriorating). Liberals and conservatives fought continuously during this period. After 1867, the history of social welfare in Mexico can be divided into three broad periods distinguished by radically different attitudes toward inequality, poverty, and the state's responsibility to modify them. The first period witnessed the birth and development of a unified national state, and began with the liberals' final victory in 1867 in their conflict with the conservatives. The *república restaurada,* or restoration of the republic (1867–1876), and the era of the *Porfiriato,* or Díaz dictatorship (1876–1911), were periods dominated by the federal government's efforts to place the formerly warring states under federal authority, resulting in the destruction of some of the existing welfare institutions, coupled with some limited efforts to construct new ones. The second period, from 1910 to 1982, began with the Revolution against the Diaz dictatorship, won in 1911 by an alliance of peasants and liberal elites seeking to reestablish the 1857 Constitution. The winners asserted the state's responsibility for achieving greater social justice, establishing in the 1917 Constitution a blueprint for a welfare state. This period represents the ascending phase of Mexico's welfare state, and the only period during which poverty declined to some degree. During the third phase, from the 1982 debt moratorium to the Vicente Fox administration (2000–2006), the authoritarian paternalist state of the preceding period experienced gradual decay, coupled with a growing buildup of pressures toward democratization. The period culminated in 2000 with the defeat of the postrevolutionary ruling party, the Institutional Revolutionary party (*Partido Revolucionario Institucional,* or PRI), which corresponds to the descending phase of an as-yet incomplete welfare state in which welfare entitlements are in practice either restricted or ignored, and the state deals only with extreme poverty.

CREATING A STABLE CENTRAL STATE AND PURSUING PROGRESS (1867–1910)

Although the peace that reigned from 1876 to 1910 allowed for substantial economic and demographic growth, it did little to improve the fate of the poor rural masses, and in fact worsened it in many respects. A major step toward pauperizing Mexico's rural population was taken, for example, when the governments that followed the liberals' victory in 1867 sought to create a new class of individual farmers by either breaking up traditional collective farms (*ejidos*) into individual plots, or distributing land that was, in principle, untilled under the Law of Unused Land (*Ley de Terrenos Baldíos*). In practice, the land was often snatched away from its lawful owners. Throughout the *Porfiriato*, this policy would lead to the wholesale theft of free peasant land by the *haciendas*, or large rural estates.

Since the colonial period, education and health services had been the responsibility of municipalities, whose chief source of revenue were *alcabalas*, or internal tariffs. Based on this system, the number of public schools increased substantially from 1867 to 1876, and nonreligious elementary education was made mandatory. Yet *alcabalas* also made it possible for individual regional *caudillos*, or military dictators, to maintain independent military forces, and hence continue fighting among themselves and/or against the elected government, as they had throughout the previous 45 years. With the elimination of these tariffs during the *Porfiriato*, the federal government's central authority and stability were strengthened, but municipalities were left powerless to offer even basic education and health services. Additionally, the former Lancastrian system, in which older students tutored younger students, was declared obsolete, but little money was made available to hire teachers. Some new schools and a teacher training school (*Escuela Normal*) were created in Mexico City, initiating a trend that would leave the provinces increasingly worse off in virtually all public services. With increasing pauperization at the end of the *Porfiriato*, school attendance began to decline.

A similar trend was visible in public health: The capital, border, and port cities received most of the resources (the latter to reduce quarantine requirements on merchandise), leaving the states and municipalities unable to build hospitals or hire physicians. Necessary sanitary public works to provide drinkable water and sewage drainage were of little interest to foreign concessionaires, unlike the railroads. Even in Mexico City, where streets were periodically inundated, deep drainage was not excavated until the very end of the nineteenth century, with the help of foreign debt and a foreign engineering firm. As a result, the "city of palaces," as it was then called, was also the "city of typhus," in the words of historian Gonzalez Navarro. In the rest of the country, yellow fever, dengue, and malaria remained firmly established.

Nevertheless, choosing France as its model, Porfirian Mexico was keen to participate in the general scramble for scientific progress. As a result, large hospitals were built and old ones modernized in Mexico City, based on an elitist view of medicine as the exercise of science rather than service to the population. Under the watchful personal eye of the dictator Porfirio Díaz, hospitals recruited the elites in each particular field who then strove to achieve excellence to bring prestige to their country.

In the last decade of the *Porfiriato*, a strong anarcho-syndicalist movement headed by the Magon brothers (hence *Magonismo*) organized strikes to demand improvements in the dismal work conditions and low wages paid to workers. The response was pitiless repression (with some help from United States troops), but also reforms instituting insurance against work accidents in those northern states where the revolt had been strongest. This inaugurated the coupling of regression and concessions toward social protest that postrevolutionary government would also adopt.

THE DEVELOPMENTAL STATE: WELFARE AS AID TO INDUSTRIALIZATION

With the victory in 1911 of the constitutionalist camp over the by-then frail dictatorial regime, grand promises of social justice were made, including land reform, free and nonreligious education for all, social insurance, public housing, and profit sharing between industrial firms and their workers. Yet most of these benefits were to go to the growing industrial force, while the rural population (at the time over 75 percent of the population) would have to be content with more public education and land distribution (often carried out by unscrupulous state governors, who generously allotted themselves large tracts of land), and a few restricted social programs.

Until 1929, when the official party, the Institutional Revolutionary Party (*Partido Revolucionario Institucional*, or PRI) was founded, social welfare stood still in the context of nonexistent international credit and a rapidly devaluating currency. Most political attention focused on the succession to power among the members of the "revolutionary family." State governments therefore continued to do what little they had been able to do during the Porfiriato, with somewhat more resources from the federal government (mainly for education), upon which they had become totally dependent.

From 1929 on, however, a new dynamic for the construction of the welfare state was created, accelerating after World War II, as the country began to develop its industrial capacity, based on import substitution. The PRI's domination of national politics meant more control over the presidential succession. It also demonstrated the advantage of remaining loyal for key groups in society because of tangible benefits provided through the political system. The PRI regime became plebiscitary, responsive to the perceived majority will, and welfare benefits had become the carrot to induce discipline.

Limited social insurance for public servants was introduced in 1925. Teachers were subsequently included in the social insurance program, after they loudly protested their exclusion. In 1943, the Mexican Social Security Institute (*Instituto Mexicano del Seguro Social,* or IMSS) was created. IMSS covered private sector workers, but at first only in Mexico City. This was meant to bring back into the fold labor factions that had opposed the 1940 PRI presidential candidate, who had been declared elected despite overwhelming evidence that he had lost. The scheme adopted, after years of previous fruitless bargaining between the state, employers, and labor, included insurance for work accidents, widows and orphans, health and maternity, and pension benefits. Workers were already protected against unemployment, the government contended, since the 1932 Labor Code required employers to give dismissed workers 3 months' severance pay in addition to one month for each year of service. The code also required employers to grant women workers three months' wages for maternity leave. With the founding of the Social Security Institute for Government Workers (*Instituto de Seguridad y Servicios Sociales de los Trabajadores del Estado,* or ISSSTE) in 1959, a similar plan was created for public employees. Other separate plans for selected labor and public sectors followed, resulting in the fragmentation of social insurance among diverse interest groups.

Except for sugarcane cutters, who were granted social insurance in 1954, the agricultural population was never organized enough to make strong demands. The Health Ministry (*Secretaría de Salud*) instituted a much less adequate health plan to cover the uninsured population, with no accident or retirement benefits.

Yet, owing to the limited land reform that agricultural workers received early in the period, followed by much more sweeping land reform during the presidency of Lázaro Cárdenas (1934–1940), the rural population remained unfailingly loyal to the regime. A scheme of guaranteed agricultural prices was created for major crops, ostensibly to support living standards, but it was de facto used to maintain low food prices for the growing yet poorly paid urban proletariat. Under the weight of these inauspicious policies, the fast growing but increasingly impoverished rural population began to migrate toward large cities and the United States.

As Mexico's industrial and urban proletariat grew and more groups pushed for further reforms, new welfare benefits were created, for example, profit sharing in 1961 and workers' housing through the National Institute of Housing for Workers (*Instituto Nacional de Fondo de Vivienda Para los Trabajadores,* or INFONAVIT) in 1972. Excluded from such benefits were the rural population, as well as the growing pool of the urban poor who worked outside the formal economy and received a much poorer public housing scheme. Yet, the policy of subsidizing the prices of basic foods (tortillas, milk, rice, sugar) helped sustain living and health standards. In 1977, as new oil reserves were discovered, the López Portillo administration established the General Coordination of the National Plan for Depressed Zones and Marginal Groups (*Coordinación General del Plan Nacional de Zonas Deprimidas y Grupos Marginales,* or COPLAMAR), a large financial umbrella for social programs aimed at the "marginalized." COPLAMAR programs included food stores operated by the National Company of Popular Subsistence (*Compañía Nacional de Subsistencias Populares,* or CONASUPO), a state agricultural enterprise, health clinics, and rural hospitals operated by COPLAMAR in association with IMSS and *Sistema Nacional de Alimentos,* or SAM, a national nutrition program. With the combined impact of COPLAMAR programs, the growth rate of poverty began to slow down, becoming negative by 1980 (see Figure S.3). After 1982, the poverty rate would climb again as a result of macroeconomic policies that aimed at achieving financial stability and international competitiveness.

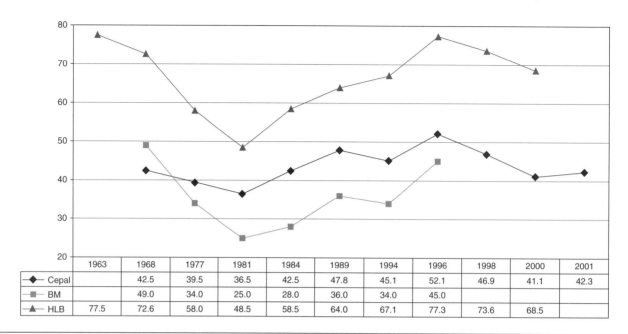

Figure S.3   *Percentage of Poor in Mexico, 1968–2003: Three Alternative Measurements*

CEPAL = Economic Commission for Latin America (Comisión Económico Para America Latina)

BM = World Bank (Banco Mundial)

HLB = Hernández-Laos, 1992, and/or Damián & Boltvinik, 2003

Sources: Damián, A., & Boltvinik, J. (2003). Evolución de la pobreza en México. *Comercio Exterior,* 53(6); Hernández-Laos, E. (1992). *Crecimiento económico y pobreza en México: Una agenda para la investigación.* Mexico City: Universidad Nacional Autónoma de México.

THE NEOLIBERAL STATE: WELFARE AS A SUBSIDIARY TO MARKET

The last period began with the financial debacle of 1982, triggered by a sudden decline in the international price of oil, the principal source of revenue for Mexico's welfare programs aimed at the poor. The decline in the price of oil forced Mexico to declare a debt moratorium, and it received its first international rescue package. Thereafter, welfare reforms resulted from agreements with international financial bodies to reduce public expenditures. Despite efforts to maintain some welfare safety nets and create new ones, the social consequences of the economic measures launched during this period included unprecedented income polarization and general pauperization of the bottom deciles of the income distribution.

Before 1982, pro-business policies (mainly high tariffs and low wages) had been tempered by measures aimed at sustaining minimum living standards. These counteracting measures, however, were gradually reduced to programs targeted first to the poor (from 1982 to 1994) and subsequently only to the extremely poor. Simultaneously, Mexico opened its borders to international competition, yet wage controls were left in place to attract foreign investment. The result was a precipitous fall in real wages, the growth of a non-wage (informal) economy, a rise in unemployment and underemployment, and a general lowering of living standards throughout the country. To counteract these tendencies, COPLAMAR continued from 1982 to 1988, despite fiscal constraints, and was renamed the National Solidarity Program (*Programa Nacional de Solidaridad,* or PRONASOL) in 1988. PRONASOL, which continued until 1994, spent a large proportion of its budget on nonpoverty-related infrastructure such as toll roads, bridges, water towers, and street paving despite its designation as an antipoverty program. In 1994, PRONASOL was renamed the Program for Education, Health and Nutrition (*Programa de Educación, Salud y Alimentación,* or PROGRESA) and was downsized to target only the extremely poor. With renewed economic growth from 1996 to 2000, the proportion of the poor began a slow descent, thereafter

Table S.1 Essential Health Services Package (PAB) Delivered by the Secretary of Health to the Uninsured Poor, 1994-2004

Interventions

- Family hygiene and waste disposal
- Family planning
- Prenatal care and birth delivery
- Nutritional and growth surveillance of children
- Immunization
- Home management of diarrhea
- Antiparasitic treatment for family unit
- Acute respiratory disease management
- Prevention and control of pulmonary tuberculosis
- Prevention and control of diabetes mellitus and high blood pressure
- Prevention of accidents and early management of injuries
- Community participation for self health care
- Prevention and control of cervical cancer

growing again after 2000 with the return of economic stagnation. During the Vicente Fox administration, PROGRESA became Opportunity (*Oportunidad*), which made few changes in programs for the poor.

COPLAMAR and its successors were new programs, and were therefore vulnerable to economic and political change. Social insurance and Health Ministry coverage, in contrast, were firmly entrenched. In 1996, however, the pension system switched from intergenerational redistribution to individual capitalization, and the minimum period of active labor force participation to qualify for benefits jumped from 9.6 to 24 years. This excluded a very large proportion of workers with only sporadic formal employment (especially women) from the pension system. Likewise, the Health Ministry reduced its services to the uninsured poor, nearly 50 percent of the population (see Table S.1). Both reforms were carried out in the context of increased tolerance of the violation by employers of the obligatory social insurance registration of their workforce, so that by the last decade of the century, over 60 percent of the economically active population had de facto no access to social insurance or other wage-related benefits.

With the defeat of the PRI in 2000, which ended the hegemonic party system, little change took place in the welfare system because it had been weakened by previous reformers. Economic stagnation and recession in the United States during the early 2000s

made matters worse. In addition, the National Action party (*Partido Acción Nacional,* or PAN), the victorious party of President Vicente Fox, was openly market oriented, although keen to reduce extreme poverty within the limits of social welfare policies. By the beginning of the twenty-first century, Mexico's comparatively late and incomplete welfare system had been partially dismantled, and no plan for its reconstruction had yet been envisaged, resulting in the exacerbation of ongoing social inequalities.

—*Viviane Brachet-Márquez*

See also Food Assistance Policy (Mexico); Labor Movement and Social Welfare (Mexico); Mother and Family Programs (Mexico); Philanthropy (Mexico); Poverty (Mexico); The Rockefeller Foundation and Public Health (Mexico); Social Reform and State-Building (Mexico); Social Security (Mexico); Welfare Capitalism (Mexico); Welfare Ministries in the Twentieth Century (Mexico)

Current Comment

Álvarez Amézquita, J., Bustamante, M. E., López Picazos, A., & Fernández del Castillo, F. (1960). *Historia de la salubridad y de la asistencia en México* (Vols. 1–4). Mexico City: Secretaría de Salubridad y Asistencia.

Cortés, F. (2000). *La distribución del ingreso en México en épocas de estabilización y reforma económica.* Mexico City: Centro de Investigaciones y Estudios Superiores en Antropología Social; Miguel Ángel Porrúa.

Further Reading

Aldrete Haas, J. A. (1991). *La desconstrucción del estado mexicano: Políticas de vivienda, 1917–1988.* Mexico City: Alianza Editorial.

Brachet-Márquez, V. (1994). *The dynamics of domination: State, class and social reform in Mexico, 1910–1990.* Pittsburgh, PA: Pittsburgh University Press.

Brachet-Márquez, V. (forthcoming). Mexico's welfare developmental state: Birth, growth and retrenchment, 1823–2003. In M. Riesco (Ed.), [Title to be determined]. New York: Palgrave Macmillan.

Brachet-Márquez, V., & Sherraden, M. S. (1994). Political change and the welfare state: The case of health and food policies in Mexico, 1970–1993. *World Development* 22(9): 1295–1312.

Cortés, F. (2000). *La distribución del ingreso en México en épocas de estabilización y reforma económica.* Mexico City: Centro de Investigaciones y Estudios Superiores en Antropología Social.

Fox, J. (1992). *The politics of food in Mexico: State, power and social mobilization.* Ithaca, NY: Cornell University Press.

Ochoa, E. C. (2000). *Feeding Mexico: The political uses of food since 1910.* Wilmington, DE: Scholarly Resources.

SOCIAL WELFARE (UNITED STATES): BEFORE THE SOCIAL SECURITY ACT

Several themes are important in the development of social welfare in the United States before the Social Security Act of 1935. First, the responsibility for the provision of social welfare services shifted from the local level—the town or county—to the state. (The Social Security Act would make the federal government, as well, an important actor in social welfare.) In addition, the purposes of social welfare programs shifted. At times, social welfare services were designed to relieve and control the poor. At other times, social welfare services compensated veterans who had contributed to the preservation, expansion, and development of the nation. During the late nineteenth century, the development of the rural West provided an important objective. By the Progressive Era, the prevention of social problems became an important objective.

Abundant land and its rapid development characterized North America from the time of the European invasions of the sixteenth and seventeenth centuries until the early twentieth century. Congress followed a social investment strategy during the nineteenth century, resulting in the rapid development of the West. The history of social welfare in the United States is, in part, a story of the transfer of the location and control of social welfare services from rural areas to metropolitan areas. The United States was an agricultural nation before the twentieth century, and most people lived in rural areas. During the nineteenth and early twentieth centuries, the nation grew as the result of land purchases, international agreements, and conquests. The use of steam technology, at first on boats plying rivers and canals and later on railroads, bound the growing nation together. The proportion of Americans living in urban areas increased steadily. State governments provided an increasing range of social services and funded and regulated many services delivered at the local level.

The financing and control of social services shifted as population shifted from rural to urban areas, in a process that some social scientists have called modernization. At the same time, the economic and communal development of rural areas was an objective of national policy during the nineteenth century. Development implied the transfer of assets to prospective settlers and investment by the state or federal government in education, transportation, and community development. Thus, asset-building and social investment to meet the needs of immigrant families, often to the detriment of indigenous populations, dominated American social policy before 1900.

COLONIAL PERIOD

Land policy in many of the British colonies in North America during the eighteenth century was liberal. The availability of land on easy terms made landowning feasible for ordinary people migrating from the British Isles and Europe. Thus, access to assets and asset accumulation explained much about the appeal of the Americas even before independence.

The British colonies in North America, however, faced chronic labor shortages. Attempts to enslave Native Americans were met with frustration, so colonial landowners were forced to look elsewhere for laborers to cut the trees, plant the crops, load the ships, and perform a variety of other jobs in the New World. As a result, colonial authorities turned to bound laborers, including African slaves, convicts and paupers from the streets of English cities, and indentured servants from the British Isles and the continent of Europe. Those indentured worked for a term of years to repay their passage from Europe to North America. Contracts for indentured service in the middle colonies often provided for land ownership at the conclusion of the period of service. The prospect of land ownership also provided a major incentive for these immigrants.

A locality's level of development affected its social welfare programs. The English Poor Law, affirmed by the colonial legislatures, made poor relief a local responsibility. Masters were responsible for providing care or discipline when slaves or indentured servants were involved. Otherwise, it was up to colonial towns and counties to devise programs for the poor, frail, and deviant, programs that were appropriate for their level of social and economic development. In many rural areas, poor relief arrangements were informal. Often, local authorities used households to deliver services by boarding the dependent poor. Eventually, poorhouses, jails, and in some cases schools and hospitals, operated by town or county governments, opened as commercial farming and towns succeeded subsistence farming. Local governments added these amenities to provide more efficient handling of the increasing numbers of poor that accompanied economic development.

EARLY NATIONAL PERIOD

After the American Revolution, Congress maintained a liberal land policy to promote settlement. A land-rich and cash-poor federal government used public land sales to finance a variety of public projects, subsumed under the summary appellation of "internal improvements." These included transportation—roads and canals and later railroads—and schools, including common schools and state universities. The Land Ordinance of 1785, which provided for surveying the public domain into 6-mile-square townships, reserved a one-square-mile section in each township for the support of the common schools. States admitted to the union after 1800 received grants of land to support state universities and other state services.

Espousing a Jeffersonian ideal that emphasized the superiority of the yeoman farmer and the benefits of the family farm, and facing pressures from western settlers and developers, Congress repeatedly liberalized land policies to make it easier for individuals to acquire and work the land. Although land sales provided a major revenue source for the federal government, the pressure for liberal terms for land ownership proved irresistible. Congress also provided free land for soldiers who fought in the Revolutionary War, the War of 1812, and the Mexican-American War. Because the benefit was often provided in scrip that could be exchanged for land, many veterans sold the scrip to speculators, who held the land for increased prices. These veterans' measures began a tradition of generous benefits for veterans that continued with pensions for Civil War veterans and twentieth century programs for veterans of World Wars I and II.

Towns and counties continued to provide basic social welfare services, support for the dependent poor, increasingly in small institutions such as almshouses and poor farms. But the campaigns of Dorthea Dix, a noted reformer, and others for expanded state services, usually institutional care for specific categories of poor people—the insane, the retarded, children, and criminals—increased the power and prominence of state government in the provision of social welfare services. Indeed, as social welfare provision became more specialized, more targeted upon persons with identifiable physical, emotional, or cognitive impairments, states began to expand their social welfare activities. Although county and town services continued to be important as a first line of defense for the "undifferentiated poor," some state leaders argued the superiority of state services as opposed to the backward, often patronage-ridden town or county services.

THE CIVIL WAR AND AFTER

A half century of agitation for a more liberal land policy culminated in the successful passage of four "western measures"—the Homestead Act, the Morrill Land Grant College Act, the Department of Agriculture Act, and the Pacific Railroad Act—by the first Civil War Congress in 1862. The four measures determined to an extent unforeseen in 1862 the subsequent development of the western United States. Between 1863 and 1912, the federal government distributed over 239 million acres of free land to homesteaders (although settlers claimed final title to only 150 million acres). In addition, the states received nearly 100 million acres in land grants for agricultural and mechanical colleges and railroad companies received nearly 350 million acres. The four western measures were the culmination of an increasingly liberal land policy and embodied a social investment approach to the development of the western United States. The federal government distributed assets in the form of land to settlers and invested in research, education, and a transportation infrastructure through direct appropriations and land grants to states and railroads. The four laws, as modified by subsequent legislation, were to provide the basic structure for the development of the western United States.

Also in 1862, Congress passed the Pension Act, providing pensions for disabled soldiers and the survivors of deceased soldiers. Initially designed as an aid to Union Army recruitment, Congress repeatedly liberalized the provisions of the pension system. By the early twentieth century, the American Civil War pension system rivaled European old-age pension programs in coverage and generosity. By 1910, more than one fourth of men over the age of 65 received Civil War pensions.

States began to centralize social welfare and correctional services during the late nineteenth century. Following Massachusetts' lead in 1863, many states created boards of charities and correction to organize state institutions on a businesslike basis. State social welfare provision expanded as state boards examined outcomes of institutionalization. Specialized mental health services, correctional services, and a variety of other institutional services were provided under state auspice, rather than by towns or counties. The view that services administered by state governments were believed to be less patronage-ridden and corrupt than local government services was even more widely accepted after the Civil War. The widely imitated New York State Care Act of 1890 gave the state responsibility for providing care to all of the insane poor. In some states, commissioners visited township and county institutions and recommended improvements in local programs. Wisconsin went further, mandating that counties provide care for chronically mentally ill residents in county institutions. In 1869, Congress created a Board of Indian Commissioners, similar to the state boards of charity, to oversee federal Indian programs.

THE PROGRESSIVE ERA

By the twentieth century, the United States had become an urban nation. Urban population, only a quarter of the total in 1880, increased to 40 percent in 1900 and to half of the population in 1920. Rural areas began to be seen as problem areas. In comparison to cities, rural areas had fewer specialized services and less economic opportunity. Following European precedent, in 1908 President Theodore Roosevelt organized a Country Life Commission, which celebrated rural life, but criticized farmers' excessive individualism. It called for the development of cooperative enterprises and focused attention on the problems of farm wives and the difficulty of keeping children on the farm. Toward the end of his term, Roosevelt called social workers and child welfare workers to Washington for the first White House Conference on Dependent Children, which met in

1909. Family life rather than institutional care for children should be supported, the conference attendees declared. The conference also called for the establishment of a federal Children's Bureau, which Congress created in 1912.

A major agenda of the Progressive Era was the expansion of state regulation and state social welfare services. Social workers campaigned for state social welfare measures, in particular for the children's codes, and expanded their scope to include mothers' pensions and juvenile courts as well as child labor restrictions and compulsory school attendance laws. Quite often, however, the reforms were limited to urban areas. For example, Missouri's Mothers' Pension Law, the first in the nation, applied only to St. Louis and Kansas City when it was enacted in 1911. (The Illinois law, however, enacted a few months later, applied to all sections of the state.) State social welfare legislation had the potential to influence rural areas by establishing standards for children and families, but often it was only a potential. Problems of funding, inadequate resources, and rural resistance frustrated reformers.

WORLD WAR, PROSPERITY, AND DEPRESSION

During World War I, the American Red Cross organized the Home Service, a national social service program. Red Cross workers attempted to link servicemen, many of whom were away from home for the first time, with their families on the home front. For the first time, social workers attempted to organize services in rural areas as well as in cities. The U.S. Children's Bureau, created to "investigate and report on all matters pertaining to the welfare of children," focused on investigations of infant mortality during the 1910s. The U.S. infant mortality rate, the bureau found, was higher than in any other industrial country. High rates of infant mortality prevailed in the rural South and in slum areas of big cities. In 1921, Congress passed the Sheppard-Towner Act, which provided federal funds to the states for health and welfare services. Although physicians who feared socialized medicine criticized the act, it proved to be popular with the states, which initiated new child health programs with the federal money.

Drought and agricultural depression in the 1920s accelerated the move to the cities that began during World War I. The war ended large-scale immigration from Europe. The buildup of wartime industry, however, created new demands for workers, resulting in increased internal migration from rural areas to the cities. Immigration legislation in 1924 severely limited immigration from eastern and southern Europe, creating new industrial employment opportunities for domestic migrants displaced by the agricultural depression or fleeing rural poverty. Rural states in the Great Plains lost population as homesteaders abandoned their claims and sought work in growing industries such as automobile manufacturing. African Americans and poor Whites left the South, moving to eastern and midwestern cities in search of opportunity.

For social welfare administrators, public welfare seemed to have come of age during the 1920s. All of the states adopted workmen's compensation programs. The Sheppard-Towner Act provided the first direct federal funding for state social welfare services and stimulated the development of such programs. The children's code movement succeeded in state after state, and state child welfare laws extended social services into the rural areas of even the most backward states. States from Alabama to Minnesota established county child welfare boards to enforce child labor and school attendance laws, to establish juvenile courts and juvenile probation services, and to provide support to dependent children. By 1935, all but two states had enacted mothers' pension laws and smaller numbers of states had pension programs for the blind and elderly poor.

The Great Depression of the 1930s, which resulted in business failures, drastic declines in stock prices, and high unemployment, threatened to stall the growth of welfare programs. Congress ended the controversial Sheppard-Towner program in 1929. Increasing need, however, led Congress to enact the Emergency Relief and Construction Act in 1932, authorizing the Herbert Hoover administration to loan funds to the states for unemployment relief. The new administration of Franklin Delano Roosevelt went further. Upon taking office, Roosevelt called for an emergency relief act, providing grants, not loans, to the states for unemployment relief. In response, Congress enacted the Federal Emergency Relief Act in 1933. A plethora of other relief acts followed. In 1935, a new era in social welfare began with the Social Security Act, which provided a federal old-age insurance program and federally assisted and regulated state programs of unemployment insurance, public assistance for dependent children, the aged, and the blind, and social services. Henceforth, it seemed that the federal government would be at the forefront of social welfare in the United States.

—Paul H. Stuart

See also Homestead Act (United States); Poor Law (Unites States); Poverty (United States); State Boards of Charities (United States)

Primary Sources

State archives are the place to study the development of social welfare provision in the states before and after 1935. The Social Welfare History Archives, University of Minnesota, Minneapolis, holds the records of the National Conference on Social Welfare, a meeting place for state officials involved in public welfare during the late nineteenth century. The Rockefeller Archives Center, Sleepy Hollow, NY, holds the records of a number of organizations involved in social welfare during the early twentieth century, notably the Commonwealth Fund, the Russell Sage Foundation, and various Rockefeller family charities. The *Proceedings* of the National Conference of Charities and Correction and its successor organizations (1874–1982; www.hti.umich.edu/n/ncosw/) provide a useful and accessible source of current comment on developments in social welfare.

Current Comment

Mink, G., & Solinger, R. (Eds.). (2003). *Welfare: A documentary history of U.S. policy and politics.* New York: New York University Press.

Further Reading

Katz, M. B. (1986). *In the shadow of the poorhouse: A social history of welfare in America.* New York: Basic Books.
Skocpol, T. (1992). *Protecting soldiers and mothers: The political origins of social policy in the United States.* Cambridge, MA: Harvard University Press.
Trattner, W. I. (1999). From poor law to welfare state: *A history of social welfare in America* (6th ed.). New York: Free Press.

SOCIAL WELFARE (UNITED STATES): SINCE THE SOCIAL SECURITY ACT

The history of social welfare since the 1935 Social Security Act divides into two distinct periods. The first period, from 1935 to 1968, expanded social welfare; the second, 1969 to the present, has contracted it. In each period, political and economic factors combined with powerful social movements to foster expansion or contraction.

EXPANSION: 1935–1968

The Great Depression of the 1930s spurred the expansion of the first era. In the wake of the 1929 stock market collapse, the unemployment rate reached 25 percent in 1933, and the economy shrank to half its former size. The magnitude of this crisis overwhelmed private charities and demonstrated the inadequacy of measures like the Federal Emergency Relief Administration, which, beginning in 1933, had distributed grants to the states. When the Democrats swamped the Republicans in the 1934 congressional elections, their victory closed the "first New Deal" and set the stage for more decisive action.

This decisive action crystallized in the form of an omnibus Social Security Act. Enacted in 1935, the Social Security Act incorporated social welfare provisions that social movements had long demanded. Its social insurance provision for the aged traced its origins to reformers like Isaac Rubinow of the American Association of Labor Legislation, who had long hoped that pensions granted to Civil War soldiers could be expanded into a form of universal social insurance, as well as to the popular Townsend movement of the early 1930s, which promised $200 a month to every person over 60. Likewise, the provision for Unemployment Insurance, which dated back to the Populist party platform of the late nineteenth century, responded to the formation of "unemployment councils" seeking to organize against the high levels of unemployment during the Great Depression. Finally, Aid to Dependent Children, the welfare legislation in the act, built on the small mothers' pensions programs that already existed in many states. It grew out of the support of some female reformers, in particular, for assistance to children whose mothers had lost a male breadwinner.

Although the Social Security Act created the foundation for the modern American welfare state, the strength of the "Solid South" within the Democratic party severely limited its scope and progressivism. With southerners occupying the chairmanships of many key congressional committees, the legislation bowed to states' rights. Its retirement program barred domestic and agricultural laborers—African American maids and plantation workers in the South. To ensure that welfare payments did not rise above their low wages, the states set minimal need and benefits levels for public assistance and got considerable latitude to design the eligibility requirements for their own unemployment programs. Social Security also excluded health insurance and funded the retirement program out of a tax on payroll rather than a progressive tax on all income. Most important, however, the legislation handed future generations of reformers a two-track legacy. One track drew on an earned benefit to offer a social insurance program that, over time, would expand to include unstigmatized and nearly universal coverage. The other track, public assistance, gave stigmatized aid to the "unworthy poor"—women and children who, either alone or through their husbands, had insufficient contact with the labor market. Into the early twenty-first century, public assistance, and the food, housing, and health care programs with which it was associated, would prove much more vulnerable to retrenchment.

Other New Deal social welfare legislation accompanied the Social Security Act. Work relief programs like the Civilian Conservation Corps and the Work Projects Administration stimulated the economy by hiring the unemployed to prevent soil erosion, construct public facilities, and initiate cultural projects like collecting oral histories from former slaves. In 1937, the Franklin D. Roosevelt administration also enacted the first housing law that provided federal funds for housing projects. As with so much other New Deal legislation, however, this act deferred to private interests by insisting on the destruction of one unit of housing for every new unit that was built.

Yet, despite these social welfare measures and the first deliberate deficit spending to stimulate the economy, the Depression lingered on. After declining to 14 percent in 1935, unemployment climbed again to 18 percent in 1937. It only declined after that with the preparations for World War II. The war brought the unemployment rate down to one percent by 1944.

In addition to reducing unemployment, World War II also subtly altered gender and race relations. Gender relations were altered because with so many men in the military, a shortage of male workers obligated Congress to reconsider its opposition to the provision of day care. The result was the Lanham Act of 1941 that enabled thousands of 'Rosie the Riveters' to get jobs in factories. Although Congress ended its funding immediately after the war, the act demonstrated the potential of comprehensive day care and firmly implanted an image of female resourcefulness and independence in the public's mind.

The war also created the preconditions for powerful changes in race relations. The mechanization of southern agriculture had already sparked the great migration northward. As the system of tenant farming declined, and White southerners needed fewer Blacks on the plantations, African Americans headed toward the cities of the industrial North, where, despite persistent racial discrimination, they could work and vote. Although a segregated military lasted throughout World War II, it proved harder to maintain in the face of these conditions and the dedication of African American soldiers As a result, President Harry Truman desegregated the military in 1948, and the Supreme Court desegregated the schools 6 years later.

The victory of the United States in World War II precipitated a great debate about the continuation of New Deal social policies. Uneasy in the knowledge that only rearmament had ended the Great Depression, many progressives worried that demobilization of the military would return the unemployment rate to depression levels. This concern led them to push for passage of the Full Employment Act of 1946, which would have created an employment planning mechanism within the federal government. When conservatives and the business community mobilized successfully to prevent such an expansion of the federal government's economic role, the act lost its enforcement powers, and post–World War II social welfare policy followed a different trajectory. Now, instead of significant new policy initiatives, social welfare moved slowly forward under the banner of cold war liberalism.

The rise of McCarthyism and the arms race with the Soviet Union dictated the pace of social welfare reform. Although Senator Joseph McCarthy, a Republican from Wisconsin, began his political ascendancy by focusing on "communists" in the State Department, scrutiny soon spread throughout American society to anyone who advocated significant social reforms. With the arms race siphoning off money for domestic needs, policymakers had neither the inclination nor the resources to address many pressing domestic issues. The federal government did fund hospital construction under the Hill-Burton Act of 1946, urban renewal and suburban development through the Housing Reform Act of 1949, and disability insurance through an expanded Social Security Act in 1956. For the most part, however, social welfare policy in the immediate postwar era lacked the boldness that marked the height of the New Deal.

Over time, however, this timidity gave rise to restlessness. Borne first of a concern for civil rights, this restlessness soon extended to include issues of poverty, housing, and urban decay. With the civil rights movement gaining momentum through the Reverend Martin Luther King, Jr.'s successful 1956 campaign to boycott the segregated Montgomery, Alabama, bus system, the Senate under the leadership of Democratic Majority Leader Lyndon Johnson passed the first civil rights bill since Reconstruction (1957). The bill quickened the pace at which African Americans shifted their allegiance from the Republicans—the party of Abraham Lincoln—to Democrats like 1960 presidential candidate John F. Kennedy, who saw the potential for a majority electoral bloc in the cities of northeastern states, with their new concentration of African Americans.

Despite Kennedy's reputation for dynamism, he adopted a cautious approach to civil rights and most other social welfare issues. Pressed by trade unions concerned about the effects of automation, he signed the 1962 Manpower Development Act, the first real job training initiative since the New Deal. In the same year, Kennedy also pushed for an amendment to the Social Security Act that expanded the federal government's authority to reimburse the states for social services. Although he admired books like Michael Harrington's *The Other America* (1962), his concern for Appalachian poverty did not find a legislative focus. Under mounting pressure from liberals outraged by violent resistance to the integration of the University of Mississippi and the Freedom Riders who were seeking to integrate the interstate bus system, he did not acquiesce to the need for an omnibus civil rights bill until after Martin Luther King's "I Have A Dream" speech at the Lincoln Memorial in August 1963.

Yet it was only his assassination 3 months later that paved the way for the passage of the bill. In a legislative wave unmatched since the New Deal, a spate of other social welfare measures soon followed. This Great Society legislation included the Voting Rights Act of 1965, the Older Americans Act of 1965, Medicaid and Medicare (1965), as well as a number of programs launched under the auspices of the Office of Economic Opportunity as part of the War on Poverty. Coming after the urban riots of the mid-1960s, these community action programs—the Neighborhood Youth Corps, Head Start, and VISTA (Volunteers in Service to America, the domestic peace corps)—have always been controversial. Conservatives contend that they unfairly benefited racial minorities and demonstrate the clumsiness of government intervention. Liberals respond that such judgments are premature, because, with the exception of Head Start, most of the antipoverty programs were severely underfunded and did not last very long.

RETRENCHMENT: 1969 TO THE PRESENT

In fact, these programs did not last very long because their targeting of racial minorities quickly produced a racial backlash. Defining this group of Whites as the "silent majority," Richard M. Nixon won a narrow plurality in the 1968 presidential election. Although his administration continued to expand social welfare, the Nixon presidency marked the end of the New Deal. To be sure, he proposed a Family Assistance Plan, which, while it failed to pass Congress, was the closest the United States has ever come to a guaranteed income; consolidated the states' programs for aged, blind, and disabled into Supplemental Security Income (SSI, 1972); increased Social Security by 20 percent and indexed it to inflation (1973); and enacted the Comprehensive Employment Training Act (1973), the largest job training program since the Great Depression. By centralizing power within the federal government, however, he put the brakes on

the diffusion of social welfare. For the next three decades, justifications of social welfare would depend on their use for conservative ends.

Beset by high unemployment, rising inflation, and mounting competition in the global economy, the American electorate was increasingly receptive to this conservative critique. At its core, this critique insisted that the Great Society's reckless expansion of social welfare created dependency among the poor and interfered with the private sector's natural productivity. From this perspective, policymakers should either contract social welfare or emphasize work programs and make it more marketlike.

Social welfare retrenchment began in earnest during the administration of President Jimmy Carter, who cut housing subsidies and restrained spending. When Carter's cutbacks angered liberal Democrats, without addressing the concerns of the Republican party's conservative wing, Ronald Reagan, the governor of California and a true tribune of the conservative movement, swept into power. Defining government social programs as the problem rather than a solution, Reagan slashed social services, cut the housing budget by three-quarters, tightened work requirements for welfare recipients, and pushed nearly a half million people off the disability rolls. Moreover, as federal spending shifted into the military and an arms race with the Soviet Union, the skyrocketing budget deficit further lowered the ceiling on domestic spending and made it harder to propose new social policy initiatives.

By the end of the Reagan administration, the conservative critique of social welfare pervaded the public's consciousness. Social welfare was, by definition, for other people—the poor, persons of color, and women who refused to stop having babies. Such a definition underlay further cutbacks like the first major welfare reform, the Family Support Act of 1988, which, in exchange for one year of transitional day care and health coverage, demanded that any mother with a child more than 3 years old find work or register in a work training program.

President George H. W. Bush's focus on international affairs created a domestic policy vacuum that Bill Clinton (1993–2001), the first Democratic president in 12 years, rushed to fill. Against the opposition of Republicans wary of any federal intervention in the job market, the Clinton administration did pass a law providing for unpaid family medical leave. But otherwise, Clinton's policy model relied on the private sector to effect most of his social reforms. Conservatives succeeded in blocking his 1993–1994 health care initiatives, because no existing social movement pushed for a proposal in which the government would only supplement the health care funded by a rationalized health insurance industry. Likewise, after campaigning for an "end to welfare as we know it," Clinton yielded in 1996 to the Personal Responsibility and Work Opportunity Reconciliation Act, a more conservative bill that lacked the social supports the administration desired, but ended the entitlement to public assistance, limited its lifetime receipt to 5 years, and required most welfare recipients to get a job within 2 years. In employment training, too, Congress enacted and Clinton signed the 1998 Workforce Investment Act, which defined clients as "customers" and demanded "work first" before offering services. Although these efforts to harness the private sector for the goal of policy reform did make social welfare more marketlike, some policy analysts criticized them as disguised retrenchments—a market solution for poor people who had already lost out in a market economy.

Elected on the promise of compassionate conservatism, President George W. Bush has combined proposals for a market-based approach with a renewed emphasis on direct cutbacks in social welfare spending. His proposals for direct cutbacks include extending the workfare requirements from 30 to 40 hours a week and tightening eligibility for public housing. But he also proposed privatization of Social Security and the provision of a drug prescription benefit on the condition that the elderly leave Medicare for a private insurance plan. Enactment of these proposals would further dramatize the difference between the New Deal and the Great Society's expansion of social welfare and the contraction that has occurred under the increasingly conservative policies that have dominated for the last three decades.

—Joel Blau

See also Aid to Dependent Children/Aid to Families With Dependent Children (United States); Poverty (United States); Social Security (United States); Supplemental Security Income (United States)

Primary Sources

The Papers of Franklin Delano Roosevelt, Franklin D. Roosevelt Presidential Library, Hyde Park, NY; the Papers of Lyndon Baines Johnson, Lyndon Baines Johnson Presidential Library, Austin, TX.

Current Comment

Harrington, M. (1962). *The other America.* New York: Macmillan.

Further Reading

Abramovitz, M. (1996). *Regulating the lives of women* (2nd ed.). Boston: South End Press.
Katz, M. B. (2001). *The price of citizenship.* New York: Metropolitan Books.
Noble, C. (1997). *Welfare as we knew it.* New York: Oxford University Press.

SOCIAL WORK PROFESSION (CANADA)

The history of social work in Canada spans more than a century. With its roots in private charity, and influenced by developments in Great Britain and the United States, it evolved into an indigenous profession in 1926, guided by the Canadian Association of Social Workers. Schools of social work, which began as early as 1914 in Canada, continued to grow to meet the increasing demand for professionally educated social workers following the Great Depression of the 1930s. Throughout the century, the number of social workers has grown significantly and the profession has evolved in response to economic, social, and political changes in society, a trend that continues to the present day.

EARLY ROOTS IN PRIVATE CHARITIES

The social work profession in Canada has its roots in the social dislocation and extreme poverty that resulted from industrial capitalist development in the second half of the nineteenth century. Strongly influenced by developments in England and the United States, Canada responded to these social problems with a voluntary system of relief for the deserving poor provided by churches, benevolent societies, and private charities.

As poverty persisted and demands for financial assistance increased, the charities began to coordinate their services. Modeled after the charity organisation societies in England, the Associated Charities appeared in Canada in 1881 with their attendant "friendly visitors." Based on the longstanding view that poverty resulted from personal failings, friendly visitors saw themselves as role models that the deserving poor were expected to emulate if they were serious about alleviating their poverty.

The settlement movement provided important training opportunities for the incipient social work profession. Originating with Toynbee Hall in London's East End, the settlements were based on the notion that rich and poor should coexist in one community. Settlement workers, often motivated by Christian values, lived among the urban poor and promoted improved conditions of work and housing as well as access to recreation. Jane Addams was the founding member of Hull House in Chicago (1889), and it was here that J. J. Kelso (one of Canada's foremost child welfare advocates of the 1890s) and William Lyon Mackenzie King (future prime minister of Canada in the 1920s, 1930s, and 1940s) were first introduced to problems of the poor. In Canada, two important settlement houses were affiliated, from the outset, with universities (Women's University Settlement at McGill University in Montreal in 1891 and University Settlement at the University of Toronto in 1910), providing opportunities to work with the poor as part of students' education.

At the turn of the century, a shift occurred away from private charity toward more public support. This was accompanied by a trend replacing untrained charity workers with social workers who were prepared to approach social problems rationally and scientifically. Many of Canada's first salaried social workers received their education in the United States, belonged to American professional associations, and attended the National Conference of Charities and Correction.

In the history of social work in Canada, there are clear distinctions in the roles of women and men. For the most part, women were educated in social work and played primary roles in social work practice and service delivery. Men, often trained as economists or political scientists, secured leadership positions in universities, were employed as government consultants, and were more prominent than women in developing social policy positions related to social work and social welfare. The contributions of numerous female social work pioneers have yet to be acknowledged fully, although local histories are beginning to recognize their work. Joy Maines, for example, was executive director of the Canadian Association of Social Workers for most of its developmental years and had a profound impact on the direction of the new profession. Laura Holland also made significant contributions to the development of child and social services in Toronto, Ontario; Vancouver, British Columbia; and Edmonton, Alberta in the 1930s.

EDUCATION

In the first decades of the twentieth century, increased demand for educated social workers in Canada led to the development of university-based social work programs. The first one was established at the University of Toronto in 1914, followed by McGill University in 1918. In 1928, the University of British Columbia offered social work education for students in western Canada and, in 1939, a bilingual program was started at the Université de Montréal. The Maritime School of Social Work (Halifax, Nova Scotia) was established in 1941 and, in 1943, schools were developed at Université Laval in Montreal, Quebec, and the University of Manitoba in Winnipeg.

A combination of influences from Great Britain and the United States gave a distinctive character to Canadian social work education. It was strongly influenced by the casework approach popularized by Mary Richmond, a leader in social work in the United States. Moreover, the Council on Social Work Education (United States) accredited Canadian schools of social work until 1970; the Canadian Association of Schools of Social Work now accredits Canadian schools. The English influence came largely through prominent social work educators such as John Howard Toynbee Falk, head of McGill University's School for Social Workers (1918–1924). Born in England, Falk was the nephew of Arnold Toynbee, a social reformer at Oxford University and for whom the first university settlement was named. Similarly, Edward J. Urwick, director at the University of Toronto School of Social Work (1927–1937), was born in England and had worked in Toynbee Hall and Oxford House. Dorothy King, the influential director of the Montreal School of Social Work (1933–1950) was also born in England.

In 1945, representatives of the Canadian schools of social work established the National Committee of Canadian Schools of Social Work to address severe shortages of social workers brought on by the depression of the 1930s. The committee's plan to solicit federal financing for social work education materialized when, in 1947, the federal Department of National Health and Welfare made its first financial contribution. Over the next decades, several new social work programs developed across Canada with a current total of 34.

CANADIAN ASSOCIATION OF SOCIAL WORKERS FORMED

By the close of the nineteenth century, salaried social workers were replacing volunteer friendly visitors and by the end of World War I they began to identify themselves as professionals with specialized skills. Opportunities for social workers increased following the war. Canada suffered staggering casualties in World War I, and a new appreciation for life, and particularly for children, materialized. Child welfare work was given high priority, providing new opportunities for social workers.

The demand for skilled social workers continued to grow and after a few years of debating the need for an indigenous organization, the Canadian Association of Social Workers (CASW) was established in 1926. It began with branches in Toronto and Montreal followed by British Columbia; Hamilton, Ontario; and Manitoba. Among other functions, the CASW was involved with setting professional standards, recruiting members, brokering social work positions, and promoting adequate professional training. In 1928, the annual Canadian Conference on Social Work was formed and in 1932 the CASW established a journal, *The Social Worker.*

Throughout its development, the CASW was plagued with issues of unity and cohesiveness. Vast distances, a sparse population, limited resources, and provincial/regional differences presented challenges

to the nascent association. As membership increased, the branches were replaced with semiautonomous provincial/territorial associations directly affiliated with the national organization.

The Great Depression brought unprecedented levels of unemployment and poverty and a more critical examination of their root causes. The League for Social Reconstruction (LSR) and the Cooperative Commonwealth Federation (CCF) were two organizations formed in 1932 that adopted radical critiques of capitalism. The LSR, headed by social reformers and social work educators Leonard Marsh (author of the 1943 *Report on Social Security for Canada*) and Harry Cassidy (author of *Social Security and Reconstruction in Canada*, 1943), focused on research and education. The CCF (forerunner to the New Democratic party) was formed as an alternative political party. Its first president was J. S. Woodsworth, social gospeller and former superintendent of the All People's Mission in Winnipeg.

A number of female practitioners with Marxist orientations played central roles in the profession following the Great Depression. Women, including Mary Jennison, Dora Wilensky, Margaret Gould, Hazel Wigdor, and Bessie Touzel, infused the profession with an explicitly socialist and action-oriented perspective. Based mainly in frontline community organizing, this group of women not only spoke out but also acted on their convictions and regularly challenged government and the profession to adopt more Left-leaning positions. Some of these women lost jobs or were driven underground for their political views and actions, particularly during the cold war era. In the late 1930s and into the next several decades, the CASW began to contribute actively to government policy development on various topics related to social welfare. In 1938, it presented its first brief to the Royal Commission on Dominion-Provincial Relations (the Rowell-Sirois Commission), followed by several others on topics that included unemployment insurance, postwar reconstruction, Social Security, Indian affairs, health, taxation, old age security, the death penalty, the Canada Pension Plan, revisions to the criminal code, housing, abortion, young offenders, and the nonmedical use of drugs.

World War II followed closely on the heels of the depression, placing new and expanded demands on social workers during and after the war. Following the war, Canada entered into the construction of a welfare state with a range of government programs and services designed for the collective well-being of Canadians. Social workers increasingly entered into government jobs that were developed as a result of the state's expanded role in Social Security. Since the late 1970s, however, there has been a decline in state funding for social programs and services and fewer social workers are employed in these sectors of the economy.

Since its inception, the social work profession has grown significantly. There are an estimated 37,470 social workers in Canada with over 15,000 active members of the CASW. There are 10 provincial associations and one representing the three northern territories. Canadian social workers are also members of the International Council of Social Work (formed in 1928) and the International Association of Schools of Social Work (formed in 1929).

—Therese Jennissen and Colleen Lundy

See also Canadian Association of Social Workers; Small Systems Social Work (Canada)

Primary Sources

Records of the Canadian Association of Social Workers (MG 28 I441), Library and Archives Canada, Ottawa, ON; Records of the Montreal Council of Social Agencies (MG 2076); Records of the School of Social Work (Record Group 66), McGill University Archives, Montreal, QC; Social Welfare History Archives, University of Minnesota, Minneapolis; Records of the Faculty of Social Work (A85-0002); Papers of Harry Morris Cassidy (B72-0022), University of Toronto Archives, Toronto, ON.

Current Comment

Canadian Association of Schools of Social Work. (2001). *In critical demand: Social work in Canada, final report.* Ottawa, ON: Author.
Cassidy, H. (1932). *Unemployment and relief in Ontario, 1929–1932.* Toronto, ON.
Irving, A., Parsons, H., & Bellamy, D. (Eds.). (1995). *Neighbours: Three social settlements in downtown Toronto.* Toronto, ON: Canadian Scholars' Press.
Maines, J. (1953). Through the years. *The Social Worker, 22*(2), 3–10.

Further Reading

Burke, S. Z. (1996). *Seeking the highest good: Social services and gender at the University of Toronto, 1888–1937.* Toronto, ON: University of Toronto Press.
Hill, K. (1984). *Oral history of social work in Canada.* Ottawa, ON: Canadian Association of Social Workers.
Pitsula, J. (1979, Spring). The emergence of social work in Toronto. *Journal of Canadian Studies, 14*(1), 35–42.
Wills, G. (1995). *A marriage of convenience: Business and social work in Toronto, 1918–1957.* Toronto, ON: University of Toronto Press.

SOCIAL WORK PROFESSION (MEXICO)

Social work is a profession created and defined within the modern image of the world; therefore, its purposes and goals have been strongly linked to resolving the interests and disputes of the prevailing social and economic system. Historically, social work has been a social discipline that legitimates the capitalist state, that is interested in addressing the social needs and problems of the population, in particular of those most affected by poverty, inequity, and marginal conditions. In the case of Mexico, this professional activity has gone through several stages.

THE EMERGENCE OF SOCIAL WORK IN MEXICO, 1920–1930

In Mexico, the roots of social work can be traced to the social practices enforced by the post-revolutionary governments that emerged from the Mexican Revolution. To strengthen the new revolutionary state, these governments implemented several kinds of social programs to instill the values and behavior needed to rebuild the country. These activities were not developed from a professional plan but from a naive framework of good will, mainly carried out through public institutions and primarily in fieldwork done directly in the places where the population lived, long before the official recognition of social work as a profession or career. In this context, the focus of this incipient social function was stimulating education, health, and charity tasks, such as the work done by the newly created Secretariat of Public Education (*Secretaría de Educación Pública*, 1923), known as *misiones culturales* (cultural missions), whose main effort was to train rural teachers to develop communitarian jobs.

These missions traveled throughout the country and were composed of a physician, a farming expert, a teacher, and a household promoter. The household promoter was dedicated to disseminating information on hygiene, domestic economy, and family relationships. In 1923, the secretariat sent some of its personnel to the University of Chicago in the United States to study social work. These Chicago-educated social workers immediately influenced the training of nurses, doctors, and lawyers. This was an important precursor to the foundation of the first school of social work in Mexico.

INSTITUTIONALIZATION OF SOCIAL WORK IN MEXICO, 1930–1970

Social work emerged in 1933 as a technical career, with the creation of the School of Domestic Instruction and Social Work (*Escuela de Enseñanza Doméstica y Trabajo Social*) of the *Secretaría de Educación Pública*. Since the creation of this institution, its study plan has been updated and it remains an important school of technical education for social workers. Social work was introduced as a university-based discipline in 1940 and developed into a bachelor's degree at the *Universidad Nacional Autónoma de México* in 1969, and at other institutions throughout Mexico.

During this period, different theoretical assumptions and approaches that sometimes merged and mixed concepts and categories without much thought nurtured the academic preparation of social workers. Before 1950, the education of social workers was centered on the case method, and occasionally on the group method. Social work education also stressed the development of a basic understanding of law, medicine, and psychology. Because of this eclectic training, social work was considered to be an auxiliary activity of other professions (especially medicine and law) that was practiced primarily in health and welfare institutions.

During the 1950s and 1960s, professional education for social work was modified. As the result of the development model promoted by the United States, and through various development programs culminating in the Alliance for Progress program, the social communitarian work method became important in education for social work. This method, based in a positivist philosophy of reality, sought to develop an outlook that sees human evolution as a natural and harmonious process such that any manifestation of disagreement or human despair was assumed to be due to a lack of social adjustment. In time, this approach gave social work a social adaptive and adjustment role; and the social worker was considered to be a technical, practical, and eclectic professional.

THE RECONCEPTUALIZATION OF MEXICAN SOCIAL WORK, 1970–1980

From the late 1960s to the early 1970s, in a Latin American context of increasing underdevelopment and economic dependency manifested by increased poverty and inequality, many social work professionals seriously questioned the traditional paradigms, theories, and methodologies of social work from a dialectical materialist perspective. A movement called *reconcepción* became important to these social workers. This movement is certainly the most important Latin American trend and the one that has had more repercussions in social work than any other. In Mexico, this trend influenced social work during the 1970s with its emphasis on academic training of qualified professionals able to do research and analysis of social problems as well as to be agents of social change.

In this period, many social workers abandoned the case method of social work and adopted knowledge theory as a research method. Consequently, social work became a social science discipline oriented toward promoting community organization and participation in social transformations, to contribute to the integral development of different population segments, based on a critical perspective of the communitarian development methodology.

There is no doubt that the *reconcepción* process contributed to the social work profession's improvement, mainly because the traditional social work approaches, the case and group methods and the social adjustment approach, were outdated. *Reconcepción* resulted in a more scientific and engaged professional approach. Nevertheless, new social workers discovered that there were gaps between academic training and the demands of the social institutions that employed them. The gap between academic preparation and professional practice frustrated many social workers and hindered their progress in welfare institutions.

NEW PARADIGMS OF SOCIAL WORK, 1980–2000

After the advances and setbacks sparked by the reconceptualization of the previous period, social work was suddenly immersed in a sui generis situation. In the working environment, social workers who had been educated under the traditional approach continued performing traditional practices in health, penitentiary, and social assistance, which was to maintain roughly the same conditions. The new generation of social workers moved into the labor market with the distinctive reconceptualization influence and looked forward to broadening their perspectives in the traditional institutions. At the same time, they were opening new practice settings, such as private and civil institutions, and nongovernmental organizations.

Social workers began to develop other professional activities, such as conducting social research, making communitarian diagnoses, generating strategies to solve social problems, promoting the community's participation in the solution of social problems, preparing and developing social programs and projects, working with the vulnerable groups of the society, and advising in the political decision-making process, among other activities.

In Mexico, social work education includes technical training institutes and institutions offering bachelor's degrees. The *Escuela Nacional de Trabajo Social* of the *Universidad Nacional Autónoma de México* (UNAM) initiated postgraduate education in 1987 and the University of Monterrey soon followed. Some universities are expanding their study options to the master's and doctoral levels.

The 1990s were characterized by profound social transformations: In November of 1989, the Berlin Wall was demolished, in 1990 Germany was reunified, and after 1991 the USSR disintegrated, generating a major paradigmatic crisis in the social sciences that facilitated the transition toward the hegemony of neoliberal capitalist thought. The welfare state did not disappear, but it was weakened and its scope was restricted. This situation once again modified the professional practice of social workers, primarily because the institutions that promote social well-being were precisely the ones that were increasingly abandoned and had fewer opportunities to hire new social workers. Today, both schools and universities are in the process of redefining their curricula and once again the case approach and the family participation approach have been revived in academic training.

SOCIAL WORK IN THE TWENTY-FIRST CENTURY

At the beginning of the twenty-first century, social work in Mexico was quite diverse, influenced by developments in its geographical region, Latin America, by academic institutions, and by the current methodology. Social work practice differs in Mexico's different geographic regions. The North is the economically wealthier region of the country and is influenced by North American social work. Its problems and programs differ from those implemented in other parts of Mexico. The poorest and most unprotected population is found in the South. Problems in this region are related to underdevelopment and to widespread poverty. A more "balanced" situation prevails in the middle region. Even though social workers today have a broader intervention methodology, as a group, social workers have not yet achieved the social impact that other professions have.

—*Graciela Casa Torres, Teresa Zamora Díaz de León, Eli Evangelista Martínez*

See also Philanthropy (Mexico); Social Reform and State-Building (Mexico)

Current Comment

Tello Peon, N. (1996, July–September). El Trabajo Social Contemporáneo. *Revista de Trabajo Social ENTS-UNAM, 14,* 15–22.

Tello Peon, N. (Ed., Comp.). (2000). *Trabajo social en algunos países: Aportes para su comprensión.* Mexico City: Universidad Nacional Autónoma de México, Escuela Nacional de Trabajo Social.

Valero Chavez, A. (Ed.). (1994). *El trabajo social en México: Desarrollo y perspectivas.* Mexico City: Universidad Nacional Autónoma de México, Escuela Nacional de Trabajo Social.

Zamora Díaz de León, T. (2000). *La formación del trabajador social en Latinoamérica.*

Further Reading

Evangelista Martínez, E. (Ed.). (1998). *Historia del trabajo social en México*. Mexico City: Plaza y Valdés.

Evangelista Martínez, E. (1993) Historia del Trabajo Social en México. *Revista de Trabajo Social ENTS-UNAM, 1*(3), 45–47.

Historia del Trabajo Social en México. *Revista Mexicana de Trabajo Social, 1*(3), 69. Asociación de Trabajadores Sociales Mexicanos (Eds.). (1991, March).

Revista Anales de Trabajo Social, 1, 72. Mexico City: Escuela Universitaria de Trabajo Social, UM; Escuela Nacional de Trabajo Social, UNAM. (2000).

SOCIAL WORK PROFESSION (UNITED STATES)

In the United States, the profession of social work originated in volunteer experiments in social betterment during the late nineteenth century. By the turn of the century, charity was rapidly becoming an occupation devoted to individual service and social action. Social work, as the new profession came to be called, promoted the development of social welfare measures at the state and federal levels during the Progressive Era. Ironically, social work prospered as social welfare became an accepted part of government during and after the 1930s, but the profession's influence on the evolving American welfare state waned.

Movements for reforming the poor, rescuing children, restoring community in large cities, and restructuring state charitable and correctional agencies resulted in the creation of the profession of social work. The state boards of charities and correction, child saving organizations, charity organization societies, and settlement houses of the late nineteenth century provided formative experiences for the first generation of social workers. With the exception of the state boards, which attempted to regulate state charities, these bodies were initially conceived as philanthropic associations, created, directed, and staffed by volunteers. They attempted to replace presumably haphazard methods of administering assistance to the poor with systematic and organized, but humane, methods. The early leaders called this rationalized approach scientific philanthropy and consciously imitated the forms and methods of the emerging business corporations.

By the 1890s, many of these organizations began to add paid staff members, reflecting the increasingly technical nature of their work. As reformers learned more about the problems of the poor, they began to view environmental influences as significant causes of poverty. Influencing industrial and state policy in the increasingly urban and industrial nation became an important focus of the emerging profession. The social gospel movement in American Protestantism, which emphasized the Christian's duty to improve the world, combined with the rise of social science and labor and agrarian movements, contributed to this increasing emphasis on the environments of the poor.

During the 1890s, charity organization leaders Anna Dawes and Mary Richmond called for the creation of training schools for philanthropic workers; such schools were established in Chicago and New York by the end of the decade. Additional schools of social work, as the new profession was called, were created in Boston, Philadelphia, and St. Louis during the first decade of the twentieth century. Charity organization societies established most of the early schools, but training was open to all workers in the diverse charities field. Aided by philanthropic foundations, such as the Russell Sage Foundation and later the Commonwealth Fund and the Rockefeller philanthropies, and affiliated with the emerging academic social sciences, the schools promoted a scientific, critical approach to social problems. Research, social action, and individual service provided the focus for the new professional schools.

Along with individual service, social workers in training learned how to analyze social policies and frame social legislation, how to work with community groups, how to conduct social research, and how to establish community services such as savings banks. Individual service remained at the core of the new profession, however, and new social work specializations of medical, psychiatric, and school social work incorporated the methods of individual service being used in the charity organization and child-saving fields.

Social workers promoted new services, such as juvenile courts and mother's pensions, at the state level and new agencies, such as the Children's and Women's Bureaus, at the federal level. Social workers like Jeanette Rankin were active in campaigns for women's suffrage and other electoral reforms during the Progressive Era. Social workers also attempted to influence industrial organizations, by attempting to mediate labor disputes and by promulgating standards for the treatment of workers.

During the 1910s and 1920s, the emerging social casework method began to dominate social work education as well as practice. Fueled by the publication of Mary Richmond's *Social Diagnosis* (1917) and wartime experiments with psychiatric social work and family casework, by the 1920s casework, increasingly devoted to the resolution of personal problems, was at the core of the emerging social work profession. Work with groups, the drafting of legislation, and the building of community organizations became marginalized as social work, in Porter Lee's words, "once a cause" became "a function of a well-regulated community."

The Great Depression of the 1930s led to an expansion of public social services and employment in public agencies. Social work, once mostly practiced in voluntary agencies, increasingly became a government service. The Social Security Act (1935) established a national Old Age Insurance program and federally assisted and regulated state programs of Unemployment Insurance, public assistance, and social services. At the same time, voluntary social service agencies began to focus on problems of personal adjustment, leaving work with the very poor to the public agencies. The American Association of Social Workers made professional education the minimum qualification for membership early in the decade; by 1939, the American Association of Schools of Social Work (AASSW) made graduate education the criterion for recognition. Educators at state universities in the South and Midwest created the National Association of Schools of Social Administration (NASSA) to promote undergraduate education for social work. Social workers had always practiced with community groups and organizations; the new practice methods of group work and community organization were first officially identified and defined in sessions of the National Conference of Social Work in 1935 and 1940–1941.

As had the First World War, World War II expanded opportunities for social workers in the health and psychiatric fields. Postwar public mental health programs at the state and federal levels, especially attempts to reduce public mental hospital populations, provided enhanced employment opportunities for therapeutically oriented social workers. By the 1960s, social workers provided the bulk of public mental health services in the United States. Federal public housing programs emphasized community participation, providing opportunities for community oriented social workers. The merger of AASSW and NASSA in 1952 resulted in the creation of the Council on Social Work Education (CSWE); seven professional social work organizations merged to form the National Association of Social Workers (NASW) in 1955.

By the 1960s, the social work profession seemed to be in a secure position. The election of a sympathetic president, John F. Kennedy, portended changes in public welfare, mental health services, and community action. Social workers embraced the new administration's initiatives, but had a more ambivalent response to Lyndon Johnson's Great Society programs, some of which seemed to be intended to replace professional expertise with grassroots action. Whereas some social workers embraced the new initiatives, in particular the Community Action Program, others looked askance. As the federal government replaced private philanthropic foundations as a major source of external support, social workers again became interested in empirical research. NASW promoted state regulation of social workers, advocating licensure as a consumer protection measure.

Hard times in the 1970s, combined with national administrations hostile to social work and "soft" services, resulted in retreats from community action and a turn to technical concerns and individually oriented social work. NASW recognized the baccalaureate degree in 1969, followed by the promulgation of standards for baccalaureate education by CSWE in 1971. Undergraduate education expanded during the 1970s. Educators continued to emphasize research in social work education, although some were concerned that practitioners seemed not to use research findings. The doctorate in social work, offered at only a few institutions before the 1960s, became an increasingly popular degree.

The unevenly distributed prosperity of the 1980s and 1990s did little to change these trends, even as publicly supported social services deteriorated. Many social workers were employed as private practitioners or in proprietary agencies; others were in private agencies that contracted with government to provide specified services to an identified clientele. By the 1980s, all states regulated social work practice, most by licensing social workers. Social work education experienced another period of expansion during the 1990s as many baccalaureate programs added master's programs and some MSW programs offered the doctorate. In spite of its growth, Congress and the Bill Clinton administration ignored the social work profession in 1996 as they reformed the federal-state public assistance program for families with children by imposing work requirements and time limits. By the end of the twentieth century, social work in the United States was secure, but uncertain about its mission and its relationship to the welfare state.

—*Paul H. Stuart*

See also Charity Organization Societies (United States); Child Welfare Policy (United States); National Association of Social Workers (United States); National Conference on Social Welfare (United States); Rank and File Movement (United States); Scientific Philanthropy (United States); Settlement Houses (United States); Social Gospel (United States); Social Security (United States); State Boards of Charities (United States); *The Survey* (United States)

Primary Sources

Records of the Council on Social Work Education and its predecessors, the National Association of Social Workers and its predecessors, and the National Conference of Social Welfare (formerly the National Conference of Social Work), are all held by the Social Welfare History Archives, University of Minnesota, Minneapolis; the Mary Richmond Papers, are held by the Rare Book & Manuscript Library, Butler Library, Columbia University, New York; the Sophia Smith Collection, Smith College, Northampton, MA, holds the papers of many prominent social workers.

Current Comment

Bisno, H. (1956). How social will social work be? *Social Work, 1*(2), 12–18.

Flexner, A. (1915). Is social work a profession? *Proceedings of the National Conference of Charities and Correction, 42,* 576–590.

Lee, Porter R. (1929). Social work as cause and function. *Proceedings of the National Conference of Social Work, 56,* 3–20.

Specht, H., & Courtney, M. (1994). *Unfaithful angels: How social work has abandoned its mission.* New York: Free Press.

Further Reading

Leighninger, L. (1987). *Social work: Search for identity.* Westport, CT: Greenwood.

Lubove, R. (1965). *The professional altruist: The emergence of social work as a career, 1880–1930.* Cambridge, MA: Harvard University Press.

Wenocur, S., & Reisch, M. (1989). *From charity to enterprise: The development of American social work in a market economy.* Urbana: University of Illinois Press.

STATE BOARDS OF CHARITIES (UNITED STATES)

During the last third of the nineteenth century, many state governments in the United States established state boards of charities. Called by various names, and varying somewhat in function, these new government entities all attempted to improve the standard of the administration of state charitable and correctional agencies—the prisons, mental hospitals, orphanages, and other institutions established in all of the states during the nineteenth century. Many boards also attempted to improve the local government administration of local poor relief. Although most state boards had only advisory functions, a few were given administrative control over state institutions. Together with the charity organization societies and the settlement houses, the state boards introduced a scientific and rational approach to thinking about problems of charity and correction in the United States, paving the way for the development of public welfare in the twentieth century. Since they were units of state government, the state boards of charity were important precursors of state departments of public welfare established in many of the states during the 1920s.

The early boards had supervisory but not administrative responsibilities. Composed in most cases of prominent citizens who served without pay, board members could inspect state institutions and examine institutional records, but did not have the power to order changes in administrative practice or to hire and fire personnel. In spite of their lack of administrative control, the boards were quite powerful because their recommendations were taken seriously by governors, legislators, and the public. Later in the nineteenth century, some boards were granted administrative responsibility, particularly in the Midwest. Often called boards of control, these boards exercised administrative powers over state institutions and often over county government agencies as well.

Together with state boards of health, state railroad commissions, and state bureaus of labor, the state boards of charities expanded the administrative reach of state governments in the late nineteenth century by making information available to decision makers. The members of the boards of charities also expounded a progressive, scientific approach to state government, arguing for honest and efficient public administration and expansions in state functions. Members of the early boards of charities were instrumental in organizing the American Social Science Association, the National Conference of Charities and Correction, and the American Prison Association.

The first state board, the Massachusetts State Board of Charities, was established in 1862. Samuel Gridley Howe, founder of the New England Asylum for the Blind, was the first chairman. Franklin Benjamin Sanborn, a disciple of the transcendentalist philosopher Ralph Waldo Emerson and a prominent abolitionist who was to serve the board for decades, was appointed secretary, the only paid position. The board had supervisory responsibility but no administrative powers. It could visit institutions and make reports and recommendations but it did not have the power to remove institutional superintendents. Howe, a physician who was a leader in the education of the deaf as well as the blind, was an articulate proponent of expanded state services. The states of Illinois, New York, North Carolina, Ohio, Pennsylvania, and Rhode Island established boards of charities in the 1860s, followed by Connecticut, Kansas, Michigan, and Wisconsin in the 1870s.

Sanborn was instrumental in organizing the American Social Science Association (ASSA) in 1865. Staff and members of the state boards met informally at ASSA; in 1874, Sanborn and the other board personnel organized a national conference of boards of charities that met with the ASSA. This group, which became the National Conference of Charities and Correction (NCCC), met with the ASSA until 1879, when it began to meet as a separate organization. Sanborn, who became a leader in the NCCC, continued to be active in the ASSA until it dissolved in 1909.

Although most state boards had only supervisory responsibility and were not expected to directly control the administration of state institutions, Wisconsin in 1881 established a state board of control, with administrative responsibility for state institutions. Several other midwestern states, notably Kansas, instituted boards of control during the late nineteenth century. By the 1920s, many of the state boards of charities had evolved into state departments of public welfare, with varying degrees of control over state institutions and county services.

—Paul H. Stuart

See also American Public Welfare Association (United States); National Conference on Social Welfare (United States); Poor Law (United States); Social Welfare (United States): Before the Social Security Act; Social Work Profession (United States)

Primary Sources

The records of the state boards of charities are held by state archives, usually located in the state capitals. Most boards published annual or biannual reports; a convenient checklist of reports may be found in Brock (1984), Appendix 2.

Current Comment

Conover, A. D. (1911). Supervision of state institutions by a board of control. *Proceedings of the National Conference on Charities and Correction, 38*, 27–31.

Craig, O., Slocum, W. F., Forrest, H. A., Smith, S. G., & Follett, M. D. (1893). History of state boards. *Proceedings of the National Conference on Charities and Correction, 20*, 33–51.

Kelso, R. W. (1911). State supervision by a board of state charities. *Proceedings of the National Conference on Charities and Correction, 38*, 31–35.

Wines, F. H. (1890). State boards of charities. *Proceedings of the National Conference on Charities and Correction, 17*, 63–72.

Further Reading

Bremner, R. H. (1980). *The public good: Philanthropy and welfare in the Civil War era.* New York: Alfred A. Knopf.

Brock, W. R. (1984). *Investigation and responsibility: Public responsibility in the United States, 1865–1900.* Cambridge, UK: Cambridge University Press.

Leiby, J. (1978). *A history of social welfare and social work in the United States.* New York: Columbia University Press.

Mennel, R. M., & Spackman, S. (1983). Origins of welfare in the states: Albert G. Byers and the Ohio Board of State Charities. *Ohio History, 92*, 72–95.

STRUCTURAL SOCIAL WORK (CANADA)

Structural social work emerged in Canada during the 1970s. From its inception, this approach valued history as a source of knowledge about multiple oppressions and about ways to dismantle them. Structural social work not only favored a historical perspective, but its own genesis was also visibly influenced by the pendulum of history that had swung toward widespread challenges of oppressive conditions.

The 1960s were marked by extensive student protests against the involvement of the United States in the Vietnam War. In addition, large-scale civil disobedience in the United States, led by Martin Luther King, Jr., among others, exposed the depth of racism in that country. Moreover, numerous scientists joined peace activists in public forums warning about the dangers of nuclear war. Television crews could barely keep up with the increasing pace of street demonstrations, boycotts, voter registration drives, teach-ins, and a host of other tactics against various forms of oppression in North America and elsewhere.

It was a historical epoch of turmoil and of hope. There was a sense that emancipation was feasible. After all, the global uprising against colonialism that gathered momentum after World War II resulted in over 100 formerly colonized nations declaring their independence. During this period, however, it was impossible for indigenous populations to reclaim North America as their territory, partly because so many of the original inhabitants had been killed by European settlers and their armies or had died as a result of disease or economic disruption. Furthermore, entitlement to most of their land had been extinguished, or more accurately, stolen from them.

Within Canada, aboriginal leaders scrambled to reclaim their culture and undo the severe damage from intergenerational destruction of culture, family, and community. Meanwhile, other oppressed groups, such as the Acadians in Atlantic Canada, were finding their voice. Rebelling against Anglo control over its culture and economy, the French-speaking province of Quebec threatened to separate from Canada.

GENESIS AND DEFINITION OF THE STRUCTURAL APPROACH IN CANADA

Social work in Canada felt the reverberations from the 1960s clamor for change. Inspired by the leadership of Professor Maurice Moreau, the School of Social Work at Carleton University in Ottawa, Ontario, became one of many sites of outspoken debate and intense creativity during the 1970s. These educators wanted to reclaim the authentic meaning of the word "radical" by addressing the root causes of social problems. They were influenced by numerous radical writers, including Canadian authors Ian Adams and Pat and Hugh Armstrong, Saul Alinsky and Francis Fox Piven of the United States, and Marjorie Mayo and Roy Bailey of the United Kingdom.

Maurice Moreau, along with other progressive Canadian social work educators, criticized prevailing conceptualizations of social work, including systems theory and ecological models, for their failure to address systemic inequalities. These theorists advocated a paradigm shift in the purpose of social work. More specifically, they rejected social work's social control function and its timid tinkering with change. Instead, they wanted to participate in consciousness-raising about social injustices and in mobilizing for basic change. From the 1970s onward, this form of practice became known in Canada as "structural social work."

Structural social work challenged unjust barriers created by the primary structures of oppression. These primary structures were named as colonialism, racism, patriarchal capitalism, heterosexism, ableism, and ageism. Consequently, the structural approach welcomed a diversity of radical critiques of society, ranging from a class analysis of exploited workers, to gender analysis of violence caused by patriarchy. Such critiques offered multiple visions of social justice based on communal, democratic, and feminist alternatives to oppressive structures.

The practice of structural social work changed the relationship between social workers and clients. Structural social workers built upon feminist practice as articulated by Helen Levine, a colleague of Moreau at Carleton; they also tapped into Brazilian adult educator Paolo Freire's method of conscientization. Consequently, instead of viewing social worker-client relationships as top-down, elitist, and expert-prescriptive, the structural approach emphasized power sharing. Priority was given to client survival needs, ranging from food and shelter to medical care. Using social work skills, such as critical questioning, reframing, and disputing myths, structural social workers helped clients to unmask how oppressive power relations impacted people's daily living and working conditions.

At the same time that structural social workers advocated societal change, they also helped clients to develop positive self-images by validating, for example, client fears as well as client successes in small victories against oppression. Through a process of consciousness-raising, service users were helped to change their feelings, thoughts, and behaviors when these were harmful to themselves or to others. Applying the feminist insight that the personal is political, structural social workers encouraged the formation of groups where personal experiences were shared within a climate of mutual support. Such groups fostered analysis and planning about actions to resist oppressive practices. These actions included activism with social movements to expose a variety of harmful practices and structures. Structural social workers supported alternative social services, such as shelters for women escaping abuse, where decisions, for example, about hiring, became more democratic by being shared among staff and service users. Such alternative services, in turn, became venues of support for structural practice and for further legitimation of demands for social and economic justice.

SUBSEQUENT EVOLUTION OF THE STRUCTURAL APPROACH

Given that an anti-oppression perspective had been central to structural social work, it is hardly surprising that decades after its inception this type of practice is now called "anti-oppressive" social work. With active support from the Canadian Association of Schools of Social Work, which accredits schools of social work in Canada, anti-oppressive social work has become mainstream within Canadian social work education.

As this practice approach evolved, attention was given to a diversity of identities impacting community members. Influenced by postmodern and poststructuralist analysis, progressive social workers became skeptical about universal generalizations that prescribed one "linear track" to emancipation. Continuing social work's history of attending to the subjective experiences of its clients, anti-oppressive social work probed the multi-interactive layers of internalized oppression and of internalized privilege. Today, social workers are deconstructing these subjective layers in light of the local to global span of multi-interactive structures of privilege and oppression. Such practices become empowering foundations for transformed, non-oppressive relationships and solidarities pointing toward social justice.

Regrettably, instead of welcoming this form of professional practice, most social agencies have diluted it or excluded it entirely. Usually acquiescent to conservative financial backers, social service administrators have tended to discourage workers from openly addressing the full range of systemic inequalities. Despite such obstacles, however, pockets of progressive practice have emerged throughout Canada where anti-oppressive social work is being implemented. These professionals often become part of the labor movement, which further empowers them as workers in resisting multiple oppressions.

Paradoxically, at the very time when emancipatory approaches are being legitimated within Canadian social work education, global corporations are tightening the grip of their economic colonialism over the entire world. Even as their mass media face increasing difficulties in rationalizing corporate abuses, business elites find they can still quietly and effectively impose their will upon governments. Consequences from this smoothly camouflaged corporate governance include: (1) the strangulation of the public sector and its social programs, and (2) further expansion of the ominous gap between rich and poor internationally and within many nations, including Canada. Therefore, progressive individuals within social work and other professions, alongside a diversity of activists, community networks, and multiple social justice movements, now face a monumental challenge. Will they be able to act with sufficient courage, wisdom, and humility to mobilize the political pressure required globally, to achieve sustainable development, democratized economies, and social welfare institutions responsive to human need?

—Ben Carniol

See also Race and Ethnic Relations (Canada); Social Democracy (Canada)

Current Comment

Levine, H. (1982). The personal is political: Feminism and the helping professions. In A. Miles & G. Finn (Eds.), *Feminism in Canada* (pp. 175–209). Montreal, QC: Black Rose.

Moreau, M. J. (1979). A structural approach to social work practice. *Canadian Journal of Social Work Education, 5,* 78–93.

Moreau, M. J. (with Leonard, L.). (1989). *Empowerment through a structural approach to social work.* Montreal, QC, and Ottawa, ON: Université de Montréal, Ecole de Service Social; Carleton University, School of Social Work.

Moreau, M. J., Frosst, S., Frayne, G., Hlywa, M., Leonard, L., & Rowell, M. (1993). *Empowerment II: Snapshots of the structural approach in action.* Ottawa, ON: Carleton University, School of Social Work.

Further Reading

Carniol, B. (2000). *Case critical: Challenging social services in Canada* (4th ed.). Toronto, ON: Between the Lines.

Carniol, B. (1992). Structural social work: Maurice Moreau's challenge to social work practice. *Journal of Progressive Human Services, 3*(1), 1–20.

Fook, J. (2002). *Social work: Critical theory and practice.* London: Sage.

Mullaly, B. (2002). *Challenging oppression: A critical social work approach.* Don Mills, ON: Oxford University Press.

SUBSTANCE ABUSE POLICY (CANADA)

THE FIRST PROHIBITION: ALCOHOL

Alcohol was unknown to aboriginal peoples until introduced by Europeans for trade; by 1657, however, the Roman Catholic church's concern over alcohol abuse led to the first North American Prohibition. The church promoted temperance to eliminate drinking and to increase Christianity, though, as a harbinger of the future, this initiative was quickly circumvented as First Nations groups turned to the British to trade rum for furs. Rum was imported from the West Indies, which brought "Canada" into the slave trade triangle of human lives for alcohol for beaver pelts. The British Conquest of northern North America saw alcohol become an economic vehicle. Taxation replaced Prohibition with financial benefits accruing through increased employment and licenses. Duties on imported alcohol produced 25 percent of income during the 1830s as the British focused on commerce not control.

In 1828, the first temperance meeting was held in Nova Scotia. The temperance movement, an agrarian, evangelical Protestant, middle-class phenomenon, became the most significant social movement of nineteenth century Canada. Modeled on British and American initiatives, the Canadian movement became more successful than either. By 1832, 100 temperance groups with a membership of over 10,000 existed with the Women's Christian Temperance Union being prominent in promoting both Prohibition and women's suffrage.

Between 1854 and 1859, six provincial Prohibition drives occurred but only one succeeded. In 1856, Prohibition was established in New Brunswick; revenues, however, dwindled and the law was openly ignored, leading to the government's defeat within 7 months. The next government repealed Prohibition, replacing it with liquor licensing to control alcohol sales and generate income. The first national Prohibition attempt occurred in 1898, when Liberal Prime Minister Wilfrid Laurier, who had campaigned on a pro-temperance platform, was obligated to conduct a plebiscite. The result was a 52 percent majority for Prohibition, though 81 percent of Quebecers voted against it. To avoid instituting an unwanted policy in a region of Liberal political dominance, the plebiscite was invalidated on the premise of inadequate voter turnout, forcing provinces to again establish their own Prohibition policies.

Both Manitoba and Prince Edward Island (PEI) introduced legislation in 1901. Although the Manitoba supreme court ruled that the act was unconstitutional, PEI's legislation was upheld by its supreme court on appeal though Prohibition applied only to the provincial capital, Charlottetown. This victory provided renewed inspiration to the progressive and social gospel segments of the temperance movement. Over the next decade, provincial governments became increasingly sympathetic to the activities of temperance organizations; it was World War I and the sacrifices Canadians felt were necessary, however, that led to national Prohibition in 1917. At the war's conclusion, the act was swiftly rescinded in Quebec, with British Colombia following in 1921. All provinces eventually overturned the legislation with PEI holding out until the end of World War II.

Prohibition was never fully adopted in Canada as provinces had different periods of Prohibition, allowing citizens to travel across borders to purchase spirits. While pre-Prohibition beer was typically 9 percent alcohol, 2.5 percent temperance beer was available as were locally produced wines. Physicians, along with veterinarians in Saskatchewan, were allowed to prescribe alcohol with Ontario's government selling $5 million in alcohol via 810,000 prescriptions in 1923.

During Prohibition, there was less crime and fewer health problems and deaths from alcoholism, yet Prohibition did not succeed as social policy. Substantive revenue losses combined with discrepancies between Canadian and American legislation undermined its success. Prohibition's failure was also associated with its evolution from a middle-class to a working-class movement. Once Prohibition began to garner support from working classes, the middle class grew resentful. Alcoholism was easier to use as an example of moral failure when drunkenness was attributed to marginalized groups; when outsider groups began to embrace temperance, however, it became less appealing to those of status and privilege.

The unintended consequences of Prohibition are extensively documented: Fortunes were made in bootlegging, organized crime flourished, and corruption was commonplace; thus, the retreat from complete to partial alcohol Prohibition. Provincial government monopolies were created, with liquor acts introduced to control who could sell alcohol, when, where, and at what cost, though Prohibition still exists in some First Nations communities.

THE SECOND PROHIBITION: OPIUM, NARCOTICS, AND NON-NARCOTIC DRUGS

As no distinct drug-related polices were enacted at Confederation, psychoactive substances were placed under the House of Commons' "Peace, Order and Good Government" clause. Prior to the twentieth century, there were virtually no restrictions on drugs. Opioids and cannabis were widely distributed by doctors, patent medicine companies, pharmacies, general stores, and opium shops, while cocaine was used medicinally, and

added to soft drinks, alcoholic beverages, and patent medicines. Drug abuse was not a criminal or a social issue, rather one of moral weakness, personal vice, and sinfulness. Fear, social conflict, and racism, however, produced myths that were instrumental in creating new policy.

Opium consumption, initially viewed as an upper-class indulgence, became politically valuable when linked to unwanted Chinese and Japanese immigrants. Asian workers had been necessary to supply cheap, plentiful labor for the developing mines and expanding railroad sectors of western Canada; an extended recession, however, crystallized resentment against these groups. The racially motivated 1907 Vancouver riot saw deputy labor minister and future prime minister Mackenzie King dispatched to investigate. King was astonished by the economic activity associated with opium and reported that opium smoking was increasing among young White women and men with profits accruing to Chinese merchants. King's report laid the foundation for the Opium Act (1908), which prohibited use except for medical purposes. The initial legislation was merely two paragraphs, though by 1929 it had become an 11-page document with 28 sections that would remain the foundation of Canada's drug policy through the twentieth century.

The creation of the dope fiend stereotype, associated with those of Asian ancestry and lower-status Whites, made it possible to approach opium use as a moral crusade, similar to temperance attacks on "demon rum." A societal fear was created that smoking opium facilitated sexual contact between Chinese men and White women that could lead to unwanted "mixing of the races." A similar connection was made with cocaine, except it was associated with African Canadian men. There was also a highly publicized cocaine scare in Montreal, Quebec, partially promoted by the Children's Aid Society, which led the chief of police to lobby for cocaine, a stimulant, to be added to the list of prohibited narcotics.

Cannabis, a hallucinogen, was added to the Narcotic Control Act in 1923, even though it had been a legal substance grown since the time of French colonization for medicinal and economic purposes. Cannabis quickly changed from a widely available, legal product to being portrayed as a drug that produced sexual promiscuity, insanity, and certain death.

Policy became piecemeal after the 1920s with new initiatives typically championed by the Royal Canadian Mounted Police and related interests. Internationally, Canada became a signatory of the Single Convention on Narcotic Drugs (1961), the Convention on Psychotropic Substances (1971), and the Convention Against Illicit Traffic in Narcotic Drugs and Psychotropics (1988). These treaties established the tone for contemporary Canadian prohibitionist substance abuse policy.

DEBATING PROHIBITION: FROM LE DAIN TO THE WAR ON DRUGS TO HARM REDUCTION

At the end of the 1960s, the Pierre Trudeau government appointed the Le Dain Commission, or the Royal Commission of Inquiry into the Non-Medical Use of Drugs, to examine increasing drug use in Canada. The commission's work was revolutionary as its recommendations were premised upon scientific findings and emphasized public health with a landmark proposal to decriminalize cannabis possession. The commission's work did not produce significant policy revision, though there was softening of enforcement and challenges to the dope fiend stereotype.

In the 1980s, the United States ran out of external wars to fight and turned inwards. After President Ronald Reagan declared a War on Drugs, Conservative Prime Minister Brian Mulroney proclaimed drug abuse an epidemic, undermining Canada's economic and social fabric. Surprisingly, the subsequent federal report rejected drug testing, a cornerstone of the American philosophy, in favor of Employee Assistance Programs, workplace-based counseling initiatives, as the primary mechanism for dealing with employees with drug and other personal problems in the workplace. The Canadian Drug Strategy allocated more funds for treatment, education, and prevention than for enforcement. In 1987, while the United States spent $3.9 billion fighting the War on Drugs, the Canadian government acknowledged that licit substances were a more significant drug problem than illegal drugs. Bill C-61, however, did borrow from American policy, providing new investigative powers and allowing for the confiscation of assets earned through drug trafficking.

Then came AIDS. One verified means of acquiring HIV was by sharing contaminated needles for drug injection, typically heroin or cocaine. After the delayed government response that allowed the virus to spread, methadone maintenance and needle exchange initiatives were grudgingly adopted primarily through the activism and lobbying of those infected. These harm reduction initiatives were diametrically opposed to the traditional Canadian abstinence and prohibition philosophies. At the beginning of the twentieth century, heroin had become demonized because of the association between unwanted immigrants and opium. At the end of the twentieth century, intravenous drug users and those with HIV had become the newly oppressed group partially because of the policies of nearly a century before.

Substance abuse policy has been driven by economic needs and influenced by fear, morality, and racism with supply side initiatives being the favored approach. Whereas alcohol Prohibition was rescinded because it was unworkable, other psychoactive substances have retained their illicit status and remain prohibited. Canada has come to depend upon criminal law to control drug supplies and to punish offenders. Reaction to drugs has been strict law enforcement and punitive sanctions abetted by broad police powers with resources being disproportionately channeled into these areas rather than prevention and treatment. In 2002, however, the special parliamentary committee on the non-medical use of drugs recommended that marijuana be decriminalized, safe injection sites opened, and methadone supplied to addicted prison inmates.

—Rick Csiernik

See also Health Policy (Canada)

Primary Sources

Minister of Public Works and Government Services. (1998). *Canada's drug strategy.* Ottawa, ON: Author; *Booze, pills and dope: Reducing substance abuse in Canada.* Ottawa, ON: Queen's Printer; Le Dain Commission. (1972). *The study of non-medical use of drugs in Canada.* Ottawa, ON: Information Canada; Special Committee on Non-Medical Use of Drugs. (2002). *Policy for the new millennium: Working together to redefine Canada's drug strategy.* Ottawa, ON: Ministry of Public Works; Government Services Canada.

Current Comment

Boyd, N. (1991). *High society: Legal and illegal drugs in Canada.* Toronto, ON: Key Porter.

Erickson, P. (1980). *Cannabis criminals: The social effects of punishment on drug users.* Toronto, ON: Addiction Research Foundation.

King, W. L. M. (1908). *The need for the suppression of the opium traffic in Canada.* Ottawa, ON: S. E. Dawson.

Spencer, R. (1919). *Prohibition in Canada.* Toronto, ON: Dominion Alliance.

Further Reading

Csiernik, R., & Rowe, W. S. (Eds.). (2003). *Responding to the oppression of addiction: Canadian social work perspectives.* Toronto, ON: Canadian Scholars' Press.

Giffen, P., Endicott, S., & Lambert, S. (1991). *Panic and indifference: The politics of Canada's drug laws.* Ottawa, ON: Canadian Centre on Substance Abuse.

Smart, R., & Ogborne, A. (1996). *Northern spirits: A social history of alcohol in Canada.* Toronto, ON: Addiction Research Foundation.

Warsh, C. (1993). *Drink in Canada: Historical essays.* Montreal, QC, and Kingston, ON: McGill-Queen's University Press.

SUBSTANCE ABUSE POLICY (MEXICO)

After a long period of relatively low rates of drug use, with the major problems derived from illegal production and trafficking, Mexico's drug use has increased, resulting in significant health and social problems.

TRENDS IN DRUG ABUSE

Drug use in Mexico existed well before the arrival of the Spaniards. Use of hallucinogens was linked to cultural traditions among the indigenous populations that inhabited the country. It has been estimated that knowledge of the hallucinogenic effects of different plants is as old as the farming of such crops as corn, beans, and cotton, and that their use was linked to shamanic practices. The first evidence is seen in murals painted in Teotihuacán between the third and eighth centuries. Today, some Indian communities still include plants with hallucinogenic properties in their religious rituals. They are considered sacred and to have healing properties. They are used to communicate with the supernatural world, and they are widely available throughout Mexico.

In some communities, cannabis has been used since the eighteenth century. By the beginning of the twentieth century, however, cannabis use was limited to soldiers and to a small group of people linked to the production of this crop. Some sixteenth century documents refer to antidotes for opium, providing evidence of its use since then. There are reports of addiction to morphine in the nineteenth century, but there is no evidence of its widespread diffusion.

The first attempts to study the demand for drugs in Mexico from a public health perspective date from the 1970s. Since then, population-based surveys, studies conducted among special populations, and statistics derived from treatment have documented drug use in the country.

During the 1970s, the inhalation of industrial solvents among children and adolescents and marijuana use among adolescents and young adults characterized the Mexican drug problem. Inhalants were used predominantly by the more unprotected segments of the population—boys, girls, and adolescents from the poorest sectors of society. Today, inhalants are the drug of choice of children who work on the streets, a phenomenon that results from economic crises when all members of poor households, including children, are expected to work, often in the informal economy, as a survival strategy. Between 1976 and 1978, school surveys of high school students showed an increase in the inhalation of substances from 0.9 percent to 5.4 percent. The first evidence of abuse of heroin also dates from this period. In the northern border city of Tijuana, there was an increase of nearly 7,000 percent in demand for drug treatment between 1970 and 1976. Interestingly, use of cocaine by high school students in Mexico City was relatively low, varying between 0.5 percent in 1976 and 0.7 percent in 1979.

In the 1980s the use of inhalants, previously seen in students attending schools in poor communities, expanded to include all social levels, and, by 1986, the rates of use were similar at all social levels—about 4.7 percent. Marijuana was still popular, with use rates of 3.5 percent in 1980 and 4 percent in 1989, and experimentation with cocaine increased considerably during the decade, from 0.7 percent in 1979 to 1.6 percent in 1989.

More recently, in the period between the 1990s and 2003, the rate of experimentation with cocaine among the adult population (18 to 65 years of age) increased by nearly 300 percent from 0.33 percent in 1988 to 1.45 percent in 1998 and by 400 percent among high school students from 1.6 percent in 1989 to 5.2 percent in 2000. The growth in cocaine use in Mexico was probably linked to changes in distribution, as Colombian drug traffickers began to look for a market within Mexico.

The rate of increase in cocaine use during the first part of the 1990s was much more rapid (one percent in 1990 as compared to 3.9 percent in 1997) than that observed between 1997 and 2000, when it reached 5.2 percent of the student population. This might suggest a trend toward stabilization. In fact, a National Household Survey conducted by the Health Ministry (*Secretaría de Salud*) in 2002 showed no significant changes in the proportion reporting drug use in the 12 months prior to the survey (0.45 percent in 1998 as compared to 0.38 percent in 2002). On the other hand, specialized treatment centers for drug users showed an increase in demand, from 12 percent of patients in 1990 to 71 percent in 2001. Use of heroin seems to be more frequent in regions close to the border with the United States, where more than 25 percent of drug treatment demand in 2002 is due to this substance as compared to a national average of 5 percent. Inhalant abuse diminished among high school boys between 1998 and 2002 from 7.4 percent to 5.5 percent; treatment demand nationwide showed the same trend with a decrease from 55.8 percent in 1990 to 32.6 percent in 2001.

Between 1994 and 2001, demand for treatment for users of amphetamine-type stimulants increased from 2.7 percent to 9.3 percent of the patients seeking treatment nationally. In three cities on the border with the United States—Tijuana, Mexicali, and Ciudad Juárez—the numbers increased from 29.6 percent to 49.9 percent during the same period. The prevalence rate of stimulant use nationwide is estimated to be 0.1 percent of the adult population. It has been estimated that 0.7 percent of the adult urban population meets the criteria for substance dependence. This rate is lower than the rates reported for the United States (7.5 percent), Germany (2.1 percent), and the Netherlands (1.8 percent).

ASSOCIATED FACTORS

Since the 1980s, researchers have attempted to explain why some people do not use drugs in spite of their widespread availability. Their research has focused on factors that increase a person's vulnerability to substance abuse and those that protect a person when he or she is at risk. One of the first questions asked was whether differences existed in the choice of type of drug. A national survey of high school students revealed that boys were more likely to use nonmedical drugs. Girls preferred prescription drugs. Although drug use is rapidly increasing among high school girls, boys are still consuming more drugs. Students under 15 years of age and unemployed or living in a household whose head had a low educational level were more likely to use inhalants. Persons older than 15 years of age and those from higher socioeconomic levels were more likely to use cocaine.

The increased availability of drugs is a major predictive factor for increased substance use; tolerance and use within the family and by friends are also significant predictors. Among working minors, living with the family is a strong protective factor. School enrollment is a protection factor for boys and drug use but plays a less important role in drug involvement for girls. Among boys, living with the family is a more potent protector; working in high-risk environments is related to drug use in both genders and puts girls at risk for sexual abuse.

Problems with the police are related to boys and drug use. Among girls, problems with the police are more related to the specific community; girls working in places with high police involvement were likely to have problems with the police, regardless of whether or not they consumed drugs.

Emotional problems also play an important role. Suicide in adolescents is an increasing problem in Mexico. The suicide mortality rate in 1970 for the 15- to 24-year-old age group was 1.9 percent per 100,000 inhabitants. In 1997, the rate was 5.9 percent, an increase of 212 percent. Substance abuse may increase the probability of suicide. The 1998 National Survey on Addictions found that 1.34 percent of urban adolescent respondents between the ages of 12 and 17 years had attempted suicide. This statistic was almost twice as great, 1.8 times higher, for those who consumed alcohol, 5.7 times greater for those who used drugs, and 4.5 times greater for those who reported having problems with alcohol or drugs.

These data show a rapid increase in substance abuse and in associated problems. Increasing substance abuse has required a major shift in social response, which had been mainly devoted to prevention, to include enhanced treatment and rehabilitation programs. Though the number of specialized treatment centers has increased and new modalities have been created, a high proportion of persons with dependence receive treatment (17 percent). The main challenge is to have the national health system include addictions as chronic diseases that could be treated cost effectively through a more integrated system of care from general practice to specialized hospitals and community services, with adequate case referral and follow-up.

The data presented show a trend from low rates of use to a period of rapid increase, followed by a period of stabilization. Not only the prevalence of the problem has changed, but also the types of substances abused and the characteristics of the population that abuse them, including the use of substances with a higher addictive potential and more girls abusing substances. The impact of this problem on the individual and on society is important. Data suggest a need to increase the availability of services that attend the multiple needs of individuals.

—Elena Medina-Mora

See also Economic Crises, Family and Gender, 1980s to the Present (Mexico); Medicine and Popular Healing Practices in Colonial Mexico

Current Comment

Consejo Nacional Contra Las Adicciones (CONADIC). (2001). *Observatorio epidemiológico en drogas*. Mexico City: Secretaría de Salud.
Consejo Nacional Contra Las Adicciones (CONADIC). (2002). *Observatorio Mexicano en tabaco, alcohol y otras drogas*. Mexico City: Secretaría de Salud.
El fenómeno de las adicciones en México. (2001). Mexico City: Secretaría de Salud.
Encuestas nacionales de adicciones. (1993, 1998, 2002). Mexico City: Secretaría de Salud.

Further Reading

Medina-Mora, M. E. (2000). Abuso de sustancias. In DIF-DF & UNICEF (Eds.), *Estudio de niñas, niños y jóvenes trabajadores en el Distrito Federal* (pp. 119–137).
Medina-Mora, M. E., Cravioto, P., Villatoro, J., Fleiz, C., Galván-Castillo, F., & Tapia-Conyer, R. (1998). Consumo de drogas entre adolescentes: Resultados de la Encuesta Nacional de Adicciones. In *Salud del Adolescente* [Special issue]. *Salud Pública de México, 45*(Suppl. 1), 16–25.
Solis, F. (2001). El uso de los alucinógenos en el México prehispánico y colonial. In J. Bali (Ed.), *La drogadicción en México, indiferencia o prevención* [Special issue]. *México Desconocido*, 33–42.
Suárez-Toriello, J. E. (1989). Análisis de 800 casos de farmacodependencia a heroína. *Heroína, 2*(1), 123–137.

SUBSTANCE ABUSE POLICY (UNITED STATES)

The history of attitudes and policies in the United States concerning the use of substances such as tobacco, alcohol, and other drugs is replete with conflicting claims about the their benefit or harm to users as well as their impact on society. Attempts at substance abuse control have involved efforts to restrict the supply of harmful substances and efforts to reduce the demand for harmful substances. Supply-side efforts involve attempts by opponents of consumption of alcohol or other drugs to decrease their availability through restrictive legislation or other means. Alternatively, demand-side efforts involve attempts by the medical community and others to rehabilitate substance abusers and to educate the public about the dangers of drug use.

THE COLONIAL ERA

During the colonial era, the prevailing medical opinion was that people benefited medicinally from beer. Pregnant women especially were advised to drink beer to maintain optimal health, and children were rationed small quantities on a daily basis as an essential health measure. Beer, rum, and hard cider were all thought to contain health-promoting properties.

Taverns, inns, and ordinaries were constructed conveniently alongside public facilities to provide for the alcohol needs of travelers. The first beer brewery was established at New Amsterdam around 1633, followed by the first distillery in 1640 on Staten Island. Taverns commonly brewed their beers and strove to achieve higher qualities than their competitors. Among the most popular alcoholic beverages were beer, hard cider, and applejack.

While moderate drinking was generally considered acceptable, steps were underway to curb drunkenness and rowdiness. With Puritan clerics' influence, considerable pressure was exerted on the legislatures of New England and Massachusetts to enact laws prohibiting the sale of liquor to Indians in the early 1630s. These laws were soon repealed to accommodate colonists engaged in commercial trade with Indians. In 1643, the legislature of New Netherlands enacted a law to prohibit the sale of liquor to Indians with fines ranging from corporal punishment for recidivists to banishment from the colony.

With excessive drinking widespread, Cotton Mather and other like-minded Puritan clerics denounced drunkenness. With additional support from Native American tribal leaders, colonial legislatures were pressured to legislate against drunkenness and rowdiness, only to have their brief success marred by an appeal of the law in 1644. Throughout the colonies, tobacco also gained widespread popularity with no concern for its health risks. Some medical professionals even regarded tobacco as medicinal, and spittoons were commonly placed in homes and business establishments to accommodate tobacco chewers.

When the new federal government imposed an excise tax on whiskey, grain farmers marched in protest, emphatically demanding its repeal, in what became known as the Whisky Rebellion of 1794. Public opinion encouraged drinking; young men were socialized to equate drinking with manhood. The overall attitude among the colonists was that alcohol protected against poor health, and even the Puritans proclaimed that moderate drinking was a godly practice.

THE TEMPERANCE MOVEMENT

A number of factors contributed to excessive alcohol consumption in the new nation. Rum and whiskey were used to purchase slaves. Liquor distillation, in effect, promoted slavery. Payment for hides purchased from Indians was typically in the form of liquor. General George Washington ordered that Revolutionary War soldiers be provided with liquor, ostensibly as a viable food substitute because liquor, unlike food, was not apt to spoil.

A temperance movement gained increasing support in response to continued excessive drinking. In 1785, Dr. Benjamin Rush, surgeon general of the Continental Army and a signer of the Declaration of Independence, identified excessive drinking as a precipitating factor for social problems, namely crime, poverty, and moral degeneration. Coupled with support from Rush, Calvinist clerics and reform-minded Indian leaders provided opposition to the prevailing pro-drinking attitudes of the late 1700s.

Rowdiness and drunkenness, considered an inevitable outgrowth of excessive drinking, set the stage for the temperance movement that at first promoted moderate and respectable drinking, rather than abstinence, as a societal norm. But between 1825 and 1850, the main thrust became abstinence and the enactment of legislation prohibiting alcohol consumption was the movement's legal strategy. By the mid 1800s, about a third of the states had enacted prohibition legislation.

In the late nineteenth century, intense anti-Semitic and anti-Catholic sentiments gave impetus to a keen sense of nativism and opposition to immigration. The American Protective Association was clearly the outgrowth of xenophobic sentiment directed toward German immigrants in part because of their association with beer brewing. Some immigrants embraced temperance as a means of self-improvement.

Two diametrically opposed approaches to substance abuse control had emerged by the end of the nineteenth century. Some, including Calvinist clerics, advocated curtailing the supply of alcoholic beverages through stringent legislation. These antialcohol campaigners attempted to restrict the supply of alcohol. On the other hand, others, including the medical community, emphasized educating citizens to the medical risks associated with excessive drinking. Reducing demand would result in widespread abstinence or moderation. These approaches continued to inform substance abuse policy into the twenty-first century. Law enforcement agencies generally promoted supply-side strategies, and treatment and prevention services promoted demand-side approaches.

Even more than alcohol, tobacco was painfully slow in gaining recognition as a health risk. By the late nineteenth century, approximately half of all tobacco consumed in the United States was chewed. Adverse health effects were not recognized, and the nation would have to wait over half a century before the surgeon general recognized tobacco as a major health risk.

THE PURE FOOD AND DRUG ACT OF 1906

Aside from alcohol and tobacco, other drugs were used widely and indiscriminately, particularly opiates. Even though the medical community recognized that opiate use could result in medical problems, especially addiction, there existed virtually no regulations governing their use. Moreover, the use of patent medicines was rampant and disclosure of their ingredients, typically containing addictive properties, was not legally required. The Pure Food and Drug Act of 1906 regulated opiates for the first time. Despite the medical community's recognition of the addictive properties of opiates, they continued to be included in many drugs and prescribed indiscriminately as painkillers and tranquilizers for numerous ailments.

MEDICINE SHOWS AND "SECRET FORMULAS"

From about 1875 to the early 1900s, medicine shows replete with court jester-like musicians, jugglers, and a motley assortment of other entertainers were likely to enter rural towns with a fanfare. Led by a salesman who had taken the liberty to conveniently add the prefix "doctor" to his name, the shows provided entertainment to rural communities. The salesman would boldly make the claim that his magical tonics would cure any disease from rheumatism and dysentery to dyspepsia.

Rural America, deprived of entertainment, enthusiastically welcomed these charlatans. Interspersed with entertainment, the sales pitch would begin with a few bottles of tonic sold. Predictably, a planted voice would then cry out "I've been cured," and that would likely stimulate a mad frenzy of purchases of products that would have as their main ingredient, alcohol, or rather, the "secret formula."

Medicine show sales remained a risk until 1906, when the Pure Food and Drug Act required that ingredients be listed on product labels. Even though the law curtailed the patent-medicine industry and the accompanying "medicine shows" their popularity continued. When the automobile was introduced, allowing rural denizens to shop the large cities that stocked their cure-all medicines, the popularity of medicine shows declined. No longer were rural Americas dependent upon medicine show "doctors" to fulfill their hunger for patent medicines. Sales of patent medicines lingered into the 1950s only to be dealt a final blow with the advent of television advertising that systematically replaced the medicine show and patent medicines once and for all.

PROHIBITION: 1920–1933

Concern with excessive alcohol consumption continued well into the 1900s. Following the adoption of the Eighteenth Amendment to the Constitution in 1919, Congress enacted the Volstead Act, also known as the National Prohibition Act, in 1920. From Prohibition's infancy in 1920 to its repeal in 1933, the crime rate, and organized crime, increased dramatically. The Prohibition era in the United States provided the optimal conditions for crime syndicates to flourish. Al Capone's organization provided a classic case study of government enabling business enterprises controlled by organized crime families. Not surprisingly, the crime rate declined substantially with the adoption of the Twenty-First Amendment, which repealed the Eighteenth Amendment and ended Prohibition in 1933. In brief, the U.S. experiment with Prohibition ended in utter failure. Most voters overwhelmingly supported the Volstead Act in 1920, but realistically it was a protest vote against the enormously powerful alcohol and saloon industries and not against alcohol consumption per se.

After Mexican farmworkers introduced marijuana (*cannabis indica*), Congress enacted the Mexican Stamp Tax Act (1937), ostensibly to control its sale and use. In addition, scare tactics in the form of propaganda films were produced and federally subsidized to lower the demand by preventing and/or stopping marijuana use. *Tell Your Children* (1938), reissued as

Reefer Madness in 1947, the best known of the propaganda films, depicted an exaggerated illustration of the debilitating effects of marijuana use that warned the public that its continued use would inevitably lead to insanity. A more subtle target may have been the Mexican farmworker.

POST WORLD WAR II

After World War II, the United States experienced a sharp increase in illicit drug use, especially heroin use in poor areas. Heroin use increased sharply again during the Vietnam War due largely to the lower prices in Southeast Asia and the high-grade quality of virtually pure heroin available there. Heroin is a highly addictive drug that also poses serious health problems. In addition, needle sharing by HIV/AIDS–infected users spread what was soon to become one of the world's most horrific disease epidemics.

Perhaps contrived as a convenient diversion to the unpopular Vietnam War, President Richard Nixon waged a war on the domestic front. The "War on Drugs," as this ambitious undertaking was called, emphasized a supply-side strategy; the bulk of expenditures were for efforts to limit the availability of drugs. Only about 30 percent of the total monies were designated for the demand side, prevention and treatment-related services. Through several presidential administrations, including both Republicans and Democrats, several billion dollars was expended to combat this scourge, yet no appreciable victories have been recorded as substance abuse-addiction cases mount. In the early twenty-first century, U.S. jails and prisons continue to hold large numbers of drug-related offenders with victory, tragically, nowhere in sight.

—Michael Beechem

See also Criminal Justice Policy (United States); Health Policy (United States); Immigration Policy (United States); Mental Health Policy (United States); Rush, Benjamin

Current Comment

London, J. (1913). *John Barleycorn*. New York: Century.
Schaler, J. (2000). *Addiction is a choice*. Chicago: Open Court.
Stevens, S. J., & Morral, A. R. (Eds.). *Adolescent substance abuse treatment in the United States: Exemplary models from a national evaluation study*. New York: Haworth.

Further Reading

Abadinsky, H. (2001). *Drugs: An introduction*. Belmont, CA: Wadsworth/Thomson Learning.
Beechem, M. (2002). *Elderly alcoholism: Intervention strategies*. Springfield, IL: Charles C. Thomas.
Mancall, R. (1995). *Deadly medicine*. Ithaca, NY: Cornell University Press.
Van Wormer, K. (1997), *Alcoholism treatment: A social work perspective*. Chicago: Nelson-Hall.

SUPPLEMENTAL SECURITY INCOME (UNITED STATES)

The Supplemental Security Income (SSI) program is an important component of social welfare in the United States. This means-tested, public assistance program provides a federal guarantee of cash aid to individuals with little or no income who are aged or disabled. Historically, these individuals have been called the "deserving poor."

SSI had two major predecessors: (1) state and local aid for poor aged or disabled individuals and (2) the federal-state public assistance programs called Old Age Assistance (OAA), Aid to the Blind (AB), and Aid to the Permanently and Totally Disabled (APTD). Prior to 1935, a number of state and local governments had old age assistance or pension programs and similar programs for people who were blind. Elderly individuals generally had to be financially destitute and meet residency and citizenship requirements. Individuals with relatives deemed capable of supporting them could be denied aid, and programs might claim any assets of recipients at the time of their death. Payments were meager. Individuals who were blind were treated somewhat more generously. Programs for individuals with other disabilities were less common.

The 1935 Social Security Act was a milestone for people with limited incomes who were aged or blind. In addition to Social Security retirement benefits, the act contained OAA and AB. States could participate in OAA and AB by sharing program costs with the federal government. All states participated. In 1950, Congress added APTD for people younger than age 65 who were disabled due to conditions other than blindness. Nevada was the only state that never adopted APTD.

The federal government required that OAA recipients be aged 65 or over and AB and APTD recipients aged 18 or over. The states administered the programs and determined most eligibility requirements (definitions of disability and blindness, terms of residency, income and asset limitations, relative support, and property liens). Benefits were modest, and benefits and eligibility requirements varied considerably among states.

President Richard Nixon wanted to replace the federally supported cash public assistance programs with a graduated, guaranteed annual income that would encourage people to work and treat them the same regardless of their state of residence. As a result, OAA, AB, and APTD became SSI under Title XVI of the Social Security Act in 1972. The SSI program began operating in 1974.

The Social Security Administration (SSA), rather than the states, administers SSI to promote uniform treatment of recipients and reduce the stigma of receiving public assistance. Thus, eligibility requirements and basic payments are the same in all states. In addition to the aged, children as well as adults with disabilities are eligible for assistance. The federal government pays the full cost of benefits, though states may supplement payments and include additional recipients at their own expense. State supplements are generally intended for special care needs or the higher cost of living in some geographic areas. SSI remains a program of last resort because eligibility is determined only after applicants claim all other income and benefits due them.

The SSA uses the following definitions to determine who qualifies for SSI: (1) age is 65 years or older; (2) blind means 20/200 vision or less using a corrective lens in the better eye or tunnel vision of 20 degrees or less; (3) a disabled adult is unable to engage in "substantial gainful activity" (i.e., in 2003, any work at which the individual can earn at least $800 per month of income not counting disability-related work expenses or $1,330 a month if the individual is blind); (4) a disabled child is someone under age 18 (or age 22 if a student) who has "marked and severe functional limitations." To qualify as disabled, children and adults must have a "medically determined physical or mental impairment expected to result in death or that has lasted, or can be expected to

last, for a continuous period of least 12 months." SSI does not assist with partial or temporary disability. In determining eligibility, allowances are made for living expenses but other resources cannot exceed $2,000 for individuals and $3,000 for couples. Parents' income is considered in determining a child's eligibility. Since 1996, individuals disabled due to alcohol or drug addiction are ineligible for SSI. Other eligibility rules also apply.

The federal SSI payment in 2003 was $552 per month for an individual and $829 for a couple. Payments are adjusted annually based on the Consumer Price Index. If the recipient resides in another's household, payments are reduced by one-third. Federal payments currently equal about 75 percent of the poverty level for individuals and about 90 percent for couples. Recipients who reside in a facility in which more than half the costs of care are borne by the Medicaid program (e.g., a nursing home) receive a fixed federal payment of $30 per month for personal items. Individuals residing in public state or local facilities (e.g., mental hospitals, prisons) are generally not entitled to SSI.

In December 2001, nearly 2 million SSI recipients were aged 65 or older, 3.8 million were aged 18 to 64, and 882,000 were under age 18. About 1.3 million received payments on the basis of being aged, 78,000 based on blindness, and 5.3 million based on other disabilities. The most common disabilities of SSI recipients are mental retardation and mental illness. About 5 percent of recipients with disabilities work. Many individuals who consider themselves disabled are initially denied SSI and use the appeals process to establish eligibility.

The SSA is concerned about several issues in the SSI program. They include improving the method of determining disability and seeing that determinations are conducted consistently across jurisdictions, simplifying the complex application process, and developing strategies to encourage more of the growing number of recipients with disabilities to work.

—Diana M. DiNitto

See also Aging Policy (United States); Aid to Dependent Children/Aid to Families With Dependent Children (United States); Disability Policy (United States); Social Security (United States); Social Welfare (United States): Since the Social Security Act

Current Comment

Committee on Ways and Means of the U.S. House of Representatives (*Green Book* and committee hearings). The Social Security Administration is the primary source of data and reports on Supplemental Security Income (www.ssa. gov).

Further Reading

Berkowitz, E. D. (1987). *Disabled policy: America's programs for the handicapped.* Cambridge, UK: Cambridge University Press.

Moynihan, D. P. (1973). *The politics of a guaranteed income.* New York: Random House.

Myers, R. J. (1975). *Social Security.* Bryn Mawr, PA: McCahan Foundation.

Turnbull, J. G., Williams, C. A., & Cheit, E. F. (1973). *Economic and Social Security* (4th ed). New York: Ronald Press.

THE SURVEY (UNITED STATES)

The Survey was a national journal of social work and social welfare published from 1909 to 1952. *The Survey* was progressive in its outlook and methodology. It advocated reform, social planning, and a national system of social insurance as means to combat poverty and related problems. The journal investigated a wide range of issues and directed its findings to both professionals and the socially conscious public. *The Survey* also facilitated the evolution of professional social work and linked social welfare to reform. Half a century after its demise, *The Survey* remains one of the best sources for the study of social conditions and programs during the first half of the twentieth century.

The Survey and its predecessors were part of a transformation in social welfare during the early decades of the twentieth century. As social and economic forces were recognized to be the root causes of poverty, the response to social problems shifted from alleviation through charity to eradication through reform. The realization that education, training, and research were needed to combat complex social problems helped establish social work as a profession. The *Survey*'s philosophy, subject matter, and methodology both reflected and influenced these trends.

The Survey pursued reform by investigating and interpreting social problems. It presented the facts surrounding an issue, offered explanations, and explored potential solutions with the goal of informing and inspiring social change. The journal often used graphics and photographs to present and interpret information. It also printed expert commentary and provided a forum for discussion. *The Survey* offered writers an opportunity to reach an influential, socially active audience. Its contributors included social workers and other professionals as well as politicians, reformers, and philanthropists.

The Survey tackled issues and proposed solutions that were ahead of their time or foreshadowed the formation of government welfare programs. For example, it studied race relations and proposed social insurance decades before the passage of civil rights legislation or the institution of Social Security. A small sample of other topics explored in *The Survey* includes: child labor, industrial working conditions, housing, unemployment, public health, and labor relations.

In addition to promoting reform, *The Survey* facilitated the development of professional social work. Before specialized journals were formed, *The Survey* and its predecessors were a source of information and cohesion for charities, reformers, philanthropists, and members of the nascent social work profession. The journal disseminated new ideas. It provided information about agency activities, reform campaigns, legislation, and professional conferences. As social work became more specialized, *The Survey* incorporated emerging theories and practices such as casework and psychology. It related new developments to social work as a whole as well as to broader issues in social welfare. In doing so, it connected social workers across practice area boundaries and maintained the links between social work and reform.

The Survey's predecessors were charity organization and settlement house journals. In 1891, the New York Charity Organization Society established *Charities Review* to communicate with board members and volunteers. In 1897, the society created *Charities* to advise and unite organizations. Edward T. Devine, secretary of the society and a co-founder of the New York School of Philanthropy, edited the weekly publication. *Charities* merged with *Charities Review* in 1901.

In 1902, Paul U. Kellogg began his 50-year association with the journal when he joined the staff of *Charities Review* as an assistant editor. He was appointed editor in 1912 and held the post until 1952. Kellogg was a staunch believer in the application of expertise, social planning, and progressive reform, and was a pioneer spirit in the elimination of social ills. Due in part to Kellogg's influence, the journal placed a greater emphasis on the prevention of poverty and began reaching out to a broader audience during the early 1900s.

In 1905, *Charities* merged again, this time with the *Commons,* a settlement house journal, to form *Charities and Commons.* In 1909, the journal was renamed *The Survey.* The name was inspired by the recently completed Pittsburgh Survey, an in-depth study of conditions in the city that had been headed by Kellogg. The new name distanced the journal from the old ideas of charity and reflected its focus on investigation and interpretation. In 1912, Survey Associates was formed as an independent body to conduct investigations of social issues and produce *The Survey.*

From 1922 through 1948, *The Survey* was issued as two separate publications, *Survey Midmonthly* and *Survey Graphic. Survey Graphic* was aimed at the socially active public. It emphasized illustrations as a means of conveying information and discussed social welfare topics in accessible terms. *Survey Midmonthly* was directed to professional social workers, regardless of their practice area, and took a more technical approach to social issues.

The Survey's longtime support for social planning and national insurance gained new momentum during the Great Depression. It quickly recognized and publicized the extent of the crisis and argued for a national system of government relief, planning, and social insurance. The *Survey* hailed the New Deal, but eventually became critical of it for not establishing more comprehensive programs.

During the 1940s, circulation decreased as *The Survey* struggled to define its focus and faced competition from specialized social work journals as well as popular publications that dealt with social issues. Ongoing financial and operational troubles also plagued the journal. In 1952, the remaining members of the Survey Associates board voted to cease publication. The last issue appeared in May 1952. For over 40 years, *The Survey* had explored social conditions and espoused the progressive ideals of reform and social planning. *The Survey* and its predecessors had influenced the evolution of social work and the formation of social welfare policies and programs throughout the first half of the twentieth century.

—*Linnea M. Anderson*

See also Progressive Era (United States); Social Work Profession (United States)

Primary Sources

Paul U. Kellogg Papers and *The Survey* Associates Records, Social Welfare History Archives, University of Minnesota, Minneapolis.

Current Comment

Charities, 1897–1905
Charities and Commons, 1905–1909
The Survey, 1909–1952

Further Reading

Chambers, C. A. (1971). *Paul U. Kellogg and* The Survey*: Voices for social welfare and social justice.* Minneapolis: University of Minnesota Press.

Finnegan, C. (2003). Social engineering and photographic resistance: Social science rhetorics of poverty in *Survey Graphic.* In *Picturing poverty: Print culture and FSA photographs.* Washington DC: Smithsonian Books.

Finnegan, C. (n.d.). Social welfare and visual politics: The story of *Survey Graphic. New Deal Network* [On-line]. Available: http://newdeal.feri.org/sg/index.htm

Trattner, W. I. (1999). *From poor law to welfare state: A history of social welfare in America* (6th ed.). New York: Free Press.

T

TAX EXPENDITURES (UNITED STATES)

Although direct expenditures for social welfare have been extensively analyzed, far less attention has been devoted to forgone tax revenues, often called tax expenditures, which indirectly fund social welfare activities through the tax code. Tax expenditures subsidize a vast array of social welfare activities that include education, housing, health, income, job training, child care, and pensions by tax concessions to individuals or corporations. They also promote charitable contributions by allowing citizens and corporations to deduct them from their income taxes.

DEFINITION OF TAX EXPENDITURES

Unlike social welfare programs that are subsidized as line items in government budgets, social welfare tax expenditures fund specific social welfare activities through exemptions, deductions, and credits in the tax code, as well as deferred taxes that depart from the normal tax structure. "Exemptions," which allow citizens not to pay taxes on some of their income, enhance resources of low-income persons who would otherwise find all of their income subject to taxes. (Millions of citizens who fall beneath specified levels pay no federal income taxes at all.) "Deductions" allow citizens to reduce their taxable income by subtracting from it some or all of certain kinds of expenditures, such as mortgage interest payments, payments into pension funds, and health care costs. Corporations deduct from their taxable income such expenses as the cost of their employees' health insurance and corporate pensions. "Tax credits," which give citizens or corporations tax rebates, include the Earned Income Tax Credit (EITC) and tax credits for certain corporate job-training programs. "Deferred taxes" allow citizens to postpone taxes on income that is placed in private pensions. The fiscal magnitude of specific tax expenditures is determined by calculating the extent to which they reduce tax revenues.

States, too, provide social welfare tax expenditures. They subsidize not-for-profit organizations by exempting them from property taxes. They sometimes encourage corporations to place their operations in areas with high unemployment by reducing their property taxes. They subsidize not-for-profit organizations by not taxing their revenues. States with income taxes provide various exemptions and deductions.

SIZE OF TAX EXPENDITURES

Relatively little attention was given to tax expenditures by social policy experts until Stanley Surrey popularized the label in President John F. Kennedy's cabinet-level pension reform committee in the 1960s as well as in his book, *Pathways to Tax Reform* (1973). Surrey and colleagues at the Treasury Department produced the first credible estimates of forgone tax revenues from tax entitlements. In the Congressional Budget Act of 1974, Congress mandated that a "tax expenditure budget" be produced annually beginning in 1975.

From the time when the government first kept records on their magnitude in 1975, the federal government has spent $12.8 trillion on tax expenditures in constant 1992 dollars. Tax expenditures for individuals grew from $169 billion in 1975 to roughly $569 billion in 2004, while corporate tax expenditures rose from $33 billion in 1975 to more than $63 billion in 2004. Comparing these tax breaks with expenditures of large social programs reveals the sheer size of these tax expenditures. The cost from 1975 through 2004, for example, is only slightly less than the nation's combined expenditures for Social Security, Medicare, and Medicaid from 1965 through 2004.

The United States is unique in the extent of its use of the tax code to fund social welfare. Tax expenditures currently account for one third of all social welfare expenditures in the United States as compared with less than one tenth in other industrialized nations. Although many policy analysts have contended that American funding of social welfare activities has been considerably lower than other industrialized nations, aggregate American social welfare spending falls in the mid-range of these nations when the cost of tax expenditures is added to direct funding of social welfare.

Several factors account for the sheer number of tax expenditures in the federal tax code. If proposals to initiate social programs or to expand their funding often become engulfed in polarization between liberals and conservatives, tax expenditures are usually enacted in the relatively secretive politics associated with tax proposals. Tax expenditures are often popular because they can be efficiently administered through the tax code rather than requiring program structures to implement them. The political appeal of tax expenditures is enhanced in the United States by bipartisan support of proposals that cut citizens' taxes.

EVOLUTION OF TAX EXPENDITURES

Tax expenditures have always been integral to the federal tax code. When a federal income tax was first enacted during the Civil War to defray the war's costs, Congress immediately enacted various exemptions and deductions, such as provisions that exempted many low-income citizens from paying income taxes and a provision that allowed taxpayers to deduct rent payments. Congress terminated the Civil War income tax in 1872. Some legislators contended that the Constitution did not specifically give the federal government the power to levy income taxes. Congress enacted another income tax in 1894, but the Supreme Court ruled it unconstitutional in 1895 for technical reasons.

With the enactment of the Sixteenth Amendment to the Constitution in 1913, a federal income tax was finally institutionalized. Congress immediately enacted various exemptions and deductions, such as allowing citizens to exempt their first $3,000 in income plus an additional $1,000 for married persons, interest on state and local bonds, proceeds of life insurance policies, and public assistance, as well as to deduct state and local taxes, mortgage interest, and interest on consumer credit.

Many tax expenditures were enacted from 1913 to 1943, including exclusion of workmen's compensation and military benefits (1918); employer-furnished meals and lodging (1918); some capital gains from taxes (1921); employer contributions to employees' life insurance (1920); and unemployment compensation (1938), as well as the deduction of charitable contributions (1917). Private pensions provided by employers greatly expanded between the two World Wars, partly in response to exclusion of employers' contributions to pensions in 1926.

Relatively few citizens realized tax entitlements prior to 1943 because few of them paid income taxes. Only about 5 percent of wage earners paid an income tax in the 1930s, for example, when the United States levied only about 5 percent of GDP in aggregate tax revenues as compared to roughly 18 percent from 1950 to 2000.

All this changed with the extension of the federal income tax to most wage earners during World War II. Major new tax expenditures were added in the 1950s, including exclusion of disability pay, scholarship and fellowship income, and employers' contributions to employees' health plans as well as a retirement and child care tax credit. Congress excluded contributions of self-employed persons to pensions, interest on housing bonds, and capital gains on the home sales of the elderly in the 1960s. It enacted the Earned Income Tax Credit (EITC), general and targeted jobs credit, and investment credit for housing rehabilitation in the 1970s, as well as an exclusion of employer educational assistance. With the enactment of the Employer Retirement Income Security Act (ERISA) in 1974, Congress allowed citizens to defer taxes on payments to Individual Retirement Accounts (IRAs). It enacted deduction of adoption expenses and certain income of two-earner couples in the 1980s, as well as an exclusion of employer child care benefits. During the 1990s, Congress greatly expanded the Earned Income Tax Credit, enacted HOPE scholarships that gave tax credits to students in the first two years of postsecondary education, as well as a lifetime learning tax credit in the last two years of college or in graduate school if their parents fell beneath specific income levels.

SOME POLICY ISSUES

If some tax expenditures redistribute resources to low-income persons, such as the EITC, many others favor affluent Americans. Mortgage interest deductions assist homeowners but not renters. The value of deductions increases with taxpayers' income: a person with a top marginal tax rate of 39 percent gains $3,900 from a $10,000 deduction as compared with only $1,500 for a person with a top marginal rate of 15 percent.

Tax expenditures are both supplements and rivals to public programs. Supported by tax subsidies, employers' private health insurance supplements Medicare and Medicaid. Subsidized by favorable tax policies, private pensions supplement Social Security. Yet, some conservatives tout private health insurance as an "alternative" to public programs. They would provide public subsidies to allow medically uninsured Americans, as well as some Americans currently receiving Medicare and Medicaid, to purchase private health insurance. Private health insurance, which fails to insure tens of millions of Americans, diminishes public support for universal national health insurance by offering a private alternative to most American workers. Some conservatives support proposals to privatize Social Security by expanding tax-subsidized individual retirement accounts that would supplant or reduce conventional Social Security pensions—an approach that could sustain or increase current inequities in pensions.

—*Bruce S. Jansson*

See also Economic Policy (United States); Health Policy (United States); Voluntarism (Unites States)

Primary Sources

Roy Blough Papers, Harry S Truman Library, Independence, MO; U.S. Congress, Joint Committee on Taxation. (1993). *Estimates of federal tax expenditures for fiscal years 1994–1998*, 103d Cong., 1st Sess. Washington, DC: Government Printing Office. Available: www.house.gov/jct/s-6-93.pdf; Office of Management and Budget. (1999). *Budget of the U.S. government, Fiscal year 2000: Analytic perspectives*. Washington, DC: Government Printing Office. Available: http://www.gpoaccess.gov/usbudget/fy00/browse.html; Social Security Administration. (1950–1994). *Social welfare: Expenditures series*.

Current Comment

Rose, R. (1991). Welfare: the public/private mix. In S. B. Kamerman & A. J. Kahn (Eds.), *Privatization and the welfare state* (pp. 73–95). Princeton, NJ: Princeton University Press.

Surrey, S. S. (1973). *Pathways to tax reform: The concept of tax expenditures*. Cambridge, MA: Harvard University Press.

Surrey, S. S., & McDaniel, P. R. (1985). *Tax expenditures*. Cambridge, MA: Harvard University Press.

Witte, J. F. (1985). *The politics and development of the federal income tax*. Madison: University of Wisconsin Press.

Further Reading

Hacker, J. S. (2002). *The divided welfare state: The battle over public and private social benefits in the United States*. Cambridge, UK: Cambridge University Press.

Howard, C. (1997). *The hidden welfare state: Tax expenditures and social policy in the United States*. Princeton, NJ: Princeton University Press.

Jansson, B. S. (2001). *The sixteen-trillion-dollar mistake: How the U.S. bungled its national priorities from the New Deal to the present*. New York: Columbia University Press.

Johnston, D. C. (2003). *Perfectly legal: The covert campaign to rig our tax system*. New York: Portfolio.

TOUZEL, BESSIE (1904–1997)

Long recognized by the Ontario social work community, Bessie Touzel was a true leader of vision to the emerging profession of social work for over 40 years, in a career that traversed many points between the Red River Valley in Manitoba and Tanzania. The one constant theme throughout her career was that of advocacy for the poor and dispossessed, especially mothers and their children. Born in Killaloe, Ontario at the beginning of the twentieth century, she became a fighter at an early age when she contracted polio as a toddler.

At the age of 24, Touzel began her lengthy career in social work after graduating from a 2-year diploma course at Canada's oldest school of social work, the University of Toronto. Her first social work position was working with new immigrants in a downtown Toronto settlement house. As a member of the newly formed Canadian Association of Social Work (CASW), Touzel became a social policy advocate. She was active on the Service Standards Committee, where she led the fight for standards of practice that respected the dignity of clients, such as increased relief rates. Touzel continued to promote a social advocacy agenda within the CASW, and in 1954, she was elected its president.

Touzel opposed the firing of a number of female social workers by the City of Ottawa. She resigned from the Toronto Welfare Council after persistent conflicts. In the latter half of the 1930s, as the depression years waned on, the City of Ottawa hired Touzel to set up an emergency relief department. She balanced private donations and public support to provide supplementary relief to clients of relief-giving agencies. An even thornier issue was looming: sex-typing and professionally trained workers. The Canadian Welfare Council argued for relief investigations conducted by men, whereas Touzel thought professionally trained women were best suited because they would consider "the humanitarian aspects of working with people on relief." The conflict culminated in the dismissal of many female colleagues. In the face of these dismissals and the destruction of relief policies she had worked so hard to establish, Touzel resigned.

Touzel took her leadership experiences and zeal for welfare reform to the Toronto Welfare Council (TWC). She worked with other social reform activists to make the adequacy of welfare allowances part of Toronto's political agenda. The struggle between fears of perpetuating idleness reemerged when the Cost of Living Study suggested an upward revision of relief allowances. In 1947, when the funding arm of the TWC demanded the withdrawal of the Cost of Living Study, Touzel resigned.

While conducting a poverty study, Touzel helped organize relief efforts after flooding in New Brunswick in the late 1940s. When Manitoba's Red River Valley flooded in 1950, the Red Cross called on her expertise. Ever the activist, Touzel traveled to Tanzania for the United Nations. Returning to Canada, Touzel started her teaching career in the Faculty of Social Work, University of Toronto. At the end of this long and industrious career, the University of Toronto recognized Touzel as most distinguished graduate of the School of Social Work, the Ontario government bestowed her with the Order of Ontario, and the Ontario Association of Social Workers established the Bessie Touzel Award to acknowledge social workers demonstrating leadership and vision. One of her last public speeches, delivered to a packed audience of students, faculty, and alumni celebrating the Faculty of Social Work's 75th anniversary, was an eloquent and deeply moving insistence that tomorrow's generation of social workers continue the long and important fight for social justice. Bessie Touzel died at age 92 in 1997, but her legacy of social advocacy is deeply ingrained into Canada's social welfare landscape.

—*Cathryn Bradshaw*

See also Cassidy, Harry; Social Welfare (Canada): Since the Marsh Report

Current Comment

Davis, K. (1997, April 27). Obituary: Bessie Touzel: Feisty social worker fought 1950 flooding of Red River. *Ottawa Citizen* (Final ed.), p. A4.

Maines, J. (1959). Through the years in the CASW. *The Social Worker, 27*(4), 5–45.

Shookner, M. (1998, November 4). *90 years of social action.* Speech given at the 90th anniversary celebration of the Ontario Social Development Council, November 4, 1998, Toronto, ON. Available: www.osdc.org/90yr.html

Further Reading

Moscovitch, A., & Albert, J. (1987). *The "benevolent" state: The growth of welfare in Canada.* Toronto, ON: Garamond.

Struthers, J. (1994). *The limits of affluence: Welfare in Ontario, 1920–1970.* Toronto, ON: University of Toronto Press.

Tillotson, S. (1997). Class and community in Canadian welfare work, 1933–1960. *Journal of Canadian Studies, 32,*(1), 63–92.

Wills, G. (1995). *A marriage of convenience: Business and social work in Toronto, 1918–1957.* Toronto, ON: University of Toronto Press.

U

URWICK, EDWARD JOHNS
(1867–1945)

Edward Johns Urwick combined an international reputation as a respected scholar with a firsthand appreciation of social work. He was born into a well-to-do family, with his father serving as a prominent British Congregational minister. Urwick studied at Wadham College, Oxford, where he won a first-class degree in *Literae Humaniores* in 1890, and was awarded an MA two years later.

From 1893 to 1904, Urwick held a number of social work-related positions in England, including resident and sub warden of Toynbee Hall, London (1897 to 1903), poor law guardian in Whitechapel (1896 to 1902), and board member of the Charity Organisation Society. The same year he published *Studies of Boy Life in Our Cities* (1904) under the auspices of the Toynbee Trust, Urwick was appointed director of the London School of Sociology and Social Economics, a position he held until 1920. Subsequent appointments included the Tooke Professor of Economic Science at King's College, London (1907 to 1914), professor of social philosophy at the University of London (1914 to 1924), and director of the Department of Social Science and Administration at the London School of Economics (1910 to 1923). He helped establish social work courses at the Universities of Liverpool, Edinburgh, Birmingham, and Glasgow, and remained active in social development initiatives within the London community. His scholarship was greatly influenced by early social work experiences working and living among London's poor and immigrant populations. He maintained a strong commitment to cohesion among the social classes and to the less fortunate throughout his life. He was deeply influenced by Plato, the spiritual philosophy of the Vedanta, and a number of Indian writers and teachers, among them Vivekanananda, Sri Ramanathan, and Ananda Acharya. A prolific author, his major works included *A Philosophy of Social Progress* (1912), *Luxury and Waste of Life* (1906), *The Message of Plato* (1920), *The Social Good* (1927), and the posthumous *The Values of Life* (1948). The last work was based on lecture notes from undergraduate courses in social philosophy, in which social work students at the University of Toronto were enrolled.

Leaving England for Canada in 1924, Urwick took up the position of special lecturer to social work students at the University of Toronto. Within the year, he was chosen as acting director of the Department of Social Service. In 1927, Urwick assumed the position on a permanent basis, was appointed professor of political science, and invited to head the Departments of Political Economy and Social Service (the latter he renamed Social Science in 1929). Urwick remained with the two departments until his retirement in 1937, at age 70. More than any other University of Toronto social work scholar, Urwick was able to pioneer new ways of looking at the world and to inspire students and colleagues alike. He endorsed the view that university education means primarily the education of the soul, not just the intellect. This rested on a practical wisdom that ideals of love, virtue, and social responsibility must undergird any commitment to the profession. He was also wisely suspicious of "ephemeral . . . fashions of thought." To Urwick, life contained greater complexity than what many prevailing scholarly trends might have claimed. His written work strongly reflects these sentiments.

During his tenure at the University of Toronto, Urwick remained active in academic administration and community work. He helped found and became president of the Canadian Political Science Association and was appointed fellow to the prestigious Royal Society of Canada. Within the local community, Urwick was instrumental in preparing the report of the lieutenant governor's Committee on Housing Conditions (1934); organized the Citizen's Housing Association to advocate housing reform; helped establish, in 1937, the Toronto Welfare Council; served on the board of the University Settlement House; and was actively involved in the Canadian Association of Social Workers. In both academic and community capacities, he always stressed the primacy of ideas, and pointed to the lack of idealization as one of the reasons for society's slow social progression. A man of depth, complexity, principle, and intellect, he is remembered for many things, including his status as one of Canada's most distinguished social work scholars.

—*John R. Graham*

See also Bowers, Frank Swithun Barrington; Cassidy, Harry; Hendry, Charles Eric; Small Systems Social Work (Canada); Social Work Profession (Canada)

Further Reading

Moffatt, K. (2001). *A poetics of social work: Personal agency and social transformation in Canada, 1920–1939*. Toronto, ON: University of Toronto Press.

Urwick, E. J. (1927). *The social good*. London: Methuen.

Urwick, E. J. (1948). *The values of life*. Toronto, ON: University of Toronto Press.

V

VAN KLEECK, MARY (1883–1972)

Mary van Kleeck was a prominent social scientist, reformer, feminist, and social worker. From her base as a social science researcher with the Russell Sage Foundation from 1909 to 1948, van Kleeck was an important national and international figure in efforts to address issues regarding women in industry, the relationship between capital and labor, child labor, social work, organized labor, New Deal policy, economic business cycles, scientific management, and technology in the workplace. Frustrated with the slow rate of improvement in working conditions and standards of living, van Kleeck made the transition from liberal-technocratic-progressive to New Deal–era radical. She advanced the notion of a scientifically managed society and economy characterized by social-economic planning that integrated Marxist economic policy with American democratic principles. Van Kleeck possessed a sharp wit, a powerful speaking voice, strong leadership skills, and a tenacious reform spirit. She lived most of her adult life in New York City and Amsterdam with friend and Dutch social reformer Mary Fledderus.

Mary Abby van Kleeck was born in 1883 in Glenham, New York, the daughter of wealthy descendants of Dutch settlers. Her father, the Reverend Robert Boyd van Kleeck, was an Episcopal priest. Her mother, Eliza Mayer van Kleeck, was the daughter of a founder of the Baltimore and Ohio Railroad. Mary van Kleeck received an AB from Smith College in 1904 and, with the aid of a fellowship in 1905, became a resident in New York's College Settlement, where she was trained in the technique of social investigation by Florence Kelley, a noted researcher, settlement house resident, and women's and children's advocate. Van Kleeck made a name for herself in New York City by conducting studies of the conditions of working women and children in New York factories and tenements. Her work at the College Settlement led to the establishment of the Alliance Employment Bureau (AEB) in 1907. She continued to investigate the industrial trades for women and women's lodging. By 1910, the AEB and its staff became a formal unit of the expanding Russell Sage Foundation. In 1917, the foundation established a Department of Industrial Studies, with van Kleeck as its director. Influenced by the works of economists Thorstein Veblen and Simon Patton, and business consultant Frederick Taylor, van Kleeck's investigations convinced her that the difficult working and living conditions of women and children demonstrated the need for more and stronger government-sponsored factory regulations and the inclusion of Taylor's scientific management techniques as a means to improve economic efficiency. In 1918, van Kleeck took a leave of absence from Russell Sage to accept a position as director of the women's branch of the industrial service section of the federal government's Ordinance Department. During her tenure, van Kleeck convinced the War Labor Policies Board to adopt her proposed standards for the employment of women in defense industries. In 1921, she was selected to sit on Commerce Secretary Herbert Hoover's Committee on Unemployment and Business Cycles, which struggled to identify policies to reduce unemployment and destructive business cycles that were acceptable to both capital and labor. In the mid 1920s, van Kleeck turned her attention to the International Industrial Relations Institute (IIRI), an independent, Left-wing academic research institute that examined issues of social and economic planning. Van Kleeck met friend and colleague Mary Fledderus through the IIRI. She served as its associate director and was an active participant in the organization through the late 1940s.

During the Great Depression of the 1930s, van Kleeck was an outspoken critic of capitalism and of New Deal policy. After accepting an invitation from her friend, Secretary of Labor Frances Perkins, to serve on the Federal Advisory Council of the United States Employment Service in 1933, she resigned after one day of service upon hearing President Franklin D. Roosevelt's decision to eliminate a clause that protected organized labor's right to strike in industries covered by National Recovery Administration (NRA) codes. Van Kleeck was a coauthor of the Frazier-Lundeen Bill, a more generous and inclusive countermeasure to the administration-backed Social Security Act. She joined the left-wing American Labor party in 1936. She supported the Loyalist cause in the Spanish Civil War, denounced efforts by Congress to institute an oath of allegiance in the United States, criticized government efforts to deport the British writer John Strachey for allegedly belonging to the Communist party, advanced the cause of the Fair Standards and Labor Act of 1938, advocated for a liberalization of benefits and eligibility requirements for Aid to Dependent Children (ADC), and traveled to Russia and published in Russian journals. In her book, *Miners and Management* (1934), she advanced the notion that industry would have to be socialized if poverty was to be reduced and the standard of living improved for all Americans. In *Creative America* (1936), she outlined plans for a new social system termed social-economic

planning that featured a collective economy built on the principles of scientific management and political democracy.

At the National Conference of Social Work in Kansas City in 1934, van Kleeck energized the rank and file movement (RFM), a burgeoning left-wing movement in social work, when she criticized capitalism and New Deal policy and encouraged social workers to align themselves with labor. Van Kleeck became a leader of the RFM and served as an editor and contributor to its journal of social criticism and social work, *Social Work Today,* during its publication years, 1934 to 1942. She supported the unionization of social workers, and urged social workers to infuse social and political analyses in their work.

In 1939, van Kleeck supported the Nazi-Soviet Pact based on her belief that Russia had no genuine interest in fascism and was acting only to defend its political interests within a complex international arena. She lost support within much of social work and the American Left for her decision and found herself increasingly on the margins of political power. Regardless, van Kleeck continued to write and do research. She published *Technology and Livelihood* (1944) with Mary Fledderus and in 1948 she ran unsuccessfully for the New York state legislature on the American Labor party ticket. In 1953, she received a subpoena from the United States Senate Permanent Subcommittee on Investigations, chaired by Senator Joseph McCarthy, which aimed, unsuccessfully, to prove she had been a member of the Communist party. Mary Abby van Kleeck died of a heart attack in Kingston, New York, on June 8, 1972.

—Patrick Selmi

See also Labor Movement and Social Welfare (United States); The New Deal (United States); Rank and File Movement (United States); War and Social Welfare (United States)

Primary Sources

Mary van Kleeck Papers in the Sophia Smith Collection, Smith College, Northampton, MA, and at Reuther Library, Wayne State University, Detroit, MI.

Current Comment

Van Kleeck, M. (1913). *Women in the bookbinding trade.* New York: Russell Sage Foundation.

Van Kleeck, M. (1934). Our illusions regarding government. *Proceedings of the National Conference on Social Work, Sixty-First Annual Session* (pp. 473–486). Chicago: University of Chicago Press.

Van Kleeck, M. (1936). *Creative America.* New York: Covici, Friede.

Further Reading

Alchon, G. (1991). Mary van Kleeck and social-economic planning. *Journal of Policy History, 3,* 1–23.

Selmi, P., & Hunter, R. (2001). Beyond the rank and file movement: Mary van Kleeck and social work radicalism in the Great Depression, 1931–1942. *Journal of Sociology and Social Welfare, 28,* 75–100.

VOLUNTARISM (UNITED STATES)

Voluntarism became a fundamental aspect of life in the United States soon after independence. In the early 1800s, a famous French traveler, Alexis de Tocqueville, noted the American propensity for forming purposeful associations and considered such activity vital to democracy in this country. Although the praxis of voluntary association is currently spreading around the world and has a long tradition in other Anglo-Saxon countries (like England and Australia), the scope and influence of voluntarism in the United States remains unparalleled. It is embedded in major philanthropic institutions, in universities and schools, in child care organizations, in hospitals and health care, in associations for music and the arts, as well as in numerous civic and neighborhood groups.

The term voluntarism covers a range of conceptual views and definitions. To begin with, voluntarism is often defined by what it is not: it is not activity carried out by government or business. Accordingly, diverse numbers of voluntary organizations are defined as constituting a "third," nonprofit, sector, distinguished by organizational difference from the other two sectors (government and business). Voluntary activity is directed outside the family, but is usually related to community needs. In a legal context, voluntarism refers to a sector in which organizations are incorporated under state laws as "not-for-profit" and are considered exempt from federal income taxes under the Internal Revenue Code. Voluntarism also characterizes the spirit of mutual aid and collective activity carried out by informal groups that may not be formally incorporated. In other countries, the term "nongovernmental organization" is often used to refer to voluntary associations. In general, the terms "voluntary sector," "third sector," and "nonprofit sector" tend to be used interchangeably. More recently, voluntary activity has been conceptualized in terms of the social capital, networks of association, and norms of trust that altogether constitute the essence of a civil society.

SCOPE AND SIZE

The size and scope of the nonprofit sector are determined from estimates based on imperfect knowledge. Calculations usually begin with the number of organizations listed as Tax-Exempt Entities (under Section 501 (c) of the Internal Revenue Code) in the Master File of the Internal Revenue Service (IRS). In the year 2002, the IRS listed 1,444,905 tax-exempt nonprofit organizations under the 501 (c) section of the tax code. This probably includes organizations that are no longer active; it also omits many religious congregations (churches, synagogues, and mosques) and small organizations (with revenues under $25,000) that are not required to register.

Of the 27 subsections of the 501 (c) category, two are particularly related to social welfare purposes: the 501 (c) (3) category, often referred to as "charities," and the closely related 501 (c) (4) social welfare-civic association group. In 2002, these groups included, respectively, 909,574 and 137,526 organizations; they have been described as constituting the American "independent sector." Calculations of the independent sector also generally include approximately 300,000 (of an estimated total of 350,000) religious congregations not registered with the IRS. Some scholars also argue that more attention should be paid to the important role played by small grassroots groups and civic associations not counted in the IRS figures.

RATIONALE AND JUSTIFICATIONS FOR THE SECTOR

Nonprofit organizations in the 501 (c) category are exempt from federal income taxes and from various state and local taxes. As tax-exempt entities, they are expected to operate in the public interest and to be self-governed by an accountable governance system (e.g., a board of directors). They are legally prohibited from distributing profits to shareholders or other individuals. Organizations in the 501 (c) (3) subsection benefit from a separate, second tax exemption given to donors who contribute to these organizations. This additional tax benefit is provided to donors because the organization receiving the contribution is presumed to be operating for religious, charitable, scientific, literary, or educational purposes; this delineation has its origins in the Statute of Charitable Uses, enacted by the English Parliament in 1601. In comparison with 501 (c) (4) organizations, publicly supported "charitable" 501 (c) (3) organizations have limitations on activities related to lobbying.

No one comprehensive theory of the nonprofit sector exists, but scholars have proposed some convincing theoretical explanations for its existence. One economic argument suggests that voluntary services develop as a result of a government-market failure. Failure in government provision of collective-consumption goods—for example, open space—results in a market substitution of private goods; voluntary provision of such goods offers an effective balance. The alternative of non-market, non-governmental provision of social goods like child care or education also meets the demand for diversity and choice in American life. Moreover, when the government is unwilling to pay for services at a level that voters desire, voluntary organizations can fill the gap; donations from consumers of services also help solve the "free rider" problem. Further theoretical justification for the sector is based on the concept of contract failure: Voluntary services may be preferable to for-profit services where there is a lack of information or asymmetrical knowledge about the quality of the service, as in nursing care arranged for by the children of the consumers. The consumer chooses a nonprofit institution because of trust in its operators; in the absence of a profit motive, there will be less reason to take advantage of the consumer.

SUBSECTORS

Social welfare organizations in the nonprofit sector may be grouped into subsectors according to their major focus of activity, such as health, social services,

civic organizations, and so on, which shapes their function, sources of revenue, and other characteristics. Another crosscutting categorization applicable to social welfare organizations would differentiate advocacy groups, service providers, and intermediary or supporting organizations that provide funds to other organizations. The first group of advocacy organizations includes lobbying groups like the American Association for Retired Persons (AARP), or the National Committee to Preserve Social Security (NCSSP), which are generally 501 (c) (4) organizations. This group also includes social action/social change (oppositional) activity. Examples of the second group, 501 (c) (3) service providers, are family service agencies, day care centers, and hospitals. The third group, also defined as 501 (c) (3) under the code, are intermediary (supporting) organizations, such as federated fund-raising groups, like the United Way or a host of "alternative funds" (Black United Funds or Women's Funds). The functions of these groups certainly overlap: AARP and the United Way may provide some services directly, and most service-providing agencies also advocate (and lobby) for their clients' needs. Religious organizations and congregations may also provide social welfare services.

ECONOMICS AND FINANCES

The voluntary sector constitutes a significant part of the American economy; it includes about 6 percent of all organizations in the United States, and without including estimated values of volunteer time, its share of national income was 6.7 percent in 1998. Thus defined, the independent sector had an estimated 10.9 million paid employees and included work contributed by an additional 5.8 million (full-time equivalent) volunteers.

Even in an uncertain economic year, total contributions to the nonprofit sector in 2002 amounted to $240.92 billion (slightly more than for 2001): Of this amount, educational institutions received an estimated $31.64 billion; human services, $18.65 billion; health organizations, $18.87 billion; and public benefit organizations, an estimated $11.60 billion. Estimates vary, but one major source suggests that for independent sector organizations (1997) an average of 38 percent of revenues came from dues and services; 31 percent from government; 20 percent from private contributions; and 11 percent from other sources (e.g., interest).

Larger institutions (hospitals, universities, museums) have a disproportionate share of revenues of the sector; some subsectors, such as health, benefit from greater amounts of government funding.

ISSUES FACING THE SECTOR

The conservative climate of the late twentieth century brought new challenges to the voluntary sector, both in terms of threatened decreases in government funding and proposed regulations on sector activities. Cutbacks of federal funding in the early 1980s (under President Ronald Reagan) were eventually less draconian than expected, but still led to increased privatization and more commercialization of nonprofit activity (e.g., more use of for-profit instruments, fees, and sales of products). Profit-making organizations also presented increased competition. Yet by the late 1990s, social welfare subsectors (health and social services) had increased their total government revenues, including federal, state, and local sources. Serious threats in the mid 1990s to restrict or prohibit lobbying by nonprofit organizations (the Istook Amendment) were also defeated by 1996, but only with great effort.

As the twenty-first century begins, the voluntary sector demonstrates resilience, but also appears to be facing a crisis of identity. Uncertainty about government funding and a new business-dominated paradigm have been accompanied by a stronger philosophy of social entrepreneurship; some even consider this a positive direction. But commercialization intensifies questions about organizational purpose, legitimacy of the sector, and location of accountability. Increased use of public-private partnerships (business, voluntary, and government) is a closely related issue. Although such partnerships allow for more leveraging of scarce resources, they may undermine the mission-driven (and autonomous) public-purpose function of nonprofit organizations.

New federal funding for services provided by faith-based organizations, originally formalized in the 1996 Welfare Reform Act and embraced by President George W. Bush in 2001, is another unresolved issue. Although contracting between public agencies and nonprofits has a long history in the United States, this new direction opens the way for religious congregations to provide services directly, without limits on their religious messages. Although religious institutions have not yet responded extensively, concerns have been expressed about the constitutional problems entailed.

Finally, new technologies, (including the Internet) with far-reaching and direct means of communication, will increasingly affect nonprofit development, requiring expertise and funding resources that smaller organizations currently lack. In order to protect the role of smaller organizations in promoting social change and addressing community concerns, efforts must be made to provide them with the resources and technical capacity needed for survival in an increasingly complex, global world.

—Eleanor L. Brilliant

See also Mutual Aid (United States); Philanthropy (United States); Tax Expenditures (Unites States)

Primary Sources

Council of Foundations Records, Rockefeller Archive Center, Rockefeller University, Sleepy Hollow, NY; John D. Rockefeller III Papers, Rockefeller Archive Center, Rockefeller University, Sleepy Hollow, NY; Adam Yarmolinsky Papers, John F. Kennedy Library, Boston, MA; and Manuscript Collections: Philanthropy, Indiana University-Purdue University Indianapolis (IUPUI) University Library, Indianapolis.

Current Comment

Commission on Private Philanthropy and Public Needs [Filer Commission]. (1975). *Giving in America: Toward a stronger voluntary sector.* Washington, DC. Available: http://india-mond.ulib.iupui.edu/PRO/

Giving USA 2003: The Annual Report on Philanthropy for the Year 2002. (2003). Indianapolis, IN: American Association of Fundraising Counsel (AAFRC) Trust for Philanthropy.

Internal Revenue Service. (2003). *2002 Data Book* (Publication 55B). Washington, DC: Government Printing Office.

Weisbrod, B. A. (1988). *The nonprofit economy.* Cambridge, MA: Harvard University Press.

Further Reading

Brilliant, E. L. (2000). *Private charity and public inquiry: A history of the Filer and Peterson commissions.* Bloomington and Indianapolis: Indiana University Press.

Hammack, D., & Young, D. R. (Eds.). (1993). *Nonprofit organizations in a market economy: Understanding new roles, issues, and trends.* San Francisco: Jossey-Bass.

Salamon, L. M. (Ed.). (2002). *The state of nonprofit America.* Washington, DC: Brookings Institution Press.

Smith, S. R., & Lipsky, M. (1993). *Nonprofits for hire: The welfare state in the age of contracting.* Cambridge, MA: Harvard University Press.

WALD, LILLIAN D. (1867–1940)

Lillian Wald made a unique contribution to the development of North American social welfare as a leader in public health nursing, public education, and social work. A lifelong activist for social justice, civil rights, women's rights, and peace, she was subjected to political attacks throughout her career. Nevertheless, she was honored for her contributions to social welfare toward the end of her life and received numerous posthumous awards.

She was born in 1867 in Cincinnati, Ohio, to middle-class German Jewish immigrants who had fled Europe to escape religious persecution. After she graduated from the New York Hospital Training School for Nurses in 1891, she moved to the Lower East Side of Manhattan, which was at the time the most densely populated neighborhood and one of the poorest communities in the Western world. With the backing of millionaire philanthropist Jacob Schiff, who became Wald's longtime patron, she founded the Henry Street Settlement, one of the first settlement houses in the United States, and the Visiting Nurses Service of New York, which pioneered public health nursing. She helped develop Columbia University's Department of Nursing and Health and the Department for Special Education in the New York City school system. Wald was also involved in the hiring of the first school nurses for New York City schools and the creation of the first nursing care insurance program in the nation. In 1912, in recognition of her stature and accomplishments, she was elected the first president of the National Organization of Public Health Nursing, an organization she helped to found.

Lillian Wald made the Henry Street Settlement a center of community service for the area's diverse residents and a catalyst for social activism and social reform. In 1902, Henry Street opened the first children's playground in the nation and in 1909 it hosted the National Negro Conference, which led to the establishment of the National Association for the Advancement of Colored People. Wald made the Henry Street Settlement a locus for cultural activities and political debate, and a safe place for the discussion of controversial issues.

An outspoken supporter of labor, she organized the Women's Trade Union League, in conjunction with other settlement leaders, such as Jane Addams. With another settlement leader, Florence Kelley, Wald made a major contribution to the expansion of workers' rights by providing written testimony for the landmark Supreme Court case of *Muller v. Oregon* (1908). This decision established the right of state governments to regulate the number of hours in a workday. In partnership with Kelley, Wald also organized the

New York Child Labor Committee and helped establish the U.S. Children's Bureau.

In 1915, on the eve of World War I, Wald cofounded and was elected president of the American Union Against Militarism (AUAM), which opposed war and militarism. She consistently argued for peaceful solutions to international problems rather than war and saw socialism as an answer to many social problems. That year she also helped form the Women's Peace party, which eventually became the Women's International League for Peace and Freedom. From its inception, the AUAM was active nationally in an unsuccessful attempt to block U.S. participation in World War I and a successful effort to thwart a U.S. invasion of Mexico. United by their social feminism and anti-imperialist philosophies, Wald forged alliances with radicals such as Crystal Eastman and Emma Goldman around domestic issues, too, such as prostitution and White slavery. Although her pacifist views were often criticized by conservative patriotic organizations, she retained the respect of mainstream political leaders. After World War I, she was appointed an adviser to the League of Nations Child Welfare Division in Paris and was asked by President Woodrow Wilson to participate in an industrial conference to discuss postwar reconstruction.

During and after World War I, even though politicians, the press, and some philanthropists virulently attacked her antiwar views as unpatriotic and pro-German, Wald continued her political activism. In 1919, the Lusk Committee of the New York state legislature investigated her antiwar activity. In a report issued two years later, the committee accused her of being "anxious to bring about the overthrow of the government and establish in this country a soviet government on the same lines as in Russia." In the same period, the Overman Committee of the United States Congress, a predecessor to the House Un-American Activities Committee of the 1950s and 1960s, labeled her an "undesirable citizen" and the U.S. Military Intelligence Bureau included her in a "Who's Who in Pacifism," an attempt to publicize the danger to the nation of those who opposed American involvement in World War I.

Defiant and even dismissive of these attempts to repress her, Wald led efforts in the early 1920s to obtain diplomatic recognition for the newly formed Soviet Union, organized protests against U.S. military intervention in Nicaragua, and served on the committee to free the famous anarchists, Nicola Sacco and Bartolomeo Vanzetti. She also played a leading role in the movement to obtain women's suffrage and opposed the Ku Klux Klan as it grew in power in the 1920s. She joined other antiestablishment organizations such as the American League to Abolish Capital Punishment and the American Anti-Imperialist League for Independence of the Philippines from the United States.

Her tireless work for social justice eventually took a toll on her health. In 1925, Wald had emergency surgery and never fully regained her former strength and energy. During the late 1920s and 1930s, she played the role of an elder stateswoman. Wald was pleased that former protégés like Frances Perkins were appointed to leadership positions in the administration of President Franklin D. Roosevelt. She supported New Deal, social welfare, and labor policies that were consistent with her values and beliefs.

In the mid and late 1930s, Lillian Wald was honored by the New York state legislature and the United States Congress, which had attempted to silence her less than two decades before because of her strong opposition to many domestic and foreign policies. She died at her home of a cerebral hemorrhage in September 1940, at the age of 73. In the late 1950s, she was installed in the Hall of Fame of Great Americans.

—*Michael Reisch*

See also Addams, Jane; Perkins, Frances; Settlement Houses (United States)

Further Reading

Coss, C. (Ed.). (1989). *Lillian D. Wald: Progressive activist.* New York: Feminist Press of the City of New York.

Wald, L. D. (1915). *The house on Henry Street.* New York: Holt.

Wald, L. D. (1934). *Windows on Henry Street.* Boston: Little, Brown.

WAR AND SOCIAL WELFARE (CANADA)

Canada made a significant contribution to the Allied cause in both the First and Second World Wars. Between 1914 and 1918, approximately 630,000 men and women volunteered with the Canadian

Expeditionary Force; 60,000 died and over 135,000 were wounded. In the Second World War, about 1 million men and women served in Canada's armed forces; 45,000 were killed. In the country's response to the problem of returned soldiers and veterans during the First World War, public policy changes prompted the federal government to embark on significant social welfare reform. Canada's wartime experience with its citizen soldiers illustrates the shift from welfare based on charity and voluntarism to state intervention and support in the lives of its citizens. Veterans and their dependents, by their suffering and loss, rewrote the definition of social entitlement. It was not a battle won during the war, it was evolutionary and incremental, but through the next three decades, policymakers and ordinary Canadians created a broad social welfare system in Canada, the origins of which can be traced to the federal government's response to veterans of the First World War.

The Military Hospitals Commission (MHC) was established in June 1915 by the federal government to provide hospital accommodation and convalescent homes for returned soldiers and to develop programs for the rehabilitation and reemployment of the disabled. Its early work is indicative of prevailing attitudes at the time—private citizens donated facilities for convalescent homes, and nongovernmental organizations were encouraged and expected to offer their support. At the outbreak of war, the Canadian Patriotic Fund was established to provide financial assistance to soldiers' families and dependents and, in 1915, a Disablement Fund was launched to raise money for invalid and disabled soldiers. Both funds relied on public contributions. The Military Hospitals Commission itself was a hybrid, combining traditional forms of charity and voluntarism with a small measure of state involvement; by the end of 1915, it had launched a series of initiatives to provide returned soldiers and invalids with the means to become economically self-sufficient. This was uncharted territory for the government. Only with caution and over time did the government assume greater responsibility for the sick and disabled. As more wounded were returned to Canada, MHC officials recognized and accepted that a fundamental change was taking place in the relationship between the state and its citizens. MHC Secretary Ernest Scammell (1872–1938) acknowledged

as early as October 1915 that the government had an obligation to those who volunteered to serve. By extension, this included the dependents of both the disabled and those who had been killed.

By the end of 1916—with no end of the war in sight—the Military Hospitals Commission had assumed increasing responsibility for returned soldiers and had developed policies and programs for the medical treatment of the sick and disabled, for the retraining of the blind, and for those who suffered amputations. It was, by any measure, a huge undertaking and government officials recognized that the state's obligation to the returned soldier required an unprecedented commitment of resources.

Treatment of those suffering from tuberculosis (TB) is a case in point. The first contingent of the Canadian Expeditionary Force (CEF), consisting of 30,000 men, departed Quebec in October 1914. Several thousand men were rejected by medical boards because of ailments including heart disease, pneumonia, and, especially, TB. Even though few if any would ever serve in the CEF, the government assumed responsibility for their health and welfare. It was a landmark decision. Many of those who suffered from TB, for example, never donned a uniform, yet they received free medical treatment, convalescent care, and pensions. Some were eventually well enough to join the CEF but many others could not.

The sick and disabled who returned to Canada during the war were the responsibility of the Military Hospitals Commission, but by 1918, the government faced an even greater challenge: the demobilization of Canada's army at the end of hostilities. A Department of Soldiers' Civil Re-establishment (DSCR) was established in February 1918 to develop plans for the postwar reintegration of Canadian veterans in society. At the same time, the MHC was renamed the Invalid Soldiers Commission with ongoing responsibility for the rehabilitation and retraining of the disabled, and was absorbed by the new department—the DSCR. Although there would be a continuing role for nongovernmental agencies in the care of war veterans, the development and coordination of policies and programs were now centralized, as never before, within the federal government.

Medical treatment, vocational retraining, and assistance in finding employment represented only one aspect of the government's overall program for returned soldiers. Pensions for the dependents of those who been killed or disabled were important if Canada was to meet its obligation to its citizen soldiers. Pensions for soldiers permanently disabled and for the widows and children of those killed on active service had a long tradition in Canada, but the number of pension awards made to those who had served in the military, as members of the Permanent Force, as volunteers in the War of 1812, in the Fenian Raids of 1866 and 1870, or in the Northwest Rebellion of 1885, were few in number. They were administered by the Department of Militia and Defence. By the time Canada's World War I soldiers reached England in October 1914, a Pensions and Claims Board had been established, but pension awards, based on militia regulations that dated from the 1880s and earlier, were now considered inadequate. Following extensive research and debate, the government appointed a Board of Pension Commissioners (BPC) in June 1916 under the direction of Dr. John L. Todd (1876–1949) of McGill University. Todd studied the pension systems of several countries, including Great Britain, France, and the United States, and developed a policy that compensated veterans for disabilities. Support for war widows and dependents was another matter, but the BPC quickly adopted the principle that the state should assume legal responsibility for the survivors of those whose death was attributable to war service.

In a few short years, Todd and his fellow commissioners acquired extensive experience in the theory and practice of pensions as tens of thousands of disabled soldiers returned home. Rules and regulations were finally codified in September 1919, when Canada's first pension act took effect. In 1918, the board reported that 15,335 disability pensions were in force, a figure that would rise to 69,000 2 years later. Pensions for dependents experienced marked increase, too, from 10,488 in 1918, to 17,800 in 1920. By March 1938, close to 98,000 pensions were administered by the BPC, including 18,105 for dependents. Total war pension liability exceeded $40 million, and approximately 300,000 men, women, and children received benefits.

The significance of the pension scheme created during and after the First World War lies in the fact that it altered the relationship of the individual and the state and in doing so, it changed the concept of social entitlement. No longer could an individual be left to the uncertainties of charity-based social welfare. Those who volunteered their services in time of war had earned the right to be treated in a fair and just manner by their fellow citizens. The state accepted this obligation, thus creating a system that would eventually benefit all Canadians. Pension awards may have been criticized as small and insufficient, but an important principle had been established: Widows and dependent children and the disabled were provided with state financial support that had simply not existed in prewar Canada.

The battle for social justice did not end with the war. Issues affecting veterans, especially pensions, were constantly before the government throughout the 1920s and 1930s. In 1920, again at the urging of Todd, the government instituted a returned soldiers' life insurance scheme, and 2 years later, a royal commission headed by Col. J. L. Ralston (1881–1948) made an exhaustive study of the pension act. In 1930, the government introduced a war veterans allowance to provide pensions to those who had aged prematurely—so-called "burnt out" veterans—because of physical or mental disability attributable to war service.

If the rehabilitation and reestablishment of veterans had not been a popular success, the lessons of the past were heeded a generation later. Although the policies and programs for veterans had been roundly criticized and often disparaged during the interwar years, at the outbreak of the Second World War, the federal government was well versed and experienced in matters affecting veterans. Over the course of 20 years, officials of the Department of Soldiers' Civil Re-establishment and its successor, Pensions and National Health, had become experts in preventive medicine, vocational rehabilitation, and had gained valuable experience with the needs of an aging population. Pioneering work had been done in occupational therapy, retraining of the disabled, pension administration, and overall social policy, expertise that could be and was shared with the nonveteran population.

Drawing on the experience of the First World War and cognizant of the difficulties and criticisms voiced by veterans in the two decades since the end of the war, the government was quick to act in 1939. In December, three months after the declaration of war, the federal cabinet appointed a Committee on Demobilization and Rehabilitation. Its subcommittees examined every aspect of the rehabilitation question, devised new programs, modernized existing legislation, and created by the end of the war a federal "Veterans Charter" that enshrined a comprehensive program to meet the needs of returning soldiers, widows, their families, and dependents.

The origins of social welfare in Canada are not found exclusively in the experience of the First World War, but the war, as a national undertaking, had a profound effect on Canadian society, on individuals, on families, and on communities. During and after the war, the state assumed increasing responsibility for the individual, recognizing and acting on its obligation to the men and women and their dependents who had suffered because of the war. As the war stretched into years, the philanthropic or voluntary approach to social welfare was doomed, replaced by government intervention in the lives of its veterans, their dependents, and survivors. Only the state had the financial resources equal to the task at hand. The experience focused attention on the marginalized in society as never before, the disabled, widows, children, all those unable to provide for themselves. Even at the end of the war, Canadians were not accustomed to state-managed social welfare, although the work of the Military Hospitals Commission, the DSCR and its successor, and the Board of Pension Commissioners created for Canadians a new concept of state-supported social services. And it was the war that had forced the issue: The reality of disabled soldiers, unemployed veterans, and desperate families required the intervention of the state. The evolution of federal government administration to meet the challenge is instructive. A Department of Health was created in June 1919, and was administered by the minister responsible for the DSCR, and in 1928 the two departments were merged as the Department of Pensions and National Health. The department was split again during the Second World War to become the Department of Veterans Affairs and the Department of Health and Welfare in October 1944. Within these administrative structures, one finds the cradle of Canada's postwar welfare system.

Although the policies and programs developed for veterans of the First World War pale in comparison with what was achieved in the Second World War, the 1914–1918 experience—and the debates that continued through most of the next two decades—had a significant impact not only on veterans and their dependents but on the Canadian population generally. From medical treatment to pensions, the concept of social entitlement had been redefined. The state acknowledged that the sick, the disabled, and their dependents—the less fortunate in society—had a right to be treated justly and humanely, and it was the acceptance of this fundamental idea that would cement the foundation for further social welfare measures in the decades to follow. Various private and religious initiatives existed before the war to care for the poor and indigent, yet few recipients could claim continuing state support. But the demands on the government during the First World War led to a reexamination of the right of entitlement, and it was this shift, from charity to entitlement, that is, in the words of James Struthers, the "central metaphorical turn in the construction of the welfare state" (quoted in Neary & Granatstein, 1998, p.179) and would become the fundamental principle for Canada's social programs.

—*Glenn Wright*

See also Labour and Social Welfare (Canada); Social Welfare (Canada): Before the Marsh Report; Social Welfare (Canada): Since the Marsh Report; Welfare Capitalism (Canada)

Current Comment

England, R. (1943). *Discharged: A commentary of civil re-establishment of veterans in Canada*. Toronto, ON: Macmillan.

Woods, W. S. (1953). *Rehabilitation, A combined operation*. Ottawa, ON: Queen's Printer.

Further Reading

Guest, D. (1997). *The emergence of Social Security in Canada* (3rd ed.). Vancouver: University of British Columbia Press.

Morton, D., & Wright, G. (1987). *Winning the second battle: Canadian veterans and the return to civilian life, 1915–1930*. Toronto, ON: University of Toronto Press.

Neary, P., & Granatstein. J. L. (Eds.). (1998). *The Veterans Charter and post World War II in Canada*. Montreal, QC, and Kingston, ON: McGill-Queen's University Press.

Snell, J. G. (1996). *The citizen's wage: The state and the elderly in Canada, 1919–1951*. Toronto, ON: University of Toronto Press.

WAR AND SOCIAL WELFARE (UNITED STATES)

A nations's involvement in armed conflict influences not only its position on an international level; it also affects the "home front" in significant ways, both during the conflict and afterward. This essay provides an overview of developments in social welfare in the United States during the Civil War, World Wars I and II, and the Vietnam War.

THE CIVIL WAR AND RECONSTRUCTION

The Civil War occasioned the first significant involvement of the federal government in social welfare. The war resulted in the creation of pensions for Civil War veterans, the establishment of the Freedmen's Bureau, and an expansion of voluntary effort. Numerous voluntary social welfare programs were created, including the nation's first major public health organization—the United States Sanitary Commission—and the United States Christian Commission.

The U.S. Sanitary Commission was a voluntary organization in spite of its name. Founded in New York in 1861, the commission was staffed mainly by women. Commission volunteers initially engaged in preventive work, in particular educating Union soldiers about the importance of hygiene. As the war expanded, the commission's nursing staff also provided medical supplies, trained physicians in proper sanitary procedures, and facilitated communication between servicemen and their families. The American Red Cross, which undertook much of this work in subsequent conflicts, was founded in 1881 by Clara Barton, who had been a volunteer nurse during the Civil War.

Members of the YMCA founded the U.S. Christian Commission in 1861 to provide chaplains to Union troops. Meeting in New York in November of that year, YMCA representatives formed the organization to meet the spiritual needs of the troops. Over time, the commission extended its work to provide material assistance as well.

Federal developments in social welfare that occurred during the Civil War included the creation of the first federal old age and disabilities pension program. In 1862, Congress enacted the Pension Act to provide benefits to Union veterans disabled during the conflict and their dependents. Congress expanded the program in 1890 to include any disabled veteran, whether or not the disability resulted from war-related injuries. A 1906 amendment included old age as a qualifying disability.

Congress created the first federal social welfare agency, the Bureau of Refugees, Freedmen, and Abandoned Lands, in 1865. Congress created the bureau to assist the former slaves in the transition to freedom. Though never adequately funded, the bureau provided direct relief to the destitute, as well as educational, medical, and legal services during its 7-year period of operation.

WORLD WAR I AND ITS AFTERMATH

The entry of the United States into World War I in April 1917 also brought about significant developments in social welfare. These included the establishment of psychiatric social work to address the needs of servicemen with mental health problems, the Red Cross Home Service, which provided services to both soldiers and their families, and the Women in Industry Service, which was created to address the needs of women entering the workforce during the war.

Growing awareness of the emotional toll of war on soldiers led the army to establish a neuropsychiatric division to treat soldiers suffering from mental disorders, to screen prospective recruits, and to facilitate soldiers' return to civilian life after discharge. Psychiatric social work developed during this period, as social workers formed an alliance with psychiatrists, who were, for the first time, treating soldiers with mental conditions in large numbers. After the war, medical services for veterans expanded. Congress created the Veterans Administration in 1930 to coordinate the federal government's expanded veterans services.

Several private organizations provided a wide range of social welfare services to soldiers and their families during the war. One of these, the Red Cross Home Service, offered medical, legal, employment, and educational assistance to families. The YMCA provided services to servicemen; its Department for Colored Troops served African American soldiers. The 85 YMCA department's "secretaries," often working in the face of virulent racism, organized educational programs, facilitated communication between the troops and their families, and advocated for African American soldiers' right to services when the program was threatened with extinction.

During the war, social service agencies, public and private, suffered losses of funds and professional staff. The U.S. Children's Bureau spearheaded an effort to address this problem in April 1918 with its call for a "Children's Year," a program designed to call attention to the needs of children and their families brought on by the war. The bureau focused its efforts on developing community support to address four areas of concern: the prevention of infant mortality, the provision of economic assistance to children in their own homes, further regulation of child labor, and the creation of recreational opportunities for children.

The war also saw significant government involvement in economic matters. In April 1918, President Woodrow Wilson established the National War Labor Board to stem labor unrest in industries critical to the war effort. The board, consisting of representatives of both organized labor and industry, was the first federal agency to issue comprehensive policies governing working conditions in the private sector. Such policies were the forerunners of the labor legislation of the New Deal.

Women entered the workforce in large numbers during the war as men left civilian employment for military service. Mary van Kleeck, director of industrial studies for the Russell Sage Foundation, accepted an appointment as head of the Women in Industry Service (WIN) in the Department of Labor in July 1918. Van Kleeck's charge was to develop standards to govern the employment of women in war-related industries. The professed goal was to safeguard women in the workplace, addressing such issues as health and safety, and wages and hours. Van Kleeck remained with WIN through the summer of 1919. WIN became the Women's Bureau in 1920. After the war, the Women's Bureau investigated women's working conditions in both the public and private sectors and made recommendations concerning women's employment.

WORLD WAR II

By the time the United States entered the Second World War in December 1941, the federal government's role in social welfare was well established as a result of Franklin Roosevelt's New Deal. The war created needs not envisioned by the social planners of the 1930s, however. To respond to those needs, Congress created several new programs. These new initiatives included the provision of federal funding for community services (Lanham Act, 1941), the creation of the Office of Community War Services (1943), and the passage of the Servicemen's Readjustment Act or "G.I. Bill" (1944).

The massive entry of women into the workforce raised the issue of child care for working mothers. The federal government responded with the Community Facilities (Lanham) Act of 1941, which provided federal funds for the building of child care centers, hospitals, schools, and recreational facilities. In 1943, the Office of Community War Services was created to assist states and communities in providing basic services for families, including health care, recreational programs, and housing assistance.

The postwar era brought forth the prospect of reintegrating millions of former servicemen and women into the civilian labor force. Congress responded with the Servicemen's Readjustment Act of 1944, the "G.I. Bill," which provided educational and job training assistance, as well as low-interest housing loans, employment services, medical services, and unemployment insurance to veterans. Some said that this law, which expanded the scope of the services provided by the Veterans Administration, completed the New Deal.

THE VIETNAM WAR

A major expansion of the welfare state occurred in the 1960s with President Lyndon Johnson's Great Society programs, including the War on Poverty. Medicare, Medicaid, and job training and education programs were a part of this effort. At the same time, the United States was escalating its involvement in Vietnam and the antiwar movement was gathering momentum. Antiwar activists often worked across movements, supporting the struggle for civil rights, and second-wave feminism, as well as the War on Poverty. Public opposition to the war eroded public support for President Johnson's domestic agenda, including social welfare programs. Though many Great Society programs are still in existence today (Medicare and Medicaid, the Older Americans Act programs, Head Start, Job Corps), the War on Poverty was largely stalled by 1968, the year that Johnson chose not to seek a second term in office.

The Veterans Administration (VA), originally created in 1929, expanded its programs both during and after the war. The Veterans' Readjustment Benefits Act (the "Vietnam G.I. Bill"), passed in 1966, provided educational assistance to Vietnam War veterans. The VA also created new outreach programs. Beginning in 1967, it established Veterans Assistance centers in 21 cities. In 1968, the agency implemented Operation Outreach to ensure that veterans were aware of the benefits available to them. During the postwar period, the VA continued to provide services to disabled veterans, including those suffering from the effects of Agent Orange. The VA became a cabinet-level agency, the Department of Veterans Affairs, in 1989.

CONCLUSION

The social, economic, and political disruptions created by war often necessitate changes in social institutions to meet the needs of both the civilian and military populations. Over the course of U.S. history, significant new social welfare policies and programs have been created during periods of major armed conflict. Many of these changes have been institutionalized, and have contributed to the development of the American welfare state.

—Ike Burson

See also Disability Policy (United States); Housing Policy (United States); Van Kleeck, Mary

Primary Sources

Records of the Department of Veterans Affairs (Record Group 15), Records of the Bureau of Refugees, Freedmen, and Abandoned Lands (Record Group 105), Records of the Women's Bureau (Record Group 86), National Archives & Records Administration, Washington, DC, and College Park, MD.

Current Comment

Barton, C. (1906). *The Red Cross in peace and war.* Washington, DC: American Historical Press.

Oliver, J. W. (1917). History of Civil War military pensions, 1861–1885. *Bulletin of the University of Wisconsin*, History Series, *4*(1).

Titzel, M. E. (1919). Building a child welfare program in wartime. *American Journal of Sociology, 24*(4), 411–422.

Further Reading

Black, W. G. (1991). Social work in World War I: A method lost. *Social Service Review, 64*, 379–402.

Skocpol, T. (1992). *Protecting mothers and soldiers: The political origins of social policy in the United States.* Cambridge, MA: Harvard University Press, Belknap Press.

Summerfield, P. (1998). *Reconstructing women's lives: Discourse and subjectivity in oral histories of the Second World War.* Manchester, NH: Manchester University Press.

WELFARE CAPITALISM (CANADA)

Since the creation of Canada as a nation in 1867, legislative responsibility for social and workplace welfare has been shared between the federal and provincial or territorial governments, and between the public and private sectors. Despite the prevailing ideological commitment to freedom of contract in employment relations, governments have intervened to impose minimum wages, maximum hours, and health and safety standards. Governments have also stepped in to provide basic necessities when remuneration from employment is inadequate, including old age and disability pensions, unemployment insurance, paid employment leave for new parents, state-funded health insurance, and publicly funded education and job training—what some call the "social wage." By the First World War, three of the main processes of modernization—immigration, industrialization, and urbanization—had disrupted the possibility that families and communities could maintain those whose earnings were inadequate to support themselves and their families. The war emergency added to the problem, but also added to the legitimacy of state intervention.

When Canada followed the United Kingdom to war in August 1914, many men who volunteered for overseas service left behind dependent wives, children, or parents. The government provided a minimal separation allowance. A charitable organization, called the Canadian Patriotic Fund, raised money to provide the difference between the separation allowance and a decent living. Fund organizers emphasized that the payments were not charity but fulfillment of the country's obligations to the men in the trenches. Pensions for disabled soldiers or dependents of those killed in the war were also presented in terms of entitlement rather than charity, as were government allowances to women who, through no fault of their own, were fulfilling the important social responsibility of child rearing without the assistance of a male breadwinner.

When postwar unemployment and runaway inflation dashed expectations that wartime sacrifices would be rewarded with improved wages and working conditions, workers turned to collective action to secure wartime wage gains. In the Winnipeg General Strike of 1919, workers briefly constituted an alternative government. The strike was crushed through the deployment of federal troops, arrests, and deportations, but employers and governments also sought less overtly coercive ways to ensure that Canadian workers did not launch a Bolshevik revolution. In the resource sector, for example, employers offered subsidized housing and recreation facilities for their workers. A company selling lumber pre-cut to the lengths needed for building modest bungalows offered its product in an advertisement with the slogan, "Kill Bolshevism by Erecting Homes" (*Industrial Canada*, November 1920, p. 1) In many single-industry towns, employer-provided public utilities, schools, stores, and other essentials reinforced the employer's dominance and the workers' dependence, adding to the risks for workers who resisted wage cuts or unfair hiring practices. Leases for employer-owned housing in coal mining towns, for example, sometimes prohibited tenants from holding meetings in their homes.

Employers sometimes offered welfare benefits to undercut employee support for unions or to forestall legislation to provide these benefits out of payroll taxes. In this way, the employer provided as a gift what would otherwise have become a right. Employment pensions were usually ad hoc payments made entirely at the employers' discretion. Even in heavily unionized sectors such as rail transportation, employees could lose their pension rights for participating in strikes. Formal pension plans became more common

after 1917, when their cost was recognized as a deductible business expense in calculating federal income tax obligations. The Cape Breton–based British Empire Steel and Coal Corporation (BESCO) introduced noncontributory employee pensions in 1923, the same year that BESCO requested assistance from federal troops to suppress a strike for union recognition. Reporting on the pension plan 5 years later, just before the company collapsed under its debt load, BESCO characterized the plan as good business rather than charity; although it gave the workers no legal rights, it inspired loyalty, improved morale, reduced labor turnover, and facilitated the dismissal of older employees.

Group life insurance plans were a popular supplement or alternative to employee pensions, once the government approved group insurance in 1919. For employers, the plans provided a fixed-cost benefit that the employer did not have to administer. As with many other state- and employer-sponsored welfare programs, the plans provided a higher benefit payment for men's dependents than for women's.

Despite the attention given to employment pensions and group life insurance in the business press, most Canadians who were too old to find work had to live on their savings, or the charity of family members and the community. In 1927, under pressure from labor representatives who held the balance of power in Parliament, the federal government, in cooperation with the provinces, instituted minimal old age pensions for the indigent. Contributory pension plans were an alternative for employers who were concerned about the demoralizing effect of charity, with the added advantage of reducing the employer's costs. Pension plans initiated in the 1930s usually required employee contributions, and existing employer-funded plans were converted to contributory plans.

Profit sharing and stock-purchase plans, like contributory pension plans, gave employees a direct stake in the success of the enterprise, and gave employers another means to compel employee loyalty. In most of the stock-purchase plans, the employees' shares did not give them voting rights at shareholders' meetings. Getting workers to identify with the employer rather than with other workers was the motivation behind various workplace improvement programs, from clean locker rooms to company picnics. Even time clocks for workers were advertised in *Industrial Canada* (September 1921, p. 80) as being for the workers' advantage; they were "the faithful employee's best protection against the filching of his reward by the slothful, careless co-employee."

In the Second World War as in the first, the federal government assumed authority over many areas of labor relations and social welfare that in peacetime would come within provincial or territorial jurisdiction. The war also facilitated federal-provincial cooperation on a national Unemployment Insurance program. First enacted by the federal government during the Great Depression, the legislation was declared unconstitutional by the Supreme Court because it belonged within provincial jurisdiction. After a constitutional amendment, and with the war ensuring full employment, the federal government created an Unemployment Insurance fund based on compulsory contributions from employers and employees. Limited coverage and miserly benefits notwithstanding, unemployment insurance met some longstanding labor demands. In contrast, the Family Allowance program—a monthly check mailed to every mother of young children, with the amount based on family size, which was quickly dubbed "the baby bonus"—was introduced to stifle labor protests against a wartime wage freeze.

Labor historians use the label "postwar compromise" for government support for collective bargaining and an enhanced social wage, in exchange for restrictions on workers' right to strike. The social wage included enhanced state-funded old-age pensions, a national employment-based pension plan funded by compulsory contributions from employers and employees, and publicly funded hospital and medical insurance. The latter, pioneered in Saskatchewan by the Co-operative Commonwealth Federation government led by Tommy Douglas, was implemented across the country by 1970. Federal government guarantees to encourage the private sector to offer student loans, introduced in 1964, along with expansion in the number of institutions offering university-level training (from 30 in 1945 to 60 in 1970), created unprecedented access to university education.

Worker gains at the bargaining table and in the political realm were eroded in the 1980s and 1990s by governments and employers promoting deregulation and deficit reduction. Some governments repealed legislation that had limited the use of strikebreakers.

Expanded access to education, health care, and public welfare benefits, matters within provincial jurisdiction, had been stimulated by federal funding for specific programs. In 1977, the federal government moved away from conditional grants to block funding, and by the mid 1980s, it significantly reduced its share of funding for health and social programs. In 1993, the federal government replaced the universal family allowance with a child tax credit intended to benefit the working poor. With implementation of the Canada-U.S. Free Trade Agreement (1989), followed by the North American Free Trade Agreement (1994), business stepped up its campaign for union-free workplaces, and demanded that Canadian wages, working conditions, and social benefits be lowered to meet standards prevalent beyond the border. Some unions negotiated benefits to ease the pain of "downsizing." For example, the Canadian Auto Workers contracts with the "Big Three" Canadian subsidiary automakers in 1999 provided for early retirement packages and scholarships for postsecondary education for the sons and daughters of union members.

Through workplace and political struggles, Canadians in the twentieth century developed a relatively stable mix of public and private welfare policies that maintained employer freedom to set the terms and conditions of the employment relationship while making some provision for universal access to subsistence income, health care, and education. These social rights will be maintained in this century only through continued struggle.

—*Margaret McCallum*

See also Economic Policy (Canada); Social Democracy (Canada); Social Welfare (Canada): Before the Marsh Report; Social Welfare (Canada): Since the Marsh Report; War and Social Welfare (Canada)

Primary Sources

Labour Gazette, publication dates 1900–1978; *Industrial Canada*, publication dates 1900–1973.

Current Comment

Canada, Department of Labour. (1921, March). Report of Conference on Industrial Relations. *Labour Gazette, 21*(3; Suppl.), 483–545.

National Employment Commission. (1937). *Report on phases of employment conditions in Canadian industry.* Ottawa, ON: Author.

Ontario, Department of Labour. (1929). *Survey of industrial welfare in Ontario.* Toronto, ON: Author.

Scott, F. R. (1972). Labour learns the truth. In J. L. Granatstein & P. Stevens (Eds.), *Forum: Canadian life and letters, 1920–70: Selections from the* Canadian Forum (pp. 234–236). Toronto, ON: University of Toronto Press. (Original work published 1946)

Further Reading

Chernomas, R., & Black, E. (1996). What kind of capitalism? The revival of class struggle in Canada. *Monthly Review, 48*(1) 23–34.

Grant, H. M. (1998). Solving the labour problem at Imperial Oil: Welfare capitalism in the Canadian petroleum industry, 1919–1929. *Labour/Le Travail, 41,* 69–95.

McCallum, M. E. (1990). Corporate welfarism in Canada, 1919–39. *Canadian Historical Review, 71,* 46–79.

Tudiver, N. (1987). Forestalling the welfare state: The establishment of programmes of corporate welfare. In A. Moscovitch & J. Albert (Eds.), *The "benevolent state": The growth of welfare in Canada* (pp. 186–202). Toronto, ON: Garamond.

WELFARE CAPITALISM (MEXICO)

Welfare capitalism is distinguished by the balance between social welfare programs and state efforts to influence social and economic stratification within a capitalist economy. In Mexico, the shifting contours of welfare capitalism have been critically influenced by the country's legacy of Catholic-inspired corporatism. The origins of welfare capitalism lay in shifts that accompanied the rise of liberal, large-scale industrialization and the extension of state authority during the reign of Porfirio Díaz (1876–1911). Yet, it was the Mexican Revolution (1910–1920) and postrevolutionary political and social conflicts that ultimately fostered the consolidation of a ruling party, the Institutional Revolutionary party (*Partido Nacional Revolucionario,* or PRI), committed to protected capitalist development underpinned by conservative corporatist welfare. By the late 1960s, however, the failures of protected development engendered a crisis of legitimacy for the PRI and provoked a reevaluation of corporatist welfare capitalism. The subsequent rise of neoliberalism has been accompanied by targeted forms of welfare aimed at diminishing the social and economic fallout accompanying a return to market-driven growth strategies.

SOCIAL STABILITY AND WELFARE IN THE POSTREVOLUTIONARY ERA

Political stability and Porfirian policy encouraged an influx of foreign investment and sudden expansion of exports that fueled rapid capitalist transformation in the late nineteenth century. Yet, although the rise of full-scale capitalism brought a mild increase in wages and an expansion of the middle classes, it did little to improve national welfare. Education and health care remained the province of elites, and overall standards of living remained low. Moreover, the state, with the support of owners, regularly repressed peasant and labor uprisings in an effort to foster capital accumulation. Further weakening popular groups was the vast dispossession of communal land, which undermined local and familial forms of welfare and intensified social stratification by forcing peasants and workers into dependent forms of labor. The Porfirian regime supported this form of capitalist expansion with positivist ideals that reinforced traditional corporatist notions of welfare as a familial, local, or religious concern.

The Mexican Revolution, and its legacy in the radical 1917 Constitution, transformed welfare in Mexico by integrating an ideal of social equality into national welfare debates. Epitomized in provisions for land redistribution and labor rights, the Mexican Constitution threatened traditional corporatist relations by empowering peasants and the working class. Yet, in the immediate postrevolutionary period, Presidents Álvaro Obregón (1920–1924) and Plutarco Elías Calles (1924–1928) subordinated social equality to the demands of ending political instability and fostering industrial and agricultural expansion after the economy's decimation during the Revolution. For example, during this period, the state redistributed land in response to specific uprisings or regional threats, rather than as a means to achieve agrarian transformation. Furthermore, the creation of state-sponsored labor organizations aimed less at emancipating workers and improving their living standards than at countering labor's growing power and autonomy.

Continuing unrest, the lack of a coherent industrial bourgeoisie, and the diminishing role of large land-owners, however, limited economic recovery and political consolidation in the 1920s. In response, popular demands became increasingly important in forging a consensus between peasants, workers, and the state. By the 1930s, the ruling party saw the pacifying possibilities of social reform, including its potential to promote state legitimation through incorporating popular groups into state-building and economic expansion. Revolutionary redistribution soon became a hallmark of welfare capitalism in the 1930s. For example, President Lázaro Cárdenas (1934–1940) hailed communal agrarianism as the best route to capitalist economic growth. The ruling party also promulgated the 1931 Federal Labor Code, which shifted responsibility for labor to the state. Moreover, during the 1930s, state price controls and distribution companies expanded the state's role in directly alleviating poverty amid capitalist expansion. Despite these gains, by the late 1930s, disruptions accompanying rapid industrial growth and urbanization, including the postrevolutionary empowerment of peasants and workers coincident with the failure of economic growth to radically alter overall living standards, continued to feed popular unrest. Furthermore, established industrialists in industrial centers such as Monterrey and Puebla joined to challenge expanding state authority over owner-labor relations, contending that it threatened to upset the paternalistic relations between workers and owners that, while preserving social stratification, ensured social order and worker welfare.

THE RISE OF STATE-LED CORPORATIST WELFARE CAPITALISM

World War II and the postwar economic crisis soon provided the context to confirm welfare and capitalist growth as state concerns. Conflicts among industrialists over state intervention in the economy, however, slowed this transition. Established industrialists continued to favor liberal growth with minimal state intervention. They added that market-driven capitalist social justice would ensure worker welfare. Though newer industrialists countered that economic recovery could only be accomplished with state protections, they agreed that a liberal welfare regime would

eventually have a leveling effect in society. While welcoming industrial protections, they stated that social protections would breed laziness and drunkenness, thus preventing the market from enabling each worker to maximize his or her individual welfare in free competition with others.

In contrast, the Monterrey Group, a powerful coalition of business people from Monterrey, Nuevo León, supported Catholic-influenced corporatist welfare. Backed by Pope Leo XIII's 1891 *Rerum Novarum,* the Monterrey Group viewed the factory as a social family wherein owners had an obligation to ensure worker welfare, which would in turn foster class cooperation. They thus opposed the commodification of labor that would occur under a liberal welfare regime because it jeopardized their authority over workers. The Monterrey Group also challenged the expansion of state authority into the economy and welfare, which they contended was an assault on free enterprise, private property, and the corporatist roots of their historic authority over and responsibility to workers.

In the postwar period, however, economic problems and the reticence of the international lending community to grant loans and aid to Mexico fueled a fragile accord between industrialists and the state in support of state economic intervention. Consequently, Keynesian ideas that had provided a radical, though short-lived, counterpoint to classical liberalism as a means to pull the developed world out of the Great Depression now enjoyed growing support in Mexico. The PRI soon built a model of state-sponsored corporatist development aimed at underpinning protected, albeit dependent, capitalist growth. By the 1950s and 1960s, social welfare became embedded within elaborate relations of political patronage dominated by the PRI. Many have argued that state-led corporatist welfare capitalism supported the PRI's long-term power, because most programs were administered or regulated by the central government. Yet, the PRI, with broad industrialist support, also hoped to enforce the social conditions and class cooperation viewed as a precondition for economic growth. For example, benefits, such as Social Security, often were targeted at relatively privileged workers engaged in stable, urban, formal-sector employment. Under the PRI's influence, industrialization was accompanied by state-led corporatist projects customized to meet the demands of the new industrial class arrangement arising amid average annual growth rates of roughly 6 percent. This growth in turn justified the PRI's abandonment of revolutionary commitments to redistribution, as most contended that economic growth would eventually engender an overall improvement in living standards.

THE SHIFT TO NATIONAL SOLIDARITY AND THE PRIVATIZATION OF WELFARE

Although standards of living improved during the 1950s and 1960s, inequality and status differentiation were preserved and even worsened. In fact, industrial growth failed to absorb the rapid influx of migrants to the cities, and rural areas remained largely excluded from any gains. Scholars quickly realized that wages and social expenditures were responding to more than just economic growth. For example, the PRI had adopted capital-intensive growth strategies in the 1950s and 1960s that hindered the expansion of labor opportunities and wages.

Many scholars and policymakers blamed the developmental failures of the 1950s and 1960s on state economic intervention. Focusing on the lack of a concern of state-led corporatist welfare capitalism with market efficiencies, they began clamoring for a return to liberalism. Dependency theorists, in contrast, contended that Mexico's developmental difficulties stemmed not from protections but from dependency on international markets and investment. They added that foreign influence had hindered the autonomy of the state to enforce welfare provisions, while impeding individuals from pursuing their welfare freely in the market. By the 1980s, then, the PRI had abandoned its protected economic miracle in favor of a return to economic liberalism. Yet, at the same time, the state approached poverty with a renewed vigor, partly in an effort to reestablish legitimacy in the fallout of the political and social convulsions that shook Mexico in the late 1960s and early 1970s.

Since the 1980s, the state has redefined its corporatist welfare strategy to mitigate the social costs that market-led policies have brought to Mexico, including growing income inequality and diminishing living standards. These residual or targeted welfare efforts to alleviate poverty climaxed in the national Solidarity strategy

under President Carlos Salinas de Gortari (1988–1994). Yet, increased exposure to international influences, including to austerity measures attached to international aid, has restricted the impact of these changes.

Moreover, the economic crises of the 1980s and 1990s ensured that the fulfillment of the neoliberal goal of improving market efficiencies and expanding free trade would occur at the expense of programs for social welfare and distributional equity. Even the rapid expansion of the *maquiladora* (export-oriented factories) sector, codified in the North American Free Trade Agreement, has failed to compensate for the lower priority placed on social welfare by the state. Despite strong job growth in that sector, the combination of labor deregulation, ineffective or nonexistent union representation, and owner collusion has had a regressive impact on wages since the 1990s. Moreover, pressure to retain a labor cost advantage over other countries has curbed the amount of social services provided by companies. Instead, many companies have used benefits, such as child care and housing, to control the labor force—for example, by denying benefits to punish absenteeism or labor organizing. Neoliberalism consequently has brought distributional deterioration and a diminished standard of living for Mexico's poorest. Most recently, the state has taken tentative steps to transfer the burden of welfare to private sources, including the traditional nuclear family. But with the recent trend among companies to shift production from Mexico to Asia, the promise of economic growth and job creation proffered by neoliberalism is under threat, narrowing the chances of success for the privatization of social welfare.

—Susan M. Gauss

See also Economic Policy (Mexico); Labor Movement and Social Welfare (Mexico); Neoliberalism, Social Programs, and Social Movements (Mexico); Social Reform and State-Building (Mexico); Social Welfare (Mexico): Since 1867

Primary Sources

Records on welfare capitalism in Mexico are in the *Fondo Gonzalo Robles* held at the *Archivo General de la Nación*, Mexico City. The library at the *Banco de México* in Mexico City has a range of published primary sources relevant to twentieth century economic policy. The private holdings at the *Archivo Manuel Gómez Morín* in Mexico City include documents relating to industrialist relations.

Current Comment

Colín, J. R. (1945, October). *Requísitos fundamentales para la industrialización de México.* Presentation at the Third National Congress of Industrialists, Mexico City.

Confederación Patronal de la República Mexicana. (1949). *Modernización de las relaciones de trabajo: Aspectos de una nueva conciencia patronal.* Mexico City: Author.

Hope, P. H., Carrillo Flores, A., & Sáenz, J. (1950). *Conferencias a técnicos, hombres de empresa, y dirigentes obreros por una mejor producción y un mayor consumo de artículos nacionales.* Meeting of the Movimiento Económico Nacional, Mexico City.

Partido Nacional Revolucionario. (1934). *Plan sexenal del P.N.R.* Mexico City: Author.

Further Reading

Esping-Anderson, G. (1990). *The three worlds of welfare capitalism.* Cambridge, MA: Polity Press.

Filgueira, C. H., & Filgueira, F. (2002). Models of welfare and models of capitalism: The limits of transferability. In E. Huber (Ed.), *Models of capitalism, lessons for Latin America* (pp. 127–157). University Park: Pennsylvania State University Press.

Goodin, R. E., Headey, B., Muffels, R., & Dirven, H.-J. (1999). *The real worlds of welfare capitalism.* Cambridge, UK: Cambridge University Press.

Knight, A. (1994). Solidarity: Historical continuities and contemporary implications. In W. A. Cornelius, A. L. Craig, & J. Fox (Eds.), *Transforming state-society relations in Mexico: The national Solidarity strategy* (pp. 29–45). La Jolla: University of California, San Diego, Center for U.S.-Mexican Studies.

WELFARE CAPITALISM (UNITED STATES)

The United States has a phenomenon of welfare capitalism that dates to the late nineteenth century. Although always more common in the core sectors of the economy and stable professional work, it has been presumed to set the model for employment terms in the United States. Welfare capitalism refers to social welfare benefits and health, safety, or leisure programs offered through the workplace. These are programs established and directed by the employer. Welfare capitalism is also a political tactic: Since its inception, it has been a management strategy for heading off further development of the regulatory state or demands by organized workers' movements. Therefore, welfare capitalism usually is on the rise when government is extending its involvement in labor and social welfare matters.

The two decades of violent confrontations between capital and labor in the late nineteenth century had neither stopped the emergence of a national labor movement nor quelled reformers' attempts to enact industrial regulatory laws. Hence, by the end of the century, corporate leaders sought a new set of responses to what was then known as "the labor question." Leading industrialists decided that the best way to achieve a harmony of interests between workers and managers was not through collective representation for workers but through each firm assuming some obligation for their workers' well-being, either inside or outside the workplace. This "welfare work" program relied on employee benefits that ranged from company cafeterias and lunch plans to athletic activities, picnics, English-language and home economics classes, company housing, and company doctors. Some employers offered pecuniary forms of welfare work—loans, savings plans, profit sharing, or accident relief funds. There were company owners, such as George Pullman, who established entire towns—complete with company housing, stores, churches, and athletic teams. Companies offered different mixes and approached welfare work with a variety of motivations and expectations. Some executives believed welfare work improved productive efficiency: These programs would inspire the employee to become a better worker, whether more efficient, healthy, or loyal. Others sought to avoid labor upheaval and discourage unionization; still others hoped to attract and keep skilled workers. In all cases, however, welfare work was a strategy to retain complete managerial control over the terms of employment, and to assure legislators that there was no need for state intervention.

In the first few decades of the twentieth century, welfare capitalism emphasized efficiency more than security. Often, company welfare benefits were meant to be the carrot that would convince workers to accept the stick of faster, mechanized production systems, such as the assembly line. Qualifying for Henry Ford's famed $5-dollar day, or profit-sharing bonuses, entailed conforming to proper social and deferential behavior both inside and outside the workplace. Pension consultants and welfare capitalism proponents urged firms to adopt pensions as a means to eliminate superannuated, less fit employees who could not run the machinery as fast as others. But until the 1930s, firms with industrial pension programs provided in-house plans. Neither actuarially based nor funded annuities, they were not a reliable source of economic security.

In the 1920s, as the threat of social insurance seemed to supplant that of protective legislation, welfare capitalist employers shifted emphasis toward pecuniary welfare benefits. One of the most effective and long-lasting of these benefit programs was group insurance, a new type of private insurance policy that would become the basis of the modern employee benefits system. Insurers devised group insurance for employers to provide life insurance coverage for a large group of employees under one group risk factor. Welfare capitalists presented private group insurance as a solution to economic insecurity that was apolitical, rational, and organized. Managers and actuaries could make the decisions on behalf of working people but without the interference of the masses or the state. Group insurance indeed brought life insurance and funeral benefits to many workers who did not have any life insurance, or who could not maintain industrial policies over a number of years. Previously, low-wage industrial workers had been considered "uninsurable risks" along with African Americans, Asians, and Mexicans. Group insurance, however, benefited White male workers, who were more likely than non-Whites to work in companies that made some effort to regularize employment and stabilize production—laying down a cleavage that would persist for the rest of the century.

Both group insurance and company pensions rested on long-term and uninterrupted employment. Thus, women workers were far less likely to qualify for insurance benefits, because they worked in part-time or seasonal jobs that regularly laid off workers at particular points in the year. Women periodically removed themselves from the paid labor market to take care of children or sick relatives. Therefore, as long as insurance remained tied to workforce participation—essentially the rest of the twentieth century—women had a great deal of trouble qualifying for benefits.

Amidst the Great Depression of the 1930s, social insurance took center stage on the national agenda. In this climate of political upheaval, grassroots political movements—especially movements of the old-aged unemployed—and the Franklin D. Roosevelt administration pushed for federal economic security legislation. Far from disappearing, welfare capitalism persisted as a strategy business used to adapt to pressure from workers and the state during the New Deal era. Insurers convinced employers that the most effective political response to this upheaval was to enhance the promises of welfare capitalism and thereby demonstrate that government solutions could certainly be avoided if business made private options more dependable and realistic.

With the passage of the Social Security Act, the grassroots movements and New Dealers generated an "ideology of security," as well as a new policy of government intervention in the wage relation. Insurers and welfare capitalist employers quickly adapted to the new welfare state, offering private, company plans as "supplemental social security"—particularly as a way to keep a lid on the new public pension program. Rather than rejecting or fighting the welfare state outright, welfare capitalists instead disseminated the concept of the "basic welfare state"—wherein the state provided a minimal, basic level of protection, which would not cover all needs, and thus left the rest to private institutions.

The rest of the 1930s marked a period of growth and adaptation of private pensions and welfare capitalism. This new wave of industrial pensions helped preserve the notion of the paternalistic employer who cared for his employees' needs beyond the workplace. Although more likely to be insured and funded than before the depression, new pensions still retained the unilateral characteristics of their predecessors. Management chose to implement them; chose what the amounts would be; chose the carrier; and retained the right to discontinue them.

The New Deal not only created the Social Security Act but also gave the ascendant union movement new legal backing. Under the terms of the National Labor Relations Act, employers would have to negotiate with unions and sign labor-management contracts. Yet, although business executives of the 1940s and 1950s did have to make decisions about labor policy in a different political-economic context than before the New Deal, they chose the same strategy for generating employee loyalty: their own private welfare state.

For employers, welfare capitalism proved the key to containing further expansion of the New Deal state and union power and union political goals after World War II. Commercial insurers had now expanded group insurance to include hospital insurance, surgical insurance, disability wage compensation, and medical insurance. Because the employer was the only legal policyholder, employers could unilaterally choose the insurance carrier, type of policy, benefits, and the percentage paid by the workers. Insurance companies helped rejuvenate postwar welfare capitalism by offering to "tailor" health insurance policies to fit the needs of each employer, and herein lay the roots of the United States' balkanized system of health insurance coverage. The employer could select exactly what it did and did not want: what hospital services would be covered, the percentage of reimbursement, and the amount of an employee's contribution. Indeed, in both unionized sectors and nonunionized sectors, management could make these decisions unilaterally, without input or revision from a union or employee representation group.

The postwar employee benefits system retained the essential aspects of welfare capitalism. It tied workers to a particular company, and made all other family members dependent on the worker. Such a welfare system was inherently patriarchal since it depended on a man's employment. Because health insurance was designed as part of the family wage ideal—a single breadwinner and dependent family—insurers forged a health care system in which numerous persons had no direct claim to medical care. Their only claim to medical coverage was through a wage earner. Managers and insurers became partners in defining what constituted health security, shifting its focus away from the New Deal emphasis on national standards and toward a multitude of isolated, firm-specific welfare sites. More than ever, welfare capitalism could highlight the difference between security inside the firm and insecurity in the outside labor market.

For a generation, welfare capitalism brought many workers an unprecedented level of economic security and access to health care, but the employment-based benefits system soon widened wage and income disparities between workers rather than closed them. Inequality was inherent in coverage for family members, who usually received lesser benefits, such as fewer days in the hospital and more excluded medical procedures and stricter rules about preexisting conditions. Even within unionized sectors, coverage for family members varied from place to place. Among the vast majority of the American workforce, the lags in family coverage have persisted into the present.

To benefit from a supplemental security system, one had to work in industries covered by both the public and the private social security systems. Until the 1970s, the majority of African American women worked in industries that were covered by neither. In the mid 1950s, African American men and some women had begun to move into urban manufacturing jobs and thus within the umbrella of the New Deal Social Security system. Yet, just as they had the possibility to obtain union-negotiated health insurance, life and disability insurance, and pensions, employers embarked on a new labor strategy: automation and business relocation. For African Americans, the limited welfare state and private supplementation would both mirror and solidify unequal patterns of economic opportunity.

The patterns of racial and regional inequality inherent in welfare capitalism remained in place throughout the entire twentieth century. As a rule, the industries that did not offer private welfare benefits prior to World War II still do not. The South still lags behind the Northeast and Far West in offering employment-based welfare benefits. Nor did benefits ever fully extend to African Americans or Latinos; fewer than half receive private, employment-related health insurance. As long as labor markets remain segmented, private employment-based social welfare has not compensated for those inequalities and it has reinforced them.

With each round of collective bargaining by unions in the 1950s and 1960s, employers granted enumerated increases—adding on a few more surgical procedures, additional hospital days, physician's office visits, maybe coverage for eyeglasses and root canals—within a limited framework that foreclosed labor's capacity to challenge any existing economic relationships, whether in industrial relations or the delivery of health care. As long as business executives faced a countervailing weight—unions or the state—the incentive to bargain upward remained. In the 1970s, the tables turned and bargaining started going in the other direction; "bargaining for security" became a downward spiral of concessions and losses.

Business firms increased their commitment to corporate social welfare programs when government itself expanded its social welfare and labor intervention roles. For two generations, the public and the private welfare systems grew in tandem, offering a greater level of benefits to millions of Americans. After 1979, this trend would reverse and the number of Americans covered by private pensions and health insurance began a steady, uninterrupted decline. After dropping to 38 percent of private sector workforce in 1980, private pension coverage fell to 31 percent by 1987 and below 30 percent in the 1990s. By 2001, American workers carried a larger portion of the financial burden of employment-based pensions than their employers, reminiscent of the welfare capitalism of the 1920s.

Although only public Social Security old-age pensions have become universal, most of the public policies enacted in the last 30 years have been aimed at propping up or patching up the leaky private welfare system. Yet, neither private health insurance nor private pensions have moved any closer to universal coverage; nor will they. Health insurance coverage has never extended beyond 69.6 percent of the workforce. The historical ideological legacy of American welfare capitalism—that of the basic welfare state, contained and limited, with all other needs met by private sources—continues to dominate policy proposals and legislation up to the present day.

—*Jennifer Klein*

See also Health Policy (United States); The New Deal (United States); Poverty (United States)

Further Reading

Jacoby, S. M. (1997). *Modern manors: Welfare capitalism since the New Deal*. Princeton, NJ: Princeton University Press.

Klein, J. (2003). *For all these rights: Business, labor, and the shaping of America's public-private welfare state*. Princeton, NJ: Princeton University Press.

Tone, A. (1997). *The business of benevolence: Industrial paternalism in progressive America*. Ithaca, NY: Cornell University Press.

Zahavi, G. (1983, December). Negotiated loyalty: Welfare capitalism and the shoeworkers of Endicott Johnson, 1920–1940. *Journal of American History, 70*(3), 602–620.

WELFARE MINISTRIES IN THE TWENTIETH CENTURY (MEXICO)

The year 1920 marked the end of the Mexican Revolution, although challenges still existed for the new postrevolutionary government. Banditry in the countryside abounded, and peasants remained dissatisfied with the new regime's limited agrarian reform. Additionally, the economy was in chaos due to the multiple currencies printed and distributed by various armies, as well as a drop in industrial and commercial production. Bad harvests resulted in shortages in both the countryside and the cities. The government moved to shore up legitimacy through the promotion of public health and welfare programs—leaders hoped to combat the poverty and unrest created by the war. Indeed, throughout the twentieth century, the government would use a variety of public welfare agencies to combat poverty, quell labor unrest, and consolidate political authority and legitimacy. Although the names of the agencies changed frequently with various administrations, their fundamental purpose remained the same.

The 1917 Constitution officially mandated that all charity and welfare organizations, both private and public, were to be under state control. The administration reestablished the federal Department of Public Welfare (*Departamento de Asistencia Pública*) in Mexico City, with the task of coordinating all public and private welfare activities. Many postrevolutionary welfare activities focused attention on mothers and children. In 1921, reformers convened the First National Child Congress. The congress greatly influenced policymakers, who in turn created the School Hygiene Service in 1922 and two hygiene centers for children in 1923. These programs focused on health care, and instituted vaccination programs. By 1927, the Mexico City Department of Public Welfare had added a children's shelter for the homeless.

In addition to public sector programs, private women's societies organized on behalf of mother-child welfare. In 1929, a national group, the Association for the Protection of Childhood (*Asociacón Para la Protección de la Infancia*), was established. Female charity workers focused on distributing school breakfasts and creating centers for the prenatal care of pregnant women. The activities would become a model for later state-run welfare programs, such as the National Institute for Child Protection (*Institut National de la Protección Infantil*). Reformers also turned their attention to rural areas. Between the violence of the Revolution, the continuing *caudillismo* (regional boss rule), and, in the 1920s, the direct threat to government authorities posed by rural uprisings, such as the Cristero Rebellion, welfare workers viewed the taming of the recalcitrant countryside as an important order of business. The postrevolutionary regime's newly created Secretariat of Public Education (*Secretaría de Educación Pública,* or SEP) sent cultural missions to the countryside to teach peasants proper health and hygiene, and to show peasant mothers proper child rearing techniques. In the 1930s, the SEP's socialist education project continued the work of the cultural missions with the goal of remaking the peasants into modern participants in a capitalist society. SEP's rural socialist education projects would continue until 1940.

President Lázaro Cárdenas established the Secretariat of Public Assistance (*Secretaría de Asistencia Pública*) in 1937 to consolidate welfare programs, particularly urban welfare programs previously administered by Mexico City's Department of Public Welfare. In 1943, the government merged the Secretariat of Public Assistance with the Health Ministry (*Secretaría de Salud*) to create the Secretariat of Health and Welfare (*Secretaría de Salubridad y Asistencia*). Over the next two decades, the secretariat would dramatically expand both public health and welfare agencies and programs in Mexican cities and rural areas. Programs included mother-infant centers, foster care programs, family dining halls, school breakfasts, volunteer societies, as well as rural welfare centers and a variety of public health and sanitation campaigns. The secretariat greatly expanded the number of hospitals and clinics under its control. In 1943, the government also established a Social Security program to cover the health and welfare of workers.

During this period, the government also created a number of agencies designed to help the working classes and the poor. In 1954, the National Housing Institute was established to create and subsidize public housing. Although the name of the agency changed with successive administrations, it remained an important force in building affordable housing through the 1990s. Mexican governments also supported agencies

dedicated to the provision of inexpensive food for the urban poor and working classes. Established in 1937, the first agency purchased grain for the poor. The agency expanded its mission throughout the twentieth century and had several name changes, but remained fundamentally dedicated to feeding the poor and working classes.

In 1961, the government created the National Institute for the Protection of Childhood (*Institut National de la Protección Infantil*) to consolidate and differentiate welfare services from health and medical programs. The institute's services focused on the health, nutrition, and education of children and their mothers and had as its first goal the provision of school breakfasts. In 1968, the Mexican Child Welfare Institute was also established to aid and protect abandoned children.

The decade of the 1970s witnessed population growth combined with severe economic dislocations. Government policymakers recognized the need to offer more integrated assistance not just to children, but also to their families and communities. Previous agencies, along with other government programs targeting the poor, were combined into the state ministry, the National System for the Integral Development of the Family (*Sistema Para el Desarrollo Integral de la Familia,* or DIF) in 1977. Many of these programs were reorganized in the 1990s under the National Solidarity Program (*Programa Nacionale de Solidaridad*). The Integral Development of the Family agency along with Social Security and other agencies and programs dedicated to providing affordable food and housing continue to be committed to the health and welfare of poor rural and urban families in Mexico today.

—Nichole Sanders

See also Constitution of 1917 (Mexico); Social Reform and State-Building (Mexico); Social Welfare (Mexico): Since 1867

Primary Sources

Archivo Histórico de la Secretaría de Salubridad y Asistencia and *Ramos Presidenciales,* both in the *Archivo General de la Nación,* Mexico City.

Current Comment

Amezquita, J. A., Bustamente, M. E., López Picazos, A., & Fernández del Castillo, F. (1960). *Historia de la Salubridad y de la Asistencia en México.* México City: Secretaría de Salubridad y Asistencia.

Further Reading

Bliss, K. (2001). *Compromised positions: Prostitution, public health and gender politics in revolutionary Mexico City.* University Park: Pennsylvania State University Press.

Fuentes, M. L. (1998). *La asistencia social en México: Historia y perspectivas.* Mexico City: Ediciones del Milenio.

González Navarro, M. (1985). *La pobreza en México.* Mexico City: Colegio de México.

Vaughan, M. K. (1997). *Cultural politics in revolution: Teachers, peasants and schools in Mexico, 1930–1940.* Tucson: University of Arizona Press.

Villarespe Reyes, V. O. (2001). *La Solidaridad, Beneficencia y programas: Pasado y presente del tratamiento de la pobreza en México.* Mexico City: Universidad Nacional Autónoma de México.

WELLS-BARNETT, IDA B. (1862–1931)

Ida B. Wells-Barnett was one of the most celebrated African American civil rights leaders of the twentieth century. Called controversial, uncompromising, a fierce defender, a lonely warrior, and a crusader for justice, Wells-Barnett gained a national and international reputation for her antilynching campaign at the beginning of the twentieth century. She is credited with being one of the first to bring accurate statistical accounts of this "southern horror" to the public eye. Wells-Barnett was an accomplished investigative journalist, newspaper publisher, clubwoman, and settlement house worker. She was a founding member of the National Association for the Advancement of Colored People and the Alpha Suffrage Club, the first African American women's suffrage organization in Chicago. Wells-Barnett was active in civic, legal, and civil rights affairs in Chicago and nationally. Her activism and her quest for social betterment for African Americans mark her as a significant figure in American social welfare history.

Born in 1862 in Holly Springs, Mississippi, to Jim and Elizabeth Bell, Ida was the oldest of eight children. She grew up in a home where discipline, education, and self-determination were valued. Ida learned a great deal from her father, Jim Wells, a master carpenter in the post–Civil War South; he lost his job with a major contractor when he did not vote for White supremacy and the Democratic ticket. He eventually opened his own business and was recognized as a leader in the local African American community.

Ida received her early education at Rust College. When she was 16, tragedy struck the Bell family. Both parents and a baby brother died when the yellow fever epidemic hit Holly Springs in 1878. Rather than separate as a family, Wells became a schoolteacher and supported the surviving members of her family. After passing qualifying exams in 1884, she taught school in Memphis, Tennessee, for several years and took summer courses at Fisk University.

Two events shaped Ida Wells's life's work. In 1884, she filed the first antidiscrimination lawsuit against the Chesapeake, Ohio and Southwestern Railroad when she refused to give up her seat to a White passenger and move to the racially segregated section of the train designated for African Americans. She won her case and received damages of $500 but the Tennessee Supreme Court overturned the ruling. This injustice would spur her lifelong fight against unfair and unequal treatment of African Americans.

A second event was life altering for Wells. By 1892, she was a well-known journalist and part owner of the *Free Press* in Memphis, Tennessee. That year, her friend and grocery store owner, Thomas Moss, was lynched with two other men. Moss's business had competed with a store owned by a local White and Moss had refused to be intimidated. His lynching propelled Wells to launch her lifelong antilynching campaign. Wells's newspaper editorials called for an economic boycott of White-owned businesses in Memphis. Eventually, thousands of Black Memphis residents left the city and migrated west. Though her life was threatened, Wells traveled across the South, investigating and documenting over 700 lynchings that had occurred over the preceding decade. She wrote that the main justifications for lynching Black men—that they raped White women—were simply lies. She published her findings in "Southern Horrors: Lynching in All Its Phases" and the "Red Record," pamphlets that were widely distributed. She traveled to England in 1883 and 1884 where she spoke about lynching. Antilynching societies were formed because of her advocacy. She met with Presidents William McKinley and Herbert Hoover to argue for antilynching legislation

At the age of 32, Ida Wells married attorney and newspaper publisher Ferdinand Barnett in 1895 in Chicago. After her marriage, she signed her name

"Wells-Barnett" to retain her own identity. She and her husband had four children, two boys and two girls. Ida Wells-Barnett was a devoted mother, who found a way to be attentive to her family while being actively engaged in community work. This was not always easy for her because she felt pulled by the demands of family and the community.

Less well known, but equally important is her role in the development of social welfare agencies and services for African Americans in Chicago. Wells-Barnett brought the same fierce determination and self-help philosophy to the building of social settlements for African Americans as she did to fighting for their rights. She was instrumental in planning the Frederick Douglass Center and starting the first kindergarten for African Americans in the city. In addition, Wells-Barnett began the Negro Fellowship League Reading Room and Social Center in her home in 1908, which opened as a social service agency in 1910. She served as its director for nearly 10 years. Its purpose was to address problems relating to race and racial discrimination. It sheltered homeless men, provided employment services, spearheaded legal defense work for Blacks wrongly accused of crimes, and educated residents on race matters in Chicago. It had one of the finest reading rooms in the city. Books, magazines, and newspapers were provided for male migrants and it published a newsletter, *The Fellowship Herald.* It served as a meeting place for groups concerned with economic and social issues. When an early benefactor stopped his donation, Wells-Barnett used her $150 salary as a juvenile probation officer to support the agency. The agency closed after 10 years of operation.

Ida B. Wells-Barnett is one of the most multifaceted and complex activists of the twentieth century. A nationally recognized crusader against lynching, she was an accomplished journalist, newspaper publisher, and active clubwoman. She was active in many race organizations of the day, including the Negro Press Association, the Afro-American Council, the National Association of Colored Women, and the National Equal Rights League, where she held executive responsibilities. Defiant and vigilant on racial matters, Wells-Barnett was a contemporary of W. E. B. DuBois, Jane Addams, Thomas T. Fortune, Booker T. Washington, Mary Church Terrell, Grace and Edith Abbott, and Mary White Ovington. She did not see the problem of race as being one of race inferiority, which was a popular scientific and political notion of the day. Instead, she framed the problem as one of social injustice and inequality. Never one to bite her tongue or "make nice," she was fearless in seeking justice and fairness for African Americans.

Ida B. Wells-Barnett died in 1931 in Chicago. She left a fascinating legacy of social change, advocacy, and social service innovation.

—*N. Yolanda Burwell*

See also African Americans and Social Welfare (United States)

Further Reading

Duster, A. M. (Ed.). (1970). *Crusader for justice: The autobiography of Ida B. Wells.* Chicago: University of Chicago Press.

Holt, T. C. (1982). The lonely warrior: Ida B. Wells-Barnett and the struggle for Black leadership. In J. H. Franklin & A. Meier (Eds.), *Black leaders of the twentieth century.* Urbana: University of Illinois Press.

Myrick-Harris, C. (2002, July). Against all odds. *Smithsonian, 33,* 70–77.

Tucker, D. M. (1971, Summer). Miss Ida B. Wells and Memphis lynching. *Phylon, 32,* 112–122.

WHITTON, CHARLOTTE (1896–1975)

Charlotte Whitton was a pioneer in the social service sector in Canada. A social worker, politician, champion of women's and children's rights, and a fierce conservative, she is known as one of Canada's most outspoken, flamboyant, and energetic figures of her time. Born in Renfrew, Ontario, in 1896, she attended Queen's University during the First World War where she received an MA in history and English. Her time and accomplishments at Queen's foreshadowed the leadership roles she would go on to take in the Canadian voluntary and social service sector. She received the Queen's medals in both history and English. She was also the first woman editor of the *Queen's Journal.* Her entry into the field of social welfare began with her first position as an assistant secretary for an interchurch group known as the Social Service Council of Canada from 1918 until 1922. In 1920, she helped to form the Canadian Council of Child Welfare (later called the Canadian Welfare

Council). She ran this organization as a volunteer out of her own home while employed as a private secretary to the federal minister of trade and commerce. She served as the full-time director of the Canadian Welfare Council (known today as the Canadian Council on Social Development) from 1926 until her resignation in 1941. In the 1920s, she advocated for professional standards in the delivery of social welfare programs, particularly relief administration and the protection of children. She was also a strong proponent of research, particularly the social survey as a means of informing and improving social welfare policies. Throughout her life, she fought for equal pay and equal rights for women in both the private and public sectors. Despite this, her views were considered to be quite conservative. Although she believed in improving the social welfare state, she was also concerned with containing and not expanding it. Whitton believed in the importance of personal responsibility and resourcefulness in the achievement of social justice and well-being. She did not believe in married women working outside the home and held conservative views on abortion and divorce. After leaving the council in 1941, she worked as a consultant and newspaper columnist. During this time, she was responsible for several studies and reports, two of which have become well known. One report of note was "Dawn of Ampler Life" (1943), commissioned by the leader of the Conservative party. In the report, she compared several designs for government policy following World War II. A more controversial report was her 1947 study of social welfare in Alberta. Despite threats of legal action and a ban on cooperation from the provincial government, she uncovered poor and shocking conditions in the care of the elderly and children and in child protection. In the 1950s, Whitton entered the world of politics. In 1951, she was elected as the first female mayor of Ottawa, becoming the first female mayor in Canada. She was reelected in 1952, 1954, 1960, and 1962. Although she was defeated in 1964, she served as an alderman for the city until 1972. Her career came to an end late in 1972 after a fall resulted in a broken hip from which she never fully recovered. She died in January of 1975, several weeks after a heart attack. Throughout her life, Charlotte Whitton was recognized for her accomplishments in many ways. She was awarded a CBE (commander of the

Order of the British Empire) from King George V, honorary doctorates, and was voted Canada's "Woman of the Year" on six occasions.

—Peter Donahue

See also Child Welfare Policy (Canada)

Further Reading

Rooke, P. T., & Schnell, R. L. (1987). *No bleeding heart: Charlotte Whitton, a feminist on the Right.* Vancouver: University of British Columbia Press.

WOMEN AND POVERTY (CANADA)

Women have historically experienced higher rates of poverty in Canada according to relative measures such as Statistics Canada's low-income cut-offs (LICOs) as well as absolute measures such as level of wealth and earnings. One in five Canadian women, roughly 2.8 million women, was living in poverty in the year 2000. The main causes included limited access to well-paid, full-time, secure employment, social expectations that women should undertake the majority of care giving and domestic labor in the family, and little or no control over family finances within heterosexual families.

Canadian women of most classes have been expected to provide unpaid work within the home in the form of child care, care of dependent adults, housework, and, until commercialized, production of many of the goods and products needed in everyday life. These unpaid domestic responsibilities often limit their capacity to gain and retain full-time employment, or pursue upwardly mobile career paths where these opportunities are available. The low-wage, often part-time, jobs in which women are employed generally lack provisions for sick time, vacation, or family responsibility leaves; hence women with heavy family obligations often lose their employment when the care of their dependents intrudes on the work world. In the long and short term, this undercuts women's earnings, pension accumulation, career path, and eligibility for workplace and unemployment benefits, all of which have helped to keep men out of poverty.

Antipoverty activists argue that the existence of universal, high-quality, accessible, nonprofit child care would expand women's opportunities to be more equal participants in the workplace. From time to time, this policy proposal has found considerable support among the public and politicians but has not resulted in legislation, sustained funding, or widespread, quality services.

With the exception of the World War II years, when women were pulled into the workforce in record numbers, it was not until the 1980s that economic conditions compelled the majority of women to work outside the home for wages. By the year 2000, the proportion of women (41 percent) in the paid labor force was very close to that of men (42 percent). Workforce participation, however, did not significantly relieve women's poverty because women do not currently, and have not historically, entered the labor market as equals. Since the 1990s, close to equal rates of participation in postsecondary education among men and women suggest that it is not a lack of skills and education that keep women in financial hardship. Rather, it is the segmentation of women in low-wage sectors such as clerical, retail, and service and the failure of the market to generate adequate incomes in those sectors. Female workers are concentrated in part-time, casual, and contract employment characterized by low wages, low skill, few or no benefits, temporary and insecure terms of employment, nonunion work sites, and few opportunities for advancement or skill development.

Government strategies to increase female wage levels, such as the Pay Equity and Employment Equity legislation of the 1980s and 1990s, resulted in an increase in women's wages in some job categories, particularly in the public sector, although men remain overall better paid and less likely to fall into poverty. Critics of equity policy claim that a more effective strategy would be a legislated increase in the minimum wage as women and youth make up 83 percent of minimum wage earners and both are overrepresented among the poor. After the 1990s, the wage gap between men and women narrowed. Ironically, this resulted from a fall in male wages rather than equity legislation or voluntary initiatives among employers.

Other government strategies to combat poverty among women have met with limited success and often reproduce class and gender discrimination.

Early government programs, such as municipal relief projects, provided short-term, negligible support in conjunction with strong moral messages aimed at changing the habits and character of those who suffered in poverty. The Mother's Allowance was the first provincial income program to specifically target women and their children. It made assistance available to the worthy widows of soldiers, whereas divorced women and never-wed mothers were excluded from benefits for the better part of four decades. Social assistance in Canada continues to be imbued with moralist judgments about recipients as exemplified in welfare rates that are 20 percent to 70 percent below the poverty line, in the disentitlement of single mothers after their child reaches the age of 6, and in depictions by elected officials of welfare recipients as lazy, promiscuous, and irresponsible.

Other income support programs established and expanded during the 1970s have also failed to provide poverty protection for women, in part, due to ongoing funding cuts and restructuring. In the early 1980s, 70 percent of women qualified for Unemployment Insurance whereas by the year 2002, 31 percent of unemployed women qualified, and only 15 percent of young women. Since the 1980s, federal and provincial cuts to social housing budgets and the dismantling of tenant protection acts have worsened the difficulties women face in finding safe, affordable housing, creating a growing number of women and children among the long-term homeless.

Women are vulnerable to poverty later in life as they are unlikely to have workplace pensions or private savings, particularly those who have worked primarily in the home or in low-wage jobs. Changes to pension laws providing wives with access to their husband's pensions even when divorced or deserted has improved this situation somewhat although 49 percent of sole-support, elderly women live in poverty, making this group overrepresented among the poor and almost poor. Even where women have pension plans in their workplaces and have contributed to the federal government pension plan, their overall lower lifetime earnings often result in inadequate levels of benefits.

Race and ethnicity are predictors of poverty, with visible minority women experiencing higher rates of poverty whether born in Canada or elsewhere. The enduring negative impacts of European colonization can be seen in the ongoing higher poverty rates among aboriginal people. Single, aboriginal mothers and their children experience incomes lower than non-aboriginal women or aboriginal men.

Women with disabilities are also significantly over-represented among the poor as they rarely have access to the key benefits associated with good, full-time employment, such as long-term disability, comprehensive medical plans, long-term rehabilitation, and drug plans. Instead, they must bear the full burden of these health-related costs, falling back on welfare when they deplete their personal resources. To be active members of the workforce, women with disabilities often require workplace supports. Very few employers offer such supports, however, leaving women with disabilities with extremely limited opportunities for employment, and few options for income except social assistance.

Women raising families without the presence of a male income have been and continue to be the most likely group of women to fall into poverty. Contrary to public opinion, these women are not exclusively those who are unemployed. They may work outside the home, generate income within the home (babysitting, sewing, taking in boarders), and most certainly perform unpaid caring and domestic labor. This underscores the claims of antipoverty analysts who assert that the complex interplay of unpaid caring labor and insecure, low-wage, low- or no-benefit, paid work, as well as the failure of governments and markets to generate adequate incomes for women, must be addressed in order to successfully relieve women's poverty and produce more equitable results.

—Donna Baines

See also Aging Policy (Canada); Economic Policy (Canada); Family Violence (Canada); Poverty (Canada); Social Security (Canada); Social Welfare (Canada): Before the Marsh Report; Social Welfare (Canada): Since the Marsh Report; Women and Social Welfare (Canada)

Current Comment

Income Statistics Division, Statistics Canada. (2004). *Low income cutoffs from 1994 to 2003 and low income measures from 1992 to 2001* (Income Research Paper Series). Ottawa, ON: Author.

National Task Force on the Definition and Measurement of Poverty in Canada. (1984). *Not enough: The meaning and measurement of poverty in Canada.* Ottawa, ON: Canadian Council on Social Development.

Further Reading

Little, M. (1994). "Manhunts and bingo blabs": The moral regulation of Ontario single mothers. In M. Valverde (Ed.), *Studies in moral education* (pp. 233–247). Toronto, ON: Centre of Criminology.

Lochead, C., & Scott, K. (2000). *The dynamics of women's poverty in Canada.* Ottawa, ON: Status of Women Canada.

Morris, M. (2002). *Women, poverty and Canadian public policy in an era of globalization.* Ottawa, ON: Canadian Research Institute for the Advancement of Women.

WOMEN AND SOCIAL WELFARE (CANADA)

Women have always occupied a unique position relative to men in the field of social welfare. The heart of this difference flows from the historic division of labor between men and women that has resulted in women bearing the primary responsibility for care-giving work in our society. With the onset of industrialization and the division of life into public and private spheres, women have been primarily responsible for the quality of life within the private sphere. As a result, a woman's relation to the public sphere and the world of paid work has always been contingent upon the status of her care-giving role. Until very recently, this has meant that women were either excluded from or marginalized in the world of paid work. In societies in which wage labor is the primary means of self-support and self-sufficiency, women were overrepresented in positions of dependency. These two realities of women's lives, primary care givers and disproportionately dependent, locate women as central actors in social welfare: as clients, as reformers, and as employees of the welfare state. Although women are the primary recipients and employees of the social welfare system, they are seldom the architects of the system. The ultimate decision makers, political leaders, are disproportionately male and the primary architects of Canada's major social programs have historically been men. As a result, their standpoint, their experience, and their agenda have not been the same as those of women.

A GENDERED PERSPECTIVE

Although early charities and later government programs were clearly designed to "save" desperate women from destitution, they did so with the presumption that support implies the right to regulate or control the dependent person. This philosophy mirrored the patriarchal relationship between husband and wife, breadwinner and dependent that characterized family relations at the time. In a very real sense, early social welfare programs took on the role and assumed the authority of the "absent" patriarch, husband, or breadwinner. To this day, women are the majority of clients of means-tested social assistance programs, which retain this paternalistic and regulatory character. The Canadian social welfare system has three tiers. The top tier is composed of universal programs, such as Medicare, which are most comprehensive and embody the principle of entitlement. Access to these universal programs is based on citizenship. The second tier provides benefits to people based on participation in the paid labor force, such as the Canada Pension Plan, Employment Insurance, and Workmen's Compensation. These programs are based on an insurance model in which benefits are based upon contributions. The bottom tier is accessed by people who are disconnected from the labor force and make claims based on "dependency," or family status, rather than employment status. Individuals accessing bottom tier programs, disproportionately women, receive less generous benefits and are subject to stringent eligibility requirements and considerable scrutiny. The top two tiers exemplify the usual male experience of the welfare system, based on the principle of entitlement, whereas the bottom tier, most typically accessed by women, is based on the ability to prove eligibility and subservience to regulation. The following brief history exemplifies the paradox of women's location within the welfare system, which is simultaneously central and second class.

THE EARLY YEARS: 1880–1940

From the earliest times, Canadian women were much more likely to be dependent on charity than men. The reports of the Inspector for Charitable Institutions in Ontario from 1884 to 1912 consistently showed that women and children made up 80 percent or more of the residents in "houses of refuge." The women who were in these institutions were usually there because they had lost their husbands, regarded as the "breadwinners," through death, disability, or desertion. During this period, welfare services evolved from dispersed charities to organized government programs at the provincial level. Provincial social welfare programs were meager, means tested, and associated with a high degree of scrutiny and control of recipients. Women and children were the focus of the emerging welfare bureaucracies. The first government-administered social assistance program, Mother's Allowance, was introduced in the province of Manitoba in 1916 and was followed by similar programs in other provinces at later dates. The Manitoba legislation provided a monthly allowance for mothers without economic support due to death or permanent incapacitation of their husbands. The members of the board who administered the funds were advised to treat the allowance like wages for which only the most worthy of mothers would be eligible. Thus, women deemed unworthy, regardless of how desperate their need, would be denied. The largest category of women excluded were unwed mothers who were deemed ineligible due to their "poor moral character," exhibited by their unwed status. The other major social welfare program that had a substantial impact on women during this period was the child welfare system. Although clearly admirable in its intent to protect children, it was frequently experienced by women, especially poor women, as more focused upon policing their parenting than supporting it. Regulation and control were primary features of social welfare programs specifically directed to women. In contrast, the social welfare programs primarily accessed by men, Workmen's Compensation, introduced in 1915, and Unemployment Insurance, introduced in 1940, provided much more substantial benefits. They were based on the principle of entitlement and did not involve substantial regulation or control. The tiered nature of the Canadian social welfare system dates back to the earliest days of its development.

THE GROWTH OF THE WELFARE STATE: 1940–1980

This period marks a dramatic growth in the Canadian welfare state. Between 1946 and 1978, Canada's gross national product (GNP) increased four-fold, total government expenditure increased six-fold, and social welfare expenditures increased eighteen-fold. This period is perceived by many to be the golden age of the welfare state. The philosophy of entitlement predominated and two new universal welfare programs were introduced. The first, the Family Allowance Act, introduced in 1944, was the only universal welfare program specifically paid out to women. Family Allowances marked a radical departure from the provincial Mother's Allowance programs because they were not means tested and the concept of entitlement was, uniquely, attached to the status of mother. Millions of Canadian women became unconditional recipients of a monthly payment determined by the number of children in care. The second universal program began 24 years later, when Medicare was introduced in 1968. In both of these programs, women enjoyed the same status of entitlement that men experienced in accessing employment-based social insurance. In this period of increasing social expenditures, even the means-tested programs became more benevolent and less paternalistic. In 1966, the federal government introduced the Canada Assistance Plan. It provided for 50 percent cost sharing by the federal government for all provincial social-welfare programs. In 1967–1968, for example, the Ontario Department of Public Welfare reported a recovery of $115 million on a budget of $190 million. Under these circumstances, provinces could afford to be less restrictive in their eligibility criteria for social assistance and more generous in their benefits.

A PERIOD OF RETRENCHMENT: 1981–2001

In the late 1980s and throughout the 1990s, political attention shifted from social welfare concerns to concerns about fighting deficits and cutting taxes. Under these pressures, willingness to finance existing social welfare programs declined and they began to be reengineered. In 1990, the federal government removed its financial support for Unemployment Insurance, making the program fully funded by employer and worker contributions. Increasingly, restrictive eligibility criteria and shortened benefit periods were enacted. In 1996, the name of the program was changed to "Employment Insurance" and

reductions in eligibility and benefit periods continued. Although women were becoming more integrated in the paid labor force, their greater concentration in part-time employment resulted in lower eligibility for benefits than men. In 1993, the universal Family Allowance program was eliminated and replaced by various "targeted" tax benefit programs that focused on benefits for the working poor rather than recognizing the needs of all low-income families. As a result, one of the largest categories of families in need, families headed by single mothers on public assistance, receive no benefit from tax-based programs. The next reduction in the social welfare system was the elimination of the Canada Assistance Plan, which was replaced by the Canada Health and Social Transfer Act. It eliminated the federal government's commitment to 50 percent cost sharing with the provinces for social welfare expenditures. As federal contributions plummeted, social welfare programs contracted throughout the country. Finally, federal support for Medicare declined from 50 percent cost sharing in the 1960s to less than 13 percent by 2000. This retrenchment has exaggerated the tiered nature of the Canadian welfare system and has disproportionately disadvantaged women. Further, retrenchment has brought the one remaining universal program, Medicare, perilously close to demise.

CONCLUSION

Despite the expansion and contraction of the social welfare system in Canada, women have retained their unique position relative to men. Although women are the primary recipients and employees of the social welfare system, they have made little progress as architects of the system. Women remain underrepresented in political office in Canada. Despite the centrality of women, they continue to be disadvantaged in their ability to access programs based on participation in the labor force, which have generous benefits and are less regulatory. Women continue to be disproportionately concentrated in programs in which claims are based on "dependency," or family status, which have less generous benefits, and are more likely to regulate personal behavior. When social services shrink, women are called upon to absorb the personal and social costs of these reductions. Cutbacks in care for the elderly, day care, social assistance, or Medicare translate directly and immediately into more work and responsibility for daughters, mothers, and wives. It is ironic that women's disproportionate responsibility for "caring" work in Canadian society is the very condition that restricts women's access to the "care" provided by the Canadian social welfare system.

—*E. Jane Ursel*

See also Social Reform Movements (Canada); Social Security (Canada); Women and Poverty (Canada)

Primary Sources

Reports of the Inspector of Charitable Institutions for the Province of Ontario. Ontario Sessional Papers, 1884 (No. 19), 1885 (No. 40), 1892 (No. 6), 1897 (No. 35), 1904 (No. 40); *Report of the Superintendent of Neglected Children for the Province of Ontario,* Ontario Sessional Papers, 1911 (No. 26), pp. 101–102; *Manitoba Inquiry on Child Welfare* (the Whitton Report); Manitoba Sessional Papers, 1928 (Part III), p. 65; Ontario Department of Public Welfare *Annual Report 1967–1968.*

Current Comment

Hougham, G. M. (1962). *The relationship between unemployment and Canada's other employment maintenance programs* [Royal Commission of Inquiry into the Unemployment Insurance Act.] Ottawa, ON: Queen's Printer.

Marsh, L. (1975). *Report on Social Security for Canada.* Toronto, ON: University of Toronto Press.

Pickersgill, J. (1960). *The Mackenzie King record.* Toronto, ON: University of Toronto Press.

Social Insurance and Allied Services. (1942). *Beveridge Report.* New York: Macmillan.

Splane, R. (1965). *Social welfare in Ontario 1791–1893.* Toronto, ON: University of Toronto Press.

Further Reading

Evans, P., & Werkle, G. (1997). *Women and the Canadian welfare state: Challenges and change.* Toronto, ON: University of Toronto Press.

Graham, J., Swift, K., & Delaney, R. (2003). *Canadian social policy* (2nd ed.). Toronto, ON: Prentice Hall.

Moscovitch, A., & Albert, J. (1987). *The benevolent state: The growth of welfare in Canada.* Toronto, ON: Garamond.

Ursel, J. (1992). *Private lives, public policy: 100 years of state intervention in the family.* Toronto, ON: Women's Press.

WOMEN AND SOCIAL WELFARE (MEXICO)

Women have been integral to the construction of a Mexican welfare state, both as welfare providers and as recipients. In both capacities, they have helped to reify symbolic and real links between women, femininity, maternity, welfare provision, and the Mexican state. In particular, the relationship between women and the welfare state in Mexico has rested upon use of the concept of maternalism, the glorification of motherhood for political ends, highlighting women's roles as mothers and the values associated with motherhood, such as nurturance and moral virtue, to justify women's political roles. In Mexico, many have used maternalism to argue for women's qualifications as welfare providers and recipients, particularly in child and maternal welfare programs.

FEMALE WELFARE INITIATIVES AND STATE FORMATION FROM THE *PORFIRIATO* TO THE REVOLUTION

Women played central roles in the Mexican government's gradual usurpation of welfare functions from the Catholic church and other private beneficent organizations from the mid nineteenth century on, as they came to predominate in care-giving professions such as schoolteaching and nursing at the same time that the state welfare apparatus began to emerge. First ladies, the wives of Mexican presidents, also constituted important patrons of state welfare services, thereby associating the most prominent female representatives of presidential administrations with maternal roles. This is seen as early as the *Porfiriato* (1876–1911), when Carmen Romero Rubio de Díaz, the second wife of President Porfirio Díaz, founded the *Casa Amiga de la Obrera* to provide day care for the children of working mothers in 1877.

By 1910, women had created, funded, and administered a number of welfare institutions, including shelters to reform prostitutes, networks of mothers' clubs to train poor women in hygiene and child care, and child care centers and orphanages. Likewise, during the Mexican Revolution, women's action as welfare providers increased in importance on and off the battlefield, especially as nurses, teachers, and *soldaderas* (female combatants and camp followers). As hospitals, shelters, orphanages, and schools became militarized, sanitary brigades proliferated to serve troops throughout the republic. As the numbers of Mexicans, especially children, served by such institutions grew, women complemented and replaced male welfare providers.

WOMEN'S ROLES IN POSTREVOLUTIONARY WELFARE REFORM

After the Revolution, women became the foot soldiers of new social programs. They continued to dominate the corps of schoolteachers, building Mexico's new schools and carrying out cultural missions, literacy campaigns, and workshops in public health and job training. It was a woman, feminist, journalist, teacher, and labor organizer, Elena Torres Cuellar, who founded and managed the country's first school breakfast program, which was operated by the Secretariat of Public Education (*Secretaría de Educación Pública*) from 1921 to 1923. Between 10 and 20 percent of the delegates to the First and Second Congresses of the Child (in 1921 and 1923, respectively) were women. They were instrumental in creating some of the revolutionary state's first public health clinics and child and maternal welfare institutions, and they joined male medical professionals, eugenicists, social workers, and teachers to identify welfare policy priorities for the following decade.

Some of the female delegates to the child welfare congresses also attended 1920s feminist conferences, which gave significant attention to social welfare. At two 1923 congresses organized by Pan American women's organizations and at the 1925 Congress of Women of the Race, delegates secured government funding to print child welfare pamphlets and highlighted women's roles in administering and utilizing nurseries and schools, clinics and hospitals, playgrounds, free food programs, and "*gotas de leche*," milk stations for children without access to breast milk.

Delegates to these congresses argued that welfare would be better administered by women because of their "natural" maternal capacity. They argued that granting women political rights to vote and their election to office had resulted in the improvement of public welfare administration, suggesting that woman's maternal influence justified her attainment of political rights.

Women competed and cooperated in welfare provision across private and public, church and state spheres. For example, in 1926, both feminist and Catholic philanthropists treated prostitutes interned for venereal disease in the Hospital Morelos's *silifcomio* (syphilis ward). At the same time, Mexico's first ladies continued to patronize welfare projects emerging from private and public initiatives. María Tapia Monte Verde de Obregón, wife of President Álvaro Obregón (1920–1924), visited *hospicios* (asylums for the poor), orphanages, and school breakfast programs. Hortensia Calles, wife of Obregón's successor, Plutarco Elías Calles (1924–1928), inaugurated Mexico's first chain of free cafeterias for children. In the 1930s, Carmen García de Portes Gil created a National Committee of Child Protection (*Asociación de Protección de la Infancia*), which was succeeded by Josefina Ortiz de Ortiz Rubio's National Association for the Protection of Children (*Asociacón Nacional Para la Protección de la Infancia*). These organizations created *gota de leche* stations, maternity and children's homes, child care centers, and clinics for children and mothers throughout Mexico. Both García de Portes Gil and Ortiz de Ortiz Rubio received Red Cross awards for their efforts. Amalia Solorzano de Cárdenas established an office for women to direct their petitions for social action as well as associations for indigenous and Spanish refugee children.

Women's involvement in welfare as providers and recipients grew significantly in the 1930s. Women helped to run two Houses of the Mother established in Mexico City in 1931 and 1938 through cooperation between private benefactors and government welfare programs. They provided women with access to health care, classes in domestic and job training, and access to cooperative sewing machines and bathrooms. Meanwhile, two privately administered women's groups, the *Confederación Mexicana Femenina* and the *Frente Único Pro Derechos de la Mujer,* as well as the official party's Feminine Sector, established sewing workshops and health clinics, offered courses in literacy and hygiene, and promised to provide day care and instruction for working women's children.

WOMEN'S INVOLVEMENT IN THE SOLIDIFICATION OF THE MEXICAN WELFARE STATE

Welfare services in general, especially for women, were expanded in the late 1930s and early 1940s. President Lázaro Cárdenas created the Secretariat of Public Assistance (*Secretaría de Asistencia Pública,* or SAP) in 1937. In 1943, the SAP merged with the Department of Health (*Departamento de Salubridad*) to form the *Secretária de Salubridad y Asistencia* (SSA). The SSA provided assistance to those not covered by Social Security, including many women.

First ladies continued to promote the link between women and welfare. Soledad Orozco de Avila Camacho gave her husband two ideas for celebrating Mother's Day. In 1942, she advised allowing mothers to reclaim sewing machines pawned in the national pawnshop (*monte de piedad*) with exemption from repayment of the collateral acquired for them. President Avila Camacho carried out this initiative in cooperation with the SAP, which agreed to reimburse the pawnshop up to 800,000 *pesos* for the cost of lost profits and helped to identify women in need of the program. In 1943, Orozco suggested giving gas stoves to 17,000 female heads of family, clearly favoring the now state-owned petroleum industry to promote state-led industrialization. Beatriz Velasco Mendoza de Alemán continued the Mother's Day initiatives introduced by her predecessor, and also conceived of the idea of the *Asociación pro Nutrición Infantil* to distribute school breakfasts alongside the SSA and to educate mothers in health, hygiene, and nutrition.

In addition to first ladies, women in feminist coalitions cooperated with the SSA and Department of the Federal District to provide welfare services for women. The *Liga Central Femenina, Liga de Defensa de la Mujer,* and the *Bloque Nacional de Mujeres Revolucionarias* created schools and women's and mothers' centers with cooperative sewing and washing machines, bathrooms, and child care facilities for

their members; organized fund-raising campaigns to collect toys for poor children at Christmastime; and petitioned for land grants, water service, and local medical service.

LATE TWENTIETH CENTURY REORGANIZATIONS AND REDEFINITIONS OF WELFARE SERVICES

In 1961, First Lady Eva Samano de López Mateos engineered the transformation of the National Committee of Child Protection, created by Portes Gil in 1929, into the National Institute for Child Protection (*Instituto Nacional de Protección a la Infancia,* or INPI), a fully funded state program. Initially, the INPI's most important function was to expand school breakfasts. Later, it created child care centers and health clinics for women and families.

Guadalupe Borja de Díaz Ordaz promoted the creation of the National Institute for the Attention of Children (*Institución Mexicana de Asistencia a la Niñez,* or IMAN) to aid abandoned minors and orphans. The IMAN and INPI coexisted, attending to different sectors of the child population. María Esther Zuno de Echeverría oversaw the INPI's name change to the Mexican Institute for Children and Family (*Instituto Mexicano Para la Infancia y Familia,* or IMPI), reflecting her view that it was impossible to attend to children without addressing entire families, including their main pillar: women. With this change, Zuno de Echeverría laid a base for her successor, Carmen Romano de López Portillo, to unify the INPI and the IMAN into one organization, the National System for the Integral Development of the Family (*Sistema Para el Desarrollo Integral de la Familia,* or DIF), in 1977, which exists today as the major coordinating institute for family welfare services, working in cooperation with the SSA, and the Social Security organisms, *Instituto Mexicana de Seguro Social* (IMSS) and *Instituto de Seguridad y Servicios Sociales de los Trabajadores del Estado* (ISSSTE). It is still the responsibility of the first lady to oversee the DIF on a national level and it is expected that the wives of governors and municipal presidents will oversee state and local affiliates and their projects.

Women's organizations that have worked independently from and in cooperation with state-sanctioned programs have continued to expand and solidify welfare services. Second-wave feminism allowed women to combine work for women's rights and broader social services in a variety of ways. The 1985 earthquake gave rise to new social movements, which have supported independent civil and state-run welfare organizations.

CONCLUSION

The identification of women with welfare provision that was promoted by maternalist assumptions and the increased participation of women in politics and the workforce have resulted in women assuming roles closely resembling women's unpaid, domestic care giving. Women are most highly represented in service industries, including domestic labor, food preparation, and expanding education and health care professions. Men dominate the workforce in industry, manufacturing, and highly paid professions. In politics, women have dedicated themselves to traditional activities and have been excluded almost entirely from the executive branch, which has dominated Mexican political decision making. Women's government roles in cabinet level and subsecretary positions have also been concentrated in care giving and service fields such as tourism, education, labor, and foreign relations.

—Sarah A. Buck

See also Child Welfare Policy (Mexico); Mexico City Poor House; Mother and Family Programs (Mexico); Philanthropy (Mexico); Social Reform and State-Building (Mexico)

Primary Sources

See the correspondence between women welfare organizers and providers, government agencies, and government officials, in the *Ramo Presidenciales* and the records of the *Secretaría General de Gobierno*, *Archivo General de la Nación*, Mexico City. Statistics on welfare institution construction were compiled for *Anuario Estadístico Nacional*, published, successively by the *Departamento de la Estadística Nacional*, 1926–1932, and the *Secretaría de la Economía Nacional*, 1941–1968, Mexico City.

Current Comment

Secretaría de Asistencia Pública (1940). *La asistencia social en México: Sexenio 1934–1940*. Mexico City: Author.

Further information on women's organizing and welfare services can be found in newspaper articles from *El Heraldo de México*, *El Universal*, *Excelsior*, and *El Nacional*.

Further Reading

Camp, R. A. (1998). Women and men, men and women: Gender patterns in Mexican politics. In V. E. Rodríguez (Ed.), *Women's participation in Mexican political life*. Boulder, CO: Westview.

Fuentes, M. L. (1998). *La asistencia social en México: Historia y perspectivas*. Mexico City: Ediciones del Milenio.

Guy, D. (1998). The politics of Pan American cooperation: Maternalist feminism and the child rights movement, 1913–1960. *Gender and History, 10*(3). 449–469.

Macias, A. (1982). *Against all odds: The feminist movement in Mexico to 1940*. Westport, CT: Greenwood.

WOMEN AND SOCIAL WELFARE (UNITED STATES)

The traditional literature on the U.S. welfare state focused nearly exclusively on the needs of male workers, labor markets, and the class struggle. This changed once the intellectual revolution sparked by feminism revealed that the study of gender, like that of race and class, uncovers previously ignored information and introduces new understandings of social interactions. As scholars applied a "gender lens," they discovered that women played a central role in the origins of the welfare state and that the welfare state affected the well-being of women in contradictory ways.

THE ORIGINS OF THE WELFARE STATE

The welfare state arose to cushion the adverse effects of industrialization on individuals and families, to create the basis for social solidarity, and to mute social unrest. It also emerged to subsidize family maintenance because wider society depended on the family to reproduce the next generation of workers; to maintain a healthy, productive, and properly socialized workforce; to consume goods and services; and to provide for those unable to support themselves. The market economy, however, did not always yield the needed resources. As the requirements of profitable economic activity (low wages and high unemployment) increasingly undercut successful family maintenance, the state stepped in with social provision to mediate the conflict. In so doing, it replaced patriarchal control of women in the home with a more diffuse collective control of women by the male-dominated state.

Women reformers—middle and working class, White and Black—concerned about the impact of industrialization and urbanization upon the have-nots, contributed to the development of the welfare state. Middle-class women of both races fought for protective labor laws, mothers' pensions, maternal and child health programs, and against child labor and low living standards—without necessarily challenging prevailing patriarchal structures. Black reformers also sought to mediate the impact of racial discrimination on their communities. Drawing on the extensive women's club movement, the settlement houses, and church organizations, the women reformers pressed for and won national, state, and local social welfare programs—although the unbridled racism of the period ensured segregated, if any, public programs for Black households.

Low-income women also shaped the welfare state. They demanded that employers, landlords, merchants, and local governments improve the standard of living of their communities. Often militant, their early calls for social, economic, and racial justice exposed the limits of the market economy and prefigured the goods and services that the welfare state would eventually have to provide. The welfare rights movement of the 1960s helped to expand the welfare state; and since 1980, grassroots activism has defended programs against punitive policies and large budget cuts.

THE DESERVING AND UNDESERVING POOR

The welfare state—a system of cash benefits and social services—modifies the play of market forces by protecting individuals and families against the loss of the breadwinner's income due to old age, illness, disability, death, joblessness, or absence. But because the United States never endorsed universal social provision, from the start even its most widely used programs have distinguished between those "deserving" and "undeserving" of aid based on compliance with the work and the family ethics.

Since colonial times, social welfare policy has incorporated the work ethic by setting benefits below the lowest prevailing wage so that only the most desperate people would choose welfare over work. It has also treated applicants differently based on a perception of their willingness to labor. Retired, laid-off, disabled, or ill workers believed to be jobless through no fault of their own were regarded as "worthy" and granted more generous benefits than able-bodied adults deemed lazy and unmotivated for work. These strategies did more than lower welfare caseloads. They pressed wages down and increased the supply of cheap labor.

From the start, the welfare state has also incorporated the family ethic—those social norms that tell women that their proper place is in the home, married, mothering, and, economically dependent on a husband. With this, the welfare state rewarded the heterosexual, two-parent, one-earner family and penalized other types. Its programs also treated applicants differently based on their marital status. Married or previously married women—believed to lack a breadwinner through no fault of their own—such as widows, wives of sick, disabled, or temporarily unemployed men were regarded as "deserving" and granted more generous aid than divorced, separated, or never-married women viewed as willfully departing from prescribed wife and mother roles. These strategies stigmatized single motherhood while upholding the traditional gender division of labor and women's economic dependence on men. To this day, despite massive employment, women still bear near-exclusive responsibility for family maintenance and still are blamed when things go wrong at home.

ENFORCING THE WORK AND FAMILY ETHICS

The U.S. welfare state has sustained the work and family ethics from the colonial poor laws through the 1935 Social Security Act to the 1996 federal welfare reform. Throughout its history, regardless of gender, able-bodied recipients faced a work test that either penalized impoverished but able-bodied adults or rewarded long years of employment.

Social welfare policy has also imposed a marriage test on women, treating them differently based on their compliance with the family ethic. Colonial era communities that willingly aided destitute widows in their own homes often sent single mothers to the local almshouse or the workhouse in exchange for aid. The "undeserving" later became overrepresented among inmates in the institutions (hospitals, prisons, asylums) built during the nineteenth century. Children of "unfit" single (often immigrant) mothers and those whose parents could not feed or shelter them filled the orphanages.

Early in the twentieth century, many states enacted mothers' (or widows') pension programs to enable poor single mothers to stay home rather than work or institutionalize their children for reasons of poverty alone. The program subsidized "deserving" widows but routinely denied aid to separated and never-married women as morally "unworthy."

The 1935 Social Security Act—the core of the modern welfare state in the United States—enforced the work and family ethics throughout its two-tiered system composed of universal and popular social insurance programs for the middle class and means-tested and stigmatized public assistance programs for the poor. Like the earlier twentieth century protective labor laws and maternal and child health programs, which also regarded women as the biological producers of the species and socializers of the next generation, both social insurance and public assistance ceased supporting women once their caretaking work ended. Unless the mother became disabled, reached age 65, or qualified for local relief, no program covered her needs.

The welfare state upholds the family ethic as well by favoring full-time homemakers over working wives and unmarried women. The Social Security retirement program provides benefits to employed wives based on their own work record or a proportion of their retired or deceased husband's pension—whichever is higher. Due to low wages and time out for family care, workingwomen do better as dependent spouses than as paid workers. They were penalized further because full-time homemakers received the same benefit but did not pay Social Security taxes.

Husbandless women also lose out. The original Social Security pension excluded divorced women. Despite subsequent reforms, they still have a harder time collecting death and retirement benefits on their husband's record than their married counterparts. The family ethic, however, falls hardest on single mothers on welfare. The 1935 Aid to Dependent Children (ADC) program sought to help poor single mothers stay home with their children. Stigmatized at the outset, the program received less governmental support than the other means-tested programs. The states took longer to implement ADC. It received less per capita federal funding and included no funds for the mother's needs until 1950. The states conditioned aid on moralistic behavioral standards that linked nonmarital births to "unfit" motherhood and on the mother's "willingness" to work—even though prevailing societal norms defined good mothers as stay-at-home moms. The behavioral supervision intensified in the 1950s, when poverty and racial discrimination led never-married women and women of color to become overrepresented on the rolls. By 1996, when more women of all races and classes worked for wages, Congress transformed welfare from an income support into a "temporary" program (Temporary Assistance for Needy Families) and insisted upon work, marriage, and time-limited assistance. Welfare policy has consistently punished single mothers and supplied employers with cheap labor. The greater emphasis on work requirements since the 1970s has meshed well with the growing demand for low-paid women workers in the expanding service sector. The current family values and marriage mandates continue the pattern of upholding patriarchal controls.

DIFFERENTIAL TREATMENT OF WOMEN AND MEN

Ostensibly gender neutral, the welfare state reproduced male/female labor market inequities. Because most welfare state programs mirrored the work patterns of (White) men and applied them to women (and men of color) as if no differences existed, women (and persons of color) have had a harder time maximizing their benefits. Initially targeted to White male industrial workers, both the Social Security retirement program and Unemployment Insurance excluded many of the occupations open to women and persons of color. Because their husbands were not covered, for many years, few widows of color qualified for Social Security benefits.

Congress eventually covered these jobs in education, charity, farm, and domestic service, but did not stop mirroring the male-female (or racial) differentials built into the labor market. The Social Security program rewarded higher wages and longer work histories. This disadvantaged women who were more likely to be hired for low-paid jobs and to reduce their labor force participation to fulfill family responsibilities. Caretaking also made it harder for women to accumulate the 10 years of work needed to qualify for their own Social Security benefits. Similarly, the Unemployment Insurance program does not cover part-time, temporary, or intermittent jobs that many women "choose" in order to care for their families. Nor does it provide benefits for spouses who leave a job to follow their mate to another city—a practice more common among women than men.

Finally, the welfare state does not cover many of the risks to loss of income faced by women but not men. Women lose earned income due to pregnancy, time needed for care giving, sexual harassment, and sex-segregated jobs. Although women depend on marriage as well as the labor market for support, the welfare state barely covers income lost due to divorce, desertion, lack of child support, and violence in the home.

WOMEN AND WELFARE STATE PROGRAM CUTBACKS

By the end of the twentieth century women had become the majority of both welfare state workers and clients. Two decades of budget cutbacks had cost many women the public sector jobs that had moved them into middle class. The cutbacks also increased women's domestic work by shifting the costs (time and money) of caretaking back to women at home. By tying benefits to investment yields and market fluctuations, the proposed plans to privatize Social Security risk women's retirement and survivor's income.

AN ARENA OF STRUGGLE

Standard theories highlight the historical relationship between the market and the state and argue that the welfare state upholds class power. The gender lens reveals the complex historic relationship between the family and the state. The welfare state helped women—however minimally—by providing jobs, assisting families, and reducing the costs of caretaking. At the same time, its programs have subjected women to patriarchal controls. Paradoxically, a more fully developed welfare state contains a liberatory potential. Access to income outside the market and marriage could reduce women's economic dependence on both marriage and the market, increase their bargaining power at home and on the job, and enhance women's capacity to form and maintain independent households. For women, then, the welfare state represents an arena of struggle as well as a site of social control.

—Mimi Abramovitz

See also Aid to Dependent Children/Aid to Families with Dependent Children (United States); Mothers' Pensions (United States); Roosevelt, Anna Eleanor; Sanger, Margaret Higgins; Social Reform Movements (United States); Social Security (United States)

Primary Sources

Social Welfare History Archives, University of Minnesota, Minneapolis; Wisconsin Historical Society, Madison (www.wisconsinhistory.org); Social Security Online (official website of the Social Security Administration (www.ssa.gov/history/history.html).

Current Comment

Axinn, J., & Stern, M. (2000). *Social welfare: A history of the American response to need* (5th ed.). Boston: Allyn & Bacon.
Baxandall, R., & Gordon, L. (Eds.). (2000). *Dear sisters: Dispatches from the women's liberation movement: Broadsides, cartoons, manifestos, and other documents from the twentieth century's most influential movement.* New York: Basic Books.
Langley, W., & Fox, V. C. (Eds.). (1994). *Women's rights in the United States: A documentary history* [Primary documents in American history and contemporary issues]. Westport, CT: Greenwood.

Further Reading

Abramovitz, M. (1996). *Regulating the lives of women: Social welfare policy from colonial times to the present* (2nd ed.). Boston: South End.
Gordon, L. (1994). *Pitied but not entitled: Single mothers and the history of welfare.* New York: Free Press.
Kessler-Harris, A. (2001). *In pursuit of equity: Women and men and the quest for economic citizenship in 20th century America.* New York: Oxford University Press.

WORK RELIEF (UNITED STATES)

When governments accept responsibility to help people who are unable to support themselves, they can help directly with money, food, and shelter or they can give them public jobs so they can earn those things themselves. The latter is work relief. The policy has both economic and moral dimensions that have changed over time but remain intertwined.

Following the Elizabethan Poor Law tradition of distinguishing between the "deserving" and "undeserving poor," elders, widowed mothers, and people with disabilities were seen as deserving of help and not expected to work in colonial America. A county "workhouse" or "poor farm" provided a place for the others to sweat out their subsistence. To be idle voluntarily was immoral.

In the nineteenth century, it occurred to some that people who were unemployed might not be so by choice. Business cycles were recognized wherein the economy sometimes boomed and sometimes collapsed. People who wanted jobs couldn't always find them. Work relief became available during all the depressions after the Civil War, but increased considerably in the depression of 1893.

The charity organization society (COS) entered this depression with the belief that poverty was caused by individual weaknesses and that relief encouraged indolence. Charity workers preferred setting a moral example. But they also believed in making home visits to the recipients of relief and in keeping careful records of their experiences, which soon produced evidence that did not fit their assumptions. Leaders like Josephine Shaw Lowell came to believe that, in the words of Amos Warner, the problem might in some cases be "misfortune, not misconduct." The COS began to provide its own work relief projects: cleaning streets, sewing clothes, and whitewashing tenements.

Recognizing causes of unemployment in the economy rather than the individual did not erase moral concerns. If misconduct did not cause unemployment, it still might lead to it. Getting direct relief, "the dole," might be demoralizing. People would lose their work skills and habits. They might try to escape their shame in drunkenness or desertion. Therefore, work relief was preferable even if more expensive.

A parallel development to work relief was the public works program. Governments need to build things like schools, courthouses, and parks that the private sector does not provide. Such projects can also be a supplement to private employment. In the 1920s, they came to be seen as an agency for smoothing out the business cycle by offering jobs and purchasing materials when private enterprise could not. They were not work relief programs because they were not organized just for the unemployed. They simply reduced the numbers of people who might become unemployed. But the policy was not put into practice quickly or extensively enough to avoid the Great Depression of the 1930s.

By the time Franklin Roosevelt was elected president in 1932, the unemployment rate was approaching 25 percent, with men of all ages, even whole families, roaming the highways and railways seeking work. A variety of programs that combined public works and work relief were begun by the New Deal administration to counteract this widespread misery and despair.

The Civilian Conservation Corps (CCC) put young men to work replanting depleted forests and eroded farmland, fighting forest fires, and developing state and national park systems. The Civil Works Administration (CWA) brought work relief to a broad spectrum of the unemployed, skilled and unskilled, white and blue collar. It lasted only four and a half months but put four million people to work. The Works Progress Administration (WPA) concentrated on labor-intensive work-relief projects, though some of their projects rivaled in size and complexity those of the Public Works Administration (PWA), a more traditional public works program. The National Youth Administration (NYA) gave after-school jobs to high-school students and dropouts to keep them in school or get them back in. Together these and other "alphabet soup agencies" built a huge amount of the country's physical and cultural infrastructure, much of which is still in use.

The New Deal tried to integrate these efforts into a broad social policy to provide everyone with work, relief, and security in retirement. Its leaders hoped to deal with the dual challenge of keeping the economy working smoothly and meeting individual human needs. But broad policies gradually fragmented into a jumble of specific programs separating economic adjustments from human services and dividing participants by class, race, and gender.

After World War II, there were periodic efforts to revive general "manpower" policies to provide temporary employment for those thrown out of work and also help those who were left out of the economy to gain entry. But because unemployment was no longer a widespread worry but rather one experienced in special segments of society, these initiatives did not gain wide support. Emphasis shifted from work relief for those temporarily displaced in the economy to training for those not yet in it.

President Lyndon B. Johnson's War on Poverty in the 1960s spawned the Job Corps and the Neighborhood Youth Corps (NYC). Both were patterned after the CCC in some respects, though they emphasized training over public work. After a rocky start, the Job Corps developed organizational stability and political support. It still exists. The NYC was briefly popular as an antidote to the frustration building up among unemployed urban youth in the early 1970s. It was regarded as "riot insurance." Though terminated in 1974, its stress on summer jobs was maintained in local programs.

With an economic downturn in the 1970s, public jobs were made available to a wider range of the population. The Comprehensive Employment and Training Act (CETA) of 1973 was eagerly embraced by cities whose revenue base was being bled by taxpayer revolts and suburban migration. Under CETA, another soup bowl of alphabet agencies poured forth, including several youth training programs, most not lasting long enough to be properly evaluated. General public service employment dominated CETA. Unlike the work relief programs of the New Deal, CETA jobs were used to keep basic services running rather than to build new facilities. The Richard Nixon administration placed responsibility for the program at the local level with little federal guidance or oversight. Local agencies were unprepared for the expansion of the program ordered by President Jimmy Carter, and CETA became associated with mismanagement and corruption.

Presidents Ronald Reagan, George H. W. Bush, Bill Clinton, and George W. Bush all backed away from any economic interventions in unemployment problems. Neither broad policy to counter business cycles nor specific training programs were supported. All that remains is the moral imperative to work. Work relief has now shrunk into "workfare" programs

requiring mothers requesting public assistance to seek jobs in the private sector. Many leave the welfare system but few escape poverty.

A problem with all work relief programs is that their jobs can be a threat to current public employees and private employers. The availability of relief workers may cause governments to lay off current employees. Private employers may fear that public jobs will drive up wages. One response is to make public jobs inferior in conditions and compensation to public ones. Another is to concentrate relief work on things that would not otherwise be done, commonly known as "make-work." In practice, the competition with private employment has not been a problem when employers offer decent wages and benefits. The displacement of public workers happens mainly when public agencies are underfunded. During the Great Depression and under CETA, the supposed make-work was actually quite useful. It is primarily a limited conception of what needs to be done in public life that allows work relief projects to be defined as make-work. The economic wisdom and the moral obligation of providing public jobs for people who cannot find work in the private economy will continue to be debated.

—*Robert Leighninger*

See also Charity Organization Societies (United States); Hopkins, Harry Lloyd; Lowell, Josephine Shaw; The New Deal (United States); Poverty (United States); Roosevelt, Franklin Delano

Primary Sources

Records of the Works Progress Administration (Record Group 69), Records of the Public Works Administration (Record Group 135), and Records of the Employment and Training Administration (Record Group 369), National Archives & Records Administration, College Park, MD.

Current Comment

Bakke, E. W. (1940). *The unemployed worker: A study of the task of making a living without a job.* New Haven, CT: Yale University Press.
Federal Works Administration. (1946). *Final report on the WPA program, 1935–1943.* Washington, DC: Government Printing Office.
Public Works Administration. (1939). *America builds: The record of the PWA.* Washington, DC: Government Printing Office.

MacMahon, A. W., Millett, J. D., & Ogden, G. (1941). *The administration of federal work relief.* Chicago: Public Administration Service.

Further Reading

Amenta, E. (1998). *Bold relief: Institutional politics and the origins of modern American social policy.* Princeton, NJ: Princeton University Press.

Howard, D. S. (1943). *The WPA and federal relief policy.* New York: Russell Sage Foundation.

Rose, N. E. (1995). *Workfare or fair work; Women, welfare, and government work programs.* New Brunswick, NJ: Rutgers University Press.

Schwartz, B. F. (1984). *The Civil Works Administration, 1933–1934: The business of emergency employment in the New Deal.* Princeton, NJ: Princeton University Press.

YOUNG, WHITNEY (1922–1971)

The unexpected and sudden death of Whitney M. Young by drowning in Lagos, Nigeria, in March 1971 cut short the life of one of the most engaged and dynamic leaders of the civil rights and social uplift movements of the twentieth century. Dedicated to improving race relations and conditions in urban America and expanding economic, employment, and housing opportunities for the least advantaged, Whitney Young used his role as executive director of the National Urban League to negotiate with government, corporate, philanthropic, and grassroots organizations to achieve those ends. As executive director of one of the major social service agencies for African Americans between 1961 and 1971, Young heightened the presence and prominence of the Urban League during one of the most volatile periods in recent history. He infused new thinking about how to ameliorate social problems using his skill at negotiation, mediation, fund-raising, and advocacy with prominent business, philanthropic, and government leaders. For many, Whitney Young was a moderate voice of reason and pragmatism between Black Power activists and proponents of nonviolent social change during the modern civil rights movement. He offered clear thinking around creation of jobs, decent housing, health care, and racism in America.

Whitney Young was born in 1922 to middle-class, educated parents in Lincoln Ridge, Kentucky. His father directed the Lincoln Institute, a preparatory school for African Americans in racially segregated Kentucky. Young earned his undergraduate degree from Kentucky State University. He married Margaret Buchner in 1944 and later became the father of two daughters. After completing military service, he earned a MSW in 1947 from the University of Minnesota and then worked for the Urban League in Minneapolis/St. Paul and Nebraska. While in Nebraska, he taught courses at Creighton University and the University of Nebraska. These experiences supported Young's selection as the dean of the School of Social Work at Atlanta University in 1954. As leader of the Atlanta school, he increased enrollment, expanded financial aid opportunities for students, and broadened field education training. During the early years of the modern civil rights movement, Young became known for his exceptional skills in race relations and research on desegregation. Throughout his career, he was much sought after as a public speaker at conferences and public forums.

In 1961, he succeeded Lester Granger as the executive director of the National Urban League and served in this position until his death. Under his leadership, Young strengthened the Urban League by expanding its offices across the nation. He obtained funding from major philanthropies such as the Rockefeller and Carnegie foundations and worked with major corporations to provide training, employment, and management opportunities for African

Americans. Young spearheaded efforts to bring African Americans and Whites together to work cooperatively on race relations. He was able to work effectively with coalitions of grassroots civil rights organizations, labor groups, and businesses. A skilled negotiator, Young was adept at finding the "middle ground" among divergent perspectives on how best to achieve opportunities for social betterment for urban African Americans. Young's prestige enabled him to work effectively with the leaders of other major civil rights organizations such as the Congress of Racial Equality (CORE), the National Association for the Advancement of Colored People (NAACP), the Southern Christian Leadership Conference (SCLC), and the Student Non-Violent Coordinating Committee (SNCC). He was a contemporary of Martin Luther King, Jr., Roy Wilkins, John Lewis, James Farmer, Ella Baker, Bayard Rustin, and A. Phillip Randolph. Young's reputation as a civil rights leader enabled him to meet with Presidents John F. Kennedy, Lyndon B. Johnson, and Richard M. Nixon to discuss what government could do to improve the lives of African Americans. Young understood that his involvement in civil rights actions could help focus public attention on social problems. He helped organize and spoke at the famous March on Washington, D.C., in 1963, which brought civil rights issues to the nation's attention. In the often-polarizing atmosphere of debates about how best to achieve civil rights for African Americans, Young argued pragmatically for tangible outcomes. He wanted more jobs, better access to decent housing and schools, and improved social services, which he felt would provide opportunities and support for African Americans and ameliorate the long-standing effects of racism and discrimination. His work with dominant and powerful businesses, major philanthropies, and government bodies made him controversial with other more militant civil rights leaders and groups. Some accused him of "selling out" because of his pragmatism.

Young's leadership was evident within the profession of social work. He was president of both the National Association of Social Workers (NASW) and the National Conference on Social Welfare (NCSW) during the late 1960s. Ironically, racial tensions crystallized within these influential organizations while he was their leader. African American social workers were disenchanted and disgusted by what many saw as institutionalized racism within them. In 1968, the African American social workers walked out of the National Conference on Social Welfare's annual meeting in San Francisco and formed their own organization, the National Association of Black Social Workers.

Whitney Young was at the center of major efforts to improve racial and social equality during the civil rights era. He authored two books: *To Be Equal* and *Beyond Racism.* His status and prestige resulted in his being asked to serve on important presidential commissions during the John F. Kennedy and Lyndon B. Johnson administrations, and in 1969 he received the Medal of Freedom, one of the nation's most prestigious awards for civilians. His life serves as a reminder of how an intelligent, gifted, and socially committed activist can improve the social welfare of all Americans.

—*N. Yolanda Burwell*

See also African Americans and Social Welfare (United States); King, Martin Luther, Jr.; National Association of Social Workers (United States); National Conference on Social Welfare (United States)

Primary Source

Whitney M. Young, Jr., Papers, Columbia University, New York.

Further Reading

Dickerson, D. C. (1998). *Militant mediator: Whitney M. Young Jr.* Lexington: University Press of Kentucky.

Lewis, J. (1998). *Walking with the wind: A memoir of the movement.* New York: Simon & Schuster.

Young, W. M. (1964). *To be equal.* New York: McGraw-Hill.

Young, W. M. (1969). *Beyond racism: Building an open society.* New York: McGraw-Hill.

APPENDIX A

Research Guides

Resources for Social Welfare History

Research on the history of a subject as broad as social welfare in North America is oftentimes much like good detective work. Writing good history most often requires careful examination of primary sources, documents produced by participants—contemporary observers of the events being described—or other sources, such as oral histories, unpublished memoirs, or even photographs. Throughout North America there are archives or libraries where primary source materials are available for use by researchers. Such materials may include manuscript materials, such as correspondence, memoranda, and unpublished reports, as well as printed materials, such as government documents, conference proceedings, and scholarly journals. Information on primary sources and printed materials is included after many of the entries in this volume in a section labeled Primary Sources, where collections are listed, and in the Current Comment section, where a selection of published writings by contemporaries of the events described in the entry are listed. For those readers who want to investigate primary sources more fully, the following Research Guides provide information about archival resources and their locations in Canada, Mexico, and the United States.

CANADA

This essay will discuss and define archival sources as they pertain to the study of social welfare history in Canada, the structure of the Canadian archival system, and examples of relevant sources to be found therein.

Social welfare history encompasses many areas. It includes the history of organized activities or interventions, and official policy and programs that have improved the well-being of vulnerable classes of persons, such as the economically disadvantaged, the ill, children, the aged, and the disabled. It involves the work of charitable, religious, and philanthropic organizations; government departments; social reformers; and welfare workers. Beyond these are topics not traditionally included in a narrow definition of social welfare, such as parenting and family planning; community planning; preventive health; the social work profession; and sexuality-related areas such as birth control, the sex trade, and sexually transmitted diseases. Before beginning archival research into one of the above, however, it is advisable that the researcher be familiar with the historical background of the selected subject. A wide variety of published sources are available in libraries to provide excellent starting points for research. Examples are provided in the Further Reading sections that follow each entry in this volume.

Archives are repositories for recorded memory. Recorded memory includes every medium from textual records to sound and moving images, graphic materials, cartographic material, architectural and technical drawings, documentary art, and electronic data. In most Canadian archives, a set of records originally produced or gathered by a specific individual or organization is called a "fonds," which is considered to be the whole of the records. Each fonds is unique. It reflects the life and work of the creator, and may hold material unavailable anywhere else. It may consist of only one medium, such as textual records, or it may include several media. Intellectual access to fonds is provided by finding aids, some available on-line, that contain descriptions of the fonds's dates, extent, types of documents, and other valuable data.

When commencing archival research, it is important that researchers know the creator of the records they are seeking. Is the creator a private individual or organization, or government department or official? Government records are important for studying health and welfare policies in the public sphere. Examples of such records that might be useful include government statutes and legislative acts; operational files of government departments; institutional records of mental hospitals, asylums, poor farms, municipal homes, youth and/or correctional facilities; and educational facilities (e.g., schools of social work). Private-sector sources are important for revealing the impact of independent activities on the formulation and implementation of social welfare policies in the public sphere. Examples of private-sector sources that are helpful are records of nonprofit associations and organizations directly aimed at assisting disadvantaged groups (e.g., Poor Man's Friend Societies, Child Welfare Leagues, the Society for the Prevention of Cruelty). Many other organizations that promoted social reform (e.g., Local Councils of Women), religious and temperance organizations (Sisters of Charity, Women's Christian Temperance Union), missionary societies, and Protestant evangelical groups also provided assistance to the disadvantaged, and their records are often available in Canadian archives. Finally, the papers of philanthropists, social workers, national social welfare associations, and specialized service organizations (e.g., Public Welfare Associations) can provide valuable perspectives on service delivery and conditions of client populations.

Knowledge of the structure of the Canadian archival system and individual archives' mandates and acquisition policies is equally important in undertaking archival research. In the past 20 years, the number of archives in Canada has increased fivefold, with over 800 archival repositories now in existence. They range from the national archives and provincial/territorial archives to university, religious, municipal, community, medical, business, and many specialized private archives. Because of recent advances in computer technology, access to archival collections has been revolutionized to the point that most Canadian archives now have websites that allow researchers to easily obtain information concerning the repository's acquisition holdings and policies.

The Library and Archives Canada (formerly the National Archives of Canada), located in Ottawa, Ontario, is the nation's largest archive, with a mandate to "preserve the collective memory of the nation and the government of Canada, and to acquire, conserve and facilitate access to private and public records of national significance" (Library and Archives Canada website: www.archives.ca/08/08_e.html). Some relevant examples of its holdings that are described on-line include: the Company of Young Canadians fonds, the National Council of Women of Canada fonds, and the Canadian Association of Social Workers fonds. There are also 12 provincial and territorial archives, and their common mandate is to acquire records created by the individual province or territory and, in most instances, private-sector records of provincial or territorial significance. For example, Nova Scotia Archives and Records Management (www.gov.ns.ca/nsarm) in Halifax, Nova Scotia, has both valuable government records and private-sector sources, such as the Department of Social Services fonds, 1921–1981 (50.2 meters of textual records), and the Canadian Mental Health Association, Nova Scotia Division fonds, 1947–1983 (7.5 meters of textual records). The Department of Social Services fonds document the provision of services relating to social welfare, public charity, old-age pensions, mothers' allowances, juvenile delinquency, reformatories, and other topics. The Canadian Mental Health Association, Nova Scotia Division fonds document the promotion of mental health through education, research, and advocacy.

There are over 70 university and college archives in Canada. Generally, their mandate is to acquire the official records of the university as well as records related to faculty. Some have other specialties. For example the *Centre d'études acadiennes* at the *Université de Moncton* in New Brunswick (www.umoncton.ca/etudeacadiennes/centre/cea.html), acquires and preserves records relating to all aspects of the Acadian French experience in the Maritime region. Other university archives focus on societal groups, such as the Canadian Women's Movement Archives located at the University of Ottawa (www.biblio.uottawa.ca/archives/collection-e.html). This archive collects the records of the contemporary Canadian women's movement, with the focus on documenting grassroots or community-based organizations as opposed to institutional or government groups.

Similarly, the archives of religious institutions and agencies have extensive holdings relating to social welfare history. Most Christian denominations have websites that link to their archives. For example, the Anglican and United churches have archive networks, such as the Anglican Church Archives Network in British Columbia (http://aabc.bc.ca/aabc/anglican.html), and the United Church of Canada's United Church Archives Network (www.united-church.ca/archives). Also, the Canadian Jewish Congress's National Archives and Reference Centre in Montreal has large holdings of records of institutions, associations, and individuals pertaining to all aspects of Jewish history in Quebec and Canada (see www.cjc.ca/template.php?action=archives&Type=0&Language=EN).

For health- and medical-related archives, researchers should consult the Historical Health Information Locator Service, Canada, a national research service that provides access to historical resources relating to Canadian health care and medicine (see www.fis.utoronto.ca/research/ams/hilscan). An example of one of their links is to the Archives of Canadian Psychiatry and Mental Health Services in Toronto, which holds archival material relating to the history of the Canadian Psychiatry and Mental Health Services (see www.utoronto.ca/museum/museums/archive/canadianpsychiatryar.html).

Finally, many specialized private archives have important holdings related to social welfare history. An example is the Canadian Lesbian and Gay Archives in Toronto, whose mandate is to acquire, preserve, organize, and give public access to information and materials by and about lesbians and gays (see www.clga.ca). One of its key holdings is records of the AIDS Committee of Toronto, which is Canada's largest community-based AIDS organization.

On-Line Tools and Directories

The National Database (CAIN). The Canadian Archival Information Network is a searchable network of networks linking Internet users with information about Canadian archives and descriptions of archival documents. Each provincial/territorial network and the national archives make descriptive records accessible through the national database (www.cain-rcia.ca).

Provincial/Territorial Networks

Archives Network of Alberta (ANA). The Archives Network of Alberta Database consists of fonds-level descriptions of archival records held in Alberta's archival institutions (see www.archivesalberta.org/general/database.htm).

Archway: Nova Scotia's Archival Database. An electronic finding aid for archival descriptions of original archival documents held in archives throughout Nova Scotia (see www.councilofnsarchives.ca/archway).

Canadian North West Archival Network. Descriptions of records held in publicly accessible archives in Alberta, British Columbia, and the Yukon (http://aabc.bc.ca/aabc/icaul.html).

British Columbia Archival Union List (BCAUL). A database that consists of descriptions of records held at publicly accessible archival repositories in the province of British Columbia (see http://aabc.bc.ca/aabc/bcaul.html).

Réseau de diffusion des archives du Québec (RDAQ). The RDAQ is a searchable database of archival descriptions from Quebec repositories (see www.rdaq.qc.ca/cgi-bin/home.cfm).

Saskatchewan Archival Information Network/Manitoba Archival Information Network (SAIN/MAIN).

The Saskatchewan/Manitoba Archival Information Networks consists of descriptions of archival material held at publicly accessible repositories in Saskatchewan and Manitoba (see http://lib74123.usask.ca/scaa/sain-main/).

Yukon Archival Union List (YAUL). The Yukon Archival Union List consists of descriptions of archival material held at publicly accessible repositories in the Yukon Territory (see www.whitehorse.microage.ca/yca/sections/yaul/yaul.html).

Directories of Canadian Archives

Directory of Archives. The Canadian Council of Archives website (www.cdncouncilarchives.ca/directory.html).

Canadian Archival Resources on the Internet. University of Saskatchewan Archives website (www.usask.ca/archives/menu.html).

—*Wendy L. Thorpe*

MEXICO

Researchers interested in the history of public welfare and social reformism in twentieth century Mexico may wish to start their investigation by consulting Moises González Navarro's *La Pobreza en México* (Colegio de México, 1985) or Miguel E. Bustamante et al.'s *La Salud Pública en México, 1959–1982*, published by the *Secretaría de Salubridad y Asistencia* in 1982. González Navarro's work introduces some of the major themes and institutions concerned with relieving poverty in Mexico; *La Salud Pública en México* offers the reader detailed descriptions regarding specific federal social service campaigns, synopses of major conferences, and summaries of relevant legislation. Those seeking background on the history of welfare initiatives in Mexico will want to consult Sylvia Arrom's *Containing the Poor: The Mexico City Poor House, 1774–1871* (Duke University Press, 2000), which analyzes the transformation of one institution from a religious charity to a state-supported assistance program over the period from the late Bourbon era through the Wars of Reform. Ann S. Blum's article on "Conspicuous Benevolence:

Liberalism, Public Welfare and Private Charity in Porfirian Mexico City, 1877–1910" (*The Americas,* vol. 58, no. 1, 2001) offers an analysis of the intellectual and social foundations of late nineteenth and early twentieth century Porfirian-era philanthropy and documents the proliferation of public welfare programs in the capital city by the early decades of the twentieth century.

Archival material regarding the origins and development of welfare agencies in Mexico can be found in a variety of public collections. For data on twentieth century federal programs, investigators may want to start at the *Archivo General de la Nación* (Mexico City), where the document collections pertaining to the *Secretaría de Gobernación,* the *Presidencia de la República,* and the *Consejo Tutelar Para Menores Infractores* offer information regarding the themes of concern to Mexican public officials from the revolutionary period onwards. The material contained in the section pertaining to the *Secretaría de Gobernación* documents the founding and administration of a variety of institutions, including some health and assistance agencies. Files in the *Archivo General's Presidencia de la República* section offer insight into major executive-branch initiatives and contain correspondence between public officials and citizens relating to specific themes, including social services. These files, which are organized by presidential administration, contain correspondence from all over the country. The files of the *Consejo Tutelar Para Menores Infractores* contain the case files for juvenile offenders in the capital and offer insight into the lives and social conditions of adolescents in the capital city. Because they are organized according to case, however, they offer less insight into the organization's *raison d'être* or its directors' relationship with the federal government.

The collection at the *Archivo Histórico de la Secretaría de Salubridad y Asistencia* (Mexico City) contains material regarding the public health ministry's transformation from the Porfirian-era *Consejo Superior de Salubridad Pública* into the *Departamento de Salubridad Pública* and its later integration with the *Secretaría de Asistencia Pública,* which itself developed out of the older *Junta de Beneficencia Pública* in the capital. Although many of the documents do relate specifically to the Federal District, the files encompass correspondence and documentation regarding initiatives in the states as well. Of particular interest will be the collections regarding major campaigns against venereal disease, begging, alcoholism, and tuberculosis, as well as files regarding infant feeding, adoption practices, and a visiting nurse program. The *Archivo Histórico de la Secretaría de Salubridad y Asistencia* also houses material pertaining to the Federal District's *manicomio*, or mental asylum, and the public hospital for indigent women, including prostitutes, the Hospital Morelos. Collections pertaining to the *Casa de Niños Expósitos* and *Junta de Beneficencia Pública* will also be of interest. Most of the information in this archive centers on the early part of the twentieth century. For the later period, the archives at the *Secretaría de Salud* (Mexico City) headquarters may be useful, although they are not necessarily designed for historical research. For information about health care and social insurance in the period after 1945, researchers may also wish to consult the nearby *Centro de Documentación* at the *Instituto Mexicano del Seguro Social* (Mexico City).

On the campus of the *Universidad Nacional Autónoma de México* (Mexico City), the *Hemeroteca Nacional* contains collections of periodicals, including the official publications of the *Departamento de Salubridad* (*Boletín de Salubridad*) and the *Junta de Beneficencia Pública* (*Asistencia*). The *Hemeroteca* also houses more popular magazines such as *Mujer, Nosotras,* or *Eugenesia*, which offer insight into how feminists, eugenicists, and other groups in the 1920s and 1930s thought about reform and welfare. The *Biblioteca Nacional*, also located on the campus of the National University, houses theses presented by students in law and social work and sheds light on the themes and issues of concern to researchers involved in social service work throughout the century.

Researchers may also wish to consult the *Biblioteca Miguel Lerdo de Tejada*'s (Mexico City) collection of historical newspaper clippings. This collection, which is organized by theme, offers investigators a database of journalistic articles regarding major federal welfare campaigns and initiatives from a variety of perspectives.

In the United States, published laws and treaties are held at Harvard University's library at Langdell Hall (Cambridge, Massachusetts); the International Law Collection offers information regarding the institutional framework in which welfare initiatives developed. At Countway Library of Medicine at Harvard Medical School (Boston, Massachusetts), researchers may locate volumes of early twentieth century health and welfare periodicals as well. In Chicago, Illinois, the Center for Research Libraries, located near the campus of the University of Chicago, houses some mid-twentieth century Mexican welfare publications; the Newberry Library in downtown Chicago contains bulletins and published memoranda from early twentieth century municipal collections. Finally, researchers may want to consult the collection of theses and social work tracts housed at the Library of Congress in Washington, D.C.

—Katherine Elaine Bliss

UNITED STATES

Archives are defined as the records of an organization or institution that are no longer required for current use but have been selected for permanent preservation because of their enduring value. They represent the tangible link between past and present that informs historical research and understanding. Themselves the direct by-product and surviving evidence of human and institutional activity, they provide raw material in the form of firsthand accounts for studying past events, activities, and conditions. At one level, they are a source of information to be reported, analyzed, and interpreted. At another, the surviving physical documents often inspire a more intense appreciation of the past, whether to celebrate the legacy of a person or institution, or to seek a better theoretical understanding of present conditions. Effective use of archival materials requires an understanding of their basic nature, how they are administered and made available, and how to locate them.

The Nature of Archives

Individuals, agencies, and organizations create records as a part of the process of planning, delivering, and evaluating social services. Later researchers will find the resulting records to be a unique body of evidence that provides an intimate picture of the records' creators as well as a window on surrounding conditions.

Several characteristics define the nature of records and distinguish them from published books and articles that are the more familiar starting point for most historical researchers. Unpublished documents are usually created to communicate with a very specific and immediate audience on a need-to-know basis. Having been produced spontaneously and not having undergone the editorial process accorded to published materials, they represent a rougher, less self-conscious account of events.

Records tend to be part of a process. Individual items must be studied in the context of other materials related to the same activities if all possible information is to be derived from them. Simply, the whole is greater than the sum of its parts. That concept underlies all office filing systems, and it is retained when records are transferred to archival custody.

Records go through a life cycle that includes creation, a period of active use for current activities, retirement to inactive storage, and either destruction or transfer to an archives for long-term preservation. The archival institution represents a distinct second stage of life for selected records, offering specialized management that facilitates use by different users and for different purposes. Three perspectives—those of creators, keepers, and users of archives—will contribute to an understanding of what they offer and how they must be approached.

Creators of Archives

The creators of records naturally focus on current programs and operations. For them, conscious attention to record-keeping requires a practical payoff in terms of operating efficiency. A few large institutions that place high value on their historical legacy employ historians or archivists to ensure that a representative and accurate set of records is selected and retained. More often, though, selection for retention is unsystematic, with fate and circumstance playing too large a role. This is particularly true for welfare and service organizations, whose resources are hard-pressed to support basic programs.

The nature of an organization's programs shapes its records. Direct service providers are likely to assemble detailed information about clients, whereas standard organizations focus more on the nature of practice and the need for improvements. Coordinating bodies' records offer evidence of interaction between various organizations in attempts to address common issues.

Governmental agencies—federal, state, and local—leave records reflecting their respective societal roles. Since the advent of Social Security and New Deal–based welfare programs, federal records have documented the lives of individual citizens to a much greater degree than have records of national voluntary organizations. Researchers on pre-1930 topics must rely more heavily on state and local relief programs. In general, the bureaucratic, hierarchical nature of governmental programs mandates extensive official reporting of at least overall administrative concerns.

National voluntary organizations emerged in the late nineteenth and early twentieth centuries, dedicated to a rational analysis and planning process that would promote better, more effective services offered by affiliated local agencies. Their records are eminently usable because they are far less voluminous than governmental records, are focused on a particular type of service or issue, and reflect the value these organizations placed on intimate knowledge of social conditions.

Local agencies devoted to providing direct service to clients are the most likely to provide an intimate picture of the condition of client populations and of social work as actually practiced. This can correct the understanding informed by the prescriptive literature of social work journals and conference proceedings.

Individual social work leaders and practitioners leave papers that supplement the records of organizations and agencies, often filling gaps where the latter records have not been fully preserved.

Keepers of Archives

From a researcher's perspective, archivists add value to records in three ways: selection, preservation of context, and description. Archival resources are seriously limited, making it vital to select the records most worthy of permanent retention so that available resources can be concentrated most effectively.

Archivists preserve context by keeping together the records received from a particular creator and by maintaining the natural groupings within a body of records. Only in this way can the researcher properly interpret and take full advantage of the interrelatedness of documents.

Archival description provides an intellectual roadmap to the records. The most important component of the archival system of finding aids is the descriptive inventory prepared for each collection. Of necessity, it provides multiple levels of description, recognizing that a researcher may be interested in the collection as a whole, or in a particular segment (known as a series), a folder, or even an individual document. All of this interpretive activity aims not to list and describe each individual item, which would in itself present an undecipherable mass, but to provide summary descriptions of patterns and groupings that allow the researcher to identify the most likely location of desired information.

Archival finding aids were once confined to typed sheets of paper and index cards that could be consulted principally in the archives. Now, most archives maintain their own websites with at least general information about their holdings and policies governing use. Many library-based archives have brief records describing their collections in the host library's on-line catalog. Increasingly, the full detail of descriptive inventories is being presented over the Web as well, making it possible for researchers to plan their research trips much more intelligently and arrive prepared to make more efficient use of available time.

For the most part, archival research requires "going to the source." Because archival collections are unique and irreplaceable, they do not circulate, except sometimes to a limited degree within a small network of related institutions. Occasionally, a collection of exceptional value is replicated on microfilm, which allows other institutions to purchase a copy or obtain portions temporarily through interlibrary loan. Digital technology allows scanned images to be made available over the Web, but this is unlikely to be implemented on more than a highly selective basis.

In general, the American archival universe is divided into two spheres: institutional archives where the records remain in the custody of the institution that created them; and collecting repositories that take on responsibility for records created elsewhere.

The archives of the federal and state governments are the most relevant examples of institutional archives for social welfare history researchers. Records of federal social programs belong in the National Archives in or near the District of Columbia; the main home for federal agency records is in College Park, Maryland. Records from federal field offices are dispersed to a network of federal records centers across the country. Beginning with Herbert Hoover, each U.S. president has had a presidential library devoted to preserving the papers of the president along with cabinet officers, advisers, and other key officials from his administration. Each state operates a state archives, usually in the capital city and sometimes a part of the state historical society, with responsibility for state and, to some degree, local government agency records.

Very few private social work agencies and organizations operate their own institutional archives. The Salvation Army National Archives and Research Center in Alexandra, Virginia, is the most significant exception to this rule. Religious-affiliated social program records are generally the responsibility of denominational or diocesan archives. Most universities operate institutional archives that could be expected to contain the records of their social work schools or departments. This represents an important resource for the study of social work education.

The records of most voluntary-sector social work agencies and organizations, along with personal papers of individual leaders, are preserved, if at all, by collecting repositories. This category includes state and local historical societies, college and university libraries, public libraries, and a variety of other specialized libraries, archives, and research centers. Most collecting repositories focus on defined geographic areas. A number of university-affiliated urban-area archives have significant social agency and social reformer holdings. Among the cities that are best documented are Boston (Simmons College, University of Massachusetts–Boston, and Northeastern University), Chicago (Chicago Historical Society, University of Illinois at Chicago, and University of Chicago), Cleveland (Western Reserve Historical Society), Los Angeles (California State University, Northridge, and University of Southern California), Minneapolis-St. Paul (Minnesota Historical Society and University of Minnesota), New York City (Columbia University, New York Public Library, New York University, and LaGuardia Community College), New Orleans (Tulane University), and Philadelphia (Temple University).

Other collecting repositories define their scope by subject rather than geographic area. The University of Minnesota's Social Welfare History Archives was the first to focus exclusively on social work and social welfare. Several colleges and universities, most notably Columbia University, Smith College, and the University of Chicago have assembled the papers of eminent early social work leaders who were associated with their schools of social work, either as faculty or alumni. Other theme collections whose scope includes significant social welfare history materials include Radcliffe College's Schlesinger Library on the History of Women, Indiana University-Purdue University-Indianapolis's Philanthropy Center, the Rockefeller Archive Center (Rockefeller Foundation and other philanthropies), and Wayne State University's Walter Reuther Library of Labor and Urban Affairs.

Users of Archives

In the 1950s, Ralph and Muriel Pumphrey, Verl Lewis, Karl and Elizabeth de Schweinitz, Robert Bremner, Blanche Coll, and Clarke Chambers formed the Social Welfare History Group, in large part as an attempt to correct the then-severely-limited archival collecting in the social welfare field. Today, thanks in part to their pioneering efforts, the problem facing researchers is not a dearth of records so much as sorting through the extensive, diverse holdings found in numerous institutions.

There is no one-stop resource for identifying available sources. A historical researcher has three basic options. Following the trail of citations and source notes left by previous researchers is a good beginning step, leading at least to what has been interpreted before.

Second, archival finding aids provide an ever-growing set of access points for identifying relevant materials. The key is to find pointers to all of the unique collections spread across the country, each with its own descriptive inventory. At the time of this writing, two national on-line resources provide an index to tens of thousands of collections in thousands of repositories. *ArchivesUSA*, produced by Chadwyck-Healey, and *RLG Archival Resources*, maintained by the Research Library Group, provide parallel, overlapping coverage. Both are available only by subscription, meaning that

they must be used in or through major research libraries. Similar on-line interinstitutional resources may be anticipated in the future, particularly at the state and regional levels.

Many archival materials, likely the majority now and into the foreseeable future, are not included in any integrated index. Adept use of the search engine in one's Web browser is one effective way to locate such collections. In addition, in such cases the researcher must engage in informed speculation about the possible location of a desired source. Such an approach requires familiarity with the full range of possible record creators and the pattern of possible archival repositories. Put simply, the operative questions become "who would have had reason to record the information I need, and where might those records have ended up?"

In any event, archival research requires as much familiarity with the subject matter as possible. Recognition of basic concepts, events, and names associated with the topic provides access points and a basis for distinguishing between significant and extraneous materials.

Selected Resources

Unpublished Primary Sources: Selected Repositories

Out of the lengthy list of repositories discussed here, several deserve mention for the extent of their social welfare history holdings. Detailed information about these, and many other, repositories is available on-line at their respective websites. Searches on the repository's name in a Web browser will locate the sites easily.

The U. S. National Archives & Records Administration is responsible for the historical records of the federal government. Its archives at College Park, Maryland, house the records of most civilian agencies, including the Women's Bureau, the Children's Bureau, the Social Security Administration, and the Department of Health, Education, and Welfare.

The Library of Congress Manuscript Division (Washington, D.C.) is America's preeminent collecting repository, containing the papers of many of the nation's government officials and other public figures. Included are records of organizations like the National Urban League and the National Child Labor Committee and the Roy Wilkins papers.

The Social Welfare History Archives at the University of Minnesota (Minneapolis) contains the records of many national voluntary social service organizations, personal papers of individual leaders, and records of selected local agencies, particularly settlement houses. It is the only national repository focused exclusively on social welfare history.

The Sophia Smith Collection at Smith College (Northampton, Massachusetts), one of the nation's preeminent women's history collections, includes extensive materials documenting the social work profession, particularly papers of persons associated with the Smith College School for Social Work.

The Columbia University Rare Book & Manuscript Library (New York City) contains many social work collections that are particularly rich for the early twentieth century origins of the profession, when much of the national leadership came from persons associated with the New York School of Philanthropy (later the Columbia University School of Social Work).

The State Historical Society of Wisconsin (Madison) contains many progressive reform and social action collections that transcend the state's borders. Particularly important are the papers of numerous individuals associated with the development of Social Security in the United States.

Published Primary Sources

Not all firsthand historical sources are unpublished. The published professional literature provides a useful perspective as evidence of discourse among practitioners in an earlier era. These materials are more widely available in various research libraries and occasionally on the Web.

The U.S. Congressional Serial Set published by the Government Printing Office is a complex, extensive compilation of hundreds of thousands of reports and documents submitted to Congress by congressional investigative committees, executive departments, and independent organizations. This collection contains much information about federal social programs. Copies are maintained in research libraries across the country that are designated as federal depositories.

The National Conference on Social Welfare (which underwent several name changes) was the chief meeting place for social welfare leaders from the 1870s through the 1970s. The published proceedings of its annual meetings provide a comprehensive wide-angle snapshot of programs and mindsets at a given time. The University of Michigan Library has made the full set of proceedings, from 1874 to 1982, available on the World Wide Web (www.hti.umich.edu/n/ncosw/).

—David J. Klaassen

Further Reading

Hill, M. (1993). *Archival strategies and techniques.* Newbury Park, CA: Sage.

Klaassen, D. J. (1995). Archives of social welfare. In R. Edwards (Ed.), *Encyclopedia of social work* (19th ed.; pp. 225–231). Washington, DC: NASW Press.

Stuart, P. H. (1997). Historical research. In R. Grinnell (Ed.), *Social work research and evaluation* (5th ed.; pp. 442–457). Itasca, IL: F. E. Peacock.

APPENDIX B

Chronologies

Social Welfare History, Canada

Complied by Joan E. Esser-Stuart

1639   Establishment of the Hotel Dieu, a general hospital, that provided care for "indigents, the crippled, idiots, and lunatics."

1763   The Royal Proclamation of 1763 created the colony of Quebec, acknowledged First Nations' land rights, partitioned lands for hunting grounds and European settlements.

Treaty of Paris ended the Seven Years' War and ceded New France to Great Britain.

1774   The Quebec Act left untouched much of the social fabric of French Canada; the Canadians were free to use the French language in local (and eventually in provincial) government, in their schools and in business, to retain their system of civil law, and to practice their religion.

1799   The Orphans Act of 1799 provided for orphaned children to be indentured.

1827   Poor Man's Friend Society established in Halifax to assist the poor and disabled.

1833   British Emancipation Act of 1833 ended slavery in Canada.

1840   The 1840 Act of Union unified the colonies of Upper and Lower Canada, which were inhabited primarily by English and French speaking populations, respectively.

1845   Beauport, or the Quebec Lunatic Asylum, established to treat the mentally ill.

1847   The New Brunswick Lunatic Asylum established; the first asylum in English Canada.

1850   The Toronto Lunatic Asylum established.

1857   Gradual Civilization Act Indians were to abandon Indian status and life ways in favor of British Canadian citizenship and political rights.

1864   Delegates to the Charlottetown Conference agreed that education should be a provincial rather than a federal responsibility.

1866   Delegates to the Quebec Conference agreed that education should be a provincial rather than a federal responsibility.

1867   British North American Act (BNA) established the Canadian State as a federation of four provinces: Ontario, Quebec, Nova Scotia, and New Brunswick. The federal government was accorded powers including the regulation of trade and commerce, postal service, defense, navigation, shipping and taxation. Provincial governments were accorded matters of "local concern" such as the management and sale of provincial public lands, the running of hospitals and asylums, municipal institutions within the province, education, and direct taxation for provincial purposes.

1869   The Department of Indian Affairs attempted to regulate tribal affairs by assuming the power to depose chiefs and councilors and overseeing band council meetings.

The enfranchisement legislation was broadened so that any woman with Indian status who married a male without it would lose her status, as would their children and descendants.

1871   The Toronto Trades Assembly established, became one of the more successful of the local labour movements.

The Municipal Code gave the cities and towns of Quebec some responsibility for the relief of the indigent.

1872   The Trade Union Act confirmed the legality of unions in Canada.

The Toronto Trades Assembly (1871) helped launch the Nine Hours league which campaigned for a reduction in the working day.

1873   The Canadian Labour Union attracted support for a program of labour reform in the industrial towns of southern Ontario.

1874   The Act Respecting Industrial School of 1874 attempted to define a neglected child.

1879   The Provincial Workmen's Association in Nova Scotia was established as a regional labour movement.

1880   Charity organization societies (COS) established in Canadian cities, based on English charity organisation societies formed in 1869.

1880s   The Knights of Labour entered Canada from the United States, organized workers from many trades into 450 assemblies, mainly in Ontario, Quebec, and British Columbia.

1881   The Miner's Mutual Protective Association in British Columbia was established as a regional labour movement.

1883   The Trades and Labour Congress (TLC) of Canada aimed to become an inclusive national organization of labour but did not establish a strong presence across the country until after 1902, when it defined itself primarily as a federation of the Canadian branches of unions affiliated with the American Federation of Labor (AFL) in the United States.

1885   The Indian Act, a comprehensive legislative effort to regulate all aspects of First Nations peoples' lives, passed.

Completion of transcontinental Canadian Pacific Railroad (CPR), not only an impressive engineering achievement but also a significant joint public-private sector economic undertaking.

The Chinese Immigration Act, passed after the completion of the railroad, introduced the head tax system, making it more difficult for Chinese people to enter Canada. The head tax system continued in force until 1947.

1888   Severalty Policy, a copy of the American Dawes Act (1887), enacted, encouraged the conversion of Indian reserves to freehold properties.

The Act for the Protection and Reformation of Neglected Children (Children's Protection Act) established the principle that representatives of the State could remove a child from a family if provisions of care were found unsuitable.

1889   The Prison Reform Commission concluded that the care of young children at risk was critical for the prevention of adult crime, and that children at risk were better served in family foster homes than in larger institutions.

1891   The first Children's Aid Society (CAS) in Canada was founded in Toronto with J. J. Kelso in the volunteer position of president.

Manitoba abolished public funding for Roman Catholic schools.

1892   Toronto CAS opened the first children's shelter to provide temporary room and board for destitute and neglected youth.

1893   The Ontario Act for Prevention of Cruelty to and Better Protection of Children (The Children's Act) outlined a new approach to child welfare and established the position of Superintendent of Neglected and Dependent Children. J. J. Kelso was appointed to this position and held it for the next 41 years.

Children's Aid Societies were established in Ottawa and Petersborough.

The National Council of Women (NCWC), formed as an association of associations, sought to bring women together in a united front to provide leadership on social issues affecting women and families.

1894   Children's Aid Society established in Hamilton, Ontario.

1902   Department of Temperance and Moral Reform established by the Methodist Church.

1905   Radicals and revolutionaries joined Canadian branches of the Industrial Workers of the World.

1906   Parliamentary committees began to study the concept of old age pensions, although the effort lacked strong government support.

1907   The Methodist Church's Department of Temperance and Moral Reform renamed the Department of Evangelism and Social Service.

1908   Farmers formed the Saskatchewan Grain Growers Company (SGGC) to ensure justice for farmers, advocated for reforms like a graduated income tax, nationalization of utilities and food processing plants, tariffs favorable to farmers, women's and universal health care.

Board of Moral and Social Reform established by the Presbyterian Church.

1910   The Immigrant Act emphasized the prospective newcomer's country of origin, favored immigrant workers from Great Britain, the United States, and northwestern Europe; other racial groups were deemed "unsuitable" based upon the belief that they could not adapt to Canada's climate.

1914   The Social Service Congress raised Canadians' awareness of the need for social security programs, including those that protected citizens from the poverty associated with old age. Reformers argued that no child should be removed from his or her home on grounds of poverty alone.

Workers' Compensation legislation introduced in Ontario.

Saskatchewan was the first province to experiment with a form of medical care insurance when a rural municipality offered physicians a retainer to practice in the area. The success of this plan allowed municipalities to levy property taxes to retain physicians. Manitoba and Alberta adopted similar plans.

National Council of Women (NCWC) membership included twenty affiliated associations at the national level and thirty-two local councils. The NCWC was legally incorporated by an Act of Parliament.

1916   Mothers' Pension legislation enacted in Manitoba.

1917   Saskatchewan authorized municipalities to create hospital districts in order to build and maintain hospitals and to collect taxes for financing hospital care.

1918   The Hospital for the Insane in Whitby, Ontario was converted to a military hospital to treat mentally ill military personnel returning to Canada from World War I.

Department of Social Study and Training founded at McGill University.

1920s   Labour Wars in the coalfields of eastern and western Canada.

Quebec enacted the Public Charities Act committing the government of the province to a measure of financial support to persons in need.

1921   *Conferation des Travailleurs Catholiques du Canada*, a conservative and nationalist labor organization, established in Quebec.

1923   Immigration of the Chinese into Canada was completely banned.

1926   The Canadian Association of Social Workers (CASW) established.

1927   Parliament passed the Old Age Pension Act, which involved a partnership with provinces, to provide pensions for the elderly.

An amendment to the Indian Act, which remained in force until 1951, made it illegal to raise or contribute money for pursuit of a claim, effectively barring Indian leaders from using lawyers and making political organization and activity on a large scale extremely difficult.

1929   Child Labour Legislation enacted.

The British Privy Council, on behalf of five Alberta women who were members of NCWC, decided to interpret the word "person" in the British North America Act (1867) to include women.

1930   The Canadian Royal Commission concluded that Provincial Psychiatric Hospitals, though somewhat better than jails and poor houses in treating the mentally ill, were found wanting from a therapeutic or humane accommodation perspective, recommended twenty million dollars of capital expenditures to upgrade existing facilities, but this was unrealistic due to the worldwide economic Depression.

1930s   The Progressive Education Movement (strongest in Alberta) included a new social studies curriculum (combining history, geography, and civics), the "enterprise" system of inquiry-based learning, and the junior high school.

Provincial psychiatric institutions were deteriorating due to overcrowding and a lack of resources.

1931   The federal government enacted legislation that prohibited immigrants from all classes and occupations, with the exception of farmers with capital, British and Americans with sufficient resources to maintain themselves until employment could be found, and persons with financially secure relatives in Canada. This legislation, however, did not apply to individuals of any Asian race.

Quebec became the last province to legislate a program of Workers' Compensation.

1932   The League for Social Reconstruction was established to advocate for social reforms to alleviate the problems created as a result of the Depression.

Harry Cassidy's study of relief administration in Ontario, entitled *Unemployment and Relief in Ontario 1929-1932: A Survey and Report* published.

1935   Employment and Social Insurance Act enacted to collect taxes and to provide social security benefits, including health benefits. The Act failed since it trespassed on provincial jurisdiction.

Protests against unemployment in the Great Depression culminated in the On to Ottawa Trek.

Church Conference of Social Work founded to provide a forum for clerical social workers.

1937   The automobile workers strike against General Motors in Oshawa.

The Needy Mothers Assistance Act of 1937 established in Quebec.

1939   Humanitarian petitions for Canadian acceptance of a fair quota of Jewish refugees fleeing the threat of extermination were ignored.

1940   The Rowell-Sirois Commission (the Royal Commission on Dominion-Provincial Relations) recommended equalization transfers from the federal government to the provinces and a federal unemployment insurance system.

1941   National Unemployment Insurance program adopted.

1942   Forced evacuation of Japanese-Canadians from west coast areas, confiscation of their property, and confinement of them as "enemy aliens" in heavily guarded internment camps.

1943   The Marsh Report offered a broad overview of existing social security legislation and practice at both the Dominion (federal) and provincial levels of government, made suggestions for improvement and expansion of these programs, and argued for the creation of a planned, integrated, and comprehensive system of social security.

1944   Family Allowance Act (also known as the baby bonus) passed providing monthly checks for each child in each family from 1945 until the program was replaced by the Canada Child Tax Benefit (CCTB) program 1993.

1948   The *National Health Grants Act* provided grants-in-aid for hospital construction, laboratory services, and professional training for public health and mental health professionals.

Industrial Relations Disputes Investigation Act and equivalent provincial laws established the worker's right to representation and recognition in collective bargaining.

1949   Quebec Asbestos Strike.

1951   The Old Age Security Program (OAS) created a universal program that was managed and financed by the federal government.

The Old Age Assistance Act, cost-shared with the provinces, provided means-tested assistance for persons aged 65 to 69.

A revision of the federal Indian Act ended many of the colonial strictures on Aboriginal people and allowed them to organize effectively.

1957   Hospital Insurance and Diagnostic Service Act (HIDS) provided for 50% federal cost-sharing of hospital services (excluding physician services) for provinces with a universal hospital insurance plan. Five provinces immediately joined and by 1961, HIDS was operating in all provinces and territories.

The innovative Saskatchewan Plan was a forerunner of the federal government's ambitious mental health policy.

1961   Saskatchewan implemented compulsory, government-sponsored medical insurance. Between 1963 and 1966, several other provinces developed similar medical insurance programs.

Department of Family and Social Welfare established in Quebec.

1962   Canadian immigration policy underwent major changes in 1962 when criteria based upon skills, education, and training were developed and decreased emphasis was placed on the long-held practice of preferential treatment of individuals from certain parts of the world.

1963   Report of the Study Committee on Public Assistance, the Boucher Report, recommended a liberal public assistance program for the province of Quebec.

Royal Commission on Bilingualism and Biculturalism created to study language issues in Canada.

1965   The Canada Pension Plan (CPP) and Quebec Pension Plan (QPP) were designed as contributory pension plans in which workers paid a percentage of their salary and received benefits after retirement. The plans include survivor's pensions for the spouses of the deceased pensioners, disability benefits, children's and death benefits.

The Company of Young Canadians (CYC) emerged as a federal government initiative aimed at putting the energy of youth to work in communities across Canada. It evolved into a nationwide, grassroots approach to community development with projects centered on civil rights, anti-poverty, food co-ops, youth issues, drop-in centers, and outreach projects addressing drugs, alcohol, and violence.

The Royal Commission on Health Care (the Hall Commission, under Justice Emmett Hall) undertook a comprehensive review of health services in Canada and recommended strong federal leadership and financial support for medical care to ensure adequate coverage for all Canadians. The Commission also recommended sweeping reforms in mental health treatment and services.

"More for the Mind" advocated the treatment for mental illness on the same basis as physical illness and demanded that the standards of care and facilities for anyone with any illness should be equal.

1966   The Medical Care Act provided payments to provinces for physicians' services and some dental and chiropractic services.

Guaranteed Income Supplement (GIS) was introduced to provide a guaranteed minimum income for retired persons on the basis of an income test.

The Canada Assistance Plan (CAP) was introduced. Under CAP, federal and provincial governments shared costs on a fifty-fifty basis for health insurance, education, and welfare.

The Report of the Royal Commission of Inquiry on Education in the Province of Quebec (the Parent

Commission) recommended greater local autonomy in decision-making, broadening curriculum through thematic and interdisciplinary approaches, organizing learning through individual timetables, and the abolition of grades.

The White Paper on Immigration was published by the federal government and reaffirmed that immigrants should be selected based upon an established set of criteria rather than designating certain countries for more favorable treatment.

1967   Quebec established its own family allowance system.

The Canada/Quebec Pension Plans were introduced in 1967 to provide a public pension based upon contributions related to earnings throughout one's lifetime.

The federal government replaced several programs that supported provincial categorical programs with the Canada Assistance Plan, which encouraged a shift away from categorical to generalized means and income tested programs.

A revised immigration policy adopted using a point system to assess individuals applying to immigrate to Canada. Points were awarded for personal suitability, education, specific vocational preparation, occupational demands, arranged employment, language, relatives, and specific destination in Canada.

1968   The Report of the Provincial Committee on Aims and Objectives of Education in the Schools of Ontario (Hall-Dennis Report) recommended greater local autonomy in decision-making, broadening curriculum through thematic and interdisciplinary approaches, organizing learning through individual timetables, and the abolition of grades.

1969   Church-managed residential schools for First Nations children phased out.

National Farmers Union (NFU) established by merging similar farmer organizations.

The federal government partially decriminalized male homosexual activity.

Report of the Royal Commission on Bilingualism and Biculturalism resulted in the Official Languages Act.

Quebec Social Aid Act of 1969 integrated the pre-existing categorical welfare programs (aged, long-term unemployed, needy mothers, etc.) into a single needs-based program.

1971   Prime Minister Pierre Elliott Trudeau announced Canada's first official policy on multiculturalism.

1972   Alberta's Report of the Commission on Educational Planning (Worth Report) recommended greater local autonomy in decision-making, broadening curriculum

through thematic and interdisciplinary approaches, organizing learning through individual timetables and the abolition of grades.

Multicultural Directorate established to assist ethnic and cultural groups in dealing with issues such as racism, human rights, citizen involvement, and immigrant services.

Shelters for battered women established in British Columbia and Alberta.

The Common Front in Quebec helped to develop a modern social democracy in the province.

1973   The Canadian Consultative Council on Multiculturalism was introduced to monitor implementation of the federal government's initiative on multiculturalism.

1975   Human Rights Commissions established in all Canadian provinces to administer anti-discriminatory legislation.

1976   New Dawn Development Corporation incorporated in Sydney, Nova Scotia, to promote local economic development and provide technical and financial assistance, including capital, to projects.

Immigration Act amended to reaffirm the principle that the selection of immigrants should not be based on race, nationality, or country of origin. Three classes of immigrants would be admitted into Canada — family class, refugees, and independent immigrants who have the financial resources to provide for themselves and create jobs for others.

Canada ratified the United Nations Covenant on Economic Social and Cultural Rights, which guarantees the human right to food.

1977   Quebec was the last province to develop child protection legislation since the child protection function had previously been vested in the Catholic Church.

The Human Resources Development Association (HRDA) was founded in Halifax, Nova Scotia, to create small businesses that are labour intensive and do not require high skill levels. The goal of these businesses was to provide an alternative to social assistance.

Quebec formally prohibited discrimination in both the public and private sectors.

The Federal-Provincial Fiscal Arrangements and Established Programs Financing Act (EPF Act) was passed, providing a federal financial contribution for extended health care services (such as nursing homes, adult residential care, and ambulatory health care) but changing the funding formula for federal contributions so that hospital insurance and medical care were no longer directly related to provincial costs. Instead, EPF was a block-funded system tied to economic growth. The Act also affected postsecondary education.

The Canadian Human Rights Act established a federal Human Rights Commission.

1980   The National Advisory Council on Aging was established to assist and advise the Canadian government on policies related to the aging of the Canadian population.

The Hall Report called attention to the issue of heatlh care accessibility, suggesting that extra billing by physicians was threatening access to services for some patients.

1981   Food bank established in Edmonton, Alberta.

1982   The Constitution Act repatriated the BNA of 1867, included the Canadian Charter of Rights and Freedoms and guaranteed linguistic choice for French-language minorities.

National Clearinghouse on Family Violence established to provide national information and consultation services for professionals as well as a base for public education.

1984   The Canada Health Care Act (CHA) provided universal health care coverage for all Canadians including the aging population.

The Badgley Report detailed a high rate of sexual abuse of Canadian children and resulted in new legislative and policy attention to this issue. Sixteen offenses were added to the sexual assault provisions of the Criminal Code of Canada ranging from unwanted touching to assault with a weapon.

1985   An amendment to the Indian Act was passed which ended gender discrimination against Indian women and their descendants.

1986   Bill C-96 reduced the annual per capita escalator under EPF to 2% below GNP growth.

Many physicians went on a 25 day strike when legislation was introduced in Ontario to ban extra billing by physicians.

The Ontario French Language Services Act assured French language provincial services in designated areas where the majority of Franco-Ontarians live.

Employment Equity Act enacted to address the exclusion of particular groups from the Canadian workforce by removing discriminatory barriers and implementation of protective measures to accommodate differences.

1987   The Meech Lake Accord recognized Quebec as a distinct society but failed since Manitoba and Newfoundland did not pass the referendum by the specified date.

1988   The federal government initiated a Child Tax Credit program replacing child income tax deductions.

The Canadian Association of Food Banks established.

The Canadian Multiculturalism Act of 1988 established Canada as the first country in the world to enforce multiculturalism as a federal law.

Public assistance program in Quebec modified to reduce benefits for single persons fit to work and impose financial responsibility on families for young adult family members.

1989   Two years after the failure of Meech, constitutional negotiations resumed.

1991   The federal Goods and Services Tax reformed the consumption tax.

The Toronto Food Policy Council in the Toronto Board of Health was created along with a network of food policy organizations across the country.

1992   Health Canada, in collaboration with the Social Sciences and Humanities Research Council as well as other organizations, established five research centres on family violence and violence against women in Canada.

The Charlottetown Accord achieved consensus among governments, yet was rejected by Canadians, including the citizens of Quebec, in a national referendum.

Canada signed the World Declaration on Nutrition.

The Fraser Institute introduced a "Basic needs" measure, arguing that poverty as understood by the public related solely to basic needs. It included funds for shelter, food, and clothing but excluded books, magazines, toys, or a television.

1993   The Child Tax Benefit and Work Income Supplement replaced family allowances and the Child Tax Credit.

The election of the liberal government resulted in the reorganization of federal departments; the activities of the multiculturalism department were distributed to the Departments of Canadian Heritage and Citizenship and Immigration.

1994   The National Framework on Aging (NFA) assists governments at all levels to respond to the needs of the aging population and to recognize the valuable contributions of seniors.

At the Annual Premiers' Conference, concern was expressed over what was perceived as the lack of efficiency and effectiveness of national social programs. Premiers agreed to pursue an agenda of social policy reform.

1995   The federal budget announced major changes to federal fiscal transfer programs to provinces. The federal government merged the Established Programs Financing (EPF) and the Canada Assistance Plan (CAP) into the Canada Health and Social Transfer (CHST). As a part of the reform, federal conditions about how provinces could spend funds were reduced.

At the Annual Premiers' Conference a Ministerial Council on Social Policy Reform and Renewal was established.

The Report of the Gove Inquiry into Child Protection (Gove Report) detailed problems and errors leading to the death of Matthew Vaudreuill in British Columbia and recommended changes in the child protection system.

Quebec voters rejected sovereignty by only a few percentage points.

British Columbia recognized adoption rights for same-sex couples.

1996   Bill C-69 reduced the escalator and froze transfer payments for two years. As a result of these restrictions and a concomitant cost-cutting effort of provincial governments, there were cutbacks and restructuring of health care services.

1997   The Afghan Women's Catering Group was established in Toronto to alleviate the economic and social hardship experienced by Afghan women and their families, particularly as a result of cutbacks in social assistance and services.

Canadian Law Reform Commission became the Law Commission of Canada.

1998   National Child Benefit System (NCBS) created by combining the federal Canada Child Tax Benefit (CCTB) and provincial programs for low-income families with children.

Canada's Action Plan for Food Security (CAPFS) to reduce food insecurity released

1999   Social Union Framework Agreement (SUFA), increasing federal transfer payments to the provinces, signed by the federal government and all provinces and territories except for Quebec.

A national Food Security Bureau within Agriculture and Agri-Food Canada was created and charged with overseeing the implementation of CAPFS recommendations and coordinating food security activities at the federal, provincial, and civil society levels.

A Supreme Court Ruling in 1999 (M. v. H.) was a clear victory for equity advocates, essentially treating any differentiation of same-sex couples and heterosexual de facto couples as unconstitutional.

2000   The Seniors Policies and Programs Database (SPPD) was established to assist governments and other organizations review and develop policies and programs related to seniors.

2001   The Commission on the Future of Health Care (The Romanow Commission) formed to examine Canadian health care and to make recommendations to ensure service delivery associated with the growth of the aging population.

2002   The report of the Romanow Commission reaffirmed the commitment to publicly funded health care and the principles of the Canada Health Care Act (CHA) and recommended new funding arrangements which would increase federal funding to provinces and included provisions for rural and remote access, home care services, and catastrophic drug coverage.

Quebec implemented a comprehensive "civil union" registration, open to same and opposite sex couples

The Act Respecting Social Security and Exclusion, passed unanimously by the Quebec National Assembly, emphasized social *exclusion* as well as material *insecurity* as the business of social welfare.

2003   National Child Benefit Supplement (NCBS), intended to support the working poor, established.

Social Welfare History, Mexico

1504-1650	200,000 to 450,000 Spaniards migrated to the Americas, the majority to New Spain (Mexico)	1821	Independence of Mexico from Spain achieved.
1517	First New World office of the *Protomedicato,* a Spanish institution to regulate physicians, established in Santo Domingo.	1824	Constitution authorized federal and state educational institutions. Spaniards asked to leave Mexico.
1519	Spanish conquest of Mexico begins.	1828	Expulsion of Spaniards from Mexico ordered.

1504-
1650   200,000 to 450,000 Spaniards migrated to the Americas, the majority to New Spain (Mexico)

1517   First New World office of the *Protomedicato,* a Spanish institution to regulate physicians, established in Santo Domingo.

1519   Spanish conquest of Mexico begins.

1521-
1650   Indigenous population declines by up to 95% due largely to diseases that came with conquest.

1532   Father Vasco de Quiroga established two experimental hospital-pueblos to provide medical care and education.

1553   Royal and Pontifical University of Mexico established.

1555   First Mexican Council ordered that hospitals be established in every parish in Mexico.

1556   Bernardino Alvarez, a wealthy Spaniard, founded first of many hospitals in Mexico.

1572   Hospital San Lazarus (for the care of lepers) founded by Dr. Pedro Lopez.

1582   Hospital of the Epiphany (for the care of blacks, mestizos, and mulattoes) founded by Dr. Pedro Lopez and supported by the confraternity of Our Lady of the Forsaken.

1590s   *Alhóndiga* (public granary) and *Pósito* (grain reserve) established in Mexico City to insure consistent food supply and avoid price hikes.

1646   *Protomedicato* established in Mexico City to regulate physicians.

1760s   Bourbon reforms, designed to stimulate the economy and boost the export of Mexico's raw materials, begun.

1767   Spain expelled the Jesuits from Mexico.

1774   *Hospicio de Pobres* (Poor House) founded in Mexico City, begging outlawed.

1806   The Patriotic School, a boarding school established within the Mexico City Poor House to educate children in the institution.

1810   Mexico declared its independence from Spain, initiating Mexico's war for independence.

1821   Independence of Mexico from Spain achieved.

1824   Constitution authorized federal and state educational institutions.

Spaniards asked to leave Mexico.

1828   Expulsion of Spaniards from Mexico ordered.

1833   Attempts to secularize education, frustrated by inadequate funding.

1841   Superior Sanitation Council created; its jurisdiction was at first limited to the Federal District.

1842   National network of teacher training institutions established.

1845   Society of St. Vincent de Paul, a volunteer charity, established in Mexico.

1856   A liberal reform government took power; legal reforms mandated secular public primary education and transferred charitable institutions to public administration.

Ley Lerdo, a law for the disentailment of corporate property, including property belonging to the Catholic Church and indigenous communities (*ejidos*), enacted.

1857   A new constitution emphasized unleashing market forces and the sanctity of private property, provided for academic freedom and state control of licensing requirements for teachers.

1861   Secularization of welfare institutions and centralization of welfare activities in the federal government.

1863   French occupation of Mexico began, continued until 1867. Emperor Maximilian installed as ruler.

Empress Charlotte created Associations of Ladies of Charities to establish, fund, and administer welfare institutions.

1867   French occupation ended; *República Restaurada* (restoration of the republic) began.

1871   Begging legalized in Mexico City.

1876   *Porfiriato* (dictatorship of Porfirio Díaz) began, lasted until 1911.

First National Congress of Physicians held in Mexico City.

1877 *Casa Amiga de la Obrera* founded by Carmen Romero Rubio de Diaz, wife of President Profirio Diaz, to provide daycare for the children of working mothers.

1879 *Consejo Superior de Salubridad* (CSS; Superior Sanitation Council) reorganized and made answerable to the federal Ministry of the Interior; separate commissions made responsible for surveillance of the quality of medicines, food, and beverages, as well as the sanitary conditions of hospitals, jails, and industrial establishments.

1881 A federal law grouped beneficence centers into three categories: hospitals, orphanages, and educational/correctional facilities.

1883 Colonization and Naturalization Laws enacted to encourage settlement in sparsely populated areas and to promote development.

1884 Mexico City Poorhouse became a boarding school for orphans and was renamed the *Hospicio de Niños* (House of Children).

1885 Dr. Eduardo Liceaga became director of the Superior Sanitary Council and continued in this office until 1914.

1886 The Immigration and Naturalization Law conferred Mexican citizenship on immigrants who owned property and did not intend to maintain their foreign nationality. Mexican women deprived of Mexican citizenship if they married foreigners. The law remained in force until 1934.

1888 Mexico and Japan signed a Treaty of Friendship, Commerce, and Navigation; the first "equal" treaty negotiated with a non-Asian country by Japan, it facilitated the immigration of Japanese to Mexico.

1891 Sanitary Code of the United States of Mexico approved; first comprehensive public health legislation. The code was revised in 1894 and 1903, and continued in force until 1926.

1893 Mexico and China signed a Treaty of Amity and Commerce.

1902 Mexico hosted the Second International Congress of American States.

A general convention of the health organizations of the American republics met in Washington, D.C.; established the International Sanitary Bureau.

1904 First state laws for work accidents enacted.

1905 General Hospital of Mexico opened in Mexico City.

1906 Strike at the Cananea Copper Company.

Hospicio de Niños closed.

1908 Economic difficulties led Porfirian government to re-examine its liberal immigration policy; immigrants likely to require public support prohibited.

Elementary Education Law for the Federal District and Territories promulgated.

1909 Mexico adhered to the International Treaty of Rome (1907), which established the *Office International d'Hygiène Publique*.

1910 Mexican Revolution began, continued until 1917.

La Castañeda, Mexico's first mental hospital, opened in Mexico City.

Popular Hygiene Exhibition organized in Mexico City.

National University of Mexico reestablished.

1911 Over 300 Chinese murdered by soldiers and civilians in Torreón, Coahuila.

1912 Textile workers won a 10-hour workday, holidays, and uniform wages across the industry.

1913 Rockefeller Foundation established in the United States.

1914 Mexico City Department of Public Beneficence established Sanitary Brigades to treat those wounded in revolution.

1915 Department of Aid established to build shelters for the homeless and educational centers for children orphaned by revolution.

1917 Mexican Constitution of 1917 adopted, placed all charity and welfare organizations under state control, limited child labor and mandated universal public secular education, limited immigration.

Department of Anthropology created in the federal government by President Venustiano Carranza, first of a series of agencies that sought to solve the "Indian problem."

1921 First National Child Congress convened to discuss state's role in training "fit" mothers and educating children.

Secretaria de Educación Pública (SEP, Ministry of Public Education) established; José Vasconcelos became first Secretary of Public Education.

Voluntary worker pension funds consolidated by the federal government.

Rockefeller Foundation's Special Commission for the Eradication of Yellow Fever in Mexico initiated cooperative health programs with the Mexican public health programs, which would continue until 1951. Yellow fever eradicated by 1923.

1922 SEP Secretary José Vasconcelos sent normal school graduates to rural areas to stimulate interest in education, recruit teachers, and establish schools; *misiones culturales* (cultural missions) established to serve indigenous communities.

School Hygiene Service established.

Fee structure imposed on applicants for immigration.

1923   Second National Congress of the Child; two hygiene centers for children established.

1924   *Departamento de Salubridad Pública* (DSP; Department of Public Health) created.

1925   Limited social insurance for public servants (teachers subsequently added after protests) and veterans of the revolution; retirement age set at 65.

   Dirección de Pensiones Civiles created to provide housing for government employees.

1926   *Consejo Tutelar para Menores Infractores,* which oversaw the *Tribunal para Menores* (Juvenile Court), established in Mexico City.

   Medical reasons for excluding immigrants added to existing immigration restrictions.

   Sanitary Code gave DSP authority to implement new programs fusing treatment and prevention programs.

   National Agricultural Credit Bank established.

1927   Shelter for homeless children constructed by Mexico City Department of Public Beneficence.

   Immigration from Syria, Lebanon, Palestine, Arabia, and Turkey restricted.

   Rockefeller Foundation inaugurated local health units in Veracruz.

1929   Official Revolutionary Party established, to be re-named the Institutional Revolutionary Party (PRI) in 1946.

   Asociación de Protección de la Infancia (Association for the Protection of Childhood) established, focused on nutrition programs for children and prenatal care for pregnant women.

   Mexico City Child Hygiene Service established.

   All immigration to Mexico temporarily suspended.

   Dr. Miguel Bustamante, a physician and former Rockefeller Foundation fellow, named director of a health unit in Veracruz, pursued an ambitious public health agenda.

1930s   Campaign Against Begging conducted in Mexico City.

1931   Federal Labor Code provided for state regulation of unions and labor conflicts, facilitated the growth of unions allied with the government, and restricted child labor, incorporating educational and medical criteria for improving child development.

   Dr. Miguel Bustamante promoted to head the Rural Hygiene Service of the *Departamento de Salubridad Publica.*

   Narciso Bassols became Secretary of *Secretaria de Educación Pública* (SEP, Ministry of Public Education), supported "socialist" education and anti-clericalism.

1932   Labor Code enacted, required employers to give three months' severance pay in addition to one month for each year of service to dismissed workers; women were granted three months' wage for maternity.

   Banco Nacional Hipotecario Urbano y de Obras Públicas (BNHUOP) established.

1933   *Escuela de Enseñanza Doméstica y Trabajo Social* (School of Domestic Instruction and Social Work), a technical school, established by the *Secretaria de Educación Pública* (SEP, Ministry of Public Education).

1934   Administration of President Lázaro Cárdenas began, right to public assistance articulated, public child welfare linked to national economic development, 18 million hectares of land distributed to rural Mexicans. Cárdenas administration ended in 1940.

   Workers secured the right to a minimum wage, set by Minimum Wage Commissions that included unions.

1935   Seventh International Pan America Child Congress held in Mexico City, resulting in a proliferation of child and family services.

1936   General Population Law prohibited immigration of alcoholics, drug addicts, prostitutes, anarchists, and salaried foreign workers, banned most commercial activities by foreigners.

   National Bank for Ejidal Credit (BNCE) established to support recipients of redistributed land.

1937   Federal Ministry of Public Assistance (SAP) created.

1938   President Lázaro Cárdenas expropriated Mexico's petroleum reserves.

   President Lázaro Cárdenas made the Confederation of Mexican Workers (CTM), which represented three quarters of all unions, one of four organizations that officially represented Mexican society within the Institutional Revolutionary Party (PRI).

   Comié Regulador del Mercado de Subsistencias (CRMS) established to purchase grains from small producers, to control prices, and maintain supply.

1939   CRMS opened first stores to provide low-cost food staples to the working poor.

   Refugees from fascist Spain welcomed.

After Subsequent presidential administrations adopted a
1940   conservative program of capitalist modernization and
       industrializing the nation.

1942   *Ley Orgánica de Educación* (Organic Education Law).

1943   *Instituto Mexicano del Seguro Social* (IMSS, Mexican
       Institute of Social Security) created, beginning the Mexican
       Social Security System; *Secretaria de Salubridad y
       Asistencia* (SSA; Ministry of Health and Welfare) created
       by merging the *Secretaria de Asistencia Social* (SAS;
       Ministry of Public Assistance) with the *Departamento de
       Salubridad Pública* (SAP; Ministry of Public Health).

       Rockefeller Foundation invested in Mexican Agricultural
       Program, designed to increase food production through
       new biotechnologies.

       U.S. State Department's Office of the Coordinator of
       Inter-American Affairs initiated a massive health and
       sanitation program in Mexico.

1945   Volunteer social service required for college graduation.

1946   An amendment to Article 3 of the Constitution defined
       national commitment to compulsory, free, and secular
       education.

1947   A second Population Law enacted; attempted to resolve
       discrepancies resulting from the 1936 General Population
       Law.

       Age of retirement for government employees reduced to
       55 years of age.

1948   *Instituto Nacional Indigenista* (INI, National Indigenous
       Institute) created to stimulate education and integration of
       indigenous population.

1949   *Unión General de Obreros y Campesions de México*
       (UGOCM, General Union of Workers and Peasants of
       Mexico) formed to mobilize peasants independent of the
       states and demand the redistribution of land.

1953   *Banco Nacional Hipotecario Urbano y de Obras Públicas*
       (BNHUOP) and the *Dirección de Pensions* completed
       Unidad Modelo, a public housing complex with 3,639 units.

       United Nations Children's Fund (UNICEF) began spon-
       soring public health initiatives directed toward children
       and pregnant mothers.

       Sugar cane cutters included in social insurance system.

1954   The *Instituto Nacional de Vivienda* (INV National
       Housing Institute) established to subsidize public
       housing.

1959   Social Security Institute for State Workers (ISSSTE)
       established; centralized pensions and health services for
       government workers and their families.

1961   State food agency renamed *Compañia Nacional de
       Subsistencias Populars* (CONASUPO, National Company
       of Popular Subsistance), established to control prices and
       distribute, store, and sell rural products.

       Instituto Nacional de Protección a la Infancia (INPI,
       National Institute for the Protection of Childhood) estab-
       lished to operate maternal and child health programs.

1962   The *Instituto Nacional de Vivienda* (INV) completed
       the *Conjunto Habitacional Tlatelolco*, a large planned
       community of 11,016 units.

1968   *Institución Mexicana de Asistencia a la Niñez* (IMAN,
       Mexican Child Welfare Institute) established to organize
       and direct welfare activities for children.

1970   Administration of President Luis Echeverria began, new
       resources committed to indigenous communities, contin-
       ued to 1976.

1972   *Instituto Nacional de Fondo de Vivienda para los
       Trabajadores* (INFONAVIT; National Institute for the
       Construction of Worker Housing) created to provide
       workers' housing.

1973   *Ley Federal de Educación* (Federal Education Law)
       enacted.

1975   At a Congress in Pátzcuaro, Michoacán, indigenous leaders
       from throughout Mexico demanded cultural autonomy,
       official status for Indian languages, representation in
       government for ethnic groups, and an Indian University.

       National Bank for Rural Credit (BANRURAL) created to
       provide loans to small farmers.

       Instituto National de la Senectud (INSEN) created as
       part of the Health Ministry to coordinate aging policy
       in Mexico; became the *Instituto Nacional de Personas
       Adultas Mayores* (Older Persons National Institute,
       INAPAM) in 2000.

1977   *Coordinación General del Plan Nacional de Zonas
       Deprimidas y Grupos Marginales* (COPLAMAR, the
       General Coordination of the National Plan for Depressed
       Zones and Marginal Groups) established to provide social
       programs aimed at the marginalized.

       Integrated Family Development ministry, *Sistema para el
       Desarrollo Integral de la Familia* (DIF) established to
       coordinate programs for families and children.

1979   Rural organizations formed *Coordinadora Nacional Plan
       de Ayala* (CNPA, National Coordinator Plan de Ayala) to
       promote land redistribution.

1980   *Sistema Alimentario Mexicano* (SAM, Mexican Food
       System) created to provide credit, fertilizers, seeds, and
       crop insurance to small farmers.

1982   Mexican state responsible for over half of the Mexican economy; Mexican economy crippled by debt crisis leading to devaluation of the peso, defaulting on foreign debt, and reductions in social spending.

1983   Massive civil strikes called to protest austerity policies.

1985   Mexico City earthquake stimulated voluntary philanthropy.

1986   Mexico signed the General Agreement on Tariffs and Trade (GATT).

1987   CTM union leader Fidel Velásquez signed a "social pact" with government and business that constrained wages.

       Escuela Nacional de Trabajo Social established by the *Universidad Nacional Autónoma de México* (UNAM), initiating graduate education for social work.

1988   *Centro Mexicano para la Filantropia* (CEMEFI; Mexican Center for Philanthropy) established to promote a culture of philanthropy.

1989   International Labour Organisation Convention 169 on Indigenous and Tribal Peoples adopted by Mexico.

       Programa Nacional de Solidaridad (PRONASOL, National Solidarity Program) established by President Carlos Salinas. A new Secretariat for Social Development (SEDESOL) created to manage social development programs.

1990   Constitution amended to recognize Mexico as a multicultural nation and give indigenous peoples the right to protect and preserve their cultures.

       Mexico ratified the United Nations Convention on the Rights of the Child and amended the constitution to include child rights.

1991   International Lesbian and Gay Association (ILGA) met in Acapulco, first ILGA meeting outside of Europe.

1992   Salinas administration ended land redistribution, allowing market mechanisms to determine land ownership.

1993   North American Free Trade Agreement (NAFTA) signed, implemented beginning in 1994; neo-liberal economic policies ascendant in Mexico.

       Ley General de Educación (General Education Law) made secondary education compulsory.

1994   Mexico joined the Organisation for Economic Co-operation and Development (OECD).

       Mexican peso crisis.

       The *Ejercito Zapatista de Liberación Nacional* (EZLN, *Zapatista* Army of National Liberation) rose in rebellion in the state of Chiapas.

1995   IMSS privatized the social security pension system.

1995   National Program for the Well-Being and the Incorporation of Individuals with Disability initiated by the Federal Government.

1996   The pension system switched from intergenerational redistribution to individual capitalization, and the minimum period of active labor force participation jumped from 9.6 to 24 years excluding a large proportion of workers with sporadic formal employment (especially women).

       The health ministry reduced its services to the uninsured (nearly 50% of the population) to 12 key interventions.

1997   Social Security Law created administrators of retirement funds to manage privatized contributions for pensions

       Programa de Educación, Salud y Alimentación (PROGRESA, Program for Education, Health and Food) replaced PRONASOL, decentralized responsibility from the federal to the state level.

1999   Mexican Senate committed itself to adhere to International Labor Organisation Convention 159, Vocational Rehabilitation and Employment of Disabled Persons.

       Tortilla Subsidy Ended; liquidation of CONASUPO.

2000   Vicente Fox of the National Action Party (PAN) elected president, established *La Oficina de Representación para la Promoción e Integración Social para Personas con Discapacided* (ORPISPCD, Office for the Representation, Promotion, and Social Inclusion of Persons with Disability); term ends in 2006.

       Instituto National de la Senectud (INSEN), established in 1975, renamed the *Instituto Nacional de Personas Adultas Mayores* (INAPAM, Older Persons National Institute) and became part of the *Secretaria de Desarrollo Social* (SEDESOL, Ministry of Social Development).

2001   National Program for the Attention to Persons with Disability and National Consultative Council for the Social Inclusion of Persons with Disability established; federal Law for Deaf Culture enacted.

       Oportunidades (Opportunities), a new anti-poverty program supported by the United States and the World Bank, established by President Vicente Fox.

2002   Farmers on horseback occupied Congress protesting NAFTA provisions that would end most agricultural tariffs in 2003.

2003   National Program for Accessibility proposed, Federal Law for the Social Inclusion of Persons with Disability enacted.

2004   Congress Passes Law Reforming the National Social Security System. New employees will contribute 10% (up from 3%), can retire after 35 years of employment (up from 28 years), and will receive 100% of their pay (down from 130%).

Social Welfare History, United States

1601   Elizabethan Poor Law enacted by Parliament in England.

1641   Massachusetts became the first English colony in North America to recognize slavery as a legal institution.

1646   Elizabethan Poor Law first introduced in the American colonies in Virginia.

1650   Connecticut recognized slavery as a legal institution.

1661   Virginia recognized slavery as a legal institution.

1733   First Masonic Lodge opened in the American colonies in Boston.

1776   New Jersey granted suffrage to single women and widows but this was an isolated event as women made little progress in securing the vote for the next 100 years.

1778   First treaty between the United States and Native Americans (the Delaware Tribe).

1785   The Land Ordinance of 1785 provided for surveying the public domain into six-mile square townships, reserved one square mile in each township for the support of the common schools. States admitted to the union after 1800 received grants of land to support state universities and other state services.

1792   First union founded in the United States (the Cordwainers in Philadelphia).

1818   Federal government granted pensions to veterans who had served at least nine months and required assistance.

1819   First Independent Order of Odd Fellows Lodge established in the United States. It was a fraternal trendsetter since it established a clear schedule of guaranteed benefits whenever a member became ill and was unable to work.

1824   New York State appointed a commission to study poor relief and transferred primary responsibility to county governments and required that each county establish a poor house.

1825   First House of Refuge, an institution for juvenile offenders, created in New York.

1828   Andrew Jackson developed a plan for Indian Removal.

1830   Congress passed Indian Removal Act.

1833   Congress appropriated funds for a United States Naval Home.

1841   John Augustus, a Boston boot maker, asked the Police Court to release convicted juveniles and adults into his custody as an alternative to incarceration, a system that is now called probation.

1846   Mexican American War (1846-1848) began.

1848   Treaty of Guadalupe Hidalgo accomplished the dual purpose of annexing Mexican territory and expanding United States citizenship.

1851   Congress appropriated funds for a Soldier's Home.

1861   United States Civil War began; The United States Sanitary Commission established in New York as the nation's first public health organization. The commission, which provided sanitary services to Union Army soldiers, was a voluntary organization and was staffed primarily by women.

       Members of the Young Men's Christian Association (YMCA) founded the United States Christian Commission to provide chaplains to Union troops.

1862   Congress passed the Morrill or Land Grant College Act, which provided for the founding and maintenance of agricultural and mechanical colleges in the United States; the Homestead Act, which distributed free land to homesteaders, the Pacific Railroad Act, which provided land grants to railroads to develop a transportation infrastructure, and established the Department of Agriculture.

       Congress passed the Pension Act, which provided pensions for disabled Union Army soldiers and the survivors of deceased soldiers. Initially designed to aid Union Army recruitment, Congress repeatedly liberalized the provisions of the pension system.

1863   President Lincoln signed the Emancipation Proclamation, ending slavery in the rebelling states.

       Massachusetts created a Board of Charities to organize state institutions on a businesslike basis.

1865   Civil War ended when the Confederate Army surrendered.

The Thirteenth Amendment to the Constitution abolished slavery. Slavery in the rebelling states.

Congress established the Bureau of Freedmen, Refugees and Abandoned Lands in the War Department (known as the Freedman's Bureau). The Bureau was the first social welfare agency and provided direct relief to the destitute as well as educational, medical, and legal services during its seven year period of operation.

1867   First Black Odd Fellows lodge established in the United States.

1868   The Fourteenth Amendment to the Constitution extended citizenship rights to freedmen.

Formation of the Ancient Order of United Workmen signaled the onset of a new phase of American fraternal development, the national life insurance order.

1869   Congress created a Board of Indian Commissioners to oversee federal Indian programs.

Knights of Labor, an early labor union, founded.

1870   Massachusetts law required that juvenile offenders under the age of 16, would have their cases heard "separate from the general and ordinary criminal business" but they were still handled in adult courts.

1872   Freedman's Bureau was closed.

Congress terminated the Civil War income tax.

1873   Economic Depression.

1874   The Conference of Boards of Public Charities, later renamed the National Conference of Charities and Correction (1882), the National Conference of Social Work (1917), National Conference on Social Welfare (1956), began as a section of the yearly conference of the American Social Science Association (ASSA).

1876   The Sioux War (Battles of the Rosebud and Little Bighorn).

Apache War in the Southwest and Navajo War and Nez Perce War.

1877   First Charity Organization Society in the United States founded in Buffalo, New York.

1881   The American Red Cross founded by Clara Barton.

1882   The Chinese Exclusion Act of 1882 prohibited Chinese immigration for a decade.

Josephine Shaw Lowell founded the Charity Organization Society of the City of New York (COSCNY) which pioneered research on poverty, developed and refined the "casework" approach to social welfare, and promoted the professionalization of social work.

Lowell founded the Consumer's League of the City of New York.

1886   American Federation of Labor founded.

1887   General Allotment Act divided nearly 200 Indian reservations into individual allotments granted to tribal members.

1889   Jane Addams and Ellen Gates Starr founded Hull House, Chicago's first settlement house. Hull House was among hundreds of settlements in the United States that were designed to bridge the distance between social classes through fellowship, recreation, social reform, and political influence.

1890   Wounded Knee Massacre, South Dakota.

Second Morrill Act of 1890 provided funds to states to support land grant colleges, permitted separate segregated institutions for African Americans.

New York State Care Act of 1890 gave the state responsibility for providing care to all of the insane poor.

Congress expanded the Pension Act to include any disabled veteran, whether or not the disability resulted from war-related injuries.

1891   The New York Charity Organization Society started *Charities Review* to advise and unite charity organization societies.

1894   Congress enacted an income tax, ruled unconstitutional in 1895 by the Supreme Court for technical reasons.

1896   The Supreme Court upheld segregation that was widespread in the southern states in *Plessey v. Ferguson*.

1898   United States government intervened on behalf of the Cuban revolutionists which precipitated the Spanish-American War.

Puerto Rico transferred to the United states at the end of the Spanish-American War.

The New York Charity Organization Society established a Summer School in Philanthropy.

1899   The first juvenile court was established in Chicago, Illinois.

1900   National Association of Colored Women founded as an advocacy organization.

1901   New York City enacted a Tenement House Law.

Russell Sage Foundation, founded by Olivia Slocum Sage, widow of financier Russell Sage, became the first true philanthropic foundation in the United States.

English reformer Joseph Rowntree developed an absolute deprivation notion of poverty by estimating an income threshold that is required to obtain a minimum standard of living; households with incomes below that threshold were defined as poor.

1902   Henry Street Settlement opened the first children's playground in the nation.

1906   The Pure Food and Drug Act of 1906 regulated opiates and other dangerous narcotics for the first time.

Congress passed the Meat Inspection Act.

An Amendment to the Pension Act included old age as a qualifying disability.

1907   The Alliance Employment Bureau (AEB) was established to investigate the industrial trades for women and women's lodging. By 1910, the AEB and its staff became a formal unit of the expanding Russell Sage Foundation.

1908   President Theodore Roosevelt organized a Country Life Commission which celebrated rural life but criticized farmers' excessive individualism. It called for the development of cooperative enterprises and focused attention on the problems of farm wives and the difficulty of keeping children on the farm.

The landmark Supreme Court case *Muller v. Oregon* established the right of state governments to regulate the number of hours in a workday.

1909   Roosevelt called social workers and child welfare workers to Washington for the first White House Conference on Dependent Children. Conference attendees supported family life, rather than institutional care for children; the creation of federal children's bureau (created in 1912); and focused attention on the impact of a father's death or desertion on the entire family.

The Henry Street Settlement hosted the National Negro Conference, which led to the establishment of the National Association for the Advancement of Colored People (NAACP).

The Survey began publication.

1910   The National Association for the Advancement of Colored People (NAACP) founded.

1911   Psychoanalysis introduced in the United States as the result of Sigmund Freud's lectures at Clark University.

State legislatures in Illinois and Missouri enacted Mothers' Pension laws.

1912   Congress authorized pensions for any Union Army soldier who had served 90 days and was at least 62 years old.

The federal Children's Bureau was established to conduct research on the welfare of women and children.

Massachusetts enacted a minimum wage law for women and children in private industry.

1913   The Sixteenth Amendment to the Constitution authorized a federal income tax.

The Cleveland Chamber of Commerce established the first Community Chest, an organization which consolidated the many annual fund drives conducted by the city's charities into a single annual appeal. The process assured that donated dollars were put to the best and most efficient use by vetting recipient charities in advance.

1914   The first community foundation was established in Cleveland to enable large and small donors to create endowment funds and place them under common management.

1916   Margaret Sanger, an advocate for women's health, opened the first birth control clinic in the United States.

Jeanette Pickering Rankin elected to the House of Representatives from Montana, the first woman to serve in the United States Congress.

1917   The United States entered World War I in April.

The Army established a Neuropsychiatric Division, staffed by psychiatrists and psychiatric social workers, to treat soldiers suffering from mental disorders, to screen prospective recruits, and to facilitate soldiers' return to civilian life after discharge.

The Red Cross Home Service established to provide services to soldiers and their families.

The Women in Industry Service was created to address the needs of women entering the work force during the war.

The Jones Act of 1917 eliminated legal barriers to migration from Puerto Rico to the United States.

Forty-one states had laws to protect women workers with shorter working hours and safer working conditions; these laws constricted women's occupational choices since they prohibited women from working in occupations considered unsafe.

1918   Social caseworkers in medical settings established the American Association of Medical Social Workers (AAMSW).

The United States Children's Bureau spearheaded a "Children's Year" to call attention to the needs of children and their families as a result of the war.

The National War Labor Board established to reduce labor unrest in industries critical to the war effort. The Board, consisting of representatives of both labor and industry, was the first Federal agency to issue comprehensive policies governing working conditions in the private sector.

1919   The Eighteenth Amendment to the Constitution ratified; made manufacturing, sale, or transportation of intoxicating liquors illegal; Congress enacted the Volstead or National Prohibition Act, which prohibited the manufacture and sale of alcoholic beverages.

The National Association of School Social Workers (NASSW) established.

1920   The Nineteenth Amendment to the Constitution ratified; gave women the right to vote throughout the United States.

1921   Congress enacted the Emergency Quota Act, limiting the number of allowable immigrants to a percentage of the number of immigrants from that nation living in the United States in 1910. This "quota system" governed immigration policy until 1964.

The Sheppard-Towner Maternity and Infant Act of 1921 provided health education and services through federal grants-in-aid to the states. Congress ended the controversial program in 1929.

The American Association of Social Work (AASW) founded by social work leaders to establish professional standards in training and practice and to bring a common identity and high standards to a broad group of practitioners.

1924   National Origins Quota Act extended the application of the Emergency Quota Act.

1926   Social workers organized the Association of Federation Social Workers in New York City, a precursor to the Rank and File Movement, a social movement would attract young, radical social workers who fought to improve their own working conditions so they could better serve their clients.

Psychiatric social workers formed a separate organization, the American Association of Psychiatric Social Workers (AAPSW).

1929   New York Stock Market crashed.

League of United Latin American Citizens (LULAC) founded to represent the Hispanic community in the United States.

1930   Congress created the Veterans Administration to coordinate the federal government's expanded veterans' services.

1931   Jane Addams received the Nobel Peace Prize.

1932   The Federal Home Loan Bank was established to create a home loan banking system to support the provision of home mortgages.

The Emergency Relief and Construction Act in 1932 authorized the Hoover Administration to loan funds to the states for unemployment relief.

The Norris-LaGuardia Act denied the federal courts the right to forbid strikes, peaceful picketing, and other actions not illegal of themselves that unions employed in their dealings with employers.

1933   Federal Emergency Relief Administration (FERA) distributed grants to states for unemployment relief.

The Twenty-first Amendment repealed the Eighteenth Amendment and ended Prohibition.

The Civil Conservation Corps (CCC) stimulated the economy by hiring unemployed young men to work in conservation projects located in national and state parks.

1934   Indian Reorganization Act (IRA) permitted tribal communities to form tribal governments and loans were made available to tribal communities.

National Housing Act of 1934 stimulated the housing market by making credit available for the repair and construction of housing. It also established the Federal Housing Administration (FHA) which issued mortgages to prospective homeowners.

Social Work Today launched to provide a voice for the Rank and File Movement.

1935   Congress passed the Social Security Act, which provided social insurance, public assistance, and social service programs.

The Works Progress Administration (WPA) stimulated the economy by hiring unemployed workers to construct public facilities and cultural projects were initiated.

The Wagner or National Labor Relations Act (NLRA) guaranteed the right of collective bargaining and strengthened organized labor.

1936   The American Association of Group Workers (AAGW) was formed.

1937   The National Housing Act (Wagner-Steagall Act) created the first public housing program and established the United States Public Housing Authority to provide federal funds for public housing projects. Unemployed workers were hired to clear slum areas to build affordable housing for the working class.

Congress enacted the Mexican Stamp Act to control the sale and use of marijuana.

1938   The Fair Labor Standards Act (FLSA) prohibited child labor, established a forty hour work week, a minimum wage and required payment of time and a half for any hours worked in excess of forty.

1939   Social Security amendments added survivors' benefits to Old Age Insurance Program, which changed from a full reserve model to a modified reserve basis for paying benefits to recipients.

The American Association of Schools of Social Work (AASSW) made graduate education the criterion for membership.

1940   Congress passed the Lanham Act to provide federal funds for community services; enabled thousands of women to get jobs in the factories and demonstrated the potential of comprehensive day care during World War II.

1941   The United States entered the Second World War in December.

1943   The Office of Community War Services established to assist states and communities provide basic services for families, including health care, recreation, and housing assistance.

1944   Congress enacted the Servicemen's Adjustment Act, also known as the "G.I. Bill," to support services to veterans such as education and job training, low-interest housing loans, employment services, medical services, and unemployment insurance.

1946   Congress enacted the Full Employment Act.

Congress enacted the Hill-Burton Act to provide federal funding for hospital construction.

Congress enacted the National Mental Health Act of 1946.

Community organization practitioners founded the Association for the Study of Community Organization (ASCO).

1947   The Taft-Hartley Act guaranteed the right of individuals to refuse to join unions and addressed problems with labor practices that employers regarded as unfavorable.

1948   President Truman desegregated the military.

1949   Congress enacted the Housing Reform Act of 1949 to provide for urban renewal and suburban development.

The Social Work Research Group (SWRG) was formed by persons doing research on social work and social services.

1950   An Amendment to the Social Security Act created Aid to the Permanently and Totally Disabled (APTD) for individuals younger than age 65 who were disabled due to conditions other than blindness.

1952   The merger of the American Association of Schools of Social Work (AASSW) and the National Association of Schools of Social Administration (NASSA) resulted in the creation of the Council on Social Work Education (CSWE).

1953   The Refugee Act encouraged defection from all communist nations and key personnel from Soviet satellite countries.

1954   The Supreme Court decision in *Brown v Board of Education* outlawed racial segregation in public schools and declared the doctrine of "separate but equal" unconstitutional.

House Concurrent Resolution 108 called for the termination of federal responsibilities to the Indian tribes.

1955   National Association of Social Workers (NASW) founded when five specialist organizations merged with the American Association of Social Workers.

The Joint Commission on Mental Health and Illness created.

1956   Congress created a disability insurance program through amendments to the Social Security Act.

Rosa Parks began the campaign to boycott the segregated bus system in Montgomery, Alabama; national attention increased when Reverend Martin Luther King, Jr., supported this boycott as the civil rights movement gained momentum.

1957   Congress enacted the first Civil Rights Bill since Reconstruction.

1959   National Security Council memorandum and the 1953 Refugee Act implemented with regard to Cuba when Fidel Castro imposed a communist government there.

1961   The Peace Corps created.

The Joint Commission on Mental Health and Illness published its influential *Action for Mental Health*.

The Presidential Commission on the Status of Women energized the women's movement.

1962   The Manpower Development Act initiated the first real job training program since the New Deal.

The Services Amendments to the Social Security Act reimbursed the states for social services.

The Keogh Act set guidelines for individual retirement plans.

1963   The March on Washington highlighted civil rights issues.

The Omnibus Civil Rights Bill enacted.

The Community Mental Health Centers Act. A victory for the advocates of a community-oriented approach to mental health services, since it strengthened community facilities and diminished the role of mental hospitals.

1964   The Civil Rights Act of 1964 mandated desegregation of public facilities and outlawed discrimination in hiring on the basis of race, color, religion, gender or national origin. The act also established the Equal Employment Opportunity Commission (EEOC) and outlawed discrimination in private employment. Title VII prohibited racial discrimination in the hiring, firing, compensation, terms, conditions, and privileges of employment.

The Economic Opportunity Act created the office of Economic Opportunity.

1965 Congress enacted the Voting Rights Act of 1965 was designed to extend to all citizens equal voting rights. The act abolished literacy tests and provided federal examiners to monitor elections.

Congress established the Medicaid program to provide medical services to lower income citizens and long term care for the disabled and aged poor.

Congress enacted the Medicare program to provide hospital insurance and physician fee reimbursement to social security beneficiaries.

War on Poverty Programs launched under the auspices of the Office of Economic Opportunity.

Mollie Orshansky developed a mathematical formula called the poverty line to define poverty in the United States.

Congress enacted the Older Americans Act which created the Administration on Aging.

Congress enacted the Housing Act of 1965 which created the first cabinet-level agency, United States Department of Housing and Urban Development (HUD), to deal with housing and urban renewal.

Congress enacted the Hart-Cellar Act, which eliminated the national origins quota system established by the 1921 and 1924 Immigration Acts.

1966 The Supreme Court in *Kent v United States* granted juveniles some of the due process guarantees afforded to adults.

The National Organization for Women founded.

The Veterans' Readjustment Benefits Act (the "Vietnam G.I. Bill") provided educational assistance to Vietnam War veterans.

1967 The Supreme Court, in *In Re Gault,* provided additional rights to juveniles such as the right to counsel, the right to confront witnesses, and the right to timely notice of charges.

The President's Commission on Law Enforcement and the Administration of Justice recommended the decriminalization of status offenders, the diversion of juvenile offenders from official court processing, and the deinstitutionalization of juvenile offenders.

The Veterans Administration established Veterans Assistance Centers in twenty-one cities as a part of its outreach program.

1968 The Fair Housing Act prohibited housing discrimination and legislation established the Government National Mortgage Association (Ginnie Mae) to expand the availability of mortgage funds for moderate income families.

The United States Bureau of the Budget used the poverty line developed by Orshansky in 1965 as an official measure of poverty.

The American Indian Movement (AIM), an activist organization, established.

The Veterans Administration implemented Operation Outreach to insure that veterans were aware of the benefits available to them.

1969 The Stonewall Riots of 1969 in New York City provided the impetus which led to the emergence of the modern lesbian, gay, bisexual, and transgendered (LGBT) civil rights movement.

NASW decided to extend membership benefits to individuals with undergraduate degrees in social work.

Congress enacted the Tax Reform Act of 1969 to ensure that organized philanthropy was more responsive to the public interest.

1972 Congress enacted a Social Security Amendment that added a cost of living index to Old Age Insurance benefits and established the Supplemental Security Income (SSI).

NASW moved its headquarters to Washington, D.C. to be more effective in advocating for national policy changes.

Congress passed the Equal Rights Amendment but the amendment ultimately fell three states short of the required 35 for ratification when the time limit expired in 1982.

1973 Congress increased social security benefits by twenty percent and indexed them to inflation.

The American Psychiatric Association deleted homosexuality from its official nomenclature of mental disorders.

The Comprehensive Employment Training Act (1973) provided the largest job training program since the Great Depression.

The Comprehensive Services Act gave states more discretionary power in allocating funds through the creation of a network of Area Agencies on Aging.

1974 The Employee Retirement Income Security Act (ERISA) established fiduciary standards for larger pension systems; Congress allowed citizens to defer taxes on payments to Individual Retirement Accounts (IRAs).

Congress established the National Institute on Aging.

In the Congressional Budget Act, Congress mandated that a "tax expenditure budget" be produced annually beginning in 1975.

The Housing and Community Development Act of 1974 created the Community Development Block Grant (CDBG) program to provide federal funds for housing to be administered by cities and states. The act also created the Section 8 program to provide low-income persons with rental assistance vouchers.

The Juvenile Justice and Delinquency Prevention Act of 1974 was designed to prevent delinquency and remove children from adult jails and lock-ups.

California and New York moved to decriminalize homosexual acts between consenting adults.

1975   Congress passed the Indian Self-Determination and Education Assistance Act.

1976   NASW created Political Action and Candidate Election (PACE) to endorse candidates for office and contribute to their campaigns.

1977   The Juvenile Justice and Delinquency Prevention Act of 1974 was amended to make it more controlling of juvenile behavior.

1978   The term Hispanic as a label was first introduced by the Office of Management and Budget to better administratively operationalize the idea of persons of Mexican, Puerto Rican, Cuban, Central or South American, or other Spanish heritage regardless of race.

1983   Amendments to the Social Security Act raised the retirement age and increased payroll taxes.

1984   The Comprehensive Control Act included "get tough" measures to deal with juvenile delinquency.

1986   The Tax Reform Act of 1986 authorized a Low Income Housing Tax Credit that provided tax incentives to developers to build low-income housing.

1987   The Stewart McKinney Act of 1987 provided community-level funding to address homelessness.

March on Washington for Gay and Lesbian Civil Rights.

1988   The Family Support Act of 1988 mandated that all mothers with a child less than three years of age find work or register in a job training program in exchange for one year of transitional day care and health coverage.

1989   The Veterans Administration became a cabinet level agency, the Department of Veterans Affairs.

1990   The Cranston-Gonzalez National Affordable Housing Act of 1990 authorized housing for special needs populations including people with AIDS.

1993   Family and Medical Leave Act (FMLA) of 1993 provided unpaid family leave for childbirth and medical emergencies.

President Clinton compromised and enacted the landmark "Don't Ask, Don't Tell" policy which was designed to stop the discharge from the military of men and women based solely on their sexual orientation.

March on Washington in response to Clinton's broken promises and lack of effective policies for gay men and lesbians in the military.

1994   Multiethnic Placement Act (MEPA) increased opportunities for transracial adoption and prohibited any foster care or adoption agency that receives federal funds from denying a placement solely on the basis of race.

1996   Personal Responsibility and Work Reconciliation Act (PRWORA) of 1996 eliminated the welfare entitlement program Aid to Families with Dependent Children (AFDC) and replaced it with Temporary Assistance to Needy Families (TANF) and limited its lifetime receipt to five years, required most welfare recipients to get a job within two years. As a part of welfare reform, public welfare benefits including food stamps and Supplemental Security Income (SSI) were curtailed for legal immigrants.

1998   Workforce Investment Act defined clients as "customers" and demanded "work first" before offering services.

1999   The Supreme Court in Hawaii ruled that recognized marriage could not be denied to people based on their sexual orientation which caused the United States Congress to pass legislation prohibiting any state from recognizing any marriage not involving a man and a woman.

2004   President Bush argued undocumented illegal aliens be given opportunities for residency which could culminate in citizenship.

APPENDIX C

Master Bibliography

Abadinsky, H. (2001). *Drugs: An introduction*. Belmont, CA: Wadsworth/Thomson Learning.

Abbott, E. (1939, September). Grace Abbott: A sister's memories. *Social Service Review, 13,* 351–407.

Abbott, E. (1940). *Public assistance*. Chicago: University of Chicago Press.

Abbott, E. (1942). *Social welfare and professional education* (Rev. ed.). Chicago: University of Chicago Press.

Abbott, E., & Breckinridge, S. (1921). *Administration of mothers' aid law in Illinois* (U.S. Children's Bureau Publication No. 82). Washington, DC: Government Printing Office.

Abbott, G. (1917). *The immigrant and the community*. New York: Century.

Abbott, G. (1938). *The child and the state: Legal status in the family, apprenticeship, and child labor*. Chicago: University of Chicago Press.

Abbott, G. (1939, June 20). [Obituary]. *New York Times*, p. 21.

Abbott, G. (1941). *From relief to Social Security: The development of the new public welfare services and their administration*. Chicago: University of Chicago Press.

Abel, C., & Lewis, C. M. (Eds.). (2002). *Exclusion & engagement: Social policy in Latin America*. London: Institute of Latin American Studies.

Abramovitz, M. (1996). *Regulating the lives of women: Social welfare policy from colonial times to the present* (2nd ed.). Boston: South End.

Abu-Laban, Y., & Gabriel, C. (2002). *Selling diversity: Immigration, multiculturalism, employment equity and globalization*. Peterborough, ON: Broadview.

Achenbaum, W. A. (1978). *Old age in the new land: The American experience since 1790*. Baltimore: Johns Hopkins University Press.

Acuna, R. (1988). *Occupied America: A history of Chicanos* (3rd ed.). New York: Harper & Row.

Adams, H. (1977). *Harry Hopkins*. New York: Putnam.

Adams, I. (1971). *The real poverty report*. Edmonton, AB: M. G. Hurtig.

Adams, T. (2001). Philanthropic landmarks: The Toronto Trail from a comparative perspective, 1870s to the 1930s. *Urban History Review, 30*(1), 3–21.

Addams, J. (1902). *Democracy and social ethics*. New York: Macmillan.

Addams, J. (1909). *The spirit of youth and the city streets*. New York: Macmillan.

Addams, J. (1910). *Twenty Years at Hull House*. New York: Macmillan.

Addams, J. (1930). *The second twenty years at Hull House*. New York: Macmillan.

Addams, J. (1974). *My friend, Julia Lathrop*. New York: Arno. (Original work published 1935)

Addams, J. (1990). *Twenty years at Hull House* [With autobiographical notes]. Urbana: University of Illinois Press. (Original work published 1910)

Addams, J., Balch, E., & Hamilton, A. (1915). *Women at The Hague: The International Congress of Women and its results*. New York: Macmillan.

Agostoni, C. (2002). Discurso médico, cultura higiénica y la mujer en la ciudad de México al cambio de siglo (XIX–XX). *Mexican Studies/Estudios Mexicanos, 18*(1), 1–22.

Agostoni, C. (2003). *Monuments of progress. Modernization and public health in Mexico City, 1876–1910*. Calgary, AB: University of Calgary Press; Boulder: University Press of Colorado; Mexico City: Instituto de Investigaciones Históricas.

Aguayo Spencer, R. (Ed.). (1939). *Don Vasco de Quiroga: Documentos: Biografía de Juan Jose Moreno, Ordenanzas de los hospitals, testamento, informacion en derecho, juicio de residencia, litigio por la isla de Tultepec*. Mexico City: Editorial Polis.

Aguirre Beltrán, G. (1992). *Teoría y práctica del la educación indígena*. Mexico City: Fondo de Cultura Económico. (Original work published 1973)

Aikin, W. M. (1942). *The story of the eight-year study, with conclusions and recommendations*. New York: Harper & Brothers. Available: www.8yearstudy.org

Alchon, G. (1991). Mary van Kleeck and social-economic planning. *Journal of Policy History, 3,* 1–23.

Aldrete Haas, J. A. (1991). *La desconstrucción del estado mexicano: Políticas de vivienda, 1917–1988.* Mexico City: Alianza Editorial.

Allen, R. (1973). *The social passion: Religion and social reform in Canada, 1914–1928.* Toronto, ON: University of Toronto Press.

Allen, R. (1990). *The social passion: Religion and social reform in Canada, 1914–1928* (2nd ed.). Toronto, ON: University of Toronto Press.

Alsop, J., & Kintner, R. (1971). *Men around the president.* Lincoln: University of Nebraska Press. (Original work published 1939)

Altmeyer, A. J. (1932). *The Industrial Commission of Wisconsin.* Madison: University of Wisconsin Press.

Altmeyer, A. J. (1966). *The formative years of Social Security.* Madison: University of Wisconsin Press.

Álvarez Amézquita, J., Bustamante, M. E., López Picazos, A., & Fernández del Castillo, F. (1960). *Historia de la salubridad y de la asistencia en México* (Vols. 1–4). Mexico City: Secretaría de Salubridad y Asistencia.

Álvarez Amézquita, J., Bustamante, M., Picazos, A. L., & del Castillo, F. F. (1960). *Historia de la salubridad y de la asistencia en México.* Mexico City: Secretaría de Salubridad y Asistencia.

Ambrose, L. M. (2000). *Women's institutes of Canada: The first one hundred years 1897–1997.* Gloucester, ON: Tri-Co Printing.

Amenta, E. (1998). *Bold relief: Institutional politics and the origins of modern American social policy.* Princeton, NJ: Princeton University Press.

America's Second Harvest. (2001, October). *Hunger in America 2001* [National Report]. Chicago: Author.

American Public Welfare Association. (1941). *APWA: Our autobiography.* Chicago: Author.

Ames, H. B. (1972). *The city below the hill.* Toronto, ON: University of Toronto Press. (Original work published 1897)

Amezquita, J. A., Bustamente, M. E., López Picazos, A., & Fernández del Castillo, F. (1960). *Historia de la Salubridad y de la Asistencia en México* (México City: Secretaría de Salubridad y Asistencia.

Anderson, R., & Bone, R. M. (2000). First Nations economic development: The Meadow Lake Tribal Council. *Journal of Aboriginal Economic Development, 1*(1), 13–34.

Angers, F. A. (1955). *La sécurité sociale et les problèmes constitutionnels.* Quebec: Commission Royale d'Enquête sur les Problèmes Constitutionnels.

Armitage, A. (1988). *Social welfare in Canada* (2nd ed.). Toronto, ON: McClelland & Stewart.

Armitage, A. (1996). *Social welfare in Canada revisited: Facing up to the future.* Toronto, ON: Oxford University Press.

Armitage, A. (2003). *Social welfare in Canada* (4th ed.). Toronto, ON: Oxford University Press.

Arrom, S. M. (2000). *Containing the poor: The Mexico City Poor House, 1774–1871.* Durham, NC: Duke University Press.

Arrom, S. M. (2002, Spring). Philanthropy and its roots: The societies of St. Vincent de Paul in Mexico. *ReVista: Harvard Review of Latin America,* 57–59. Available: http://drclas.fas.harvard.edu/publications/revista/Volunteering/tcontents.html

Ash, R. (1972). *Social movements in America.* Chicago: Markham.

Assessing ACCESS (A Convention on the Canadian Economic and Social Systems): Towards a new social union. (1997). *Proceedings of the Symposium on the Courchene Proposal.* Kingston, ON: Queen's University, Institute of Intergovernmental Relations.

Axinn, J., & Stern, M. (2000). *Social welfare: A history of the American response to need* (5th ed.). Boston: Allyn & Bacon.

Bakke, E. W. (1940). *The unemployed worker: A study of the task of making a living without a job.* New Haven, CT: Yale University Press.

Bakvis, H., & Skogstad, G. (Eds.). (2002). *Canadian federalism: Performance, effectiveness, and legitimacy.* Don Mills, ON: Oxford University Press.

Ball, R. M. (1952). *Pensions in the United States.* Washington, DC: Government Printing Office.

Ball, R. M. (1978). *Social Security today and tomorrow.* New York: Columbia University Press.

Ball, R. M. (2000). *Insuring the essentials: Bob Ball on Social Security.* New York: Century Foundation.

Ball, R. M., & Bethel, T. N. (1989). *Because we are all in this together: The case for a national long term care insurance policy.* Washington, DC: Families USA Foundation.

Ball, R. M., & Bethel, T. N. (1998). *Straight talk about Social Security.* New York: Century Foundation.

Banco Nacional de México. *Review of the economic situation of Mexico* [On-line]. Available: www.banamex.com/eng/esem/index.html

Bane, M. J., Coffin, B., & Thiemann, R. F. (Eds.). (2000). *Who will provide? The changing role of religion in American social welfare.* Boulder, CO: Westview.

Banting, K. G. (1987). *The welfare state and Canadian federalism* (2nd ed.). Montreal, QC, and Kingston, ON: McGill-Queen's University Press.

Barber, W. J., Rutherford, M., Medema, S. G., Johnson, M., & Samuels, W. J. (Eds.). (2000–2003). *Early American economic thought* (Vols. 1–15). London: Pickering & Chatto.

Barkin, D., & Suárez, B. (1985). *El fin de la autosuficiencia alimentaria mexicana.* Mexico City: Ediciones Océano.

Barman, J., Sutherland, N., & Wilson, J. D. (Eds.). (1995). *Children, teachers and schools in the history of British Columbia.* Calgary, AB: Detselig.

Barry, T. (1995). *Zapata's revenge: Free trade and the farm crisis in Mexico.* Boston: South End.

Barton, C. (1906). *The Red Cross in peace and war.* Washington, DC: American Historical Press.

Baumohl, J. (Ed.). (1996). *Homelessness in America.* Phoenix, AZ: Oryx.

Baxandall, R., & Gordon, L. (Eds.). (2000). *Dear sisters: Dispatches from the women's liberation movement: Broadsides, cartoons, manifestos, and other documents from the twentieth century's most influential movement.* New York: Basic Books.

Beaudoin, G. A., & Mendes, E. (1995). *The Canadian Charter of Rights and Freedoms* (3rd ed.). Toronto, ON: Carswell.

Beechem, M. (2002). *Elderly alcoholism: Intervention strategies.* Springfield, IL: Charles C. Thomas.

Beers, C. W. (1908). *A mind that found itself.* New York: Longmans, Green.

Beito, D. T. (2000). *From mutual aid to the welfare state: Fraternal societies and social services, 1890–1967.* Chapel Hill: University of North Carolina Press.

Bell, W. (1965). *Aid to dependent children.* New York: Columbia University Press.

Bella, L. (1995). Gender and occupational closure in social work: Registration initiatives of Canada's anglophone social work associations. In P. Taylor & C. Daly (Eds.), *Gender dilemmas in social work: Issues affecting women in the profession* (pp. 107–124). Toronto, ON: Canadian Scholars' Press.

Bella, L. (1996). Profession as ideology: Doctors, nurses and social workers. In W. Kirwin (Ed.), *Ideology, development and social welfare: Canadian perspectives* (pp. 145–164). Toronto, ON: Canadian Scholars' Press.

Benería, L. (1992). The Mexican debt crisis: Restructuring the economy and the household. In L. Benería & S. Feldman (Eds.), *Unequal burden: Economic crises, persistent poverty, and women's work* (pp. 83–104). Boulder, CO: Westview.

Benítez-Zenteno, R. (1988). *Población y política en México.* Mexico City: Miguel Ángel Porrúa; Universidad Nacional Autónoma de México, Coordinación de Humanidades, Instituto de Investigaciones Sociales.

Berkowitz, E. D. (1987). *Disabled policy: America's programs for the handicapped.* Cambridge, UK: Cambridge University Press.

Berkowitz, E. D. (1991). *America's welfare state.* Baltimore and London: Johns Hopkins University Press.

Berkowitz, E. D. (1995). *Mr. Social Security.* Lawrence: University Press of Kansas.

Berkowitz, E. D. (2003). *Robert Ball and the politics of Social Security.* Madison: University of Wisconsin Press.

Berkstein Kanarek, C. B. (1981). *El hospital Divino Salvador.* Unpublished master's thesis, Universidad Nacional Autónoma de México, Mexico City.

Beveridge, W. H. (1943). *The pillars of security and other war-time essays and addresses.* New York: Macmillan.

Bickenbach, J. E. (1993). *Physical disability and social policy.* Toronto, ON: University of Toronto Press.

Birn, A.-E. (1998). A revolution in rural health? The struggle over local health units in Mexico, 1928–1940. *Journal of the History of Medicine and Allied Sciences, 53*(1), 43–76.

Birn, A.-E. (2003). Revolution, the scatological way: The Rockefeller Foundation's hookworm campaign in 1920s Mexico. In D. Armus (Ed.), *Disease in the history of modern Latin America: From malaria to AIDS* (pp. 158–182). Durham, NC: Duke University Press.

Bisno, H. (1956). How social will social work be? *Social Work, 1*(2), 12–18.

Bissondath, N. (2002). *The selling of illusions: The cult of multiculturalism* (Rev. ed.). Toronto, ON: Penguin.

Black, A. (1996). *Casting her own shadow: Eleanor Roosevelt and the shaping of postwar liberalism.* New York: Columbia University Press.

Black, A. (Ed.). (1999). *Courage in a dangerous world: The political writings of Eleanor Roosevelt.* New York: Columbia University Press.

Black, W. G. (1991). Social work in World War I: A method lost. *Social Service Review, 64,* 379–402.

Blank, R., & Haskins, R. (Eds.). (2001). *The new world of welfare.* Washington, DC: Brookings Institution Press.

Bliss, K. (2001). *Compromised positions: Prostitution, public health and gender politics in revolutionary Mexico City.* University Park: Pennsylvania State University Press.

Blom, D., & Sussman, S. (1989). *Pioneers of mental health and social change, 1930–1989.* London, ON: Third Eye.

Blondin, M. (1971). Animation sociale. In J. A Draper (Ed.), *Citizen participation: A book of readings* (pp. 159–170). Toronto, ON: New Press.

Blum, A. S. (2001, July). Conspicuous benevolence: Liberalism, public welfare, and private charity in Porfirian Mexico City, 1877–1910. *The Americas, 58*(1), 7–38.

Blum, A. S. (2004). Cleaning the revolutionary household: Domestic servants and public welfare in Mexico City, 1930–1950. *Journal of Women's History, 15*(4), 67–90.

Boltvinik, J. (2003). Welfare, inequality and poverty. In K. Middlebrook & E. Zepeda (Eds.), *Confronting development* (pp. 385–446). Stanford, CA: Stanford University Press.

Bowe, F. (1992). *Equal rights for Americans with disabilities.* New York: F. Watts.

Bowers, S. (1949, October). The nature and definition of social casework: Part I. *Social Casework, 30,* 311–317.

Bowers, S. (1949, November). The nature and definition of social casework: Part II. *Social Casework, 30,* 369–375.

Bowers, S. (1949, December). The nature and definition of social casework: Part III. *Social Casework, 30,* 412–417.

Bowers, S. (1950). The nature and definition of social casework. In C. Kasius (Ed.), *Principles and techniques in social casework: Selected articles, 1940–1950* (pp. 97–127). New York: Family Service Association.

Boyd, N. (1991). *High society: Legal and illegal drugs in Canada.* Toronto, ON: Key Porter.

Brace, C. L. (1973). *The dangerous classes of New York and twenty years' work among them.* Silver Spring, MD: National Association of Social Workers. (Original work published 1872)

Brace, E. (Ed.). (1894). *The life of Charles Loring Brace told chiefly in his own letters.* New York: Scribner.

Brachet-Márquez, V. (1994). *The dynamics of domination: State, class and social reform in Mexico, 1910–1990.* Pittsburgh, PA: Pittsburgh University Press.

Brachet-Márquez, V. (forthcoming). Mexico's welfare developmental state: Birth, growth and retrenchment,

1823–2003. In M. Riesco (Ed.), [Title to be determined]. New York: Palgrave Macmillan.

Brachet-Márquez, V., & Sherraden, M. S. (1994). Political change and the welfare state: The case of health and food policies in Mexico, 1970–1993. *World Development 22*(9), 1295–1312.

Braddock, D. (Ed.). (2002). *Disability at the dawn of the 21st century and the state of the states.* Washington, DC: American Association on Mental Retardation.

Branch, T. (1988). *Parting the waters: America in the King years 1954–63.* New York: Simon & Schuster.

Bremner, R. H. (Ed.). (1970). *Children and youth in America: A documentary history* (Vols. 1–3). Cambridge, MA: Harvard University Press.

Bremner, R. H. (1980). *The public good: Philanthropy and welfare in the Civil War era.* New York: Alfred A. Knopf.

Breton, M. (1990). Learning from social group work traditions. *Social Work With Groups, 13*(3), 21–34.

Brilliant, E. L. (1990). *The United Way: Dilemmas of organized charity.* New York: Columbia University Press.

Brilliant, E. L. (2000). *Private charity and public inquiry: A history of the Filer and Peterson commissions.* Bloomington and Indianapolis: Indiana University Press.

Brinkley, A. (1995). *The end of reform: New Deal liberalism in recession and war.* New York: Vintage.

Brock, W. R. (1984). *Investigation and responsibility: Public responsibility in the United States, 1865–1900.* Cambridge, UK: Cambridge University Press.

Broughton, J. (2001). *Silent revolution: The International Monetary Fund, 1979–1989.* Washington, DC: International Monetary Fund.

Brown, J. C. (1940). *Public relief, 1929–1940.* New York: Henry Holt.

Brown, L. (1972). *How we got where we are now: A short history of the farmers' movement in Saskatchewan.* Saskatoon, SK: National Farmers' Union.

Brown, L., Roberts, J., & Warnock, J. (1999). *Saskatchewan politics: From Left to Right '44–'99.* Regina, SK: Hinterland.

Bruno, F. J. (1957). *Trends in social work: 1874-1956* (2nd ed.). New York: Columbia University Press.

Bruce, S. (Ed.). (1992). *Religion and modernization: Sociologists and historians debate the secularization thesis.* Oxford, UK: Clarendon.

Bryan, M. L. M., & Davis, A. F. (Eds.). (1990). *100 years at Hull House.* Bloomington: Indiana University Press.

Bryden, P. (1994). The Canadian Charter of Rights and Freedoms is antidemocratic and un-Canadian: An opposing point of view. In M. Charleton & P. Barker (Eds.), *Crosscurrents: Contemporary political issues* (2nd ed., p. 108). Scarborough, ON: Nelson.

Bucknill, J. C. (1876). *Notes on asylums for the insane in America.* London: J. & A. Churchill.

Buffington, R., & Aguirre, C. (Eds.). (2000). *Reconstructing criminality in Latin America.* Wilmington: DE: Scholarly Resources.

Bullen, J. (1991). J. J. Kelso and the "new" child-savers: The genesis of the children's aid movement in Ontario. In R. Smandych, G. Dodds, & A. Esau (Eds.), *Dimensions of childhood: Essays on the history of children and youth in Canada.* Winnipeg: University of Manitoba, Legal Research Institute.

Burke, S. Z. (1996). *Seeking the highest good: Social services and gender at the University of Toronto, 1888–1937.* Toronto, ON: University of Toronto Press.

Burkhauser, R. V., & Haveman, R. H. (1982). *Disability and work: The economics of American policy.* Baltimore, MD: Johns Hopkins University Press.

Burns, E. M. (1956). *Social Security and public policy.* New York: McGraw-Hill.

Bustamante, M. (1931). Local public health work in Mexico. *American Journal of Public Health, 21,* 725–736.

Butler, R. N. (1975). *Why survive?* New York: Harper & Row.

Butterfield, L. H. (Ed.). (1951). *Letters of Benjamin Rush* (Vols. 1–2). Princeton, NJ: Published for the American Philosophical Society by Princeton University Press.

Cairns, A. C. (2000). *Citizens plus: Aboriginal peoples and the Canadian state.* Vancouver: University of British Columbia Press.

Cámara de Diputados. (2001). *Violencia en casa.* Mexico City.

Camp, R. A. (1998). Women and men, men and women: Gender patterns in Mexican politics. In V. E. Rodríguez (Ed.), *Women's participation in Mexican political life.* Boulder, CO: Westview.

Canada, Department of Labour. (1921, March). Report of Conference on Industrial Relations. *Labour Gazette, 21*(3; Suppl.), 483–545.

Canada, House of Commons, Select Standing Committee on Industrial and International Relations. (1928). *Report.* Ottawa, ON: King's Printer.

Canadian Association of Food Banks (CAFB). (2002). *Facts about food banks in Canada* [On-line]. Available: www8 .cpr.ca/cms/English/General+Public/Community/Holiday+T rain/Facts+About+Food+Banks+In+Canada.htm

Canadian Association of Schools of Social Work. (2001). *In critical demand: Social work in Canada, final report.* Ottawa, ON: Author.

Canadian Association of Social Workers. (2001, October). *Toward sector collaboration in social work.* A report on the Social Work Forum, Montreal, Quebec. Available: www.casw-acts.ca/ SW-Forum/CdnSWForum-TowardSectorCollaboration.htm

Canadian Centre for Philanthropy [On-line]. Available: www.ccp.ca/

Canadian Council on Social Development. (1984). *Not enough: The meaning and measurement of poverty in Canada.* Ottawa, ON: Author.

Canadian Council on Social Development. (2000). *The Canadian fact book on poverty.* Ottawa, ON: Author. Available: www.ccsd.ca/pubs/2000/fbpov00/index.htm

Canadian Institute for Health Information. (2000–2002). *Health care in Canada: Something to talk about* [On-line]. Available: www.cihi.ca

Canadian Mental Health Association, (1963). *More for the mind.* Toronto, ON: Author.

Cárabes Pedroza, J., Reid Rodríguez, M., Pardo Zepeda, F., & Flores García, J. (1979). *Fundamentos político-jurídicos de la educación en México.* Mexico City: Editorial Progreso.

Carlton-LaNey, I. (Ed.). (2001). *African American leadership: An empowerment tradition in social welfare history.* Silver Spring, MD: NASW Press.

Carnegie, A. (1889). Wealth. *North American Review, 148,* 653–664; *149,* 682–698.

Carniol, B. (1992). Structural social work: Maurice Moreau's challenge to social work practice. *Journal of Progressive Human Services, 3*(1), 1–20.

Carniol, B. (2000). *Case critical: Challenging social services in Canada* (4th ed.). Toronto, ON: Between the Lines.

Carp, E. W. (Ed.). (2002). *Adoption in America: Historical perspectives.* Ann Arbor: University of Michigan Press.

Carr, H. P. (1926, July). Observations upon hookworm disease in Mexico. *American Journal of Hygiene, 6*(Suppl.), 42–61.

Carr, M., & Chen, M. A. (2002). *Globalization and the informal economy: How global trade and investment impact on the working poor* (Working Paper). Geneva, Switzerland: International Labour Office, Employment Sector.

Carrier, J. (1995). *De los otros: Intimacy and homosexuality among Mexican men.* New York: Columbia University Press.

Carrillo, A. M. (2002). Economía, política y salud pública en el México porfiriano (1876–1910). *História, Ciências, Saúde—Manguinhos, 9,* 67–86.

Carrillo, H. (2002). *The night is young: Sexuality in Mexico in the time of AIDS.* Chicago: University of Chicago Press.

Carson, M. (1990). *Settlement folk: Social thought and the American settlement movement, 1885–1930.* Chicago: University of Chicago Press.

Cassidy, H. (1932). *Unemployment and relief in Ontario, 1929–1932.* Toronto, ON.

Cates, J. R. (1983). *Insuring inequality: Administrative leadership in Social Security, 1935–1954.* Ann Arbor: University of Michigan Press.

Chairman of the Council of Economic Advisors. (1950–). *Economic report of the president.* Washington, DC: Government Printing Office. [On-line 1995–]. Available: www.gpoaccess.gov/eop/

Chambers, C. A. (1971). *Paul U. Kellogg and* The Survey*: Voices for social welfare and social justice.* Minneapolis: University of Minnesota Press.

Chambers, J. W. (2000). *The tyranny of change: America in the Progressive Era, 1890–1920.* New Brunswick, NJ: Rutgers University Press.

Chandler, S. K. (2001). E. Franklin Frazier and social work: Unity and conflict. In I. Carlton-LaNey (Ed.), *African American leadership: An empowerment tradition in social welfare history* (pp. 189–202). Washington, DC: NASW Press.

Charles, S. F. (1963). *Minister of relief: Harry Hopkins and the Great Depression.* Syracuse, NY: Syracuse University Press.

Chao, L. (1997). *Beyond silence: Chinese literature in English.* Toronto, ON: TSAR Publications.

Charleton, M., & Barker, P. (Eds.). (1994). *Crosscurrents: Contemporary political issues* (2nd ed.). Scarborough, ON: Nelson.

Chauvet, F. de J. (Ed.). (1951). *Cartas de Fray, Pedro de Gunte.* Mexico City: Fray Junipero Serra.

Che, J., & Chen, J. (2001). Food insecurity in Canadian households. *Statistics Canada Health Reports, 12*(4), 11–22.

Chernomas, R., & Black, E. (1996). What kind of capitalism? The revival of class struggle in Canada. *Monthly Review, 48*(1), 23–34.

Chesler, E. (1992). *Women of valor: Margaret Sanger and the birth control movement in America.* New York: Simon & Schuster.

Children's Aid Society of New York. (1971). *Annual reports, 1854–1963.* New York: Arno Press.

Christie, N., & Gauvreau, M. (1996). *A full-orbed Christianity: The Protestant churches and social welfare in Canada, 1900–1940.* Montreal, QC, and Kingston, ON: McGill-Queen's University Press.

Coady, M. (1939). *Masters of their own destiny.* New York: Harper & Brothers.

Coates, K., & Morrison, W. (1992). *The forgotten North: A history of Canada's provincial norths.* Toronto, ON: Lorimer.

Código Sanitario de los Estados Unidos Mexicanos. (1891). Mexico City: Imprenta del Gobierno Federal en el ex Arzobispado.

Cohen, W. J. (1957). *Retirement policies under Social Security.* Berkeley: University of California Press.

Cole, T. R. (1992). *The journey of life.* New York: Cambridge University Press.

Colín, J. R. (1945, October). *Requísitos fundamentales para la industrialización de México.* Presentation at the Third National Congress of Industrialists, Mexico City.

Collier, G. (1999). *Basta! Land and the Zapatista rebellion in Chiapas.* San Francisco: Food First Books.

Colonial Office. (1864). *Report No. 885/3.* London: Her Majesty's Stationery Office.

Comisión Económica Para América Latina y el Caribe (CEPAL). (2003). *Panorama social de América Latina, 2002–2003.* Santiago, Chile: Naciónes Unidas. Available: www.eclac.cl/

Commission on Private Philanthropy and Public Needs [Filer Commission]. (1975). *Giving in America: Toward a stronger voluntary sector.* Washington, DC. Available: http://indiamond.ulib.iupui.edu/PRO/

Commission on the Future of Health Care in Canada. (2002). *Building on values: The future of health care in Canada* (Final Report to Canadians). Ottawa, ON: Author. Available: www.hc-sc.gc.ca/english/care/romanow/index1.html

Committee on Sexual Offences Against Children and Youth. (1984). *sexual offences against children* [Badgley Report]. Ottawa, ON: Department of Supply and Services Canada.

Committee on Ways and Means of the U.S. House of Representatives (*Green Book* and committee hearings).

Confederación Patronal de la República Mexicana. (1949). *Modernización de las relaciones de trabajo: Aspectos de una nueva conciencia patronal.* Mexico City: Author.

Conkin, P. K. (1995). *The uneasy center: Reformed Christianity in antebellum America.* Chapel Hill: University of North Carolina Press.

Connecticut Bureau of Labor Statistics. (1892). *Annual report.* New Haven: CT: Author.

Conover, A. D. (1911). Supervision of state institutions by a board of control. *Proceedings of the National Conference on Charities and Correction, 38,* 27–31.

Consejo Nacional Contra Las Adicciones (CONADIC). (2001). *Observatorio epidemiológico en drogas.* Mexico City: Secretaría de Salud.

Consejo Nacional Contra Las Adicciones (CONADIC). (2002). *Observatorio Mexicano en tabaco, alcohol y otras drogas.* Mexico City: Secretaría de Salud.

Conway, J. K. (1971–1972, Winter). Women reformers and American culture, 1870–1930. *Journal of Social History, 5,* 164–177.

Cook, B. W. (1992). *Eleanor Roosevelt: A life.* New York: Viking.

Cook, M. L. (1996). *Organizing dissent: Unions, the state, and the democratic teachers' movement in Mexico.* University Park: Pennsylvania State University Press.

Cook, R. (1985). *The regenerators: Social criticism in late Victorian Canada.* Toronto, ON: University of Toronto Press.

Cornelius, W. A., & Myhre, D. (Eds.). (1998). *The transformation of rural Mexico: Reforming the* ejido *sector.* La Jolla: University of California, San Diego, Center for U.S.-Mexican Studies.

Cornelius, W., Craig, A., & Fox, J. (Eds.). (1994). *Transforming state-society relations in Mexico: The national solidarity strategy.* San Diego: University of California Press.

Cortés, F. (2000). *La distribución del ingreso en México en épocas de estabilización y reforma económica.* Mexico City: Centro de Investigaciones y Estudios Superiores en Antropología Social.

Coss, C. (Ed.). (1989). *Lillian D. Wald: Progressive activist.* New York: Feminist Press of the City of New York.

Costin, L. B. (1983). *Two sisters for social justice: A biography of Grace and Edith Abbott.* Urbana: University of Illinois Press.

Coughlin, T., Ku, L., & Holahan, J. (1994). *Medicaid since 1980: Costs, coverage, and the shifting alliance between the federal government and the states.* Washington, DC: Urban Institute Press.

Craig, O., Slocum, W. F., Forrest, H. A., Smith, S. G., & Follett, M. D. (1893). History of state boards. *Proceedings of the National Conference on Charities and Correction, 20,* 33–51.

Crichton, A., & Jongbloed, L. (1998). *Disability and social policy in Canada.* Toronto, ON: Captus.

Cruikshank, M. (1992). *The gay and lesbian liberation movement.* New York: Routledge.

Csiernik, R., & Rowe, W. S. (Eds.). (2003). *Responding to the oppression of addiction: Canadian social work perspectives.* Toronto, ON: Canadian Scholars' Press.

Cueto, M. (Ed.). (1994). *Missionaries of science: The Rockefeller Foundation and Latin America.* Bloomington: Indiana University Press.

Cunningham, H., & Innes, J. (Eds.). (1998). *Charity, philanthropy and reform: From the 1690s to 1850.* New York: St. Martin's.

Currie, E. (1993). *Reckoning: Drugs, the cities, and the American future.* New York: Hill & Wang.

Currie, E. (1998). *Crime and punishment in America.* New York: Metropolitan Books.

Cypher, J. (1990). *State and capital in Mexico.* Boulder, CO: Westview.

Cypher, J., & Dietz, J. (2004). *The process of economic development* (2nd ed.). London: Routledge.

D'Elia, D. J. (1974). *Benjamin Rush: Philosopher of the American Revolution.* Philadelphia: American Philosophical Society.

Dacks, G. (Ed.). (1990). *Devolution and constitutional development in the Canadian North.* Ottawa, ON: Carleton University Press.

Damián, A., & Boltvinik, J. (2003). Evolución de la pobreza en México. *Comercio Exterior, 53*(6)

Daniels, C. R. (Ed.). (1997). *Feminists negotiate the state: The politics of domestic violence.* Lanham, MD: University Press of America.

Daniels, R. (1990). *Coming to America: A history of immigration and ethnicity in American life.* New York: HarperCollins.

Daniels, R. (1997). No lamps were lit for them: Angel Island and the historiography of Asian American immigration. *Journal of American Ethnic History, 17*(1), 3–18.

Davis, A. F. (1984). *Spearheads for reform: The social settlements and the progressive movement 1890–1914* (2nd ed., with a new introduction by the author). New Brunswick, NJ: Rutgers University Press.

Davis, A. F. (2000). *American heroine: The life and legend of Jane Addams* (Rev. ed.). Chicago: Ivan Dee. (Original work published 1973)

Davis, K. (1997, April 27). Obituary: Bessie Touzel: Feisty social worker fought 1950 flooding of Red River. *Ottawa Citizen* (Final ed.), p. A4.

Dawley, A. (1991). *Struggles for justice: Social responsibility and the liberal state.* Cambridge, MA: Harvard University Press.

Day, R. (2000). *Multiculturalism and the history of Canadian diversity.* Toronto, ON: University of Toronto Press.

De la Garza Toledo, E. (1994). The restructuring of state-labor relations in Mexico. In M. L. Cook, K. J. Middlebrook, & J. M. Horcasitas (Eds.), *The politics of economic restructuring* (pp. 195–217). La Jolla: University of California, San Diego, Center for U.S.-Mexican Studies.

De Vos, P. (2001). *The art of pharmacy in seventeenth- and eighteenth-century Mexico.* Unpublished doctoral dissertation, University of California, Berkeley.

Deacon, B., Hulse, M., & Stubbs, P. (1997). *Global social policy: International organizations and the future of welfare.* London: Sage.

Deber, R. B. (2000). Getting what we pay for: Myths and realities about financing Canada's health care system. *Health Law in Canada, 2,* 9–41.

Deichmann Edwards, W. J., & De Swarte Gifford, C. (Eds.). (2003). *Gender and the social gospel.* Urbana: University of Illinois Press.

Derthick, M. (1979). *Policymaking for Social Security.* Washington, DC: Brookings Institution Press.

Deutsch, A. (1948). *The shame of the states.* New York: Harcourt, Brace.

Devine, E. (1904). *Principles of relief.* New York: Macmillan.

Devine, E. T. (1922). *When social work was young.* New York: Macmillan.

Dewey, J. (1966). *Democracy and education: An introduction to the philosophy of education.* New York: Free Press. (Original work published 1916)

Díaz Polanco, H. (1997). *Indigenous peoples in Latin America: The quest for self-determination.* Boulder, CO: Westview.

Dickerson, D. C. (1998). *Militant mediator: Whitney M. Young Jr.* Lexington: University Press of Kentucky.

Dimock, H .S., & Hendry, C. E. (1931). *Camping and character: A camp experiment in character education.* New York: Association Press.

Dorfman, J. (1946–1959). *The economic mind in American civilization* (Vols. 1–5). New York: Viking.

Drummond, J. (1894). Co-operation as shown in associated charities. In *Women workers of Canada: Being a report of the proceedings of the first annual meeting and conference of the National Council of Women of Canada.* Ottawa, ON: National Council of Women.

Dubois, W. E. B. (1903). *Efforts for social betterment among Negro Americans.* Atlanta, GA: Atlanta University Press.

Duffy, A. D., & Momirov, J. (1997). *Family violence: A Canadian introduction.* Toronto, ON: Lorimer.

Dumont, F. (1993). *Genèse de la societé québécoise.* Montreal, QC: Boréal.

Durst, D. (Ed.). (1999). *Canada's national child benefit: Phoenix or fizzle?* Halifax, NS: Fernwood.

Dussel, E. (1984). *Historia de la iglesia en America Latina: Vol. 5. México.* Mexico City: Ediciones Paulistas.

Duster, A. M. (Ed.). (1970). *Crusader for justice: The autobiography of Ida B. Wells.* Chicago: University of Chicago Press.

Dyck, N. (1991). *What is the "Indian problem"? Tutelage and resistance in Canadian Indian administration.* St. John's, NL: Memorial University, Institute for Social and Economic Research.

Dyson, M. E. (2002). *I may not get there with you: The true Martin Luther King, Jr.* New York: Free Press.

Ebenstein, W. (1960). *Great political thinkers: Plato to the present* (3rd ed.). New York: Rinehart

Eccles, W. J. (1990). *France in America.* East Lansing: Michigan State University Press.

Edwards, G. F. (Ed.). (1968). *E. Franklin Frazier on race relations.* Chicago: University of Chicago Press.

Eisinger, P. (1998). *Toward an end to hunger in America.* Washington, DC: Brookings Institution Press.

El Cotidiano. Mexico City: Universidad Autónoma Metropolitana, Itztapalapa. Available: http://dcsh.azc.uam.mx/cotidiano/

El fenómeno de las adicciones en México. (2001). Mexico City: Secretaría de Salud.

El Primer Congreso Femenista de Yucatan, convocado por el C. Gobernador y Comandante Militar del Estado de Yucatan, General D. Salvador Alvarado, y reunido en el Teatro "Peon Contreras" de esta Ciudad del 13 al 16 de enero de 1916. Merida, Yucatan: Talleres Tipograficos del Ateneo Peninsular.

El sistema de escuelas rurales en México. (1927). Mexico City: Talleres Gráficos de la Nación.

Elias, P. D. (1991). *Development of Aboriginal people's communities.* North York, ON: Captus.

Elshtain, J. B. (2002). *Jane Addams and the dream of American democracy.* New York: Basic Books.

Encuestas nacionales de adicciones. (1993, 1998, 2002). Mexico City: Secretaría de Salud.

England, R. (1943). *Discharged: A commentary of civil re-establishment of veterans in Canada.* Toronto, ON: Macmillan.

Enns, H., & Neufeldt, A. H. (2003). *In pursuit of equal opportunity: Canada and disability at home and abroad.* Toronto, ON: Captus.

Erickson, P. (1980). *Cannabis criminals: The social effects of punishment on drug users.* Toronto, ON: Addiction Research Foundation.

Esping-Anderson, G. (1990). *The three worlds of welfare capitalism.* Cambridge, MA: Polity Press.

Evangelista Martínez, E. (1993, October-December). Historia del Trabajo Social en México. *Revista de Trabajo Social ENTS-UNAM, 1*(3), 45–47.

Evangelista Martínez, E. (Ed.). (1998). *Historia del trabajo social en México.* Mexico City: Plaza y Valdés.

Evans, P., & Werkle, G. (1997). *Women and the Canadian welfare state: Challenges and change.* Toronto, ON: University of Toronto Press.

Evans, S. (1979). *Personal politics: The roots of women's liberation in the civil rights movement and the New Left.* New York: Alfred A. Knopf.

Executive director's report. (1926). *Canadian Child Welfare News, 2*(2).

Fantasia, R., & Isserman, M. (1994). *Homelessness: A sourcebook.* New York: Facts on File.

Federal Works Administration. (1946). *Final report on the WPA program, 1935–1943.* Washington, DC: Government Printing Office.

Ferrero, R., & Altmeyer, A. J. (1957). *Estudio economico de la legislacion social Peruana y sugerencias para su mejoramiento.* Lima, Peru.

Filgueira, C. H., & Filgueira, F. (2002). Models of welfare and models of capitalism: The limits of transferability. In E. Huber (Ed.), *Models of capitalism, lessons for Latin America* (pp. 127–157). University Park: Pennsylvania State University Press.

Fine, S. (1956). *Laissez faire and the general-welfare state.* Ann Arbor: University of Michigan Press.

Finnegan, C. (2003). Social engineering and photographic resistance: Social science rhetorics of poverty in *Survey Graphic.* In *Picturing poverty: Print culture and FSA photographs.* Washington DC: Smithsonian Books.

Finnegan, C. (n.d.). Social welfare and visual politics: The story of *Survey Graphic. New Deal Network* [On-line]. Available: http://newdeal.feri.org/sg/index.htm

Fisher, J. (1936). Rank and file movement, 1931–1936. *Social Work Today, 2,* 5–6.

Fisher, J. (1980). *The response of social work to the Depression.* Cambridge, MA: Schenkman.

Fitzpatrick, E. (2003). Social welfare. In T. M. Porter & D. Ross (Eds.), *The Cambridge history of science: Vol. 7. The modern social sciences* (pp. 608–620). New York: Cambridge University Press.

Fixico, D. L. (2003). *The American Indian in a linear world: American Indian studies and traditional knowledge.* New York: Routledge.

Flanagan, T. (2000). *First Nations? Second thoughts.* Montreal, QC, and Kingston, ON: McGill-Queen's University Press.

Fleras, A., & Elliot, J. L. (1992). *Multiculturalism in Canada: The challenge of diversity.* Scarborough, ON: Nelson.

Fleras, A., & Elliot, J. L. (2002). *Engaging diversity: Multiculturalism in Canada.* Toronto, ON: Thomson Nelson.

Fleras, A., & Elliot, J. L. (2003). *Unequal relations: An introduction to race and ethnic dynamics in Canada* (4th ed.). Toronto, ON: Prentice Hall.

Flexner, A. (1915). Is social work a profession? *Proceedings of the National Conference of Charities and Correction, 42,* 576–590.

Flores-Briseño, G. A. (1999). El modelo médico y el modelo social de la discapacidad: Un análisis comparativo. In M. Ribeiro & R. E. López (Eds.), *Políticas sociales sectoriales: Tendencias actuales* (Vol. 2). Monterrey: Universidad Autónoma de Nuevo León.

Flores-Briseño, G. A. (2003). *Societal attitudes toward persons with disabilities in the metropolitan area of Monterrey, Nuevo León.* Unpublished doctoral dissertation, University of Texas at Arlington.

Foner, P. S. (Ed.). (1970). *W. E. B. DuBois speaks* (Vols. 1–2). New York: Pathfinder.

Foner, P. S. (1975). *The history of the labor movement in the United States* (2nd ed., Vols. 1–8). New York: International Publishers.

Fontan, J.-M., & Shragge, E. (1996, October). Chic Resto-Pop: New community practice in Quebec. *Community Development Journal: An International Forum, 31*(4), 291–301.

Fontan, J.-M., & Shragge, E. (1998). Community Economic Development organizations in Montreal. *Journal of Community Practice, 5*(1, 2), 125–136.

Fook, J. (2002). *Social work: Critical theory and practice.* London: Sage.

Forsey, E. (1982). *Trade unions in Canada, 1812–1902.* Toronto, ON: University of Toronto Press.

Fox, D. M. (1993). *Power and illness: The failure and future of American health policy.* Berkeley: University of California Press.

Fox, J. (1992). *The politics of food in Mexico: State, power and social mobilization.* Ithaca, NY: Cornell University Press.

Franklin, J. H. (1993). *The color line: Legacy for the twenty-first century.* Columbia: University of Missouri Press.

Franklin, J., & Moss, A. (1994). *From slavery to freedom.* New York: Alfred A. Knopf.

Fraser, S. J. (2002). An exploration of joint ventures as a sustainable development tool for First Nations. *Journal of Aboriginal Economic Development, 3*(1), 40–44.

Freire, P. (1972). *Pedagogy of the oppressed.* Harmondsworth, UK: Penguin.

Friedman, L. J., & McGarvie, M. D. (Eds.). (2003). *Charity, philanthropy, and civility in American history.* New York: Cambridge University Press.

Friedman, L. M. (1993). *Crime and punishment in American history.* New York: Basic Books.

Friedman, M. (1962). *Capitalism and freedom.* Chicago: University of Chicago Press.

Friedman, M., & Friedman, R. (1984). *Tyranny of the status quo.* New York: Harcourt, Brace, Jovanovich.

Fuentes, M. L. (1998). *La asistencia social en México: Historia y perspectivas.* Mexico City: Ediciones del Milenio.

Fujiwara, L. H. (1998). The impact of welfare reform on Asian immigrant communities. *Social Justice, 25*(1), 82–104.

Galbraith, J. K. (1973). *Economics and the public purpose.* Boston: Houghton Mifflin.

Gann, L. H., & Dunnigan, P. J. (1986). *The Hispanics in the United States: A history.* Boulder, CO: Westview.

Garcia, F. C., & de la Garza, R. (1977). *The Chicano political experience: Three perspectives.* North Scituate, MA: Duxbury.

García Cruz, M. (1961). La seguridad social. In *México, cincuenta años de revolución: Vol. 2: La vida social.* Mexico City: Fondo de Cultura Económica.

Garrow, D. J. (1986). *Bearing the Cross: Martin Luther King, Jr. and the Southern Leadership Conference, 1955-1968.* New York: Morrow.

Garza, G. (2003). *La urbanizacíon de México en el siglo XX.* Mexico City: Colegio de México.

Gastelum, B. J. (1926). La persecucion de la sifilis desde el punto de vista de la garantia social. *Boletin del Departamento de Salubridad Publica, 4*(8).

Gates, P. W. (1936, July). The homestead law in an incongruous land system. *American Historical Review, 41,* 652–681.

Gates, P. W. (1968). *History of public land law development.* Washington, DC: Government Printing Office.

Gates, P. W. (1996). *The Jeffersonian dream: Studies in the history of American land policy and development* (A. G. Bogue & M. Beattie Bogue, Eds.). Albuquerque: University of New Mexico Press.

Gerson, M. (1996). *The essential neoconservative reader.* New York: Addison-Wesley.

Gibbins, R., & Laforest, G. (Eds.). (1998). *Beyond the impasse: Toward reconciliation.* Montreal, QC: Institute for Research on Public Policy.

Gidney, R. D. (1999). *From Hope to Harris: The reshaping of Ontario's schools.* Toronto, ON: University of Toronto Press.

Giffen, P., Endicott, S., & Lambert, S. (1991). *Panic and indifference: The politics of Canada's drug laws.* Ottawa, ON: Canadian Centre on Substance Abuse.

Gil, D. (1998). *Confronting injustice and oppression: Concepts and strategies for social workers.* New York: Columbia University Press.

Gilbert, N. (1995). *Welfare justice: Restoring social equity.* New Haven, CT: Yale University Press.

Giles, K. S. (1980). *Flight of the dove: The story of Jeannette Rankin.* Beaverton, OR: Touchstone.

Gillespie, W. I. (1991). *Tax, borrow and spend: Financing federal spending in Canada, 1867–1990.* Ottawa, ON: Carleton University Press.

Gilly, A. (1997). *Chiapas: La razon ardiente.* Mexico City: Era Press.

Ginsberg, L. (1998). *Conservative social welfare policy.* Chicago: Nelson-Hall.

Giugale, M. M., Lafourcade, O., & Nguyen, V. H. (2001). *Mexico: A comprehensive development agenda for the new era.* Washington, DC: World Bank.

Giving USA 2003: The Annual Report on Philanthropy for the Year 2002. (2003). Indianapolis, IN: American Association of Fundraising Counsel (AAFRC) Trust for Philanthropy.

Gladden, W. (1892). *Applied Christianity: Moral aspects of social questions.* New York: Houghton Mifflin.

Gledhill, J. (1991). *Casi nada: A study of agrarian reform in the homeland of cardenismo.* Albany: State University of New York, Institute for Mesoamerican Studies.

Glenn, J. M., Brandt, L., & Andrews, F. E. (1947). *The Russell Sage Foundation, 1907–1947.* New York: Russell Sage.

Godfrey, D., & Watkins, M. (Eds.). (1970). *Gordon to Watkins to you, a documentary: The battle for control of our economy.* Toronto, ON: New Press.

Gomes, C. (1997). Seguridad social y envejecimiento: La crisis vecina. In C. Rabell (Ed.), *Los retos de la población* (pp. 297–339). Mexico City: Facultad Latinoamericana de Ciencias Sociales; Juan Pablos.

Gomes, C., & Montes de Oca, V. (in press). Aging in Mexico: Families, informal care and reciprocity. In P. Lloyd-Sherlock (Ed.), *Living longer: Aging, development and social protection.* London: Zed Publishers.

González de la Rocha, M. (1988). Economic crisis, domestic reorganisation and women's work in Guadalajara, Mexico. *Bulletin of Latin American Research, 7*(2), 207–223.

González de la Rocha, M. (1994). *The resources of poverty: Women and survival in a Mexican city.* Oxford, UK: Blackwell.

González de la Rocha, M. (2000). *Private adjustments: Household responses to the erosion of work* (Conference Paper Series No. 6). New York: United Nations Development Programme.

González de la Rocha, M. (2001). From the resources of poverty to the poverty of resources: The erosion of a survival model. *Latin American Perspectives, 28*(4), 72–100.

González Navarro, M. (1985). *La pobreza en México.* Mexico City: Colegio de México.

González Navarro, M. (1994). *Los extranjeros en México y los mexicanos en el extranjero, 1821–1970* (Vols. 1-3). Mexico City: El Colegio de México.

Goodin, R. E., Headey, B., Muffels, R., & Dirven, H.-J. (1999). *The real worlds of welfare capitalism.* Cambridge, UK: Cambridge University Press.

Goodman, N. G. (1934). *Benjamin Rush: Physician and citizen, 1746–1813.* Philadelphia: University of Pennsylvania Press.

Goodwin, J. L. (1997). *Gender and the politics of welfare reform: Mothers' pensions in Chicago, 1911–1929.* Chicago: University of Chicago Press.

Gordon, L. (1976). *Woman's body, woman's right: Birth control in America.* New York: Viking.

Gordon, L. (1988). *Heroes of their own lives: The politics and history of family violence.* New York: Penguin.

Gordon, L. (1994). *Pitied but not entitled: Single mothers and the history of welfare, 1890–1935.* New York: Free Press.

Gostin, L. O. (2000). *Public health law: Power, duty, restraint.* Berkeley: University of California Press; Milbank Memorial Fund.

Gove Commission. (1995). *Report of the Gove Enquiry into Child Protection in British Columbia* (Vols. 1–3). Vancouver, BC: Author.

Graham, J. R. (1994). Charles Eric Hendry (1903–1979): The pre-war formational origins of a leader of post–World War II Canadian social work education. *Canadian Social Work Review, 11*(2), 150–167.

Graham, J. R., Swift, K., & Delaney, R. (2003). *Canadian social policy: An introduction* (2nd ed.). Toronto, ON: Prentice Hall.

Grant, H. M. (1998). Solving the labour problem at Imperial Oil: Welfare capitalism in the Canadian petroleum industry, 1919–1929. *Labour/Le Travail, 41,* 69–95.

Greeley, D. (1995). *Beyond benevolence: Gender, class and the development of scientific charity in New York City, 1882–1935.* Unpublished doctoral dissertation, State University of New York at Stony Brook.

Greer, T. H. (2000). *What Roosevelt thought: The social and political ideas of Franklin D. Roosevelt.* East Lansing: Michigan State University Press.

Griffiths, N. E. S. (1993). *The splendid vision: Centennial history of the National Council of Women of Canada, 1893–1993.* Ottawa, ON: Carleton University Press.

Grob, G. N. (1994). *The mad among us: A history of the care of America's mentally ill.* New York: Free Press.

Guest, D. T. (1997). *The emergence of Social Security in Canada* (3rd ed.). Vancouver: University of British Columbia Press.

Guillermo, M. B. B. (Ed.). (1993). *Simbiosis de culturas: Los inmigrantes y su cultura en México.* Mexico City: Fondo de Cultura Económica.

Gurteen, S. H. (1882). *A handbook of charity organization.* Buffalo, NY: Author.

Gutiérrez, L. M. (Ed.). (1996). *Salud del adulto mayor en México, estrategias y plan de acción.* Mexico City: Grupo Intersectorial de Salud del Adulto Mayor; OPS; Secretaría de Salud, Dirección de Enfermedades Crónico Degenerativas.

Gutierrez Casillas, J. (1984). *Historia de la iglesia en México* (2nd ed.). Mexico City: Editorial Porrua.

Guy, D. (1998). The politics of Pan American cooperation: Maternalist feminism and the child rights movement, 1913–1960. *Gender and History, 10*(3), 449–469.

Guy, D. J. (1998, July). The Pan American Child Congresses, 1916 to 1942: Pan Americanism, child reform, and the welfare state in Latin America. *Journal of Family History, 23*(3), 272–291.

Haber, C., & Gratton, B. (1994). *Old age and the search for security.* Bloomington: Indiana University Press.

Haber, S., & Bortz, J. L. (2002). *The Mexican economy, 1870 to 1930: Essays on the economic history of institutions, revolution, and growth.* Stanford, CA: Stanford University Press.

Haber, W., & Cohen, W. J. (Eds.). (1948). *Readings in Social Security.* New York: Prentice Hall.

Haber, W., & Cohen, W. J. (Eds.). (1960). *Social Security: Programs, problems and policies.* Homewood, IL: Irwin.

Hacker, J. S. (2002). *The divided welfare state: The battle over public and private social benefits in the United States.* Cambridge, UK: Cambridge University Press.

Hall, G. S. (1922). *Senescence.* New York: D. Appelton.

Ham Chande, R. (2003). *El envejecimiento en México: El siguiente reto de la transición demográfica.* Mexico City: Colegio de la Frontera Norte; Miguel Ángel Porrúa.

Hamilton, A. (1943). *Exploring the dangerous trades.* Boston: Little, Brown.

Hammack, D., & Young, D. R. (Eds.). (1993). *Nonprofit organizations in a market economy: Understanding new roles, issues, and trends.* San Francisco: Jossey-Bass.

Handy, R. T. (1966). *The social gospel in America, 1870–1920: Gladden, Ely, Rauschenbusch.* New York: Oxford University Press.

Hannon, J. U. (1984, January). Poor relief policy in antebellum New York State: The rise and decline of the poorhouse. *Explorations in Economic History, 22,* 243–247.

Harrington, M. (1962). *The other America: Poverty in the United States.* New York: Macmillan.

Harrington, M. (1988). *The long distance runner: An autobiography.* New York: Holt.

Harris, M. (1986). *Justice denied.* Toronto, ON: Macmillan.

Harrison, D. (2002). *The first casualty: Violence against women in Canadian military communities.* Toronto, ON: Lorimer.

Hartley, I. S. (Ed.). (1882). *Memorial of Robert Milham Hartley.* Utica, NY: Press of Curtis & Childs [Printer].

Hartley, R. M. (1842). *An historical, scientific, and practical essay on milk as an article of human sustenance; with a consideration of the effects consequent upon the unnatural methods of producing it for the supply of large cities.* New York: J. Leavitt. (Available: Rare Book & Manuscript Library, Butler Library, Columbia University, New York)

Harvey, J. (2001). Dealing with the "destitute and the wretched": The Protestant House of Industry and Refuge in nineteenth-century Montreal. *Journal of the Canadian Historical Association,* New Series, *12,* 73–94.

Harvey, N. (1998). *The Chiapas rebellion.* Durham, NC: Duke University Press.

Haslip-Viera, G. (1986). The underclass. In L. S. Hoberman & S. M. Socolow (Eds.), *Cities and society in colonial Latin America* (pp. 285–312). Albuquerque: University of New Mexico Press.

Hawke, D. F. (1971). *Benjamin Rush: Revolutionary gadfly.* Indianapolis, IN: Bobbs-Merrill.

Hawkins, F. (1991). *Critical years in immigration: Canada and Australia compared.* Montreal, QC, and Kingston, ON: McGill-Queen's University Press.

Hayek, F. (1976). *The road to serfdom.* Chicago: University of Chicago Press. (Original work published 1944)

Hayek, F. A. (1976). *The mirage of social justice.* Chicago: University of Chicago Press.

Health Canada. (2002). *Canada's aging population.* Ottawa, ON: Ministry of Public Works and Government Services Canada. Available: www.hc-sc.gc.ca/seniors-aines/pubs/fed_paper/pdfs/fedpager_e.pdf

Health Canada. (2004, January 26). *Canada Health Act: Overview* [On-line]. Available: www.hc-sc.gc.ca/medicare/chaover.htm

Health Canada. (2004, July 8). *Seniors policies and programs database* [On-line]. Available: www.sppd.gc.ca

Health Canada. (2004, September 19). *Principles of the national framework on aging: A policy guide* [On-line]. Available: www.hc-sc.gc.ca/seniors-aines/nfa-cnv/pdf/aging_e.pdf

Health Canada, Division of Aging and Seniors, National Advisory Council on Aging. (2003, September 30). *Interim report card: Seniors in Canada 2003* [On-line]. Available: www.hc-sc.gc.ca/seniors-aines/index_pages/naca_e.htm

Healy, L. M. (2001). *International social work: Professional action in an interdependent world.* New York: Oxford University Press.

Heath, J. (1998). The impact of Mexico's trade liberalization: Jobs, productivity, and structural change. In C. Wise (Ed.), *The post-NAFTA political economy: Mexico and the Western Hemisphere* (pp. 171–200). University Park: Pennsylvania State University Press.

Held, V. (1995). *Justice and care: Essential readings in feminist ethics.* Boulder, CO: Westview.

Henchey, N., & Burgess, D. (1987). *Between past and future: Quebec education in transition.* Calgary, AB: Detselig.

Hendry, C. E. (1933). *Youth inspects the New World.* Chicago: Roy Sorenson.

Hendry, C. E. (1969). *Beyond traplines: Does the church really care? Towards an assessment of the work of the Anglican church of Canada with Canada's Native peoples.* Toronto, ON: Ryerson.

Herman, E. E. (1998). *Collective bargaining and labor relations* (4th ed.). Upper Saddle River, NJ: Prentice Hall.

Hernández Saénz, L. M. (1997). *Learning to heal: The medical profession in colonial Mexico, 1767–1831.* New York: Peter Lang.

Hernández-Laos, E. (1992). *Crecimiento económico y pobreza en México: Una agenda para la investigación.* Mexico City: Universidad Nacional Autónoma de México.

Heron, C. (1996). *The Canadian labour movement: A short history.* Toronto, ON: Lorimer.

Herron, G. D. (1968). *Social meanings of religious experience.* New York: Johnson.

Hewit de Alcántara, C. (1978). *La modernización de la agricultura Mexicana, 1940–1970.* Mexico City: Siglo XXI.

Hill, K. (1984). *Oral history of social work in Canada.* Ottawa, ON: Canadian Association of Social Workers.

Hindus, M. S. (1980). *Prison and plantation: Crime, justice, and authority in Massachusetts and South Carolina, 1767–1878.* Chapel Hill: University of North Carolina Press.

Historia del Trabajo Social en México. *Revista Mexicana de Trabajo Social, 1*(3), 69. Asociación de Trabajadores Sociales Mexicanos (Eds.). (1991, March).

Historias, 33. (1994, October–1995, March). Mexico City: Instituto Nacional de Antropología e Historia.

Hobbs, M., & Sangster, J. (Eds.). (1999). *The woman worker, 1926–1929.* St. John's, NL: Canadian Committee on Labour History.

Hodges, D. (1995). *Mexican anarchism after the Revolution.* Austin: University of Texas Press.

Holt, M. I. (1992). *The orphan trains: Placing out in America.* Lincoln: University of Nebraska Press.

Holt, T. C. (1982). The lonely warrior: Ida B. Wells-Barnett and the struggle for Black leadership. In J. H. Franklin & A. Meier (Eds.), *Black leaders of the twentieth century.* Urbana: University of Illinois Press.

Hoover, H. (1934). *The challenge to liberty.* New York: Scribner.

Hope, P. H., Carrillo Flores, A., & Sáenz, J. (1950). *Conferencias a técnicos, hombres de empresa, y dirigentes obreros por una mejor producción y un mayor consumo de artículos nacionales.* Meeting of the Movimiento Económico Nacional, Mexico City.

Hopkins, J. (1999). *Harry Hopkins: Sudden hero, brash reformer.* New York: St. Martin's.

Horn, M. (1976). Leonard Marsh and the coming of a welfare state in Canada: A review article. *Histoire Sociale, 9*(17), 197–204.

Hougham, G. M. (1962). *The relationship between unemployment and Canada's other employment maintenance programs* [Royal Commission of Inquiry into the Unemployment Insurance Act.] Ottawa, ON: Queen's Printer.

Howard, C. (1997). *The hidden welfare state: Tax expenditures and social policy in the United States.* Princeton, NJ: Princeton University Press.

Howard, D. S. (1943). *The WPA and federal relief policy.* New York: Russell Sage.

Howe, R. B., & Johnson, D. (2001). *Restraining equality: Human rights commissions in Canada.* Toronto, ON: University of Toronto Press.

Hsiao, A. (1998). The hidden history of Asian-American activism in New York City. *Social Policy, 28*(4), 23–31.

Hunter, G. (2002). Child poverty and the Saskatchewan child poverty initiatives. *Prairie Forum, 27,* 45–57.

Hurd, H. M. (1916). *The institutional care of the insane in the United States and Canada.* Baltimore, MD: Johns Hopkins University Press.

Hyman, H. M. (1986). *American singularity: The 1787 Northwest Ordinance, the 1862 Homestead and Morrill Acts, and the 1944 G.I. Bill.* Athens: University of Georgia Press.

Illinois Health Insurance Commission. (1919). *Report.* Springfield: Illinois State Journal.

Internal Revenue Service. (2003). *2002 data book* (Publication 55B). Washington, DC: Government Printing Office.

International Labour Organization (ILO). [Working papers]. Available on the ILO website, www.ilo.org

International Labour Organization. (2002). *Women and men in the informal economy: A statistical picture.* Geneva, Switzerland: International Labour Office, Employment Sector.

Irving, A. (1981). Canadian Fabians: The work and thought of Harry Cassidy and Leonard Marsh, 1930–1945. *Canadian Journal of Social Work Education, 7*(1), 7–28.

Irving, A. (1983). *A Canadian Fabian: The life and work of Harry Cassidy.* Unpublished doctoral dissertation, University of Toronto, ON.

Irving, A., Parsons, H., & Bellamy, D. (Eds.). (1995). *Neighbours: Three social settlements in downtown Toronto.* Toronto, ON: Canadian Scholars' Press.

Ismael, J. S. (Ed.). (1985). *Canadian social welfare policy: Federal and provincial dimensions* (Canadian Public Administration Series No. 12). Montreal, QC, and Kingston, ON: McGill-Queen's University Press.

Jacoby, S. M. (1997). *Modern manors: Welfare capitalism since the New Deal.* Princeton, NJ: Princeton University Press.

Jansson, B. S. (2000). *The reluctant welfare state: American social welfare policies—past, present, and future* (4th ed.). Belmont, CA: Wadsworth.

Jansson, B. S. (2001). *The sixteen-trillion-dollar mistake: How the U.S. bungled its national priorities from the New Deal to the present.* New York: Columbia University Press.

Jaramillo, R. (1967). *Autobiografía.* Mexico City: Editorial Nuestro Tiempo.

Johnston, D. C. (2003). *Perfectly legal: The covert campaign to rig our tax system.* New York: Portfolio.

Johnston, P. (1983). *Native children and the child welfare system* (Canadian Council on Social Development Series No. 147). Toronto, ON: Lorimer.

Jones, A., & Rutman, L. (1981). *In the children's aid: J. J. Kelso and child welfare in Ontario.* Toronto, ON: University of Toronto Press.

Jones, M. (1992). *American immigration.* Chicago: University of Chicago Press.

Josephson, H. (1974). *Jeannette Rankin, first lady in Congress: A biography.* Indianapolis, IN: Bobbs-Merrill.

Kaestle, C. F. (1983). *Pillars of the republic: Common schools and American society, 1780–1860* (American Century Series). New York: Hill & Wang.

Kallen, E. (2003). *Ethnicity and human rights in Canada: A human rights perspective on ethnicity, racism and systemic inequality* (3rd ed.). Toronto, ON: Oxford University Press.

Kappler, C. J. (Ed.). (1904). *Indian affairs: Laws and treaties* (Vols. 1–2). Washington, DC: Government Printing Office.

Katz, M. B. (1996). *In the shadow of the poorhouse: A social history of welfare in America* (Rev. ed.). New York: Basic Books.

Katz, M. B. (2001). *The price of citizenship.* New York: Metropolitan Books.

Kaufman, J. (2002). *For the common good? American civic life and the golden age of fraternity.* New York: Oxford University Press.

Kaufman, S. B. (Ed.). (1986). *The Samuel Gompers papers* (Vols. 1–4). Urbana: University of Illinois Press.

Kealey, G. S. (Ed.). (1973). *Canada investigates industrialism: The Royal Commission on the Relations of Labour and Capital.* Toronto, ON: University of Toronto Press. (Original work published 1889)

Kelly, N., & Trebilcock, M. (1998). *The making of the mosaic: A history of Canadian immigration policy.* Toronto, ON: University of Toronto Press.

Kelso, R. W. (1911). State supervision by a board of state charities. *Proceedings of the National Conference on Charities and Correction, 38,* 31–35.

Kennedy, A. E. (1934). *The Ohio Poor Law and its administration.* Chicago: University of Chicago Press.

Kennedy, D. M. (1970). *Birth control in America: The career of Margaret Sanger.* New Haven, CT: Yale University Press.

Kessler-Harris, A. (2001). *In pursuit of equity: Women and men and the quest for economic citizenship in 20th century America.* New York: Oxford University Press.

Kim, H.-C. (1994). *A legal history of Asian Americans, 1790–1990.* Westport, CT: Greenwood.

King, M. (1943). *King diaries.* Ottawa, ON: King's Printer.

King, M. L., Jr. (1958). *Stride toward freedom: The Montgomery story.* New York: Harper & Row.

King, M. L., Jr. (1964). *Why we can't wait.* New York: New American Library.

King, M. L., Jr. (1967). *Where do we go from here: Chaos or community?* New York: Harper & Row.

King, T. (2003). *The truth about stories: A native narrative.* Toronto, ON: House of Anansi.

King, W. L. M. (1908). *The need for the suppression of the opium traffic in Canada.* Ottawa, ON: S. E. Dawson.

Kinsman, G. (1996). *The regulation of desire: Homo and hetero sexualities* (Rev. ed.). Montreal, QC: Black Rose.

Kirk, R. (1955). *The conservative mind: From Burke to Eliot* (4th ed.). Washington, DC: Regnery.

Kitchen, B. (1986). The Marsh Report revisited. *Journal of Canadian Studies, 21*(2), 38–48.

Kitchen, B. (1987). The introduction of family allowances in Canada. In A. Moscovitch & J. Albert (Eds.), *The benevolent state: The growth of welfare in Canada.* Toronto, ON: Garamond.

Kleibard, H. M. (2002). *Changing course: American curriculum reform in the 20th century.* New York: Teachers College Press.

Klein, J. (2003). *For all these rights: Business, labor, and the shaping of America's public-private welfare state.* Princeton, NJ: Princeton University Press.

Knight, A. (1986). *The Mexican revolution* (Vols. 1–2). Cambridge, UK: Cambridge University Press.

Knight, A. (1994). Solidarity: Historical continuities and contemporary implications. In W. A. Cornelius, A. L. Craig, & J. Fox (Eds.), *Transforming state-society relations in Mexico: The national Solidarity strategy* (pp. 29–45). La Jolla: University of California, San Diego, Center for U.S.-Mexican Studies.

Knowles, V. (1997). *Strangers at our gates: Canadian immigration and immigration policy, 1540–1995* (Rev. ed.). Toronto, ON: Dundurn.

Koc, M., MacRae, R., Mougeot, L. J. A., & Welsh, J. (1999). *For hunger-proof cities: Sustainable urban food systems.* Ottawa, ON: International Development Research Centre.

Kochman, A. (1997). Gay and lesbian elderly: Historical overview and implications for social work practice. In J. Quam (Ed.), *Social services for senior gay men and lesbians* (pp. 1–10). New York: Haworth.

Kopinak, K. (2004). *The social costs of industrial growth in northern Mexico.* La Jolla: University of California, San Diego, Center for U.S.-Mexican Studies.

Koven, S., & Michel, S. (Eds.). (1993). *Mothers of a new world: Maternalist politics and the origins of welfare states.* New York: Routledge.

La Botz, D. (Ed.). *Mexican Labor News and Analysis* [On-line serial]. Available: www.ueinternational.org/

Lader, L. (1955). *The Margaret Sanger story and the fight for birth control.* Westport, CT: Greenwood.

Lalonde, M. (1973). *Working paper on Social Security in Canada* (2nd ed.). Ottawa, ON: Department of National Health and Welfare.

Lang, T. (1997). *Food policy for the 21st century: Can it be both radical and reasonable?* (Discussion Paper No. 4). London: Thames Valley University, Centre for Food Policy.

Langley, W., & Fox, V. C. (Eds.). (1994). *Women's rights in the United States: A documentary history.* Westport, CT: Greenwood.

Lanning, J. T. (1985). *The royal Protomedicato: The regulation of the medical professions in the Spanish Empire* (J. J. TePaske, Ed.). Durham, NC: Duke University Press.

Lasch-Quinn, E. (1993). *Black neighbors: Race and the limits of reform in the American settlement movement, 1890–1945.* Chapel Hill: University of North Carolina Press.

Latapí Sarre, P. (Ed.). (1998). *Un siglo de educación en México.* Mexico City: Consejo Nacional Para la Cultura y las Artes.

Lathrop, J. (1918). *Provision for the care of families and dependents of soldiers and sailors.* New York: Academy of Political Science.

Laurell, A. C. (2000). Structural adjustment and the globalization of social policy in Latin America. *Journal of the International Sociology Association, 15*(2), 306–325.

Laws relating to "mothers' pensions" in the United States, Denmark, and New Zealand (U.S. Children's Bureau Publication No. 7). (1914). Washington, DC: Government Printing Office.

Layton, J. (2004). *Speaking out: Ideas that work for Canadians.* Toronto, ON: Key Porter.

Le Dain Commission. (1972). *The study of non-medical use of drugs in Canada.* Ottawa, ON: Information Canada.

Lebel, L. (1928). *Le problème de la famille nombreuse: Sa solution, les allocations familiales.* Montreal, QC: Imprimé par Le Devoir.

Lee, P. R. (1929). Social work as cause and function. *Proceedings of the National Conference of Social Work, 56,* 3–20.

Leiby, J. (1978). *A history of social welfare and social work in the United States.* New York: Columbia University Press.

Leiby, J. S. (1992). San Hipólito's treatment of the mentally ill in Mexico City, 1589–1650. *Historian, 54*(3), 491–498.

Leighninger, L. (1987). *Social work: Search for identity.* Westport, CT: Greenwood.

Leighninger, L. (1999). The service trap: Social work and public welfare policy in the 1960s. In G. R. Lowe & P. N. Reid (Eds.), *The professionalization of poverty: Social work and the poor in the twentieth century* (pp. 63–88). New York: Aldine de Gruyter.

Lerner, G. (Ed.). (1972). *Black women in White America: A documentary history.* New York: Vintage.

Leuchtenberg, W. E. (1963). *Franklin D. Roosevelt and the New Deal.* New York: Harper & Row.

Leuchtenberg, W. E. (1993). *In the shadow of FDR: From Harry Truman to Bill Clinton* (2nd ed.). Ithaca, NY: Cornell University Press.

Levine, H. (1982). The personal is political: Feminism and the helping professions. In A. Miles & G. Finn (Eds.), *Feminism in Canada* (pp. 175–209). Montreal, QC: Black Rose.

Levine, P. (2001). The legitimacy of labor unions. *Hofstra Labor & Employment Law Journal, 18,* 527–571.

Lewis, D. L. (2000). *W. E. B. DuBois—The fight for equality and the American century, 1919–1963.* New York: Holt.

Lewis, J. (1998). *Walking with the wind: A memoir of the movement.* New York: Simon & Schuster.

Lewis, O. (1961). *The children of Sánchez: Autobiography of a Mexican family.* New York: Viking.

Lewis, S. E. (2002). Ghosts and the machine: Teaching Emiliano Zapata and the Mexican Revolution since 1921. In J. Marten (Ed.), *Children and war: An historical anthology* (pp. 147–159). New York: New York University Press.

Li, P. (Ed.). (1999). *Race and ethnic relations in Canada.* Don Mills, ON: Oxford University Press.

Lieberman, R. (1998). *Shifting the color line.* Cambridge, MA: Harvard University Press.

Lightman, E. (2003). *Social policy in Canada.* Toronto, ON: Oxford University Press.

Lindenmeyer, K. (1997). *"A right to childhood": The U.S. Children's Bureau and child welfare, 1912–1946.* Urbana: University of Illinois Press.

Ling, P. (1988). *Martin Luther King, Jr.* New York: Routledge.

Linn, J. W. (1935). *Jane Addams: A biography.* New York: Appleton-Century.

Little, M. (1994). "Manhunts and bingo blabs": The moral regulation of Ontario single mothers. In M. Valverde (Ed.), *Studies in moral education* (pp. 233–247). Toronto, ON: Centre of Criminology.

Lochead, C., & Scott, K. (2000). *The dynamics of women's poverty in Canada.* Ottawa, ON: Status of Women Canada.

Lomas, J., Woods, J., & Veenstra, G. (1997). Devolving authority for health care in Canada's provinces: 1. An introduction to the issues. *Canadian Medical Association Journal, 156,* 371–377.

Lomelí, E. V., Gendreau, M., & Tepichín, A. M. (Eds.). (2000). *Los dilemas de la política social: Como combatir la pobreza?* Mexico City: Universidad Iberoamericana.

Lomnitz, C. (2001). *Deep Mexico, silent Mexico: An anthropology of nationalism.* Minneapolis: University of Minnesota Press.

London, J. (1913). *John Barleycorn.* New York: Century.

Lotz, J., & MacIntyre, G. (2002). *Sustainable people: A new approach to community development.* Sydney, NS: University College Cape Breton Press.

Lowell, J. S. (1884). *Public relief and private charity.* New York: Putnam.

Lowitt, R., & Beasley, M. (Eds.). (2000). *One third of a nation: Lorena Hickok reports on the Great Depression.* Urbana: University of Illinois Press.

Lubove, R. (1959). The New York Association for Improving the Condition of the Poor: The formative years. *New York Historical Society Quarterly, 43,* 307–327.

Lubove, R. (1965). *The professional altruist: The emergence of social work as a career, 1880–1930.* Cambridge, MA: Harvard University Press.

Lubove, R. (1968). *The struggle for Social Security, 1900–1935.* Cambridge, MA: Harvard University Press.

Lumsden, I. G. (1991). *Homosexuality, society and the state in Mexico.* Toronto, ON: Canadian Gay Archives.

Lundberg, E. O. (1928). *Public aid to mothers with dependent children* (U.S. Children's Bureau Publication No. 162). Washington, DC: Government Printing Office.

Lurie, H. L. (1931). Review of *A changing psychology in social case work*, by Virginia Robinson. *Social Service Review, 5,* 488.

Lurie, H. L. (1932). Spreading relief thin. *Social Service Review, 5,* 223–234.

Lurie, H. L. (1935). The dilemma of the case worker. *Social Work Today, 3,* 13–15.

Lyon, D., & Van Die, M. (Eds.). (2000). *Rethinking church, state, and modernity: Canada between Europe and America.* Toronto, ON: University of Toronto Press.

Macias, A. (1982). *Against all odds: The feminist movement in Mexico to 1940.* Westport, CT: Greenwood.

MacLachlan, C. M., & Rodríguez O., J. E. (1980). *The forging of the cosmic race: A reinterpretation of colonial Mexico.* Berkeley: University of California Press.

MacLeod, G. (1986). *New age business: Community corporations that work.* Ottawa, ON: Canadian Council on Social Development.

MacMahon, A. W., Millett, J. D., & Ogden, G. (1941). *The administration of federal work relief.* Chicago: Public Administration Service.

Magat, R. (Ed.). (1989). *An agile servant: Community leadership by community foundations.* New York: Foundation Center.

Maines, J. (1953). Through the years. *Social Worker, 22*(2), 3–10.

Maines, J. (1959). Through the years in the CASW. *Social Worker, 27*(4), 5–45.

Mancall, R. (1995). *Deadly medicine.* Ithaca, NY: Cornell University Press.

Mann, H. (1851). *Slavery: Letters and speeches.* Boston: B. B. Mussey.

Manzer, R. (1994). *Public schools & political ideas: Canadian educational policy in historical perspective.* Toronto, ON: University of Toronto Press.

Marmor, T. R. (1987). Entrepreneurship in public management: Wilbur Cohen and Robert Ball. In J. W. Doig & E. C. Hargrove (Eds.), *Leadership and innovation.* Baltimore, MD, and London: Johns Hopkins University Press.

Marsh, L. C. (1975). *Report on Social Security for Canada.* Toronto: University of Toronto Press. (Original work published 1943)

Marshall, D. B. (1992). *Secularizing the faith: Canadian Protestant clergy and the crisis of belief, 1850–1940.* Toronto, ON: University of Toronto Press.

Martin, E., & Martin, J. (1985). *Helping tradition in the Black family and community.* Silver Spring, MD: NASW Press.

Martin, G. W. (1976). *Madam secretary, Frances Perkins.* Boston: Houghton Mifflin.

Martin, R. (1994). The Canadian Charter of Rights and Freedoms is antidemocratic and un-Canadian. In M. Charleton & P. Barker (Eds.), *Crosscurrents: Contemporary political issues* (2nd ed., p. 105). Scarborough, ON: Nelson.

Martínez Dominguez, G. (1950). *Intentos de control de precios en México.* Mexico City: Secretaría de Educación Pública.

Martinson, R. (1975). *The effectiveness of correctional treatment: A survey of treatment evaluation studies.* New York: Praeger.

Masters, D. C. (1947). *The rise of Toronto, 1850–1890.* Toronto, ON: University of Toronto Press.

Maurutto, P. (2003). *Governing charities: Church and state in Toronto's Catholic archdiocese, 1850–1950.* Montreal, QC, and Kingston, ON: McGill-Queen's University Press.

McCallum, M. E. (1990). Corporate welfarism in Canada, 1919–39. *Canadian Historical Review, 71,* 46–79.

McClellan, B. E. (2002). *Moral education in America: Schools and the shaping of character since colonial times.* New York: Teachers College Press.

McCullagh, J. (2002). *A legacy of caring: A history of the Children's Aid Society of Toronto.* Toronto, ON: Dundurn.

McFarlane, P. (1993). *Brotherhood to nationhood: George Manuel and the making of the modern Indian movement.* Toronto, ON: Between the Lines.

McGilly, F. (1998). *An introduction to Canada's public social services.* Don Mills, ON: Oxford University Press.

McJimsey, G. (1987). *Harry Hopkins: Ally of the poor, defender of democracy.* Cambridge, MA: Harvard University Press.

McKay, I., & Jackson, L. (Eds.). (1996). *For a working-class culture in Canada: A selection of Colin McKay's writings on sociology and political economy, 1897–1939.* St. John's, NL: Canadian Committee on Labour History.

McLean, F. (1901). Effects upon private charity of the absence of all public relief. *Proceedings of the 28th National Conference of Charities and Correction, 28,* 139–146.

McRoy, R., Oglesby, Z., & Grape, H. (1997). Achieving same-race adoptive placements for African American children: Culturally sensitive practice approaches. *Child Welfare, 76,* 85–104.

McShane, M. D., & Williams, F. P., III. (Eds.). (2003). *Encyclopedia of juvenile justice.* Thousand Oaks, CA: Sage.

Mechanic, D. (1999). *Mental health and social policy: The emergence of managed care.* Boston: Allyn & Bacon.

Medina-Mora, M. E. (2000). Abuso de sustancias. In DIF-DF & UNICEF (Eds.), *Estudio de niñas, niños y jóvenes trabajadores en el Distrito Federal* (pp. 119–137).

Medina-Mora, M. E., Cravioto, P., Villatoro, J., Fleiz, C., Galván-Castillo, F., & Tapia-Conyer, R. (1998). Consumo de drogas entre adolescentes: Resultados de la Encuesta Nacional de Adicciones. In *Salud del Adolescente* [Special issue]. *Salud Pública de México, 45*(Suppl. 1), 16–25.

Melnick, R. S. (1994). *Between the lines: Interpreting welfare rights.* Washington, DC: Brookings Institution Press.

Mendieta, G. de. (1993). *Historia eclesiastica indiana: Obra escrita a fines del siglo XVI* (4th ed.). Mexico City: Editorial Porrua.

Mendiolea, G. F. (1957). *Historia del Congreso Constituyenente de 1916–1917.* Mexico City.

Meneses Morales, E. (1988). *Tendencias educativas oficiales en México, 1934–1964.* Mexico City: Centro de Estudios Educativos and Universidad Iberoamericana.

Mennel, R. M. (1973). *Thorns and thistles: Juvenile delinquents in the United States, 1825–1940.* Hanover, NH: University Press of New England.

Mennel, R. M., & Spackman, S. (1983). Origins of welfare in the states: Albert G. Byers and the Ohio Board of State Charities. *Ohio History, 92,* 72–95.

Mensah, J. (2002). *Black Canadians: History, experience and social conditions.* Halifax, NS: Fernwood.

Mesa-Lago, C. (1978). *Social Security in Latin America: Pressure groups, stratification, and inequality.* Pittsburgh, PA: University of Pittsburgh Press.

Mesbur, E. S. (2002). Social group work practice: The Canadian experience. In F. J. Turner (Ed.), *Social work practice: A Canadian perspective* (pp. 282–300). Toronto, ON: Pearson Education Canada.

Middlebrook, K. (Ed.). (1991). *Unions, workers and the state in Mexico.* La Jolla: University of California, San Diego, Center for U.S.-Mexican Studies.

Middlebrook, K. (1995). *The paradox of revolution: Labor, the state and authoritarianism in Mexico.* Baltimore, MD: Johns Hopkins University Press.

Middlebrook, K., & Zepeda, E. (Eds.). (2004). *Confronting development: Assessing Mexico's economic and social policy challenges.* Stanford. CA: Stanford University Press.

Midgley, J. (1997). *Social welfare in global context.* Thousand Oaks, CA, and London: Sage.

Miller, J. C. (1913). *Rural schools in Canada.* New York: Teachers College Press.

Miller, J. G. (1996). *Search and destroy: African-American males in the criminal justice system.* New York: Cambridge University Press.

Miller, J. R. (1996). *Shingwauk's vision: Canada's Native residential schools.* Toronto, ON: University of Toronto Press.

Miller, J. R. (1997). *Canada and the aboriginal peoples, 1867–1927.* Ottawa, ON: Canadian History Association.

Miller, J. R. (2004). *Lethal legacy: Current Native controversies in Canada.* Toronto, ON: McClelland & Stewart.

Milloy, J. S. (1999). *A national crime: The Canadian government and the residential school system, 1879 to 1986.* Winnipeg: University of Manitoba Press.

Minister of Public Works and Government Services. (1998). *Canada's drug strategy.* Ottawa, ON: Author.

Mink, G., & Solinger, R. (Eds.). (2003). *Welfare: A documentary history of U.S. policy and politics.* New York: New York University Press.

Minville, E. (1939). *La législation ouvrière et le régime social dans la province de Québec.* Ottawa, ON: J.-O. Patenaude.

Minville, E. (1939). *Labor legislation and the social regime in the province of Quebec* (Annex to the Report of the Royal Commission on Dominion-Provincial Relations). Ottawa, ON: J.-O. Patenaude, Printer to the King.

Mishel, L., & Walters, M. (2003, August). *How unions help all workers* (Economic Policy Institute Briefing Paper No. 143 [On-line]). Available: www.epinet.org

Moffatt, K. (2001). *A poetics of social work: Personal agency and social transformation in Canada, 1920–1939.* Toronto, ON: University of Toronto Press.

Mogrovejo, N. (2000). *Un amor que se atrevió a decir su nombre: La lucha de las lesbianas y su relación con los movimientos homosexual y feminista en América Latina.* Mexico City: Centro de Documentación y Archivo Histórico Lésbico.

Moley, R. (1939). *After seven years.* New York: Harper & Row.

Mongeau, S. (1967). *L'evolution de l'assistance au Quebec.* Montreal, QC: Montréal Éditions du Jour.

Monkkonen, E. H. (1991). *Crime and justice in American history* (Vols. 1–2). Westport, CT: Meckler.

Monsiváis, C. (1998). El mundo soslayado. Prologue of S. Novo, *La estatua de sal.* Mexico City: Consejo Nacional de Cultura.

Montes de Oca, V., & Gomes, C. (2003). *Envejecimiento y políticas públicas para adultos mayores: México y Iberoamerica ante un nuevo siglo.* Mexico City: Universidad Nacional Autónoma de México, Coordinación de Humanidades, Instituto de Investigaciones Sociales.

Montes de Oca, V., & Gomez, C. (Eds.). (in press). *Envejecimiento demográfico y políticas públicas para personas adultas mayores: México en Iberoamérica ante el nuevo siglo.* Mexico City: Universidad Nacional Autónoma de México, Coordinación de Humanidades, Instituto de Investigaciones Sociales.

Morales Camarena, F. J. (2004). *Volunteerism in Mexico.* ServiceLeader.org: International [On-line]. Available: www.serviceleader.org/new/international/articles

Morales-Gomez, D., & Torres, C. A. (1990). *The state, corporatist politics, and educational policy making in Mexico.* New York: Praeger.

Moreau, M. J. (1979). A structural approach to social work practice. *Canadian Journal of Social* Work *Education, 5,* 78–93.

Moreau, M. J. (with Leonard, L.). (1989). *Empowerment through a structural approach to social work.* Montreal, QC, and Ottawa, ON: Université de Montréal, Ecole de Service Social; Carleton University, School of Social Work.

Moreau, M. J., Frosst, S., Frayne, G., Hlywa, M., Leonard, L., & Rowell, M. (1993). *Empowerment II: Snapshots of the structural approach in action.* Ottawa, ON: Carleton University, School of Social Work

Moreno, S. R. (1940, September–November). Anexos psiquiátricos en los hospitales generales. *Revista Mexicana de Psiquiatría, Neurología y Medicina Legal, 8,* 75–76.

Mörner, M. (with Sims, H.). (1985). *Adventurers and proletarians: The story of migrants in Latin America.* Pittsburgh, PA: University of Pittsburgh Press.

Morris, M. (2002). *Women, poverty and Canadian public policy in an era of globalization.* Ottawa, ON: Canadian Research Institute for the Advancement of Women.

Morrison, J., & Zabusky, C. F. (1980). *American mosaic: The immigrant experience by those who lived it.* New York: Dutton.

Morton, D. (1998). *Working people: An illustrated history of the Canadian labour movement.* Montreal, QC, and Kingston, ON: McGill-Queen's University Press.

Morton, D., & Wright, G. (1987). *Winning the second battle: Canadian veterans and the return to civilian life, 1915–1930.* Toronto, ON: University of Toronto Press.

Moscovitch, A., & Albert, J. (1987). *The "benevolent" state: The growth of welfare in Canada.* Toronto, ON: Garamond.

Moser, C. (1996). *Confronting crisis: A comparative study of household responses to poverty and vulnerability in four poor urban communities* (Environmentally Sustainable Development Studies and Monographs Series No. 8). Washington, DC: World Bank.

Moynihan, D. P. (Ed.). (1969). *On understanding poverty: Perspectives from the social sciences.* New York: Basic Books.

Moynihan, D. P. (1973). *The politics of a guaranteed income.* New York: Random House.

Mullaly, B. (2002). *Challenging oppression: A critical social work approach.* Don Mills, ON: Oxford University Press.

Mullaly, R. (1993). *Structural social work: Ideology, theory and practice.* Toronto, ON: McClelland & Stewart.

Muncy, R. (1991). *Creating a female dominion in American reform, 1890–1935.* New York: Oxford University Press.

Muriel, J. (1956). *Hospitales en la Nueva Espana.* Mexico City: Universidad Nacional Autónoma de México, Instituto de Investigaciones Historicas.

Murray, C. (1984). *Losing ground: American social policy, 1950–1980.* New York: Basic Books.

Musto, D. F. (2002). *Drugs in America: A documentary history.* New York: New York University Press.

Myers, R. J. (1975). *Social Security.* Bryn Mawr, PA: McCahan Foundation.

Myrick-Harris, C. (2002, July). Against all odds. *Smithsonian, 33,* 70–77.

Narváez, G. C. (1966). Hospitales psiquiátricos de México: Desde la colonia hasta la actualidad. *Revista Mexicana de Neurología y Psiquiatría, 7*(3).

National Advisory Commission on Criminal Justice Standards and Goals. (1976). *Report of the Task Force on Juvenile Justice and Delinquency Prevention.* Washington, DC: Government Printing Office.

National Alliance to End Homelessness. (1998). *The ten year plan to end homelessness.* Washington, DC: Author. Available: www.endhomelessness.org/pub/tenyear/

National Clearinghouse on Family Violence [On-line]. Available: www.hc-sc.gc.ca/nc-cn

National Conference on Social Welfare [and its predecessors]. (1872-1982). Proceedings. Available at www.hti.umich.edu/n/nocsw/

National Conference on Social Welfare. (1985). *The report of the Committee on Economic Security of 1935* and other basic documents relating to the development of the Social Security Act. Washington, DC: Author. Available: www.ssa.gov/history/reports/ces/ces5.html

National Council of Women of Canada. (1894). *Yearbook.* Ottawa, ON: Author. Available: www.ncwc.ca

National Employment Commission. (1937). *Report on phases of employment conditions in Canadian industry.* Ottawa, ON: Author.

National Farmers' Union. (1969). NFU statement of purpose. Available: www.nfu.ca/misc_files/NFU_Statement_of_Purpose.pdf

National Task Force on the Definition and Measurement of Poverty in Canada. (1984). *Not enough: The meaning and measurement of poverty in Canada.* Ottawa, ON: Canadian Council on Social Development.

Naylor, D. C. (1986). *Private practice, public payment: Canadian medicine and the politics of health insurance, 1911–1966.* Montreal, QC, and Kingston, ON: McGill-Queen's University Press.

Neary, P., & Granatstein. J. L. (Eds.). (1998). *The Veterans Charter and post World War II in Canada.* Montreal, QC, and Kingston, ON: McGill-Queen's University Press.

Nesbitt, F. (1923). *Standards of public aid to children in their own homes* (U.S. Children's Bureau Publication No. 118). Washington, DC: Government Printing Office.

Niemeyer, E. V., Jr. (1974). *Revolution at Querétaro: The Mexican Constitutional Convention of 1916–1917.* Austin: University of Texas Press.

Nixon, R. M. (1969, July 14). Special message to the Congress on control of narcotics and dangerous drugs. In *Public papers of the presidents: Richard M. Nixon* (pp. 513–518). Washington, DC: Government Printing Office. Available: www.nixonfoundation.org/Research_Center/PublicPapers.cfm

Noble, C. (1997). *Welfare as we knew it.* New York: Oxford University Press.

Nord, M., Andrews, M., & Carlson, S. (2002, October). *Household food security in the United States, 2001* (Food Assistance and Nutrition Research Report No. FANRR29). Washington, DC: U.S. Department of Agriculture, Economic Research Service. Available: www.ers.usda.gov/publications/fanrr29/

Norrie, K., Owram, D., & Emery, J. C. H. (2002). *A history of the Canadian economy* (3rd ed.). Scarborough, ON: Nelson Thomson Learning.

Novo, S. (1979). Memoir. In W. Leyland (Ed.), *Now the volcano: An anthology of Latin American gay literature* (pp. 11–47). San Francisco: Gay Sunshine Press.

O'Connor, S. (2001). *Orphan trains: The story of Charles Loring Brace and the children he saved and failed.* New York: Houghton Mifflin.

O'Gorman, F. (1973). *Edmund Burke: His political philosophy.* London: Allen & Unwin.

Observatorio Ciudadano de la Educación [On-line]. Available: www.observatorio.org/

Ochoa, E. C. (2000). *Feeding Mexico: The political uses of food since 1910.* Wilmington, DE: Scholarly Resources.

Ochoa, E. C. (2001). Coercion, reform and the welfare state: The campaign against begging in Mexico City during the 1930s. *The Americas. 58*(1), 39–64.

Oficina de Representación Para la Promoción e Integración Social Para Personas con Discapacidad. (2003). Ley federal para personas con discapacidad. *Boletín de la Oficina de Representación Para la Promoción e Integración Social Para*

Personas con Discapacidad, 2(6). Available: www.disca pacidad.presidencia.gob.mx

Oliver, J. W. (1917). History of Civil War military pensions, 1861–1885. *Bulletin of the University of Wisconsin*, History Series, *4*(1).

Ontario, Department of Labour. (1929). *Survey of industrial welfare in Ontario.* Toronto, ON: Author.

Organization of American States. (1994). *Inter-American Convention on the Prevention, Punishment, and Eradication of Violence against Women, "Convention of Belém Do Pará"* [On-line]. Available: www.oas.org/main/main.asp? sLang=E&sLink=http://www.oas.org/documents/eng/ documents.asp

Oriol, W. E. (2002, January/February). Olmstead decision brings major shift in disability care. *Aging Today 23*(1). Available: www.agingtoday.org/home/archives.cfm

Orlebeke, C. J. (n.d.). The evolution of low-income housing policy, 1949–1999. *Housing Policy Debate, 11*(2), 489–520.

Ormsby, R. (1969). *A man of vision: Francis H. McLean, 1869–1945.* New York: Family Service Association of America.

Orshansky, M. (1965). Counting the poor: Another look at poverty profile. *Social Security Bulletin, 28,* 3–29.

Ostrey, A. (2001). The roots of North America's first comprehensive public health insurance system. *Hygiea Internationalis, 2,* 25–44.

Packer, G. (1968). *Introduction to criminal law* (3rd ed.). Toronto, ON: Methuen.

Palmer, B. D. (1992). *Working–class experience: Rethinking the history of Canadian labour*, 1800–1991. Toronto, ON: McClelland & Stewart.

Parsons, T. (1951). *The social system.* Glencoe, IL: Free Press.

Partido Nacional Revolucionario. (1934). *Plan sexenal del P.N.R.* Mexico City: Author.

Penner, N. (Ed.). (1973). *Winnipeg 1919: The strikers' own history of the Winnipeg General Strike.* Toronto, ON: Lorimer.

Perkins, F. (1946). *The Roosevelt I knew.* New York: Viking.

Perry, J. H. (1989). *A fiscal history of Canada: The postwar years* (Canadian Tax Paper No. 85). Toronto, ON: Canadian Tax Foundation.

Peters, E. D. (2000). *Polarizing Mexico: The impact of liberalization strategy.* Boulder, CO: Lynne Rienner.

Peterson, P. (1995). *The price of federalism.* Washington, DC: Brookings Institution Press.

Pezzoli, K. (1998). *Human settlements and planning for ecological sustainability: The case of Mexico City.* Cambridge: MIT Press.

Pickersgill, J. (1960). *The Mackenzie King record.* Toronto, ON: University of Toronto Press.

Pifer, A., & Chisman, F. (Eds.). (1985). *The report of the Committee of Economic Security of 1935.* Washington, DC: National Conference on Social Welfare.

Pilcher, J. M. (1998). *¡Qué vivàn los tamales! Food and the making of Mexican identity.* Albuquerque: University of New Mexico Press.

Pitsula, J. (1979, Spring). The emergence of social work in Toronto. *Journal of Canadian Studies, 14*(1), 35–42.

Piven, F. F., & Cloward, R. (1971). *Regulating the poor: The functions of public welfare.* New York: Pantheon.

Piven, F. F., & Cloward, R. A. (1977). *Poor people's movements: Why they succeed, how they fail.* New York: Pantheon.

Pla, D., Zárate, G., Palma, M., Gómez, J., Cardiel, R., & Salazar, D. (1994). *Extranjeros en México (1821–1990)* [Bibliography]. Mexico City: Instituto Nacional de Antropología e Historia.

Platt, A. M. (1977). *The child savers: The invention of delinquency* (2nd ed., enl.). Chicago: University of Chicago Press.

Platt, A. M. (1991). *E. Franklin Frazier reconsidered.* New Brunswick, NJ: Rutgers University Press.

Platt, A., & Chandler, S. (1988). Constant struggle: E. Franklin Frazier and the African-American tradition in social work. *Social Work, 33,* 293–297.

Pleck, E. (1987). *Domestic tyranny: The making of social policy against family violence from colonial times to the present.* New York: Oxford University Press.

Poppendieck, J. (1986). *Breadlines knee-deep in wheat: Food assistance in the Great Depression.* New Brunswick, NJ: Rutgers University Press.

Portes, A., & Sassen, S. (1987). Making it underground: Comparative material on the informal sector in Western market economies. *American Journal of Sociology, 93,* 30–61.

Portes, A., Castells, M., & Benton, L. A. (Eds.). (1989). *The informal economy: Studies in advanced and less developed countries.* Baltimore, MD: Johns Hopkins University Press.

Poulin, G. (1955). *L'assistance sociale dans la province de Québec, 1608–1951* (Memoir). Quebec: Commission royale d'enquête sur les problèmes constitutionnels.

Poverty in Canada: Report of the Special Senate Committee. (1971). Ottawa, ON: Information Canada.

Powers, M. E. (1979). *The pattern of emergence of social services in housing programs.* Unpublished doctoral dissertation, Brandeis University.

President's Commission on Law Enforcement and the Administration of Justice. (1967). *The challenge of crime in a free society.* Washington, DC: Government Printing Office.

Prieur, A. (1998). *Mema's house, Mexico City: On transvestites, queens, and machos.* Chicago: University of Chicago Press.

Programa Nacional de Atención a las Personas con Discapacidad. Available: www.discapacidad.presidencia.gob.mx

Proulx, J., & Perrault, S. (Eds.). (2000). *No place for violence: Canadian aboriginal alternatives.* Halifax, NS: Fernwood.

Province of Quebec, Comité d'Étude sur l'Assistance Publique. (1963). *Report of the Study Committee on Public Assistance.* Montreal, QC: Author.

Provincial Committee on Aims and Objectives of Education in the Schools of Ontario. (1968). *Living and learning* [Hall-Dennis Report]. Toronto: Ontario Department of Education.

Prucha, F. P. (1984). *The great father: The United States government and the American Indian.* Lincoln and London: University of Nebraska Press.

Public Works Administration. (1939). *America builds: The record of the PWA.* Washington, DC: Government Printing Office.

Puttee, A. (Ed.). (2002). *Federalism, democracy and disability policy in Canada.* Montreal, QC, and Kingston, ON: McGill-Queen's University Press.

Quarles, B. (1969). *The Negro in the making of America.* New York: Collier.

Rakowski, C. A. (Ed.). (1994). *Contrapunto: The informal sector debate in Latin America.* Albany: State University of New York Press.

Ramírez de Aguilar, F. (2002, August 14). En la decimal economía del mundo, 53.7% de la población vive en la pobreza. *El Financiero,* p. 44.

Ramírez Solórzano, M. A. (2002). *Hombres violentos. Un estudio antropológico de la violencia masculina.* Mexico City: Plaza y Valdés.

Ramirez, J. M., & Regalado, J. (Eds.). (1997). *Los cuatro actores socials: El debate nacional.* Mexico City: Diana Press.

Ramos, S. (1977). *Obras completas.* Mexico City: Universidad Nacional Autónoma de México.

Rauschenbusch, W. (1912). *Christianizing the social order.* New York: Macmillan.

Rauschenbusch, W. (1917). *Christianity and the social crisis.* New York: Macmillan.

Rawls, J. (1999). *A theory of justice* (Rev. ed.). Cambridge, MA: Harvard University Press, Belknap Press.

Rayback, J. G. (1966). *A history of American labor.* New York: Free Press.

Rayside, D. (1998). *On the fringe: Gays and lesbians in politics.* Ithaca, NY: Cornell University Press.

Reed, U. (1994). *Postwar immigrant America: A social history.* New York: St. Martin's.

Reid, J. G. (1984). Health, education, economy: Philanthropic foundations in the Atlantic region in the 1920s and 1930s. *Acadiensis, 14*(1), 64–83.

Reisch, M., & Andrews, J. (2001). *The road not taken: A history of radical social work in the United States.* Philadelphia: Brunner-Routledge.

Rello, F. (1986). *El campo en la encrucijada nacional.* Mexico City: Secretaría de Educación Pública.

Renzetti, C. M., Edelson, J. L., & Kennedy Bergen, R. (Eds.). (2001). *Sourcebook on violence against women.* Thousand Oaks, CA: Sage.

Report of the superintendent of Indian schools. (1897/98–1903/04). Washington, DC: Government Printing Office.

Research Committee of the League for Social Reconstruction. (1935). *Social planning for Canada.* Toronto, ON: Thomas Nelson.

Revista Anales de Trabajo Social, 1, 72. Mexico City: Escuela Universitaria de Trabajo Social, UM; Escuela Nacional de Trabajo Social, UNAM. (2000).

Reynolds, B. (1951). *Social work and social living: Explorations in philosophy and practice.* New York: Citadel.

Rice, J. J., & Prince, M. J. (2000). *Changing politics of Canadian social policy.* Toronto, ON: University of Toronto Press.

Rich, M. (1956). *A belief in people: A history of family social work.* New York: Family Service Association of America.

Riches, G. (Ed.). (1997). *First world hunger: Food security and welfare politics.* New York: St. Martin's.

Richmond, M. (1917). *Social diagnosis.* New York: Russell Sage.

Richmond, M. (1922). *What is social case work?* New York: Russell Sage.

Riis, J. (1890). *How the other half lives.* New York: Scribner.

Riis, J. (1971). *How the other half lives: Studies among the tenements of New York.* New York: Dover. (Original work published 1890) Available: www.yale.edu/amstud/inforev/riis/title.html

Risse, G. (1987). Medicine in New Spain. In R. L. Numbers (Ed.), *Medicine in the New World: New Spain, New France, and New England* (pp. 12–63). Knoxville: University of Tennessee Press.

Ristock, J. (2002). *No more secrets: Violence in lesbian relationships.* New York: Routledge.

Roberts, J. V. (2000). *Criminal justice in Canada: A reader.* Toronto, ON: Harcourt Brace.

Robinson, A. (1981). *George Meany and his times.* New York: Simon & Schuster.

Rodriguez Cabo, M. (1931). *Estudios sobre la delicuencia e infancia abandonada.* Mexico City: Imp. Compania editora "La Razon."

Rodriguez, C. E. (1997). *Latin looks: Images of Latinas and Latinos in the U.S. media.* Boulder, CO: Westview.

Romanow, R. (2002). *Building on values: The future of health care in Canada.* Ottawa, ON: Commission on the Future of Health Care in Canada. Available: www.hc-sc.gc.ca/english/care/romanow/

Ronfeldt, D. (1973). *Atencingo: The politics of agrarian struggle in a Mexican ejido.* Stanford, CA: Stanford University Press.

Rooke, P. T., & Schnell, R. L. (1983). *Discarding the asylum: From child rescue to the welfare state in English-Canada (1800–1950).* Lanham, MD: University Press of America.

Rooke, P. T., & Schnell, R. L. (1987). *No bleeding heart: Charlotte Whitton, a feminist on the Right.* Vancouver: University of British Columbia Press.

Roosevelt, E. (1948, April). The promise of human rights. *Foreign Affairs, 26,* 470–477.

Rose, N. E. (1995). *Workfare or fair work; Women, welfare, and government work programs.* New Brunswick, NJ: Rutgers University Press.

Rose, R. (1991). Welfare: The public/private mix. In S. B. Kamerman & A. J. Kahn (Eds.), *Privatization and the welfare state* (pp. 73–95). Princeton, NJ: Princeton University Press.

Rosenberg, C. E. (1997). Science, society, and social thought [Introduction]. In C. E. Rosenberg (Ed.), *No other gods:*

On science and American social thought (2nd ed., rev. and enl.; pp. 1–21). Baltimore, MD: Johns Hopkins University Press.

Rosenberg, C. S. (1971). *Religion and the rise of the American city: The New York City mission movement, 1812–1870.* Ithaca, NY: Cornell University Press.

Ross, D. P., Scott, K. J., & Smith, P. J. (2001). *The Canadian fact book on poverty—2000.* Ottawa, ON: Canadian Council on Social Development.

Ross, E. (Ed.). (1978). *Black heritage in social welfare, 1860–1930.* Metuchen, NJ: Scarecrow.

Ross, M. (1951). *The YMCA in Canada.* Toronto, ON: Ryerson.

Royal Commission on Health Services report. (1963). Ottawa, ON: Queen's Printer. (Original work published 1930)

Rubinow, I. M. (1934). *The quest for Social Security.* New York: Arno.

Ruiz, L. (1903). *Cartilla de Higiene. Profilaxis de las enfermedades transmisibles para la enseñanza primaria.* Paris: Viuda de Charles Bouret.

Ruiz, L. (1904). *Tratado elemental de higiene.* Mexico City: Oficina Tipográfica de la Secretaría de Fomento.

Ruiz, R. E. (1963). *Mexico: The challenge of poverty and illiteracy.* San Marino, CA: Huntington Library.

Ruíz, R. E. (1992). *Triumphs and tragedy: A history of the Mexican people.* New York: Norton.

Salamon, L. M. (Ed.). (2002). *The state of nonprofit America.* Washington, DC: Brookings Institution Press.

Sánchez, G. I. (1936). *Mexico: A revolution by education.* New York: Viking.

Sanderson, S. E. (1981). *Agrarian populism and the Mexican state.* Berkeley: University of California Press.

Sanger, M. (1920). *Women and the new race.* New York: Truth Publishing.

Sanger, M. (1969). *My fight for birth control.* New York: Maxwell Reprint. (Original work published 1931)

Sanger, M. (1971). *Margaret Sanger: An autobiography.* New York: Dover. (Original work published 1938)

Sarlo, C. A. (1996). *Poverty in Canada.* Vancouver, BC: Fraser Institute.

Schaler, J. (2000). *Addiction is a choice.* Chicago: Open Court.

Schell, P. (1999, Winter). An honorable avocation for ladies: The work of the Mexico City Union de Damas Catolicas Mexicanas, 1912–1926. *Journal of Women's History, 10*(4), 78.

Scherlock, P. L. (Ed.). (2003). *Aging, development and social protection.* Thousand Oaks, CA: Sage.

Schlesinger, A. M., Jr. (1957–1960). *The age of Roosevelt* (Vols. 1–3). Boston: Houghton Mifflin.

Schmalleger, F., MacAlister, D., McKenna, P., & Winterdyk, J. (2000). *Canadian criminal justice today: An introductory text for the twenty-first century.* Toronto, ON: Pearson Education Canada.

Schneider, D. M. (1938). *The history of public welfare in New York State, 1609–1866.* Chicago: University of Chicago Press.

Schwartz, B. F. (1984). *The Civil Works Administration, 1933–1934: The business of emergency employment in the New Deal.* Princeton, NJ: Princeton University Press.

Scotch, R. K. (1989). *From good will to civil rights.* Philadelphia: Temple University Press.

Scott, F. R. (1972). Labour learns the truth. In J. L. Granatstein & P. Stevens (Eds.), *Forum: Canadian life and letters, 1920–70: Selections from the* Canadian Forum (pp. 234–236). Toronto, ON: University of Toronto Press. (Original work published 1946)

Sealander, J. (1997). *Private wealth and public life: Foundation philanthropy and the reshaping of American social policy from the Progressive Era to the New Deal.* Baltimore, MD: Johns Hopkins University Press.

Secretaría de Asistencia Pública. (1940). *La asistencia social en México: Sexenio 1934–1940.* Mexico City: Author.

Secretaría de Desarrollo Social, Secretaría de Educación Pública, Secretaría de Salud. (2002). *Un México apropiado para la infancia y adolescencia: Programa de acción, 2002–2010.* Mexico City: Author.

Secretaría de Educación Pública [On-line]. Available: www.sep .gob.mx

Secretaría de Salud. (1993). *La atención materno infantil: Apuntes para su historia.* Mexico City: Author.

Selmi, P., & Hunter, R. (2001). Beyond the rank and file movement: Mary van Kleeck and social work radicalism in the Great Depression, 1931–1942. *Journal of Sociology and Social Welfare, 28,* 75–100.

Semo, E. (1993). *The history of capitalism in Mexico: Its origins, 1521–1763.* Austin: University of Texas Press.

Sen, A. (1997). *Resources, values and development.* Cambridge, MA: Harvard University Press.

Shaw, R. L. (1957). *Proud heritage.* Toronto, ON: Ryerson.

Shookner, M. (1998, November 4). *90 years of social action.* Speech given at the 90th anniversary celebration of the Ontario Social Development Council, November 4, 1998, Toronto, ON. Available: www.osdc.org/90yr.html

Shortt, S. E. D. (1986). *Victorian Lunacy: Richard M. Bucke and the practice of late nineteenth-century psychiatry.* Cambridge, UK: Cambridge University Press.

Shragge, E. (Ed.). (1997). *Community Economic Development: In search of empowerment* (2nd ed.). Montreal, QC: Black Rose.

Sicherman, B. (1984). *Alice Hamilton: A life in letters.* Cambridge, MA: Harvard University Press.

Sicherman, B., & Green, C. H. (Eds.). (1980). *Notable American women, The modern period: A biographical dictionary.* Cambridge, MA: Harvard University Press, Belknap Press.

Siembieda, W. J., & Moreno, E. L. (1999). From commercial banking systems to non-commercial banking systems in Mexico. In K. Datta & G. A. Jones (Eds.), *Housing and finance in developing countries* (pp. 75–88). London: Routledge.

Silva, M. (1917). *Higiene popular. Colección de conocimientos y consejos indispensables para evitar las enfermedades y prolongar la vida, arreglado para uso de las familias.* Mexico City: Departamento de Talleres Gráficos.

Silver, A. I. (1997). *The French-Canadian idea of Confederation, 1864–1900* (2nd ed.). Toronto, ON: University of Toronto Press.

Simkhovitch, M. K. (1926). *The settlement primer.* Boston: National Federation of Settlements.

Simmons, H. G. (1989). *Unbalanced mental health policy in Ontario, 1930–1989.* Toronto, ON: Wall and Thompson.

Simpson, E. N. (1937). *The ejido: Mexico's way out.* Chapel Hill: University of North Carolina Press.

Sinclair, U. (1906). *The jungle.* New York: Jungle Publishing.

Sissons, C. B. (1917). *Bi-lingual schools in Canada.* Toronto, ON: J. M. Dent & Sons.

Siurob, J. (1936, December). La sanidad en México. *Boletín de la Oficina Sanitaria Panamericana, 15*(12), 1148–1153.

Skocpol, T. (1988). *The politics of social policy in the United States.* Princeton, NJ: Princeton University Press.

Skocpol, T. (1992). *Protecting soldiers and mothers: The political origins of social policy in the United States.* Cambridge, MA: Harvard University Press, Belknap Press.

Smart, R., & Ogborne, A. (1996). *Northern spirits: A social history of alcohol in Canada.* Toronto, ON: Addiction Research Foundation.

Smith, A. (1991). *The wealth of nations.* New York: Everyman's Library. (Original work, *An Inquiry Into the Nature and Causes of the Wealth of Nations,* published 1776)

Smith, M. (1999). *Lesbian and gay rights in Canada: Social movements and equality-seeking, 1971–1995.* Toronto, ON: University of Toronto Press.

Smith, S. R., & Lipsky, M. (1993). *Nonprofits for hire: The welfare state in the age of contracting.* Cambridge, MA: Harvard University Press.

Smith, T. L. (1958). *Revivalism and social reform in mid-nineteenth-century America.* New York: Abingdon.

Snell, J. G. (1996). *The citizen's wage: The state and the elderly in Canada, 1919–1951.* Toronto, ON: University of Toronto Press.

Snyder, R., & Torres, G. (Eds.). (1998). *The future role of the* ejido *in rural Mexico.* La Jolla: University of California, San Diego, Center for U.S.-Mexican Studies.

Social Insurance and Allied Services. (1942). Beveridge Report. New York: Macmillan.

Social Security Administration. Available: www.ssa.gov

Social Service Council of Canada. (1914). *Proceedings of the Social Service Congress of 1914.* Ottawa, ON: Author.

Soederberg, S. (2001). From neoliberalism to social liberalism: Situating the National Solidarity Program within Mexico's passive revolutions. *Latin American Perspectives, 28*(3), 104–123.

Solis, F. (2001). El uso de los alucinógenos en el México prehispánico y colonial. In J. Bali (Ed.), *La drogadicción en México, indiferencia o prevención* [Special issue]. *México Desconocido,* 33–42.

Solomon, B. B. (1976). *Black empowerment: Social work in oppressed communities.* New York: Columbia University Press.

Solórzano Ramos, A. (1997). *¿Fiebre dorada o fiebre amarilla? La Fundación Rockefeller en México, 1911–1924.* Guadalajara, Mexico: Universidad de Guadalajara.

Soss, J., Schram, S., & Vartanian, T. (2001). Setting the terms of relief: Explaining state policy choices in the devolution revolution. *American Journal of Political Science, 45,* 378–395.

Sowell, T. S. (1995). *The vision of the anointed: Self-congratulation as a basis for social policy.* New York: Basic Books.

Spano, R. (1982). *The rank and file movement in social work.* Lanham, MD: University Press of America.

Specht, H., & Courtney, M. (1994). *Unfaithful angels: How social work has abandoned its mission.* New York: Free Press.

Speisman, S. (1973). Munificent parsons and municipal parsimony: Voluntary vs. public relief in nineteenth century Toronto. *Ontario History, 65,* 33–50.

Speisman, S. A. (1979). *The Jews of Toronto: A history to 1937.* Toronto, ON: McClelland & Stewart.

Spencer, R. (1919). *Prohibition in Canada.* Toronto, ON: Dominion Alliance.

Splane, R. (1965). *Social welfare in Ontario 1791–1893.* Toronto, ON: University of Toronto Press.

Splane, R. B. (1996). *75 years of community service to Canada: Canadian Council on Social Development, 1920–1995.* Ottawa, ON: Canadian Council on Social Development.

Splane, R. B. (2003). *George Davidson: Social policy and public policy exemplar.* Ottawa, ON: Canadian Council on Social Development.

Spring, J. (2000). *The American school 1642–2000.* New York: McGraw-Hill.

Stanley, T. J. (2000). Why I killed Canadian history: Towards an anti-racist history in Canada. *Histoire Sociale/Social History, 33*(65), 79–103.

Starr, P. (1982). *The social transformation of American medicine.* New York: Basic Books.

Statistics Canada. (2004, April 4). *2001 Census of Canada* [Online]. Available: www.statcan.ca/

Steinberg, S. (2001). Race relations: The problem with the wrong name. *New Politics, 8, 2*(30), 57–61.

Steiner, G. (1966). *Social insecurity: The politics of welfare.* Chicago: Rand McNally.

Stephen, L. (2002). *Zapata lives! Histories and cultural politics in southern Mexico.* Berkeley: University of California Press.

Stern, A. M. (1999). Responsible mothers and normal children: Eugenics, nationalism and welfare in post-revolutionary Mexico, 1920–1940. *Journal of Historical Sociology, 12*(4), 369–397.

Stevens, R. (1998). *American medicine and the public interest: A history of specialization.* Berkeley: University of California Press.

Stevens, S. J., & Morral, A. R. (Eds.). (2002). *Adolescent substance abuse treatment in the United States: Exemplary models from a national evaluation study.* New York: Haworth.

Stewart, W. R. (1974). *The philanthropic work of Josephine Shaw Lowell.* Montclair, NJ: Patterson Smith. (Original work published 1911)

Stoner, M. R. (2002). The globalization of urban homelessness. In M. J. Dear (Ed.), *From Chicago to L.A.* Thousand Oaks, CA: Sage.

Struthers, J. (1987). "Lord give us men": Women and social work in English Canada, 1918–1953. In A. Moscovitch & J. Albert (Eds.), *The benevolent state: The growth of welfare in Canada* (pp. 111–125). Toronto, ON: Garamond.

Struthers, J. (1994). *The limits of affluence: Welfare in Ontario, 1920–1970.* Toronto, ON: University of Toronto Press.

Suárez, L. (1984). *Lucio Cabañas. El guerrillero sin esperanza.* Mexico City: Grijalbo.

Suárez-Toriello, J. E. (1989). Análisis de 800 casos de farmacodependencia a heroína. *Heroína, 2*(1), 123–137.

Sullivan, N., & Mesbur, E. S. (in press). Groupwork practice. In F. J. Turner (Ed.), *Canadian encyclopedia of social work.* Waterloo, ON: Wilfrid Laurier University Press.

Summerfield, P. (1998). *Reconstructing women's lives: Discourse and subjectivity in oral histories of the Second World War.* Manchester, NH: Manchester University Press.

Surrey, S. S. (1973). *Pathways to tax reform: The concept of tax expenditures.* Cambridge, MA: Harvard University Press.

Surrey, S. S., & McDaniel, P. R. (1985). *Tax expenditures.* Cambridge, MA: Harvard University Press.

Sussman, S. (1998). The first asylums in Canada: A response to neglectful community care and current themes. *Canadian Journal of Psychiatry, 43,* 260–264.

Sutherland, N. (1976). *Children in English Canadian society.* Toronto, ON: University of Toronto Press.

Swanson, J. (2001). *Poor bashing: The politics of exclusion.* Toronto, ON: Between the Lines.

Swift, K. (1995). An outrage to common decency. *Child Welfare, 74*(1), 71–91.

Swift, L. (1934). *New alignments between public and private agencies in a community family welfare and relief program.* New York: Family Welfare Association of America.

Takaki, R. (1989). *Strangers from a different shore: A history of Asian Americans.* New York: Penguin.

Takaki, R. (1993). *A different mirror: A history of multicultural America.* New York: Oxford University Press.

Takaki, R. (1994). *From different shores: Perspectives on race and ethnicity in America* (2nd ed.). New York: Oxford University Press.

Taylor, C. L. (1978). *El ambiente: Male homosexual social life in Mexico City.* Unpublished doctoral dissertation, University of California, Berkeley.

Taylor, I., Walton, P., & Young, J. (1975). *The new criminology: For a social theory of deviance.* London: Routledge & Kegan Paul.

Teeple, G. (1995). *Globalization and the decline of social reform.* Toronto, ON: Garamond.

Tello Peon, N. (1996, July-September). El Trabajo Social Contemporáneo. *Revista de Trabajo Social ENTS-UNAM, 14,* 15–22.

Tello Peon, N. (Ed., Comp.). (2000). *Trabajo social en algunos países: Aportes para su comprensión.* Mexico City: Universidad Nacional Autónoma de México, Escuela Nacional de Trabajo Social.

Tester, F., & Kulchyski, P. (1994). *Tammarniit: Inuit relocation in the eastern Arctic.* Vancouver: University of British Columbia Press.

The National Low Income Housing Coalition (NLIHC). Available: www.nlihc.org/.

Thériault, J. Y. (1999). *Francophonies minoritaires au Canada.* Moncton, NB: Éditions d'Acadie.

Thomas, L. H. (Ed.). (1982). *The making of a socialist: The recollections of T. C. Douglas.* Edmonton: University of Alberta Press.

Thompson, F., & Dilulio, J., Jr. (Eds.). (1998). *Medicaid and devolution: A view from the states.* Washington, DC: Brookings Institution Press.

Tillotson, S. (1997). Class and community in Canadian welfare work, 1933–1960. *Journal of Canadian Studies, 32*(1), 63–92.

Titzel, M. E. (1919). Building a child welfare program in wartime. *American Journal of Sociology, 24*(4), 411–422.

Tokman, V. E. (Ed.). (1992). *Beyond regulation: The informal economy in Latin America.* Boulder, CO: Lynne Rienner.

Tomes, N. (1984). *A generous confidence: Thomas Story Kirkbride and the art of asylum-keeping, 1840–1883.* New York: Cambridge University Press.

Tone, A. (1997). *The business of benevolence: Industrial paternalism in progressive America.* Ithaca, NY: Cornell University Press.

Torres Falcón, M. (2001). *La violencia en casa.* Mexico City: Croma Paidós.

Torrey, E. F. (1988). *Nowhere to go: The tragic odyssey of the homeless mentally ill.* New York: Harper & Row.

Trabajos especiales del servicio de higiene rural, a cargo del Señor Dr. Henry P. Carr. (1932). *Salubridad, 3*(2), 443–445.

Trattner, W. I. (1999). *From poor law to welfare state: A history of social welfare in America* (6th ed.). New York: Free Press.

Trent, J. W., Jr. (1994). *Inventing the feeble mind: A history of mental retardation in the United States.* Berkeley: University of California Press.

Tresierra, J. C. (1994). Mexico: Indigenous peoples and the nation-state. In D. L. Van Cott (Ed.), *Indigenous peoples and democracy in Latin America* (pp. 187–210). New York: St. Martin's.

Tucker, D. M. (1971, Summer). Miss Ida B. Wells and Memphis lynching. *Phylon, 32,* 112–122.

Tudiver, N. (1987). Forestalling the welfare state: The establishment of programmes of corporate welfare. In A. Moscovitch & J. Albert (Eds.), *The "benevolent state": The growth of welfare in Canada* (pp. 186–202). Toronto, ON: Garamond.

Turnbull, J. G., Williams, C. A., & Cheit, E. F. (1973). *Economic and Social Security* (4th ed.). New York: Ronald Press.

Turner, F. J. (1996). *Social work treatment* (4th ed.). New York: Free Press.

Turner, F. J. (2002). *Social work practice: A Canadian perspective* (2nd ed.). Toronto, ON: Prentice Hall.

U.S. Commissioner of Indian Affairs. (1824–1949). *Annual report(s)*. Washington, DC: Government Printing Office.

U.S. Department of Commerce. (1984). *Federal and state Indian reservations and trust areas*. Washington, DC: Government Printing Office.

U.S. Department of Commerce, Bureau of the Census. (1913). *Benevolent institutions*. Washington, DC: Government Printing Office.

United Electrical, Radio and Machine Workers International. *Mexican Labor News & Analysis* [On-line serial]. Available: www.ueinternational.org

United Nations Division for the Advancement of Women, Department of Economic and Social Affairs. (1979). *Convention on the Elimination of All Forms of Discrimination Against Women* [On-line]. Available: www.un.org/women watch/daw/cedaw/cedaw.htm

United Nations, Office of the High Commissioner for Human Rights. (1959). *Declaration of the rights of the child*. Available: www.unhchr.ch/html/menu3/b/25.htm

United Nations, Office of the High Commissioner for Human Rights. (1989). *Convention on the Rights of the Child* [On-line]. Available:www.unhchr.ch/html/menu3/b/k2crc.htm

Ursel, J. (1992). *Private lives, public policy: 100 years of state intervention in the family*. Toronto, ON: Women's Press.

Urwick, E. J. (1927). *The social good*. London: Methuen.

Urwick, E. J. (1948). *The values of life*. Toronto, ON: University of Toronto Press.

Vaillancourt, Y. (1988). *L'evolution des politiques sociales au Quebec, 1940–1960*. Montreal, QC: Presses de l'Université de Montréal.

Valero Chavez, A. (Ed.). (1994). *El trabajo social en México: Desarrollo y perspectivas*. Mexico City: Universidad Nacional Autónoma de México, Escuela Nacional de Trabajo Social.

Valverde, M. (1991). *The age of light, soap, and water: Moral reform in English Canada, 1885–1925*. Toronto, ON: McClelland & Stewart.

Van Kleeck, M. (1913). *Women in the bookbinding trade*. New York: Russell Sage.

Van Kleeck, M. (1934). Our illusions regarding government. *Proceedings of the National Conference of Social Work, 61*, 473–485.

Van Kleeck, M. (1936). *Creative America*. New York: Covici, Friede.

Van Stolk, M. (1972). *The battered child in Canada*. Toronto, ON: McClelland & Stewart.

Van Wormer, K. (1997), *Alcoholism treatment: A social work perspective*. Chicago: Nelson-Hall.

Van Wormer, K., Wells, J., & Boes, M. (2000). *Social work with lesbians, gays, and bisexuals*. Needham Heights, MA: Allyn & Bacon.

Vasconcelos, J. (1982). *The memoirs of José Vasconcelos: Vol 2. El desastre* in *Memorias*. Mexico City: Fondo de Cultura Económica.

Vaughn, M. K. (1982). *The state, education, and social class in Mexico, 1880–1928*. Dekalb: University of Northern Illinois Press.

Vaughan, M. K. (1996). *Cultural politics in revolution: Teachers, peasants, and schools in Mexico, 1930–1940*. Tucson: University of Arizona Press.

Villafuerte Solis, D., Díaz, S. M., Franco, G. A., del Carmen García Aguilar, M., Rivera Farfán, C., Lisbona Guillén, M., & Morales Bermúdez, J. (1999). *La tierra en Chiapas: Viejos problemas nuevos*. Mexico City: Plaza y Valdés.

Villarespe Reyes, V. O. (2001). *La Solidaridad, Beneficencia y programas: Pasado y presente del tratamiento de la pobreza en México*. Mexico City: Universidad Nacional Autónoma de México.

Villavicencio, J. (2000). La política habitacional en México: ¿Una política con contenido social? In R. Cordera & A. Ziccardi (Eds.), *Las políticas sociales en México al fin del milenio* (pp. 263–288). Mexico City: Universidad Nacional Autónoma de México; Miguel Ángel Porrúa.

Viswanathan, N. (1961). *The role of the American Public Welfare Association in the formulation and development of public welfare policies in the United States: 1930–1960*. Unpublished doctoral dissertation, Columbia University, New York.

Wald, L. D. (1915). *The house on Henry Street*. New York: Holt.

Wald, L. D. (1934). *Windows on Henry Street*. Boston: Little, Brown.

Ward, P. (1986). *Welfare politics in Mexico: Papering over the cracks*. London: Allen and Unwin.

Ward, P. W. (2002). *White Canada forever: Popular attitudes and public policy toward Orientals in British Columbia*. Montreal, QC: McGill University Press.

Ware, S. (1981). *Beyond suffrage: Women in the New Deal*. Cambridge, MA: Harvard University Press.

Warner, A. G. (1894). *American charities: A study in philanthropy and economics*. New York: Thomas Y. Crowell.

Warner, M. (Ed.). (1993). *Fear of a queer planet: Queer politics and social theory*. Minneapolis: University of Minnesota Press.

Warner, T. (2002). *Never going back: A history of queer activism in Canada*. Toronto, ON: University of Toronto Press.

Warsh, C. (1993). *Drink in Canada: Historical essays*. Montreal, QC, and Kingston, ON: McGill-Queen's University Press.

Washburn, W. E. (1971). *Red man's land, White man's law: A study of the past and present status of the American Indian*. New York: Scribner.

Watkins, M. H. (1963, May). A staple theory of economic growth. *Canadian Journal of Economics and Political Science, 29,* 141–158.

Watson, F. D. (1922). *The charity organization movement in the United States: A study in American philanthropy.* New York: Macmillan.

Waugh J. (1997). *Unsentimental reformer: The life of Josephine Shaw Lowell.* Cambridge, MA: Harvard University Press.

Waugh, J. (2001, Summer). "Give this man work!" Josephine Shaw Lowell, The Charity Organization Society of the City of New York, and the depression of 1893. *Social Science History, 25*(2), 217–246.

Weaver, R. K. (2000). *Ending welfare as we know it.* Washington, DC: Brookings Institution Press.

Webb, S., & Webb, B. (1927). The old poor law. Part I of *English local government: English Poor Law history.* London: Longmans, Green.

Weir, G. M. (1934). *The separate school question in Canada.* Toronto, ON: Ryerson.

Weisbrod, B. A. (1988). *The nonprofit economy.* Cambridge, MA: Harvard University Press.

Weismiller, T., & Rome, S. H. (1995). Social workers in politics. In R. L. Edwards & J. G. Hopps (Eds.), *Encyclopedia of social work* (19th ed., Vol. 3). Washington, DC: NASW Press.

Weller, G. (1993). Hinterland politics: The case of northwestern Ontario. In C. Southcott (Ed.), *Provincial hinterland: Social inequality in northwestern Ontario* (pp. 5–28). Halifax, NS: Fernwood.

Wenocur, S., & Reisch, M. (1988). *From charity to enterprise: The development of American social work in a market economy.* Urbana: University of Illinois Press.

Wharf, B., & Clague, M. (Eds.). (1997). *Community organizing: Canadian experiences.* Toronto, ON: Oxford University Press.

White, J. E. (2000). *Democracy, justice, and the welfare state: Reconstructing public care.* University Park: Pennsylvania State University Press.

White, R. C., Jr., & Hopkins, C. H. (1976). *The social gospel: Religion and reform in changing America.* Philadelphia: Temple University Press.

Whitton, C. (1943). *The dawn of ampler life.* Toronto, ON: Macmillan.

Wilensky, H. L., & Lebeaux, C. N. (1958). *Industrial society and social welfare.* New York: Russell Sage.

Wilkie, J. W. (Ed.). (1990). *Society and economy in Mexico.* Los Angeles: University of California, Los Angeles, Latin American Center Publications.

Williams, H. (1996). *Planting trouble: The* Barzón *debtors' movement in Mexico.* La Jolla: University of California, San Diego, Center for U.S.-Mexican Studies.

Williams, H. (2001). *Social movements and economic transition: Markets and distributive protest in Mexico.* New York: Cambridge University Press.

Wills, G. (1995). *A marriage of convenience: Business and social work in Toronto, 1918–1957.* Toronto, ON: University of Toronto Press.

Wilson, B. (1993). The institutional capacity of the court. In F. L. Morton (Ed.), *Law, politics and the judicial process in Canada* (2nd ed., p. 287). Calgary, AB: University of Calgary Press.

Wilson, B., & Tsoa, E. (2002). *HungerCount 2002: Eating their words: Government failure on food security.* Toronto, ON: Canadian Association of Food Banks.

Wilson, J. D., Stamp, R. M., & Audet, L.-P. (Eds.). (1970). *Canadian education: A history.* Scarborough, ON: Prentice Hall.

Wilson, T. D. (Ed.). (1998). The urban informal sector [Special issue]. *Latin American Perspectives, 25*(2).

Winder, D. (2001, Fall). Mexican philanthropy breaking new ground: The Bajio Foundation. *ReVista: Harvard Review of Latin America,* 24–25. Available: http://drclas.fas.harvard.edu/publications/revista/mexico/tcontents.html

Winder, D. (2004). *Innovations in strategic philanthropy: The case of Mexico* (Paper prepared for the International Network on Strategic Philanthropy). New York: Synergos Institute. Available: www.synergos.org/globalphilanthropy/04/insp mexico.pdf

Wines, F. H. (1890). State boards of charities. *Proceedings of the National Conference on Charities and Correction, 17,* 63–72.

Winks, R. W. (1997). *The Blacks in Canada: A history* (2nd ed.). Montreal, QC: McGill University Press.

Wise, C. (Ed.). (1998). *The post-NAFTA political economy: Mexico and the Western Hemisphere.* University Park: Pennsylvania State University Press.

Witte, E. E. (1962). *The development of the Social Security Act.* Madison: University of Wisconsin Press.

Witte, J. F. (1985). *The politics and development of the federal income tax.* Madison: University of Wisconsin Press.

Wohl, R. R. (1969). The "country boy" myth and its place in American culture: The nineteenth century contribution. *Perspectives in American History, 3,* 77–156.

Wong, K. (2001). *Voices for justice: Asian Pacific organizers and the new labor movement.* Los Angeles: Center for Labor Research and Education.

Woods, W. S. (1953). *Rehabilitation: A combined operation.* Ottawa, ON: Queen's Printer.

Woodsworth, J. S. (1911). *My neighbour: A study of human conditions, a plea for social service.* Toronto, ON: Missionary Society of the Methodist Church.

Woodsworth, J. S. (1972). *Strangers within our gates.* Toronto, ON: University of Toronto Press. (Original work published 1909)

World Bank. (1993). *World development report 1993: Investing in health.* New York: Oxford University Press.

World Health Organization. (1997). *Violence against women: A priority health issue* [On-line]. Available: www.who.int/gender/violence/prioreng/en/

Wright, C. E. (1992). *The transformation of charity in postrevolutionary New England.* Boston: Northeastern University Press.

Wright, H. (1954). Three against time: Edith and Grace Abbott and Sophonisba Breckinridge. *Social Service Review, 28,* 41–53.

Yelaja, S. A. (1985). *An introduction to social work practice in Canada.* Toronto, ON: Prentice Hall.

Young People's Forward Movement Department, Research Committee of the League for Social Reconstruction. (1935). *Social planning for Canada.* Toronto, ON: Thomas Nelson.

Young, R. (Ed.). (1999). *Stretching the federation: The art of the state in Canada.* Kingston, ON: Queen's University, Institute of Intergovernmental Relations.

Young, W. M. (1964). *To be equal.* New York: McGraw-Hill.

Young, W. M. (1969). *Beyond racism: Building an open society.* New York: McGraw-Hill.

Zahavi, G. (1983, December). Negotiated loyalty: Welfare capitalism and the shoeworkers of Endicott Johnson, 1920–1940. *Journal of American History, 70*(3), 602–620.

Zamora Díaz de León, T. (2000). *La formación del trabajador social en Latinoamérica.*

Ziliak, S. T. (2002, June). Pauper fiction in economic science: "Paupers in almshouses" and the odd fit of *Oliver Twist. Review of Social Economy, 60*(2), 159–181.

Ziliak, S. T. (2004). Self-reliance before the welfare state: Evidence from the charity organization movement in the United States. *Journal of Economic History, 64*(2), 433–461.

Index